POP WENT THE PIRATES II

POP WENT THE PIRATES II

Keith Skues

PERSEVERANTIA ET PRUDENTIA

LAMBS' MEADOW PUBLICATIONS

27 - 11 - 20.

ISBN 978-0-907398-05-9
EAN 9780907398059

Main text set in Classical Garamond 10pt and Swiss 721 BT, by
Graficas Design, Cwmbach, Glasbury-on-Wye, Powys HR3 5LU

Printed in Great Britain by MPG Books Group,
Bodmin and King's Lynn

Published by Lambs' Meadow Publications,
Horning, Norfolk NR12 8PJ England

British Library Cataloguing in Publication Data
A catalogue record for this book is available
from the British Library

Contents

'He's off a radio pirate ship—they have
a girl on every wavelength.'

For I am a Pirate King. You are!
Hurray for our Pirate King!
And it is, it is a glorious thing
To be a Pirate King. Hurrah!!
Hurrah for our Pirate King

Pirates of Penzance, W.S. Gilbert and Arthur Sullivan

The opera's official premiere was at the Fifth Avenue Theatre, New York City,
31 December 1879, where the show was a hit with both audiences and critics. The London
premiere was on 3 April 1880, at the Opera Comique where it ran for 363 performances,
having already been playing successfully for over three months in New York.

An
Illustrated
History of
Pirate Radio by
KEITH SKUES

Original artwork and Front Cover design of first edition by
Bridge Barn Studio, Hindhead, Surrey, England.

A potted history of Pirate Radio as seen through the eyes of The Daily Sketch, October 1966

FOCUS ON FACT—*The Pin-striped Pirates* (1) By Gary Keane & Neville Randall

NEXT MONTH'S BIG FIGHT. **GOVERNMENT** v. **PIRATE RADIO**. TEN UPSTART STATIONS CLAIM **25 MILLION LISTENERS**. THE GOVERNMENT HAS SERVED SUMMONSES ON THREE. IS PLEDGED TO SILENCE THEM ALL.

FROM **ANCHORED SHIPS** AND **ABANDONED FORTS** THEY BROADCAST NON-STOP MUSIC FROM DAWN TO TELLY TIME — SOME THROUGH THE NIGHT. TO LONELY HOUSEWIVES AND YOUNG POP ADDICTS.

THEY MAKE THEIR MONEY PLAYING PERMUTATIONS OF THE CURRENT TOP POP DISCS—WITHOUT PAYING FEES. AND CHARGING UP TO £100 A MINUTE FOR ADVERTISEMENTS BETWEEN TUNES

FOCUS ON FACT—*The Pin-striped Pirates* (2) By Gary Keane & Neville Randall

1964. MARCH 27. A 763 TON SHIP DROPPED ANCHOR OFF HARWICH. IT WAS EQUIPPED WITH AN AERIAL 168 FT. ABOVE DECK-LEVEL. *THE FIRST PIRATE RADIO*

MARCH 28. NOON. DISC JOCKEY **SIMON DEE** ANNOUNCED: "THIS IS RADIO CAROLINE BROADCASTING ON 199, YOUR ALL-DAY MUSIC STATION". THREE WEEKS LATER IT HAD SEVEN MILLION LISTENERS.

APRIL 27. ANOTHER SHIP, FORMERLY THE MV MI AMIGO, ANCHORED 14 MILES AWAY. BEGAN BROADCASTING ON MAY 9 AS **RADIO ATLANTA**.

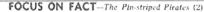

JULY. BOTH SHIPS MERGED. CAROLINE SAILED TO THE ISLE OF MAN, BECAME **CAROLINE NORTH**. ATLANTA BECAME **CAROLINE SOUTH**. TODAY THEY CLAIM 13½ MILLION LISTENERS TOGETHER, MAKE MORE THAN £½ MILLION A YEAR.

FOCUS ON FACT *The Pin-striped Pirates* (3) By Gary Keane & Neville Randall

1964. MAY. SELF-STYLED POP SINGER "SCREAMING LORD SUTCH" SAILED FROM THE POOL OF LONDON. FOR A DERELICT WARTIME GUN-TOWER ON SHIVERING SANDS IN THE THAMES ESTUARY.

HE INSTALLED A 63 FT. AERIAL. IMPROVISED A STUDIO IN THE RUSTY STEEL-PLATED TURRET AND INTRODUCED THE FIRST PROGRAMME OF **RADIO SUTCH**

NEXT SEPTEMBER. SUTCH'S MANAGER REG CALVERT TOOK OVER. RE-NAMED IT **RADIO CITY**. WAS SOON TRANSMITTING NON-STOP POP TO 3½ MILLION LISTENERS — AND BOOKING ADVERTISING AT £ A SECOND.

FOCUS ON FACT —The Pin-striped Pirates (4)

By Gary Keane & Neville Randall

DECEMBER, 1964. A 1,000 TON EX-U.S. MINE-SWEEPER ANCHORED FOUR MILES OFF HARWICH. PURVEYING PIRATICAL POPS AS RADIO LONDON. CLAIMS THE BIGGEST—AND MOST PROFITABLE AUDIENCE OF 12 MILLION.

SEPTEMBER, 1965. TED ALLBURY FORMER ADMAN, SET UP RADIO 390 ON RED SANDS TOWER OFF WHITSTABLE. SPECIALISES IN SWEET MUSIC AND SYMPATHY FOR LONELY WIVES AND WIDOWS. CLAIMS FOUR MILLION DEVOTEES.

JUNE 1966. ANOTHER FREIGHTER OFF HARWICH, BACKED BY A MILLION POUNDS, LAUNCHING ANOTHER TWO STATIONS. BRITAIN RADIO—WALLPAPER MUSIC AND OLDIES. AND RADIO ENGLAND—LATEST RECORD HITS—AND A GROWING AUDIENCE OF 4 MILLION.

FOCUS ON FACT—The Pin-striped Pirates (5)

By Gary Keane & Neville Randall

1964. SUMMER. PIRACY SPREAD TO HOLLAND. A PLATFORM ON STEEL STILTS APPEARED OFF NOORDWIJK NEAR THE HAGUE. TV NOORDZEE OFFERED THE FIRST DUTCH COMMERCIAL RADIO AND TELEVISION. IT WAS EAGERLY ACCEPTED.

DEC. 17. DAWN. TWO DUTCH HELICOPTERS HOVERED OVERHEAD, DROPPED TEN POLICEMEN ON DECK. A NAVAL PILOT BOAT CLOSED IN. EQUIPMENT WAS SEIZED. TV NOORDZEE WENT OFF THE AIR.

IN BRITAIN WEDGWOOD BENN, THEN SOCIALIST POSTMASTER-GENERAL, MADE THREATENING NOISES, DID NOTHING. BRITISH RADIO PIRATES CONTINUED TO GROW, AND PROSPER.

FOCUS ON FACT—The Pin-striped Pirates (6)

By Gary Keane & Neville Randall

JULY 28, 1966. EDWARD SHORT, NEW LABOUR P.M.G. ANNOUNCED BRITAIN'S ANTI-PIRATE BILL TO MAKE IT A CRIME TO WORK FOR PIRATE STATIONS, SUPPLY THEM, OR ADVERTISE ON THEM. EXPECTED TO KILL THEM BY MARCH, 1967.

SHOULD THEY BE KILLED? RECORDING COMPANIES SAY YES. PIRATE RADIO PLAYS RECORDS CONTINUOUSLY, REDUCES SALES PAYS THEM NO ROYALTIES. ONLY FOUR PAY PERFORMING RIGHTS— FAR LESS THAN THE BBC. ALL BROADCAST WITHOUT PERMISSION OF THE PERFORMING RIGHTS SOCIETY.

EUROPEAN STATIONS SAY YES, COMPLAIN PIRATES INFRINGE THEIR WAVELENGTHS, SPOIL RECEPTION. 25 MILLION WHO LISTEN TO PIRATE RADIO SAY NO.

NEXT WEEK: INCIDENTS JUST HAPPEN!

Illustration Acknowledgements

The publishers would like to thank the following for kindly supplying the photographs and line drawings used in this book. Whilst every attempt has been made to trace copyright in some cases this has been impossible.

To David Kindred, who has supplied over 50 per cent of the pictures.

To: Ted Allbeury, David Allan, Associated Newspapers, Olive Baker, Greg Bance, Vivien Barnard, BBC, Karl Beattie, Beer Davies Publicity, Johnny Beerling, Tony Benn, Colin Berry, Dave Berry, Eric Brett, Olive Burgess, Paul Bumett, Andy Cadier, Capital Radio, Linda Carter, Coastal Cards, Edward Cole, Roger Day, Decca Records, East Anglian Daily Times, East Anglian Productions, Chris Edwards, Tom Edwards, Chris Elliot, Steve England, Foto Flite of Kent (formerly Skyphotos), Roger Gale, Philip Gotlop, Paul Graham, Paul Gunniford, Jo Gurnett, Barbara Hadler, Harwich Printing Company, John Hatt, Dezo Hoffman, House of Commons Public Information Office, Imperial War Museum, Melvyn Johnson, Hans Knot, Bob Leroi, Keith Martin, Doug McKenzie, Tony Meehan, Steve Merike, Richard Morecraft, Tom Mulder, Colin Nicol, Offshore Echo's, PAMS, Popperfoto, Press Photos Ltd., Barry Pritchard, Iain Quick, Tony Ray, RNLI, Bill Rollins, John Ross-Barnard, Paul Rusling, Keith Skues, Mark Sloane, Square Photographic Service, Martin Stevens, Universal Pictorial Press, Vicky (Evening Standard) and Paul Young.

Second Edition
Copyright of the pictures in Chapter 14 are credited to BBC, Mike Brand, Sue Davies, John Forman, Angela Lander, Jaqui Lazelle, Bob Le-Roi, Jenny Matthew, Pauline Miller, Colin Nicol, Tony O'Neil, Chris and Mary Payne, Radio London Limited, Tom Read, John Ross-Barnard, Keith Skues, Dr Martin van der Ven, Ron Vick, Charlie Wallace, Chris Woodward and Annie Wright.

Music Acknowledgements

The writer is grateful to the following publishers for allowing a short extract of one of their songs to appear in this book:

Acuff Rose Opryl and Music Ltd; Blossom Music; Bregman, Vocco and Conn; Cat Music; Dump Music; Eaton Music; EMI Music Publishing Ltd; Essex Music; Northern Songs; Queen Music Ltd; Rondor Music (London) Ltd; Springfield Music; Story Songs Ltd., and B.F. Wood. The chapter numbers are followed by title of the song, artist, writer, music publisher, record company and number.

Chapter 1
Times They Are a-Changin"
Bob Dylan
Bob Dylan
Blossom Music
CBS BPG 62251

Chapter 2
Caroline
Fortunes
Hille, Ford
B.F. Wood
Decca F 11809

Chapter 3
This Could be the Start
Steve Lawrence and Eydie
Gorme Allen
Bregman, Vocco and Conn
HMP CLP 1372

Chapter 4
A Whiter Shade of Pale
Procol Harum
Keith Reid/Gary Brooker
Essex Music
Deram DM 126

Chapter 5
Ship to Shore
Chris de Burgh
Chris de Burgh
Rondor (London) Ltd.
A & M AMLH 64815

Chapter 6
Wonderful Radio London
PAMS radio jingle

Chapter 7
W.O.L.D.
Harry Chapin
Harry Chapin
Story Songs Ltd.
Elektra K 12133

Chapter 8
I'm Gonna Get me a Gun
Cat Stevens
Cat Stevens
Cat Music
Deram DM 118

Chapter 9
When I'm Sixty-Four
Kenny Ball and his Jazzmen
Lennon/McCartney
Northern Songs
Pye 7N 17348

Chapter 10
I Fought the Law
Bobby Fuller Four
Sonny Curtis
Acuff-Rose Opryland Music
London HL 10030

Chapter 11
The Carnival is Over
Seekers
Tom Springfield
Springfield Music
Columbia DB 7711

Chapter 12
Radio Ga Ga
Queen
Roger Taylor
Queen Music Ltd
EMI Queen 1

Chapter 13
Rock'n'Roll
Status Quo
Rossi/Frost
Dump Music/Eaton Music
Vertigo QUO 6

Chapter 14
The Last Time
Rolling Stones
Richards/Jagger
Mirage Music
Decca F 12104

List of Abbreviations

AM	amplitude modulation
BBC	British Broadcasting Corporation
BFBS	British Forces Broadcasting Service
BFN	British Forces Network
BigL	Radio London
Capt.	Captain
CID	Criminal Investigation Department
COMM	Command Headquarters
DPP	Director of Public Prosecutions
DTI	Department of Trade and Industry
EAP	East Anglian Productions
FBS	Forces Broadcasting Service
FCC	Federal Communications Commission
Fg.	Off.Flying Officer
FM	frequency modulation
GLC	Greater London Council
IBA	Independent Broadcasting Authority
IBC	International Broadcasting Corporation
ILR	Independent Local Radio
ITU	International Telecommunications Union
jgj	unior grade
kc/s	kilocyclesk
Hz	kilohertz
kW	kilowatt
LSA Co.	Lifesaving Apparatus Company
MeBO	Marine, Etc., Broadcasting (Offences) **Act**
MHz	megahertz
MoD	Ministry of Defence
m.v.	motor vessel
NZBC	New Zealand Broadcasting Corporation
OCD	Opsporings Controle Dienst
PLO	Palestine Liberation Organisation
PTT	Postal, Telephone and Telegraph Administrations
RADA	Royal Academy of Dramatic Art
RAF	Royal Air Force
RAFVR	Royal Air Force Volunteer Reserve
RIS	Radio Investigation Service of the **DTI**
RNLI	Royal National Lifeboat Institution
RNVR	Royal Naval Volunteer Reserve
RSL	Restricted Service Licence
RTE	Radio Telefis Eireann
SAS	Special Air Service
Sgt.	Sergeant
TSW	Television South West
USN	United States Navy
USNR	United States Naval Reserve
USS	United States Ship
VHF	very high frequency
YTV	Yorkshire Television

Foreword

WHATEVER THE OCCASION, an anniversary is always worth a celebration. The year 1988 marked the 21st anniversary of the Marine Etc., Broadcasting (Offences) Act which came into operation at midnight on 14 August 1967. The 30th anniversary of Radio Caroline commencing regular transmissions off the Essex coast, which marked the birth of British offshore radio, was celebrated at Eastertime 1994 when the First Edition of this book was published.

Much of the book was written during the three years I worked as a disc jockey on Radio Caroline and later Radio London (1964-1967).

A major British film, *Rock the Boat*, was to have been produced in 1988 with many of the events of the pirate era included. Sadly the backers 'pulled the plug' financially and the film was scuppered. Fast forward 21 years and another film, *The Boat That Rocked*, made the big cinema screens with worldwide distribution. The film was not based on any one disc jockey or radio station but was set in the Swinging Sixties.

This era was, in my humble opinion, the best time to have been a disc jockey in Britain. Fashion and pop music was at its best. We had the Mary Quant phenomenon, Carnaby Street, the John Stephen 'boutiques', the Beatles, hair stylist Vidal Sassoon, top fashion model Jean 'The Shrimp' Shrimpton, photographer David Bailey and flower power. *Ready Steady Go's* Cathy McGowan, top model Twiggy, films like *Saturday Night and Sunday Morning*, *The Good, The Bad and the Ugly*, *Bonnie and Clyde* and *The Pink Panther* and the whole music explosion. Everyone appeared to have more money and much of it was spent on clothes. It was fashionable to eat at Trader Vic's. National Service was a thing of the past. Girls were on the pill. It was good to be young. We had telephone exchanges with names like Mayfair, Maida Vale and Hyde Park - even Budleigh Salterton, Fenton Claypole and Hurstbourne Tarrant - not just a string of impersonal numbers. Some young men backcombed, tinted and lacquered their hair, whilst the girls wore knee-length socks, backcombed their hair and used huge amounts of eye liner, mascara and shocking pink lipstick. We were into the era of Mods and Rockers. The Rockers preferred black rivet-studded leather jackets and motor bikes. Mods dressed in suits and other clean-cut outfits and preferred driving scooters. Musically they were poles apart. Mods enjoyed the 1960s British rhythm and blues groups like the Who, the Yardbirds and Small Faces. Some enjoyed soul and ska from black singers, whereas the rockers preferred rock'n'roll music from white American artists of the 1950s including Elvis Presley, Gene Vincent, Eddie Cochran and Bill Haley.

One of the most controversial events of the 1960s was the birth of offshore, or as it was to become affectionately known, pirate radio. For listeners it was the realisation that pirate ships and forts, operated by young people who were doing their own thing and fighting against the forces of the Establishment, were providing a service for the very first time which made music available any time of the day or night. From the freedom of international waters the pirate radio stations changed the face, and indeed the shape, of British broadcasting.

At a similar time we experienced, through modern technology, the birth of the transistor radio. Electrically heated valves gave way to the minute 'tranny.' For the first time in our lives radio was a portable medium and you could take it anywhere with you - in the car, the bathroom, to work. It was with us twenty-four hours a day.

The Sixties were a very important time for young people who were growing up. Music was an important part of their lives. The words of songs expressed their feelings as young teenagers came to terms with themselves. Maybe their parents couldn't understand them and they did not identify with teachers at school, but the pirate stations had that special 'something' which teenagers did identify with and they loved it!

There was more freedom and no talk of sending our British troops to Northern Ireland, the Falklands, Iraq, Bosnia or Afghanistan. There was the freedom of being yourself and having fun, and for those of us working in radio, the freedom of the airwaves.

It was, as W.S. Gilbert wrote in the *Pirates of Penzance*, "a glorious thing, to be a Pirate King."

Someone once likened the pirates to a tap. When you turn it on out comes the water and people rely upon it - in the case of the pirates it was music and chat you heard when you turned it on.

I believe one of the main attractions of the pirates was their illegality. Turntables could wow or records suffer from repeating grooves, transmitters could go off air from time to time; DJs may misread commercials. None of this seemed to matter at the time. Illegality spelt excitement. The music interspersed by singing jingles and DJ banter added to the exhilaration. However, there was a certain air of respectability about being a pirate DJ before the Marine Offences Act was talked about in Parliament. Yes, you were a pirate, but at that time in history you were not breaking any laws because no laws were in place to break until midnight on 14 August 1967, the 22nd anniversary of the greatest fight for freedom (VJ Day) when the Japanese surrendered, thus ending World War II. The Postmaster-General chose this day to strike a blow against freedom of the air. I was proud to have been in the United Kingdom in the mid-1960s, not only to have been alive and kicking at that time, but to have been a small part of the offshore story. My ambition then was gently to help persuade the Government of the day to introduce some form of commercial radio in Britain. In those halcyon days of the mid-Sixties, if you ignored the pirates, there was only Radio Luxembourg worth listening to for pop music. The BBC had the Light Programme, but very few record programmes existed. Instead of the hundreds of disc jockeys who are making a living today in radio there were just a handful, including David Jacobs, Brian Matthew, Pete Murray, Alan Freeman, Keith Fordyce and Don Moss. Britain was light years behind the rest of the western world which had enjoyed commercial radio for a long time.

The pirates helped new recording artists, songwriters, new record labels, young independent record producers, and promoted new styles in music. They played a large number of LP tracks which helped shift the taste of many people from the Top 20. The pirates may have 'waived the rules', but in the 1960s they 'ruled the waves!' From their concept of radio, Britain's first legal pop station was created - BBC Radio 1. In retrospect most people tend to ignore the faults of the pirates and only remember their good points, rather like they look back on a summer holiday. The stereotyped image of pirate radio was lying on a beach in the summer, listening to the latest pop records.

The original text of *Pop Went the Pirates* was written in 1968 and took three years to compile. The manuscript was never published due to a clause in the Marine Etc., Broadcasting (Offences) Act 1967 which made it an offence to publicise pirate radio stations. My solicitor joked "You could publish your book and spend three months in prison…it may become a best-seller." I declined his kind offer. The manuscript lay in his office for almost a quarter of a century. Following the introduction of the Broadcasting Act in 1990 - which effectively put an end to pirate radio as we knew it on the high seas - I believed it was time to resurrect the now sepia coloured text and photographs, bring the book completely up to date and include the pirate stations off the coasts of the United Kingdom and Europe in historical terms. This revision took a further three years.

Pop Went the Pirates was not written in a country cottage whilst being waited on hand and foot, but in a variety of places ... in the cabin of a former minesweeper three miles off the Essex coast during many a force 9 gale ... in reference libraries up and down the country ... in my then London flat ... at my parents' home in Dorset ... in my room in various officers' messes around the United Kingdom ... on a London to Norwich train ... in the University of East Anglia ... even on board an aircraft returning from the Falkland Islands. Neville and Sheila Rofaila kindly loaned me their flat in Marbella, Spain, in 1986 for two weeks so that I could check the text of "Pirates."

The buzz words 'pirate radio' conjure up shoddy gangsterism and seedy goings-on, when brawls broke out at sea and on rusty forts in the Thames Estuary as rival gangs fought for possession of their radio station. We sample shipwrecks, sudden death on land as well as at sea, numerous attempts to find loopholes in the law, and the opportunity for swashbuckling managers to make a lot of money. These features would make a good novel. However, although 99% of the time disc jockeys played popular music to a huge listening audience throughout the United Kingdom there was, sadly, the murkier side of the pirates which culminated in the shooting of the boss of Radio City. This incident sounded the death knell for British pirate broadcasters.

As with any book an author relies on help - and I am no exception to the rule. I was given so much help in producing the text that it might have been more tactful to have omitted my name as author.

A number of the people who helped me in the early days have now sadly died. Nevertheless their contributions and names will stay for posterity. I should now like to thank the following for their co-operation in the First Edition:

Members in both the House of Lords and House of Commons, including the Rt. Hons. Tony Benn, Reginald Bevins and Edward Short; Hugh Beech for information relating to radio in the 1930s; The Controller of Her Majesty's Stationery Office for allowing me to quote so freely from Hansard and to reproduce the Marine Etc., Broadcasting (Offences) Act of 1967, amended 1990; the Radio Services Department of the Post Office; the Radio Investigation Service of the Department of Trade and Industry; Trinity House; the station directors and staff of all the offshore radio stations; the 250 disc jockeys to whom I either spoke or wrote, or who were kind enough to give me a quotable 'sound bite'; numerous housewives who contributed 'large amounts of home produced stanzas'; Jean Sutton, Maggie Stevens and Susie Lansom for so bravely taking on the task of typing and retyping over 1,500 pages of manuscript in 1967 and 1968; Nancy Tym for reading the first 1,000 pages of typed manuscript, looking for spelling errors, long before we had the luxuries of the computer spell check; to Chris Shepherd for 'proofing' the updated manuscript after I had made many alterations to the original text; to Ronan O'Rahilly, Frances van Staden, Richard Morecraft and Ken Evans of Radio Caroline; Wilf Proudfoot and Maggie Lucas of Radio 270; Philip Birch, Des Brown and Roger Seddon of Radio London; the late Ted Allbeury and Peter James of Radio 390; and Roy Bates of Radio Essex.

All the national newspapers of the 1960s were most helpful, especially the *Daily Mail, Daily Sketch, Daily Express, Daily Mirror, The Times, Guardian, Daily Telegraph, Sun* and their Sunday equivalents, plus *News of the World, The People* and *The Observer*. All these papers, together with many regional and local press, have allowed me to extract various quotes about the pirates.

The East Anglian Daily Times also receives an honourable mention as the staff were most helpful, especially David Kindred who supplied a large proportion of the photographs for inclusion in the book.

The British music press are not ignored. They gave wide exposure to the offshore stations - *Melody Maker, Disc and Music Echo, Record Mirror* and *New Musical Express*.

My thanks also to the Walton and Frinton, Clacton and Southend lifeboat personnel, HM Coastguard and auxiliary coastguards who kept their eyes and ears scanned along the Essex coastline. They were lifesavers in more ways than one between the years 1964 and 1967. To Russ Godwin from the Rescue Records Department of the Royal National Lifeboat Institution in Poole, who was most helpful in pinpointing dates and times of all the rescues from the offshore ships and forts, and for bringing me up to speed with all the RNLI stations around our coastline.

I am indebted to John Ross-Barnard and Steve England for their first-hand accounts of life at the 'sharp end.'

To Paul Rusling, an expert in matters technical regarding pirate stations from the 1960s to 1990s, for supplying his contribution to Chapter Thirteen, and granting me access to his many scrapbooks on the subject. Also to pop stars who have talked to me about what pirate radio meant to them. They include P.P. Arnold, Beach Boys, Dave Berry, Petula Clark, The Fortunes, Freddy Garrity, Tom Jones, Gerry Marsden, the Overlanders, Gene Pitney, Brian Poole, Reg Presley and Twinkle.

I acknowledge the many talents of Ray Anderson, Maxine Mitchell, Paul Graham, Richard Walker and Christopher Minter for their help in updating many of the facts and figures. Likewise to the late Howard Rose of *Radio Magazine*, and Chris Edwards of *Offshore Echo's* and his wife Stephanie, who must have the largest collection of press cuttings and photographs on the subject of pirate radio. Also François Lhote of France and Boudewijn Dom of Belgium. To the late Roland C. 'Buster' Pearson and the team from *Monitor* magazine who, fastidiously, kept a log of all comings and goings of people on the ships and forts. Hans Knot of Groningen, Holland, was most helpful in enabling me expand Chapter Thirteen, and to Les Livermore of Steggles Palmer for supplying the legal clearance.

Chris Elliot and Jonathan Wolfert gave me much information on the origins of the Radio London, Radio England, Britain Radio and Radio 1 jingles recorded by PAMS of Dallas, Texas. To PAMS of Dallas for permission to reproduce their logo in Chapter Six.

Disc jockeys have been helpful in many cases and I thank Mike Ahern, David Allan, Mike Allen, Andy Archer, John Aston, Greg Bance, Colin Berry, Tony Blackburn, Tony Brandon, Paul Burnett, Dave Cash, the late Edward Cole, Roger Day, Simon Dee, Chris Denning, Pete Drummond, Tom Edwards, the late Kenny Everett, Roger Gale, Guy Hamilton, Keith Hampshire, Peter James, Duncan Johnson, the late Paul Kaye, Martin Kayne, Keith Martin, Tony Meehan, Steve Merike, the late Ed Moreno, Colin Nicol, Dick Palmer, Richard Park, Tony Prince, the late Mike Raven, Bill Rollins, Mark Roman, Mark Sloane, Bryan Vaughan, Johnnie Walker, Willy Walker, Graham Webb, the late Tony Windsor, Paul Young and Steve Young for their help in allowing me to update their biographies. Others have not been so helpful with the result that their biographies may be out of date. I did my very best to contact them - even enclosing a stamped addressed envelope. When no reply was forthcoming I contacted their agents. Again no reply.

Robin Scott, former Controller of BBC Radio 1, and the BBC Publicity Department made Chapter Twelve possible, much of which was previously contained in my 1968 book *Radio Onederland*. My thanks to Johnny Beerling, former Controller, Radio 1, from 1985-1993, for his contribution regarding the network during that period.

The original typewritten text was transferred to computer in 1992. 'Brad' Bradbury was an expert on technical matters with my Dell computer for page layouts and fonts. I am indebted to Brad, and his wife Garielle, who allowed him to spend so many hours of his spare time on this project which was originally to have been 250 pages with 80 pictures. The book is now double that size ... and then some!

Eunice Goodwin of Bridge Barn Studio, Hindhead, Surrey did a magnificent job on the art work with photos and diagrams. These were produced with Adobe Photoshop 2.1® software on an AppleMac computer. Karl Beanie, also of Bridge Barn Studio, designed the cover which encapsulated all the fun and excitement of the 'Swinging Sixties' with the more recent events in 'The World of Watery Wireless.'

Gavin Markham and Ruth Chaloner carried out the image-setting at Desktype Ltd, Cambridge. The First Edition of this sizable tome was printed by Black Bear Press Ltd., Cambridge. They have since been taken over.

Listeners also played a big part in this book. They are mentioned by name individually throughout the book, but one or two names spring readily to mind: Barbara Apostolides, the late Olive Burgess, Barbara Hadler and Clive Moore.

Many others have helped including John Adamson, the Baker family, David Clayton, Derrick Connolly, Chris Dannatt, Alex Dickson, Jo Gurnett, Melvyn Johnson, Martin Lee, Brian Long, Rob Olthof, Alan Ross, Stuart Russell and Gloria Bristow. I am most grateful to them all.

To the dozens of people left unmentioned, I thank you too. This book is dedicated to all those who worked on the pirate stations, but more especially to the many millions of everyday folk who listened to the stations and gave us all encouragement. Without listener loyalty there would be no means of sustaining radio stations, whether they be pirate, BBC or independent.

Pirate radio, by name, has carried on into the new millennium. There are numerous land-based pirates operating around the country, but this book is about the pirates of the watery wireless days.

Cornwall's legalised independent local radio station is called Pirate FM and on race courses around the country in the 1990s we saw a racehorse named Radio Caroline! I spotted it running at Carlisle on 12 May 1990. It was in fact the first outing for this two-year old. Sadly it lost the race and I lost a fiver! Subsequent races brought me no winnings either. Nevertheless it was fun to see a horse with a really good name.

By the time the First Edition of *Pop Went the Pirates* went to press in 1994 the pirates of the high seas were broadcasting no more. This did not stop reunions and anniversary celebrations taking place at Eastertime and around 14 August. Five, ten, twenty, thirty, thirty-five, forty and now forty-five years since Radio Caroline went on air there is huge interest from an audience that in most cases have retired, although it is encouraging to see youngsters taking an interest in how radio used to be.

Pop Went the Pirates sold steadily over a 15-year period, but by the end of 2008 both softback and hardback editions had sold out. I decided it was time to bring out a Second Edition, with an additional chapter containing more recent photos of the DJs. This was partly prompted by the publicity surrounding the 2009 film *The Boat That Rocked*.

In the First Edition I tried to concentrate on both the history and the excitement of the pirate radio era. I hope I have preserved that in this updated and revised edition. Some of the facts in this edition are obviously outdated, but rather than destroy the atmosphere which was recreated over 40 years ago, I have left things as they are. The main area of change will be Chapter 7 featuring biographies of DJs. I have added an extra chapter at the end which lists those personnel who have sadly died since the Marine Etc., Broadcasting (Offences) Act took effect. Some DJs are still working in the United Kingdom, Australia, Canada and the United States. Others have retired, but most still have an interest in anniversaries and reunions and have made every effort to meet up with colleagues with whom they worked in the 1960s.

A lot of water has passed under many bridges since the 1960s and all of us have stories to tell. I was honoured in 2004 when I was presented to HM The Queen on two occasions within three months – one to collect the MBE at Buckingham Palace and a second occasion at the RAF Club in Piccadilly in connection with the Royal Air Force Volunteer Reserve and Royal Auxiliary Air Force. What does this have to do with pirate radio? In Chapter 2, "Turn Your Radio On," I tell the story of an 'unofficial' visit to Radio Caroline in June 1965 of Prince Richard of Gloucester. The visit was given wide coverage by the press following his arrival at HM Customs and Immigration. An officer asked the Prince, who was wearing a suede coat with lamb wool collar, if he was English. At the time he was eighth in succession to the English Throne. Fast forward 40 years to London. I and a number of colleagues were representing 7644 Public Relations Squadron. A few yards away was Prince Richard, now Duke of Gloucester, and the most senior agnatic descendant of Queen Victoria and Prince Albert, making him the most senior exclusively male-line-male in the House of Windsor. He was there as Honorary Air Commodore of 501 (County of Gloucester) Squadron, Royal Auxiliary Air Force. After the official ceremony I managed to have a few words with the Duke reminding him of his visit to Radio Caroline. He still had fond memories of the day. However he was 'spoken to' by a senior member of the Royal Household about the visit. "When I was at Cambridge University my colleagues and I used to listen to the offshore stations during our off-duty hours."

I am sure many other DJs have equally interesting stories to relate about people they have met since coming ashore.

For this edition I should like to thank the following for their help in making this Second

Edition possible. In alphabetical order: Tom and Jane Allwright, Mike Barraclough, BBC Essex, BBC Norfolk, Colin Berry, Tim Bishop, Peter Brady, Mike Brand, Gloria Bristow, Paul Burnett, Candy, Dorothy and Susan Calvert, Dave Cash, Ray Clark, David Clayton, Robbie Dale, Ian Damon, Roger Day, Trevor Dann, Claire Dickenson, Chris Edwards, Tom Edwards, Paul Elvey, Tim Gillett, John Hatt, Dermot Hoy, Nigel Hunter, Katie Ives, Duncan Johnson, John Kerr, Hans Knot, Angela Lander, David Lander, Bob Le-Roi, Greg Lunnon, Ian MacRae, Celia Mason, Jenny Matthew, Pauline Miller, Peter Moore, Jon Myer, Colin Nicol, Pearl O'Brien, Tony O'Neil, Chris and Mary Payne, Tom Read, Hans Rip, Mike Roberts, Mark Roman, Emperor Rosko, John Ross-Barnard, Paul Rowley, Stuart Russell, Steve Scruton, Norman St. John, Ed Stewart, Ray Teret, Mike Terry, Alan Thompson, Carl Thomson, Alan Turner, Dr. Martin van der Ven, Johnnie Walker, Graham Webb, Dr. Jonathan Wilson and Gerry Zierler.

Radio stations may come and radio stations may go, but I believe that pirate radio will long remain in the memories of the baby boomers and before. As this edition goes to press we learn of celebrations being arranged for the 45th anniversary of Radio Caroline going on air. I am sure there will be a 50th and possibly more; I just hope I am still on this earth to help celebrate those unforgettable days.

KEITH SKUES
Easter, 2009,
Norfolk

Note: *Pop Went the Pirates II* - readers may notice some typographical and punctuation errors, caused by the scanning of the text of the first edition, for which we apologise.

"That seems to have taken care of the acknowledgements. Now can we get on with the book!"

Chapter One

BRINGING ON BACK
THE GOOD TIMES

Come writers and critics who prophesise with your pen
And keep your eyes wide the chance won't come again
And don't speak too soon for the wheel's still in spin
And there's no telling who that it's namin'
For the loser now will be later to win
For the times they are a changin'

Times They Are A-Changin', Bob Dylan, 1965

FOR CENTURIES BRITANNIA ruled the waves! That was until 1964 when, on 28 March, she was rocked with pop music which has been constantly pumped out ever since. Britain's first pirate radio station operating from sea was actually on the air. Her name was *Caroline.*

Her founder was Ronan O'Rahilly, a young man who owned London's Scene Club, and also managed blues singer Georgie Fame. By chance Ronan met a Mr Allan Crawford, a music publisher, in Soho in January 1964.

Crawford had completed plans to launch Britain's first offshore commercial radio station - Radio Atlanta. He told O'Rahilly of the details, but Crawford, a former Australian fighter pilot, was in for a shock just two months later. He was pipped at the post by O'Rahilly who could foretell the British pop scene and, combining his business mind with his likes for popular music, predicted that the "beat" was becoming more and more part of the nation's life.

Allan Crawford took O'Rahilly into his confidence and thought he had a prospective backer. Ronan told the Australian that his father owned the Port of Greenore in southern Ireland, nestling under the Mountains of Mourne, which was a perfect place to fit out a pirate ship. The port had a giant crane which would make easy work of the complicated radio mast.

Both men firmly believed they were the first with the idea of offshore broadcasting, beamed to Britain. But, in fact, pirate radio was not exactly new to the western world, although admittedly it was to these shores. Quite a number of people have tried their hand at pirate broadcasting - and been caught!

On 15 October 1934, the *Daily Mail* reported "A pirate radio station was closed yesterday. Post Office officials have tracked down a mysterious broadcaster in Brockwell, Norwich, and dismantled the transmitter run by Gerald H. Barker who announced himself over the air as the 'Old Pirate.' He transmitted on 342 metres medium wave."

From the *Daily Mail* - 1 July 1935: "Radio Pirates Sunday Concert." "A pirate radio station is operating in the London area on 285 metres in the medium wave. A selection of gramophone records of Ambrose and Henry Hall and his BBC Dance Orchestra were linked by a mysterious broadcaster who calls himself 'Station Z.' There have been several instances of piracy in the last eighteen months."

On 18 September 1936, one pirate hauled down his flag! In a letter to the *Daily Express* we read "Dear Sir, The owner of station GRC begs to inform you that, owing to the fact that he has fallen in love with the sweetest girl on earth, pirate radio station GRC is closing down for ever."

The Channel Islands became involved in the pirate broadcast world in 1937. Every day between noon and 1.00pm during November a woman's voice broadcasting from a mysterious station in Alderney gave the introduction, "Channel Islands speaking" - French patois of the 2,000 inhabitants was featured in the programme.

In June 1939, the *Daily Herald* said there was an alarming increase in the number of pirate radio stations which have caused the Government to institute a more intensive watch on certain wavelengths. Pirate stations that have been caught in the past have been heavily fined and had their apparatus confiscated.

On 25 February 1940 a station announcing itself as the New British Broadcasting Station began transmissions at night. The programme opened with *Loch Lomond* played on the piano. An English announcer then said "You are listening to the New British Broadcasting Station which you will hear four times a night. We address ourselves to every Britisher who loves his country, no matter what party he belongs to." The transmissions closed with *God Save the King*. The BBC said it was impossible at that time to establish from where the broadcasts were coming.

Other 'pirate' broadcasters have been caught like Alan Walker who, in March 1955, was fined £5 with 3 guineas (£3.15) costs at Nottingham for operating his home-made radio transmitter without a licence. He played requests and get well messages. Post Office engineers eventually tracked Alan down and confiscated his equipment.

In April 1959 Graham King was fined £20 at Kingston-on-Thames in Surrey. He lasted for a whole year before Post Office detector vans tracked him down. He played pop music and jazz for friends throughout Surrey. Graham admitted "I was no Jean Metcalfe".

On 21 December 1962 Cyril Forrester of Rush Green Road, Romford, Essex, was fined £20 for being a "member of a group of radio pirates."

From the *Daily Mail* on 12 April 1963 we read "A Pirate Radio station operated by Aberdeen University students has been breaking into Radio Luxembourg programmes. Known as Radio Rox, it gives information about the present charities campaign. The Post Office is trying to trace them."

Radio Rag, apparently Britain's smallest pirate radio station, transmitted its first programme on 27 October 1964 from a tiny motor boat three miles off the north- east coast. No more was heard of it after that date.

Another Radio Rag appeared on the scene on 6 February 1967 when a group of Manchester University students set up a secret transmitter and broke into Radio Caroline North transmissions on 259 metres, advertising their university rag week.

On Saturday 15 May 1965 the day after the Government had declared 'war' on the pop pirates, an Essex businessman announced he was going to start a new pirate station named Radio Pamela on a 20ft. motor cruiser anchored near the Gunfleet Sands. Transmitting on 220 metres, 1367 kHz, it had an aerial wire suspended from a helium balloon, some 19 years before Laser 558 tried this idea. The station's owner was Reg Torr, (36) of Clacton, Essex, who managed a chain of radio and television shops. The range of Radio Pamela during test transmissions was put at about 20 miles, covering Walton, Clacton, Harwich, Ipswich and Mersea Island. However, due to rough weather, the station never really got 'off the ground' and ceased test transmissions.

Yet another pirate! On 1 September 1965 it was reported that a Radio Manchester was to start transmissions from a former United States minesweeper moored 3½ miles off Fleetwood, Lancashire. Transmissions were expected to be made on 300 metres on the medium wave band. The programmes would be transmitted from six in the morning until eight each evening. However, this station never succeeded in broadcasting.

The Post Office succeeded in prosecuting 19-year-old William James of Wilne Road, Sawley, Derbyshire, on 18 April 1967. He was found guilty of transmitting without a licence and fined £10 with 5 guineas (£5.25) costs.

James, an apprentice electrician, broadcast pop records from his garden shed and his transmitter was said to cover an area of 50 miles. His last record was *They're Coming to Take Me Away Ha Ha*.

Pirates popped up off the coast of New Zealand in October 1966. Hundreds of spectators lined the Auckland waterfront on 23 October and booed police when they boarded the country's first pirate ship to arrest the crew.

The police were enforcing a Government detention order placed on the 169 ft. vessel *Tiri* to prevent it from anchoring in the ocean and setting up a radio station.

A police inspector jumped aboard the ship as it left a wharfside in Auckland harbour, attempting to put to sea. A police launch pulled alongside, more police clambered on board and a scuffle started on the foredeck.

As the crowds cheered, the *Tiri* rammed its way through the drawbridge at the entrance to the basin with a smash which splintered the rear mast and sent pieces of timber crashing to the deck.

The ten men aboard were taken ashore in a police launch, and later charged with obstructing Marine Department inspectors.

On 7 April 1967 came news of another pirate in New Zealand when Radio Ventura made plans to commence operating.

In Auckland the co-managing director Antonio Fernandez said "The station would operate for 24 hours in an American manner with quick fire presentation." It would broadcast from the 550 ton converted weather ship which had sailed over from San Francisco. The power of Radio Ventura was to be a maximum of 7kW.

There would be eight disc jockeys (Canadian and American) supplemented by three presenters from New Zealand.

A pirate on a much smaller scale was 21-year-old Terry Vacani of Waller Road, New Cross, London, whose pirate transmitter was confiscated by the Post Office after he was found guilty of transmitting without a licence on 25 April 1967.

Terry broadcast records of Glenn Miller and Tommy Dorsey to South London and called his station Radio Kent. He broadcast from his bedroom on a home-made transmitter that cost him £3.15.0d (£3.75) to build.

Terry succeeded in fooling the Post Office for nine months. His nightly transmissions lasting two hours were transmitted on 180 metres medium wave.

He was fined £25 with 8 guineas (£8.40) costs. After the court case Terry said:

My transmissions were heard best of all in Deptford, Blackheath, Dulwich and Camberwell. I want to show that the local radio stations being set up by the BBC need not cost the ratepayer extra money. I shall most certainly carry on. I have found a way of beating the GPO and shall change my frequency and location. Should the Postmaster-General wish to contact me, I will show him how to start a radio station for less than £4.

In July 1967 a blind pop enthusiast who operated a pirate station from his garden shed was fined £25 at Redditch, Worcestershire. The station. Radio Freedom, was run by 21-year-old Robin Wood of Station Road, Alverchurch, Worcestershire, who said that his ambition was to be a disc jockey, but he was turned down because he was blind. His mother sat in court with a petition bearing 2,000 signatures to let the station remain open. However, Robin lost the case and his equipment was confiscated by the Post Office. He had previously been tracked down for operating Radio Christina in 1966. This station was also silenced.

On 12 February 1968 there was news of another pirate radio station operating off the coast of Britain. Transmissions were picked up on 213 metres in the medium wave and the station called itself Radio Atlantic South. One person who heard the test transmissions, Richard Barnett of Chesterfield in Derbyshire, said "The signal was clear for about six hours, and the disc jockey referred to the station as 'Your number one independent commercial radio station'."

Commercial radio on land, and broadcasting from the Continent, dates back to the 1920s, and one of the earliest programmes broadcast in English occurred in 1925.

Captain Leonard Plugge persuaded Selfridges to organise a fashion show which would be broadcast from the Eiffel Tower in Paris.

In 1928 a programme of Sunday concerts of light music originated from Radio Hilversum. Played by the de Groot Orchestra these concerts heard fortnightly were sponsored by a firm of radio manufacturers. The shows continued for two years.

Radio Toulouse successfully broadcast during 1929, 1930 and 1931 but found it difficult to operate after 1933. However, five years later the station reopened with an address by Winston Churchill.

It was in 1930 that Radio Paris (broadcasting on the long wave) joined in the competition following the formation of Radio Publicity Limited, a company which arranged contracts in Great Britain. It was eventually taken over by the French Government in April 1933 and all sponsored shows ceased in November the same year.

In March 1930 the International Broadcasting Company was registered under the leadership of Captain Leonard Plugge who was both founder and president. It had its headquarters at 11 Hallam Street, London (their studios still turn out some of today's best pop music). Plugge has been described as 'the father of commercial radio in Britain.' He died in 1967.

At exactly the same time as the IBC registration, a French company was formed to transmit programmes from Luxembourg. It was known as Societe Luxembourgeoise d'Études Radiophoniques which in June 1931 changed to Compagnie Luxembourgeoise de Rediffusion.

In 1931 the International Broadcasting Company commenced transmissions in English from Radio Normandy. Although the power of the transmitter was only 10 kilowatts, signals were picked up all over the British Isles, especially along the south coast of England.

Looking at the IBC programme sheet for 17 December 1933 (Volume 1 - N° 38) we see that it was 'Berkshire Week.' The programme sheet also listed other radio stations including Radio Athlone (called Radio Eireann from 1938), which broadcast on 413 metres on a power of 60 kilowatts. Details of programmes relayed by Radio Dublin on 217 metres and Radio Cork, 224 metres, both of which transmitted on a power of 1 kilowatt, were also included. On Sundays Radio Athlone broadcast from 1.00pm to 4.00pm and programmes consisted of dance music, concert music, and a special show sponsored by Littlewoods Football Pools. The announcer for Radio Athlone was C.P. Hope.

Also under the IBC banner was Poste Parisien, a 60 kilowatt station that transmitted on 328 metres for just half an hour on Sunday evenings - normally a variety concert. Poste Parisien began transmissions in November 1933.

Radio Normandy broadcast on 226 metres with a power of 20 kilowatts from 8.45am on Sundays to 2.00am the following day and programmes ranged from military band music, dance music and orchestral music to an IBC Members' Request Hour, an organ recital and regular news broadcasts. The announcers for Radio Normandy included T. St. A. Ronald, B. McNabb, Miss N. Crown, Roy Plomley and Stephen Williams.

Weekday broadcasting for Radio Normandy commenced at 11.00am usually for an hour's long orchestral concert, then closed down until 3.30pm when they came on the air for two and a half hours of military band music, nursery corner and light music. The final transmission of the day was heard from 10.00pm until 2.00am, normally dance music and request shows.

During weekdays more IBC stations were operational; namely Radio San Sebastian (453 metres) with a power of 1 kilowatt and E.A.Q. Aranjuez which was a short wave transmission on 30 metres at 20 kilowatts.

Union Radio Madrid broadcast for an hour from 1.00am - 2.00am on 424 metres at a power of 15 kilowatts and Radio Ljubljana (7 kilowatts) on 574.4 metres. There was also Radio Barcelona on 348 metres on 8 kilowatts, not forgetting Radio Cote D'Azur on 249.6 metres with a power of 10 kilowatts.

It is interesting to note that announcers from one radio station would also appear on others around the Continent. For example Bob Danvers Walker was listed in the programmes for E.A.Q. Aranjuez, Union Radio Madrid, Radio San Sebastian and Radio Barcelona.

The BBC made little comment on the stations broadcasting from the Continent until the Radio Normandy signals were picked up in London. When news was announced that a station in Luxembourg was to open in 1933 with a power of 200 kilowatts they complained to the Post Office who in turn wrote to the Luxembourg Government about the station which was to broadcast on 1250 metres long wave.

The BBC further complained that experimental transmissions on 1250 metres did, in fact, infringe the Washington Convention. Luxembourg, they said, was also interfering with British aircraft wireless services. The station was really a pirate.

However, the interloper, broadcasting from the Villa Louvigny near Luxembourg city centre, went on the air with programmes proper in the summer of 1933 much against the wishes of the BBC, the International Broadcasting Company and the Post Office. Radio Luxembourg changed its frequency from 1250 metres to 1304 in January 1934.[1]

The Post Office refused permission for land lines to be used for recordings of sponsored 'live' shows. So programmes had to be pre-recorded in London. The tapes were then shipped out to Luxembourg for transmission.

Although the BBC could not officially ban Luxembourg's broadcasts, they arranged certain blockades. In February 1936 they refused permission to allow the station to broadcast the King's Speech.

Radio Luxembourg programmes appear to have been printed in very few newspapers. However, during 1934 and 1935 the *Sunday Referee* carried the schedules and from November 1935 so did the Communist-backed *Daily Worker*.

A survey undertaken at the end of 1935 showed that there was definitely a need for commercial radio with one out of every two people interviewed listening regularly to Radio Luxembourg. Listening figures for Radio Normandy were also very high.

In 1936 Radio Lyons came on the air. Its director was Tony Melrose, a well-known announcer, whose voice was heard at Radio Olympia in 1935. He was later under contract to the BBC but, like so many at that time, opted for commercial radio, joining Radio Normandy and then transferring to Radio Lyons.

Radio Lyons, during weekdays, broadcast from 4.00pm to 6.00pm and from 7.00pm to midnight. Amongst the stars to appear on the station regularly were Arthur Tracey the Street Singer, Carroll Gibbons, Peter Dawson, Alfredo Campoli and his Orchestra and Jack Hylton

---

1. Luxembourg was probably the most famous commercial radio station in Europe. In June 1933 it was broadcasting in English on long wave. Stephen Williams launched the English service and became its first disc jockey. During the Second World War, Luxembourg was invaded and occupied by Germany, who relayed, on medium wave, the infamous Nazi propaganda broadcasts of William Joyce, better known as Lord Haw-Haw. He was captured at Flensburg, Germany, tried and convicted of treason at the Old Bailey and hanged in 1945.

Soon after the Second World War ended the long wave was, once again, used for English language broadcasts. In 1951 the English language programmes moved to medium wave. The station styled itself 'Two-O-Eight: Your Station of the Stars.'

In its most popular years, between the mid-1940s and the mid-1960s, Luxembourg broadcast popular programmes like *The Ovaltineys*, *Opportunity Knocks*, and *Take Your Pick*. Horace Batchelor was heard nightly spelling out his famous infra-draw pools system, located at a town near Bristol spelt K-e-y-n-s-h-a-m.

English language programmes on Radio Luxembourg ended in December 1991, but they continued to be broadcast on the Astra satellite until 30 December 1992 when that service also closed down.

Radio Pictorial magazine published the programmes of commercial radio stations broadcasting from the Continent during the 1930s

and his Orchestra.

By 1939 Radio Normandy had changed its frequency to 274 metres but retained its original power of 20 kilowatts. Transmission times on Sundays were 7.00am - 11.45am; 1.30pm to 7.30pm and from 10.00pm to 1.00am. During weekdays programmes could be heard from 7.00am - 11.30am; 2.00pm - 6.00pm; and 12 midnight to 1.00am. Chief announcer was David Davies.

Amongst the many big names that broadcast on Radio Normandy were Donald Peers, Helen Clare, Donald Watt, Tom Newman, Bob Danvers Walker, George Formby, Peter Yorke, Billy Cotton, Ted Ray, Wilfred Thomas, Vic Oliver, Carroll Levis, Jack Jackson, Roy Plomley, Bebe Daniels, Ben Lyon, Tommy Handley, Joe Loss, The Radio Revellers, Neal Arden, George Melachrino, Cyril Fletcher, Philip Martell and Stephen Williams.

Unfortunately the future of Radio Normandy was very uncertain. On 4 January 1938, the French Government said they intended banning the broadcasting by French radio stations in English.

Strong representations about sponsored programmes had been made by the British Foreign Office to the French Government. The ban incorporated Radio Toulouse, Radio Normandy, Poste Parisien, Radio Lyons and Radio Mediterranean where English transmissions would cease. The Foreign Office said in January 1938 that they were going to renew similar representation to Luxembourg. They did. However, the station closed in September 1939 on the outbreak of the Second World War. Luxembourg outlasted all other English language programmes on commercial stations from the Continent.

On 12 March 1965 some of the men who ran Radio Normandy during the 1930s held a reunion in London and they included Bob Danvers Walker, Roy Plomley and Philip Slessor, all of whom later worked for the BBC. Many readers will presume that Pirate Radio is a description given to British offshore radio ships since 1964. But in fact, it was going strong in 1935.

Mr Hugh Beech who was at Caius College, Cambridge University, wrote an article in *Varsity Weekly* on 16 November 1935, and with his permission we reproduce it.

UP COMMERCIAL RADIO - Pirate Radio Defended

"This is the Radio Normandy programme; wavelength 269.5 metres, frequency 1113 kilocycles, sent to you by the International Broadcasting Company of London."

Those of us who have wireless sets are almost certain to have heard, at some time or other, the above announcement.

Maybe we are getting bored with BBC programmes and aimless knob-twiddling brought us in touch with an IBC station.

It is my task to tell you some more about the organisation which sends out sponsored programmes in the English language from continental stations.

Some ten years ago the International Broadcasting Company came into being to give English listeners a change from the rather stereotyped home product and at the same time to provide advertisers with a new medium.

In the early days Radio Paris, Fécamp, and sometimes Toulouse and Rome were among the chief stations to radiate their programmes. The concerts were often given by the various gramophone record companies.

The state of affairs has changed considerably since then. The record manufacturers, badly hit by the depression, abandoned this form of publicity several years ago, while of the four stations mentioned Fécamp is the only one still transmitting English programmes. Radio Paris was taken over by the French Government towards the end of 1933, while Rome is not now interested in sending out 'entertainment' for British consumption.

At the present moment we are treated to sponsored programmes on the following lines as regards times of transmission:

Sundays

Radio Luxembourg:	8.15am	-	midnight
Radio Normandy:(Fécamp)	8.00am	-	11.00am;
	2.00pm	-	7.00pm
	9.30pm	-	2.00am
Juan-les-Pins : (Nice)	10.30pm	-	1.00am
Poste Parisien :	4.00pm	-	7.00pm;
	10.30pm	-	midnight
Madrid (short wave):	12.00 midnight -		12.30am

Weekdays

Radio Luxembourg:	8.30am	-	8.45am;
	12.00 noon	-	12.30pm
	6.00pm	-	7.30pm
Radio Normandy: (Fécamp)	8.00am	-	10.00am;
	3.30pm	-	6.00pm
	12.00 midnight -		2.00am
Ljubljana : Tuesdays only	9.30pm	-	10.00pm
Poste Parisien:	10.30pm	-	11.00pm

All these come from the IBC, except some of the Luxembourg transmissions, which are controlled by another company, Radio Publicity. There is also a sponsored concert every night between 9.30pm - 10.30pm from Athlone.

During the second week in October there were 100 hours of commercial broadcasting and there is every possibility of this total being repeated throughout the winter. The same time last year there were only about 70 hours per week.

What has brought about this very creditable advance?

There must be something persuading listeners to tune into these programmes, in spite of the advertising, which many are inclined to find repellent.

That many people do listen is evident by the increases in membership of the International Broadcasting Club. This club was formed with the purpose of estimating the number of listeners to IBC programmes in order to show prospective advertisers that their concerts will be sure of a large audience.

At present about a quarter of a million listeners belong to the club. This means that about one set in every two dozen is flying the IBC banner.

Admittedly, the IBC does not cater adequately for the highbrow, but herein lies, I think, the reason for the success of the enterprise!

Radio time has to be apportioned out according to the wants of the listening public. The fact that operatic selections only fill about half an hour a week while dance music and light orchestral music are represented to the extent of four-fifths of the programme time reduces itself merely to an example of the principle of supply and demand. This is, after all, the essential difference between IBC and BBC.

The former has, for obvious reasons, to give the public what it wants, if it is to succeed, while the latter, popularity or otherwise being of less importance, contents itself with trying to give the public what it ought to want. In passing it may be observed that the IBC's choice of orchestral music is far more calculated to raise the tastes of the lowbrow and low class listener than the programmes looked on by such listeners as emblems of musical apathy and uninspiration such as are given by the Studio Orchestras.

The IBC definitely scores over the BBC in that we are not told "The National programme will follow almost at once" and then kept waiting for two minutes. Now we are entertained for periods up to ten minutes by the original and vastly entertaining strains of Bow Bells. Time means money and consequently the programmes follow one another without even an intermission of more than a few seconds.

The human touch is a marked characteristic of the Anglo-French programmes. There is none of that "I will now put on a gramophone record" stuff which so exasperates one. The friendly spirit which the announcers cultivate means a lot to thousands of people, particularly those who lead lonely lives.

The same spirit is very evident in the Children's Corner.

The school mistress idea of talking down to the children is completely abandoned; rather do the 'uncles' try and infuse a real atmosphere of carefree camaraderie into these programmes, whilst Flossie is a most amusing example of the awful child.

The Goodnight Melody and Epilogue with which the IBC programmes conclude are worthy of mention. Ted Lewis' special rendering of the Goodnight Melody is renowned far beyond the ranks of IBC listeners, while the short closing announcement is put over with a simplicity and sincerity which the BBC might well emulate. Light-house keepers and night-watchmen are among those given special goodnight wishes.

There is no lack of well-known artistes in the sponsored programmes. Featured in a recent Sunday's listening were: S.P. Mais, Sir Malcolm Campbell, Geoffrey Gilbey, Anona Winn, Hildegaarde, Harry Hemsley, Claude Hulbert, Nelson Keys, Johnny Green, Debroy Somers, and Carroll Gibbons' bands, Alfredo Campoli's Salon Orchestra, and the Orchestra from the Theatre Royal, Drury Lane, not to mention Mr Christopher Stone, who is now connected with the English programmes at Luxembourg

That article by Hugh Beech made interesting reading. Many points also applied to offshore radio, especially with regards lo presentation and likes in music. Commercial radio in the thirties tended to feature more dance music whereas the pirates of the sixties went for pop music.

In the late 1930's there had been plans to set up a ship offshore and broadcast in English to the United Kingdom. This was abandoned due to a variety of problems. One was the imminence of the Second World War. The second related to equipment which in those days was very bulky. Tapes were not available and all gramophone records were 78s. Equipment was not as portable as it was in the 1960s.

Canadian John Thompson worked on a newspaper in Slough. In 1961 he visualised a radio station and called it GBLN - GB for Great Britain and LN after his wife Ellen. It was to be on 216 metres. The registered address was 365, Beechwood Gardens, Slough. Pre-recorded programmes were made by Keith Martin and Roger Gomez, but they were never broadcast. Thompson felt he was being hounded by the law and he spent an increasing amount of time looking for the right kind of ship. Keith Martin suggested making use of the forts in the Thames Estuary. His advice was not acted upon *this* time and the project faded. He later moved to Folkestone, Kent, where he planned another radio station, this time on one of the forts in the Thames Estuary, with a 10 kilowatt RCA transmitter. It was to be known as Radio King, which did eventually go on air in 1965.

In 1962 Arnold Swanson came on the scene and set about preparing a station to be called GBOK broadcasting on 388 metres. A glossy prospectus, published on 15 January 1962, gave us a little more information:

Radio Station GBOK is a commercial broadcasting station operating in international waters, located at the Nore in the Thames Estuary. The minimum power of GBOK's transmitter is 5000 watts which operates on a frequency of 388 metres, being one of the few clear channel frequencies now being used. For the first time in history, English listeners will be able to listen to well-programmed music and news for a full twenty-four-hours each day. This is made possible by GBOK having a stand-by transmitter while regular servicing is carried out on the main unit.

There are two main features to GBOK's Public Service function, the first being its actual physical structure and location in that GBOK is situated on a lightship and pilot station at the Nore in the Thames Estuary and that this lightship will perform all the functions and duties of a lightship to sea traffic and, secondly, that GBOK will supply a twenty-four-hour-a-day news service to listeners, plus the usual public service feature broadcasts. Religious material announcements will not be charged for and in the main will consist of Thoughts for Today, paragraphs of religious comment from all church denominations and strategically placed throughout each day's programming, rather than a crammed weekly effort on Sunday.

GBOK's policy in respect to programming is based on a time-block scheduling system, wherein other than five-minute news broadcasts, programmes are from two to eleven hours duration. This type of block programming of music and news has proved to be highly successful, both in Canada and the United States for over a period of twenty years. This method allows the station to retain complete control over its programming, rather than subjecting the schedule to a myriad untried programme idea, by persons not qualified in capturing mass-listening audiences.

The Amalgamated Broadcasting Company, located at Notley Abbey, Long Crendon, Bucks, has exclusive rights over all commercial time sales on GBOK. Other than this, the Amalgamated Broadcasting Company has no rights or control over Radio Station GBOK.

Programmes were to include *Wake Up Show*, *The Bandwheel*, *Motorway Special*, and *All-Night Dance Party*. GBOK's radio signal was to be non-directional covering a area of 150-mile radius from the Nore in the Thames Estuary. However, as with GBLN, the project failed as Swanson encountered problems purchasing a suitable ship. Keith Martin did suggest making use of the forts in the Thames Estuary, but again his advice was not taken.

Commercial radio in the offshore form as we came to know it began in 1958 with Radio Mercur broadcasting from international waters off the Danish coast. The station transmitted from the ship *Cheeta*, and later in 1962 from *Lucky Star*. In 1962 armed Danish police with customs men escorted the ship *Lucky Star* into port. The Danish Government had brought a court injunction against the radio station which was closed down.

The name we associate with pirate radio away from the British shores was Mrs Britt Wadner who, in 1961, was a 47-year-old Swedish grandmother who bought a ship and began broadcasting to Sweden in competition with the rather dull programmes that were being heard on land.

The station became Radio Syd. On 1 August 1962 Sweden outlawed the pirate radio ship, but Mrs Wadner and her colleagues remained at their turntables and continued broadcasting. The Swedish Government was not amused to say the least and to practise what they preached jailed Mrs Wadner in 1964. Her Swedish audience organised protest marches demanding her release from jail - they gatecrashed Hinsberg Prison where she was housed and near riots broke out. Ten thousand Radio Syd fans went wild in the streets of Malmo. Mrs Wadner had been jailed for three months, but she was released after completing just four weeks.

Pirate radio had begun as early as 1960 in Holland. A group of conscientious partisans formed a new station, Radio Veronica, which commenced transmissions in Dutch from a lightship off Scheveningen, and beamed its broadcasts to Holland at a power of 2 kilowatts. Within weeks it was reported in the Dutch press that their audience ran into millions.

English transmissions began on 16 February 1961 on 192 metres between 7.00am and 12.00 noon and from 11.00pm to 1.00am. The DJ on the first test transmission was John Michael. On Sunday transmission times were 8.00am to 12.00 noon and from 11.00pm to 1.00am. Disc jockeys were Doug Stanley, Paul Hollingdale and Bob Fletcher. The station operated from the m.v. *Borkum Riff*, Radio Veronica, five miles off the Dutch coast, opposite The Hague, and broadcast under the callsign CNBC (Commercial Neutral Broadcasting Company) based in Dean Street, London. The advertising agency was at Ross Radio Productions, 23 Wimpole Street, London W1. Programmes were pre-recorded onto tape. There were no English disc jockeys on the ship. CNBC transmitted on a power of 1,000 watts. The service only lasted throughout the summer months of 1961.

Radio Nord was founded by Jack Kotschack (who died 9 December 1988) and broadcast from the Panamanian registered ship *Magda Maria*. Transmissions to Sweden began on 8 March 1961. The ship suffered damage in a storm in December 1961 and she put into Sandhamn for repairs.

In London Allan Crawford was on the look-out for backers for Project Atlanta and his search had taken him to both sides of the Channel. He appeared to be making good progress until the news of Mrs Britt Wadner being jailed for illegally broadcasting pop music. His potential backers lost interest and withdrew their offer. Crawford, down but not out, approached the American company which backed Radio Nord which had just ceased operations when the Swedish Government made it illegal for their subjects to serve on the radio ships.

Crawford was determined to launch offshore radio to British listeners. Amongst many other reasons, this would enable him to exploit his own songs from Merit and Southern Music, and the artists he owned on his Carnival, Sabre and Crossbow record labels.

The battle of the British pirates was hotting up. All the time that Allan Crawford dithered, the conscientious Ronan O'Rahilly was making progress fast. He had already found seven millionaire backers including Mr Jocelyn Stevens, editor of *Queen* magazine (who became deputy chairman of the Independent Television Commission in 1991, chairman English Heritage 1992 and was made a CVO in the New Years Honours List, 1993); Mr John Sheffield (chairman of the Norcross group of companies) and Mr Jimmy Ross.

O'Rahilly formed a company which was registered in Ireland and known as Planet Productions, but he had an office at 52 Fetter Lane, London EC4. He made himself a director - the company was worth £350,000. Radio Caroline was owned by Alrana and registered in Liechtenstein.

One up to O'Rahilly. But Crawford wasn't down for long. It was his idea of starting offshore radio in Britain and he had been working on plans for close on four years - and he was determined to win the day. He came fighting back with the news that the Americans had decided to sail Radio Nord to Galveston, Texas. Crawford offered to buy the ship which was built by Deutsche Werft A.G. in Kiel in 1921. She has been known by a number of names over the years. As a three masted schooner she was the *Margarethe* and owned by Simon Ernst. Six years later she passed into the ownership of Heinrich Koppelmann and renamed *Olga* after his wife. At this stage she was converted into a motor vessel by the addition of a four-cylinder engine. For this it was necessary for her to be 'stretched' when a new centre section increased her length from 98ft. to 134ft., and her gross tonnage from 156 tons to 247 tons. During the Second World War the *Olga* was commandeered to serve the German Navy from 9 June 1941 to 18 November 1943 and served in the Baltic. Heinrich Koppelmann died in 1951 and ownership passed to his wife and son. By 1959 the *Olga* was registered to the Superior Shipping Corporation of Nicaragua. Her name was changed to *Bon Jour,* and she became the home of Radio Nord, broadcasting to Sweden from the Baltic Sea.

The Swedish Government were not too impressed with an unauthorised radio station off its shores and put pressure on the Nicaraguan authorities who in turn, in 1961, withdrew the ship's registry. Panama agreed to re-register her providing there was a name change. She became the *Magda Maria* and was registered to International Tug in Panama. The Swedish Government introduced legislation against the pirate ships in 1961 and Radio Nord closed down on 30 June 1962. The *Magda Maria* was taken into port. In 1963 she was acquired by the Radio Atlanta project and renamed *Mi Amigo.* Under the registry of Atlantic Services Ansalt, Liechtenstein, she sailed to Galveston, Texas, for a refit.

The Americans agreed that the aerial should be fitted in Ireland and the ship set sail for Greenore. Whilst she was sailing across the Atlantic Allan Crawford succeeded in finding 38 investors including Major Oliver Smedley, M.C., Miss Kitty Black, a wealthy South African lady, Captain 'Sandy' Horsely, Mr Frank Victor Broadribb, Major Cecil Lomax and Mr R.J. Deterding, a grandson of Sir Henry Deterding. Radio Atlanta issued some 150,000 shares at £1 each. Everything looked rosy for Crawford again.

It should be said here that Kitty Black was the driving force behind Allan Crawford - one disc jockey, Colin Nicol, went as far as saying "she was the unsung heroine of British pirate radio. A very intelligent woman she worked as a publisher, a writer and translator."

Major Oliver Smedley, writing in *The People* on 6 November 1966, said he was approached by Allan Crawford and Kitty Black "as someone who could organise some capital investment in their scheme. I was able to raise the sum of £160,000 among my City friends with relatively little trouble. At the same time I agreed to become chairman of a company we three formed. Project Atlanta."

Allan Crawford continued to be a little ponderous in the way he proceeded, trying to ensure he did not upset either his backers or the British Government. By now he realised that O'Rahilly had a few weeks lead. His ship *Caroline,* the former Baltic ferryboat the *Fredericia*

(763 tons), could well be the first pirate off the shores of Britain. Crawford was led to believe that O'Rahilly would anchor off the west coast of Britain somewhere around the Isle of Man. But Crawford wasn't unduly worried for he had set his mind on the Essex coast for Project Atlanta from where he would beam his programmes into the thickly populated London area.

He who plays the pirate king first will undoubtedly find the treasure chest. Ronan O'Rahilly appeared to have all the key points marked out on the Treasure Island map. History, too, was on his side. His grandfather was one of the leaders of the Easter uprising in Dublin and was shot by the English when storming a British machine-gun post outside the Post Office in Dublin in 1916. Son of Aodogan O'Rahilly, Ronan was right for the "pirate part."

Allan Crawford on the surface portrayed a much milder image. In 1964 he was 42 years of age whereas as O'Rahilly was only 24.

Crawford learned that the information relating to the anchorage point for Radio Caroline was wrong. Not only had he been 'pipped at the post,' but it now seemed certain that O'Rahilly was after Crawford's audience as well.

In March 1964 Caroline sailed and anchored in international waters 3½ miles off Harwich, on the Essex coast. En route she had aroused interest from the Royal Navy and shore radio stations who requested information from Caroline. Captain Conrad Baeker simply replied "Caroline heading south. Destination - Spain!"

The authorities became suspicious when Caroline passed Plymouth going east. A Royal Navy destroyer went alongside for a while. The captain and crew had taken professional advice as to the exact anchorage. They were well aware of the necessity for not causing any danger to shipping along the busy east coast routes.

Harwich was close by. It was a helpful and convenient port with full customs facilities and within reasonable reach of London where Radio Caroline was to have its office headquarters.

Caroline arrived on Good Friday 1964, and started a series of test transmissions in the evening. John Junkin was the first pirate voice over the Caroline airwaves on tape. Many people thought Simon Dee was the first broadcaster. This was not the case. Simon did, however, make the first 'live' announcement.

Ronan O'Rahilly, remembering that it was Easter time when his grandfather made his name, followed on in true family tradition. He related "It would appear that I was taking an Easter revenge against English authority. I guess I was!"

The slim, grey-haired Irishman was to go down in history as making the most important step forward in British radio for over forty years - he broke the BBC monopoly!

Regular programmes began at noon the following day when listeners to Radio Caroline heard the record *Round Midnight* played by Jimmy McGriff at the organ - this later became the Caroline "Anthem" which was also played at closedown each evening following the programme *Sunset Serenade*. The record was followed by the Caroline Bell and an announcement by Simon Dee which said "This is Radio Caroline on 199, your all-day music station. We are on the air every day from six in the morning till six at night. The time right now is one minute past twelve and that means it's time for Christopher Moore." He began his programme by saying:

Hello and a Happy Easter to all of you. This is Christopher Moore with the first record programme on Radio Caroline. The first record is by the Rolling Stones and I'd like to play it for all the people who worked to put the station on the air and particularly for Ronan.

Then followed the very first record on Radio Caroline - *Not Fade Away* by the Rolling Stones. A number of newspapers reported *Can't Buy Me Love* by the Beatles was the first record. Not so!

On Easter Sunday an armada of ships surrounded the first lady of British offshore radio which was flying the Jolly Roger flag. The Caroline ship was commanded by Captain George Mackay, a 50-year-old Lancastrian from Chorlton-cum-Hardy; there were yachts, motor boats, catamarans, helicopters and planes. Almost 100 pressmen came out to the radio ship on special launches. Pirate radio had hit Britain and the national press gave it wide acclaim.

The programme side of Radio Caroline was controlled by 23-year-old Christopher Moore. Bom in Washington DC, in 1941, he was of Irish American extraction. He arrived in the United Kingdom at the age of eight and was educated in England. After a time in the Merchant Navy, which he joined at 18. he returned to England and initially worked for an advertising agency, and later entered the music business. As programme director he was ably supported by disc jockeys and production staff including Gerry Duncan, Doug Kerr and Simon Dee. Carl and Jenny Conway recorded their music programmes for the ship on tape in London.

Simon Dee, relating that the Caroline boys had their first visit from the tender on that Wednesday after Easter, says "We received sacks of mail. In fact I actually counted nine huge sacks being hoisted onto the ship and we had only been broadcasting regular programmes for a period of four days."

At the Caroline offices in London more than 20,000 letters were received during the first ten days on the air.

A Gallup poll took place and it was learned that nearly seven million regular listeners tuned into Radio Caroline on 199 metres in just three weeks. And this survey did not include persons under the age of 17 years. Caroline had a prospective listening audience of some 19 million people. The Conservative Government didn't take too kindly to Radio Caroline coming on the air, and within a few days questions were asked in the House of Commons. The 7 April 1964 was the first day the pirates came under fire ... and it wasn't the last!

Mr Roy Mason, Labour MP for Barnsley, asked the Postmaster-General if he would make a statement on the activities and broadcasts of the radio station Caroline; and furthermore was the Postmaster-General aware of the inherent dangers of allowing such a station to continue, and whether he would either jam all broadcasts or prepare legislation to make pirate radio stations illegal off the coastline?

The Right Honourable Reginald Bevins as Postmaster-General replied to the effect that he was quite aware that a station calling itself 'Caroline' had been broadcasting programmes of music during the daytime from a ship beyond territorial waters off Harwich. Mr Bevins stated that he recognised the dangers of the situation, and he went on to say that he was relying on British advertisers not to use this medium to exploit their products.

Answering Mr Paul Williams, Conservative MP for Sunderland South, as to whether 'Caroline' interfered with any other station, Mr Bevins said it did. The station was causing interference with a Belgian station which communicated with ships at sea, and also with British maritime services.

Further discussions took place in the Commons on 14 April. Lieutenant-Colonel Marcus Lipton, Labour MP for Brixton, asked the Postmaster-General what action he had taken to dissuade advertisers from using Radio Caroline? Mr Bevins replied:

> On three occasions during the past two years I have invited the attention of the principal advertising associations to report on plans to establish broadcasting stations on ships - not 'Caroline' specifically - outside territorial waters and I have sought their co-operation in dissuading their members from supporting such ventures. The answers they have given me are encouraging.[2]

Mr Brian Harrison, Conservative MP for Maldon, asked Mr Bevins to consider the British public and asked him to do nothing to deprive the people of East Anglia of the first decent radio programme they have had for a long time. Mr Bevins added that the Government was still examining the possibility of legislation and also making a technical examination of the possibilities of jamming.

Captain John Litchfield RN, MP for Chelsea, continued the debate by stating that he

---

2.   Hansard House of *Commons Parliamentary Debates*, 14 April 1964

understood that Radio Caroline had no flag of registration, and asked the Postmaster-General what was the position regarding liability for seizure or other deterrent action on the high seas.

Mr Bevins said that he understood that the Panamanian Government had withdrawn the ship's registration which created a number of practical difficulties.

Mr Lipton said that he was very unsatisfied with the Postmaster-General's reply and would raise the matter on the adjournment at the earliest possible opportunity.

The final mention of Radio Caroline in the House of Commons for the month of April 1964 came on the 16th when under 'Written Answers' Mr Bevins told Mr Roy Mason that he had no further comment to add to what he had said on 7 April but went on to say that he would take whatever action he could against the permanent establishment of pirate radio stations.[3] Broadcasting on the high seas was specifically forbidden by the International Radio Regulations to which nearly all countries of the world subscribed. Mr Bevins said that an agreement on the subject was being considered by the Council of Europe.

Six weeks after Radio Caroline had commenced transmissions, Radio Atlanta sailed in and anchored some fourteen miles from Caroline on 27 April 1964. She had encountered some trouble on her journey from Greenore when one of the aerial mast stays came adrift and the *Mi Amigo* put into dock in Falmouth, Cornwall.

This was an interesting situation for it was obvious to the Port Authorities that she was a pirate ship full of broadcasting equipment. By rights the captain of the *Mi Amigo*, Polishman, Mark Oldokowski, was perfectly in his right to ask for a rigger as the ship was not broadcasting from within the three mile limit.

Permission for an aerial rigger was granted, the job completed, and once again the ship set sail on the high seas bound for a location off the Essex coast.

Radio Atlanta went on the air with test transmissions on 9 May on 1520 kHz, switching on when Radio Caroline closed down for the night at 6.00pm. Regular broadcasts commenced on 12 May when the frequency was changed to 1493 kHz. Test transmissions were conducted by Bob Scott and Johnny Jackson, two Texans with a wide experience of commercial radio in the States but whose stay on board the *Mi Amigo* was about a month.

The first scheduled programme over the Atlanta airwaves was the *Breakfast Show* with Australian Colin Nicol who later joined Radio England.

The disc jockeys for Radio Atlanta during its first week of transmission were Colin Nicol, Richard Harris (who acted as general manager), Clive Burrell, Mike Raven, Neil Spence and Tony Withers. Ken Evans was programme manager.

Keith Martin had taken an interest in offshore radio and had visited Radio Mercur in Denmark. "They informed me that Radio Syd would begin broadcasting off Stokholm in 1961. Little did I realise that a few years later I would be broadcasting from that very ship when she became Radio Caroline South. I made myself known to Allan Crawford during the winter of 1963 on the back of knowing the people at CNBC. He took me into his confidence because of my background and enthusiasm for radio. I later worked for Project Atlanta."

The week prior to Atlanta broadcasting regular programmes Ken Evans and Tony Withers went around the city of London and collected tape greetings from many stars including Alma Cogan, Harry Secombe, Frank Ifield, Cliff Richard, The Shadows, Victor Silvester, Edmundo Ros, Peter Finch and Rolf Harris. All these were transmitted on opening day.

Ken Evans adds "We did not have too many refusals, but one does spring to mind. That was when Tony and I went along to the BBC Playhouse where we wished to obtain a recording with Tommy Steele. Both Tommy and his manager, Ian Bevin, had reluctantly to say no to recording a greetings message. It would have put Tommy in a rather embarrassing situation. However, when Atlanta became more well known they both co-operated to the full."

---

3.   Hansard House of *Commons Parliamentary Debates*, 16 April 1964

Radio Atlanta programmes were taped in the studios of Project Atlanta at 47 Dean Street, London W1. It was a freezing building before the studios became operational and all hands, disc jockeys included, helped to build the studios ... laying lino, building shelves and installing equipment. When Project Atlanta was looking over the offices for possible lease, the main room, which later became the studio, was full of tin cans and rubbish. Weeks had to be spent clearing up and preparing the studio for transmission.

During these days Atlanta had about 150 long playing records and about 500 singles. Their music format was for a family type of programme consisting of pop and ballads.

Ken Evans (who later joined BBC Radio 2) was responsible for scheduling all the discs and running the record library. He was assisted by Marion Cochrane and later Maureen Blackburn. There were two panel operators, Terry Saunders and Dermot Hoy, who later became DJ Bryan Vaughan.

Others who worked for Project Atlanta included Michael Chetham-Strode, Erica Crone, Eugene Gomeche, Toni Gomeche, George Harris, Richard Harris, Ted King, Keith Martin, Ross Mackenzie, Leslie Parrish, Arthur Pelteret, Alan Phillips, John Ridley, Peter Shaylor, R. St. Abbs and Jillian Walsh.

Disc jockey Colin Nicol recalls:

I became involved with the Atlanta project as early as November 1963, four months before Caroline went on the air. At that time nobody had heard of commercial radio, other than Luxembourg. Together with Allan Crawford and Ken Evans, I was in the front rank of people who were 'in the know.' We were working in a small studio at the top of a building in Soho which was the Merit Music office. Radio Atlanta was going to be styled on Radio Veronica, off Holland, which in itself was based on Radio Syd off the Swedish coast. It was intended that Atlanta would broadcast all taped programmes and we devised a system so that when it came out on the air it would sound fresh, as if it had been done that day. My job was to record the breakfast shift, which was a matter of sitting and panelling in a little booth in the corner of a large room full of records, with Ken basically lining up records and passing them through. They would come through to the desk, we would play them and then recycle them. Later on we had someone to panel for us because the equipment was so clumsy and crude. We would record onto reel-to-reel tape at 7½ inches per second. The tapes would be stacked up and carefully numbered and named so that when they went out on the air they would be in the right sequence. The ship itself was crucial to the whole operation. There were long delays with it being refitted in America, so I took a short holiday in Spain. On return, early in 1964, new faces were on the scene.

A gentleman I had never heard of - none of the others had heard of him either - a Mr Ronan O'Rahilly was very much to the forefront. Initially he had been brought in as a probable investor, but he decided he could do it better himself, I think quite rightly, so he obtained a former North Sea ferry, the *Fredericia*, and started to fit her out in Greenore, Ireland.

Suddenly we were no longer working together as a group. There were two ships and the two sides had split apart. One of the ships had to come off second best, and that was to be the *Mi Amigo*. It nearly went aground on a sandbank off Greenore in a Force 11 storm. Caroline, in the meantime was fitted out. She set sail and went very close to the location that Radio Atlanta was planning to occupy near Clacton-on-Sea, Essex. They did not quite find the right location, but they did use the radio frequency that was intended for Atlanta. That was one of the major reasons it was Caroline and not Atlanta which started to broadcast first, at Eastertime 1964.

After the first week of transmission listeners sent in records and offered many of their own private and personal record collections for the new station.

As well as being geographically closely situated Radio Atlanta and Radio Caroline were next to each other on the radio dial.

Caroline broadcast on 199 metres on the medium wave band whereas Radio Atlanta was heard on 201 metres. It had to be said that the figure '199' was used to rhyme with 'Caroline.' If fact the station broadcast closer to 194 metres. The battle of the airwaves was on! The east coast listeners had never had it so good. But whilst the Top 50 records were being churned out minute by minute, hour by hour, day by day, the British Government was still planning to rid the shores of pirates. The House of Commons had a fairly busy month discussing the problem.

Mr Roy Mason still hammered away asking the Postmaster-General when he intended introducing legislation. Mr Ray Mawby, sitting in for Mr Bevins said, on 5 May:[4]

> "New legislation which would effectively deprive pirate broadcasters of material support is the most suitable action to take and the Postmaster-General was considering it."

Six days later Mr Mason asked the Postmaster-General to what extent the BBC sound broadcasts had been subject to interference during the test transmission period of Radio Caroline and since its subsequently established broadcasting hours.

Mr Bevins said[5] "I understand that, except for some slight interference when Radio Caroline began broadcasting, transmissions from this station have not caused interference to reception of the BBC services."

Mr Mason asked the Postmaster-General under which national flags Radio Caroline and Radio Atlanta were operating and what communications he had had with the Governments of the nations concerned?

The Postmaster-General replied "Radio Caroline was registered in Panama but the Panamanian Government cancelled the registration when they were informed that the ship had been used for broadcasting. I understand that the other ship is registered in Panama also. If so, and if she similarly contravenes international and Panamanian Law, I have no doubt that her registration also will be cancelled."

Mr Mason then asked the Postmaster-General if he would list the occasions when transmissions from pirate ships had interfered with signals sent from coastguards and shore-based stations to ships at sea, what representations he had received regarding the type of interference, and if he would make a statement.

"Transmissions from Radio Caroline," the Postmaster-General went on, "caused interference to British and Belgian maritime services during the first few days she was broadcasting. Interference to maritime services since then has been negligible. Serious interference to maritime radio could recur at any time if the powerful transmitting equipment on the ship is not properly maintained." Mr Bevins said that he had received complaints from the Belgian Government that Radio Caroline was interfering with reception to the Belgian Broadcasting Service from Brussels on 198½ metres.

In the House of Commons the following day Captain H.B. Kerby, Conservative MP for West Sussex asked Mr Bevins what representations he had received drawing attention to the popularity of Radio Caroline's transmissions in the South East of England, especially amongst younger persons, and furthermore if he would give an assurance that these views would be taken into account before the Postmaster-General took further action to restrict this example of free enterprise in broadcasting. Mr Bevins promised he would.

On 15 May Mr Bevins said in answer to a question put by Roy Mason that jamming Radio Caroline's transmissions would be technically possible, but at the same time would raise complicated issues relating to the use of the radio frequency spectrum.

Roy Mason further pressed the Postmaster-General as to what information had been forwarded to him by the Secretary of the International Telecommunications Union advising

---

4. Hansard House of *Commons Parliamentary Debates*. 5 May 1964
5. Hansard House of *Commons Parliamentary Debates*. 12 May 1964

him what action has been taken by members of the union against offshore pirate radio stations.
Mr Bevins then gave the following summary:[6]

DENMARK, SWEDEN and FINLAND
Copy of Decree (1961) forbidding ships of all nationalities to receive or carry in Danish water apparatus intended for broadcasting. Notice (1961) that Denmark's Radio Stations have ceased to exchange radio correspondence with offending ships.

NORWAY
Radio stations forbidden (1961) to exchange radio correspondence with offending ships.

FRANCE
Copy of decree (1961) regulating transmissions in French territorial waters. Notice (1962) that radio stations forbidden to exchange correspondence with ships broadcasting at sea.

BRAZIL
Notice (1961) that action had been taken to prevent broadcasting from ships or aircraft outside the limits of national territories.

DENMARK, FINLAND, SWEDEN and NORWAY
Copy of laws (1962) prohibiting broadcasting on the high seas and penalising financial or technical support for such activities, including ordering transmitters via the offending stations or preparing programmes for them.

BELGIUM
Copy of law (1962) forbidding operation of broadcasting stations on ships or aircraft inside or outside Belgian waters and penalising co-operation in the supply of apparatus or the execution or financing of programmes for such stations.

INDIA
Notice (1963) that the prohibition in the international radio regulations on broadcasting from ships had been specially brought to the notice of Indian ship owners.

PANAMA
Copy of Decree (1962) forbidding operation of broadcasting stations on ships or aircraft flying the Panamanian flag and outside Panamanian waters.

General information had also been circulated from Argentina, Australia, Congo, Hungary, Iran, Morocco, New Zealand, Vietnam and Yugoslavia to the effect that none of these countries would permit broadcasting from its own ships.

There was no other business concerning the pirates during May 1964 in the House of Commons. Meanwhile back in the North Sea there was some action on 6 May when a Government Customs launch drew alongside. A young officer requested permission to board Radio Caroline. "Refused" shouted the Dutch Merchant Navy captain Conrad Baeker. "We are in international waters." After a large amount of bickering and bargaining the Captain said that one of the Customs officers could come on board, but instead he and his colleagues returned to Harwich.

Simon Dee dramatically described the incident over the air down to the last detail, so literally the entire south east of England were informed about this drama. Listeners heard:

---

6.   Hansard House of *Commons Parliamentary Debates*, 15 April 1964

At 12.20pm today, Wednesday 6th May, Her Majesty's ship *Venturous* flying the blue ensign drew close to Caroline's port side. Permission was asked for them to board and see our bonded stores. The captain of the Caroline stated that this was against the law as we were in international waters, but would allow one man to come across in a lifeboat. This offer was not accepted. At 12.33pm the *Venturous* drew off and after some moments, turned and steamed away. We shall, of course, interrupt any scheduled programmes at any time to bring you news as and when it happens. But right now everything's all right.

Simon Dee's announcement was followed by the record *Everything's All Right*, by the Mojos.

On 12 May Radio Caroline was featured in the Granada Television programme *The World in Action*.

The month of June was a busy one in the House of Commons with the Government still doing its best to bring in legislation. But the pirates came through with flying colours. On 2 June the Postmaster-General, Mr Bevins, made a statement about the radio ships.[7]

Broadcasting frequencies are agreed by the International Telecommunications Union. Pirate radio ships select their own frequencies. This is an infringement of international agreements. If no action is taken against the pirates, such transmissions from ships outside territorial waters may increase, with the result that radio communications with ships and aeroplanes would be interfered with and human life endangered. Also, such transmissions could well lead to massive interference with the reception of existing radio programmes both in Britain and Europe. As it is, protests of interference have already been received from Belgium and France.

The Council of Europe has been studying this problem and a draft convention is now in an advanced stage of preparation. What is required to deal with the problem is concerted action. The Government, therefore, propose to await the conclusion of this convention and then consider legislating on lines proposed by the Convention.

The Government cannot accept the establishment of pirate radio ships as a reason for making precipitate decisions on local sound broadcasting in this country. To legislate for a national service of local sound broadcasting and to establish the necessary machinery for supervision during the remaining months of this Parliament is clearly not practical. In the next Parliament the Government will undertake the review of the situation foreshadowed in the White Paper on broadcasting published in 1962 (Cmnd 1893).

After this statement by the Postmaster-General in May 1964, Mr Ian Gilmour, Conservative MP for Norfolk Central, asked Mr Bevins if he was aware that a survey had been taken of the number of people who listened to Radio Caroline. He said that the survey showed that 14 per cent of the people interviewed would approve of Government action against the pirates, but 74 per cent would not.

Mr Bevins said in reply that he didn't know who took the poll, but surely the thing that a poll of that sort illustrated was undoubtedly the fairly widespread demand, not only in East Anglia, but in other parts of the country, for more music on sound radio.

On 24 June 1964 Jeremy Thorpe, Liberal Member for Devon North, made a speech to the House of Commons. Amongst other things he said:

One might admire their legal ingenuity, their capacity to make tax free profits and, not least, their capacity to provide this sort of programme that appears to fill a need. But I suggest there are four main objections to pirate radio stations. First is that 123 nations, of which we are one, have decided to share out radio frequencies on a rational basis rather than leave congested wavelengths to jamming and confusion. It is clear that the

---

7.   Hansard House of *Commons Parliamentary Debates*, 2 June 1964

pirates care nothing for this. The second reason is that there is no legal recourse in connection with the contents of broadcasting by pirate radio transmitters. The content may be innocuous now, but it could just as easily be defamatory, seditious, obscene or undesirable in some other way without any protection, for the public or for this House.

The third objection is that, unlike the BBC, the ITV Companies, Radio Luxembourg and Radio Manx, these stations are exploiting the products of record companies without any recompense. This is doubly unfortunate since these recording companies recognise the interests of the musical profession and the performers in making their livelihood in these ways. I do not believe any "ex gratia" payments by these pirate radio stations are any substitute for payments as of right.

The fourth objection to the stations is that by broadcasting outside the jurisdiction, they are not liable to tax on their profits and I believe that it is not unreasonable to expect that when money is made out of this country something should be paid back in return. If any proof is needed of the unsatisfactory state of existing legislation, I would point out that every person who listens to an unauthorised broadcast commits a criminal offence, for which he can be fined £10, and £50 for every subsequent offence. In fact the Postmaster-General has been condoning a series of criminal breaches of law by not withdrawing the licences of offenders.

Radio Caroline has already had its registration withdrawn by Panama. It is not now registered in any country and is accorded no protection from visit or seizure by a warship of any country. It is, in certain circumstances, liable to seizure, and in certain other circumstances individuals broadcasting from it are liable to arrest, under the Wireless Telegraphy Act.

Radio Atlanta is in a somewhat stronger position because the Postmaster-General has not yet asked the Panamanian Government to withdraw its recognition on the ground of the breach of the International Telecommunications Union which is being committed by that Panamanian-registered ship.

In fact the only executive act so far adopted by the Postmaster-General is to divert a helicopter on a training flight to collect a food-poisoned disc jockey who was suffering the ill effects of eating tinned salmon squatting on Crown property and broadcasting therefrom.

On 2 July Allan Crawford, managing director of Radio Atlanta, and Ronan O'Rahilly, managing director of Radio Caroline, announced that they were merging operations and would broadcast in future under the one call sign, 'Caroline,' but from two different positions - off the coast of Essex and the Isle of Man.

M.V. *Caroline* was to sail to the Isle of Man on 3 July and anchor at a position five miles off Ramsey. It would continue to broadcast Radio Caroline programmes on the way to its new destination and would remain on 199 metres on the medium wave band.

M.V. *Mi Amigo* (Radio Atlanta) would remain in its present position off the Essex coast but would broadcast to the Greater London area and south east England under the Radio Caroline call sign also on 199 metres. Radio Atlanta closed down on 2 July at 8.00pm. Crawford and O'Rahilly said that the decision to merge was taken in view of the enormous interest from the public and advertisers in parts of England outside the broadcasting area. The new network would cover the most populous areas of Britain.

Caroline North would be heard in the North, the Midlands, Ireland, Scotland and Wales. Caroline South would be heard not only in south east England but also Holland, France, Belgium, Norway, Sweden and Finland.

The "Caroline-Atlanta" merger represented a floating investment of £500,000. Disc jockey Colin Nicol describing his view on the new merger says:

The first we knew of the merger was when the tender drew alongside and Simon Dee and Doug Kerr said they were coming on board to take over. There had been an amalgamation. They had a note in Dutch from their Captain authorising the takeover using the name "Caroline."

I was in charge at the time, and I hadn't received any information and my first thought was that it was a trick to take over Atlanta.

Colin Nicol let Dee and Kerr on board, at the same time telling one of the English engineers to lock the studio and transmitter room, and see that all external equipment was locked away.

Simon Dee sent a telegram (via the tender) to Ronan O'Rahilly in London requesting him to hold up the moving of Radio Caroline to its new northern location until the matter had been clarified.

Next day Colin Nicol, Simon Dee and Doug Kerr disembarked from the *Mi Amigo* and were met at Brightlingsea wharf by Ken Evans, Marion Cochrane. Keith Martin, Tony Withers and Bryan Vaughan.

Keith Martin says:

The main reason Radios Atlanta and Caroline amalgamated was the lack of advertising for both ships. It made business sense not to compete for the limited amount of advertising that was at that time available. The reason why the original Radio Caroline, *Fredericia*, sailed to the north was because she had a slightly weaker signal than the *Mi Amigo*, which enjoyed a much better signal into London. One has to remember that Radio Caroline was born out of Allan Crawford's enthusiasm for the pirate radio project. Ronan O'Rahilly stole the thunder of Allan Crawford because he was more of the traditional pirate, yet a modern day buccaneer.

Ronan O'Rahilly and Allan Crawford after the merger of Caroline and Atlanta

Due to the merger a number of disc jockeys resigned including Richard Harris, Clive Burrell, Mike Raven and Neil Spence. The new team of disc jockeys for Caroline South comprised Simon Dee, Keith Martin, Tony Withers, Peter Du Crow and Bryan Vaughan.

It was only a matter of hours before Caroline North set sail. On 6 July the north of England received its first blast of pirate broadcasts from Radio Caroline - radio sets were picking up transmissions on 199 metres.

The Manx Government officials were silent about the threat to their hopes of launching the island's proposed independent radio station.

The m.v. *Caroline,* under the command of Captain Hangerfelt, sailed into Ramsey Bay shortly before 3.00pm and her programmes were heard from early morning all over the north of England, North Wales, Scotland and Ireland. She had broadcast non-stop pop music since leaving her original anchorage off Harwich, Essex, on the Saturday morning. DJs on board were Tom Lodge, Jerry Leighton and Alan Turner.

When the ship approached the Manx coast a message was broadcast saying that she had come not to disturb the peace but to make friends. When Caroline neared Douglas, car owners were asked to switch on their headlights seawards in welcome. The sky was a glare of light.

Both Radio Caroline North and South adopted the song *Caroline* by the Fortunes as their theme tune. It remained as the stations' theme through to their final chapter in 1990.

Founder member Rod Allen says "The song became a turntable hit, but it never made the charts, although it has sold very well over the years. It has also been played regularly on the radio over the last 25 years and, although we never made any money out of it, radio stations have always mentioned the Fortunes. And thirty years later we are still in business, performing around the world. Sadly we were never invited out to visit Radio Caroline."

In the early days of Caroline the advertising rates ranged from £50 to £110 a minute. One of the earliest advertisers was the Duke of Bedford who used a special May Day spot urging the public to visit Woburn Abbey. He reported that instead of 4,000 people turning up the next day he had 4,500 even though it was pouring with rain. Advertising cost him almost £2 a second and he said that reception of Caroline had been picked up as far away as Lagos, but this was perhaps just a little too far for people to travel to Woburn. However, the Duke proved to be a very satisfied customer.

Comparing the advertising rates of Caroline with Radio Luxembourg, they were much cheaper. Luxembourg had an average of 6 million adults in England each evening and charged £90 - £193 for a 60 second spot before midnight.

It was at this time that Radio Caroline commenced advertising stick-on labels for cars, motor cycles and scooters with the message "I Love Caroline on 199". Prior to the amalgamation Atlanta had a similar car sticker which read "I Prefer Atlanta on 201."

Another Radio Atlanta appeared on the air in 1966 but this time it was run by two Birmingham schoolboys on land. Clive Price, aged 17 of Selly Oak and a colleague were branded by Birmingham magistrates as 'pirates' and ordered to 'Walk the Plank' to the tune of £25. They appeared in court on 10 October 1966 and were reported as transmitting a two hour pop show every Sunday morning from a 10 watt transmitter which was purchased for £10. Post Office officials tracked down the equipment with detector vans and silenced Radio Atlanta. Clive said that his ambition was to be a disc jockey on Radio Caroline!

In the House of Commons the Assistant Postmaster-General, Mr Ray Mawby, said on 14 July 1964 that a new pirate station had been transmitting from a disused fort in the Thames Estuary since 28 May and there had been reports of attempts to establish stations off the Lancashire coast, the Yorkshire coast, and another fort in the Thames Estuary.

Three days later Mr Mathews, Secretary of State for Foreign Affairs, said in reply to Mr Thorpe's question asking what representations he had made to the Panamanian Government in connection with the registration of Radio Atlanta, that he did not know of any ship by that name. Mr Mathews said that he knew of a Radio Atlanta broadcasting from a Panamanian registered ship *Mi Amigo.*

He went on "It is usual for alleged breaches of the International Telecommunications Convention or of the Regulations made, to be taken up, in the first instance, by one telecommunications authority direct with the competent authority in the other country. In the case of the *Mi Amigo* the GPO reported to the competent Panamanian authority on the 13 May and again on 3 July saying that the ship had been broadcasting since 9 May from a position just outside the United Kingdom territorial waters, in contravention of the International Radio Regulations. No reply had yet been received from the Panamanian

Authorities."

Mr Mathews said that on 31 March the GPO had notified the Director General of Telecommunications and Radio in Panama saying that a ship called *Caroline* using a Panamanian call sign had been broadcasting daily to the United Kingdom since 28 March. On the 3 April the Panamanian authorities cancelled their registration of the *Caroline*.

James Green, writing in the *Evening News* on 29 May 1964, was complimentary towards the pirates. He said "The BBC was dying. The arrival of the pirates on the air is exactly what the BBC planners needed to jerk them into life and action."

Green went on to say he thought that the BBC's future radio side should be that the Light Programme would become all music, and that the Third and Home would be amalgamated to handle talks, plays and serious programmes.

Just one year and two months after James Green wrote that article the BBC announced that they were planning to sink the pirates by capturing the bulk of their audiences when the Light Programme opened from 5.30am in August 1965. The BBC thought they had really got the message as the pirates didn't come on the air until 6.00am. They hoped to attract the whole of the early morning audience and furthermore keep it. The latest radio survey had shown that early morning, when people are getting ready for work, was the most popular time for radio. Alas, the BBC did not win that round, for the pirates retaliated by opening at 5.30am and in certain cases commenced twenty-four hour broadcasting. But we are jumping ahead a little too far.

On 16 July 1964, Radio Caroline received recognition from the police when they broadcast an advertisement at peak listening time for the Police National Athletic Championships at Southend-on-Sea.

The four 15-seconds adverts were placed by Sgt. Wickenden of Southend police. He was the secretary of the Southend-on-Sea Constabulary Recreation Club. This was Radio Caroline's first advertisement from a public body.

On 24 August Radio Caroline broadcast a police message - until then the monopoly of the BBC.

The disc jockey asked Mr Douglas Stedman of Heath Road, East Bergholt, Suffolk, to ring the police because his father Mr Andrew Stedman, 64, was dangerously ill in a hospital at Lowestoft after a road accident. The message on the air did not tell Mr Stedman that his mother, Mrs Beatrice Stedman, 63 was killed in the accident, and that his aunt Hilda, 65, was seriously ill.

Douglas Stedman was touring southern England on a motor scooter, YRT 134, with his son. A police spokesman said that "The message was sent out through Caroline because we believe Mr Stedman listens to that station."

But the SOS nearly didn't go out... a Post Office radio station refused to send the message out to the ship. The message was finally written out and given to a fisherman who ferried it out and threw the paper aboard.

The House of Commons was very silent, probably due to its summer recess, and the word 'pirate' was not heard from 17 July until 10 November when there had been a change of Government from Conservative to Labour and, hence, a change of Postmaster-General. In a written answer to Mr Kenneth Lewis, Conservative MP for Rutland and Stamford, the new Postmaster-General, Mr Anthony Wedgwood Benn said he was thinking of introducing legislation.

Meanwhile, up in the north of England, Blackpool GPO engineers, looking for a compère for their ball took on Tom Lodge who was then a disc jockey on Radio Caroline North to organise the evening's entertainment.

Manx Radio, Britain's first land-based commercial radio station, went on air for the first time on 8 June 1964 for five minutes and then closed down because of a last minute refusal by the Postmaster-General to grant it a licence.

Listeners who were tuned to Manx Radio on 91.2 megahertz VHF heard announcer

David Davis say - "We shall not be broadcasting programmes, as no licence has been received from the Postmaster-General for broadcasting on the medium wave."

Later, in July, Manx Radio protested to the Postmaster-General and also the Prime Minister about Radio Caroline stealing their listeners, thus "precluding all possibility of obtaining revenue for operation of existing VHF local broadcasting station."

Radio Caroline North

Manx Radio broadcast at this period from 8.00am - 10.00am and from 12.00 noon to 2.00pm. The programmes consisted of recorded music and local news flashes, weather forecasts and information for holiday makers.

Radio Caroline was on the air 18 out of 24 hours playing mainly pop music, but also news broadcasts, weather forecasts and adverts for the Isle of Man.

Manx Radio station cost £20,000 to build and equip and was situated just two miles out of Douglas. The Postmaster-General told Manx Radio in answer to their protest that he was taking no immediate action against Radio Caroline.

In August 1965 Radio Caroline received a pat on the back from the Isle of Man tourist board. Their northern ship had been giving the Isle of Man free publicity for several months, and the tourist board expressed their wish that Caroline could be brought ashore to carry on the good work. Unfortunately, the people in Whitehall did not have the same outlook.

Five Manx MPs suggested a marriage between Radio Caroline North and Manx Radio. They praised both Caroline and Manx Radio for the part they both played in the tourist drive. The annual report which was published on 24th August went on to say:

How desirable it would be if events made It possible for Manx Radio to make an honest woman out of Caroline and bring her ashore so that a land-based commercial radio station operating on high power was available to further the varied interests of the island.

Manx Radio, run by Mr Richard Meyer, formerly with IBC, could only be picked up on the island.

On 27 July 1964, disc jockey Bryan Vaughan was taken ill with suspected food poisoning and what could have turned out to be a straightforward transfer from ship to shore via the tender turned out to be a controversial, widely publicised 'mutiny'.

The Dutch captain of the *Mi Amigo* accused Simon Dee, then chief disc jockey of mutiny, and refused to have him back on board. At first the captain refused permission for Bryan to be taken off the ship, so Simon interrupted his programme and broadcast an SOS message appealing to listeners to get a boat out to Radio Caroline as soon as possible. Police and lifeguards were flooded with calls and the Walton and Frinton lifeboat was launched. Simon relates:

> A terrific argument arose when the lifeboat drew alongside. The captain of the *Mi Amigo* was furious and immediately accused me of mutiny. I went back to the studio and put on an LP - I think it was Barbra Streisand, and then went down to Bryan's cabin. He looked all horrible and green. I thought at first he had acute appendicitis.The Captain said 'Don't fuss! There's nothing wrong.' But how could he be so sure? I suggested he be sent to hospital. I appreciated that he was the captain of the ship but I was chief disc jockey and in charge of all the radio personnel. The captain replied saying that 'I was only a disc jockey and nobody goes off the ship unless I say so.'

Simon Dee then warned the captain that if Bryan should die, he was still the captain of the ship. Simon went on: "I spoke to Bryan and asked him if he wished us to send him to hospital and he said 'Yes.' I then went back to the microphone. Listeners throughout southern England then heard: "One of our chaps isn't feeling too good. I wonder if there's anyone listening who would be good enough to come out and pick him up?"

Bryan Vaughan was eventually taken off the *Mi Amigo* aboard the Walton and Frinton lifeboat and detained in Clacton Hospital for two weeks, apparently none the worse for wear. He later returned to Radio Caroline.

As for Simon Dee? He was ordered off the ship in disgrace and went back to Caroline House in London where he was used for production work. He eventually moved onto the BBC.

On 6 August 1964 Radio Albatross was reported to be another pirate radio station to start operating off the coast of eastern England by October. A 30-year-old television engineer, Robert Tidswell, of Gosberton near Spalding, Lincolnshire, announced his plans to broadcast programmes to East Anglia from a converted minesweeper. It would use an American type transmitter that he was modifying and have a range of approximately 50 miles reaching Peterborough, Mablethorpe and Hunstanton. Tidswell said that £12,000 would be needed initially. But east coast listeners never heard any more about it.

At this time in offshore history most people managed to pick up Caroline transmissions on their radio sets, but a Mr R. Howes of Shotley, near Ipswich, Suffolk, decided to go one better! He could pick up Radio Caroline every time he lifted his 'phone to make a call. This was in August 1964 when Post Office officials were baffled as to how the transmission came to get tangled up in the wires. Eventually the mystery was solved and Mr Howes then had to tune in on the radio if he wanted pop music, but at least he could make his phone calls in peace!

'Officialdom' went slightly wrong when the Egg Marketing Board placed £27,000 worth of advertising with Radio Caroline towards the end of 1964. The state-backed Board, which had four Government appointed members, sponsored an hour-long *Breakfast Show* aimed at young people and housewives between seven and eight every morning. "Go to work on an egg," they said. Twelve advertisement spots were included in each show. The programmes, which were described as "cracking" (no pun intended), ran daily for thirteen weeks.

On 28 September a survey showed that Radio Caroline had a bigger afternoon audience in the areas it covered than all the BBC programmes put together. The figures showed that there was a substantial audience for Radio Caroline during most transmission hours, particularly during the late morning period, when housewives in particular appeared to choose Caroline to listen to during their housework.

The information was obtained by Attwoods who said that the two ships were reaching a potential audience of about 39,000,000 people. Attwoods obtained the information by two methods.

First of all a questionnaire was despatched to 3,000 housewives in the south of England and 3,298 in the north asking whether they or any member of the household had listened to Caroline, Atlanta (as it was) and Luxembourg over the previous four weeks. They were then asked to indicate the quality of reception on the following scale - Very Good/Good/Fair/Poor/Very Poor/Variable. The rate of the return of questionnaires in the north was 93.5% and in the south 90.3%.

A BBC spokesman said he had "No comment to make on the survey."

The battle of the airwaves had really been hotting up since the birth of Caroline and then the BBC's subsequent decision to challenge both Caroline and Luxembourg. The *Melody Maker* music paper published a survey they had taken during December 1964 which interviewed a hundred teenagers throughout Britain. Luxembourg had an almost unassailable lead. Fifty-seven of the hundred persons interviewed chose 208 metres. Radio Caroline had twenty-one votes to their credit and the BBC received only seven. The remaining eleven voters (four did not vote) listened regularly to two or more stations. Of these eleven, six agreed that they would listen to Caroline most of all if it remained on the air throughout the evening instead of closing transmission at 8.00pm.

A new offshore floating commercial radio station came before the eyes of the British public towards the end of November 1964 anchored in the Thames Estuary. In December she commenced test transmissions on 266 metres, 1133kHz, and went on the air on 23 December. Her name? Radio London. But more about her can be found in Chapters Four and Six.

During the Christmas period 1964, the BBC refused to allow Radio Caroline to broadcast the Queen's Speech on Christmas Day. The BBC claimed that they owned the copyright of the pre-recorded speech and said that because Radio Caroline was not an authorised station she was not entitled to a copy.

A Buckingham Palace spokesman said he honestly thought the broadcast was available to all radio stations. "Buckingham Palace didn't specify who should or should not broadcast it. The BBC made the decisions."

Immediately after Christmas, the Postmaster-General, Mr Anthony Wedgwood Benn, who succeeded Reginald Bevins in October 1964 following a Labour Party victory at the polls said that the Government was expected to act against the pirates operating from around British coasts early in 1965.

An agreement of the Council of Europe against offshore radio stations outside international waters was to come into force on 25 January. It was expected to signal the move to silence Radios Caroline North and South, London, Invicta, City and others.

On New Year's Day 1965 Radio Caroline wished a "Happy New Year" to many people including Mr Anthony Wedgwood Benn, who is now better known as Tony Benn.

Chapter Two

TURN YOUR RADIO ON

There is a girl, she really is fine, so fine,
I know one day she's going to be mine, be mine.
She is so fine - I'll make her mine,
Her name is CAROLINE.

Caroline, The Fortunes, 1964

THE RADIO SHIPS were scattered around the shores of the British Isles but the more popular ones like Caroline South, London, England and Britain were off the Essex coast.

To reach the ships from London town one normally met fellow disc jockeys and engineers at Liverpool Street Station and travelled down on the 8.30am Norwich train, changing at Manningtree, Essex, for Parkeston Quay, Harwich. That was from 1964 until June 1966 when British Rail asked the tender servicing crew to leave because work on a £8,000,000 development caused a shortage of berths at Parkeston Quay. So the tender *Offshore I* changed her affections to Felixstowe Dock in Suffolk which meant that staff caught the same train from Liverpool Street, but this time continued to Ipswich and took a taxi to Felixstowe, some twelve miles east.

My very first visit to the office of Radio Caroline was on the day of the merger between Caroline and Atlanta in July 1964 when I signed a contract to work on the south ship. My initial trip to the *Mi Amigo* was on Monday 31 August 1964 when I travelled down to Harwich with Doug Kerr, Keith Martin and Tony Blackburn to serve my first fortnight aboard a pirate radio ship.

We arrived at Parkeston Quay just after 10.00am and were met at the station by the Caroline liaison officer, Percy (known as 'Bill') Scaddan, a former CID inspector at Scotland Yard, who then became chief of security for the Apapa and Lagos Wharfs, West Africa, in connection with the Nigerian Ports Authority. Scaddan was with the police for 25 years.

He asked us all if we had passports. Tony, Keith and myself were British - Doug Kerr was Canadian. As I was the new boy (Tony Blackburn had completed a previous trip), Bill Scaddan went on to tell me that going out to the radio ships was a very complicated business on paper.

This was because we were officially leaving the country and it involved passing through HM Customs and Excise, HM Waterguard, HM Immigration and the Special Branch of the CID. Also involved were British Rail, Trinity House, the Board of Trade, the Ministry of Transport, the Port of Health Authority and the local Harbour Board. Quite a complicated set-up every time the tender took people out to the radio ships.

We boarded the scarred diesel tender, *Offshore I*, a former Dutch fishing boat weighing some 60 tons, registered in Baarn, Holland - a tender that was built for utility rather than for comfort. It was manned by three Dutchmen.

The tender was owned by the Offshore Tender and Supply Company of Holland and the Agents were the Harcourt Shipping Agency of Foster Road, Parkeston Quay.

The journey out to *Mi Amigo* took just under two hours and we were accompanied by twenty or so seagulls flying and crying overhead. I had not done any travelling on ships

Above: Caroline DJ Keith Martin *saying goodbye to Bryan Vaughan as he prepares to go on shore leave for one week aboard Offshore I.*

Below: Offshore II *arriving with provisions at Radio Caroline South.*

previously (except once from Harwich to the Hook of Holland in 1959) and I was a little concerned to say the least realising that one had to stay on board for fourteen days and fourteen nights fighting whatever weather happened to come along. I wondered if the life at sea would suit me! All my previous travels around the world had been by air.

Keith Martin, a former employee at Granada TV, told me he was quite often seasick. He had joined Caroline in April 1964 just when the merger had taken place, but was employed initially by the Project Atlanta team, who in fact also employed me.

The journey out to Radio Caroline had been somewhat of a marathon. I had travelled from a London railway station to a port at Harwich, been processed through numerous Government departments, and finally sailed on a small tender for nearly two hours.

Just a few minutes before 1.00pm we pulled alongside the *Mi Amigo,* formerly Radio Atlanta, and prior to that Radio Nord. My very first impression of the radio ship was that it was extremely rusty; originally a silver hulled schooner-like ship. All on board the tender had a perilous jump from the *Offshore I* into a crowd of eager hands on the *Mi Amigo.*

We were welcomed aboard by the captain, chief disc jockey Mike Allen, and fellow disc jockeys Bob Brown, Eddie Anthony and Bryan Vaughan. Ken Evans, assisted by Marion Cochrane and Maureen Blackburn, represented the programme planning department. And from the panel operators' section there was Terry Saunders, a slim, long-haired Australian youth. In fact Australia appeared to have the monopoly - there was Ken Evans, Bryan Vaughan, Marion Cochrane and Terry Saunders - just on one shift! All were extremely pleasant.

The sea, on this occasion, looked placid and inviting. Later, in my Radio Caroline career, I was to witness, many times, the *Mi Amigo* floating in a cold sea, grey and gale-swept.

Throughout my life I have gone around 'cracking funnies' and 'sending up people' in joke form. Sooner or later I was going to say the wrong thing. I guess this happened on my very first day aboard.

I distinctly remember saying as a joke, but with a perfectly straight face "Programme Director, Chris Moore, has sent me out to sort you out and liven up proceedings!" This classic clanger from the Skues repertoire acted as a black mark against me for many a long day until the ship's personnel learned of the humour relating to one RKS.

As it happened morale on board was low the day I arrived, for the captain had said a definite "No" to all the staff going off for a party that night. A motor launch had earlier in the day come out from Clacton-on-Sea with twelve beautiful girls on board inviting the disc jockeys to a party to be held on the launch which would anchor just off Caroline. However, the captain refused permission for anyone to leave the radio ship. "If anyone did," he said "they would be sacked instantly."

To spend a fortnight on a ship cut off from the rest of the world seemed like a life sentence and, I have to be honest, my first fortnight appeared to drag. I was still finding my sea-legs!

Jane Wilson, writing in *Town* magazine in January 1965, hit the nail on the head when she wrote "There was isolation, claustrophobia and a kind of deprived hip euphoria on the *Mi Amigo.*" And she was only on board for two hours!

I appeared on air 1 September 1964 the day after my arrival and presented *The Sound of Music* from 9.00-11.00am, followed by *Lunch Date* 12noon-1.00pm.

Fortunately I soon made friends and everything began to fall into place and I really enjoyed myself, in spite of the rather changeable weather.

The first two weeks mail-wise was the most interesting for I must have read every single word of every letter. Many remembered me from BFN Germany - others from Forces Broadcasting Service in Kenya and Aden. Mail was undoubtedly a morale booster and every time the tender visited - which was three times a week - I was there waiting to collect our delivery of letters, sent on from Caroline House in London.

The *Mi Amigo* was captained by a Dutchman, and the seven crew including a chief engineer. They normally worked six weeks on the ship and then had two weeks leave in Holland. And we thought we were suffering with two weeks on and one off!

Radio Caroline South, off Frinton-on-Sea, Essex, 1966

Mind you they were getting well paid. A steward was collecting more in his wage packet than a disc jockey. The Dutch could claim overtime, which of course we couldn't. I started off at under £20 a week, but fortunately had a rather attractive pay rise after a few weeks on board. Everything was found whilst at sea ... accommodation, food, etc, etc. All disc jockeys paid National Health and Insurance. Some, like myself, had the upkeep of a London flat - even when on board. So the money soon dwindled away. One tended to spend a lot of money when on land - but it was a great life!

There was always someone on the lookout for small boats and pleasure craft. Sometimes, even during the summer months, the sea became rough and trouble followed.

For example, on 2 August 1964 four boys rowed out in a dinghy to Caroline from Walton-on-the-Naze to request a top ten record, but on the way back the current carried them out to sea. A second dinghy, this time motorised, was launched to assist but was unable to cope. A disc jockey broadcast an appeal and the Walton and Frinton lifeboat was launched. The four boys, Ron Beecham, George Lewin, Alex Foster and Graham Hodges, all 18 years old, in the first dinghy, were landed at Walton pier. The second dinghy was also towed in by the lifeboat. The record that was played for them was *A Hard Day's* Night by the Beatles.

One of the complaints of working on a ship was that you could not get a great deal of exercise with the result you tended to become rather lazy. Fair enough, during the summer you could walk up and down the deck, but during the winter the idea was very soon forgotten.

Caroline South - registered as the merchant vessel *Mi Amigo* (My Friend) - was the ship used by the Swedish station Radio Nord until 1962. She weighed 470 tons, was 150ft. in length, had a beam of 24ft. and was capable of a speed of 8 knots. The ship was propelled by a 200 horsepower diesel engine with a single screw.

Off the Isle of Man, Caroline North was a much larger ship; 763 tons - 188 ft. in length and had a beam of 32ft. The m.v. *Caroline* could reach 14 knots and was propelled by a 1000 horsepower diesel engine with a single screw.

Both ships were fitted out for broadcasting in Greenore, southern Ireland. Here they were also fitted out with very important and unusual pieces of equipment - heavy anchors. The anchors were effective in keeping the ships steady in bad weather, although in January 1966 they dragged, which in turn resulted in Caroline South running aground (see Chapter Five).

On Caroline South, shortly after she was settled in the North Sea off Frinton, the Dutch crew laid three big anchors and attached them by a swivel junction to the single heavy chain which was secured to the bow of the ship. A forty-gallon drum was used to mark the position of the anchors, and was attached to the junction of the three sea-anchors.

The first night after the work had been carried out, the ship wound round and round the anchor chains, and finally rode over the big drum which bumped its way down one side of the hull, under the ship, and up the other side by the next day.

In the meantime it had knocked a small hole in the engine room hull which had water pouring into that very vital part of the ship in quite large amounts. Disc jockey Colin Nicol reported that the water was at least a foot deep inside and coming up to the generators. This was discovered when the duty engineer made his regular inspection and gave the alert. Everyone on board manned the buckets and hand pumps. Meanwhile the captain supervised a patching job which saved the day. The drum was removed the next day and no buoy was used again.

Radio England/Britain had a similar system when they first anchored off the Essex coast and experienced exactly the same trouble.

Meanwhile, back on Radio Caroline, both the North and South ships had completely self-contained broadcasting units. Arthur Carrington was responsible for heading the team that installed the equipment on Radio Caroline North. He was formerly with the BBC and also worked for the Government on radar. Another ex-BBC man designed and installed the equipment on Caroline South. He was A.N. Thomas. On both ships there were two generating sets, each capable of producing 80 kilowatts at 220 volts (3 phase).

Above: Paul Noble in Radio Caroline South transmitter hall
Below: Panel operator Terry Saunders in the main on air studio, Radio Caroline South

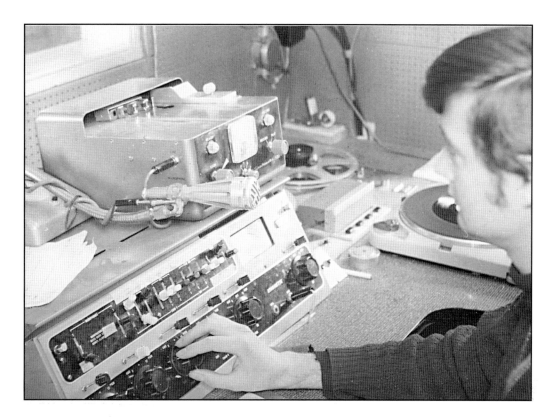

Caroline North had a transmitter power of 10 kilowatts - Caroline South was also 10 kilowatts until she went aground in 1966, although with a combining unit both ships could reach 20 kilowatts. Later Caroline South stepped up her power to 30 kilowatts. The transmitters originated from Continental Electronics of Dallas, Texas.

The studio and control room was completely self-contained with two Gates turntables and two Ampex tape machines. The 10-channel mixer was made by Gates. There were three Spotmaster cartridge machines for jingles.

During the early days a panel operator was used to spin in the discs and jingles, but on the South ship, when Terry Saunders returned to Australia, there was a unanimous vote amongst the disc jockeys that we should in future spin in our own records, cartridges and taped commercials - this meant we had to have roughly three hundred and one pairs of hands. To a newcomer this was slightly confusing, to say the least. Fortunately my training with the British Forces Network had taught me the art of self-operating which I found a great asset.

A three hour programme, which disc jockeys normally did in one spell, required a great deal of concentration. In many instances commercials had to be broadcast at a specific time: for example 10.02am. This meant that records had to be pre-faded. Offshore radio did not enjoy fading records like Luxembourg. If the records contained a natural fade, fair enough - but not if they had a recognised ending. Today most records have a fade ending. So the boys lived up to their name 'disc jockeys.' On certain BBC programmes and at Luxembourg records were spun in by a studio manager, but even that system changed in the late 1960s to one of self-operation.

One is in complete control of the programming should anything go slightly wrong. If a record should develop a repeating groove, you can simply open the microphone and utter a few words of wisdom, whilst at the same time fading down the disc channel and moving the stylus on the turntable arm forward a few grooves, and bringing the volume up again.

On Radio Caroline the programme made its way from the studio to the transmitter room, through the 10 kilowatt transmitter and up to the aerial which consisted of a folded dipole, of which the mast was one leg, and a sausage aerial the other. Caroline North's aerial height was 168ft. above the deck whereas Caroline South's was 157ft. The Caroline aerial was designed and manufactured in Southampton and rigged at Cowes on the Isle of Wight. Ideally the height of the aerial should approach a quarter of a wavelength, which roughly means that on 200 metres in the medium wave the aerial length should be some 150ft.

On the *Mi Amigo* there were three decks. The top deck was where the two lifeboats were housed, and where, during the summer months, disc jockeys and engineers basked in the sun, if and when the sun broke through.

The middle deck was the largest and here were the two studios, the control room, the central mess, the galley, toilets and showers.

The bottom deck housed the transmitter and also the sleeping quarters, the stateroom (which was later transferred into the library), the provision store and fridges; also the captain's quarters.

Disc jockeys shared cabins, normally two per room, although the custom for new boys was to spend two tours in the forecastle (the front end of the ship) which was undoubtedly the worst place on the ship to sleep. In addition to the vessel's constant pitching and tossing, there was the slow monotonous creaking of the anchor chains. The particular cabin that I remained in for three tours (had to be one up on everyone else!) was old, smelly (it was situated next to the paint store) and only had a dim light shining. There was an aura of creepiness about the whole place. An ideal situation and perfect surroundings if a person were writing a novel about a haunted cabin! Added to this was a very strong rumour that a Swedish engineer had died on board some four years previously. This cabin was not the most pleasant place to spend one's leisure hours on the ship, so most of mine were spent in the library! The Dutch crew were accommodated aft on the middle deck.

It may surprise you to know that there were two girls on board Caroline South - Marion

Above: DJs and engineers sit down for an evening meal
Below: DJs and Dutch crew watch local English television

Cochrane and Maureen Blackburn (no relation to Tony) - both of whom helped with the programming. They remained on board until Caroline House came into being in the autumn of 1964, and then returned to land-based jobs in London.

You can conjure up all sorts of pictures when you learn that there were at least six programme men, two engineers and a Dutch crew and two ladies 'at sea' for fourteen days at a time. But everything was 'above board.' The captain made sure of that!

Apart from the cabin mentioned earlier, all the others were very modern and more central (ship-wise) so didn't pitch and roll so much. They were a pleasure to live in.

The stateroom, originally held for round-table conferences and such like, was used as the general programming office and library. There were about 2,000 singles and 500 long playing albums, ranging from rock 'n' roll to symphony. Records were indexed alphabetically by artist under the general classification of female singer, male singer, group or instrumental. Only one artist had a special section to himself in the library and that was Ray Conniff who had so many albums featuring his orchestra and the Conniff Singers! The records were sorted and filed by Ken Evans, Marion and Maureen, but when they returned to Caroline House in Mayfair, London, the job was done by the disc jockeys.

There were so many records coming on board each and every week (at least 200 singles) that space was rapidly running out. The captain authorised new shelves to be built to house another 8,000 records. In July 1964 the stateroom had three small shelves on one of the walls. By the time the *Mi Amigo* went aground in 1966 all four walls had at least four shelves each. I remember working in the stateroom, one evening, selecting my records for the following day's programme. Outside there were shrieking winds and tumultuous seas. It was a strange sensation hearing the sound of the storm, with the howling wind and feeling the booming explosions of huge waves smashing into the *Mi Amigo*. It wasn't very long before the records parted company with the shelves, as LPs and singles by the hundred crashed to the floor. This was not helped by the fact that the ventilation shaft had been left open so there was flooding as well.

Directly above the cabins was the central mess - the Dutch and radio staff shared the mess which had one television set. They also shared the same cooks.

Sometimes there were two cooks on board - at other times, just one. They were all known by their Christian names like Arnold, Rudi, Jan and Bill. By and large the food was good. Obviously being on board there were limitations to variety. More often than not the food was English but cooked in a Dutch manner, therefore including a lot of grease. Nutmeg was used in abundance, even on cornflakes!

There were two sittings: one for the English followed by another sitting for the Dutch. For the radio people breakfast was from 8.00am - 9.00am; lunch from 1.00pm - 2.00pm and tea 5.30pm - 6.00pm.

If a disc jockey was on the air during meal times, say he was presenting the 3.00pm to 6.00pm show, he would officially miss out on a meal. But this problem was solved by letting him eat with the Dutch. This applied for all meals.

It may be interesting to see an example of the weekly provisions for 17 personnel aboard Caroline South which comprised:

One pig, one hindquarter of beef, 5lb. of lamb, 5lb. sausages, 15lb. of bacon, 10lb. of fish, six chickens, 18 dozen eggs, 48 tins of baked beans, 3lb. of lettuce, 12lb. of tomatoes, one hundredweight of potatoes, 12lb. of bananas, 28lb. of butter, 24 tins of orange juice, 5lb. of cheese and six packets of breakfast cereal. In addition there were apples, tea, coffee, beer and cigarettes brought on board, together with gallons and gallons of fresh water. Luxuries like cake, biscuits and chocolate were usually sent in by listeners.

Next door to the mess was Studio One from where the news was broadcast. There was no equipment housed there - just a microphone, a desk and a chair. Next door to that was the main studio and control room from where the disc jockey controlled the programme of records, commercials and jingles.

Although this was the main studio it was still very small and if three people, including the disc jockey, were standing then it would become terribly crowded.

There were two portholes so the disc jockey could see what was going on out at sea. Portholes could be opened to let in fresh air as there was no air conditioning. The only problem here was that the noise from the cooling fans coming from the transmitter room normally succeeded in making such a din that a certain amount of this sound was picked up on the microphone.

During the summer months small craft from Walton-on-the-Naze, Frinton-on-Sea, Harwich, Felixstowe and Clacton used to come and pay us a visit.

No visitors were allowed on board, but we used to talk to them over the side of the *Mi Amigo* and play them requests. Some people brought presents - others came with newspapers. During the early days of Caroline we never had a visit from the tender at weekends. It was a great thrill seeing and talking to these people who were good enough to come out as we were cut off from all communication with the outside world. Our eyes scanned the horizon daily during the spring and summer months.

As people learned of Caroline's existence they tried to make their way out to 'have-a-look-see.' But in certain cases our listeners (mainly holiday makers during the summer months) did not own boats of their own.

Soon it became a business to operate tours aboard the *Lady Kent* from the Albion breakwater at Walton-on-the-Naze to the radio ships.

When the *Lady Kent* arrived we used to say 'Hello' to the dozen or so people on board and sign autographs. Most of those who came out brought their own cameras so we put on an act, clowning around. In some cases, like a Miss Vivien Barnard, they would make a few visits out to Radio Caroline. I remember seeing Vivien seven days out of seven. She was good enough to send all the disc jockeys copies of the photographs she took. Vivien was 17 at the time and lived at West Avenue, Chelmsford, Essex. She recalls:

> The first time I heard Radio Caroline was on Easter Monday, 30 March 1964. Caroline was different. There was the novelty that it was being broadcast from a ship in the middle of the North Sea, but I listened to the station because of the DJs. They made you feel they were talking TO you as if they were friends - and not AT you. They were amusing to listen to. They used to tell funny stories and crack jokes and I used to enjoy listening to them just as much as listening to the music. They were more than just a link between each record. In a word they were 'entertaining.' Radio Caroline was so refreshing after listening to Auntie BBC! I joined the Caroline Club for 5 shillings (25p) in June 1964.
>
> My first visit to the *Mi Amigo* was on 27 July 1964. My mother and I went to Walton-on-the-Naze in order to go out on the pleasure boat, the *Lady Kent,* which made trips to Radio Caroline. Whilst waiting on the pier for the *Lady Kent* we saw the Walton and Frinton lifeboat go out to Radio Caroline to collect Bryan Vaughan who was suffering from a gastric complaint. At 5.00pm we boarded the *Lady Kent* and started the journey to the *Mi Amigo.* We passed the returning lifeboat with Bryan aboard. He was taken to Clacton hospital. When we reached the ship I noticed the hull was painted dark green and the cabins and deck were white. Simon Dee was on deck with a few other men. One of the DJs played "Have I the Right" by the Honeycombs for all the girls on board the *Lady Kent.* We didn't go close to the ship, just slowly cruised by.

---

1. In the late 1960s these enthusiastic visitors became known as 'fanatics' or "freaks'. By the summer of 1973, Caroline DJ Andy Archer had invented a new name - 'anorak' - which became popularised by DJs and given to dedicated fans of pirate radio stations. They were given this name because of their habit of visiting radio ships in pleasure craft to see their favourite DJs, often in appalling weather conditions. Most of the time the visitors, carrying transistor radios, duffle bags and cameras, wore anoraks. The name is applied to all those who still have an affection to the watery wireless days.

The very first personal request which was played for me was *You'll Never Get to Heaven* by Dionne Warwick. This was the record I had requested and it was played by Doug Kerr on 30 July 1964 for "Vivien, Jim and Mr and Mrs Barnard of Chelmsford who have been sunbathing on Frinton cliffs."

I first met Keith Skues in August 1965. I was on holiday staying at Kirby Cross, near Frinton-on-Sea, Essex. I was with my parents. I got up and had breakfast and on the Radio 1 of the DJs said Keith was wearing a red polo neck sweater. I had intended to go out on the pleasure boat the *Lady Kent* that day, but she only sailed when the weather was good. Fortunately, on that particular day, the weather WAS good and we sailed from Walton-on-the-Naze to Radio Caroline. On deck was Keith Skues in the red polo neck sweater, so I recognised him immediately. I said are you Keith Skues and he replied "Yes." I did take a picture of the occasion - in black and white! It was my first attempt at photography and it was a bit out of focus.

I visited Radio Caroline 21 times altogether aboard the *Lady Kent* between 1964 and 1967 during the summer months. It was very disappointing if sometimes we went to Walton-on-the-Naze and found the weather was so bad we couldn't go out to the ship. There were two men who jointly owned the *Lady Kent* - Frank Bloom and Les Wall. Sometimes they would both come out on the boat - on other occasions there would be just one of them. I got to know them very well. They used to let me go free sometimes. Their charge was normally 10 shillings (50 pence). Often, when I passed over the money, the skipper used to pass it back as if he were giving me change just so that everyone else sitting on the boat wouldn't notice. Sadly Les Wall died in 1992.

Going out to Caroline was very exciting. I used to love being near the sea - I'm a water sign - Pisces. To meet the DJs at the end of the trip was most interesting because you felt they were more like friends, and it was very nice meeting them and getting to know what they looked like.

We were not allowed to go on board Radio Caroline as we would have been breaking the law. One day I almost got on board when I asked to see Keith Hampshire, one of

Vivien Barnard points to the entry on the wall of Walton and Frinton lifeboat station recording the rescue of Radio Caroline DJ, Bryan Vaughan, which she witnessed in July 1964

my favourite DJs. Robbie Dale said "He's asleep in his bunk." And he put his hand out and said "Come on board and you can come and wake him up." I got one foot on the ship Caroline ready to be hauled aboard and the skipper of the *Lady Kent* said "No. Sorry, but the coastguard will be watching. I can't allow you to go on board." He was very apologetic because he knew how disappointed I was not being allowed on board. I would dearly have loved to have seen what the conditions were like.

I have met Robbie Dale, Dave Lee Travis, Keith Skues, Bryan Vaughan, Colin Nicol, Tony Blackburn, Paul Noble, Carl Conway, John Peel, Pete Drummond, Simon Dee and many more.

I have also been to a number of venues to see Caroline disc nights including 100 Club, Uppercut Club at Forest Gate and Wimbledon Palais.

During the summer months of 1965 a larger boat, the *Viking Saga*, from Clacton-on-Sea appeared. She made nightly trips reaching Radio Caroline around six o'clock. Sometimes the owner of the Viking Saga, Dick Harman, threw bottles of beer on board in exchange for requests played over the air. This made a welcome change from the Dutch beer we drank on the *Mi Amigo*.

Whether we soaked up the sunshine or suffered the showers the disc jockey crew decided on a series of pranks to entertain the many people who came out to see us. Many's the time that we would skim old useless records across to them in the *Viking Saga*. It was quite entertaining watching the visitors' faces as many of them nearly fell overboard making a brave attempt to try and catch some of the records.

On one occasion during July all on board decided to walk around the ship wearing 12 inch record sleeves on our heads. The sightseers across the water thought we had gone completely berserk - come to think of it, we probably had! Even the disc jockey on air, who was visible from the *Viking Saga*, entered into the spirit.

However, I think the highlight of 'prankery' came at the end of July when a similar stunt was played, and the pleasure launch which normally stayed about twenty feet away came very close indeed to the *Mi Amigo*. The visitors on board were beginning to think they had been 'had' (there was no-one visible on the ship) when suddenly disc jockeys, engineers, Dutch crew ... all emerged from their places of hiding, dressed as pirates in towels, odd appropriate pieces of clothing, carrying broom sticks and mops. The disc jockeys prodded Roger Gale along the deck with a sign attached to him which read "I played Mozart" ... and made him walk the plank which had been rigged up over the side of the *Mi Amigo*.

Roger (he was a former RADA student who went on to become a member of parliament in Kent) acted very well indeed and fell headlong into the racing tide. Even the disc jockeys on board became worried for he seemed to spend ages under water. There was a shocked silence from the sightseers. He finally appeared at the stern of the ship and was helped aboard by Colin Nicol.

"I think you overdid it just a little," Colin went on to the dripping, but jolly, Roger. "Might as well give them a good show," retorted Roger. "They came a long way and paid a fortune for the trip!"

Wisely or unwisely, the captain subsequently forbade any further pranks, and bathing from the ship at any time.

One of the most popular disc jockeys on Caroline South was Tony Blackburn who began to tell jokes in between records. He says[2] "My jokes marked me out. The public became aware of me because of them. So I invented what I called the 'groan factor.' Only the most terrible jokes were bad enough for my shows. I was on my way to achieving the crown as King of the Corn. Love me or hate me, the public would never in future be indifferent to me."

How many listeners have groaned to jokes like "I fancied my chances at singing ... until I

2. Tony Blackburn *The Living Legend*, W. H. Allen, London 1985, page 19

once sang in the New Forest. Even the trees got up and walked out." Or perhaps "I keep seeing double, doctor." Said the doctor "Lie down on the couch then." "Which one?"

As disc jockeys we were entitled to two free bottles of beer per day. They were kept in a fridge in the stateroom. We could draw further rations from the captain for a price. The same principle applied to cigarettes after the free ration of 100 for each disc jockey had run out. However, we were not allowed to take any cigarettes onto land. Normally when one goes abroad he or she is entitled to bring into Britain 200 cigarettes without paying tax but, basically, we were 'pirates' and therefore entitled to no concessions whatsoever, in spite of the fact that we were outside the three mile limit. If we were found 'smuggling' cigarettes or cigars by the Customs, then the management stood firm - instant dismissal for the offender. One abided by the law of the land ... and the sea!

During the summer months of 1964 and 1965 we at Radio Caroline South were honoured when a water-skiing team from Southend came out to demonstrate their skills around the ship. We gave special mentions to this event over the air, and during successive weekends teams from London, Felixstowe, Clacton and other coastal resorts surrounded the ship. It was truly fantastic to watch and all those participating were spectacular in their performances.

Although Radio Caroline sounded more varied with its output of music, there was a format to which DJs had to adhere. In September 1965 programme director Bill Hearne said "Considerably increased emphasis is to be laid on the charts, drawing particularly from Sounds '65 (65 hit records representing the year 1965), supported with the American Hot 100 and supplemented with new releases, picks-to-click, blasts from the past and selected cuts from Caroline Spotlight albums." Bill suggested an active turnover in the chart material to maintain freshness. Records on the decline were eliminated when they reached the 20 or lower position, thus making room for newer material to be introduced in place of those records which had been 'played to death' on their way up the charts. Music on Caroline had to be current, bright and cheerful, well paced and this format had to be strictly adhered to without exception.

The format comprised: Sounds '65 Top 10; Sounds '65; American Hot 100; Sounds '65; New release; Sounds '65; Blast from the past; Sounds '65; Top 20 album or 'Spotlight.'

Taking into consideration commercial time, news, announcements and station identifications the routine would cover half an hour. This format was repeated each half hour over the length of the three-hour programme.

During the 9.00am - 12.00 noon show, which I presented, the pace was slowed down after the first half-hour. About 11.30am the tempo increased to anticipate the *Lunch Show*.

To avoid duplication of any particular chart record in the final half-hour of a show disc jockey "A" would draw only upon even numbers in both the Sounds '65 and American Hot 100. In turn disc jockey "B" would use only odd numbers from the charts for his first half-hour. Disc jockey "B" would stay with the odd number for his final half-hour and when disc jockey "C" took

Tony Blackburn

over he would use records from the even numbers!

We were encouraged to be 'personality DJs.' A personality established himself not by dulcet tones and crystal clear pronunciation (although it helped), but by being his good old ever-loving self. That, coupled with a unique presentation, the ability to emerge vocally as flesh and blood in the presence of the listener and to communicate together comprised a force with which to be reckoned.

I remember a few do's and don'ts which I jotted down in a diary in 1964: 1) Keep your announcements to a minimum; 2) Don't wait for a record to fade before speaking; 3) Don't, under any circumstances, knock either the product or the sponsor; 4) Have a good sense of humour; 5) Give regular times checks; 6) Exercise good taste; 7) Do not swear; 8) Do not "talk down" to your audience; 9) Give frequent updates on the weather and 10) At all times be enthusiastic, positive and loyal to the management of the station.

When Radio London and other stations came on the air in late 1964 we certainly had competition. I believe that competition is stimulating and progressive. Because of the competition all radio stations became more professional and the person to benefit was the listener - exactly as it should be!

Talking about mail ... which we weren't... this was probably the biggest morale booster. The amounts varied enormously depending on the individual disc jockey. One tended to receive

DJs Tom Lodge, Emperor Rosko and Rick Dane reading fan mail

more mail when the DJ was on air for a fortnight rather than when he was on shore leave. Some disc jockeys received 20 letters a week - others 2,000. To strike a happy average throughout, the disc jockeys on pirate stations could attract a figure of 1,000 per week. These included requests. Lots of fan letters required a reply, the sender having enclosed a stamped addressed envelope. They would ask straight forward questions, requesting a photograph ... asking your age ... were you married ... your favourite pop stars and many other questions.

To answer all these letters took a very long time. If each letter required five minutes that would eventually take the disc jockey 1000 x 5 minutes ... roundabout 83 hours non-stop typing, without food, drink or sleep. Fan mail to a new disc jockey was like gold dust to a digger, but the novelty soon wore off when you had to reply. If listeners enclosed a stamped addressed envelope they were entitled to a reply! It was great receiving such large numbers of letters and reading the contents. If one answered the letters it would not be too long before the listener eventually answered yours. You would then be back to square one. Sadly we did not have any secretaries for such work.

Many listeners wrote in asking advice. I have received letters from good ladies asking me what colour they should paint their kitchen ... what to buy their husbands for their birthday ... what colour to choose for a new dress ... what style of dress, etc etc. Some have even written and said they were going to name their children after me, and these are people you have never met! One could write a book on the interesting letters received from listeners.

Presents came in large quantities as well ... gonks, scarves, socks, handkerchiefs, gloves, woolly hats, sweaters and food parcels.

One of the most interesting letters I ever received came from a prisoner inside HMP Wormwood Scrubs. For obvious reasons his name cannot be mentioned. For the benefit of this book we'll call him Tony. He wrote in 1964 to say how much he enjoyed Radio Caroline, and also made a few suggestions as to programmes.

He said that one programme could review pop records of 10 years ago, ending up with the top ten tunes of the present week. This would give the people in the 20-30 age group an opportunity of hearing Elvis Presley, Buddy Holly, Bill Haley and Little Richard. At the same time this would show the present teenagers the changing trends in pop music.

Tony's suggestions were all very constructive. Another idea suggested the current hit tune of, say the Beatles, followed by the very first record ever made by the fab four from Liverpool - thus showing listeners the way singers tended to change their style. He didn't like the way Radio Luxembourg faded records halfway through and pleaded for Radio Caroline not to follow suit - which I am pleased to report we never did.

I replied to Tony thanking him for all his interest (incidentally his favourite record was *Jailhouse Rock* by Elvis Presley) and a correspondence soon got underway. In subsequent letters he offered more criticism of Caroline programmes, and the ways he thought we might improve listenership. He said there were a lot of Caroline fans in Wormwood Scrubs, and there was no audience more critical than a prison audience. We only had to ask either Adam Faith or Dickie Henderson both of whom had performed in front of a prison audience.

The correspondence between Tony and myself came to a halt after three months when I wrote suggesting that I visit the prison and say hello. The governor of the prison wrote telling me that it was not possible and that correspondence with Tony must now cease. And that was the last I ever heard from him. I did not know why he was sent to Wormwood Scrubs. All I will say is that on paper he appeared to be a pleasant young chap with a striking personality. His letters were intelligent and constructive.

Letters were received from all over the world - from as far away as Tripoli where an Arab gentleman wrote in regularly; Pakistan was another far-flung place where devotees to Radio Caroline have listened when atmospheric conditions were right. Besides the large European audience which ran into millions there was also a giant audience behind the Iron Curtain where foreign pop music was very much in demand.

On 14 January 1966 Freice Rokuskova wrote from Czechoslovakia to the *New Musical Express* saying she enjoyed reading an article about Radio Caroline from Andy Gray (the then editor) who wrote a whole page about the ship on 5 November 1965. Freice went on to say that she picked up Caroline South transmissions.

During 1965 Thomas A. Sundstrom writing in *Barron's Newspaper*, New York, said he was assistant editor of the *Newark News Radio Club* monthly bulletin. He said that Radio Caroline South operated with 20,000 watts on 1520 kilocycles and could be heard on Monday mornings signing on at 1.00am. Radio Caroline was heard every Monday during the winter of 1964 until 2.30am or 3.00am when it faded out.

During late night broadcasts I often used to ask people who were listening a long way from England to drop us a line. On one occasion in September 1964 a K.J. Butler who was a navigator apprentice on the *SS British Engineer* wrote and told me that he picked up Radio Caroline South, then on 199 metres, from Lisbon to Finisterre at strength 4 at sunset.

Perhaps the most incredible occurrence happened in September 1965 when a David Auld of Raleigh Street, Greymouth in New Zealand, sent me a tape saying that he had recorded part of the transmission from Radio Caroline South at 6.00am New Zealand time the previous week (6.00pm our time) and forwarded the tape on for archival purposes. The tape contained the final ten minutes of an afternoon show I was doing and also the first quarter of an hour of the Caroline Club Request programme which was introduced on that particular evening by Bryan Vaughan. The reception was so clear it could have been recorded in Colchester, Essex. But there it was, 12,500 miles away from the transmitter. Quite incredible!

However, a job as a disc jockey at sea is far less romantic than it sounds. I can assure you there is no fun in tossing about in a force nine gale. Spending two weeks on board one has to keep up a façade of friendliness, not only to the listeners but to one's colleagues on the ship. Life is more or less a hermitage.

Perhaps one of the most worrying sides of spending life at sea was the danger of becoming ill. It is easy to say "Walton and Frinton lifeboat is only a few miles away." But why should we have to put the already overworked RNLI boys, for whom I have the greatest admiration, to more trouble? They were called out thirty six times to the radio ships and forts off the coastline of Britain to give assistance between 1964 and 1990.

On 27 July 1964 disc jockey Bryan Vaughan was taken off the *Mi Amigo* by the Walton and Frinton lifeboat with food poisoning. The incident was covered in Chapter One.

In October 1964 during a force 9 gale I became involved in an accident on board the *Mi Amigo*. I had just finished a *Caroline Club Request* programme and decided to take the back way down to the library rather than go through the mess as everyone was watching television and I would have to disturb them to pass.

Unfortunately, one of the giant steel doors swung wide open and almost off its hinges as the ship pitched. A metal stake somehow splintered and severed itself from the door and part of the metal penetrated my right eye. I can't remember too much about what happened afterwards but the *Offshore I* made an emergency trip and I was taken to hospital in Harwich, then transferred to Myland Hospital in Colchester, Essex, where I stayed for a fortnight.

I lost the sight of my right eye for almost a week, and was very lucky indeed to regain it. Even now many years later I get lots of trouble from it. The eye never did get back to normal but at least I could see again.

On 13 February 1966 disc jockey Graham Webb was taken off by the Walton and Frinton lifeboat because he had a serious bout of flu. The lifeboat answered the SOS call and Graham was taken to Walton Hospital by ambulance.

But whilst there was the danger of illness on board the pirate ships there have been other occasions when the radio ship's tender *Offshore I* has helped out.

On 27 May 1965 Martin Skipper (18) from Walton-on-the-Naze was rescued by the *Offshore I* after his canoe became waterlogged when he was going out to Radio Caroline for a day's trip.

Perhaps the greatest rescue for the *Offshore I* came on Tuesday, 20 April 1965. I was returning with Bryan Vaughan to Caroline after a week's leave and we were dropped at the *Mi Amigo*. The tender then went on to Radio London to take some relief disc jockeys, and as it was going over an F-101 Voodoo tactical fighter jet crashed into the North Sea between Caroline and London narrowly missing the tender. One of the crew members saw a parachute falling into the sea - the tender went full steam ahead.

The pilot was Lieutenant John C. Wynn Jnr who had flown from his base in Laon, France, and freed himself from his parachute in the air, dropping into the sea. He cut his boots off with a knife, and started swimming in the ice cold water. A strong current carried him some distance from where his parachute had landed. He was given some attention at Radio London and changed into dry clothes. On the way back he was given tea at Radio Caroline. From

Above: A Dutch crew member in the galley on board Radio Caroline South, 1965
Below: DJ Graham 'Spider' Webb spins another yarn in his Cobweb Corner on Radio Caroline South, 1966

what I could see of him, John Wynn was suffering from shock and had an injury behind his left ear.

The tender made a radio call to Harwich and arrangements were made for Harwich Hospital to have an ambulance waiting at the quayside when *Offshore I* docked. Disc jockeys Keith Martin and Doug Kerr accompanied the pilot to land.

The ambulance arrived well ahead of the tender, to be followed by another from the U.S. Air Base at Bentwaters, Suffolk, with a medical officer on board. The crew of the *Offshore I* were skipper Captain de Reuver, engineer Ted van Ovwekerk and navigator Frank Heilbrink. Radio Caroline dedicated a record to Lieutenant Wynn - *Voodoo Blues*.

Another upset in the North Sea came in 15 May 1966 when disc jockey Rick Dane helped to rescue two girls after their Italia Yachting World catamaran capsized near to Radio Caroline. With members of the crew he lowered a lifeboat for Pamela Nightingale and Margaret Soulsby, both 21. The girls had set out from Clacton Sailing Club and, said Pamela, a hairdresser, "We turned the wrong way, got into the wind, jibbed and capsized." Coincidence that thirteen months later she should marry a captain of the *Offshore I* - Willem In't Veld. The wedding took place at Walton-on-the-Naze Parish Church, Essex, on 15 July 1967.

Margaret, then a stockbroker's secretary, went on "We were on Caroline for about six hours and had a fabulous time. Everybody made us very comfortable and gave us a wonderful meal." The two girls were taken off by Walton and Frinton lifeboat later in the day. Willem was killed in a motor cycle accident in St. Osyth, Essex, in 1985.

A rescue of another kind occurred on 12 April 1966 when a racing pigeon landed exhausted on the deck of the *Mi Amigo*. It was cared for and fed by members of the crew. Don Allen was on the air at the time and read out the number on the tag attached to the pigeon's leg and appealed over the air for its owner to contact Caroline agents, Harcourt Shipping of Harwich. Within two hours, George Dutton of Fryatt Avenue, Dovercourt, owner of the pigeon, made contact with the agents. Later that evening George collected the pigeon from the *Offshore I* tender, which had taken the bird from Radio Caroline to Harwich.

Rick Dane before he rescued two girls from a capsized catamaran in the North Sea

As disc jockeys we used to pride ourselves in playing a particular record (preferably by an unknown artist or group) and see if we could make the record 'happen.' Pirate radio has succeeded in bringing into the public eye (and ear) artists like Wayne Fontana & The Mindbenders, The Byrds, Jonathan King, Unit Four Plus Two, Neil Christian, Chris Farlowe, Paul and Barry Ryan, Crispian St. Peters, Twinkle, The Moody Blues, The Rolling Stones, The Animals, Tom Jones, Georgie Fame, The Fortunes, Pinkerton's Assorted Colours, The New Vaudeville Band, Episode Six, Guy Darrell, Normie Rowe, The Easybeats, Barry McGuire, The Toys, Los Bravos, Sandy Posey, Ike and Tina Turner, Percy Sledge, The Honeycombs, Kiki Dee, Peter and Gordon, Spencer Davis, The Small Faces, David and Jonathan, The Walker Brothers, The Move, Cat Stevens, Dave Dee, Dozy, Beaky, Mick and Tich,

The Cream, Graham Bonney, Sonny Childe and the TNT and David Garrick.

There are many others as well. In certain cases pirates have been instrumental in choosing a particular record which has later become a big hit record. For example: *Um Um Um Um Um*, Wayne Fontana and the Mind Benders, *Il Silenzio*, Nino Rossi; *In the Midnight Hour*, Wilson Pickett; *Concrete and Clay*, Unit Four Plus Two and *Hey Joe*, Jimi Hendrix. In other instances famous artists of years gone by who had not been in the public eye in recent times were given a new boost - examples included *Paper Tiger*, Sue Thompson; *Price of Love*, Everly Brothers; and *Rag Doll*, Four Seasons. All the pirate stations promoted American records since they came on the air and two notable songs stand out during the latter end of 1966 and the beginning of 1967, *Summertime*, Billy Stewart and *98.6*, Keith.

I well remember the time I received an American pressing of *Mr Tambourine Man* from The Byrds. I was 'knocked out' by it, and played it every day. Within a week I must have received over 100 letters from listeners asking where they could buy it. Eventually it was released by CBS Records in London and it became a national hit. CBS gave credit to Radio Caroline in the *Daily Mail Handbook of Golden Hits*. My theme tune from then on was changed to *Mr Tambourine Man*, but this time an instrumental version by the Golden Gate Strings which over the years must have sold a few thousand copies, if letters received were anything to go by.

As has been mentioned already a fortnight on board at one stretch was quite a long spell, so we were always delighted to learn when visitors were coming out from London. There were quite a number of pop stars who visited Radio Caroline from 1964. They included: Susan Hampshire, Manfred Mann, Julie Grant, Graham Bonney, Denny Laine (of The Moody Blues), Mark Richardson, Marie Vincent, Mike d'Abo, David Garrick, Rolf Harris, Los Bravos, Guy Darrell, Twinkle, Dave Clark, Adam Faith and Mitch Murray. Organist Jimmy Smith not only visited the ship but presented a live lunchtime show from the poop deck introduced by Simon Dee on 5 May 1965. The show also featured Tony Crombie on drums and Tony Thorpe on guitar. Outside broadcast technician was Martin Newton.

Disc jockey Jimmy Savile visited Caroline North off the Isle of Man in August 1965, and commented "We land-based DJs don't know we're born, except me, as I was never so pleased

DJ Bryan Vaughan interviews French singer Marie Vincent who flew into Britain from Paris. The 30-year-old singer was promoting her 1965 record release "Chip Chip"

to see that marvellous land as when I eventually got back. And I was only at sea for a few hours."

Undoubtedly the most noble person to visit the pirates came in June 1965 when we were honoured with royalty. Unbeknown to Bryan Vaughan and myself we were asked to return to Radio Caroline a day later than usual. Neither of us expected anything out of the ordinary, but thought it was Caroline House giving us an extra day off in lieu of days we forfeited on board due to bad weather. At Harwich, the liaison officer, Bill Scaddan, asked us both to look after three students from Cambridge with extra care - they were studying architecture. There was Brian, Bernard and Richard. No other details were given. We introduced ourselves on the

'STUDENT PRINCE' VISITS POP PIRATES

By MIRROR REPORTER

THE Student Prince paid a surprise visit to the pirate radio ship Caroline yesterday.

Prince Richard of Gloucester, 20, went aboard the ship off the Essex coast with two chums from Cambridge University where he is studying architecture.

They took cameras and notebooks and got first-hand material for an article they are doing for the students' magazine Granta.

The party arrived at Harwich in the Prince's car in time for a trip in Caroline's supply tender Offshore.

A sticker on the side of the Prince's car read: "I prefer B B C Third on 464."

This was a reference to the metre wave-band of the programme which puts out classics and jazz—but never Pop.

Request

Two of the Caroline's team of disc jockeys—Keith Skues and Bryan Vaughan —made the 17-mile trip with the Prince.

Usually Caroline dee-jays announce special visitors.

But listeners did not get a hint that Prince Richard was aboard yesterday.

A Caroline spokesman said : " There was a request that there should be no fuss."

POP STAR GORDON —NOT GUILTY PLEA

Singer Gordon Waller, of the pop pair Peter and Gordon, is to plead not guilty to assaulting Louisa McKenna (or Holden), it was stated at Dundee yesterday.

Gordon, aged twenty, is alleged to have spat on her in the street. The hearing was fixed for July 15.

Story in Daily Mirror, Wednesday 9 June 1965

tender, which also had the Radio London relief disc jockeys and a special guest, Gene Pitney, on board.

On arrival at Radio Caroline I took over the microphone from Mike Allen who was going off for his week's leave. Around one o'clock I called the three guests into the studio and had an informal chat with them on the air about Cambridge. They said they were gathering information for the University magazine *Granta*. The penny had still not dropped as to who our famous guest was. Bernard gave his surname as Hunt - Brian as Walters - but Richard just said "Call me Richard." So I did.

We all sat down for lunch at 2 o'clock, spoke about life on board, cracked numerous jokes, showed the visitors around the ship, and then all too soon it was time for the tender to leave.

As was usual on a changeover day for disc jockeys we all waved goodbye: shouted fond farewells and generally clowned around.

When the tender went out of sight towards Radio London the captain of the *Mi Amigo* came up to Bryan Vaughan and myself and said "You know who that was, don't you?"

"Three university students," replied Bryan.

"One of them was Prince Richard of Gloucester" he said with raised voice!

I have to say we didn't believe him. And then he showed us the visitors book which all three had signed. Sure enough there it was "Prince Richard of Gloucester, 8 June 1965; Bernard Hunt and Brian Walters."

I must have turned scarlet. I immediately thought back to the broadcast where we were all cracking jokes and sending each other up. I must be fired for this!! Would my days be numbered? Would I be frogmarched to the Tower? I drank a couple of beers to drown my sorrows. What would Caroline House authorities be saying? Later it began to fall into place ... the reason why Prince Richard didn't want his surname mentioned ... Scaddan asking us to look after the three students with extra care ... But why weren't we told Prince Richard was paying us a visit?

A couple of days later we found out when he wrote and thanked us for an informative visit to Caroline. He didn't want any fuss. If people had known he was coming out, there would have been the red carpet treatment. Prince Richard and his two colleagues saw us in our true light and as we normally behaved.

On returning to Parkeston Quay, Harwich, dressed in a suede coat with lamb wool collar, Prince Richard was asked by a Customs officer "Are you English?" The Prince, who was then 20, was eighth in succession to the English Throne. We were all delighted to learn he passed his finals before leaving Cambridge.

One comment that all visitors made coming out to the radio ship was the danger of 'leaping' from the tender to the *Mi Amigo*. To say the least one had to be fairly agile, especially in the high jump or the long jump, as the tender and *Mi Amigo* were not on the same level. The ships were never stationary and normally rock and rolled towards and away from each other. Andy Gray, the then editor of the *New Musical Express*, who also paid us a visit said "To get from the tender to Caroline I had to do a death defying leap ... and that just about sums it up." He was absolutely right!

In September 1965, press officer Frances Van Staden's assistant, Wendy Barber, paid us a visit and brought a tape made by the Merseybeats. It was broadcast, and then Wendy put it in her handbag with the intention of sending it up to Caroline North the following day. But when she arrived at Parkeston Quay Customs point, on her return journey, she was searched by a Customs officer who also looked into her handbag and seized the tape. It was a complete mystery why they took it. Tapes were being sent to and from the boat every other day, and there had never been any trouble until that occasion.

A Customs official at Harwich said "It is our job to search everyone who comes in from the pirate stations. They have all been warned about bringing goods back into the country."

However, as Wendy told the Customs officer, "I took the tape out with me personally this morning." The tape was still held by officials.

When we transferred to Felixstowe Customs we found the officers far more friendly, although extremely thorough in their job. They would talk to us as human beings - even ask us what conditions had been like at sea.

As Radio Caroline was at sea for 365 days a year, it was not unnatural for her crew members, disc jockeys and radio engineers to know about the technical set up of the ship should she get 'into deep water.' Lifeboat drill was a necessity. Perhaps the captain who was most keen on Radio Caroline South was Peter Klokkers who used to spring lifeboat drill on us all at varying times. All those not immediately involved on air were expected to take part.

The Dutch crew lowered one of her two lifeboats and, once aboard, a few Dutchmen, disc jockeys and engineers sped off to some unknown destination. We then stopped the small engine and took to the oars. Captain Klokkers told us it was important to know all about rowing and sailing should the engines of the lifeboat either break down or run out of fuel.

During the summer months it was great fun taking part in lifeboat drill, but in the winter months it was a 'little draughty around the knee caps,' to say the least.

With lifeboat drill ringing in the ears of all disc jockeys it was obvious, I suppose, when new members came aboard to tell them about it soon after their arrival. On one occasion we carried out a send-up mock lifeboat drill during the middle of the night. This I well remember with regard to Norman St. John, a new boy to Caroline in the winter of 1965. As I was chief disc jockey at the time it was my job to tell him about lifeboat drill. On his first day on board he went to bed around 10.00pm. We told the captain of our intention to hold a 'send-up' around midnight and he approved. At midnight engineer George Saunders woke up Norman and told him that lifeboat drill was on! "Get your life jacket fitted and be on the top deck within two minutes," Saunders said with some urgency. Needless to say Norman did panic slightly having trouble fitting his life jacket on the correct way around. All the lights fused (on purpose) and everyone raced around with torches. I was on the top deck pretending to organise the broadcasters. Norman eventually came up and I told him to hold a wheel of the lifeboat until such time we told him to release it. It was important to put a great deal of pressure on it. It was a very cold night, and Norman only had pyjamas on with a thick sweater and life jacket. I then disappeared from the top deck as did everyone else who happened to be around, and returned to bed. About 45 minutes later Norman popped into my cabin and found me supposedly asleep. He then proceeded to wake me up by asking "What the **** was going on?"

He had stood there on the top deck literally freezing to death holding this ******* wheel, and no one had said a word.

He was then let into the secret and took it very well. It wasn't too long before he was taking an active part in send-up lifeboat drills himself!

It may seem unfair to have exploited Norman, but he was undoubtedly the record holder lasting for 35 minutes. Most of us smelt a rat after about four or five minutes when we originally went through 'the drill.'

As well as our 'humour side' we could also be very serious. Take the death of Sir Winston Churchill, whom we all admired and respected. Keith Martin instigated a programme looking back on his career, which was narrated by Simon Dee. Radio Caroline received hundreds of letters of praise following the station's decision to play sombre music on the day of his death in 1965, followed by tracks from the film based on his war career. Among the many who wrote were Valerie Price of Willow Way, Ewell, Surrey; Alan R. Johnson, Lincoln Avenue, Cheltenham, Gloucester; Mrs R. Firth, Wickham Street, Welling, Kent; and Patricia Hunter of The Shambles, Otterham Quay, Rainham, Kent.

Many listeners were good enough to keep us informed of their own activities regarding the continuation of 'Offshore Radio.' Many people like Mrs Rose Montgomery of Frog Street, Kelvedon Hatch, near Brentwood, Essex, wrote to their local MP (in her case John Biggs-Davidson). Another was Miss Barbara Cook of High Road, Trimley-St.Mary, Ipswich, Suffolk, who wrote to Keith Stainton. In each case the MP forwarded their letters on to the Postmaster-General. The main objection to the pirates, according to the Postmaster-General's letters, were international obligations. The existing pirate stations were making it difficult for people in France and Belgium to hear their own radio stations.

At least three days a week we on board Radio Caroline were kept in touch with what was happening in the outside world by our courier - Richard Swainson who brought us mail, tapes, food parcels and amendments for radio commercials. Richard was an excellent lad for he always passed on messages to people and, if necessary, would phone up and say "So and so sends his regards." Every so often Caroline House would have a clear out of staff when numerous people suffered the 'chop.' Unfortunately the powers that be thought it would be more economical if they didn't have a courier and poor old Richard was 'axed' in January 1966.

But Radio Caroline's loss was Radio London's gain. Richard was a talented song-writer and knew many important people in the record business. Radio Caroline didn't exploit him in the slightest. But Swainson went on to show Caroline that he was capable of holding a good position. Programme director Alan Keen and former chief disc jockey Tony Windsor offered him the job in charge of administration on board the m.v. *Galaxy*. He accepted the challenge and there he remained until the end of Radio London's days. He then joined MGM Records in the exploitation department, and later still Radio Luxembourg.

During the earlier days of Caroline none of us on board realised the power of the spoken word. In September 1964 I remember mentioning the birthday of a young man living then in Shepherd's Bush, London - Roger Aspinall. I read out his address and wished him well from all the disc jockeys on board. Within the next week he received almost a hundred and fifty cards from listeners wishing him a happy birthday. Both Roger and I were stunned by the response. I wonder how many cards he would have received had I *asked* people to send him a card.

Earlier in the Chapter I mentioned that there were two girls helping out in the programming side of Caroline: Marion Cochrane and Maureen Blackburn. Marion is now back in Australia, her homeland, and Maureen went for an extended holiday in Italy and liked it so much that she decided to remain over there. The next girl ever to stay on Radio Caroline South was a young Yorkshire-born singer named Sylvan Whittingham. Sylvan, aged 21, came out for the day on 19 September 1965 with the intention of promoting her record *We Don't Belong*, and saying hello to the disc jockeys. But she became stormbound as high winds sprang up and the tender which took her out from Harwich was forced to return to land urgently, just as Sylvan was appearing on the radio. She spent the weekend of 18 - 20 September 1965 on board with the captain, crew and broadcasting personnel. As far as I know she is the only singer to have stayed over on board in those early days. Sylvan was the daughter of Jack Whittingham who wrote the screenplay of the James Bond film *Thunderball*. She said "It was very rough when I went out but after lunch, when I should have gone back, it grew worse and the tender was rising up and down beside Caroline. I knew I would be sick, so I locked myself in the lavatory and just refused to leave. The tender hooted at me for half-an-hour but eventually left without me." As there was no tender on the Sunday, Sylvan had to wait until the Monday, and a quiet sea, before returning to Harwich.

A listener, Mrs Monni Aldous of Catherine Close, Pilgrim's Hatch, Brentwood, Essex, remembers Sylvan's ordeal as follows:

Keith Skues (left) and Richard Swainson looking at a new Caroline Top '65 before the Saturday transmission

Have you e'er heard the tale, which now must be told
How sweet Sylvan was captured by pirates so bold
A blonde so attractive, a gorgeous young thing,
And to add to her talents she really can sing.
She came out on the tender one fine Saturday,
And rough weather prevented her getting away
Two days she was kept, though not chained to the floor,
And Roger Gale howled at her cabin door.
Of her beautiful frame Patrick caught just one glimpse,
And poor scientist's never been quite the same since.
On Caroline party time, Saturday night,
The listeners could near her and pity her plight
Held fast in the studio by Blackburn and Gale,
She couldn't escape, only sit there and wail
"Stand aside let me get off this ship," she did roar,
"No, never," cried Roger, as he locked the door.
On Sunday she kept all the good guys in order,
And monkeyed about with the tape recorder,
Recording some gimmicks, as listeners well know,
To enliven the Tony Blackburn show.
But Monday dawned fine and clear once more,
And our heroine was able to go ashore,
Avowing out loud as she stepped off the boat,
That never again would she set foot afloat.

Storms sprang up very quickly in the North Sea. I distinctly remember coming to the end of a fortnight's stint on board at the latter end of October 1965. I had packed my case, had a shower, a shave and was all 'dolled up' for a week's leave. The tender was due on the Monday around 1.00pm. I had to present the lunchtime show from midday to 2.00pm. As expected the tender came alongside and dropped off the various disc jockeys, including Tony Blackburn, then went off to Radio London. The crew from the tender had lunch on Radio London and returned to Caroline to take us off at 1.45pm. I was still on air. The tender came alongside. On jumped Bryan Vaughan, Paul Noble and engineer Patrick Starling. No-one checked the whereabouts of young Skues. The captain had said it was becoming a little rough and suggested the tender did not tie up. When I came off the air at 2.00pm the tender was on its way to Harwich. I, too, became stormbound and remained so for four more days.

The weather remained extremely rough as winds of storm force howled around the *Mi Amigo*. Torrential rain drove horizontally across the black water from Frinton-on-Sea. One evening the sky was torn by a violent electrical storm with fork lightning, accompanied by thunder. I recalled the famous mariners' hymn, words by William Whiting; "Eternal Father strong and brave; Whose arm doth bend the endless wave; Who bidd'st the mighty ocean deep; Its own appointed limits keep; O hear us when we cry to thee; For those in peril on the sea." I thought of all the ships that were at sea that October evening. I eventually stepped ashore on the Friday! Was I paid any extra money? No chance!

During the time the pirate ships were anchored off the Essex coast there have been numerous occasions where bad weather played havoc with shipping in that area. Two notable wrecks near to Radio Caroline and Radio London happened in 1965 and 1966.

In September 1965 the 1,317 ton sand dredger *Boqueen* sank and four people were drowned. The Trinity House pilot cutter *Peloxros* rescued seven crew members.

The other wreck involved the Panamanian-registered ship *Ypapanti* which broke up near Gunfleet Sands in November 1966. The Walton and Frinton lifeboat rescued all the men on board.

Coincidence stories sometimes happened through names we read out on the air or people that we interviewed. During our afternoon programmes in the summer we had a school spot where we interviewed schoolchildren, and during one of these programmes in August 1965 I was talking to a Miss Jackie Woollard of Clacton-on-Sea. A few days later I received a letter from a Veronica Williams of Sutton in Surrey who related that Friday the 13th was usually unlucky - but in this case it was lucky! Veronica happened to be listening to the programme and in her own words "nearly fell over backwards". Jackie's sister, Barbara, was Veronica's bridesmaid six years previous. Apparently both the Woollards and the Williams had moved houses during the six years that had elapsed and subsequently lost touch with each other. So, in brief, six years and two children later we managed to put both families in touch again.

There was a rather amusing "In Memoriam" board which measured six feet long by three feet wide and listed the disc jockeys who had been with Radio Atlanta and Radio Caroline South. Sadly it was lost during the time the ship was washed up on Great Holland beach in January 1966. Up to and including December 1965 it read:

ASK NOT FOR WHOM THE BELL TOLLS

Ted King	April - May 1964
Richard Harris	April - May 1964
Clive Burrell	April - May 1964
John Ridley	April - May 1964
Mike Raven	April - May 1964
Neil Spence	April - May 1964
Colin Nicol	April - June 1964 and
	September 1965 - February 1966
Bob Scott	May-June 1964
Johnny Jackson	May - June 1964
Tony Withers	May - July 1964
Keith Martin	June - August 1964
	Eastertime, 1965
Peter du Crow	June - August 1964
Terry Saunders	May - November 1964
Bobby Brown	August - December 1964
Eddie Anthony	July - September 1964
Ed Moreno	May - September 1964
Errol Bruce	August 1964 - January 1965
Peter James	December 1964 - January 1965
Simon Dee	April 1964 - February 1965
Doug Kerr	April 1964 to April 1965
Bob Stewart	April 1965
Don Allen	April - June 1965
Gary Kemp	December 1964 - September 1965
Jon Sydney	March 1965 - September 1965
Roger Gale	June - September 1965
Don Dwight	Two days from 22 - 24 September 1965
Mike Allen	July 1964 - September 1965
Bob Walton	August 1965 - September 1965
Mel Howard	August 1965 - December 1965
Bryn Vaughan	April 1964 - December 1965
Paul Noble	January - December 1965
Keith Skues	September 1964 - December 1965

At close down and on the Early Show we shall remember them!

'Daffy' Don Allen

The departure of engineers was on a much smaller scale - Ted Walters, Joe Neal, Patrick Starling (the Child Scientist), George Saunders, Carl Thomson, Paul Noble (who transferred to the broadcasting side), Martin Newton, 'Topmaster' Sallon, Trevor Grantham and Jack Havey.

During its time on the air Radio Caroline had numerous people writing in wanting to organise "Hands off the Pirates". Some of the more energetic people were Miss Pamela Hayward of Colchester; Dallas Willcox of Tiptree, Essex, and David Hughes of Loose, near Maidstone, Kent.

In June 1965 we learned that boys at England's oldest public school were trying to save the pop pirate stations from any Government ban. About 60 boys at the King's School, Canterbury, (fees then were £436 a year) signed a petition that was sent to the Prime Minister. The petition deplored any Government ban to bring in legislation to run the pirates out of business.

The petition organiser was 16-year-old John Hamp, son of a solicitor of Croydon. He said:

> I am a Radio Caroline Club member and I think they have marvellous programmes - far better than the BBC. Although this was a 'Hands off Caroline' petition, we were trying to save all the pop pirates. We all had transistor radios in our rooms and used to tune in regularly.

The headmaster of the school, the Rev. J. P. Newell, said he had no comment to make on the boys' attitude towards the pirates.

On the subject to schools, John Dancy, a master of the £561-a-year Marlborough College, said in November 1965 that the boys at the school had two accents "One for talking with their parents and teachers." Perhaps you could call it their Oxford accent. The other was a classless Radio Caroline accent. Dancy said he found the state of affairs "healthy and encouraging."

As well as music on Radio Caroline we used to delight in setting competitions. Each Sunday during 1965 I was fortunate in presenting a lunchtime comedy show which also slotted in present and past hit records. An imaginary character helped me with the programme. He was known as Flying Officer Dingleweed. He had a voice likened unto Donald Duck. In actual fact it was my voice recorded slow and then played back at double speed. Dingleweed used to come along and interview guest stars and introduce records. Slowly but surely his mail was growing larger each and every week. It soon overtook mine, so I decided to make him even more controversial and pre-recorded a few phone calls on land with the help of a Barbara Sainsbury, who went under the radio name of 'Elsie Hatchett.' Barbara now lives in Cardiff. Ninety-nine per cent of the people who wrote in enjoyed Dingleweed's weekly antics, but I had to kill off the Elsie Hatchett romance when a young lady from Hillview Road, Rayleigh, Essex, wrote in and drew my attention to a few facts. She was Miss Carol Watts who suggested I should devote more time to playing records instead of chatting to girls on the telephone, especially during a record programme. After all, people tuned in for the music, not lots of talking. Carol went on to say that in her opinion this sort of performance might encourage more teenagers to phone up and talk to disc jockeys as if they were old friends.

I wrote back to Carol in June 1965 explaining that the whole episode concerning Flying Officer Dingleweed was harmless; we did not have a telephone on board in real life! - and the feature was meant to be taken "with a pinch of salt." I did eventually meet Carol in London and agreed to drop the Dingleweed/Hatchett romance. After all the last thing I wanted to do was to offend our listening public. Dingleweed as such continued until the end of my time on Caroline. He was going to be reintroduced when I later joined Radio London, but some other producer beat me to the punch and used a similar idea (but with a different name) in the Curry's programme. So we had to forget poor old Dingleweed. Other competitions we ran also brought great amounts of mail. Every two months I jumbled up thirty or so different hit parade records - making a completely new record out of them - and asked listeners to name them. In certain cases there may have only been a couple of words of the song.

Listeners then started to send in their own tapes, and we did broadcast one or two which were worthy of transmission. One name readily springs to mind - a Clive Moore of Woodbridge, Suffolk, who decided to go one better. Instead of linking records, he edited together disc jockeys' speech. Taken over a period of a fortnight he would record off the radio and cut in sentences from every disc jockey on board to make a rather amusing imaginary story. Very clever editing and an extremely novel idea.

Another interesting competition consisted of asking listeners if they remembered any amusing incidents on Radio Caroline - or perhaps an incident that stuck in their memory. Among the many entries received included:

Miss Jackie Hetherington of Seeshill Close, Sydney Road, Whitstable, Kent, wrote to say she was listening to *Party Time* on a Saturday night when literally everyone was in the studio - disc jockeys Tony Blackburn, Paul Noble, Dave Lee Travis, Norman St. John and engineers Trevor Grantham, Jack Havey and the Child Scientist (Patrick Starling). Apparently the show consisted of every person in turn sending requests to their respective girlfriends or wives ... some read poetry ... and I could hardly get a word in edgeways (it was meant to be my show). We were due to close down at 12.00 midnight, but in fact didn't succeed until 12.30am. Jackie, together with a large number of her friends, found this the most amusing incident ever to happen on Radio Caroline. 'Real enjoyable broadcasting!'

Other letters included Mrs Barbara Apostolides of Rush Green, Essex, who remembered Bryan Vaughan and 'Mad' Mel Howard committing the trousers they wore on the ship to the sea with full military honours. The ceremony was described to listeners over the air at the actual time. Barbara also remembered the time when Bob Walton was reading the weather forecast and said "There will be fisty mog tonight." And on another occasion Mr Walton said "There will be frog and fost later this evening." Another instance concerned Graham Webb who came to read the news after the elections. He said "*Caroline Newsbeat* starts with details of the elections (long pause ... rustle of paper) ... Oh I do believe I left it on my bunk before falling asleep. I'll go and get it." There was laughter from the studio next door where Tommy Vance continued with music until Graham obtained the necessary news sheet. It was moments like this that made listening to pirate radio such a pleasure," Barbara Apostolides went on. "We enjoyed this kind of informality."

Pamela Alridge of Merlin Grove, Hainault, Essex, remembers the time that Norman St.

John was reading the news on a day that there were rough seas. Halfway through the news broadcast a giant wave swamped the studio and washed away his news script. What other news reader (especially on BBC) in this position would describe in detail what had happened and why he couldn't continue?

From Wolseley Road, Hornsey, London N8, Mrs Rita Ignatius commented on the writer broadcasting a series of limericks during the morning show. One of them went:

> There was a DJ called Vaughan,
> Who was an Australian born,
> He had a girlfriend named Jean,
> On which he was terribly keen,
> That Australian born Vaughan with the corn.

Rita says that just before the limerick was read out on the air her insurance man called and listened with particular attention. He asked what station produced such wit and added "I'm an Aussie, too."

Another memorable incident which concerned Bryan Vaughan was remembered by Mrs Helen Harlow of Palmerston Avenue, Walmer, Deal, Kent. Bryan, according to Helen, had a "dishy chocolate voice." She said she was rather surprised when Bryan once said on his morning show which came live from a studio on a ship three and a half miles off Frinton-on-Sea ... "I've just seen a car go past the porthole without a driver at the wheel."

"I thought I had gone completely berserk," Helen went on. "However, it turned out to be a car strapped securely down on a passing ship."

Miss Sheila Webber of Street Farm, Bandwell, Bury St. Edmunds, Suffolk, remembered the time when Simon Dee was on the air during a period of rough weather. The tender had just drawn alongside with a spare copy of P. J. Proby's record, *Hold Me*, which was thrown onto the *Mi Amigo*. Unfortunately the record missed by a couple of inches and ended up in the North Sea. Simon announced "P. J. is going down, and that if listeners paid particular attention they would hear Mr. Proby singing *Hold Me*," which was followed by a large gurgle, gurgle. And that was that!

Bob Walton was the disc jockey whom Martin Pike of Graydon Avenue, Chichester, Sussex, described as a memory-maker. Bob made an announcement one lunchtime: "You have just heard *Soundtrack* ... No! ... er ... *Spin Around*. Yes, you have been listening to *Spin Around* and the time is 1 o'clock ... No! 2 o'clock ... No! 1 o'clock; The time is two o'clock and now I can at least get this right. We present *Soundtrack*." "Can you imagine the BBC saying this? Very human, most amusing and definitely good informal radio," says Martin Pike.

Miss Mary Hopman went back to the early days of pirate history for her contribution to the memory game. It concerned the time when Radio Atlanta had just amalgamated with Radio Caroline. One ship (Caroline) was to sail round to the Isle of Man to, in future, be called Radio Caroline North. Radio Atlanta was to become Radio Caroline South. "Simon Dee had been transferred to Caroline South and his friend Neddy (Alan Turner) was left on Caroline North. Neddy didn't want Caroline (North) to leave her moorings so he tied the anchor chains around him and threatened to jump overboard. When he discovered that no one minded if he did jump overboard he 'mooched' around the ship in a depressive mood muttering how unfair it was. Every time he moved his chains would move, and the rattle could be heard by the listeners. Every time the chains rattled I burst into laughter."

Mary Hopman also remembered "the time a gallon bottle of ink fell off its position on top of a wardrobe and smashed into a million pieces staining the entire cabin and ruining Bryan Vaughan's pyjamas and Keith Skues' suit."

Mrs Winifred Poulter of The Folly, Tangham, Woodbridge, Suffolk, recalled the time Doug Kerr was broadcasting when an American jet fighter "buzzed" Caroline. Doug, deafened by the noise, said on air "Come a little closer, fella, then I can see the whites of your eyes."

Those were just a few of the incidents that listeners remembered from Radio Caroline.

Above: 'Admiral' Robbie Dale enrolls Mickey Dolenz of the Monkees in his 'Beat Club'
Below: Emperor Rosko about to spin in some rock'n'roll greats on Radio Caroline South

Most people who were regular listeners were, in fact, human beings. But in November 1965 it was reported that Radio Caroline had increased its number of fans by 4,000 who listened to nonstop pop for eight hours a day at Minsterly near Shrewsbury. Nothing odd in this? Odd would be an understatement - the listeners were all hens! Their owner, farmer David Jones, claimed that the music helped to relax the birds.

From hens to fish! In November 1964 the port of Fleetwood, Lancashire, celebrated a bumper catch of fish which were caught around Radio Caroline North. The skipper of the 40-foot trawler *Faith Star,* 35-year-old Wilf Clark, and his two- man crew had caught 480 stone of codlings in eighteen hours which brought a price of £16 for less than four days at sea.

Wilf Clark, who is married and has ten children, said "My theory is that the fish feed from the waste food thrown overboard from the radio ship."

It's generally believed that fish can sense sound waves or vibrations on their lateral lines. I wonder if they had a local Top 10? ... *Theme from a Summer Plaice, Cod Only Knows, Perchance to Bream, Whale Meat Again, How Much is that Dogfish in the Window, O Sole Mio, Hey Mr Bassman, Salmon Chanted Evening, Tiddler on the Roof* and *Fillet of Plaice Reminds Me of You.*

In November 1965 four fishermen visited the Radio Caroline South ship. They were writing an article for *Creel* magazine and they were catching cod from Caroline. Les Moncrieff, John Nixon, Michael Prichard and Dennis Wilkinson came on board and set up camp on the poop deck of the *Mi Amigo.* A floodlight was set up so that they could fish after dark. Les told me "It was more of an endurance test. We were fishing in a force 8 gale, which was coming from the south, and the rain was freezing on the handrails. It was bitterly cold."

The first cod went to Mike Prichard, speedily followed by one to Dennis Wilkinson, and the ensuing scraping noise had been ship's cook, Martin Schuit, sharpening his knife in the galley below. Later Les Moncrieff, the 1965 champion fisherman of Gibraltar, pulled in another plump cod which was brought into the studio whilst I was on air. As I was a great nephew to the fisherman and author, G.E.M. Skues, the lads thought I ought to see their catch. I had to apologise to listeners as the fish slapped its tail against the microphone. The fishermen decided to call it a day as it was very stormy. The following morning they caught another dozen cod, in addition to whiting and dabs which they kindly presented to the ship's cook. They left at lunchtime, leaping at risk of life and limb onto the deck of the *Offshore I,* rising and falling twelve feet at a time alongside the *Mi Amigo.*

An incident which made all the national newspapers occurred in September 1966 when a Radio Caroline North disc jockey was married on board ship.

Mick Luvzit was married to Janet Teret by the Dutch Captain Martin Gipps on board m.v. *Caroline* on Tuesday 20 September. The ship was registered in Panama so it made the marriage ceremony, performed by a ship's captain, quite legal.

Mick and Janet, both 23, were introduced by Janet's brother, 'Ugli' Ray Teret who was also a disc jockey on Caroline North for a while. Ray was best man at the wedding.

Mick wore a black velvet jacket, pinstriped trousers and high heeled boots. The bride, two hours late because of fog, arrived by motor launch, barefoot and wearing hipster slacks with bare midriff. A mod wedding with a difference!

Many listeners were good enough to write to newspapers. One such letter from the *Daily Mirror* in November 1964 was sent in by Mrs Dylis Calver of Felixstowe, Suffolk, - "I think the boys on Radio Caroline deserve a medal for sticking to their duties during the recent very rough seas, especially as they are not professional sailors."

Reading letters in the press made us realise how genuine were our listeners.

On board we quite often received letters of a technical nature telling us that during winter nights Caroline transmissions carried a whistle. In business circles this was known as heterodyne which occurs when two radio signals (i.e. the radio frequency energy upon which the modulation is impressed to carry the signal) are located on the same or near the same wavelength. A note is produced, the intensity of which is dependent on relative strengths of two signals: pitch directly dependent on the radio frequency difference of the two carriers. However, if the stations are on exactly the same frequency there is no heterodyne. Caroline South had a heterodyne on 199 metres on their 10 kilowatt transmission.

There were two occasions when the Caroline ships moved their positions. In the case of Caroline South, on 2 November 1964 she moved some 20 miles south into the Thames Estuary, but it was so choppy that many of the disc jockeys, engineers and crew were sick, and furthermore the records refused to remain on the turntable. The constant rocking and pitching of the *Mi Amigo* forced Caroline off the air on numerous occasions on weekend tests. However, during the time she was on the air reception was infinitely better in the London area. But as conditions were so rough she returned to her original anchorage point off Frinton.

Caroline North, at a similar time, also tried for a better reception area. She sailed a short distance but got caught in the tide, and nearly ended up in Liverpool harbour. Caroline just managed to get out of the tide-race in time and hurried back to her old location.

The majority of the programmes on Radio Caroline were live, although the religious sections of broadcasting were taped. Sometimes, tapes tended to go slightly wrong due to mains fluctuations. Presenters refer to them as 'wowing.' Colin Nicol recalls an instance when he was duty announcer and sitting in the studio should the tape suddenly stop or troubles occur. The take-up spool suddenly (for no apparent reason) stopped and Colin had to pull the tape through by hand for twenty-seven minutes, adjusting the speed manually. When the sponsor's report came through there was no hint of a noticeable difference on transmission. One up to Colin, who had it more or less taped, one could say!

During the summer months when we went on shore leave we sometimes travelled by car. On all other occasions we let the train take the strain. There were times when we set competitions over the air. Around lunchtime we would mention that we would be driving to London, leaving Harwich around 4.00pm. If people could recognise the car in which we were driving (Tony Blackburn's car - an MGB was used in the majority of cases) and wave us down successfully, we would give them a record. On the return journey we had to pass through the Customs department at Harwich who checked every individual to see if he had brought back any cigarettes or spirits.

After that formality (and sometimes we had to wait at the quayside at Parkeston for over an hour for the Customs men to come and see us) we were on our own. Memorable incidents abound during the summer of 1965 when Tony and myself made the trip to London by road.

DJ Dave Lee Travis having a swinging time on board the tender Offshore I as he prepares for one week ashore. In the background m.v. Galaxy, Radio London

Normally there were about twenty or thirty people waiting at Harwich before we could get on to the London road. Cars were parked in lay-bys and followed us, eventually overtaking and finally waving us down and demanding a pop record. Quite often we had run out of records, so towards the end we promised to play the people a record over the airwaves.

When we went through the big towns there were always people lying in wait ... like in Colchester, Chelmsford, Brentwood, Romford and Ilford.

Perhaps the biggest surprise came once when we thought we had been delayed too long by people (we reached Brentwood just five hours after leaving Harwich, and it was dark), but lo and behold on entering the outskirts of the town we were waved down by a boy leaning against a bicycle. We got talking and signed a few photographs and were all set to move on when a car screeched to a halt and out jumped two young men and two girls. They invited us for a drink in Brentwood.

On other occasions we would return to London by train. We set similar competitions, but asked people to be at the main railway stations when we would have a quick natter out of the carriage window. On one Monday in November 1965 there were so many people who had come to the station at Manningtree, Colchester and Chelmsford, that the train arrived in Liverpool Street twenty minutes late.

The *Essex County Standard* reported that teenagers had held up the Norwich-London train when they went onto the station to see Radio Caroline disc jockeys.

Vivien Barnard of Chelmsford, Essex remembers:

When the disc jockeys were going on their week's leave they would very often mention they would be travelling on a certain train going to London. So my brother and I had the idea that we would travel to Colchester on the train on which we knew Keith Skues, Tony Blackburn and perhaps one or two others would be travelling.

We did this about three times just so we could meet the broadcasters, talk to them and ask them to play us a record on their return.

I used to log all the dedications that I had on Radio Caroline - I know that I had 30 written down, but I am sure there were many more.

DJ Keith Skues tucking into a plate of cornflakes whilst
presenting the Morning Show on Radio Caroline South 1965

It was all great fun. But most of all we were surprised when we reached Liverpool Street (there was Tony Blackburn, Norman St. John and the author) to find at least twenty people waiting to meet and greet us. We used to receive a terrific kick out of this sort of friendliness from listeners. At the same time I hope it proved to them that we were not stuffy individuals who no-one ever saw, but humans with whom you could have a conversation.

Most listeners at some time or other visit the dentist. A large proportion do not particularly look forward to their appointment with the man who tends to 'fill you in.'

However, in 1967 a novel idea came from Mr Ralph Neal, a 53-year-old children's officer for Cumberland. He asked his county council to buy transistor radios for the county's twenty school surgeries. Furthermore he recommended tuning them to Radio Caroline. Mr Neal said: "Modern children react most favourably to pop music. Transistor radios in clinics could be of immense value in helping children to relax."

Experiments have been undertaken in Whitehaven and Workingham where music like *Oklahoma!* and *The Sound of Music* failed to make the patient relax. However, pop music did the trick. The teenagers tapped their feet even whilst having their teeth out. Mr Neal went on: "Radio Caroline will be the station to listen to. It's not my kind of music - it jars me. But in this case, the customer is right!"

On my final day with Radio Caroline South in December 1965 I was in such a panic to catch the tender that I inadvertently left my transistor radio in my cabin. Perhaps a fitting finale to this chapter would be a poem sent in by a listener, Mrs Monni Aldous of Pilgrim's Hatch, Essex, whom we met in print earlier.

FOND FAREWELLS

'Twas Saturday morning, 11th December
A day that Skues' listeners will ever remember
For Skues was departing for life on the shore;
And Caroline listeners would hear him no more.

He woke up that morning, a little off-key,
For at yesterday's party they drank more than tea,
(Corks were popping all over the studio
But listeners weren't supposed to know).

His very last programme so warm and sincere,
Took a piece of our hearts - from our eyes jerked a tear;
Then he took off his headphones and said his farewell
To the friends he had worked with so long and so well.

The tender toot-tooted and Skues was away,
Whether sorry or joyful I really can't say.
Then Norman St. John went downstairs to find
If anything might have been left behind.

What did he notice? A cardboard shoe?
Or poor little Dingleweed locked in the Loo?
No, none of these dear little things remained,
For only one item the cabin contained.
A transistor radio belonging to Skues
Which Norman took to London the following Tues.

If you are wondering what disc jockeys did during their week's leave ... read on!

Sunset from Radio Caroline

Chapter Three

HOUSE OF THE RISING SUN

You suddenly hear a bell
And right away you can tell
This could be the start of something grand!

This Could be the Start of Something, Steve Lawrence and Eydie Gorme, 1960

CAROLINE HOUSE, a large palatial building in the heart of London's Mayfair, had the appealing address of 6 Chesterfield Gardens, London W1. It enjoyed the most luxurious offices of all the offshore radio stations. Originally the Radio Caroline personnel were housed in a small office in Regent Street, London.

Caroline House came into being on 14 September 1964 when furniture and carpets were moved into the 45-roomed mansion. To enter the building one passed between two large double pillars, which were situated either side of a rather flamboyant archway, into the entrance hall with a staircase reminiscent of a manor house. A switchboard and reception desk was situated just inside the hall.

There were over 60 yards of plushly fitted carpets in the six storey headquarters where one bumped into recording artists, producers, directors, journalists, secretaries, administrative people, news readers, technical experts, salesmen and disc jockeys.

Caroline House was a busy enterprise when it became operational in 1964 with an active staff of forty that handled over 2,000 telephone calls a day. But in 1966 the staff was cut by half, and they moved out of the top two floors of the building.

In Caroline House there were two studios for recording purposes and on 23 October 1964 Radio Caroline went transatlantic. Disc jockey Simon Dee in studio 'A' spoke 'live' to Terry Knight of Station WKLW in Detroit, the home of the famous Tamla Motown people. Every other week the stations got together for a chat and an exchange of records and pop stars. Amongst the British artists to participate were the Animals, Bachelors, Nashville Teens, Ronnie Jones, Georgie Fame, Barry St. John and Susan Maughan. The programmes were broadcast live in America across 27 states.

In December 1964 Caroline opened an American office at 1697 Broadway, New York, headed by George Bernard.

When Radio Caroline commenced transmissions off the Essex coast, sacks of mail flooded into their offices asking for information on the disc jockeys, how to have records played and how to visit the ship. They asked for information of a technical nature and many other queries. So it was decided to start a Caroline Club which was launched on 1 July 1964. It was run by Rikki Stein and later taken over by Derek Kavanagh. The first programme which dealt specifically with Caroline Club requests took to the airwaves on 11 July 1964. Members paid 5 shillings (25p) annually, but in 1965 the membership went up to 10 shillings (50p). By April 1967 Club membership amounted to no fewer than 60,000 members scattered worldwide. There were members as far away as Scandinavia, France, Germany, Holland, Norway, Sweden, Canada and the United States of America.

Members received many price discounts, also an illustrated brochure containing information about Caroline, an identity bracelet, pictures of the disc jockeys and also a car sticker.

Caroline House, 6 Chesterfield Gardens, London W1

A number of times disc jockeys tried to find out who was Caroline Club member number one ... apparently the original three names had been lost from the register as they were overseas members. But thanks to Mrs Olive Burgess, who lived in Houghton Regis, Bedfordshire (but who has since died) the name and address is to hand. He was Martin Groenhorst of Boerhaarelaan, Schiedam, Holland. In a letter to Caroline in November 1964 Martin wrote:

> Radio Caroline is the favourite radio station for me and many other Dutchmen, and that's why I am member number one of the Caroline Club. The reception is very good in a very big part of Holland, and the programmes are for many people more pleasant than those of our national ship "Radio Veronica."
> I am convinced that it should be a great pleasure for many Dutch people if you would broadcast a bilingual programme for a few hours in a week. If you need a Dutch disc jockey it should be a great honour to me, if you would engage me for it. I am twenty years old and studying mathematics at the University of Leiden.
> Yours faithfully,
>
> Martin Groenhorst.

There were many changes of staff at Caroline House during its time. In 1964 the two joint managing directors were Ronan O'Rahilly and Allan Crawford, but in December 1965 Crawford resigned and Barry Ainley (who had been general manager for several months) became joint managing director with O'Rahilly. In February 1966 Philip Solomon came as a full-time working director. Later that year Barry Ainley resigned which left Ronan O'Rahilly and Philip Solomon as joint managing directors.

Barry Ainley, when he was in operation at Caroline House, was an executive director and his responsibilities were on the administrative and financial sides of Caroline. Bom in London in 1934 he was educated at Sorbonne and Madrid Universities as well as the London School of Economics where he graduated with a B.Sc. (Economics). Before joining Radio Caroline he was a merchant banker.

Executive director Philip Solomon came into Caroline to help boost the advertising revenue. He was born in Northern Ireland in 1926, stemmed from a family that already had connections with the record industry, and was managing director of Major Minor Records which recorded artists like David McWilliams, O'Brien Brothers, Frankie McBride, Raymond Lefevre Orchestra, Odin's People, The Gibsons and Jane Birkin and Serge Gainsbourg, and licensed pop stars like Kim Weston, Tommy James and the Shondells and Johnny Nash. Solomon, who also managed the Dubliners and Los Bravos, took an interest in the breeding of racehorses, and came to England in 1961. His wife, Dorothy, ran an agency and managed artists including Twinkle, the Gibsons and the Bachelors.

But the key figure at Caroline House was Ronan O'Rahilly whose main interest lay in the programming and sales departments. Ronan was bom in Dublin of an Irish father and American mother. His father, Aodhogan O'Rahilly, was the operator of the Preston to Greenore ferry service located at Greenore, Eire. Ronan came to Britain in 1961 and took an interest in the management of pop groups. He was also a director of Roar Music Publishing Company. He managed the Scene Club and gave the Rolling Stones their first break. Ronan 'discovered' the Animals and Georgie Fame.

He puts the success of Radio Caroline down to the disc jockeys and says "Unlike the BBC these boys were human. They came over as flesh and blood - people who breathed fresh air and not artificial respiration. They made human mistakes and they were even embarrassing. But whatever you say they did emerge as personalities and people and not as BBC automatons." Politically Caroline was very strong, especially Caroline North which became the centre of comment in the crucial Isle of Man General Elections (see Chapter One).

Radio Caroline compliment slip, 1964

In January 1965 it was learned that 50,000 voters were asked to decide whether the island should defy Whitehall by not banning supplies of food and other essentials to the Caroline North ship off Ramsey. The ban had been agreed by the Council of Europe.

However, the Isle of Man made its own laws in Tynwald, one of the oldest parliaments in the world.

Sir Edward Callister, the leader, said "Radio Caroline have given free publicity - an important matter to a holiday island."

The Isle of Man came into the news again in a similar situation in March 1967.

On 7 March the Manx Parliament turned down the Marine Offences Bill with 19 people voting against it, and only three in favour of the Bill. The three in favour were committed to it by virtue of their official positions.

The Chairman of the Broadcasting Commission, Roy Macdonald, who introduced the Bill, said "In my personal capacity I would fling the Bill out, but as Chairman of the Broadcasting Commission I am forced to support the Bill. I am not even sure on whose behalf I am introducing the Bill."

Clifford Irving warned the Prime Minister, Harold Wilson, that he was going to have his "One big bite" and vote against the Bill.

Sir Henry Fogden, a member of the Tynwald, said "Advertising on radio is probably the best medium there is today. Let us keep Radio Caroline. They are here, and putting out the cause for the Isle of Man."

He called on the Tynwald to reject the bill and introduce another bringing Radio Caroline on shore and forbidding any other station from operating on the island.

Throughout the debate constant reference was made to Radio Caroline as 'our station'; most members who spoke against the Bill referred to the rejection as an opportunity for the island to fight against 'Big Brother' and show the Labour Government that they could not impose their own personal prejudices against the Isle of Man.

Caroline was described by the Post Office as a 'pirate', therefore not eligible for any help from their sources. But the GPO delivered thousands of letters daily to all the offshore stations. Many letters were just addressed to 'Radio Caroline' or 'Big L' - yet they reached their destination!

In 1964 Caroline applied for a telephone. Lines were granted on Hyde Park 9721, but they were not listed in the telephone directory. This was quite absurd when one considers the extra revenue enjoyed by the Post Office as a result of people writing or phoning in to the offshore stations' offices.

After much argument the Post Office allowed the station to be listed. Not as Radio Caroline - but, in fact, Caroline Sales.

A Post Office spokesman said that he did not consider it proper for Radio Caroline to be included in a Government publication, nor to give 'Enquiries' the number of an organisation that was, in the official view, making illegal broadcasts.

"However, services to various companies on land which were connected with them was rather a different matter. The company existed to sell advertising time on the stations and to promote their activities. It was difficult in some cases to prove that these companies were actually operating the broadcasting."

Many listeners presumed they would find Radio Caroline listed under Caroline House. There was a Caroline House located in Bayswater, but many people did not check the address and duly phoned through. A receptionist on this Hyde Park number told the author that she used to receive an average of twenty calls a day for Radio Caroline. After two years, she was getting "A little cheesed off. I have suggested to management we have our number changed."

On the subject of telephones, in April 1964 the GPO refused to allow radio telephone communications between the ship and shore except in cases of emergency, in which the captain alone was allowed to deal. The radio telephone was not to be utilised for any routine matter connected with the radio station. Even then only the ship's captain was allowed to use the equipment.

In the *London Gazette* in February 1962 a Notice from the Postmaster-General gave formal warning that radio telephony services would not be available to ships used as illicit radio stations. The only link between ship and shore for the radio stations off the Essex coast was the tender *Offshore I*.

In October 1964 it was learned that the BBC were to drop their longest running variety programme *Workers' Playtime* which began as a morale-booster during the last war. The idea of 'axing' the programme was part of the BBC's new-look plans featuring lighter shows in answer to the pop programmes of Radio Caroline.

Douglas Marlborough, writing in the *Daily Mail* on 3 October 1964, said that the last *Workers' Playtime*, from a corrugated case manufacturers at Hatfield, Hertfordshire, was to star Anne Shelton, Cyril Fletcher, Val Doonican and the Four Ramblers. *Workers' Playtime* had been compèred and produced by Bill Gates for 23 years.

In November 1964 Eamonn Andrews' younger brother Noel (31) was signed by Radio Caroline to compère a daily *Housewives' Choice* record request show from December, called *The Andrews Show* and sponsored by Andrews Liver Salts. Noel, a freelance broadcaster, had been heard on Radio Eireann for the past 14 years. The fifteen minute show on both Radio Caroline North and South toured the British Isles asking housewives to pick their favourite discs.

The Caroline House studios were used for taping interviews with the stars and also recording commercials prior to their being sent out to the ship for transmission.

Caroline's first big production from their studios in Chesterfield Gardens was broadcast on Caroline North and South during the Christmas period in 1964.

The 120 minute programme called *Around the World* had guests participating from all over the globe who spoke about their present activities and gave Christmas greetings. Amongst the many stars who appeared were: The Beatles, Karl Denver Trio, Val Doonican, Bachelors, Fourmost, Ronnie Carroll, Max Bygraves, Merseybeats, Edmund Hockridge, and Susan Maughan representing the British Isles and Wout Steenhuis (Holland), Heidi Brühl (Germany), Roberto Cardinali (Italy), The Cousins (Belgium), Robert Goulet, Betty Everett (America), Millie (Jamaica), Spotniks (Sweden), Jeremy Taylor (South Africa), Tsai Chin (The Far East), June Bronhill and Keith Michell (Australia) and Inia Te Wiata (New Zealand).

The programme, transmitted on Boxing Day 1964, was edited by Martin Newton and produced and introduced by Keith Skues.

Christmas broadcasting also incorporated a programme when disc jockeys Keith Martin and Carl Conway, helped by Cilla Black and Gerry Marsden (of the Pacemakers), visited the Great Ormond Street Children's Hospital in London and the Alder Hey Children's Hospital

Liverpool. They talked to some of the children who requested records for their families and friends during the Christmas holiday. The programme was broadcast on both the North and South ships on Christmas Day. Keith remembers: "Cilla called me chuck! After we had completed the interviews, in London, I can vividly remember a very large lady, assistant to the equally large programme director of Radio Caroline, Chris Moore, telling Cilla that she should have formal singing lessons or she would damage her vocal chords if she carried on singing the way that she did. I'm delighted to say I still see Cilla, but what happened to the large lady, I know not!

*Doug Kerr (left) and Simon Dee selecting
cards for Christmas dedications, 1964*

"It was at a similar time I remember going with Keith Skues, who was compiling another special programme for Christmas, to interview the highest paid barman in London at the Roof Garden bar of the Hilton Hotel."

One of the busiest offices in Caroline House was the programme office which housed the programme director (Chris Moore and later, Bill Hearne). Here too, was Ken Evans, the chief librarian ably assisted by Marion Cochrane and Maureen Blackburn, and later Dorothy White.

There was an excellent team spirit in this office which, to say the least, was always a hive of activity, with people racing around answering one or more of the five phones.

Here, too, one could find numerous pop stars and personalities from the world of show business. Amongst the many who visited Caroline House have been:

Adam, Mike and Tim, The Animals, The Applejacks, Eddie Arnold, The Bachelors, Joe Baker, Beau Brummel, Cilla Black, Graham Bond, Los Bravos, June Bronhill, Joe Brown, Eric Burdon, Chad and Jeremy, Checkmates, Petula Clark, Alma Cogan, Russ Conway, Peter Cook and Dudley Moore, Ray Coussins, Cream, Jim Dale, Troy Dante, David and Jonathan, Billie Davis, Spencer Davis, Dave Dee, Dozy, Beaky, Mick and Tich, Johnny Devlin, Diana Dors, Donovan, Val Doonican, Alan Drew, Marianne Faithfull, Georgie Fame, Andrew Faulds, Peter Fenton, Billy Fury, Snuff Garrett, Gerry and the Pacemakers, Goldie and the Gingerbreads, Bobby Goldsboro, Bobby Graham, Harbour Lites, Anita Harris, Rolf Harris, Herman's Hermits, The Hollies, The Honeycombs, Frank Ifield, Jimmy James and the Vagabonds, Bruce Johnson (of the Beach Boys), Ronnie Jones, Jonathan King, Kinks, Kathy Kirby, Billy J. Kramer, Cleo Laine, Harry Leader, Gary Lewis, Mia Lewis, Hank Locklin, Kenny Lynch, George Maharis, Henry Mancini, Manfred Mann, Susan Maughan, Chas McDevitt, Cathy McGowan, Barry McGuire, Merseybeats, Keith Michell, Millie, Miracles, Moody Blues, Stirling Moss, Mitch Murray, Nashville Teens, New Faces, Paramounts, Peter and Gordon, Peter, Jan and John, Wilson Pickett, Robbie Porter, Alan Price, Quiet Five, Tommy Quickly, Johnnie Ray, Cliff Richard, Righteous Brothers, Tommy Roe, Freddie Ryder, Mike Sarne, The Seekers, The Shadows, Sandie Shaw, Small Faces, Sonny and Cher, Sounds Incorporated, Dorothy Squires, Barry St. John, The Supremes, Sylvan, Jimmy Tarbuck, Johnny Tillotson, Twinkle, Walker Brothers, Billy Walker, Dee Dee Warwick, Nancy Whiskey, The Who, Danny Williams, Mark Wynter and Jimmy Young.

Caroline employee Richard Morecraft, reminiscing about the artists to visit Caroline House, relates that in his opinion Val Doonican was the most genuine. "One day in 1964 Val came in to record an interview but the studio was out of action due to some technical fault, so the interview was recorded on a portable tape machine in the kitchen with Keith Skues. On transmission the programme sounded as if it came from a plush studio. In fact Val squatted on a bucket to do the interview. Some artists would have walked out in disgust, but Val took it all in good part."

Gary Leeds of the Walker Brothers recalls "We toured Britain in 1964 with P.J. Proby and suggested to Scott and John that we ought to try our luck in London. We recorded at the Philips studios with producer Johnny Franz. We had recorded *Love Her* in the States, but our first recording in London was a number one hit, *Make It Easy On Yourself*, in August 1965. We went along to both Radios Caroline and London to be interviewed and they really played our record a lot. Our next record was dedicated to the pirate stations, *My Ship Is Coming In*. We were one of the first American groups to have long hair."

Gerry Marsden, of Gerry and the Pacemakers, who enjoyed three consecutive hits in 1963 says: "Although we were well established a year before Radio Caroline came on air, we certainly listened to the pirate stations. They played all the latest records and the DJs sounded enthusiastic. It was a great boost to the music industry for singers, songwriters and music producers."

Rick Wild, lead singer with the Overlanders, whose best selling record was *Michelle*, recalls

"I used to listen to Radio Caroline North in bed with an old pair of RAF headphones. I have a great admiration for the pirate radio stations as they were the forerunner of the commercial radio we have today. Had the pirates not happened we would probably still have the BBC monopoly. What was so interesting about the pirates was their style - so relaxed and laid back. I was a musician in the pop music business and with the pirates you could keep track of what was happening throughout the industry and hear all the latest music produced."

Freddy and the Dreamers had enjoyed four hits in the Top 20 by the time the pirates began transmitting in 1964. Their lead singer, Freddy Garrity, said: "With Radio Caroline on the waves we were getting lots of plays with our records. One evening I remember hearing our records no less than nine times. I was interviewed for the Radio Caroline North ship when The Dreamers and I were appearing in a summer season at a theatre on the Isle of Man in 1964."

Dave Berry was another northerner, who graced our charts on eight occasions, between 1963 and 1966. "The pirate stations were very important for people like myself. It was the first time we had radio stations playing music all day for our age group. Before, we had to hope that maybe we would get on the playlist of *Saturday Club* or *Family Favourites* on the BBC Light Programme. It may sound strange now, so many years on, when it is normal for DJs to talk to you on your wavelength. They would be similar to the people you would get deejaying at your local club. There was only one person doing that before and that was Jimmy Savile.

"Along with the Cruisers, I visited the Radio Caroline North ship and was interviewed live on the air. In 1966 we did a tour with Crispian St. Peters and the Small Faces, which was promoted by Radio London. All of the pop pirate radio stations were interested in promoting the music of the day. They will long be remembered."

Peter Noone of Herman's Hermits recalls: "When Radio Caroline North began in 1964 it was modern pop music they played all day. It was all needle time, with no 'live' music like on the BBC. For us it was great as they picked on our records because we were local."

Dave Berry

The Searchers, like Freddy and the Dreamers, had four chart records in the Top 20 before pirate radio came along. Founder lead singer, Mike Pender, says "In those days we used to drive to and from gigs, with our road manager, in an old van. We used to tune in to Caroline and London and they kept us going through the night. Together with Radio Luxembourg they certainly helped us with our songs. We were well established at that time, but if you were a new group or artist, and you couldn't get your record played on either the BBC or Luxembourg, you counted on airplay on the pirates. I don't think the pirate radio stations will ever be forgotten."

Dave Dee of Dave Dee, Dozy, Beaky, Mick and Tich recalls: "Had it not been for the pirates our group would not have had any chance of our records being heard at all. I don't know what the BBC music policy was at that time, but they definitely didn't want to play our records. If it hadn't been for the pirates I might still be a policeman!"

One person who was very much involved with the music played on Radio Caroline was Ken Evans. He always had time for music publishers, record pluggers and even fans. All this was in addition to his fixing interviews, compiling record programmes, arranging, sorting and filing records.

Born in Newcastle, New South Wales, Ken had a wealth of radio experience. He had been a studio manager at 2CH in Sydney, Australia, and then joined 2GB, the Mcquarie Network as overseas interviewer. After the pirates closed Ken moved to Radio Luxembourg and was responsible for the production of the entire output of all EMI programmes on the radio station, working with disc jockeys Alan Freeman, Tony Blackburn, Simon Dee, Jimmy Young, Mike Raven, Pete Brady and David Jacobs. He was promoted to programme controller under Alan Keen on 1 August 1970. After seven years with Luxembourg Ken moved to ABC Records and on 1 May 1979 joined BBC Radio 2 as a producer. It is rewarding to see good people succeed in the radio business, and the author has not come across one person with a bad word to say against Ken Evans. In 1987 almost every name in the music business turned up to 'honour' him at a party when he retired from the BBC. The party had been kept a secret from Ken who was 'stunned' when he walked into a large banqueting suite in London's West End to find names representing over 30 years in the business.

Recalling his time with Caroline, Ken says: "They were great days, but one thing I didn't like was bad weather. On one occasion I arrived at the Caroline North ship just as Jimmy Savile was leaving after a day's visit. Everything was peaceful ... blue skies, soft breeze - and then up came a force 10 gale. It appeared to get worse as the night wore on. I held onto either side of the bunk in the cabin. The next day, whilst in the record library, attempting to type an inventory, a table came lurching at me and for ages I had a beauty of a bruise on the left thigh as a result.

"Working in Caroline House was a great pleasure. One could say the place was somewhat extravagant. There were huge chandeliers in the main offices with large mirror panels down this blue, carpeted staircase. The rooms were enormous. Forty people could easily have worked in the space which accommodated maybe three or four. When I reported for work each day I felt like a million dollars. The building was quite cheap to rent in those days. I believe it was somewhere around £500 a week."

When programme director Bill Hearne left Radio Caroline, along with Ken Evans and his programme girls, on 27 January 1966, Alison Muir then took an active interest in answering mail and looking after the disc jockeys' commitments.

Letters flooded into Caroline House from all over the world. They came from as far away as New Zealand, China, Italy, USA, Canada and most Continental countries.

Alison Muir says that one of the most interesting letters she received came from Estonia in the former Soviet Union. Written in English the letter said:

> It is difficult to find words to express thanks to you for the astonishingly good tunes. I have never find so many humanity around me than in your songs. It is a part of only man's dream to see ones self in the best exist in the world. English is the most beautiful language for me. If I am able to marry with English woman I shall learn English for ever.

According to a National Opinion Poll, published in January 1965, an estimated 12,500,000 people tuned into Caroline each week. Profits for the station amounted to £9,000 a week.

Also in January Ronan O'Rahilly was quoted in the *Daily Express* as saying "There's only one thing the Government can do that would put us off the air - declare war on the country whose flag we fly under."

This statement was prior to the Council of Europe signing an agreement to outlaw all the offshore stations.

Ronan said that Caroline had recovered its original £500,000 investment. The station had spent over £ 10,000 on legal fees.

In the Commons Mr Anthony Wedgwood Benn, Postmaster-General, cited 19 instances where pirate radio stations had interfered with communications between ship and shore. Caroline was the offender in seven cases.

Shel Talmy, writing in *Music Echo,* on 13 March 1965 said that in Los Angeles alone he could count 40 commercial stations, most of them running twenty four hours a day providing a music service that ranged from Bo Diddley to Beethoven.

Radio London and Radio Caroline were trying to provide a similar service, on a much diminished scale, in an area roughly ten times the size of Los Angeles and they were getting slapped down for it at every turn. The figures showed that without a doubt the general public wanted diversified radio programming. Unfortunately this did not coincide with the benevolent wisdom of the Government. Roll on 1984!

All references to Radio Caroline in Government debates can be found in Chapter Ten.

In 1964 Simon Dee was the first pirate disc jockey to appear on ITV's *Ready Steady Go.* In March 1965 three offshore boys appeared as guest disc jockeys on the ABC Television network *Thank Your Lucky Stars,* all on separate weeks: Ed Moreno, Simon Dee and the author. Tony Blackburn was the fourth pirate to break through on television.

As Caroline's first birthday was to be celebrated in March 1965 a live show was arranged for the beginning of the month at the Fairfield Halls, Croydon, called *The Sounds of 65.* Compèred by Caroline disc jockeys Simon Dee, Bryan Vaughan and Keith Skues the show had a galaxy of pop names - The Moody Blues, The Yardbirds, Ronnie Jones and the Nightimers, The Mark Leeman Five and Jimmy James and the Vagabonds. This was the very first time that Radio Caroline had presented a 'live' show.

Radio Caroline celebrated its first birthday on 28 March 1965 and claimed an audience of 12 million people. Commenting, Ronan O'Rahilly said "Should the Postmaster-General wipe us out we would take the matter to the Court of Human Rights."

A *Times* correspondent spent the night on board Caroline North off the Isle of Man, and reported:

Everyone tunes into 199 metres at some time - particularly in rough weather to hear that the boys are all right. Caroline's frequent references to the Isle of Man's beauties and bland weather are appreciated by the tourist trade. Caroline is a foreign country to the authorities and every voyage of the *Essex Girl* is scrutinized. The nation need have no fear of some elaborate smuggling plot. Mr Robinson, Customs officer at Ramsey, is assiduous in his duties.

To mark its first birthday Radio Caroline announced the winners of the Bell Award for the best records and artists for the year 1964 - 1965 in four categories.

Petula Clark won her award for the best female recording artist for her version of *Downtown.* She was presented with her 'Bell' by disc jockey Simon Dee on 28 March 1965, Caroline's birthday. Pet had flown in from Paris for twelve hours to record a BBC television programme. The presentation was made in the Park West offices of her British agent, Alan A. Freeman.

Talking with the author on Classic Gold Radio in November 1989, Petula updated listeners about the Caroline Bell award.

My family and I lived in a large chateau in France, but in 1987 sold it to an Arab prince, who wanted to buy everything, including the loo rolls! A couple of months later I went back to see what they had done to it. They had totally revamped the accommodation, and only lived in it for about two weeks a year. I was being shown around and walking up the stairs when I noticed, in one of the alcoves, my Radio Caroline Bell. I said to the servant showing me around 'I have been looking for that bell for two months. Can I take it?' He said 'No! The Prince likes it so much when he comes home from ski-ing, he rings the bell so that everyone knows the Prince is home' So that's where it is today!

SOUNDS OF SIXTY FIVE!

On behalf of Radio Caroline, thank you for coming.

This is an exciting and important evening for all of us as it is the first time that Radio Caroline has presented a live concert. We are hoping that tonight's concert will be the forerunner to many more Radio Caroline land-based activities. We want to convey our appreciation to the artists on the bill tonight. They, and the disc jockeys who are compering the show have made a special effort to come and join in the celebrations tonight. And celebration it is. Because this is the first time we have met you, our listeners, in person. Tonight is also the first of the series of events which we have planned for our birthday celebrations. Yes, on March 28 we are a year old.

Time has really flown since the good ship Caroline dropped anchor off the coast of East Anglia, and started its broadcasts to the South of England. You may remember the time when, last July, Radio Caroline joined forces with its then rival, Radio Atlanta. After the merger the original Caroline sailed North to broadcast from off the Isle of Man, and Radio Atlanta became Radio Caroline South. From that moment the Caroline network covered a population of over 39,500,000 people in this country! We have recently learned that the station is almost as big on the continent. The signal roaches a population of 25,000,000.

We knew when we started that although our organisation was 100% legal, that there would be some difficulties. We had to fight on our hands. We won the fight for existence for one important reason. That reason was! and is, YOU. Radio Caroline became so popular with its mlllions of listeners that it virtually guaranteed its own survival.

In the coming years we will continue with this policy. It is what YOU want to listen to that matter with Radio Caroline.

Again, thank you for coming, and thank you forty million times for your support.

GUEST STARS

THE YARDBIRDS   BARRY ST JOHN   THE MOODY BLUES   RONNIE JONES

THE MARK LEEMAN FIVE   JIMMY JAMES AND THE VAGABONDS

Front cover of 1964 brochure sent to Caroline Club members

The award for the best and most consistent artists went to the Beatles, and Simon Dee made the presentation on 6 April 1965 at Twickenham film studios, where the four Liverpool lads were filming *Help.*

The Animals received Radio Caroline's first birthday Bell Award at London Airport as they left for New York. The presentation, made by Ronan O'Rahilly, was for the best group record of the year, *House Of The Rising Sun.*

The award for the best male vocal of the year was made to Tom Jones for his record of *It's Not Unusual* by composer and orchestra leader Burt Bacharach on 26 April. Talking to the author about the pirates in a radio programme on Radio Hallam in April 1987, Tom said:

> Radio Caroline made a hit out of *It's Not Unusual.* They played it a long time before the BBC picked up on it. I still have the Radio Caroline award, which is a fine brass bell on a wooden trestle. Had Caroline and the other pirate stations not been as adventurous as they were maybe BBC pop radio may never have seen the light of day.

Back at Caroline House in Mayfair, Michael Parkin was sales director from 1964 to 1966 before starting his own company, Caroline Films. He was assisted by Tony Welsh who later joined Radio Scotland.

Parkin recalls the amusing incident concerning 'a close friend' Mr Anthony Wedgwood Benn, the former Postmaster-General. He said in June 1965: "We haven't met at all since the election. I have known him for some time. We were introduced by Lora Kennett. Tony Benn appreciates that a friendship between a Minister and one of his official opponents could be embarrassing for the Government. I know he listens to Caroline in more ways than one. His wife's name is Caroline, but he listens to Radio Caroline in the bath, I believe."

The first sales executive was Josie Scudder who handed over to Michael Parkin when she left for Grampian Television.

By May 1965 the record industry was smarting because record sales were down from 1964. Board of Trade figures showed that the production of 45rpm discs were down to 4,700,000 in February 1965 compared with nearly 6,500,000 for a similar period in 1964. At the 1965 conference of the Gramophone Record Retailers Association there was a strong feeling that the pirate radio stations were partly responsible because they broadcast all the pop music which fans required, so instead of buying records the public simply tuned in to the

The Beatles collect their Caroline Bell Award from Simon Dee

pirate stations.

Ron White of EMI Records accused the pirates of making a living out of records and paying nothing to the companies in return.

Moody Blues manager, Harry Fenton, disagreed: "The existence of the pirates meant that new young artists were getting exposure and that surely must be good. They simply didn't get enough airtime before. We had to have all that influx of new talent or the whole business would have become stagnant." Fenton said he had not seen any evidence that the pirates were causing a slump in record sales.

George Melly, writing in the *Daily Mail* on 5 May 1965, said: "To own up that a situation may be of your own making requires, it would seem, more moral courage than the industry can call on. It prefers to blame the pirate ships, to put up £1,000,000 to boost sales, and to demand the Government take action on its behalf.

"What it should do is to take a cool look at the product it is selling, and to take into account that it is possible to kill golden geese by over-feeding. What I think they have got on their plates is Pate de teenager grass."

Decca Records promotion man of the 1960s, Tony Hall, recalls: "The pirate stations gave much exposure to new artists who would otherwise never have been heard of. So record sales were spread over a greater variety of artists. The actual volume of sales remained the same. People used to say that a number 1 record sold in much less quantity in 1965 and blamed the pirates. I don't believe there is any such thing as overexposure. You can play a record 100 times a day and if it hasn't got it in the groove, it will never sell, however much you brainwash the public.

"Let's take an example. Tom Jones' *Green Green Grass Of Home*. That record was played on the hour every hour on Radio London, or if you pressed your car radio channel selector you could hear it maybe four or five times an hour. But it was such a great record of its kind that it sold 1,000,000 copies in England, in three months. You can't knock that!"

On 24 June 1965 Radio Caroline challenged a council to stop it ferrying 2,000 teenagers to the island of Dalkey, nine miles south of Dublin, for a Saturday night party. Charter planes were booked to fly staff and youngsters from London and Manchester into Dublin. It was reported that Bing Crosby had made tentative arrangements to attend. The Dun Laoghaire Borough Corporation tried in vain to stop the party taking place.

In the *Evening Standard* on 19 July 1965 Max Hastings said:

At Caroline House, professionalism has replaced the initial cheerful amateurishness. The pirates sift public opinion polls to achieve balanced programme planning and sponsor competitions to help their advertising. The Performing Right Society, which represents composers, artists and producers has reached agreement with Caroline who are to pay them royalties.

The first fan club to be organised for a pirate disc jockey was centred around Simon Dee and run by Mrs Olive Burgess of Houghton Regis, Bedfordshire.

It started in December 1964. Olive relates "I was a great fan of Simon's. I first met him in Basildon, Essex, when he attended a carnival ceremony."

Fans received a membership card, and a signed photo of Simon. Letters were sent out letting fans know where he was appearing, and also other schemes that were being organised.

Other pirate disc jockeys to have fan clubs included Tom Lodge, Tony Blackburn and Mike Ahern.

Caroline travel bag, purchase price 24/- (£1.20), produced in 1965 by a Dewsbury, West Yorks. firm

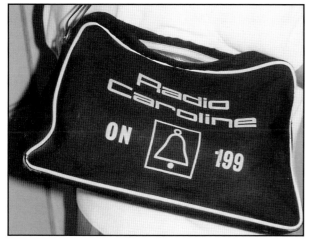

The press officer at Caroline House was Frances van Staden. She replaced David Block who left to form his own publicity company. Frances was one of the original Caroline girls starting as office administrator and receptionist in the early Caroline House days. As press officer she also had a say in the programme side of Radio Caroline. Frances' assistant at Caroline House was Carolyn Irvine.

When a disc jockey returned from the high seas for a week's shore leave he was expected to check into Caroline House at regular intervals to keep in touch with the 'pop scene.' Truthfully, broadcasters had very little spare time to themselves for they were expected to attend programme meetings at Caroline House, sign countless autograph books, record interviews with pop stars, meet fans, compère disc nights at Leyton Baths; the 100 Club; Notre Dame, Leicester Square; Wimbledon Palais and the Cavern Club; all this in addition to opening fêtes, giving talks and delivering lectures. It was all go. Many disc jockeys openly admit they went back to the ship for a fortnight's rest!

When they were on land, regular meals were missed. Late nights were incurred because of various invitations to parties and clubs. It was a busy life, but most certainly an enjoyable one. If disc jockeys chose that kind of life, they had only themselves to blame if they didn't like it. Lots of DJs did in fact 'give it up,' but the stalwarts remained.

In the north of England disc jockeys also had their share of the shows both in the Isle of Man, and along the Lancashire coast at resorts such as Blackpool and Morecambe.

The author kept a small blue book which was housed in his car, the *Skuesmobile,* and whilst driving around the countryside could check on any village or town that listeners had written from and made invitations for coffee - or tea. Quite often he would call in and say 'hello' if he had a few spare moments.

Let's face it, listeners were the most constructive people and could say what they enjoyed listening to and what did *not* appeal to them. They offered helpful suggestions for programme ideas and forecast their predictions in records. Most disc jockeys who are human are interested to know what their listeners look like just as listeners are curious as whether the face of the presenter matches his voice. A disc jockey could be far more personal if he knew to whom he

Left: Christopher Moore, the first disc jockey to broadcast on Radio Caroline, on Easter Saturday 1964. He was also the station's first programme director

Below: Rolling Stones and "Not Fade Away" was the first record to be played on Radio Caroline at 12.00 noon on Easter Saturday 28 March 1964

Singer Donovan about to "Catch the Wind" outside
Caroline House with DJ Simon Dee in May 1965

was talking. A great deal of the success of offshore radio disc jockeys was the fact that they spoke *to* listeners and not *at* them.

Perhaps the best opportunity disc jockeys had of meeting their audience was at disc nights. This would be true most certainly in the cases of teenagers. Mums and Dads would probably not bother to go along - after all what was a disc night? As its name suggests - a night of playing discs where a personality would present records from the hit parade, and also introduce guest stars who made personal appearances.

Take for example the contents of a page from the diary of Roger Horton (manager of London's 100 Club in Oxford Street) in 1965 ...

23rd September
Radio Caroline Disc Night. Guest appearances of Mike Sheridan, Sonny Childe, The Pack, Tornados, Russ Loader, Charles Dickens and Applejacks - Compère, Colin Nicol.
or
30th September
Radio Caroline Disc Night. Trendsetters, Peter Jay and the Jaywalkers, Jonathan King, Cymbaline, Cherokees, Knack, Valerie Mitchell, and Mojos. The Peddlers would be playing 'live' for an hour. Compère, 'Cardboard Shoes,' Keith Skues.

The Caroline Disc Nights at the 100 Club began in July 1965, when the opening night featured guest stars Millie, Walker Brothers, Goldie and the Gingerbreads, Twinkle, Doris Troy and the Who, with DJs Tony Blackburn, Bryan Vaughan and Keith Skues. Disc Nights were also held at the Cavem Club, Leicester Square, London. During 1965 guests included The Who, Georgie Fame, Pretty Things, Paul and Barry Ryan, Sonny and Cher, The Walker Brothers, Jonathan King and Hedgehoppers Anonymous.

At a disc night a 'viewer' would meet one or two unknown artists accompanied by some famous names.

This 'viewer'[1] could also talk to the artist and add a few more names to his or her autograph book. Disc nights were run on similar lines up and down the country. The number of people that attended these functions varied immensely, anything from 200 to 2,000 depending on the size of the venue.

Caroline Disc Nights moved to the Wimbledon Palais in 1966. DJs were Robbie Dale, Dave Lee Travis (DLT), Rick Dane, Emperor Rosko, Keith Hampshire and Steve Young. During 1966 a variety of guests appeared including Los Bravos (6 August), The Vogues and Glenda Collins (27 August), Carol Keys, Pussyfoot, Los Bravos, Rothchilds and Twice as Much (17 September), Dave Davies of the Kinks, Long John Baldry and Twice as Much (26 November), Donovan, Pretty Things and the Move (24 December).

Other disc nights were held at Harry Owen's Club in Hammersmith. On 16 September 1966, DLT and Robbie Dale introduced Diana Dors, Soundtrekkers, Los Bravos and Rothchilds.

Pop group Los Bravos were very popular in 1966 at Caroline Disc Nights.
Their most successful record was "Black is Black"

---

1. I always referred to listeners as viewers in order to be different from other DJs. I also invented my own phrases, clichés and sayings. A married lady was referred to as Mrs Woman. Other words and phrases included Fantasmagorical, Have a Large, Talking about 'x' … which we weren't, Lurking Locally, 'x' … Who doesn't Want His Name Mentioned, Making a Mental Note on Paper … and many more.

Apart from disc nights, disc jockeys were asked to open fêtes. For example in May 1965 the author had the pleasure of opening the Billericay Fête in Essex, and whilst in the same county with the help of Kenny Lynch, the Brentwood Fête in July 1965. Kenny found time to judge a 'Cardboard Shoes' competition which invited listeners to make a pair of cardboard shoes to be worn by me at personal appearances. The winner was the Baker family (Olive, Carol, Teresa and Louise) of Richmond Road, Ipswich, Suffolk.

Some disc jockeys were asked to give talks to youth groups, Young Conservatives and Young Liberals throughout the British Isles. I don't remember receiving any invitations from the Labour movement, although many who voted for Harold Wilson were Caroline listeners. One such 'talk' sticks in my memory when I was asked to speak to the Young Conservatives at Wembley in Middlesex, along with publicity officer David Block. The billing went something like:-

"Horace Batchelor couldn't make it, so we have asked Skues of Radio Caroline instead to talk about commercial radio in Britain."

It was not until occasions like this, when one met the general public, that we realised what a fantastic following offshore radio had. There was also a definite lack of 'heckling.' Normally at every political rally or speech some bright 'Charley' decries the speaker. Not so with offshore radio talks. It seemed that everyone who went along was genuinely interested in the subject.

So many listeners were kind enough to take the trouble to write to the Postmaster-General between 1964 and 1967 objecting to his proposed ban on pirate radio stations that Mr Anthony Wedgwood Benn took the unprecedented step of replying to them in a duplicated letter that was headed 'Dear Listener.' He went on to say:

> The pirate stations themselves won't give you the reasons why, so perhaps I can do so. The unhappy fact is the pirate stations have simply taken over wavelengths that belong to other countries. These wavelengths were divided up between the countries of Europe by International agreement, an agreement to which Britain pledged its word. In disregard of this agreement the pirates are causing serious interference with the enjoyment of people on the Continent who now find that they cannot hear their own local stations clearly.

On 24 May 1965 Radio Caroline adopted the 'Good Guys' image, which was styled on radio stations WMCA in New York and 2SM in Sydney, Australia. The idea was to 'do away' with the term 'disc jockey', and to go out and encourage goodwill and courtesy in all programmes and personal appearances. We all wore identical clothing which consisted of blue and white check shirts, light grey trousers and a double breasted mod style yachting jacket.

As 'Good Guys' we broke into two shifts: A Shift) Bryan Vaughan, Don Allen, Jon Sydney and Keith Skues. B Shift) Gary Kemp, Mike Allen, Tony Blackburn and Bob Walton. In London we fulfilled personal appearances, met pop stars and groups and discussed new programme ideas at Caroline House.

In a National Opinion Poll of July 1965 it was learned that 6,000,000 listened to Radio Caroline and Radio London daily, and they were the housewives' favourites.

The peak audiences in any half hour at lunchtime was 2,500,000. Of these, 750,000 were housewives. In East Anglia the pirate stations were heard by 77.6% of the population. The BBC had no comment to make on the survey, but in the following month Caroline officials learned that the BBC was to extend its long running *Housewives' Choice* by 30 minutes daily to compete with the offshore stations. *Housewives' Choice,* with a daily audience of 8,250,000, was given a new look for the first time in 19 years. This programme had the BBC's second largest audience. *Family Favourites* linking Britain with the Forces in Germany and overseas was the number one programme with a Sunday lunchtime audience of 14,000,000.

Pirate radio is believed to have been instrumental in an election issue. Julian Holland, writing in the *Daily Mail* on 5 October 1965, relates:

At Leyton in January, Patrick Gordon-Walker lost Labour a safe seat, dropping an 8,000 majority. A lot of reasons have been advanced for this defeat. One of them is that a pressure group with the slogan "Don't vote Labour, they're going to kill Caroline," joined in the fray.

Radio Caroline and Radio London also played a large part in the Greater London elections when the Labour Government suffered heavy defeats in 1967.

In the House of Commons on 8 December 1965 the Postmaster-General once again threatened to kill off the pirate stations (see Chapter Ten). At the very moment he was announcing the news to Parliament a trainload of excited pop fans and musicians was pulling out of Euston Station for Radio Caroline North's first 'pop' ball.

On arrival at the *Zowie One* show, which was held in the New Brighton Tower Ballroom, the stars were asked for their comments on the Postmaster-General's threat to the pop stations. Amongst the many stars there included The Searchers, Yardbirds, Four Pennies, Brian Poole and the Tremeloes, Paul and Barry Ryan, Honeycombs and Twinkle, Disc jockeys included Tony Blackburn, Mel Howard, Tom Lodge, Jerry Leighton and Ray Teret.

Pop singer Twinkle succeeded in making headline news by saying "nuts to Mr Wedgwood Benn." She went on to say:

> Pirate radio had made many names famous, and it was the best thing to ever hit Britain this century. The BBC was old hat and stuffy. At the BBC they have hundreds of people -- Radio Caroline uses just one disc jockey to do all the work. But at the BBC there are studio managers, producers, script writers, tape operators and loads of other people. Radio Caroline sounded far more friendly.

Twinkle actually knew what she was talking about for she had visited the radio ship on two occasions during 1965.

Brian Poole, who with the Tremeloes had achieved four Top 10 records by 1965, including a No 1 hit *Do You Love Me,* remarked:

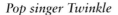

Pop singer Twinkle

We do not approve of the Postmaster-General's announcement. Pirate radio does far more for groups and pop music than the BBC. Any move to stop them would be a very bad thing so far as the industry goes.

In spite of the Postmaster-General's threat to offshore radio the *Zowie One* show was a fantastic success.

A couple of days prior to Radio Caroline South going aground in January 1966, disc jockey Colin Nicol set up a competition, but was stumped as to how to let the listeners know who had won. So he decided to advertise the names of the winners in the *Times* personal column. Commenting at Caroline House, Colin said at the time:

> I don't suppose for one moment that the winners would actually take the *Times* daily, but it was effective as local papers picked up the story and the winners were all informed. They also picked up a useful bit of publicity.

I did of course write and congratulate the winners personally.

One of the founder members at Caroline House was ex-RAF man Gerry Duncan whose job it was to produce all the commercials used on transmission. 30-year-old Gerry had the occasional programme of his own on Radio Caroline - his speciality was jazz. He also worked as an assistant to film director Lewis Gilbert and helped in the making of films such as *Light up the Sky* and *Sink the Bismark*. He later became an assistant ATV cameraman. Gerry remained with Caroline for two and a half years before leaving in January 1967. He died in the 1970s. His job at Caroline was taken over by pop singer, Freddie Ryder.

Another face that was always wearing a smile around Caroline House was that of Carl Conway who had been a disc jockey on the ship in the earlier days, but didn't take too kindly to the sea, although he thoroughly loved the job.

So he became land-based and presented programmes such as the *Chappell Show*. His voice was heard regularly on commercials on both Caroline North and South and was probably the deepest one ever on the station. Listeners thought he had 'the sexiest voice in the business.'

Carl has appeared in several television plays (he's very good at impersonating German officers). He has presented numerous radio programmes and taken part in films both in front of the camera and in 'voice-overs.' In March 1967 he hosted the BBC's *Swingalong*.

Born in Ramsgate, Kent, Carl attended St. Lawrence College and then broke into television. Like Ken Evans, he was one of the most genuine people at Radio Caroline. He has made countless personal appearances up and down the country.

Top-rating disc jockey Pete Murray hit the headlines when he 'joined' the pirates in December 1965. He pre-recorded a series for Currys which was heard by an estimated 15,000,000 people on Radio Caroline North and South, and also Radio London. Pete lost a BBC series on Saturday nights through this move, although this was denied at the time.

The BBC said they would not engage disc jockeys who were currently working on offshore stations.

When Pete completed his contract in 'piratesville,' he returned to his old time slot with the BBC Light Programme, and who replaced him during the time Pete was on the commercial stations? Ex-pirate disc jockey Simon Dee!

In February 1966, just after Caroline had gone aground, 40-year-old Philip Solomon bought a £200,000 interest in Radio Caroline - his 20 per cent interest was the largest single one.

On the return of the *Mi Amigo* from Holland and its change of frequency from 199 to 259 metres, 1187kHz, it was decided to bring down a few disc jockeys from the North ship off Ramsey. They included Mike Ahern and Rick Dane. Tom Lodge was the first Caroline North man to join the South ship a month before.

Caroline South was the first ship to broadcast 24 hours with regular transmissions following a tremendous demand for all-night music from truck drivers, factory workers and other all-nighters. However, the first offshore station to commence round-the-clock music was Radio Essex (see Chapter Four).

Caroline House had its accounts department in Chesterfield Gardens and on one occasion in February 1966, twenty-one-year-old accounts clerk, Ian Richards, was attacked and robbed of £1,000 after leaving a bank in North Audley Street in Mayfair while returning to Caroline House.

In the basement of Caroline House was the traffic office which was the final department with whom an advertiser liaised before his product was broadcast. Transmission spots were logged into quarter hours stating the product, the tape or cartridge number to be used on the air, and the exact length of the commercial.

The commercial logs were made up about a fortnight in advance and despatched to the ships. During Caroline's early days the manager of the department was Arthur Pelteret who had three assistants in the office, namely Colin Berry, assistant traffic manager, Margaret Webster, typist and Robin Boston, co-ordinator and chartist.

Caroline blazer badge, 1965

As time went by, people left or were replaced. In January 1967 Arthur Pelteret left to join Grampian Television. The management post was taken over by Colin Berry who ran more or less as a 'one-man operation.' Colin is now a BBC Radio 2 presenter.

The logs, instead of being typed, were written out in longhand, photocopied and then sent to Caroline North and South.

Talking about the Beatles - which we weren't - Radio Caroline and Radio London were the only representatives of British radio that covered the Beatles' tour of America in August 1966. From Caroline, Jerry Leighton made the tour, and Kenny Everett was chosen to represent Radio London. Jerry sent daily reports that were phoned through, and the disc jockey on duty read the text over the air each day.

The increase in power of Radio Caroline's southern transmitter to 50kW in May 1966 was dramatically reflected in the findings of an audience survey carried out for the station by National Opinion Polls Ltd.

STATION	FIGURES (All adults)
RADIO CAROLINE (NORTH AND SOUTH)	8,818,000
RADIO LUXEMBOURG	8,818,000
RADIO LONDON	8,140,000
RADIO 390	2,633,000
RADIO ENGLAND	2,274,000
RADIO SCOTLAND	2,195,000
BRITAIN RADIO	718,000
Commercial Radio listeners	33,596,000
TOTAL Number of listeners to Radio	39,900,000

The poll was taken between 6 - 11 July 1966 and showed that Radio Caroline South had nearly doubled its audience in the previous four months from 15 per cent of all adults to 28 per cent.

This survey showed that 45 per cent of the adult population listened to a commercial radio station sometime during the week.

78 % listened in the 16 - 24 age group
55 % listened in the 25 - 34 age group
45 % listened in the 35 - 44 age group
44 % listened in the 45 - 54 age group

Another survey undertaken by National Opinion Polls Ltd in August 1966 showed that Radio Caroline had a larger female audience than any other commercial radio station. The survey was for the period 9-13 August.

Front cover of "Radio Caroline and its Stars" booklet, published in 1965

The percentage figures for female listenership showed:

RADIO CAROLINE	18.9%
RADIO LUXEMBOURG	18.3%
RADIO LONDON	13.3%
RADIO SCOTLAND	5.0%
RADIO ENGLAND	4.7%
RADIO 390	3.7%
RADIO BRITAIN	2.3%

1,215 interviews were carried out with women as follows: 123 in Scotland, 328 in the north of England, 189 in the Midlands, 152 in Wales and the south-west and 423 in the south-east. Names were drawn at random from the electoral roll.

From surveys to programmes, and Radio Caroline came out with a winner in October 1966 when they introduced *Caroline Cash Casino* to the two ships North and South.

Listeners were invited to enter the *Caroline Cash Casino* by sending in proof of purchase from any of the four participating products along with their answer to the current Casino question.

Fifteen letters were selected each day from the thousands of letters received. Five programmes, lasting a quarter of an hour each, were broadcast daily and three letters were chosen for each programme. For each incorrect answer to the Casino question, the jackpot was increased by £10. If no winner were found, it increased by £150 a day. The programme was introduced by Bill Hearne.

The programme was the brainchild of Terry Bate, with cash prizes which were the largest ever on Caroline, or any other offshore station at that time.

Joan Barton of Vulcan Road, Barrow-in-Furness, Cumbria, was the first winner collecting £460. She sent an Alberto VO5 shampoo label.

Davidson, Pearce Berry and Tuck Ltd, advertising agents for Alberto, said:

The fantastic frequency to be gained through this scheme made this one of the most exciting media buys of the year. During the thirteen-week period of the campaign, Alberto received over 1,200 name mentions and commercials, plus, of course, the immediate promotional value in stimulating product movement.

On another occasion Mrs Shirley Monserat of Albion Crescent, Chalfont St. Giles, Buckinghamshire, won £3,330 by sending a label from Findus garden peas and answering the question correctly.

The four firms participating in *Caroline Cash Casino* were Alberto Culver, Findus Frozen Foods, Libby's Canned Fruit and Weetabix.

The Casino programme produced the biggest ever mail response to Caroline House with over ten large sacks arriving each day of the week.

Two other successful series were *Partners in Profit*, sponsored by Weetabix and at other times by Ajax, and *Lucky Birthday Bonanza*, sponsored by Golden Wonder Peanuts and Halex Tooth Brushes.

News that stunned the music business broke in February 1967 when Radio Caroline admitted they were accepting £100 a week to plug records not in their Top 50.

Caroline played the Top 50 based on the best selling charts published in the music press. There was no charge for these plays. Among the twenty other singles plugged each week were discs bought in at £100 a week.

The payola storm surfaced after a new Cliff Bennett single was dropped after a fortnight's plugging. Said Cliff "As a matter of principle, I don't think any artist should pay cash to a radio station to have a record broadcast. If it's worth broadcasting it should be played. Caroline thought *I'll Take Good Care of You* was good enough to go on the air regularly before they started their new policy of charging for airplay which began at the end of January."

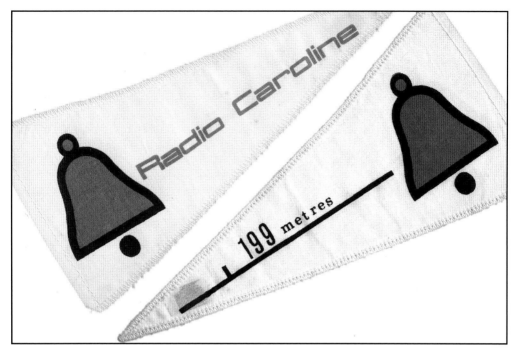

Each side of a Radio Caroline pennant, 1965

Commenting on the £100 charge, Philip Solomon, joint managing director, said "By this method we were giving the smaller companies and artists a chance. As for dropping a disc after two weeks, if it's not going to do anything, why not? Who does Cliff Bennett think he is?"

Cliff Bennett and the Rebel Rousers had enjoyed one Top 10 hit in 1964, *One Way Love* and another in 1966, *Got To Get You Into My Life*.

On Radio Luxembourg all record companies used to buy time for their shows. Two other radio stations, London and 390, said they had no intention of adopting Caroline's system.

During 1967 many listeners wrote to the Prime Minister, Harold Wilson, about the banning of the pirates. These letters were just passed onto the Postmaster- General, Edward Short, who, in turn, passed them onto Miss E.E. Frankham, his private secretary, to deal with. A copy of the note which was enclosed with a standard response letter is reproduced here:

PUTTING AN END TO PIRATE BROADCASTING

Many people have been very disappointed to hear that pirate broadcasting is to be stopped. It seems so harmless, and is enjoyed by so many people. In fact, despite the repeated claims of the pirates, their broadcasts are far from harmless. The pirates are using wavelengths which we have undertaken to leave clear for the broadcasting services in other countries. By so doing, they prevent people in those countries from hearing their own domestic programmes. They also represent a danger - slight but ever-present to the radio services - on which safety at sea depends. Moreover, broadcasting from the high seas is forbidden, all over the world, by international law, and the pirates make almost unlimited use of recorded material, threatening the livelihoods of the musicians and other performers whose work they use without permission or payment.

To date twelve European countries have complained to the Postmaster-General about the pirates' interference with their broadcasting services. And communications between ships and the shore have often been seriously interfered with. If the pirate stations were allowed to continue unchecked, there would soon be so much interference that broadcasting as we know it would become impossible.

This threat to the future of broadcasting has caused the maritime countries of the Council of Europe to agree to legislate on common lines to deal with it. The Bill, which is being considered by Parliament, carries out our obligations under the European Agreement. Many people feel that an easy solution would be to "bring the pirates ashore," that is, to licence them to operate on land. That is just not possible. There are no unused wavelengths on which powerful stations like the pirate stations could operate without causing interference.

In any case, if they operated within the control of the copyright laws, they could not transmit the sort of programmes that they have been transmitting. The Government's plans for the future of sound broadcasting, which have recently been announced, are designed to match our broadcasting services more closely to our needs without interfering with other people's rights. But the most pressing need is to silence the pirate stations, which are flouting international regulations, earning us such a bad name abroad, endangering shipping and threatening to make broadcasting end in chaos, not only in Britain but over most of Europe.

By March 1967 it seemed as though Caroline House would have to close, once the Marine Offences Bill became an Act of Parliament. Ronan O'Rahilly said he would be setting up an office in Holland. He told *Time and Tide* magazine on 16 March 1967:

Most of the thinking people in Britain are unaware of what the Marine Etc., Broadcasting (Offences) Bill will do. It will make Radio Caroline international; internationally recognised and legal. For the public it does this: If a British shopkeeper sells cigarettes to a Radio Caroline announcer he (the shopkeeper) becomes a criminal. If the Archbishop of Canterbury or Cardinal Heenan or the Chief Rabbi gave a sermon on Radio Caroline they would become criminals. If a journalist writes a newscast or talks on Radio Caroline, he becomes a criminal. If a British advertiser advertises on Radio Caroline, he becomes a criminal. If, on the other hand, the Pope were to write a sermon for Radio Caroline he would not be a criminal, nor would any foreign figure who wanted to use the medium to voice publicly something he wanted to say. In other words it is stifling the freedom of speech of the British subject to speak where he likes about what he likes.

The Marine Offences Bill became an Act of Parliament at midnight on 14 August 1967. Maintenance manager, Richard Morecraft, had been given instructions to close down Caroline House after furniture and carpets had been removed and sent to their new office in Holland. Richard completed his task early in September 1967, almost three years to the day after Radio Caroline moved into Chesterfield Gardens. He recalled some of the people he worked with at Caroline House between 1964 and 1967. First he takes us on a tour of the building when it was buzzing with staff:

I can do no better than quote from the 1965 booklet *Caroline and Its Stars* to describe one's arrival at 6 Chesterfield Gardens. "You go through double pillars, flanking an ornate archway, into an entrance hall with a staircase that would not disgrace a Hollywood spectacular. It is deeply carpeted in rich blue, all the way to the top floor. As you climb the stairs, you pass half-open doors emitting noises of typewriter and telephone, avoid people rushing past clutching sheaves of paper, and eventually enter one of the score or so busy offices.

"The discreet portico of the building in Chesterfield Gardens hides a practically non-stop industry. Here are all the secretaries and typists, the business organisers, the programmers and off-duty DJs, the advertising men, the sales people, the accounts department and post office of a radio station.

"It is from here that a sales department allocates air time for advertisers through an advertising agency. There is also a department for direct selling to advertisers. Here chief DJ and programme director, Chris Moore, decides on the records to be used on

Caroline, and plans the format of programmes like *Caroline Club Hour,* a feature show. "Here Gerry Duncan, programme producer, wins a battle with the clock every day, slotting in records, disc jockeys' announcements, time checks, commercial spots and, all the time, keeping a sharp eye on the running of Caroline's general programmes. Here conferences are held, headed by Ronan O'Rahilly and Allan Crawford, the joint managing directors, to think up new ideas, evolve new programmes and new tie-ups for Caroline."

With the passing of the Marine Broadcasting Offences Act in 1967, Caroline's London headquarters closed and operations were moved to Amsterdam. Caroline House at 6 Chesterfield Gardens remained empty for many years afterwards and it was not until 1984 that the building was redeveloped.

These are the staff I remember working with at Caroline House. There were others who came and went and whose stay was short. Sadly their names I do not remember. The following are those who left a lasting impression. Their names are in alphabetical order: Barry Ainley, general manager; Alex Anderson, production department; Andrew Arden, record library; Patricia Atkins, Chris Moore's secretary; Terry Bate, sales manager; Sally Beecham, sales office; Colin Berry, DJ and commercials; Kitty Black, director of Project Atlanta and secretary to engineering; Maureen Blackburn, secretary to Ken Evans; Robin Boston, commercial traffic department; Geoff Brown, engineer; Marion Cochran, record library; Robin Courage, sales office; Allan Crawford, managing director; Paul Dale, engineer, Caroline North; Annette Downey, traffic secretary; Gerry Duncan, producer and commercial recording; Ken Evans, programme department; George Gale, North ship link man; John Gilman, chief engineer; Denise Goldfinch, Caroline Club; Eugene Gomeche, accountant; Toni Gomeche, Allan Crawford's secretary; George Hare, North ship liaison with Caroline House; George Harris, engineer; Caroline Irvine, assistant to Frances van Staden; Eddie Jenkins, Caroline Club; Shirley Jones, assistant press officer; Mary Josephine (Blaney after marriage), receptionist; Oonagh Leigh, Ronan O'Rahilly's secretary; Colin Leighton, accounts; Marina Martin, personnel officer; Margaret McKenzie, sales office; Carolyn Miller, sales office; Chris Moore, programme director; Richard Morecraft, building services and maintenance; Doreen Mottau, tea lady; Alison Muir, Gerry Duncan's secretary; Martin Newton, chief engineer; Ronan O'Rahilly, managing director; Michael Parkin, sales director; Arthur Pelteret, commercial traffic manager; Ian Richardson, commercial traffic department; Ian Ross, sales office; Freddy Ryder, dubbing and commercials (he was also a singer on Mercury Records); Chris Sandford, sales office; Carol Sax, personnel office; Brian Scudder, sales office; Josie Scudder, sales office; Frances van Staden, press officer; Ricky Stein, Caroline Club organiser; Philip Solomon, director; Heather Strachan, sales office; Richard Swainson, music library and assistant to Ken Evans; Linda Thorston, commercial production; Malcolm Vaughn, sales office; Jo Wright, Philip Solomon's personal assistant, and Delia Zimmerman, personal assistant to Oonagh Leigh.

Richard Morecraft with Johnnie Walker

Also in Caroline House were Track Records and the Who with Kit Lambert, The Moody Blues and Denny Cordell. In another office was the actor Terence Stamp, and at the top of Caroline House was a photographic studio run by Ralph von Bronzig.

Richard Morecraft concludes: "I was the last person to leave Caroline House a few weeks after the Marine Offences Act came into force. My job was to dismantle and remove all office equipment. However, there was no activity going on. I had to do a lot of tidying up. There were no authorities looking over my shoulder. Come to think of it, no one ever came around."

As you, the reader, may have realised, the off-duty hours for a disc jockey on shore leave for a week were none too many. Most of the disc jockeys, who were single, wished to further their career during their few days on land.

Mrs Barbara Apostolides of Rush Green, Romford, Essex, realising that DJs led hectic lives, was tempted to send the following poem to the author just prior to his leaving Radio Caroline.

THE CANDLE BURNER

This is the story of a very dear friend,
Who came to a rather untimely end.
He led a 'fantasmagorical' life
No time to eat, or take a wife,
Now he's raising hell below,
Because he had so far to go.
His career was the only thing in his head.
He 'had a large[1] and now he's dead.
So heed this warning all you friends
Don't burn your candle at both ends.

Chapter Four

ROCK AROUND THE CLOCK

BRITISH PIRATE RADIO STATIONS 1964-1967

We skipped the light fandango
And turned cartwheels cross the floor.
I was feeling kind of sea-sick
But the crowd called out for more.

A Whiter Shade of Pale, Procol Harum, 1967

BRITAIN RADIO
KING RADIO
RADIO ATLANTA
RADIO CAROLINE
RADIO CITY
RADIO ENGLAND
RADIO ESSEX
RADIO INVICTA
RADIO LONDON
RADIO SCOTLAND
RADIO SUTCH
RADIO 270
RADIO 355
RADIO 390
TOWER RADIO

TECHNICAL TALK

DURING THE 1960s it was fashionable to announce the radio station's wavelength on air and quote it in promotional material. However, some poetic licence was taken as many stations did not, in fact, transmit on the exact wavelength. For example. Radio Caroline South said, at one stage, they were broadcasting on 259 metres when they were actually on 252 metres, 1187 kHz, but it rhymed with Caroline 259.

Metres still exist, but since the early 1980s the frequency (in kilohertz) was given rather than the wavelength (in metres). In the 1960s we referred to medium wave, long wave, short wave and VHF. Long and short wave are still known by their respective name, although medium wave is known as AM. VHF is now popularly referred to as FM.

AM stands for amplitude modulation and FM for frequency modulation. Amplitude modulation causes the carrier to vary rapidly in power according to the audio signal. Frequency modulation causes the frequency of the carrier to vary according to the magnitude of the audio signal.

On AM the signals are prone to electrical interference, which is known as static, but tend to travel a long distance with limited power, whereas VHF (FM) signals are immune to electrical interference, but their range is restricted to roughly line of sight, even with relatively high transmission power.

The majority of the pirate stations transmitted on medium wave between 187 metres (1605 kHz) and 570 metres (525 kHz). Caroline did use short wave for a brief period in the 1980s.

All electromagnetic waves travel at the speed of light - about 186,000 miles (300,000km) per second. Frequencies are measured in units called Hertz, named after Heinrich Hertz, the German physicist who, in 1888, demonstrated that electrical signals could be sent through the air. Take an example of 390 metres, 773 kHz. The signal comprises the complete number of waves which pass the receiver per second. So in the case of 390 metres, this would go up and down 773,000 times in one second.

The speed of light (which always remains constant) = frequency x wavelength. So 300,000,000 metres per second = 388.09, near enough to 390 metres, x 773,000.

Between 1894 and 1896 the Italian scientist, Guglielmo Marconi, developed a method of using Hertzian waves to send signals in Morse code, better known as wireless telegraphy. By 1901 Marconi had improved the system so much that he was able to send wireless telegraph signals across the Atlantic from Cornwall to Newfoundland.

In the early days of wireless telegraphy listeners used to tune in on a set of earphones linked to receivers that used crystal to pick up radio waves. Later, crystals gave way to diode valves and more powerful receivers with loudspeakers.

By the late 1950s valves were superseded by transistors, and radio receivers became very compact and portable. Operated by either battery or mains, transistor radios went on sale in the early 1960s.

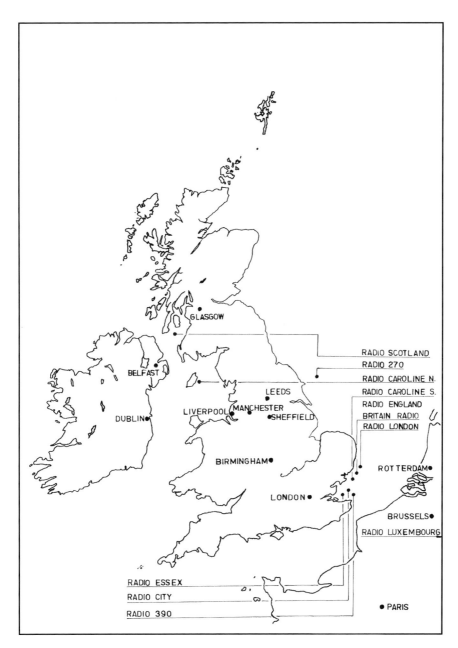

Location of offshore radio stations, 1967

BRITAIN RADIO

THE SISTER station to Radio England, Radio Dolfijn and Radio 227, she later changed her name to Radio 355. The station broadcast from the m.v. *Olga Patricia,* later renamed *Laissez-Faire,* anchored off the Essex coast on 355 metres, 845 kHz.

Test transmissions began on 3 May 1966 and regular programmes commenced on 18 June 1966.

Her disc jockeys included Gordon Bennett, Alan Black, Woolf Byrne, Roger Day, Ted Delaney, Graham Gill, Sheldon Jay, Phil Martin, Dave McKaye, Jack McLaughlin, Ed Moreno, Colin Nicol, Brian Tylney, Johnnie Walker, Alan West and Tony Windsor.

The format for Britain Radio was directed primarily at the housewife and broadcast 'middle-of-the-road' music from artists like Tony Bennett, Dean Martin, Percy Faith, Ray Conniff, Frank Sinatra, Johnny Mathis and Peggy Lee.

Britain Radio had her aerial broken in two during a gale on 28 February 1967, and she broke her anchor on 4 May 1967.

History was made on 29 September 1966 when M.M. McLaren, a local by-election Ratepayers candidate, advertised himself on Britain Radio. He won by 260 votes and was elected to Harwich Town Council.

Although very popular, Britain Radio failed to attract both audiences and revenue. Consequently on 22 February 1967 it closed down and was replaced by Radio 355.

For a description of the ship and the studios see Radio England.

PROGRAMME SCHEDULE - BRITAIN RADIO

January 1967

6.00am	Breakfast Club with Ted Delaney
7.00am	World Tomorrow
7.30am	Breakfast Club
9.00am	Request Show with Alan Black
12.00 noon	Musical Carousel with Graham Gill
12.30pm	World Tomorrow (repeat)
1.00pm	Musical Carousel
4.00pm	Rush Hours with Woolf Byrne
6.00pm	Evening Spin with Alan West
8.00pm	Late Date with Woolf Byrne
12.00 midnight	Close Down

News and Weather, every hour on the hour

Radio mast being erected on Olga Patricia
in Miami, Florida, 1966

KING RADIO

THE STATION commenced broadcasting regularly on the weekend of 9 March 1965. It was housed in a group of forts on Red Sands in the Thames Estuary and was the successor to Radio Invicta. It was named after a radio station in Seattle, USA.

The station was given £7,000 plus financial backing by a group of six Kent businessmen. John Thompson, a fast-talking persuasive Canadian, who had tried to pioneer offshore radio in 1961, was the brains behind the station. There were eight disc jockeys, a technical staff and a full-time cook. The transmitters were shipped out to the forts during February.

KING Radio transmitted on 238 metres, 1289 kHz. Music consisted of standards performed by the likes of Ella Fitzgerald, Frank Sinatra and Ray Conniff. When the station first went on air around 24 March 1965, it hoped for an audience of 40,000 listeners a day, but achieved only half that figure.

Advertising revenue was very small indeed and nowhere near the running costs, so the owners decided that drastic action was necessary if the station was to continue, and outside advice was obtained.

In order to attract advertising in volume during daytime hours, it was considered essential to aim primarily at the audience who would most interest advertisers, namely housewives. While there were not sufficient funds available at this time to carry out a detailed market research programme, there was enough evidence to suggest that a programme for housewives should not be based on continuous pop music, but rather easy-to-listen-to background music with a sweet flavour. .

As a result, the two main recommendations made to the owners of KING Radio were that the programmes should be sweet in flavour and soft in presentation.

Among the disc jockeys who worked on KING Radio were John Ross-Barnard, Clive Berry, Brian Cullingford, Bruce Ford, Roger Gomez, Jonathan Harvey, Ed Hinkins, Bruce Holland, Sheldon Jay, Eddie Jerold, Paul Leevey, John McGowan, Mike Raven, John Stewart, Jay Thompson, Jeff Tyse and Stephen West.

KING Radio closed down on 22 September 1965. Its successor, Radio 390, went on the air on 25 September 1965. See Radio 390 for further story.

PROGRAMME SCHEDULE - KING RADIO

April 1965

7.00am	Rise and Shine
8.00am	Mike and Mandy Raven's Breakfast Show
9.00am	Country Style
9.30am	South of the Border
10.00am	Mail Beat
11.00am	Music from the Shows
11.30am	Our Kinda Folk
12.00noon	Lunch Box
2.00pm	Melody Hour
3.00pm	Memory Lane
3.30pm	Lucky Numbers
4.30pm	Stateside '65
5.00pm	Up and Coming
6.00pm	Raven Around - Mike Raven
7.00pm	Close Down

RADIO ATLANTA

THE FORERUNNER of Radio Caroline South. Operated from the m.v. *Mi Amigo* off the Essex coast. She arrived off Frinton-on-Sea on 27 April 1964 and commenced regular programmes on 26 May 1964.

Disc jockeys were Richard Harris (who was killed in a lorry crash in Norfolk in January 1993), Johnny Jackson, Ted King, Keith Martin, Ed Moreno, Colin Nicol, Mike Raven, Bob Scott, Bryan Vaughan and Tony Withers, who later changed his name to Tony Windsor when he joined Radio London.

The station transmitted on 201 metres, 1493 kHz, but closed on 2 July 1964 becoming Radio Caroline South. For Radio Atlanta story see Chapter One.

RADIO CAROLINE

THE WORLD'S most famous pirate radio station comprised two ships - North and South. Both ships originally transmitted on 199 metres, 1520 kHz but switched to 259 metres, 1187 kHz during 1966.

Radio Caroline continued transmitting in defiance of the Marine, Etc., Broadcasting (Offences) Act which came into operation in August 1967, and broadcast on 319 metres, 963 kHz, and other frequencies, under the names of Radio Caroline, Radio Seagull, Radio Atlantis and Radio Mi Amigo. Radio Caroline was eventually silenced in 1990.

Disc jockeys who broadcast after 14 August 1967 included Glenn Adams, Don Allen, Andy Archer, Bud Ballou, Ross Brown, Gerry Burke, Robbie Dale, Roger Day, Stevi Merike, Carl Mitchell, Henry Morgan, Spangles Muldoon and Johnnie Walker.

Without exception all the Caroline disc jockeys travelled in and out of Britain freely from August 1967 although some were fined by magistrates at Southend.

For full story of Radio Caroline North and South see Chapters One, Two and Three.

PROGRAMME SCHEDULE - RADIO CAROLINE NORTH

Commencing Saturday 22 May 1965

6.00 - 9.00am	THE EARLY SHOW
	Current pops from both the British and American charts, and 15% up-tempo popular standards by top recording artists e.g. Tony Bennett, The Searchers and Dionne Warwick.
9.00 - 11.00am	CAROLINE CLUB REQUESTS
	Current pop material featured, with a sprinkling of standards.
11.00-11.15am	TRAFFIC JAM
	A programme for motorists with occasional interviews. Fast driving sounds, mainly instrumental.
11.15 - 1.00pm	ALL SYSTEMS GO
	The format for this two-hour time slot heavily accentuates the British and American Top 50 selections (in preference to the Top 100) in company with the best rhythm and blues.
1.00-4.00pm	SOUNDS OF '65
	As with All Systems Go, this three-hour show leans heavily on new material, comprising highlights from the Caroline Top 100; predictions, new releases, etc.
4.00 - 6.00pm	THE AMERICAN TOP FIFTY
6.00 - 8.00pm	DOWN BEAT
	Comprises the hip, up-tempo sounds from the Caroline Top 100; rhythm and blues, plus the great soul standards by such artists as Ray Charles, Wes Montgomery and Della Reese.
8.00 - 8.02pm	REVIVAL TIME

| 8.02 - 8.30pm | THE WORLD TOMORROW |
| | Religious programme |

MONDAY to FRIDAY

6.00 - 9.00am	THE TOM LODGE SHOW
9.00 - 12.00 noon	THE MIKE AHERN SHOW
	Current pops and favourite standards.
12.00 - 1.30pm	SPIN AROUND
	In contrast to the Mike Ahern Show the sounds of this ninety-minute programme are very up-tempo and swinging. Predominately a DJ 'Hip Show.'
1.30 - 1.45pm	THE ANDREWS SHOW
	Request programme compèred by Noel Andrews.
1.45 - 4.00pm	BOB STEWART SHOW
	The musical content covers the widest possible range. Current pops, standards - material somewhat in a lower key - and wherever possible by artists in the news. Also accent on chart numbers.
4.00 - 6.00pm	THE BIG LINE UP
	Features tunes from the British and American Top 100 - also predictions about numbers heading for the Top 50, and new releases.
6.00 - 7.00pm	CAROLINE CLUB REQUESTS
	A miscellany of requests and news for members of the Caroline Club.
7.00 - 8.00pm	THE JACK SPECTOR SHOW
	Top American material and interviews with stars straight from the States. Sponsored by Roulette Records.
8.00 - 8.02pm	REVIVAL TIME
8.02 - 8.30pm	THE WORLD TOMORROW

SUNDAY

6.00 - 9.00am	THE EARLY SHOW
9.00 - 11.45am	CHART TIME
	Features tunes from the British Top 50, American Top 50, predictions etc.
11.45 - 12.15pm	BULOVA STAR CHOICE
12.15 - 12.30pm	DOWN MEMORY LANE
	Compèred by Anne Shelton, this show is sponsored by Fynnon Salts.
12.30 - 1.45pm	IT'S ALL HAPPENING
	Rhythm and Blues, new releases.
1.45 - 2.00pm	THE MINERS MAKE-UP SHOW
	Compèred by Vera Lynn.
2.00 - 4.00pm	CAROLINE TOP FIFTY
4.00 - 5.00pm	CAROLINE CLUB REQUEST
5.00 - 6.00pm	THE TOP ALBUM SHOW
	Selected tracks from the Caroline Top 20 Albums.
6.00 - 7.00pm	CAROLINE CLUB REQUESTS
7.00 - 8.00pm	THE R'n'B SHOW
	Top current R'n'B material
8.00 - 8.02pm	REVIVAL TIME
8.02 - 8.30pm	THE WORLD TOMORROW
	Religious programme

PROGRAMME SCHEDULE - RADIO CAROLINE SOUTH

Commencing Monday 14 June 1965

| 6.00 - 9.00am | THE BRYAN VAUGHAN SHOW |
| | Featuring Caroline Top 10 discs, English new |

releases, English or American standards, U.S. chart disc, folk or similar disc, Caroline Top 50, and instrumentals.

9.00 - 10.00am	THE DON ALLEN SHOW
	opening with the SOUND OF MUSIC. Upbeat standards
10.00 - 10.15am	THE ANCHOR SHOW
	Sponsored by Anchor cigarettes. Containing smooth current music.
10.15 - 11.00am	ON THE TRACKS
	Tracks from currently popular LPs.
11.00 - 12.00 noon	TOP DECK
	Pops, avoiding the Top 50.
12.00 - 1 30pm	THE KEITH SKUES SHOW
	Straight English and American pop music.
1.30 - 1.45pm	ANDREWS SHOW
	Sponsored show by Andrews Salts. Taped introductions with request records.
1.45 - 2.00pm	THE NEW ONES
	Newly released pops.
2.00 - 3.05pm	GOING LIVE
	Live performances on disc, from theatre, television and show material.
3.05 - 4.00pm	GOOD GUY PREDICTION TIME
4.00 - 5.45pm	THE BIG LINE UP with KEITH SKUES
	Combination of British and American pops, new and current.
5.45 - 6.00pm	THE CHAPPELL SHOW
	Sponsored by Chappell Pianos. Standards including show music.
6.00 - 7.00pm	CAROLINE CLUB MAGAZINE
	Messages, requests and promotions for Caroline Club members.
7.00 - 8.00pm	THE JACK SPECTOR SHOW
	Fast moving, up-tempo show from New York. Compèred by top American disc jockey Jack Spector.

STATION CLOSE Closing theme - *Round Midnight* by Jimmy McGriff

SATURDAY

6.00 - 9.00am	THE BRYAN VAUGHAN SHOW
	English and American pops
9.00 - 11.00am	THE DON ALLEN SHOW
	Opening with ON THE TRACKS. Tracks from currently popular LPs.
11.00 - 11.15am	THE MOTOR SHOW with GARRY KEMP
	A programme for motorists with occasional interviews. Fast driving sounds, mainly instrumental.
11.15 - 12.00 noon	TOP DECK
	Pops, avoiding the Top 50.
12.00 - 2.15pm	CAROLINE TOP 50 with KEITH SKUES
2.15 - 4.00pm	THE NEW ONES
	British new releases.
4.00 - 6.00pm	THE BIG LINE UP with KEITH SKUES
	Combination of pops, new and current releases from England and United States.
6.00 - 7.00pm	CAROLINE CLUB MAGAZINE
	Messages, requests and promotions.
7.00 - 8.00pm	DOWNBEAT with JON SYDNEY
	Specialising in R & B, modem, mainstream and traditional jazz, soul and any other form of music for specialised audiences.

STATION CLOSE Closing theme - *Round Midnight* by Jimmy McGriff

SUNDAY

6.00 - 9.00am	THE BRYAN VAUGHAN SHOW
	Featuring Caroline Top 10 discs, English new releases, English

	or American standards, U.S. charts, folk, Caroline Top 50 and instrumentals.
9.00 - 10.00am	CAROLINE CONTINENTAL Continental requests and records.
10.00 - 11.45am	THE AMERICAN TOP 50
11.45 - 12.15pm	BULOVA STAR CHOICE Sponsored by Bulova Watches. Containing new and current British releases. Compèred by Ted Frances.
12.15 - 12.30pm	DOWN MEMORY LANE Sponsored by Fynnon Salts. Introduced by Anne Shelton.
12.30 - 1.45pm	THE KEITH SKUES SHOW Straight English and American pop.
1.45 - 2.00pm	GUEST SPOT Interview time, featuring a different artist every week.
2.00 - 3.00pm	AROUND THE WEST END Music from the shows, clubs etc., in London's West End, also interviews.
3.00 - 6.00pm	THE BIG LINE UP with KEITH SKUES Combination of British and American pops, new and current.
6.00 - 7.00pm	CAROLINE CLUB MAGAZINE with DON ALLEN Messages, requests and promotions for Caroline Club members.
7.00 - 8.00pm	DOWN BEAT with JON SYDNEY Specialising in R & B, modern, mainstream and traditional jazz, soul and any other form of music for specialised audiences.

STATION CLOSE Closing theme - *Round Midnight* by Jimmy McGriff.

A listening report card (QSL) sent out to listeners who received Caroline transmissions outside the United Kingdom

MV CAROLINE

RADIO CITY

THIS STATION took over from Radio Sutch. It first went on the air in September 1964 and was run by Reginald Calvert, who managed a number of pop groups. The station transmitted from a group of derelict forts on Shivering Sands in the Thames Estuary. It broadcast music and chat from 6.00am until midnight, with four disc jockeys on board at any one time, each doing an average of 4½ hours per day. The station broadcast on 299 metres, 1003 kHz.

The transmitter had a power of 2 kilowatts and the aerial was a 200ft. mast which was referred to as 'The Tower of Power.' Although it was a mere 2kW the radio station put out an extremely potent signal as the modulation level was kept high. The main transmitter, which was 'home made,' was supervised during its building by Ian West and took some two months to build.

In June 1965 a dispute began over some of the equipment which had been provided second-hand by another pirate radio backer. The studio equipment, which was assembled by Phil Perkins, consisted of three Connoisseur turntables, two replay decks made by Brenell, two microphone inputs and a control panel. The rusty steel-plated studio measured 12ft. by 10ft.

Radio City occupied two towers as working and living quarters, and the remainder were used for housing empty fuel drums. A sixth tower, (occupied by the Port of London Authority), was knocked down by a Norwegian tanker in 1956 killing three men on the tower. When the tide is out one can still observe the side of this fort jutting out of the sea.

The forts were serviced by a tender, owned by local fisherman Fred Downes, which came out from Whitstable, Kent, twice a week. He was later to die in a fishing accident at sea. His boat, *Harvester II,* was found but the body of Downes was never recovered.

By November 1965 more trouble was brewing at Radio City, when the station landed test gear on Knock John Tower, another derelict fort, 4 miles from Shivering Sands. There were heated exchanges between Radio City staff and workers from a Southend-based venture group hoping to start a new pirate station on Knock John.

Roy Bates had his plans drawn up to use Knock John Tower for his own pirate station, Radio Essex. Calvert landed some £3,000 worth of broadcasting equipment on Knock John, and the two men representing Bates were sent packing to Whitstable. Bates, not unnaturally, came to hear of the raid and, in turn, forcibly evicted Calvert's men who returned to Shivering Sands. Calvert conceded defeat.

Amongst the disc jockeys who worked on Radio City were: Karol Beer, Colin Brian, Tony Brandon, RWB (Ross William Brown), Wolf Byrne, Candy Calvert, Tony Carroll, Chris Cross, Alan Clark, Ralph Cooper, Cliff Cottell, Rick Dane, Tony Daniels, Terry Dawson, Alex Dee, Keith Delmont, Dick Dickson, Peter Dolphin, John Edward (Johnny Flux), 'Tatty' Tom Edwards, Paul Elvey (engineer), Martin Green, Mike Hayes, Ben Healy, Peter Jamieson, Eric Jay, Phil Jay, Peggy Knight, Paul Kramer, Bob Le-Roi, Adrian Love, Trevor Lucas, Dave MacKay (Dave Gilbee), Ian MacRae, Eric Martin, Rick Michaels, Ed Moreno, Janice Nicholls, Brian Paul, Mac Peters, Mike Proctor, Martin Ross, Neil Spence, Bob Spencer, Gary Stevens, Martin Stevens, Dennis 'the Menace' Straney, Gordon Swan, Leon Tippler, Graham Wallace (who later became Mark Roman of Big L), Ian West (engineer), Jeremy Wilde, Geoff Woods and Peter York.

The record format was mainly Top 60 records with the *Five by Four* show at 5 o'clock in the evening, a thirty minute show of records by the Rolling Stones and the Beatles ... *Auntie Mabel Hour* with Alan Clark and Ian MacRae ... and a *Late Date* between 11 o'clock and 12 midnight, which broadcast softer more romantic music. The station always closed down at midnight with the national anthem.

Mark Roman remembers his short stint with Radio City. "I worked for just one week on Shivering Sands. We had to wash in sea water. Conditions were very primitive and every time we walked past the radio transmitter it 'spat' at you. Reginald Calvert (known as Uncle Reg) insisted that the DJs played a record by the Fortunes on the hour every hour. Calvert was their manager. Tony Brandon and I had a few laughs during our time with Radio City. I left in March 1965 to join Radio London."

On 29 December 1965 there was a collision drama at Shivering Sands when Tom Edwards interrupted a tea-time show on Radio City to announce dramatically "A boat is about to hit us!" Then the station went off air. But within minutes, as listeners telephoned police, it resumed broadcasting. A two-masted fore-and-aft rigged sailing boat, with a mizzenmast

DJs with Radio City. Left to right: Eric Martin, Alan Clark, Phil Jay,
Paul Kramer, Ed Moreno, Tom Edwards and Ian MacRae

stepped forward of the rudder, had drifted in rough seas towards the wartime fort firing distress signals. The ketch, the *Scarab*, with a crew of three, had got into difficulties on a voyage from Gosport in Hampshire to London.

Shipping, and the Southend lifeboat, were already looking for her when she scared the Radio City staff. Coastguards had spotted red flares 20 minutes earlier. The lifeboat was launched at 6.38pm in a south-westerly storm force wind and a very rough sea. It was two hours after high water.

The 295-ton Dutch coaster, *Westland Trader,* eventually took the *Scarab* in tow as it headed for Sheerness with a lifeboat standing by. The ketch's two masts snapped in the gale.

With great difficulty the coxswain managed to take the lifeboat alongside twice, rescue the three men, and then, in mountainous seas, made for Sheerness where they were landed. The lifeboat remained at Sheerness until the weather had moderated, before returning to her station which she reached at 1.45am.

Reg Calvert said "There was a bit of panic because, at first, we thought the vessel might be so big it could wreck the fort."

Asked if the food was good on Radio City, Tom Edwards commented "We had a chef who had so much Brylcreem on his hair I am sure he threw half of it into the frying pan to cook food. He used to serve up "Crud Pie" and then wondered what went into it. But beggars can't be choosers and we had to eat it.

"The best cook was Leslie Dunn who was a qualified chef and prepared us very good food. All water had to be boiled first before we could drink it.

"There was no alcohol allowed on board. Reg Calvert was very strict in this respect. However, when we were working over Christmas in 1965 there were just three of us on duty. There was Alex Dee, who is now a born-again Christian, Phil Perkins, the engineer, and myself. We were allowed a celebration drink. However one has to remember that the studio was 90ft. above sea level and it would have been completely out of order to have got drunk."

In high winds, or when the tide was very rough, the forts used to sway a lot. Tom Edwards likened the forts to an aeroplane's wings. "If they were strictly rigid the plane would crash because the wings of the aircraft would fall off. It was the same with the towers at Shivering Sands. They would move with the wind and shudder from time to time. When I experienced this for the very first time, it was very nerve-wracking. However, the forts are still standing in 1993, minus the connecting catwalks which had collapsed into the sea, so they must be pretty strong."

Engineers who worked on Radio City included Phil Perkins, Paul Elvey, Ian West, Dick Dickson and Don Witts.

At the end of 1965 negotiations took place with Radio Caroline with a view to their taking over the City operation, and a new transmitter was delivered to the fort. This deal fell through. In June 1966 it was announced that Radio City was being taken over by an anonymous group of backers from Britain, Canada and the United States of America, working through a trust registered in the Bahamas. That deal also fell through.

The next takeover bid for Radio City was by Radio London who wanted to run a middle-of-the-road music station, United Kingdom Good Music (UKGM), from the fort (see Chapter Eight). That, too, did not happen as Reg Calvert had not paid the £10,000 owing to Major Oliver Smedley and Project Atlanta for the transmitter, and the latter were planning to claim it back.

In the early hours of 20 June 1966, Oliver Smedley led a boarding party of riggers and took control of the station. After a few hours Smedley left the fort and returned home to his Essex cottage leaving the riggers in charge. The following evening Reg Calvert visited Smedley at his home in Wendens Ambo, near Saffron Walden. The door was opened by Smedley's secretary/housekeeper who did her best to stop Calvert gaining access to the cottage. A scuffle developed and Smedley appeared with a shotgun and killed Calvert.

Smedley appeared in court at Saffron Walden accused of the murder of Reg Calvert. The jury took three days to decide that no court would convict on a murder charge. He was sent for trial at Chelmsford. On 18 October he was found not guilty of 'unlawfully' killing Reg Calvert on 21 June 1966 and was completely discharged.

Radio City was taken over by Reg Calvert's widow, Dorothy. On 9 February 1967 she appeared before magistrates at Rochford accused of operating a radio station without a licence. She said that Radio City, based on a fort at Shivering Sands, was outside territorial limits. However, the magistrates disagreed and she was fined £100. That evening the station closed down at midnight. All station staff took part in Radio City's final hour, including Paul Kramer, Ian MacRae, Alan Clark and Ross Brown (RWB). The final record played was "The Party's Over". Each of the DJs said goodbye and the station closed down with the national anthem.

In the Spring 1972 issue of *Monitor* magazine, Dorothy Calvert wrote a short letter regarding her involvement with Radio City:

It amazes me that there is still so much interest in free radio after all this time. Looking back now on those few short years I think the thing that stands out most was the amount of energy that was radiated from all concerned in Radio City. I cannot mention everyone who was concerned but I will try to give a little more information than has come to be written before.

My husband, Reg Calvert, had been interested in radio for many years and when Radio Caroline started transmissions he was delighted. At the time we were very involved in our business in the entertainment field, but there were light hearted discussions with Screaming Lord Sutch about him starting a joke radio station as a publicity stunt. Little by little this idea grew and Reg started looking for a boat. Eventually we arrived at Southend one day for a trip to the old sea forts in the Thames. I only went for the drive as I was a very poor sailor but I was taken on board for the trip. Going out was all right and the sight of the towers for the first time was like something from a science fiction film. We went past what was eventually Radio 390 as we were informed that they were definitely inside the limit and Shivering Sands were boarded.

I went on the towers a few weeks after transmissions started and was petrified by the climb up the ladders. Occasionally I used to go out in the boat but never went on board again until Good Friday 1966. Meanwhile things had slowly improved but I wasn't very involved with things until my second visit. Reg had asked me to take over administration of broadcasting while he still handled the technical side. On that trip there was a hoist to go up to the towers. That absolutely terrified me and how I managed to hold a conversation with Ian MacRae I don't know. After talking to Ian while he was on air and watching the procedure, and then going over with Tom Edwards how things worked, I went back and literally thought up 'format radio.' Having been in the pop world so long was a big help in understanding the requirements of pop radio. Luckily it worked very well. Of course, the event that really put Radio City on the map was my husband's death. The news flashed round the world but my world was shattered. If Radio City had disappeared at the same time I think I should have completely lost my mind but, in the face of such a tragedy, other people's welfare just had to come first. Radio City had to go back on the air and I was determined that no one else should take over. The people around me at that time were wonderful. I expected them to give of their best and they were determined to make Radio City the best. We immediately extended the hours of transmission, and *Auntie Mabel* was born. Ian MacRae and Alan Clark really worked hard on that programme and everyone was pulled into the Christmas pantomime. If we had had more time I wonder just how far we would have evolved. Time was short. It hung over my Christmas and in January I was served with a summons. What a waste of talent. What a travesty of justice. What an indictment of Britain when, in the two cases I was personally involved in, such a mockery was made of everything I believed that British justice stood for. How I wish now that I had used Radio City to expose the truth of those events, but if I had tried I wonder what would have happened. I am still here and working hard, but how and when would I have been silenced if I'd spoken out then? By the way, my daughter Candy was the first girl disc jockey. She was thirteen at the time, and she went out over the air in May 1964 - she did broadcast after that from time to time during her school holiday.

Disc jockey Paul Kramer, nicknamed 'Kinky', was run over and killed by a car on Putney Bridge on 5 December 1968. In addition to working on Radio City, he also spent time with Radio 270, Caroline North and Caroline South. He produced a short 8mm film (black and white) of Radio Caroline taken aboard *Mi Amigo* in 1965.

Eric Martin, at one time manager and station controller of Radio City, died on 20 August 1992, aged 72 years.

See Chapter Eight for the shooting of Reginald Calvert and the fort takeover.

PROGRAMME SCHEDULE - RADIO CITY

17 January 1967

MONDAY to SATURDAY

6.00am	Early Bird Show
7.30am	Voice of Prophecy
8.00am	Breakfast Break
8.30am	Allen Revival Hour
8.45am	Up and About
10.00am	Just Go
10.45am	Coffee Break
11 00am	Just Go

12.00 noon	Gary Stevens Show
1.00pm	Breakaway
5.00pm	Five by Four
5.30pm	Sixty Minute Special
6.30pm	Voice of Prophecy
7.00pm	City by Night
11.00pm	Late Date
12.00 midnight	Close Down

SUNDAY

6.00am	Early Bird Show
7.30am	Voice of Prophecy
8.00am	Breakfast Break
9.30am	Basildon Request Show
11 00am	Just Go
12.00 noon	A La Carte
2.00pm	Aunty Mabel Hour
3.00pm	Breakaway
4.30pm	Discamania
5.30pm	Cobweb Corner
6.30pm	Voice of Prophecy
7.00pm	Top Twenty
8.00pm	City by Night
11 00pm	Late Date
12.00 midnight	Closedown

Extra: 11.00am Monday, Wednesday and Friday - Radio Doctor 4.30pm
Saturday - Discamania

News and Weather together on the hour, every hour

RADIO ENGLAND

KNOWN AS "Swinging Radio England", the station came on the scene in June 1966 operating from the 186ft. long ship, m.v. *Olga Patricia*, later renamed m.v. *Laissez-Faire*. Nearly £100,000 had been spent on re-equipping the ship in Miami. The m.v. *Olga Patricia* was launched in America. It had an American managing director, an American director of programmes and a predominantly American team of disc jockeys ... and it had the cheek to call itself "Swinging Radio ENGLAND"!

Managing director was William Vick. It was the sister station to Britain Radio which broadcast good music, whereas Radio England transmitted much more music in the pop idiom. The two stations used a transmitter with a joint power of 110 kilowatts. On board the m.v. *Olga Patricia*, a former World War II Liberty ship of 480 tons, were two Englishmen, two Australians, and four American southerners, representing the broadcasting side. There were 13 seamen from Nicaragua, Salvador, Colombia, Jamaica, Spain and Cuba.

Radio England's first test signal was a recording of *The Yellow Rose Of Texas*. Test transmissions began on both stations on 3 May 1966, Radio England on 355 metres, 845 kHz and Britain Radio on 227 metres, 1321 kHz. Exactly one month later there was a transmitter failure, and a new one had to be obtained from Dallas, Texas. At a similar time Italy complained that the test transmissions were interfering with Rome II, so Radio England switched to 227 metres and Britain Radio to 355 metres. Due to the complaint, Britain Radio's transmitting power in the evening was reduced to less than a quarter of its daytime power. Regular programming began on Radio England on 18 June 1966, and the frequency was changed again to 225 metres. It was then we were introduced to the jingle *Swinging Radio England*. The following day programmes began on Britain Radio, "Hallmark of Quality".

Advertising for the station was handled by Radio-Vision Broadcasts (International) Ltd., a company in the Pearl and Dean Group. The cost of launching Radio England along with her sister station, Britain Radio, was estimated at around £1,450,000.

In what appeared to be a "fantastic" champagne party to other offshore commercial stations, Radio England/Britain Radio held a "do" at the Hilton Hotel in the autumn of 1966 when hundreds of guests put in an appearance including Dusty Springfield, Madeleine Bell, Tom Jones, Small Faces, Dave Berry, Neil Christian, Chris Farlowe, Zoot Money, Vanessa Redgrave, Paul and Barry Ryan, Walker Brothers, Limeys, Dave Clark Five, Koobas, John Lennon, Sandie Shaw, Crispian St. Peters, Geno Washington, Ray Ellington, Herman's Hermits, Manfred Mann, Frank Chacksfield, Jackie Trent, Tony Hatch, Benny Hill, Sir Donald Wolfit, The Moody Blues, Patrick Wymark, Alyn Ainsworth, Sir Peter Rawlinson QC MP, Joan Regan, Alma Cogan and Alan Price. But could the company really afford such an elaborate party? Obviously not! On 14 March 1967 Peir-Vick Ltd., the company which backed the station, went broke to the tune of £110,000.

They vacated their luxurious offices in Curzon Street, which had the whole of Mayfair talking, and moved into Berkeley Street. At 32 Curzon Street there used to stand a beautiful walled garden. At one end stood a large mock-Roman facade complete with pillars and a statue of a nymph as its centrepiece. But, with the downfall of "Swinging Radio England," all the glitter and gold had gone.

Both stations transmitted their programmes through two separate aerials held aloft by a 210ft. mast. One aerial was secured to a small mast on top of the bridge, and the other attached to a deck insulator. This was a novel idea in offshore radio. The radio station was unusual in other ways too; for instance, she had a staff of announcers who would have gladdened the heart of any large commercial station in the United States of America ... Ron O'Quinn from a top Florida station, Larry Dean from a top New York station, Jerry Smithwick, a capable and experienced disc jockey. Boom Boom Brannigan from a top Philadelphia station and Chuck Blair from top stations all over the States. Boom Boom Brannigan was tragically killed in a car accident shortly after returning to the States.

The Radio England side of transmissions were 'loud' in presentation and disc jockeys tended to shout at their audience rather than talk to them. This kind of presentation was acceptable in the States, but the British people were not ready for this style of radio. Her problem was too many American disc jockeys and not enough English on-air personalities.

The rich Texas owners were obviously good at making money by other means, but not by this type of broadcasting. They did not heed the advice of any of the station's experienced personnel. The company blamed its failings on Ron O'Quinn who was then programme director - he left and Larry Dean and Jerry Smithwick followed. Chuck Blair, with ten years experience in broadcasting, was hired as programme director and then general manager, but even this was not enough. Radio England arrived too late on the scene to compete with Radio London and Radio Caroline with a similar format in record presentation.

The station lacked advertising which was handled inadequately by Radio-Vision, lacked adequate support from the shareholders and, finally, suffered loss of support from her listeners. In locking the stable door after the horse had bolted, the company began severe cost cutting. Chuck Blair and several key men were dismissed to make way for lesser paid and inexperienced personnel. Jack Curtiss, a man with little radio experience, took over the helm and immediately fired disc jockeys Johnnie Walker, Roger Day and Bill Berry. From then onwards it was downhill all the way for the mismanaged company. Radio England had great potential but financial disaster torpedoed her five months after her entry into pirate waters.

Her disc jockey staff, shared between Radio England and Britain Radio (later Radio 355), comprised David Allan, Gordon Bennett, Bill Berry, Alan Black, Chuck Blair, Boom Boom Brannigan, Errol Bruce, Woolf Byrne, Tom Cooper, Jack Curtiss, Johnny Dark, Roger Day, Larry Dean, Tel Delaney, Dave Gilbee (Dave McKaye), Graham Gill, Jim Henry, Sheldon Jay, Martin Kayne, Phil Martin, Jack McLaughlin, Tony Meehan, Tony Monson, Ed Moreno, Colin Nicol. Ron O'Quinn, Rick Randall, Mark Sloane, Jerry Smithwick, Gary Stevens, Brian Tylney, Johnnie Walker, Greg Warren, Bruce Wayne, Alan West, Stephen West and Tony Windsor.

The m.v. *Laissez-Faire* was equipped with two studios and two transmitters. Each transmitter sent out 55 kilowatts and they were made by Continental Electronics of Dallas, Texas. In February 1967 the radio mast buckled during a force 9 gale, and the ship had to go to Holland for refitting which took just a week. In each studio (one for Radio England - the other for Britain Radio) there were two record turntables, three tape machines, and a 'carousel' which worked on the juke box principle, selecting and playing tapes secured in cartridges.

Following the close down of Radio England, the m.v. *Laissez-Faire* transmitted programmes in Dutch under the station name Radio Dolfijn. It commenced transmissions in November 1966 through until March 1967 when, once again, she changed her call sign, this time to Radio 227. The station closed on 21 July 1967 at 6.00pm. The *Laissez-Faire* sailed for Flushing in Holland on 19 August 1967 where its mast was due to be removed. However, when she arrived in Miami on 22 September 1967 the mast was still visible, although buckled due to gale force winds.

The transmitters were sold to Swazi Radio, Mbabane, Swaziland, and Trans World Radio, Swaziland. The Continental Electronics 3170, 50 kilowatt medium wave transmitter is in daily use on 1377 kHz. The other, also made by Continental Electronics of Dallas, is used by Trans World Radio.

PROGRAMME SCHEDULE - RADIO ENGLAND

July 1966

6.00am	Ron O'Quinn Show
10.00am	Larry Dean Show
2.00pm	Jerry Smithwick Show
6.00pm	Roger Day Show
10.00pm	Rick Randall Show
2.00am	Graham Gill Show

News at 15 minutes past the hour
Weather at fifteen minutes to and fifteen minutes past the hour

RADIO ESSEX

RADIO ESSEX was the only localised offshore station in the British Isles and the first to operate around the clock.

The station commenced test transmissions on 27 October 1965 on 222 metres, 1351 kHz, and was directed, as its name suggested, to listeners in the county of Essex, although it could be heard much further afield. A listener reported picking up the transmissions in Cologne, Germany. Regular programmes began on 7 November 1965 on 1353 kHz, announced as 222 metres.

The station itself was housed in Knock John Fort in the Thames Estuary. The journey out to the fort took about four hours. Unlike the forts of Radio 390 and Radio City, Knock John

The Laissez-Faire at anchor off the Essex coast, 1967

(which was six miles from land) was constructed of concrete and steel and had hollow legs, two or which supported the main structure. To get on board one had to climb a seaweed and slime-covered rusting ladder to a single plank 50ft. above the North Sea. On board were two generators, one studio with a record library, a mess room and living and sleeping quarters.

The fort extended 110ft. above sea level. On the outside of the fort one was greeted by the white painted sign "Radio Essex - 222 metres." This job was undertaken by Dick Palmer.

At each end of the platform, which was sixty feet above sea level, there were two old 4.5-inch anti-submarine, anti-aircraft guns - non operational, of course!

The broadcasting studio measured approximately 9ft. by 5ft. wide. It contained two Garrard 401 turntables, two Vortexion tape machines and a Vortexion mixer with studio console controls.

The walls of the studio were decorated with record covers and pictures of pop stars. There was no daylight in the studio and the electricity was provided by the fort's own generating system. Constant fresh air was passed through the studio which had numerous red blankets draped around the room to act as sound-proofing.

The captain of the fort was Dick Palmer who also acted as chief disc jockey. He worked in close liaison with fellow disc jockeys Vince Allen, Johnny Caine, Dick Dickson, Guy Hamilton, Graham Johns (real name Graham Dubber, who later went under the name of Tim Yale on Radio Caroline), Martin Kayne, John Knight (cook), Tony Mandell, Roger Scott (real name Greg Bance), David Sinclair, Chris Stewart, John Stewart (who later became John Aston), Van Stirling, and Mark West (also known as Mark Wesley).

Radio Essex had one American RCA transmitter with 50 watts output. Says Dick Palmer "Although our signal was only of low power, our transmissions were picked up in Germany. Within a year we managed to have the power increased to about 200 watts."

Elsewhere on the fort, disc jockeys and engineers could use the excellent mess room and the fort"s television set.

The shift rosters meant that disc jockeys worked for three weeks and had a week's leave. That was in theory. In practice it very rarely worked. Dick Palmer remembers doing a stint of eight weeks without a break on one occasion. It was not unusual for DJs to work continuously up to six weeks at a time. The DJs made up their own programmes and, unlike Radio London and other stations, did not like duplicating their records. If a record were played twice within six to eight hours it was a mistake.

Radio Essex supported charities, organised dances and held competitions.

Disc jockey Guy Hamilton looks back on his days spent on Fort Knock John:

I had signed on as a DJ, but free of charge. I was trained in peeling spuds, washing up (or throwing the worst over the side, in reality), loading diesel and flushing loos with a bucket of seawater (after twenty feet even a bucket felt heavy).

Sleeping below sea level in the dormitory decks of this old wartime naval fort was an experience: you could hear ships' screws a long way off, and appreciated submariners' desire for silence. The foghorn on Mid-Barrow lightship was a kind of friend: you were glad it was there in fog, but wished it would shut up.

Forts had their advantages: there was plenty of room compared with ships, but living was basic. Getting seasick was difficult (except on the tender, which made up for it) but getting homesick was easy, especially when the lights of towns round the estuary twinkled at night and reminded you of worldly pleasures left behind in dedicating your life to the turntable.

Radio Essex was tiny and hard up but, in retrospect, produced some really good programmes musically. The only pirate, in fact, to have such a catholic taste: mostly easy listening, but with real old rock and roll slots, as well as jazz, folk, country and big bands, the direct descendants of these shows went on to BBC Radio.

The fort was haunted. There were still postcards from home with wartime pin-ups on the

RADIO ESSEX IS **MY** STATION 24 HOURS A DAY **222** METRES

walls of the lower floors down near the seabed. It was spooky there, with wartime remains where the ammunition lockers were. The engineers swore that they'd put down their tools in one place, and have to pick them up elsewhere. But it seemed to be a friendly spirit.

I experienced its effects on one occasion when presenting a programme at about 3.00am. Without warning, my on-air studio door burst open to reveal an ashen-faced chief engineer demanding to know whether I'd left the studio: I hadn't. He went away sharpish: he knew his colleague, Mike Brereton, hadn't moved when he'd gone to the tank room to fill a kettle with fresh water for tea before plugging it in the mess room, the only place that was possible. Nonetheless, he'd returned a little later to find the kettle, boiling hot but unplugged, in the same place he'd filled it, which was devoid of electricity. Mike, a good friend to this day, said that they'd checked and all the remaining crew were asleep in their bunks - in any case you'd have heard them move. Funny, but scary!

The aerial was a long wire between two scaffold poles, and used to arc prettily to the top of the fort's superstructure in damp weather, reducing our coverage area from nearby parts of Essex and Kent, even east London on a good day, to just the Mid-Barrow lightship, Foulness and the very tip of Southend pier. One day a plan was hatched: we would remove the top of the fort (this while standing on it). This was duly achieved after incredibly daring feats of sawing and jumping clear. The entire top floor, a searchlight or anti-aircraft gun turret, made of inch-thick steel, keeled over and almost went cleanly over the side of the deck below. It hit the main deck and the whole place reverberated: how it didn't fall apart we'll never know. We somehow eased the wrecked turret over the side, and made the best splash I've ever seen.

The signal strength didn't really improve. Why on earth we didn't just raise the aerial masts so it didn't arc, I forgot to ask. Perhaps we couldn't afford another scaffold pole. The transmitter was home-made and tinpot. A new bigger model was constructed out of old Hoover parts and washing-up bowls (to catch the rain) and to celebrate the massive upsurge in power from 50 to 200 watts, a new programme schedule was devised and a change of name planned. Thus was born the snappy title, Britain's Better Music Station, or BBMS. We launched. Minutes later the new transmitter melted ... perhaps the Hoover had needed emptying! Soon after that the station was prosecuted and the name was irrelevant.

Aged 18, I grew up on Knock John, very rapidly. You learned not only how to DJ and crank diesels and cook, but also how to live at close quarters with unusual people, and not to criticise the cooking. One night, the entire supper for the whole crew was slung over the side by the day's maître D, all because someone had rashly said, "Not bloody meat pie again!"

When stocks were low - storms kept little ships at bay - we learnt to improvise. Drink was limited to sterilised milk at one point. Jam in sterilised milk made a nice change, as did marmalade on cheese - really quite gourmet, though it didn't seem that way at the time. Fried corn flakes was probably the nadir. Smokers got desperate when cigarettes ran out. Realising that profit-taking was better than smoking, I almost gave up myself at this point, preferring to alleviate the suffering of fellows in distress (especially if they had money). Tea leaves rolled in toilet tissue were known to have been smoked on occasions. The more amusing part, looking back, was the intended 'discreet' coded messages for our 'head office' (a modest flat in Southend) whenever supplies were low. A letter signifying a particular commodity, say food for instance, was mentioned on air (no radio service was allowed us by the Post Office) followed by a number which was the days' supply left. Rough weather for a fortnight would thus result in an increasingly mutinous crew sweetly announcing, "Here is a special message for our head office: A 0; B 0; C 0;" and so on.

To rub this in, tracks with suitable titles were played ad nauseam, for example *Last Chicken in the Shop*, *One Last Cigarette*, and we found at least 13 pleasingly different versions of *Cool Clear Water*. One day, when the weather had seemed pleasant enough for a boat for just a little too long, the entire repertoire of the station was limited to these titles and nothing much else. I have never seen a man so apoplectic as when the owner arrived an hour later.

Programme content, in retrospect, was excellent. A rich and fully stocked library had quantities of most forms of good music. Various programmes had specific music themes, such as musicals, or jazz, or big bands. I personally started a rock & roll hour on the overnight pop show *Essex Beat Club,* with some success judging by the mail. It was clear we were appreciated as the only English-speaking station overnight: amazing but then true. Bakers would send out the most spectacular cakes with their requests. I can remember a splendid iced picture of the fort on one, and a 3-foot long Swiss roll in a wooden box from another happy earlybird listener.

The Radio Essex station was the brainchild of Roy Bates, a Southend businessman. He thought of starting an offshore station before Radio Caroline became operational, but didn't succeed. In the early days when Roy was preparing the fort for broadcasting, it was apparently raided by Radio City men. However, Radio City said they were on the fort first.

Roy Bates recalls: "I chose a fort rather than a ship because it made much better sense from an economic point of view. It is easier to maintain. It doesn't pitch and roll like a ship, so there was a much more stable situation, which made it easier for the DJs and engineers. When we began broadcasting conditions were primitive to say the least, but after a few months they improved. We then put a full-time cook on the fort which pleased the DJs. A tender went out to Fort Knock John twice a week."

Officially record companies would not service the pirate ships and forts, but most stations admitted they did receive the latest releases - if not from the record company then from the music publisher or the artist's manager. As Radio Essex was outside British jurisdiction they did not pay performing rights for the use of the records.

Commenting on the Marine Offences Bill to rid the shores of Britain of the pirates, Roy Bates added in 1966: "The Bill is quite unrealistic and takes no account of the mass of the people of all tastes and ages, and also the marketing requirements of modem industry and business.

"Commercial radio has to come to Britain, so why not be realistic and allow it by setting up local and regional stations now, and by using the knowledge of the offshore radio people? All have proved they can make an audience and do the job in a responsible manner."

The Post Office served a summons on Roy Bates on 28 September 1966, alleging that on 16 August 1966 he had contravened Section One of the Wireless Telegraphy Act 1949 by operating without a licence.

Radio Essex was summoned to appear in court at Rochford, Essex, on 30 November 1966 (see Chapter Eleven). The station was fined £100 and, against the advice of its solicitors, carried on broadcasting having changed its name to Britain's Better Music Station. However, the money had run out and the station closed. Dick Palmer (who also opened Radio Essex) presented the final programme and closed BBMS on Christmas Day 1966.

The equipment was dismantled and taken to Roughs Tower where Roy Bates later set up the Independent State of Sealand.

PROGRAMME SCHEDULES - RADIO ESSEX

November 1965

6.00am	Get Up and Go
9.00am	Good Morning Show
12.00noon	Afternoon Spin
3.00pm	Sound of Music
6.00pm	Big Bands
7.00pm	Essex Goes Pop
8.00pm	An Evening with Essex
11.00pm	Essex Beat Club
3.00am	Night Owl

News on the even hour between 8.00am and 8.00pm
Sunday on the odd hour from 9.00am to 9.00pm
Weather on the half hour

RADIO INVICTA

THE STATION made its first regular broadcast on 29 July 1964 and was the fourth pirate station to become operational off the British shores. It transmitted from seven ack-ack forts on Red Sands near Princess Channel in the Thames Estuary on 306 metres in the medium wave, 985 kHz. It had a range of 75 miles, and broadcast from 6.00am to 6.00pm when it became blocked out by Radio Algiers.

The leader of Radio Invicta was Tom Pepper (real name Harry Featherbee), a tugboat skipper well-known in Folkestone harbour. He dressed like a pirate and wore a single gold earring. He was assisted by Kent businessmen John Thompson and Charles Evans.

Test transmissions were heard on a number of frequencies including 266 metres, 1126 kHz, 306 metres, 980 kHz, 305 metres, 985 kHz, 303 metres, 991 kHz and 228 metres, 1319 kHz. Regular broadcasts commenced on 17 July on 306 metres, 985 kHz. The station built up a small but loyal listenership.

On 24 July 1964 two men on the forts signalled passing ships with mirrors and SOS signs. An air sea rescue helicopter from Royal Air Force Manston in Kent arranged to go and visit the forts. Kent coastguards had received a message from the ship *American Champion* that there was a problem on the forts. Fort staff were suffering from lack of water, so 100 gallons were later sent out.

Less than a month later Tom Pepper claimed that saboteurs had caused engine damage to the tune of £1,000 to his supply tug and trawler in Folkestone Harbour.

Radio Invicta put out more SOS calls in its short time of operation than most of the other offshore stations put together. On 28 September 1964 the station sent an SOS for a doctor, and the Southend lifeboat was launched to take Doctor Patrick Collins of Chalkwell to the forts where he treated one of the radio staff for a badly injured foot.

Radio Invicta claimed, on 6 October 1964, they were the first all night radio station in the country.

Thirteen days later disc jockey Ed Moreno, head DJ on the fort, made a startling announcement: "We are being invaded." In fact the invaders turned out to be a naval survey team making a friendly visit.

The Southend lifeboat was called out once again. Pat Collins, who appeared to be the fort's regular doctor, paid a visit on 7 November to treat disc jockey Simon Ashley who was suffering from suspected appendicitis. The station had sent out an SOS over the air to which the Southend lifeboat was asked to respond. Doctor Collins took off Ashley who was later transferred to hospital for treatment.

Disaster struck the station on 17 December 1964 when the body of 38-year-old Tom Pepper was washed ashore near Reeves Beach, Whitstable. Pepper left Faversham on the previous day in his 36ft. launch, the *David*, named after his son. He had travelled out early in the morning with Ed Moreno. On arrival at Red Sands, Ed instructed 21 year-old DJ Simon Ashley and engineer Martin Shaw (18) to return to land with Pepper. Simon (real name Barry Hoy) was known for his *Pot Luck* show. He had intended spending Christmas with his girl friend and there was talk that the two might become engaged over the holiday period. It was to be Simon's first shore leave since his appendicitis in November 1964. Martin came from Northwood in Middlesex. They had left Red Sands fort shortly after 11.00am.

Parts of the wreckage of the launch were washed ashore at Whitstable on 17 December and examined by police. The following day more wreckage, including fuel barrels and a water tank, was washed up.

It was later learned that Pepper sailed from Faversham Ore on the Wednesday morning about 7.30am to take out chief disc jockey Ed Moreno to the Red Sands fort, and was on his way back with Hoy and Shaw when their launch overturned in rough seas. Neither Hoy nor Shaw could swim. Furthermore they were not wearing life jackets.

Commenting, Ed Moreno said that Pepper was not well, but insisted on making the return journey to land. The seas were rough and Pepper was already suffering from an attack of flu.

On the Red Sands fort on 18 December a programme of hymns and solemn music was broadcast in memory of Pepper, Hoy and Shaw.

Police did not rule out the possibility of sabotage. They said that radio equipment and the hulls of other boats owned by Pepper were found smashed earlier in the year. On this occasion the sea was calm (in spite of Ed Moreno's saying it was rough) and there was no fog. A friend of Pepper said "Tom was a masterly seaman and a very strong swimmer. It seemed impossible he could have wrecked the *David* on a sandbank - he knew them all."

In late December, police frogmen were all set to make an underwater search off Whitstable for the bodies of Hoy and Shaw. Wreckage of the boat had been found, but the search was called off due to bad weather and rough seas. A helicopter searched the Thames Estuary on 18 December but with no success.

An open verdict was recorded at the inquest on Pepper in Herne Bay, Kent, on 22 December 1964. The East Kent Coroner, Wilfred Mowll, said evidence was insufficient to establish what had happened to the boat in which the trio had been travelling.

The actual wreck of the *David* was found by divers the following June, but there was no sign of the bodies of Hoy and Shaw. It was believed that the launch went down near the Street Buoy about 2 miles from land. Writing in the *News of the World* on 30 October 1966, DJ Mike Raven said "One other body may have been swept all the way to Spain, for all there was to identify it was a three-inch spool of recording tape. When they dried it out and played it ... it was part of a programme from Invicta!"

There was another call on the RNLI on 21 December 1964 when the Southend lifeboat was launched to carry stores to Radio Invicta. The station's supply ship was held up by heavy seas at Sheerness and permission was given for the lifeboat to carry food and other supplies to the radio staff. A Whitstable fishing boat, *Mallard*, loaded with food and fuel also reached the forts.

Lack of oil for the generators caused the station to go off air on Sunday afternoon, 20 December. The three man crew had no light, heat nor cooking facilities.

More SOS calls! On 21 January 1965 an SOS was picked up by the Post Office Radio Station at North Foreland - it was a request for water. London promoter Monty Schulberg, who took over the business side of the station from Pepper, contacted the supplies depot in Folkestone.

Just over a week later the station called for a doctor. On 29 January North Foreland radio dictated medical advice and a doctor took off in a helicopter for the forts. Disc jockey Bruce

Holland (25) had fallen and injured his head. He had seven stitches put in the wound.

It was reported that Françoise Pepper took over control of Radio Invicta after her husband's death, along with John Thompson, an ex-journalist and Canadian broadcaster, who had tried earlier to set up a pirate radio station, GBLN, in 1961, but the project failed. Advertising rates on Radio Invicta varied from six to ten pounds per ten seconds.

The station prided itself in finding new talent, and amongst the groups they signed up were the Mission Bells who went on a nationwide tour with the Bachelors during 1965.

On 5 February 1965 Kent coastguards claimed that Radio Invicta jammed the international radio distress frequency for two hours with complaints that their heating system had broken down.

A rumour that Radio Invicta was to be sold to the pop group The Bachelors was denied by Francoçise Pepper who said she was not selling the station.

Disc jockeys who worked on Radio Invicta included Chris Allen, Simon Ashley, Gary Brandem, Johnny Caine, Jeff Godfrey, Bob Graham, Bruce Holland, Eddie Jerold, Ed Laney, Johnny Lark, Ed Moreno, Pete Ross, Tony Silver, Neil Spence, Lee Taylor and Paul Wayne. Engineers included Phil Perkins, a radio amateur, Martin Shaw and Phil Silver.

The station closed down halfway through February 1965 and a new station, KING Radio, took over the forts on Red Sands and commenced test transmissions on 25 February 1965.

PROGRAMME SCHEDULE - RADIO INVICTA

January 1965

5.00am	Early Morning Spin
7.00am	Breakfast Show
9.00am	Top Sticks
10.00am	Mail Call
11.00am	Strictly for Highbrows
11.30am	Pot Luck
12.55pm	Information Desk
1.00pm	Lunch Box
2.00pm	Date with Romance
3.00pm	Memory Lane
4.00pm	Afternoon Session
4.30pm	Kiddies' Corner
5.00pm	Music for the Evening
6.00pm	Close Down

Saturday and Sundays: 2.00pm A Seat in the Stalls

RADIO LONDON

RADIO LONDON started transmitting from the m.v. *Galaxy*, a 780-ton former United States minesweeper, on 23 December 1964. It broadcast music in the pop idiom under a general heading of Top 40, in the medium waveband on 266 metres, 1133 kHz.

The original team of disc jockeys were Tony Windsor, Paul Kaye, Pete Brady, Earl Richmond, Dave Dennis and Kenny Everett.

The ship itself, which was crewed by 22 men, was the largest of all the offshore radio stations. During its teething period life aboard was described as "rough." It took 2½ years to rebuild inside of the entire ship, and what had been a mass of pipes, wires, air vents, lockers and paint stores became a neatly decorated 'home' with adequate cabin accommodation. The majority of disc jockeys had single cabins - the less fortunate shared with another person.

In July 1965, Radio London claimed 50.9% of all commercial radio listeners in East Anglia according to a National Opinion Poll survey.

Many guest artists visited the ship including Gene Pitney, Spencer Davis, Jonathan King, Marianne Faithfull and Geno Washington, together with almost every name from the newspaper world ... nationals, locals, magazines and pop papers! All were dined in the *Galaxy's* mess.

Radio London was represented by Radlon (Sales) Ltd. who had their offices at 17 Curzon Street in Mayfair, London. Managing director was Philip Birch.

The station operated from 5.30am each day until 2.00am the following day.

Radio London ran some very successful land-based promotions including disc nights at Greenford, Lowestoft, Forest Gate, Catford, Slough and Bishop's Stortford. They had a stand at the Racing Car Show and Camping and Outdoor Life Exhibition in 1967, and ran a pop show at Brands Hatch and Biggin Hill, both in 1966 and 1967.

Radio London ceased broadcasting at 3.00pm on Monday 14 August 1967 following an announcement from the Government that it would be illegal to continue broadcasting from ships after midnight on the 14th.

For the complete story about Radio London, see Chapter Six.

PROGRAMME SCHEDULE - RADIO LONDON

Commencing Wednesday 8 March - Tuesday 14 March 1967

WEEKDAYS

5.30am	Chuck Blair Breakfast Show
9.00am	Keith Skues Show
11.00am	Coffee Break
11.15am	Keith Skues Show
12.00 noon	Kenny Everett Show
3.00pm	Ed Stewart Show
6.00pm	Pete Drummond Show
7.00pm	The World Tomorrow
7.30pm	Pete Drummond Show
9.00pm	Lome King Show
12.00 - 2.00am	London After Midnight

Plus: News and Weather every half hour

SATURDAYS

5.30am	Chuck Blair Breakfast Show
8.00am	Keith Skues Show
11.00am	Ed Stewart Show
2.00pm	Kenny Everett Show
5.00pm	Pete Drummond Show
7.00pm	The World Tomorrow
7.30pm	Pete Drummond Show
8.00pm	Lome King Show
11.00 - 2.00am	London After Midnight

Plus: News and Weather every half hour SUNDAYS

5.30am	Chuck Blair Breakfast Show
7.30am	Herald Of Truth

8.00am	Keith Skues Show
11 -00am	Fab Forty Show Ed Stewart
2.00pm	Kenny Everett Show
5.00pm	Pete Drummond Show
7.00pm	The World Tomorrow
7.30pm	Pete Drummond Show
8.00pm	Lome King Show
11.00 - 2.00am	London After Midnight

Plus: News and Weather every half hour

NEWS CENTRAL
Released through: Radlon (Sales) Ltd., 17 Curzon Street, London W1
Telephone: MAYfair 5361

RADIO SCOTLAND

ON NEW YEAR'S EVE 1965 Radio Scotland was waiting for their ship to come in. Disc jockeys and engineers waited patiently for hours in a hotel at Dunbar, East Lothian. The ship had expected to arrive at noon the previous day ... then at four o'clock. But bad weather delayed the 500-ton converted lightship, the *Comet*, as she was towed at four knots up the east coast from the English Channel.

Patrick Heartgreaves, the technical director, said "We need a certain amount of time to get everything ready. A great deal of technical work requires to be done before we can broadcast. If everything goes right once the ship arrives we might just make it."

The cost of the project up to that time was £200,000 which was provided by Glasgow casino operator Alan Carr, London financier Stanley Jackson, and Radio Scotland managing director, Tommy Shields.

The *Comet*, a former lightship built at John Brown's famous yard on the River Clyde, did arrive in the early hours of New Year's Eve and engineers worked hard to ensure that the station went on the air at Hogmanay as the bells were ringing in the New Year for 1966. Paul Young, well known for his television appearances in Scotland, made the opening announcement which was followed by a short talk from the managing director, Tommy Shields, about the company's intentions.

Radio Scotland transmitted on 242 metres, 1241 kHz, later adjusted to 1259 kHz but retaining its 242 identification. The programmes were heard all over Scotland as well as Scandinavia. At night Radio Scotland could be clearly received in the city of London. The station theme was *Black Bear*. The first advertisement was for the *News of the World*. The *Comet* had been originally towed from Dublin to St. Sampson's Bay, Guernsey, to be equipped with transmitting apparatus.

A few months after Radio Scotland came on the air the company running the station, City and County Commercial Radio (Scotland) Ltd., was receiving complaints from listeners in the western part of Scotland that her signal was not coming in very strongly.

So the *Comet* completed a 1,000 mile trip around the north of Scotland. As the vessel was a hulk without engines she had to be towed all the way and moored off Troon in the Firth of Clyde. On her journey she encountered storms and the ship almost caught fire at one stage.

In a survey undertaken by National Opinion Polls and published on 13 April 1966, of the 246 people who replied to questions, Radio Scotland had been heard by 48% of them. And that did not include listeners under the age of 16. The BBC's Scottish Service said it would be surprising if 48% of the people or more had not heard Radio Scotland transmissions for her frequency was very close indeed to the Light Programme wavelength, and that sometimes confused listeners.

Radio Scotland was the first station to have its own magazine. Called *242* it was a monthly entertainment magazine covering the musical and show business scene, particularly in Scotland. The magazine was edited by Jim Blair, a former reporter with the *Evening Times*.

A Radio Scotland fan club, the "242 Clan", was formed to answer queries about disc jockeys and the station. Listeners requested car stickers, pin badges and photographs of the DJs. The "Clan" was handled by Cathy Spence, a former beauty queen. Its mascot was Jock, a West Highland terrier.

The managing director of Radio Scotland, Tommy Shields, created the station from a dream. Born in Glasgow, he was a former newspaper reporter and war correspondent. For a time he was publicity manager for Lord Thomson of Fleet. At that time he was preparing a biography of his employer and found out that the Thomson empire was, in fact, founded on commercial radio. Shields saw the birth of offshore commercial radio in England and decided to plan a similar enterprise to serve Scotland.

Radio Scotland had their headquarters at Cranworth Street, Glasgow. Its 'gimmick' name on the air was "Big S" (presumably copied from Big L) which was later changed to "Super S."

The *Comet* was about 90ft. in length and weighed 500 tons. She had two diesel generators, presented by the chairman of Radio 270, Leonard Dale. These drove the transmitters which were RCA BTA-lOJs employing the Ampliphase system of phase modulation. Each transmitter had a power of ten kilowatts and, when combined, gave a total output of twenty kilowatts.

The studios at the headquarters in Glasgow were equipped with a Pye sound mixing desk and accessories so that interviews and light entertainment shows could be recorded.

Some of the people involved in the Radio Scotland operation were: Jim Blair, editor of the *242* magazine; Alan Carr, joint managing director; Bill Fleming, promotion and public relations; Errol Gardiner, head of sales; Brian Holden, co-ordination executive; Stanley Jackson, joint managing director; Tony Jackson, promotions; Liz Kearsley, secretary; John Lumsden, senior engineer; Pat O'Reilly, commercial scheduling; David Sandilands, sales; John Stephens, sales; and London- based Tony Welch, sales.

The Comet off Dunbar, Scotland

Disc jockeys on Radio Scotland during its operation period included Tony Allan, Alan Black, Peter Bowman, Roger Gale, Drew Hamlyn, Ben Healey, Stuart Henry, Mel Howard, John Kerr, Jimmy Mack, Peter Mallan, Brian McKenzie (Brian Webb), Jack McLaughlin, Tony Meehan, Stevi Merike, Richard Park, Michael Speake, Bob Spencer, Bryan Vaughan and Tim Yale.

Just prior to the Marine Offences Bill having its second reading in the House of Commons, Tommy Shields said:

> Never in my life - and that's been quite a while - has there been such public demonstration of protest as there has been against the decision to ban the pirates. Schoolchildren, teenagers, young men and women, and the majority of the older generation as well have put their names to our "Save Radio Scotland" petition.
> The 250,000 people who have signed the petition forms are not concerned with the "unlawful use of wavelengths."
> What concerns them is the decision to deprive them of a service they have become accustomed to, and want to keep. In my

office are many many thousands of letters from people pledging their support in my fight to legalise Radio Scotland.

I have always tried to mould Radio Scotland into a responsible unit because irresponsibility on the air will not attract advertising revenue, and commercial radio must present a dependable image to both advertisers and listeners.

The people who run all the pirate stations expect pressure of public opinion is going to force the Government to produce some kind of plan for an alternative service to the BBC.

At Radio Scotland we have plans for complete radio coverage of local news and views, sport, current affairs and localised information bulletins such as traffic warnings, weather forecasts and shopping prices ... and, of course,local entertainment.

It is still not too late for the Government to save face. Let them reprieve the pirates and put forward proposals for local commercial radio.

Shortly after this statement was issued, Radio Scotland received a summons which was returnable at Ayr on 13 March 1967. The station was fined £80 for transmitting within territorial waters.

Radio Scotland ceased transmissions almost immediately and moved her ship, first off Ballywalter, County Down, and then to its former anchorage off Dunbar. She resumed programmes at the beginning of April. Her broadcasting day began at 6.00am and continued until 2.00am the following day.

Tommy Shields said that by the beginning of August 1967 he and the six directors of Radio Scotland had lost roughly £100,000. Had the station operated until the end of the year, they would have come out of the 'red' with a little bit to spare because advertisers were beginning to rally round. He described his twenty-two-month campaign to maintain a commercial pop station as "a great adventure," and said it was a shame they had lost the battle.

Due to the Marine Offences Act coming into operation from midnight on 14 August 1967 Radio Scotland closed down at the last possible moment - midnight! For story of closing, see Chapter Eleven.

PROGRAMME SCHEDULE - RADIO SCOTLAND

"Your All Day Sunshine Station"

January 1967

6.00am	Rooster Call
9.00am	Snowball Requests
11.00am	Apron Strings
12.00noon	Swing Across Midday
2.00pm	Lazearound
4.30pm	All Systems Go
6.15pm	McLaughlin's Ceilidh
7.00pm	World Tomorrow
7.30pm	Lucky Dip

9.30pm	Sophistikat
10.15pm	Destination Midnight
12.00 midnight	Night Owls
2.00am	Close Down

RADIO SUTCH

THIS STATION was operated by pop singer and Parliamentary candidate, David Sutch, from May to September 1964. He was better known as "Screaming Lord Sutch," who unsuccessfully contested John Profumo's old constituency, Stratford-on-Avon, as an Independent in the by-election of August 1962. In the Sixties Sutch stood as a "Teenage Party" candidate and later created the Official Monster Raving Loony Party.

Said David Sutch: "After my Stratford experience I decided, unlike other politicians, to practise what I preached. As I believed in commercial radio and thought it should be legalised as it was in America and Australia, I started up Radio Sutch as a protest."[1]

On 25 May, less than a month after Caroline began broadcasting, Screaming Lord Sutch set off on the former fishing boat, the *Cornucopia*, from Leigh-on-Sea, Essex. Many thought this was purely a publicity stunt. Sutch was dressed in a purple velvet cape and bright blue trousers and waved a cutlass. His group, the Savages, were dressed in caveman outfits.

Sutch said that the fishing boat was only insured for fishing and not music, so he had to abandon this idea in favour of a group of old wartime anti-aircraft forts which stood on rusty iron legs eight miles off the coast near Herne Bay at a location known as Shivering Sands.

Radio Sutch made its first broadcast on 27 May 1964 on 197 metres, 1542 kHz. The first record played was *Jack the Ripper* by Screaming Lord Sutch. On the fort Sutch was assisted by Reginald Calvert and Brian Paul, who was a member of Sutch's backing group, the Savages.

The first female voice heard on Radio Sutch was that of Tamara Harrison, a niece of Reg Calvert. She joined the station in June 1964.

The first pirate station to be established on a fort, Radio Sutch, 1964

---

1. *Life as Sutch*, David Lord Sutch, Harper Collins, London, 1991, page 43

A harbour patrol boat from Sheerness investigated the occupation of the forts, but Sutch, who was armed with a .410 shotgun, did not allow them on board. Commenting afterwards, Sutch said, "I shouted to them from the catwalks - the Army had left the forts, and did not want them. I had offered to buy them. No-one came aboard Radio Sutch unless I said so."

A Ministry of Defence spokesman said that "Screaming Lord Sutch" was trespassing. Although the forts were unmanned they remained Government property.

Radio Sutch was noted for its readings from "Lady Chatterley's Lover" and "Fanny Hill."

The station broadcast from noon to 2.00pm; 5.00 to 8.00pm and from 12.15am to 2.15am. Programmes ranged from *Candy's Pop Shop* to *From Me To You* and *Programmes for the Under Sixteens* to *Saucy Bedtime Stories.*

Disc jockeys included Candy Calvert, Chris Cross, Dick Dickson, Brian Paul and Screaming Lord Sutch.

The transmission area of Radio Sutch was about 40 square miles.

I was working with Screaming Lord Sutch at a show in Scarborough in 1989 and he told me: "The format we had on the radio station caused eyebrows to be raised, and because of the enormous depth of my political appeal, the authorities had to silence me. I was finally forced to surrender in order to avoid bloodshed. I was satisfied that I had made my point. At the time I was planning Sutch Island which was to have been a nudist colony. We would have issued our own stamps and currency." A variation of that idea was perfected by Roy Bates, Prince of Sealand, four years later.

Radio Sutch was taken over in September 1964 by Reginald Calvert who changed the name to Radio City.

RADIO 270

THE STATION went into the planning stage in November 1965. Six months later the company, Ellambar Investments Ltd., had purchased and converted the *Oceaan 7* into a radio ship.

The ship, a Dutch lugger, was built by A. Vuijk & Zonen of Holland in 1939 for the Dutch fishing fleet. The ship was captured by the Germans who made use of her during World War II. When hostilities ceased she was returned to the Dutch fishing fleet and completely overhauled. She was then put back into service and operated very successfully until the end of 1964, when the economics of fishing proved rather difficult.

The *Oceaan 7* was then laid up for a while but purchased in 1965 by Radio 270 whereupon both engines were overhauled in Holland. She then sailed to Britain where her interior was partly stripped and converted into a radio station. She flew the Honduras flag and was registered in Puerto Cortes.

Although the ship was cheap to purchase, the refitting and equipping of a radio ship was a most expensive exercise. A number of Scarborough businessmen came to hear of the project and invested money.

Radio 270 (which broadcast on 270 metres, 1115 kilocycles) adopted the Top 40 format similar to Radio London's, but called it the Fun 40. They broadcast hourly news bulletins, sports flashes, weather forecasts and community announcements.

The managing director of the station was Wilf Proudfoot, Conservative Member of Parliament for Cleveland between 1959-1964. He became Parliamentary Private Secretary to the Minister of Housing and Local Government, and Minister for Welsh Affairs. He introduced a Private Member's Bill for decimal coinage. An ex-RAF sergeant who served in India during the war years, Wilf was the owner of a chain of supermarkets which he built up from one small shop. He believed the BBC needed competition as it was a monopoly.

"I read in the local paper about a Don Robinson, whom I did not know, and some colleagues who had bought a ship. So I rang him up and said 'When it goes on the air I want to buy advertising.' Within half an hour he came to visit me asking me to be involved with the station. He basically had three sets of figures on the back of a cigarette packet and that was it. He had paid £1,300 for the *Oceaan 7*. Later we called a meeting of anybody we could think of interested in offshore radio, to be held in the Pavilion Hotel, Scarborough. When the meeting took place about 60 people turned up. I told them that offshore radio was a high risk business and they might as well go on the cliffs and throw their pound notes in to the air. However, this did not deter them and they were keener than ever to put money into the project. We raised £28,000 for Radio 270 at that meeting."

Chairman of Radio 270 was Leonard Dale, AMIEE, MAmlEE, then aged fifty, who was also managing director and chairman of the Dale Group of Companies, a thriving electrical concern which exported British-made goods. Today his firm of Dale Generators are well-known worldwide. They are still powering radio stations the world over, including many in Europe. British Telecom use Dale Generators at their Woolwich teleport, from where all satellite radio signals are beamed into space.

In addition to Dale, the board members were Don Robinson, Tony Rylands of Whitby, Tim Jackson, Peter Asquith, who started Asda, bandleader Cyril Stapleton, farmer Roland Hill and fisherman Bill Pashby.

Wilf Proudfoot, an adventurous man with a dynamic personality and inexhaustible enthusiasm for radio, said "I went out to Honduras, Central America, having obtained my travel documents from the American Embassy. I travelled via Mexico to the capital of Honduras which is Tegucigalpa. Everyone appeared to be selling bananas to each other. It is a capital without a railway line, but there were more private aeroplanes than I have ever seen anywhere in the world. Honduras was happy to register the *Oceaan 7* and its port of registration became Puerto Cortes. We had to have the ship's papers translated from Dutch into English and then into Spanish. I then went to see the Minister of Shipping and everything was agreed."

Oceaan 7 sailed into British waters on 1 April 1966 and anchored outside the three-mile limit off Scarborough, Yorkshire, later moving to Bridlington, in December 1966. It had been planned to go on air on 1 April at midday, but the aluminium aerial mast, which had been erected in Guernsey, snapped off the ship. Sitting in the Grand Hotel, Scarborough, were members of the press, but all they heard was ... silence!

Breakfast show DJ, Paul Burnett, who had been recruited from the Top Rank venue in Darlington, was the first disc jockey signed up by Don Robinson. He was on board the ship on 31 March 1966: "Suddenly a storm blew up, and one of the worst that part of the North Sea had ever experienced. There was over 100ft. of aluminium crashing around the bridge, like a pendulum. I shall never forget that day because there was a clear blue sky. You would normally expect storms to be accompanied by heavy clouds. The seas were unbelievably rough. The broadcasting staff all stayed below deck being very ill. I was so ill that I wasn't scared. I would have quite happily gone down with the ship at that time. It was awful! The Dutch crew very bravely hacked down the antenna and it was last seen disappearing into the North Sea."

The ship was then taken to Grimsby to have the aerial mast repaired. Wilf Proudfoot says: "The Board of Trade threw the book at us. It cost a few thousand pounds to have other repairs. I was on the ship at the time, along with my son Mark, when the authorities said we could sail. We got the crew together and off we went. I stayed on the ship all night until we arrived at Scarborough when I was taken off."

Radio 270's first broadcast was on 4 June 1966. Its station identification was: "This is the super hit sound of Radio 270." The first record played was *Strangers in the Night* by Frank Sinatra.

The ship which was commanded by two captains who alternately worked a month on and a month off, was 139ft. long; 22ft. wide; weighed 160 tons and her aerial mast was 154ft. above sea level. The galley was equipped with every modern appliance. She had navigational and life saving aids including radar and a radio telephone. The transmitter had a power of 10 kilowatts and was manufactured by RCA. The aerial mast, of aluminium aerofoil section, was

Right: Radio 270 logo

Below: Oceaan 7 anchored off Bridlington, 1966

of vertical birdcage construction.

Under the wheelhouse was the main four cylinder 240hp propulsion engine which was run every evening, after transmission had ended, to ensure that the ship could sail anywhere under her own steam.

The main generating room housed two 45kVA Dale Marine generating plants which supplied all the electricity. Two tanks held the diesel fuel: one with a 6,000 gallons capacity, the other of 600.

The crew quarters were originally designed to hold 12 seamen. They comprised two tier bunks, a table in the centre, electric heating, hot and cold water, storage cupboards and wardrobe.

The galley was fitted with a large oil burning stove, complete with cooker, hot plates, large refrigerator and deep freeze, sink cupboards and hot and cold water.

Disc jockeys slept in the large dining/sitting room in separate curtained bunks.

An electrical engineer reported that there was more than a mile of wire installed inside the *Oceaan 7*. The wheelhouse was fitted with radio and radar and the captain's cabin had a wardrobe, hot and cold water, as well as a folding chart table.

The crew and technical staff worked two weeks on the ship and two weeks off, whereas the disc jockeys spent a week at sea and had a week on dry land.

Food on board was described as good. A typical menu read: Fruit juice; tomato soup; roast lamb with baked potatoes and vegetables; apple croissant with ice cream; tea or coffee.

A tender visited the *Oceaan 7* daily and took out books, magazines, mail, supplies and provisions. Managing director, Wilf Proudfoot, normally managed to visit the *Oceaan 7* at least once a fortnight.

Radio 270 had two studios which were equipped with EMI tape decks, Spotmaster cartridge machines and two Garrard 401 turntables, which were stabilised and fitted in gimbals in preparation for any bad weather at sea. The studios were soundproofed and air conditioned. The disc jockey operated all the controls in the studio. The programmes went through a Pye limiter, which kept music and speech gain levels constant, to the transmitter. Chief engineer was Keith Robinson.

Amongst the staff who broadcast on Radio 270 were Vince 'Rusty' Allen, John Aston, Mike Baron, Robin Best, Pete 'Boots' Bowman, Paul Burnett, Alex Dee, Bob Dewing, Roger Gale, Guy Hamilton, Albert Hart, Mike Hayes, Phil Hayton (who later became Philip Hayton, BBC TV newsreader), Julian Hewitt, Alan Ives, Jeff Jones, Roger Keene (Roger Gomez), Roger King, Andy Kirk, Paul Kramer, 'Neddy' Noel Miller, Ed Moreno, Brendan Power (who left to go to the West Indies), Ross Randell (formerly Alan West of Radio London and Radio 390), Roger Scott, Dave Sinclair, Bob Snyder, Dennis (the Menace) Straney, Steve Taylor, Leon Tippler, Mark West (previously on Radio Essex) and Hal Yorke.

Radio 270's first programme controller was Noel Miller, a 23-year-old Australian who was noted for his *Neddy Noel Show*. Prior to joining 270, six-foot Noel worked on several top stations in Australia. After the pirates closed he returned to Australia and worked in radio in Melbourne.

Paul Burnett was Noel Miller's successor. Aged 23, Paul originated from Manchester and had previously spent five years in the Royal Air Force. Vince Allen replaced Paul Burnett as programme controller in 1967.

For information on DJs Paul Burnett, Guy Hamilton, Ed Moreno, Mike Hayes, Bob Snyder, Brendan Power, John Aston and Vince Allen see Chapter Seven.

At the Radio 270 headquarters in Scarborough the office manager was Stella Ellis, who now lives in Spain. The first programme assistant to the controller of programmes was Carole Miller who returned to Australia in 1966 and was programme co-ordinator of 2GB in Sydney in 1979. Her successor was Maggie Lucas who was born near the famous 'pier' in Wigan, Lancashire. She was the 'right hand woman' to the controller and, prior to entering the radio world, was a political agent! Maggie left for Australia in July, 1967. Some of her most

FIGHT
FOR
FREE RADIO
IN BRITAIN

Offshore commercial radio is now too strongly entrenched and popularly supported to be treated lightly.

At a time when the audience of the commercial stations together is larger than the audiences of the BBC Light and Home Programmes combined, the government seeks to ban offshore commercial radio, leaving Britain, alone, the only democratic country in the world to tolerate a monopoly of broadcasting.

There is nothing new in the hostility of officialdom to commercial broadcasting. It is simply the reflex action of Established interests to adventurous competition.

The success and popularity of offshore commercial radio is dependent entirely on the goodwill of the public. But the government's proposed Bill to ban commercial stations (with no provision for a real substitute) clearly shows the government's disregard for the public, and the extremely one-sided viewpoint brought about by pressures and false arguments from the existing monopoly.

The case for licensing commercial radio rests on the very demonstrable fact that an impressive majority of the people want the entertainment it brings.

Radio 270 does not want a monopoly for itself - but we do claim the right to broadcast competitively, side by side with the BBC to the British public.

It is you, the public, who should have the final say!

If you believe in Freedom of Speech, then you must join in the Fight for Free Radio in Britain: Write to your Member of Parliament, House of Commons, London ... and make your opinion count.

A Fight For Free Radio leaflet distributed to Radio 270 listeners inviting them to write to their MP to support the offshore stations

memorable days at Radio 270 were spent sorting mail and she relates that she had nightmares at least three times a week wondering if, in fact, she would be buried alive by the thousands of letters.

Radio 270 took a great interest in motor sport sponsoring a car, and a driver, named Charles Ratcliffe.

Car stickers were sold for a penny each and all the proceeds went to the British Wireless for the Blind Fund. Many hours of free time were given to charities and universities. In fact Radio 270 taped half-hour programmes with universities and colleges which were transmitted on Sundays at 1.30am and were not edited nor censored.

The station carried political advertisements for all parties if they wished to take up the offer, but did stipulate that none of them must inspire race hatred.

Amongst the many visitors to the *Oceaan 7* was the former Shadow Postmaster-General, Paul Bryan (later Sir Paul Bryan), who visited Radio 270 in the autumn of 1966. Sir Donald Kaberry (later Lord Kaberry), a Leeds MP, also went out to the ship. Whilst on board he broadcast to his constituents over the air.

All members of Parliament were invited to visit the ship including the Postmaster-General, but the latter declined!

By June 1967 Radio 270 claimed 4 million listeners. Its transmission area was vast - from the counties of Northumberland and Tyneside in the heart of industrial Britain, the woollen mills of the West Riding, Sheffield's steel furnaces, the Potteries, Derby's engineering works and the hosiery industries of Nottingham and Leicester. However, the majority of mail came from Scarborough and Bridlington.

Disc jockey Guy Hamilton remembers "Scarborough was fun, and the people were friendly, especially the girls. This was the Swinging Sixties, and the area was small enough to be infamous in. I shared a large flat with two other jocks, and since we alternated weeks on 270, three other DJs made a mess there when we were afloat.

"We changed shift usually after transmissions ended on a Tuesday night at 2am; the radio ship would sometimes up anchor and sail in to meet us! Otherwise, the trip of three and a half miles was usually made in an open Yorkshire boat called a coble, and was very invigorating!

"Living quarters were cramped and not very private. DJ bunks were separated only by curtains from the large mess room. My first shift on 270 was over Christmas 1966, and I wasn't due on air till New Year. I squeezed into the crew's quarters in the fo'c'sle. There you really *felt* like a pirate of the old school.

"The 270 ship, *Oceaan 7*, rolled like a drunk. Even a tap from the tiny tender was enough to set it going like a pendulum for an hour. Hardly surprising, because it *was* a pendulum: a huge transmitter mast counterbalanced by concrete in the hull. In a force nine, it was truly breathtaking to see the seas smashing over the side. I was the only DJ brave enough to go on deck in a North Sea storm - I realise now the others were older and perhaps wiser!

"The station had a huge following, but was not so good as Caroline and Radio London in exploiting it. They were a late starter, had teething problems, and were quickly faced with the need to make their money back before the plug was pulled for all the pirates by the then Government."

Radio 270 closed down at midnight on 14 August 1967, the last possible moment before the Government's Marine Offences Bill became law.

The duty disc jockey was 'Rusty' Allen. As chief disc jockey he had regularly presented the 9.00am - 12.00 noon show each day, with an extra slot from 6.00pm to 9.00pm. He was a Canadian with a unique 'bronco' style, complete with a theme tune of cowboys and cattle riding through the studio crying 'Whoa Horse,' which ended with a very sexy voiced girl saying, seductively, 'Hallo Rusty.' But on the final night of Radio 270 'Rusty' was in no mood for humour. He was playing taped messages from former 270 personalities. That Monday, the weather was not rough - it was pretty atrocious!

Whenever the weather was bad, or looked like it might be, the captains sailed 18 miles south of Scarborough Bay to a location in Bridlington Bay - in the lea of Flamborough Head, which provided some shelter from the northerly and NE gales. On 14 August 1967, none of the pleasure boats left Bridlington so the disc jockeys could not travel out to the ship. The alternative plan was to sling the bag of tapes in one pass over the ship from the tender. Big pleasure boats, such as the *Boys Own* and *Yorkshire Belle,* could not get alongside. Small fishing boats (270 used one called *Monica Two,* owned by local skipper Ted Newby) could not get out of the harbour as it was so rough. So another plan was conceived. Ex-RAF man Mike Hayes decided to enlist the help of the Royal Air Force at Leconfield, north of Beverley, Humberside. More taped messages were required on the ship for 'Rusty' Allen to play. Mike Hayes gave a number of tapes to Tony Harrison, the helicopter pilot, who agreed to help. The 'chopper' set off from Leconfield at 8 o'clock in the evening. He gave the navigator a waterproof bag containing the tapes to drop on the deck. The pilot gave instructions to drop the bag, but it promptly missed the ship by inches, and fell into the sea. The tapes were lost for ever. In the bag was a note which said "Under no circumstances mention how this bag got out to the ship." The arrival of the helicopter was mentioned at least half a dozen times. The helicopter crew were reportedly given a reprimand by the Government for helping out a pirate ship. However Parliament was on summer recess from 28 July 1967 to 23 October 1967 and there are no references to the event in Hansard for the year 1967.

At ten minutes to midnight a message was read out from Leonard Dale, chairman of Radio 270, which said "It is very distressing that my company will not be able to provide you with the kind of radio programme that you have become used to. However, the Government in office at the moment sees fit to make this form of entertainment illegal when offered by other than the state-owned monopoly. We sincerely hope and trust that in the years to come we may have the opportunity of serving you, our listeners, from a land-based station.

"During the 15 months in which we have been operating, we have tried to give you all the very best in light entertainment, and we will attempt to do this again. One must bear in mind that this has cost you nothing, and on this our closing day, I would like to say a few thank you's ... first of all to our many advertisers who have made everything possible. Also I would like to say thank you to the people of Scarborough and Bridlington, and especially to those who have helped us in our maritime enterprise. In particular I should like to say thank you to the lifeboat service in Bridlington, and also the air sea rescue organisation from Leconfield who kindly helped us when our captain was taken ill and when a small accident happened to one of our crew members. Furthermore I would like say a big thank you to all our sea crew, both past and present, and also to our staff of DJs, engineers and technicians. Finally, thank you to our suppliers of foodstuffs and various commodities. We appreciate the co-operation you have given us. Therefore it is my sorry duty to say goodbye, but with the hope that we shall meet again when Britain has free commercial radio like every other freedom-loving country."

'Rusty' Allen closed the station at midnight. Following the record *Land of Hope and Glory* by Vera Lynn, his final words were: "I'm gonna miss you one hell of a lot. I hope that maybe someday soon in the not too distant future we'll meet on the air again. This is Radio 270, broadcasting on 1115 kilocycles in the medium wave band. The time is one and a half minutes before midnight and we're now closing down. On behalf of the 270 men, the radio technicians, the captain and crew and everybody onshore concerned with Radio 270, this is 'Rusty' Allen, wishing you God bless and God speed. Goodnight and Goodbye. Radio 270 is now closing down." Then followed the national anthem and ... silence. The *Oceaan 7* sailed into Bridlington harbour in the early hours of the morning.

Said Wilf Proudfoot "On the day we closed down I was on the Costa Brava, Spain, and heard the station close. It was a little crackly, but the station was audible. It was a very sad occasion. At the end of the day we did not come out with a profit. However, none of our creditors was hurt and all were paid off in full. The only people who lost money were the shareholders. I did not receive any wages or expenses from Radio 270. It was a totally honest company.

"Pirate radio gave the listeners what they wanted. It was not in a rut like the BBC. The most impressive thing which came out on 270 was that the DJs never had to be told not to swear. Nobody said it to them. There were no written rules. The DJs respected good taste. I also learned that people are more literate than numerate. Members of the public would come up to me and say 'You were Radio Caroline.' They could remember names, but not numbers like 270. Radio Caroline came to represent all the pirate radio stations in the public mind. Looking back I feel a sense of achievement with what we succeeded in doing with 270 and helping to break the BBC monopoly. I would like to see a campaign run to get the BBC to sell all their local stations. The BBC are carrying huge overheads with local radio. Pirate radio will have a place in the history of broadcasting in this country."

The ship *Oceaan 7* was put up for sale for £25,000 by estate agents, Tuckley and Company of 16 Pavilion Square, Scarborough. On 15 August 1967 first mate Ken Lester, from Bridlington, took the ship into Whitby harbour and left her moored up. Looking back to the pirate days Ken says:

> They were really exciting. The disc jockeys were not sailors and had to work under difficult conditions, especially when there was a force 9 easterly gale blowing. They were heroes having to broadcast whilst being thrown around the studio by the bad weather. When I took the ship into Whitby I was heartbroken. It was the end of an era. I knew *Oceaan 7* was going to her grave, and it was a wet and muddy one! After the pirates were closed I went on to trawling and retired at 65 back in 1983.

Wilf Proudfoot returned to politics and was elected MP for Brighouse and Spenborough in 1970. He contributed to the Sound Broadcasting Bill, published in 1972, which proposed the introduction of an alternative local radio service financed by advertising. The Government's plans envisaged that the IBA would provide a service of up to sixty local stations which would serve about 65% of the population of the United Kingdom by day and night on VHF, and 70% by day and 25% by night on MF.

Proudfoot said in the House of Commons that he could not agree with the amendment which stated that for local sound broadcasting the minister and the IBA should, from time to time, draw up and publish a statement setting out the criteria they should adopt on programme content and quality, advertising duration and nature, and the extent to which news programmes and minority interest programmes should be catered for.

Wilf Proudfoot said the amendment would have the effect of stopping commercial radio dead in its tracks.

> Commercial radio would maximise its audience by local involvement programmes. It would give business to those companies lucky enough to get licences, but the amendment assumed there would be only one radio station in any one locality. He hoped there would be competition between local radio stations.
>
> Listeners were mostly interested in local sport and other local activities which the BBC had never been able to give them. The amendment, if one recognised what local radio was to be like, was unnecessary.
>
> When local commercial stations were in competition, one with another, they would, like newspapers, have to strike the right balance. If they put in too many commercials they would lose their audience.

There was a strong rumour circulating in north Yorkshire during March 1968 that Radio Caroline was thinking of buying the Radio 270 ship. But it was not to be. The *Oceaan 7* was sold for scrap for under £5,000 and broken up at Blyth, Northumberland. The aerial mast was removed at Whitby. The technical equipment was sold to Capital Radio in 1970.

Paul Harris, author, publisher and offshore radio authority, recalls "We had known for some time there was an RCA 10 kilowatt transmitter in store near Scarborough which had been used on Radio 270. Although the radio ship, the *Oceaan 7*, had since been scrapped, I knew the valuable transmitter had been removed. Its owners, Ellambar Investments Ltd., were only too glad to part with it. A sum was negotiated and we made arrangements for it to be collected."[2]

Harris helped set up the offshore Capital Radio which began broadcasting test transmissions off the Dutch coast on 14 June 1970. It broadcast on 270 metres, 1115 kilocycles, from aboard the m.v. *King David*. Regular programmes began on 1 September 1970. She drifted on 10 November 1970 and ended up on Noordwijk beach, just 200 yards from the Palace Hotel. Capital Radio never returned to the air, and eleven months later the *King David* was sold.

PROGRAMME SCHEDULE - RADIO 270

6.30am	Leon Tippler Breakfast Show
	Paul Burnett Breakfast Show
9.00am	Dennis the Menace Show
	Roger Keene Show
12.00 noon	Neddy Noel Show
	Boots Bowman Show
2.00pm	Dennis the Menace Show
	Roger Keene Show
4.00pm	Neddy Noel Show
	Boots Bowman Show
7.00pm	Hal Yorke Show
	Paul Burnett Show
9.00pm	Andy Kirk Show
	Alex Dee Show
12.00 midnight	The Midnight Hour
1.00am	End transmission

RADIO 355

THE SUCCESSOR to Britain Radio, the 'good music' station broadcasting from the m.v. *Laissez-Faire* anchored off the Essex coast, which broadcast on 355 metres, 845 kHz. It became Radio 355 in March 1967 after the company, Peir-Vick Ltd., went broke.

Ted Allbeury, ex-managing director of Radio 390, ran the new station with John Withers, another ex-Radio 390 man. The station format was identical to that of Radio 390's but was later altered to a more mid-tempo style. The station ceased broadcasting in the early hours of 6 August 1967.

For information relating to the ship and its staff, see Radio England.

PROGRAMME SCHEDULE - RADIO 355

	July 1967
6.00am	Breakfast Club
7.00am	World Tomorrow
7.30am	Breakfast Club
7.50am	Revive Your Heart
7.55am	Breakfast Club
9.00am	Tony Monson Show

2. *Broadcasting from the High Seas*, Paul Harris, Paul Harris Publishing, 1977, page 287

10.30am	Pause for Prayer
10.45am	Tony Monson Show
11.00am	Coffee Break
11.15am	Tony Monson Show
12.00 noon	Mark Sloane Show
12.30pm	World Tomorrow (repeat)
1.00pm	Mark Sloane Show
3.00pm	Dave McKaye Show
6.00pm	Kayne's Kingdom
7.00pm	355 Countryfield
7.30pm	John Aston Show
9.00pm	Dave McKaye Show
10.30pm	A.P. Spree
11.55pm	Epilogue
12.00 midnight	Close Down

RADIO 390

HOUSED IN SEVEN Thames Estuary ack-ack forts, known as Red Sands Tower, Radio 390 made its first broadcast on 25 September 1965 at 7 o'clock in the evening, transmitting on 390 metres, 773 kHz.

The staff on the forts, 8 miles off Whitstable, consisted of a station controller, nine announcers, three librarians, five engineers and two cooks.

Says presenter Edward Cole "Red Sands Tower was a wartime coastal defence fort, comprising seven separate buildings each perched on four massive legs embedded in concrete below the water, and interconnected by catwalks 50 feet above.

"We were all mad, of course; I realise that now. We must have been; why else would we risk our lives on a crumbling rusty structure 8½ miles from land? It certainly wasn't the salary that attracted us, nor the working conditions, although these had improved considerably since the early months when we sat huddled round one electric fire while the bitter November gales swept up the Thames Estuary. Now there was a modern studio, central heating, television and ping-pong - but the fort still shook in the wind, and if anyone had fallen over the rail into the sea there was little hope of rescue."

Presenter David Allan confirms that the forts were comfortable. "The central heating system was still working. There was hot and cold running (fresh) water, showers, loos and an excellent kitchen. The sleeping quarters were also excellent. We each had a proper bed, fresh linen and no more than three people to a room. There was plenty of space everywhere."

Initially the station had an investment of £150,000 and was owned by four businessmen who had interests in civil engineering. Managing director was Ted Allbeury, then aged 48, a former Intelligence Corps lieutenant-colonel and poultry farmer who described his new station as a service in which he provided "wallpaper music, slightly romantic, slightly nostalgic."

The directors of the company were listed as Christopher Blackwell of Essex, Michael Mitcham of Cambridge, John La Trobe and Morris Gething of Kent, the latter formerly owning KING Radio.

The tender which serviced Red Sands Tower was the *Mallard*, a 39-foot Whitstable fishing boat, captained by Vic Davis. Says Edward Cole "The tender called twice a week, normally on the Wednesday and the Saturday. The shifts changed midweek. At weekends the tender would bring out supplies. It was quite dramatic getting off the tender as, one by one, we were winched up onto the fort while the *Mallard* circled, pitching and tossing, below."

Radio 390's programmes were beamed primarily to the housewife. The station initially described itself as *Eve - The Women's Magazine of the Air,* but this was later dropped. Says Ted Allbeury "I was concerned that the newspapers would not indicate where you could find the radio station on the dial, so I decided that the wavelength of 390 metres would be easier for listeners to identify."

There was a five-minute family doctor talk, a series named *Doctor Paul* which had been running in Australia for 14 years, *Playtime,* children's favourites, a horoscope time, *Memory Lane* and for the city gent *The Voice of Business.* There were specialist programmes: *Masters of the Organ, Jim Reeves Show, Keyboard Cavalcade* and *Countrystyle.*

Shifts for the broadcasters consisted of two weeks on the forts followed by one week on leave. Each presenter broadcast for around six hours a day, but normally divided into two-hour shifts. The result was a variety of voices and styles throughout the day and evening.

During the first few weeks of transmission the station received over 500 letters a day. Office staff included Carol Hewitt and Jean Payne.

The equipment on the forts consisted of an effective RCA transmitter with a power of 35 kilowatts. Also on board were four Gardner diesel generators. The transmitting mast was 200ft. high and fixed to the centre fort which was 90ft. above sea level.

Announcers through its period of transmission included: David Allan, Paul Beresford, Woolf Byrne, Christopher Clark, Edward Cole, Gary Courteney (Keith Martin), Brian Cullingford, Lee Gilbert, Graham Gill, Roger Gomez, Jonathan Hall, Mark Hammerton, Peter James, Sheldon Jay, Gordon Johns, Dominic Lefoe, Jack McLaughlin, Robert Randall, Mike Raven, John Ross-Barnard, Roger Scott, Clement Shaw, David Sinclair, John Stewart, Alan West and Stephen West. They were all paid at the same rate - £25 a week.

Presenters were not allowed at first to give their names, although this policy changed later. Ted Allbeury insisted on only employing males (no ladies) who sounded like real gentlemen. They were expected to be smartly dressed on the fort. Alcohol was officially forbidden but, entering into the Noel Coward spirit, several presenters would insist on a couple of Martinis before embarking on an evening shift.

Advertisements on Radio 390 cost £60 a minute. In order to obtain advertising in volume during daytime hours, it was considered essential to aim primarily at the audience who would most interest advertisers, namely housewives. There was enough evidence to suggest that a programme for housewives should not be based on continuous pop music, but easy to listen to background music with a sweet flavour instead. There was also some indication that the more mature audience which the programme would be aimed at did not like the brash, pseudo-American presentation which had been adopted by some commercial stations at this time.

Due to the success of the station there was no problem in securing interviews with major popular stars of the day. Russ Conway and Anita Harris were just two artists who reckoned they owed a lot of their success to the station. Radio 390 was run by Estuary Radio Ltd. of Queens House, Folkestone, Kent, and had its headquarters at 35a Bessborough Place, London SW1.

From 21 March to 7 April 1966, M.W. Electronics Ltd. conducted a survey in 112 towns and districts.

In two, Radio 390 tied with its main competitor, but in ninety-nine of the remaining one hundred and ten the station had a stronger signal than its principal commercial rival, and in many cases a very much stronger one than from any other station including the BBC Light Programme.

The following is a condensed survey showing a cross section of towns. The figures are recorded in microvolts.

Town	Radio 390	Competitor	Light
Ilford	2,000	600	3,200
Wembley	200	120	2,000
Finchley	800	220	7,500
Paddington	120	45	2,000

Dartford	1,200	550	1,200
Dagenham	1,000	450	1,600
Maidstone	2,000	750	200
Margate	8,500	6,000	200
Brighton	325	175	350
Guildford	350	200	550
Portsmouth	95	60	95
Southampton	75	25	85
Cambridge	550	400	500
Huntingdon	460	220	150
Norwich	320	350	75
Nottingham	200	130	35
Lincoln	200	170	30
Oxford	250	180	200
Windsor	300	200	3,000
Colchester	2,500	3,000	900

Although Radio 390 did not state the wavelength (long or medium) on which they measured the BBC Light Programme readings, one must presume it was 247 metres medium wave.

Reception reports came from all over the country representing the whole of the south and east of England up to Newcastle and down to Bournemouth, as well as a large part of the Midlands. Due to the design of the aerial installation on Red Sands Fort, where the 200ft. aerial was sited on the highest point of the tower, evening reception was remarkably free from interference.

The station's audience was extremely loyal, for in December 1966 when the Postmaster-General made one of his many threats to prosecute the forts, allegedly 10,000 listeners wrote to the GPO in defence of Radio 390.

The station was fined £100 on 25 November 1966 after being found guilty of broadcasting without a licence. The magistrates at Canterbury decided that by reason of the existence of Middle Sands, the territorial waters of the United Kingdom could be extended, and thus the Red Sands Forts were situated in the jurisdiction of the County of Kent. The company was therefore, subject to the provisions of the Wireless Telegraphy Act 1949. Subsequently Radio 390 lodged an appeal to the Divisional Court on a point of law, but this case was decided against them by a majority of two judges to one. For a more detailed account of the court case story, see Chapter Eleven.

The directors of Radio 390 then decided, after having obtained further professional advice, that a hydrographic survey should be conducted over Middle Sands. This was carried out during the last week of December 1966 and, as the hydrographers' report confirmed, Middle Sands were no longer a low tide elevation within the meaning of the Order in Council, 1964. Red Sands Forts were situated outside territorial waters. In view of this survey. Radio 390 commenced broadcasting again on 31 December 1966.

However, in February 1967 the Post Office issued further summonses against Radio 390 and all its directors which were heard before magistrates at Rochford on 22 and 23 February. The company was fined £200.

Managing director, Ted Allbeury, left Radio 390 in February 1967 and joined Radio 355, also as managing director.

Radio 390 ceased broadcasting at 5.10pm on 28 July 1967. Graham Gill read the news which was followed by *On the Scene* with Christopher Clark. However he had only played one record by the Alan Price Set, *The House that Jack Built*, when Edward Cole came into the studio. As chief announcer he had been handed a sealed envelope delivered by the *Mallard* to Red Sands Tower. Edward read out a farewell message by David Lye, the managing director, and the station played all three verses of the national anthem, after which came silence.

Radio 390 located on Red Sands forts in the Thames Estuary

"We had a group of journalists on board that day - in for the death of Radio 390 - so we were all a little sad," said Edward Cole. "Two weeks later the Marine Offences Bill became an Act of Parliament. During the 22 months with the station I had enjoyed great comradeship. It was a unique adventure. I am delighted that many of the 390 presenters are still broadcasting. Looking back it was quite remarkable what we achieved. I don't think I would do it again. But I am so glad I did it once."

Says presenter David Allan, who is now a television announcer with BBC1, "Radio 390 was an antidote to the pop pirates and is, I would suspect, sadly missed today."

Red Sands was used in an episode of *Danger Man* entitled *Not So Jolly Roger,* starring Patrick McGoohan as John Drake, broadcast on ITV in 1965. Drake became a disc jockey when death struck pirate radio station Jolly Roger. One asked whether the hostility Drake met from the crew hid a sinister flip side to the station's identity? Filming took place whilst Radio 390 were in residence. There were some interesting external shots of the towers and superstructure.

PROGRAMME SCHEDULE - RADIO 390

January 1967

WEEKDAYS

6.30am	Bright and Early
7.00am	Morning Melody
9.00am	Stars on Discs
9.30am	Light and Blue
10.15am	Masters of the Organ
10.35am	Pause for Prayer
10.45am	Keyboard Cavalcade
11.00am	LP Special
11.15am	Doctor Paul
11.30am	Music from the Shows
12.00 noon	Lunchbreak
1.00pm	From Me to You (requests)
2.00pm	Playtime
2.10pm	Moonmice
2.15pm	Melody Fair
3.15pm	Spotlight
3.30pm	Intermezzo
4.00pm	Memory Lane
4.30pm	Tea Time Tunes
5.00pm	Music Bound
6.00pm	Scene at Six
6.30pm	Rendezvous with Rhythm
7.00pm	Country Style
7.30pm	From Me to You
8.00pm	Dinner at Eight
8.30pm	Continental Cabaret
10.00pm	Serenade
12.00 midnight	Close Down

SATURDAY

6.30am - 10.30am	As Weekdays
10.30am	South of the Border
11.00am	Keyboard Cavalcade
11.30am-6.00pm	As Weekdays
6.00pm	Six o'clock Singalong
6.30pm - 9.00pm	As Weekdays
9.00pm	Serenade
12.00 midnight	Close Down

SUNDAY

6.30am - 10.30am	As Weekdays

10.30am	South of the Border
11.00am	Russ Conway at the piano
11.15am	Voices in Harmony
11.30am	Music from the Shows
12.00 noon	Lunch Break
12.30pm	Jim Reeves Show
1.00pm - 9.00pm	As Weekdays
9.00pm	Red Sands Rendezvous
9.30pm	Serenade
12.00 midnight	Close Down

TOWER RADIO AND TELEVISION

The first announcement of this station was on 22 October 1965. Eric Sullivan of Vision Products, Colchester, Essex, was named as controller. He said: "I have sunk every penny I have into this venture - I have even sold my bungalow. If the station is **not** a success then **I'll** end up in the workhouse."

Directors were named as Eric D. Sullivan, a Colchester businessman; Peter G. Reeves, formerly with Conde Nast Publications and Southern Television; Eric Goldschmidt, origins unknown; Dave Simser, originally from Florida, USA, who came to England with the United States Air Force and, following discharge, became the proprietor of a general store in Newmarket, Suffolk.

Programmes commenced from Sunk Head Tower on 15 October 1965 on 215 metres medium wave. 'Dynamite Dave' Simser was named as chief disc jockey. Also on Sunk Head Tower, off Felixstowe, were two other disc jockeys, a maintenance man and an engineer.

Disc jockeys were Chris Gosling, Bill Rollins, George Short, Dave Simser, Graham London (Graham Smith), Eric Sullivan and John Waters. Transmitter engineers were George Short and Derek Massen.

The Walton and Frinton lifeboat took off George Short from the tower on 28 October 1965 after a request for help. On 2 December 1965 the station sent an SOS for water - Radio Caroline and Radio London refused permission for their tender to go to the rescue. The next day the tug *Agama* sailed from Harwich with 300 gallons of water.

Another SOS call came in February 1966 when the station once again ran out of water - the station was the "Tower with no Shower!"

Tower Radio had experimented on various frequencies in its early days; 197, 210, 212, 215 and 220. It moved to 236 metres, 1268 kHz, in January 1966 - their gimmick call sign was "Get a fix on 236!"

The owners of Tower Radio, Vision Projects, were based at 15 Trinity Street, Colchester, Essex. Towerad (Sales) Ltd., were at 2 Tilney Street, Park Lane, London Wl, and 5 Dawson Street, Dublin 2. Advertising manager for local sales was Robin Garton of Walton-on-the-Naze. Eric Sullivan said the cost of advertising on the station was between £5 and £10 for a 15-second commercial. The station had a potential audience of 2½ million reaching as far north as Sheringham, Norfolk; south to Hastings, Sussex, and west to Watford, Hertfordshire. Advertising placed in 1965 included *News of the World,* Bulova and the Seventh Day Adventists. About £180,000 worth of advertising was "in the bag."

Sullivan contacted a colleague, John Waters, in 1965, and asked if he was interested in joining Tower Radio. John answered in the affirmative and went on: "He asked if I could go out at the weekend. I said 'Yes.' I travelled out from Burnham-on-Crouch in the fishing smack *Girl Betty,* but on that occasion I couldn't climb onto the fort. I stared up and saw John Boulter and Terry Lambeth looking like a couple of hermits. I thought to myself 'Oh God, I can't climb up there." It was a very frightening experience because you see this giant monster protruding out of the North Sea. Anyway, they put this ladder down, which was hooked over a gantry on the top of the fort. The ladder, which dropped below sea level, was about 9 inches wide and you had to get on the bow of the boat to step onto the bottom rung. When someone shouted '*Jump!*', you jumped, or you would have ended up in the drink."

Bill Rollins tuned into the test transmissions from the station and he told his family and friends that he was thinking of applying for a job as a disc jockey. He recalls "They thought I had gone potty! I made a demonstration tape and took it in to Eric Sullivan in Colchester. He played it back and said it was quite acceptable. One week later, on 7 December 1965, I was standing on the deck of a tug called *The Agama* from Felixstowe and we are pulling along the Sunk Head Tower. I thought to myself 'What am I doing in a situation like this? I shouldn't be here.' Down came the ladder and I clambered to the top. Once I reached the fort I had expected something a little more plush, but there were these untidy people standing around. They hadn't shaved for days."

Eric Sullivan explained how Dave Simser became a director: "I met this western type gentleman with a beard and wearing a sombrero who said he had seen a news item on Anglia Television about Tower Radio and that he wanted to invest money in the project. He had a carrier bag full of pound notes. So who was I to say 'no'? From that day on we hit it off. He was more interested in the practical side. *He* wanted an 'in' and *I* wanted the money."

Dave Simser, the man with the beard and sombrero, went on: "I saw the romantic side of becoming a disc jockey. Because it was the 'in' thing everybody was interested in a local radio operation, and I wanted to be a part of it."

Bill Rollins, the youngest member of the team, takes a historical look at the Tower Radio story:

The concept for local North Essex radio was the original idea of Reg Torr and George Short. Reg Torr was a local businessman in Clacton-on-Sea. He ran a TV shop called TD Television. In May 1965 Reg and George decided to start a weekend pirate station called "Radio Pamela," named after George Short's wife Pamela, from an 18ft. boat called *Pamela.* There were, allegedly, a couple of weekends when transmissions were carried out. In July 1965 George Short met Eric Sullivan.

A former Canadian Army Wireless Set No. 52, manufactured by RCA Victor in 1943/1944, was obtained and originally tests were carried out on land in the Colchester area. The next step was to hire a fishing boat, *Girl Betty,* from Burnham-on-Crouch and go either to the Roughs Tower off Felixstowe, or the Sunk Head off Walton-on-the-Naze. For various reasons they could not board the Roughs Tower so they tried the Sunk Head Tower instead and successfully got aboard.

In September 1965 three men, John Boulter and Terry Lambeth, together with transmitter engineer, George Short, were left aboard to erect the antenna and install the transmitters.

In late October 1965 John Waters joined the team on the fort. Test transmissions at this stage had just commenced. There were rumours of something completely different from offshore radio around this time - offshore pirate television! This was not, in fact, a completely novel innovation as the REM Island off Katwijk-on-Zee, Holland, had already been the location of the short-lived radio and television RTV Noordzee project. The original idea was to transmit on the VHF 405 line system on Channel 5. Despite press stories that were circulating at this time, *no* television signal was ever transmitted from the fort. However press stories at the time described in graphic detail the reception of a test card by somebody who was watching their TV at 4.00am. However, the idea to do TV was there ... at least there was a Tower TV test card and a closed circuit television camera. The end of Tower TV came on 8 January 1966 when Eric Sullivan announced that no more TV experiments would be done from the Sunk Head Tower after he had been told by the then Postmaster-General, Tony Benn, that there would be big trouble if the project went ahead. Advertisements were placed in local newspapers to say that, in future, Tower would concentrate on local radio.

People who joined the Tower Radio at the same time as myself, 7 December 1965, were Chris Gosling, Dave Simser and Graham London (Smith). Dave Simser had invested about £2,000 in the project.

The original idea for Tower Radio was for a *local* station (although not according to their rate card) which would concentrate on local features like farming programmes, keep fit, and in general locally-sponsored ideas and programmes. However, while things on the fort were muddling along, on land things were really underway with promises of advertising coming in, new offices opening in Colchester, London and Dublin, plus the services of Towerad (Local Sales) Ltd., at Walton-on-the-Naze, multilined switchboards, new carpets ... you name it, they had it... all on land and very little on the place that mattered ... the fort! Numerous problems were also encountered with tendering. There was one instance when, after 'dropping' a few quid in the pocket of Kees Romas (the captain of the *Offshore I* tender), we, the Tower staff, were taken via the *Galaxy* (Radio London), the *Laissez-Faire* (Radio England) and the *Cheeta II* (the temporary home of Radio Caroline) to the Sunk Head Fort (most of us hiding under canvas on the deck. The *Offshore I* was heading back after her 'drop' at the other ships to her home port of Ijmuiden in Holland for some mechanical work to be done. However, due to an incident, in which the vessel got trapped against Sunk Head Tower, the front mast became damaged shortly after the Tower staff shinned up our ladder on to the fort and to safety. On arrival in Holland the front mast smashed down, crushing the wheelhouse in the process. Kees Romas was fired by the Wisjmuller Company almost immediately ... probably helped by the fact that under the deck canvas were numerous articles addressed to "Tower Radio, Sunk Head Tower."

Eric Sullivan then contacted Kees Romas in Holland and between them they bought an old Icelandic fishing boat, the *Maarje,* which was to be the permanent tender. Shortly after purchase this vessel was filled with diesel and food to be dropped off at the fort en route to Brightlingsea. Essex. There was also some stock of Dutch Heineken beer, gin, cigars and cigarettes intended for delivery to Eric Sullivan's Colchester offices. However, due to a misunderstanding, all the stores were deposited at The Sunk Head fort ... It must be said that we did not complain!

The saga of Kees Romas and the *Maarje* was not to end there. In early April 1966 a new Oman diesel generator of 15kVA was purchased by the company to be delivered to the fort by the *Maarje.* However, on Good Friday, 8 April 1966, the *Maarje* turned up and, during the attempted loading of the generator, it was damaged and had to be returned to land for repair. This was duly carried out and the generator was returned to the fort, this time by Billy Bennett's boat, the *Venus,* from Harwich. The *Maarje* was, within a few days, impounded by HM Customs at Ipswich and was later sold by them for unpaid dues owing. By now time was running out for Tower Radio. The "official" on air date of Thursday 21 April was nearly on us and there we were still doing spasmodic low power test transmissions. There was no communication between land and fort at this time, so the fort-based staff had no idea what was going on in Colchester nor London. The money which had been invested in the company had, by now, run out. The only tangible asset left was a Bedford van. Eric Sullivan contacted Billy Bennett, in Harwich, and offered him the van in return for a trip to the fort to remove the staff who, by now, had not had any contact with the outside world for over two weeks.

It was on Thursday 28 April 1966 that Billy Bennett collected all the remaining staff from the fort and returned them to Harwich. The staff on board mainly took only their personal possessions leaving all the equipment ... generators, records, microphones, turntables and tape recorders ... on board the fort. Sadly that was the end of Tower Radio.

At Harwich the DJs and engineers had to clear Customs. John Waters recalled: "As it was the end, I decided it was time to have a final fling on the journey back on the tender. I drank a bottle of Scotch and had a few packets of cigarettes in my bag. On arrival at Harwich, Customs officers were waiting and we were requested to empty our bags. I refused. So *they*

Above: Dave Simser

Below: Aerial shot of top of Tower Radio and TV

emptied my bag for me! In the bag were a number of foreign-made cigarettes. The Customs officer remarked sarcastically 'You are a naughty boy. You are not supposed to have these. Where did you get them?' I said I had bought them at a shop in the North Sea somewhere. I was then asked to accompany him to their main Customs office. Consequently I was fined £12.00 for smuggling. I asked what would become of the cigarettes? The Customs officer replied "They go to The Queen." I replied: "I am sure The Queen doesn't smoke this bloody rubbish!"

Bill Rollins remembers not being paid for 15 weeks with no chance of getting the money when he arrived on land. The same applied to a greater or lesser extent to all the other staff. Says Bill: "We later found out that the tender had been impounded due to various legal troubles. A writ nailed to its mast, in true pirate tradition, thus blocked our only chance to recoup wages ourselves."

Sunk Head Tower was back in the news again on 9 November 1966 when two squatters, C.T. Payne of Bexley, Kent, and Dexter Stoneham of London, were rescued by the Walton and Frinton lifeboat after Coastguards had been alerted that there was smoke billowing from the fort. The reason for their being on the fort was never made public. However, the Coastguards at Walton-on-the-Naze said that a film director, David Hart, had told them that he was placing two squatters on board, but that it was nothing to do with a radio station.

On Friday 18 August 1967 a team of twenty Royal Marines boarded the fort and, after several small explosions and three days work, the final charge of 2,200 pounds of explosive was set. Having checked first that no-one was living on the fort, they blew up Sunk Head Tower. All that remains of the fort today are the stumps of the legs which are still used as navigational aids to shipping entering the Thames Estuary.

Today Eric Sullivan owns an old peoples' home in Clacton-on-Sea. Looking back he says it was a great challenge and something he will never regret doing: "It was a part of my life, which was a major experience." Robin Garton runs a video production company in Walton-on-the-Naze; Derek Massen lives in East Bergholt, Essex; Bill Rollins is still involved with radio in Essex and John Boulter works as an engineer with British Telecom. George Short died of cancer in 1967 and John Waters worked for the Royal Mail until his death in February 1993.

Tower Radio advertising poster

SEA FORTS

A NUMBER of sea forts were erected around the Thames Estuary during the Second World War. The War Office, working with the Admiralty (now both Ministry of Defence), combined to construct a series of static gun platforms. They came into existence to meet the special needs of the military, which arose when Britain, standing alone, had to bear the full force of the German onslaught by the Luftwaffe who flew across London and the Home Counties. The forts were placed in isolated positions in the open sea where, addition to the ordinary hazards of distance, tide and tempest, they were also exposed to attack by the Luftwaffe and enemy surface and submarine craft.

Four forts were located and manned by sailors and marines at Knock John, Roughs, Sunk Head and Tongue Sands.

Each fort consisted of a boat-shaped reinforced concrete pontoon 168ft. long, 88ft. wide and 214ft. deep from which arose two cylindrical reinforced concrete towers 24ft. in diameter and 60ft. high. On the top of these towers a four-deck steel superstructure was erected which contained the guns. They were designed by G.A. Maunsell and built at Gravesend. The Navy forts were painted with the wavy camouflage reminiscent of the great battleships of the 1914-1918 War.[3]

Each fort was towed into position during the night and slowly sunk into place. There was trouble when Tongue Sands Fort was being placed in position when a German Luftwaffe aircraft attacked and gravely damaged it. Slowly it sank, and the sailors and marines on board were rescued.

Three other forts were manned by the Army and sunk into position at Nore, Red Sands and Shivering Sands. This was a much larger operation as there were seven separate towers connected by catwalks. Each was 90ft. high and consisted of an octagonal steel building on four concrete legs. The layout of the towers was similar to a land-based anti-aircraft site. Each of them was towed into position separately, the central tower containing the Bofors gun. These forts were abandoned in 1956, and the Nore Fort demolished in 1961 as it was

Roughs Tower, 7 miles east of Harwich, Essex, during World War II

---

considered a hazard to shipping.

These were not the first forts to be erected in the sea off the British coast. Between the years 1850 and 1956 some £50,000,000 was spent on the construction and operation of forts. In the mid-nineteenth century there was concern over the vulnerability of the waters around the Isle of Wight to enemy attack. Concern, too, about the deep-water entrance to Portsmouth and Southampton. Between 1868 and 1871 four forts were built at Horse Sands, No Man's Land, St Helen's and Spitbank. St Helen's was abandoned in 1900, No Man's Land in 1925 and Horse Sand and Spitbank in 1956 when the MoD decided that under modern war conditions such defences would be useless.[4]

Two forts were built in the Humber on Bull Sands and Haile Sands. Bull was manned from 1916 to 1956 and Haile Sands from 1916 to 1949.

The forts were built on land and were pushed out to sea in 1941/1942. On board were 100 Royal Artillery gunners and naval ratings who spent a month at sea, then two weeks ashore.

Six of the forts survived until the advent of the pirate radio stations when they proved a great embarrassment to the Government.

Screaming Lord Sutch set up Radio Sutch on Shivering Sands in May 1964. A number of battles took place in the years that followed. Confusion has reigned since the Second World War as to who bears the exact responsibility for the forts.

Reference has already been made (under the station name) to Radio Sutch setting up on Shivering Sands, Radio Essex on Knock John and Tower Radio on Sunk Head.

Although strictly not a pirate radio station, mention should be made of Roughs Tower, seven miles east of Harwich, upon which is based the Principality of Sealand.

The self-proclaimed Prince of Sealand is 71-year-old Roy Bates, a former 8th Army Royal Fusiliers major and later managing director of Radio Essex, who acquired the world's smallest "state" by simply boarding the Roughs Tower in 1967 and not moving away. Prior to setting up Radio Essex, Bates ran one of the biggest fleets of inshore fishing vessels in the United Kingdom. His wife, Joan, is a former beauty queen. Their son, Michael, was just 15 years old when his parents took over Roughs Tower.

Sealand, which has its own flag - Red for Roy. white for purity and black for the pirate radio days - has not all been smooth sailing. The business tactics employed in a long history of diatribe have been unscrupulous, bordering on piracy in a number of instances.

On 11 August 1965 Jack Moore (54), a ship's stoker from Harwich, together with his 16-year-old daughter, Jane, landed on Roughs Tower to "claim" it. They took with them tinned food, blankets and a liquid gas-stove, and became squatters on top of the gun bastion, set in Roughs Sands. They claimed they were establishing squatters' rights for Radio Caroline. It was rumoured that Ronan O'Rahilly was planning to use the fort as a casino. O'Rahilly was reported to have spent £15,000 on building a helipad on the Roughs Tower. A few months later there was another "battle" and this time it was won by Bates.

In August 1978 Sealand was invaded. Roy Bates was away from the Roughs Tower on business. He had been planning a £35 million hotel and casino complex on Sealand. He had been negotiating the deal with a wealthy German businessman, but the talks had broken down. Whilst he was away from the fort an armed raiding party, which included a German lawyer, captured both the fort and its only occupant at the time, Michael Bates.

At dawn on 16 August, Roy Bates and his team of three flew in by helicopter. They slid down ropes about 100ft. above the sea because it was not possible to land the helicopter due to bad weather. As Ray landed on the fort he saw two Germans and a Dutchman running out of the building, so he and his colleagues got in amongst them before the Germans could organise themselves. He recaptured Sealand after fierce hand-to-hand fighting. The raiding party were eventually released with the exception of Gernot Putz, a 34-year-old German lawyer, who also was a passport holder of Sealand. He was held in Sealand's prison charged

4. *Offshore Radio.* Gerry Bishop, Iceni Enterprises, Norwich. 1975, pp 120-122

with treason, because he held a Sealand passport. He was also fined 75,000 Deutschmarks (about £20,000). The German embassy in London demanded that the British Government act to free Putz, but the Foreign Office said they could not intervene. However, they did not recognise Sealand as an independent state. After representation from Putz's wife, Frau Hannelore Putz of Dusseldorf, to the German Foreign Office, Dr Christoph Niemoller, head of legal and consular affairs at the London embassy, then flew by helicopter to Sealand to try to secure the lawyer's release, but he was short-changed by Roy Bates.

A number of journalists visited Sealand by helicopter including London *Evening News* man, Barry Gardner, who was allowed to speak with Putz who told him: "I'm lonely and frightened ... I regret ever getting involved." Gardner said that Putz and his two colleagues were thrown into a dungeon, formerly an ammunition store down in one of the tower's huge concrete legs.

Putz was held prisoner for seven weeks before being given a 'royal pardon' and released on 28 September 1978. He was taken to Harwich by Joan Bates who said "I think he has been there long enough as a punishment. He was misguided and now he realises what he did was wrong. He was very sorry." Roy Bates told the *Southend Evening Echo* on 28 September "Putz was hoodwinked and conned by certain people who are jealous of what I have in mind for Sealand. He now realises the errors of his ways ... I have not waived the fine. It will be taken out of his fees. I'm very disappointed that a Sealander could be involved in an invasion like this."

A week later, on 3 October 1978, police launched a dawn swoop on Roy Bates' Westcliff-on-Sea flat and took away radio equipment owned by Michael Bates. A second raid took place at one of his factories in Wickford Road, Westcliff-on-Sea. Both raids were carried out by police and Post Office investigators.

Questions were asked in the House of Lords on 5 December 1978. Lord Kennett raised the question "Whether a British national is occupying a wartime gun platform called 'Sealand', seven miles off Harwich; whether he is, or at any time has been, holding a German national prisoner there; and whether Her Majesty's Government will make a statement on the facts of the matter, and on their legal and political implications."

The Minister of State, Foreign and Commonwealth Office, Lord Goronwy-Roberts replied: "My Lords, a British national, Mr Roy Bates, is living on a wartime gun platform called Roughs Tower, seven miles off Harwich. The gun platform remains the property of the British Crown, but it lies outside British territorial waters. In October we were informed by the Embassy of the Federal Republic of Germany that a German national was believed to be held prisoner there. To the best of our knowledge the German national in question left Roughs Tower some time ago."

Lord Kennett: My Lords, is it not the case that what this time may be a harmless and colourful escapade could next time, in law, be a moderately dangerous act by an unfriendly foreign power? What is the argument for not extending our territorial waters now to 12 miles, as has already been done by the majority of the states in the world?

Lord Goronwy-Roberts: My Lords, United Kingdom territorial waters at present extend to three miles, but we support the text now under discussion at the United National Law of the Sea Conference, which would recognise the right of coastal states to declare a territorial zone of up to 12 miles in breadth as part of an internationally accepted regime for territorial waters. If the United Kingdom extended its limits from three to twelve miles - and I repeat that we would seek to do so within an international regime - Roughs Tower would be brought within them. I take full note of what my noble friend has said about the possibilities of much more serious incidents on Roughs Tower than have so far proved to be the fact. I can assure him that my Department and others are watching the situation very carefully indeed.

Lord Pargiter: My Lords, may I ask my noble friend whether or not it is a fact that, if Crown property happens to be outside the three-mile limit, anyone can occupy it without let or hindrance?

With an anti-aircraft gun close by, Gordon Wilkinson puts a ring on the finger of his bride, Miss Karen Huxistable. The couple were married on Sealand by Reverend Jim Chelton on 5 May 1979

Lord Goronwy-Roberts: My Lords, I think that the noble Lord is quite right. We have proportional rights to this platform. It was set up in 1942 for defence purposes by Departments acting for the Crown. It is now occupied by an individual who asserts a right to the platform by, I presume, occupation. The position has not yet been tested in the courts, but I can imagine that if there was a reason to do so, there would be ample grounds for the British Government to move into the matter and to assert what they believe to be the position, namely that this platform belongs to the Crown of the United Kingdom.

Lord Hailsham of St. Marylebone: Quite seriously, my Lords, is not such an installation a danger to navigation, and so many years after the War? Is it not time that it was sunk or demolished in some other way?

Lord Goronwy-Roberts: My Lords, that may well be so. I have no information about the possible dangers to navigation. So far such hazards have not proved to be present. But certainly the point which the noble and learned Lord has made is one to be very carefully considered. As I said, we are considering every aspect of the situation and I have no doubt that the point made by the noble and learned Lord is included.

Lord Kennett: My Lords, is it not the case that the British national on this tower has been reported in the Press as having taken actions which, if they had been committed in a place where there was jurisdiction, would have been crimes; but as there is no jurisdiction on this tower no action has been taken to restrain him from capturing or kidnapping people and holding them to ransom?

Lord Goronwy-Roberts: My Lords, I think that the noble Lord puts the position fairly. I understand that in 1968 there was a case which, to some extent, was heard in Chelmsford. However, it could not be pursued since at the time of the incident then in question - which took place on Roughs Tower - the defendant was held to be outside the area of the court's geographical jurisdiction. What has been said this afternoon, of course, supports the case for an appraisal of the position on this installation, and I shall convey to my right honourable friend the feeling, which I think is general to the House, that, small and incidental as the position may be now, it should be reappraised and any necessary action taken.

Lord Hawke: My Lords, will the Minister say whether or not the right of occupation varies in any way from that of any uninhabited island outside our territorial waters?

Lord Goronwy-Roberts: My Lords, I did not accept that view. I said that that was probably the view of the present occupant of this installation, and that if anybody occupied an actual island it might be very possible that after a lapse of years he would claim that by sheer occupation he had a right to that island. We do not accept that view. I merely quoted it as probably being the view of the present occupant on this installation."[5]

On 11 June 1979 Roy Bates was before magistrates at Southend to answer three charges of "using a radio transmitter without a licence." Mr Anthony Bentnall, prosecuting, said "Some of the calls were of a personal nature and on one occasion vegetables were ordered to be taken out to Sealand." The magistrates were suitably shocked that precious frequencies owned by the Post Office should be used for such purposes. Bates was fined £200 plus £100 costs. The £2,000 worth of radio equipment which was seized in the raid by the Post Office in October 1978 was confiscated.

Thirty nine years previously. Roughs Tower had been built at Gravesend, a 168ft. long by 88ft. wide lozenge-shaped pontoon. It was topped by two concrete cylinders each 24ft. in diameter. Finally the top deck, control room and lantern house were added before the fort was towed to Tilbury for fitting out. The guns, generators, pumps, air conditioning and furniture were fixed and the fort was commissioned at the fitting out basin. In February 1942 three tugs pulled the 4,500-ton monster to its site. At this time the fort was fully manned and ready for action. It was sunk into its position in harsh conditions - fog, snow and bad weather.

During the war the forts were credited with shooting down 22 enemy aircraft, destroying

---

5. Hansard *House of Lords Parliamentary Debates*, 5 December 1978

an E boat and damaging another, in addition to destroying about 30 flying bombs.[6]

The Royal Navy, using Roughs Tower as its first sea fort, kept a lookout for German submarines and aircraft. They abandoned the fort in 1946. Twenty years later conditions on board were primitive. Doors had huge holes in them. Windows were shattered and there were numerous dead birds on the fort.[7]

A wedding with a difference took place on 5 May 1979 when Sealand's security officer, Gordon Wilkinson from Westcliffe-on-Sea, married Karen Huxstable of Rochford, on Roughs Tower. Gordon was manager of Roy Bates' Air Fern factory at Wickford, Essex, which processed decorative seaweed. Karen flew out to Sealand in a Bell 47G helicopter owned by Highland Helicopters. Waiting for her on the 932 square yards of the Principality of Sealand were her parents, Ted and Joan, her youngest brother Stephen, her elder sister Suzette and about 50 guests.

The wedding ceremony was performed by the vicar of St. Nicholas Church, Harwich, Reverend Jim Chelton, who was also chaplain for the Mission to Seamen. Permission had to be granted by the Archbishop of Canterbury for the wedding to take place. Doctor Donald Coggan had written to the couple to say the wedding could go ahead. As long as the couple were free for a legal marriage there was no reason why it could not be performed on Sealand. Although Sealand was outside the United Kingdom territorial waters, Lambeth Palace said that "the marriage would still be valid in the eyes of the church."

Over the years Sealand is said to have cost Roy Bates more than a million pounds, reportedly financed by the sale of at least half a dozen of his companies in Essex. *Sunday Telegraph* writer, Charles Alverson, visited the Roughs Tower in June 1980, and says that Roy Bates told him that officialdom was getting a little worried as he was staying on the fort for so long that the Ministry of Defence sent a retired naval commander, with a discreet offer to buy him out of Sealand. The price climbed from £5,000 to £30,000, and he told the commander "The Ministry does not have enough money to get me off Sealand."

Alverson said: "The Bates have transformed the old artillery tower's severe, metal-walled rooms into eclectically-furnished but comfortable quarters along a long corridor. They include a sitting-room, complete with a wall full of paperback books, a dining-room made homely with framed hunting scenes on the bulkheads, a well-equipped kitchen, small cell-like bedrooms for the security staff, shower and radio room.

"Climbing down the ladders into the 30ft. round concrete legs of the tower, one finds that the disused naval quarters and ammunition-storage rooms have been utilised to house Sealand's two diesel generators, the fuel stores and - more esoterically - a makeshift jail. In the other leg of the tower, just below Sealand's post office, where stamps and coins[8] are sold to visitors. Princess Joan has an entire floor devoted to her bedroom, complete with oak wardrobes, dresser and queen-size bed. The rusty drab-green walls contrast strangely with Princess Joan's frilly bedcover and feminine accoutrements."

There was talk of selling Sealand to a Greek shipping line from Saudi Arabia who wanted to use the fort for Muslim religious broadcasts. Two consortia wanted to erect a hotel and casino on Roughs Tower. In 1986 the trade press announced that Roughs Tower would shortly be launching three radio stations.

Music Week said on 2 August 1986 that the island's residents, Prince Roy and Princess Joan Bates, would build a small island alongside Sealand to provide a service harbour and base for commercial activity. A 200ft. aerial would broadcast a 50kW signal for each of the three medium wave frequencies. The radio stations would be franchised by Sealand State Corporation which had the Bates family as its principal shareholders. The Corporation itself comprised businessman John Addie and South African-born Hal Shaper, group chairman of Sparta Florida Music.

6. *Sealand* by Chris Edwards. *Offshore Echo's*, January 1987
7. *North Sea Island State* by John Sutherland. *Daily Telegraph Magazine*, 17 January 1969
8. Sealand passports were issued in 1969 and coins minted in 1970.

Joan and Roy Bates, formerly of Radio Essex, now rulers of the Principality of Sealand

Shaper was quoted as saying "I realise that many people so far see Sealand as an eccentric English joke, but we couldn't have raised the finance for the whole project if it weren't a serious commercial venture. I believe it could become one of the most successful maritime developments ever."

In an interview with *The Scotsman* on 4 August Shaper said "The DTI and British Government cannot take action against us, but I do not underestimate the ability of the British authorities to find some way of getting at us, but in legal terms we are untouchable."

Not one of the three radio stations ever commenced transmissions.

In a letter to Chris Edwards of the magazine, *Offshore Echo's,* dated 27 October 1986, Roy Bates explained the origins of the wartime fort: "Roughs Tower was established on the high seas by Britain during the 1939-1945 War. During that time Britain exercised her authority and sovereignty over the area by force of arms. After the war the UK abandoned the site which, with time, became derelict.

"This was an illegal act because the fort should have been destroyed when it was abandoned. The fort was occupied by us, and we reactivated the abandoned sovereignty for Sealand."

Bates has won a court ruling that Sealand is outside British territorial waters and therefore not subject to jurisdiction. The British Government has been content to let those living on Roughs Tower carry out their activities. He has repulsed seven boarding parties since 1967.

Roy Bates said "Sealand is, and will remain, a micro state. We have not applied, nor do we propose to apply, for de jure or diplomatic recognition from any State. Neither Sealand nor any other micro state indulges, or can afford to indulge, in this expensive luxury.

"Also, to make the point, neither Sealand, San Marino, Monaco, Liechtenstein, Andorra nor Naura are members of the United Nations.

"Micro states are what they say they are. Small. They are unimportant militarily and financially in the world with very small populations, and, rightly considered to be unimportant as far as world events are concerned. However, they do exist, and de facto recognition is on record. The international legal requirement for territory is a portion of the globe, and that Sealand literally sits on. Size is immaterial.

"When the German and Dutch Governments complained to the UK that Sealand was holding some of their nationals imprisoned, and demanded that Britain must arrange their release, the British Government had to inform them that they had no authority in Sealand, and that they must negotiate directly with Sealand themselves.

"The German ambassador sent a senior diplomat to Sealand, and the German Government accepted the decision."

Roy Bates' claim to sovereignty was reinforced as long ago as 1968 when his son, Michael, was charged at a court in Essex with firing a shotgun over the heads of unwelcome visitors. These visitors were, in fact, maintenance men from Trinity House, based in Harwich, who went out on the vessel *Siren* to service a buoy, close to Sealand.

Michael Bates, who was then under age, went along with his father, and represented by counsel, to contest the charge of possessing a firearm without a licence and discharging the same. However, the judge ruled that the case was outside his jurisdiction because Sealand lay beyond Britain's three-mile territorial limit.

Roy and Joan Bates spend two thirds of the year on Sealand. The remainder of the time they are to be found travelling around Essex visiting family members. They go shopping in either Harwich or on the Continent. The journey, in an inflatable boat, powered by a 55hp outboard engine, takes about a quarter of an hour to Harwich.

Expected visitors travelling to the fort by boat have a tricky time on arrival at Roughs Tower. They have to be winched up from a boat deck in a three-foot-square wooden box, which swings alarmingly as it is hauled up to the platform.[9] "Visitors are then greeted by shotgun-carrying guards and a barking Alsatian. They are searched before their passports receive a Sealand stamp."

Since the Territorial Sea Act came into force in 1987, Sealand has now been placed within the boundaries of the new 12-mile territorial waters limits.

The DTI has said that Sealand is now "within the criminal jurisdiction of the United Kingdom courts, and would consider taking action if broadcasting started from the Roughs Tower."

The Department of National Heritage, which is now responsible for broadcasting policy in the United Kingdom, said, in a letter to the author, on 30 September 1993, that "Roughs Tower is the property of the Crown under the management of the Crown Estate Commissioners and lies within United Kingdom territorial waters and within the United Kingdom jurisdiction. The Government does not recognise 'Sealand.' "[10]

Discussing the Principality of Sealand with the author in February 1994, Roy Bates said: "Our rights and claims of sovereignty over this island and its territorial waters have been ratified time and again by national courts and international jurists.

"Over the years more and more international lawyers and leading jurists became fascinated with the Sealand story, and declared that Sealand fulfilled all the legal requirements of a state and that its sovereignty was absolute.

"We have brought a measure of freedom of choice to people, and I for one have always been immensely proud of that."

9. *A Law Unto Its Tiny Self,* by Charles Alvereon. *Sunday Telegraph Magazine,* 8 June 1980
10. Letter from Mr R. L. Lacey, Broadcasting Policy Division, Department of National Heritage, 30 September 1993

Chapter Five

RIDERS ON THE STORM

Ship to shore, do you read me anymore?
The line is bad and fading.
Ship to shore, answer my call,
Send me a signal ... a beacon to bring me home.

Ship to Shore, Chris de Burgh, 1982

THE TWO MAJOR offshore stations almost arrived on land in January 1966! The cause, natural elements. Gale force winds were outside their control. First off was Radio London which went for a trip, unintentionally, round Clacton Pier on 12 January.

The m.v. *Galaxy* broke adrift in the early hours of the morning. Eric Hartley, one of the Walton coastguards, said she was "going like the devil." At 1.30am he informed the honorary secretary of the Walton and Frinton lifeboat. Half an hour later the *Galaxy* was 171 degrees still dragging her anchor. He alerted the Clacton lifeboat which was launched at 2.40am. Forty-five minutes later the lifeboat was within a mile of Radio London and by 3.40am was alongside. The lifeboat returned to its base at 8.30am.

There were 25 men aboard the *Galaxy* including disc jockeys Tony Windsor (senior DJ), Paul Kaye, Ed Stewart, Mark Roman and Mike Lennox. The English engineers were Russell Tollerfield and Martin Newton and Belgian engineer Paul Peeters. The ship was under the captaincy of Bill Buninga. Chief Officer was P.R. Dekker, chief engineer, Van de Zee and 2nd engineer, K. Van Duyn.

Radio London had closed its transmissions on 11 January at 9.00pm and she had started drifting around midnight after the anchor chain holding two anchors snapped.

A Radio Caroline lookout said the *Galaxy* had come within a hundred metres of the *Mi Amigo*. They tried to signal her but with no luck.

At 3.30am the ship was reported to be four miles off Clacton Pier still dragging badly. She was due back on the air at 5.30am but stayed off because of uncertainty about her exact position.

Apparently the ship was only 2½ miles off the Essex coast around dawn and should Radio London have transmitted, it would have been committing an offence under the Post Office Wireless Telegraphy Act. The station staff could have been fined up to £100 and also receive three months imprisonment.

The m.v. *Galaxy* was towed back to her original position by the tug *Kent* at 2.16pm. The *Galaxy's* engines were working perfectly, but the steering gear had become damaged in the storm. They refused help from a Dutch salvage vessel.

The ship had made the journey across the Atlantic from Miami to the east of England in 1964. Managing director Philip Birch said "We could have gone on the air at the scheduled time, but we realised we would have been breaking the law."

As Radio London passed its 'opposition,' Caroline disc jockey Dave Lee Travis said "An old warship is just being towed past flying the surrender flag."

Surrender flag? Most definitely not! Radio London resumed transmissions at 1.00pm on that day, 12 January.

Eight days later the smile on the face of Dave Lee Travis disappeared when the cruel sea claimed another victim. This time it was Radio Caroline South which went one better by actually running aground in the early hours of Thursday morning 20 January after she had dragged her anchor in a freezing force 9 gale.

The 470-ton ship began to drift at 9.00pm the previous evening. The station had ceased transmission as usual at 8.00pm. However, no one aboard seemed to know anything about the drifting. Visibility at this time was seven to eight miles.

Radio London was the first to spot Caroline drifting and signalled her, but with no success. They then contacted the coastguards at Walton-on-the-Naze. At a similar time Coastguard 'Ginger' Ward had observed the *Mi Amigo* dragging her anchor. A gale was blowing from the south-east. He had tried to contact the ship by Aldis lamp and other means, but without response. Both the Clacton and Walton and Frinton lifeboats were informed. North Foreland Radio tried to contact the *Mi Amigo*. The Anglia Television news staff prepared a bulletin about the ship dragging her anchor, but this was not seen. Bill Scaddan, Caroline's liaison officer, drove over from his house in Frinton-on-Sea and flashed his car lights on Caroline but with no luck. At 10.10pm two green maroons were fired to alert the Walton and Frinton lifeboat followed by a white maroon to muster members of the Walton Lifesaving and Apparatus Company (LSA Co.) who assembled at 10.45pm. The *Mi Amigo* by this time was drifting south, about half-a-mile offshore from the Frinton-on-Sea Golf Club House. Shortly before 11.00pm the district officer and a coastguard set off for Holland Haven as an advance party taking with them a searchlight, followed five minutes later by the station officer, two coastguards and twenty auxiliaries, who took the necessary equipment with them. The *Mi Amigo* was only a few hundred yards offshore, using her engines, but making no headway in the gale force winds and heavy seas.

In sharp snow and sleet squalls the gear was manhandled along the back of the sea wall, near Frinton-on-Sea Golf Club, and at five minutes to midnight the *Mi Amigo* grounded on a wave-lashed Great Holland Beach at Chevaux de Frise Point. At a similar time the ship's tender, *Offshore I*, set out from Harwich, but arrived too late to be of any assistance. By half-past-midnight a whip had been secured on Radio Caroline.

Abreast the *Mi Amigo* the rocket apparatus and whips were hauled up and over the seventeen-foot sloping sea wall, then covered in snow and ice, and the rescue gear was rigged and made ready in the tight confines of a beach between the heavy breaking seas and the sea walls.

On board Radio Caroline South were Captain Willy Wrury and an eight-man Dutch crew, five disc jockeys and three engineers. The disc jockeys were Tom Lodge, Tony Blackburn, Graham Webb, Norman St. John and Dave Lee Travis. Engineers were Carl Thomson, George Saunders and Patrick Starling.

The tug *Kent*, which had towed Radio London back to position the previous week set out from Felixstowe but returned to base after being told that she could be of no assistance.

Walton and Frinton lifeboat waited an hour in the gale before the crew could launch her from the pier head. They reached Caroline after she had grounded.

No. 1 of the Walton Lifesaving and Apparatus Company (Rocket Section) was Eric Brett who supervised the setting up of the breeches buoy. "The idea is to rig up a tripod with lines secured to the ship and then run a buoy from one to the other so you bring the people back safely on shore. Before any rescue can be attempted the ship has to haul our whip and lines out to her to make them secure, and then we can start getting the breeches buoy into place. It took ten minutes in the howling gale to get the people on the ship to react. No one moved out of the wheelhouse. A number of us were on top of the sea wall and then all of a sudden 'whoosh', a rocket went across the top of our heads. The captain of the ship had fired *his* rocket across the top of us. I had fired *our* rocket which had landed on top of the wheelhouse, but everyone preferred to stay indoors. We had to set up the tripod at three separate locations as the ship kept moving further down the beach. Eventually the lines were secured and we began to rescue those on board."

Disc jockey Norman St. John is rescued at night by breeches
buoy on Great Holland Beach at Chevaux de Frise Point

Norman St. John was the first person to be brought ashore at 12.35am. Remembering the incident he says:

> I had gone to bed around 11 o'clock. Dave Lee Travis came into the cabin some ten minutes later and said that we were drifting. Using some words to the effect that he was taking the mickey, I decided to get dressed and have a look, as it was an extraordinarily rough night. When I arrived on the deck the ship was engulfed in lights. At this stage we thought that we were still some two and a half miles offshore. We found out later that this was in fact untrue. The captain came down from the bridge and gave orders that we should put on warm clothing and life jackets as we may have to abandon ship. By this time the ship's engines were started but all to no avail in a force 9 gale. On the bridge at this time the engineers were repairing the ship's spotlight and finally when they got it working, it revealed that we were only some thirty yards from a concrete wall on the beach. Moments later the ship that had built up a name all around the world as Britain's first pirate radio ship was on the ground. Realising the danger of the ship breaking up, coastguards at this time fired rockets with ropes attached in order to fix the breeches buoy. The first rocket missed and exploded on the deck of the *Mi Amigo,* the second was quite successful. We then prepared to leave the ship.

Norman St. John came ashore wearing his famous trilby hat... Tom Lodge carried a large picture of his wife, Romy. As huge breakers smashed against the *Mi Amigo* other disc jockeys followed ... Tony Blackburn, Dave Lee Travis, Graham Webb, as did engineers Carl Thomson, Patrick Starling and George Saunders. The only Dutchman to come ashore was steward Thys Spyker. For Thys it was his second disaster. He was on Radio London the previous week when she drifted. The 19-year-old Dutchman had joined Caroline on the Monday. "I am becoming quite used to travelling the English coastlines," he said. The other crew members remained on board. By 1.35am the Walton and Frinton lifeboat was in the area, but later returned to base. Coastguards and the Coast Rescue Company remained on duty throughout the time the *Mi Amigo* was on the beach. A shift system was operated.

Coastguard Dennis Street related "The first person I saw come ashore was disc jockey

Above: Ronan O'Rahilly talks with a member of HM Coastguard at Chevaux de Frise Point

Below: Liaison officer Bill Scaddan (3rd from right) with the survivors from the Radio Caroline ship at Walton-on-the-Naze the morning after the rescue. Left to right, Carl Thomson, Norman St. John, Patrick Starling, Tony Blackburn, Thys Spyker, Graham Webb, Tom Lodge, Dave Lee Travis and George Saunders.

Tony Blackburn carrying a teddy bear. Instead of getting into the breeches buoy, as he was told to do by me, he put one leg into the breeches buoy itself and the other leg was dangling over the other side. We did manage to haul him ashore. He was then taken away by a local businessman Ray Hall for a bath and was given a change of clothing. After coming ashore Tony Blackburn said:

> At first I thought it was all a joke. Norman St. John woke me and told me to go on deck. As I was on the *Breakfast Show* I told him to go away as I needed all the sleep I could get. Eventually the captain came down to say we were really in trouble. I got up, put on some clothes and went on deck to find car lights and houses on the shore coming nearer and nearer. It was very cold and dark. We missed the television warning news flash because our TV aerial was not correctly turned and the news faded just at the time the announcement was made. Waves were crashing over the ship and there was this terrible crunching sound as she ran aground. There was no panic.

Graham Webb said "Only last week we were laughing at Radio London when she broke anchor, but now the joke's on us."

Ironically three hit records in the Radio Caroline Top 20 that week were: *My Ship Is Coming In*, *The Water Is Over My Head* and *Let's Hang On*.

Engineer Carl Thomson recalls "I went ashore in the breeches buoy, but was not really dressed for the occasion. By the time I landed on the beach my trousers were soaking. I had lost my socks and slippers in the sea. As I was walking up the beach I thought 'We must be famous as they have laid out the red carpet. I can't feel the stones.' It wasn't until I scrambled up to the top and looked down with the headlights of the ambulances, I saw it was so soft because I had been walking on six inches of snow! My toes turned blue, and I actually got frostbite."

The rescued were taken first to Frinton Golf Club House and then to Walton-on-the-Naze police station where they were given a change of clothing and cups of tea all round. The clothing was taken to the police station by a Frinton outfitter, Ray Hall, and the bill paid for by the Distressed Mariners' Fund. The clothing consisted of T-shirts, jeans and plimsolls.

Some of the disc jockeys spent the night at liaison officer Bill Scaddan's house. Others were accommodated at the Gables Hotel in Dovercourt.

The regular coastguards who took part in the operation were District Officer Ken Curtis, Station Officer Ted Shreeve and Coastguardsmen Tom Sayer, Dennis Street and Eric Hartley. Auxiliaries who took part were Eric Brett, Don Barber, Don Barrett, Gordon Birks, Cecil Chaplin, Bernard Field, Jack Griffiths, Bob Hazel, J. Jackman, Les Jarman, Len Lacey, Bert Oxley, Douglas Parmenter, Leslie Scales, George Sharman, David Speight, Robin Tott and Bill Chapman.

Others who assisted were Roger and David Todd, Barry Duller, John Hall, Robert Hipkin, Bernard Norman, John Oxley, John Steer and John Rowland.

On the beach a desperate race against time and tide to save Caroline was made throughout the night and day of Thursday. There were fears that she would break up or be flung against the sea wall.

The *Mi Amigo* suffered a serious list at midday and was taking a terrific hammering and battering from the flood tide.

A tug and a tender were standing by at Harwich and another tug, the *Titan*, was on its way from Holland to help refloat the ship.

Coxswain Frank Bloom, who has been awarded both a silver and bronze medal for his courage spanning many years as coxswain of the Walton and Frinton lifeboat, said:

> On 19 January we received a message to say that the *Mi Amigo* was drifting and coming towards the shore. We assembled at the head of Walton-on-the-Naze pier. On

m.v. Mi Amigo aground at Chevaux de Frise Point, Great Holland Beach, January 1966

that occasion the lifeboat we had was on relief and was a petrol engine boat, whereas our main lifeboat had a diesel engine. Water had gone down the funnel and was giving a lot of engine problems. It was the failure of the boat to get underway that caused the delay in us getting to Radio Caroline before she ran aground. We boarded that night in dreadful conditions. We then had more engine problems on the way up. Had we gone in our regular boat I am certain we would have rescued the Caroline crew before she hit the beach. I must say that the disc jockeys were very cheerful in spite of the freezing weather and didn't appear too worried when they came on shore.

The members of the Walton and Frinton lifeboat were Frank Bloom (coxswain) Dennis Finch (2nd coxswain), Robert Kemp (bowman), Ron Wyatt (assistant mechanic), Ken Haggis (signalman), Tony Warnock (travelling mechanic) and Arthur Cole, Jack Barratt, Brian Oxley and Keith Richardson.

When managing director Ronan O'Rahilly made the trip from London to Frinton-on-Sea with director Barry Ainley, Caroline had become embedded in three feet of sand and shingle. They went aboard with Bill Scaddan. Two coastguards were on board with the Dutch captain and crew. O'Rahilly and Ainley returned to London in the afternoon.

Early on Friday morning 21 January, an attempt to refloat Caroline with the tug *Titan* failed when a steel hawser snapped. The long battle to save the pirate radio ship was watched by 300 people in driving rain on the Essex coast.

The captain of the *Mi Amigo*, Willy Wrury, asked for two volunteers to help crew the vessel as most of the Dutch crew were stewards. A launcher from Clacton-on-Sea lifeboat and David Speight from the Coast Rescue Company both volunteered. David lived at Kino Road, Walton-on-the-Naze, and was a lifesaving member and a ex-naval man.

Said David "My job was to get the ship off the beach. This was done by running a wire from the ship to the anchor cable which had been dropped by the ship. The anchor and all the cable had run out of from the ship and was running on the beach. We walked along and picked up the end of the anchor cable and took that to the bows of the ship and then to the winch. This winch hadn't been used for a very long while and was solid. With a large hammer we freed it and then with a great deal of effort we got the diesel engine to start. Once the bows were pointing in the right direction off we steamed. After about half an hour we were taken off by the supply tender *Offshore I* which came out from Harwich. That was the last we saw of the *Mi Amigo*."

Also on duty was the Customs and Excise officer Albert Richardson who was alerted as soon as the *Mi Amigo* broke her moorings. He relates:

Radio Caroline was a *pirate* radio station, so the crew who were on board were aliens. Therefore they were due Customs interrogation should they be landed on shore. I was standing by in blizzard conditions on Holland Haven beach when the *Mi Amigo* ran aground. When Tony Blackburn came ashore he was treating the whole affair as a joke. It was no joke to any of us on the beach early that morning. As a Customs officer I had to enforce the health rules which meant that anyone from aboard should go through immigration. The first question I asked 'Was everyone well on board?' My main concern was to see that those who were rescued were not suffering from any disease or were injured in any way. After I was assured they were fit, if a little wet, the disc jockeys and engineers were rescued by breeches buoy. The Walton Lifesaving Company did a marvellous job. I had to climb aboard the Radio Caroline ship to seal up and secure the duty-free stores.
There were a large number of boxes of cigarettes, together with spirits. I was surprised no-one tried to take any off the ship when they were rescued, but they didn't. I remained on board until she set sail on 22 January.

Engineer Carl Thomson tells a different story "The first person to greet me was from the

British Customs. 'Anything to declare?' So I put my cigarettes that were all wet and soggy straight into his right hand and said 'Yes!'. He said 'Oh, thank you very much!' and threw them down. We were then looked after by the coastguard people."

Another who was in attendance at Holland Haven was a police officer from Walton-on-the-Naze who asked Tony Blackburn to accompany him to the local police station where particulars were taken from him.

The GPO, for all its plans to outlaw the pop pirates since 1964, could do nothing officially about Radio Caroline, although the ship was within the three-mile limit (inside territorial waters) - the station was off the air!

At 11.00am on 21 January Caroline freed herself from a sandbank some 50 yards from the beach at Frinton-on-Sea by kedging - putting an anchor into deep water and then winching herself free at high water. Within an hour the Coast Rescue Company had recovered all their kit from the beach and stood down at 12 noon, as did Walton Coastguards.

No. 1 in the Walton Lifesaving and Apparatus Company (Rocket Section), Eric Brett of Walton Road, Walton-on-the-Naze, said "The rescue of the Caroline people was the last time a breeches buoy was used in the Thames District. It is unlikely that breeches buoys will ever be used again. Coastguards and rescue companies today are search and patrol, not apparatus companies like we were."

Speaking in 1993 Eric (70), a former ambulance driver/attendant, said "I retired from the Walton Lifesaving Company in 1984 after 36 years service. All the equipment belonged to the coastguards who always backed us up on any rescue. We were all auxiliaries. The Chief Coastguard was always in charge of the rescue team. The Walton Lifesaving Company was eventually disbanded because of modem technology taking over and there was no need for us to carry on. The rescue of the Caroline disc jockeys and engineers was the most exciting in which I had taken part. It tested all of us to the hilt in freezing conditions. We were awarded a shield for the best wreck service of the year in 1966." Later Eric Brett was awarded the Coastguard Auxiliary Service Long Service Medal and Clasp.

In January 1966 Paul Graham, of Frinton-on-Sea, was a schoolboy and remembers the beaching of Caroline very clearly.

What amazed everyone including Ronan O'Rahilly, the coastguards and everyone involved in the rescue was that the ship escaped serious damage. All the way along the east coast there are rows of groynes - large, tough wooden posts or metal sheeting driven into the sand and held together by giant cast iron posts.

Anybody who had hit that on a ship would have been in big trouble. The miracle of it all was that the *Mi Amigo* arrived on the beach side on, which was the worst scenario. If she had come in either bow on or stern on she would not have had a problem. By some pure fluke she managed to miss the concrete jetty and the groyne. I remember that night there was a blizzard and it was 8 or 9 degrees below freezing. If she had hit the groyne it would have certainly driven a hole into the hull of the *Mi Amigo*. With the force of the waves the hull could have been punctured and immediately filled with water. Then one of two things could have happened:

1. She could have gone over on her side, impaled on the metal groyne. Eventually she would have been pushed over by the sea and become a total loss, or:

2. She would have simply broken in two. The force of the sea would have driven her further into the metal stakes on the beach. Without sounding too dramatic all those on board could have easily been drowned. Fortunately by sheer good luck they were rescued in time.

The Board of Trade set up an inquiry into the beaching of Radio Caroline. A coastguard report was sent to the Board and was concerned with whether the drifting of the *Mi Amigo* could have caused danger to shipping and if there was any negligence on the part of the Dutch captain and his crewmen. Radio Caroline said that the captain and crew were provided by a

Dutch company while the ship was owned by another foreign company.

On 22 January a message reached managing director Ronan O'Rahilly from Mrs Britt Wadner of Radio Syd in Sweden offering him her radio ship in the Baltic off Gothenburg.

Because of ice and snow the ship had to be moved from its usual position for the months of February and March 1966 and it was for this period that Mrs Wadner made her offer. By chance, the *Cheeta II* moved from the Baltic, almost within an hour of Caroline going aground.

Ronan O'Rahilly said "We are delighted at this offer and the expression of unity. We could continue to broadcast Caroline programmes from her ship off the Essex coast."

The *Mi Amigo* was towed by the tug *Titan* to IJmuiden and thence up the North Sea Canal to Zaandam, a town just before Amsterdam. Engineers Carl Thomson and Patrick Starling were asked by Bill Scadden to sail with the ship. It was a rushed decision. Said Carl: "We had a short time to get on board with *Offshore 1* from Harwich, and as soon as we were onboard we were under way. At first the tow went well, the *Titan* moved at a good rate of knots. However in the morning of the next day when I went to the transmitter hall to sort things out, I found some large pumps and hoses pumping water from the water and diesel storage tank room next door. During the night it had been discovered that some rivets had been damaged during the grounding. I seem to remember the tow took a lot longer than the crew had predicted. The arrival at IJmuiden some time in the afternoon was something I will always remember, it seemed like the whole population of Holland had turned out to welcome us. Every vantage point had crowds of people. The berth at the shipyard in Zaandam was by a side canal, which was iced over."

Disc jockeys were retained by Caroline and they had a holiday with pay, although they had to phone into Caroline House daily to keep abreast of all the latest movements.

It is interesting to note that Radio Caroline North also drifted twice during the early part of 1965. As soon as she realised she had drifted inside territorial waters she ceased transmissions. She remained inside the three-mile limit during the night but returned to her original position the following morning when the seas had calmed.

The *Cheeta II* arrived off the British shores on time and was picked up by the tender *Offshore I* and guided into position where the *Mi Amigo* normally anchored. A 1924-built passenger ship, *Cheeta II* was slightly bigger than the m.v. *Mi Amigo* in tonnage, but not in length. The main difference between the *Cheeta II* and the *Mi Amigo* was the accommodation created by the extra width in the former. She had 20 cabins and could accommodate 40 crew

Disc jockey Colin Nicol with Britt Wadner and Ronan O'Rahilly on board m.v. Cheeta II

and radio staff. There were some 7,000 records on board but many of them were in Swedish ... not unnatural as she was a Swedish ship broadcasting Swedish records to Sweden!

Disc jockey Colin Nicol was the first announcer to go aboard the Swedish ship with Britt Wadner and Ronan O'Rahilly. He recalls:

The day I first went aboard the *Cheeta It* was the first occasion I formally met Mrs Wadner - the ship's owner, boss of Radio Syd and the first lady of pirate radio. We met on the wharf at Harwich - she, Ronan O'Rahilly and I ... along with a gaggle of journalists and photographers.

Mrs Wadner was a striking woman. Full of charm and with a commanding personality she obviously controlled her staff and crew through the affection and respect she commanded. Certainly, in her own country (Sweden) she was known as the 'Viking Lady' and was a national celebrity ... as much for the number of times she went to prison for operating a pirate radio ship, as for the fact that it was hers entirely, and was well-known as a radio personality on the ship. There were times shortly after when she and her son, Kalle, fascinated me for hours with the stories of their adventures as the world's first commercial radio buccaneers, and of the enormous success they enjoyed in Scandinavia.

After introductions were made at Harwich, on a rather cool and damp morning, we boarded the tender waiting for us and made for the open sea.

As is often the case in those seas, a heavy mist was up, and visibility was very bad. We chugged for what seemed like many hours, vainly searching for the ship which was to be the new temporary home of Radio Caroline South. I began to doubt if *Cheeta II* had arrived at all. The captain of our tug admitted he was lost, and didn't know where the elusive Swedish vessel was - when the mist curtains parted for an instant over our bows, suddenly there she was ringing her ship's bell to guide us alongside.

My first impressions were that she looked a homely kind of ship. My landlubber's eyes saw what appeared to be a fairly typical, old ferry (which indeed she was) - set fairly high out of the water, but with no visible sign of any radio masts or equipment.

We pulled alongside, to the accompaniment of greetings shouted in Swedish, Dutch and English. A rope ladder was thrown down, and I helped Mrs Wadner up to be the first aboard. Ronan followed, with me trailing third, and the cameras whirring.

My first impression was that the atmosphere aboard the ship was very relaxed. The people who ran her were personal friends and not employees, and nobody seemed at all troubled by a slight air of charming disarray aboard.

All the faces - though strange to me - were smiling, and I was quickly introduced to those on deck. It was several days before I discovered who the captain was, and then there seemed to be two - both of them weathered old salts.

I met Mrs Wadner's son Kalle, who was usually in charge, and who had sailed with the ship from her former location in the Baltic Sea. He said they had a smooth and quite fast journey, and were at present in a temporary mooring. Kalle was about my own age. We got on very well together, and were good company for each other during the time I was aboard. Despite missing his young wife (who worked for their firm in Sweden) he was excited to be in England (or almost) and like the rest of the crew, anxious for shore leave and a look at London. Most of them had been aboard for a long stretch, and a replacement crew was expected before many days were out. They did arrive, but rather later than hoped.

The purpose of our expedition to the ship that day was to look her over, decide how suitable she would be for our needs, and to discover what was needed to get the radio side operative as soon as possible.

The first thing that crossed my mind was that we'd need a mast to start with ... all that was visible was two 10ft. high lattice masts, set well apart on the superstructure of the middle of the ship. "That won't do," I thought - but it transpired that these were just the first stages of two prefabricated aerials, which could be made much higher. The masts had been taken down, prior to the ship leaving her old station in the Baltic.

Mrs Wadner led the tour of inspection of her ship, and she seemed very proud of it. Even now, long after, I can feel the friendliness and the homely warmth that seemed to characterise the old vessel. I had the feeling that many people, over many years, had enjoyed being aboard her... and I knew that I was going to feel more relaxed and at home on the *Cheeta II* than I had felt on board ship ever before. Perhaps what appealed to me most was the comparative spaciousness of her compared to my old home on Caroline South *(Mi Amigo)*. There seemed to be endless stairways and passages, and scores of doors to penetrate and explore beyond.

We went first to the lounge, and while I was still grinning with pleasure on finding so much polished wood trimming and panelling aboard, and marvellous glass swing doors into the main recreation room, Ronan was calling to me in excitement, and saying "Isn't she marvellous - what a great room."

It was, to me, a room that looked as if it would be just the haven in which a harassed ship-bound disc jockey would like to relax. Long and quite wide, and tapering in a little towards the aft end of the ship. Quite big enough to seat about forty, along the couches lining the walls, behind rows of small tables. For the second time, I told myself this was going to be fun. Just look at those little red-shaded lamps on the walls! And those big portholes!

We trailed forward, on the first level below the deck, passing a small kitchen that looked more like what one has at home than a ship's galley - and past lots of doors bearing the unpronounceable names of the crew and radio staff. Amidships, alongside the galley, was the glassed-in hold, and it was here we subsequently decided to site the medium wave transmitter that would be used for our broadcasts.

Further forward, we descended again, and in the hold discovered an almost complete television studio, littered with equipment.

Radio Syd were to have been the first with pirate television, as well as radio. In fact, they probably were the first with television since they did run a successful test broadcast before bad weather forced them to visit England. Their ingenuity had solved the problem of the movement of the ship affecting broadcasts by designing a special aerial arrangement that allowed them to broadcast television no matter which way the ship faced. Later, our transmitter stood in the middle of this studio, at the bottom of the hold. We had to bring one of our own transmitters from the *Mi Amigo* for this ship, as Radio Syd was only designed to broadcast on VHF, and this would not be suitable for the Radio Caroline arrangement. The surrounding land would also have made it difficult to get the signal to a large area.

After the television studio, a visit back on deck to the cabins and fittings on that level, and up to the bridge. Here, I was delighted to find the ship's bell, and gave it a few rings for Caroline's sake. It was going to be some time, however, before listeners heard that bell again from that ship. There was a lot to be done.

Finally, the studio. We went aft again, and found the studio in two glass-walled rooms, above the deck level, and over the saloon. On top of the studio again were store rooms for records and equipment for the radio.

It was all going to be a big adventure, I kept telling myself, and this was going to be fun. The studio was inadequate, to say the least. Ronan asked me if we could make it work, and I crossed my fingers and said "Yes." But a lot would have to be done, I told myself. Everything had been dismantled. There was not even a turntable in sight.

However, I was very impressed when, a few minutes after asking for some equipment to be brought in so that photos could be taken, the smiling Swedish radio staff had the whole room littered with tape recorders, amplifiers, turntables, wires in all directions and Swedish records. That looked good in the photos, but none of it was connected.

Cheeta II on loan to Radio Caroline South

I decided that we could adapt what equipment there was, and add some of our own from the *Mi Amigo,* and that in about a week we should be able to have the studio operating to our requirements - but it *would* be a different style of operation. The Swedes were used to having the announcer only doing the talking while an operator in the other room would play the records and run the tapes. Adapting this equipment caused some problems, but it was later made to work, after a fashion. In the end, I was rather glad I never used the equipment on the air, as I heard it was very difficult. I find myself differentiating between the crew of the ship and the radio staff. But in fact, on the *Cheeta II,* there was never really any such defining line with the original Swedish operation. For the most part, the DJ who had just done his programme was quite likely then to go down and help cook dinner, or might swing over the side and paint the ship. Everyone 'mucked-in' with Radio Syd, so I was told, and they were really a big happy family. That was to change when the English staff came aboard, but then our type of radio was quite different.

The hull of the ship was white. It seems that, not long before, they had all been very busy repainting the peeling sides of the *Cheeta II* - while she lay at anchor in the Baltic. But they painted it a bright red, thinking this to be the most noticeable and safe colour to paint a stationary ship ... and were warned by the Swedish coastguard that this was illegal. So, paintbrushes hurriedly came out again and any paint that was handy was splashed over the red in one frantic day of brush-wielding. The result was that the paint was almost the consistency of whitewash, but was the best they could do in an emergency.

Our tour of the ship was about over. We sampled the delicious Swedish coffee the crew made for us, ate a huge pile of sandwiches ... and boarded the tender for the return to Harwich - taking Kalle Wadner with us.

That night was spent at the Gables Hotel at Dovercourt, and I returned to the ship the next day with Kalle to prepare what could be done to get the studios right. I was allocated a tiny, comfortable single cabin - with a porthole. To me this was a luxury, as we shared as many as three or four to the cabin on the *Mi Amigo,* and there were no portholes as the cabins were below water level.

That ten days or more on the *Cheeta II* - just me and the Swedish crew - was one of the most pleasant times I can recall. There wasn't much to do, not much to do it with, and lots to talk about. Food was fine and well cooked. We always seemed to be eating, as four meals or hearty snacks were served up every day, in Swedish fashion. I was really on a pleasure trip, and hoped it wouldn't come to a premature ending.

I checked and helped install equipment in the studio, tried my best to make do with what was aboard, and attempted to make racks and shelves for the efficient running of the studio. But there was very little aboard to work with, and supplies from shore were slow. For a time, there was a lull, and I began to wonder if the plan was going ahead, or if I might wake up one day to find myself looking - not at Frinton, Essex - but Malmo, Sweden, on the horizon.

However, things slowly started to move, the transmitters arrived and were speedily installed by the Swedish engineer. Consulting engineers had been and gone several times, and the radio masts were extended. Power supply was a big problem. Electricity was in such short supply aboard that the electric stove had to be turned on slowly, otherwise the power supply to the whole ship - and the transmitters (which were being tested) took a sudden drop.

The *Cheeta II* was not a very stout ship, though a seaworthy one. I formed this opinion one day when sitting in the cosy little dining area as the tender came alongside.

A swell was running, as was usually the case, and the tender came heavily against the side of the ship, right where I was sitting below-decks. The wall of the room bowed in slightly as the tender struck the hull outside, and I leapt up and headed for the deck, checking safety equipment on the way.

Yet, in all seriousness, I always felt her to be a safe ship, and enjoyed a good sound sleep every night I was aboard her.

We were hardly ready for the invasion when it happened - after all, the ship was still nowhere near ready to broadcast when, one day, the tender came alongside, loaded to the gunwales with the other Caroline DJs all shouting and waving, and shattering the peaceful interlude we had been enjoying for more than a week past.

More cabins were allotted, sheets and blankets found, and I decided to go ahead with the plan I had at the time just before *Mi Amigo* went aground. After going ashore on leave shortly after this time, I resigned from Radio Caroline in the hope of working ashore, and believed (wrongly as it turned out) that I'd seen the last of the saga of pirate radio. It was quite some time after that that the *Cheeta II* first made her presence felt on the airwaves, and became an only partly successful, on-again, off-again replacement for the m.v. *Mi Amigo.*

I'll always remember those very happy evenings spent on the *Cheeta II,* with my new found Swedish friends. Those late suppers, with smorgasbrod, huge sandwiches, coffee - and listening to other radio broadcasts from all over the world on the big radio in the lounge.

She's a ghost ship now, in the Gambia River, sunk and useless. But she left a warm place in my heart, and now I understand a sailor's feeling for his ship.

In March 1966 it was learned that the Walton and Frinton lifeboat crew were to be presented with a vellum of thanks for their part in launching the lifeboat. The vellum was signed by Princess Marina, the then President of the Royal National Lifeboat Institution.

Robert Oxley, Secretary of the Walton and Frinton lifeboat, said "We were delighted by the presentation which was thoroughly deserved because on this particular night I thought the lifeboat was going to capsize."

He said in June 1966 that, in future, calls he considered irresponsible would not be answered. He said there had been several calls from pirate radio stations which could have been prevented or handled by their own tender ships. "We of the Walton lifeboat have always had good relations with Radio Caroline and Radio London, but we haven't any time for the pirates on the forts. I warned them before they went on there not to expect help unless in emergency cases. There was one occasion where they had run out of water.

We are not a taxi service. All the calls from Radio Caroline and Radio London have been genuine. You cannot have a lifeboat for commercial gain. I know some people in the Walton-on-the-Naze and Frinton-on-Sea area are saying that the money they subscribe to the RNLI is being used improperly on the pirate stations. Running errands for them could be regarded as improper use."

Robert Oxley confessed "This is not an easy matter. Should we fail to answer a call from one of the pirate ships, we might find ourselves attending an inquest. If we do answer one, we might be responding to a frivolous call. It is a catch-22 situation."

Commander Tony Wicksteed, deputy chief inspector of lifeboats for the RNLI, backed up Robert Oxley by saying "Our real function is to save lives at sea, not to run errands."

The Walton and Frinton lifeboat made its first call to the radio ships in July 1964 to take off DJ Bryan Vaughan. Other calls included 24 February 1965 to take the captain of Radio London to hospital in Clacton. A Doctor Chambers accompanied the crew ... 23 April 1965 to take Captain Buninga of Radio London to hospital in Colchester ... 20 August 1965 when Doctor Johnson went out to Radio London and took off an engineer ... and a further call to Radio London on 9 September 1965.

Walton and Frinton lifeboat visited the Sunk Head forts on 28 October 1965 and took off one man who was ill ... it went out to *Cheeta II* on 13 February 1966 to take off disc jockey Graham Webb who was suffering from a bad bout of flu.

The Walton and Frinton lifeboat towed back the *Cheeta II* speedboat which had drifted on 19 June 1966.

Another visit to the Sunk Head fort, to take out water, occurred on 9 November 1966.

The Walton and Frinton lifeboat took off four men who claimed they worked for Radio Essex on the Roughs Tower on 9 January 1967. The drama unfolded when the *Preceeder* radioed Walton coastguards that two men were flashing distress signals from the tower. Walton and Frinton lifeboat was launched on one of the coldest days for twelve months. When the lifeboat reached Roughs Tower and drew alongside, a loud hailer was used by a member of the crew to shout instructions to the men who said they wanted to be taken off. They struggled down a 15ft. rope ladder to the lifeboat. The men were frozen with cold and were hungry, having been without fuel or supplies. When they were safely aboard the lifeboat, and had been given hot drinks, they were taken to Walton Pier. They were Dick Palmer, Martin Gobal, Alistair Cheale and Ian Stroud. Disc jockey Dick Palmer said "We were expecting a relief party, but our wireless had packed up so we had to call for help. We were frozen."

On 26 May 1967 a 61-year-old Dutch engineer, Gustav Schneider, from Amsterdam who was badly burned when a stove exploded aboard Radio Caroline, was taken ashore by the Walton and Frinton lifeboat. He had been with the ship for two years. Schneider said "The stove blew up and burned my arm. This is the second explosion I have been in." The lifeboat took the man into Walton Pier where a waiting ambulance took him to hospital in Colchester. The injured man's wife caught the night boat ferry from Holland to visit him in hospital.

The crew of the Walton and Frinton lifeboat were paid 30 shillings (£1.50) for the first two hours and then a small percentage of the rate for each subsequent hour.

Robert Oxley recalled "Every time the lifeboat was launched it cost at least £25. We used to handle between 12 and 18 calls a year, so we didn't welcome any unnecessary ones. The offshore stations were not charged for our services, though sometimes they gave donations." Radio London gave free advertising to the Royal National Lifeboat Institution flag day in March 1967. Advertisements would normally have totalled over £500.

The Rt. Hon. Douglas Jay, MP, President of the Board of Trade, awarded the shield for the Best Wreck Service of the Year, 1966, to the Walton-on-the-Naze Coastguard Rescue Company for their rescue of nine men by breeches buoy from the stranded vessel *Mi Amigo*. The shield was presented by the Chief Inspector, Commander P.J.H. Bartlett, OBE, RN (Ret) on behalf of the President, at a reception held at the Royal Albion Hotel, Walton-on-the-Naze on 23 June 1966. The trophy was received by Station Officer E.P. Shreeve. Mr Barry Ainley, a director of Radio Caroline, presented a replica of the *Mi Amigo's* bell to Eric Brett, auxiliary coastguard and No. 1 of the Walton-on-the-Naze LSA Company in recognition of the part they played in the rescue of Radio Caroline personnel. The efficiency and devotion to duty of all concerned was exemplary. Despite the bitter weather, the cheerfulness and the high morale of the coastguards were an inspiration to the many spectators, not only during the actual rescue when the incentive of lifesaving makes any effort worthwhile, but also during the long hours of standby watch, which was necessary in case the *Mi Amigo* - with its high transmitting aerial - should roll over and put the lives on those board in serious danger.

Twenty-six years later Tony Blackburn was the personality in a 1992 edition of ITV's *This is Your Life* when members of the Walton and Frinton lifeboat crew were thanked for rescuing him during the 1966 beaching of *Mi Amigo*. Says Eric Brett "The Walton lifeboat did NOT rescue them from the *Mi Amigo*. The Walton Lifesaving and Apparatus Company rescued them. True the Walton lifeboat crew did help Caroline DJs on numerous occasions between 1964 and 1967. They were invited to take part in *This is Your Life* whereas not one of the Coastguards was consulted, let alone received an invitation."

The first time a lifeboat was launched on service to a radio ship after the Marine Offences Act (1967) came into force was on 5 September 1967 when the Clacton-on-Sea lifeboat was called out to stand by the Radio Caroline South ship *Mi Amigo* when she was dragging her anchor.

Going back to the arrival of *Cheeta II* off Frinton, disc jockey Norman St. John relates:

> The ship itself was very pleasant, although I can't say the same for the time I spent there. This was brought about in the early stages by the lack of fresh water, no central heating, insufficient blankets and mainly tinned food. This was mainly because the owner, Mrs Britt Wadner, ordered the tender not to come alongside in rough weather as she was under the impression that it may have damaged the ship. The sides of the *Cheeta II* appeared to be rather thin.

> After many problems on the technical side and some rather unusual station identifications (I can remember one where I received 500 letters after insinuating that it was "Radio Posterior" ... or words to that effect!) things went fairly smoothly until the morning of 25 March 1966 when I arose at 5.30am to turn on the transmitter as our engineer was ill. After leaving my cabin which was on the top deck I went below only to find four feet of water in all the starboard side cabins. 'Funny,' I thought to myself 'We must have a leak.' I woke up our non-English speaking captain and told him we were short staffed on crew and the steward who was on night watch had fallen asleep. This, as far as the captain was concerned, was quite acceptable as we had all been working 18 hours a day.

> I then phoned through to North Foreland Radio and told them that the ship was listing badly to starboard. They put me through to Bill Scaddan who, in turn, sent out the *Offshore I* immediately. The tender arrived at around 9.00am after they had breakfast at the Radio London ship and we then were tilting some 20 degrees. Owing to our

Radio Caroline director Barry Ainley presents the Caroline Bell
award to Eric Brett of the Walton Lifesaving Company

precarious situation with the Government we were not certain what would happen to the ship should she dock. Consequently, we had to make long and somewhat involved telephone calls to the ship's owner in Stockholm, Sweden. We were now using the tender's pumps to take water from the ship to supplement the *Cheeta II*'s own installations. We decided at around 12 noon that the ship would have to go into dock and the only port where a suitable berth was available was at Lowestoft, Suffolk, some seventy miles away.

Having pumped the majority of the water out, we started the ship's engines and proceeded to the port where our estimated time of arrival was around midnight. It was a beautiful sunny day and if one could have forgotten our imminent danger it would have been very pleasant indeed!

Around 8.00pm and nearing our arrival at Lowestoft harbour the winds had risen to around force 5 and a very heavy sea was running. We radioed for the pilot who was necessary in these waters, and he said he would meet us at the entrance to the Lowestoft Channel. As the *Cheeta II* did not have a depth finder working efficiently, the tender took us in tow and, having had a line across for only five minutes, proceeded to run us straight into a reef.

The ship was now in danger of being stuck fast or possibly breaking up, so the captain gave orders to detach the line and we managed using only the *Cheeta It's* engines to get off the reef. We proceeded slowly for about two miles where the pilot was waiting. He told us that under the circumstances it would probably be best to anchor there and berth in the morning.

This we did and came in to the cheers of about 400 people and a host of television cameras, press photographers and reporters. We returned to London by train.

However, engineer Carl Thomson, who was on board, had a different account: " I seem to recall that we were towed to Lowestoft by a tug from Harwich. I think the engineers were working in the engine room when a seacock became stuck. I remember doing a round railway trip from Lowestoft to Harwich to collect my car before going home."

The team of disc jockeys involved in the Caroline beaching in January also had to go through this ordeal - Norman St. John, Tony Blackburn, Dave Lee Travis and Graham Webb.

Cheeta II went into Lowestoft harbour to the Richards Ship Builders for repairs. The manager, J. Bell, said it was almost certain that the ship would have to go into dry dock but the decision was to be made at a meeting of the owners on 28 March. From what he could see the *Cheeta II* had not suffered any serious damage.

It was later decided after a meeting with the owners to carry out only a temporary repair, and the ship returned to its original position off Frinton-on-Sea the following Thursday. She resumed transmissions on the Friday morning.

Radio Caroline's own ship, the *Mi Amigo,* returned from Holland in April and commenced by relaying the programmes from *Cheeta II* on 199 metres. Caroline officials had not been satisfied with the output on that frequency and went further up the dial experimenting with various frequencies. The best quality of signal and most successful reception reports came from an experiment carried out on 259 metres. This was a very clever move on the part of Caroline who positioned themselves midway between Radio London and the BBC Light Programme on the medium wave band. Caroline South remained on this frequency until she ceased broadcasting.

Cheeta II eventually closed down transmissions, but she remained anchored between Radio Caroline and Radio London until 21 July 1966 when she got carried away! Carried away as in drifting. In storm force winds, drenching rain and high seas she radioed for help after she had broken away from her moorings and started drifting towards the Gunfleet Sands. Walton and Frinton lifeboat was alerted and a tug from Felixstowe put to sea. *Cheeta II* refused the offer of assistance from the lifeboat. The tug, the *Agama,* eventually reached the radio ship which had drifted almost a mile off position and a line was put aboard and she was taken in tow. This prevented *Cheeta II* going aground on Gunfleet Sands.

Cheeta II had three crew members aboard and was towed into Harwich harbour where she anchored to two buoys in the river between Shotley and Parkeston Quay.

A few days later a warrant of arrest was tied to its mast by the Customs authorities in Harwich. The ship remained in Harwich harbour for the next five months with various rumours circulating as to its future. There was talk of Radio 390 taking it over ... but it remained at anchor, its transmitter silent.

On 23 January 1967 a second summons warrant was nailed to its mast. The ship had remained under arrest by Customs authority pending a court hearing to decide who were the owners.

The warrant was issued by solicitors of the London and East Anglia Ships Supply Company Ltd. of Harwich. The managing director, L.G. Martin, said the warrant was in respect of tender service, supplies and wages to the *Cheeta II* since August 1966 which amounted to approximately £3,000.

Waterguard officers of HM Customs served the warrant on the ship which was then moored on Harkstead Buoy in the River Stour, off Wrabness, and nailed it to the mast.

It was assumed that the owner of *Cheeta II* was Mrs Britt Wadner who lent the ship to Caroline when *Mi Amigo* had drifted in January 1966. Mrs Wadner was responsible for discharging the writ for salvage taken out against the ship by Gaselee and Sons Ltd., tug owners of Felixstowe.

The East Anglian press reported on 27 February 1967 that *Cheeta II* left Harwich the previous day towed by a tug. The writs which had been served on the ship had been lifted. It was believed that the *Cheeta II's* destination was Flushing in Holland.

Mrs Britt Wadner died in Sweden on Friday, 13 March 1987, aged 72 years.

ROYAL NATIONAL LIFEBOAT INSTITUTION

Originally known as The Royal National Institution for the Preservation of Life from Shipwreck, the Royal National Lifeboat Institution was founded in 1824 as the first organised lifeboat service in the world, with the purpose of saving life at sea. Its function is to provide, on call, a 24-hour lifeboat service necessary to cover search and rescue requirements to 50 miles from the coasts of the United Kingdom. Today the RNLI maintains some 260 lifeboats in Britain and Ireland of which about 140 are high-speed inflatable boats. Over the years, RNLI lifeboat crews have been responsible for saving 124,799 lives (latest figure October 1993).

Each lifeboat station is organised at local level and, as on the east coast, forms the focal point of the seaside town. An honorary secretary is responsible for the authorisation of each lifeboat launch. However, every station is linked into a central headquarters of the RNLI which is located at Poole on the south coast.

The RNLI is a registered charity, and is entirely funded by voluntary contributions. The money raised goes towards designing new boats as well as purchasing, supplying and maintaining equipment. Lifeboat Day is one of the best supported charities in the United Kingdom. In addition, bequests and legacies provide a sometimes unexpected bonus.[1] In October 1993, Roy Barker, a former agricultural businessman of Grantham, left the RNLI £6,500,000 in his will - the largest single donation ever made up to that time.

The earliest mechanically propelled lifeboats were steamboats and the RNLI's first steamboat was completed in 1890. Before that rescues were carried out by oars and sail.

Radio-telephony was introduced in lifeboats in 1927. Radar was installed on a number of lifeboats in 1963. Since the Second World War we have seen echo sounders, radio direction-finding equipment and Decca navigators introduced and more modem craft include Arun, Mersey, Severn, Trent and Tyne class lifeboats.

The RNLI comprises a voluntary service of men and women who are ready and willing to put to sea to save the lives of others who live on the sea and those who sail for work or pleasure.

HM The Queen is the Patron, the current President is HRH The Duke of Kent KG and the Chairman is Michael Vernon.

BRIDLINGTON LIFEBOAT STATION

The station was established in 1806. Each year a memorial service is held in memory of the great gale at Bridlington on 10 February 1871 when 70 lives were lost and 30 ships were wrecked. The lifeboat saved the crews of three wrecked vessels consisting of 16 men. A private lifeboat, which had been presented by Count Batthyany, also helped, but on her sixth trip she capsized with the loss of six of her crew of nine.

Bridlington offshore lifeboat helped Radio 270 twice during 1967. The inshore lifeboat also helped Radio 270 once in 1967.

To date the crew of the lifeboat have won 14 medals, 11 Silver and 3 Bronze, the last being voted in 1979.

CLACTON-ON-SEA LIFEBOAT STATION

The RNLI decided to open a station at Clacton-on-Sea in 1877 at the request of local residents, and the first boat was sent in the following year. The first three lifeboats, all named *Albert Edward,* were gifts to the RNLI from the Freemasons of England, the first being presented in 1878 in commemoration of the safe return from his tour of India of their Grand Master, King Edward VIII, then the Prince of Wales.

Prior to this date lifeboatmen used their own private boats for rescues. The first Silver

1. *Lifeboats In Danger's Hour.* Patrick Howarth, Hamlyn, Feltham. 1981

medal was awarded to William Weekes for the rescue, with eight others, of the master, mate and ten seamen from the brig *Graf von Essen* on 1 December 1828.

Clacton lifeboat helped Radio London once in 1966, and again in 1967 and Radio Northsea International once in 1970.

To date 24 medals have been awarded to Clacton lifeboat personnel, 22 Silver and 2 Bronze, the last being voted in 1992.

In addition Clacton lifeboat collected awards from the French Government, the King of Denmark and the German Government.

HARWICH LIFEBOAT STATION

The station was established in 1876, after a meeting had been convened following the loss of the German steamer *Deutschland*. Following a further wreck the RNLI sent a lifeboat without waiting for the lifeboat house to be erected. This was built in 1876 at a cost of £250.

The lifeboat was launched on 19 January 1979 to rescue Radio Caroline staff aboard the *Mi Amigo* and the inshore lifeboat assisted Laser 558 on the m.v. *Communicator* on 16 January 1986.

To date Harwich lifeboat crew have been presented with 20 medals, 16 Silver and 4 Bronze, the last being voted in 1983.

MARGATE LIFEBOAT STATION

A lifeboat, *Hannah and Angela*, was given to the town in 1857 by Miss Burdett Coutts. The responsibility for the lifeboat was transferred to the RNLI in 1860.

A second station was opened in 1898. The No. 1 station was closed in 1927.

In 1940 the lifeboat, *Lord Southborough*, was one of nineteen lifeboats that went to Dunkirk on 30 May to help in the evacuation of the British Expeditionary Force and brought off some 600 men. Coxswain Edward Drake Parker was awarded the Distinguished Service Medal for his services at Dunkirk.

In 3 September 1940 Pilot Officer R.H. Hillary was rescued by Margate lifeboat. By coincidence he was a descendant of Sir W. Hillary, founder of the RNLI.

The lifeboat helped Radio Caroline twice, in 1975 and 1986.

At a special naming ceremony held on 21 May 1992, HRH Princess Alexandra named the Mersey Class lifeboat *Leonard Kent*.

To date Margate lifeboat crew have been awarded 6 medals - 5 Silver and 1 Bronze, the last being voted in 1952. In addition each crew member received a certificate awarded by the German Government when the lifeboat rendered assistance, on 19 December 1929, to the motor ship *Hermine* of Wilhelmshaven.

RAMSEY LIFEBOAT STATION

The station was established in 1829, five years after the RNLI itself was founded. The Institution took over the station in 1868. The following year the lifeboat house was constructed at a cost of £145. A new boathouse was completed in January 1991 to accommodate the station's new Mersey class lifeboat.

The lifeboat helped Radio Caroline North on four occasions in 1965/1966.

To date the crew of Ramsey lifeboat have been awarded 5 medals, 4 Silver and 1 Bronze, the last being voted in 1942. In addition, in 1937, the Finnish Government awarded a Silver medal to Coxswain Lord and Bronze medals to the rest of the crew for services rendered to the s.s. *Esbo* of Helsingfors on 19 October 1937.

SHEERNESS LIFEBOAT STATION

In 1969 the lifeboat *Ernest William and Elizabeth Ellen Hinde* was sent to Sheerness on evaluation trials and in 1970 the committee of management decided to establish Sheerness as a permanent lifeboat station.

A Silver medal of the RNLI was awarded to Coxswain/Mechanic Charles Bowry in recognition of the courage, determination and seamanship displayed by him when three disc jockeys and a Dutch crewman were rescued from the Radio Caroline ship *Mi Amigo* on 19 March 1980 during a force 9 gale in Black Deep near the Long Sand Bank. The lifeboat was manoeuvred alongside the *Mi Amigo* on 13 occasions to carry out the rescue of four Caroline staff, and a canary, in a strong easterly gale and a very rough sea. The Thanks of the RNLI inscribed on vellum was accorded to the remainder of the lifeboat's crew. Sheerness lifeboat went to the assistance of Radio Caroline on 31 January 1986. Coxswain Charles Bowry died in December 1990.

To date Sheerness lifeboat crew have been presented with 4 medals, 3 Bronze and 1 Silver, the last being voted in 1987.

SOUTHEND-ON-SEA LIFEBOAT STATION

The station was established by the RNLI in 1879 to assist the crews which may go ashore on the Nore and Leigh Middle Sands and other outlying banks at the mouth of the Thames. There were two stations between 1885 and 1891. The lifeboat station is situated on the seaward end of Southend Pier which is 1¼ miles long.

The outstanding figure in the history of the station was Sidney H.B. Page. He was a member of the crew from 1911 until 1933, was Bowman from February to December 1933, Second Coxswain from January to June 1934 and Coxswain from July 1934 to December 1955. From 1911 until 1955 the Southend lifeboat rescued 431 lives. Page won the Silver medal for gallantry, the Bronze medal twice and the Thanks of the RNLI, inscribed on vellum, four times. When he retired in 1955 he became honorary boathouse attendant. Page died in 1962, aged 71 years.

During the Second World War the *Greater London* was one of 19 lifeboats of the RNLI which went to Dunkirk at the end of May to help bring off the British Expeditionary Force. She was not manned by her own crew but was taken over by the Royal Navy and manned by naval ratings. The work of rescue at Dunkirk came to an end on 4 June 1940 and in the last hours of the evacuation, the *Greater London* saved a destroyer *HMS Kellett* at 1.30 on the morning of that day. *HMS Kellett* was trying to embark 200 French soldiers from the Mole, but some obstruction under water prevented her from coming alongside.

The harbour was then being cleared of what remained in it, and the block ships were to be sunk at its entrance. If she were not to be trapped, the destroyer had to leave at once. Her bows were touching the beach and her commander tried to put her astern, but again something under the water was in the way. One of her screws caught on it, and try as he would, he could not move her. There seemed no-one left to help him, when he saw a lifeboat pass full of soldiers. He hailed her and she hauled the destroyer off the beach. By its timely pluck at the last moment this lifeboat saved the destroyer and her crew from capture. She was the *Greater London* of Southend-on-Sea.

The lifeboat helped Radio Invicta three times in 1964.

To date Southend lifeboat crew have been awarded 12 medals - 4 Silver, 8 Bronze, the last being voted in 1982. In addition they received a letter of thanks to the crew from the German Government for help they gave to German aircraft in 1932.

WALTON and FRINTON LIFEBOAT STATION

There has been a lifeboat at Walton-on-the-Naze since 1884, when the RNLI received its first boat, paid for by the Honourable Artillery Company. There has been a lifeboat stationed at Walton-on-the-Naze ever since. The old lifeboat house, at the north of the sea front, still bears the plaque recording that the HAC were donors of that first boat.

The lifeboat, *E.M.E.D.*, which had been named by HRH the late Duke of Kent when he was Prince George, was one of nineteen boats of the RNLI which took part in the evacuation from Dunkirk in May 1940, but she was manned by naval ratings and not by her own crew.

She went over to Dunkirk in a small company of boats in tow of a tug. Off Gravelines, German fighter aircraft attacked them three times. The blast broke the tow ropes and threw men into the sea. One boat was sunk, others turned back, but the Walton and Frinton lifeboat carried on. The officer in command was killed by a shell, and the lifeboat returned to Dover with a rope around her propeller. A diver went down and cut it away, then she sailed again for Dunkirk. The crew were bitterly disappointed that they were not allowed to sail with her.

During the Second World War the Walton and Frinton lifeboat was launched on 57 occasions and rescued 20 lives.

There were two private lifeboats, both named *True to the Core* at Walton-on-the-Naze from 1894 until about 1911 (launched 35 times, saved 216 lives). From 1901 to 1917, two private lifeboats, both named *Sailor's Friend*, were in service at Frinton-on-Sea.

The first Silver medal was awarded to Coxswain Henry Britton in 1902 for gallant services as coxswain since 1884. In 1966 a Vellum of Thanks was awarded to Coxswain Frank Bloom and to each of his crew in recognition of the courage, skill and determination displayed in boarding the lifeboat in hazardous conditions to go to the assistance of the m.v. *Mi Amigo* (Radio Caroline) on 20 January 1966.

A Bronze medal was awarded to Coxswain Frank Bloom in recognition of the courage, determination and good seamanship he displayed when the lifeboat stood by the steam ship, *Ypapanti*, which had run aground on the Long Sand Head on 17 November 1966, and subsequently rescued eleven members of her crew on the 18th and landed the remaining five on the 19th. The Thanks of the RNLI inscribed on vellum were accorded to the other nine members of the lifeboat crew.

Walton and Frinton lifeboat helped Radio Caroline on seven occasions between 1964 and

Walton and Frinton lifeboat outbound from her station on the Essex coast

1985; Radio London four times in 1965; Tower Radio twice in 1965/1966; Radio England once in 1966, and rescued people off Roughs Tower (formerly Radio Essex) twice in 1967.

To date 15 medals have been awarded to Walton and Frinton lifeboat crew - 4 Silver and 11 Bronze, the last being voted in 1976.

WHITSTABLE LIFEBOAT STATION
One of the most recent lifeboat stations, established in 1963. It has received three "Thanks of the Institution" on vellum accorded to Helmsman David Victor Foreman in 1977, to Helmsman Michael A. Judge in 1981 and to Helmsman Michael Gambrill in 1986.

Whitstable lifeboat helped Radio City, on one occasion, on 2 July 1965.

A single storey extension to the side of the boathouse was constructed in 1989 to improve crew facilities.

HM COASTGUARD

The main role of HM Coastguard is to co-ordinate all civil maritime search and rescue operations around the 4,500 miles of coastline of the United Kingdom and for 1,000 miles into the North Atlantic. Part of the Marine Directorate of the Department of Transport, HM Coastguard is recognised as the most modern maritime emergency service in Europe.

The Coastguard was established in 1822 to crack down on smuggling. Saving lives was only a small part of the coastguard's job compared with saving money for the Inland Revenue. In those days fishing boats would come into harbour with brandy casks slung under their keels. Ships were found with false bows or false bottoms. Tobacco was even woven into hawsers. At the same time the early coastguards were expected to assist ships in distress and, in case of shipwreck, to do their best to save lives. From the mid-19th century, when smuggling was less widespread, the Coastguard acted as a Naval Reserve with a defence role under the control of the Admiralty. 3,000 Coastguards served during the Crimean War. Throughout the First World War most Coastguards were mobilised into the Royal Navy. They suffered extremely heavy losses.

Although it had no statutory obligation to save lives, the Coastguard took part in the rescue of nearly 20,000 people during the 50 years up to 1909. Their lifesaving equipment comprised rockets and line-throwing pistols, cork life jackets, cliff belt and helmets. HM Coastguard was eventually made responsible for lifesaving in 1923 when control passed to the Board of Trade and the structure and organisation of the present service was initiated. Coastguards officially took on their present day lifesaving role.

The Board of Trade established a civilian coastguard organisation covering the entire UK coastline. It consisted of well-manned stations at the main danger spots, stations with fewer staff at less hazardous points and auxiliary stations in other areas. The main stations were manned by regular coastguards, the auxiliary stations by the local population under the command of a responsible resident who received his instructions from the nearest regular station.

A major reorganisation of the service took place in the 1970s, creating the modern, efficient operation of today, which is responsible to the Department of Transport.

The UK is now divided into six major regions, each headed by a Regional Controller based at one of the Maritime Rescue Co-ordination Centres - Aberdeen, Yarmouth, Dover, Falmouth, Swansea, and Clyde. These regions are subdivided into districts, each with a Maritime Rescue Sub-Centre under a District Controller - Shetland, Pentland, Forth, Tyne/Tees, Humber, Thames, Solent, Portland, Brixham, Milford Haven, Holyhead, Liverpool, Belfast, Oban and Stornaway.

In a maritime emergency the Coastguard calls on and co-ordinates the appropriate facilities, such as RNLI lifeboats. Royal Air Force and Royal Navy fixed-wing aircraft, helicopters and ships, as well as merchant shipping, commercial aircraft and ferries.

LAUNCHES BY RNLI LIFEBOATS TO OFFSHORE RADIO STATIONS 1964 - 1990

Date	Lifeboat	Reason
27 July 1964	Walton and Frinton	Radio ship. Radio Caroline, landed sick man
28 September 1964	Southend-on-Sea	Radio Invicta on Red Sands Fort. Landed an injured man
7 November 1964	Southend-on-Sea	Radio Invicta, landed a sick man
21 December 1964	Southend-on-Sea	Radio Invicta, took out stores
26 December 1964	Ramsey	Radio ship. Radio Caroline, landed an injured man
27 January 1965	Ramsey	Radio ship. Radio Caroline, landed a sick man
24 February 1965	Walton and Frinton	Radio ship. Radio London, took out doctor
23 April 1965	Walton and Frinton	Radio ship. Radio London, landed a sick man
2 July 1965	Whitstable	Wireless transmitting station on fort. Radio City, gave help to sick man
20 August 1965	Walton and Frinton	Radio ship. Radio London, landed a sick man
9 September 1965	Walton and Frinton	Radio ship. Radio London, landed a sick man
28 October 1965	Walton and Frinton	Sunk Head Tower (radio station), landed a sick man
22 December 1965	Ramsey	Radio ship. Radio Caroline, took out a doctor
12 January 1966	Clacton-on-Sea	Radio ship. Radio London, stood by
13 February 1966	Walton and Frinton	Radio ship. Radio Caroline, landed a sick man
22 March 1966	Ramsey	Radio ship. Radio Caroline, landed an injured man
19 June 1966	Walton and Frinton	Speedboat from *Cheeta II*, saved boat and rescued two men.
4 September 1966	Walton and Frinton	Radio ship. Radio England, stood by
9 November 1966	Walton and Frinton	Sunk Head Tower (radio station), took off 2 men
5 January 1967	Bridlington	Radio ship. Radio 270, landed an injured man
9 January 1967	Walton and Frinton	Roughs Tower, took off 4 men
12 January 1967	Clacton	Radio ship. Radio London, stood by vessel
26 May 1967	Walton and Frinton	Radio ship. Radio Caroline, took off one crew member
27 June 1967	Walton and Frinton	Roughs Tower, trapped man taken off
15 July 1967	Bridlington inshore	Radio ship. Radio 270, took out doctor, rescued one man
15 July 1967	Bridlington offshore	Radio ship. Radio 270, landed a sick man
16 June 1970	Clacton-on-Sea	Radio ship. Radio Northsea International, landed 4 men
17 November 1975	Margate	Radio ship. Radio Caroline, landed 2 men
27 February 1977	Walton and Frinton	Radio ship. Radio Caroline, landed a sick man
29 August 1977	Walton and Frinton	Radio ship. Radio Caroline, landed a sick man
19 January 1979	Harwich	Radio ship. Radio Caroline, took off 5 men
19 March 1980	Sheerness	Radio ship, Radio Caroline, rescued 4 men
6 January 1985	Walton and Frinton	Radio ship. Radio Caroline, stood by vessel
16 January 1986	Harwich inshore	Radio ship. Laser 558, rescued 2 men, stood by vessel
31 January 1986	Sheerness	Radio ship. Radio Caroline, stood by vessel
31 January 1986	Margate	Radio ship. Radio Caroline, stood by vessel

Caroline Bell trophy to commemorate the rescue of nine men
from m.v. Mi Amigo on the night of 19 - 20 January 1966,
now on display at HM Coastguard, Walton-on-the-Naze.

The Coastguard maintains a 24-hour watch from strategic sites around the coastline of the United Kingdom. Rescue centres keep a constant radio watch on the international VHF distress frequency in addition to handling telephone, telex and facsimile messages through specially designed consoles. Each centre has a fully fitted operations room with emergency planning, press and staff facilities, along with storage for rescue equipment, vehicles and boats.

There are 500 uniformed regular officers who man the Coastguard Service. They have practical seagoing experience. There are some 4.000 auxiliary coastguards who back-up the regular officers. The auxiliaries, part-time volunteers from all walks of life, perform various duties, from radio watch to participating in Coastguard Response Teams.

Chapter Six

A DAY IN THE LIFE

It's smooth sailing,
With the highly successful sound
of Wonderful Radio London.

Radio London jingle, produced by PAMS, 1964

THE FIRST the British public knew of Radio London (also known as Big L) was when a former United States minesweeper arrived off the Kent coast near to Sheerness in November 1964. The ship was the m.v. *Galaxy* which had just sailed in from the Portuguese-administered island of Madeira where she had collected stores and oil.

The m.v. *Galaxy* was originally fitted out in Miami where a 50kW transmitter and a 212ft. high mast were installed. The aerial was 23ft. higher than Nelson's Column! She made the Atlantic crossing in October 1964 and was captained by Kou Walters, a very experienced American who had first-hand knowledge of troop ships and destroyers during the last war. During the crossing Captain Walters almost reached the point where he cut down the aerial mast as the storms were so rough.

Radio London was told by its lawyers that the *Galaxy* was, in fact, inside the Port of London Authority area of jurisdiction when anchored off Sheerness so she sailed around to the Essex coast off Frinton-on-Sea where she arrived on 5 November 1964. Her exact position was 51.00 degrees 47.90 minutes north; 00.10 degrees 20.55 minutes east.

Paul Kaye was the very first voice to be heard on Radio London both during the test transmissions and programmes proper, the latter of which got under way on 23 December. Paul commenced broadcasting by welcoming listeners to the new station: "Good morning ladies and gentlemen. This is Radio London transmitting in the medium wave band on 266 metres - 1133 kilocycles at a power of 50 kilowatts."

Pete Brady presented the first record show at 6.00am. His opening announcement was: "Radio London is now on the air with its regular broadcasting. This station will bring to Britain the very latest from Radio London's Top 40, along with up-to-date coverage of news and weather. Radio London promises you the very best in modern radio." The first record to be played on air was *I Could Easily Fall in Love With You* by Cliff Richard.

One of the most popular records during Radio London's first week of transmission was *Paper Tiger* by Sue Thompson which eventually became a minor national hit. Others included *Leader of the Pack*, The Shangri-Las, *You've Lost That Loving Feeling*, Righteous Brothers, *Do The Bird*, Rufus Thomas, and *Little GTO* by Ronny and the Daytonas. These and other records were played about twenty times a day as indeed were the 'B' sides of the discs.

The Radio London Top 40 became known as 'The Fab 40', and was generally about six weeks ahead of the national charts. Records enjoyed only a short life on air and were dropped once they had gone past their 'sell by' date. The format comprised the Radio London Top 40 (nothing at all to do with sales), new releases, LP tracks and golden oldies. There was a strict rotation to which DJs had to adhere. They had no say in the selection of music. The playlist was compiled by chief disc jockey Tony Windsor.

Looking at a very early Fab 40 chart for January 1965 we find the Top 10 as follows:

1.	Yeah Yeah	Georgie Fame
2.	Go Now	Moody Blues

3.	Girl Don't Come	Sandie Shaw
4.	I Feel Fine	The Beatles
5.	Somewhere	P.J. Proby
6.	Ferry Cross the Mersey	Gerry and the Pacemakers
7.	Terry	Twinkle
8.	Walk Tall	Val Doonican
9.	Downtown	Petula Clark
10.	Cast Your Fate to the Wind	Sounds Orchestral

Philip Birch was 37 years old when appointed managing director. He said of the initial outlay: "We started with a capital of £500,000 of which some was American money and some British. It cost £15,000 a month to run the station, plus the cost of crewing and maintaining the ship and running the tender service."

Birch had his offices at 17 Curzon Street, London, the home of Radlon (Sales) Limited which we shall be looking at a little later on in this chapter.

The team of disc jockeys, signed up by programme director Ben Toney for the early days, comprised Tony Windsor, Paul Kaye, Pete Brady, Earl Richmond, Dave Dennis and Kenny Everett. After a few weeks Dave Cash, Duncan Johnson and Ed Stewart joined the team. A complete list of disc jockeys who worked for Radio London appears on page 180. Biographies of many of them can be found in Chapter Seven.

In their spare time all the DJs listened to recordings of KLIF Radio in Dallas, Texas, on which the Radio London format was styled. The hard-sell, jargon-filled presentation of the American station was watered down to a more modified 'British' style. Even so, Radio London was still the slickest radio station in the United Kingdom.

Describing life aboard the ship in the very early days, Paul Kaye said in 1970:

Radio London suffered agonizing birth pains including a badly organised shipping service and difficulties in obtaining spares for American equipment. The food improved during 1965. We didn't have single cabins and sometimes we slept on a mattress on the bridge. Cabins were built as from March 1965 and building continued throughout the ship until May 1967.

Before we had television on board, rummy was the most popular pastime, and pure boredom during test transmissions often ended in a sing-song in which I played guitar.

Adding to the boredom and the insecure feelings of the disc jockeys who were not used to being at sea, all sorts of rumours were rife. It was believed that living within such a close proximity to the antenna, the radiation might be causing premature baldness. It was also believed that the radiation would cause sterility.

As the ship had no proper earthing it was further believed that the vessel acted as one giant cathode, and that through the process of electrolysis the hull was gradually being etched away. Everyone on board the *Galaxy* had visions of the bottom falling away and being drowned in their sleep.

The first engineers on Radio London were Belgian who had come over from the ill-fated Noordzee television station which had been beaming programmes to Holland until police took over the platform from which they were transmitting in the North Sea off the Dutch coast (see Chapter Eleven). One of the engineers, known as 'Dutch' Marak, was actually on board the platform when the station was raided by police and Customs officials on 17 December 1964. Technically Marak could have been jailed for six months should he have ever entered Holland, but it was very unlikely the sentence would have been carried out. He later went to work for RCA in Belgium.

Police asked Marak to turn off the transmitters. He replied by saying they were highly dangerous and they should do the job themselves. They refused, and Marak was asked again. However, he fooled the police by turning off the monitor sets only. The police reported back

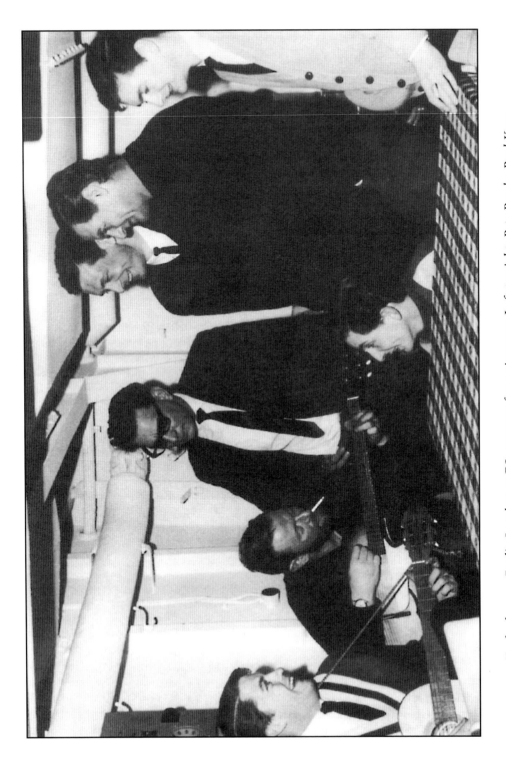

Early days on Radio London as DJs prepare for a singsong. Left to right: Pete Brady, Paul Kaye, Earl Richmond, Dave Cash (squatting), Duncan Johnson, Tony Windsor and Kenny Everett

to base that the raid had been carried out successfully. But base disagreed saying that programmes were still being transmitted. Thus Marak was forced to switch off the central control of the transmitter.

Radio London later took on English engineers, and the Belgian boys found their way onto Radio England/Britain Radio when she first commenced transmissions.

Undoubtedly the most successful disc jockey to emerge from Radio London was Kenny Everett who had no previous experience in radio before joining the station.

Paul Kaye relates the amusing story of Kenny on his first ever broadcast, alone.

It coincided with the eve of his 20th birthday on Christmas Day and, as an added birthday present, he was allowed to present a special show from 6.00 - 9.00 in the evening. This was the first time that he had been on the air 'solo.' My last piece of advice to him was not to forget the public service announcements with particular reference to drinking and driving. After playing his first record Kenny said 'If you are a motorist at a Christmas Eve party I suggest you drink, drink, drink until you can't even find your car.' That gag made us realise that we had a natural on our hands.

Representing the Radio London engineering side, David Hawkins says:

We always found that though Kenny didn't have any technical training he was interested in both the operation and theory of operation of all electronic equipment on the ship. In fact sometimes his questioning was so detailed that it made us refer to our text books.

The Radio London transmitter was reported to have given a range of 250 miles and covered an area in which 37 million people lived. The station broadcast Top 40 pop records from 6.00am until 9.00pm. It had news and weather reports every hour.

In January 1965, after the Government made one of its many threats to 'kill off the pirates,' managing director Philip Birch added "We do not anticipate being forced off the air for a long time in spite of the declaration of the Council of Europe. We have our own way of keeping going."

The programme director for the station during its first two years was Ben Toney, a Texan, who had first class knowledge of American stations. He had also been at sea for many years and at one time served with the USS *St. Paul*. He was aboard the *Galaxy* when she sailed across the Atlantic in 1964 helping out with the navigation. Alan Keen replaced Ben Toney as programme director in 1966.

Chief disc jockey was Australian Tony Windsor, a personality famed for his sincerity and his greeting "Hello." He remained with Radio London from November 1964 until February 1967 when he left the ship and joined Radio 355. His position on board was taken over by Ed Stewart.

During the early days of Radio London, visitors to the *Galaxy* were few and far between, normally members of the press. *Daily Mirror* reporter Clifford Davis, describing his visit to the ship in January 1965, said:

Below deck the quarters are cramped with little comfort. Steel walls are painted white and battleship grey. There's a smell of damp seaweed. The men sleep in bunks, two to a cabin. Wash basins are rusty, the showers primitive. There are no baths.

Not everyone could be a disc jockey at sea. Many people who went out to visit the *Galaxy* were sick on the tender taking them from Harwich or Felixstowe. That was through spending one hour at sea. Disc jockeys spent 340 hours at a stretch in the North Sea which was no joke during rough weather. *Daily Mail* columnist Olga Franklin was seasick just looking at Radio London. She recalls:

Actually I never got as far as seeing round the ship because by the time we reached it, our tender was thrown smack against Radio London's side. I don't remember after that.

Galaxy, Radio London, anchored off the Essex coast

When I woke up we were back in Harwich.

In May 1965 Radio London extended their programmes from 5.30am until 2.00am the following day. Many factories in the east of England piped Radio London programmes around their works. The Post Office jumped in and said: "We have ordered firms not to relay programmes from pirate ships. Under the terms of the licence, relay companies must only provide subscribers from the BBC and other authorised radio stations."

In a National Opinion Poll taken in July 1965, Radio London appeared to be well ahead of Radio Caroline South. During the peak listening time of 12.30pm - 1.00pm an average of 1,630,000 people listened to London, whereas only 500,000 tuned into Caroline.

Radio London's audience was drawn from two age groups, 12 to 15 and 25 to 34 whereas those between 16 and 24 preferred Radio Caroline. In a straight battle between London and Caroline South, Radio London won hands down with an average of 1½ million listeners to Caroline South's half million. In East Anglia, where both stations were received at top strength, London claimed 50.9% of listeners to Caroline's 26.7%.

On board the *Galaxy*, which was anchored 3½ miles off Frinton-on-Sea, Essex, there were 22 men who controlled the ship for twenty-four hours a day. She had a Dutch captain and a crew of 12 who worked three weeks on board and a week in Holland. British disc jockeys and engineers worked two weeks on board with a week in London.

The m.v. *Galaxy* (gross tonnage 780 tons - dead weight 1,100 tons) was originally a United States minesweeper. She was 180ft. in length and 33ft. wide.

As Radio London she comprised a flying bridge, the bridge deck, the main deck and the studio deck. Although the flying bridge was not used (except for sunbathing and for housing television receiver aerials) this part of the ship was used in wartime as a ranging and plotting station for the guns and attack weapons.

The wheelhouse was situated on the bridge deck and contained the steering gear, compass and the main controls, all of which were kept in working order and checked every day. There was a Decca navigator and an echo-sounder with three gyro repeaters.

Also on the bridge deck was the newsroom and stationery (which was also stationary except in rough weather) office originally used in wartime days as the radar room. In 1967 the radar plotting chart was still intact.

News director was Paul Kaye. Commenting on why a Top 40 pop music station broadcast news, he said:

> Radio London decided to embark on a news service at half past every hour, firstly because it is a known fact that listeners who hear nothing but music acquire a guilt complex at not being well informed, and secondly, that they might decide to seek this information from other sources - namely the BBC Light Programme.

Radio London was the first station to incorporate news in their schedules which was later followed by Radio Caroline and Radio 390.

On the bridge deck was the radio telephone which was only allowed to be used by the captain in cases of emergency and not for radio work.

One deck below was the boat deck where the captain had his cabin and office as did the chief engineer and mate.

Outside on the boat deck was the anchor winch, two life rafts and an electric derrick.

The *Galaxy* had two anchors attached to the anchor hawse, one of which weighed one-and-a-half tons, the other, one ton. In addition, and resting on the sea bed, was a pair of three ton anchors which were attached by two swivels and one anchor chain to the ship which moved on the swivel with the tide usually twice a day.

Descending the companionway, one came to the main deck. Here was the fo'c's'le which housed a lot of the ship's gear like paint, wires and ropes.

There were two messes - one for disc jockeys and engineers and the other for the Dutch crew. The captain, chief engineer and mate used the DJs' mess which, during wartime days, was the wardroom.

The galley used to be all electric with a steam boiler, but during the offshore era it had an oil stove. Normally one cook (sometimes there were two) was responsible for the welfare of twenty two men, English and Dutch, which was a difficult job. Jan Visser (christened 'Pancake' for his perpetual love of making pancakes) was the regular Radio London cook assisted by Bill Oudenhoven.

The showers and toilets ran adjacent to the galley. Towards the stern of the *Galaxy* was the transmitter room which housed the RCA 50 kilowatt BTA 50H set which employed phase to amplitude modulation on a frequency of 1137.5 kilocycles. The original frequency was 1133 kilocycles. Many frequencies had been tried over the operational life of Radio London including 1115 kc/s, 1124 kc/s and 1139 k/cs, but all produced heterodyne interference with other European stations, in some cases those from behind the Iron Curtain.

Radio London's standby transmitter was an RCA BTA IOJ 10 kilowatt set which again employed phase to amplitude modulation. Both Ampliphase transmitters gave excellent linearity and were quite reliable in service.

The aerial was shunt-fed through a series capacitor, and at 1137.5 kilocycles, the impedance was approximately 35 ohms.

On numerous occasions the Postmaster-General accused all offshore stations of stealing wavelengths belonging to other countries. The wavelengths are divided between the countries of Europe by international agreement which the British Government has endorsed. The Postmaster-General stated that the pirates caused serious interference on the Continent and listeners there could not hear their own stations clearly. Did Radio London interfere with Continental stations, and furthermore, did she just steal her wavelength of '266' metres (113.5 kHz) without thinking? Mike Howell, chief engineer in charge of the transmitters aboard Radio London, said in 1967:

> There was certainly no question of any offshore radio station taking a frequency without thinking. A great deal of investigation is needed to find a good transmission frequency in the medium waveband, grossly overcrowded as it is. Unfortunately, there are overwhelming technical and other reasons why the long wave and VHF are unsuitable for a ship-borne station, and so we were forced to find some kind of space on the medium waveband.
>
> While it is true that the frequencies used by the offshore stations were not allocated by any international agreement (e.g. Copenhagen Plan 1948) it is only fair to point out that this applies also to several hundred so-called 'authorised' land-based stations which have started up or moved frequency without consultation with other countries. Great care was taken to ensure that the transmissions from Radio London caused no interference with any other service - especially the international distress channels, essential to safety at sea, in which we ourselves, after all, had considerable interest!

Also on the main deck, apart from the transmitter room, galley, messes, showers and fo'c's'le that have already been mentioned, were the disc jockeys' and British engineers' cabins. The majority were built between 1965 and 1967 by Karel van Aken, the ship's carpenter. He was assisted for part of the time by Leo Schuitema. In some cases cabins had twin berths, in others they were single.

The Dutch engineers had their workshop on the main deck, and there was also the hot water boiler which gave constant hot water for twenty four hours. The linen cupboard was situated next to the boiler room.

Each of the messes had a television set which could pick up transmissions from BBC and ITV (Anglia). Television played a large part in the off-duty hours of the disc jockeys, engineers and crew members.

Descending from the main deck one came to the studio deck. Here was the high tension transformer with a potential of 15,000 volts. On one side of the transformer were the engineers' stores, and on the other side the main record library which housed about 5,000 single records and 500 LPs.

Aft of the library were the studios. When transmissions first commenced in December 1964, Radio London operated from a single studio comprising two 16-inch Gates turntables, three RCA cartridge machines, an Ampex tape recorder and a Scully tape reproducer. Mixing facilities were provided by an RCA four channel mixer.

In the spring of 1966 engineer Martin Newton built an additional studio incorporating a ten channel mixing console with quadrant faders.

Three turntables were provided together with three cartridge machines, a Scully tape reproducer and an Ampex recording machine. An AKG microphone and a Grampian artificial reverberation unit completed the new installation. The studio output was fed via a Gates limiter to the transmitter.

In February 1967 it was decided to rebuild the original studio which was then being used for recording purposes and standby only. By May this studio had been smartly reconstructed using the same basic components but with the addition of a jack field and some extra facilities. The work was done under the supervision of Mike Howell, assisted by Russell Tollerfield and David Hawkins. Mike Howell died in 1991.

Behind the studios was the remainder of the ship's steering gear which was attached to the rudders which, in turn, was synchronised to the bridge.

In the forward part of the studio deck were the Dutch crew quarters. What used to be the ammunition stores during the last war had been converted and seven new cabins built.

Further below these, there were the bunker tanks and finally the propeller shaft. Here also were the ship's engines. In the forward engine room there was a 900 horsepower Cooper-Bessemer engine, along with a Fairbanks and Cummins generator.

In the aft engine room there was another Cooper-Bessemer (900hp) engine with General Motors and Cummins generators. In theory any of these generators could provide either the transmitter or ship's power, but in practice the transmitter was powered by either the General Motors or 175kW Cummins, but latterly following the acquisition of a deck-mounted 270kW Rolls Royce generator in August 1966, these reverted to standby.

Obviously when a ship is anchored at one point for over two years a large number of barnacles and cockleshells accumulate on the parts of the ship underwater. Divers visited the m.v. *Galaxy* at regular intervals, and in July 1967 Bill and John Milner of Felixstowe made an investigation underwater. They reported that there were at least five inches of cockleshells attached to the propellers and rudders. Cockleshells had also become attached to the eleven intakes for generators. A fishing line, with four inches of cockleshells clinging to it, had wound itself around the propeller. The divers faced the unenviable task of removing the accumulated cockleshells and tangled fishing line from the twin propellers and twin rudder blades which took them four hours. The keel of the ship was about 35ft. from the sand bed.

That just about completes the tour of the m.v. *Galaxy* both above and below water, as she was with Radio London, except to mention that about £650 a month was spent on food, the captain, assisted by the chief cook, being responsible for ordering provisions.

The *Galaxy* was not exactly a steel Alcatraz, but at the same time she had a long way to go to compete with the plush and roomy Broadcasting House of the BBC in London which, from the air, resembles a larger version of the Radio London ship.

The former minesweeper, which was registered in Honduras, consumed 1½ tons of diesel fuel and four tons of water daily. The maintenance of the ship was carried out by Dutch crewmen. Electricity on the *Galaxy* was 115 volts 60 cycles AC.

The regular captain of the *Galaxy* was Bill Buninga who had a colourful past as a seaman. He started with Shell Tankers in 1933 and was a chief officer until 1939, the outbreak of war. He was involved in the Battle of the Atlantic and was torpedoed by a German cruiser. Thirty

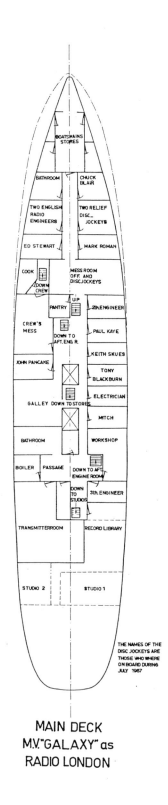

MAIN DECK
M.V. "GALAXY" as
RADIO LONDON

Plan of Main Deck of the Galaxy as Radio London.
The names of the disc jockeys were on board, July 1967

seven of the crew were lost, but Buninga managed to get to Penzance. He saw, and took part in, the invasion of North Africa and was chief officer of the *Antonio,* a supply ship for the 8th Army. Sir Winston Churchill, remembering the ship in one of his books, describes her as the "Old Dependable."

Buninga was made a captain with Shell Tankers in 1949 and he remained with them until 1962, then returned to Holland to be with his family in Soest. He travelled to all parts of the world including Hawaii, the Black Sea, Singapore, Hong Kong, the United States and South America.

Captain Buninga took a break from the sea and joined the Dutch Government as a motor vehicle examiner for three months. But he longed for the sea, and decided to return. He became a captain of a Dutch tanker for two years travelling to Japan and back.

Bill Buninga then joined the company of Wijsmuller for whom he sailed ships all over the world. Following this he joined Wijsmuller's sister company. The Offshore Company, before taking over as captain of Radio Caroline North off the Isle of Man for three months and then Radio Caroline South, as well as serving as captain of the tender *Offshore I.* In October 1965 he became captain of Radio London. His shift meant he worked three weeks on board with a week in Holland. Married in 1929 to Marie de Kreuk, Captain Buninga had three sons. One was an engineer, the other two were at school at the time.

In his spare time he is a great collector of guns and lists as one of his favourite hobbies "dabbling with electric trains."

Captain Buninga's most memorable occasion on Radio London was at Christmas time 1966 when he was presented with a suede jacket by the disc jockeys. "It was totally unexpected but warmly appreciated," he said at the time.

When he was on leave in Holland his place was taken by Acting Captain Wilhelm Theodoor Angenent who was born in Bandung. Indonesia. He moved to Holland in 1952. His life at sea was spent mainly sailing on deep sea ships travelling to the Mediterranean, West Africa, northern Europe and the British Isles. He died in 1993.

An interesting 'find' occurred on board the *Galaxy* in October 1966 when carpenter Karel van Aken was stripping one of the 'original' wartime cabins in the officers' quarters, then used by disc jockeys. As he was pulling down one of the wooden wallside lockers he found some old papers which, in fact, turned out to be a *Time* magazine for 12 February 1945, a Christmas card and a photograph.

The Christmas card came from Valerie and was addressed to Lieut. Alex L. Curtis, U.S.S. *Density* (AM 218), c/o Fleet Post Office, San Francisco, California. It carried an Atlanta postmark for 10.00pm, 13 December 1945.

Dear Alex,

Aunt Mac told me that she had heard from you recently.
She gave me your address so I wanted to send you a Christmas card. I hope that by this time next Christmas you will be back in your home. Come to see us and bring your wife.

Sincerely,

Valerie Wise.

When the author's cabin was being rebuilt an old Incoming Mail Log for February 1946 was found which contained such entries as:-

1st February 1946. Pamphlet on Japanese Warships that have been sunk.
7th February 1946. Deutschendorff. Paul Joseph, Cox, U.S.N. request for discharge. Disapproved.
13th February 1946. Transfer to shore duty. Request from Chief Mach. J.D.

Owen, 364792 via C.O.M.M.
18th February 1946. Cukmore, James Wilburn, Fie U.S.N.-l (SA) request for discharge. Disapproved.
18th February 1946. Copy of orders for Lt.(jg) Paul A. Drummond D.(L) U.S.N.R. 369618.
20th February 1946. Lt. Walter A. Smith Jnr, 194155, D.U.S.N.R. Release from active duty. Order for.

Apparently when Radio London first took over the *Galaxy* many old books, papers and records were found but thrown overboard, and the aforementioned items were the only ones still available, with the exception of the *Time* magazine dated 12 February 1945 which carried a picture of the Nazi leader Himmler on the front cover.

There was an interesting coincidence in that the magazine contained an article about victory in Manila during World War II, and the day the *Time* magazine was found President Lyndon Johnson had visited the same city on 30 October 1966.

In the news from England section we read:

> In London last week a Liberal Party Conference called to draft election plans produced two assets that Liberals badly needed - a policy and a personality. The Policy included the Beveridge plan for full employment; and a housing programme calling for 750,000 new houses a year for five years.

The personality was Lady Violet Bonham Carter, then aged 57, the brilliant daughter of the late great Liberal Prime Minister, Herbert Asquith.

An amusing paragraph was contained in the section of *Time* magazine referred to as 'Under Milestones.'

> Lois de Fee, 25, 1801b. towering (6ft. 2ins.) Amazon, one time night club bouncer, and Lieut, Hugh M. Roper, A.A.F., 23, - she was to be married for the fourth time - he for the first in Annapolis, Md. Pleasantly vague about her three previous husbands (including a midget), she is certain that this time her husband is taller (6ft. 3ins.) than she is.

New films for release that week included *Tonight and Every Night* starring Rita Hayworth and *Hangover Square* with George Saunders.

The m.v. *Galaxy* was formerly the USS *Density* (AM 218). Her keel was laid on 27 October 1943. Built by the Tampa Shipbuilding Company in Florida, she was launched on 6 February 1944. *Density* was sponsored by Miss M. Farmward for $3,000,000 and was commissioned on 15 June 1944. Lieutenant Commander R. R. Forrester Jnr, USNR, was in command.

Density (an "Admirable' class steel-hulled minesweeper) arrived at San Diego on 23 September 1944 to serve as a training ship for the Small Craft Training Centre at Terminal Island, until 2 February 1945, when she sailed for Pearl Harbour and Utithi.

As background information as to why *Density* sailed to Pearl Harbour it should be remembered that the Japanese made a surprise attack on the main United States naval base at Pearl Harbour in Hawaii on 7 December 1941, which in turn brought America into World War II. 353 Japanese carrier-borne aircraft, from a fleet which had secretly left the Kurile Islands twelve days previously, attacked the anchorage without a declaration of war. Ninety four ships of the US Navy were anchored in the harbour. The attack began shortly before 8.00am and was over in two hours. 2,400 Americans had lost their lives, another 2,000 were injured and most of the American fleet destroyed or damaged. Fortunately for the Americans there were no US aircraft carriers in port at the time. America declared war on Japan the following day. By March 1942. Japan had conquered Hong Kong, Siam (Thailand) and Malaya (Malaysia); the Dutch East Indies, the Philippines, the Andamans and Burma were later overrun.

Density sortied from Utithi on 19 March 1945 to sweep mines preparatory to the invasion of Okinawa, the largest and most important of the Ryukyu Islands some 330 miles (531 kilometres) SSW of Kyushu, Japan, on 1 April. Okinawa was the scene of bitter fighting between American and Japanese forces in 1945. Patrolling off Okinawa for its capture and occupation, *Density* fired on the enemy during several Japanese suicide attacks. On 6 April she splashed several of the huge *kamikaze* force which struck the fleet, then assisted *Rodman* (DMS 21) picking up 16 of her survivors and towing her to Kerama Retto. On 22 April she splashed an enemy attacker which cleared her bridge by only 10ft., then rescued three survivors from the stricken *Isherwood* (DD 520) before resuming her patrol. Five days later she recovered the body of an enemy officer from a plane she had downed and thus obtained valuable intelligence material including a secret codebook and photographs. Whilst sweeping mines she sank an enemy suicide boat off Naha (capital of Okinawa) on 4 May.[1]

Density sailed from Okinawa on 4 July to join a group of minesweepers supporting the 3rd Fleet strikes against the Japanese homeland. From 9-28 August she was in San Pedro Bay, Leyte, in the Philippines, for brief overhaul, and on 8 September put out from Okinawa to sweep mines in Japanese waters. She remained in the Far East on occupation duty until 20 November when she sailed for the West Coast, arriving at San Diego on 19 December. On 29 January 1946 she reached Galveston, Texas, to provide services to the reserve fleet at Orange, Texas, and was placed in commission on reserve on 14 May 1946. *Density* was decommissioned on 3 March 1947.

The minesweeper received three battle stars for World War II service. She was reclassified MSF 218 on 7 February 1955, and later sold to a Greek company as a cargo ship and renamed *Manoula*.

Line drawing depicting USS Density, during World War II, on patrol off the Pacific island of Okinawa, the scene of bitter fighting in 1945

1. *Dictionary of American Naval Fighting Ships Volume II,* 1963. Navy Department, Naval History Division, Washington. USA, pp 262-262

By August 1964 she had been sold for $80,000 to Americans Don Pierson and Tom Danaher who wanted to operate her as a radio ship off the English coast. The ship was converted, with the installation of RCA equipment, for $350,000. In the planning stage the radio station was to be called either Radio Galaxy, a name thought up by Philip Birch, or KLIF after the Texas radio station on which Big L was styled. This was the suggestion of Don Pierson.

By the autumn of 1964, after much debate, a decision was taken.[2] The station was to be known as 'Radio London, the Big L' and the *Density/Manoula* ship was to be renamed *Galaxy*.

There now follows a complete list of the disc jockeys who served aboard the m.v. *Galaxy* from 1964 to 1967, in the order they joined Radio London:

TONY WINDSOR
DAVE DENNIS
PAUL KAYE
KENNY EVERETT
EARL RICHMOND
PETE BRADY
DAVE CASH
DUNCAN JOHNSON
ED STEWART
JOHN SEDD
MARK ROMAN
MIKE LENNOX
JOHN EDWARD
KEITH SKUES
WILLY WALKER
ALAN WEST
GRAHAM GILL
BILL HEARNE
RICHARD WARNER
TONY BLACKBURN
CHRIS DENNING
NORMAN ST. JOHN
PETE DRUMMOND
CHUCK BLAIR
LORNE KING
JOHN PEEL
TONY BRANDON
JOHN YORK
IAN DAMON
TOMMY VANCE

Amongst the many guest artists who have visited the *Galaxy* during her stay off the Essex coast were: Gene Pitney, Spencer Davis, Marianne Faithfull, Guy Darrell, Twice As Much, Barry Benson, Geno Washington, Frank Ifield, David Garrick, Normie Rowe, Rolf Harris and P.P. Arnold.

Away from the glamour and bright lights, Marianne Faithfull donned bell-bottoms for a visit to Radio London on 12 May 1965 during which she broadcast her opinion on various pop records.

Gene Pitney, who enjoyed 21 hit records in the British charts, visited Radio London on

2. *The Wonderful Radio London Files*, Chris Elliot. 1986. Bexleyheath. Kent

Dave Dennis

Chief disc jockey Tony Windsor

Dave Cash

Ian Damon

Kenny Everett

11 June 1965. He told me: "Whilst on the ship I climbed up into the crow's-nest to take photographs. I was shown around the *Galaxy* and was interviewed on air. In all I took something like five rolls of film including shots inside DJs' cabins. It was all very interesting. It was one of the things I wanted to do whilst in Britain. They even got me sweeping the deck. It was a pretty rough day, weather-wise, but I couldn't turn down such an opportunity. I also travelled on the tender with a member of the British Royal Family. Prince Richard of Gloucester."

Pat Arnold, who was one of the backing voices on Ike and Tina Turner's *River Deep, Mountain High*, had a Top 20 hit record of her own with *The First Cut is the Deepest*. She visited Radio London in 1967. Interviewed on Classic Gold Radio by the author in April 1990, she recalled, "As an American I had heard a lot about the British pirate radio stations. They were very popular and played the records which listeners wanted to hear. I was invited out to Radio London in April 1967 to be interviewed by Tony Blackburn. The journey out to the ship on the tender was traumatic and by the time I reached Radio London I was feeling ill as the sea was very choppy. But the disc jockeys made me very welcome. Radio London certainly helped my record become a hit."

Jonathan King, who enjoyed great success with *Everyone's Gone to the Moon* in 1965, was the first pop singer to stay for a weekend and present live programmes. These two shows occurred on 8 and 9 April 1967. In his temporary cabin aboard the *Galaxy* he told me: "The pirates have given records a sense of vital importance and they pushed the whole feeling of music up and up and up. When I happened with *Moon*, I became a huge national star. Because of the excitement from the pirate radio stations who virtually discovered and pushed the record, plus the fact that pop music means a lot, national personalities were suddenly made out of ordinary people through the pop music world. The greatest thing pirate radio has done for the pop music scene is to create an atmosphere of excitement and adventure which hasn't really existed up to now. By doing all this 'out on the ocean, going up and down, struggling through enormous odds' to get music to their public, the whole music spectrum has taken on a new sort of feeling of necessity. If somebody is really prepared to go through sheer hell just to play you a Tremeloes record, then that Tremeloes record has to be a particularly important thing in your life."

Brian Poole and the Tremeloes

The Tremeloes celebrated their first time at the top of the charts on Monday 15 May 1967 by visiting the m.v. *Galaxy*. Alan Blaikley, Dave Munden, and Chip Hawkes boarded the ship armed with champagne. Unfortunately the fourth member of the group, Ricky West, was feeling under the weather so didn't make the journey out to the ship.

The Tremeloes appeared on the air and thanked Radio London for their support. Without Big L's help they would not have been No. 1 nationally on that day with the record *Silence is Golden*, written by American songwriters Bob Crewe and Bob Gaudio of the Four Seasons. The record remained at the top of the national charts in Britain for three weeks, and also reached No. 9 in the USA with big sales there and around the world. The record sold 250,000 copies in Britain and was the group's biggest hit. Their previous record was *Here Comes My Baby*, written by Cat Stevens.

On 8 June Lord and Lady Arran paid a courtesy visit to the *Galaxy*, had lunch on board with disc jockeys and later spoke to them on air. Lord Arran watched the presentation of a record programme and a news broadcast and also operated some of the controls. Before leaving the ship he told the writer:

> I had a wonderful day with my wife and was delighted to see everyone on board so very happy. I like seeing contented people in a community, and pop radio has brought a great deal of joy to many people.

Lord Arran said he had not previously formed an opinion as to what the Radio London ship would look like, but he went on to say that he was surprised how so many people could get on with each other in such small surroundings.

Radio London promoted new groups, records, songwriters and record producers and new independent record labels which emerged at the time. One such producer/songwriter was Miki Dallon: "A lot of small independents can look back to the pirates and thank them for where they are today. They were more progressive than the BBC stations at that particular time. They were always trying to find something new to identify with the public.

"When you look at the business nowadays you realise just how talented they were in picking individuals like myself, who couldn't get into the BBC at that time. Radio London, and stations like it, gave everyone a chance. I had written a song called *That's Nice* which I gave to an unknown singer called Neil Christian to record. We gave a copy of the record to Radio London. They liked it and hammered it. It made the Top 20 nationally in 1966."

Other people were also forming new companies like Denny Cordell who, with the help of music publisher David Platz of Essex Music, found an outlet for his productions:

> Decca advanced us £1,500 to make six singles for them. The last record I made under the Decca contract was *A Whiter Shade of Pale* by Procol Harum, based on *Air on a G String* by Bach. They brought me the demo. The only thing that was wrong with that demo was the time. The arrangement was already there, Matthew Fisher had done his organ bit perfectly. The words were there. There was a middle verse as well which made the record over seven minutes long. My contribution, outside getting the sounds together and reducing the overall length to under four minutes, was the suggestion that Bill Eyden, who was Georgie Fame's drummer, should play drums on the record. We used to try and crib the Stax sound. With *A Whiter Shade of Pale* I was trying to copy *When A Man Loves a Woman* by Percy Sledge.

The record was released on the newly-formed Deram label. Global sales were in excess of six million. It is a record one always associates with the watery wireless days and it remained in the British charts for 15 weeks. I never found out who the 'miller' was in the song or indeed the names of '16 vestal virgins who were leaving for the coast.' I guess the words were not important. What was created on the record was a haunting, evocative atmosphere. Each time I played that record on Big L in 1967 a tingle went down my spine. Even today when I play the record as a 'golden oldie' I become carried away listening to Keith Reid's teasing lyrics. Producer Denny Cordell went on to form his own label with artists including the Move, T-Rex and Joe Cocker.

What Becomes of the Broken Hearted was recorded by Jimmy Ruffin in the States in the summer of 1966. Jimmy looked back to his first chart success in Britain: "The song was originally down for the Spinners to record, but I convinced producer William Stevenson that I should record it. I came across to Britain to promote it. At that time I had not heard of the pirate radio stations, but then I met some of the DJs from Caroline, London and other stations, who used to play a lot of Tamla Motown records. I know they broke my record in England." The record reached the Top 10 in October 1966.

The Radio London transmitter had a power of 50 kilowatts, one of the most powerful in offshore radio. Programmes were primarily radiated to East Anglia, the Greater London area and southern England, but good reception reports were received from Cornwall, Scotland, Wales and Ireland. When darkness fell, reception appeared to improve as far as foreign listeners were concerned. Here are a selection of listeners' letters from outside England.

Kenneth J. Poole Jnr, a member of the International Radio Club of America, picked up Radio London transmissions in August 1966, eighty-eight miles south-west of Frankfurt-am-Main in Germany. His receiver was a Braun T1000. Kenneth was an airman with the United States Air Force stationed in Germany.

Hal Robie wrote from South Street, Medfield, Mass., USA, in November 1966 saying that Radio London reception was best between the hours of 21.45 to 22.00. His receiver was a Hallicrafter's S20R which he used with a Heathkit Q-Fl "Q" Multiplier. Hal used an aerial which had 20ft. of long wire running north-west to south-east and mounted 20ft. above the ground.

Robert F. Leamy Jnr picked up the opening transmissions of Radio London when he heard dogs barking (Tony Blackburn's theme tune) in October 1966. Transmissions were picked up on 1137 kilocycles in Erie, a town situated in the north-west corner of the state of Pennsylvania, midway between Cleveland, Ohio, and Buffalo, New York. Robert said that he had also picked up the BBC on 1214 kilocycles and Radio Caroline on 1520 kilocycles. Robert's receiver was a Hammarlund HQ-100 and he had a 30ft. aerial consisting of wire running from north to south.

Gregg A. Calkin of Waterloo Street, St. John, N.B., Canada, heard Radio London in November 1966 on a Hallicrafters S-108 Communications set with a 75ft. 'long-wire' aerial suspended 40ft. above ground level beaming north-east to south-west. Gregg also said that when he was in Rome during 1965 he picked up Radio London transmissions on a small portable receiver and preferred the programmes to those put out by the BBC.

Goren Eklund of Forstadsvagen, Sweden, heard Earl Richmond reading the Radio London news on 17 November 1965. Reception was good on a Japanese transistor radio.

F.N. Ham Jnr, of Pinagbarilan Street, Pasay City in the Republic of the Philippines, said he was in the Gulf of Suez, Egypt, and heard the news and weather read on the Lome King programme on 10 March 1967. This was followed by the record *Feeling Groovy* with Harpers Bizarre.

George Craibheimer of Kew Road, Mowbray, Cape Town, South Africa, heard Radio London on 17 September 1966. He picked up the signal on 1133 kilocycles with a di-pole aerial 65ft.in length, suspended 25ft. above the ground on an RCA AR 88 communications receiver.

Carl Durnavich of Riverdale, Illinois, USA, was tuning around the dial of a Hallicrafters SX-110-2 receiver which he bought for $50 and heard Radio London news and weather on 15 February 1967. His aerial was a 75ft. long wire running north to south with a lead in of 30ft., which was end-fed. Carl's call sign in America was WA9SX9.

P. Franken of St. Augustine's Road, Kimberley, South Africa, said the first time he ever picked up a pirate station was on 29 April 1966 and it was Radio London. He only heard the signal for about five minutes and then it was blotted out by a Portuguese station.

Martin Buckman, a deckhand on the P.& O. liner *Orsova*, sent the author a card on 28 February 1967 when he heard Radio London at 03.00 hours local time in Aden with fair reception.

Those were just ten of the many reception reports from overseas letters and cards received at the Radio London office.

In May 1966 an ITN film camera team came on board the *Galaxy* to film sections for the programme *Reporting '66*. Amongst those seen on the televised programme were Mike Lennox, Tony Windsor, Mark Roman, Martin Newton, Dave Hawkins, Dave Dennis and the author.

The previous September Radio London was the set for a film called *Dateline Diamonds* in which Kenny Everett, Ben Toney and Tony Windsor made brief appearances.

The Government persistently made accusations that the pirate stations were not paying royalties on records to the Performing Right Society. In fact the majority of them did.

Radio London agreed in February 1966 to pay royalties based on a percentage of advertising revenue. The sum ran into thousands of pounds and the agreement was backdated eight months. Commenting, the Performing Right Society said:-

> We oppose pirate radio broadcasts on principle because they do not come to us and ask if they may use our property - they grab it, and some come back to us and say they will make an ex-gratia payment.

The Society accepted the money however, but did not authorise use of the records or enter into a formal agreement with the pirates.

On 13 April 1966 a National Opinion Poll was published which gave Radio London a weekly audience of 10,330,000. Of the 2,360 people who replied to questions on daytime commercial radio, 20.9% had tuned into Radio London in the previous seven days compared with 15.6% for Radio Caroline; 4.2% for Radio 390 and 6.1% for Radio Scotland.

The Radio London ship was the target of some practical jokes, but surprisingly enough none actually managed to come off. They normally resulted in disappointment for the originators of the 'stunt.'

On 19 June 1966 thirty-two university students set out on a mock commando raid to capture the *Galaxy* with a small fleet of boats. The students had been planning the attack for weeks, but it ended in a flop. They congregated on the beach at midnight near Walton-on-the-Naze, dressed as commandos with blackened faces, and armed with ladders, handcuffs, torches, flares and a radio.

They put to sea in hired boats intending to board Radio London, take over the ship and broadcast publicity on behalf of the Cancer Research Fund by advertising a stock car race meeting at King's Lynn. Norfolk.

It was not long after putting to sea that the so-called commandos were in trouble. The first motor dinghy broke down near Walton Pier and the raiders had to return to shore. An outboard rubber dinghy with four men aboard ran into choppy seas and was swept out to sea until the crew of another boat managed to get a line aboard and tow the boat back to the beach. It landed about half a mile off the Naze end of Walton.

In the meantime, Station Officer Edward Shreeve, on duty at Walton Coastguard Station, spotted red parachute flares being fired about four miles off Walton-on-the-Naze, which resulted in the Walton and Frinton lifeboat being launched.

Two Swedish crew members from the Radio Caroline ship *Cheeta II*, Karl Ake Thore, chief engineer, and Cristen Rode, deck hand, were fishing from a small motorboat when the engines and steering failed. They were drifting away from the *Cheeta II* and, failing to attract attention from Radio Caroline, fired distress signals, totally unaware of the students' planned raid on Radio London. By this time one of the students' boats had reached the m.v. *Galaxy* and they climbed aboard in the early hours when most of the crew and disc jockeys were asleep. They did not succeed in getting into the radio studio.

At 6.00am the Walton and Frinton lifeboat brought the *Cheeta II* speedboat into Walton Pier where Thore and Rode were checked by a Customs officer, and then taken to the Radio Caroline ship.

On the return journey the lifeboat fetched four students, Ross Forsyth, Peter Roberts, Tony Cobb and Phil Willmot, and their craft, *Bags of Wind*, and took them to Walton Pier.

Four teenage boys on holiday at Walton-on-the-Naze took a dinghy and rode through a strong wind to Radio London on 5 August 1966. When the boys did not return, the Walton and Frinton lifeboat and a helicopter from RAF Manston, Kent, were sent to search for them, and ships in the area were asked to keep a lookout. The boys were eventually found safe on board the m.v. *Galaxy* and were taken ashore by the Walton and Frinton lifeboat.

The quartet were Robert John Hyde, and his brother, Keith, of London, Geoffrey Neale of Buntingford, Hertfordshire, and a friend.

It was the last day of their holiday and they thought it would be a clever idea to visit Radio London. They took it in turn to row and reached the ship, but when they tried to row back they could not make headway and called out to the Dutch crew on Big L for help. Members of the crew grabbed the dinghy and hauled the boys on board.

Mrs Lily Phillips, grandmother of the Hyde brothers, became worried when the boys did not return and rang Walton Coastguard who called out the Walton and Frinton lifeboat and an RAF helicopter.

The boys were taken off Radio London by the tender *Offshore I* which proceeded towards Felixstowe. The coastguards then instructed the tender to rendezvous with the lifeboat off the Naze. This was carried out and the boys were transferred to the lifeboat and delivered to Walton Pier.

At the pier the boys were met by Albert Richardson, Customs officer, and Eric Hartley, Coastguard officer, who lectured the boys on the foolhardiness of their venture!

Robert Hyde said afterwards "DJ Chris Denning asked if we would like tea or a meal, and then he showed us around the Radio London ship."

Another raid on Radio London was planned for Friday 17 March 1967. However, it went 'pear-shaped' after a group of students were rescued when a home-made raft that the boys were on got into difficulty half-a-mile from land. When the students were brought ashore at Walton-on-the-Naze they were greeted by cries of "Pity they didn't drown" and "Drop them overboard."

The coxswain of the lifeboat, Frank Bloom, said "They were crazy to attempt such a stunt. If they had travelled another mile the raft would have broken into pieces."

Car loads of male and female students, along with a 10-ton lorry with a raft balanced on the roof, had arrived on Walton beach at lunchtime. The students, who had come from Hertford College of Education, prepared to 'take over' Radio London.

Eight of the students put to sea. They were skippered by John Somers, and also on board were Bob Graham, Peter Rowe, Murray Lowe, Kevin Walsh, Mike Stephens, Alan Parker and Steve Bamber. The raft was named *Big L*.

Commenting on the so-called 'raid', the captain of Radio London, Bill Buninga, said:

If the raid was a result of further education I would suggest the students should try and study psychology. My crew are always on the look out and the students would have met with immediate action had they tried to board the *Galaxy*.

So much for the students and raids on radio ships. Turning to a more serious note - many thousands of Radio London listeners wrote to the prime minister requesting him not to ban the offshore stations, but in fact bring them on shore and make them legal. One such letter was sent to Harold Wilson from David Turtle of Fremantle Road, Belvedere, Kent, who was good enough to send the author a copy of his letter:

Dear Sir,

As a poor, underprivileged voter of this declining country, which was known as Great Britain, I feel I must take this unusual step of writing to you personally to air a small quantity of my disgust and shame of being part of what is slowly becoming a Police State and Dictatorship.

My complaint comes with regard to your amendments to the Wireless Telegraphy Act which you, I think, consider a foregone conclusion. Commercial radio is nothing new in this world and in fact commercial television has been established for many years. The offshore radio stations that we have available to us in this country have now conclusively proved that the 'establishment' is wrong. 'Auntie' is unable to cater for all tastes.

You may well look upon private enterprise as the Devil in your Godly eye, as other Socialists tend to look upon successful businessmen who, by hard work and honest competition, are able to earn a good wage.

Getting down to a few facts about commercial radio stations, what is wrong with what they are doing? They are unlicensed, so, alright, they are outside your jurisdiction; but they are using frequencies which are not being used in this part of the globe as they have no wish to cause trouble as they would prefer to be officially recognised. You hint that they pay no royalties on their records, but how can you explain that some of the stations at least are run by, or with, recording companies and that they play records in advance of their release date? That in itself must answer the question. All your objections have a good explanation, but let me ask one question - to what extent has Mr Callaghan benefited from commercial radio by all forms of direct and indirect taxation?

Leaving this particular subject, this Bill is phrased to give the Postmaster-General a *carte blanche* case to say what forms of wireless equipment can and cannot be used in this country without giving any indication as to what limitations he may have in his sweeping powers. Presumably the next step will be to say what can and cannot be received with wireless equipment.

I enclose, for your attention, a licence reminder. I intend to continue to use my wireless equipment as I see fit and intend to support commercial radio in any way possible. I see your actions as a further limitation upon free speech within this country. I wonder why you don't tear up the Magna Carta - at least then we would all know where we stand.

So far as the enclosed is concerned, I have no objection to paying my due into the Treasury, provided you are able to assure me and others that my listening pleasure and freedom will not be affected by any action that you may take.

Yours faithfully,

D.G. Turtle. (Signed)

In theory David Turtle, like any listener to offshore radio, could have received a fine of up to £50, although in practice this appears to have been kept undercover.

The majority of letters written to the prime minister on the subject of commercial radio were referred to the Post Office for action, although some people, like David, were fortunate enough to receive a reply from Downing Street thanking them for writing, but without addressing the contents of their letters.

With much criticism being levelled at the Labour Government about the banning of offshore radio, many listeners were upset about the Government's intention.

One listener, Mick Hazell of Kingston Road, Ipswich, Suffolk, looked on the light- hearted side of it, and suggested that Radio London should take over Parliament if and when they were closed down. A new Government could be formed from Big L personnel:

Prime Minister   TONY WINDSOR
Because he was the leader of the disc jockeys on Radio London for two years
Foreign Secretary   PAUL KAYE
He spoke Greek, French and Swahili
Minister of Law & Order   Marshal MIKE LENNOX
He came to England to keep the disc jockeys in order
Minister of Agriculture   DAVE DENNIS
He once worked on a farm and claimed to be an authority on pigs
Minister of Education   ED STEWART

He thought of the 'School Spot'

Minister of Health	KEITH SKUES

After his long appendix operation he knew everything about British hospitals

Minister of Food	TONY BLACKBURN

He was always referring to cheese and tomato sandwiches - in fact he lived on them

Minister of Transport	MARK ROMAN

Apart from driving fellow disc jockeys round the bend, he was reported to have owned a 1951 Bentley

Minister of Trade	NORMAN ST. JOHN

After selling Binatone radios, and racing car courses, he couldn't go wrong

Radio London listeners never missed a trick. The author remembers making a comment to the effect that he couldn't remember the first record he played on Radio London, although *Big Man* by the Four Preps was the very first he played as announcer with the British Forces Network, Germany, in 1959. A young lady, Cherry Wyborn of Gaston Bridge Road, Shepperton, Middlesex, happened to be listening and replied saying that it was *Mr Tambourine Man* recorded by the Golden Gate Strings followed by *Shotgun Wedding* by Roy C.

Quite often disc jockeys gave names over the radio following letters from listeners requesting pen pals. Sometimes this friendship went further. For example in the case of Donna Strachan of Carlton Hill, St. John's Wood, London NW8, who said:

> I met my fiancé, Phil Goodenough, through Radio London. I had a row with my boyfriend and was feeling rather upset with life, and I heard Tony Windsor mention that Phil, who was then in the Navy, wanted someone to write to him. After many letters we finally met, and it was then that we decided that we wanted to be more than pen pals. We became engaged on 22 April 1967 and plan to marry in the not too distant future.

Jean of Teesdale Court, London Road, Isleworth, answered a plea from a lonely RAF boy,

Norman St. John in Big L studio

RADIO LONDON FAB 40

Week ending 1 June 1966

Last week	This week	Title	Artist
13	1	Wild Thing	The Troggs
5	2	Love Around the World	David Bowie
10	3	Sorrow	The Merseys
8	4	Come on Home	Wayne Fontana
20	5	Hey Girl	Small Faces
7	6	I Hear Trumpets Blow	Episode Six
22	7	When a Man Loves a Woman	Percy Sledge
2	8	Shotgun Wedding	Roy C
16	9	I Love Her	Paul and Barry Ryan
1	10	Sloop John B	Beach Boys
15	1	I Come See Me	Pretty Things
18	12	How Does That Grab You Darlin'	Nancy Sinatra
24	13	Monday Monday	Mamas and Papas
29	14	I Go to Sleep	The Truth
19	15	Nothing's Too Good For My Baby	Stevie Wonder
3	16	Pretty Flamingo	Manfred Mann
17	17	Can't Live Without You	Mindbenders
-	18	Paint It Black	Rolling Stones
26	19	Strangers In the Night	Frank Sinatra
-	20	Rainy Day Women Nos 12 and 35	Bob Dylan
31	21	Promises	Ken Dodd
4	22	(You're My) Soul & Inspiration	Righteous Brothers
28	23	I Take What I Want	The Artwoods
-	24	Nothing Comes Easy	Sandie Shaw
-	25	Not Responsible	Tom Jones
-	26	Twinkie Lee	Gary Walker
32	27	Under My Thumb	Wayne Gibson
37	28	Gonna Put Some Hurt on You	Philip Goodhand-Tait
-	29	What'cha Gonna Do Now	Chris Andrews
40	30	Message to Michael	Dionne Warwick
30	31	Mother's Little Helper	Gene Latter
35	32	Sad Songs	Ed E. Lynch
-	33	Gotta Find Another Baby	Force West
9	34	Daydream	Lovin' Spoonful
-	35	Look Before You Leap	Dave Clark Five
-	36	I've Got So Used to Loving You	Marty Wilde
-	37	Love's Made a Fool of You	Bobby Fuller Four
39	38	You Can Go	Valerie Mitchell
-	39	Wonder Boy	Bruno
-	40	Stay a Little While	Barry Benson

Analysis of Radio London Fab 40: David Bowie was being played three years before he had his first national hit record. 16 of the Fab 40 for the week ending1 June1966 did not enter the national charts.

Jim in Aden, and they became engaged in July 1967.

Sheila Smith wrote to Radio London asking for a pen pal. Following the broadcast, Sheila received over a hundred replies. She met a number of the pen pals, and later married the most persistent, a Mr Landseidel, in April 1966 and went to live in Cambridge.

In August 1966 the record *Winchester Cathedral* was prominent in the Radio London Fab 40. Drummer Henry Harrison of the New Vaudeville Band recounts: "Radio London made the Geoff Stephens song, *Winchester Cathedral*, a hit. Make no mistake about that. They played it on the hour for about a week, which made it pick up sales. Then all the other radio stations played it and it went to No. 4 in the national charts the following month. It all happened so quickly. Without Radio London I doubt if it would have been a hit." The record became a monster smash in America where it became No. 1 for three weeks and was America's biggest British hit of 1966. Global sales of the record were over three million.

In the author's opinion one of the most memorable weeks of Radio London history was Christmas week 1966. Normally at Christmas married disc jockeys and engineers were allowed to spend time with their families. There was a completely different atmosphere on board. The messes were bedecked with Christmas trees, thousands of Christmas cards from listeners and countless decorations. The broadcasting side of the station still continued twenty four hours a day.

One of the highlights of the festive season was on Christmas Eve when the captain, disc jockeys and engineers went into the studio and sang Christmas carols. Then the following day there was the Christmas dinner. The author was fortunate to work over the 1966 festivities, along with fellow disc jockeys Tony Windsor, Ed Stewart, Mike Lennox, Kenny Everett and Chuck Blair, administrator Richard Swainson and engineers David Hawkins and Russell Tollerfield.

A look at the menu for Christmas day as printed by the cook.

DINNER

18.00 hrs.	Apéritif with little snack
19.00	Hors D'Oeuvre Varié - Wine
19.30	Consommé Julienne
20.00	Bouche à La Reine
20.30	Canard à l'Orange with sauce - Pommes Noiselles - Aluminettes
21.30	Orange fruit cocktail - Christmas pudding
22.00	Café - Ase Fromages - Brandy

Thee cooks, Jan Pancake and R. Verburgt, did everyone proud. On Boxing Day there was another enormous meal - Stewards Michel (Mitch) Philistin and Johannes Simonnes served up:

18.00	Apéritif
19.00	Crab Cocktail
19.30	Consommé Agnàs Sorel
20.00	Stuffed Turkey. Fried and baked potatoesToroiene
21.30	Omelette Siberienne
22.00	Café - Cognac

One wonders if the officers of the USS *Density* ate as well during the wartime.

Paul Kaye, reminiscing in 1970 about his most memorable incident with Radio London related:

Actually there were two ... one concerning the 1966 Le Mans ... the other involving the Beatles' tour of America.

Awaiting the arrival of the tender from Felixstowe. L to R: Mitch (steward), DJ Tony Blackburn, engineer Dave Hawkins, DJs Norman St. John and Mark Roman and engineer Russell Tollerfield

The 24 hour Le Mans race was undoubtedly the most exciting programme that I have done for the station. We faked the soundtrack in the studio on the *Galaxy* and we were receiving coded details of the race via a yacht's radio that shall remain nameless. The material was written by Bob Stanners in such a way that I felt I was commentating live from Le Mans.

The Beatles' tour of America was a milestone in Radio London history. Kenny Everett accompanied the Beatles in the autumn of 1966. He recorded conversations with the four Liverpool lads. Amongst the cities they visited were San Francisco, Chicago, Los Angeles, Dallas, New York, and Toronto, Canada.

I was the link man in Harwich and we had Beatle records to make up a fortnight's programmes. They were broadcast each evening and were thirty minutes in duration. I spoke to Kenny in America every night.

During its stay in the North Sea the m.v. *Galaxy* was serviced by the *Offshore I* and *II* who were based in the ports of Harwich and Felixstowe. The tugs *Ocean Cock* and *Agama* also helped out on occasions. When Radio London first came on the scene in December 1964, disc jockeys and engineers boarded the tug *The Hooligan* and sometimes *The Rana* in Ipswich, a rather long and tedious journey out to the *Galaxy*. The port of embarkation was changed to Harwich in 1965 and Felixstowe in 1966.

Once on board, the disc jockey received maximum exposure and far more than he could possibly hope for had he been legal. Let us compare a legal disc jockey who may have presented two BBC programmes a week … a forty-five minute *Midday Spin* and a *Late Night* programme lasting two hours. The disc jockey may also have been fortunate to present three separate quarter-hour programmes on Radio Luxembourg. This would bring his total air time each week to 3½ hours. This would be very good exposure! It would be highly unlikely that the DJ retained his programme for four broadcasting quarters, but we'll be generous and give him the benefit of the doubt. This would give him exposure totalling 182 hours a year. Now, compare this to a pirate disc jockey who would probably have a three hour disc show, also read half a dozen news broadcasts and, in addition, 'sit in' on someone else's show for three hours a day. But this time we'll be hard to the offshore boy and just allow him three hours a day, spending two weeks at sea followed by a week's leave. This would give him 21 'air' hours a week; 1092 per 52 weeks, but he's only at sea for eight out of the twelve months. This reduces his total to 756 hours a year. During his stay with offshore radio the author boasts that he clocked up 2,500 'air' hours.

Arriving at the Galaxy, August 1966, aboard Offshore I for crew changeover

One of the most colourful characters aboard Radio London was Mitch, the abbreviated name for Michel Philistin, a Haitian, who was then 22 years old. He came over on the *Galaxy* from Miami, and was the original crew member.

Mitch, who was the *Galaxy's* steward, recalls that his most memorable moment on board was the trip from Miami in October 1964 when the weather was so bad that he, and everyone on board, was very sick, even Captain Kou Walters. There was no hot water on board and the ship was in a very dirty state.

When he arrived in sight of Britain, Mitch could speak no English at all, but mastered the language in under two years. He appeared on the air in *Coffee Break* many times and received a lot of fan mail which he religiously answered.

One of his fans was Barbara Hadler of Sittingbourne, Kent, who was a firm follower of pirate radio from the beginning. She knew all the disc jockeys by name, and almost everything about them. In November 1966 she sent the author the following - a sort of listeners' popularity poll ...

Most perfect	Paul Kaye
Most successful combination of facts and humour	Keith Skues
Most dramatic	Dave Dennis
Most casual	Pete Drummond
Most happy	Tony Blackburn
Most successful combination of facts and mistakes	Norman St. John
Most speedy	Ed Stewart
Most slow	Tony Windsor

In September 1966 I developed appendicitis whilst on board the *Galaxy* and had to be taken ashore by the tender *Offshore I*. I was admitted to hospital at Heath Road, Ipswich, but later transferred to Foxhall Hospital, Ipswich. The incident caused interest both among the press and with listeners.

This inspired Barbara Hadler, of Sittingboume, Kent to pen the following poem as a get well message to the author.

APPENDECTOMY - No. 6589
or
HOW TO SPEND THE SUMMER WITH A GRUMBLING APPENDIX AND TEN
THOUSAND GOOD WISHES

One grim day back in July
D.J. Keith Skues, said "Goodbye."
He had the dreaded cardboard grott
Carry on? - he really could not.

Viewers noted his faltering word
That last morning he was heard.
The irrepressible Cardboard Shoe
Had, at last, met his Waterloo.
The sky was grey, the seas were rough
When the tender came to take him off.
He felt so ill he didn't care -
A last pale grin was all he could spare.

Another day or three went past,
Then news of Skues came through, at last.
Suspected Appendicitis, they said -
He was now tucked up in a hospital bed.

Mrs Women and Viewers, too
All decided what they would do,
If they couldn't visit him, they would send
Letters and cards and gifts, without end.

Daily bulletins were announced on the air -
All his agonies we could share.
Then, surprisingly, word had come,
The hospital had sent him home.

Alas, he wasn't well again -
We'd wait for his return, in vain.
Complications meant he'd have to wait,
They would operate on a later date.

The weeks passed by, so slowly now,
Big L just wasn't the same, somehow.
They call him the dreaded Skues, and yet
He's the kind of person you can't forget.

No messages came for quite a while,
And then something happened to make us smile.
Norman had been to see Keith, to make
A recording we heard during "Coffee Break."

Well, another week or two went past.
And then we got the news, at last.
An operation for Keith was due,
And soon he'd feel as good as new.

A jubilant Big L Dee-Jay
Announced to all the world next day -
"The appendectomy was a great success,
We'll have Keith back in a month or less."

Just another few weeks wouldn't be so bad,
All his listeners were, at last, so glad -
To know their beloved Cardboard Shoes
Would return to his show and read the news.

So now, as the longed-for date grows near,
We listen, with bated breath, to hear -
The words, guaranteed to dispel the blues,
"Hi there, Viewers - It's me, Keith Skues."

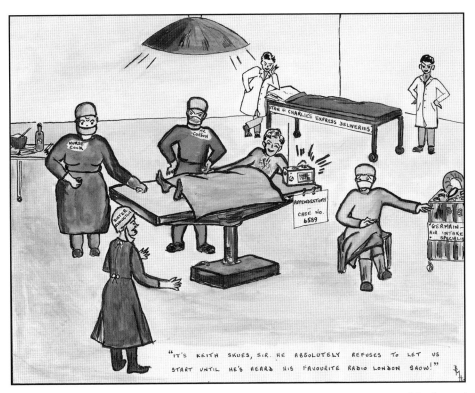

It's Keith Skues Sir! He absolutely refuses to let us start the operation until he hears his favourite Radio London show. illustration by Barbara M. Hadler.

In addition to the previous poem, I received from another listener, Barbara Apostolides, of Rush Green in Essex the following:

As the 'Most Dishonourable Member of the Cardboard Shoe'
I feel there's something I ought to do.
And that's to say (from the 'viewers' and me)
"How dare you nearly get buried at sea?"
You could get the scourge of the 'Dreaded Knees'
Or the 'Glockenspiel Grott' ... whichever you please.
'Fantasmaritis' ... which is caused by leaping.
Or the 'Or something' disease, would be more in keeping.

When you gotta go ... you gotta go,
It comes to us all in the end ... you know.
But appendicitis ... come off it Skues.
It's far too normal ... for the 'Dreaded Skues.'

One wonders, if there had been some competition for the best poems, whether either of those would have won awards. However, some awards that were announced in February 1967 were the *Disc and Music Echo* Valentine's Day presentations in which Kenny Everett was voted 5th most popular disc jockey in Britain and Tony Blackburn, 8th.

For programmes, Radio London took third place with the *Fab 40 Show* followed by the *Kenny Everett Show* in slot No. 8. Radio London was ahead of all the other offshore stations in the entire poll.

During the past few pages we have had a good look around the *Galaxy* to find out what life was like on board. We have met some of the personalities who kept Radio London working like clockwork at sea.

But where did the idea of Radio London originate? The answer was Eastland, Texas, USA, where, in 1964, businessman Don Pierson. a car agency boss and owner of Abilene National Bank had been installed as mayor of the city. He had visited London on a number of occasions and noticed how dull British radio sounded in comparison to American radio. Pierson had read a newspaper article about Ronan O'Rahilly's plans to launch a commercial radio ship off the English coast. He made another visit to England and hired a light aircraft to fly over the proposed anchorage for Radio Caroline. The more he thought of it, the more he was convinced it could be a very good financial investment.

Back in the States he phoned a number of colleagues. One of the first to show interest was Mac McIlwaine from the MacIlwaine-Cadillac Company in Abilene. A meeting was arranged and a number of important people gathered around a table including McIlwaine, and Texan businessmen Tom Danaher and Jack McGothlin. Danaher owned an airport and was a car dealer in Wichita Falls; McGothlin, a Texan oil mogul.[3]

All agreed it could make a most profitable enterprise. The four contacted other colleagues. Within a short space of time seventeen shareholders, whose interests were automobiles, construction and banking, put up $1½ million (approx £½ million). The station's investors had their money in a trust fund in the Bahamas, which was free of US tax obligations.[4] This ensured enough money to purchase the radio ship and broadcasting equipment.

Pierson co-ordinated the whole project. McIlwaine was responsible for the sales organisation; McGothlin dealt with legal and financial operations and Danaher supervised the outfitting of the station's broadcasting vessel which was owned by Panavess Incorporated of Panama and purchased for £28,000.

Mac McIlwaine knew of Philip Birch who was at the time working for the J. Walter Thompson advertising agency in London. He was hired by the four Texans to set up the company. Birch's first task was to secure satisfactory office accommodation in London and by the middle of August 1964 had done so, in the heart of Mayfair, a stone's throw from Radio Caroline. 17 Curzon Street was a plush former showroom for a fashion house and its owner agreed to Birch renting it at the figure of £1,450 per annum. A bargain even in those days! There was a total space of 2,000 square feet located on the ground floor and basement.

British by birth, Philip Birch was reputed to have been the youngest commissioned officer in the Second World War. At 18 he served with the Royal West Kent Regiment. When demobbed he went to the United States of America where he took up a position with the vast J. Walter Thompson advertising agency, becoming media director in New York and Detroit.

Eleven years later Birch returned to England and became an account executive before he

---

3. *The Wonderful Radio London Files*, Chris Elliot. 1986. Bexleyheath. Kent
4. *Selling the Sixties*. Robert Chapman, Routledge, 1992, London and New York, pp 74-80

left to form various companies that looked after the interests of Radio London including Radlon (Sales) Ltd. and the Philip Birch Agency.

He now lives in the United States of America. Commenting on the offshore scene in January 1965, Philip Birch told the author:

> We are not, and have no intention of becoming, law breakers. Our aim and objective is to become a land-based station. Our commercial relations, our programme content, and our station behaviour proves we are responsible, reliable business people supplying what the public likes and wants. Offshore commercial radio has given radio a new image. For the man in the car, driving alone, and the lonely housewife, they provide constant companionship. To the teenager they mean instant 'beat' presented by a happy disc jockey with a pleasant patter which includes a package of pops and plugs.

As early as the end of September 1964, three months before the station was launched, Philip Birch had noted that the two Radio Caroline ships were taking sales orders at the rate of £500,000 a year. For his part Ronan O'Rahilly had been very aware of the speed and professionalism with which both Radio London and Radlon (Sales) Ltd had been set up. To stave off this new competition he had approached Philip Birch with a view to a merger. Birch suggested that O'Rahilly chartered the *Galaxy* for a year at a rate of £5,000 a week, plus additional payments of 5% of gross advertising revenue from combined activity exceeding £500,000 to £750,000 and 10% over that. Birch would also be general manager of Caroline Sales.[5]

Not surprisingly Ronan O'Rahilly did not go along with the idea and no more was heard of the proposed merger.

Radlon (Sales) Limited represented Radio London in Great Britain and their job was to sell 'air space.' They moved into 17 Curzon Street on 1 September 1964. Their team of personnel comprised Alan Keen, Dennis Maitland, Margaret Greville, Roger Seddon, Eddie Blackwell, Godfrey Morrow and Desmond Brown. The company (colours were red, black and white) officially opened its sales operation on 21 September 1964. A public relations campaign was handled by Patric Baker Ltd.

Prior to joining Radio London as senior sales executive in September 1964, Alan Keen spent sixteen years in the advertising profession, twelve of them with the Daily Mirror Group. He was also assistant advertising manager for *Woman's Mirror,* having studied marketing at London University Institute of Marketing. Other jobs included working in the editorial department of the *Daily Telegraph* as editorial assistant in the House of Commons press gallery, and three years in the Royal Air Force with the Air Ministry Manpower Unit carrying out time and motion study assignments.

A 'keen' (pardon the pun!) follower of modern jazz (addicted to Blossom Dearie and Bill Evans), he was appointed a director of Radlon (Sales) Limited on 1 January 1966. Alan later became programme director of Radio London.

Dennis Maitland, a former copy man for the *Daily Mail,* started his commercial life as a reporter for *Boxing News.* He later became a sales representative on the *Daily Mail* and *Daily Sketch.* Dennis was later promoted to classified manager of the *Sunday Dispatch* and from there moved to senior sales executive with *Woman.* Prior to joining Radlon (Sales) Limited in October 1964, he held a post as assistant advertising manager with *Housewife.* Dennis was appointed a director of Radlon (Sales) Limited in March 1966. He is married with two sons.

Margaret Greville was the personal secretary to the managing director, Philip Birch. Prior to this she had worked for Philip Birch at the J. Walter Thompson advertising agency. Margaret was the first secretary at Radlon (Sales) Limited.

5. *The Wonderful Radio London Files.* Chris Elliot. 1986. Bexleyheath. Kent

Above and below: The Radio London advertising rate card, effective October 1965

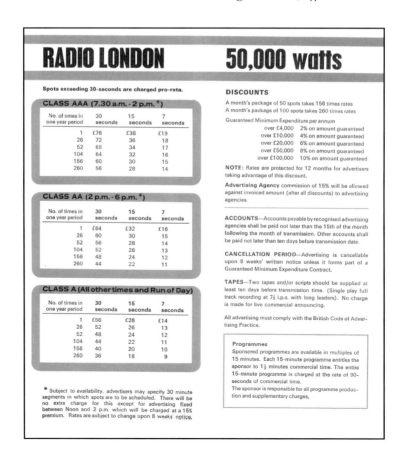

Roger Seddon was the assistant company secretary and, like Desmond Brown, was jointly responsible for public relations. He joined the staff in November 1964 as commercial controller from the sales administrative section of Educational Publicity Limited. Prior to this Roger worked in the sales promotion department in the technical and educational group of publishers, Macmillan and Co. Ltd. He joined the company in the capacity of an assistant to the advertising manager, and dealt with all aspects of design and production.

Edwin Blackwell (Eddie to his friends) was the senior sales executive of Radlon (Sales) Limited which he joined from the National Magazine Company where he had been a senior sales representative with *Good Housekeeping*. His previous experience included working in the advertisement departments of Fleetway Publications, formerly as an administrator, and then as a senior sales executive with *Woman's Mirror*. He qualified as a member of the Advertising Association in 1955. Eddie was famous for his cheery smile. A close relation who doesn't want to be identified (his wife) relates the story that he even smiles in bed when he's asleep. Eddie, a keen follower of jazz, has a son and daughter.

Godfrey Morrow was the sales executive responsible for audience research. Born into an advertising-minded family (his father and brother were both in the business), Godfrey commenced his working life as a planner and buyer with Mather and Crowther. After three years he moved to Graham and Gillies as assistant media manager in control of the planning and buying for several major accounts.

Desmond Brown was responsible for public relations with Radlon (Sales) Limited. He first entered advertising when joining Westward Television where he worked for two years. After this, Des went for a holiday in France combining work with pleasure. He stayed there six months and then joined Olympia Business Machines just prior to 'signing up' with Radlon (Sales) Limited in July 1966. He took an almost fanatical interest in pop music and listed among his favourite artists Sam and Dave, Otis Redding, Arthur Conley, Wilson Pickett and all soul recording stars.

The secretaries who worked for Radlon (Sales) Limited included Annabel, Judy, Alison, Shelly, Lynn, Margaret, Jane, Hazel, Sue and Joanna.

Commenting on the Radio London format, Alan Keen relates:

Radio London was built around 'Formula Broadcasting' which has been tried and proved all over the world. This did not mean that the station churned out records from 1 to 40 in the 'Radio London Fab 40' every day. The system worked on selected records from the hit parade, a new release, a 'revived 45,' an overseas hit and the occasional track from LPs. On the half hour there was a newscast and weather forecast and the disc jockeys gave very regular time checks.
That method of broadcasting ensured that no record was played more than once in the three-hour programme presented by the disc jockey.

Dennis Maitland gave a list of some of the companies that had advertised with Radio London:

J.S. Fry and Sons, Mars, Cadbury's, Walls Ice Cream, Rael Brook, Borough of Ramsgate, Brands Hatch Circuits, Twentieth Century Fox, Warner Brothers, Brooke Bond, Crosse and Blackwell, Findus Frozen Foods, Huntley and Palmers, Kraft Foods, Maxwell House Coffee, Meredith and Drew, Nestle, Horlicks Ltd., Lever Brothers, H.J. Heinz, Regent Petrol, Gibbs Props Limited, Beechams, Cheseborough Ponds, Firestone Tyres, Shell Mex and B.P. Limited, Colgate Palmolive, F.W. Woolworth, Richard Hudnut, The Toni Company, Gallaghers, W.D. & H.O. Wills, Lyons, Martini Rossi, Reveille, Sunday Mirror, S.C. Johnson, News of the World, Wrigleys, Old Oak, Swell Products, Binatone, Bauer, Corono, Nabisco, John West, Spedeworth, Green Shield Stamps, S. & H. Pink Stamps, Aquavelva, J. Walter Thompson, Camp Coffee, Oxo, The Cheese Bureau, Elida, Bassetts Jelly Babies, Harry Fenton, San Raphael, Peter

Left: DJ Keith Skues interviews the Everly Brothers in a laundry basket on the 7th floor of the Dorchester Hotel, London

Right: Chief DJ Tony Windsor interviews Connie Francis at a Big L Disc Night

Stuyvesant, Players Cigarettes, Trecto and Bravo.

The World Tomorrow, with Garner Ted Armstrong, broadcast seven days a week at 7.00pm, was paid for by the Worldwide Church of God of Pasadena, California. They paid £300 per half-hour show on Radio London.

The Radio London promotional activities were handled by the Philip Birch Agency and represented by Gordon Sheppard, Jimmy O'Dey, Brenda Cogdell and Lynda Kattan. Radio London promoted and covered many pop tours including The Beatles in America, The Rolling Stones, Georgie Fame and The Everly Brothers.

Motor racing played a big part in Radio London which promoted meetings at Brands Hatch and Mallory Park. At the Brands Hatch meeting in June 1966, hundreds of girls mobbed the Walker Brothers and other pop stars and disc jockeys when they spilled on to the race track while racing was still in progress. An ITV newsreel cameraman, Rowan Bulmer, was hurt when the Walker Brothers arrived by plane. Fans rushed the plane and spun the cameraman into the propeller. There were near riots in the grandstand and one girl was taken to hospital. Amongst the pop stars there were Tom Jones, Susan Maughan, Paul and Barry Ryan, David Garrick, Chris Farlowe, David Bowie, The Small Faces, Episode Six and The Pretty Things. The disc jockeys included Ed Stewart, Mike Lennox, Mark Roman, Duncan Johnson and Keith Skues.

Amongst the drivers to represent Radio London were Keith St. John, Harry Stiller and Tony Lanfranchi. Motor Racing Stables, Brands Hatch, taught novices to drive racing cars and gave them expert tuition and first-hand experience on the tracks.

Radio London was present at the 1966 and 1967 Biggin Hill Air Displays when disc jockeys Mark Roman and Tony Blackburn were in attendance.

The station was also represented at the 1967 International Racing Car Show at Olympia in January, and had a modern stand from where disc programmes were broadcast. Numerous pop stars attended and signed photographs. Over 120,000 people visited the show. The author had the honour of being resident disc jockey, helped by Brenda Cogdell and Gordon Sheppard. Other disc jockeys, Tony Blackburn, Norman St. John, Ed Stewart, Paul Kaye, Mike Lennox, Pete Drummond, Dave Cash, Chris Denning, Chuck Blair, Johnnie Walker and Bryan Vaughan also visited the show.

The pop stars to appear on stage and be interviewed included: The Action, P.P. Arnold, The Bata, Barry Benson, Bitter End Singers, Graham Bonney, The Bunch, Ray Cameron, Sonny Childe and the TNT, Neil Christian, Creation, Cymbaline, Kenny Damon, Guy Darrell, David and Jonathan, Spencer Davis, Carol Deane, Roger Dennison, Donovan, Julie Felix, Chris Farlowe, Claire Francis, Herbie Goins, Gnomes of Zurich, Jimi Hendrix, Engelbert Humperdinck, Samantha Juste, Laurie London, Merseys, Meggido Dancers, Millie, Zoot Money, Moody Blues, John Mayall's Bluesbreakers, Nashville Teens, Roy Orbison, Oscar, Peddlers, Lance Percival, Brian Poole, Duffy Power, Normie Rowe, The Riot Squad, James Royal, Marshall Scott, Nicky Scott, Helen Shapiro, The Silvera, Spellbinders, Cat Stevens, Sue and Sunny, Symbols, Mick Tinsley, Tremeloes, Tuesday's Children, Twice As Much, Geno Washington and Young Idea.

The following month Radio London was present at the Camping and Outdoor Life Exhibition at Olympia and presented a similar pop show from their stand as at the International Racing Car Show. However, after the first weekend, Brenda Cogdell walked

Presenting
BIG L NITE
at The Hermitage
All the D.J.s say this Club's
Here to Stay

RADIO LONDON
presents

Sunday 28th May
Top Radio London D.J.

Keith Skues
Pye Records, Radio, T.V.
EPISODE SIX
A Really Big Sound
plus The Spectrum

Free Membership
The Club with the Fantastic Atmosphere
Admission: Members 4/6, Guests 5/6
7.30 till 11 p.m.
Licensed Bar Every Sunday

HERMITAGE BALLROOM
HITCHIN, HERTS.
Apply NOW for your free Membership
—call, or send s.a.e.

into the Exhibition on Monday morning, 6 February 1967, to find that the studio had been broken into and all the equipment stolen comprising gramophone decks, tapes and records to approximately £1,000 in value. Detectives from Hammersmith Police Station were called in, but the equipment was never recovered.

The Philip Birch Agency also sent out disc jockeys to the regular Big L Nights, and amongst the venues at which these were staged were The Wimbledon Palais; The Carlton Ballroom, Slough; The Marquee Club, London; Pleasurama, Ramsgate; The Witchdoctor Club, Catford; Uppercut Club, Forest Gate; Starlite Ballroom, Greenford; Nautilus Club, Lowestoft; Industrial Club, Norwich; Kingsway Theatre, Hadleigh; The Rhodes Centre, Bishops Stortford; The Hermitage Club in Hitchin and many others. The agency also dealt with personal queries when an organisation like a university requested a disc jockey for a particular evening.

Radio London made regular recordings at the Marquee Club in Wardour Street, London for transmission on air. Among the artists to appear and be interviewed by Earl Richmond and Norman St. John were the Spencer Davis Group, David Bowie, David Essex, Julie Felix, The Fenmen, Harbour Lites, The Limeys, Mindbenders and Twice As Much.

Johnny Moran, who had been on Radio Luxembourg, introduced a special *Terylene Club* on 28 August 1966. He was also compère for the *Elida Show*, sponsored by Elida Hair Products. Theme music was by Acker Bilk, *The Girl with the Sun in Her Hair*. Guest artists included: The Animals, Easybeats, Fortunes, Four Pennies, Crispian St. Peters and The Who.

Harry Fenton Menswear sponsored another half hour programme during 1966 in which Johnny Moran interviewed film stars and also went to film studios at Shepperton and Pinewood and on location. Among those he interviewed included Gene Barry, Honor Blackman and Roger Moore. He visited RAF Hendon (now the RAF Museum) where the film *Dirty Dozen* was being made and interviewed Trini Lopez, Lee Marvin, Telly Savalas and Clint Walker. Johnny interviewed Susan Hampshire, Robert Morley and Cliff Richard on the set of *Finders Keepers*, and James Garner, Françoise Hardy and Eva Marie Saint in *Grand Prix*.

At the Radio London office in Curzon Street members of the public could walk in and make enquiries about disc jockeys, or see some of the products advertised on Radio London. Many joined the Big L Club.

During the summer of 1967 many young people visited the office on the first stage of their visit to Estartit on the Costa Brava, for their 'Holidays With DJs.' Radio London listeners (thanks to Big L's Gaby Collins) went on a holiday in the sun for a week which included a flight from Gatwick Airport in a Dan Air Elizabethan airliner to Perpignan in France, thence by coach to Estartit, a quaint fishing village situated at the foot of two pine-covered hills at one end of a sandy bay. There was a Radio London discotheque where they could dance from 11.00pm to 2.00am. There were numerous night clubs and, during the daytime, sunny beaches, water skiing, underwater swimming and many other attractions. Estartit possessed the rugged beauty common to all that part of the coast. The cost of the holiday was £28. Accommodation was at the Pension Montgri.

The disc jockeys who went on these 'holidays' were Ed Stewart, Mark Roman, Keith Skues, Tony Blackburn and Chuck Blair.

Radio London supported various charities; these included Oxfam, Talking Books for the Blind, Cancer Research, Polio Research, the National Institute for the Deaf, and the Royal National Lifeboat Institution.

Hundreds of pounds have been collected through listeners donating to various causes. Radio London also broadcast 'free ads' in support of walks and rag weeks when the money went to charity.

In January 1967 Paul Kaye became the first news director in commercial radio to be sent on a mission to report the Common Market negotiations between the Prime Minister, Harold Wilson, and President de Gaulle. In addition, Paul presented two disc shows, one in Lille, France, the other in Menin, Belgium. He interviewed disc jockeys from Europe

One for Radio London.

In March 1967 Big L put out the following announcement, voiced by Ed Stewart:

Radio London needs your help to put Free Radio to the public vote. For nearly three years now, Radio London has been bringing you free entertainment at no cost to you, the taxpayer. Radio London has also helped British manufacturers to sell their products at home and abroad. We have helped such organisations as The Institute for the Blind, Oxfam and the British Empire Cancer Campaign gather funds to help the people they serve.

Now, the Postmaster-General has submitted a Bill to Parliament which attempts to stop this station broadcasting by imposing sanctions against us. The PMG levels three charges:

1. We steal their copyrights. This is not true. Radio London pays full royalties for its music.

2. The PMG says we interfere with emergency services at sea, yet in nearly three years there have been close to 3,000 emergency calls around Britain but not one case of interference has occurred during that time.

Beach Boys

3. The PMG says we interfere with Continental stations. In nearly three years Radio London has yet to receive its first complaint.

Technical experts agree that Great Britain could have dozens of free stations using directional signals pointed away from Europe. Public Opinion Polls have shown that a majority of the British Public want us to continue broadcasting. We say put Free Radio to the Public Vote and we ask you to write to the Prime Minister and ask for his help. The address is: The Rt. Hon. Harold Wilson, Prime Minister, 10 Downing Street, London SW1.

All we are asking for is fair treatment. We say again, Put Free Radio to the Public Vote ... write today.

A similar message was broadcast five times a day on all offshore stations and it was the first attempt that Free Radio made in trying to influence the public at all in taking any action about the Postmaster-General's Bill. It was expected that millions of letters would arrive at No 10, but less than 10,000 were actually written, posted and delivered.

Radio London always managed to 'scoop' most other radio stations with Beatles' records. They were heard first on Radio London. In May they had a 'scoop' with *Sergeant Pepper's Lonely Hearts Club Band* and played the entire LP a week before the BBC were allowed to play the record.

Also in May, Radio London had another scoop' with the *Beach Boys' Show*, which was originally intended as a *Coffee Break* interview but ended as a full sixty minute show which had a repeat broadcast within the month by popular request from listeners. Roger Easterby of the Arthur Howes Agency which handled the tour says:

Bruce Johnston of The Beach Boys, at Ipswich railway station, on his way to Radio London. Seen with L to R: Teresa Baker, Louise Baker and Keith Skues

The Beach Boys were so knocked out by the standard of Radio London, they allowed Keith Skues every facility to record an hour's programme. The Beach Boys wanted to visit the ship, but couldn't fit a visit in during their itinerary. Instead they obtained a copy of the broadcast.

Bruce Johnston of The Beach Boys did manage to pay a visit to the *Galaxy* in August 1967.

Radio London asked National Opinion Polls to prepare a poll on commercial radio during April 1967. It proved that nearly three out of four Londoners approved of the pop stations. The figures released proved that 71 per cent said they should be allowed to continue, 17 per cent said they should be banned and the 'don't knows' totalled 12 per cent. Interviews were obtained with 2,092 electors in 100 Parliamentary constituencies.

Back to Philip Birch for a word about the organisation in London:

Radio London broadcast from off the Essex coast for over 2 years and, during that time, we never received a single complaint about interfering with foreign stations. As far as we knew there existed not one station in the world that operated on the same frequency as Radio London. The Postmaster-General accused us of interfering with shipping. During the time that we broadcast we were on a ship, behind a sandbank and a long way from the shipping lanes. We had a fine relationship with all local shipping authorities. The Postmaster-General also accused Radio London of not paying royalties. We did pay the full amount to the Performing Right Society.

The Marine, Etc. Broadcasting (Offences) Bill made it illegal for British subjects to serve on the radio ships. A disc jockey was liable to a £400 fine and/or two years imprisonment.

A disc jockey who did go to jail, but didn't stay behind bars, was John Edward who went along with singer Just Jane, and the pop group The Style, to Wandsworth Prison on 25 January 1967 to present a Radio London pop show.

Commenting afterwards, John said "It was a great show, and the prisoners made a very appreciative audience, but I wouldn't fancy being on their side of the fence."

Radio London commissioned the British Market Research Bureau Limited to compile a day-to-day listenership survey of Radio London, Radio Caroline South and Radio 355.

Data was collected by means of a diary which covered 48 quarter-hour periods, between 6.00am and 6.00pm on seven consecutive days. The diaries were mailed to 2,500 people aged 12 years and over who lived in England and Wales. The survey showed that Radio London was well in the lead of the other two stations, enjoying an approximate weekly audience of some 12,000,000.

During the weekday transmissions, *The Breakfast Show* (5.30am - 9.00am) was the most popular with the *Lunchtime Show* (12.00 noon - 3.00pm) running a close second. At the weekend the 9.00am - 12.00 noon show swept into the lead with the 12.00 noon - 3.00pm running second.

One of the most memorable days in the history of the station was 1 April 1967 when morning transmissions were interrupted by a Radio East Anglia. Listeners complained to their local GPO and many phoned the papers with the result that the story broke in nearly every national newspaper. Two of Radio London's engineers, Dave Hawkins and Ian West, pretended they were a new station operating on 267 metres with a signal so powerful that it wiped Radio London off the dial. From all the letters that people wrote, this episode proved one thing; Radio London followers were very faithful. Many wrote to the address given over the air, and tore Radio East Anglia to shreds. Of course, it was all an April Fool! I have to admit that I was 51% responsible for the hoax. Ed Stewart, who doesn't want his name mentioned, was 49% responsible as we had to interrupt his show. We both got into serious trouble with Radio London management, even to the stage where we were almost sacked!

Writing in his book *Offshore Radio* in 1975, Gerry Bishop says:

> For April Fool's Day 1967 a hoax was devised which would involve the aid of Radio Caroline DJs, but they backed out for fear of being dismissed. Instead Radio London thought up a very clever hoax. Just after 9.00am the *Keith Skues Show* was interrupted by what appeared to be a new station, Radio East Anglia, testing. As the morning progressed the tests continued from time to time, interrupting not only the records but commercials and news as well. The 10.30am Radio London news should have enabled listeners to deduce what was going on. Lead item concerned the extension of Felixstowe Pier to two miles, so that the offshore stations would be brought within the three-mile limit, and there followed a number of other fake items including an impossible weather forecast. The signal from East Anglia gradually improved and just before 11.30am completely drowned Radio London. It was announced by the DJs, Bob Parkin and Aspley Guise, that Radio East Anglia was broadcasting from Norfolk on 267 metres with a power of 50kW. Advertisements for various businesses were aired and it really sounded like the start of a new station. Just before noon Radio London faded in and Radio East Anglia was never heard again. The whole thing had been broadcast from the *Galaxy by* clever mixing and very good production work.[6]

Colleague David Kindred, who worked at the *Evening Star,* Ipswich, as a photographer was actually travelling out to the *Galaxy* on the day of the hoax. What he didn't know was that we gave out his address to where all irate fans could write and complain.

Said Dave afterwards "I received more than 100 letters, mostly abusive, asking for Radio East Anglia to get off the air. It's the April Fool that worked. Everybody took it so deadly serious, that's the funniest thing. I did not hear the original broadcast, so Keith, whom I have known since he returned from Aden in 1964, played it back to me on tape."

David is now picture editor of *Evening Star* in Ipswich, and looking back says: "Another amusing incident that happened with the newspaper on 1 April 1967 was that they sent a reporter to my address, but he went to the wrong house!"

There now follows a selection of letters from listeners who relate their memories of Big L: Mrs V.M. Webb of Cherry Gardens, Herne Bay in Kent, remembers the time when Radio London's tender, *Offshore I*, rescued an American pilot, Lieutenant John Wynn, when his plane crashed into the North Sea. Mrs Webb says "This should be pointed out to the Postmaster-General. The officer would most certainly have died had the *Offshore I* not been in the vicinity." Mrs Webb enjoyed the first-hand commentary by Paul Kaye and she congratulated the station for an excellent piece of broadcasting.

Michael Worthington lived at Pusehill, Westward Ho!, North Devon, and was a firm follower of Radio London from the beginning. He sent many revived 45s to the station.

> The most amusing incident in my life occurred with Radio London when I wrote to Keith Skues asking him to call up a Miss Rosemary Norris who had come to stay with us. He

---

6. *Offshore Radio*, Gerry Bishop. 1975, Iceni Enterprises, page 71. Author's note: It was, in fact, the Ed Stewart programme which was interrupted, not that of Keith Skues. who read the news on the half hour.

David Kindred of the Ipswich Evening Star checking his "fan mail"

kindly played the dedication but stated over the air she was my girl friend. I would just like to add she was 88 years old at the time and I was 25! Ever since then it has been a standing joke in the Worthington household.

Miss Diane Butt of Rectory Grove, Clapham Old Town, London SW4, relates that her most memorable incident concerned Dave Cash and Kenny Everett. During their *Kenny and Cash* programme one day, the two of them were playing a game of draughts over the air. Says Diane "It's not the type of incident that will go down in the annals of history, but it always stays fresh in my memory."

Kenny and Cash brought in many letters, but space won't allow us to reproduce them all. However, Marion Hicks of Barham Road, Chislehurst, Kent, is brief and to the point.

It was during 1965 that Kenny and Dave put a long playing record on the turntable and then decided to go off for a swim. When they returned to the studio, they were dripping water over all the equipment and everyone was breaking up with laughter. It was the funniest moment I can ever remember on Radio London.

John Mann of Old Road, Frinton-on-Sea, writes:

The most amusing event in the life of Big L was when 'Stewpot' thought he had time to dash upstairs for some cigarettes whilst a record was playing ... but he hadn't. The record came to an end and then there was a deadly hush. He returned some thirty seconds later rather puffed and apologised.

Mrs Marguerite Collier writes from Carstairs Avenue, Park South, Swindon, Wiltshire:

There are several incidents which remain in my mind, but they are not what you would call 'earthshakers.' They are just simple things that amused and interested me. For example during the first few weeks of Radio London I heard Sue Thompson singing *Paper Tiger* about 20 times a day. What a fantastic record it was but it never reached the national charts' Top 10 for some strange reason.
I remember Christmas Eve 1966, when everyone on board came down to the studio around midnight, sang Christmas carols and wished all the listeners a 'Happy Christmas.' That was very nostalgic.
But the best 'gag' of all time was the April Fool's Day incident concerning 'Radio East Anglia.' I, for one, was never really sure whether it was Radio London fooling around or the real thing. I frantically tried to separate 266 metres from 267; I really must say the 'gag' was superbly done. Not a giggle or a 'slipped voice.' The news broadcast by Cardboard Shoes was hilarious, and read with such a serious voice. It took ten minutes to sink in that it was not a genuine newscast.

The next letter from Miss Barbara Cook of High Road, Trimley St. Mary, Suffolk, was more a personal letter to the author:

The most memorable incident was on the morning of 20 July 1966 when we suspected you had appendicitis. All the other disc jockeys changed over except you. You carried on for another three days and then suddenly you stopped in the middle of your programme and didn't come back. The tender came out to take you ashore. It was like being cut off from a telephone and not being able to get through again. I remember dashing down to Felixstowe Docks to see if you had got off safely.
The second most memorable incident was some ten months later (the day you were due off) and you had washed a shirt at 5.15 in the morning and hung it on a line to dry. You checked at various intervals during your show and kept us informed, and then at 11.30am you came back with the news that a wind had started to blow, and it had

blown your shirt off the hanger into the sea. I laughed so much at the hilarious, obviously spontaneous poem that you made up about it.

David Bradley of Bower Street, Bedford, says that Radio London DJs rarely made reference to items in the news which, he believed, was company policy. However, on one occasion in June 1966, he remembers:

To hear on the radio news that someone has been accused of a murder is no laughing matter. To make it worse it involved two pirate radio stations! Major Oliver Smedley, a shareholder in Radio Caroline, had been arrested by police and accused of shooting dead Reg Calvert, managing director of Radio City. After the news Keith Skues played a record from the Lionel Bart musical 'Oliver!' and said "Now we come to our daily feature 'Music from the Shows.' Today a 'Smedley' of a hit from 'Oliver'!" I had to smile

News broadcasts appear to be the most popular memories. Audrey Lydia Jones of Oakfield Road, Hawley, Camberley, Surrey, writes: "I remember the time when Paul Kaye in his just so voice had read the 12.30pm news and he inadvertently left the microphone open when suddenly we heard "Oh God! Dave, what's for afters? I'm starving!"

Mrs Marjorie Sheldon, of Devonshire Road, London NW7, relates:

Keith Skues was reading the 3.30pm news in the *Chris Denning Show* ... it was read in his typical BBC voice ... we heard ... "The meeting took place today in Salisbury. Mr. Ian Smith told the British Prime Minister... 'I refuse to throw in the sponge.'" There was a 'splot' followed by a pause and a certain amount of tittering in the background. Then Keith said "I'm sorry. I have just been hit in the face with a sponge which had been soaked in water... I'm sorry I'll continue ... the meeting took place in Salisbury. Mr Ian Smith told ...

From Carlisle Avenue, St. Alban's, Herts, Derek Evans writes:

My most long-remembered incident was when they 'broke-in' Stewpot. Ed Stewart was once a deadpan Auntie-style newsreader. Then one day he was sent to read the news in the *Kenny and Cash Show* which was a presentation of ruined adverts, records played sideways and general pandemonium. Stewpot was reading the news in all seriousness when he suddenly cried out "Ahhhhh! Get that chap out of here." and was carried off laughing by Dave Cash while Kenny read the news.

Still on the news, Anne Needon of Selworthy Road, Catford, London SE6, sent in a letter about Mark Roman.

Mark was very new to the station and was reading the news on the Double D. Show. He started, and then broke into fits of uncontrollable laughter. He managed to stop, but every time he started a new sentence he collapsed into hysterical giggles again. Dave Dennis later apologised and said that the poor fellow was reading under difficulties.

Another letter involving news break-ups involved Norman St. John and Tony Blackburn. It comes from Mrs Lynda Rathborne of Abbey Road, St. John's Wood, London NW8.

Two news broadcasts will stick in my memory for as long as I live. In March Kenny Everett and Keith Skues were doing a double show and they fixed the various cassettes for Norman St. John when he came to read the news on a Saturday afternoon at 3.30pm. Apparently his earphones were put out of commission, so he couldn't hear what was going out on transmission. Kenny and Keith had fixed all sorts of rude noises and sound effects instead of the news blips. It sounded even funnier when Norman

John Peel

Norman St. John

Paul Kaye

Mark Roman

Tony Blackburn

read it very straight not suspecting that anything was wrong.

A similar occasion happened when Tony Blackburn read the news. His headphones had been broken. Instead of the news blips he got the 'weather forecast jingle' every time, and no one could hear what he said as the jingle was much louder than Tony's voice. All terrific broadcasting.

Barbara Hadler of Cortland Close, Sittingbourne, Kent, refers to a late show on Radio London - *London after Midnight*. She relates:

It is very difficult to pinpoint one occasion in the life of Big L which can be classed as the most memorable - there have been so many. However, there is one incident which I won't forget in a hurry, although it is purely personal and would not have affected anyone else. I was listening to *London after Midnight*, which was presented by Keith Skues, one night during the autumn of 1966 and because of the late (or should I say 'early') hour, was picking up the station through my earplug while lying in bed.

Suddenly, at about 1.15am, he gave me a call and included some highly amusing remarks. This triggered off an attack of the giggles which shook the bed and consequently woke my husband who wondered what on earth was happening. Apparently my explanation, accompanied by subsequent chuckles, was not appreciated by John who retaliated by pushing me out of bed causing me to yell loud enough to wake the whole neighbourhood. I now keep my late night laughter under control as I don't want to be accused of causing a breach of the peace.

The final letter comes from David Winter of Rock Avenue, Gillingham, Kent.

There have been so many memorable incidents in the life of Radio London. The greatest thing that happened to offshore radio was Kenny Everett, Dave Cash, Tony Windsor, Dave Dennis, John Edward, Ed 'Stewpot' Stewart, Keith 'Cardboard Shoes' Skues, John Peel, Chuck Blair, Lome King, Tony Blackburn, Chris Denning, Mike Lennox, Paul Kaye, Pete Drummond and Mark Roman - in other words, Radio London! The saddest thing that ever happened to Radio London was the splitting of Kenny and Cash, and also when Radio London disc jockeys left the station for other jobs.

The brightest idea on Radio London was the Kaye Club when Paul Kaye invited people to speak at 10.00pm each night on various subjects.

The sickest things on Radio London were Tony Blackburn's jokes in the early morning.

During the summer of 1966 a song called *We Love the Pirate Stations* was released by members of the Ivy League working under the alias "The Roaring Sixties". (A copy of the disc was sent to the Prime Minister, Harold Wilson, on 10 August 1966. However, the record, which could have been a smash hit, had been refused distribution by Selecta Gramophone, a subsidiary of Decca Records.) The song was written by Messrs Carter, Stephens and Kennedy, published by Carter Lewis Music and released on the Marmalade label 598001. Some of the lyrics are reproduced below:

> The Government wants to close them down
> But we want them to stay.
> They are playing sounds that we all like
> So don't take them away.

> When you're walking down the street with your transistor radio
> Everybody has a good time.
> You can dance to the beat of your transistor radio
> Even when the sun don't shine.

You can hear your favourite rock 'n' roll
Rhythm and blues with a lot of soul.

There are some swinging DJs playing Top 40 records
They can really turn you on.
Now the Government's trying to close down the stations
What'll happen when they're gone,
You won't hear the music that you like
Any old time of day or night.

We love the pirate stations
Don't let them take 'em away.

But take 'em away they did. Inevitable that the Government was to win. On 1 August 1967 Radio London issued the following statement from managing director Philip Birch:

It is with deep regret that I have to announce that, after nearly three years of broadcasting, Radio London will be closing down on 14 August. It is unfortunate that this Government's attitude towards independent radio has consistently been one of suppression as part of a determined plan to continue the Government's monopoly of radio broadcasting. Radio London has repeatedly pointed out that the British public could benefit from dozens of independent radio stations operating under licence on land, but the Government has said no. This, in spite of the fact that the Prime Minister has in his possession a study by National Opinion Polls that shows that 69% of the population are in favour of allowing the free radio stations to continue broadcasting. We understand that the new Government programme, which is to be called Radio 1, is largely modelled on Radio London and will employ many Radio London DJs. We receive hundreds of thousands of letters from listeners but possibly this Government's imitation is the greatest tribute of all.

Monday 14 August - execution day for Radio London - was in fact Black Monday. At sea it was a bleak, cold and rainy day. Seas were rough. As usual Chuck Blair presented the *Breakfast Show*.

During his show and the following one (presented by Pete Drummond) pop stars broadcast farewell messages to Radio London. These included Guy Darrell, Kenny Damon, P.P. Arnold, Spencer Davis, Twice As Much, Warm Sounds, Young Idea, Johnny Young, Episode Six, The Fortunes, Helen Shapiro, and Tremeloes. Former disc jockey, Earl Richmond, said 'goodbye' as did administrator Richard Swainson, radio personality Tony Hall and promoter Gloria Bristow.

More stars appeared between 12.00 noon and 1.30pm and included: Paul and Barry Ryan, Dave Clark Five, Stevie Winwood, Traffic, Chantells, David Garrick, The Shadows and Ray Davies and the Kinks. Among those who appeared in the final sponsored show on Radio London, the *Juicy Fruit Show*, presented by disc jockeys Tommy Vance and Lee Peters, were Tony Hatch, Engelbert Humperdinck, Eric Burdon, Ken Dodd, and Gary Brooker of Procol Harum. The show was broadcast from 1.30pm to 2.00pm.

Ed Stewart joined Paul Kaye for the final hour on 266. The programme incorporated records made hits through the help of Radio London. Many of the station's 'old' disc jockeys in addition to the present staff also said their goodbyes to Big L. Pop stars, too, had their final say. The complete list in order of appearance was: Cliff Richard, Lulu, Mark Roman, Tony Windsor, John Walker, Mick Jagger, John Peel, Bruce Johnston, Duncan Johnson, Cat Stephens, Kenny Everett, Pete Drummond, Tony Blackburn, Madeleine Bell, Chuck Blair, Chris Denning, Dave Cash, Jonathan King, Keith Skues, Tommy Vance, Dusty Springfield and Ringo Starr. The final commercial broadcast was for Consulate Cigarettes.

Just before three o'clock, managing director Philip Birch made a speech, the contents of which can be found in Chapter Eleven. This was followed by the last record to be played on Radio London, the Beatles' *A Day in the Life*, a track off *Sergeant Pepper's Lonely Hearts Club Band* which sold over seven million copies worldwide and which had been banned by the BBC.

Paul Kaye then made history. He was the very first voice ever to be heard on Radio London. He was also to be the last. He said: "Big L time is three o'clock and Radio London is now closing down." The station's theme, *Big Lil* followed, the 50 kilowatt transmitter was switched off and 266 metres became silent.

DJs and engineers were taken ashore by the *Ocean Cock* to Felixstowe which, by coincidence, berthed alongside a ship marked *The Wilson Line*. Many of them returned to London to be given a tumultuous welcome at Liverpool Street Station.

The Top Ten records from the Radio London Fab 40 for the final week were:

1	Even The Bad Times Are Good - The Tremeloes
1=	Heroes and Villains - The Beach Boys
3	The Day I Met Marie - Cliff Richard
4	Long Legged Girl - Elvis Presley
5	The House That Jack Built - Alan Price
6	A Girl Like You - Young Rascals
7	Excerpt from A Teenage Opera - Keith West
8	Love Years Coming - Strawberry Children
9	Time Seller - Spencer Davis
10	Sticks and Stones - Warm Sounds

Radio London's farewell dedication to the Postmaster-General (which was played about five times daily during the final week of transmission) was sung by Frankie Vaughan, *There Must Be a Way*. At this point, what could be more fitting than a lament from Barbara Hadler of Sittingbourne which was written a week before the station closed?

LONDON LAMENT

Goodbye, farewell my faithful friend,
The time has come to part.
At last, it seems, our joy must end
And heavy is my heart.

The countless hours of fun we've had,
And happy music, too.
Because of these my mood is sad -
The moments left are few.

Who could have thought the end would come,
Your future seemed so sure.
Success was yours and great the sum
Of sounds we'll hear no more.

Shows we missed were soon forgot...
Always more to be heard.
Now, as the hours fly by, we stop
And hang on every word.

With skill your DJs did impart

Their mirth and music bright.
Always gay and eager to start
They gave the day new light.

Never again the jokes and fun
Can we tune in to hear.
Remarks about the Stewpot's turn
Or Myrtle's "Hello, Dear."

No more the Perfumed Garden's scent,
With gentle, 'loving' Peel.
And where was it that Blackburn went
With Keith Skues at his heel.

Where could we hear another Kaye
With voice so deep and calm?
And what about the Bird Brain's way
Of joking, without harm.

Your DJs' names are known by all...
The Wombat, Dum-Dum, Blair.
No matter if they're short or tall
They're loved upon the air.

So many voices from the sea
Recalled in 'London's' past.
Like Everett and Double D,
Their memory will last.

Who could forget the big "Hello,"
T.W.'s favourite call.
Everybody loved him so,
The 'Daddy' of them all.

These people, and so many more,
Pass through my reverie.
Such memories I have in store
Of Big L on the sea.

And though your days are numbered now,
And your closing date is set,
Dear London, proudly take your bow
We never will forget.

Ten years after Radio London ceased broadcasting from her anchorage off the Essex coast I met Philip Birch in his office in Manchester. At the time he was chief executive of the independent station, Piccadilly Radio, which began broadcasting to the Manchester area in 1974. I asked him to explain the policy behind Big L's Top 40 format.

I felt for a commercial station to succeed the first thing is that it has to have a very large audience so that advertisers will be keen to support it to put their sales messages on air. To do this we felt we had to do something entirely different. Not just a pop station,

Philip Birch, managing director Radio London, 1964 - 1967

but a pop station with a special personality of its own. So we adopted what we now call the Top 40 format and the only idea was to play the 40 records that were the most interesting records of the week. This had nothing at all to do with the charts. Our disc jockeys would select 40 records collectively - what they thought were the best 40 records of the week and that would be our sound for the following week. The other thing we felt was very important was professionalism. We wanted Radio London to move very fast in a happy way and for the listener to feel that the station itself was dynamic and alive. We did this by using jingles, which had not been used by anyone very much up till that time. We introduced the jingle "Wonderful Radio London". In 1967 BBC Radio 1 introduced a series of jingles based on the Radio London package and using the slogan "Wonderful Radio 1". The whole pace of Radio London was rapid but pleasant.

By selecting the 40 best records of the week and not relating them to sales we were a little concerned about payola. Certain record pluggers were keen to have their records played. Certainly to my knowledge we never had a problem with payola because the records were chosen not by individuals, but by a committee of DJs who in a sense guarded each other. We did help make hit records. Take, for example, *Winchester Cathedral* by the New Vaudeville Band which became a big hit. The group who put that record together had done nothing before. We liked the sound of the record so brought it into the Fab 40. The audience loved the record, and it became one of the biggest selling records not just in this country, but all over the world. I remember going into a little cafe in southern Italy, and there was *Winchester Cathedral* playing on the juke box. Another example was Jonathan King who came into my office once and played me *Everyone's Gone to the Moon* which just had a touch of magic which really big selling records do have. It was obvious Jonathan King had what it takes, so we said fine and we would play it. He even went out to the radio ship to act as a disc jockey on one occasion.

In the beginning we won over the teenage audience. From there it was a fairly short step to get the housewives to listen because what teenagers are interested in, the young housewives are interested in. Teenagers soon become housewives - at least the female ones!

Radio London helped to expand the total radio audience. The total audience measured in terms of time listening to the radio in this country was roughly 8 to 10 hours in a week. In the United States of America it was twice that amount. During the pirate era it grew very rapidly. These were new listeners who were not getting what they wanted

RADIO LONDON

Have you heard....
WONDERFUL
RADIO LONDON 266 M.
rl

FIGHT FOR *FREE*
RADIO LONDON 266

RADIO LONDON NEEDS YOU!
TO ENLIST IN A GROWING ARMY OF
PEOPLE TO FIGHT FOR FREE RADIO.
WRITE TO HAROLD WILSON TODAY!

WONDERFUL
RADIO LONDON
BIG L CLUB 266

to hear from other radio stations. The Government asked the BBC to create a programme to replace the pirates in order to continue to provide the service that people had become accustomed to. Radio 1 was modelled on Radio London. It obtained its jingles from PAMS, an organisation in Dallas, Texas, where Radio London had its jingles recorded and used the same music. By and large, Radio 1 followed the same format with jingles and put its news out on the half-hour exactly as Radio London did. It also hired most of Radio London's disc jockeys including Ed Stewart, Keith Skues, Kenny Everett and Dave Cash. Radio 1 was Radio London without the commercials!

Whilst we were on air for three years, Radio London was never involved in any litigation. We were absolute model citizens in every way. We had very strict rules with our staff who realised we were broadcasting outside of the law rather than against the law, and that we behaved ourselves and ran our organisation in a model way. We paid a Performing Rights copyright fee for the music. We offered to pay Phonographic Performance Limited, another royalty organisation, but, in fact, they were not prepared to accept our money.

I look back to the pirate era with much pleasure. It was very worthwhile. I am pleased as a direct result of pirate broadcasting that we now have commercial radio in this country. Commercial radio is important because it is another system. It takes away the problems of the BBC that always had a monopoly in broadcasting. Monopolies are not healthy. The BBC has become a better service as a result of the commercial stations, and I think the BBC believes this as well. Pirate radio was great fun. We did something very worthwhile and for which we can be proud.

RADIO JINGLES

MUSICAL JINGLES on British radio were popularised by Radio London at the latter end of 1964 with familiar refrains like Wunnnderful Radio Lunn-Dunn ... Biggest Sound Around ... Big L."

The role model for Radio London was KLIF 1190 Radio in Dallas, Texas, USA. The company called PAMS (Promotions, Advertising and Merchandising Services) supplied KLIF with its jingles. So it was no surprise when KLIF owner, entrepreneur Gordon McClendon, pointed Radio London founder Don Pierson in the same direction. McClendon later became involved with Jack Kotschack and Bob Thompson in setting up Radio Nord off the Swedish coast.

The original incorporation papers dated 16 August 1951 indicate that PAMS had been set up by Dallas saxophone player, Bill Meeks, Jr, Charles H. Meeks (Bill's brother), and William Meeks, Sr (Bill's father). All three were founder directors and shareholders.

It was common practice at the time for radio stations in America to have their own bands and singers performing 'live' on sponsored programmes.

While rehearsing these live shows, Meeks and the other musicians started to record (onto disc) commercial jingles for local merchants advertising on KLIF. It occurred to Meeks and his team that if jingles for advertisers could be done in this way, then why not jingles for KLIF itself? Although individual radio stations had experimented with ID jingles since the 1930s, this was the first time the idea was seriously pursued. Meeks and McClendon conferred, and on 11 November 1947 KLIF began broadcasting for the very first time. Later the first KLIF jingles package was broadcast.

As post-network music radio gained momentum, Meeks and McClendon realised the potential of setting up a company specialising in the production of both commercial and ID jingles.

The success of PAMS was immediate and, as the '50s progressed and competition between radio stations intensified with more and more stations adopting all-record formats, so the demand for PAMS jingles grew. Employing only the cream of Dallas writers, arrangers, musicians and singers, PAMS jingles were unusually arranged and elaborately engineered, becoming, more than anything else on Top 40 radio, the synthesis of rock with big-band era music.

The real breakthrough, however, came in 1960 with the arrival of Series 14 'The Dramatic Signatures.' The package revolutionised jingle writing techniques of the day by introducing the 'variable logo.' Prior to this, every station had been locked into using the same melody for their call letters and frequency, regardless of whether they fitted that melody or not! Now, however, PAMS could write a special melody for each station name, or set of call letters (77 WABC, KLIF 1190, WLS in Chicago etc.), tailor-made to fit the appropriate place on the jingle backing tracks. Thus, Series 14 is recognised as the start of radio ID jingles as we know them today.

Other Series 14 innovations were the use of multi-track vocals and natural auditorium reverberation (PAMS was probably the first studio in Dallas to introduce multi-track machines. It definitely had one of the first Moog synthesizers in 1967, and the city's first 16-track machine in 1970). This led to the reverb craze that swept American Top 40 radio in the early to mid-1960s with stations falling over themselves to get studio reverb units.

Series 15 'Living Radio' (1960) and Series 16 'Sound Of The City' (1961) followed with yet more innovations. Series 15 (much pirated by Radio London) introduced jingles with positioning statements long before they became an accepted part of jingle vocabulary, while Series 16 introduced the record-length jingle for the first time - in this case two songs with customized lyrics about the town or city where the radio station was based. One of the songs, *Hometown*, crossed the Atlantic three years later as "London - my Hometown" for the start of Wonderful Radio London.

The year 1961 also saw the release of Series 17 'The New Frontier' and Series 18 'Sonosational', both very relevant to Radio London. The New Frontier was named after Kennedy's famous presidential address and based on popular show tunes of the day. Sonosational introduced the 'Sonovox' electronic voice effect first popularised in the 1941 Disney film *Dumbo* (remember the talking train?) and, later. *Sparky's Magic Piano*. Bill Meeks' idea was to fool the radio audience into thinking that musical instruments playing the station musical logo were actually singing. It was a simple yet highly effective gimmick. The Sonovox could be best described as a couple of small speakers held hard on either side of the throat, just below the jawline. Single instruments such as trombone, trumpet, alto-saxophone, flute, piano, organ and Alvino Rey's steel guitar were fed through the mixing board into the Sonovox units, causing them to vibrate. Once placed against the throat, the units' vibrations would replace the function of the vocal chords, allowing the Sonovox operator (PAMS baritone bass singer Dan Alexander) to mouth the required lyrics in sync with the instrument feeding the units and generating the necessary tones. Thus the instruments would appear to talk or sing. When amplified by the studio microphones and fed back through the control room board, the resulting 'sound' would be balanced against the Series 18 backing tracks. A good number of regular vocal cuts (some 'answering' the Sonovox or vice versa) made up the balance of the package. Series 18 remained a PAMS best-seller for many, many years and it's still popular today among Gold format radio stations.

Don Pierson booked the Series 18 package for Radio London. The music tracks had originally been recorded in 1961 (package registered 20 December 1961) and in three years it came to be heard on all top stations in America, including KLIF in Dallas.

The success of the Series was undoubtedly due to singer Dan Alexander's use of the 'Sonovox' electronic voice - a PAMS exclusive - and it was clever thinking on the part of Don Pierson to bring this highly distinctive feature to British shores for the very first time. Like the top American stations, Radio London would identify itself with a superlative, in this case 'Wonderful.'

So, after adapting one of the most popular PAMS musical logos, came the familiar refrain of "Wunnnderful Radio Lunn-dunn."

Chris Elliot is an Associate of the International Division of PAMS. He says:

Don commissioned the complete set of Series 18 and this included Radio London's theme (nicknamed *Big Lil* by the disc jockeys, but officially titled *The Sonowaltz* being written in waltz time) and the legendary news, weather and 'Spanish' jingles. I'm afraid I can't recall the name of the male bass singer featured on several Series 18 cuts (Biggest sound around, Big L etc.). I'm pretty sure he died - as did Billy Ainsworth - and current bass singer, Jim Clancy, certainly replaced him quite early on.

Jonathan Wolfert, president of JAM Creative Productions, Inc., of Dallas, Texas, worked at PAMS for a number of years. He says: "The original bass singer was Bill Simmons." He disagrees with Chris Elliot by saying that Jim Clancy did not sing on the Radio London jingles as he only worked for PAMS in the late 1960s.

Completing the Radio London package were selected cuts from Series 17 'The New Frontier' (package registered 31 August 1961), including Jean Oliver's *Smooth Sailing* and the church jingle; Series 26D 'The Beatles' (Big L chose two cuts - one based on *I Saw Her Standing There* and the other *It Won't Be Long*); and, finally, the popular record-length *Hometown* song from Series 16 'The Sound of the City' (package registered 14 November 1961) given new lyrics as *London - My Hometown*. Terry Lee supplied the vocals with the PAMS chorus adding their 'oohs' and 'aahs' on the final verse.

Finding their way out to the ship with the above were a number of PAMS jingle demos - most notably Series 15 'Living Radio' recorded for WABC New York, although never used by that station. The Big L DJs wasted no time getting the scissors into these to create more jingles to play (Here's Yours Truly with the Weather, Remember You Heard It, All the Deejays say, 1.2.3 jumps ahead etc.). Other PAMS demonstration tapes to have the same treatment in Big L's short life were Series 25 'The Happy Difference,' Series 26 'Let's go America,' Series 27 'The Jet Set,' Series 28 'Happiness Is' and Series 29 'Go Go.'

Says Chris Elliot "Avid Big L fans may also remember the much used 'You're a pussycat, you're where it's at, the one's that's in on every play' jingle 'cut-up.' This came from Gwinsound of Dallas and not PAMS, although when founder Tommy Gwin retired in the mid-1980s, he leased the entire Gwinsound library to us!"

Radio London returned to PAMS in late 1966 to have a good number of cuts from the then recently released Series 31, 'The Music Explosion' (package registered 20 June 1966). The distinguishing features of Series 31 were the powerful all-male harmony vocals (Marvin Shaw did the amazing high parts!), the Sonovox 'Muuusic' pre-record punctuations and the bright, brassy backing tracks. Top 40 formats were becoming tighter, so many Series 31 cuts were designed to end *a cappella*, enabling the DJ to smoothly and rapidly 'segue' from jingle to disc. Best known of the Big L Series 31 jingles were 'The London Sound' (later to appear on Radio 1 as "The Voice of Radio 1'), 'Music that's our middle name,' 'Much more music every morning' and *The Stripper* instrumental.

Don Pierson's next venture, after leaving Radio London, was the setting up of Radio England and Britain Radio. He returned to PAMS and purchased Series 27 'The Jet Set' for Radio England. The exciting music tracks were first recorded for WABC at the end of 1963 (package registered on 3 January 1964) and to this day it remains another PAMS best-seller.

Don commissioned the package (and the Britain Radio jingles) for $6,000 in March 1966. All the cuts were purchased, adopting the logo "Swinging Radio England." Says Chris Elliot:

The real secret ingredient of Series 27 was the use of girl singer Glenni Rutherford (actually an Indian girl called 'Bright Eyes Longknife') whose incredible high range vocal 'scat' was synchronised with the trumpet players to give the backing tracks a very distinctive and unique flavour. As regards the orchestration, there were no baritones, bass-trombones or anything in the lower range. Everything was 'high' except for the rhythm - the bass player being left unencumbered and uncluttered to give the tracks a feeling of movement. Alvino Rey's exciting steel guitar 'sweeps' also

PAMS baritone singer Dan Alexander. He sang on the Radio London, England, Britain and BBC jingle packages. Dan was aalso responsible for the PAMS 'Sonovox' throughout the 1960s.

punctuated many of the tracks.

Contrasting with these distinctive tracks were powerful all-male unison vocals (Dan Alexander, Frank Bloebaum, Marvin Shaw and Jody Lyons), while Glenni was responsible for the 'Whees' and 'Whoopees' that punctuated some of the cuts. Series 27 was topped off with the 'sounds' of the Jet Set. Diving board, water splash, surf, jets, motor boats and racing cars gave the package a summery, open air 'life is for living' feel.

Many PAMS 'cut-ups' also found their way to Radio England, most notably from packages made for WFUN Miami, some of the Radio England disc jockeys having worked there.

Incidentally, Radio England had an extremely 'loose' on air use of their PAMS jingles during test transmissions, so loose that Radio Caroline pirated the whole package, immediately editing them for their own broadcast use ahead of Radio England's official launch! Later in 1966, and as a result of Caroline's actions, Radio England returned to Dallas, to a smaller jingle company, Spot Productions, for a set of their new 'Batman' jingles recorded to coincide with the Batman craze. Many people believe the Batman set came from PAMS, but no, it was Spot, a company that went out of business quite a few years ago now, sadly destroying all their backing tracks in the process.

To suit the middle-of-the-road format of Britain Radio, Don Pierson chose PAMS "The Smart Set'. Piloted for WFAA in Dallas, Smart Set was originally recorded in early 1964 (package registered 12 March 1964) as an easy listening companion to the Top 40-orientated Series 27 'Jet Set', and was over two years old before it was re-sung for Britain Radio adopting the slogan 'Hallmark of Quality'.

The distinguishing features of the package - apart from the obvious catchy melodies - were the big band style music tracks, some very reminiscent of Glenn Miller. Sophisticated mixed group vocal harmonies, courtesy of the PAMS regulars, gave the package its rich 'velvet' feel.

Baritone Dan Alexander sang the cheeky 'Music for this, that and the other' cut.

Britain Radio purchased the complete 'Smart Set' package. Jingle historians will know that 5 years later (in 1971) it reappeared, re-sung for BBC Radio 2 as part of a jingles composite.

The occasional PAMS 'cut-up' also featured on Britain Radio, as did a set called 'Global Medium,' not a PAMS package and origins unknown.

The BBC, influenced by the popularity and success of the Radio London jingles and the lack of a 'home-grown' jingles industry, commissioned PAMS of Dallas to make the identifications for Radio 1 when the new service began on 30 September 1967.

For the launch, the station chose a composite of Series 31 'Music Explosion' (1966, package registered 20 June 1966 and previously used by Big L), Series 32 'Swiszle' (1966, package registered 31 October 1966), Series 33 'Fun Vibrations' (1967, package registered 1 June 1967), plus *A Cappellas* based on the PAMS 'Voices' demo (1967).

Shortly afterwards, Radio 1 also selected many cuts from Series 34 "The 10th Dimension' (1967, package registered 22 September 1967 and more popularly known as 'Music Power').

The Radio 1 jingles used the musical logo 'Radio 1 is Wonderful' to the familiar tune of *London Bridge is Falling Down*. The slogans, catchphrases and lyrics owed much to Kenny Everett and Radio 1 promotions man, James Fisher.

The first jingle heard on Radio 1 (The Voice of Radio 1) came from Series 31.

In Series 32 soloist Trella Hart made her début on such jingles as 'Let the Good Times Roll,' 'Mornings are Fun on One,' etc. She was backed by the PAMS male group, now known as 'The Good Timers.'

Chris Elliot of PAMS recalls that Series 33 'Fun Vibrations,' influenced by the Beach Boys' recording of *Good Vibrations*, was co-written by Euel Box.

Many cuts included the 'therimin' electronic effect used by The Beach Boys. Again, Trella Hart dominated the package with the PAMS male group, most cuts ending with a shimmering vocal 'Funnnnl' effect recorded in different keys to match each respective music track. However, Radio 1 only had one Series 33 jingle, sung with the full group, 'Merry-go-round of musical fun').

Jonathan Wolfert says that Series 34 - '10th Dimension' was so named because PAMS had custom-built an Ampex ten-track tape machine. This was the first series to be recorded on that machine, and thus moved PAMS' production into the '10th Dimension.'

Chris Elliot continues:

The '247 Music Power' jingles came from this package, as did Radio 1's most famous jingle of all time 'Music hour by hour on your Tower of Power' (lyrics Kenny Everett). 'Music lovin' Keith Skues,' (and other DJs) came from Series 34. Also, many 'cut-up' PAMS jingles from demos, and the Big L and Radio England packages, were frequently aired on Radio 1 by DJs like Tony Blackburn, Rosko, Pete Brady, Dave Cash and others. I don't know if this practice had PAMS' blessing!

For the record, the first set of Radio 1 jingles were aired from September 1967 to October 1968 when, sadly, and coinciding with the launch of *Radio 1 Club,* the BBC strayed to other American jingle companies: first, Pepper-Tanner (1968) and then, Audio-Producers (1970). By October 1971, however, Radio 1 was back at PAMS, in the company of Radio Two paying their first visit. PAMS jingles dominated Radios One and Two from October 1971 to September 1976 when the networks changed their allegiance to the comparatively new JAM Creative Productions of Dallas ... In 1993 they are still with JAM.

As for PAMS, throughout the 1960s and early 1970s, they produced thousands of innovative, exciting and unique jingles for radio stations all over the world. These sounds made pop radio much more than just records and DJs.

The writers/arrangers for PAMS were: Brian Beck, Euel Box, Bob Farrar, Ray Hurst, Jody Lyons, Bill Meeks, Bob Piper and Marvin Shaw.

The best known names of the female singers were: Jackie Dickson, Mary Jo Grogan, Trella Hart, Terri Lee, Susie McCune, Jean Oliver, Judy Parma, Carol Piper, Tinker Rautenberg, Glenni Rutherford, Claire Stewart and Libba Weeks.

Male singers included: Billy Ainsworth, Dan Alexander, Brian Beck, Frank Bloebaum, Jim Clancy, Tommy Loy, Jody Lyons, Peyton Park, Marvin Shaw and Charlie Thompson.

Sadly, in 1976, it all started going wrong. Believing that ID jingles were on the decline, PAMS moved into other broadcasting areas (including automated programming) and this caused some financial stretching. However, companies like TM and JAM were coming to the fore so clearly jingles were not losing their popularity. But for PAMS it was too late. Serious financial problems were growing within the company, morale slumped and key creative people left to join the competition. Failure to pay tax led to the Internal Revenue Service seizing PAMS' assets. After the collapse of just one serious rescue attempt, PAMS finally disintegrated in 1977.

The highly prized jingle master tapes were split between Ken R. Deutsch and Toby Arnold. In 1984 CPMG subsequently went after, and acquired, the actual PAMS trademark, name and print logo.

CPMG remains a New York State corporation, but operates PAMS Productions from Dallas. Overseas sales are handled by PAMS International in Kent. President of the 'new' PAMS is Ben Freedman, although Bill Meeks (now 71) has a small, token role in the company. Many PAMS originals remain on the books, including writer/arranger Bob Piper and baritone bass singer Dan Alexander.

Jonathan Wolfert, of JAM Creative Productions in Dallas, says: "Sadly, there is still some legal controversy over who owns the rights to the old PAMS material. By obtaining the trademark, CPMG did acquire the ability to use the PAMS name. But they did not acquire the actual corporation. In June 1990, JAM Productions Inc., did buy all rights, title and interest in PAMS, Inc. (the original Texas corporation which began in 1951). Since there is no clear documentation to indicate that PAMS ever sold or transferred its copyrights to any other party, it is our position that PAMS, Inc., still owns and controls all of the PAMS musical copyrights.

"It is unfortunate that the legalities involved are so confusing, and that the documentation is so bad. It will probably never be resolved to everyone's satisfaction. This is truly a sad ending for a once marvellous organisation which contributed so much to the world of radio and jingles."

Chapter Seven

THE IN CROWD

I am the morning DJ at W.O.L.D
Playing all the hits for you
Wherever you may be

W.O.L.D. Harry Chapin, 1974

THERE WERE more than 250 disc jockeys broadcasting to Britain in 1967 alone. Most of them were *pirate* DJs - some working on ships in the North Sea and Irish Sea, whilst others squatted on forts in the Thames Estuary.

What is the definition of a *pirate disc jockey?* One well-known dictionary describes *pirate* as a 'sea-robber' and *disc jockey* as 'an announcer of a radio programme of recorded music'

The spontaneous style of the pirate DJs was fresh and exciting and caught the mood of the time. Novelist John Winton, writing in *Nova* in April 1965, went further by describing a disc jockey as: "a gregarious amphibian with a seductive mating call. He is as agile as a chimpanzee. He is indefatigably cheerful (or at least sounds cheerful) even at six o'clock on a cold wintry morning with a force 9 gale blowing. He is young, probably in his twenties, and is still a bachelor. He had previous experience on Commonwealth or American radio, or on the stage, or as an MC in dance halls and clubs. He wears clothes so casual they might almost be called *negligée.* And he sometimes attempts to grow a beard, but with only occasional success."

Radio presenter Brian Matthew, who gained his broadcasting experience with the British Forces Network in Germany, and who later joined the BBC, says that some of the pirate disc jockeys were very good, but others could best be described as "talented bingo callers."

Virginia Ironside, writing an article in the *Daily Mail* in June 1965, said that pirate disc jockeys were "a race as weird as switchboard operators - disembodied voices, faceless joke machines."

The late Tommy Shields, former managing director of Radio Scotland, said in 1966: "A pirate disc jockey must be a young, adventurous man with a theatrical turn of mind. He must have a pleasant personality and a warm and friendly voice."

Radio News said in January 1967 that the criterion for selecting a pirate disc jockey "is the ability to project his personality. He must carry the audience along practically on his own for a full three hours. Among the basic requirements are a good clear voice, and experience in broadcasting which will enable him to operate his own panel whilst transmitting. At any one moment he can call upon more than a dozen different sources of sound and sound effects, and of course his own voice. A disc jockey must be willing to work unusual shifts, because of the peculiarity of the position of the broadcasting station. A disc jockey works two weeks at sea and spends a week on land."

Peter Lewis, writing in the *Daily Mail* on 22 August 1967, described the man at the microphone as follows:

He is rich. He is, in his way, famous. He is the latest development of that familiar figure of the open market place, the salesman with an endless stream of patter and spiel. Only he is not selling substandard blankets or tea trays or sides of pork, but lengths of music.

It is some sort of comment on our mechanical civilisation that the star is not the singer, not the song, but a man who puts on records well.

The final description of a pirate disc jockey comes from the late Lois Hollands, former

Mike Allen

Don Allen

Andy Archer

Greg Bance

Alan Black

Chuck Blair

Tony Brandon

Paul Burnett

Roger Day

president of the Ray Conniff fan club, who said in 1967: "Happiness is commercial radio and her disc jockeys; voices of the day and age; the voices which give you the music you want to hear when you want to hear it. They genuinely sound interested in the difficult job they are doing.

"Pirate disc jockeys are happy voices playing happy music on their desert island ships ... they all swing and sway the commercial DJ way."

DJ Tommy Vance says that the BBC would introduce records ('introduce' being the key word). "The pirate radio disc jockey would gently cajole you into listening to a record."

The world's very first disc jockey was Christopher Stone - or to give him his full title - Christopher Reynolds Stone, DSO. MC. He was born in Eton in 1882 and commissioned into the 22nd Royal Fusiliers in 1915.

Christopher Stone presented the first programme of gramophone records from the BBC's Savoy Hill studios on 7 July 1927 and regularly broadcast until 1960. He appeared on television many times. Stone died on 22 May 1965.

A list of disc jockeys and newsreaders connected with the British offshore stations between 1964 and 1967 now follows - some two hundred and fifty of them. Some stayed for a few days and disappeared, never to be heard of again, whereas others remained and made a name for themselves. We shall look in a little more detail at some of the more famous names. In certain cases, when a DJ moved from one radio station to another, he changed his name. In this instance the former name, or nickname, appears in brackets.

DJs who appeared on pirate radio stations after the Marine Offences Act came into force can be found in Chapter Thirteen.

Glenn Adams, Mike Ahern, David Allan, Chris Allen, 'Daffy' Don Allen, Mike Allen, Tony Allen, Vince 'Rusty' Allen, Eddie Anthony, Andy Archer (Terry Dawson), Simon Ashley, John Aston, Bud Ballou, Mike Barron, Nick Bailey, Mike Baron, Fred Beare, Karol Beer, Paul Beresford, Bill Berry, Clive Berry, Colin Berry, Robin Best, Alan Black, Tony Blackburn, Guy Blackmore, Chuck Blair, Peter 'Boots' Bowman, Pete Brady, Gary Brandem, Tony (Bird Brain) Brandon, Boom Boom Brannigan, Stacey Brewer, Colin Brian, Bobby Brown, Ross William Brown (RWB), Lord Charles Brown, Errol Bruce, Gerry Burke, Paul Burnett, Clive Burrell, Woolf Byrne, Johnny Caine, Candy Calvert, Susan Calvert, Doug Carmichael, Tony Carroll, Dave Cash, Alan Clark (Christopher Clark), Edward Cole, Carl Conway, Ralph Cooper, Ray Cooper, Tom Cooper, Chris Cross, Peter Du Crow, Gordon Cruse, Brian Cullingford, Jack Curtiss, Cliff Cuttelle, Robbie Dale, Ian 'Wombat' Damon, Rick Dane, Tony Daniels, Johnny Dark, Roger 'Twiggy' Day, Larry Dean, Alex Dee, Simon Dee, Ted Delaney, Keith Delmont, Chris Denning, Dave Dennis (Neil Spence), Bob Dewing, Dick Dickson, Peter Dolphin, Pete Drummond, Don Dwight. John Edward (Johnnie Flux), 'Tatty' Tom Edwards, Paul Elvey, Kenny Everett, Bruce Ford, Paul Freeman, Roger Gale, Stevie Gee, Lee Gilbert (Bob Walton), Graham Gill, Jeff Godfrey, Roger Gomez (Roger Keene), Jim Gordon (Guy Blackmore), Chris Gosling, Bob Graham, Martin Green, Jonathan Hall, Guy Hamilton, Drew Hamlyn, Keith Hampshire, Richard Harris, Dee Harrison, Tamara Harrison, Albert Hart, Jonathan Harvey, Tom Hatala, Mike Hayes, Phil Hayton, Ben Healy, Bill Hearne, Stuart Henry, Julian Hewitt, Ed Hinkins, Bruce Holland, Paul Hollingdale, Mel Howard, Shaun Howard, Alan Ives, Johnny Jackson, Peter James, Peter Jamieson, Eric Jay, Phil Jay, Sheldon Jay, Eddie Jerold, Duncan Johnson, Gordon Johns, Ric Johns, Jeff Jones, John Junkin, Paul Kaye, Martin Kayne (Michael Caine), Gary Kemp (Gordon Bennett), Doug Kerr, John Kerr, David Kinnaird, Jerry King, Lome King, Roger King, Ted King, Andy Kirk, John Knight, Peggy Knight, Paul Kramer, Ed Laney, Johnny Lark, Bob Larkins, Paul Leevey, Dominic Lefoe, Samantha Leigh, Jerry 'Super' Leighton, Mike Lennox, Bob Le-Roi, Tom Lodge, Graham London (Graham Smith), Trevor Lucas, Mick Luvzit, Adrian Love, Jimmy Mack, Allen Mackenzie, Peter Mallan, Tony Mandell, Mike Marriott, Eric Martin, John Martin, Keith Martin (Gary Courteney), Phil Martin, John McGowan, Brian McKenzie (Brian Webb), Jack McLaughlin, Ian MacRae, Dave McKaye (Dave Gilbee), Tony Meehan, Wally Meehan, Steve Merike, Howard Michaels, Rick

Duncan Johnson

Lorne King

Martin Kayne

Jerry Leighton

Mike Lennox

Tony Meehan

Jon Sydney

Bryan Vaughan

Willy Walker

Michaels, 'Neddy' Noel Miller, Carl Mitchell, Tony Monson, Chris Moore, Ed Moreno, Henry Morgan (Gerry Burke), Spangles Muldoon (Kilroy, Chris Cary), Jim Murphy, Janice Nicholls, Colin Nicol, Paul Noble, Ron O'Quinn, Richard Palmer, Richard Park, Brian Paull, John Peel, Mac Peters, Brendan Power, Tony Prince, Mike Proctor, Harry Putnam, Rick Randall, Robert Randall, Ross Randell (Alan West), Mandy Raven, Mike Raven, Earl Richmond, John Ridley, Bill Rollins, Mark Roman, Emperor Rosko, Martin Ross, John Ross-Barnard (JRB), Larry Pannell, Pete Ross and Peter Barraclough), Sheena Russell, Bob Scott, Mike Scott, Peter Scott, Roger Scott (Arnold Layne, Greg Bance), John Sedd (John Cross), Clement Shaw, Mike Shaw, George Short, Tony Silver, Dave Simser, David Sinclair, Keith 'Cardboard Shoes' Skues, Mark Sloane (Mark Hammerton), Jerry Smithwick, Bob Snyder, Michael Speake, Jack Spector, Bob Spencer, Norman St. John, Mark Stephens, Gary Stevens, Martin Stevens, Bob 'Baby' Stewart, Chris Stewart, Ed Stewart, John Stewart, Dennis 'The Menace' Straney, Eric Sullivan, Screaming Lord Sutch, Gordon Swann, Jon Sydney, Keith Taylor, Lee Taylor, Steve Taylor, Ray Teret, Jay Thompson, Shawn Tilley, Leon Tippler, Dave Lee Travis, Alan Turner, Brian Tylney, Jeff Tyse, Tommy Vance, Bryan Vaughan, Guy Vernon, Johnnie Walker, Willy Walker, Bob Walton, Richard Warner, Greg Warren, John Waters, Bruce Wayne, Paul Wayne, Brian Webb, Graham Webb, Alan West, Ian West, Mark West (Mark Wesley), Mike West, Stephen West, Charlie White, Eddy White, Jeremy Wilde, Dave Williams, Tony Windsor (Tony Withers), Doug Wood, Jason Wood, Geoff Woods, Tim Yale (Graham Johns), John York, Peter York, Hal Yorke, Paul Young and Steve Young.

Cartoon of pirate radio disc jockey, circa 1964

Cartoon of BBC radio presenter, circa 1964, drawn by an anonymous pirate radio fan, from the same source

MIKE AHERN

Mike Ahern was born in Waterloo, Liverpool, on 30 September 1942 and was educated at St. Bede's Secondary Modern School where he stayed until he was 15. He had met Kenny Everett at St. Edmund's Primary School, Waterloo, and both went on to St. Bede's Secondary Modern School.

Mike remembers those days: "It was at St. Edmund's that Kenny chucked a brick over a wall. I was on the other side and he split my head open!!"

His first appearance on stage was aged 11 when he led the singing at the children's Saturday morning matinee at the Odeon Cinema, Waterloo ... "Here we are again, happy as can be, all good pals and jolly good company ..."

Mike's first job was in a menswear shop but, due to a serious mishap involving a suit worth 30 guineas (£31.50), he moved to another job after just three months. A variety of jobs followed including barman, clerk and factory hand. A colleague of his opened a club, 'The Teen-Beat', and Mike acted as compère. He was also part-owner. He worked at two legendary venues in Liverpool as compère, Litherland Town Hall and the Jive Hive at St. Luke's Hall. He has worked at the Cavern Club, Liverpool, with disc jockey Bob Wooler.

Shortly afterwards Mike applied for a job with Radio Caroline. "I bombarded the radio station with letters and phone calls. In the end they got fed up with me and told me to go to London for an audition. I borrowed the bus fare from my mum. I had never been to London before and nearly got lost trying to find Chesterfield Gardens. I recorded the audition tape and waited for three weeks but heard nothing. I kept ringing them. Then one day my mum called at the shop where I was working and said 'This Radio Caroline, or whatever it's called, wants you to ring them ...' I did, and reversed the charges from a phone box in Liverpool. They asked me if I could join the North ship in four days. Could I? It was one of the best days of my life. My first stint on board was three weeks in November 1964. I was sick before my first programme because of nerves. I still get nervous before a radio show even after

Mike in 1964

nearly 30 years." He moved to the South ship in April 1966 and took over the 9.00am to 12.00 noon show.

Mike says he does not have any hobbies outside of work. His job is his hobby. However, he enjoys reading non-fiction books. His favourite books are "Deadly Carousel" by Monica Porter; all Philip Ziegler's works and biographies of famous people.

Looking back to those halcyon days of the Swinging Sixties, Mike says of his time working for Radio Caroline: "It was a marvellous experience and I'm thankful I was a part of it all. There are so many stories to tell. One which vividly sticks in my mind concerns Emperor Rosko's mynah bird, Alfie. I was given the job of looking after the bird for a week when Rosko went on shore leave. He really did love the bird. I decided to rig up a continuous tape which said 'Rosko's a bastard!' This was relayed through a small speaker in his cage. The bird chatted away but never said the words I had recorded ... until three weeks later. Rosko had taken Alfie to the Royal Garden Hotel in Kensington, London, and put him on a window-ledge in his room behind the curtains. Sometime later that evening he entertained a lady guest in his room. The story goes that it was all very romantic with wine and soft music, when suddenly Alfie piped up from behind the curtain 'Rosko's a bastard!' The lady apparently freaked out as she did not know who or what it was uttering the words. Rosko lost one bird who flew out of the room but kept the other, Alfie. Boy, was he mad!"

Mike had a successful fan club during the pirate era, through which he used to receive proposals of marriage.

He made his television début on Granada in June 1966 as presenter of *New Faces.*

He was one of the original team of disc jockeys on BBC Radio 1 when the station opened on 30 September 1967. He co-presented one show *Top Gear,* and achieved a record as being the disc jockey who survived Radio 1 for the shortest possible time. "They didn't ask me back because I was awful," says Mike "so I left for Australia. I was told that I would never get a job on radio in Australia because of my pommy accent. I did!"

Mike joined radio station 4BC in Brisbane. He was with them from 1968 to 1981 with short breaks at 6PM, Perth. Other stations he worked on in Australia were 3UZ, Melbourne, 2KO, Newcastle and 7HT, Hobart. Mike was the only British-born presenter to make it successfully on commercial radio in Australia ... pommy accent or not!

Mike Ahern, who has two children, 'stopped being married in 1981,' returned to Britain in the summer of 1988 and joined Essex Radio. This was followed by short attachments to Radio Aire and Piccadilly Radio. In August 1990 he moved to Capital Gold in London where he now presents the Monday to Thursday 10.00pm to 2.00am show and Saturday morning *Breakfast Show.* He describes this as "my best ever radio job."

DAVID ALLAN

Born in 1940, David began his radio career in 1966 on Radio 390, the sweet music station - with the now celebrated thriller writer Ted Allbeury in command. The radio station was based on anti-aircraft forts in the Thames Estuary.

Says David: "My first impression after having been winched up some 60ft. from the

David Allan

small tender (based in Whitstable) was that - all in all - it was rather a comfortable place. The central heating system was still working. There was hot and cold running fresh water, showers, proper toilets and an excellent kitchen. The sleeping quarters were also excellent. We each had a proper bed, fresh linen, and we slept no more than three to a room. There was plenty of space everywhere.

"Shifts consisted of two weeks on and one week off (subject to weather conditions), and each presenter broadcast for around six hours a day. We opened at 6.00am and closed at midnight. There were usually only three presenters on the fort, an engineer, a librarian and - most importantly - a cook.

"We all got paid the same rate - £25 a week, so there was no sort of one upmanship. Everyone was equal. This was in marked contrast to the vast profits the station was making in its heyday. Apparently just one sponsored programme - Herbert V. Armstrong"s celebrated *The World Tomorrow* - paid all the station's weekly expenses. The rest was profit."

Programming was middle-of-the-road 'sweet' music with certain types of music being featured in regular slots ... *Masters of the Organ, Jim Reeves Show,* and *Countrystyle* which, in little over a month, became Radio 390's most successful specialist programme. This, in turn, led to David being given a country music programme on Radio 2 in 1968.

David continues: "Compared with life on a pirate ship (I did a very brief spell on Radio 355), it was a cushy number. Records were selected from a huge library (housed in one of the forts) by the librarian who would be waiting, with a full running order, outside the studio prior to one's shift. We never broadcast for more than two hours at a time, so there was a variety of voices and styles throughout the day and evening.

"Apart from *Countrystyle*, my favourite programme was *Dinner at Eight*, sweet music designed to be listened to whilst taking a leisurely dinner. It was something very few listeners were likely to be doing, but it was exactly this sense of a civilised, gentlemanly lifestyle that appealed to so many of the listeners. I can well recall one letter I had from a listener in Birmingham (Yes, we had a wide reach) describing her pretty horrendous life in slum-like conditions trying to bring up a family on very little money. 'Your programmes,' she wrote 'offer me a glimpse of another kind of life and I am so grateful that for a few hours a day at least I can be a part of that. To be spoken to by such gentlemen and to listen to such lovely music is a great pleasure ...'"

David concludes: "Radio 390 was an antidote to the pop pirates and is, I would suspect, sadly missed today."

When the pirates closed he joined the BBC and from 1968-1982 regularly presented country music shows on Radio 2. For many years he hosted the Sunday morning *Breakfast Show* on Radio 2 until 1992.

He is now a television announcer with BBC 1 as well as doing a similar job with British Forces TV (SSVC). David has kept the country music connection going with current programmes on five international airlines (including British Airways), and BBC World Service.

In 1990 David Allan received the award of "Most Popular European Country Music DJ" in a poll organised by the journal *Country Music Roundup* and voted for by listeners in seven European countries. He holds that award to this day.

DON ALLEN

'Daffy' Don Allen joined Radio Caroline in March 1965. He originally came over to England in December 1964 to meet his in-laws shortly after marrying his English wife, Sandra, in Canada. He had planned a short stay but, upon looking into the 'Caroline adventure', decided he would give it a try, and thoroughly enjoyed his job.

Don worked with Radio Caroline South as well as in Caroline House, London, but in 1966 he moved to the North ship and held down the 9.00am - 12 noon show. He also presented a country and western show on both Radio Caroline North and South.

"I am a great C & W fan", says Don "and I hope that one day this kind of music will make a big impact in the British Isles."

Don recalls that to get to the North ship from his Surrey home before the Marine, Etc., Broadcasting (Offences) Act became law, he had to go by cab, then train, cab again, coach, plane, car and boat. He was thankful it was not a daily occurrence.

Before coming to Britain he worked in Canadian radio and television, America and Mexico, but said that working for offshore radio had been one of the most exciting times and interesting ventures of his career.

Don and his wife, Sandra, became the parents of a son, Gary, in 1967. They were divorced on 20 July 1976.

He remained with Radio Caroline North after the Marine, Etc., Broadcasting (Offences) Act became law in the Isle of Man on 1 September 1967.

Two years later he joined Manx Radio as chief announcer, resigning in 1972 to take up a post with Radio Northsea International. Whilst with RNI he also pre-recorded a weekly country music show for BBC Radio Merseyside.

Don decided to quit radio in 1976 and took up industrial engineering which he continued to do until 1980. By chance he rang ex-Caroline DJ Robbie Dale who was working in Ireland. Don was offered a job in Ireland where he has been ever since. He is the regular presenter of *Country and Western*

Jamboree on Radio 3M, from Tullamoore, County Offaly. Ireland.   (He has since died)

MIKE ALLEN

Mike Allen was born Alan Zeffert, son of Charles and Adelaine Zeffert, in Portsmouth, Hampshire, on 15 May 1931.

He was educated at Portsmouth Grammar School and, after leaving, had a total of thirty one jobs including digging ditches and buying plastics.

Mike teamed up with colleague Tony Day who broadcast on Radio Caroline under the name Eddie Anthony. Since he left the ship Tony has been writing, arranging and playing music in both the USA and in England. He now lives in Portsmouth. Together Mike and Tony have written over 200 songs, as well as instrumental and cabaret material. About 60 songs have been recorded by such artists as Mark Murphy, Ray Ellington, Cleo Laine, Gerry and the Pacemakers, Billy Cotton, Lord Sutch and Millicent Martin.

Day and Zeffert were given a three-year contract with Merit Music in London as staff writers during which time they instigated the famous West Indian 'Carnival' label. They found the artists, wrote the songs, supervised the recording sessions and then went out and sold the records themselves. One of their records - Sugar 'n' Dandy's *What a Life* - sold over 30,000 copies.

Mike joined the staff of Radio Caroline South (although it was Radio Atlanta in those days) and made his début on the air during the afternoon of 27 June 1964.

He left full-time broadcasting in October 1965 but continued freelancing for Radio Caroline with shows like *Star Choice* and jazz programmes. He also interviewed many of the day's top pop stars.

In February 1966 Caroline changed its broadcasting format and went all pop. Mike decided he had just about had enough and could stand no more. For the sake of his wife and family he left Radio Caroline.

His first wife's name was Rhoda (Red), they were married in 1956 and have two children, Leigh and Jo.

Mike's likes in jazz, a subject on which he is an authority, cover the spectrum. From Armstrong and Morton through the big band "swing era", bebop (his favourite period), and modern jazz. His particular favourites are Charlie Parker, Miles Davis, Stan Getz, Bud Powell and Bill Evans.

Mike presented a series of programmes called *Triple Crown* for the BBC Light Programme during June and July 1966 in which he devised, scripted and selected the music himself.

His hobbies are records, writing jazz articles, reading and playing football and tennis. His personal ambition is to live in peace at his own pace. He ran a successful business called "Discoveries" where he dealt with rare and deleted LPs for collectors.

Mike married for the second time (wife's name Gillian) in 1972, returning to Portsmouth in 1985 where he is now a freelance writer and broadcaster.

VINCE ALLEN

Sometimes known as 'Rusty' because of the colour of his hair, Vince started broadcasting in offshore history with Radio Essex, later moving to Radio 270 where he presented a breakfast show.

Six feet tall and an ex-paratrooper, Vince, who was born in 1937, lists among his favourite artists Mary Wells, Beach Boys, Little Richard, Jerry Lee Lewis and all Tamla Motown stars.

He became programme controller of Radio 270 in April 1967 and remained with the station until it closed at midnight on 14 August 1967. Vince officially closed down Radio 270. The last record he played was *Land of Hope and Glory* by Vera Lynn.

His hobbies include photography and, when he has a few spare moments, delving into the history of railway engines. Amongst Vince's likes are Chinese food, travel and central heating.

He is currently employed by Southend Council. Essex.

ANDY ARCHER

Andrew Anthony Dawson was born in Terrington St. Clement, Norfolk, on 22 January 1946 and educated at Terrington St. Clement High School and West Norfolk College of Art and Technology.

He first took an interest in radio when he

heard DJ Tom Lodge on Radio Caroline. Andy recalls: "From then on I decided I wanted to be a disc jockey. I was given a small transistor radio for Christmas which I used to listen to Caroline, and then in December 1964 along came Big L."

He visited London and called in at the offices of Radio City in Denmark Street, which was known in those days as Tin Pan Alley. He was offered a trip out to the forts in 1965. "I had already signed on to join the Royal Air Force and I was awaiting my joining instructions. However, I did go out to Radio City with Tom Edwards. Alan Clark was on board and I stayed with the station for just one week, then returned to land and joined the RAF. I became an assistant air traffic controller stationed at RAF Shawbury and later RAF Tern Hill and RAF Ballykelly. I had signed on for 9 years but decided to buy myself out after two. I went to see Ronan O'Rahilly who was working at Mid Atlantic Films in London's West End. I hung around for two days before I eventually met him.

"He said I could go out to Radio Caroline. This was just after the Marine Offences Act had come into force. He rang Philip Solomon's office and I met his assistant, Joan Thirkettle (who later went on to television news), who gave me £10 and a single air ticket to Schiphol Airport, Amsterdam. I travelled out with Caroline DJ Bud Ballou.

"We arrived at the Caroline office, which was located at Singel 160, Holland, and run by Nan Richardson, wife of an engineer, Don Richardson, who worked on the *Mi Amigo*. No one seemed to know who we were. Eventually, two days later, we sailed from IJmuiden on the *Offshore I*. It was a horrendously long journey which took some 19 hours to reach Radio Caroline.

"Once on board I was given a radio show and had to play about 18 records an hour, all of which were paid for. The DJs had no say in their choice of music on air. The adverts centred around Phil Solomon's cabaret acts who were promoted regularly.

"Incoming mail was unbelievable. I used to receive between 1,000 and 2,000 letters a week. I have never seen anything like it

before - nor since! However, that was nothing to Johnnie Walker's 5,000 letters a week."

Andy was on board Radio Caroline South when she was forcibly towed into Amsterdam in March 1968.

He worked for Radio Northsea International from 1970 until the station had its first closedown. He reappeared on it again in 1971 and then joined Radio Caroline for two years when the ship was rescued from the scrapyard in 1972.

On 18 September 1975 Andy Archer went into the history books as being the first disc jockey to be prosecuted under the Marine Etc., Broadcasting (Offences) Act 1967. He was fined £100 with £50 costs.

Andy joined Radio Orwell, in Ipswich, in 1975, two years after ILR came to Britain, and also worked as a continuity announcer for Tyne Tees Television and Television South West.

In 1980 he worked for Devonair Radio before going to Ireland where he was programme controller on Nova and Radio ERI. He was also employed by Centre Radio, the first ILR station to go bankrupt!

Andy returned to Radio Caroline in 1983 for a short time before coming on land again with County Sound in Guildford in 1984. A year later he was back with Radio Orwell as head of music where he stayed until 1990, moving to Invicta Supergold as programme controller. He was also at the opening of Mellow 1557 in Frinton-on-Sea.

More recently he was with CNFM in Cambridge as programme controller. Now a freelance broadcaster, he lives in the Norfolk countryside.

Looking back on the watery wireless days Andy recalls: "The whole period was enlightening. We were living in rather bizarre circumstances spending two or three weeks on a ship. We could very clearly see the shore with cars and motor bikes zooming along the coast road, but we were not allowed ashore. I certainly enjoyed the camaraderie and bonhomie. I didn't take life too seriously. Our job was to produce light entertainment. We were all young. When we went ashore after three weeks on board we would pick up about £400, spend it and then go back and do it all again."

Andy is the only disc jockey to have worked with offshore stations during three of the four eras of pirate radio.

JOHN ASTON

John Aston (real name John Hatt) entered the world of radio in 1965. Following a two hour audition with Mike Raven in London. John joined the former World War II sea fort-based KING Radio as a disc jockey. He had been taken on board for the build-up to a new high power station, at the time not yet named.

Following the installation of a 10kW transmitter and 200ft. high radio mast, KING Radio closed down and Radio 390 was bom; John broadcast under the name John Stewart on KING, changing to Chris Stewart for 390 (this was due to Equity already having a John Stewart on their books). In November 1965, he left 390 and moved further out of the Thames Estuary to Knock John Fort, home of Radio Essex. This station gave a whole new meaning to the word 'basic' and was quite a challenge. At a later date, he took over from Vince Allen as programme director. Towards the end of his time with Radio Essex, John would typically start work at 11.00pm. continue to 6.00am, compile and read the news from 7.00am to 9.00am, go back on air from 9.00am to 12 noon, grab some sleep, and then start all over again. He would remain on the fort for up to 4 or even 5 weeks before taking a single week's leave. On one occasion John remembers: "At about 5.30am on a Sunday morning in 1966 I was talking about the record I had just played, when there was an almighty crash. I put on the next record and rushed out on deck. And there it was, our aerial mast no longer up in the air, but now hanging over the side of the fort, dangling in the Thames Estuary." John left Radio Essex at the end of May 1966.

After a short break, he was employed by Caroline North as a newsreader/relief disc jockey. After a couple of weeks on board, another name change became necessary due to mail mix-ups with Bob Stewart; from then on he was John Aston.

In October 1966, Caroline's advertising

John Aston

revenue dropped (mainly on the South ship) and, as a result, the company made some cutbacks - John was one of them! However, all was not lost as Graham Webb introduced John to Chuck Blair at Radio England/Britain Radio. As the stations were fully crewed at that time. Chuck referred John to Pearl & Dean's Radiovision Broadcasts (International) Ltd, where John spent a few weeks selling advertising time on Radio England/Britain Radio.

In November 1966 he rejoined Caroline, now on the South ship *(Mi Amigo)*, again working on the news. After the North ship, the *Mi Amigo* was very cramped and lacked the stability of the m.v. *Caroline* so, at the end of January 1967, after a very severe storm. John resigned from the South ship. The following month he joined Radio 270 presenting the 9.00am to 12 noon slot, plus a couple of hours in the evening. All went well aboard the *Oceaan 7* until he went down with flu whilst on shore leave. During this time he was approached by Mark Sloane (ex-390) who said that Tony Windsor required an extra presenter on Radio 355.

In April 1967 John joined 355 aboard the *Laissez-Faire*. He recalls: "This was a great station to work on as the studios were very well equipped and living standards were almost as good as on Caroline North, not to mention the transmitters (two 50kW units, one for 355, the other running Radio 227, a Dutch pop station). 227 was shut down in the month preceding the Marine Offences Act coming into force, so at first 355 was broadcast on both frequencies; then 227 frequency was disconnected from the antenna system and 355 was able to transmit on full power (prior to this neither station could transmit on full power due to cross-modulation)."

About 6 weeks before 14 August 1967, a new page in the history of Radio 355 was turned with a live broadcast by José Feliciano. As both studios were in use, the venue was John's four-berth cabin, the top bunk beds being removed to accommodate their guest. Says John: "Following the Feliciano broadcast we had a lot of trouble with one very drunk member of the Dutch crew, who had a compelling desire to attack the captain of the *Laissez-Faire*. Reading about the incident the following day in the tabloids, I was amazed at one press statement claiming that they, the disc jockeys, were all locked in their cabins for their protection. Even 26 years later I remember the incident very clearly, we all stayed up late, playing cards and humouring the offending Dutchman, until the supply tender arrived in the early hours of the morning to take him back to Holland. My cabin had no door, just a curtain and there were definitely no locks on that. 355 shut down just before 14 August and the Marine Offences Bill. It had been John's intention to rejoin Caroline North, but a couple of weeks in getting urgent dental repairs carried out resulted in John literally missing the boat!

After a short spell of unemployment, John started working on voice-overs for documentaries and sales training films. In 1970, he joined a film production company as assistant production manager. In 1975, he briefly returned to radio on the technical side, providing and setting up his own studio equipment in commercial locations for Swansea Sound Outside Broadcasts.

He set up a small audio visual production studio at Bray Film Studios, Berkshire, located within the main sound recording studio complex owned by Adam Francis. Although several promised contracts were not forthcoming, in 1977 he was approached by Nick Allder and Brian Johnson, who had just finished the special effects on *Space 1999* at Bray Studios. They invited him to join their effects crew on *Medusa Touch*. This led to work on *Revenge of the Pink Panther, Alien, The Empire Strikes Back, Sea Wolves, Dragonslayer, Nighthawks, Return of the Jedi (Star Wars III), Krull,* and then *Dune*. Located in Mexico City for 16 months, *Dune* brought about 35 seconds of screen stardom with a brief speaking role as a five star general.

In 1985, John again worked with Nick Allder, this time on *Jewel of the Nile*. The effects crew built a full sized F-16 fighter out of fibre glass, steel and alloy sheeting. He says: "To make it suitable for filming, the aircraft was powered by a 7½ litre Chevy Camero engine driving the aircraft's main wheels. The driving position was located inside the air intake and was best suited to a driver around 5ft. in height. Anyway, it's a long story, but the Italian stunt co-ordinator felt that it would not be possible to drive the aircraft, so as I (all 6ft.3ins. of me) had driven the vehicle for a couple of miles to the location, guess who was asked to undertake the stunt driving?"

John also worked on *Haunted Honeymoon* directed by Gene Wilder, *Aliens, Princess Bride, The Rescue, Leviathan, Russia House* and *Hudson Hawk,* not to mention on numerous TV commercials. He was, in 1993, working on Kenneth Branagh's *Frankenstein.*

John is married to Christine, and they have two children, Caroline and Christopher. The family lives in Berkshire.

GREG BANCE
When the offshore stations began in 1964, Gregory Edward Bance was still at grammar school in London and had set his mind on becoming a radio 'jock'. Once he left school he compiled an audition tape and sent it to Radio Essex, one of the smaller offshore stations. He was accepted, and joined the station in February 1966 under the name Roger Scott.

Says Greg: "In the Sixties it was the vogue

for anyone in the public eye or ear to change their name. Roy Bates, the station owner, wanted his 'chaps' to bear strong, resolute names. I became the first Roger Scott to be heard in Britain and it was a name I used professionally for a number of years."

Greg remembers his first task on the Knock John Fort, Radio Essex. It was filling up the oil tank. "Oil came on board in small cans and had to be transferred to an old aircraft tank on deck. This was a sort of initiation rite for the newcomer and I copped it on a very cold, windy day. I was soon drenched in diesel oil. Showers on Radio Essex were unheard of, baths too, or any water at all sometimes. Over a quarter of a century later, a whiff of diesel fumes instantly transports me back to my training as a disc jockey!"

Greg remained with Radio Essex for nine months. He says: "I was only 17 and my approach to presentation was described as 'bubbly.' It was certainly very lively and uninhibited. Conditions on board were primitive. When we stopped being paid for our fun and found ourselves being left on the fort for weeks on end, it was time to make a move."

The next port of call was Radio 270 off Scarborough. He did not enjoy his four months there. "For one thing, the owner didn't give the impression of having a great love for DJs and for another, the *Oceaan 7*, the station's home, was a horribly cramped tub. It wasn't without its amusements, largely thanks to Aussie jock, Dennis Straney, who had a great personality."

By March 1967 Greg was, once more, on the move: "Time was running out as the Government were getting very shirty about us naughty *pirates*. The Postperson-General at the time, Edward Short, was determined to nail us so that the airwaves would be nice and dead and boring again!" Greg joined the 'sweet music station,' Radio 390. However, the station was obliged to close down on 28 July and he was "forced by the Government to be unemployed," as he puts it. With malice? "Oh yes, quite a lot of it!"

The state of unemployment didn't last long, and Greg joined Radio Caroline North off the Isle of Man. The Marine etc.,

Broadcasting (Offences) Act had come into effect by now and the future of the only remaining offshore station beamed to the UK didn't seem bright. "Radio Caroline was a legend and I was glad to have had an opportunity to work there before it disappeared for a few years," says Greg. "The m.v. *Fredericia* was a comfortable vessel and what made it different from the rest was that it actually had a real staircase which was very civilised! I like staircases. They're an endangered species in the elevator age! One Sunday evening in March 1968, the *Fredericia* left her anchorage and was towed to Amsterdam, arriving there the following Saturday. Although this was a forced repatriation, it meant another dead-end for me."

So Greg left offshore radio behind for the time being to spend more time with his staircase, as he puts it. He didn't stay home for long as he was hired by the fledgling Harlech TV as a continuity announcer. He says that the silliest thing he did at HTV had nothing to do with his professional performance. "One of my beautiful colleagues, Elizabeth Carse, with whom at work I was perfectly friendly, one day suggested that we might together do nothing in particular. I don't know whether my imagined telly-star status had done my brain in, or whether I'd been looking at too many staircases but I heard myself say that I was too - wait for it - 'busy'. She went on to marry a BBC Television newsreader."

After a few months freelancing, Greg went to Anglia TV in Norwich in October 1969 for a year. Since then he has spent a short time with Tyne Tees TV until his hankering after offshore radio became uncontrollable.

Radio Northsea International provided a lifeline for Greg's yearning for the high seas. Early in 1972, he shipped out to the *Mebo II* anchored off the Dutch coast. Now 23, he changed his name to Arnold Layne, after the Pink Floyd hit which was one of his all-time 'faves.'

"One of the great thrills of being on RNI was that listeners would write in. Not just for namechecks or to enter competitions but to express opinions on what I'd said on-air. I mostly jocked a midnight to three slot, which in a pan-European setting is a perfect time to be on the radio. Co-channel interference was minimal, so the signal reached far and wide and, of course, at that time of day, listeners do tend to listen rather than to hear something on in the background. The music around at that time was excellent. A sort of mixture of Marc Bolan glitz and navel-gazing concept albums. Barclay James Harvest were a mainstay, I'm afraid. "There was always something going on on board, so there were seldom dull moments. Sadly it all had to end when I crossed swords with a fellow jock who held great sway at HQ. So I suddenly wasn't there any more."

Upon leaving offshore radio for the last time, Greg was not offered a star billing with the BBC, nor did Capital Radio, which was just about to start in 1973, come up with anything either. Worst of all for him was the arrival on the UK airwaves for the first time of another Roger Scott. "I used to call him the 'Other Roger Scott',", says Greg, "but he maintained that it was his "real' name, so there was nothing I could do about it. As he quickly became a very high profile, extremely talented jock, I changed my name at Equity to Greg Bance and I've been that way ever since. It's my 'real' name, so woe betide anyone who nicks it!"

There followed two productive years of freelancing, especially , on commercial voice-overs and audio-visual narrations for 'corporates' and 'industrials'. There was TV announcing work, too, at Granada, Southern, ATV and LWT. At LBC and IRN he presented network news bulletins, hosted the occasional magazine slot and conducted interviews.

He then joined Radio Orwell in Ipswich. From October 1975 until early 1980 he learned most of what there is to know about local radio and its audience. He left Orwell at the right time and proceeded to hoover up much freelance voice work and some presentation.

Throughout the 1980s and 1990s Greg turned his talents to every kind of radio communication - journalist, scriptwriter, presenter, producer, freelance voice-over man for radio, television, 'corporate' videos and audio visual presentations.

He has worked for both BBC and ITV, including HTV and Anglia, and on radio for BBC Radio London, Essex Radio, Beacon IRN, LBC, Two Counties Radio, Radio Orwell and BFBS.

PAUL BERESFORD

Paul Beresford was the longest serving disc jockey on Radio 390 having started with the station at its inception.

His ambition in life was to become a farmer, but he changed his mind suddenly the day he set fire to a tractor by mistake.

He moved to the City of London and signed up for a two-year acting course. After this he tried his hand at being a stunt man with an equal lack of success. Other jobs included a milk bar attendant and a watch salesman. He joined the staff of Radio 390 in September 1965 and later became its chief announcer. Paul married a French girl named Annick.

In May 1967 he was struck by lightning on the Red Sands Fort off Whitstable ... and lived! Now working in South Africa.

(He has since died)

COLIN BERRY

Son of a company director, Colin was born in Welwyn Garden City on 29 January 1946 and educated at Wembley Grammar School.

He began his media career working in the advertising department at Granada Television and Westward Television.

Colin joined Radio Caroline in 1964 working in the traffic department where radio commercials were scheduled for transmission. He graduated to an 'on air' newsreader and relief disc jockey.

Commenting on his time aboard *Mi Amigo* he says: "From an early age I had always wanted to be a broadcaster, but appreciated it was a difficult job in which to get a break. Working in the traffic department of Radio Caroline was a useful step forward. I was asked to do an audition tape which the programme people accepted. I found the rough seas impossible to cope with and, apart from occasional stints on board mainly for newsreading, my 'on air' work consisted of recording the odd

Colin Berry

commercial; reading weekly bingo numbers for Charlie Drake's *Ognib* programme which was sponsored, and being the regular presenter for the Weetabix-sponsored *Partners in Profit* proof-of-purchase game - a sort of weekend equivalent of *Caroline Cash Casino* which Bill Hearne presented on weekdays. These were pre-recorded in Caroline House studios so there were no rough seas to cope with.

"When on board *Mi Amigo* I used to read the news. Many people wondered where we got our news. I suppose it would spoil a best kept secret if I said we taped it off the BBC Light Programme, rearranged the wording and read it!"

Asked what memory stands out above all others about his time on the ship, Colin says: "Sharing a cabin with Dave Lee Travis, the 'hairy monster' - and choking on his Right Guard deodorant spray every morning as he rose and carried out his ablutions at 5.30am. I shall always remember the smell."

He also has two memories of travelling out to the *Mi Amigo* aboard the tender *Offshore I*. "On one occasion I went out with Olga Franklin who was writing an article for the *Mail*, I think. She was so ill, poor thing, that she spent the whole time resting or being sick!

"Another occasion I was escorting Susan Hampshire to the ship. She was fairly new to the scene, rather aloof and not at all friendly. I am sure maturity has seen her grow into a delightful person, but all she wanted to do that day was sunbathe!

"There was an offer of a presenter's job on board made to me. 'Would I care to join Robbie Dale and Johnnie Walker?' mainly for newsreading, I recall, but programme presenting would inevitably be available. It wasn't easy to make a decision, but good sense and an uneasy stomach made me decline!"

Returning to dry land in 1967, Colin continued to host some "disc nights" and went on to do club/ballroom work in a much bigger way. He had a short spell setting up the advertising side of Yorkshire TV in London and then moved into music publishing for a while.

He joined HTV as an announcer in Cardiff in 1971, but within twelve months was working at BBC Radio Medway (now Radio Kent). He later moved to London in the promotions department of Radio 1.

By September 1973 he had become an announcer on Radio 2, as well as a newsreader. Over the years he has presented numerous programmes including *Two's Best*, *Radio 2 Top Tunes*, *Band Parade*, *Gala Night*, *Music Through Midnight*, *Golden Days*, *Europe 70/80*, *European Pop Jury*, *You the Night and the Music*, *Night Ride* and *The Happy Hour*. He has deputised for Terry Wogan, Ray Moore, David Hamilton, John Dunn, Charlie Chester, Steve Jones and Jimmy Young. His voice is heard worldwide each year on *Eurovision Song Contest*. He has co-presented *Top of the Pops* on BBC TV and appeared in *The Generation Game*, *Going Live*, *Blankety-Blank* and *Wogan*.

He was the commentator for Barry Humphries Variety Club lunch, 1988. Colin has presented shows for BBC Bedfordshire and BFBS, and more recently for Inflight, providing programmes for the airlines.

Of his work at Radio 2, Colin says: "The most time I have spent on a particular programme slot has been the *Early Show* ... for about two years in the mid '70s when it ran from 6.00am; and for over four years in the mid-to-late '80s when it began at 4.00am."

He married Sandra Barker on 4 July 1981 and they have two children, Marina and Jonathan. Colin lists as his enjoyments Wimbledon Fortnight, Thai and Szechuan cuisine, oysters and real ale, not necessarily in that order!

ALAN BLACK

Born in Rosyth in the "Kingdom of Fife', Scotland, on 15 January 1943, Alan was educated locally and studied with a view to going to art college to specialise in fine art. When the time came he underwent a radical change of mind - immediately upon leaving school he spent six months with an itinerant band of gypsies.

Alan followed this by joining a commercial art studio as an illustrator where he "learnt how to wash paint brushes with the best of them." He decided to terminate his employment with the firm after the senior partner told Mr Black that he would be unable to raise his salary from thirty shillings (£1.50) - "You shouldn't think of your career in terms of money." he said, flicking the ash of a corona from a neatly-suited knee.

So Alan picked up his easel and "brushed" out. He travelled as far as the Leith Docks and spent several idyllic months playing at sailors on various coasters and even a couple of ocean-going vessels. After deciding to think about a serious job, Alan joined a publishing firm in Dundee, turning out cartoon strips and small features for the company's various publications.

He gravitated to London in early 1963 and worked for different agencies and firms as a commercial artist, later going freelance.

"Through doing some 'bit' work in films and advertising for television, I became interested in radio and began broadcasting in 1966 at the outset of the offshore Radio Scotland. In September that year I made a move south and joined the ill-fated Radio England. When this closed I stayed with her doomed sister station, Britain Radio, and had the dubious honour of being programme director when it eventually folded." When pirate radio came to a close in August 1967,

Alan turned his affections to animations for films and television, and he was one of the team who produced the new Beatles' cartoon film *Yellow Submarine*.

He made his BBC début on 18 July 1968 on *Midday Spin*.

Alan has had various cartoons published in the *Radio Times*.   (He has since died)

TONY BLACKBURN

One of Britain's most popular disc jockeys, he received maximum exposure on the two principal pirate stations, Radio Caroline and Radio London.

Tony Blackburn was born on 29 January 1943, the first child of Dr Kenneth and Mrs Pauline Blackburn, then of Guildford, Surrey. The Blackburns moved to Poole in Dorset in 1948. Tony was educated at Millfield Public School in Street, then received private tuition for a couple of years, ending up with six GCE subjects to his credit at "O" level. From 1961 to 1964 he studied at Bournemouth College of Further Education where he received a business diploma.

Tony's father was a medical practitioner in Poole and he has one sister, Jacqueline.

His ambition from a very early age was to be a singer and a disc jockey, the latter he put out of his mind as it was too difficult a business to get into. Instead, during his spare moments from Bournemouth College, he practised his singing. To this end, and to prove his enthusiasm, he joined the Jan Ralfini Band as resident singer at the Bournemouth Pavilion.

In 1964 Tony was offered a job as a singer with the Johnny Howard Band - at the same time he had spotted an advert in the *New Musical Express* asking for potential disc jockeys for Radio Caroline. He sent a tape and was accepted by programme director, Chris Moore.

Tony Blackburn joined Caroline South in July 1964. Thus he achieved his ambition of wanting to become both a singer and a DJ. Had the pirates not come along, Tony would have most certainly remained a singer.

When he joined Caroline Tony projected a happy style, a teenage sound and a completely new image. This was frowned upon by Caroline authorities who didn't like the personality of a disc jockey to come over the air. However, he finally proved his point and won the battle. Proof enough when he was voted 13th most popular disc jockey in Britain in the *New Musical Express* polls of 1965 (14th in the *Record Mirror);* in 1966 he moved up to slot No. 10 in the *New Musical Express* poll (13th in the *Record Mirror)* and in the 1967 *Disc and Music Echo* Valentine polls, he was No. 8. On the Continent, in the Dutch polls, Tony came 5th in 1964; 5th in 1965 and No. 3 in 1966.

In the summer of 1965 Tony was offered a job on Radio London, but turned it down because Big L wanted him to change his name to Mark Roman; and why should he? After all, it was Tony Blackburn who made the charts! He resigned from Caroline and suddenly found himself without a job. However, Caroline took him back. He was one of the disc jockeys who "almost made it on land" during the winter gales of January 1966   when Caroline ran aground on the Essex coast.

Tony achieved another ambition during his Caroline days - he broke into the recording business; he signed a contract for Fontana Records in 1965 and recorded *Don't Get Off That Train* (1965), *Is There*

Another Way to Love You (1965) and *Green Light* (1966). He has written over 200 songs, but has only had one published, *Winter is Through*, which was the flip side to *Green Light*.

He changed his affections to MGM Records and recorded *So Much Love* (1968) which reached No. 31 in the national charts in January 1968; *She's My Girl* (1968), *It's Only Love* (1969), which reached No. 42 in the national charts in March 1969, and *Blessed Are The Lonely* (1969), Polydor. He also recorded five songs on RCA Records: *Is It Me, Is It You, Chop-Chop, Paper Song, Fairy Tales* and *Cindy*. In addition, he released *Paper Song* (1972) on RCA. Tony has also released the following LPs: *Tony Blackburn Meets Matt Monro* (Fontana), *Tony Blackburn Sings* (MGM) and *Tony Blackburn* (Polydor and RCA).

During the summer of 1965 he introduced a series of *Discs A Go Go* from Bristol on ITV, and appeared on the 'box' a further ten times to promote his first record. Due to illness Tony went into hospital in Bournemouth in May 1966 and resigned from Radio Caroline. He never even said goodbye to his audience. One month later he was offered a job with Radio London and accepted it, retaining the name Tony Blackburn. He presented the *Breakfast Show* and in 1967 successfully brought the programme into the top ratings in commercial radio.

Tony Blackburn joined the BBC Light Programme on contract in August 1967 and presented *Midday Spin*. When BBC Radio 1 commenced on 30 September 1967 he broadcast a daily *Breakfast Show* and was the first disc jockey to appear on the new network where he remained until 1984.

Tony was married to actress Tessa Wyatt, and later divorced. He has one son, Simon. He married Debra Thomson in June 1992 and there was a blessing of the marriage at St Margaret's, Westminster.

He worked as a regular presenter on BBC Radio London from 1984 until June 1988. He joined Capital Radio in London on their Gold service in July 1988 and is a daily presenter of the *Breakfast Show.*

CHUCK BLAIR

Like an intercontinental ballistic missile, Chuck Blair was launched into this world in Boras, Sweden, in the year something or other. If we rapidly subtract, divide, and multiply we can come to a speculative but hazardous guess as to the exact date of the project. In his youth he was scrawny, shy, well-read and well-educated.

He lived in Sweden for only three years while his gadabout industrialist papa flitted between continents, and then was transferred to Swampscott, Massachusetts, (25 miles from Boston) which is a small seaside resort village.

His main ambition was to be a football player much to the dismay of his concert pianist mum and the mystification of his high school football coach who deemed him too undernourished. But by pure courage in devouring tons of American milk shakes and other paraphernalia, our hero went from 12 stone to 15 stone. He then flexed his new biceps and became the tornado of the schoolboy football world and went on via a scholarship to the University of Maryland, to play yet more football. After successive breakages of ankles, wrists and noses, he decided the Korean War was much safer and joined the United States Air Force for two reasons: 1) to avoid the draft and the army marching exercises, and 2) to ride in aeroplanes. From his none-too-safe vantage point on the defence perimeter of Kimpo airfield, he was sometimes allowed to peek at the aircraft he never flew or rode in. He was decorated a few times for successfully confusing the enemy with his running and ducking prowess.

After this happy-go-lucky adventure was over, he returned to his old university and, after graduation, tried his success at professional football. Take tons of scarred brute force, add one missile with a shrapnel filled leg, and subtract one football career.

At this point in life our hero thought of radio as a square box from which *Amos 'n' Andy* and news emitted themselves. After he made known his feelings about industry, stuffy offices, and arithmetic to his dad, he went back to school, this time it was the Emerson College of Dramatics and Broadcasting. He paid his way by touring through the States during his holidays and summer months as a cocktail lounge pianist and jazz musician. Some of mum's talent, not quite the same style, however, rubbed off and he was fairly successful at it, but more importantly it paid the bills.

He also appeared in many plays at college and in summer playhouses, but since Broadway and Carnegie Hall weren't quite convinced of his talents, he sought refuge, on the advice and peculiar insistence of his teachers, and took another look at the square boxed wireless. From then on in, it was all systems go-go-go. From small radio stations in the wilds of America to the top stations of the big cities ... from medium stations of the south to the Columbia Broadcasting Network, Chuck continued.

Dissatisfied with the relative security of a beautiful home on a lake in delightful New England, a wife and two lovely children, two automobiles, and a sizeable bank account, Chuck looked excitedly to the pirate-infested waters of Britain. Never having had the opportunity of wearing an eye-patch, spending doubloons and capturing Spanish women, he accepted an offer from Radio England with its lucrative promises of riches of booty and plunder. It took Chuck three months to become Radio England's general manager but, unbeknown to him, Radio England was in debt up to her stern and was foundering miserably.

After subtracting a secure past and one fed-up wife, multiplying many headaches, and adding numerous debts accrued to the piratical mismanagement of Radio England's hierarchy, we come up with a very disillusioned missile whose rockets did not fire. Hence Radio London became a God-sent refuge for this wild colonial boy. It was his immediate replacement for a happy family.

Chuck can reject the pleas of maidens in five languages, and he can pound hell out of three instruments with complete bliss. In the midst of his then contented state (lots of spaghetti fills the cravings of his big frame) one wondered whether, just like a ballistic missile, Chuck Blair would fizzle or actually go off.

He did go off - but it was for a holiday in the United States of America on 9 June 1967. He returned to England for a short while, but finally decided to settle down in Boston, Massachusetts at the latter end of 1967.

Chuck is currently working in radio in the United States of America. (He has since died)

PETE BRADY

Pete was born in Montreal, Canada, in 1942 and began his disc jockey life with Radio Jamaica. He later decided to come to Britain and his first job was as an assistant film producer. During the evenings he worked as a disc jockey in a club.

He applied for a job with Radio London, was accepted and became one of the original disc jockeys on the m.v. *Galaxy,* holding down the *Breakfast Show* every morning of the week.

He left Radio London in September 1965 to freelance. He acted as compère on the *Star Scene '65* tour with the Everly Brothers and Cilla Black, a joint Brian Epstein/Radio London package. During 1966 and 1967 Pete Brady was heard over the airwaves of Radio Luxembourg in the EMI programmes, and he also broadcast for the BBC on *Midday Spin, Swing into Summer* and *Newly Pressed.*

In the years 1967 and 1968 he presented the *Pete Brady Show* on Radios 1 and 2 and became one of the hosts on the ITV children's programme, *Magpie.* In 1971 he returned to radio and presented an afternoon show on Radio 2, but it did not work out. He always enjoyed broadcasting to the younger age group. Radio 2 was not the right slot for him and his show was dropped.

Pete is a great follower of water skiing. He represented both the West Indies and England in major water skiing championships. He also likes flying and motor racing. His likes in music are directed towards the folk slant, although he admires the talents of Dusty Springfield.

Pete married 25-year-old showjumper Judith Humble on 15 December 1966. Guests included fellow disc jockeys Dave Cash, Simon Dee and David Jacobs.

After living in both Dorking and Winchester for a time, he returned to London in 1982 and has since been running a corporate video company in Shepherd's Bush.

TONY BRANDON

Tony was born on 12 December 1933 in Portland, Dorset. Being third in line to the Brandon fortunes it was his mother's express wish that she would have him at home - in fact it was only after he finally arrived that his mother was taken to hospital. The house in which young Tone was first exposed to the traumas and rigours of life was right next door to a Borstal institution, which could possibly account for the fact that he showed criminal tendencies at a very tender age ... for at only six months he pinched ... his father's arm!

When Tony was still only eighteen months old, the family moved to Portsmouth and it was only after considerable pressure had been brought to bear that Anthony managed to persuade his family to take him along.

The years that followed in Pompey were very happy indeed, though Tony didn't take too kindly to the strict discipline at Portsmouth Grammar School where he was educated. He relates: "What nostalgic days they were - or perhaps sickening is a better word!" A hopeless scholar (Tony's own words), and even more unforgivable, an absolutely abysmal sportsman, he was at last granted his school leaving certificate, "but only because they wanted my desk," he admits.

On leaving school Tony had two burning

ambitions, one to take up journalism - the other, to set his old school alight! However, discretion being the better part of valour he elected for the former. For the next two years his life held all the excitement of a latter-day James Bond - covering such daring events as Women's Institute garden fetes, parish council meetings and on one occasion, an interview with an old lady had who batted 100 years not out. Unfortunately the poor soul expired before the story got into print.

The turning point in Tony's career came when Carroll Levis brought his *Discovery Show* to the Theatre Royal at Portsmouth, and along with 4,000 other hopefuls he went to audition for the great impresario.

To cut a long story sideways, he was engaged on the spot and duly 'discovered.' Tony stayed with the show for about two years during which time he broadcast and appeared on television doing a comedy impression act - a sort of 'poor man's Peter Cavanagh,' he recalls. The natural progression was to cabaret, revue, pantomime and what are known colloquially as 'one night stands.'

Tony goes on: "It's no fun living out of a suitcase - especially as it had several pairs of my socks in it at the time ... so I thought I'd keep my one good eye open for something more settled."

His chance came early in 1966 just after returning home from a Combined Services Entertainment tour of Malta, Libya, Cyprus, Aden and the Persian Gulf. How's that for country dropping!

Having learned that two disc jockeys were leaving Radio Luxembourg, he decided to try for a job. He managed to convince the powers-that-be at '208' that they would be foolish not to employ him. He was taken on. and within a week was on his way to the Grand Duchy of Luxembourg. He remained in Luxembourg for a year before being troubled by itchy feet again. Experiencing a great deal of frustration at not being able to spin his own choice of records, he decided 'to take the plunge and apply for a job with Radio London. He joined the 266 team in April 1967, having spent a very brief spell on Radio City.

Says Tony: "I shall always be very grateful to Radio Luxembourg for giving me my start in radio, but I really did feel that the only way to progress was to have complete control of one's own programmes, and by joining Big L I couldn't have been happier." Known as the 'Bird Brain', Tony remained with Radio London until its closing day on 14 August 1967.

He joined the team of Radio I disc jockeys in November 1967 and presented Tuesday's *Midday Spin.*

In March 1968 he released a record on MGM called *Candy Kisses.* Other records Tony has recorded include *Sleep Little Children* on Chapter One label with Les Reed; *Myrtle's Birthday* with Ed Stewart ("I'm still awaiting the royalties," he adds); *Just Leave It To Me* (1967); *Misty the Mischievous Mermaid* (LP, Walt Disney) and various storytelling EPs (also for Walt Disney).

Other radio shows Tony presented for BBC Radios 1 and 2 included *Family Choice, Radio 1 Club, Tony Brandon Show* and *Tony Brandon Meets the Saturday People.* He also starred in the situation comedy series, *The Family Brandon,* and *Watty Who?* For seven years he wrote and presented *Acker's Half 'Our* featuring Acker Bilk.

Television appearances have included hosting Southern TV's magazine programme, *The Brandon Exchange;* the long-running children's programme *The Learning Tree; Harry Secombe Show, Definition, Babble, Chance in a Million* and *Miss Marple - Murder at the Vicarage.*

His most recent stage appearance was with the UK tour of the record-breaking Ray Cooney farce *Run For Your Wife,* which included a visit to the National Art Centre, Ottawa, Canada. He loves the theatre and always looks forward to the pantomime season when he usually plays a 'Dame'.

Tony is currently involved with independent radio and presents a daily show on Britain's very first all-oldies radio station, First Gold/County Sound, which is currently based in Crawley, Sussex.

Apart from his DJ role he is also sought after to record radio commercials and is a familiar voice behind many advertisements heard throughout the country.

Away from work, Tony lives in the Surrey countryside with Jill (nee Wells), whom he married in 1968. They have a golden labrador, Buster.

PAUL BURNETT

Son of Paul and Alice Burnett, variety artists, Paul was bom on 26 November 1943 in Manchester.

His first job after leaving school was as a salesman in a shop in Darlington. In 1961 he joined the Royal Air Force and began his broadcasting career whilst stationed at Khormaksar, Aden, in 1964. He worked voluntarily for the Aden Forces Broadcasting Association, which had a listening audience of about 5,000 servicemen and women, and enjoyed the job so much that after two years he bought himself out of the RAF and returned to England in search of a job in radio. He did not look around for long.

Whilst working as a resident DJ at the Top Rank Club. Darlington, he was the first disc jockey to be signed up for Radio 270, hired by Don Robinson. He was on board the ship on 31 March 1966. the day before the station was due to begin regular broadcasting, when: "Suddenly a storm blew up, one of the worst that part of the North Sea had ever experienced. There was over 100ft. of aluminium mast crashing around the bridge, like a pendulum. I shall never forget that day because there was a clear blue sky. You would normally expect storms to be accompanied by heavy clouds. The seas were unbelievably rough. The broadcasting staff all stayed below deck being very ill. I was so ill that I wasn't scared. I would have quite happily gone down with the ship at that time. It was awful! The Dutch crew very bravely hacked down the antenna, and the last we saw was it disappearing below the waves into the North Sea."

So how did Paul adapt to his life at sea-broadcasting with a bucket between his legs? "I was ill almost every day. I had read somewhere that Admiral Nelson was also a very bad sailor. Eventually you have to concentrate the mind and live with it and it just becomes part of your life. It is amazing how you can adapt to it without too much difficulty."

One of the great practical jokes on board *Oceaan 7* was thought up by Paul. It involved the senior DJ, Noel Miller.

Said Paul: "We had this cylinder-type vacuum cleaner on board. One day one of the guys poured some self raising flour he obtained from the galley down the tube of the vacuum cleaner. He placed the nozzle, out of view, behind the microphone in the main on-air studio. The vacuum cleaner was left behind the turntables, and the electric cable went through into another room. All we had to do was to flick the switch. Noel was sometimes a little pompous, and we thought it was time to bring him down a peg. So when he went on air with his opening announcement the vacuum cleaner switch was turned on, but nothing happened. All you could hear was the cleaner humming and the power building up behind this tightly packed flour. The bad news was that the flour was *too* tightly packed with the result there was an almighty roar and Noel was covered from head to foot in flour - he looked like a ghost. Talk about flour power! He was not amused at first, but later accepted it as a joke."

Some time later, when Noel Miller left the ship and returned to Australia, Paul took over as station manager for a while before he, too, left Radio 270, in March 1967, to join Manx Radio on the Isle of Man. This was followed by Radio Luxembourg in 1967 where he presented the *Top 20* show for six years. DJ Pete Murray had eased the way for Paul to join Luxembourg. He joined BBC Radio 1 in March 1974 and later worked for Radio 2, BBC World Service and Independent Local Radio. He hosted the *Miss World* TV show, 1978, and appeared on BBC TV's *Top of the Pops*. He was nominated Pye Industries and TV Writers Guild Best Newcomer to TV 1978.

At one stage in his career Paul was working simultaneously for BBC World Service, Capital Radio, Southern Sound, Viking Radio and Radio Nova (satellite), and each station had a different radio control panel which he had to operate.

In 1976 he enjoyed success with fellow DJ Dave Lee Travis when they had a hit record *Convoy GB*, working under the name

Laurie Lingo and the Dipsticks. The record reached No. 4 in the British charts.

Looking back to pirate days Paul says: "I must be the only DJ to be physically sick halfway through a radio commercial. On Radio 270 I had to do a commercial for Wilf Proudfoot's supermarket and describe the delights of sizzling Danish bacon. At the time I was presenting the *Breakfast Show* and the ship was rolling about a great deal, so much so that I couldn't reach the microphone fader, and I vomited all over the continuity desk which, I must say, was not very conducive to buying bacon.

"Being a disc jockey in those days was great fun. I feel rather sorry for the younger generation trying to get the break into radio nowadays. The job has now become much more respectable. Management want university degrees or 'O' and 'A' levels. It is regarded as a form of journalism. What we lack now is 'personality' radio. You can't teach anyone personality at school. You either have it, or you don't. It's as simple as that."

Paul is married to Nicole and they have two sons, Darren and Philip.

He joined Capital Radio as part of the weekly satire show, *Brunch,* which included Josie Lawrence, Angus Deayton, Tony Slattery, and was something of a commercial radio first. The show won a number of international radio awards.

In 1992 he presented a weekly show with the legendary Cousin Brucie in New York, although Paul was in London. He said it was great fun and the show received good audience ratings. He is currently working for Capital Gold, London.

DAVE CASH

Son of a Royal Navy 'medic', Dave Cash was born in Bushey, Hertfordshire, in 1942. He attended the Royal Naval School, Greenwich, before leaving for Canada at the age of sixteen. There he enrolled in the University of British Columbia for a year before deciding that show business was the life for him and joining the world-famous Calgary Stampede where he made his first public appearance as an assistant in the bronco-busting events.

Deciding that life was too tame, Dave took up motor racing and drove a Formula Junior Lotus on the Westward race track. Four broken ribs later, he understandably decided that a quieter life might be more appropriate after all. So he enrolled at the Lome Green Theatrical School for two years after which he packed his bags and headed south down to Los Angeles in California to break into radio. Luckily one of his next door neighbours was Red Robinson who was top DJ on CFUN and got Dave a job on the station.

He spent two years on CFUN presenting the late show from 12 midnight to 6.00am before moving on to New York.

After a short spell in the 'Big Apple', Dave received a letter from an old school chum in England telling him about pirate radio, the Beatles and the whole media explosion.

As a result Dave decided to take a holiday in England and whilst over here was offered a job on Radio London where he proved so successful that he was voted 5th most popular DJ in Britain by the *New Musical Express*. Together with Kenny Everett, he enjoyed tremendous success with the *Kenny and Cash Show*.

Success continued to follow him after leaving Big L when he was offered two regular shows on Radio Luxembourg, first with CBS Records and then with Polydor.

He had his own show on BBC radio called *The Dave Cash Show,* and he was also compère of Radio 1's *Monday Monday*. During the Sixties he presented *What's New* and *Midday Spin*. He inherited the afternoon Radio 1 show from Pete Brady, losing it in turn to Terry Wogan.

Dave attended the opening of BBC Radio Brighton in February 1968 and BBC Radio Durham in July 1968.

The BBC still employed him on chat shows on Radios 1 and 2 which he presented for six months. Guests included Cliff Richard, Spike Milligan, John Cleese and Peter Sellers.

Dave then went to work for Radio Monte Carlo along with Kenny Everett and Tommy Vance. He says: "I helped programme the English service and in six months learned more about radio than in the previous six years."

In 1970 Dave wrote and presented a six-month series for HTV and. whilst in Bristol, met his wife, actress Monica Evans. She had recently returned from America where she had starred in *The Odd Couple* on Broadway for two years. She later appeared in the film with Jack Lemmon and Walter Matthau. Dave and Monica have two children, Emma and Simon.

When Independent Local Radio was introduced to Britain in 1973, Dave joined Capital Radio and has since worked for Radio West and Invicta Radio. He later returned to Capital Radio where he still works.

In June 1992 he launched his first novel, *The Rating Game*, which gave readers a glimpse into the world of present day prime-time radio.

One year later his second novel appeared called *All Night Long* about life during the pirate radio era. It set out to describe life as seen through the eyes of fictional characters, thereby allowing more sex, drugs and rock 'n' roll to feature than really happened, but still giving a feel for the era and the music.

He lives in an oast house in Kent, and in his spare time is a keen Chelsea football supporter.

ALAN CLARK

Born in Wales and educated in Croydon, Surrey, Alan left school in July 1965. In September of that year he heard an announcement over Radio City asking for would-be DJs to send in audition tapes.

Commenting in *Monitor* magazine in spring 1972, he said: "For some reason, probably visions of fame and fortune, I decided to apply. I had never done any disc jockey work of any kind and certainly did not know the first thing about radio deejaying. On the strength of the audition tape which I submitted I was invited out to the station for a trial period.

"I arrived at City's office in Oxford Street, Whitstable, and met American DJ Rick Michaels, and the owner of the record shop which served as the radio station's base at Whitstable, Eric Martin - not to be confused with DJ Eric Martin. This was the beginning of sixteen months of thrills and spills on 299."

At the end of his trial period he was driven back to London by Reg Calvert who gave him £5 expenses. But young Mr Clark had been bitten by the broadcasting bug. He pestered Reg Calvert, and his secretary Jill Wileman. until they finally offered him a permanent job with Radio City.

Alan believes that 1966 was the best time for the station. In a further extract from the spring 1972 *Monitor* article, he said: "We had a fairly good signal, due to our monster mast (the tallest of all the stations) and a good crew working together with some professional broadcasters from Australia, plus the relatively new English jocks. We were on air for 18 hours a day. We had City discos in place during the week, where DJs made personal appearances, plus two cooks fresh out of catering school preparing all kinds of delicacies for the crew's stomachs. The London office moved into better premises and the engineers worked wonders with the equipment. At this point, given a larger power output, City would have seriously challenged the big stations with some revamping of the programmes."

Alan was on board when the boarding party took over Radio City in June 1966. He later learned of the death of Reg Calvert with immense shock.

Together with Ian MacRae, he presented the *Auntie Mabel Hour*.

When Radio City closed in early 1967, Alan joined Radio 390. He said: "Some people thought I might not like the music played on the station but I soon got used to it. The most outstanding thing about Radio 390 was its professionalism. We received mail from all over the country."

Alan was only with 390 for a short time before that station, too, closed down due to the High Court decision that it was broadcasting within British territorial waters.

He decided to try his luck with the club circuit and worked for three months at London's Flamingo Club in Wardour Street. As there was no opening in radio in Britain he moved to Holland and succeeded in securing a job with the Dutch World Radio Service, Radio Nederland. He presented a

Edward Cole in the studio of QEFM, 1993

Saturday show. *What's New*, which could be heard in Britain on short wave. Alan was voted 15th most popular disc jockey in the *Record Mirror's* DJ Poll in 1970. He now works with Meridian TV in Southampton.

EDWARD COLE
Born on 20 April 1939 in London, Edward was educated at Highgate School.

He considers himself to be a pioneer twice over - first on pirate radio, and now on satellite radio. After leaving law school, he joined Radio 390 in November 1965. He was accepted after being auditioned by Mike Raven. He later took over as chief announcer and 'closed' the station at 5.00pm on 28 July 1967.

Edward remembers: "Radio 390 made its début in September 1965. We were the first pirates to specialise in sweet music, instead of mindless pop, with civilised announcers instead of raving DJs. Our audience weren't teenyboppers but housewives, and all daytime programmes began with the words 'Radio 390, presenting *Eve*, the woman's magazine of the air ... 'My own regular show was *Memory Lane* every afternoon. About eight million tuned into the station from many parts of England, as our signal was very strong."

After the closure of 390, Edward worked as a freelance newsreader for BBC Television in Southampton, as an announcer for HTV in Cardiff, and as a freelance disc jockey for BBC Radio Brighton. In 1974 he joined the BBC staff in London as an announcer/newsreader on Radio 4. He also compiled and presented many series including *The Unforgettables* and *Up to the Hour*. In 1985 he devised the format for *Counterpoint*, Radio 4's musical quiz chaired by Ned Sherrin, and wrote the questions for the series.

Edward left the BBC staff in 1991, and became managing director of Quality Europe FM, a new easy-listening music station based in Camberley, Surrey, which broadcasts around the clock to the whole of Europe on the Astra 1A satellite.   (He has since died)

ROBBIE DALE
A North Country man, Robbie (born in Littleborough, Lancs, on 21 April 1940) joined Radio Caroline as a disc jockey without any previous experience.

He attended Lancaster Secondary

Modern School. His first job in London was as a bellboy at the Mayfair Club. Robbie was then 15. He later became an antique dealer, a press agent and finally joined the Army for five years, three of which were spent in south-east Asia in the Army Air Corps. He returned to Britain in 1962 and took a job with a plastics and machine manufacturing company.

Robbie Dale made his first public appearance in January 1966. He joined Radio Caroline in April 1966.

His hobbies include motor racing, horse riding, modern art, swimming and listening to good music. His ambition is to be a top entertainer and he admits he is somewhat of an exhibitionist.

The 'Admiral', as he was known on Caroline, was famed for *Robbie Dale's Diary*. He formed the 'Beat Fleet' and persuaded many famous members of show business to feature amongst its ranks including The Monkees, Petula Clark, Sandie Shaw, Brenda Lee and The Rolling Stones.

In February 1967 Robbie was nearly arrested by police in Trafalgar Square, London, whilst posing for photographs for his 'fan club'. He was dressed in the uniform of an admiral which was a genuine original from Portobello Road. The uniform cost £100 and took four weeks to retailor to his size.

He has released two records; *Soul Mama* (Pink Elephant), and *Hey You're Crazy* (Philips).

With Johnnie Walker he remained on board the *Mi Amigo* on 14 August 1967 when the Marine Offences Act came into force at midnight.

Robbie left Caroline in 1968 after the *Mi Amigo* was towed into Holland by the Wijsmuller's. He worked for a short time on Radio Veronica and later ran a successful cleaning business in London, including a contract with Capital Radio. He subsequently started up Sunshine Radio in Ireland with Spangles Muldoon (Chris Cary). This ran from 1980 for eight years until outlawed by the Irish Government. He is now a broadcaster in Dublin.

ROGER DAY

Roger 'Twiggy' Day was born on 29 March 1945 in Cheltenham, Gloucester. He began his show business career in the dance halls of Kent as a disc jockey.

In May 1966, he applied for a job on Radio England and was lucky. Says Roger: "I got the job on Radio England because I was lucky enough to be the first English disc jockey they met. I was one of those horrible people who come up and say 'How do I get a job on your station?' Dave Cash was very kind and pointed out that Radio London didn't have any vacancies, but the Yanks from America who had just flown in to set up Radio England were in need of jocks. They must have just ordered their first gin and tonic when I knocked on the door. They hired me because they liked my cute English accent. I did not have any radio experience so they could train me in their own ways. The next person they hired was Peter Dee from Birmingham who had to change his name because it was too similar to mine - the name he chose was 'Johnnie Walker'. I often wonder what would have happened had the situation been reversed."

Roger stayed with Radio England from May until November 1966. Eight months later he joined Radio Caroline shortly before the Marine Offences Bill became an Act of Parliament. He went on to defy the Government and was one of the first to risk prosecution. He booked a holiday in Spain and flew from Gatwick Airport, but there were no problems. However, he didn't take any chances for a few months and spent his shore leave in Holland. In December 1967, Roger plucked up the courage to fly into Heathrow. "This time, a keen Customs officer asked me to open my bag. The thing was, I had brought a lot of my letters home to show mum and dad what a popular boy their son was. He noticed these letters and asked what they were. I was waiting for the handcuffs to be slapped on my wrist. I said: 'Letters from friends'. He smiled and said: 'It must be nice to have so many friends. Play us a record next time you're out there'."

In August 1968 Roger married Jenny, and they have two children: a daughter, Michelle Caroline (1979), named after his favourite

Beatles' song and the radio ship, and a son Michael (1989).

Says Roger: "The atmosphere on Caroline after the Marine Offences Act came into force was wonderful. You had the genuine feeling everybody, apart from the Government, was on your side. We thought it would last until we were given a licence to broadcast on land."

Roger remained with Radio Caroline until March 1968 and then went to work in Luxembourg for six unhappy months before leaving to compère the Beach Boys' European tour. In January 1970 he joined Radio Northsea International, stayed for six months and became a major 'pirate DJ pin-up'. The name 'Twiggy' came about when the Dutch crew spotted him sunbathing - a fellow disc jockey mentioned it on the air - and the name stuck.

Whilst on RNI Roger had a spot of trouble with the press. "It was around the time when RNI was being jammed. I was at home in Surbiton and another disc jockey had given my address to *The People* newspaper. This reporter threatened me that if I didn't give him a story his editor would get nasty. It was a farce, as the article which appeared bore no relation to the truth. As a result, the police came to see me, but no action was taken."

His career then brought him back to London where he worked for three years with the industrial United Biscuits Network.

When independent radio came to Britain, Roger moved north to Manchester and worked for Piccadilly Radio, being on 2 April 1974, the station's first disc jockey on air. He was also music producer.

In the *Record Mirror* poll of 1973, Roger Day was voted Top Disc Jockey in the country. Around the same time he became the No. 1 Piccadilly Radio personality.

In 1975 he clocked up a seventy four hour marathon during which he was allowed only three hours sleep a day. He slept in a special bed set up in the studio. Rumour has it that a Bunny girl from Manchester's Playboy Club served him a prepared diet each day!

Roger's stint on Piccadilly Radio was followed by four years in Birmingham with

BRMB, thence to Radio West in Bristol in 1983, Invicta Radio when the station was launched in October 1984 and, finally, to Pirate FM in Cornwall where he presented the daily *Breakfast Show* until 1993 when he returned to Kent to be with his family. He joined Jazz FM, London in July 1993 where he broadcast regularly for three months. He now works with Kent and Sussex Radio.

Looking back on his days with offshore radio, Roger recalls: "The pirates attracted many undesirables, but without them the public would not have known what commercial radio was like. We would have been stuck with the old system without good music radio. Basically we created a demand and, personally speaking, it was a lot of fun that ended, for me, too soon."

SIMON DEE

Born Carl Nicholas Henty-Dodd on 28 July 1935 in Manchester, Simon Dee was educated at Shrewsbury School. His first appearance in public actually concerned pirates. He played a genuine pirate in Gilbert and Sullivan's *Pirates of Penzance* at the ripe old age of eight.

He had a variety of jobs before turning disc jockey including a photographer in the Royal Air Force, theatre ticket salesman, designer of toilets, a navvy, a vacuum cleaner salesman, an actor, model, husband, father, clerk and drama student.

He recorded a commercial for Players cigarettes in 1956, but had no experience in radio until he joined Caroline in 1964.

Writing in *Reveille* on 22 May 1969 about his early days with Radio Caroline before the ship began regular programmes. Simon related: "I was auditioned by Chris Moore, an ex-putter-on of records in a discotheque, who told me that I was obviously good. Well, I had been a radio addict for years; in school I had often been punished for listening when I should have been studying. I could talk about music, but the thing farthest from my mind in October 1963 was being a disc jockey.

"The thought was interesting though, and the job quickly got exciting when we shipped to Ireland the entire collection of taped radio shows which both sides had been working on together at Allan Crawford's headquarters. (Note: Allan Crawford was the managing director of Radio Atlanta, who later teamed up with Ronan O'Rahilly of Radio Caroline).

"Crawford's suspicions were not aroused, however, for his ship *(Mi Amigo)* was due in Greenore to complete her final preparations.

"I remember my first sight of Greenore. We had checked in at a hotel in Dundalk, 52 miles north of Dublin, then driven another 13 to the entrance of a beautiful sea lough, with the Mountains of Mourne rising out of the rippling water just opposite.

"Caroline was tied up at the quay, her immense aluminium mast, piercing the late evening sky. A skein of geese was flighting overhead.

"I felt a sudden quickening of my pulse rate as the car stopped before the hush-hush ship in that deserted little port. The atmosphere was right for the work afoot. It was like stepping on to the set of a real-life thriller at a moment of it being acted out."

Simon sailed on the Radio Caroline ship, the m.v. *Fredericia,* from Greenore to a location off the Essex coast. The ship dropped anchor on Good Friday, 1964 at 7.00pm. That night he pre-recorded an opening announcement for a test transmission broadcast at midnight. Following the Radio Caroline signature tune *Round Midnight* by Jimmy McGriff, Simon announced "Good morning everybody. This is Radio Caroline on 199 metres, your all day music station ..." History had been made.

During his days on the high seas Simon promoted the Tamla Motown sound, and lists among his favourite artists the Supremes, Martha and the Vandellas and the Four Tops. His tendency in music was to big band, his favourites being the Tommy Dorsey Orchestra (Simon's Caroline theme was *On the Sunny Side of the Street*), and the orchestras of Count Basie, Neal Hefti and Don Costa.

Many people are curious as to his name. How did Carl Nicholas Henty-Dodd come to be called Simon Dee? As the former was too much of a mouthful for the name of a DJ, he adopted his eldest son's forename and the initial of the last part of his own surname.

Simple ... but effective!

Simon's first television appearance came on *Ready Steady Go* in 1964. He split from Radio Caroline on 7 May 1965 and turned freelance. His first BBC programme was *Midday Spin* which came his way in July 1965. Shortly afterwards he was signed by EMI Records for a series of Radio Luxembourg programmes including *Simon's Scene.* Other BBC programmes followed like *Stay Late* and *Swing Into Summer.*

Fame came to Simon Dee quickly and he was voted the second most popular disc jockey by the *New Musical Express* at the end of 1966 and also won the *New Musical Express's* 'Cat's Whisker Award'.

He released the record *Julie* on the Chapter One label in 1969. The song was written and directed by Les Reed, but failed to make the charts.

Simon first became known on the television screen through his Smith's Crisps commercials and introducing *Top of the Pops.* He progressed to having his own television show from Manchester on BBC, *Dee Time,* which was regularly watched by 15 million people. The show later moved to London to replace *Juke Box Jury* and was shown early Saturday evenings. It was a meteoric rise to fame, but sadly his downfall was equally as swift. His personal and professional life has been surrounded with controversy.

Newspapers, which had given Simon many column inches of positive publicity, went on the attack and were swift to criticise his lifestyle. He learned all too quickly that he was 'public property', and not allowed a private life. The press reported he had been sued for libel, had been in prison, and had publicly criticised politicians.

The BBC axed his television show. London Weekend Television signed him up, but that was short-lived. He tried broadcasting with local radio stations with little success then headed for Australia. That, too, was not successful. He returned to Britain and joined the dole queue.

Simon, who has two sons and a daughter, has been married twice to the former model Beryl 'Bunny' Cooper and to another former model, Sarah Terry. Both marriages ended in divorce.

In 1987 the BBC booked him for a couple of radio programmes presenting music of the Swinging Sixties. The programmes were well received, but even then he 'had a go' at Bill Cotton who was at the time Head of BBC TV.

In April 1988 Simon made a triumphant return to BBC Radio 2 when he hosted a thirteen-week series *Sounds of the Sixties* on Saturday mornings. However, the programme was taken over at a later date by Brian Matthew.

CHRIS DENNING

Chris Denning was born in Hayes, Middlesex at 10.00pm on 10 May 1941, the last night of the Blitz. One can only surmise that Hitler took one look and gave up! He began his radio career with a talk on Radio Moscow! This was whilst he was on a tour of East Europe at the age of 16 and, as a result of this trip, on his return to London Chris also landed a series of talks for the BBC Home Service about his experiences abroad.

A few weeks after his return from Moscow, he was visited by MI5. They thought he was a Russian 'sleeper.' Chris convinced the authorities that he hadn't 'slept' with anyone, let alone Russians. MI5 returned to base.

For the next four years he had a varied career. In turn he was a furniture salesman, an encyclopaedia publisher's representative calling on American servicemen in Germany, and a tyre salesman in London. Between jobs he also organised, and took part in an overland car trip to Ceylon and back!

However, bitten by the radio bug, Chris was determined to get back on the air, and landed himself a job with the British Forces Broadcasting Service in Kenya where, among other things, he went on big game safaris, and climbed Mount Kilimanjaro, but had to give up just a few feet from the summit. Work-wise, he had opportunity to try everything from TV and radio newsreading to classical concerts and pop shows. He also featured often as the voice on many of East Africa's TV commercials, and had his own pop music column in one of the national daily newspapers.

Chris recalls: "First I was offered a job with BFN in Germany, but this was cancelled shortly afterwards on instructions from MI5. Instead I was sent to Kenya."

It was in Nairobi where he met the writer. But, after two years in East Africa, Chris was itching to get home once again to London and his friends. On holiday in England, he rang up the head of BBC2, which was just about to open, and talked himself into a job as the new channel's very first announcer.

After some months on BBC2 an offer came to join Radio Luxembourg as one of the resident DJs - which Chris most readily accepted. And, during nearly two years with 208, he built up an audience for his *Music in the Night* show and weekly *Beatles* programme, numbered in millions. He stayed with Radio Luxembourg until March 1966, when he finally left to return home to England. But he was not to remain in London for very long. On the same night he returned from Luxembourg he met Ed Stewart in a disco in London. Says Chris: "Ed told me that Johnny Moran had rejected a Radio London job offer at the very last minute. I went to see programme director Alan Keen the next morning - and the day after that I was on my way to join the DJs and crew aboard the *Galaxy*."

His months as a pirate DJ broadcasting to Big L's twelve million listeners gained him more and more fans in all parts of the country, and invaluable experience for the future. He also thoroughly enjoyed himself!

Does Chris have any memories of his days on the *Galaxy*? "I remember the night Kenny Everett tried gambling for the first, and only, time", he says. "Not knowing what he was doing, he was soon in huge debt (i.e. £150, some four weeks' wages!) playing liar dice. To some general anger, he announced he could not and would not pay. Since he was well ahead on the week's gambling -and to avoid murder at sea - Tony Windsor offered to cut some cards for £10 a time, then £20, £50, £100 etc. But, to everyone's dismay, Kenny lost *every* time. Soon he owed £900. There were dangerous mutterings around the ship. Other people who had been gambling on credit all week were not about to let him off the hook."

It was then that Chris Denning had a brainwave. He remembers: "I suggested to TW that all debts for the week (which had all been on credit) be reduced by 90%, so that we just pretended that when we had been playing for £1, we had really been playing for one tenth of that amount (at the time 24 old pence). Everyone thought about it and finally it was decided this was a solution that enabled Everett to extricate himself with honour. He had to pay back £90, but that was better than the £900 of a few minutes previously.

"I was congratulated warmly by everyone for coming up with such a fair solution. And, to my relief, nobody noticed that I had similarly reduced my own debt - from £50 to £5!"

Just when he had found his sea legs, Chris decided to be a landlubber again and to become a freelance deejay.

After a quick six-day trip to New York in August 1966 he started a series of regular shows on the BBC Light Programme.

To date he has presented *Midday Spin*, *Swing into Summer*, *What's New*, *Swingalong* and *Where It's At* and has guested on the panel of BBC TV's *Juke Box Jury* and introduced several editions of *Top of the Pops*. He had his own BBC1 quiz show *Look Where You're Going*, produced in Bristol by a former FBS Nairobi man, John King. Chris also presented CBS and Decca record shows on Radio Luxembourg. "I was also booked to record some special records introducing an unknown duo," he says. "They were called Simon and Garfunkel."

He was present at the official opening of BBC Radio Leicester in November 1967 and BBC Radio Merseyside in November 1967.

For a while in the 1970s he was director of promotion for Decca Records; director of marketing and promotion for Bell (later Arista); and general manager of UK Records (and Jonathan King's then partner). During his tenure of these posts, he was responsible for over 60 Top 10 hits and the launching of many stars, including Gary Glitter, the Bay City Rollers and Dawn.

During the 1980s and 1990s he specialised in voice-over work and was heard on radio commercials on independent radio throughout the country. He also recorded international TV commercials (i.e. Coca Cola, Philips etc) on the Continent, mainly in Holland. He frequently travelled to the radio stations in a luxury motor caravan, complete with his dog. Max, and a video, carphone, shower and freezer. Chris claims to be the only man in Britain to have received a parking ticket whilst taking a shower!

DAVE DENNIS

Real name Neil Spence, Dave's original ambition was to be a farmer. He attended Leighton Park School near Reading and boasts he was not only bottom of his class, but of the whole school during his entire stay. He took up farming when he left school until bitten by the acting bug.

After three years at the Central School of Speech and Drama, he worked in repertory until 1964 when he decided to try his hand as a DJ and joined Radio Invicta as Neil Spence, followed by Radio Atlanta in April 1964. In December 1964 he joined Radio London as Dave Dennis.

In 1966 he recorded *Yes Virginia, There Is A Santa Claus* on the Go label. The song was written by Tony Windsor (Withers).

Dave became programme organiser for the cable network, United Biscuit Network, in the early 1970s.

He helped set up the National Broadcasting School in London when independent radio arrived in 1973. He later spent time as a broadcaster with Radio Trent in Nottingham and worked for the Independent Broadcasting Authority for a short while.

He is now believed to be out of radio altogether.   (He has since died)

PETE DRUMMOND

Pete Drummond was born on 29 July 1943 at Bangor, North Wales. His great beauty, he assures the author, achieved him the 'bonniest baby' title when he was a few weeks old at a contest held in the town. This was mainly because there were only three entrants ... himself, a goat and a chicken.

At the age of three Pete and his family went to Australia where they lived for 7½

Pete Drummond

years in Sydney, New South Wales. It was there he learnt the arts of surfing, skiing, wombat baiting, and kangaroo flounging and chundering, an art which he considers to be one of the hardest to perfect because of the tremendous effort involved.

Pete returned to England in 1954, stopping off in France for nine months to study the French in their natural surroundings. Although only eleven at the time, his perceptiveness led him into many difficult situations and, whilst attending school at Bormes, by the Mediterranean, he acquired the French language, specialising in idiomatic phrases. It was this constant use of French slang that eventually forced his parents to remove him from the country in the hope that the French police would be unable to arrest him in England. As it happened they were perfectly correct, and Pete was very soon firmly ensconced in one of the more exclusive schools in the country - namely Millfield in Somerset.

And it was at Millfield that he met one Tony Blackburn, a hairy-chested rugger player who Pete was later to meet again on the m.v. *Galaxy*, this time disguised as a disc jockey. However, Tony was recognised at once ... yes, it was those hairs that gave him away.

On leaving Millfield at the age of 15, Pete had acquired eight 'O' levels and looked like becoming one of the greatest geniuses of our time, but for the fact that he had one very minor fault... he was bone idle! (Pete Drummond has given the author full permission to reproduce that statement!)

After attending the High Wycombe School of Art for three months, he decided to make acting his career and won a grant to attend the Royal Academy of Music and Drama. The drama department transferred to the New College of Music and Drama after Pete's first year. He continued to study at the college, completing his course in 1964 after playing many varied parts from an old man of 96 to a young virgin of 17. He says it was difficult to portray the latter because he was 20 at the time!

During his time at the college he worked in just about every theatre in London in many diversified jobs. From scene shifter he graduated all the way up to... scene shifter! On leaving college, he took a job for a few weeks as a guide for the National Union of Students, showing Americans around England, France, Italy, Switzerland and Austria. As he only spoke French he had a little difficulty when in the other countries and lost his charges and his way on numerous occasions.

In October 1964 a friend in Wichita. Kansas, offered him a part in a play that was being presented in one of the city's three theatres, and he flew to the States the next day. On arrival in Wichita he started rehearsals and the play *The Private Ear and The Public Eye* was quite a success. He worked for the theatre playing various roles for the next three months until he suddenly tuned in to Radio one day and realised that although every station was playing British music at the time, there were no English announcers - the American disc jockeys were trying to talk in English accents.

"Aha," he thought. "Now's my chance to speak on the wireless!"

Pete went to the top station and asked the programme director for a job.

"Are you... English?" asked the programme director.

"Yes," replied Pete.

The American went on: "Ever worked in radio? No? Don't worry, we can train a monkey to do this in 24 hours!"

From that moment he was hired. After three months, his show was the top-rated one in the southern half of the state. It was at this time Pete decided to ask for a raise - but what a mistake! So, taking his pride in both hands, he quit and was forced to earn his living helping to run a friend's coffee house-cum-jazz club for the next five months. During this time he read poetry, put on short plays, waited at tables and was punched in the mouth by people who didn't like his long hair. Pete relates: "They thought I was a communist because I had long hair and was trying to disrupt the American way of life, apple pie and Mom."

Pete also cleaned out the lavatories at the club when it closed at nine o'clock in the morning. He painted pictures and was justifiably paid very little for the results.

Finally everything got on top of him and he decided to leave Wichita (known as the Air Capital of the World, mainly because it had more hot air than any other city) and move to the Kansas state capital of Topeka just outside Kansas City. Here he got a job with the big Top 40 station where he remained until August 1966.

It was in Topeka that Pete married Carolyn, a girl whom he met soon after his arrival in the States. Eventually, however, he got rather bored with the American way of life and decided to show Carolyn what Britain was like. Arriving in London in August 1966, he joined Radio London as a staff disc jockey on 28 September.

The Drummonds had a daughter, Samantha, who now has a son. Jack. Pete is now married to his second wife, Celia, and they have a son, Luke.

Affectionately known as 'Dum Dum' on Radio London, Pete says he invented the name himself and it has no connection with the word "Dumb!" That's his story and he's sticking to it.

Following the closure of Radio London in August 1967, Pete joined Radio 1 and became a regular voice on the network. He has presented *Midday Spin* and *Top Gear* and worked in the Radio 1 promotions department, together with writing continuity announcements for Radios 3 and 4. This was followed by *Sounds of the 70s* and *The Sequence,* which in turn got him voted No. 2 DJ in the *Melody Maker* poll, even though he used to talk briefly after every third record. Says Pete: "The voters obviously thought that the less you heard of a DJ, the better you liked him."

Pete was heard on *In Concert* for many years as well as specials. *The Island Story* and *The U2 Story.*

He appeared on BBC TV in the *Disco 2* series, *Sight and Sound In Concert* and for two series of *Rock Goes to College* where he had the pleasure of "being insulted and yelled at by students from Dundee to Plymouth."

In 1972 Pete appeared as a guest vocalist on *The Old Grey Whistle Test*, together with his second wife Celia (lead singer with the folk rock band Tress), backed up by various producers and engineers from Radio 1, as The VHF Band. Their song was *Rockin' at the BBC* which was released by Warner Brothers Records as a stereo 78rpm (the only one ever issued in this format!). This coincided with the 50th anniversary of the BBC.

Pete also worked on the BBC World Service for two years presenting the *Morning Show* (African Service). Nowadays he is a freelance doing voice-overs on television and radio adverts, videos and films (including dubbing foreign films).

TOM EDWARDS

Tom Edwards was bom in Norwich on 20 March 1945 and, after leaving school, began his working career as a journalist. As is often the case, having spent a while in journalism one wishes to break into show business. Tom was fortunate and obtained a job as an announcer with Border TV's pop show *Beat Up the Border.*

In September 1965 he sent an audition tape to Radio City and, on the strength of that, was given a week's trial. He later joined City's staff and became the station's chief disc jockey. He moved into a house at West Beach, Whitstable. Speaking at the time, he said: "It had to be something with a sea view." Tom discounted rumours that off-duty DJs dash to London for a series of wild parties. "If Radio City suddenly finished I would still live in Whitstable."

Having made the grade, however, it was still possible to make the occasional faux pas. Says Tom: "I well remember the time in 1965 when I was asked to play a Swinging Blue Jeans record from husband to wife for their wedding anniversary. I played *You're No Good*!

"It used to take up to four hours to travel the ten miles from Whitstable Harbour to Shivering Sands.

"Those people who think that all DJs have to do is to speak in between discs are wrong! In actual fact we were 'cueing' up records on turntables and lining up the tape machine for commercials, as well as keeping the output volume at the correct level. We did not work from scripts.

"Each DJ broadcast for an average of three hours and, as for the rest of the day, we had plenty of time to ourselves. There was a television lounge and always a radio relaying Radio City on 299 metres.

"What amazed me was that the time passed very quickly over the two weeks we spent on the forts. We then had a week's leave on land."

Asked what was the music format on Radio City, Tom replied: "If Reg Calvert had a new record out for release by Pinkerton's Assorted Colours or the Fortunes, they obviously took priority as he was their manager.

"I remember there were dozens of new records being released each week. The DJs would sit around and decide which to play. We compiled our own Top 40 which bore no resemblance to the national charts.

"We used to listen to Caroline and London a great deal and, if we heard them playing a record very often, we thought it must be good so we'd play it as well. One record certainly springs to mind - that was *That's Nice* by Neil Christian which, through persistent playing on the pirates, reached the Top 20 in national charts in April 1966."

Tom remained with the station during its troubled periods with the Reginald Calvert shooting incident and when the forts were taken over. He was employed by Radio City until the station closed in February 1967.

One month later he joined Radio Caroline South as a disc jockey where he stayed until the beginning of August 1967.

Tom takes a great interest in clothes and is always dressed in the latest fashion. One of his main hates concerns the way women dress - but only those who wear short skirts and white stockings combined.

His ambition was to be a TV director of a top pop show or, failing this, to own his own radio station.

Commenting on the Government's attitude to offshore radio, Tom said in 1967: "The thing which really amazes me is that when the late Reginald Calvert learned of the boarding party on Shivering Sands he, together with his wife Dorothy, went to Scotland Yard to ask if the men could be made to get off the station and, if not, whether the City staff could be given any kind of protection.

"The official reply was that as the station was outside territorial waters nothing whatsoever could be done. Why then, only a few months later, did the law courts in Southend fine the station £100 resulting in us having to go off the air ... if this is British justice, I have no faith in it at all."

Tom Edwards joined the long list of ex-pirate DJs who were offered a BBC series in January 1968 - the Monday edition of *Midday Spin* on Radios 1 and 2.

Later he became a staff announcer on Radio 2. On television he has appeared on *Look East, Pebble Mill, Nationwide* and *Come Dancing*. He has been an announcer with Thames Television and Harlech TV.

Looking back to the pirate days Tom said in 1993: "What an era ... one that can never be repeated ... where *are* all my DJ mates now? Twenty five years and more have passed, but those days will remain in memory for ever.

"My lasting memory of the pirate days will be the very first time I went out to Radio City and saw this enormous set of structures in the middle of the ocean; then being hoisted 90ft. up in a cheese crate to the studios. 'Is this what broadcasting is all about?' I asked myself.

"All the time I was on Radio City I never got over the fear of being winched up to the forts - or crossing the catwalk, one of which we used all the time. It comprised planks of wood and pieces of rope.

"The staff knew I was terrified of walking across this catwalk up in the sky. I would sneak half way across if I thought nobody was looking, but invariably they were. There would be disc jockeys and engineers at either end of this catwalk jumping up and down making it shake. That was frightening and it was a mean thing to do. Furthermore, I can't swim. Even after 29 years I still get the collywobbles when I think about it."

In 1988 Tom moved to Hollywood, Los Angeles, to work where he was host on TV shows *Hollywood Stars, A.L.M.A., The Name Game* and *L.A. in the Morning*. He also appeared in *Around the World in 80 Days* and *Face to Face*.

He has presented TV and radio programmes worldwide including Holland, Australia, Barbados, Antigua. Germany and France.

He returned to his home city of Norwich in 1990 and has since appeared in *Breakfast News, Look East Extra* and *Day-Time UK*. He has also presented *Across East Anglia* on Sunday evenings on BBC Radio Norfolk.

KENNY EVERETT

Kenny started life in Liverpool on the rather unfortunate date of 25 December 1944. Mrs Everett (who doesn't want her surname mentioned!) upon seeing the young lad, said: "Actually, all I wanted was a pair of socks or a year's subscription to the *Radio Times*, but no! I got 'im instead."

Young Everett's ambition was to grow and by the age of four he was led screaming by the left lug (or was it 'leg'?) into his first school, St. Edward's Primer, in the outside world. Still screaming twelve years later, he left the world of scholastic indoctrination and entered another kind. As the world watched on with bated 'spron'. Ken entered a life of humiliation and sacrifice ... the St. Peter Clavier School for Budding Missionaries in South Africa. Ken relates: "I had all the go required, but for some reason they wanted me to be a first class

mathematician. I failed this in an exam and was out by the next camel to Liverpool. Still, it was lots of fun and my last encounter with fresh air as it was out in the country."

Ken found that during the ensuing years being shifted around through several jobs was a little soul destroying, but as it was in the north of England, with little chance of anything great happening, he battled on regardless. He developed a healthy love of tape recording and consequently (through a newspaper round) bought two machines.

Nights at home were not spent in front of the television, but working with his tape recorders knocking out tapes in the likeness of one Jack Jackson. He sent these off to friends up and down the country. Kenny goes on: "In *Tape Recording Magazine,* a certain columnist, one Alan Edward Beeby, suggested that readers should send him tapes of themselves just 'muckin abaht'. So ... we became great all time buddies and, as I took to his sense of humour and apparently 'vickey verkay', he suggested that I should bombard Broadcasting House with mad tapes which I did."

But alas for dear Ken, the great white

Auntie showed no interest at first, and all he received was the usual stereotyped letter: 'Your enquiry is currently passing through our administration department and will be dealt with in due course; see *Radio Times* for further details."

So Ken waited and waited until one day ... our hero continues the story ... "Yes, folks one day Zoweearootie!!! A telegram arrived saying: 'Come quick, we wants yer fer an interview on the British Wireless and we'd like ter play yer tape over the air. Yours, Auntie.' So it went over the air, the first time I believe that a four track tape recording made at 3¾ inches per second (gungey quality) has ever been broadcast on the quality wireless - the BBC Home Service, no less."

Young Everett had tasted his first sip of show business. He yearned for more, so he went around to various famous people, none of whom he can remember, until one day Kenny was called to Mr 'X's office. The next part of our dialogue must be read in an Etonian accent.

"Now. er, er Mr Evernards, we'd like you to introduce this heap of recordings by the Northern Dance Orchestra".

Kenny faltered - "Cor, this ain't my cup of teath". Up he jumped and said to the man with the Etonian accent: "I am not the man for you. The Northern Dance Orchestra indeed!"

Our Etonian friend went on: "Why don't you go to one of those pirate wireless boats? You'd be far better off there." There was a touch of scorn in his voice.

Pirate radio had only recently begun in 1964, and in December Radio London had just sailed in from America. Kenny sent them the same tape he had compiled for BBC and was accepted more or less immediately. He was one of the original Big L disc jockeys. But was he happy at sea?

"The first month on board was the most miserable that I have ever spent anywhere," Kenny commented. "I think I was solidly ill for about a week eating nothing. Considering the first meal I was offered was pancakes and syrup it's not really surprising. I couldn't even get off the ship because the tender service in those days was so diabolical that

we didn't see it for weeks at a time, so I was stuck with my turn.

"I got fired from Radio London for going on regardless about how awful one of our religious programmes was - *The World Tomorrow*. Happily I landed a job with Radio Luxembourg which kept the bread roiling in at a satisfactory rate. Unfortunately Luxembourg had a lot of drawbacks for a 'jock' who's been used to wireless at sea. At sea the disc jockey operated his own controls which, as you might imagine, makes you a lot sharper. No one can press a button better than the person who's thinking about it at the time. Also I was on the CBS show, which meant that I could only play CBS records. It was at this time that I met the author of this book - the dreaded 'Cardboard Shoes' - who was doing exactly the same thing. Another drawback of Radio Luxembourg was that we had to pre-record everything because the transmitter was in Luxembourg and we were in London. Ninety per cent of Lux's stuff was recorded in this way, so you couldn't do weather and time checks up to date - dragsville!

"I managed to wangle my way back on to the wireless of Big L about six months later as did Skues, but he joined London instead of Caroline, Wise move, lad!"

Kenny released a number of records - *Knees* (1966), *The Edge* (1967), *It's Been So Long* (1968), *Now For a Little Train Number*, *Happy Birthday from Cuddley Capital*, *Captain Kremmen -Retribution* (a hit which reached No. 32 in the national charts in November 1977) and *Snot Rap*, which reached No. 9 in the national charts in March 1983.

Millions of listeners were heartbroken in February 1967 when they learned that Kenny had decided to quit the sea life again. He wanted to try his luck with the BBC. His first programme was on 20 May when he presented a special preview of a new Beatles album.

From the top of Broadcasting House, supping a cup of the Wireless Corporation tea, and holding a picture of producer (later controller of Radio 1) Johnny Beerling in both hands. Ken reminisces: "Radio London will always occupy (cue strings) a big place in my heart (increase volume on strings) as it provided me with my start in the business and made me some of the best friendships like the Double D (Dave Dennis), TW (Tony Windsor), Hermione Hawkins (private jockey) and many other great people. Salud to a great station!"

Kenny joined the Radio 1 team in October 1967 presenting a weekly *Midday Spin*. He also appeared each Saturday in Chris Denning's *Where It's At* programme.

In January 1968 he took over a two-hour slot on Radio 1 each Sunday when he combined his various talents into *The Kenny Everett Show*.

In 1970 he was fired by the BBC after he made a joke on radio (following a news broadcast) about the wife of the then Minister of Transport bribing the examiner so she would pass her driving test! Again, in 1984, for a joke about Margaret Thatcher.

He joined Capital Radio, but has been regularly seen on BBC TV in *The Video Show* and *The Kenny Everett Show*. He created a world of comic characters. There was Sid Snot, the Hell's Angel biker; Marcel Wave, the French hair stylist; Maurice Mimer, the mime artist; Gizzard Puke, the skinhead, and starlet Cupid Stunt.

In between spells at Capital Radio he has appeared on Radio 2. In 1988 he joined Capital Gold.

Kenny wrote *The Custard Stops at Hatfield* published in 1982.

In April 1993 he announced to the world he was HIV positive saying: "I am not angry, but resigned. We all have death hanging over us. It's just that I'll probably get there that bit sooner than most." He went on: "I am really enjoying life at the moment so I am hoping I have got ages yet."   (He has since died)

ROGER GALE

The first DJ to become an MP. Roger was born in Poole, Dorset, on 20 August 1943, son of Richard Byrne and Phyllis Mary Gale.

He was educated at Southborne Preparatory School, Hardye's School, Dorchester, and the Guildhall School of Music and Drama in the City of London.

He has been married three times. First in 1964 to Wendy Dawn Bowman (marriage dissolved 1967); secondly to Susan Sampson in 1971 with one daughter (marriage dissolved), and thirdly to Susan Gabrielle Marks. They have two sons.

Roger was a freelance broadcaster from 1963-1967, during which time he joined Radio Caroline South in June 1965 and remained with the floating station for three months. He was also programme director, Radio Scotland, and personal assistant to the general manager of Universal Films.

Roger became a freelance reporter with BBC Radio London, 1972-1973; a producer with Radio 1 *Newsbeat* and Radio 4 *Today*, 1973-1976; producer/director with Children's Television 1976-1979; producer/director Thames TV, and editor Teenage Unit, 1979-1983.

He joined the Conservative Party in 1964. His appointments comprised: Member, Home Affairs Select Committee; Special Select Committee on televising House of Commons; All Party Group, Fund for Replacement of Animals in Medical Experiments; Vice-Chairman, All Party Group for Animal Welfare; Chairman, Backbench Media Committee; Delegate,

Council of Europe, 1987-1989; PPS to Minister of State, Armed Forces, 1992 to present day.

He contested Birmingham Northfield in October 1982. He has been Conservative MP for Thanet since 1983 and is a founder member of the East Kent Development Association.

In his spare time he enjoys swimming, sailing and canoeing.

Roger is a member of the Garrick Club and Kent County Cricket Club.

GUY HAMILTON

Reared in Woodford Green, Essex, Guy Hamilton (real name Gerry Zierler) was hooked on radio even before the pirates sailed in. After having the nerve to deejay at a school dance, Guy thought he could tackle anything. He sent a tape to the newest, smallest, least heard-of pirate of them all, Radio Essex.

He was offered a job and the day after, while attempting to concentrate on GCE A-levels, sailed out to the uttermost Thames Estuary in a fishing smack to become *really* famous. Famous for making the filthiest tea imaginable, that is.

So, 20 miles out from Southend, Guy became a DJ at the age of 18 in July 1966,

presenting up to six hours of shows daily and learning the hard and fast way. From the graveyard shift to the breakfast show in a few months!

Then a new ship arrived off Yorkshire: Radio 270. Prosecution threatened the fort-based stations down south, so he presented himself up north and walked straight into a fun job when the station had a few teething problems. Teatime and lunchtime, it was music for munchtime, with the Wise Guy (Hamilton, that is).

The thing about working at sea in a little ship is actually getting off the ship and having even more fun. This was the Swinging Sixties, and so were the girls! Scarborough was one of those places that had a higher proportion of women than almost anywhere else. He did not see too much of the countryside!

The Government of the day was threatening the extinction of the pirates, and Auntie BBC's starting a pop station seemed about as likely as a four-bob note at the time. So Guy Hamilton became Gerry Zierler again and went into the ad biz, working as a media man at one or two leading West End advertising agencies. But twice a week the hair grew on the backs of his hands again and Guy Hamilton terrorised dancehall audiences for as much as £5 a throw. Even *Radio 1 Club* wasn't safe, and the money hit £6. Even so, he says "it beat working!"

Guy returned to Yorkshire in 1968 to look at the old ship, *Oceaan 7*, laid up on the mud in Whitby harbour. He recalls: "It was truly a very sad and moving sight. I climbed on board - it wasn't an easy matter at 45 degrees. One or two souvenirs came off with me, but I wish that I'd had the presence of mind to keep the DJs'' log book, signed by all manner of names as they had passed through the studios, and full of wonderful dramatic reports. The best was 'Ship sinking. I'm off!'"

The day job took over, and then things eventually went full circle when Gerry Zierler helped start and eventually run Britain's biggest radio ad sales agency. When nobody was looking, he was known to disappear at roughly the same time as Guy Hamilton appeared on such new stations as

Piccadilly, BRMB, Orwell and, by kind permission of the programme director, Hallam! He later opted for the easy life in the country and set up Wiltshire Radio, now GWR, before succumbing to the delights and, as he quaintly puts it, the dosh, of TV.

Gerry Zierler, now in his prime, runs his own commercial TV airtime sales outfit, Zierler Media. Guy Hamilton, now in his dotage, is content to help him out occasionally, voicing commercials and, indeed, making them whenever a client wants to spend money wisely.

KEITH HAMPSHIRE

Keith Laurence Hampshire (Keefers) was bom in Lewisham, London, on 23 November 1945. He lived there until he was six, and then moved with his mother, father and only sister to Calgary in Alberta, Canada.

His first public appearance was at the age of four in a dancing show in London. He sang professionally for fifteen years, firstly in a boys' choir. He later won nine diplomas. He then went on to sing with pop groups for five years with the intention of making some pocket money. Keith sang 'live' in the opening act of a Roy Orbison show and also appeared in a cross-Canada television series every fortnight.

Keith recalls: "I got into broadcasting by sheer fluke. I needed a job and because of my entertainment past became a television cameraman at a local station in Canada. I then progressed to singing jingles for the radio side of the station. This was followed by a job as a disc jockey and presenting the all night programmes at the weekends."

He returned lo England on 5 May 1966. Asked why he left Canada, he replied: "I got five speeding tickets, but the police hadn't caught up with me; a pop group that had gone dead on me, and a girl friend who nagged me persistently to marry her. Basically I needed a change so I came across to England and joined the staff of Radio Caroline in July 1966."

On the subject of free radio, Keith had this to say in 1967:

"This country is definitely trying to break away from tradition as seen in today's youth. It feels it is a world power, yet it is not. The people narrow mindedly think they have got the best life. However, their Government holds them back from advancement in many fields. The brain drain is one example and commercial radio is another.

"Regional stations could easily be set up under some sort of governing body on the same lines as Independent Television. There could be four stations in each region -
1) BBC
2) a 24 hour Top 40 station
3) a 24 hour good music station
4) some sort of FM station

"Introducing this form of radio would affect no-one but the BBC. There would be some stimulating competition between stations, and power could be restricted so that the stations involved did not crowd out each other. In this way, and I firmly believe *only* in this way, can successful commercial radio bring the British population what they have a right to hear."

He released the record *Millions of Hearts* on King Records in 1967. It was produced by Mike Berry who had associations with Radio Caroline in 1964/1965.

Once the Marine Offences Act came into force in the United Kingdom, Keith went to Majorca for a month to "recharge my batteries." On return to London he listened to the new Radio 1, didn't like what he heard, and flew to Canada. In Montreal he listened to local radio and ... didn't like what he heard, so moved to Toronto where radio was much more exciting.

Keith joined station CKFH in 1967 and stayed there for three years. Whilst at the radio station he made useful contacts in the record industry and, early in 1971, made preparations to record an LP of songs which had been hits in the UK but not in Canada.

The album was recorded in 1972 and the first single taken off the LP, *Daytime Nightime*, became a Top 10 hit in Canada and also appeared in the US Top 100. The follow-up release, in 1973, was *The First Cut is the Deepest* which reached the coveted No. 1 spot in Canada. That was followed by *Big Time Operator* which also reached No. 1 in both Canada and South Africa.

Keith was the host of a CBC network show from coast to coast called *Keith Hampshire's Music Machine* from 1974-1975.

He married Cathy on 1 August 1971, and they have a son, Christian, and a daughter, Laura.

Keith still appears in radio plays and records voice-overs for television and radio, as well as recording jingles and cartoon voices.

In 1983 he was presented with a gold disc for *Okay Blue Jays*, a record he made with the Canadian basketball team. Also in 1983 he became a very successful quarter horse breeder and in 1993 owned 10 horses.

Does Keith have any memories of the offshore radio days? "Many. I visited England in 1992 and met up with a number of jocks from the class of '67 ... Mike Ahern, John Aston, Mark Sloane, Tommy Vance and Johnnie Walker. We gathered in the Red Lion, just around the corner from Chesterfield Gardens in London's Mayfair, and exchanged stories. Although twenty five years had elapsed, all of us could remember so many memorable incidents aboard the ship and the occasions we spent ashore during our time on land.

"One of the funniest I remember occurred on Radio Caroline South in 1967. Each time Mike Ahern came on board the *Mi Amigo*, he went to his cabin and changed into his ship's clothes, which included a pair of carpet slippers. He was always squeaky clean. However, after he had been wearing these slippers for more than a week they began to ... should we say ... smell! One night Mike fell asleep in front of the television in the messroom. Steve Young and I took off his slippers and filled them with lighter fuel and set them alight and dropped them overboard. They were given an official burial at sea. As they were sailing towards Frinton-on-Sea, still burning brightly, Mike woke up and saw the remains of his slippers heading towards England. He appeared quite upset, but never again did he wear slippers on the ship!"

Today Keith and his family live in Churchill, Ontario, Canada.

MIKE HAYES
Mike Hayes started his career as a radio announcer like many young broadcasters in their day - whilst in the Royal Air Force. He was stationed in the Middle East and during his off-duty moments helped out with the Aden Forces Broadcasting Association. He worked up from announcer to head of programmes.

The Aden Forces Broadcasting Association was run by the Royal Air Force and was not connected to the British Forces Broadcasting Service which had its studios at Steamer Point, Aden.

After he was demobbed Mike returned to this country and tried his luck as a 'civvy' disc jockey - but he was out of luck until 1966 when he landed a temporary job as a summer relief on Radio City.

From there he went to Radio 270 as a DJ and presented *Mickey Mo Early Morning Sleepwalkers' Show* and *M.H. Evening Showgramme*.

STUART HENRY
Son of William and Mary Henry, Stuart was born in Edinburgh on 2 February 1944. He found his way into broadcasting through a variety of jobs ranging from selling ice cream to reading poetry in a cellar.

In 1966 he joined Radio Scotland as a disc jockey on board *The Comet*, but was so violently sick after two days at sea that he was sent back to the Cranworth Street offices

in Glasgow to tape programmes for transmission. This caused vehement complaints from the other disc jockeys who accused him of having an easy time recording shows on land whilst they were roughing it in force 9 gales at sea.

Stuart, who calls the author a Sassenach, left Radio Scotland after nine months just before the Marine Offences Act became law. He set his mind on presenting 'live' disc shows around various Scottish towns and cities.

His favourite colour is tartan, favourite food, curry and favourite drink, water! His likes in dress take in Eastern kaftans, Indian handbags and brass necklaces. "My clothes are happy as against hippy," he says.

Stuart joined the BBC at the start of Radio 1 in September 1967 by presenting the Friday edition of *Midday Spin*. The show was heralded by wailing bagpipes. He also appeared in *Radio 1 Club, Pop Inn* and *Disc Jockey Derby*. He was given his own Sunday morning show in June 1968.

Relating an amusing story when he had shoulder-length black hair, Stuart adds: "I was asked to go to the BBC for an audition and my agent, Bunny Lewis, warned me to get my hair cut. But on the very day, I had to rush down from Glasgow and didn't have time for a trim. Bunny ordered me to stay in the car as he didn't want certain people to see me like that. When all was clear I was ushered into an empty third floor office where I made my initial recording."

He was sacked by the BBC because of rumours of drink and drug problems. Unbeknown to Stuart or the BBC, he was suffering from multiple sclerosis which accounted for his lack of co-ordination.

He was offered a job as a disc jockey on Radio Luxembourg and went to live in the Grand Duchy with his attractive wife, Ollie.

Over the years both Stuart and Ollie have given moral support to many other sufferers from multiple sclerosis and raised thousands of pounds for research into the disease.

He stopped broadcasting regularly in 1985. Stuart and Ollie still live in a purpose-built house in a forest not too far from the capital of Luxembourg.   (He has since died)

MEL HOWARD

Mel Howard, who describes himself as 'an unsung hero', wandered over to Britain in late 1961 and through determined effort and great human drive ... remained unemployed for five whole months. EMI Records were the first to spot this lively lad - not for a recording contract - but for a post at the headquarters in Hayes, Middlesex. However, as the position for Mel (described as 'horribly overweight' at the time) was an uncomfortable one, and London was only fifteen miles to the east of his boarding house, he was forced to quit the area and move to Spain. He lived there for six months with a French tenor saxophone - they are still good friends!

He returned to England, and Air Canada begged for his services late in the year of 1963 whilst he reluctantly turned down a job with the BBC (he didn't have the necessary van driving experience or licence!). Working around Air Canada took him home several times over the following year - Mel is a Canadian - and there in Winnipeg, Manitoba, he dug up some old friends who owed him paltry amounts of money at two of the city's best radio stations, CKY and CKRC. Conversations with his radio mates and visits to the studios whetted his appetite for the vocation. Thus, when he returned to Britain, he quickly placed himself in an obvious position in the waiting room of Radio London's plush Mayfair office. Mel describes the office as a 'bedsitter.' There he waited ... and waited and waited ... It's an embarrassing story to relate but he remained there during his lunch breaks for nearly two weeks until, unfortunately, he was asked to leave by an irritated floor walker. Luckily, Mel had befriended the station's former programme director and occasionally broke down and bought the wretched man a beer or sweets in one of Shepherd's Market automats. The man (whose name has long been forgotten) couldn't help Mr Howard but promised to 'get him in' round the corner at Radio Caroline. No sooner said than done.

Within two months, and many terrible auditions later (the words of Mel), he took to the boats and went to work on Radio Caroline South in September 1965. Life was good on the *Mi Amigo* whilst Mel was there, but his luck changed and by the New Year he found that he was faced with coping with land labour once more as his contract with the station expired. Caroline was found, shortly after he left, on the beach near Frinton-on-Sea in Essex. Mel was deeply moved over this incident.

January and February of 1966 found Mel working amongst friends at the 100 Club in Oxford Street ... friends who have now all gone their different directions ... Bryan

Vaughan, Colin Nicol and even the writer, Keith Skues. "Oh, those wonderful memories," Mel would say if you could catch him recalling his joyous past.

March came, and so did a phone call ... from Radio Scotland this time and Glasgow's Tommy Shields (Mr 242). He thought that Mel might be interested in a job. He was hired as senior disc jockey and there he continued as one of Scotland's most popular radio personalities.

For the record, Mel Howard was born in 1941, is six ft. tall, and lists as his favourite likes tongue sandwiches.

He has now returned to Canada where he is a successful disc jockey as well as presenting a regular TV series.

PETER JAMES

Former programme director of Radio 390, he joined the station in its second week as an announcer. Peter was born in New Zealand where he worked for the NZBC for four years before setting sail for the land of his ancestors.

He arrived in Britain in January 1965 and found himself again afloat two weeks after his arrival working for Radio Caroline together with Bryan Vaughan, Keith Skues and Don Allen.

Peter recalls: "This very happy combination inevitably broke up and each went his respective way."

In September 1965 he joined Radio 390, not long afterwards was made chief announcer and, in August 1966, became programme director based in London. At a similar time he embarked on a television series for ITV - an educational programme for young children called *Seeing and Doing* which was networked throughout the country.

Peter joined the BBC as a staff producer in September 1967, being responsible for *Family Choice* which replaced *Housewives' Choice*. He later worked on *Midday Spin*, *What's New* and *Pick of What's New*.

From the BBC he moved to Capital Radio for a short while before returning to the BBC where he took up the post of Head of Transcription Service in 1990.

Says Peter: "Looking back all those years ago, pirate radio now has assumed a somewhat rosy hue. But being much younger (and certainly more energetic) then, it was an experience not to be missed. Friendships made during those heady days have lasted and there are stories to be retold."

In November 1993 he went to live in Australia and joined ABC Radio in Sydney as a senior executive.

DUNCAN JOHNSON

Duncan Johnson was born in Toronto, Canada, on 17 August 1938. He decided to leave school at the age of 14 because his brothers (one younger, one older) always received better marks!

The first exciting period in Duncan's life was at the age of 18 when he journeyed to Havana with the intention of looking around but, in fact, spent a whole week avoiding pro-Castro demonstrations.

He moved to Vancouver Island off the coast of British Columbia and secured a job in which he carried machinery up and down mountains for lumberjacks. "I must have been the only person never to have seen a tree actually felled," Duncan relates, "but at least I was very fit at the end of a day's work."

His shortest assignment lasted for six hours when he took a job driving a tractor on a farm - his longest was with Radio London. Other jobs he did included an oil rigger and a truck driver. Duncan goes on: "I only worked when it was absolutely necessary."

In September 1960 he joined a radio station in Swift Current, Saskatchewan, and he admits that it was the easiest job he ever held down. "I spent five months sitting in front of a microphone (not all at the same time) reading news, presenting record programmes and writing commercials. There was a total staff of 12."

Duncan then moved to Lethbridge, Alberta, with a radio and television station (CJOC) but found that the weather was too cold for him so he embarked on a visit to Bermuda. There he stayed for a year and a half and met such characters as Mike Lennox and Willy Walker, two lads who later teamed up with him on Radio London.

Duncan Johnson then set his sights on England and sailed from Bermuda, arriving on British soil on 1 August 1963. "I didn't do anything of interest for well over a year - just looked around and got a few jobs doing voice-overs on commercials. I even worked as a barman. However, in January 1965 I decided to join the staff of Radio London. My most memorable incident about pirate radio was the day I arrived on the m.v. *Galaxy* and found that I didn't have a bed to sleep in. It was a very rough night and I thought the ship would sink, but we all survived."

Duncan goes on: "Another memorable incident was the time Radio London was thinking of taking over Radio City as a good music station and I went out to the Shivering Sands Fort to look the place over with Reginald Calvert and a few other people. It seems unbelievable that Calvert was shot dead within a few hours of our meeting. Major Oliver Smedley was accused of his murder, but was later acquitted."

Duncan quit radio for a while in July 1966 and spent his time developing (if you'll pardon the pun) a new photographic studio in London's West End with colleague Brian Ward. He produced radio and television commercials, and in May 1967 produced his first record, *Lace Covered Window*, recorded by the New Faces.

He returned to radio in October 1967 presenting a weekly *Midday Spin* on Radio 1. For a similar period he broadcast a thrice daily *Crack the Clue*. Both series ended in December 1967.

Duncan released his own record, *Big Architect in the Sky*, in February 1968, but alas, it didn't sell a million. "At least if it did, nobody told me," Duncan adds.

He married Lynne Grout on 7 December 1968 at Kensington Register Office, London, and they jointly ran a ladies' clothes business in Epsom, Surrey, from 1977 to 1984. They were divorced in 1988.

In 1971 Duncan became label manager with EMI Records promoting material produced by Mickie Most with artists like Hot Chocolate and Suzi Quatro. He also promoted records produced by the rock group Deep Purple.

"Whilst working with EMI", says Duncan, "my main claim to fame was signing up the Simon Park Orchestra to record the theme music from the successful TV series. *Van der Valk*. No one wanted that record. It was my secretary, Barbara, who finally convinced me it would sell. She said her mother fell in love with the music. She was proved right. The record, under the title *Eye Level*, sold a million copies. Sadly I was not on commission!"

Duncan never gave up his photographic skills and has worked on record sleeves with such names as David Bowie and Jethro Tull.

In September 1973 he left EMI and joined Radio Luxembourg as production manager working with his old Radio London colleague, Alan Keen. He remained at Luxembourg for 2½ years before joining Capital Radio in London at Eastertime 1976, where he stayed for eight years presenting such shows as *Afternoon Delight* and numerous late night programmes.

Another move came in the autumn of 1984 when Duncan moved to Invicta Radio, Kent, when it commenced broadcasting on 1 October. Here he hosted a daily evening radio programme as well as a Saturday afternoon show. In addition he voiced and produced many commercials for the station.

He quit Invicta in September 1988.

Today Duncan lives on the edge of a golf course near Otford, Kent and is the financial controller of David Knight Advertising in London.

PAUL KAYE

Paul Kaye (real name Paul Kazerine) was bom on 17 February 1934 at Barnstaple. north Devon. His mother (nee Indina Scott-Gatty) was an English actress and authoress of four books. His father was Russian and came to England at the time of the 1917 Revolution. He was one time Russian correspondent for *The Times*.

Paul's education was at Avisford School in Arundel, Sussex. He then moved on to Ampleforth College in Yorkshire which is a Catholic public school run by Benedictine monks. He passed School Certificate and Matriculation and obtained distinctions for English, French and Greek in Higher Certificate. He left college at sixteen and went straight into repertory companies in England, first as an assistant stage manager/actor and later as stage manager/actor. He has worked in Windsor, Salisbury, Perth, Warrington and Basingstoke! Whilst in Salisbury he became a colleague of actor Richard Burton.

At the beginning of 1952 Paul went overseas to Kenya and joined the Donovan Maule Players in Nairobi as stage manager. He volunteered for the Kenya police and saw active service against the Mau Mau. He joined the Kenya Department of Information in 1953.

The African Broadcasting Service (later the Kenya Broadcasting Service and now the Voice of Kenya) was then only a section of the Department of Information. His early duties with ABS included editing and production of Swahili programmes, the training of an all-African dance band, dictation speed newscasts and educational programmes in English, and several documentaries in both English and Swahili. After three years in Nairobi with ABS, Paul was promoted, put in charge of their regional station at Nyeri and later started a regional station in Kisumu.

He went to Canada in 1957 and worked

for a year with CBC on contract as a drama producer in Toronto. He sold three radio plays of his own at that time.

Paul returned to Kenya at the beginning of 1958 and joined the Forces Broadcasting Service in Nairobi where he was programmes officer.

Two years later he was on tour again, this time to Cyprus with the Forces Broadcasting Service where he worked for 3½ years. He carries on his story: "A broken marriage, a certain amount of debt, and social contact with the Tass correspondent in Cyprus resulted in my being a security risk which meant that FBS could not renew my contract, although I was allowed to work six months over the odds due to shortage of staff. I would probably have remained with FBS but for this little incident."

Paul returned to London towards the end of 1963 and obtained work as a narrator/interviewer with BBC2. His favourite programme in which he appeared was *Late Night Line Up*. He has also appeared in other programmes including *Stars and Garters* in which he played the piano. He admitted that he was never happy in television so jumped at the chance to join Radio London as news director in November 1964.

When the offshore stations were closed down in August 1967 Paul decided to look around for a land-based job in radio. Six months later he moved to Radio Luxembourg as head of news in the British department.

Paul returned to England in the 1970s and became a freelance broadcaster for Yorkshire TV, including *Miss YTV* and continuity announcing. He presented a jazz programme on Radio Hallam, Pennine Radio and Radio Tees.

Paul died in hospital in Stevenage, Hertfordshire, on 4 November 1980. He was 46 years old and is buried in Northallerton.

Paying tribute to Paul, his old friend Alan Keen said: "Paul Kaye was the very first voice to broadcast on Big L in December 1964 as, indeed, he was the last voice to be transmitted in August 1967. I also knew the other side of Paul. He was a very fine

guitarist and his roots were in the field of jazz. He was particularly keen on the Belgian guitarist Django Reinhardt. When he came on leave from the ship, Paul would team up with Ed Stewart and myself and we would play 'live' jazz. Paul was a most professional broadcaster who will be remembered for a very long time to come."

MARTIN KAYNE

Martin Kayne (real name Andy Cadier) was born 27 October 1943, at Gravesend, Kent, and educated at St. Edmund's College, Ware, Hertfordshire. He joined the Royal Air Force as a boy entrant in 1959, trained in catering at RAF Cosford and later RAF Hereford. In 1961 he worked in the Officers' Mess at RAF Stanbridge, Bedfordshire. Martin also served at RAF Tangmere, Sussex, and RAF Episkopi, Cyprus, when he worked on the personal staff of an air vice-marshal, and also did spare time work for BFBS.

After returning to England in 1965 he heard transmissions from Radio Caroline and decided he wanted to be a part of the offshore radio scene. At that time he was working at RAF Uxbridge. He purchased his discharge for £200 and was released in October 1965. He then sent an audition tape to Radio Essex, and on the strength of that was offered a job on Knock John Fort which he joined in January 1966.

Martin says that life with Radio Essex was a daily adventure. There was always something happening, including the distractions of the Knock John ghost. There were no luxuries like television on the fort so one had to do painting and decorating to make the place more habitable.

The station was well serviced, unofficially, by record companies for new releases.

He earned £12 a week for starters. "Nobody did the job for money," he recalls. In addition to his radio work, Martin also ran the catering facilities which included feeding the half dozen staff on board and ordering provisions. Deliveries arrived on an 'if and when' basis depending largely on the weather and the availability of the tender - a fishing boat called the *Kestrel*.

"Personnel, supplies, diesel and water

were all hauled aboard by a manual 4 DJ-powered winch," says Martin. "Items and people left in the same manner! DJs slept in bunks, left by the MoD, in the circular bedrooms contained in the legs of the fort. Some pin-ups still remained attached to the walls. However time and progress ... like bikinis and miniskirts reduced their sexual or sensual attraction a great deal.

"Sometimes manpower levels were on the low side, but I do recall cooking lunch whilst monitoring the BBC Home Service news. This was recorded on a machine in the kitchen/dining area, so it was a question of peeling the potatoes, recording the news, then rewriting it to fit the 3 minute time slot, making the pudding, then on the hour, rushing into the studio to read on air before the peas boiled over.

"Night time programmes included *Essex Beat Club* and the *Night Owl Show* for which the presenter was expected to hoover the studio and empty the ashtray. I have always been interested in long distance radio reception and those night time shows had a clear frequency after midnight.

"I received much mail from Scandinavia, Scotland and a young lady at the Dog and Duck at Pluck's Gutter near Canterbury. This I discovered was a pub in the back of beyond in the Kent countryside, the young lady being the landlord's daughter. I have to say I am not a music fanatic. What gave me the biggest buzz in pirate radio was the communication aspect of it. I do remember whilst working on Radio Caroline North at a later date having to explain to George Hare, their shore agent, why I spoke for close on 15 minutes. I think I was close to being fired."

Martin left Radio Essex for Radio 355 in 1967. He recalls: "Unfortunately the station was not a success, nor were the stations that preceded it. Swinging Radio England and Britain Radio failed in rather spectacular circumstances. Radio Caroline and Radio London had become part of the youth culture revolution that was taking place. The presentation of Swinging Radio England and Britain Radio was primarily American and I believe people thought it sounded false. Radio 355 was intended to be an up-tempo version of Radio 390. However, it was possibly too similar to the Light Programme and Radio 390. With hindsight it would have been a roaring success as possibly an oldies or country and western station."

When Radio 355 closed down five months later, Martin moved to Radio Caroline North close to when the Marine Offences Bill became law. The Manx Parliament, however, had refused to accept the Bill so Caroline had a stay of execution for a month before it received the Royal Assent.

Martin joined Radio Caroline North the same day as Mark Sloane. He stayed with the station until the ship was towed away to Holland in March 1968 by the Dutch firm Wijsmuller because money owed to them by Radio Caroline had not arrived.

After a brief time running a discotheque in Folkestone, Kent, Martin joined RNI at a similar time to getting married. He says: "I was certainly in a tug of war love situation, half of me wanting to be at home with my wife, Heather, the other half really enjoying doing the radio job. Life on board the *Mebo II* was very comfortable indeed, each cabin having a small speaker by the bed so you could listen to the station's output."

The marriage won. Martin left RNI and returned to the catering trade but found little or no money. He now writes for a regular page for *Short Wave Magazine*, also works for a catering contractor (and is currently based) in a nursing home for mentally disabled people.

Looking back to the watery wireless days Martin adds: "I certainly enjoyed my time on the pirates but I don't think the situation would be the same today. On land we have commercial stations, but they do lack that certain amount of excitement. I was privileged to have been part of an era when so much excitement was taking place. I managed to fulfil my ambition, being in the right place at the right time."

LORNE KING

Lorne King was born on 1 February 1943 at Edmonton, Alberta, Canada. He comes from a family of nine children which accounts for his always being late ... his mother set the alarm for 8!!

In his school years, as a boy treble, Lorne appeared in the lead part in operettas such as the *Red Mill*. *Naughty Marietta* and *Snow White and the Seven Dwarfs*.

He began his radio and television career at CKSA in Lloydminster, Alberta, at the age of 19, before moving on to CKRD radio and TV in Red Deer, Alberta. There he did the *Sign-On* show on radio from 6.00am - 9.00am, also the lunchtime TV spot called *Noontime Nonsense* along with an afternoon teenagers' programme.

By the time Lorne reached the age of 23 the wanderlust had struck and he hit the travelling road for some five months which included seeing Toronto, Montreal, Detroit, Chicago, Cleveland; then abroad to Sweden, Denmark, Germany, Austria, Yugoslavia, Greece, Turkey. Italy, Sicily, Tunisia, Algeria, Morocco, Spain, Gibraltar, France, Belgium and finally England.

Lorne King began on radio in Britain with Radio London which he joined in February 1967 returning to Canada four months later.

At the time he listed among his favourite artists, Bob Dylan, Four Tops, Dusty Springfield and the Beatles.

BOB LE-ROI

Born in Canterbury, 5 May 1949. He became involved in offshore radio whilst still at school. The station manager of Radio City, Eric K. Martin, asked Bob if he would help with the "tender tapes." These were pre-recorded programmes which were played over the air whilst the supply tender was visiting the forts. Everybody was needed to help unload the boat which carried provisions and haul the produce up to the tower, so the DJ on air had to abandon his programme and play a tape instead.

Aged 15 years Bob was invited out to Radio City to present his first live shows. He was the youngest male offshore DJ at the time.

During the 1970s Bob provided some taped programmes for Radio Caroline. He has since been heard on BBC local radio and a number of commercial stations. For a while he was programme director of Medway FM.

He was involved with reunions for Radio Sutch and Radio City and spent some time on Roughs Towers (Sealand) in 2002. Much of his time these days is devoted to voice-over work and producing radio commercials.

JERRY LEIGHTON

Jerry started off his working life as a comedy script writer.

He was born in London in 1936 but moved with his parents to Canada where he completed his education by graduating at the University of British Columbia.

On returning to England in 1955, he had a series of jobs including comedy script writer, compère, singer and fashion designer.

He was one of the original disc jockeys on Radio Caroline off the Essex coast in 1964. He travelled round with the ship to the Isle of Man with colleagues Tom Lodge and 'Neddy' Turner.

Known as Jerry 'Super' Leighton, he accompanied the Beatles to America in 1966 to provide reports for Radio Caroline on their American tour.

Jerry left Caroline in June 1967 and joined his wife's antique business in Southampton.

MIKE LENNOX

A six-feet-two Canadian who was born in Winnipeg in 1942, Mike (real name Mike Graham) is one of the few disc jockeys to have studied to be a DJ. Whilst at the Sam Houston State College in Texas studying business administration, he took a drama course in his spare time to cure shyness. Part of the curriculum was to tape and present a radio programme. On returning to Winnipeg he became a disc jockey on a local station earning £10 a week before going south to Bermuda to be compère of a daily radio show. *Housewives' Choice,* when listeners could phone him direct and talk on the air."Everything was great until a finance company phoned one day about some money I owed them - and it came through on the 'live' radio telephone line." Mike also hosted a television sports programme.

Whilst in Bermuda he met colleague Duncan Johnson who helped Mike land a job on Big L when they both came to England. Mike joined Big L in November 1965 and presented the 12.00 noon to 3.00pm show. He says: "My wages began at £35 a week, which I believed was a lot of money in those days. All the food and accommodation were free. We were also paid for our week on leave. During our time on land I used to do lots of personal appearances ranging from disc nights to stock car races. My most memorable appearances were at the Starlight Ballroom, Greenford, and the Witchdoctor Club, Catford."

Mike clearly remembers the final day on Big L. "The arrival at Liverpool Street Station, London, will always remain in my mind. I have never seen so many people. We were mobbed by thousands of people, and the story and pictures hit the front pages of most of the daily newspapers."

He has appeared on numerous television commercials and also in films including *The Bedford Incident* and *Doctor Who and the Daleks.* In May 1967 he landed a part as a DJ in *A Smashing Time,* a film with Rita Tushingham and Lynne Redgrave.

Following the closure of Radio London in August 1967, Mike was taken on by BBC Radio 2 where he presented *Late Night Extra* on Tuesdays until February 1968. He failed to convince the Radio 1 bosses he was the right mould for a regular show on the network. "I used to take part in soccer matches for the BBC. I know various producers wanted to use me on *Radio 1 Club,* but it never happened, although I did present *What's New* for one week."

Asked what his ambition was in 1967, Mike said: "To make money and be famous. I love being recognised in the street and signing autographs."

He released the record, *Images of You,* on the Decca label in February 1968. Later that year Mike went to Ireland and worked on the film *Alfred the Great,* after which he came back to London and worked for Phonogram Records in the artists and repertoire department for two years.

He returned to Canada in 1972 to see his parents. He worked with his father and brother who owned a number of horses. He got his trainer's licence and moved onto a ranch in California. He married in 1977 but was divorced in 1991. He has two sons who live with him in Vancouver.

In 1984 Mike became a stockbroker. Today he is out of the media altogether but says he enjoyed his days on Big L and at the BBC.

TOM LODGE

Tom left England for Virginia, USA, at the age of four. By 17 he had become a cowboy on an Alberta ranch and at 19 embarked on an Arctic expedition. He returned to England via the West Indies and wrote a book about his two years in the Arctic called *Beyond the Great Slave Lake.*

He then joined the Canadian Broadcasting Company as a disc jockey, later returning to Britain as a freelance broadcaster.

He joined the staff of Radio Caroline in March 1964, and was one of the original disc jockeys. He sailed with the ship to the Isle of Man and became chief disc jockey on Radio Caroline North. He later moved to Caroline South in 1966 and with a unique form of programming he was able to substantially increase Caroline's total audience share.

Tom's grandfather. Sir Oliver Lodge (1851 - 1940), played a considerable part in the development of wireless telegraphy.

Although Tom reached the ranks of the BBC in January 1968 compèring *Radio 1*

Tom Lodge on board m.v. Mi Amigo, 1966

O'Clock featuring the Johnny Howard Band, he only lasted as presenter for two months.

He left England for London, Ontario, Canada and became the rock DJ star on CHLO.

In 1970 he joined Fanshaw College, London, Ontario and established Music Industry Arts, the world's first training for recording engineers and record producers. The success of this course was such that many of the top Canadian music industry people are Tom's former students.

In 1979 he travelled to India, where he lived for two years and then set out on a world travel which included a year in Costa Rica. This experience led to his second book *Success Without Goals* and the establishment of the International Breatherapy Association which he runs from California.

In 1988 he was managing his son's pop group. The Corndogs, in Canada.

He is now working on his third book which covers his personal experiences with Radio Caroline and some of the behind the scenes details. Tom says "I have spared no detail, no matter how personal."

MICK LUVZIT

Mick, born 24 February 1944, joined Radio Caroline in June 1966. Two weeks on the northern ship and over 1,000 fan letters in the first week was enough to convince the management that this was a very special DJ - two weeks was enough to make him one of Radio Caroline's top broadcasters.

Mick was not only a DJ but also a singer, songwriter, musician, actor and radio programme producer. His first record in Britain as a single was on Decca, *A Long Time Between Lovers*. The 'B' side, *Tho' I Still Love You*, he wrote himself.

Before joining Caroline he appeared as an actor, singer and even guest interviewer in Canada and California. One wonders how Mick found time to foster so many talents, but his rather secluded and strict childhood and upbringing led to hours of songwriting and singing lessons, and learning to play the guitar, drums, piano, electric bass and violin. He won the Manitoba violin solo contest at age 14 but, instead of taking up the offer of free study in Vienna, Mick turned to rock music. He gained his first radio show on CKY, Winnipeg, singing with his own rock 'n' roll band at the age of 16. On the same station Mick became a DJ and worked on general production. He then moved to CHWO, CHIC and CHUM - the latter being Canada's top station - before joining CFGM, the No. 1 country station in Canada, with whom he produced his own show before coming to Britain.

Mick Luvzit had the unique experience of being the only pirate disc jockey ever to be married at sea - and with it went wedding guests totalling 4 million. Mick (Real name William Brown) married pretty, auburn-haired Janet Teret, aged 23, from Wythenshawe, Manchester, on board Radio Caroline North on 20 September 1966.

Mick Luvzit in Radio Caroline North studio, 1966

The ten-minute ceremony was broadcast live over the Radio Caroline airwaves to an estimated 4 million listeners. The wedding ceremony was conducted by the Dutch captain, Martin Gipps. Janet wore a white silk trouser suit with a nine-inch bare midriff, a lace veil and coat and head-dress. She was barefoot with her toe nails painted crimson. Mick wore pin striped trousers, a velvet jacket, Chelsea boots and a yellow cravat. Best man was Ray Teret, the bride's brother who was a former Radio Caroline disc jockey.

Mick and Janet divorced in the 1970s and he returned to Canada.

IAN MacRAE

Ian MacRae started his radio career in Melbourne, Australia, with 3AW in 1958 as a record librarian assistant and control operator. After five years he moved to country station 3CS, Melbourne as a production manager, coupled with general announcing and organising outside broadcasts. During this time he wrote radio scripts for several networked dramas.

He came to Britain and joined Radio City in February 1966, presenting the *Aunty Mabel Hour* with Alan Clark. The show was voted one of the top radio shows by *Record Mirror*. Ian was on the fort during the unfortunate take over by boarders in June 1966. When Radio City closed in February 1967, he joined Radio Caroline South as a DJ and newsreader.

Ian was born in Melbourne in 1943 and enjoys every possible kind of music - pop, jazz and classical. In his spare time he likes to play golf, go bowling and gliding.

Travel is another of his hobbies, and in 1967 he commented: "I have a ridiculous urge to travel all the time. One day I hope to return to Australia overland through India, then do a trip around the Pacific Islands. I enjoyed my fight for free radio in Britain and tend to rebel against officialdom."

Ian MacRae *did* return to Australia where he became a household name on radio at 2SM in Sydney presenting the *Breakfast Show*. In addition he worked on station promotions and commercials. Since then he has worked for various radio stations in Adelaide including 5AD and 5KA. Since 1988 he has lived in Sydney where he now works for 2WS.

He released the record *The Ballad of Lady Di* in Australia in 1981.

Looking back to his pirate days Ian recalls: "I shall never forget the day I first clambered aboard Radio City on those shaky towers. I remember thinking 'Ah well, they look pretty grotty outside but they can't be that bad inside. After all, it is a radio station.' I was wrong on both counts. The equipment was straight out of the ark, held together with chewing gum and bits of string ... we couldn't afford wire in those days! But, surprisingly it worked ... most of the time. I suppose you could say it was homely, like a cosy slum. In winter, when the winds reached gale force 10, the towers shuddered and swayed. The tender could not get out to us for days, and often we would live on porridge and black coffee for ages. Regardless of all this I'd do it all again. It was a great experience."

KEITH MARTIN

Son of Stanley and Floris Martin. Keith was born in Sandwich, Kent, and attended Sir Roger Manwood's Grammar School. During his school days he was the 'biggest knob-twiddler in the world' listening to stations around the radio dial. At this time Keith made his first broadcast on radio from Paris, France, in English!

After leaving school, Keith trained as a hotelier and caterer in order to enter the family business but: "It was about this time I decided I wanted to learn more about radio, so I moved to London and descended on Broadcasting House," said Keith. "I didn't have an appointment, but realised if you looked confident you could get anywhere. I used to sweep into BH wearing a suit and carrying a few papers in my hands which looked like scripts. The only occasion on which I was challenged was whilst eating in the staff restaurant." Eventually Keith was to make his first BBC broadcast in *Roundabout*, hosted by Colin Hamilton, on the Light Programme in 1963 with a short talk on bottles!

In the meantime, Keith's mother thought it would be much better if her son got a job on the RMS *Queen Mary*. "But being a rebel I decided to go for P & O (the company which popularised the word POSH - Port Outward Starboard Home!). I joined them on the 28,000-ton *Chusan* and cruised around the Mediterranean. What a life, but unfortunately I developed glandular fever and ended up in an isolation hospital in Southampton which ended my days in the Merchant Navy."

Keith then joined Granada Television in their sales and advertising department based in London. During this time, around 1961, he met John Thompson who was keen to start a ship-based pirate radio station called GBLN. Keith had been on a holiday to Denmark where he visited Radio Mercur and was told about a new radio ship about to begin broadcasting off Stockholm named Radio Nord, later to become Radio Atlanta and Radio Caroline South.

He also had a connection with CNBC, the English language service of Radio Veronica, which transmitted off the Dutch coast and was owned by the three Verwey brothers who ran a hosiery business in Holland.

Keith recalls: "CNBC failed because it had a very low-powered transmitter, less than one kilowatt, and broadcast on a frequency below 200 metres which was not available on many current domestic radio receivers, a point which Radio Caroline, when it first started, did not take on board."

1964 was the year Keith began his full time broadcasting career with Radio Atlanta which later became Radio Caroline South. He says: "The pirate stations gave an informality which was rather refreshing to British ears. We heard a variety of accents which some listeners complained about including, without doubt, mine! Generally the pirate DJs talked *to* their listeners and not *at* them. Another bonus with the pirate stations was that they played music all day long. And because what we were doing appeared to be dangerous, it was also exciting to listen to these pirate ships and forts and the antics that used to go on. Listeners loved it! I'm sure that if the rest of Europe spoke English, broadcasting in this country would have changed much more rapidly than it did, but the pirates certainly brought about the radio revolution."

Keith became the first land-based broadcaster from a pirate station, joining ABC Television as a vision announcer in 1965, working out of Manchester and Birmingham. He performed weekend duties until the company closed in 1968.

Says Keith: "During my ABC TV days I received a phone call from Mike Raven who asked me if I would like to join him on a new radio project. I was fascinated that somebody should be asking me to join them after all my pleading with the BBC! Mike said there was no worry about being seasick as it was going to be on a fort. The project was Radio 390 which had a very powerful signal that went straight up the Thames Estuary. I worked on 390 as a relief announcer, presenting the *Breakfast Show,* as well as turning the many pages of *Eve,* the woman's magazine programme of the air under the name Gary Courteney. Colleagues at that time included David Allan, Stephen West and Lee Gilbert."

When not on Radio 390 and ABC Television, Keith extended his freelance work to include commercials for television, radio and the cinema, as well as narration for documentary films and other announcing duties. For BBC Radio he compèred a topical magazine programme, *South East*; compiled and introduced an extended record series, *All Time Hits,* and was one of the readers for *Listening Post.*

In 1968 Keith emigrated to Canada and began work as an operator/producer with CFRB/CKFM-stereo in Toronto. He then moved to CHOO Radio where he hosted a daily four hour programme plus a six hour shift on Sundays. Other duties at CHOO included newsreading, interviewing, selling airtime, copywriting and production. Before returning to England he toured North

America by car, a journey of over 11,000 miles, which offered many opportunities of visiting and sampling small as well as major market radio and television stations.

In 1970 he resumed his freelance work with Anglia, ATV, Border, HTV, TVS, LWT, Southern, Thames and Yorkshire Television. He says: "The nice thing was, I always appeared to be asked back!"

From 1971 to 1974 Keith was employed by Standard Broadcasting as a 'consultant/representative - to anglicise their Canadian Radio expertise' in the planning, programming and operation of local radio for their British clients.

During this time he was an active member of the Local Radio Association, a pressure group, who campaigned for legal, local commercial radio as early as 1962.

In 1974 he joined BBC Television for an extended contract as an announcer. Little did the BBC know that he continued to work for Anglia Television. Two years later he returned to his freelance work for ITV and again established himself in the highly competitive commentary and commercial voice-over market.

Keith joined Radio Orwell on 14 March 1977 and stayed with them for a month working on the project called *Up Your Resort* - his answer to *Down Your Way.*

Keith joined the British Forces Broadcasting Service for a fortnight's freelance work in 1981, but was still there, on and off, four years later!

The 1980s saw him making use of his extensive experience in broadcasting, with Media and Self-Awareness courses for British Gas, lawyers, academics, clerics, business executives and politicians.

In 1983 he established the Television Presenter Course for the Polytechnic of Central London - now the University of Westminster. The course was also the foundation for his individual training of candidates selected by ITV and BBC TV.

In 1988 he lectured students of the Inns of Court Law School on the 'pompous and pedantic image' of their profession. In 1989 he was a tutor at the City University School of Broadcast Journalism and lecturer at the University of Hertfordshire.

One of the delicate aspects of Keith's work has been to reiterate the principles of broadcasting to professionals who have been working in the industry for many years. Whilst a stream of invitations to lecture actors, producers and directors testifies to his diplomacy and success in this specialised field, Keith Martin remains active as a commentator and television presenter, and has been seen, in cameo roles, when he wears another of his many caps - his actor's hat!

TONY MEEHAN

Son of Edward Joseph and Mary Meehan, Tony was born in London on 24 August 1943. He was educated at St. George's, Maida Vale, London. His father, who worked for the GPO, was transferred to Glasgow and the family moved to Scotland in 1962. From leaving school up until 1965 Tony had embarked upon a career in insurance. Having studied for the ACII exams and achieved the elevated position of new business inspector with the Scottish General Insurance Company in Glasgow, part of the General Accident Group, by the time 1965 came around he knew the insurance world was not for him. In the same year he visited America for the first time on holiday and was exposed to commercial radio. During visits to London he became aware of pirate stations and realised that there was more to life than the BBC Light and Home Programmes.

A chance meeting with a friend of Tommy Shields, the managing director of Radio Scotland, led to an introduction to Shields himself, following which, according to Shields later, Tony Meehan was offered a job to sell ads for the station, due to his American experiences. Little did Tony realise that selling ads meant writing and producing the commercials and, on occasions, doing the voice-overs.

Following the launch of the station on 1 January 1966, Stuart Henry, a 'Top Jock' in the station, discovered he was a chronic sufferer of *mal de mer* and could not survive on the boat. As a short term replacement, Tony was sent out for two weeks to fill in.

The 'Boss Jock' - Station Manager - was Roger Gale, who in his log book at the time recorded: "I have deep concerns over the suitability of Meehan and his long term future as a broadcaster." He was kind enough to write six months later that his initial fears had been misplaced and that Tony was doing an okay job which was just as well because both are still close friends today. What was initially thought to be a short term break finished as a sixteen month enlistment as a DJ of Radio Scotland.

On most stations there were some DJs who were prone to mishap, and it must be said that Tony was possibly Radio Scotland's *faux pas* expert.

Whilst announcing Frank Sinatra over a sixty nine second introduction, Meehan was heard to say before Sinatra began to sing, "the King of Swing ... Mr Frank Sinatra ... from the show Kiss Me Kate, Baubles, Bangles and Shite Briny Beads." There were many other occasions when the mouth worked quicker than the brain! Tony was fired and hired four times. The reasons are not memorable but like a bad penny Meehan always made a comeback.

During his latter period with Radio Scotland he was responsible for promotions and ran the 'Clan Balls' which, as history shows, was good training for his business some seven years on.

After the closure of Radio Scotland, Meehan like many others found himself unemployed with not too many land-based companies interested in employing an ex-DJ pirate. However, he got a job as an advertising executive with a small Scottish plastics company and, in 1970, moved to the Rex Stewart Advertising Agency as a copywriter where once again he began to write and produce advertisements.

In 1971 he heard that familiar phrase, "We would like you to fill in for a short time," this time it was three months and the 'fill in' was in the public relations department at Rex Stewart. Needless to say, the 'fill in' period was extended, and two years later he became a director of the company which he subsequently left in 1975 to start his own public relations company, Tony Meehan Associates Limited.

One of his first clients, when he opened his company, was Radio Clyde, and for the next seven years he managed Radio Clyde DJs and established the Radio Clyde Roadshow, an ancient cry from the past. Also during this time he managed people such as Kenny Dalglish, Steve Jones, Richard Park, Ken Bruce, Paul Coia and Dougie Donnelly, all of whom started or developed their careers in Scotland.

In 1984 he reviewed his business, which was really two businesses in one, a management business and a public relations business. Tony decided to forego the pleasures of personal management in order to concentrate and focus on his PR interest. During the past eighteen years he has established his company as one of the top three in Scotland with a client list including such names as Safeway, Burton Group, Debenhams, Bank of Scotland, Scottish and Newcastle Brewers and T & R Theakston, to name a few. Today the company employs eighteen people in Glasgow and is amongst the most highly regarded public relations consultancies in Scotland.

Tony Meehan has become more 'establishment' than could be considered possible, a Fellow of the Institute of Public Relations and a Member of the Institute's National Council, a Freeman of the City of Glasgow, Deputy Chairman of the Scottish Public Relations Consultants Association, Honorary Fellow of the Strathclyde Institute, a Deacon Master of The Incorporation of Weavers and a Member of the Master Court, and he still finds time to present lectures at one of Scotland's newest universities.

He is also a member of Stirling University MSC, Public Relations Advisory Board: a member of the Stirling University Steering Committee for Distance Learning Programmes - Public Relations, The Western Club and Scottish Society of Epicureans.

Does Tony still go to the States? "The answer is yes, regularly two or three times a year, mainly for social reasons."

He married Linda Jane Stone on 24 October 1974. They have a son, Michael Anthony, and a daughter, Clare Louise, and live in Stirlingshire. Tony lists his interests as walking, reading and cooking.

On reflecting over the past twenty seven years of a career in the communications industry which started off by accident but continues to develop with a purpose, Tony reflects on his pirate days: "The time spent between October 1965 and August 1967 has had a profound impact on the years between then and now. I established good friendships which still remain today. Whilst most people thought that life on the ocean waves was full of fun and frolic, it was a hard school. You grew up very quickly and learned to identify the people you could trust and those you couldn't, and without that God only knows what I'd be doing today."

STEVE MERIKE

A Londoner, born on 23 October 1945 in Lewisham (real name Michael John Willis), he went to the Royal Naval School at Talhandqu in Malta. At the age of 15 he joined - not the Navy - but the Royal Air Force where he spent six years travelling the world.

When he left the RAF he worked in discos on the south coast, including Bognor Regis and Portsmouth.

Working under the name Tony Merrick, Steve recorded *Lady Jane* (on Columbia Records) which reached No. 49 in the British charts in June 1966.

He became an offshore DJ in July 1967 joining Radio Scotland. But the job was short-lived because the radio station was forced to close down due to the Marine Etc., (Broadcasting) Offences Act.

Steve was offered a job on Radio Caroline. He joined the *Mi Amigo* in August 1967 where he stayed presenting the mid-afternoon shows until the ship was towed away in 1968.

Many of his colleagues had joined Radio 1 when the pirates closed. Steve followed them in 1970 presenting *Pop Workshop* and *Radio 1 Club*. He stood in for Tony Blackburn for two months.

He was one of the few DJs to return to the pirates when offered the post of programme director with Radio Northsea International for six months.

It was then back to the Beeb - and local radio. In September 1971 he joined Radio Sussex as senior producer, followed by LBC in London from 1973-1974, Piccadilly Radio Manchester (1974-1975) and Pennine Radio, Bradford (1975-1977).

In 1976 he branched out into television and was the host for YTV's *Pop Quest*. He also worked at Radio Trent as senior producer, speech/music programmes and deputy programme controller.

Steve then taught media studies to BTEC standard from 1988-1990 and ran production and presentation courses. In addition he ran media courses for businesses at South Notts College. In Leicester he supervised radio training unit media courses from *ab initio* to experienced professionals, and business courses for using the media.

He then quit Britain for Australia working at ABC Regional Radio in Brisbane, 4QR and 4QB as acting regional programme manager. Off the radio he ran motivation courses for the Queensland Arts Council. He remained in Australia for a year, then returned home to Britain where he is now a producer/presenter for the afternoon programme on BBC Radio Leeds.

Steve has a private pilot's licence for UK and Australia on fixed wing aircraft, and is currently studying to obtain his commercial pilot's licence. He is computer literate.

ED MORENO

Ed Moreno was born on 19 June 1933 in

Wimborne, Dorset. He went to America in his teens and later attended Columbia University, New York, for four years as a medical student.

Six-ft. Ed started his life in radio in 1951 whilst at university, and has since worked on over 50 stations all over America, Japan and Australia.

He spent three years in the United States Air Force attached to the American Forces Network in Stuttgart.

Ed played the harmonica when he had spare time on his hands, and enjoyed listening to records by Andy Williams, Barbra Streisand and Tony Bennett.

Ed was first introduced to radio in the UK by a Canadian, Arnold Swanson, who lived near Notley Abbey, Thame, Buckinghamshire. He had made his fortune by inventing a car seat belt, and he wanted to start a pirate radio station from aboard an 84-year-old lightship, the *Lady Dixon*, but the venture was sunk by the GPO in 1962. It was due to transmit on 388 metres and would have been called GBOK radio. Ed recorded light music programmes in Swanson's studio at Notley Abbey. He was employed for a month and paid for his work.

In Britain Ed, who held a private pilot's licence, worked on almost every offshore station ... Invicta, Atlanta, Caroline, City,

Britain, England and 270.

He joined Radio Caroline in May 1964 but because of a medical problem (he suffered from diabetes) gave up the job after five days.

Tom Pepper offered Ed his next job, with Radio Invicta, at £25 a week.

Ed recalled his first impression of the fort: "We had sailed from Faversham Ore on the small tender, the *David*. When we arrived the fort was a disgrace. There was rust ... there was dirt. Having been a medical student I didn't take too kindly to this situation. But the staff were good fun. The living conditions were appalling. True, we had beds and blankets, but no sheets. The central heating system did not work."

On Invicta, where he had been chief disc jockey and in charge of the fort, it was Ed who insisted that DJ Simon Ashley and engineer Martin Shaw leave with Tom Pepper aboard the tender, the *David*, on 16 December 1964. All three were drowned and it left its mark on Ed for many years.

He was the first pirate disc jockey to appear on television taking part in *Thank Your Lucky Stars* (ITV) in February 1965.

He made personal appearances with pop groups in dance halls up and down the country. It was whilst working with Screaming Lord Sutch that it was suggested Ed might work for Radio City, but he did not want to work on a fort again. Manager Reg Calvert said he could pre-record the programmes on tape on land. This is exactly what he did, presenting daily *What's New* and *Last Date*. Those carried on until another death in the family - that of Reg Calvert in June 1966.

Next stop was Radio England/Britain Radio. Whilst on board the *Laissez-Faire* his medical knowledge came in useful when he helped DJ Errol Bruce who had developed glandular fever. Ed still wanted to continue his medical studies, but there were more students than places at medical school. He quit Britain Radio, returned to shore and was offered a job with Radio 270 by Wilf Proudfoot. He remained with the station until it closed on 14 August 1967.

After the Marine Offences Act came into force Ed was employed by Radio Northsea International for a short while before joining Radios 1 and 2 where he presented a film music programme. He stayed at the BBC until he decided to quit broadcasting altogether and returned to the medical profession.

Ed Moreno graduated as a general practitioner in the 1970s. He worked under his real name of Dr Norman Brian Cole. He was found unconscious in his flat at Curbar Cave, Inkersall, Chesterfield, by his girlfriend, Elizabeth Else of Duke Street, Staveley. She had called at his flat and saw the newspaper was still at the door. She contacted the police who found Ed unconscious in his bed. There were a number of syringes and empty drug phials close by. There were also two letters and a tape recording. He was taken to Chesterfield Royal Hospital, but never regained consciousness and died two days later, on 4 August 1980, from pneumonia caused by an overdose of insulin. Ed was 47 years old.

JIM MURPHY

Pole-squatting was Jim Murphy's speciality, having done this regularly since he was 17 when he spent 39 days at the top of a pole waiting for a record to become a hit. His longest "squat" was for 49 days.

Born by the Gulf Stream of Texas, "Murph the Surf" has lived with water all his life - he would have us believe he could surf before he could walk! KAML. WAKY, KILT and KIBL are just four of the Texas radio stations where he worked at different times. He completed his national service with the military police. He has been in radio all over the world as a disc jockey, programme director and sales manager. Born in 1943, he is one of three children. He weighs 13 stone, is 6ft. 5ins. tall and has brown hair and brown eyes.

His tastes in music centre round the country and western style but he says that he likes 'anything well-done.' He came to England early in 1965 to 'pole-squat' until the Cannon Brothers' *Turn Your Eyes to Me* reached the Top 20. By rights he should still be up the pole as the record failed to reach the charts.

With the sea in his blood to such an extent it was only natural that when he wanted a job he should think of Radio Caroline, and within a short while of going on the air enquiries were pouring in from all over the country. He broadcast from the North ship with his *Midnight Surf Party*.

In 1965 Jim said: "Everything is happening here in Britain. People are alive! Anybody under 35 has more opportunity to make it here than anywhere else. It's a young man's country and I want to be part of it. The young set the pace, make the changes and call the tune."

Like many Americans, he's never given much thought to Britain. For him it was 'funny cops, pubs and squares.' He stopped off in London on his way to Spain, took a quick look around and decided to stay for a couple of years.

As well as being on the air everyday, Big Jim Murphy had his own country and western programme every Saturday night which he handed over to Don Allen on Radio Caroline North.

He married an English girl, Anna, in 1966, and went to live in the United States of America.   (He has since died)

COLIN NICOL

Now in Australia running a city centre

shopping precinct, worked with radio ships at different times representing four stations - Atlanta, Caroline South, England and Britain Radio.

He was born in Perth, Western Australia, on 29 December 1936 and is the eldest of four children, having two sisters and a brother. His father was an electrical contractor and engineer with his own business. Colin was all set to follow in his father's footsteps, but his first 'love' was broadcasting. His first job as a radio announcer was with station 6PM-AM in Perth.

Two years later he moved to 6KY, also in Perth, where he later became the most popular announcer and programme director. Colin travelled the length and breadth of Australia meeting people throughout the continent.

He compèred many live fashion shows and broadcasts featuring such artists as Cliff Richard, Pat Boone, Bobby Rydell, Everly Brothers, Crickets and Australia's top acts.

In his own mind Colin realised in 1963 that he had gone as far as he wanted in Australia and wished to make the break in either England or America. He tossed a coin and America's loss was England's gain.

He set sail in March 1963 along with two musicians he had worked with on his 'live' shows around Western Australia. On arrival Colin, with his Australian friends, did a few 'gigs' in and around London. Unfortunately during the summer his friends went down to South Africa. At this stage Colin had just begun a breakthrough into radio in this country. After all. this was his ambition. By luck and by accident he happened to bump into fellow Australian Ken Evans who had been in radio in Sydney. Ken said he was preparing for the birth of Britain's first offshore commercial radio station - Radio Atlanta - and through managing director, Allan Crawford, asked Colin to join them. The station was 'happening' in Dean Street in the heart of Soho, London. Although Radio Atlanta was beaten by Radio Caroline to broadcast first to Britain, Colin managed to be the first disc jockey on that station to present a complete show. He presented the *Breakfast Show* on the station's first regular transmitting day on 12 May 1964. He was later part of the transfer to Radio Caroline (when Caroline and Atlanta amalgamated in July 1964) where he spent a period as chief announcer. He remained with the *Mi Amigo* until February 1966 just after the station went aground off Frinton-on-Sea.

The day Radio Caroline South went aground, the m.v. *Cheeta II*, Radio Syd, off Sweden, had to leave the Baltic Sea , partly because of Swedish Government harassment but mainly because of the sea icing up during a particularly bad winter. Ronan O'Rahilly made a deal to use the ship to replace Caroline South while she was refitted in Holland, and Colin was put aboard to take care of the fitting out of the studios - equipment for the transfer from FM to AM transmissions on 199 metres. Colin says that these couple of months were his happiest at sea. He and two technicians were the only British aboard the Swedish-crewed *Cheeta*.

Although he had enjoyed life as a pirate he badly wanted a break from the sea life and decided to try his luck on land. However, the land life didn't last too long for he joined Radio England and Britain Radio in May 1966 for a period of three months. An offer later came from Radio Luxembourg and he transferred his affections to a legal land-based life as relief announcer for the station,

leaving on the day of the first reading in Parliament of the Marine, Etc., Broadcasting (Offences) Bill, 27 July 1966.

Not only did Colin's broadcasting improve immensely but his health did too. Luxembourg officials were so delighted with his performance that they asked him to join the permanent staff.

Colin Carlyle Nichol, to give him his correct name and spelling, is 5ft. 10ins. tall and has brown hair and blue-grey eyes. The Carlyle in his name originates from his mother's side and descends from the historian Thomas Carlyle. On the genealogy side, Colin descends from the Scots. Both his mother and late father's ancestors came from north of the border. On his father's side, the family originated from around Hawick and fought the English in the Border wars. His sept is Nicholson of Nicholson, and his forebears lie buried at Borthwick Walls, near Ettrick Forest, which they once owned. Before recorded history his raiding ancestors - the Nords - landed on the northern coast of Scotland in about 850AD! The leader's name was Nic, hence Nic-ol or McNic-ol, being "son of.'

On a personal kick Colin likes people who know how to make the best of themselves, and their abilities, especially people with a real talent who do all the things he would like to be able to do if time and talent would permit. He likes London in the winter time; tall buildings; music in any form; the King's Road in Chelsea, and the English way of life.

Colin's ambition to work for the BBC was realised in 1968 after leaving Radio Luxembourg in October that year. He joined as a staff announcer presenting shows and reading news bulletins on Radios 1 and 2. He then spent five years with the British Forces Broadcasting Service in Malta and Gibraltar.

He returned to Australia working on Radio 6KY in Perth, but decided to quit the radio business and, by chance, broke into management of shopping precincts, first in Perth and later in Adelaide and Sydney, but is now resident again in Perth.

DICK PALMER
Dick Palmer broke into a new career in

Dick Palmer tucking into an early morning breakfast

September 1965 when he became one of the first DJs on Radio Essex which later became known as BBMS (Britain's Better Music Station).

After joining Radio Essex as a disc jockey in the station's early days, Dick was immediately recognised by its bosses as a potential leader and promoted to fort captain.

Shortly afterwards he became station manager and, in February 1966, only five months after joining the organisation, he was given the added responsibility of programme controller.

Born in Wimbledon, London, on 29 March 1943, Dick has a dry and very English sense of humour. He spent the early part of his childhood in Wimbledon and moved to Kent at the age of nine.

He was educated at a variety of private boarding schools, including the Royal Merchant Navy School in Berkshire. This meant following in the family footsteps, for Dick's father chose a profession in the Merchant Navy in which he was chief engineer.

Indeed, Dick's background proudly boasts an ancestral line of seafaring people, both in the Royal and Merchant Navy, which probably gave him his great love of, and fascination with, the sea. On leaving school at the age of 16, Dick took an apprenticeship in engineering having been interested in anything mechanical from an early age. He studied at college and obtained a degree in engineering. During his apprenticeship he was engaged in design and research projects at one of Britain's major motor manufacturers. Later he became involved in racing car design, and worked on rally cars for famous personalities in the racing world.

When he started his new career. Dick was intrigued by the involvement of free enterprise in commercial radio, a new concept in British broadcasting. The technicalities and difficulties of running a radio station at sea and operating expensive and highly complicated technical equipment presented a challenge which he felt would suit his personality and abilities admirably.

Dick has always had a keen interest in music. In his early teenage years he preferred classical, but grew to like and appreciate, in particular, rhythm 'n' blues, soul and black spiritual music.

Apart from cars and music, his other main hobby is the technical side of radio and television. Dick used to make his own radio sets, and once built a television set which actually worked. He has always enjoyed travelling, and has journeyed through most of Europe, the United States of America, Canada and Mexico. Photography is another of his pastimes, and he has many colour photographs to remind him of his travels.

After pirate radio was outlawed, Dick worked as road manager for Pink Floyd from 1967 - 1969. At this time the group were enjoying two hit records, *Arnold Layne* and *See Emily Play*.

In 1969 he went overland on a 20,000-mile trip to Europe, Turkey, India, Nepal, Afghanistan and Iran. This was, in fact, a research expedition on behalf of Kew Gardens and the British Museum collecting animal and plant samples. On return to this country he was "headhunted" to join Radio Caroline aboard the *Mi Amigo* where he stayed for a year, having become ship's captain.

He fitted out another radio ship *Deep River* in Lame, Northern Ireland and sailed her to Oporto, Portugal, and back to British waters, except en route she broke down and had to be towed into the Isles of Scilly.

Browsing through the *Daily Telegraph* at a later date, Dick spotted an advert for an engineer in the Oman. He applied for the job and became the personal engineer to the Sultan with responsibility for looking after a fleet of 2,000 vehicles, all belonging to the Sultan of Oman. During this time he was present for the official visit of Her Majesty the Queen to Oman in 1978.

Says Dick: "Whilst in Muscat, Oman, I got to know the people who ran the television service and became a newsreader for four days, but was politely told that I was only contracted for one job - and this was not appearing on television."

Dick resigned his post with the Sultan in 1981 and was immediately offered a job as an engineering officer in the Omani Navy. He returned to England in the acting rank of lieutenant commander.

Today he runs his own engineering business in East Sussex.

RICHARD PARK
Bom 10 March 1948, at Kirkcaldy, Fife, Scotland, Richard attended Kirkcaldy High School and later Edinburgh University, after which he joined the *Fife News* as a reporter from 1964-1966 and from 1968-1973. In between stints on the local paper he became a DJ on Radio Scotland, off Troon, from 1966-1967.

Guesting on BBC *Radio 1 Club* between 1967-1969, Richard joined Radio Clyde, Glasgow, in December 1973 and remained

with this station for fourteen years attaining the position of head of music.

Married to Brenda, they have a son, Paul, and daughter. Jennifer. His hobbies include football, rugby, cricket, and squash.

He became programme controller with Capital Radio in 1987. Richard has broadcast from all over the world including Russia, Australia and Mexico.

JOHN PEEL

Born 30 August 1939 in Heswall, Cheshire, he was christened John Robert Parker Ravenscroft and set out to find a solution.

He went to Miss Jones' Kindergarten in Neston at the age of four where he spent most of his time scaring girls and refusing to eat leeks. At this time he invented a device for detecting the presence of bagpipes in deserted gymnasiums. His mother sang it as a Christmas oratorio as she sank slowly in the west.

His parents then sent him to Woodlands School in Deganwy near Conway in north Wales. At this school, for the sons of gentlemen, he distinguished himself by leaving at the age of thirteen for Shrewsbury - one of Britain's proudest (until that bizarre moment) public schools, and that, dear readers, is how the badger got its swollen ankles.

He settled down well into the convivial life of Riggs Hall under the direction of one of the unsung great men of all time - the Rev R.H.J.Brooke. His career was fairly grotesque for his first two years at Shrewsbury and he owed his continued presence there only to the infinite patience of Mr Brooke (who was not at this time of the Church). He admired Brooke enormously for that worthy's eccentricities and flouting of convention. He attended a Convention Flouting Picnic and Pig-sticking on the lower banks of the Brahmaputra in 1951. The lowest bank at that time was the Fourth City Bank of Tunbridge Wells.

He failed more GCE "O" levels than he passed, but gained his house football colours because the house captain of football was a good friend and because he could kick a football with terrifying power and almost total absence of accuracy. This latter was an ability that was to stand him in good stead when he later went over Niagara Falls in a paper bag handcrafted by the members of the Chocolate Church of the Slightly Damp Pamphlet.

Some time previously John had accumulated two brothers, Francis Houghton Leslie Ravenscroft and Alan Watson Ravenscroft.

At the age of fourteen his voice broke and became, for three glorious weeks, a pure basso profundo - which he thought was an illegal operation. He owned two dogs called Tension and wrote a book called *Moroccan*

Taxation Systems in the Seventeenth Century Vols. 14 and 15.

Upon John's leaving school his father, with rare insight sent him to work for one of his competitors in the Liverpool Cotton Exchange.

His first public appearance was at a National Service medical at which he was called upon to prance about lightly, in front of four lumpy doctors, without any clothes on. He was considered warm enough to serve his country and joined the Royal Artillery in the spring of 1958.

His basic training, as an indoor harpoonist, took place at Oswestry. Here he learned to run about very fast and pointlessly, how never to admit being able to ride a bicycle and how to deflect bullets with a pick-handle. Following this he was transferred to Larkhill from which a man of considerable strength and little ambition could throw a stone and hit Stonehenge. This appealed to him but little so he arranged a posting to Ty Croes camp in Anglesey where he whiled away the rest of his two years.

He learned how to paint radar sets and how to play hockey, the latter because no one else would play goalkeeper. He made the camp team and, being the only non-officer on the team, travelled to away games in lonely majesty in the back of a three-ton truck.

However, bearing in mind that Napoleon never saw a giraffe until he was 48, he set out, following his demob, to investigate the persistent murmurings about the metallic content of road surfaces on the blunt side of the Atlantic. He found himself living in Dallas, Texas, surrounded by enormous people who sang songs mainly concerned with the untimely deaths of dogs in wells. He learned that people regarded him as a whimsical novelty and were prepared to grant him unlimited credit as soon as he mentioned that he was 26th in line of succession to the throne. Consequently he settled in Dallas for four years. He bought two pairs of falcon-feather trousers with certain foreign patents pending. Angry crowds sang selections from *The Student Prince* in protest.

In 1964 the Beatles made all those born

within soot-fall of Liverpool into minor gods of intermittent showers. He went to work for Radio Station KLIF in Dallas where it was his function to conduct research into the colour of Paul McCartney's eyes. His life became a mad round of personal appearances at which pubescent females tore at his clothes, begged him to touch them, fainted, cried, vomited and called him the only man in the world with built-in aftershave comfort.

At this time John was working as a computer programmer for an insurance company. This work he found boring to an extent considered impossible ten years before. He considered communication with human beings more rewarding than communication with machinery and thus went to work for KOWA in Oklahoma City. He also forced one Shirley Ann Milburn of Dallas to marry him by reciting to her from a history of sheep and their inner meanings and secret deaths.

John spent a year with KMEN in San Bernardino where he lived a life of startling beauty and understanding. He sent a group called The Misunderstood to England where they vanished swiftly into the subsoil. He spent his waking hours laughing in the sunshine, riding camels and ostriches, trying to look like David McCallum, singing the *Dead March from Saul* through a hollow log and proving that early Florentine sculpture was seldom filled with raisins.

He wrote a poem called "It is not necessary to have a licence to be a rhinoceros" which he read once and then threw away. Then, recalling the Ravenscroft family motto, "Brake-linings, not words", he wrapped his wife in their asbestos garage, packed his priceless collection of aftershave lotions and returned to England.

Radio London beckoned, being an appealing alternative to starvation, and he manifested himself aboard the m.v. *Galaxy* in the spring of 1967. John Peel, as he had become at the suggestion of a girl at 17 Curzon Street (with nice legs), says the world is divided into two camps, in his estimation, Love and Hate and he knows that Love will eventually win.

John joined the BBC Radio 1 team in

September 1967 and was one of the compères of *Top Gear*. He eventually took over the show full time in February 1968. A quarter of a century later he was still a regular presenter with the network and in 1993 qualified as the longest-serving disc jockey on Radio 1.

The Peel family - John, Sheila and two sons, William and Thomas, and two daughters, Alexandra and Florence - live in the Suffolk countryside.

John was voted National Broadcaster of the Year in the Sony Radio Awards, 1993.

(He has since died)

BRENDAN POWER

Brendan Power has the nickname 'Brenge' and he was born in the Republic of Ireland in September 1944. He had a variety of jobs before entering the radio disc jockey world which included being a pop group manager, a ballroom disc jockey, a demolition worker, a truck driver and a swimming pool attendant.

Brendan openly admits that he chased round numerous radio stations with tapes looking for a job as a DJ before finally being in luck with Radio 270 in December 1966 earning £11 a week.

He recalls: "Working on 270 was great fun and I wouldn't have missed it for the world. But on the ship we worked very hard. I used to start work at 5.00am on news until about 10.00am, then on at midday for a couple of hours presenting a show, then back to news for a few hours. Finally I presented another programme in the evening. The station went off the air at 1.00am for four hours. During this time I would be producing promotional tapes and commercials. In between times, if I had five minutes, I'd have a sleep."

In 1967 Brendan said: "With the Government hotting up on people who serve on radio ships, I shall probably go overseas - maybe the States. The Marine Offences Bill is quite ridiculous really."

In 1967 he did go overseas to the British West Indies and joined Radio Antilles as a disc jockey.

He returned to Britain in 1974 and joined BRMB in Birmingham where he worked as

production manager for five years.

Brendan is now believed to be out of the radio business and selling insurance.

TONY PRINCE

Real name Thomas Richard Whitehead, he was born in Oldham, Lancashire, on 9 May 1944. He attended Henshaws Secondary Modern School where a day off school to enter an art college exam seemed a good idea. This led to him passing the exam and using his formative teens, 13-15, to wield a palette at Oldham Municipal Art School.

In 1959 he persuaded himself that his potential stature in the arts didn't quite match up to his physical stature and potential to be a winning jockey! Tony left Oldham at 15 to take up a pitch fork at the Gerald Armstrong racing stables in Middleham, Yorkshire. After 6 months he decided the odds were too long and he returned home to Oldham. Another apprentice with whom Tony shared a bedroom stayed the course and went on to become the Queen's jockey. His name? Willie Carson!

At 16 Tony met another future superstar. On holiday at Butlins in north Wales, he bumped into a drummer cleaning his cowboy boots in the camp's Rock 'n' Jive ballroom. Tony by then was a real fan of pop music, knew all the lyrics and was always singing the hits for his friends. "You should enter our weekly talent competition," said the drummer Ringo Starr!

Tony did. He sang *Mean Woman Blues*

with Ringo's first group, Rory Storm and the Hurricanes. In the middle of the song the small Prince tried doing a Gene Vincent by kicking his leg over the microphone stand but his legs wouldn't reach. His boot flew off his foot hitting someone in the audience on the head. Tony fell over the microphone and off the stage onto the dance floor below.

No one who saw it will ever forget it. Least of all Tony who was given 2nd prize!

Fate moved quickly then. He was approached that night by some boys who had a group in his home town and needed a new vocalist. The Jasons were born, and Tony's job as an apprentice toolmaker soon became secondary in importance. The group toured the north of England extensively in 1961.

The following year the Jasons were given the opportunity to turn professional and, when the rest of the band turned down the season at Butlins where they'd first met the Prince, Tony left the band to go solo.

As Brian Epstein was hawking the Beatles around London record companies, Tony was joining a 15-piece Top Rank dance band. Whilst the Beatles were completing their last tour of Hamburg, Tony began spinning the records at the Oldham Top Rank venue. The regular DJ hadn't arrived so the manager gave Tony a bonus £2 a night to sing, play guitar and spin the records during the band break. The night the Beatles' record *Please Please Me* went to No. 1 on the NME chart, they were introduced on stage by Tony Prince.

Tony and the band were moved to Bristol to open a new Rank venue. Here the Musicians' Union expelled him because their rules ('Keep music live') did not permit members to play records.

Now he was a DJ full time. It was the mid-60s and he was miles away from home.

One of his girlfriends took him to a recording of TWW's *Discs-a-Gogo*, the nation's first audience participation pop show where the fans mingled in the studio with the Yardbirds, Animals, Sonny and Cher, Paul Simon and compère Kent Walton.

Tony met the producer who, six months later when Kent had to miss some shows in favour of commentating on the wrestling at the 1964 Olympics, offered the job to Tony

who deputised. The kid was a hit and stayed on with Kent for 1½ years.

In 1965 he met Tony Blackburn who guested on the show with his record *Don't Get Off That Train*. It was Tony B who told Tony P about his wonderful new job as a DJ on Radio Caroline.

When *Ready Steady Go* took the spotlight from *Discs-a-Gogo* and that show was canned, the Princely platter player turned to Radio Caroline where he spent 'two glorious years'.

One of his great memories was when, on Caroline South just before Ronan O'Rahilly sent him to the North ship, he and Tony Blackburn climbed the 180ft. mast in a force 6 storm to release a rogue cable at the top which was short circuiting the transmissions. "We'd been off air in a storm for four days and were pretty frustrated," recalls the by now 'Royal Ruler'. "Blackburn was the first to try the climb, then Norman St. John and finally me. It was very dangerous beyond the halfway point as here the new mast was welded to the original and the rungs became too thick for the clip on your safety belt. Blackburn went all the way. He was a very insane person. But then we were all driven with a wild passion for radio in those days!"

When Caroline became taboo for Brits Tony went to Radio Luxembourg to form, together with Paul Burnett, Kid Jensen and Noel Edmonds, that station's first all-live DJ team. This meant living in the centre of Europe.

Tony proposed marriage to his Oldham-born girlfriend, Christine, over the air. She accepted and during their nine years in the Grand Duchy gave birth to Daniel and Gabrielle.

In 1976 Tony was called back to Britain to become 208's Director of Programmes and Promotions, (this was the gig Skuesy turned down!). He spent seven more years with the station programming and steering it through the last days of its formidable nightly contribution to Britain's meagre pop music rationing.

After 16 years with Radio Luxembourg. Tony left broadcasting altogether to enter a new phase of his life and concentrate on a new venture with Christine. Their company,

DMC Ltd., has subsequently grown to become a powerful international organisation within the DJ and dance music industry. Their magazine. *Mix Mag,* is flourishing and they have offices and staff in New York (on Broadway of course!).

The busy couple employ 40 people, have three recording studios and manage a team of top young record producers including Brothers in Rhythm, the first British producers to be commissioned by Michael Jackson to remix his records. They also have their own record labels, FBI and Stress Records.

"By 1992 I was ten years into my separation from radio and I started to get homesickness pangs. It was like a static in the pit of my stomach," says Tony.

"Richard Park, the programme boss at Capital Gold, persuaded me that there was an important new development taking place on radio, nostalgia. So, guided by Richard's confidence, I dusted down the crown and sceptre and brought the 'Royal Ruler' back to life!"

In the summer of 1993 he moved to Extra AM as *Breakfast Show* presenter.

Tony's Top Ten Greatest Personal Accomplishments

(1) Meeting Elvis twice and introducing him on stage in Las Vegas.
(2) Becoming a vegetarian and stopping smoking.
(3) Building Radio Luxembourg when it was falling down.
(4) Creating a novel idea - a record label just for DJs to which every major club DJ in the world now subscribes, (DMC).
(5) Saving a man from drowning in the River Thames.
(6) Introducing the Beatles on stage the night it all began (February 1963).
(7) Creating The Technics World DJ Championships, staging them at the Royal Albert Hall and persuading Whitney Houston, Janet Jackson and James Brown to fly from America especially for the event.
(8) Singing with Paul McCartney at his annual Buddy Holly lunch.
(9) Saving Kid Jensen from a gorilla attack in a Luxembourg park.
(10) Managing the only UK producers to work with Michael Jackson, (Brothers in Rhythm).

MIKE RAVEN

The product of actor parents, Austin Fairman and Hilda Moore. Mike Raven was born Churton Fairman in London on 15 November 1924.

His education, which he has now almost lived down, was provided by a minor public school followed by a short spell at Oxford. This was curtailed by a combination of disgust on the part of his tutors and the arrival of his call-up papers. Mike served as an infantry lieutenant in the Second World War seeing active service throughout most of the last European campaign.

Since those war days and before becoming a disc jockey, Mike had a variety of jobs including photographer, conjuror, ballet dancer, Flamenco dancer, author, Shakespearean actor, interior decorator and television executive.

With the help of various wives (he admits openly) he has produced six children.

Mike Raven's very first attempt at broadcasting was on the BBC presenting a series of talks. He has appeared on *Woman's Hour*.

In offshore history he joined Radio Atlanta and presented a programme called *All Systems Go*.

He then moved on to KING Radio to organise a station from the remnants of Radio Invicta. He and his wife, Mandy, presented the *Breakfast Show*. In addition, he presented a daily rhythm and blues show, *Raven Around*, which was one of the highest rated shows in radio at that time.

Describing life on board Red Sands Tower with Radio Invicta in the *News of the World* on 6 November 1966, Mike said: "My day started at 6.30am with black coffee and I signed off at midnight with a cheery 'Wherever you are, enjoy yourselves.'

"The crew and I huddled down in squalor and chilly and damp depression. What with disc jockeying one-hour-on, one-hour-off, cooking, cleaning, fixing the transmitter - which often went dead on us - and running the generator slaving till we could hardly stand. And all this was for no pay at all, since there was no word from the boss ..."

KING Radio later became Radio 390 and Mike was made programme controller. He gave his final pirate broadcast on 28 November 1966.

With the opening of Radio 1 he was offered a weekly rhythm and blues show which commenced on 1 October 1967 and continued until 1971.

He produced two LPs, *The Mike Raven Blues Show* (1966) on Xtra Records, and *The Mike Raven Blues Sampler* (1969) on Transatlantic Records.

At the end of the 1970s he ran a farm on Dartmoor and a hotel in Devon.

He then moved to Cornwall where he became an actor in four horror movies including *Crucible of Terror*. He and his family live on a hill farm on Bodmin Moor.

Mike now spends much of his time enjoying his hobby, wood carving.

(He has since died)

MARK ROMAN

Mark Roman went through the usual and accepted routine of mischievous childhood during the latter days of World War II.

He started life at six o'clock in the morning, a day which he still looks back on with inherent horror. He gradually gained in stature, in spite of falling headfirst into a coal bucket, shutting a thumb in a carriage door and narrowly escaping death by a car when still only very young.

By the time Mark was three years old the gods, whose countenance smiled kindly on this fragile mortal, had saved him from drowning twice, once in a anti-personnel trench, and once in an extremely ornate fishpond in Somerset during the time he was evacuated there.

The years passed pleasantly for young Mark, and he managed to attain that lofty position of a teenager which most of us have experienced at sometime during our lifetime. As a result of his interest in music he became part owner of a jazz club in Ilford.

His father, a tailor, and his mother, a devoted wife (in spite of her offspring), spent many long hours trying to dissuade their son from the life of late nights and smoky cellars, but to no avail. He continued to pursue this way of life gaining much valuable experience in entertaining an often uninterested audience and making and losing much money.

Additionally, he enjoyed useful employment and became a salesman selling televisions, household appliances, cars, cakes and vending machines.

With time, the now mature Mark became the proud owner of a modestly youthful 1951 Mark V Bentley and, by skilful use of this splendidly opulent motor car, was able to persuade a promoter to give him a chance compèring a national beat group contest. However, this was not the immediate path to glory for him since the only subsequent employment he gained was as a disc jockey in a south London ballroom where the contest was held.

Finally, after many months of poverty, Radio London began to present weekly shows at the local ballroom in Wimbledon where Mark came to the attention of Tony Windsor, Dave Cash and Kenny Everett who suggested that when a vacancy arose on the station Mark should apply for the post.

A vacancy did arise ... Mark applied and was accepted in March 1965 ... his show became *The Roman Empire*.

Suffering violently from sea sickness, the terrors of the ship were only partially compensated for by the fame that came Mark's way. He often thought of relinquishing his 'Empire' but money, which was his fondest love, kept him striving for more.

Having been with the station for over a year, he was asked to present a nightly show for a week with the Rolling Stones reporting their activities daily to the Radio London audience. This success (he tells the author modestly) was followed almost immediately by the offer of making a guest appearance as compère of the Georgie Fame tour.

His interests were centred around photography, light aircraft flying (he qualified for his private pilot's licence in 1966) and women, not necessarily in that order!

Mark was another ex-Radio London disc jockey who broadcast over the BBC. He was given a six month contract for his own show each Saturday commencing in February 1968, sumultaneously releasing his first record - *Cuddly Toy* on Deram Records.

Mark Roman (real name Graham Wallace) left the BBC on 15 August 1968 and emigrated to Australia where, within a week, he was working for station 2UE in Sydney. "I felt that the pirate era love of radio was not being reflected in BBC programmes. In Australia it was alive and well. The atmosphere in Sydney was electric. I was fortunate to work at the key station of the major network in Australia."

He signed a contract for one year and presented the early evening drivetime programme. He also compèred top fashion shows in Sydney for big department stores.

"After my radio contract had ended I was offered work in both Brisbane and Melbourne, but I wanted to stay in Sydney. I did voice-over work for radio and television commercials and appeared in TV drama shows."

Mark then met a young lady named Susie who wanted to go to work in Adelaide. "We drove overnight in my 'Yank tank' (Pontiac Bonneville) to Adelaide. After contacting a few studios I was offered a contract with radio station 5KA and, within a year, became the highest rated disc jockey they ever had. This led to television work and guesting on *Adelaide Tonight* as co-host. I also compèred 'live' shows with the Hollies and Everly Brothers."

Whilst in Adelaide Mark met Alan Hale, a marketing man, who saw the link between radio and marketing. He encapsulated the view that radio was a product and, like Radio London, was a way of life. Working alongside Alan, he produced jingles, commercials and features which were sold to radio stations throughout Australia and New Zealand in the early 1970s.

In the spring of 1974 Mark went to work in New Zealand as a consultant programmer to the New Zealand Broadcasting Company. He spent six months in Auckland before returning to England in October 1974.

"By this time commercial radio was up and running in Great Britain and, with nine years of radio experience under my belt, I thought that radio stations would welcome me with open arms. It was not to be the case. I tried Trent, Orwell, Piccadilly and Essex, but no one was interested.

"I had been in London for six months when Alan Hale arrived to work for the agency Marden Kane who had accounts with many major companies including Shell, Batchelors foods, Pampers, Stork margarine and Crown paint. Alan offered me the job of chief executive of commercial production for Marden Kane Radio which later merged with the company, The Mouse That Roared. We were very successful and everyone was making money except us.

"Alan returned to Australia and I set up my own company - Senate. I produced a major campaign for British Airways. I spent a great deal of time creating opportunities for clients to see if advertising on radio was working for them. It was a difficult period. After two years I decided it was preferable to read other people's scripts. I was the voice on *A Year to Remember,* a collection of 40 videos, produced by Pathé. Now into the 1990s I do character voices for radio, host sales promotions and conferences, and voice audio-visuals. I am not really a star voice, but a jobbing voice. Some of my TV commercials have been shown in Sweden."

Mark Roman lives in a comfortable house, surrounded by five acres of farmland, very close to the Norfolk Broads.

EMPEROR ROSKO

Los Angeles - Paris - Sydney - London - the career of disc jockey Emperor Rosko has spanned many countries and weathered many storms - not the least of them being the unenviable chore of holding off rampaging Rolling Stones fans during a concert at the famous Olympia Theatre in Paris, while the Stones made their escape.

Michael Pasternak, to give Rosko his real name, was born on 26 December 1942 and is the son of famous Hollywood producer, the late Joe Pasternak. He was educated in Los Angeles, Paris and Switzerland.

In his teens he enjoyed the style of DJs Bill Mercer, Johnny Hayes, Wolfman Jack and Emperor Hudson.

Rosko completed his military service in the US Navy aboard an aircraft carrier. It was here that he persuaded his superiors that he would make a good broadcaster and joined the floating radio station, known as KCVA, aboard USS *Coral Sea CVA 43*. He spent time in the war zone of Vietnam. On return to civilian life, Rosko took a broadcasting course in San Francisco after which he went to live in Paris.

His achievements include a syndicated programme broadcast in Switzerland, Monte Carlo and France; holding the top rock show on Sunday on Radio Europe; co-compèring the first-ever record hop in Sydney, with the top Australian DJ Bob Rodgers, and as already mentioned, compèring at the Olympia in Paris.

Rosko came to England in 1966 and joined Radio Caroline South. His memories are that the food was terrible and the radio equipment was antiquated. Rosko caused consternation amongst the Dutch crew and Caroline disc jockeys and news readers. He brought on board a mynah bird called Alfie, which was kept in a cage in the newsroom. From time to time he would appear on radio

uttering the words "Sounds fine - it's Caroline." See Mike Ahern biography for amusing story concerning Alfie in 1967.

In 1967 Rosko accepted an offer to return to France and try out a new afternoon format on the French service of Radio Luxembourg. Within a year he was the No. 1 disc jockey in France.

Rosko was offered a weekly programme on Radio 1 which was taped in Paris and broadcast at lunchtime on Saturdays.

He presented a weekly *Midday Spin* on Radio 1 as well as *Round Table,* but in 1976 returned to the United States of America to live and work following the publication of *Emperor Rosko's DJ Book.*

He released five records *Al Capone* (1975), Trojan, *The Opposite Lock* (1969), Polydor, *Hey Sah-Lo Ney* (1976) MCA, *French Connection* (1981) Magnet and *Grabbit the Rabbit* (Philips).

Rosko returned to England in 1982 to present a Sunday morning programme on Radio 1 for 13 weeks. Ten years later he made a guest appearance on Radio 1 to help celebrate the network's 25th anniversary in September 1992.

In 1988 Rosko was offered the lead role in the British film *Rock the Boat* in which he was to play a pirate disc jockey. However, the film was never completed.

He has been heard in the UK on a pre-recorded syndicated radio show on ILR since 1984. He joined Virgin 1215AM in April 1993 presenting a weekly show, *Live From L.A.,* via satellite.

JOHN ROSS-BARNARD

John Ross-Barnard always wanted to be a broadcaster from the time he left school. The only avenues open in the early 1960s were the BBC and British Forces Broadcasting Service (BFBS).

He did not succeed in securing a job with the BBC, having received the reply "No experience, no job." He thought long and hard and decided to pester the BBC with phone calls. Eventually a kindly establishment officer, a human resources manager in 1990s speak, said "'95% of getting ON the BBC is getting IN the BBC. Take any job, but get in somehow. Get an invitation to the BBC Club for a drink and talk to as many people there as you can.' So that's what I did.

"'How do I stand for a job in the BBC? I asked one producer who was slightly worse for wear. 'About 45 degrees' came the half serious reply. Yes in those days to become a TV announcer it appeared that you had to be either Australian, catholic (with a small 'c') or queer ... or preferably all three."

The only other avenue open to potential broadcasters was BFBS, so John applied for a job and was successful. He was offered a post as an announcer in Aden where there was a lot of unrest in the Radfan area and a number of British servicemen had been killed. His wife, Connie, did not think accepting the job with BFBS was too smart a move as they had two small children.

Around this time, Easter 1964, the face of broadcasting in Britain was to change for ever with the arrival of Radio Caroline off the Essex coast broadcasting pop music all day. Within a short time two more stations arrived, Radio Atlanta and Radio Sutch.

John heard an advertisement for staff required for a new station in the Thames Estuary, Radio Invicta. He applied, having taken an audition tape down to the company secretary of the radio station who worked in Whitstable. He was successful. So began the broadcasting career of John Ross-Barnard, known on air as JRB, also Pete Ross, Larry Pannell and Peter Barraclough (pronounced on air as Barclay!).

He recalls: "I joined Invicta a couple of days after three people had died when the fishing vessel they were in capsized returning to Whitstable from Red Sands Forts. The senior announcer on board was Eddie Jerrold. He was very upset at losing three colleagues in what should have been a good boat having only recently passed its maritime test (the quality of the test, the coroner said later, had been doubtful).

"On board the only topic of conversation was the accident. My colleague Bruce Holland, who joined the same day as me, finally snapped after a few days. He asked Eddie what they all talked about before the sinking. All conversation stopped. Eddie went over to the kettle and poured hot water

on a handful of senna pods. As he went to leave the room we realised he was overcome with emotion. 'Death don't come easy to a disc jockey, Bruce,' he said and with considerable force slammed the bombproof door behind him.

"At that time we had all got into broadcasting with little thought for our futures, only a dream. Less kindly souls would have called it fantasy. It was like getting on a bus not knowing where it was going. We were going along for the ride. A magical mystery tour! The Beatles knew what they were singing about."

Radio Invicta later became KING Radio which, in turn, became Radio 390, based on Red Sands Forts in the Thames Estuary. John's final job in offshore radio was with Britain Radio/Radio England aboard the *Laissez-Faire*.

A year before the Marine Etc., Broadcasting (Offences) Act came into force, John left for the BBC in London where he became a narrator on BBC 2 TV, having found it was not a prerequisite to be Australian, catholic (with a small 'c') or queer. He graduated to BBC 1 in 1968 as a television announcer and later became network director.

In 1969 John moved to Manchester as producer/director with BBC TV News and *Nationwide*. Two years later he became assistant presentation editor, BBC 1 and 2, running the operational output of two UK-wide television networks.

Between the years 1973-1978 John took up the post as manager, foreign (now international) recordings. He was also heard as a newsreader on Radios 1 and 2.

His final BBC job was in 1978 as Head of BBC Video, BBC Enterprises, where he remained for six years. He was responsible for establishing and running what has become the fastest-growing income generator for the BBC after BBC Publications. John left to take up an appointment as Chief Executive, Thorn EMI/BT Coventry Cable Ltd., where he set up England's first broadband cable television network of 120,000 homes. He found himself acting as a diplomat and commercial catalyst between a recently privatised

Government agency, British Telecom, and an international commercial public company, Thorn EMI.

In addition he has been Executive Director Broadcasting Studies, Henley College, and is now media consultant to Coventry University.

Since 1988 John Ross-Barnard has been Chief Executive Officer to Satellite Media Services Ltd., based in the Euston Centre, London NW1, which is owned by Capital Radio, ABC Radio International (USA), Radio Clyde, Metro Radio Group and Radio City EMAP. SMS provides distribution of radio commercials, news services and syndicated programming in digital stereo audio and data. SMS was the first company to be licensed to distribute such signals in the run-up to telecom deregulation in Europe. Its service is unique. John has been responsible for setting up and running the business from scratch.

For a more detailed look at John's life with the pirates see Chapter Thirteen.

KEITH SKUES

Son of Richard and Doris Eileen (née Hughes) Skues, Keith was born on 4 March 1939. His family roots go back to 11th century Cornwall.

He began his radio career with British Forces Network, Cologne, Germany (1958-1960), Kuwait (1961) and Nairobi, Kenya, (1961-1964). Whilst in East Africa he and an RAF team from Eastleigh, Nairobi, successfully climbed to the summit of Mount Kilimanjaro (19,340ft.) on 2 October 1962. The following year he reached the summit of Mount Kenya (17,058ft.). He wrote articles for *East African Standard;* edited a weekly features page for *Sunday Post*, and compiled a pop page each week for *Daily Nation*. His radio shows *Skues Me* and *Skueball Speshall* collected awards in 1962 and 1963. When Kenya gained independence in 1963 forces radio closed down and Keith was posted to Aden early in 1964.

He returned to England after three months; resigned from BFBS and joined Radio Caroline as a disc jockey (1964- 1965) followed by Radio Luxembourg (1965) and Radio London (1966-1967).

Keith says: "The pirate radio days were probably the most exciting I have enjoyed at any time in my broadcasting career. The whole era was charismatic. Even now, over a quarter of a century later, people still talk about the good old watery wireless days. I am still in touch with at least 50 listeners from my days of Caroline and London. I was delighted to have been a part of it."

Keith was chosen as a member of the original team of disc jockeys on Radio 1 in 1967 and remained with BBC until 1974 during which time he broadcast regularly on Radios 1 and 2 as well as appearing on television. His radio shows included *Saturday Club, What's New, Album Time, Radio 1 Club* and *Night Ride*. Television shows included *Juke Box Jury, Top of the Pops, Wembley Festival of Stars, Pop the Question, Rough With the Smooth, The Kenneth Williams Show, The Ronnie Corbett Show, Thank Your Lucky Stars, Late Night Line Up, The Bruce Forsyth Show, Pop Quest* and *Calendar*. His last series with the BBC was the award winning *Story of Pop*, which ran for 26 weeks on Radio 1.

In 1972 Keith was appointed a vice-president of the National Association of Youth Clubs (now Youth Clubs UK) whose patron is HM The Queen Mother. He is actively involved in charity work up and down the country.

He is a pilot member of Aircraft Owners and Pilots Association; committee member for Stars Organisation for Spastics; Lord's Taverner; Member of the Society of Genealogists; Fellow of the International Biographical Association; Vice-President, Tideswell (Derbyshire) Silver Band and Squadron Leader, RAFVR.

In his spare time he enjoys writing and to his credit are *A Short History of Heanton Punchardon, North Devon* (1958), *Pop Went the Pirates* (1967, updated 1994), *Radio Onederland* (1968), *This is Hallamland* (1975), *Cornish Heritage* (1983) and *21 Years of the Red Arrows* (1985). In addition he has written many articles for newspapers and magazines.

Keith has written sleeve notes for LP records; appeared in the film *Sunday Bloody Sunday;* been the voice behind many television and radio commercials and film documentaries; has represented Great Britain as a disc jockey in South Africa (1971) and, at different times, been presented to HM Queen Mother, Princess Margaret, Prince Charles, Princess Anne, Prince Edward, the Duke of Edinburgh, Princess Alice, Princess Alexandra, Prince and Princess Michael of Kent and the King and Queen of Jordan.

He was appointed programme director of Radio Hallam (south Yorkshire) in May 1974 and, subsequently became a full board member. In 1977 he won the National Hit Pickers award and in the following two years compèred the National Radio Awards in London. By 1980 he was the longest serving programme director in independent radio. In June 1987 Radio Hallam merged with two other Yorkshire radio stations - Pennine and Viking - and he was made group programme consultant. In May 1989 a new service, Classic Gold, began broadcasting from the medium wave transmitters of all Yorkshire radio network stations. Keith became programme controller as well as broadcasting six days a week. His Sunday morning programme received the highest listening figures across the group (Source - JICRAR, 1990).

Always keen on travelling, he reels off the countries he has worked in or visited ... Aden, Australia, Austria, Bahamas, Belgium, Canada, Cyprus, East Africa, Falkland Islands, France, Gibraltar, Holland, Hong Kong, Italy, Kuwait, Malta, Mexico, Newfoundland, New Zealand, Oman, Pago Pago, Saudi Arabia, South Africa, Spain, Swaziland, Thailand, United States of America, and West Germany.

Keith was 'called up' for military service in the Royal Air Force at the outbreak of hostilities in the Gulf where he served in Dhahran, Saudi Arabia, as a public relations officer. Whilst on active duty his radio station made him redundant. On return to civilian life in March 1991, he was offered a daily show for BBC Radio Sheffield which he presented for six months.

As a squadron leader he attended a staff course at the NATO Defence College in Rome, Italy, in June 1991.

He is now a freelance broadcaster. In November 1991 he presented the *Celebrity Choice* afternoon show on Radio 2.

In January 1992 he was presented with a Gulf Campaign medal, and later that year returned for another tour of duty in Dhahran with the Royal Air Force.

Returning to England he has since broadcast with BBC Radio 2, BBC East and Radio Norfolk.

MARK SLOANE

Born 7 March 1942, Mark's real name is Patrick Hammerton. His interest in radio began in 1965 when he was on holiday in Europe and visited Radio Luxembourg's studios. He met Chris Denning who had attended a prep school down the road from his own school at Gerrards Cross. Says Mark: "Chris and I knew many of the same people and we struck up a friendship. He advised me that a man named Mike Raven was looking for radio announcers (not disc jockeys), who spoke Queen's English, for a new offshore radio venture (Radio 390). I visited Mike Raven at his flat in Chelsea who interviewed me and offered me a test on KING Radio. My voice test took place at their offices in Folkestone and was organised by Sheldon Jay. Following the test I was

Mark Sloane in the Radio 355 studio in 1967

offered a job on KING Radio. I consequently resigned my job as sales rep/area manager with 3M and joined KING Radio as a trainee broadcaster at approximately one-quarter of the money! KING then became Radio 390."

During his career at 390 he was offered a job on Radio Caroline. Up to this time he had been broadcasting as Mark Hammerton. Following his successful interview at Caroline he was told that he couldn't possibly use this name on air and that he needed to have a surname with a single syllable. "Cilla Black was in Caroline House and, following her interview, agreed to produce some promos. I was given 20 minutes to find a suitable surname so I ploughed through the London telephone directory and, 19 minutes later, arrived at Sloane - hence Mark Sloane."

Whilst with Caroline South he was offered, and accepted, a job with Radio Antilles. Alas, this was not all it was cracked up to be and Mark consequently returned to broadcasting in the United Kingdom with Radio 355, where he stayed until the Marine Offences Bill became law. The following day he flew to the Isle of Man and joined Caroline North where he stayed until the Manx Parliament ratified the Marine Offences Act. Mark goes on: "We were stuck on Caroline North for many weeks and unable to land at Ramsey; eventually we sailed by tender back to southern Ireland from where I flew back to the UK under my oldest school chum's name. I had every intention of returning, but I was quickly tracked down by the *Daily Mirror* and I realised that if I went back I would almost certainly be prosecuted."

That is where Mark ended his pirate radio days. He was interviewed and auditioned for Radio 2's *Roundabout*, the World Service and the British Forces Broadcasting Service, all of which failed. Consequently, he joined the sales promotion division of a major advertising agency, Masius Wynne Williams, and stayed with them until the early 1970s when, with two other colleagues, he formed a marketing company called City Marketing Group which is based in the City of London but has many subsidiary and affiliated offices around the world. The Group specialises in offering marketing advice to major corporations, banks and other financial institutions, insurance companies and shipping and maritime-related companies.

Mark retired from the Group in 1991 but still retains his original founding shares. He moved out to Milton Keynes with a small division which he now runs called City Airports Advertising International and specialises in advising companies about advertising opportunities at major airports worldwide.

He concludes: "Following the demise of the offshore stations, I have often thought about broadcasting again but have never switched on the microphone. However, I took a roadshow through Kent and along the south coast, playing at such famous venues as Sherrys, Neros, Bridge Country Club and Bearstead - and even today I occasionally wheel out the equipment for village charity discos and chums' major birthdays. Very few know of my past and are surprised at the Rosko-like antics of this staid City businessman."

BOB SNYDER

Newark-born Bob Snyder became a stage manager in repertory in Lincoln, Rotherham, Loughborough and Oxford from 1963 to 1965 and, at a similar time, was a disc jockey in clubs in Nottingham, Skegness, Lincoln, Leicester, Birmingham and Derby.

During 1965 Bob had a variety of jobs including a beach photographer, postman, chicken processor, doorman and finally became unemployed.

It was then that he decided to go to the Royal Academy of Dramatic Art "'cos he didn't talk proper, like."

Coming through the Academy with flying colours, he joined Radio 270 in April 1967 and broadcast for an average of 4½ hours daily.

From Radio 270 he joined Radio Antilles in the West Indies as an announcer and later became programme director.

On his return to Great Britain he joined the Thomson Organisation, and later Associated Newspapers. His job was the preparation of applications for newly independent radio stations.

His first appointment in Independent Local Radio (ILR) was with Piccadilly Radio where he became presentation manager in April 1974. The following year he moved to Radio Trent in Nottingham as programme controller, and remained with the station for two years.

Then followed a stint at Beacon Radio which caused problems and he lost his job. Bob emigrated to Canada in 1980 and worked for CKPG in Prince George and with CKLG in Vancouver before going to Dawson Creek in 1986 where he now works for CJDC. Bob also writes for the local newspaper.

NORMAN ST. JOHN

Norman St. John was born on 12 May 1943 at Healsville, Melbourne, Australia. He left high school with an ambition to be a farmer, but his father, who was an official in the timber business, wanted young Norman to go into some kind of professional job.

However, Norman's first job was digging potatoes and after a period of three weeks found it was too much like hard work, so he secured a job as a panel operator with radio station 3UZ, Melbourne, although he realised that this was of no use professionally.

In order to further his education he decided to go to night school and study for his matriculation, but at the same time he developed the bug for radio and joined the Lee Murray School of Broadcasting for Speech Therapy and all aspects of broadcasting. He attended the school one day and one night a week whilst continuing his educational studies. The radio school said he would never make an announcer!

After two years Norman proved them wrong and joined radio station 3CS, Colac, 100 miles west of Melbourne, as a junior announcer. The town had a population of 10,000. Before the age of 20 he had travelled to a further seven country stations.

It was then that he decided to go back to 3UZ as an announcer, and later transferred to television where he became a continuity announcer. He also appeared on a sponsored show. Soon Norman was to come to a sudden end of his radio and television career through ill health. He ended up with a nervous breakdown and doctors advised him not to work for twelve months.

He set his mind on going for a trip around the world and called in at such places as Hong Kong and Japan. He arrived in England in February 1965 with the intention of staying for a short holiday. He later took a job as a social entertainer for a shipping company, Lloyd Triestino. This entailed singing and acting as MC. He travelled to the Far East and back to Australia, eventually completing three world trips.

Norman had liked what he had seen of England, and decided to apply for a job as a disc jockey on Radio Caroline in the autumn of 1965. He was given a job as a news reader to begin with but later presented his own record show.

He was on board when the ship went aground in storms in January 1966, and lists that incident as the most memorable in pirate history.

Norman left Radio Caroline in May 1966 and one month later joined Radio London where he stayed for nine months. This was followed by a stint at Radio Luxembourg in the Grand Duchy as a staff announcer before returning to Australia where he now lives.

BOB STEWART

Now standing 6ft. 5ins. tall, 'Baby' Bob Stewart was born in Liverpool in 1939. "Ruggedly good-looking with black hair, blue eyes and a charming personality, Bob speaks with a mild mid-Atlantic accent," says an old biography released by Radio Caroline.

He was educated in his home town. Aged sixteen he took a job as a salesman. Bob completed National Service with the Army from 1960 to 1962.

His first public appearance as a compère was in Manitoba, Canada. Bob has, amongst other things, been a sales representative for both typewriter and television firms.

His hobbies are swimming, bowling and driving as well as wine, women and song.

Bob's name was put forward as a potential DJ by Pete Best, a friend, and former drummer with the Beatles. He worked as a disco DJ in various Liverpool clubs.

Bob joined Radio Caroline South in 1965 where he worked for just one week before he was transferred to Radio Caroline North and worked with colleague Don Allen.

He recalls: "When I joined Caroline I had a Liverpool dialect but the bosses wanted me to develop a mid-Atlantic accent as a Scouse sound could annoy people not living in Lancashire who tuned to Caroline."

After the Marine, Etc., Broadcasting (Offences) Act came into force, Bob joined Radio Luxembourg as a staff announcer. His country music show earned him many friends around Britain and on the Continent. He has been made an Honorary Citizen of Nashville for his services to country music.

His Luxembourg show was broadcast by satellite to America once a month.

Married to Cynthia from Texas, USA, Bob remained with Radio Luxembourg for twenty years until 1988 when he went to live in America. He returned to Luxembourg in 1990 and stayed until its close down on 31 December 1991.

Now back in Britain he presented the *Breakfast Show* on Jazz FM in London until the summer of 1993 when he joined Capital Gold.

ED STEWART

Edward Stewart was born on 23 April 1941 during an air raid in Exmouth, Devon, at a place called 'Caroline House' and as if, by some preconceived notion, fate was to play a part in his life, he joined Radio London 24 years later.

Ed (nickname 'Stewpot') was unique. He

During the summer of 1965 he was offered a job as summer relief on Radio London and he took the job "with open turntables". Ed relates: "I was the first newcomer to the original Radio London team and felt very much the new boy at school as I had ten years earlier. However, it was thanks to Big L that I got my major break. They gave me the chance to relax completely in front of a microphone and to be at ease - an opportunity which many professional broadcasters rarely experience. I became known as 'Stewpot', a name thought up by Dave Cash. One amusing moment I shall never forget on the ship - I was advertising 'Big L teeshirts, only 12/6d (62½p) including pastage and poking.' I realised what I had said and tried to cover my mistake by pressing the weather jingle and saying 'There'll be shattered scowers over East Anglia this afternoon'."

Ed goes on: "It's a great pity that land-based commercial radio didn't come to Britain much sooner because the pirates showed there was a need for this kind of entertainment. The British public have also shown their appreciation in supporting the pirates of the 1960s."

During 1967 a young lady called 'Myrtle' appeared regularly in the 'Stewpot' programme. She came on the scene thanks really to the General Post Office. "I was making a phone call to Lady Davinia Davenport," recalls Ed "when suddenly the line became crossed. I said 'Is that Lady Davinia?' ... there was a slight pause and then a small faint voice piped up 'Hello Dear!' Lady Davinia sadly vanished from the face of the earth, but as she made her exit, Myrtle made her entrance." Myrtle and Ed are still very happy together.

Ed joined BBC Radio 1 on 30 September 1967. He took over *Easy Beat* from David Symonds on Sundays, the programme being retitled *Happening Sunday* - however after 2½ months he was replaced by Kenny Everett.

He released the record *I Like My Toys* (1968) on MGM Records.

Ed appeared on the television show *Exit Way Out* on Associated Rediffusion which ran from October to December 1967. He

was born at the age of 3½ due to his mother showing off his 'tickly tum'. He had two ears ... an ear for music and an ear for jokes (most of which he pinched from other people) - suffice to say 'ear ear'. Ed was the life and death of every party (another joke he tactfully borrowed on long loan!).

His first appearance on radio was as a cherubic nine-year-old when he sang in company with his two equally cherubic brothers for the BBC North American Service. His father was a Newfoundlander and twice a year they recorded messages to relatives. He sang Christmas carols and continued to do so until the age of 21, the day he received the key to the then colony of Hong Kong. It is to Hong Kong that he owes his career in radio.

As he was some six months too young for National Service, Ed (6ft. 1ins. and 12½ stone) packed his bags and decided to see the world. A friend in Hong Kong suggested he travelled 10,000 miles to be a bass player, an instrument which he learned to play whilst at public school in Oxford. He accepted the challenge and arranged to fly out there. However, the airport authorities in London only allowed Ed to take 33lbs in weight and his bass weighed 28lbs, which left him just 5lbs for essentials.

continued to present *What's New* and *Junior Choice* throughout 1968 on Radio 1, the latter running for 12 years.

Ed says that the most exciting time in his career was flying to the Falkland Islands to record requests for his 1982 Christmas programme. This involved two mid-air refuellings during the 18 hour flight. He returned to the South Atlantic in 1993.

He was dropped from Radio 2 in 1983 so went to work in ILR at Radio Mercury for seven years. Ed returned to the BBC in 1991 and now presents a daily afternoon show on Radio 2.

He married Chiara Henney in 1974 and they have two children, Francesca and Marco.

DAVE LEE TRAVIS

Dave was born in Buxton, Derbyshire, on 25 May 1945 and was educated at the Central Grammar School in Manchester. His main interest (for which he had a talent) was art and his ambition was to become a designer when he left school. And become a designer he did with a Manchester firm, but took a part-time job as a disc jockey in the Oasis Club in the city to earn a few extra 'bob'. This was in 1963.

Dave found he liked the job of disc jockey so much that he went into it full time. He earned £1 a night. His break as a professional club disc jockey was at the Mecca Ballroom, Burnley, Lancashire. One of his earliest breaks was a tour of America with Herman's Hermits. Dave has also worked with the Beatles at the Oasis Club in Manchester.

In 1965 Radio Caroline disc jockey Ric Johns name-dropped Dave to programme director Bill Hearne who offered Dave a job with the station in September of that year.

As well as compèring his own Radio Caroline show until 1967, he also took part in *Beat Club,* one of West Germany's top TV shows.

Dave has two memorable incidents about his life on Radio Caroline: "The first was on the initial day I joined the ship. The captain took me aside and explained all the fire drills, safety regulations and so on. Should the fire bell ring we all had to assemble on the top deck and await further instructions from the Dutch crew. That night I drank more than I should have and eventually fell into the bunk bed about three o'clock in the morning.

"An hour later the fire bell went off and I raced up to the deck dressed only in a pair of underpants. As requested I stood by the lifeboat in freezing temperatures. After about five minutes I thought everything had gone very quiet. All the other DJs had returned to bed. I had been the subject of a practical joke!

"The other memorable Radio Caroline moment was on board *Mi Amigo* when she went aground in the gales of January 1966."

DLT joined the BBC Radio 1 team at the end of 1967 and was regular host of *Pop North* broadcast on Thursday lunchtimes. From 1971 to 1983 he had his own daily show. In 1976 he enjoyed success with fellow disc jockey Paul Burnett when they had a hit record *Convoy GB* for which they called themselves Laurie Lingo and the Dipsticks. It reached No. 4 in the charts.

Dave broadcast on Radio 1 at weekends until he resigned on the radio during his Sunday morning programme on 8 August 1993, having criticised the management of the BBC. He sold his story to the *Sun* newspaper and was shown the door two months before his contract expired in October 1993. Since then Dave has broadcast from QEFM to ILR stations via satellite. He was a regular broadcaster on the BBC World Service. He is an avid photographer.

TOMMY VANCE

Real name Richard Anthony Crispian Francis Prew Hope-Weston ... to name but six!

Show business runs in the Vance family. His grandmother owned a travelling repertory company. His grandfather was an executive with the National Union of Railwaymen.

Tommy was expelled from school at King's Cross, London, for non-attendance. His first job was as a trainee manager at the Hyde Park Hotel, London. At the age of 16 he ran away to sea as a cabin boy and was based in New York for two years. He then came ashore and worked in a jukebox company: "So I could listen to the music for free and not have to keep inserting money into the machine." At night he took an interest in amateur dramatics.

Tommy then embarked upon his show business career - he joined the Ulster Bridge Repertory Company (which was run by actor

James Ellis of *Z Cars* fame) as a stage manager. But he wasn't making enough money and thought perhaps his talents lay in radio, especially in America. He made the effort to raise the money and crossed the Atlantic. He drove a car from Virginia, USA, to Vancouver, Canada, where he had a girlfriend. Tommy worked for a local commercial radio station for no money at all and was 'a general dogsbody!' He worked from midnight to 6.00am helping a man, Jim Thom, who was studying for his PhD in communications and ultimately went to Columbia University, New York, as a professor in 1961.

Tommy took up residence in the USA and worked at station KEPR, followed by KARY, both in Washington State. His girl friend was still living in Vancouver so each weekend he drove to see her. Passing through Seattle he dropped off various audition tapes and was eventually offered a job working under the name Rick West.

Tommy Vance says he was America's first British DJ on station KOL in Los Angeles but within a short time was poached by KHJ, also in Los Angeles. By now he was working as Tommy Vance. How did that name come about? Says Tommy: "The radio station had already recorded its jingles. There was one for a DJ called Tommy Vance, but for whatever reason he couldn't start with the station at that time. I was asked if I would change my name from Rick West to Tommy Vance. They were paying me a lot of money to join the station, so naturally I didn't object to the name. And it's been with me ever since! In Los Angeles I became a No. 1 DJ holding down the 6.00pm to 9.00pm show daily. However, all that came to an end very suddenly when I was drafted into the US Army in 1965. I declined their kind offer! A musician friend of mine, Ian Whitcomb, lent me the money to travel back to England. I did pay him back later. I still held a British passport, arrived in London at Christmastime 1965, and went straight to Radio Caroline in Chesterfield Gardens. Programme director, Bill Heame, offered me a job on the South ship and I went out to the *Mi Amigo* on 3 January 1966."

Tommy remained with Radio Caroline

for just three months before moving to Luxembourg where he broadcast from the Grand Duchy.

Dissatisfied with the set-up at Luxembourg he returned to the high seas and Radio Caroline, rejoining the station on 5 December 1966.

Some six months later he changed his affections to Radio London and joined 266 only a couple of weeks before the station was forced to close down by the Government.

He recalls: "I joined Big L because I heard a rumour from programme director, Alan Keen, that the station was thinking of starting a land-based pop station on the Continent beaming its programmes to the UK ... similar to what Atlantic 252 does today ... However, it was only a rumour and the station never got off the ground."

Like many other disc jockeys, Tommy Vance tried his hand at the recording business and released *You Must Be the One* and *Off the Hook* on Columbia Records. Both songs were recorded in Los Angeles.

Tommy's first BBC assignment was *Top Gear* which he co-presented with John Peel, but when the show was cut in length Tommy lost out. He did a short stint with Radio Monte Carlo, along with Kenny Everett and Dave Cash.

From May to July 1968 he compèred Granada TV's *New Faces*.

Off the air, Oxford-bom Tommy says his interests vary from recordings of Dylan Thomas through to jazz.

He presented various shows on Capital Radio from 1973-1979.

He was a regular voice on Radio 1, in addition to BBC2, GLR, Sky TV, the BBC World Service and the British Forces Broadcasting Service. Over the years he has introduced *Top of the Pops, Disco 2, Top 40* and the *Friday Rock Show.*

Tommy is a founder director of the biggest digital audio post-production facility in the world. Two companies. Silk Sound and The Bridge have, between them, seven studios in Soho, London.

He joined Virgin 1215AM as the 4.00pm to 7.00pm presenter when it went on the air in April 1993 saying: "I have enjoyed presenting my rock show on Radio 1 for 14 years, but it only offered a weekly two-hour window for good, grown-up rock music and Virgin 1215 is going to be playing it 24 hours a day. That's a massive expansion and I am delighted to be a part of it."

Looking back to pirate days. Tommy recalls: "In life I enjoy a challenge. Virgin is a challenge ... so was life on board a pirate radio ship. I relished the environment of being at sea even down to thunderstorms and the rough weather.

"I had been a top DJ in Los Angeles enjoying the high life of Hollywood and earning close to $50,000 a year in 1965. Within five days, thanks to receiving my draft papers, I was in the middle of the North Sea earning £18 10s 0d (£18.50) a week on Radio Caroline. But it was good fun."

Today Tommy Vance lives in London. He is married to Stella and they have a son, Daniel, and a daughter, Jessie.

(He has since died)

BRYAN VAUGHAN

Bryan Vaughan (real name Dermot Hoy) comes from Australia where he was born on 23 February 1941 within sight of the famous Sydney Harbour Bridge. He was educated at St. Pius College, Sydney. Leaving college Bryan wanted to enter the 'radio world' and was fortunate enough in securing a post with 2GB, Sydney, first as a technician, then with 2CH as a tape editor and finally as a producer.

During his time with the station he also broadcast, mainly interviews, with leading Australian personalities; appearing on 'the live side' of the microphone was more an attraction to Bryan.

In his spare moments he continued with his favourite sports, rugby, cricket and swimming. He reminisces about relaxing on the beach after his early morning shifts had been completed.

In 1962 he decided to break with Australia and, like so many young men and women, set his mind on Britain. Bryan thought that there would be more opportunities in England in the broadcasting field. But he was in for a shock.

He arrived on the shores of Britain in

May 1962 and completed the rounds, but found that no doors were open at all. He had travelled thousands of miles to remain in broadcasting, however, and was determined to get a break sooner or later. So he decided to bide his time and took a job as a cigarette packer ... thought that was too much of a 'fag', and changed his job to barman. This job didn't last long either - he ended up as a waiter and then a night porter in a hotel.

Still not 'throwing in the towel', Bryan wrote to the BBC in pursuit of a job and much to his surprise was accepted as a studio manager. But this job was centred in the control room whereas his ambition was to be a broadcaster.

It was at this time that the plans for Radio Atlanta were bearing fruit and the station hoped to be on air in the first quarter of 1964. He was offered a job as a technician and became responsible for taping the majority of Radio Atlanta's early programmes which got underway in May 1964.

When the station commenced live broadcasting, Bryan joined the staff as a disc jockey, and then remained with the station when it changed to Radio Caroline South in July 1964, eventually working up to chief disc jockey.

He decided to return to Australia for a holiday in December 1965 and left Radio Caroline with the understanding that his job would be available if, and when, he came back to England. Whilst in Australia he made several appearances on television being the first 'live' pirate to return to their shores!

Bronzed, Bryan *did* return to England in the bleak winter of 1966, but found that his job at Radio Caroline had been taken. There had been a complete change of staff both on board and at Caroline House.

His affections turned to Radio Luxembourg with whom he was offered the *Hi Midnight* series sponsored by Polydor Records during the latter half of 1966.

He later joined Radio Scotland as assistant chief disc jockey in January 1967 where he remained for six months, but decided on returning to his native Australia during the summer of the same year. Before so doing he married Jean Roughsedge in

Kensington in May 1966. At his Roman Catholic wedding there were representatives from Radio Caroline, Radio London, Radio Luxembourg and Radio England.

Upon returning to Australia, Bryan worked for a year as professional manager for Castle Music (EMI). In June 1968 he was offered the position of product manager at Philips Records (eventually renamed PolyGram). He became interested in record producing and in early 1969 produced the first of more than 60 albums for PolyGram with a repertoire ranging from classical to jazz, country, popular and even heavy metal!

During the next fourteen years Bryan progressed to become a senior executive with the company as artist and repertoire director, responsible for all music selection, compilation and packaging. He continued to do some freelance voice-over work on commercials and documentaries.

In May 1983 he joined Reader's Digest in Sydney as repertoire manager and is currently responsible for the selection and marketing of the company's music albums.

The Vaughans have two sons, Bryan and Christopher, and a daughter, Alison, and live in Sydney, Australia.

JOHNNIE WALKER

Johnnie Walker was born in 30 March 1945 in Birmingham and educated at Solihull Public School, becoming a car salesman when he left.

His interest in pop music enabled him to work in a few clubs in Birmingham, but within one year he was a professional disc jockey with Radio England/Britain Radio.

He joined the station in March 1966. His taste in music at this time was strictly pop with a strong preference for Tamla Motown. He also liked the Beatles, the Rolling Stones, and Spencer Davis.

He joined the staff of Radio Caroline South in October 1966 and held down the 9.00pm - midnight show. His best-known gimmick was the section devoted to the 'kiss in the car' and the 'Frinton flashing' spot.

Johnnie awarded 'licences' to those couples who took part in the show. Over 20,000 were circulated to people as far away as Perth, Western Australia.

Johnnie Walker

In January 1967, when he was overlooked in the New Year's Honours list, he said in future he would call himself 'Sir' Johnnie Walker.

In his spare time he was a great fan of motor racing, and at one time enrolled at a school for racing drivers handling Lotus models with speeds of up to 130mph.

Commenting in 1966 on commercial radio in Britain, Johnnie said: "Legalised commercial radio should be introduced into the country because it won't cost the public a penny. It can provide a great public service and competition, especially amongst other stations. When Radio London came on the scene after Caroline had been successful, it caused competition, and each other station benefited by better programmes.

"The biggest tragedy in offshore radio was the Radio City incident which obviously stirred the Government to introduce legislation as soon as possible."

Johnnie Walker was one of the few English disc jockeys who remained with Radio Caroline South after the Marine Offences Act came into force in August 1967.

Says Johnnie: " Caroline was for me at that time a way of life. I had never had so much satisfaction out of doing anything else in my life and I really didn't want to leave it. If Caroline was going to continue then I wanted to be a part of it. I couldn't believe the whole Government machine and the establishment would be so concerned as to stop something that was not causing any harm to anyone and giving such a tremendous number of people such a great deal of pleasure. I really hoped that it would go on for ever.

"At 12.00 midnight on 14 August I opened the microphone, said 'Radio Caroline continues' and then played *All You Need is Love* by the Beatles. I have since been told there were about 20 million people listening all over Europe that evening. Deep down everyone wanted Caroline to continue and succeed. There were problems. It meant we as disc jockeys could not return to England and so had to spend our leave in Holland.

"There werc other problems as well like when supplies never turned up, or we ran out of food and water. Yes, it was rough, but we had to continue. We had a huge audience out there and they identified with Caroline. It was a very important part of their lives.

"The only time we really became concerned was the next day. We really didn't know what to expect. We quite expected a naval ship to arrive on the horizon, but everything just continued as normal. We were in fact coming back over to England during the time we were supposed to be in exile in Holland. The Customs knew who we were. One officer asked me for my autograph for his daughter. I don't believe they ever intended to arrest a DJ. I have to say everything was thrown at us - the whole weight of the Government, plus one of the worst winters that Caroline had ever experienced in the North Sea.

"Part of the success of Caroline was the family atmosphere. We lived on this small ship in the middle of the sea. We couldn't go anywhere and were on board for weeks at a time. All the DJs had to live for was Caroline and their radio programmes and the lives of their colleagues on board. From time to time either the captain, the cook or another DJ would come into the studio and have a chat on air which created interesting radio.

"There was a wonderful feeling of freedom on Caroline with no bosses on board. You could say what you liked - you could play what you liked. I have to say that had it not been for Caroline I would not be working in radio today."

Johnnie had a very large following and often appeared in disc jockey polls like the *Disc and Music Echo* for their Valentine's Day Award 1968 when he was voted 4th most popular disc jockey in Great Britain.

He wrote and recorded *Man's Fight for Freedom*, his dream of the Caroline ship broadcasting as she sailed up the Thames to the Houses of Parliament.

"The beginning is the past, the middle is now, the end is in the future. It is a story of sadness and triumph. 14 August as disc jockeys Robbie Dale, Johnnie Walker and Russ Brown leave Liverpool Street Station spurred on towards the sea by the hundreds of cheering people. See them now as they stand on the tender. There are tears in their eyes as their families, their homes and loved ones are left behind. Three o'clock on this Monday afternoon and on 266 Big L is heard for the last time. Caroline is alone. These three men prepare for midnight, for in a few hours' time they are to challenge the might and power of the British Government. They will become criminals. Midnight approaches and it is 15 August. Johnnie Walker announces that Caroline belongs to YOU, that she loves you and she will continue. The Beatles sing *All You Need is Love*. These men sound happy, but underneath they are sad for they now know they have passed the point of no return. They are not sad for long. They are joined by other men who also gave up so much to fight for freedom. The seas are rough and cruel, life is hard but as each day passes the moment of triumph draws nearer. The British people rally round. They send food, they send comfort and they send their love. All you need is love - and love overcomes. The British Government relents. Caroline raises her anchor and heads for England. See her now, majestically and proudly sailing up the river towards the capital that has welcomed so many victors in British history: but none so victorious as these men. They stand on the deck waving to the millions of people who line the Thames. This time the tears flooding from their eyes are tears of happiness. The insurmountable odds have been surmounted. They are reunited with their families, with their friends, with their loved ones. We near the end of our story. The London skyline has a new landmark pointing towards the heavens - Caroline's aerial, at last beaming out its love and music to a free and peaceful nation. We have overcome, the battle now over. Free radio becomes a way of life, but never taken for granted, for no man will ever forget Monday, 14 August 1967."

The song was released on a private 7-inch single by Spangles Muldoon.

In March 1968 Johnnie told the author: "We have been continuing with Radio Caroline as if nothing had ever happened. The Marine Offences Act has simply had no effect on us whatsoever from a broadcasting point of view. However, the tender trip is a bit of a drag - we have to travel by the *Offshore I* from IJmuiden in Holland and it takes 18 hours to reach the *Mi Amigo*. I have travelled in force 10 gales, and that is no joke!"

Johnnie's mother ran a 4,000 strong fan club which had members in America, Canada, Australia and all over the Continent. Commenting on Johnnie breaking the law, she added: "I was very worried at first as to what action the Government would take. Johnnie stuck by what he believed, and I agree with him all the way - in fact I think he's got my soapbox. I am very proud of him."

Radio Caroline was towed into Amsterdam harbour in March 1968 as management had not paid money to the Dutch company owned by the Wijsmuller brothers. It was there in Amsterdam where Johnnie quit Radio Caroline for good. He returned to England and for a year became a truck driver. In April 1969 he was given a job on Radio 1 where he stayed for seven years before going to work in America.

Johnnie's American experience lasted five years until 1981 when he returned to these shores slightly disillusioned with the music scene in the States.

He joined Wiltshire Radio (which later became GWR), but was taken back by Radio 1 until 1988 when, once again, he teamed up with independent radio working for Richard Branson's *Radio Radio* presenting a nightly show relayed by many of the independent stations.

When that service ceased broadcasting he again walked the corridors of power at the BBC working for Radio 1. In August 1990 Radio 5 opened up their network on the old medium wave frequencies of Radio 2 and Johnnie was offered a daily morning show. At a similar time he worked for GLR in London. He is still heard on Radio 1.

In 1993 Johnnie launched his own independent radio company. Wizard Radio Ltd.

His spare time activities are riding his Harley Davidson motor bike and sailing the canals of Great Britain in a narrow boat.

WILLY WALKER

A dental technician, charter yacht navigator and male model ... just three of the former occupations of Willy Walker (real name William Acton) before he joined Radio London in 1966. He was born in Bermuda on 25 July 1939 and began his working life in a bank, but later went to the United States to train as a dental technician. His first radio experience was with Radio Bermuda.

"It was whilst in Bermuda I met Duncan Johnson and Mike Lennox who convinced me that England was the place to be in the mid-1960s. They were right. I made my way across the Atlantic and arrived in London. I also had a sister in England at that time.

"Duncan introduced me to some of the Radio London staff, including the programme director, Alan Keen. I did not have any experience in radio, but I was asked to record a demonstration tape which was accepted by Alan who said I could join Radio London as a DJ in May 1966.

"The days on Big L were sensational. When we came on land for our week's leave I did a lot of personal appearances. We also had a very good social life. It was sad when we had to close down because of Government legislation. I shall remember that last day, 14 August 1967, because we had so many pop stars sending their good wishes. It was a very emotional time. However, once we were closed down, I opted out of the radio world and returned to modelling in London for a short time.

"I was then offered a job in a new disco in Munich, Germany. I went over there in January 1968, worked for six months in the club in the evenings and modelled during the daytime.

"In June 1968 I went to the USA to compete in the Newport, Rhode Island, to Bermuda Ocean Yacht Race. Bermuda Radio (ZBM) offered me a job so I stayed. In 1970 I left Bermuda to go to New York, thence to Florida. I have been involved in yachting ever since."

Bachelor Willy is now a yacht captain specialising in commissioning, management, brokerage and chartering. He travels the world and lives in Fort Lauderdale, Florida, USA.

GRAHAM WEBB

Son of a barber in Parramatta, Australia, Graham was born on 19 April 1936. In the 1950s he was one of Australia's first DJs in the early days of Top 40 radio and compèred many of the big shows featuring artists like the Platters, Chubby Checker, Bobby Darin and Sammy Davis Jnr.

Graham began his radio career accidentally when Hollywood actor Rod Taylor enlisted the telegram boy's help to deliver a joke telegram. Webb was to inform Taylor's colleague that he had won the lottery and was so convincing that he was advised to get professional training. There followed stints in country and city radio stations in Australia.

A decade later he was working in radio in Brisbane and Sydney. He then decided to come to England and work for Radio Caroline.

He joined the South ship in May 1965 using the catch phrase "Spinning Tops with 'Spider' Webb". He was programme controller for a time, followed by news director when he introduced *Caroline Newsbeat* bringing news to the nation. His most memorable moment with Radio

Caroline South was when the *Mi Amigo* ran aground in January 1966.

"I looked out of the porthole and saw a light which I thought was another ship about to ram us, but it was a bloke on the beach with a flashlight trying to find out what we doing on 'his' beach. We had been very lucky by the way the tide had washed us in - neatly between a groyne and a breakwater, either of which would have caused us much damage."

Graham had another ride three weeks later when he was taken off Radio Caroline by Walton and Frinton lifeboat suffering from a severe bout of flu and transferred to Walton-on-the-Naze hospital. Lifeboat secretary Robert Oxley said the rescue operation cost about £30. He went on: "Had I known it was Caroline sending out the SOS I would have asked them to provide one of their own tenders. As it turned out we didn't mind too much in this case because Mr Webb seemed genuinely to be in a pretty poor state. He was one of two men who thanked us when we took them off their old ship. *Mi Amigo*, when it ran aground three weeks ago."

When the Marine Offences Act came into force in 1967 Graham returned to Australia where he hosted the very popular *Blind Date*, which many years later was copied by ITV in Britain with Cilla Black as the hostess. Within two years of leaving Radio Caroline Graham was hosting the Australian end of *Family Favourites*, heard in this country on BBC Radio 2.

In the 1970s Graham began the first Pop-Clip TV Show in the world called *Sound Unlimited*, subsequently *Sounds* with Donnie Sutherland on the Seven Network.

Graham has been married three times. First to Peta. The couple had no children. He married again, to Margaret, and they had a son, Byron, who works on radio in Newcastle, New South Wales, and a daughter Cinnamon, who is an actress. He has two young children, Jared and Corey, by his third wife, Tina, from Wales, whom he met at a party in Australia, but it took him six years to propose.

In 1975 he was compèring his own rock video music show called *Graham Webb's Saturday Show*. But he was in the middle of

a divorce and his TV show was suffering. He later gained custody of his children, Byron and Cinnamon, and decided to wash his hands of the entire show and became a full time house-husband instead. He pressed uniforms and packed school lunches in between recording promotional videos for Channel 7 and compèring discos.

Into the 1980s Graham has taken his show into clubs, shopping centres and elsewhere whilst still involved with television and video production. He does many voice-overs and television commercials. He has produced corporate and training videos.

He spent two years on radio presenting *Webby's Weekend* on Classic Hits 2UW, and a network of some 18 stations across the east coast of Australia brought his unique style to a far wider audience.

Now into the 1990s Graham can be heard occasionally on Radio 2SM and other stations throughout Australia. His enthusiasm for the music scene is still unbounded and he adapts to varying situations, from discos of the '70s and '80s and contemporary pop back to '50s and '60s rock'n'roll.

MARK WESLEY

Martin Wesley Goble was born on 24 January 1948 in Southend-on-Sea, and was educated at King John Secondary Modern School, Hadleigh, Essex. It was there as a founder member of the school cine club and lead guitarist in the school group that the trouble started! His career since then has bounced from music through broadcasting to film production.

Mark recalls: "The first band I joined was called Their Rivals and I could play all six songs in the repertoire very well. I left and they weren't sorry to see me go. I was too bossy, something that was subsequently knocked out of me later in the close confinements of my first pirate radio station. I founded another band called The Specters which was a very raw R 'n' B band that played many pubs and clubs around south-east Essex. This was the group I left to join Radio Essex, the station whose catchphrase was 'The voice of Essex from the mouth of the River Thames'."

Mark Wesley

The manager of The Specters was Vince Allen who became the first programme controller on Radio Essex. Mark was the first on air DJ.

There were one or two scuffles before the station went on air as Radio City had sent out a boarding party, but Mark and his colleagues sent them packing. Although there was difficulty in trying to put on board a generator, it was eventually installed and test transmissions began.

Says Mark: "The first commercial was for Channel Airways (voiced by Roy Bates), which sounded more like a declaration from a town crier. It was very melodramatic and I'm sure Roy wore a black cape when he recorded it. I can't remember the first record we played. The fort itself was in a terrible state. All of us on board spent a great deal of time trying to make the place habitable. It is hard to believe now, but there were two huge concrete columns with a steel platform on top. Everything was red rust. In the legs of the fort were eight floors, one or two of them under water. I was only 17 at the time, a very impressionable age! It was good pioneering stuff, but I don't think I would opt for that kind of life today!" Whilst with

Radio Essex, Mark produced an 8mm cine film of life on board an anti-aircraft fort.

When Radio Essex closed in December 1966, he joined Radio 270 off Scarborough where he worked with three ex-Essex DJs, Vince Allen, Roger Scott and Guy Hamilton. He stayed with Radio 270 for just three months. He recalls: "I believe the *Oceaan 7* was the only ship to come into harbour after the radio station closed down. The ship would then return to be in international waters in time for the *Breakfast Show*.

In 1967 Mark went further north to join Radio Scotland where he stayed until that station closed on 14 August 1967.

Once the Marine Offences Act came into force he spent a while on the dole and then got a job with Acuff Rose Music as a record plugger in London for one year. Occasionally, he managed to persuade producers at the BBC to put records on their playlist, but it was purely on merit.

Mark then formed a songwriting partnership with a friend and they signed a deal with a music publisher and a recording contract with CBS followed. Their first record was called *Zebbedy Zak*.

Following a phone call from Roger Day,

he reappeared on radio in 1970 with Radio Northsea International where he worked as a DJ for seven months. He was then invited to join DJM Records as a plugger, prior to joining Radio Luxembourg in May 1971. He stayed with 208 until 1981 when he returned to England and joined Radio Orwell and Saxon Radio, part of Suffolk Radio.

Between 1982 and 1993 Mark developed his own commercial music production studios near Saffron Walden in Essex. This is a facility that brings together his knowledge of music and radio to a logical point whereby both skills have relevance in the commercial radio market place. The studio itself is entirely comprehensive and has produced thousands of ILR commercial jingles over the years. He has also formed a company called Media Futures that makes use of his other great interest, film making. The company produces corporate videos and has made programmes for a vast range of companies both large and small. In 1993 they produced a documentary about unlicensed taxis for Anglia TV as part of their *First Take 2* series. Additionally, in 1993 Mark joined Capital Gold and presents the weekend overnight shows.

ALAN WEST

Alan West is one of the most travelled disc jockeys on the radio ships having worked for nearly every floating station at one time or another.

He began his broadcasting career with Radio London in 1966. Prior to that he worked for Top Rank as a dance hall DJ in Sunderland. He remained with Big L for just three months and says modestly: "I don't think I was very good in those days, but it was a first class training ground. After I was dropped by Radio London I went to Radio Caroline who offered me a job on the South ship. That job did not happen so I called to see Radio England/Britain Radio."

He joined the team of DJs on board the *Laissez-Faire* and, after a month, moved to Radio 390 until the beginning of 1967 when programme controller Peter James suggested they part company. He did and Radio 270, off Scarborough, was the next stop. Alan, who also broadcast under the name Ross

Randell, stayed with the *Oceaan 7* until close down on 14 August 1967 and the introduction of the Marine Etc., Broadcasting (Offences) Act.

Alan recalls: "I suited the station and it suited me. I fitted in well with all the staff and was very happy there. Radio 270 was a Top 40 station. The DJs were fun. The people who ran the station were blunt Yorkshiremen who called a spade a spade. They were honest and told you what they thought without mincing their words. I could equate with that. The *Oceaan* 7, however, was very small … it was very cramped, but a fun station on which to work."

Alan then came ashore and joined the first local BBC station in Leicester. In 1970 it was back to sea once again, this time with RNI.

He says that the time he spent on RNI counts highly among the happiest of his life, and by far the most exciting. He joined when the station began broadcasting, and it was here on the *Mebo II* that he made news headlines around the world.

On 15 May 1971 he was broadcasting when DJ Dave Rogers popped into the studio with a cup of tea for him. Suddenly there was a terrific bang. Alan's first reaction was that the *Mebo II* must have been hit by another ship. Dave went out to investigate. He returned within two minutes and said "We have been bombed!" See Chapter Thirteen.

Alan says it wasn't until a year later that the shock hit him: "It took all that time for the events to register. I didn't know at the time, but there were a number of oil tanks in the studio. I had always believed them to be water tanks. Has those gone up, that would have been the end of my radio career … and me!"

Talking in 1993 about his days on Radio Northsea International Alan recalls: "My memories of those days are very clear … like the time when Andy Archer and I threw a bucket of ice-cold water over a slumbering David Gregory, and the time I got drunk and woke up next morning at the foot of the radio mast. Apparently I had tried to climb the mast the previous evening in a violent thunderstorm.

Alan West (right) and Steve Merike in RNI studio in 1972

"I learned most of what I know about life and living from RNI. I give credit to Erwin Meister and Edwin Bollier for creating a successful radio station in RNI. Despite their mistakes and despite the tarnished image that some have tried too hard to give them, they are two great people, kind and generous to a fault."

In 1972 Alan was asked by programme controller John de Mol to leave RNI, at a similar time to Steve Merike.

The couple returned to England and went to work for BBC Radio Brighton for a short while. Alan accepted a job as a consultant, advising potential radio companies in applying for local franchises.

The next step in the career of Alan West was as an author. He wrote a book, *Close Encounters*, not about radio but on the subject of UFOs.

More recently he has worked as a broadcaster for a number of radio stations in England, Ireland and on the Continent.

TONY WINDSOR

TW, as he was affectionately known, was one of the major personalities during the 1960s working on Radios Atlanta, London and Britain.

This is a transcript of an interview conducted by the author with TW (whose real name was Tony Withers) in 1973.

I was born in Melbourne, Australia, and was due to read law, but that didn't materialise. My father was a great radio fan and it was he who suggested I try for that occupation. I began my radio career as a sales representative for station 2SM in Sydney. I was lucky enough to become an announcer and within a year was No.1 in Australia. After nearly eight years I was invited to take over the Macquarie Broadcasting Network top radio slot, but decided against it and came to Britain instead.

I came to London mainly for health reasons, and met Allan Crawford who was managing director of Southern Music in Australia and owned his own publishing company, Merit Music, in London. He had this fantastic idea of starting a pirate radio station. I became very interested and joined him, but not on the ship in those days. We used to record at 41 Dean Street and I'd be doing a breakfast show at 2 o'clock in the morning, for instance, or maybe an afternoon show recorded at 9 o'clock in the morning. That's how it began. We went along like this for about three months without much success, it was then decided to go out on the ship (Radio Atlanta), but before very long we merged with Radio Caroline, much against my own personal wishes. I broadcast under my real name Tony Withers. I left shortly afterwards, waited for about three months and joined Radio London.

Haying talked with various members of the initial Radio London management team, I thought their ideas were very good -Top 40 format - an ambitious sales team - I was very lucky to have been one of the pioneer members. I joined the team as Tony Windsor.

Philip Birch was the managing director of Radio London. He was a most impressive man, tall and very well spoken. He brought a great professionalism to the pirates and was an excellent businessman, having been with J. Walter Thompson's.

Another great thing about Radio London were the catchy jingles. Britain had never heard anything like them before. Listeners were mesmerised - and so were all the DJs. They were produced by PAMS in America. I have since been told they were heard on a number of American stations, including KLIF, but the jingles for Big L were rewritten for a British audience. The backing tracks remained the same, but the words were changed.

People say we were responsible for making hit records. I believe that is so. One that instantly comes to mind is *Concrete and Clay* by Unit Four Plus Two. All the new records for release that week came out to the ship on Friday, if the weather was good. It was then, in collaboration with a few other people, I used to do the charts. I would have one pile I had rejected and the other pile which I would have to pick the Top 40 from, or the new entries to the Top 40. There was a rule on the ship that disc jockeys did not try to influence me, because they'd probably been wined and dined when on leave. However, Kenny Everett poked his head round in the cabin and said: Have you heard *Concrete and Clay* and which pile is it in?" I said I had heard it and it was in the reject pile. I get the credit for making that record, but in fact it was Kenny because he said "Would you mind playing it again?" and when he was gone I played it again, naturally with more attention.

People talk about the money disc jockeys earned on the ship. On Caroline Simon Dee earned £15 a week and progressed to £18 in the early days. On Radio London I started on £37 a week. That was just a bit of luck because it was the figure that first came into my head and programme director Ben Toney agreed on.

The other boys were getting £30 a week.

Critics used to say we only did three hours on the air each day. But there were lots of other things to do. You had to sort out the crates of lager - that was a ritual -otherwise the ship would not have run. You certainly had to think about what you were going to play the next day record-wise. You had to open your mail and read it, which was a great pleasure, and in some cases write a reply.

People nave asked me why I joined the pirates. It was because I honestly believed the British public should be given a wider choice of listening than just the BBC. The BBC has always been excellent in what it broadcast - there's no disputing that - but in the 1960s there was little else for listeners apart from Radio Luxembourg in the evening.

I think part of the success of Radio London was the music we played and the fact that the DJs didn't talk a lot in between records. When they did, they would play requests for people, which was important, especially to those who were lonely or infirm. The dedication would undoubtedly cheer them up. This I know because we received a huge amount of mail every week on the ship. Our DJs communicated with their audience. A lot of that person-to-person communication is missing in radio today.

We gave the listeners what they wanted musically. Disc jockeys were in touch with the record companies when they came ashore. They went to discos and gigs and that feel came across on their radio shows.

'Flower Power' was a good example. This went right through our time on air. We gave our listeners what they wanted to hear at a particular time. We were lucky because we were there at the right time, and I haven't even mentioned the whole Beatles explosion.

Looking back to the days on the high seas my memories are that I was just proud at being there. I got on very well with the fellows, and 28 guys living on a ship is a difficult thing, you know, very difficult. Everyone gave of his best, not only in his work, but as a human being as well. This was a very rewarding thing for me.

The pirates were popular because of the romance attached to the job - the sort of 'up the Government' attitude, plus the fact we were very good. We had freedom (which you don't get with the BBC). We had no telephones which is a marvellous thing, so no one could ring you up if you did a bad programme. If this happened we had a system on the ship where we would whisper to each other 'What happened to you today?',and that would be it. The person would get the message.

When the Marine Offences Bill was going through Parliament, I went along to the House of Commons with Philip Birch and we sat in the visitors' gallery. I don't think anyone knew who we were. Basically we were told that the pirates would close in 1967 and be sucked into a new pop station on Radio 1 run by the BBC. Old Harold Wilson has a lot to answer for!

I was very sad when the ships closed down on 14 August 1967, but it was good to see many of the Radio London disc jockeys be taken on by the BBC. I was not one of the fortunate few. I will go to my grave never knowing why they did not employ me, although I did guest once on national radio. BBC Local have invited me to do shows from time to time. I was not a good disc jockey technically, but I was warm and friendly. People used to think it was a gimmick playing the wrong records and jingles. If I touch anything at home my brother gets petrified, literally down to opening the fridge door, because I am accident prone with my hands. I feel so self conscious about it, too.

After the pirates closed Tony Windsor worked for Radio Luxembourg for a short time. He died in St. Stephen's Hospital, Fulham, London, on 6 June 1985, aged 65 years. His favourite saying, delivered in a deep brown voice, was "Hello" - pronounced "Hell-low" - which still lives on! Disc jockey Tony Blackburn now uses it on Capital Gold!

Says Tony Blackburn "I had been in radio two years before I joined Big L. Tony took me aside and gave me very useful advice. He was a very knowledgeable and talented disc jockey and knew how to communicate with his listeners and fellow disc jockeys.

"On numerous occasions on the *Galaxy* I used to go to the studio when he was on air, in the morning, and just sit and watch him presenting his show. It was a unique style of radio.

"He gave all the DJs plenty of his own time. He was in no way selfish. All of us were moulded into better broadcasters. I would go as far as saying I owe my career in radio to TW.

"What was sad when the pirates closed was that Tony Windsor could not get a job with the BBC. That, to me, was tragic."

PAUL YOUNG

The voice that launched not a thousand ships - but one ship, Radio Scotland, on 1 January 1966.

Paul was born and educated in Edinburgh, and has been fortunate to combine his passion for Scotland and its fishing with a successful acting career which have come together with his presentation of the television series, *Hooked on Scotland.*

His many other television appearances include *Sunset Song,* the award winning *Another Time, Another Place* and the popular comedy series with Penelope Keith *No Job for a Lady.*

Paul has appeared in several films including the title role in the delightful *Geordie;* a disaster movie, *SOS Titanic,* with David Janssen and Cloris Leachman (partly filmed aboard the RMS *Queen Mary* at Long Beach, California) and the Western, *Chato's Lad,* with Charles Bronson and Jack Palance which was directed by Michael Winner.

Shortly before leaving school, he was co-presenter of the popular Scottish children's television magazine programme, *Roundup,* to which the Beatles returned several times.

He was the first ever person to broadcast on commercial radio in Scotland, welcoming listeners to Radio Scotland on 242 metres in the medium wave on New Year's Day 1966. He is still a regular broadcaster, and frequently to be heard on film commentaries and radio and television voice-overs.

Paul has been Scottish Trout Fishing's Champion of Champions and Scottish National Champion. He is proud to have represented Scotland as a member of the Scottish Trout Fly Fishing Team several times, winning a much coveted Gold Medal.

Nowadays Paul has thrown aside the competitive mantle and lives in Glasgow with his wife. Sheila, daughters Hannah and Katie, and enjoys reading, gardening, crosswords, an occasional glass of wine and ... guess what? ... a quiet day's fishing!

STEVE YOUNG

Born in a clifftop mansion in Penarth, Wales in 1943, Steve Young moved with his family who emigrated to Canada in the early 1950s, settling in the small prairie town of Medicine Hat, Alberta. It was there that he grew up

and began his radio career, in the early 1960s, broadcasting a teen "all request" show over the local radio station.

He has always been a music lover and his listening habits cover a wide variety of musical genres. Growing up in the 50s, listening late at night to "clear channel" radio stations like WLS in Chicago, cemented his love for rock 'n' roll radio.

Steve came to England in 1965 after touring Belgium, France, Germany and Czechoslovakia. He joined Radio Caroline South in August 1966. He recalls: "Early on a Monday morning I accompanied my friend and colleague Keith 'Keefers' Hampshire on the train from Liverpool Street Station to Felixstowe where we boarded the tender for my first stint at sea. Those early images are so clear in my mind. I guess I really didn't quite know what to expect as far as the floating radio stations were concerned. Perhaps 'cruise ships' were what I somehow expected, gleaming white in the sunshine with stewards clad in their summer whites striding the decks serving deckchair-lounging passengers tall, cool drinks. The reality of that first cloudy, late winter's day was vastly different.

"Our first contact was with the *Galaxy,* home of the Big L, a converted minesweeper, painted a dull grey, with rust streaks running down its sides and the look of a hulk that had been mothballed in a military holding dock for many years. It was rather depressing in fact and, apart from one or two faces which peered out of some of the portholes, it gave no sign of the exuberant musicality that emanated from the Big L control room deep within its bowels. We stopped for a while as supplies were offloaded and then we cast-off for our final destination.

"I really didn't know what to expect at our next stop, which was to become a familiar place in months to come. It was Radio Caroline South, on board the m.v. *Mi Amigo,* a converted former coastal freighter, which was to become my place of employment and home for the next year or so. As its hindquarters loomed out of the mist and the tender drew alongside its rusted hull, chains shrieking as the two vessels met, I began to have second thoughts about this venture. This felt more like stowing away on a slow freighter to China than getting set for an exciting gig aboard the 'smallest boat to rock the nation'.

"When bodies began appearing on deck, helping to bring aboard supplies and passengers (myself and Keefers) I really began to wonder what I'd gotten myself into. Long haired leaping gnomes is the image I call to mind when I think of the first couple of people that I met as I stepped aboard, and they weren't exactly dressed to go to the Ritz. Unshaven, unkempt ... but definitely not unkind as I was quick to learn ... not an image that a teenager's mother would want her youngest daughter listening to on her transistor radio in the middle of the night. Yes, the Caroline deejays were certainly something to behold ... could I imagine I'd be looking like them within a few short months?

"Life on board those first few days was a real adventure, getting to know my surroundings, adjusting to a life on the ocean wave, familiarising myself with the control room operations and generally trying to fit into the daily rhythm of life aboard the Good Ship Lollipop. Dutch food is one of the major items I had to adjust to ... Nasi Goreng, Indonesian spices and Heineken beer were just a few of the palatables I would learn to love over time but, at first, they only aided and abetted the feeling I had of living in a totally foreign land (sea?).

"Life at sea was a challenge at first. Learning how to broadcast a radio show while the vessel tossed and heaved in a North Sea storm as I battled seasickness was my first achievement. One certainly learns how to 'go with the flow' in situations like that. There was, of course, a certain amount of tedium. Our on-air shifts were usually 3 hours, show preparation time might take another 2-3 hours, but apart from that we had plenty of spare time on our hands. We wrote a lot of letters to friends and family, answered fan mail, played cards, watched a little TV and, often, just horsed around. Probably our greatest source of enjoyment was, during the summer months, going out to greet the sightseeing vessels that would come along side, filled with autograph seekers and curiosity gazers. We were proud to consider ourselves the most 'pirate-like' bunch of all the vessels and we would usually play it to the hilt, sometimes performing skits for the punters, usually involving rough and tumble 'schoolboyish' antics. We knew that the boys from Big L were the 'cleancut' bunch and we felt that we were the 'bad guys' of rock 'n' roll and really tried hard to live up to our pirate reputations."

While broadcasting on Radio Caroline Steve was known affectionately as 'The Curly Headed Kid in the Third Row'. Host of the all-night show from midnight 'til 6.00am Steve remembers that his largest radio audience was in Continental Europe and many American GIs on tour of duty in Germany would send him letters telling him how much his show reminded them of home.

How did he come to be named 'The Curly Headed Kid in the Third Row'? "Probably the second day that I was aboard I had taken a shower to freshen up before taking over an on-air shift from the Emperor Rosko," he recalls. "I have very straight hair and it was still damp and combed back as I stepped into the control room. Rosko who was in the middle of some rhyming patter looked at me and announced to the world "whaddya know ... it's The Curly Headed

Kid in the Third Row ... coming at you next on 259" (or words to that effect)! Well, the name stuck and thereafter I was the Curly Headed Kid."

Steve returned to Canada in 1967 and continued his broadcasting career working in a number of radio and television stations in Western Canada.

Today he is happily married and lives on Vancouver Island off the West Coast of British Columbia.

In recalling the heady days of Radio Caroline, Steve remembers: "It was the crest of the wave in terms of my radio broadcasting career and I'll never forget the good times and great people who were part of the free radio movement.

"The pirates brought radio, as it's known today, to millions of listeners throughout England and the rest of Europe, we'll never be forgotten by them and we'll never forget their loyalty and support for our cause."

The biographies of the DJs have been retained from the First Edition of the book.
An update can be found in Chapter 14 - "Where Are They Now".

The POSTMASTERS-GENERAL

THE RT. HON. JOHN REGINALD BEVINS, PC, MP

THE RT. HON. ANTHONY WEDGWOOD BENN PC, MA, MP

THE RT. HON. EDWARD WATSON SHORT PC, CH, MP
(now Lord Glenamara)

THE POST OFFICE was originally concerned solely with the conveyance of written communications. In England in 1516 Henry VIII appointed Sir Brian Tuke as his Master of the Posts with the task of maintaining not only a constant link between the mobile monarch and his capital, but of maintaining a regular service along the main roads from London.

One of the earliest mentions of Postmaster-General was in 1632 when Charles I appointed Thomas Witherings, a London merchant, and already a successful "Postmaster-General for Foreign Parts", to improve the domestic services. He proved to be a most effective and ambitious officer.

Postmaster-General was to become the standard title for the Head of the Post Office from the mid-1600s. By the year 1860 the PMG earned £2,500 a year.

From 1613-1823 the office of Postmaster-General was held jointly, with a few exceptions, by two appointees; the joint holders were styled "Our Postmaster-General." There has been a single PMG since 1823.

In the 19th and 20th centuries the Post Office greatly extended its services. An Act of 1904 placed wireless under Governmental control in order to safeguard its use. This Act gave the Post Office the power to regulate the erection of stations so as to prevent duplication and undue interference.

No wireless apparatus could be set up in the British Isles or on British ships without the licence of the Postmaster-General.

Reorganisation took place in 1934 when a post of Director-General was created. The Postmaster-General was to be continued much as before as the political Head of the Post Office with the power to overrule the Board in any matters of policy.[1]

By 1950 the Postmaster-General had been made responsible for radio and television broadcasting.

A Post Office Bill was published on 31 October 1968 which received Royal Assent on 25 July 1969. From a Government department the Post Office became a public corporation on 1 October 1969. The Minister of Posts and Telecommunications took over the responsibilities for both the Post Office and public broadcasting from the Postmaster-General, whose post was abolished.

The final Postmaster-General was the Rt. Hon. John Stonehouse, MP, who authorised the jamming of Radio Northsea International. He became the first Minister of Posts and Telecommunications and was dubbed the 'vanishing MP'. In 1974 he fooled all of the people for some of the time into believing he was dead. His carefully stage-managed disappearance from a Miami beach on 20 November, which gave the impression that he had swum to a watery demise, assumed a farcical air a few weeks later when he reappeared in Australia.

Stonehouse was extradited back to Britain in July 1975 to stand trial on 18 charges of fraud, theft, forgery and conspiracy. At the Old Bailey, he pleaded not guilty to all charges,

---

I. *Britain's Past Office*, Howard Robinson. OUP. 1953

which involved some £170,000. A former MP for Walsall North, he was convicted and sentenced to seven years' imprisonment, less than half of which he had served at the time of his release from Norwich Prison on 14 August 1979, exactly twelve years to the day of the introduction of the Marine Etc., Broadcasting (Offences) Act 1967. John Stonehouse was one of Harold Wilson's young technological ministers taking up the office of Postmaster-General in 1968. After an unpopular term of office he was dropped, in 1970, after it was said he misled the Cabinet about a telegraphists' strike. He died in April 1988, aged 62 years.

THE RIGHT HONOURABLE JOHN REGINALD BEVINS, PC, MP

Reginald Bevins was born in Liverpool on 20 August 1908 and was educated at Dovedale Road Council School and Liverpool Collegiate School.

He took an interest in local politics, and at the age of 26 was elected to the Liverpool City Council of which he remained a member for fifteen years.

During the Second World War Mr Bevins served as a gunner in the Royal Horse Artillery, and was later commissioned in the Royal Army Service Corps. He served in the Middle East and Germany being demobilised in the rank of major.

Mr Bevins, a former chairman of Liverpool's Exchange Division Conservative Association, contested West Toxteth, another Liverpool division, in the 1945 general election, and the Edge Hill division at a by-election in 1947.

After the return of the Conservative Party to power in the autumn of 1951, Mr Bevins became Parliamentary Private Secretary to Harold Macmillan, at that time Minister of Housing and Local Government.

He received his first Government appointment in November 1953 when he succeeded Hugh Molson as Parliamentary Secretary to the Ministry of Works. He was later appointed as Parliamentary Secretary to the Ministry of Housing and Local Government, and, in addition, was responsible for speaking in the House of Commons for the Lord President of the Council, at that time Lord Salisbury, a member of the Upper House, and for answering Parliamentary questions on a wide range of subjects.

Mr Bevins married Miss Leonora Jones in 1933 and they have three sons.

It was in the Government changes following the general election of 1959 that he received a full ministerial appointment as Postmaster-General and at the same time was created a Privy Councillor. He remained Postmaster-General until 1964. The following year he published *The Greasy Pole*.

THE RIGHT HONOURABLE ANTHONY WEDGWOOD BENN, PC, MA, MP

The Right Honourable Anthony Wedgwood Benn was Postmaster-General from the formation of Harold Wilson's Government in 1964 until July 1966 when he became Minister of Technology with a seat in the Cabinet. At the time of his first ministerial appointment he was created a Privy Councillor.

He was born on 3 April 1925, eldest surviving son of 1st Viscount Stansgate, DSO, DFC, PC, former Labour MP and Secretary of State for India in the 1929-31 Labour Government. He was created a viscount in 1942, taking the title of Lord Stansgate, and served in Lord Attlee's Government as Secretary of State for Air 1945-6. Both his grandfathers were also Members of Parliament.

Tony Benn (as he now likes to be known) served in the Royal Air Force Volunteer Reserve (Pilot Officer) during the Second World War and later transferred to the Royal Naval Volunteer Reserve Fleet Air Arm (Sub Lieutenant), 1945-1946. He qualified for his wings on 10 March 1945 flying twin-engined aircraft.

After the war he went to Oxford, became President of the Union (the University Debating Society) and graduated as an MA. This was followed by a short spell with the BBC where he worked as a talks producer in the North American Service.

In 1949 Tony Benn married Caroline

Middleton de Camp, MA. They have four children: Stephen (b.1951), Hilary (b.1953), Melissa (b.1957) and Joshua (b.1958).

At the age of 25 Mr Benn was elected to Parliament as MP for Bristol South East to succeed Sir Stafford Cripps. He was the youngest backbencher in Attlee's Government and has taken a great interest in the United Nations, travelling to many countries including America, Africa, India and most of Europe.

He was a founder member of the Movement for Colonial Freedom in 1954 and chairman of the International and Commonwealth Labour Party Broadcasting Advisory Committee.

In 1959 the late Hugh Gaitskell, who was then leader of the Opposition, appointed Tony Benn to the front bench as principal Labour spokesman on transport.

Four years previously he presented a Bill to Parliament to allow him to renounce his becoming heir to his father's peerage. The House of Lords rejected the Bill.

Tony Benn's father died in 1960 and the Committee of Privileges of the House of Commons held that, having succeeded to a peerage, he was disqualified from membership, and its report was accepted by a majority vote of the House. When, at the ensuing by-election, Mr Benn was renominated as official Labour candidate and re-elected (with an enlarged majority), a Government motion refusing to admit him was carried in the House of Commons. The election was declared invalid by an election court, and his defeated opponent was declared MP for South East Bristol.

He had been MP for South East Bristol from 1950-1960, and after he relinquished his title, was elected again from 1963-1983. He contested and lost Bristol East in 1983.

During his time as Postmaster-General, Mr Benn was reported in the national press as having listened to the pirate radio stations ... normally in the bath. It was a coincidence that his wife's name is Caroline, the name of one of Britain's offshore pirate radio stations that he tried to force out of business during his time as Postmaster-General.

Amongst the many quotes he gave the media concerning the offshore stations was one in *The Times* on 4 March 1966: "Anyone who thought that the pirates proved a demand for local radio of that kind was deceiving himself. What were the pirate ships? They were hulks with big masts, carrying microphones, gramophones and seasick disc jockeys."

As PMG he recommended the establishment of the General Post Office as a public corporation and founded the National Giro. Subsequent appointments included Minister of Technology 1966-1970; he assumed responsibility for Ministry of Aviation, 1967, and Ministry of Power, 1969; Opposition spokesman on Trade and Industry 1970-1974; Secretary of State for Industry and Minister for Posts and Telecommunications, 1974-1975, and Secretary of State for Energy, 1975-1979. He has been Member of Parliament for Chesterfield, Derbyshire, since March 1984 and Chairman of the Campaign Group since 1987.

He is the author of *Regeneration of Britain*, 1964; *Arguments for Socialism*, 1979; *Arguments for Democracy*, 1981; *Parliament, People and Power*, 1982; *Writings on the Wall: 1215-1984, a radical and socialist anthology, 1984 (editor)*; *The Sizewell Syndrome*, 1984; *Out of the Wilderness, Diaries 1963-1967*, 1987; *Fighting Back", speaking out for Socialism in the Eighties*, 1988; *Office Without Power, Diaries 1968-1972*, 1988; *Against the Tide, Diaries 1973-1976*, 1989; *Conflicts of Interest, Diaries 1977-1980*, 1990, as well as numerous pamphlets.

Looking back on the pirate days, Tony Benn says: "In October 1964 there were certain compelling problems confronting the Post Office.

"In the first place there was the persistent illegal activity of pirate radios. In the early Sixties, radio stations such as Radio Caroline and Radio London began to appear around the shores of Britain. These were run by fly-by-night companies which employed a crew to man either a moored ship or some offshore structure from which was broadcast continuous pop music, interspersed with advertisements, and introduced by disc jockeys who became household names amongst their mainly young audience in Britain. The outgoing Conservative Government, realising that pirate radio was popular and having some sympathy with piratical entrepreneurs of that kind, decided to do nothing about it and the problem landed on my plate when Labour came to power.

"The main argument used by the Post Office against pirate radio stations was that they were breaching the international allocation of wavelengths, thereby causing interference on the Continent, and Continental countries were threatening to take over some of the wavelengths allocated to us. This would interfere with our domestic transmissions if we did not take action. It was also argued that essential police, fire and hospital services were being interfered with by pirate radio broadcasts. In addition, the Musicians' Union and some of the record companies naturally objected to loss of royalties. The Ministry of Defence were the owners of the offshore structures built during the war that were now being used for the pirate radio stations, but expressed no interest in taking action; the Board of Trade said that although they had responsibilities for shipping, they had no disciplinary powers outside the three-mile territorial limit."

In a quote from *Out of the Wilderness* which was published by Hutchinson in 1987, he said: "In dealing with the pirates one line of attack was to use the popularity of the pirate stations to persuade the BBC to schedule its own programmes so as to provide a channel of continuous popular music comparable to the pirates. BBC Radio at that time was divided into three channels - the Home Service, the Light Programme and the Third Programme - and, with its paternalistic attitude, declined to do that and said it was not there to pander to popular taste. Ultimately, the pirate stations had the effect of altering the pattern of broadcasting at home, not only in the BBC but, of course, in forming a beachhead for the development of commercially-owned radio to which I was opposed."

In his biography of Tony Benn, published by Macmillan in 1992, author Jad Adams quotes Benn as saying that in 1967: "The managing director of one of the stations decided to broadcast appeals to me to lay off the pirates. One Sunday when I was listening to a pirate station I heard, 'Mr Benn, you are a young man, you are a family man. Surely you enjoy listening to popular radio. I appeal to you to let us continue.' The phone rang and it was Harold Wilson. He had been listening to the pirates too. 'Have you heard that broadcast?' he said. I said I had. 'Well, why do you keep pursuing them?' I gave him all the arguments about wavelengths."

THE RIGHT HONOURABLE EDWARD WATSON SHORT, PC, CH, MP, now LORD GLENAMARA

Edward Short was born on 17 December 1912, son of Charles and Mary Short of Warcop, Westmorland, and educated at Bede College, University of Durham, graduating as Bachelor of Laws (LL.B).

During the Second World War he served with the Coldstream Guards and the Durham Light Infantry in which he reached the rank of captain. He is the author of *The Story of the Durham Light Infantry*, 1944; *The Infantry Instructor*, 1946; *Education in a Changing World*, 1971; *Birth to Five*, 1974; *I Knew My Place*, 1983; *Whip to Wilson*, 1989, and *The Crucial Years of the Labour Government*, 1989.

He married Jenny Sewell in 1941 and they have one son and one daughter.

Prior to entering Parliament he was headmaster of Princess Louise County Secondary School, Blyth, Northumberland, (1947). He became a councillor and leader of the Labour Group on Newcastle City Council in 1950, and Labour MP for Newcastle-upon-Tyne, 1951-1976.

Early in 1956 he was a member of a Parliamentary delegation to Western Germany, one of a number invited to go there by the President of the Bundestag to study social and health services. Later that year, as member of a Parliamentary delegation, he visited Persia (now Iran). He attended the Bermuda Conference, the NATO Parliamentary visit to Washington in 1959, and the Kenya and Zanzibar independence celebrations.

Mr Short became Opposition Whip

(northern area), 1955-1962, and Deputy Chief Opposition Whip, 1962-1964.

He was appointed Postmaster-General on 3 July 1966. He had previously been Parliamentary Secretary to the Treasury from October 1964 and, as such, Government Chief Whip in the House of Commons. At a similar time he was created a Privy Councillor.

He was the Postmaster-General responsible for seeing that the Marine Offences Bill was speeded up through Parliament, and he was in post when the Bill became law on 14 August 1967.

Edward Short became Secretary of State for Education and Science, 1968-1970; Opposition Spokesman on Education, 1970-1972; Deputy Leader of the Labour Party, 1972-1976; Lord President of the Council and Leader, House of Commons, 1974-1976. He was Deputy Leader of the Labour Party, 1972-1976.

He was made a Companion of Honour (CH) in 1976.

Edward Short was created a life peer. Baron Glenamara of Glenridding, Cumbria, in 1977. He has been Chairman, Cable and Wireless Ltd 1976-1980; President of Finchale Abbey Training College for the Disabled (Durham) since 1985; Chancellor, Polytechnic of Newcastle-upon-Tyne since 1984, and Honorary Fellow, College of Preceptors, 1965. He is a Member of the Council of World Wildlife Fund, and Honorary Doctor of Civil Law (DCL), Durham University; Honorary Doctor of Literature (D.Litt), Council for National Academic Awards and Honorary Doctorate, Open University. Made Freeman of the City of Newcastle 2001.

Lord Glenamara lives in Northumberland.

Chapter Eight

BANG BANG

So you think you can push me around
And make me run
Well, I'm gonna get me a gun

I'm Gonna Get Me a Gun, Cat Stevens, 1967

THE SHOOTING of Reginald Calvert of Radio City in June 1966 was undoubtedly one of the biggest disasters in pirate radio history. It proved that the pirates were real pirates and even willing to kill. It sent shock waves to Parliament which then speeded up the Marine Offences Bill. Had the killing not taken place there is every chance that pirate radio would have survived for a longer period of time.

Just prior to this episode fellow Radio London disc jockey Duncan Johnson, along with engineer Martin Newton and myself, learned of Radio London's plans to turn Radio City into a good music station. Radio City operated from a group of forts in the Thames Estuary and broadcast pop music for eighteen hours a day. Duncan, Martin and myself met Reginald Calvert, the boss of the radio station, at Whitstable on 7 June and went out to the forts in a small fishing boat. Also aboard was an engineer called Paul Elvey and disc jockey Ian MacRae. The forts, on Shivering Sands, were situated some seven miles off Margate and 10 miles from Whitstable. Duncan was to become programme director of United Kingdom Good Music station (UKGM), and I was to act as chief disc jockey.

Having been winched up some 90 feet in a cheese crate to the main platform, we were welcomed aboard by chief disc jockey Tom Edwards. I have to admit the four forts we looked at were in a disgusting state but there were plans to re-equip the broadcasting side and the living quarters. Disc jockeys appeared to live on dirty old mattresses. There was no sign of clean sheets or blankets. One disc jockey said "We bring out our own clobber." There appeared to be only one advantage of living on these forts and that was the stability. At least they couldn't pitch and roll in a force 9 gale. We were introduced to Alan Clark who was on air, but we requested that our visit be kept quiet. This he did.

Reg Calvert ran the station on a shoestring. He told me "It costs about £700 a week for the upkeep of the forts." He had bought Radio City from Screaming Lord Sutch for around £5,000 in September 1964.

Clearly Calvert was driven, not by financial need or artistic aspiration, but love of novelty, excitement and sensationalism. Reg came to despise the multitude of faceless beat groups with their standard suits and monotonous line-ups of three guitars and a drummer. He always demanded something different. Significantly he ignored all the major movements in rock music during the mid-Sixties, the beat boom, R & B, folk rock, the protest movement - all were deemed irrelevant in his scheme of things. Instead he gambled on novelty and visual appeal to attract an audience.

Calvert was the manager of a number of West Midlands singers and pop groups in the 1960s including Danny Storm, Buddy Britten, Mike West, The Fortunes, and the Liberators who later became known as Pinkerton's Assorted Colours. However, the pressure of administering Radio City did not leave him too much spare time for playful indulgences.

During 1965 Calvert, having approached Philip Solomon of Radio Caroline, had reached

---

1. *Starmakers and Svengalis.* Johnny Rogan. Macdonald Queen Anne Press, 1988, p.71

Above: *On the quayside at Whitstable Reg Calvert talks with Dennis Maitland, Duncan*
Johnson and Martin Newton, June 1966
Below: *Approaching Shivering Sands, the home of Radio City*

an agreement whereby Caroline's programmes were to be relayed from the fort, thus giving the station a wider coverage. I well remember receiving numerous letters from listeners asking me why I said "Caroline News," when in fact it was being pumped out of Radio City's transmitters on 299 metres medium wave? Project Atlanta (Radio Caroline South) agreed to put a transmitter on one of the forts. On Saturday 22 September the *Daily Express* reported "Radio Caroline has taken over a rival pirate station - the £150,000 Radio City. The deal means that Caroline will increase its listeners. It already claims 12 million. The network says it will cover Britain from three different points and compete with Radio Luxembourg. Details of the takeover were completed yesterday."

"I will still be in control of the station, workshops, recording studio and offices, but I will administer it on behalf of Radio Caroline," Calvert said. "I can't tell you how much I received, but I estimate Radio City was worth £150,000. Last year I spent £22.000 on the company and have ploughed back all the profits," he added.

Being winnched up to the Radio City forts

Eventually the transmitter arrived from Holland on the tender, having originally been brought over from KCUL, Fort Worth, Texas, but whilst it was being hoisted up on to the fort, part of it fell into the sea. It was recovered a few days later, much the worse for wear.

Radio Caroline engineer Carl Thomson remembers: "The infamous transmitter from Fort Worth was a home built job, in two or three cabinets. No instructions arrived with it. When it was dismantled at the station in the USA paper markings were attached to the wires. You can guess that the cabinet that went into the Thames lost all of the paper markings. Ted Walters and myself just could not figure out these connections in the time we had, as we were both due back for our normal Caroline shifts. I am not certain if Phil Perkins, the Radio City, engineer, ever got it working."

At the end of September Reg Calvert visited the *Mi Amigo* and that was the first time the writer ever set eyes on him. Radio Caroline pulled out of the deal when it was learned that the Government was to prosecute people broadcasting from the forts.

Just over a year later plans were being drawn up for an agreement between Calvert and Philip Birch, managing director of Radlon Sales, the company that represented Radio London. The idea was for a good music station where records of the Frank Sinatra, Tony Bennett, Andy Williams, Ella Fitzgerald, Peggy Lee, Ray Conniff and Percy Faith standards were to be played. The station would become known as UKGM (United Kingdom Good Music) and was hopeful of becoming operational around the beginning of July. The *Daily Express*, on 16 June 1966, reported "Radio City, the pirate pop station, has been bought by the American-backed rival, Radio London. The new set-up means a sweet music station beaming programmes from a wartime fort in the Thames Estuary."

Oliver Smedley came to hear of the agreement and became concerned about the fate of his transmitter. He had still received no payment from Calvert. The involvement of Radio London would have sounded warning bells to Smedley. By linking City to London, Radio London's listening figures would have been boosted by several million, thus winning the ratings game over rival, Radio Caroline, with its two ships. Smedley still had a financial interest in Radio Caroline.

The next stunning news I heard was when Major Oliver Smedley MC, a director of Project Atlanta, led a swashbuckling raid with a party of 17 men and women onto the Shivering Sands forts during the ink-black night of Sunday 19 June. The news hit the headlines of national newspapers throughout the world. The boarding party claimed they owned part of the equipment, and by removing the crystals from the transmitter they intended to put the radio station out of action.

The cost of the transmitter was estimated at some £10,000. Engineer Martin Newton of Radio London put the value nearer £500. Radio City man Ian West said the figure would be more correct if £50 were quoted.

Putting the whole affair into a melting pot it boiled down to the fact that Calvert was double-crossing Smedley by doing a deal with UKGM. Radlon Sales knew nothing of the Smedley/Calvert deal, and furthermore was not aware that the transmitter had not been paid for. UKGM was going to install a new transmitter anyway!

At Garden Cottage in the pretty village of Wendens Ambo near Saffron Walden, a stone's throw from the 16th century public house 'The Bull,' Oliver Smedley was dressed in rubber-soled shoes, corduroy trousers and a loose warm sweater. He travelled by train from Saffron Walden to Gravesend, Kent, via Liverpool Street, London.

It was midnight when Smedley and Kitty Black arrived at Gravesend quayside. Remembering his Army training, he had taken great care in planning his 'raid' on the forts to eliminate as much danger as possible of being spotted. According to Smedley only the barest glimmer of moonlight shimmered on the water. A tugboat rose and fell on the swell.

On board were the boarding party crew. Trinity House pilot Captain 'Sandy' Horsley had assembled three other Trinity House skippers. In addition he had recruited 13 riggers.

The weather, the tide and the wind were all exactly right. The party set sail shortly after midnight.

Smedley stood on the deck of the tug with Kitty Black, a debonair lady from South Africa, who used to work at Caroline House in London and was secretary to the chief engineer. Now dressed in black stretch pants and an anorak and carrying a bag, Kitty Black was also a television scriptwriter and generally a 'big wheel' in the show business world.

It was now 3 o'clock in the morning. They had been at sea for nearly three hours and their course to Shivering Sands had taken them through dazzlingly illuminated lanes of ships, all held at anchor by the seamen's strike.

Ahead lay the forts. In another boat Captain Horsley, the Trinity House pilots and the chief rigger. Big Alf Bullen, had been on a recce.

Oliver Smedley took up the story in *The People* on 30 October 1966:

'All right,' they called up to us. 'We can go aboard.' I jumped down into the small boat and joined the others huddled on the wooden seats round the hull. I remember thinking: 'Now we're for it! Will they let us in, or make a fight of it?'

We had no weapons. Nothing to protect us. No special clothing if we were tossed into the sea. All we took was enough to last the party two meals, plus beer and cigarettes and a Calor gas stove. That was later reported as being our oxyacetylene welding apparatus with which we were to cut down the tower, or its aerial!

Everything was dead quiet. We could hear the water lapping round the iron supports of the legs of the fort. The bottom of the ladder came within reach. I felt a heave from a strong, helpful arm and a gruff voice barked: 'Up you go, Major.' And I began to climb, hand over hand, through the darkness to whatever faced me above.

After what literally seemed like a mile-long ascent, we hauled ourselves through the open trap door. The advance party had given it a few sharp taps, and the men inside had obligingly opened up.

My impression was that nobody seemed in the least surprised to see us. Several of the men on the fort were dazed with sleep. They stood about yawning. Nobody offered the least resistance.

The radio engineer said hospitably: 'Well, I may as well put the kettle on, then. I expect you could all do with a 'cuppa'.'

Kitty was the first to be businesslike. In the back of the boat, coming out from the tug, I had seen her sitting, doing her knitting. Now she was firm.

'Would you mind giving me the crystals from the transmitter first?' She asked. 'You know what they say about kettles.' The electrician of our 'captured' garrison smiled, then went off into the control room and came back with a small, Bakelite plug-looking object about two inches square. It is this tiny unit which fashions a radio station's wavelength.

Without it, transmission was impossible. Kitty put it in her knitting bag, and snapped shut the clasp. 'Fine,' she said. 'Now what about that cup of tea?' With the burly mate from the tug, who had appointed himself her unofficial bodyguard, Kitty Black from Kensington moved into the galley and began to pour out.

Our next task was to wake up the sleeping disc jockeys and let them know their position. But at first, in the labyrinth of towers, we were unable to locate the living accommodation. After some hair-raising passages across the rusting narrow catwalks connecting one to the other, we found them.

They, too - some seven or eight young men whose melodious voices purred out over the air waves daily - seemed to have expected our arrival.

Later, there were wild and sensational reports that these men had been 'intimidated' by our raiding party. There was even an appeal to send in the Navy. This was nonsense! If there had been any threat of intimidation, I should certainly not have organised and led this raid.

Only indignation, and a sense of outrage after all these sordid dealings of commercial radio and its involvements, had forced me to adopt these methods.

As I stood on the filthy iron hoist, waiting to be winched down to our waiting boat, I looked round at some of the men who were, let's face it, my colleagues in this great enterprise of 'pirate' radio.

The ladder climbed by Major Oliver Smedley and the raiders, Shivering Sands, 1966

Shivering Sands in the Thames Estuary, 1966

The DJs for instance. At that hour of the morning they were an unattractive lot. They wore grubby pyjamas, over which some of them had pulled thick sweaters. They all looked bleary, unshaven and dishevelled.

Their quarters, which I was leaving, were squalid and untidy. Even the control room looked chaotic with spares lying around on the floor where they had fallen. At 5.00am the dawn light was beginning to highlight the dirty ironwork of the fort. It gave it the pallor of a prison. For the umpteenth time I asked myself 'What are you doing in this business?' What I wonder, would have been my answer - or my question - if I could have foreseen the fate lying in store for me only 42 hours ahead?[2]

Oliver Smedley and Kitty Black did not remain on the forts that night but left their men, led by Big Alf, to keep things under control. Very early next morning Smedley and Black went down to Philip Birch's country house in Kent and arrived there just as the Radio London boss was leaving for work in the city. They arranged for a meeting to be held at Dean Street, London, at 11.30am.

Meantime Reg Calvert threatened to remove the boarders by force by spraying the forts with a special nerve gas he had invented. A number of gas shells could be dropped onto the forts from an aircraft. The nerve gas was heavier than air so it would descend on to Radio City, thus exterminating everyone on board. Calvert may have planned to get rid of the invaders, but had he thought through a plan to save the Radio City staff?

Calvert wasted no time in visiting Project Atlanta's office in Dean Street, Soho, where the planned meeting with Smedley, Black and Birch was to take to place. By the time he reached Atlanta's office he was allegedly in a state of near hysteria. Later, when Philip Birch met Oliver Smedley and Kitty Black, he very rightly pulled out of the deal and wanted no part of the merger. "There would be no good music station for UKGM. Johnson and Skues would remain with Radio London."

According to Johnny Rogan, in his book, *Starmakers and Svengalis,* Smedley desired something much greater - a share in the profits of Radio City. Only under these terms would he remove the boarders and return the transmitter crystals. In many ways, this was an extraordinary proposition guaranteed to bring out the worst in Calvert. A half share in Radio City was worth about £100,000, precisely ten times the figure Smedley himself had calculated on the value of his precious transmitter.

On 22 June the BBC broke the news during its morning transmission that a man was to appear in court later that day in connection with the shooting of Reginald Calvert, head of the pirate radio station Radio City. He was found dead earlier that day in a house near Saffron Walden in Essex.

On Radio London I read the 12 noon news:

Dateline Wednesday 22 June. Essex: William Oliver Smedley has been charged with the murder of Reginald Calvert, the head of Radio City, who was found dead in a house in Saffron Walden this morning. Smedley was remanded in custody for a fortnight. Mr Calvert died from a gunshot wound in the chest.

In its news broadcast at 12 noon, Radio Caroline said:

Thirty-seven-year-old manager of many beat groups including the Fortunes, and owner of the offshore station Radio City, was shot dead in a country mansion near Saffron Walden in Essex early this morning. A man is reported to be helping police in their enquiries into the shooting. A cloud of mystery has surrounded the activities of Mr Calvert during the past two weeks with conflicting reports being issued as to the future of his station. Last Monday the radio chief asked detectives at Scotland Yard to investigate an alleged boarding of his radio station by unnamed people.

---

2. *Cut Throats and Racketeers,* by Major Oliver Smedley MC. *The People,* 30 October 1966

The BBC went further at 1 o'clock. It said on the Home Service:

At a special court in Saffron Walden in Essex this morning, William Oliver Smedley, an accountant and former vice-president of the Liberal Party executive, was charged with the murder of Mr Reg Calvert, head of the pirate radio station Radio City. He was remanded in custody. His solicitor said he completely denied the charge. Mr Calvert was found dead early today at a house in a village near Saffron Walden. A police superintendent said in court that he told Smedley that Mr Calvert had died of a shotgun wound. Mr Calvert, who was connected with the pop world for a number of years, took over Radio City in 1964 from the pop singer known as Screaming Lord Sutch, and when Radio City was taken over last year by Radio Caroline, he continued to run the station. Scotland Yard are looking into a complaint made yesterday to police in London that a boarding party had taken over Radio City on Monday. Radio City, which is reported to be off the air, is based in a disused Army fort off the Kent coast near

In the *World at One* on 22 June on the BBC Home Service, William Hardcastle interviewed Hugh Jenkins, Labour MP for Putney, who inspired a debate in the House of Commons that evening on "The attitude of Her Majesty's Government to pirate radio and television." Hardcastle asked him if the pirates were, in fact, not only stealing the airwaves but stealing other things like copyright. Jenkins replied:

Exactly! The Performers' Union have made their views on this matter very apparent. The BBC, of course, and other broadcasting authorities do pay reasonable fees to their performers. Now, these people are getting away with that, and not only getting away with it, but they are interfering in the general radio ability and range of international countries, and complaints have been made from abroad that Britain is allowing the pirates to impede our own air and, in so doing, interfering with the radio freedom of other countries.

Mrs Jill Wileman, who worked in Calvert's London office, told the *Daily Mail* on 23 June 1966: "Reg Calvert was a generous man and would always help anyone in need. He was a bit eccentric. He always wanted to do something different. He lived for his family."

Meanwhile over in Saffron Walden. Major Smedley, (54), was in court for only five minutes and remanded in custody until 1 July. Detective Superintendent George Brown, deputy head of Essex CID, told the special court held in Saffron Walden's town hall "At 2.40 this morning I went to the home of the accused at Wendens Ambo where I saw the body of a man. At 10.40am today I saw the accused at Saffron Walden police station. I told him the deceased had died of gunshot wounds which I understood he had inflicted.

"He said 'I don't think I had better say anything until I have seen my solicitor'."

The prosecution went on to say that "Late last night Mr Calvert called at Major Smedley's home after parking his grey Ford Zodiac in Duck Street a few yards from the cottage. Shortly afterwards Mr Calvert fell dead in the hallway of Major Smedley's home. He had been shot in the stomach with a shotgun."

Pearce Reginald Hartley Calvert was born on 24 March 1928 at 26 Sunningdale Drive, Skegness. His birth certificate says his father was unknown and lists his mother, Ada, as a musician. It is believed she moved to west Yorkshire when he was a youngster. Reg began his career as a hairdresser and lived in Huddersfield. He was also an ice cream salesman, TV engineer, clarinet player, fairground impresario and maker of popcorn before becoming a compère for dances which is how he met his future wife, Dorothy, a doctor's secretary. They married whilst he was a private (14158819) in the General Training Corps. Dorothy Rowe was the daughter of the late Harry Rowe and lived at Highcroft Crescent, Almondbury, Huddersfield. Both she and Reg were 18 when they were married at the Methodist Church, Chapel Street, Mold Green, Dalton, Hudderfield, on 20 July 1946.

Following National Service in the Army, he ran a sweet factory in Southampton and later, together with Dorothy, a printing company. The Calverts had two daughters, Susan and Candy. Reg became a professional dance organiser, a job he held for more than twenty years.

He moved his family to Clifton Hall, Clifton upon Dunsmore, near Rugby. It was a very large building with enough room for him to house and rehearse his acts.

One of them were the Fortunes. Founder member Barry Pritchard remembers:

> We were aged 16, had our little band and used to play pop music. We pestered Reg Calvert for work and, in October 1963, he invited us to go and live at Clifton Hall, where there were about five other bands living. After about three months he suggested we form one group out of the various bands. He had Glen Dale as a solo artist and heard Rod Allen and myself singing some songs in a rehearsal room. There he believed the blend would become the Fortunes. We actually began as the Cliftones. Later, American record producer Shel Talmy thought up the name the Fortunes when we went to record for Decca Records.

Rod Allen says Reg Calvert was quite a character: "He had some weird and wonderful ideas. It was Reg who thought up and orchestrated the idea of Screaming Lord Sutch running for Parliament at the Stratford-on-Avon by-election in 1963."

Barry Pritchard recalls Calvert was very much into pyrotechnics:

> We had been living at Clifton Hall for about two weeks when Reg came into our bedroom and gave us each a large cardboard box. When we opened them we found them full of rockets and the most amazing fireworks we had ever seen, most of which he had made himself. He pointed to us and said 'you are in team B.' The next night he brought out teams A and B and we spent the whole time firebombing each other in the wood at the side of Clifton Hall. That tells you all about Reg. Later he used live animals and reptiles on stage, with members of the audience who were blindfolded, singing to them ... donkeys, pigs, monkeys, ducks, baby alligators and snakes. You name it, he had them on stage. In my opinion he was the last of the old-fashioned entrepeneurs. He was also thrifty. We each earned £7 a week, but food and accommodation at Clifton Hall was free.

The Fortunes. From the left: Barry Pritchard, Rod Allen and Glen Dale

He never discussed Radio City with us, although our records were played regularly on the station, especially *You've Got Your Troubles*, when the DJs were having problems on the fort.

The night Reg was shot dead, the Fortunes had been playing at the annual Summer Ball on campus at Oxford University. There were about 20 bands on stage. I arrived home at about 5.30am and all the lights in the street were on. I was told 'Your manager is dead.' I was shocked as were the other lads in the band. Terry King, of King's Agency, then took over as manager of the Fortunes.

Calvert sold the 23-room Clifton Hall in 1965 and bought a smaller house in Rugby and a flat in London.

Son of an unsuccessful duck breeder and hotelier, Oliver Smedley was born on 19 February 1911 and educated at Monkton Combe School in Somerset before training as an accountant.

In 1939 he joined the Honourable Artillery Company, and the following year he was commissioned and posted to the 90th (City of London) Field Regiment, Royal Artillery. He served in Iraq, Sicily, Egypt, landing in Normandy on D-Day and saw action across north-west Europe. He was awarded the Military Cross.

Major Oliver Smedley was a director of several companies including Project Atlanta. During his political days he was vice-president of the Liberal Party executive, but in 1961 resigned as Liberal candidate for Walthamstow because of the party's attitude to joining the Common Market.

A week before the raid on Radio City, Smedley had appeared with daughter Emma on ITV's discussion programme, *Two Generations*.

By Wednesday 22 June 1966 there were two kinds of boarding parties on the forts at Shivering Sands - the police and the raiders who 'took over' on 19 June. The police who went out to Radio City travelled in the launch *Vigilant II* and were headed by Detective Superintendent George Brown who had, earlier in the day, attended a special court in Saffron Walden where Oliver Smedley had been remanded in custody.

Before leaving Tilbury, Supt. Brown said "It is our intention to interview everybody on the forts. I will not be making any arrests and do not intend taking anyone off Radio City."

Detectives spent three hours taking statements from the six staff of Radio City and the ten members of the boarding party. Among the Radio City staff on the forts was Tom Edwards, chief disc jockey. He was 22 years old and had been with the radio station for twelve months; disc jockey Ian MacRae who celebrated his 24th birthday the day the boarding party arrived on the forts; engineers Paul Elvey, Ian West and Phil Perkins, and Leslie Dunn, the station chef.

Tom Edwards told me shortly after Radio City had been visited by detectives, "The news that Reg was dead was quite unbelievable. I was at Radio City when the radio news suddenly came up telling us of the shooting at Wendens Ambo. I had been talking to Reg and his wife only three days previously.

"I went out to the forts the same day as the police arrived. A couple of engineers and disc jockeys went on leave as we came aboard. It was headline news with ITN and

Tom Edwards

Southern TV, and all the national papers gave the Radio City saga banner headlines. We were kept prisoners on the forts and unable to broadcast as the transmitter had been immobilised. When the boarders arrived they said they had been sent to stop us transmitting. We removed the crystals from the transmitter so that they would not be damaged. The boarders checked up on us every night. I can remember going to bed and having a flashlight from a torch shone on my face every hour to make sure we were fast asleep. After about two days we were on fairly good terms with the raiders, but there was a bit of rough stuff when we tried to continue broadcasting."

Paul Elvey confirmed that station staff were given a 'roughing up' when the raiders first arrived in the middle of the night. "Everywhere we went on the fortress we were followed by at least one of the raiders, obviously checking that we didn't reconnect the transmitter and begin broadcasting pop music again to our listeners who must have been quite concerned by our silence."

One of the raiders. Harry Foreman, (55), from Gravesend, Kent, father of seven, denied any punch-ups. "We were told not to 'rough up' the pirates. When we were called in on Sunday night we thought it was just a routine job. None of us thought we were going to be pirates as well."

Disc jockey Ian MacRae said "What a way to spend my birthday! I didn't wish to cause waves so went along with what the raiders requested."

DJ Alan Clark said that the raiders had woken up the Radio City staff who were asleep. "Some of the men wore knives in their belts so opposition was out of the question. Cameras containing film of the boarders were mysteriously smashed. Letters were sent off the station to the newspapers during this time. Messages for help were sent out on an amateur radio, unbeknown to our captors."

Radio City first went on the air in May 1964, then under the name of Radio Sutch on a power of 50 watts. It was owned by pop singer Screaming Lord Sutch who broadcast daily readings from *Lady Chatterley 's Lover*. The station engineer was Paul Elvey. It was bought by Reg Calvert in September 1964 who turned it into a pop station. It claimed 2,000,000 listeners.

Reg Calvert's widow, Dorothy, (38), said on 23 June 1966 that she intended keeping Radio City on the air. The mother of two teenage daughters said: "I am taking over as from today, and we shall be back on the air just as soon as we can get the boarding party off."

Mrs Calvert confirmed that the deal with UKGM was off. Philip Birch said he was tremendously sympathetic with her views and would give her all the support he could. He went on: "I have contacted UKGM and they do not wish to continue with the deal."

A Radio City newsreader who escaped from the forts on a press launch on 22 June was given police protection after he received a mystery phone call that threatened him.

Without a shadow of doubt the Radio City incident stirred the Government to try and speed up legislation.

Tony Benn said in the Commons within thirty six hours of the shooting of Reg Calvert that introduction of legislation only awaited a place in the congested Parliamentary timetable.

Hugh Jenkins said "These extraordinary and tragic events serve to impress on everybody that piracy is piracy in whatever aspect it occurs." He went on:

> While other countries had been able to get rid of the pirates, Britain has come to be regarded as a sort of refuge for buccaneers. The secret of the Government's inaction was that the pirates were popular. The BBC had lost its grip on audiences wanting popular music on sound radio and the Government didn't know what to do about it.

From the Radio City forts on 24 June we learned that the invaders threatened to chop down the 240ft. radio mast if there were any further attempts to board the forts. The boarders said that only Radio City relief personnel would be allowed on - the press were banned! The invaders were led by 'Big Alf' Bullen.

Ian MacRea

Mrs Dorothy Calvert received a threat after she made an appearance on television on 22 June. She sought and received police protection.

A suggestion to send in the Navy at once was made on Saturday 25 June by Sir Alan Herbert, chairman of the British Copyright Council. Sir Alan said that the towers (including Radio 390) had been inside territorial waters since 30 September 1964 under an Order in Council specially made for the purposes by the last Government. "Furthermore," said Sir Alan, "they are within the Port of London Authority's jurisdiction and all the criminal laws apply."

On the evening of Sunday 26 June the raiders left at 9.30pm, after the barge *Keyhole* delivered a note to Alf Bullen. Twenty five minutes later Radio City was back on the air and the first record played was *Strangers in the Night* by Frank Sinatra. Disc jockey Ian MacRae announced "This is Radio City. We are back on the air again. The raiders have left. I hope we will not see them again." The station remained on the air until midnight, then closed down but resumed transmissions the following morning at 6.00am.

Alan Clark commented afterwards, "As the raiders were leaving we were warned not to walk across the catwalk onto the radio station and transmitter tower until they were well away. Of course, we thought they must have planted a bomb there. We waited for a few minutes. Nothing happened, so we raced across and started a mad hunt for the transmitter crystal which had been hidden to keep us off the air. We nearly pulled the place apart, then we found it, refitted it and then went back on air. I have to say that it was a pretty emotional moment."

Alan Clark

Candy Calvert, 15-year-old daughter of Reg Calvert, said: "My mother and I had our radio tuned to 299. We heard the bleeps for 10 o'clock, followed by Radio City's signature tune. The station then played Frank Sinatra singing *Strangers in the Night*.

Alf and his boys arrived on land and before being driven off in two cars - a Mercedes Benz and a Jaguar - commented "We are not sorry to have left the forts, but we were prepared to stay another month if necessary."

Mrs Dorothy Calvert said: "I stated from the beginning that I would not come to terms with the boarding party and I haven't. When the boarding party realised we refused to be intimidated, they decided to leave the station." She thanked Radio London, and in particular managing director Philip Birch, for their help in getting the station back on the air. Radio London pulled out of the deal to broadcast good music from the forts as they did not wish to do business with people who took the law into their own hands Paul Elvey said "I have just spoken to Mrs Calvert and she tells me the boarders' tug turned up at about 9.00pm. I don't know who was in charge of the tug, but the boarders were told to leave in a hurry." On 27 June an article appeared in a Liberal magazine *New Outlook* written by Major Oliver Smedley who was charged with the shooting of Reginald Calvert. He discussed the controversy of pirate radio. He said that investors in the station stood a good chance of getting their money back, and perhaps a great deal more.

Smedley said that with his moderately respectable background as a city chartered accountant he had stipulated that "the activities of Radio Atlanta - now known as Radio Caroline South - should not be in breach of the law of any country." He went on to explain that ships were far more expensive operations than stations such as Radio 390 because the latter were located on former wartime ack-ack platforms.

Major Smedley also made the comment "If more people are now listening to the pirates than the BBC increasingly every day, it is at least *prima facie* evidence that, despite their enormous revenue from licence fees, the BBC are not providing a service which a large part of the population require."

The article in *New Outlook* was written before Smedley was charged with the shooting of Reginald Calvert.

On 27 June Gerry Reynolds, the Minister of Defence (Army), rejected a suggestion by MP Christopher Rowland (a former BBC producer) that he should order an invasion of the forts. "There is no present nor foreseeable defence purpose which would require me to exercise control over the forts," he said in a Commons answer.

The following day the British public learned that the cost of the Radio City 'raid' amounted to £2,130. The *Daily Mail* had calculated a detailed account sheet as follows:

Boarding party of 10 riggers for seven days at 24 hours a day	£1,000
Food, cigarettes, cigars and beer	£300
Taxis to take provisions and company officials to and from the harbour	£120
Tugs to take provisions to Radio City forts in Thames Estuary	£360
Boats and barges for other trips in connection with the raid	£350
	£2,130

In an interview with the *Daily Telegraph* on 28 June, 60-year-old Big Alf, who weighed 17 stone, and was a burly docker who lived in a counci house in Gravesend, said he and his men each received 50 shillings (£2.50) a day for their job on the forts. He continued:

I was told to collect 10 men and arrive at Gravesend Pier without really knowing what was on. When we arrived we met a man who introduced himself. With him was a tall thin woman of about 50 who said her name was Kitty Black. She had come to cook for us. She didn't look like a cook. We got into a tug. None of us knew where we were going. The woman called me over and told us our job was to take over the Radio City forts. It was about 3.00am when we arrived and everyone was asleep. All of us climbed onto the forts. We found that the Radio City party was seven strong. They got a bit of a shock when they saw us, but when we told them the score they realised there was not much they could do.

The man and the woman got hold of the crystals from the transmitter, climbed back into the tug and that was the last we ever saw of them.

Our adventures were far more exciting than *The Man from Uncle*!

On 27 June 1966, an inquest on Reg Calvert was adjourned for three months until 26 September at Chelmsford. Police said that a man had been charged with murder. The hearing lasted only four minutes during which Calvert's widow, Mrs Dorothy Calvert, gave evidence of identification. Dr Hugh Johnson, forensic pathologist of the Department of Forensic Medicine, London Hospital Medical College, said "Calvert died from lacerations of the lung and liver, resulting from a gunshot wound to the chest."

The funeral of Reg Calvert took place on 1 July 1966. Amongst the mourners were Screaming Lord Sutch and Pinkerton's Assorted Colours. The service, at the small parish church of St Peter, Dunchurch, was conducted by the Rev Ian Miller. Mr Calvert's widow, her two daughters, Susan and Candy, and other relatives were present. Calvert had lived in Macbeth Close, Rugby, Warwickshire.

In his will, dated 19 November 1963, and published on 5 October 1966, he styled himself 'impresario.' He left all his estate, £5,699 gross, £1,539 net, to his widow, Dorothy.

William Oliver Smedley appeared at a three-day hearing at a special court in Saffron Walden between 18 and 20 July. The prosecuting council said that the transmitter, which was worth £10,000. had been put on the forts at Shivering Sands although there had been no financial agreement. Royalties on this due to Smedley and his associates had not been paid, and when they heard that a deal was going forward, they wondered about their property. Later, when a boarding party was put on board, said the prosecution, Calvert was obviously disturbed and made a number of extravagant threats in which be mentioned a nerve gas. On the night of the murder, Calvert, accompanied by a radio engineer named Alan Arnold, who had erected the Radio City mast on the fort, went to Smedley's cottage at Saffron Walden, arriving at 10.00pm. He hammered loudly on the door which was opened by the housekeeper, Pamela Thorburn. A violent struggle took place in the hall and sitting room between Calvert and Thorburn. Mr Arnold rushed out to get help and heard a shot from the house. It was then that Smedley appeared. Arnold went back inside and saw Smedley holding a shotgun.

The prosecuting council said later that Smedley told a police constable "I shot him - I know he came here to kill me."

A small, thin pencil-shaped object was shown to the court, and was described as a gas gun which had been found on the body of Calvert. A police expert said that the weapon involved was a ball-point pen combined with a device which discharged either .22 short blank, or a gas cartridge. On the night of the shooting it was loaded with one gas cartridge. It was impossible to obtain gas cartridges legally in the United Kingdom. They were either specially made or else illegally imported. It was likely the one concerned was obtained illegally. Detective Sergeant F. Mann of Harlow said he also found gun shells and £400 in notes.

Dr Donald M. Hunter, of Newport, said that on the night of 21 June he was called to Garden Cottage, Duck Street. He arrived there and was asked by a policeman to go to Smedley's cottage. He there examined a man's body lying in the hall. The man was dead and had a large gunshot wound in the left part of his chest. He saw Smedley, who appeared shaken but was keeping himself under control. Miss Thorburn was not hysterical.

He later examined Miss Thorburn and found swelling and bruising on her left upper arm, and painful points on her shoulder and knee. The injuries were consistent with her having been physically assaulted.

Dr Hugh R. Johnson, a forensic pathologist, said he examined Calvert's body and concluded that death was due to lacerations of the lungs and liver.

Alan Arnold of Hertford said that he drove Calvert to Wendens Ambo at Calvert's request. When the cottage door opened a struggle began. While Calvert was trying to thrust his way in, a young woman was trying to keep him out. The struggle continued inside the cottage. He told the court "I became extremely apprehensive and decided possibly the best thing to do would be to go and get some help. I stepped outside the door, and stood in the street for a while deliberating whether to phone or not. Then I heard a shot. I immediately went through the door into the hall and saw Mr Calvert about to fall forward. He was in the doorway of the sitting room, then I saw a hole in his chest. I observed Smedley with a shotgun in his hand with the barrel pointing downwards."

Arnold continued: "It was a tremendous shock. Calvert fell on his face. I spoke to Smedley. I don't remember the words I said, but I did say this was murder."

Arnold told the court that he suffered from a heart complaint and that he had not gone to Miss Thorburn's aid. He did not know that Calvert was carrying a gun and ammunition.

Pamela Thorburn, who resided at The Cottage, Duck Street, Wendens Ambo, said she was Smedley's secretary and housekeeper. She had known him since she was eight years old and she was now 23. She had worked for Smedley for about two to three years. On the night of the shooting she had opened the door and known immediately it was Calvert although she had never seen him before. When she tried to close the door, he pushed her violently shouting "Where is Smedley?" Calvert used bad language and they struggled. She tried to prevent him getting in while he was trying to force his way forward into the house. During the struggle Miss Thorburn was kicked, bruised on the arm, hit with a telephone handset, and had a stone bust 'lobbed' at her, she told the court.

"He was standing in front of me and I had my back near the living room door. He picked up a statue and was holding it over his head. He said that if he could not take Smedley then he would take me. I told him not to be so stupid and that I would not go with him."

It was then that Calvert saw Smedley, and pushed past her with the statue still in his hand. Suddenly he reeled back across the hall, half turned and fell backwards on the floor.

Miss Thorburn told the court "I did not know what had happened to him. I did not realise that he had been shot. My first feeling was one of relief and it was after that when I saw Major Smedley. He was standing near me with a shotgun in his hand." She said at one stage Calvert had "looked like a raving maniac" and she was petrified with fright.

PC Christopher Kearney of Great Easton told the court that when he arrived at the cottage Smedley was in his shirt sleeves and had informed him that he had shot Calvert. Smedley told him: "I know the man and knew him to be violent. I was not surprised when he came here tonight. You see, we had an expedition the other day to do with pirate radio. I was the man who started it all off. I went to my bedroom and got my shotgun and loaded it. I knew he had come to kill me. He was about to hit Miss Thorburn on the head with a heavy thing. I could see he was mad and I knew he carried arms.

"He (Calvert) looked up and made a dive at me. I had no choice but to fire. I did not think of aiming at his legs. I just fired. What a terrible tragedy. He told me yesterday that he carried a weapon with something like gas. He was a foolish man coming like he did."

PC Kearney said that Smedley went on: "This is a joke that turned sour. It started off as a very good story and you will be able to read about it in the newspapers tomorrow. He did not come 400 miles just to have tea with me. I know I did right and I am sure I would do the same again. I did morally right. I knew he came here to kill me. I had a message yesterday to say things were getting dangerous, but I am not sure which way that meant." The police officer said that at times Smedley expressed concern for the dead man's wife and children. PC Kearney took Smedley to Saffron Walden police station at 2.00am and cautioned him to which Smedley replied "Yes, but I feel I was right." He spent the night with Smedley who rested. They did not speak again until 6.00am when Smedley said: "What a terrible thing. What a pity I did not shoot at the ceiling. The bang might have stopped him. But what could you do under the circumstances - I probably saved the girl's life."

Sergeant R. George said he went to the cottage and spoke to Smedley who said "I do not feel bad about shooting him. It is the first time I have been aggressive since the war. But in such circumstances with a man set upon harming us what can a person do? Only defend himself!"

Detective Superintendent George Brown of police headquarters, Chelmsford, said he examined the scene and later took from the dead man's clothing a pen gas gun which had the cocking device in the 'safe' position. Supt. Brown told the court that Smedley appeared to be "very highly thought of locally." He understood Smedley was the holder of the Military Cross and had been a field gunner during war service.

Mr J.H. Wiseman, chairman of the magistrates, adjourned the case for 50 minutes. He then told the court that magistrates had come to the conclusion "that no reasonable jury would convict on a charge of murder, and we will make no committal on that charge. There would be a committal on a charge of manslaughter instead," he said.

Bail was granted in the sum of £500 and two sureties, each of £500.

At Chelmsford Crown Court on 18 October 1966, Smedley was found not guilty of the unlawful killing of Mr Reginald Calvert on 21 June. He was completely discharged and awarded 250 guineas (£262.50) costs. He was acquitted on grounds of self-defence. Smedley stated: "He was the sort of chap on whose side I would have been in the normal course of events. I never felt personal animosity towards him ... I knew he came here to kill me ... I could see he was mad and I knew he carried arms ... He made a dive at me. I had no choice but to fire." The jury took less than a minute to consider their verdict.

He had spent four weeks and a day on remand in jail before he was allowed bail. After the case Smedley said "there would be no celebration." His interest in pirate radio would now be less active. The case had done a tremendous amount of damage to his personal and business career.

Writing in *The People* newspaper on Sunday 6 November 1966, Smedley said that after the hectic events leading to the raid on the fort, and its stormy sequel, he and his secretary-cum-housekeeper, Pamela Thorburn (whom he refers to in the article as Gail Thorbum) caught the 6.36pm train from Liverpool Street Station, London, to Saffron Walden. An hour later they had collected Smedley's car and driven to his cottage in Wendens Ambo.

When we got to the cottage and parked the car the phone was already ringing. The newspapers had got onto the story of the raid on the fort. Finally I agreed to talk to them. So the reporters set out from London.

At 11 o'clock, during a lull in the phoning, I suggested a drink to Gail. I was pouring them out in the dining room on the other side of the small entrance passage when the hammering sounded on the front door between us.

Gail claims feminine intuition for knowing instantly that it was something dangerous to me. She rushed to the door and opened it slightly. I watched her through the open dining room doorway. I heard her say: "What do you want?" and Calvert's almost hysterical shout of "Smedley. I want Smedley. I'm taking him to the police!" Gail was trying to push the door shut, but he was too strong for her and burst in. I caught a glimpse of another man following. My mind made an instant assessment. A crazed Calvert was breaking into my home. He had others with him, possibly a gang. I must get the police.

First I darted out of the dining room by the rear and ran down a passage, unobserved, to my bedroom. I grabbed the double-barrelled 12-bore shotgun I keep there for occasional rough shooting.

As always, two cartridges lay on my dressing-table top. I shoved them into the breech automatically. Then I rushed out of the door into the garden and into my neighbour's house.

"Ring the police," I told him "I've got big trouble."

I just had time to see the startled look on his face before turning to run back. Now my thoughts were all on how to protect Gail and stop Calvert from whatever was intended in his mind. Back I went into my dining room, with the whisky bottle and the two glasses still on the mahogany sideboard.

Through the doorway I saw the tail end of the fierce struggle Gail had been putting up to try and stem Calvert's mad rush in search of me. A heavy marble bust of Napoleon lay smashed on the floor where Calvert had hurled it at her. Now his arm was raised, menacing.

My mind flashed a warning. "He's got a gun. Beware!"

Calvert spun around, saw me, and screamed, as I believe: "Mr Smedley!" (Gail says his words were 'You bastard, Smedley!').

His black-gloved hand was threatening Gail with a bronze statuette - of Napoleon again. Then it came down and suddenly forward in a fast, underarm bowling action.

My impression was that something either hit me or whizzed past me. I thought I had been shot at.

Instinctively, a reflex in my finger pressed down on the light trigger. There was a roar, smoke, and Calvert staggered to the corner, spinning, then he fell.

We did what we could. The phone in the sitting-room had been wrenched out by Calvert in his struggle with Gail.

We rang for the ambulance from the extension upstairs. It came before the police who took 25 minutes to get to us.

When they arrived, it was all over. Calvert was dead. What more can I say about his death than has already been said? Only this: That under the same provocation - from a man who screamed in uncontrolled rage that he was going to kill the girl who was trying to protect me - I couldn't guarantee that the same thing would not happen again. Calvert is dead and I deeply regret the wastage of his life. He was a brilliant man.

But the law of self-defence in this country is clearly there to protect the rest of us from his type of maniacal intrusion.

After the shooting, I remember little in clear detail. First Gail, then I, was taken to Saffron Walden police station - she to a policewoman's room and I to a cell. We did not see each other.

Gail kept asking the police what they were going to do with me, and eventually C.I.D. Superintendent Brown said: "We don't know. It's a borderline case."

At 10.45 the next morning I was taken before Supt. Brown.

"Will you now make a statement?" he asked me. I refused to do so until my solicitor was present.

"In that case," he said "I must charge you with murder."

"Murder?" I exclaimed. "That's a bit steep isn't it?"

He looked perplexed.

"Well, the body was there and you were there. What else is it?"

In police logic, I suppose he was right.

But it took me a few moments to realise the horror of the position I was in - charged with murder, the foulest crime in the book.

They took away my necktie, one Gail had given me, for no prisoner on a murder charge is allowed to be trusted with a tie, a belt or braces, with which he might hang himself in his cell.

For the next month and a day I would get used to shaving with the only razor permitted for such as myself. A specially locked gadget with its blade held by an immovable screw.

But now I was unshaven, crumpled and dirty, for I had to leave home exactly as I was, with no luggage of any sort.I had spent the rest of that awful night on a bunk in the police cell in the light Terylene suit I had been wearing in London all the previous day. It is hard to describe my feelings. Numb is probably the nearest word.

But the constable deputed to accompany me to Brixton Prison, where I would be held on remand until the hearing of my case, was not one to feel sympathy for people on the wrong side of the law. He dangled a pair of heavy steel handcuffs in one hand and asked aggressively: "Are you coming quietly, or do I have to put you in these?"

Why some police feel they have to make a prisoner feel his absolute worst is hard for me to understand. As we came out of the station, I was told: "Here, put this blanket over your head."

"Why?" I demanded. "I'm not a criminal. I have nothing to feel ashamed of. Why should I hide my face?"

So I was not handcuffed, and I was not hidden under a blanket as I crossed the path to the Black Maria waiting to take me away.

Within an hour of my arrival at Brixton Gaol I had been bathed, measured, weighed, documented - and forced to surrender my precious watch.

For the next month and a day, as an "M/C" prisoner - on a murder charge - I would be left with nothing but my clothes to remind me of the world outside. No money, keys or papers. Everything that had been in my pockets was reduced to a single receipt.

So this was where radio piracy had led me. A far cry from the genteel tearoom scene where I had first discussed the idea.

During that first night in my cell, as I squirmed on the broken mesh-wired spring of my bed, I was smitten by the anguish of my position, and the tragedy of what had occurred at my home only a few hours before overcame me and the tears flowed.

Then I pulled myself together. I knew that I must keep up the strength of my mind.

Gail helped to maintain my health and morale by having a good lunch sent in to me each day. As a remand prisoner I was allowed that privilege.

Another privilege, it was explained to me, was that I might talk to somebody on the dreary twice-daily shuffle round and round the prison yard.

I looked hopelessly at my fellow prisoners. Among them, as I soon got to know, were several murderers, at least one gang leader, dozens of sex offenders - including one poor wretch who was changing into a woman - junkies and criminals of all sorts.

I received many letters from strangers whilst I was in Brixton, encouraging me in my belief that I was not to blame for the tragedy.

But one letter mystified me. I showed it to the Governor. It read:

"Dear Oliver. We have just come back from Malaya. Have no fear. We will have you out of there in a couple of days. Signed Colonel - and Major -."

I had never heard of any of them!

I came before the magistrates in the Town Hall, Saffron Walden, on 18 July. It amused me to remember the last time I had been there on official business.

That was during the election of 1951 when I was standing as Liberal candidate against R.A. Butler. Rather a different occasion.

At the three-day hearing, the charge against me was reduced to manslaughter. I was granted bail of £1,500 which I, my sister Pamela and a business partner put up. At last I could go home.

With three months to wait for the trial at Chelmsford, I took a quiet, restful holiday in Pembrokeshire, followed by a visit to Portugal.

Finally, on 17 October, I went to face whatever was coming to me. I was surprised to see Mrs Calvert had brought her two teenage daughters to the court. It was an awful moment when I saw them.

Later, when one of them, Susan Calvert, shouted in the court that her father had been "frightened because he knew Mr Smedley was going to shoot him," I felt deeply sorry for her. Mr Justice Melford Stevenson was right in having the girl removed from the public gallery. But I know how she must have felt.

As the trial proceeded, it was clear that the brunt of the case against me rested on what happened in just three seconds. During that time I had come into the room, fidgeted with the safety catch of my gun and shot Calvert.

At this point the judge said: "Wait a minute, this is the important part." He wrote my statement down in longhand.

Am I pleased with the verdict? Yes, of course. Pleased at being acquitted because, in my opinion, there never was a case to answer.

Pleased, too, that the court awarded me 250 guineas towards the defence costs of over £4,000.

But it has cost me dearly to prove my innocence. My life has been thrown out of gear. I have had to close down my London office.

As to the future, I intend to take a back seat for a while. I have had more than my fill of commercial pirate radio pranks and dramas.

I don't say I won't come back into the fray, if and when it becomes possible to operate a free radio station legally and properly here.

At present, the Government is committed to clearing the pirates off the air - which will probably only push them into foreign parts, with foreign staff and foreign backing - and I shall be interested to see them do it.

But after what I have been through, as a result of a cup of tea in a London hotel, I intend to keep out of the pirate-infested waters and stay where I belong. Even if the City will never look the same again.

Oliver Smedley had a wide range of interests. He helped form the National Benevolent Fund for the Aged; wrote poems; painted pictures of his beloved Algarve; and composed such Oliver Smedley had a range of interests. He helped form the National Benevolent Fund for the Aged; wrote poems; painted pictures of his beloved Algarve; and composed such songs as *When I'm All Alone Down the Bethnal Green Road*.

He made an LP privately and issued it to 500 friends, some of whom unkindly called it "Smedley's Pistols" as it shared with the Sex Pistols the distinction of being ignored by the BBC.

He was twice married: in 1944, to Eileen Faulkener, a Wren officer, by whom he had a daughter, Emma, and son, Charles, and was divorced in 1963; and in 1978, to Justine Nation.

Oliver Smedley died in November 1989, aged 78 years. Baron Ralph Harris of High Cross, Founder President of the Institute of Consumer Affairs, described him as "A high-spirited cheerful rebel against orthodoxy who relished a hard-hitting argument."

Radio City continued to transmit successful programmes throughout the remainder of 1966 - programmes like the *Auntie Mabel* shows, *The Gary Stevens Show, Five by Four* and *Top Twenty*. Ian West built a new transmitter of 4 kilowatts.

At a similar time, however, the Director of Public Prosecutions was considering whether action should be taken in the courts against the station. MPs pounced on the fact that if action was taken over Radio City because it was within territorial waters, action could also be taken against Radio 390 and Radio Essex.

All remained quiet until 27 January 1967 when Dorothy Calvert, who had been running the station since her husband's death in June 1966, was tipped off by Scotland Yard that the famous fort was about to be invaded again.

Mrs Calvert went out to the fort in a fishing boat to warn the station staff of a possible attack within a few days. She said she had heard of someone trying to sell the station. She knew the identity of the man, and furthermore, so did the police.

There were six disc jockeys and engineers on the fort, along with one cook. The only communication they had with land was by the regular supply boat operated by Fred Downes. Mrs Calvert used to visit the fort once a week. In the *Daily Express* of 28 January 1967 it was reported that 'Big Alf' Bullen had admitted that he had been asked to lead another raiding party against the station. 'Big Alf', a rigger, led the party in June 1966. Major Oliver Smedley said he knew nothing of the proposed raid and, furthermore, didn't want to.

No raid in fact took place. However, Mrs Calvert did receive another visit from the police but this time it was to receive a summons to appear at Rochford Magistrates Court, Essex, on 8 February accused of operating Radio City without a licence. She was found 'guilty' and fined £100. The magistrates held that the fort from which Radio City broadcast was within territorial waters. No order was made for costs nor confiscation of the equipment.

Mrs Calvert told the court that she had received legal advice that the fort was outside

Closeup of former Radio City broadcasting fort, 1993

territorial waters. For eighteen months she had gone through Customs procedure when visiting the fort. Asked whether she was aware that she was broadcasting on the same wavelengths as six Italian stations and one Russian (299 metres), Mrs Calvert denied she had interfered with foreign broadcasts.

After the hearing Dorothy Calvert said she had other plans for commercial radio so she would keep some of her staff together. She would have liked to carry on, but she couldn't fight the Government. Mrs Calvert did not appeal, and transmissions ceased from 'The Tower of Power' just before midnight on 8 February 1967.

The whole case of Radio City remains an unsolved mystery. In the summer of 1966 when Dorothy Calvert appealed to Scotland Yard for help she was told that the station was outside the bounds of police jurisdiction. Yet, six months later, the courts told her that the Radio City fort was within British bounds!

Radio City was the third fort-bound station to be fined £100. The others were Radio 390 and Radio Essex.

Rod Allen, writing in *Television Mail* on 18 February 1967, said he went down to the hearing with Mrs Calvert and disc jockey Adrian Love. At first they couldn't find the courthouse itself. When it was eventually found, Allen says "It resembled a modern clinical hospital, complete with refreshment room and discreet tannoy system. It made it difficult to believe that the full weight of British justice was about to be flung at Mrs Calvert. Where were the panelled walls, the bewigged justices, the grave ushers?"

Bewigged justices or not, Dorothy Calvert was ordered to pay £100. Perhaps the only consolation (and a small one) was that she did not have to pay costs, and furthermore she retained all her broadcasting equipment.

What remains of the anti-aircraft forts at Shivering Sands, former home of Radio Sutch (1964) and Radio City (1964 - 1967). Picture taken 1993

Chapter Nine

THE LETTER

Send me a postcard, drop me a line
Stating point of view
Indicate precisely what you mean to say
Yours sincerely, wasting away.

When I'm 64, Kenny Ball Jazzmen, 1967

IN ANSWER to the question "What has pirate radio given the British public?" sixteen listeners replied at the request of the author in February 1967, six months before the offshore stations became illegal.

The following are letters from: Ron Golz, Mrs Barbara M. Hadler, David Hughes, Mrs Olive Burgess, Hugh Beech, Mrs June Brooks, Miss Lois Hollands, Miss Jacky Cargill, Clive Moore, Mrs Mildred Smith, Alan Ross, Mrs Janet Ashton, Roger Faulkener, Dallas Willcox, Christopher John Minter and Mrs Barbara Apostolides.

The first letter comes from Mr Ronald Golz, a university student, who was living at Koln-Lindenthal, Stadt Waldgurtel 4, West Germany.

Even though I cannot deny that I am a pop fan, I would like to emphasise that my interest and "dedication" to the cause of the present offshore pirate radio stations lies much deeper. When the stations first took up broadcasting, I was a long way away in Germany, and therefore could not witness the effects of this new idea in public entertainment. It was only after a visit to London a few months later that my interest was aroused, in fact to such an extent that I started to scrape together all information concerning the then existing stations and their position in British social life. It was then, to my great surprise, that I realised that reception was possible even in Germany, and the first station to win me over was Radio London which had an extremely powerful signal. From that day on I became an ardent listener whenever possible, though generally in the evening when the signals came through stronger and clearer. Listening brought to me the realisation that the success of this kind of commercial radio lay in the nonchalant style of presentation. No censorship, off the cuff chatter, and in some cases an extremely good talent in choice of records. The other side of my activity and interest for this cause came when, by absolute chance, I met Keith Skues whom I had briefly been introduced to back in 1961 in Cologne, where he had been the most popular housewives' DJ on the then British Forces Network, Germany.

The meeting took place back in 1965 at a club in London where Keith was compère for the evening. A few days later I had to return to Germany, but this initial introduction to the inside world of commercial radio, British style, awakened an interest to know even more of the "backroom" news. From then on I remained in contact with the leading stations, Caroline, London, Scotland, later England and even Radio Essex, which achieved the unbelievable feat with its then 10 kilowatt transmitter of broadcasting very strong signals to Germany after midnight when the stations sharing its wavelength went off the air. Radio Essex had the enormous appeal to me that it truly was the first twenty-four hour station, and that I had non-stop music through the night, and chosen with good taste. England was next to follow, though I personally didn't like their American supply of DJs, and finally at this present time we have Caroline South, the latest twenty-four hour station, which has a DJ on for six hours solid through from midnight to six, a human feat that I will never quite grasp! We are now being faced with the threat of finding all "pop" stations banned and no compensation offered, which I consider to be necessary seeing that hardly any one in Britain can have the slightest doubt that no matter which station it is, the pirates are here to stay, or so say nearly half the population of Britain if we can take the figures of the National Opinion Poll to be correct. I state here and now quite clearly that I do not think the present status quo should be final because it would most definitely lead to pirate station anarchy all round the coast of Britain, which is not compatible with our present standards. I do not see, however, any reason why they should not become an integrated part of our everyday life, seeing that they have proved themselves sufficiently in the last three years of existence. I support one of the leading lines of opinion on this matter which suggests commercial radio on a local basis transmitting on VHF so as not to clash with already allocated wavelengths. It can only be hoped that certain institutions, such as the Musicians' Union, will change its outlook with time, and give more freedom for the use of records instead of demanding restrictions and only supporting live performances. If we want progress, then a minority must always suffer, and I'm sure that the demand for a live performance (after having heard a good record) will increase as these records reach a larger audience than at present.

Some people have suggested commercial radio on a national basis, a suggestion I cannot support, because the secret of success lies in the feeling of the audience in relationship to the DJs, and the more personal and local the news, the more they feel that it is "their" station. With such an aspect in mind, we may enter a completely new sphere of product and service advertising, limited to a small audience but with a much more personal touch.

I think it only fair that I should also state the Government's reason for wanting to ban the pirates, and give my comments to their actions. The official reasons are given as being "that these stations, whether on ships or disused forts, are transmitting without the consent of Her Majesty's Government." There is no argument for the pirates here, except to admit their willingness to apply for a licence and pay the necessary dues. Her Majesty's Government, and especially the Postmaster-General, have only recently stated on a television programme that they do not think the pirates are willing to accept terms: but how can they know when we are not even told what the terms are? Another reason for banning the pirates is "that the British Government has received over 30 complaints from various countries concerning radio interference caused by British pirates sharing the same wavelengths." People living in the London and south-east will be only too glad to tell anyone of the German Freedom transmitter in East Germany, which is extremely powerful and lies on the same wavelength as the Home Service making reception after dark virtually impossible. Has the Government sent a strongly worded message to the authorities responsible? Again the solution to the problem would be to legalise commercial radio in Britain on a local basis transmitting on VHF, a suitable type of transmission with a very small radius and very high quality reception. The third argument the Government brings up is "that some of the pirates are paying no dues (Caroline, London and Radio 390 do, I believe) to the Musicians' Union and are playing records without the permission of the record companies concerned." How can they pay dues when the musicians reject commercial radio entirely, because they incorrectly believe that they will lose their jobs? Without musicians there would be no records, so if there is a demand for records then there will always be a demand for musicians and that includes the demand for live performances as I explained a little earlier on.

In so far as records themselves are concerned, their sales may have dropped as a result of non-stop pop music, but let us consider the immense increase in the sales of transistor and other kinds of radios!

Finally we have the only argument against the pirates from the Government that sticks and it is "that these stations are non-taxpaying at present, they are taking money for advertisements and not paying their contribution to our society." This is very, very true and must be remedied as soon as possible. Only the other day, one could read that the total tax paid by ITV last year on advertisement revenue amounted to no less than £22 million! Again it is quite clear what solution will be beneficial to everyone, including the pirates, and this is that they be embedded in law and become integrated in our economy. Revenue from all the stations will well outstrip that of ITV and might save the taxpayer some of his money for other things. I would like to bring up a factor which should not be disregarded when discussing the pros and cons of commercial broadcasting - it is the immense audiences in Holland, Belgium, France, Germany and in the evening Scandinavia and Spain! Although no exact figures are to hand I would guess the audiences altogether to be well into the millions. Millions of people listening to our stations and indirectly listening to "our way of life." Must we show to these people that Britain is not moving forwards, but just stagnates in the ruins of the Establishment and tradition? Like an expectant father, whose wife is in the ninth and final month of pregnancy, all supporters of commercial radio waited in the "ninth" month of December 1966 for the Government to "give birth" to its new policies on television and radio broadcasting. It was towards the end of December that the "happy" arrival was announced, and I immediately seized my copy to take it home and study its implications in detail. It had been preceded by two court actions against Radios 390 and Essex, the first of which went off the air accordingly but returned to serve its 4.5 million listeners (estimated) at the beginning of 1967; the latter, however, disregarded the sentence of "guilty" and continued its service.

In all justice to our Labour Government, we must admit, I feel, that it has maintained its political principles as concerns the relationship between public and private enterprise in certain fields. I do not like the term "national priorities" which is the central reason why we cannot have commercial radio on a national, let alone local basis. Why should there be a two year trial period for the BBC's new service when the pirates, who have nearly all run for this length of time, have already proved what sort of demand is present within the nation? We are to see nine local stations, run by public corporations and supported by the "Open University, Chambers of Trade and Commerce (possible advertising), Church Councils, Art Associations, and other social and cultural institutions." If these people do support such stations, and receive broadcasting time accordingly, I'm sure the only popular station will be the BBC's semi-national network on the "Light Programme" wavelength, which will ensure us at least six hours of record-cum-pop music. So now we know what the signposts to Britain 1980 are: 1967 will see the gradual close-down of the offshore stations, not because of a food and supplies siege, but because of lack of advertising. 1967 will give the nation Radio 247 as it is at the moment called, and we will all be able to enjoy not only gramophone records by the Beatles and Rolling Stones, but the "swinging sounds" of Joe Loss, the Northern Dance Orchestra, and with a bit of luck, a fling from Bonnie Scotland.

Oh to be in Britain in "Swinging '67."

To return to plain facts, we all know that local authorities are nearly all in debt, and a local station will only increase their deficiencies. The taxpayer will be missing out on the opportunity of seeing his money used for better causes as a result of a nice tidy revenue to the Exchequer on advertising of commercial stations.

If we could see Independent Television in our economy, with a public board as guardian, why can't we see a "Commercial Radio System" with its public watchdog board? I'm sure everybody agrees, except the Government, which has a different conception of our nation's priorities. Let's face it: Labour has been voted into Government, they've done a lot of good things for Britain, but no Government is perfect and the idea of commercial radio in private enterprise will just have to be "frozen" until we either change Governments or our scale of priorities has commercial radio at the top. Goodbye pirates of the sea and popularity! Goodnight Britain.

The second letter is from a housewife, Mrs Barbara Mary Hadler of Cortland Close, Sittingbourne, Kent. She still lives in the same house with her husband, John.

PIRATE RADIO - these are seemingly unsavoury words in certain Governmental departments, yet in the face of so much condemnation they can boast many redeeming features. For every accusation hurled at them, they have a plausible answer, and can claim to have vastly increased sales of transistor radios, fostered many friendships between listeners and even saved lives. The hostile attitude adopted by such bureaucratic officials strongly emphasises their reluctance to investigate potentially good ideas which deviate from their archaic plans for the community. The Government's present stand against commercial radio comes after an initial disregard, which presumably stemmed from their ignorance of the needs of ordinary people like myself. They didn't foresee the popularity these stations have since gained, and, I am sure, have only taken up their resolve to dispose of them because of their enormous success. People with these attitudes cannot begin to understand just what pirate radio stations mean to us dedicated listeners, but their appeal can be measured by the fact that we obviously choose to tune into them in preference to other forms of broadcasting.

For my part, I look upon this so-called illegal activity as my real outlet from household boredom as it is a style of entertainment perfectly suited to my mood. I am not alone in this, but merely one of a large band of housewives who gain a tremendous amount of pleasure from listening to the gay informality of this type of broadcasting, which is clearly blended with slick professionalism. I find it hard to remember life prior to Radio London etc., and literally dread the thought of a possible return to the days of BBC monopoly.

It has kept me very young at heart and well informed of everything new and "with-it." The fact that I am no longer a teenager is no reason to feel out of things, and I think it is with this in mind that so much of the action is directed at us housewives. For people like me, who frequently write to favourite disc jockeys, there is the added excitement of hearing one's name given out over the air, amounting to some small claim to fame, otherwise impossible. The main attraction for me is the personalities who present these lively programmes, and at present, I feel that Radio London offers the greatest assembly of talent in this field. I realise their popularity depends upon the reaction of us listeners and would like to confirm their success with my very sincere thanks to everyone concerned for giving me so many hours of true entertainment and pleasure. May they be given the chance to continue for many years to come.

In 1993 Barbara looked back to the year 1967:

As the strains of Radio London's theme, *Big Lil*, faded into obscurity on its final transmission day, I like many other devotees, drifted into a period of morose unreality. Withdrawal symptoms lasted for several weeks, during which time I played endless tapes of Big L recordings I had made throughout its brief but joyous life, and was somewhat comforted as I constantly relived the previous few years. I reverted to Radio Caroline who continued for a few weeks longer, and was then one of the first listeners to the new BBC pop station.

Many of the pirate disc jockeys had suddenly become the BBC's new "flavour of the month," and I therefore rejoined them on Radio 1. Nowadays, in line with my more mature image, I prefer the somewhat quieter and melodic broadcasts on Radio 2. I personally believe that (with few exceptions) pop music generally was at its best during the 'Sixties, but then perhaps that is just my middle-aged judgement speaking!

David Hughes was a columnist with the *Kent Messenger* when he wrote this letter. He went on to become assistant editor of *Disc and Music Echo* followed by senior management with EMI Records based in London.

Since the first commercial broadcast was made in this country on Good Friday, 1964, from the m.v. *Caroline,* anchored 3½ miles off the Essex coast, pirate music stations have gradually increased in numbers and popularity, until today more than half the population of England, Scotland and Wales listen to them (National Opinion Poll-July 1966).

The Conservative Government, when it was in power, occasionally expressed its disapproval of the pirates, pointing out they were breaking the international broadcasting agreement set out by the Copenhagen Plan of 1948. However, it realised the value of the stations - the pleasure they were giving the listening public of the country.

Since the Labour Party has been in power, efforts to ban the stations have increased and today we are faced with a Parliamentary Bill which attempts to make it impossible for them to continue broadcasting.

However, if the pirates win the day, then the Government may well have to face the fact that many people who listen only to the offshore network could argue that they have a strong case for not paying the licence fee.

Broadcasting is not the only monopoly broken by the pirates. Until they came on the air, the four major record companies completely dominated radio, both on the BBC and Radio Luxembourg. Now, a glance at the week's top selling records is sufficient to show how much the position has changed, giving new record companies and recording artists the opportunity previously denied to them.

If the pirates are taken off the air, what alternatives is the Government offering?

Concise details showing how the Government visualises local radio are given in a booklet, *"Local Radio in the Public Interest: The BBC's Plan."*

The ideas are commendable, including programmes for schools, special courses, local news and topics, programmes "to help immigrant groups in becoming fully integrated into happy components of local society," and public services at moments of local and national crisis - but are they alternatives to Radio London and Radio Caroline?

The answer is obvious, and equally obvious is the inevitable increase in the licence fee when these stations do start broadcasting.

The pirates cost the country nothing: they give pleasure to millions of people by day and night; they benefit trade through their advertisers, and they allow the public to hear a wider selection of new records and artists.

If banned, the pirate ships will not stop broadcasting as they are outside British jurisdiction. They will merely move their offices out of the country, employ foreign disc jockeys and use foreign advertising, all at the expense of this country. For them to continue in the face of legislation would make the British Government a laughing stock.

Commercial radio is here to stay. Let it stay legally. The stations themselves want to be law-abiding. Is it not possible for the Government to take steps to make them legal?

Mrs Olive Burgess was the lady responsible for organising Britain's first pirate fan club

Simon Dee with Fan Club secretary
Olive Burgess in 1964

for Simon Dee. She now adds her own story about the early days of offshore broadcasting, when she lived in Chelmsford, Essex.

When I was first asked to give my opinion on "What has pirate radio given the British public?" many different angles crowded my mind. After considerable thought, I decided to start by giving my personal reasons for supporting pirate radio. On Easter Saturday, 1964, my family had gone off for the weekend, leaving me to my own devices. I was due to enter hospital for a major operation any day, and really wasn't fit company for the dog, let alone humans! Television had never really interested me, except for isolated viewing and even in those days I listened to the radio far more than the average person. During that Easter Saturday afternoon, I found only sporting commentaries on the BBC, and twiddled around the dial to try and find some music. I found Simon Dee broadcasting from 199 metres on the medium waveband. Radio Caroline - Your All Day Music Station!

This intrigued me. I didn't know what it was, but here from the word "Go" was something that caught my interest and made me forget my own miserable state of health. The next morning the Sunday papers carried stories of this pirate ship broadcasting off the Essex coast, also a picture. Always having loved the unconventional, the whole idea appealed to me. As a child, I'd driven my parents crazy by tuning to the then revolutionary Radio Luxembourg, but here was something better and nearer home! As the days went by I continued to listen, and Simon Dee's voice and personality came across so well that I wrote to him as, I found out later, did thousands of others. Here was someone playing records and talking as though he cared if I was listening and enjoying his choice of records. This was quite new after the impersonal programmes put over by the BBC. Even greater pleasure was to come. As the letters were received, the Caroline DJs were acknowledging them over the air and, of course, as time went by, the Caroline Club was formed.

When I came out of hospital after my operation, I spent several weeks in bed. I had been warned to expect post-operational depression, as this was quite normal. Despite the fact that my family left for work and school about 9.00am each day, returning at about 4.30pm, I never felt lonely, as I tuned in to Caroline at 6.00am until shutdown. I felt as though I had friends to listen to, request records to be eagerly awaited and even letters in answer to my own. I can honestly say that I never once sunk into self-pity or depression during this time. To my friends, my radio had become an obsession; to me, a safety valve - something that helped me through what could have been a very lonely period. In June 1964, the Basildon Carnival took place, and to my surprise and delight, I learnt that Simon Dee was to perform the crowning ceremony. That evening I met Simon and his wife, Bunny, for the first time - it was to be the start of a lasting friendship, also an opening to so much more!

My husband and I had for sometime promoted dances in various districts. The trend for disc-nites was just beginning, and I thought it would be a good idea to include in these dances Caroline DJs. At that time too I had formed The Simon Dee Official Fan Club, and this would also serve as a means of promoting Simon. We also booked Tony Blackburn, Erroll Bruce and Mike Allen. Allan Crawford, one of the directors of Caroline, ran an agency for beat groups so we thought it might be a good idea to bill them at the same time as the DJs were appearing. Naturally, nobody objected to this, as by hiring the DJs and groups both Caroline and Crawford stood to gain their commission, and at no risk to themselves. My husband has cause to remember these disc-nites. He lost approximately £400 on eight bookings!

As a direct result of these dances, official Caroline nights, also the fan club, I found myself receiving many letters from listeners. I actually met and formed friendships with both families and individual 'viewers' that a few months earlier I hadn't known existed. This was not only happening to me but to thousands of people all over East Anglia. Lonely widows and spinsters were given a new interest in life. The voice that talked to them all day got cold in winter and there were pullovers to be knitted, boxes of tissues and aspirins to be despatched at the first sign of their favourite DJ having a cold! To the housewife no longer did they have to plod on with their chores - alone and forgotten till the family returned at night; just a postcard and who knows - maybe you too could be "Homemaker of the Day!" Indeed, the DJ had become a well-loved part of the family. My own family thought that I had gone crazy in the beginning. After a while they, too, caught the 'bug' and somewhat shamefacedly, but proudly displayed autographed photographs of DJs on their bedroom walls. Pre-pirate radio days we had one radiogram. Now each member of my family, numbering seven, has his or her own personal transistor radio. Even my so respectable looking husband is to be seen each morning getting into his car complete with radio and showing offshore radio stickers on the rear window of the car. Indeed a revolution had begun!

During the first year of offshore radio other ships and forts started transmitting programmes. As human nature was involved so deeply, differences of opinion were bound to happen and of course they did! The original Caroline DJs drifted to join new colleagues on other stations. Simon Dee had proved his worth and accepted an offer to join the BBC. I feel the main reason for offering him this opening was to try and win back to Auntie BBC a portion of the listening public lost to them through the advent of commercial radio. To a degree I think this worked, but only for his programmes and not to the extent they intended. As this happened the listener was beginning to feel divided loyalties. Was it the station or the DJ that mattered most? Originally, I thought the station - as time went on I realised that the DJ either made or marred the show. Although Caroline would always be my first love, station-wise, I listened to whichever friend of mine was on at the time. I believe this applies to the majority of listeners. It is not uncommon to see 'viewers' displaying badges and car stickers relating to several stations. One thing that is for sure now that offshore radio is in peril of being closed down, the public, as one, will fight to retain this style of radio which has become a vital and very necessary part of their daily life.

Much publicity has been given to the claim that commercial radio breaks up family life, as well as unites it. When Caroline started transmitting, I lived in a semi-detached house in Chelmsford. Now my family has split up. My husband still lives in our original home. My children, all grown up, have gone their own ways. I now live in a bedsitter in London. This I don't blame on pirate radio. It would probably have happened anyway, but I have to admit that all of my present friends and associates I have met through pirate radio. It has changed my life. I have no regrets. At present I am getting as many people as possible to sign petitions to be sent to the Postmaster-General, asking him to think very carefully before banning pirate radio. If he does persist in doing this, many people once lonely, but having found companionship on their radio, will be left with nothing. In a so-called civilised society this is a terrible thing, but one that has to be faced.

I for one say "Thank God for Pirate Radio" and the pleasure it has given, and may the day be near when the Postmaster-General sees his way clear to make the stations land-based. That is the only sane answer.

In 1993 Olive Burgess reread the letter she wrote in 1968 and added:

It is now thirty years since the first era of pirate radio. Looking back over those years I feel we can never again experience the thrill or companionship we enjoyed in those pirate days. After the ships we had Radio 1. I found that it was just a poor attempt to copy offshore radio. To my mind the jingles and patter came a poor second.

In 1973 commercial radio came to Britain. I personally worked for Capital Radio in London. The first few months we had a friendly feeling with a regular listening public. That was supposedly *bad* radio, so the format was altered and now, with few exceptions, money is the name of the game to the exclusion of companionship radio. I have returned to Auntie Beeb, both locally and nationally, plus Classic FM.

Of late I find myself listening to my old records or new CDs. Maybe it's my age, who knows? That is the only way I relive those happy days. I feel sorry for people living alone and listening for a friendly voice. I don't think they are to be currently found on commercial radio, a cause for which we fought so hard.

Mr Hugh Beech of Havant Road, Bedhampton, Hampshire, wrote a number of pieces on the subject of commercial radio in the Cambridge University newspaper. *Varsity Weekly*. He also wrote a memorandum called "Hands off Offshore Radio Stations", a copy of which he sent to seventy MPs in August 1966 and also to the author from which the following has been extracted:

The new Postmaster-General, Edward Short, recently said: "These stations present a very squalid picture of which I hope no one in any part of the House is proud." 'Squalid'? This is presumably a veiled reference to events in connection with a single station, aspects of which are *sub judice*. Consequently I cannot comment, but whatever the pros and cons of that particular matter, it is surely contemptible to smear a wide set of activities bringing a lot of pleasure to millions of people purely on the strength of a single incident. One summons does not make a squalor.

Forty years of external radio: Pacesetter for the BBC
The present controversy revolves around the offshore stations (i.e. ships and forts). The sole surviving station broadcasting to British listeners from Europe, Radio Luxembourg II, escapes criticism, although its power is just as unauthorised as the frequencies of the offshore stations, and for that matter, the frequency of Radio Luxembourg I on the long wave. This was not always the case - very much the reverse when, before the war, there were not only Radio Luxembourg, Radio Normandy and, from time to time, a number of other stations broadcasting to Britain from Europe. The English broadcasts from Radio Toulouse were opened by no less a personage than the late Sir (then Mr) Winston Churchill, a fact generally ignored by his biographers. In fact, dating from the early broadcasts from Radio Paris in the Twenties, with the sole exception of the war years, there have been at all times over the last forty years broadcasts to Britain from outside her shores.

Successive British Governments have raged. The press - until recent years - has banned discussion, but these broadcasts have survived. There must be some merit in a movement which has continued to flourish against odds that have many times before seemed overwhelming.

You may well be unaware of the extent to which present BBC programmes were triggered off, in the first instance, by the transmissions reaching our shores from without. I will give just four examples.

First, the matter of early morning broadcasting; until the Thirties the BBC came to life in the region of 10.00am. The first early morning broadcast in English was from Radio Paris, who put on news of the Australian test matches at 6.30am - in due course the BBC followed suit. After midnight broadcasting, too, was only offered by the BBC as a result of Radio Luxembourg's efforts in that direction. *The Dales, The Archers,* all the other serials that you and I probably loathe but millions love, all this "soap opera" traces back to the pre-war daily serials *(Stella Dallas, etc.)* from Radio Normandy.

Most striking of all is the liberalisation of Sunday programmes; before the war, more listeners tuned to Luxembourg than to the BBC programmes which were then confined, on Sundays, to "serious" music and the spoken word. One way and another, the present pattern of BBC programmes owes much to the initiative of the competition from outside. The pop ships have already had a noticeable effect on the Light Programme, and if some present suggestions go through, it would appear that one 24-hour programme on the lines they have created would be put out on a BBC wavelength if the offshore stations should be by some means scuppered.

Price, Three Halfpence   Vol. IV. No. 318. April 30, 1939

I.B.C. Programme Sheet

APRIL 30th to MAY 6th, 1939

COPYRIGHT
RESERVED

INTERNATIONAL BROADCASTING CLUB
President : CAPT. LEONARD F. PLUGGE, M.P.

SUBSCRIPTION
RATES on PAGE
SIX

INTERNATIONAL BROADCASTING CO. LTD., 37, PORTLAND PLACE, LONDON, W.1
Telephone : LANGHAM 2000 (14 lines)   Telegrams : INTERBROAD, LONDON

REGISTERED AT THE G.P.O. AS A NEWSPAPER

RADIO NORMANDY

274 m., 1095 Kc/s., 20 Kilowatts

Sunday, April the Thirtieth

MORNING PROGRAMME	TIMES OF TRANSMISSIONS	10.45 a.m.
(7.0 a.m.—11.45 a.m.)	All Times stated are British Summer Time	GEORGE FORMBY With a strong supporting cast including

December 23, 1936   December 23, 1936   RADIO PICTORIAL

THIS WEEK AT RADIO LUXEMBOURG

SUNDAY, DEC. 27

8.15 a.m.   STATION CONCERT
9.0 a.m.
EXCURSIONS DOWN MEMORY LANE
Presented by the makers of Mother Seigel's Syrup.
9.15 a.m.   STATION CONCERT
9.30 a.m.   WAKE UP AND SING
Brian Lawrance and his Lansdowne Orchestra, with Marjorie Stedeford and The Three Ginx.—*Presented by the makers of Clarke's Blood Mixture.*
9.45 a.m.
"OLD SALTY AND HIS ACCORDION"
To-day Old Salty plays party games with Chinese Pirates.—*Presented by Rowntree's Cocoa.*
10.0 a.m.   BLACK MAGIC
A Programme of Dance Music.—*Presented by Black Magic Chocolates.*
10.15 a.m.
CARSON ROBISON AND HIS PIONEERS
Presented by Thos. Hedley & Co., Ltd., makers of Oxydol, Newcastle-on-Tyne.
10.30 a.m.   OLIVER KIMBALL
"The Record Spinner."—*Presented by Bisurated Magnesia.*
10.45 a.m.   MUSICAL MENU
With Mrs. Jean Scott, head of Brown and Polson's Free Cookery Service, who gives you a special recipe each week.—*Presented by Brown & Polson.*
11.0 a.m. LET'S ALL GO ROUND TO NORMAN LONG'S
With Flotsam and Jetsam and Sydney Jerome and his Orchestra.—*Presented by Kruschen Salts*

8 p.m. A Special Christmas Programme introduced by Christopher Stone, with Leslie Holmes and Leslie Sarony (The Two Leslies).—*Presented by the makers of Thermogene Vapour Rub.*
3.15 p.m.
THE MERRY ANDREWS PROGRAMME with Frederick Bayco at the Organ, Andy Mack, and their guest artist, Jack Simpson and his Xylophone.—*Presented by Andrews Liver Salts.*
3.30 p.m. Claude Hulbert and Enid Trevor on the PICCLETHWAITES AT HOME, entertaining Paul England.—*Presented by the makers of Virol.*
3.45 p.m.
THE DOLCIS FOOTLIGHT PARADE in step with Carroll Gibbons and his Orchestra.
4 p.m.   HORLICK'S SEA-TIME HOUR
Cruising the world with an all star cast of radio, stage and screen favourites aboard, including Max Miller, Al and Bob Harvey, Alma Vane, Ronald Hill, Sam Costa, Bernard Lee, Dorothy Kay, The Rhythm Brothers, Molly Cardew, Arthur Gomez and Debroy Somers and his Band. Bulletin from the world's cyclists.—*Presented by Horlick's, Slough, Bucks.*
5.0 to 5.15 p.m.
RAY OF SUNSHINE CONCERT
Compered by Christopher Stone.—*Presented by the makers of Betox and Phillips Yeast.*
5.30 p.m.   THE OVALTINEYS
Entertainment especially broadcast for the League of Ovaltineys, with songs and stories by the Ovaltineys and their friends. The music by the makers of Bile Beans.
6 p.m. MASTER O.K. SELECTS THE STARS
Presented by the makers of O.K. Sauce.

SUNDAY, DEC. 27—cont.

7.15 p.m.   MORE MONKEY BUSINESS
with Billy Reid and his Accordion Band, Ivor Davies and Dorothy Squires.—*Presented by the makers of Monkey Brand.*
7.30 p.m.   WALTZ TIME
with Billy Bissett and his Waltz Time Orchestra, Louise Adams, Robert Ashley, and The Waltz Timers.—*Presented by the makers of Phillips' Dental Magnesia.*
7.45 p.m.   AVA PRESENTS !
"Olga" the Radio Pianiste, with her Gipsy Girls' Orchestra, and The Girl with the Glamorous Hair.—*Programme by Ava Shampoo.*
8 p.m.   PALMOLIVE PROGRAMME
With Olive Palmer, Paul Oliver, Brian Lawrence.
8.30 p.m.   LUXEMBOURG NEWS
(in French)
9 p.m.   MACLEAN'S CONCERT
9.15 p.m.   BEECHAMS REUNION
featuring Jack Payne and his Band, with Mabel Constanduros. Compered by Christopher Stone.—*Presented by the makers of Beechams Pills, Ltd.*
9.45 p.m.   THE COLGATE REVELLERS
Presented by the makers of Colgate Ribbon Dental and Shaving Creams.
10 p.m. PONDS' SERENADE TO BEAUTY
Programme for Lovers.—Presented by Pond's Extract Co.; Perivale, Greenford.
10.30 p.m.   DANCE MUSIC
Presented by the makers of Bile Beans.
11 p.m.   THE STREET SINGER
(Arthur Tracey).—*Presented by the makers of Tokalon Powder and Cream.*
11.15 to 12 (midnight) STATION CONCERT

TUESDAY, DEC. 29

8.15 a.m.   STATION CONCERT
8.30 a.m.   VITA-CUP CONCERT
Presented by the makers of Coleman's Vita-Cup.
8.45 a.m.   STATION CONCERT
9 a.m. ROSE'S HAPPY MORNING MATINEE, with the Happy Philosopher.
Presented by L. Rose & Co., Ltd.
9.15 a.m.   STATION CONCERT
9.30 a.m.   MUSICAL MENU
With Mrs. Jean Scott.—*Presented by Brown and Polson Cornflour.*
9.45 to 10.30 a.m.   STATION CONCERT
3.15 p.m.   STATION CONCERT
3.45 p.m.   FINANCIAL NEWS (in French)
3.50 p.m.   STATION CONCERT
4 p.m.   HORLICK'S TEA-TIME HOUR
With Debroy Somers and various artistes, followed at 4.45 p.m. by the Children's Corner.—*Presented by the makers of Horlick's, Slough, Bucks.*
5 to 5.15 p.m.   STATION CONCERT
6.15 p.m.   STATION CONCERT
6.30 p.m. ROWNTREE'S SCRAP BOOK
A popular Dance Tunes.—*Presented by Rowntree's Clear Gums.*
6.45 p.m.   STATION CONCERT
7 p.m. GUEST NIGHTS, at the Mustard Club. Albert Whelan joins the Mustard Club, Mirth and Music, with Baron de Beef, Miss Di Gester, Signor Spaghetti, Lord Bacon, and other members.—*Presented by J. & J. Colman.*
7.15 to 7.30 p.m.   STATION CONCERT

The Calvert Cavalcade of Sport presents Bob Bowman, famous Canadian sports commentator, in their programme on Sunday, at 12 noon. Here's a picture of Bob giving one of his breath-taking broadcasts at the mike

THURSDAY, DEC. 31

8.15 a.m.   STATION CONCERT
8.30 a.m.   THE OPEN ROAD
3.15 p.m.   STATION CONCERT
3.45 p.m.   FINANCIAL NEWS (in French)
3.50 p.m.   STATION CONCERT
4 p.m. HORLICK'S TEA TIME HOUR with Debroy Somers and Various Artistes,

Would one pop station suffice?

Most men can only tell one woman's weekly from another by whether 'the page' is by Evelyn Home, Mary Grant or whoever ... none the less, several of these papers maintain their separate readerships of millions apiece. Woe betide the Government that said that this sort of requirement, though recognised to exist, could equally well be catered for by a single woman's magazine called, perhaps, "British Woman".

But this is precisely what many of the anti-offshore brigade are saying about the pop stations. You and I may well find the sheer corniness of the present bawl-and-twang amateur pop-merchants pretty moronic. Let's face it, though, virtually the entire teenage population adore it. And if one likes it, one will appreciate the subtle distinctions between Radio London and Radio Caroline. One station just would not fill the bill, least of all under BBC auspices. Youngsters want this stuff in the frenetic manner that the ships understand so well, not doled out patronisingly by adults pathetically trying to be 'with it', although only too obviously without it, à la *Juke Box Jury.*

BBC/Offshore/Local broadcasting

Others claim that if only local broadcasting were set up, the offshore stations would either die or would safely be suppressed. Here again there is a confusion of approach. I am entirely in favour of local broadcasting - it should have been introduced years ago - but for its own genuine purposes, not as a substitute for offshore radio. The function of local broadcasting is primarily to provide opportunities for local musicians, artists, speakers, drama groups, news, etc. and to supply a medium for local advertising - in fact to concentrate on what largely has a particular appeal to the people who live in the district. Local broadcasts on these lines could, and should, have a flourishing future and would fulfil a definite need. They are not a suitable vehicle for the programmes that the offshore stations put out, and which some twenty million widely-scattered listeners appreciate. Radio 390, in particular, carries several daily programmes which are greatly appreciated by people all over the country, and which would certainly not be available on local channels or a BBC 'pop' wavelength. At 10.30 every morning there is half-an-hour of piano music; at 3.30 every afternoon on *Memory Lane* the great pre-war bands and artists such as Jack Hylton, Bing Crosby, Cab Calloway, Al Bowlly, etc. can be heard (where else?), while from 9.00pm to midnight one has a pleasant restful programme of Cole Porter-ish music - mostly non-vocal. Can you see the BBC or local radio providing anything like this fare?

In fact there is quite a parallel between quality newspapers and the BBC, popular newspapers and the offshore stations, local newspapers and local radio stations. Each has its own functions to perform.

Before leaving local radio, a technical point. Such stations, though no doubt operating on VHF, should also operate on very low power on the international common frequencies on the medium wave band. While the radio industry would dearly love to see these stations exclusively on VHF in order to sell this type of set, there is a serious political objection to this from the long-term viewpoint.

It is a sad commentary on the supposed educational progress and the broadening of the mind that more widespread foreign holidays are supposed to bring, that the proportion of people listening to broadcasts from Europe (apart from English broadcasts from Luxembourg) has declined steeply over the last thirty years. In the Thirties there were two weeklies *(World Radio* and *Wireless World)* publishing full Continental radio programmes. Now only those within visiting distance of Charing Cross Road, London, can get details of these programmes via French or German journals. Nevertheless, the ability to hear what other nations are saying could, in certain circumstances, be very valuable. If listeners could be conditioned into buying "VHF only" sets, all opportunity to hear other than what is offered by the stations permitted by one's own Government would vanish; 1984 would in that event be brought a little closer.

What harm do the offshore stations do?

Objections to the offshore stations fall essentially into four categories, and we propose to answer each in turn.

First, we have the vested interests: the recording industry, the musicians, the Copyright Council ... and Uncle Sir Alan Cobley and all. The recording industry objects that there is "over-exposure" of records, thereby depressing sales. (In my view there was far too high a proportion of record time on the BBC devoted to 'chart chasing' at the expense of records we should all enjoy before the pop stations arrived, anyway, but that is another story). While there must be a small percentage of people 'taping' the broadcasts rather than buying the records, it does seem to be highly doubtful whether the net effect is not to increase sales rather than the reverse. I would guess, in fact, that the pop stations have extended the life of the post-war record boom at a time when it could well have fallen away in favour of some other teenage craze e.g., juvenile delinquency; (statisticians might well look for some such correlation, incidentally, between the expansion of offshore radio on transistors and what certainly to the lay eye appears to be a decline in the extent of hooliganism and thuggery). The fact is that few teenagers can be bothered fiddling about with tape after the first rush of excitement (those spools are such a nuisance!) and much prefer to buy the records - money is, for them, no object.

The Musicians' Union opposes offshore radio officially but I have yet to see any well-known musicians or pop boys complaining. This seems to be, in fact, the one thing the protest boys haven't got around to protesting about! The fact is that they know perfectly well that the extra publicity they get from these stations pays off. Furthermore, because of the ample broadcasting time, lesser known groups and minor record companies get a chance they would otherwise not have. (Perhaps that's what upsets the major record companies, but do they need your protection?).

With regard to Performing Rights, *The Times* seems to contain little else these days but a barrage of letters from Sir Alan Herbert. My heart bleeds for him as his more esoteric poems are performed day in and day out - rewardless - from Radio London! Except, of course, that they aren't, and the major offshore stations, as has been repeatedly pointed out and as repeatedly ignored, pay the appropriate amounts to the Performing Right Society. In fact, the meat of Sir Alan's case, reduced to its bare essentials, seems to amount to this: even if these stations pay, they only do so voluntarily - no one can compel them to. A nice point, certainly, but scarcely one to justify stopping the pleasure of millions.

It is worth remembering that Sir Alan Herbert has enjoyed a successful career in writing (and good luck to him for it - we enjoy the fruits of it, even if not the present somewhat spiteful letters to *The Times*) purely by virtue of the freedom of the press. That freedom did not just come naturally. We only have it today because some of our forefathers went to prison, not once but again and again, because they insisted on having this freedom, and in the end the Government of the day saw the point and retired (more or less) from the fray. It seems a little ungracious, therefore, to see him fervidly supporting the Swedish Government for having put in prison the lady who was asserting freedom of the air by way of her radio ship, and suggesting similar action here. Secondly, we are told that the offshore stations will interfere with important services and could cause loss of life. This argument is only sustained through the ignorance of the majority of technical matters. These stations all broadcast within the official medium wavebands set aside for broadcasting purposes on frequencies interleaved with BBC and European stations. If offshore stations need to close down for this reason, so do all the others. This objection is, in fact, completely phoney. The third objection concerns the matter of possible interference with Continental stations. Since such interference, if it exists, tends to operate both ways, the offshore stations have naturally chosen their frequencies with care so that any stations they clash with (and every channel has more than one occupant) are many hundreds of miles away. If any significant interference does arise, they alter their frequency to suit. It would appear that the number of Continental listeners whose enjoyment of their home stations is even occasionally reduced by the offshore stations is very small compared with the number of such listeners who tune in to our offshore stations. I was surprised last summer to find that many Belgians listen, as a matter of course, to Radio Caroline. Now we come to the fourth objection, the one which is rarely overtly admitted but which I suspect is the root objection in Members' minds, accustomed as they are to telling us (when their party is in power) what we can do and what we cannot do. There is a resentment that anything should be going on without their 'by your leave' and they feel in their hearts that such activities must at all costs be stopped!

Conclusion

So there we are - 20 million or so listeners enjoy the offshore radio stations, and those who don't get excellent programmes of other kinds from the BBC. Why disturb a situation that is a very happy one from the listeners' angle? Why should the BBC listeners have to lose some of their present broadcasts to make way for 'pop' at the same time as the 'pop' brigade has to put up with a BBC substitute which they will regard as second best, while the older Radio 390 listeners lose their Cole Porter and Al Bowlly?

Faced with the problems of the defence of the pound, the balance of payments, Rhodesia, etc. are there not enough really important items well and truly on the Government's plate without using valuable Parliamentary time in an attempt to kill a few radio stations that bring a lot of pleasure to a great number of people without harming anyone?

In 1967 Mrs June Brooks was a housewife who had a young son, and devoted a fair amount of her day listening to the radio ships. June lived at York Gardens, Braintree, Essex, and, although has since moved house, still lives in the county.

It would appear that there are the millions of us still as anxious about the banning of the radio ships as there were, in fact, this time last year. Let's hope that 1967 will knock some common sense into the stubborn-minded men who kid themselves they are running this country, and in so doing imagine themselves to be correct in telling us what to tune into. Surely we have a right to decide for ourselves what to listen to or what not to listen to.

We already appear to be "dictated" to in everything possible, and can't help feeling that the Government has more than enough to do without interfering in what little pleasures there are left in life.

I am not a teenager but a mother with a son of school age, and I am not at all ashamed to let anyone know the difference that offshore radio has made to my life, and Radio London in particular.

It isn't the music alone that makes the so-called pirate ships so very popular, but the voices of the friendly disc jockeys who talk to us seemingly as individuals. Maybe it's only the housebound who can really appreciate that!

What was formerly a very dull routine day is now brightened by the spontaneous remarks of the disc jockeys. One might assume from some of the so-called politicians that there is some kind of crime attached to one's day being somewhat brightened.

The mere thought of having the BBC thrown at me again is repugnant with its petty mindedness and its varying reception in the east of England. Surely there is a lot they can do to please the few who, I suppose, still tune into them without pestering the lives out of the majority. When will they get into their thick skulls that we tune into the pirates all day and every day because they provide what we want, and we are willing to fight tooth and nail to see it stays that way.

In recent months my husband has replaced our outdated record player (he is also on my side!) and we have bought many more records than ever before which discounts the argument that pirate broadcasts reduce record sales. It strikes me all sorts of arguments are being put forward against the pirates mainly by jealous people who didn't think of the brilliant idea in the first place. I am, needless to say, very pleased that 1966 gave my husband and I the pleasure of meeting at least one pirate disc jockey - and the author of this book. Now we know he is a friendly person and not the "ogre" that some people would like us to believe!

From Lois Hollands, secretary of the Ray Conniff fan club. Lois lived at Hurst Road, Erith, Kent, but sadly died in the early 1970s.

When asked a question like "What has pirate radio given the British public?" one has to think before one speaks or writes.

Pirate radio is a thing which was badly needed in this country. The first thing that it did was to smash the monopoly of the BBC, the only national legal broadcasting service in Great Britain. The BBC did the best they could in broadcasting but there is still an impression of the Victorian era about it. Their DJs gave, and give, the impression of being distant, cold and stiff-upper-lip types, which is fine for those who like it. Mind you, the BBC DJs are trying to become more friendly. But the BBC is good for those who like it, and the commercial stations are fine for those who like them. If you don't like commercial stations, you just don't tune into them. This criteria applies equally to the BBC. If you don't like it, you don't have to tune into it. This is a matter of personal choice.

But commercial radio has proved that the majority of people want it. They cater for the young and the housewives, giving them the type of music that they want to hear during the day and night. For the young you have the Top 50 popular records, and for those who like the standard type of music you have Andy Williams, Tony Bennett and Frank Sinatra etc. This is the type of radio that was, and is, needed in this country. It has been proved by the support that the offshore or pirate stations have received over the years from the public. There is a great future in broadcasting in this country. Commercial radio has officially come to Britain, and we will, within two to four years, have local commercial stations. Of this I am sure, and it will be thanks to our first pioneers of commercial radio, the offshore radio stations, which arrived on the scene in early 1964. The offshore stations broke the barrier with the public. The DJs acted naturally; they were, and are, themselves when broadcasting to the listeners. If they want to act a little mad, shall we say, they will, but this zany type of presentation is just part of a DJ's personality and goes down very well with the listeners. Most of the offshore DJs have a friendly manner and are always bright and cheerful when doing a show, even though the listener might be feeling miserable. Sometimes the DJs feel just as miserable, but they don't let that come over on the air. They dare not do so as it is their job to make the listener feel happy. But this kind of free and easy presentation makes the listeners feel a part of the shows; they don't feel cut off from the DJs or the shows. A feeling of personal contact with the listeners by the DJs, and vice versa, is a very good thing for it helps make commercial radio, and it's that personal contact that will make commercial radio so popular and become a big thing in this country. The first offshore stations have met that demand. So far the Government has tried to stop these stations because they are illegal and are using the medium waveband without permission. There are just 10 stations amid over 200 on the Continent that are using the medium waveband without permission. I believe that the medium waveband has legally been allocated to just over 300 stations on the Continent and Europe and there are over 500 stations using it, so why try and knock out our 10 offshore stations? If the Government sink our stations first, then it is time someone sank the other 200 illegal users of the waveband.

Why shouldn't this country have commercial radio? It has worked well in America, Canada and Australia for years. We already have commercial television, so why not radio? It is about time this country got with it and up to date by legally giving the country what it wants i.e. **Commercial Radio.** As I've stated it will come to this country sooner or later - it is just a matter of time.

Miss Jacky Cargill was a typical teenage student who tuned into the pirates in the 1960s. Jacky lived at Norman Avenue, Wood Green, north London.

Pirate radio has done much for the British public. Firstly it has "brightened up" the rather staid BBC Light Programme and, to a certain extent, Home Service. Ex-pirates, such as Simon Dee and Chris Denning, have joined the Light Programme and have injected it with bounce and spontaneity that was previously missing.

Although there are no ex-pirates with the Home Service, the BBC have recently allowed this branch of their broadcasting organisation to be much more relaxed. I think the pirates have also encouraged longer broadcasting hours by the BBC. Many ex-pirate disc jockeys have also broadcast with Radio Luxembourg like Pete Brady, Dave Cash, Keith Skues, Mike Raven and Simon Dee, and they were probably the best disc jockeys who have ever been with the station.

Pirate radio has also introduced many new and good groups, singers and record labels including the Troggs, Spencer Davis Group, Who, Small Faces and Jonathan King - the list seems endless! This completely disagrees with the accusation that many large record companies have made against pirate radio that they have cut record sales. I entirely disagree with this statement because I work part-time in a Wood Green, London, record shop and people are always coming in and asking for records that are played by the pirates. Sometimes they merely ask for "No.15 in the Fab 40" or "No.20 on the Caroline Countdown" or "so and so's climber of the week." If anything, pirates have increased record sales.

The twenty-four hour stations supply music for all sorts of people throughout the British Isles. It is an asset to overnight drivers, nurses, late shift factory workers and also people coming home from late night parties! The various selection of pirate stations has also provided the kind of music that any age group would like to hear.

Clive Moore is a young man who lived in Woodbridge, Suffolk. He had been blind for many years and derived a lot of pleasure from offshore radio. In the 1960s Clive was a professional musician.

"It must be nearly teatime," I thought, gently touching the hands of my Braille watch. It was just after five o'clock on Friday, 27 March 1964; within seconds, I was to become one of the first listeners to what may well be the greatest radio adventure in my lifetime. There are always plenty of things for a blind person to do, particularly if, as in my case, he has received encouragement to be as independent as possible, and has no other limiting handicap. Our interests are almost as diverse as those found in the sighted world in which we live; yet whoever or whatever we may be, blind or sighted, our interests are governed by the environment in which we find ourselves. For most people, sight is the predominant sense; but for us, it's sound. It is not surprising, therefore, that radio plays a more or less important part in all our lives: listening to radio (or TV sound) is the only way in which we can independently keep up to date with the news, daily Braille newspapers being impracticable; and, of course, most of us like being entertained by drama, comedy, music and so on.

My interest in radio goes considerably deeper than this. I like to know what goes on behind the scenes - both in the broadcasting studios and at the transmitters. I also enjoy the sensation of being able to listen to the world: an amateur radio operator in Italy telling an English contact about his equipment and his home; a Radio Australia commentator talking about new agricultural techniques; and strange-sounding music from India, China - from anywhere and everywhere, in fact. I have a sort of mental diagram of many portions of the radio frequency spectrum, and I can travel along the dial fairly quickly and still detect anything unexpected on the band.

Which brings me back to that Friday afternoon, sitting in front of my receiver, idly wandering around the world, looking for nothing in particular, when suddenly, a tremendously powerful station just below 200 metres took me completely by surprise, and the living room shuddered momentarily to a booming bass voice singing "Big John - Big John - Big Bad John." What could this be? The record ended, and I waited hopefully for the announcement which didn't come. Instead, another record - *Wheels* played by the Stringalongs ... then another ... then, of all the infuriating things, at 5.15pm the transmitter closed down. I wasn't going out that evening, so I resolved to keep an ear on and about that frequency. My patience was rewarded at nine o'clock when, as well as hearing records, an unknown American voice kept cutting in with the names of artists and titles of songs being played, but still no station identification. For that, I had to wait until the next day, to hear that same voice announce for the very first time: "This is Radio Caroline, your all-day music station. The time is one minute past twelve" - actually it was nearer three minutes past, but those were pioneering days - "and this is Chris Moore inviting you to stay tuned to the programmes we have for you. We're playing the first record for Ronan, the man who made this station possible ..." And offshore radio was well and truly launched. After Chris Moore, there was a programme called *Soundtrack* introduced by a new DJ with a pleasing style, Simon Dee. He was followed at three o'clock by one Carl Conway, and the day closed with Chris Moore once again, this time introducing *The Big Line-Up.* As the days went by, I found myself spending a lot of time with this new station which was already causing quite a stir in official circles. There was something different about it: no, it wasn't the unrestricted needle time - if I wanted records all day I could go from AFN to Hilversum to the Light Programme to Radio Eireann; it was something much more subtle than that. "Big ship just coming by. Hang on, I'll go and have a look what it is ... Oh, I can't read the writing. I mean ... The writing! - you know what I mean: the name on the ship. Great big one. It's the ferry, I think, Harwich to Hook of Holland. Anyway, good afternoon to you" ... "By the way, you might like to know who's up and around on Caroline at this time of day, so I shall tell you. I am. So is Patrick - Patrick is the man who helps me present this programme in the morning, as I am quite unable to operate any form of electronic equipment at twenty-five past six in the morning; now for some strange reason the captain is up" ... "While that last record was playing, I rushed down to the library for a disc I meant to bring up to the studio with me" ... "I hope you'll forgive me if we hear a bit more of the theme, because I'm not quite ready yet... Sorry, be with you in just a moment"... "I've just grabbed a few letters that arrived on board about five minutes ago. Haven't had a chance to look at them yet, though. Let's see, who's this one from?" All that sort of patter seemed ordinary enough; then what was so special about it? Just the fact that it was ordinary, and that the programme material was flexible enough to allow a sudden change of plan to coincide with immediate requirements. Of course, some of the DJs were unable to cope with this style of broadcasting, but the others who were made a pleasant change from the scripted formality of - what phrase can I use to describe them? - the professional professionals. The BBC presented announcers talking to listeners: offshore radio presented people talking to their friends. As a result, I began writing to DJs and others connected with these stations, something I had never done before. As I made clear earlier, I didn't write because time hung heavily on my hands, nor because I felt lonely and in need of friendship. I wrote to these men just as I would have spoken to someone who had come over to me at a party and introduced himself: "I'm John Jones. Can I get you another drink?" "No thanks, not just at the moment. Marvellous party, isn't it?" "Yes, but I wish they hadn't asked the Smiths along." "Oh, I think they're all right. I've always got on very well with him, but I haven't met her."

Instead of which, the dialogue went something like this: "My name's Tom Wilson. Let me know if you'd like a request." "Dear Tom, although there's no record I particularly want to hear, I'd just like to say now much I'm enjoying your shows." "Thanks for the letter, Clive. Glad you're enjoying the programmes, and we'll play this record just for you." "Dear Tom, you rotter: I disliked that disc intensely. By the way, with reference to Jim's remark about" ... and so on.

And all the time, official opposition to these stations was mounting. I quickly realised that operation from international waters for an indefinite period was undesirable. For one thing, unqualified engineers might operate inadequate equipment, causing severe interference to other broadcast and point-to-point stations. If ever proof were needed of this fact, it was provided by Eric Sullivan's short-lived Tower Radio: the engineers responsible (or should I say irresponsible) apparently knew nothing of frequency stabilisation, nor harmonic suppression. There was also just a possibility that station owners and broadcasters might abuse their complete freedom by deliberately misinforming their listeners, either about current affairs or commercial products, or by presenting material which would not otherwise have been passed by the most broad-minded censor. Whilst bearing all this in mind, I appeared to be only one of many who enjoyed what they were giving us, and I could see no reason why the organisations could not immediately be brought ashore and made answerable to the Postmaster-General. Accusations against the pirates started coming in from various groups with vested interests. Some of them were so contradictory that they cancelled themselves out. I do not regard myself as a rebel, but I was so disgusted by officialdom's attitude that I resolved to do anything I legally could to help these stations survive.

This isn't the place to go deeply into my reasons for this decision; suffice it to say that if I were to set down my arguments here, you would probably think you were reading a transcript of one of Ted Allbeury's *Red Sands Rendezvous* broadcasts. I was annoyed by allegations of wavelength stealing, copyright stealing etc. etc. The pirates stole my sympathy, but as far as I could find out, most of them stole nothing else. But perhaps some of the things which chiefly annoyed me were incidents which didn't get much publicity. The GPO became spiteful and made itself look a little ridiculous. For instance, it would not allow the pirate radio ships radio-telephone links with the shore; this action seemed to cause the stations no desperate inconvenience, but the GPO undoubtedly lost a considerable amount of revenue. Then the Postmaster-General lashed out at Radio 390 in a manner which I consider was definitely below the belt. He prosecuted the station for illegal operation: fair enough, but here's the interesting point. For legal reasons, a date of broadcasting had to be specified, and the date chosen was 16 August 1966. This was just two days after a printed letter from the Postmaster-General had been read out over the air, together with Mr Allbeury's reply to the charges contained in it. Coincidence? The BBC too adopted some rather strange tactics. They refused to allow a Radio London disc jockey to take part in *Juke Box Jury,* stating that they were not having pirates on their programmes. Sure enough, a few months later, Gary Kemp was appearing in *Pop Inn* between spells on Britain Radio as Gordon Bennett! And surprise, surprise, Dominic Lefoe, of Radio 390's *Voice of Business* programmes appeared on the *Any Questions* team.

There was another powerful anti-pirate body whose activities affected me to a much greater degree: the Musicians' Union. I am a professional musician and M.U. member, yet my views were in direct conflict with the official union policy. Ironically, the advent of those pirates, who were supposed to deprive musicians of work, may have indirectly gained me more work! I learn by ear all the music I play; by their interesting presentation, the offshore stations made me listen more carefully to the latest tunes they were playing. I therefore had an up-to-date knowledge of a fairly wide sphere of music, and was better able to satisfy the customer's wishes. But it was not for any such reason that I opposed the union's views.

I could not, and do not, accept that these stations led to any loss of work for musicians: it may be worth mentioning here that, whilst this was the union's belief, it did not bring forward any substantiating evidence. In my opinion, the M.U. sought to protect the interests of its members (very right and proper) at the expense of the general public's wishes (very wrong and stupid). Any profession which does not take into account the public it serves is committing suicide. I fully realise my good fortune at being in regular employment and remember that better musicians are not so lucky; and I know that in my chosen occupation, I may be out of a job next year when one of this year's unlucky musicians takes my place. But all this has nothing to do with how many radio stations have unrestricted needle time.

The M.U. expressed itself against any form of commercial radio, apparently believing (a) that no stations would employ musicians if they were not forced to, and (b) that unrestricted needle time on the air would mean nothing but discs everywhere else. I do not accept either point. Once a station had become financially stable, I think it would wish to employ musicians ***provided that*** they gave a service which was not merely a duplication of a gramophone record: the BBC had the right idea with its *Late Live Show,* which was shelved when the GPO found itself unable to cope with the telephoned requests coming in from all over the country. I do not accept the second point for the obvious reason that musicians will always be wanted for dances, parties and other occasions, ***provided that*** they play what their public wants to hear. As far as I am aware, there was only one reason why the pirates did not employ musicians: incredible as it may seem, the officials who made up the executive committee of the union to which I belong - those very same men who hated the idea of unrestricted needle time - forbade us to perform for any of these organisations under any conditions whatever. Fortunately, some sanity still prevailed, and we were not given a list of tunes we shouldn't play because of their association with pirate radio. I was glad about this, since I realised the potential of a catchy little theme composed as a signature tune for Radio London: not only did I like the melody and the scope it gave for improvisation, but in August 1965 I had begun regular work at an Ipswich restaurant and was looking around for an intermission theme. Waiters and customers have come to know what to expect when I play that!

But the story doesn't end here. Some time ago, I had to fill in some programme return forms for the Performing Right Society: I have often wondered since whether the composer of a tune commissioned by one of the organisations accused of stealing other people's music has himself been paid the copyright fees due to him.

Another benefit the pirates brought me as a blind person may not be immediately understood without a few words of explanation. When you walk into a shop, you will, in all probability, quickly glance at the foods on display, noticing a different brand name or colour of packet; I can't do this. When stuck in a traffic jam, your bored gaze will be drawn to a huge poster advertising bargain offers at the store across the road: I can't see this. You probably look at a newspaper every day, perhaps grumbling at the amount of space devoted to advertising. A number of Braille periodicals are available to us, but Braille is much more bulky than letterpress and every page has to be used to the greatest possible advantage; besides which, it would not be commercially worth while advertising to such a small readership. Offshore radio introduced me to an enjoyable brand of cigarette of whose existence I was unaware and that's something I couldn't even have learned about from a television soundtrack any more. Quite apart from my own limited appreciation of the commercials, they must have come as a real godsend to many blind housewives on whom the burden of shopping must often fall very heavily. Whether or not offshore radio will have had any lasting influence on the future of British broadcasting depends largely on the attitude of people who don't get much time to listen anyway, and it's too early to draw any conclusions yet. Whatever the future may bring, I shall always be grateful to the pirates: not only for the reasons mentioned already, but also for the many memories which will, from time to time, give me a good laugh. I shall remember how the author of this book unknowingly (he assures me) got larger audiences than usual when he first joined Radio London due to the fact that on two occasions when he was broadcasting, his previous employer, Radio Caroline, had break downs and many listeners retuned. And talking of Caroline break downs, I shall remember the most unorthodox station identification uttered by Norman St. John when he believed the *Cheeta II's* transmitter to be off the air. I shall remember the night when I tuned in to Shivering Sands to hear Chris Cross and Paul Elvey trying to read messages being flashed to them in Morse from a car's headlights on shore: "I think that was p. Send it again ... yes, p. Go ahead ... i. Yes, got that: carry on ... was that an s? It was? ... Good ... Eh??? ... Send that again! ... I say, are you being rude?" I expect I shall remember, too, the names not only of the DJs but of the regular correspondents to the stations, names like Mildred Smith, George Hull, Vivien Barnard, Dallas Willcox - and many others whom I have never met, and perhaps never shall meet, but all of whom joined in making that special family radio atmosphere, the spirit of the pirates.

Commenting in 1993, Clive added: "Because of wider interests, I do not listen to radio as much as I used to, but I have maintained a general interest in what's going on where, and still listen with a critical ear. As I said, or implied all those years ago, I felt I knew the offshore presenters personally. I might like them or dislike them, laugh with them or at them, respect them or condemn them - but they were, almost without exception, real people being themselves (unless of course they were exceptionally talented actors, which I don't believe). The same feeling still comes across to me today with presenters on the smaller local stations, but I get different vibes from most of what I catch on the larger regional and national frequencies. Perhaps I haven't paid enough attention, but so many presenters, particularly on Radio 1, Virgin and Atlantic, either lack individual personalities or, more probably, are not allowed to display them. I'm sure programme controllers have done their market research well: there must be an audience of millions who want plastic people with stereotyped patter, filling each frenetic nanosecond with more music. Well, I can admire them, but that doesn't mean I want to live with them. Are these guys really the same away from the microphone? I doubt it. I suspect that one of the joys of working at sea was the knowledge that by the time your boss could get a message to you that you were fired, he would have cooled down and whatever broadcasting crime you had committed would have been forgotten. There may have been a few more grey-haired executives about, but I believe it made for more interesting radio."

Mrs Mildred Smith, mentioned in the previous letter, lived in Marilyn Crescent,

Birchington, Kent. Although she has changed address, she still lives in the same town.

Pirate radio has been with us so long now that it is very difficult to remember the dull dreary days before it came into being. To its many millions of listeners it has brought music, both pop and on the sweeter side, depending on their taste, and how wonderful it is to have that freedom of choice any time of the day or night.

It wasn't until competition from the pirates that the BBC started to broadcast until 2.00am, and prior to them it used to close down at midnight and one had no alternative but to listen to stations broadcasting from the Continent.

Pirate radio caters for all age groups bringing them what they want to hear when they want it. And what could be better than that?

To millions it means more than just music; to the housewife who is alone all day, and to so many others who are always alone, it brings friendly voices and cheerful humour. In other words companionship, so that they feel a lot less lonely - in this I speak from personal experience.

I feel I owe so much to pirate radio that I would like to relate just a little of what it has meant to me, a housewife alone all day; alone but seldom lonely!

I switch on my radio each morning knowing that I will hear "my kind of music" and hoping that some time or other during the day one of my favourite disc jockeys will be on ... for like many listeners I have favourites whose programmes I especially enjoy.

To me, even more important than the records is the humour, the unexpected remarks that have me chuckling away; it's the informality which makes it all so enjoyable.

I have been fortunate in having had countless requests played over the past years and I still get a kick out of hearing each one as it comes over the air; also there are the unexpected dedications which are such a lovely surprise. It's strange for one can be doing a routine task and then suddenly one's very own record is played. It cheers me up for a long time afterwards.

It is the "Dreaded Skues" (and pirate radio) that I have to thank for three new friends, although they are not so new now ... Elizabeth, a pen friend who lives too far away to meet; Margaret, who lives nearby and whom I see every week when we go shopping or visit each other, when we share many hours of companionship and laughter which would otherwise have been spent alone ... and finally there's Joan, who, since she first wrote to me over a year ago, has now become my best friend. Our letters to one another are so long they are almost like books and occasionally we are able to meet. By these friendships my life has been enriched and they have all been due to pirate radio!

I can't imagine my days without pirate radio, It has now become part of my life ... a friend that is always welcome in my home, as it is in so many others!

It seems to me that pirate radio has, by its tremendous success, proved that the demand for it by the British public exists, and along with so many others I hope that it may long continue to fill that demand.

In 1967 Alan Ross was a schoolboy in Woodford Green, Essex. His ambition was to become a disc jockey, but he was too young to join the pirates in the mid-1960s. He did achieve his ambition in 1979 when he joined Pennine Radio in Bradford. After presenting shows on DevonAir Radio and CBC, Cardiff, he went to Humberside as programme controller of Viking Gold (1988) and, later, Pennine Radio (1990). Today he is a freelance broadcaster and lecturer and lives in West Yorkshire.

Talking of the pirates, which (sorry, Keith) we WERE ... I guess a whole generation of broadcasters has been inspired by the antics off the shores of England. My father is responsible for setting the pattern of my life when he asked me in Spring '64, "Have you heard this radio station that's on a boat?" I was eleven, and although I had enjoyed getting my first radio many years previously, I'd abandoned it for the joys of my "Elizabethan Pop 10 record changer" since the BBC hardly played any pop music at all.

I think it's impossible for today's teenagers to understand what an impact the 64-67 pirates made on us. Radio Caroline was quickly superseded in my affections by Radio Atlanta - which cheekily waited until Caroline closed each night (at 6.00pm!) and then tested on their frequency. When Atlanta and Caroline merged I was incensed, and listened to Caroline under sufferance until Christmas 1964 when something utterly wonderful and mind-blowing appeared on 266 metres.

Radio London or The Big L was perfect for its time ... a masterpiece of formatting that blew everything else off the radio dial for its $2^{2/3}$ years of life as far as I and millions of others were concerned.

Jingles are taken for granted now - but in 1964 we'd never heard PAMS jingles, let alone electronic Sonovox voices singing about "Funnnnnnnn!!!" I spent four weeks listening to Big L before I realised that the jingle didn't sing "It's just great ... for FARMERS!!!"

A quick mixed bag of memories - maybe others will remember these too!! Garner Ted Armstrong & *The World Tomorrow* from the improbably-named Radio Church of God, assuring us that "your subscription has ALREADY been paid!!!"... Mayfair 5361 ... *The Fab 40 Show* where the Radio London Club Disc of the Week was always played just before the No.1 ... the chart where a record could be No.1 one week, and No.24 the next ... one week it had 59 records in it... (payola??? perish the thought!!!) ... Kenny and Cash ... the Kenny Everett promotion for daytime programmes that had "I love Caroline on 199 your all day music station" spoken backwards in it!!! The Double D from 12.00 noon to 3.00pm ... Paul Kaye ... REPORTING!!!! ... *Big Lil* the station theme, which I discovered years later is actually called *The PAMS Sono-waltz*!!!! and *The London Song*, which had three verses, ending with *London ... that's my home town* sung in an American accent! ... the *Juicy Fruit Show ...* and *Call in at Currys,* which had the Seeburg jukebox with a hundred buttons, a hundred prizes ... and the *Oxo Show* where Katie pretended to go out to the ship twice a week to make everyone delicious nutritious meals with that elusive "Man Appeal!!!!" ... and Tony Windsor ... TW ... who was profoundly influential, and sadly never made it on the mainland ... 14 August 1967 made me, at 14, angrier than I'd ever been about anything before or since. We were on holiday in Bournemouth, and I could just hear the last hour of BIG L, through a wall of static, in my father's car where I sat for an hour, not believing this could be happening. When the carrier went off, I did something no self respecting 14-year-old male ever does - I burst into tears and was inconsolable all day. I later learned that in the heart of what I saw as the "enemy", Broadcasting House, other grown people were doing exactly the same!!! My mother, bless her, in an attempt to make me feel better, told me brightly to cheer up, "because the BBC are starting a pop service soon!!!!" It remains the one and only time I've ever sworn and thrown something at her!!! It was the day I KNEW I had to get into commercial radio, once we'd got it legalised!

In 1989, while running and programming Classic Gold, the Yorkshire AM oldies station, I had the unusual task of "controlling" the author of this book. I can report that Keith has lost nothing of the rebellious and quirky qualities I admired so much back then. I know we both enjoyed bringing back the magic of the pirates to an audience which loved them so much ... when we brought the original jingles back, resung by some of the original singers, the audience response was phenomenal. And ... even more pleasing, in a way ... people too young to remember the era loved it as well!!!

The next letter was written in February 1967 by Mrs Janet Ashton, who lived in Onslow

Village, near Guildford, Surrey. Now Mrs Jan Smith, she lives in Woking.

So it is the Government's intention to stop the pirate radio stations broadcasting.

What a pity that in this tired old country of ours they cannot do something for the public instead of going against the wishes of millions!

The pirates provide harmless entertainment for their listeners. They have helped many new groups and personalities along the road to success. Without the pirates it will be much more difficult for new talent to be heard and recognised. How many times have you heard a new release played for the very first time and hated it; but on subsequent hearings found yourself liking it, humming it and then buying it?

What chance would a newcomer have if his record were merely played once, then pushed aside because it didn't have "first play" impact?

If the Government succeeds in sinking the pirates, then the proposed successor to them will not give new artists the opportunities afforded at the present time.

It is foolish of the Government to offer present pirate listeners a second-rate replacement run by the BBC which will play a specified mixture of pop records and 'live' music. The programmes, no doubt, will be presented by "scripted" 'plum-in-the-mouth' old-fashioned so-called disc jockeys.

It has been stressed that no legal land-based radio station would be permitted to play pop records virtually all the time as the pirates do. Not permitted by the Musicians' Union? They have been against the pirate radio stations since they started, convinced that continuous record programmes would kill 'live' music. The pirates have been going strong for three years, and the call for 'live' musicians has not died a death yet! In fact the pirates are responsible for giving the music world the shot in the arm it needed. The Musicians' Union should step out of its dusty drawing room atmosphere and willingly accept the youth and new trends within its ranks.

Wouldn't it be nice if, instead of screaming "illegal" at the pirates, the Government could legalise commercial radio? The Chancellor could then arrange to dip his hands into the profits and maybe get enough money to prevent further increases in the price of radio and television licences.

If the pirates **must** go, then the best of the pirate disc jockeys should be assured that jobs will be made available to them in future broadcasting. Many of them are first class disc jockeys with personality plus who work in cramped and often uncomfortable conditions to give the public the music they want to hear.

I am disgusted by the Government's attitude, not only to commercial radio but also to commercial television, which has been refused permission to open a second channel or venture into the realms of colour television.

The Government's refusal to allow the pirates to be legalised and ITV to go ahead merely pinpoints their obvious fear of competition. Without this vital competition the public will be left with the dull BBC monopoly in radio, and without the obvious **need** for continuous record programmes being fulfilled.

In 1967 the ambition of our next listener, Roger Faulkener, was to become a disc jockey. He then lived at Duchess Road, Bedford and wrote:

A 780-ton vessel anchored three miles off the coast of Harwich. She was equipped with a 200ft. aerial mast and a 10 kilowatt transmitter. This was the start of a new concept in the form of commercial radio. Shortly afterwards another ship appeared with a more powerful transmitter and much newer ideas until finally ten stations were born.

The newspapers branded them with the name of pirates as they were illegally broadcasting. Headlines read "Offshore Pirate Network", "Pop Pirates Claim 10,000,000 listeners", "Are the Pop Pirates Here to Stay?"

The Postmaster-General could not wait to evict these intruders from the wavelengths that they had chosen after exhaustive tests. It was brought to my notice that several stations in their struggle for existence had applied to the Postmaster-General for licences and frequencies that would not interfere with shipping bands. But the Government did not make any attempt to further this matter. Instead they pushed the matter onto one man's desk who wouldn't even attempt to give the British public the right to request what they wanted.

I am quite sure the public are sick and tired with the way the BBC conducts its broadcasts which, to my mind, had far too much to say in communication regulations and the such. The BBC are so stiff and starchy I feel sure people do not want a formal introduction to the day. Keep the pirates and this will not happen!

There have been arguments time after time by the Performing Right Society saying that pop pirates do not pay royalties on discs played over the air. This is not true. Radio London, for one, pays more royalties than its fair share, I might add.

Why was it necessary to take the law into one's own hands and transmit programmes everyone enjoys? It's because the BBC has for far too long had no opposition; the British Government has had too many fluctuations and changes in policy and has not given the public the choice of what they want, instead leaving it to the Postmaster-General.

If one particular station can have a daily audience of 12,000,000 Britons and another 2,000,000 on the Continent who are not able to speak English, then this station is not only fantastic but élite!

The so-called pirates have organised social functions such as discotheques, clubs, parties, not to mention numerous offers such as cut-price radios and opportunities to drive racing cars etc. The BBC or Radio Luxembourg have never offered the latter. Agreed, the commercial network does not do this without making a profit, but does anyone nowadays run a business without a profit in mind? The BBC manage to find themselves in debt every year!

I myself would like to become a disc jockey on a pirate station. I get a great kick out of making people happy and being informal, but if the Government get their way, there will be a lot of angry people about including myself.

The United States of America has no fewer than 350 commercial radio stations; Australia has just over 200 and is planning a lot more. Britain has twelve and we are told they are illegal. My cry is Britain NEEDS commercial radio.

Our next letter comes from Dallas Willcox of Gorse Lane, Tiptree, Essex, who was at school in 1967 studying for his GCE.

Right from the outset, in March 1964, some members of the community resolved that commercial radio was not needed in Great Britain. They declared that such radio stations could not possibly be successful and that they would only be a complete menace. These people, although they may still refuse to accept the facts, have now been proved very wrong in their beliefs; commercial radio IS needed and it IS successful. What is more, commercial radio is very beneficial to Great Britain.

These benefits are too numerous to mention in their entirety, but I would like to outline those that come immediately to mind.

Independent radio has provided an additional large-scale advertising medium through which a message can reach thousands of people at a relatively low cost. This extra medium of advertising helps to stimulate trade within the community.

Through commercial radio stations, unknown talented persons are given the opportunity to become famous. This applies to disc jockeys as well as recording artists. These radio stations have provided employment for many people. Work has been found not only for disc jockeys but also for the large number of workers in the administration offices of each station.

Since Easter 1964, commercial radio has been a great help to many well-known charities by broadcasting appeals free of charge. It has also helped many religious bodies to spread the gospel throughout the nation.

Independent stations have also increased the sales of radio sets, especially transistors. Many people, particularly teenagers, never considered owning a transistor radio until the pirates arrived on the scene.

Another aspect worth remembering is that commercial radio increases the country's revenue, indirectly. Thousands of letters per week flood into the offices of the offshore radio stations at present operating around Britain's coasts. Each one of these letters bears a postage stamp (or should do!), and the revenue from the purchase of stamps benefits the Exchequer.

Above all, commercial radio has supplied Great Britain with the type of entertainment it was seriously lacking. It is also important to note that it has done this at no direct cost to the ratepayer.

In conclusion, I would like to make an appeal to any Postmasters-General who may be reading this book: please avoid sending Mr Skues to gaol for writing about the pirates - the country would have to pay!

Christopher John Minter was better known through the radio scene as Chris Cortez. He has lived in and around Cambridge all his life.

"What's the panic?" I asked myself, as through the window of my home in Trumpington, near Cambridge, I observed my friend Mike Pittock leap from his bicycle and run towards the kitchen door. "Hey Chris, have you heard this new station, Radio Caroline?" asked Mike as he entered the lounge. "No! What's its wavelength?" I replied. "It's on 199 metres, plays music all day long and it broadcasts from a ship at sea." "From a ship?" I exclaimed. "You best help me find it on my radio."

Thus it was a couple of days after Easter 1964 that I heard Radio Caroline for the first time and became a fan, which I remain to this day. However, as someone once said: "With Radio Caroline you don't just remain a fan or a listener, you become actively involved." This is certainly true in my case as Radio Caroline has now been a major part of my life for nearly 30 years. Offshore radio in general, and Radio Caroline in particular, has given me my understanding of corrupt politics and big business, plus my love of the freedom of the individual and of most types of music. Today I look back fondly at the Sixties' golden era of music radio when the offshore stations provided choice and music to suit every taste. What has gone wrong with modern commercial radio? Seems it took a wrong turn somewhere along the road! It has become fashionable to blame all the ills of modern society on the Sixties. I don't subscribe to this theory, The Sixties were simpler, happier and more freedom-loving times, when the politicians at first allowed the British people to work and play hard. I'm convinced that the whole swinging scene of a music, fashion, etc., explosion which engulfed the country and attracted valuable foreign currency, would NOT have been so big or successful without the so-called 'radio pirates.'

Back in the 'Sixties my radio was always with me, at work and at play. In 1964 my job was at Haverhill in Suffolk and I followed a very democratic listening policy whilst working. One day my Marconiphone pocket transistor radio would be tuned to Radio Caroline and the next day it would be tuned to Radio Atlanta. During my lunch breaks I would walk along Haverhill High Street and visit the market. I did not need my radio because every market stall had one blasting out music! Most of them were tuned to Radio Caroline, it must be said.

July 1964 saw me on holiday in West Sussex, munching my way through a typically British fry-up in a typically British greasy spoon 'caff'. On the café wall, sitting on a fly-ridden shelf, was an old valve radio in its wooden cabinet. From this radio came forth the amazingly clear sound of Radio Caroline. I was not to hear a clearer sound from an offshore station until some considerable time later when an almost 'VHF-like' (FM-like) Radio 390 came from my tranny during a visit to Hull! After what seemed like ages ... a coffee and a heavy fry-up could never be hurried ... in the café at Wick, near Littlehampton (no it was NOT my home!), a crowd of people rushed past down the street. I opened the cafe door, stepped outside and grabbed one guy by the arm, speaking as I did so. "Excuse me, mate. Where's the fire?" "No fire," came his reply. "It's Radio Caroline off the seafront now. Her ship is a few miles out and visibility isn't too good right now, but we might be able to see her." Soon I was with everybody else on Littlehampton seafront. I could not see Radio Caroline, but I could certainly hear her on my tranny and everybody else's! So it was that I happened to be on the south coast of England on the day that the m.v. *Caroline* sailed past en route to the Isle of Man. Since that day I have managed to obtain high quality tape recordings of transmissions from many parts of that voyage, but sadly not the portion from Brighton to Bognor Regis. My home location of Trumpington in East Anglia proved to be an ideal one for listening to the offshore stations in the 'Sixties. The powerful broadcasters, Caroline, London, England/Britain were receivable loud and clear most of the time, as indeed were Radios City and 390 with their superb aerial masts atop the Thames Estuary forts. The less powerful stations came in quite well too, thanks to the help of an aerial wire slung across the roof of my home. Radio 270 blasted in during daylight and darkness thanks to the watery path its signal was lucky to follow straight down the North Sea to the Wash and across the fens to Cambridge. Radio Scotland was only receivable well during the hours of darkness and even then with some Luxy-style fading. No such problems for Radio Caroline North which came in well day and night and absolutely thumped in when I utilised my 'special' aerial. In my garden was a 405 line television receiving aerial atop a very tall metal pole. When I connected any of my radios to either the metal pole or the TV co-ax downlead, it was a case of 'Whammo!' My 'special' aerial was not needed to listen to KING Radio, a fort-based station with a simple but amazingly effective transmission aerial. How well I remember sitting alongside the Cambridge-Bedford railway line, which ran next to my garden, with my tranny tuned to KING Radio. A loop-tape message was being broadcast inviting listeners to retune to the new and solid signal of Radio 390. A copy of this loop-tape now resides in my tape archive.

I loved the 'Sixties offshore stations because they answered your requests, took notice of what you said and played every type of music. Certainly they were and still are responsible for my wide and varying musical tastes. The memories come flooding back as if it were only yesterday that such good radio existed ... the *Caroline Club Request Hour* in the early evenings. I joined the Caroline Club and received my little blue membership card, plus my silver Caroline Bell pin badge ... the multi lingual Gary Kemp on *Caroline Continental* each Sunday morning ... country and western music programmes from the *Laissez-Faire* ... Tom Edwards with the smooth music of Radio City's *Late Date* show ... the legendary Tony Windsor as Tony Withers on Radio Atlanta ... *The Big Line Up* with a young Tony Blackburn on Radio Caroline South ... *Mike Raven's R'n'B Show* on Radio 390. A million thanks, Mike, for introducing me to obscure early rock 'n' roll and for fostering my interest in R 'n' B and the blues ... the *Jack Spector Show* from New York City on Radio Caroline ... *The Roman Empire* with Mark Roman on Big L. Why did it take so long to get rid of the night-time hetrodyne whistle on the station's signal by simply obtaining an on-channel crystal for the transmitter? ... the *Midnite Surf Party* with Jim Murphy on Radio Caroline North. The music selection was so awful, this programme became unmissable! ... Steve Young's *Nite Trip Show* with 'The Curly Headed Kid in the Third Row' on Radio Caroline South ... *The Ten Ton Yellow Mustard Seed* presented by Glenn Adams on Radio Caroline South. Eat your heart out, John Peel, in your perfumed garden! ... *Let's Motor with Moss...* Silexene Paints ... Pete Murray with the *Currys Show...* truly I could go on forever!

My usual routine in the 'Sixties was to allow my choice of radio listening to be dictated by my mood or the time of day. Caroline or Big L kept me up to date with the latest sounds, when I was feeling lively. Radio 390 helped relax me whenever I was tired and stressed. How strange it is that, even today, there is still no national radio station in the United Kingdom with a Radio 390 or Britain Radio format? Radio City, the great family station so badly affected by the more unsavoury elements of Caroline and London, never failed to cheer me up whenever I was feeling depressed. Radio Essex and the other small stations gave me the real taste of local radio, long before that wretched and overused word 'community' rose to the fore. Many different upbeat breakfast shows got me up and off to work in the mornings. The specialist music shows educated me during the early evenings. Thank God those were the days of knowledgeable DJs and not boring presenters! Johnnie Walker entertained me on Radio Caroline South late evenings and Tom Edwards on Radio City helped me to unwind at the end of each day. My routine continued unaltered until 1967 when civil servants and politicians forced various modifications! At least the two Radio Caroline International ships kept the good radio flag flying after 14 August. Then came that tragic day on 3 March 1968 when they were hijacked and towed away to Holland. On the evening of 2 March 1968 I listened as usual to Radio Caroline International (South). Among the records I recall hearing during that final evening are: *If I Had a Ribbon Bow* by Fairport Convention; *Love is Blue* by Jeff Beck, *I'll Walk Alone* by Maggie Fitzgibbon and *Legend of Xanadu* by Dave Dee, Dozy, Beaky, Mick and Tich. The next morning silence reigned on my radio as I could find no trace of the North and South Caroline ships. One day later I was awoken by my father throwing the daily newspaper containing the story of the towaway onto my bed. "It's all over," he said. How wrong he was! Today, as I conclude these writings especially compiled for one Cardboard Shoes, ... who doesn't want his name mentioned! ... it is September 1993 and a lot of water has flowed under the proverbial bridge. Since 1972 when I found myself aboard the *Mi Amigo* in Holland, just a few weeks prior to her voyage into the North Sea to return Radio Caroline to the airwaves, I have been an 'active' member of the Caroline family. However, as I am a bit too old to start a new career of sewing mailbags and a new diet of porridge, that is a story which will have to remain untold ... at least for the time being!

At present the world's most famous radio station, Radio Caroline, is silent. After nearly 27 amazing years of broadcasting, she went off-air in November 1990, the sad victim of a potent mixture of dark deeds, stupidity, bad management and bad luck. She will return one day, make no mistake about that. Her famous free sound will be heard again. Radio Brod (on a ship) co-financed by the British Government, currently broadcasting from the radioship *Droit de Parole* anchored in the Adriatic, driving a coach and horses through the highly suspect U.K. Broadcasting Act 1990 and setting a classic legal precedent as well, guarantees it. Judging by the sorry states of music, record and radio industries, that day cannot come a moment too soon.

The final letter comes from Mrs Barbara Apostolides of Rush Green, Romford, Essex, who is a housewife. She is married to a company director and in 1967 had two young children. The children have now grown up and gone their own ways, but Barbara still lives in Rush Green. She makes a comparison between the pirates and Radio 1, the BBC's pop channel, after the latter had been broadcasting for six months:

The main and most important thing pirate radio gave the British public was freedom of choice. Prior to those enterprising and much needed stations, there had only been the BBC. Although they provided light entertainment, news, views, educational programmes and a wide coverage of music ... something was missing. This something was obviously felt by the public for within three weeks of broadcasting the first offshore station was able to claim a listening audience of several million.

The basic idea behind the new Radio 1 is great. It could fill the gap left by the offshore stations. It could provide happy, cheerful music. It could give its listeners the zany, casual approach that won the pirates so many fans. It could ... but it doesn't.

The reason that it does not lies in the production ... invisible whips crack and control; one can almost hear producers consulting their stopwatches, timing every gag, message and breath the DJs take. Obviously there are problems and teething troubles in running a new radio station. One example is the Musicians' Union which forbids the continual playing of records ... fair enough, this obviously poses problems ... but does not explain why the controller of this station gives us the programmes he does. Nor does it explain his choice of compères. One wonders if he ran his auditions on Army lines ... ("Who was formerly a cook? Right, from now on you'll be the electrician" type of thing) for we have some of the brightest personalities broadcasting for two hours a week, while others drag on day after day saying nothing new and playing the same material. The old BBC image still lurks just around the corner. Radio 1 is not the new sapling we were promised ... just another branch of a very well rooted tree.

As a Mrs Woman (a name given to housewives by one of the DJs) I listened to the offshore stations because I enjoyed not only the music but also the informal atmosphere. One was aware that the choice of record and presentation of the programme was being aired for us, their listeners. Unlike other stations whose programmes, music, records and, one suspects, ad libs are planned weeks ahead ... giving the impression that they are broadcasting because that is their job, not because they have a public.

On the commercial channels many a dull day was enlivened by scatty advertisements and the remarks of the disc jockeys. Simple remarks such as "look what the silly twit has done now" ... or ..."there's water all over the place" took on great importance when they coincided with events in one's own home. An example of this was the day my two children went to school in fits of laughter, for as I plugged the toaster into the same point as the radio, the DJ said "gosh it's getting hot in this studio" ... a pointless remark, but in our case hilarious.

This informality was obviously appreciated by many, for making up the millions of regular listeners were people from all walks of life ... old folk ... young children ... hospital nurses and patients ... housewives and so on. Lorry drivers, milkmen, refuse collectors, even the occasional policeman found himself in favour of the offshore stations. These stations gave their public something that couldn't be taxed or monopolised. A happy, sunny outlook, friendship, and above all the freedom to choose. The choice of the British public was, and is, evident... to support commercial radio officially.

Commenting in 1993, Barbara says: "Regarding my observations in paragraphs 3 and 4 above, I believe those comments are more to the point now than when I made them. Maybe we've outgrown the really trivial comments from our presenters, but the informality was, and is, very important. I do wish that the powers-that-be would choose their presenters with care, then allow them to do just that ... present THEIR programme in THEIR allotted time. That way, we may again receive programmes of an hour, preferably three, of varied music, chat, discussion and listener participation. Not an hour of Willie Bloggs presents Willie Bloggs on the Willie Bloggs hour!

Chapter Ten

PAINT IT BLACK

I fought the law ... and the law won!

I Fought the Law, Bobby Fuller Four, 1966

THE GOVERNMENT planned to starve out the pirates by agreement with European countries, it was announced on 29 December 1964. The Postmaster-General, Tony Benn, said that he would try and arrange for legislation to be introduced into Parliament's heavy timetable as soon as possible. The stations to be affected would be Radio Caroline North and South, Radio London, Radio Invicta and Radio City.

On 20 January 1965 an agreement aimed at silencing the offshore stations was laid down for signing at a meeting of the European Parliament in Strasbourg. It pledged to prosecute all those supplying pirate stations with food, broadcasting tapes, records or maintenance equipment.

Britain, Belgium, Denmark, France, Greece and Sweden signed the agreement on 23 January 1965. But the following month an amendment was made to the agreement stating that action would only be taken when such broadcasting interfered with available frequencies, not the 'vested interests in broadcasting by the State or any other monopoly.' The Liberal barrister, 73-year-old Lord Grantchester, was the British representative at the 'signing.'

Prior to this amendment, out of the committee of seventeen three members voted against the resolution and three abstained. Several countries were concerned lest the agreement should be used to bolster state monopolies. Another objection was that it would endanger traditional freedom of the seas. It was these objections that were instrumental in securing the above amendment.

In the House of Commons on 4 February, Eldon Griffiths (Conservative, Bury St. Edmunds), asked the Postmaster-General what plans he now had for suppressing the pirates. Mr Benn said that this country had now signed the Council of Europe agreement.

Peter Forbes, writing for *The People* on 7 February 1965, made headlines in the paper "All Clear For Caroline."

"This is excellent news for millions of British pop fans. For the way is now clear for pirates like Radio Caroline and Radio London to carry on broadcasting provided they are careful not to jam or disturb normal services."

The International Telecommunications Union, which allocated the various wavelengths for stations to operate throughout the world, said its job would be even more complex. It was up to member nations of the Council of Europe to introduce their own legislation.

But the British Government was preparing its own legislation on the grounds that the stations *were* interfering with sea communications, and some broadcasting.

Mr Benn told Mrs Renée Short in the House of Commons on 4 March 1965 that legislation would be introduced as *soon* as was practicable.

Later in the month (22nd) Sir Knox Cunningham asked the Postmaster-General to give a list of the dates and the places where danger to shipping had resulted from broadcasts from the pirates. Replying. Tony Benn listed the instances.

RADIO CAROLINE
29 March 1964   South-east coast generally
1 April 1964 - 13 July 1964   Antwerp area.
2 April 1964   Essex coast

9	June 1964	Essex coast
11	June 1964	South-east coast generally
31	August 1964	Irish Sea
15-25	November 1964	Irish Sea

FROM OTHER PIRATE RADIO STATIONS

12	January 1965	North of Scotland
13	January 1965	Netherlands
13	January 1965	Kent Coast
14	January 1965	Netherlands
14	January 1965	East coast of Ireland
19	January 1965	Bristol Channel
19	January 1965	Kent Coast
20	January 1965	Germany
22	January 1965	North of Scotland
4	February 1965	Thames Estuary
23	February 1965	Pembrokeshire
16	March 1965	Netherlands

Mr Benn went on:

"Many of these complaints were of a routine nature, but the interruptions between ships and the shore constitute a danger to shipping. This was illustrated by the incident on 23 February last when a lightship was prevented for about 30 minutes from passing on an urgent message to the shore because both frequencies available were blocked, one of them by a pirate broadcasting station."

In a debate on broadcasting on 13 May 1965 in the House of Commons, the first since the Pilkington Report in 1962, Christopher Rowland (Labour, Meriden, a former talks producer with BBC Overseas Service 1954 - 1959), asked Sir Peter Rawlinson, Opposition spokesman for Broadcasting, "What local need has been shown to be served by Radio Caroline?"

He replied: "I am told there is a considerable and even extensive liking for this kind of programme." Bernard Floud (Labour, Acton), then asked Sir Peter if he was trying to claim that Radio Caroline was a local broadcasting station?

"I was saying that Radio Caroline shows that there is a liking for this kind of music and an audience for it should not be written off and ignored. My proposal for sound broadcasting is that there should be low-power transmissions of a local nature which should not be a burden on the licence holders, and therefore not a burden on the licence payers."

Mr Benn said in the debate that "Whatever future there may be for local sound broadcasting in this country the pirate radios have no part in it. These stations, which started last year, were designed to force the hand of this Parliament on the future development of sound radio. That has been made crystal clear many times. As I have said time and time again in the House the stealing of copyright, the endangering of the livelihood of musicians, the appropriation of wavelengths, the interference with foreign stations, the danger to shipping and ship-to-shore radio make the pirates a menace. This led the previous Government, like ourselves, to seek to negotiate with European countries a convention which would eliminate the pirates altogether. We shall certainly follow this through. The pirate stations have no future whatever in the future development of broadcasting in this country or Europe. It is sometimes said there is undoubted public demand for light music programmes through the day. It is also sometimes said that this demand has been produced by the pirate radios, but I suspect that it has always existed."

The debate continued when the Postmaster-General said: "It would be an appalling waste of the potentialities of local radio to have a multiplicity of 'pop' stations duplicating each other in different areas. In any case, neither the record companies nor the musicians could possibly tolerate the unlimited 'needle time' which would absolutely destroy the livelihood of the one and the business of the other, which, in the case of the record companies, includes a substantial export business.

"Local VHF 'pop' stations could not even be received by the 'transistor' audience who buy cheap transistor sets which are capable of receiving only the medium wave band. Therefore any idea that there is a relationship between the demand which the pirates may have revealed - and the future of local sound broadcasting in this country seems to me to be an illusion."

Sir Ian Orr-Ewing (Conservative, Hendon North) suggested that, during the daytime when there was no interference with Continental stations, the local stations could use the medium wave frequencies without interference or trouble; this had been done by the pirate stations. Mr Benn said "The pirate stations are interfering with other countries' reception, and the development of a really serious pattern of local sound stations in this country depends upon the use of VHF which makes a great number of channels available.

"What in fact is a true definition of local broadcasting is contained in the Pilkington Report of 1962 and states:

We distinguish at once between two possible definitions of local broadcasting. In one 'local' means only that a large number of stations would each serve a small area. In the other 'local' means that the material broadcast would, for a sufficient part of the broadcasting day, be of particular interest to the locality served by that station rather than to other localities. It seems to us that, if the word 'local' in the expression 'local sound broadcasting' is really to mean what it implies, the second of the two definitions is the right one.

"The BBC estimated that the capital cost of a local station would be about £35,000. On the other hand, Pye of Cambridge in their handout booklet say that such a station would be around £20,000.

"Various estimates have been made of the number of staff who would be required on each station - an average figure would be twelve."

T.G. Boston (Labour, Faversham) added:

"It is important to put on record the ways in which local broadcasting could be of help to communities. For instance, it would be of great value in reflecting local events - sporting events and social events of various types. Local broadcasting would be of particular value to a whole range of organisations, local universities, colleges and schools who would no doubt wish to contribute. There could be broadcasts of local church services. Hospitals could take part with messages to patients being broadcast, and with special request programmes for local hospitals. There could be special weather reports specially designed for the farming community. There could be special reports for holiday makers and local shopping advice could be broadcast. Clubs and societies, drama and operatic groups, for example could take part. No doubt pop groups would be encouraged by this type of broadcasting.

"One would think that news would play an important part. Local emergency announcements and local police messages could serve an important local need. Information about local traffic conditions could be broadcast."

Mr Boston then tackled the subject of local papers applying for licences. He said "There is a great danger that, if the stations were run commercially, this might endanger local newspapers. It depends on how the stations are run. The great danger which local newspapers would face, if the stations were run commercially, is that they would siphon off much of the local advertising revenue from local newspapers."

During the same debate on broadcasting on 13 May an MP was rebuked for listening to the pirates.

Postmaster-General Tony Benn repeated that legislation would be introduced to deal with the problem of pirate stations.

Richard Crawshaw, (Labour, Toxteth) said "Many people, including myself, receive a certain amount of welcome relaxation by listening to these stations."

Mr Benn replied "Though I understand your point of view, I am sure that you would not really derive any satisfaction from listening to a pirate station if you contemplated, as you should, that this is stolen copyright. It prevents other countries from listening to their radio

Above: Harold Wilson, Prime Minister when the Marine, Etc., Broadcasting (Offences) Bill was introduced into Parliament, 1966

Below: Tony Benn, as Postmaster-General, in 1965. He introduced the legislation to oulaw the pirates

stations because it is a breach of the Copenhagen Agreement and this is not the way to meet a need however great."

On 14 May 1965 it was announced that the Cabinet had decided to crush the pirates. Ministers had drawn up a plan to stop illegal broadcasting from ships and forts off the British coastlines.

Mr Benn said the pirates had no future, but he didn't give any details about what the Government would do. He agreed there was a demand for light music throughout the day and that this demand could only be met economically by use of a national wavelength.

Mr Benn repeated that there was no future for the pirates and that legislation would be introduced as soon as was practicable. He did this in the House of Commons on 30 June 1965 and again on 28 July 1965, 4 August 1965 and 27 October 1965.

On 3 December 1965 the London *Evening Standard* carried the headline "Carry on Caroline!" All other national newspapers carried the story the following day.

The various offshore stations had been given a temporary reprieve for at least twelve months. Government experts examining the future of broadcasting decided it was difficult at that stage to introduce legislation and stop their programmes.

The pirate stations were delighted with the news. Philip Birch, managing director of Radio London, said "The Government seems to have recognised that it can't simply take away a service from such big audiences."

Mr Benn scotched all rumours that the Government was to licence the pirate stations. "There is no truth whatsoever in stories that the Government has decided to licence pirate stations and permit them to provide commercial sound radio from the mainland."

The Musicians' Union added: "We do not see the Government agreeing to commercial radio in this country, so there would be no problem of needle time arising."

On 8 December 1965 the Postmaster-General Tony Benn said that legislation was being prepared that would outlaw the stations from operating outside the three-mile limit. Pirate stations transmitting from inside the limit would be prosecuted under the Wireless Telegraphy Act and could be fined up to £100 and individuals sent to prison for up to three months. He went on "Prosecutions under the law can take place quickly. This is a reminder of the position - and I don't feel we will have to give any warning of prosecution."

The aim of the Bill that was being drawn up was to stop ships from being maintained and supplied, and to ban firms from advertising with them.

Commenting, Radio Caroline said:

Not only does the Postmaster-General use false reasons against us, but contrary to his statement we do pay copyright in the form of Performing Right Society payments covering every day of broadcasting. Moreover he seems to be at loggerheads with the Prime Minister who, on 12 November, considered using our experience for broadcasting to the Rhodesian people. There is nothing recorded of us ever endangering life. We employ skilled engineers to prevent this happening, and far from it, we have actually saved life at sea.

Robert Pitman, writing in the *Daily Express* on 15 December 1965, said:

There is no need for new laws if Mr Benn, the Postmaster-General, really wants to crush the radio pirates. All he needs is a new man to replace Sir Hugh Greene at the BBC. For don't we all know the reason for the success of Radio Caroline? It is the utter failure of Sir Hugh.

In the House of Commons on 15 December 1965 Frank Allaun (Labour, Salford East) asked the Postmaster-General if he intended taking steps to stop cigarette advertising. Mr Benn replied "I have no powers over advertising by pirate radio stations, but the impending legislation will meet this point."

On 20 December 1965 Captain L.P.S. Orr (Ulster Unionist, Down South) asked the Postmaster-General what information he had about illegal radio transmissions operating from Shivering Sands Tower, Knock John Tower or Red Sands Tower, and whether they were still transmitting and, furthermore, what action had been taken to stop transmissions within territorial waters.

The Postmaster-General replied: "My information is that radio transmitters are operating from all of these towers. Inquiries are being pursued!"

The Houses of Parliament later took their recess, and the pirates succeeded in broadcasting for their second successive Christmas at sea. In the New Year, Harold Wilson, the Prime Minister, answering Paul Bryan (Conservative, Howden), in regard to replacing the pirate programmes, said on 25 January 1966: "There are discussions going on at the present time to ascertain what can be done to replace them, which are certainly popular with a great many people."

On 27 January 1966 Hector Hughes (Labour, Aberdeen North), asked the Secretary of State for the Home Department if he was aware that a disturbance had occurred on the pirate ship m.v. *Galaxy* on Christmas Day during which British police were called to the ship, and if he would call for a report on the incident indicating the place of registration of the ship, whether the event occurred in British territorial waters, and how it was dealt with.

George Thomas (Labour, West Cardiff), said: "The Chief Constable of Essex has sent a report on the incident, which occurred on a foreign ship anchored outside territorial waters. No police powers were exercised in connection with it."

On 1 February 1966, in answer to William Molloy (Labour, Ealing North), on the subject of the offshore forts, Mr Benn said that Radio 390 on Red Sands Fort, Radio City on Shivering Sands Fort and Radio Essex on Knock John Fort were inside territorial waters and legal proceedings would therefore be instituted as soon as was practicable.

On 16 March 1966 the Government produced another reason for not proceeding against the stations operating from forts in the Thames Estuary. James Callaghan, after consulting the Postmaster-General, told reporters at the Labour Party's Election news conference that the Government had been going into the question of prosecutions.

"But there are technical questions about where the powers of the magistrate begin and end. These are not entirely worked out so I cannot give any information when a prosecution will be launched."

Mr Callaghan went on "So far as the programmes are popular I think there would be responsibility to provide alternative programmes - there is no reason why you should deprive people of the programmes they like. But it would be highly irresponsible to allow people to operate who are interfering with other stations, and with ship-to-shore radio."

At another press conference, Edward Heath said:

When a pirate radio ship is outside territorial waters there are obvious difficulties. The real answer is to give people more choice inside the country. That is why we have put forward a specific proposal that we should discuss with the BBC, and others concerned with the extension of local sound radio, which will then be able to cater more for the general needs of people during the daytime and provide light music too.

Lord Byers, Chairman of the Liberal Party, said he was in favour of pirate radio stations provided they paid their proper dues and taxes.

"I worked for four years for Radio Luxembourg and I feel at the moment the pirate stations are providing for a real need among the population. Many millions are listening to them."

On 25 April 1966 Christopher Rowland asked the Postmaster-General what steps he proposed taking to prevent the operation of Radio England/Britain Radio which were scheduled to start illegal broadcasting at the end of April.

Mr Benn said "There is nothing I can do to prevent them from broadcasting - that is the problem. However, as the House knows, legislation to give us certain necessary powers will be introduced by the Government as soon as the legislative timetable permits."

The following day Mr Rowland asked the Postmaster-General what consultations he proposed having with other western European countries about the proposed operation of the two new pirates. Radio England and Britain Radio, on transmitters with a joint power of 110 kilowatts. Replying, the Postmaster-General said:

> This country has already taken part in discussions with other member nations of the Council of Europe about the best method of preventing broadcasting from the high seas. These discussions resulted in the European Agreement which the United Kingdom signed last year. Further consultations are not in prospect.

On 16 May 1966 it was announced that Sir Alan Herbert, Chairman of the British Copyright Council, had drafted a Bill to outlaw offshore stations and sought to have it introduced in Parliament. This Bill, which was to be called "Law of Piracy (Extension) Bill", would make guilty of piracy any person who broadcast unauthorised programmes from waters in and around Britain. Naval vessels would be empowered to seize pirate ships and take them to a convenient British port, and the minimum penalty on the directors of the companies would be £10,000 if found guilty of contravening the Bill. Other clauses in this Bill would make it an offence to help such broadcasters, and permit police to board vessels to inspect them. If any British-registered ship made pirate broadcasts to a foreign country, she could be arrested by the vessels of any country.

On the same day as Sir Alan Herbert's proposed Bill was announced, Eldon Griffiths spoke to the Radio and TV Retailers' Association conference in Brighton. He suggested that the BBC should stop crying about pirate radio ships and start competing for audiences. He went on "Let us not have outright banning of a service which gives pleasure to millions. The majority of people under 30 now listen regularly to the pirates because they like what they hear. The stations are providing a service the BBC has lamentably failed to provide."

In the House of Commons on 17 May 1966, Sir Arthur Vere Harvey (Conservative, Macclesfield), said: "Is not the Chancellor embarrassed by the whole situation of pirate radio? Eighteen months ago the Postmaster-General said he was going to shut down the stations. The Dutch have been able to do so. Are the Government afraid to do so because the stations are too popular?"

The Chancellor, James Callaghan, replied "I do not think it is my responsibility, but I live in an almost permanent state of embarrassment." There was laughter from other parts of the House.

Noyes Thomas, writing in the *Daily Telegraph* on 1 May 1966, said the Government appeared afraid of the pirates. He went on:

> Despite a sharp difference of opinion on the subject amongst Ministers, it was thought best not to risk upsetting 17,000,000 people. Last December, Wedgwood Benn, the Postmaster-General, was promising that the pirate stations operating from disused forts at sea would be prosecuted. As recently as February 1966 Mr Benn repeated his promise.

The Musicians' Union's war against pirate radio became more fierce on 26 May 1966 when they banned a show to be recorded at the Lyceum Rainbow Club in Bradford. T. Griffin, the union's new organiser for the north-east district, walked into the club and advised four groups not to perform. They were to have recorded four shows which would have been broadcast on Radio Caroline (North and South), Radio London, Radio Scotland and Radio City.

Mr Griffin said "The methods employed by the offshore radio stations jeopardised the livelihood of our members."

Disc jockey Tony Blackburn who worked on Radio Caroline and, later, Radio London, said:

The Musicians' Union say that non-stop music will kill live musicians and music altogether. This is absolute rot. Pirate radio has survived for over three years. Should commercial radio be introduced on land, there would be *extra* work for musicians - not less! It would give an additional outlet to the BBC. I am a member of the Musicians' Union, but they don't speak for me nor for the hundreds of pop groups that pirate radio have helped to success. Let's face it, the union is very old-fashioned. It must not dictate whether or not there should be commercial radio on land. The Musicians' Union should be flattered that the public want the commodity it is supposed to represent - music! And if the public want non-stop music, are we, the musicians, going to say no?

On 8 June 1966 Sir Alan Herbert wrote a letter to *The Times* in which he said:

Sir, while we are waiting for the Ministers to explain their legal 'doubts' about pirate forts and the magistrates, may I strike a more hilarious note? The young things, bless them, whose only comfort in these hard times is to listen to pilfered music illicitly broadcast over the water, cannot understand why stuffy folk should wish to interfere in their innocent pleasures. I have a shock for them! If, sir, you study your radio licence, you will see that you are licensed to use your 'apparatus' for 'receiving' from 'authorised broadcasting stations.' If you listen deliberately to an unauthorised station, you are, I believe, committing an offence under Section One of the Wireless and Telegraphy Act, and you are liable to a fine of £10 for the first offence and £50 for 'any other subsequent offence.' Also, your licence may be rebuked and your apparatus forfeited to the Postmaster-General. This harsh law was prompted by the Labour Government in 1949. It was recently boasted, after some sort of 'poll', that one third of the population - 17 million people - listen regularly to 'unauthorised stations.' Fines, then, I reckon of more than £800,000,000 are due most days of the week. "Why worry?", say some. Many are having fun, and a few are making money. But we are teaching 17 million citizens to think that a law they don't like doesn't matter. This sort of thing is catching. How can authors, composers, musicians - and old men of 75 - now be expected to pay income tax with patriotic promptitude?

I am, sir, yours respectfully,

A.P. Herbert,
Chairman of the British Copyright Council,
12, Hammersmith Terrace, London, W.6.

Hugh Jenkins (Labour, Putney) spoke in the House of Commons on 23 June 1966. He said there had been a tendency to dismiss pirate radio as a matter of no great importance nor great significance, but as something which was a passing episode. The extraordinary and tragic events of the past twenty four hours (he was referring to the shooting of Reginald Calvert of Radio City - see Chapter Eight) had perhaps impressed everybody - the Opposition as well as the Government - that piracy was piracy in whatever aspect it occurred.

Answering the debate, Mr Benn said that the objection to pirate radio ships did not stem from the content of their programmes. Most of them provided what had sometimes been described as audible wallpaper - a continuous series of musical items that were exceedingly attractive to a general audience and were popular. However, all European Governments had come out strongly against pirate radio organisations because they used high-powered transmitters on wavelengths that had not been allocated by general agreement. Also, the pirate ships were interfering with the reception of national stations in Europe.

The second reason was the safety of British ships at sea.

And the third reason that the pirates could not continue was that they were taking advantage of their position, stealing the work of others, and making money out of them without payment, or very little payment.

Mr Benn went on "Our Bill to deal with the pirates is ready and will come forward when the timetable permits. That is the position. It is easy and, indeed, natural for the cynics to say - I am not suggesting Mr Jenkins said it, but he hinted at it - that the Government has got cold feet and it dare not touch these stations because they are so popular."

One week later Tony Benn promised that the Bill to curb the pirates would be introduced within six weeks. The news came in a written reply to John Biggs-Davison (Conservative, Chigwell). This would be before the summer recess of Parliament.

The Bill would affect ten stations - Radio Caroline North and South, Radio London, Britain Radio, Radio England, Radio Scotland, Radio 390, Radio City, Radio Essex and Radio 270.

The *Daily Telegraph* ran an editorial on the pirates on 4 July 1966.

Just before his transition yesterday, Wedgwood Benn promised soon to put the pirate radio stations out of business. His successor, Edward Short, will presumably honour this tardily bold pledge. Before cheering we ought to see precisely how he proposes to act. These stations supply a want which, if not noble, is at least legitimate. They supply it, moreover, at the expense not of the listener but of the advertiser. Why then put them out of business? Would it not suffice to force them to return to the mainland, to submit to the law in general and to the regulation of wavelengths in particular, and to pay proper performing fees?

If Mr Short moves along these lines, he will deserve applause. He may prefer, however, merely to suppress the pirates. This would be silly; it would be worse than silly if he also instructed the BBC to fill the gap by ceaselessly broadcasting, at the listeners' expense, the sort of tripe which the pirates now purvey. This would mean that listeners would be, in effect, taxed to finance a service of which many must disapprove. If the BBC could abandon its Pharisaic prejudice against advertisements, this difficulty could be overcome. Arguments against monopoly, however, should still prevail.

The day that many of the members of Parliament had waited for finally arrived. The Bill was introduced into the House of Commons on Wednesday 27 July 1966, just twenty eight months after pirate radio commenced broadcasting off the British coasts.

Almost everybody in Britain who had anything to do with the stations would face the prospect of a two-year prison sentence, and/or a £100 fine.

The Bill, called the Marine, Etc., Broadcasting (Offences) Bill, made it illegal to broadcast from ships, marine structures or from aircraft. Masters of ships, owners, and the men who operated the stations would also be guilty of the offence. It was unlawful to provide a ship with equipment or to supply them with any goods. Everyone from disc jockeys to advertisers and from ferrymen to publishers of programme details would be caught by the legislation. The Bill was expected to become law by February 1967.

Paul Bryan, Conservative Front Bench spokesman on broadcasting, said "Twenty million listeners will have every right to protest at the Government's banning of the stations without any real attempt to provide alternative programmes."

Radio Caroline described the Bill as "spiteful, unimaginative and a negation of basic freedoms. It seems to put an outright ban on the enjoyment of 25 million regular listeners to offshore radio without submitting any alternative proposals for satisfying this legitimate demand. We do not regard the fight as over. The tussle will begin when Parliament reassembles."

Conscious of the great public popularity of the pirates, the Government was, in July 1966,

'We shall not stand idly by!'

intensifying its efforts to provide some alternative to be broadcast by the BBC.

A copy of the Marine, Etc., Broadcasting (Offences) Bill 1967 can be found towards the end of this chapter.

The Incorporated Society of British Advertisers and the Institute of Practitioners in Advertising, in a joint comment on the Bill, said on 3 August 1966 that advertisers needed British commercial radio facilities as a firm home base of knowledge to be used in overseas markets where radio was usually a substantial advertising medium. "The British public as a whole - the audience has been variously estimated as between 18 million and 25 million - has shown that with a scheme to provide a regular licensed commercial radio system, it might have made sense."

On 18 October 1966 the BBC claimed that more than four times as many people listened to the Light Programme every day as tuned to all Britain's pirate radio stations put together.

The BBC's survey showed that 16 per cent of the people questioned tuned into the pirates daily or nearly every day. But it showed that 69 per cent listened to the Light Programme daily or nearly every day, and 38 per cent to the Home Service.

Hastings Young Liberals decided to carry out their own survey into the popularity of pirate stations as they were dissatisfied with the figures produced by the BBC. Their survey covered a wide age group, the youngest person asked being 14 and the eldest over 60. Not a quarter thought the Government capable of running pop radio. Only one-seventh thought the Government had any right to tell the pirates what to do. Only a small percentage minded the advertisements, and only half those interviewed thought the stations would be improved by operating from shore bases.

Eileen Ware, editor of the Young Liberals' magazine *Gunfire,* said in October 1966 that "the Government should leave the pirates alone until they have set up a board of control which can allocate wavebands and licences to independent commercial stations. There should be no monopolies."

The National League of Young Liberals launched their "Save Pop Radio" campaign on 24 October 1966.

In the House of Commons on 5 April 1967 Eldon Griffiths said that the people who listened to 'free commercial stations' were not simply irresponsible teenagers. "They included some of the most useful productive people in the country, Wedgwood Benn was a splendid example. He had once revealed that he listened to Radio Caroline in the morning while loofah-ing his back in the bath." Mr Griffiths went on "I don't know if the present Postmaster-General, Edward Short, does that - somehow I doubt it."

Debating amendments to the Marine, Etc., Broadcasting (Offences) Bill, MPs agreed to increase the maximum penalty for offences under the Bill to £400.

Edward Short said "£100 was nothing more than petty cash to pirate broadcasters. The gamblers have been playing for high stakes, but now it is all over -the game is up and it wouldn't be worth a candle carrying on."

For the Opposition, Paul Bryan said: "The public had a brief look beyond the limits of monopoly radio - and furthermore had liked it. Now they are condemned to monopoly radio until the Conservatives get back in power."

The Bill was given an unopposed third reading.

On 7 March 1967, the Postmaster-General announced that Britain's first three home town radio stations would be on the air by the end of 1967. He listed stations for Merseyside, Leicester and Sheffield.

Each station would broadcast four hours of local programmes daily, and these would consist of record requests, news, reports on council meetings and so on.

Mr Short estimated that each station would cost about £30,000 to set up and a further £1,000 a week to run with a staff of fifteen. Local authorities would back the stations. These stations would have a range of eight to twelve miles only.

The Postmaster-General would announce six more stations later in the year. After all of them had been transmitting for twelve months the Government would then decide whether or not to extend the system of local broadcasting throughout Britain.

On 10 March - three days after the PMG's announcement - it was learned that ratepayers and local associations would have to find the £1,000 a week running costs for the stations. The names of the station managers were also announced.

Radio Merseyside would have Michael Hancock, 34-year-old BBC TV presentation editor; Radio Sheffield, Michael Barton, 35-year-old North Region TV producer, and Radio Leicester, Maurice Ennals (47) the editor of BBC's South-East News in London. These managers would earn about £65 a week.

Norfolk and Suffolk County Councils turned down suggestions from the Education Committee to have a local radio station for Norwich and Ipswich.

A National Opinion Poll survey among adults was conducted with results announced on 10 April 1967. The survey asked the question "Do you think commercial radio stations should be banned by the Government?" The results were:

Ban the stations	19%
Let them continue	69%
Don't know	12%

Nearly three out of every four Londoners approved of the pop stations said the survey which was conducted for Radio London.

On 18 April 1967 the House of Lords gave an unopposed second reading to the Marine,

Etc., Broadcasting (Offences) Bill.

Lord Sorenson, for the Government, said the regulations about wavelengths had been 'throwted' (sic) in recent years by a few artful dodgers, but the Bill would enable the Government to deal effectively with pirate stations on land, sea or air within Britain's territorial limits. The Government hoped the Bill would show the way for other countries to follow. Some of them had complained more than once of piratical broadcasting on their wavelengths.

From the Opposition front bench, Lord Denham said it was intolerable that because of a loophole in the law a number of people or countries should be able to operate on wavelengths to which they had helped themselves, although many had taken care to conduct their affairs in an otherwise unexceptional manner. The Opposition's complaint was that the Bill was too late. The delay had allowed many people to acquire a taste for light music which the BBC was unable or unwilling to provide. He spoke of rumours that a number of commercial stations on the Continent were planning to broadcast to Britain after the Bill became law.

Lord Strabolgi (Labour) said he was by no means against commercial broadcasting. The pirate stations gave pleasure to 20 million people, and their absence would leave a considerable vacuum. He would far rather hear Frank and Nancy Sinatra singing *Something Stupid* than listen to some pretentious cultural programme and French poetry read in bad translations by RADA actresses with phoney accents.

Lord Denham described the format of pirate radio stations. He said:

Broadly speaking there are two distinct types - those which play what is called 'pop' music and those which play what is technically known as 'sweet' music. Both types employ smooth-talking gentlemen known by the rather regrettable American expression of 'disc jockeys,' which has now mercifully been shortened to the initials 'DJ.' It is the job of these gentlemen to introduce the records of which their programmes are made up.

The leading 'pop' music stations are Radio London, Radio Caroline North and South and Radio Scotland. This type has at any one time a very limited repertoire. Their programmes are devoted to new records which top the sales in shops throughout the British Isles. Each week a list is prepared and published of the 40 or 50 best sellers in numerical order of popularity. These lists are known as 'The Charts.' An individual record starts its 'pop' life before it is on sale to the general public when it is played by a DJ as a record that he considers is likely to get into the charts; and at this stage it is known as a 'climber.' If a climber catches on, the public will buy it, and possibly the next week or the week after it will enter the charts at say, No.33. The following week it may climb to No.18, and so on until it reaches the peak of its popularity and therefore the lowest number, after which the sales will start declining and it will gradually lose position until it is out of the charts altogether. After that it will be heard no more until, if it has had a good run of popularity, it may eventually make the odd, fleeting reappearance as what is known either as a 'revived 45' or a 'flashback.' These are occasionally played to remind one of the happy days of one's youth, in much the same nostalgic way as the BBC will sometimes play a hit tune from *No, No, Nanette*, or *The Quaker Girl*. A 'pop' record therefore has a very short playing life. Its appearance on a 'pop' programme is entirely governed by the number of copies sold, or likely to be sold. A very important point is that it is not the song that wins a place in the charts but the individual record of that song by a particular singer or group. For instance, if a record of a song made by some obscure group should gain freak popularity for some weeks, the public would want that recording to be played, and the same song played by another group would be no substitute at all, even if the group were to be the Beatles, the Rolling Stones, the Monkees or such stalwarts as Messrs. Dave Dee, Dozy, Beaky, Mick and Tich. Very often, not even a live performance by the group themselves can reproduce the sounds on the records, many of which need devices such as over-recording or echo chambers.

Lord Denham, after being thanked by Lord Sorenson for the valuable information he had given to the House, went on to describe the 'sweet' music station.

The leading 'sweet' music pirate is Radio 390. This second type plays a much wider selection of music. They appeal mainly to the older listener and include tunes by composers such as Ivor Novello, Noël Coward, Cole Porter and Irving Berlin, and singers such as Bing Crosby and Frank Sinatra. But they also play any new 'pop' record that comes into the 'sweet' music category. Sometimes the two distinct types of pirate programmes are closer together than at others. The reason for this is that, while 'sweet' music remains constant, 'pop' music is continually changing, veering towards it, or away from it, according to the particular phase the record-buying public is going through at the moment. 'Pop' music can vary over the years from big beat, through rhythm and blues, country and western to ballads. Just at the moment, the 'pop' public is going through a ballad phase, ballads being 'sweet' music. There are a lot of ballads in the charts at the moment, and Radio 390 are playing something like 25 out of 'pop' radio's Top 40. But in six months' time the two may be poles apart.

These are the two distinct lines on which the pirate radios have developed. The public have heard them, grown used to them, and to a certain extent, adapted their lives to them. Some like one type, some like the other, and a few - but they are a very small minority - like to vary between the two. It is mainly true to say that neither the 'pop' listener, nor the 'sweet' music listener, would find the other's programme any substitute at all for their own. It would similarly be very hard to put together a programme that would appeal to both. Even when the two are fairly close together, as at the moment, there are always records which are indispensable to the 'pop' listener but which would be anathema to the 'sweet' music listener, and vice versa.

Neither type may be educational, but, then, neither type does any harm. Between the two of them they provide 20 million listeners with what they want, when they want it, at the turn of a switch. And not only is it the type of music the public want, it is presented in the way they want it. The DJs have voices, mannerisms, and catch phrases which are individually known. In these times of change, when whole communities get separated and moved to unfamiliar surroundings, the tuning in to a friendly, cheerful, recognisable voice on the wireless can be a great antidote to loneliness.

This Bill, which we all support, is designed to sink the pirate ships as they are today, leaving a void in the lives of their listeners.

Lord Denham later went on to talk about an American religious organisation that was preparing to finance a full 'pop' programme to this country once the pirate radio stations had ended. The broadcasts would come from a ship which would also broadcast to a foreign country, and would be manned by nationals of that country which as yet had not passed legislation against the pirates. This rumour was one of five he had heard in connection with the future of commercial sound radio.

One was that two commercial stations were being planned in the Pyrenees. One of them. Radio Andorra, was ready to start transmitting as soon as the Bill became effective.

Another rumour was that Radio Luxembourg would get back the listeners and advertising lost to them when the pirate radios started transmitting. It was true that Radio Luxembourg was under the control of the Luxembourg Government, but it was not under the control of our Government.

A further rumour was that foreign backers of one of the pirate stations had negotiated a merger with Europe One.

The last rumour was that some of the existing ships intended, with their present foreign backers, to carry on with broadcasts attracting revenue from foreign advertisers who exported to this country.

Lord Denham, whilst stating that his party supported the Bill, said that if a properly authorised commercial radio system were set up, none of these projects, nor the present pirates, would find it financially worthwhile to compete against it.

Lord Strange said that he had met one of the offshore men - in fact the 'Pirate King.' He did not think that Radio Caroline had been fairly treated in the debate. They had 'joie de vivre', they were 'with it' and they appealed to young people. Lord Strange went on:

> The Radio Caroline people don't intend to be sunk. They intend to fight it out, and they have all sorts of schemes which I would never give away. At the last local elections they fought throughout the country, they plugged against the Government for all they were worth; they were fighting like mad and doing everything they could to influence the election. I think the result of the election is largely due to pirate radios.

Baroness Phillips, replying to the debate, said the BBC had stated that a recent survey had shown that 16 per cent of the people listened to pirate stations while 77 per cent said they never or hardly ever listened. She quoted Sir Alan Herbert as having said that, 'If groups of people were generously dispensing free beer which they themselves had acquired without payment, no doubt there would be no complaints about this.'

That seemed to her to summarise the attitude of most people who listened to pirate stations. The allegation that the Government had allowed the demand for pirate programmes to be built up without any alternative being offered was no argument against upholding the rule of law. The pirate stations had been ingenious in giving the impression that they had been more sinned against than sinning, and that they were doing nothing more objectional than many land-based stations in Europe.

The Bill was given an unopposed second reading.

It was in April 1967 that the Institute of Practitioners in Advertising held a meeting in London. The retiring President, John Hobson, said:

> The advertising industry should press for a national radio channel supported by advertising rather than for local commercial stations. We have sampled lately the Government's attitude to commercial broadcasting - particularly commercial radio. It is very disappointing, but it is based on such a theoretical foundation - this idea of local community stations - that one wonders if the Ministers can be really serious about it.

On 13 April 1967 the GLC elections were discussed in the House of Commons.

"Pirate radio stations were attempting improperly to influence the results for the Greater London Council," said Bernard Conlan, Labour MP for Gateshead East.

Radio London and Radio Caroline gave the results over the air of a radio survey of GLC candidates' views on commercial radio. 97% of Conservative candidates favoured commercial radio; 82% of Liberals did, but only 20% of the Labour candidates.

Radio Caroline also went further by broadcasting the results of a national survey which said that the majority of Labour voters wanted free radio rather than controlled radio paid for by ratepayers.

Radio London, commenting after the discussion in the House of Commons, said: "We didn't ask people to vote for one party or another. We just asked listeners to vote for the person who was going to look after the voters' interest."

On 1 May 1967 Tory peers defeated the Government in the House of Lords by 21 votes on the Bill to ban the pirate stations. The amendment, to delay the measure until the PMG provided a suitable alternative, was carried by 65 votes to 44 against the Government.

But Lord Sorenson, the Government spokesman, then announced that the delay would be wiped out by an Order in Council. This would make the Bill effective a month and a day after it received the Royal Assent.

Earlier Lord Sorenson had said that the BBC's new 'pop' programmes would be ready six weeks after the pirates had been banned. Some five hundred letters had been received at the House protesting about the Bill. Lord Sorenson said this was a small proportion of the 10,000,000 listeners who were supposed to tune in, and it was fairly evident that the great majority of listeners were not so concerned after all.

The Marine, Etc., Broadcasting (Offences) Bill then went on to the Report Stage which was completed in the House of Lords on 31 May 1967.

Lord Colville of Culross, moving several amendments, wanted clarification of the term 'advertisement' in relation to pirate radio stations. He said that certain items which he thought might be useful in editorial comment could be considered offensive within the terms of the Bill. "The press wanted to know what it could safely publish and what it could not."

For the Government, Lord Sorenson said they thought it better to leave the interpretation of the word 'advertisement' to the courts to decide. They were not trying to penalise the publication of editorial comment or genuine news items about the pirates.

Lord Leatherland, speaking as a former news editor of a national newspaper, said this sort of thing had never been settled in the courts but might well have to be in the future. It was the editor in charge of a newspaper who decided what to publish. He would accept or reject legal advice in the interests of what he thought his readers should know.

Lord Sorenson promised to look into the matter thoroughly, and the amendments were withdrawn. The Report Stage was concluded.

The House of Commons considered the Lords Amendment to the Marine, Etc., Broadcasting (Offences) Bill on 30 June 1967. It provided that the Act should not come into operation until an order in council had been made at least one month after the Bill as passed.

Paul Channon (Conservative) moved an amendment to the Lords amendment for the Act to come into force only after an order had been approved by both Houses.

Robert Cooke (Conservative) supporting Mr Channon said that the BBC was going to do its best to fill the gap left by the pirates with Radio 247. This would no doubt be a good service, but it couldn't possibly be the same as the pirates.

Anthony Berry (Conservative) said he thought there ought to be competition, even if only for a short time, between the beginning of the BBC's new station and the end of the pirates. Otherwise, under the Bill there would be a two-month gap in the holiday period of August and September.

The Postmaster General, Edward Short, replying, said there had been general agreement on both sides of the House that the pirates must go. The only disagreement was when. The purpose of Radio 247 was not to be a substitute for the pirates but to extend the choice of the listening public. It would differ from the pirates in two ways: in accepting the restrictions on the broadcast time for gramophone records and in not ignoring the copyright laws as the pirates did. The BBC was confident that the programme would be very popular and he asked members to suspend judgement until they had heard it.

But this was not relevant to the issue of how long the pirates should be allowed to continue broadcasting. They were still interfering with wavelengths used by shipping and lighthouses, and with foreign services. The Governments of the countries concerned had been extremely patient but in fairness to them we clearly couldn't allow the pirates to go on depriving listeners in foreign countries of their services. It was the Government's intention to arrange for the Bill to come into force a month after it had received the Royal Assent.

Paul Bryan from the Opposition Front Bench said the purpose of the amendment was to give the Postmaster-General latitude in his choice of the day on which the Bill became an Act. Over 20,000,000 people were to be deprived of the programmes to which they had become accustomed, and Mr Bryan asked for an assurance that the spirit of the amendment was accepted and not merely the words.

Interior view of the House of Commons

Mr Channon's amendment was negative and Mr Short then moved the Lords amendment. He said that Lord Sorenson had made it clear in the Lords that the Government had no option but to fulfil their international obligations and to put the Bill into operation as soon as possible. The Lords amendment was approved and the debate concluded.

The *Daily Sketch* published a series of articles in which Michael Housego interviewed the Postmaster-General and Donald Currie (editor of *Radio News*). In an article on 23 June 1967 Donald Currie said that one of the PMG's objections to 'free' radio stations was that they did not pay performing rights fees to singers, musicians or composers.

This comment sparked off a great deal of controversy and on 7 July 1967 R.F. Whale of the Performing Right Society said: "The only offshore broadcasters who have ever paid us anything on what they call an *ex gratia* basis are Radio Caroline and Radio London from which we have received nothing since last year, and Radio 390, from which we last received a payment in March of this year. No other offshore broadcasters have ever offered to pay us. Our objections to the radio pirates, however, are not importantly that a few of them have ever made a show of paying for our property but, primarily, that they have taken that property without authority to do so."

The performing rights fees issue was also taken up by T.A. O'Brien, Director of Public Relations at the GPO in London, in a letter to the *Daily Sketch* on 7 July 1967. He said "So far as composers' rights are concerned, some at least of the pirates are probably in the clear, and the Postmaster-General has at no time suggested otherwise. But singers and musicians are a different matter."

Mr O'Brien further discussed Donald Currie's comments:

I think Mr Currie will find that there is not a single pirate broadcasting station which has the consent of the copyright owners for all the recordings they broadcast. Similarly on wavelengths, the Postmaster-General's objections have been twisted in such a way that they appear incorrect. 'Mr Short cannot say that the BBC use only wavelengths allocated to this country,' says Mr Currie. Mr Short has never sought to say that.

All Governments retain the sovereign right to allow wavelengths to stations under their jurisdiction, and by international agreement they are responsible to each other for doing so in a way which minimises interference.

The pirates were finally made to walk the plank! Sentence of death was passed on 13 July 1967 by Edward Short, the Postmaster-General. The execution date was fixed for midnight on 14/15 August 1967.

Mr Short said that his task of banning the pirates had been made more difficult by Tory MPs supporting the pirates. Meanwhile the Bill was awaiting Royal Assent.

On 13 July 1967 Radios 227, 270, 355 and 390 all announced they were going off the air on 14 August. Radios Caroline and London said they intended to carry on from new headquarters abroad. Radio Scotland said it might have to close down eventually. Tommy Shields, managing director, said that he had offered his station to the Postmaster-General as there were no plans for a local radio station in Scotland.

Whilst four stations were announcing their closures, the BBC said that eight local stations were to be set up in Merseyside, Sheffield, Leicester, Nottingham, Brighton, Leeds, Stoke-on-Trent and Durham. Radio 247, the BBC's pop music station, would go on the air on 30 September 1967.

Opening dates for the local stations were:

Radio Leicester	8 November 1967
Radio Sheffield	15 November 1967
Radio Merseyside	22 November 1967
Radio Nottingham	31 January 1968

Radio Brighton   14 February 1968
Radio Stoke-on-Trent   14 March 1968
Radios Leeds and Durham   June 1968

The BBC asked the Prince of Wales to perform the opening ceremony for Radio Merseyside, but the offer was declined. On the date set (22 November 1967) the Prince of Wales was in the middle of term at Cambridge.

In the House of Commons on 20 December 1967 Mr Short said that the capital cost for each station would be £30,000 to £35,000 and annual running costs about £55,000. However, for Merseyside, which would cover a much larger area, the annual cost would be around £64,000.

So the future of British broadcasting was set for the late 1960s. The pirates were to be scuttled, the BBC was to open a new pop service to replace the pirates and eight local BBC stations were to go on the air.

The pirates' battle had been a long, and in the main, a successful story. Some smaller stations had fallen by the wayside, but the more organised offshore boys made the job worthwhile from their point of view.

The complete stages of the Marine, Etc., Broadcasting (Offences) Bill went as follows:

HOUSE OF COMMONS
1st Reading 27 July 1966
2nd Reading 15 February 1967
Committee Stage in 5 sittings from 2 - 16 March 1967
3rd Reading 5 April 1967
HOUSE OF LORDS
1st Reading 6 April 1967
2nd Reading 18 April 1967 Committee Stage 1 May 1967 Report Stage 31 May 1967
3rd Reading 13 June 1967

The Bill received the Royal Assent on 14 July 1967. All the pirates were silenced by 15 August 1967 with the exception of Radio Caroline North and South.

The Post Office advertised both the new Act and the penalties involved for aiding any pirates still operating in newspapers throughout the country. In a written answer to Stratton Mills (Ulster Unionist) on the cost of the advertisements the PMG said that 135 advertisements were placed in 70 newspapers and other publications which he listed. The total sum spent was £17,754 4s 0d (£17,754.20p).

Also in the House of Commons on the same day (13 November 1967) Stratton Mills asked the Attorney-General what proceedings he was taking against Granada Television for filming operations of Radio Caroline South in breach of the Marine Offences Act.

Sir Arthur Irvine, the Solicitor-General, said he was in fact taking no action, for it would not have been in the public interest to have instituted proceedings.

Stratton Mills asked the PMG in the House of Commons on 23 November 1967 how many pirate radio stations were still broadcasting to the United Kingdom?

Mr Short replied: "There are two pirate radios still broadcasting off our shores out of the ten that were operating at the beginning of the year. The question of taking action against those concerned with these two stations for possible breaches of the Marine, Etc., Broadcasting (Offences) Act is not a matter for me."

Stratton Mills went on to ask the PMG about Radio Caroline. Did the station appear to be flourishing?

Mr Short replied: "I am sure that the party of Law and Order delights in the fact that Radio Caroline appears to be flourishing. The French Parliament recently ratified the European Agreement, the Irish Parliament is in the process of doing so and we have no doubt that the Dutch Parliament will do so very shortly."

No more matters in connection with offshore radio history were debated in the House of Commons for the remainder of 1967. It appeared that the Government had won the day and the pirates had finally been scuppered - almost four years after Radio Caroline first began broadcasting on Good Friday, 1964.

The MARINE, Etc., BROADCASTING (OFFENCES) ACT, 1967 is now reproduced by kind permission of the Controller of Her Majesty's Stationery Office.

Marine, &c., Broadcasting (Offences) Act 1967

CHAPTER 41

ARRANGEMENT OF SECTIONS

The sections are arranged as follows:

Chapter 41

Arrangements of Sections

Section
1. Prohibition of broadcasting from ships and aircraft.
2. Prohibition of broadcasting from marine structures.
3. Prohibition of acts connected with broadcasting from certain ships and aircraft, and from marine structures outside United Kingdom.
4. Prohibition of acts facilitating broadcasting from ships, aircraft, &c.
5. Prohibition of acts relating to matter broadcast from ships, aircraft &c.
6. Penalties and legal proceedings.
7. Special defence available in proceedings for carrying goods or persons in contravention of section 4.
8. Savings for things done under wireless telegraphy licence.
9. Interpretation.
10. Power to extend Act to Isle of Man and Channel Islands.
11. Short title and commencement.

1. (1) It shall not be lawful for a broadcast to be made from a ship or aircraft while it is in or over the United Kingdom or external waters, nor shall it be lawful for a broadcast to be made from a ship registered in the United Kingdom; the Isle of Man or any of the Channel Islands or an aircraft so registered while the ship or aircraft is elsewhere than in or over the United Kingdom or external waters.

(2) If a broadcast is made from a ship in contravention of the foregoing subsection, the owner of the ship, the master of the ship and every person who operates, or participates in the operation of, the apparatus by means of which the broadcast is made shall be guilty of an offence and if a broadcast is made from an aircraft in contravention of that subsection, the operator of the aircraft, the commander of the aircraft and every person who operates, or participates in the operation of the apparatus by means of which the broadcast is made shall be guilty of an offence.

(3) A person who procures the making of a broadcast in contravention of subsection (2) above shall be guilty of an offence.

(4) In subsection (2) above -

(a) "master," in relation to a ship, includes any other person (except a pilot) having command or charge of the ship;

(b) "operator," in relation to an aircraft, means the person for the time being having the management of the aircraft.

2. (1) It shall not be lawful for a broadcast to be made from -

(a) a structure in external waters or in tidal waters in the United Kingdom, being a structure affixed to, or supported by, the bed of those waters and not being a ship; or

(b) any other object in such waters, being neither a structure affixed or supported as aforesaid nor a ship or aircraft; and if a broadcast is made in contravention of the foregoing provision, every person who operates, or participates in the operation of, the apparatus by means of which the broadcast is made shall be guilty of an offence.

(2) A person who procures the making of a broadcast in contravention of the foregoing subsection shall be guilty of an offence.

3. (1) If a broadcast is made -

(a) from a ship other than one registered in the United Kingdom, the Isle of Man or any of the Channel Islands while the ship is on the high seas; or

(b) from an aircraft other than one so registered while the aircraft is on or over the high seas; or

(c) from a structure on the high seas, being a structure affixed to, or supported by, the bed of those seas and not being a ship; or

(d) from any other object on those seas, being neither a structure affixed or supported as aforesaid nor a ship or aircraft; any of the persons mentioned in subsection (3) below who operates, or participates in the operation of, the apparatus by means of which the broadcast is made shall be guilty of an offence.

(2) A person who procures a broadcast to be made as mentioned in the foregoing subsection shall be guilty of an offence.

(3) The persons referred to in subsection (1) above are the following namely:-

(a) a citizen of the United Kingdom and colonies;

(b) a British subject by virtue of section 2 of the British Nationality Act 1948 (continuance of certain citizens of the Republic of Ireland, therein referred to as Eire, as British subjects;

(c)   a British subject without citizenship by virtue of section 13 or section 16 of that Act (which relate respectively to British subjects whose citizenship has not been ascertained at the commencement of that Act and to persons who had ceased to be British on loss of British nationality by a parent);

(d) a British subject by virtue of the British Nationality Act 1965; and

(e) a British protected person (within the meaning of the 1948 c.56.   British Nationality Act 1948).

4. (1) A person who does any of the acts mentioned in subsection (3) below, while satisfying the condition as to knowledge or belief mentioned in the case of that act, shall be guilty of an offence if -

(a) he does the act in the United Kingdom or external waters or in a ship registered in the United Kingdom, the Isle of Man or any of the Channel Islands or an aircraft so registered while the ship or aircraft is elsewhere than in or over the United Kingdom or external waters; or

(b) being a person mentioned in section 3(3) of this Act, he does the act on or over the high seas.

(2) A person who, in the United Kingdom, procures another person to do, outside the United Kingdom, anything which, if it had been done in the United Kingdom by the last-mentioned person, would have constituted an offence under the foregoing subsection, shall be guilty of an offence.

(3) The acts, and conditions as to knowledge or belief, referred to in subsection (1) above are the following, namely:-

(a) furnishing or agreeing to furnish to another a ship or aircraft knowing, or having reasonable cause to believe, that broadcasts are to be made from it in contravention of section 1(1) of this Act or while it is on or over the high seas;

(b) carrying or agreeing to carry in a ship or aircraft wireless telegraphy apparatus knowing, or having reasonable cause to believe, that by means thereof broadcasts are to be made from the ship or aircraft as aforesaid;

(c) supplying to, or installing in, a ship or aircraft wireless telegraphy apparatus knowing, or having reasonable cause to believe, that by means thereof broadcasts are to be made from the ship or aircraft as aforesaid;

(d) supplying any wireless telegraphy apparatus for installation on or in, or installing any such apparatus on or in, any structure or other object (not being, in either case, a ship or aircraft) knowing, or having reasonable cause to believe, that by means of that apparatus broadcasts are to be made from the object in contravention of section 2(1) of this Act or while the object is on the high seas;

(e) repairing or maintaining any wireless telegraphy apparatus knowing or having reasonable cause to believe, that, by means thereof, broadcasts are made, or are to be made, in contravention of section 1(1) of 2(1) of this Act or as mentioned in section 3(1) of this Act;

(f) knowing, or having reasonable cause to believe, in the case of a ship or aircraft, that broadcasts are made, or are to be made, from it in contravention of section 1(1) of this Act or while it is on or over the high seas -

(i) supplying any goods or materials for its operation or maintenance, for the operation or maintenance of wireless telegraphy apparatus installed therein or for the sustentation or comfort of the persons on board of it;

(ii) carrying by water or air goods of persons to or from it;

(iii) engaging a person as an officer or one of the crew of it;

(g) knowing, or having reasonable cause to believe, in the case of a structure or other object (not being, in either case, a ship or aircraft), that broadcasts are made or are to be made, from it in contravention of section 2(1) of this Act or while it is on the high seas -

(i) supplying any goods or materials for its maintenance, for the operation or maintenance of wireless telegraphy apparatus installed therein or thereon or for the sustentation or comfort of the persons therein or thereon;

(ii) carrying by water or air, goods or persons thereto or therefrom;

(iii) engaging a person to render services therein or thereon.

5. (1)   A person who does any of the acts mentioned in subsection (3) below, and, if any intent or circumstances is or are specified in relation to the act, does it with that intent or in those circumstances, shall be guilty of an offence if -

(a) he does the act in the United Kingdom or external waters or in a ship registered in the United Kingdom, the Isle of Man or any of the Channel Islands or an aircraft so registered while the ship or aircraft is elsewhere than in or over the United Kingdom or external waters; or

(b) being a person mentioned in section 3(3) of this Act, he does the act on or over the high seas.

(2) A person who, in the United Kingdom, procures another person to do, outside the United Kingdom, anything which, if it had been done in the United Kingdom by the last-mentioned person, would have constituted an offence under the foregoing subsection, shall be guilty of an offence.

(3) The acts, and, where relevant, the intent and circumstances, referred to in subsection (1) above are the following namely:-

(a) supplying a cinematograph film or a record with intent that a broadcast of the film or, as the case may be, the recording embodied in the record may be made in contravention of section 1(1) or 2(1) of this Act or as mentioned in section 3(1) thereof;

(b) making a literary, dramatic or musical work with intent that a broadcast of the work may be made as aforesaid;

(c) making an artistic work with intent that the work may be included in a television broadcast made as aforesaid;

(d) participating in a broadcast made as aforesaid, being actually present as an announcer, as a performer or one of the performers concerned in an entertainment given, or as the deliverer of a speech;

(e) advertising by means of a broadcast made as aforesaid or inviting another to advertise by means of a broadcast to be so made;

(f) publishing the times or other details of any broadcasts which are to be so made, or (otherwise than by publishing such details) publishing an advertisement of matter calculated to promote, directly or indirectly, the interests of a business whose activities consist in or include the operation of a station from which broadcasts are or are to be so made.

(4) For the purposes of this section if, by means, of a broadcast made in contravention of section 1 (1) or 2(I) of this Act or as mentioned in section 3(1) thereof, it is stated, suggested or implied that any entertainment of which a broadcast is so made has been supplied by, or given at the expense of, a person, he shall, unless he proves that it was not so supplied or given, be deemed thereby to have advertised.

(5) For the purposes of this section advertising by means of a broadcast shall be deemed to take place as well wherever the broadcast is received as where it is made.

(6) In this section "speech" includes lecture, address and sermon, and references in this section to a cinematograph film, a record and a literary, dramatic, musical or artistic work shall be construed in like manner as reference thereto in the Copyright Act 1956.

6. (1) A person guilty of an offence under this Act shall be liable -

(a) on summary conviction, to imprisonment for a term not exceeding three months or to a fine not exceeding £400, or to both;

(b) on conviction on indictment, to imprisonment for a term not exceeding two years or to a fine, or to both.

(2) Where an offence under this Act which has been committed by a body corporate is proved to have been committed with the consent or connivance of, or to be attributable to any neglect on the part of, a director, manager, secretary or other similar officer of the body corporate, or any person who was purporting to act in any such capacity, he, as well as the body corporate, shall be guilty of that offence and shall be liable to be proceeded against accordingly.

(3)Proceedings for an offence under this Act may be taken, and the offence may for all incidental purposes be treated as having been committed, in any place in the United Kingdom.

(4) Notwithstanding anything in any enactment relating to courts of summary jurisdiction, summary proceedings for an offence under this Act may be instituted at any time within two years from the time when the offence was committed.

(5) Proceedings for an offence under this Act shall not, in England or Wales, be instituted otherwise than by or on behalf of the Director of Public Prosecutions and shall not, in Northern Ireland, be instituted otherwise than by or on behalf of the Attorney General for Northern Ireland; but this shall not prevent the issue or execution of a warrant for the arrest of any person in respect of such an offence or the remanding in custody or on bail of any person charged with such an offence.

(6) A member of a police force shall, for the purpose of the enforcement of this Act, have in external waters all the powers, protection and privileges which he has in the area for which he acts as constable.

(7) In this section "director" in relation to a body corporate established by or under an enactment for the purpose of carrying on under national ownership an industry or part of an industry or undertaking, being a body corporate whose affairs are managed by the members thereof, means a member of that body corporate.

(8) In the application of this section to Northern Ireland, the following subsection shall be substituted for subsection (6):-
"(6) A member of the Royal Ulster Constabulary shall, for the purpose of the enforcement of this Act, have in external waters all the powers, protection and privileges which he has in Northern Ireland."

7. (1) In any proceedings against a person for an offence under section 4 of this Act consisting in the carriage of goods or persons to or from a ship or aircraft it shall be a defence for him to prove -
(a) that the ship or aircraft was, or was believed to be, wrecked, stranded or in distress, and that the goods or persons carried for the purpose of preserving the ship or aircraft, or its cargo or apparel, or saving the lives of persons on board of it; or
(b) that a person on board of the ship or aircraft was, or was believed to be, suffering from hurt, injury or illness, and that the goods or persons were carried for the purpose of securing that the necessary surgical or medical advice and attendance were rendered to him.

(2) In any proceedings against a person for an offence under section 4 of this Act consisting in the carriage of goods or persons to or from an object other than a ship or aircraft it shall be a defence for him to prove - (a) that the object was, or was believed to be, unsafe, and that the goods or persons carried were carried for the purpose of saving the lives of persons therein or thereon; or
(b) that a person therein or thereon was, or was believed to be, suffering from hurt, injury or illness, and that the goods or persons were carried for the purpose of securing that the necessary surgical or medical advice and attendance were rendered to him.

(3) In any proceedings against a person for an offence under section 4 of this Act consisting in the carriage of a person to or from a ship or aircraft or to or from an object

other than a ship or aircraft, it shall be a defence for him to prove that the person carried was visiting the ship, aircraft or object, as the case may be, for the purpose of exercising or performing any power or duty conferred or imposed on him by law.

(4) The references in subsections (l)(a) and (2)(a) above to persons having been carried for the purpose of saving lives shall not be construed so as to exclude the persons whose lives it was the purpose to save and the references in subsections (1)(b) and (2)(b) above to persons having been carried as therein mentioned shall not be construed so as to exclude the person who was, or was believed to be, suffering as so mentioned.

8. Nothing in this Act shall render it unlawful to do anything under and in accordance with a wireless telegraphy licence, or to procure anything to be so done.

9.   (1) In this Act -

"broadcast" means a broadcast by wireless telegraphy of sounds or visual images intended for general reception (whether the sounds or images are actually received by any person or not), but does not include a broadcast consisting in a message or signal sent in connection with navigation or for the purpose of securing safety; "external waters" means the whole of the sea adjacent to the United Kingdom which is within the seaward limits of the territorial waters adjacent thereto;

"the high seas" means the seas outside the seaward limits of the territorial waters adjacent to the United Kingdom or to any country or territory outside the United Kingdom;

"ship" includes every description of vessel used in navigation;

"wireless telegraphy," "wireless telegraphy apparatus" and "wireless telegraphy licence" have the same meanings respectively as in the Wireless Telegraphy Act 1949.

(2) For the purposes of this section, the seaward limits of the territorial waters adjacent to the United Kingdom shall be determined by reference to the baseline established by the Territorial Waters Order in Council 1964 or by any subsequent Order of Her Majesty made in Council under Her royal prerogative for establishing the baseline from which the breadth of the territorial sea adjacent to the United Kingdom, the Channel Islands and the Isle of Man is measured.

10.   (1) Her Majesty may by Order in Council direct that this Act shall extend to the Isle of Man or any of the Channel Islands, with such exceptions, adaptations and modifications as may be specified in the Order.

(2) An Order in Council under this section may be varied or revoked by a subsequent Order of Her Majesty in Council.

11. (1) This Act may be cited as the Marine, Etc., Broadcasting (Offences) Act 1967.

(2) This Act shall not come into operation before the expiry of one month beginning with the day on which it is passed, but subject thereto it shall come into operation on a day to be appointed by Her Majesty in Council.

BROADCASTING BILL 1990

The Broadcasting Bill 1990 was preceded by the Peacock Report of July 1987, the radio Green Paper of February 1987, the Home Affairs Committee report of June 1988 and the Broadcasting White Paper of November 1988. The Bill made its way through both Houses of Parliament during 1989 and 1990. On 6 December 1989 Secretary Waddington, supporting the Prime Minister, Secretary Hurd, The Chancellor of the Exchequer, Secretary Walker, Secretary Ridley, Secretary MacGregor, Secretary Rifkind, Secretary Brook and David Mellor, presented a Bill to make new provision with respect to the provision and regulation of independent television and sound programme services and of other services provided on television or radio frequencies; to make provision with respect to the provision and regulation of local delivery services; to amend in other respects the law relating to broadcasting and the provision of television and sound programme services; to make new provision relating to the

Broadcasting Complaints Commission; to provide for the establishment and functions of a Broadcasting Standards Council; to amend the Wireless Telegraphy Acts 1949 to 1967 and the Marine, Etc., Broadcasting (Offences) Act 1967; and for connected purposes; And the same was read the First time; and ordered to be read a Second time tomorrow and to be printed. (Bill 9.)[1]

The Broadcasting Bill was read a Second time on 18 December 1989. House divided: Ayes 310, Noes 238.[2]

The Report stage of the Broadcasting Bill took place in the House of Commons on 8 and 9 May 1990. Amendments were made to the Bill in the House of Lords and debated in the Commons on 25 October 1990.[3]

David Porter (Conservative, Waveney), asked the Secretary of State for Trade and Industry if he would make a statement about the future of both offshore and land-based pirate radio stations in Britain in the light of the Broadcasting Bill. In a Written Answer, Eric Forth MP, Parliamentary Under-Secretary of State for Industry and Consumer Affairs, said, on 21 May 1990, that it remained Government policy to take vigorous action against unauthorised broadcasters, whether offshore or inland. It is essential to keep the airwaves clear for the emergency services and for the wider variety of legitimate broadcasting that we aim to foster. That is the purpose of the new enforcement provisions in the Broadcasting Bill.[4]

The Broadcasting Act of 1990 made amendments to the Marine, Etc., Broadcasting (Offences) Act 1967 and in turn put an end to pirate radio ships off the British coasts.

David Mellor, Minister of State, Home Office, said that "By the 10 May we will reach a major milestone in the Bill's progress. After its consideration on Report during the past two days, with more than 17 hours of debate on the Floor of the House, without any guillotine, we arrive at the Third Reading."

He mentioned his Hon. Friend the Member for Thanet North, Roger Gale. "He comes to the House after a career in broadcasting. He showed a remarkable grasp of the issues, and a willingness to put forward his view - never in an overweening way, and never seeking to use his experience to crush those of us who had not had the opportunity of working within the industry. He was always a tower of strength."

The House divided: Ayes 259, Noes 180. Bill was read Third time, and passed.[5]

The Minister of State, Home Office, Earl Ferrers said in the House of Lords on 5 June 1990 that the Broadcasting Bill was one of the longest Bills ever prepared by the Home Office. The Bill would replace the Broadcasting Act 1981 and the Cable and Broadcasting Act of 1984. The Bill was a hefty 217-page document, with 182 clauses and 17 schedules.

The Bill was debated in the Lords on 5 June. Lord Annan said he disliked the extraordinary amendments to the Marine Etc., Broadcasting (Offences) Act 1967 which were aimed at Radio Caroline. "The amendments proposed will make it unlawful for any foreign ship on the high seas to broadcast to the United Kingdom. It will enable the police, the Army. Customs officers and anyone who is authorised by the Secretary of State to board and search these foreign ships and seize documents.

"It is another example of the Government putting on their Clause 28 'bovver boots.' Exceptional cases such as hijacking or drugs could justify seizure or detention of a foreign vessel and confer immunity on the officers who boarded it. I realise that the Home Office regards Radio Caroline as a maddening wasp and infuriated that its attempts over the years to swat it have failed. However, surely this station is not a wasp but a common or garden cabbage white. Why break a butterfly on the wheel? Why run the risk of an embarrassing

---

1. Hansard *House of Commons Parliamentary Debates* 6 December 1989
2. Hansard *House of Commons Parliamentary Debates* 18 December 1989
3. Hansard *House of Commons Parliamentary Debates* 25 October 1990
4. Hansard *House of Commons Parliamentary Debates* 21 May 1990
5. Hansard *House of Commons Parliamentary Debates* 10 May 1990

diplomatic confrontation? That could perfectly well happen if the vessel turned out to be under an American flag."[6]

Lord Colwyn said "I have received a submission from supporters of Radio Caroline who are surprised that the additional powers proposed cover all vessels on the high seas whose broadcasts are capable of being received or causing interference in the United Kingdom. I am informed that the conventional way of dealing with an authorised broadcast from a foreign registered vessel on the high seas would be for the Government to make the appropriate representations through diplomatic channels to the flag state of the vessel.

"Although I would wish to see an end to radio piracy, it is not clear to me whether those powers may be used extra-territorially on the high seas against vessels flying a foreign flag."

The Earl Ferrers, in summing up, said "The noble Lord, Lord Annan, and my noble friend. Lord Colwyn, referred to pirate radios. The noble Lord, Lord Annan, said that they were not wasps that should be swatted off but just harmless butterflies. He said that it was absurd to send the Army, the Navy, the Customs and Uncle Tom Cobbleigh and all after these pirate stations. The provisions on pirate radio are justified and necessary. The radio spectrum is a valuable resource and its use has to be carefully planned. Unauthorised transmissions have put the safety of life channels at risk and at times of emergency could cost lives. Moreover, by interfering with the wider variety of channels they also reduce listener choice.

"The provisions in the Bill are in accordance with international law. The United Nations Law of Sea Convention allows states to act against ships on the high seas of any nationality, or none, if broadcasts from them can be received on their territory or cause interference. Of course, the powers will be exercised with moderation and restraint in the case of foreign flag vessels to avoid the diplomatic controversy which the noble Lord feared."[7]

On 25 July 1990 in the House of Lords during the Committee Stage Lord Monson said that "It is an open secret that the purpose of Clause 159 and its associated schedule, Schedule 14, is to smash Radio Caroline. This is a so-called pirate radio station which has been harmlessly operating for 26 years ... Clause 159 has alarming implications both for international law - in particular, maritime law - and for civil liberties. The powers which Her Majesty's Government are seeking against Radio Caroline, astonishingly, are very much greater than the powers which they have, in the past, sought and obtained against hijackers, smugglers and drug traffickers ..."

Lord Annan considered Section 7A, which empowers servants of the Crown to seize property and detain persons, to require the crew to produce documents and - this is most extraordinary and reprehensible - to grant officials immunity who are engaged in search and seizure. He gave an example of a vessel boarded in the way now to be permitted: "A member of the crew resists and is knocked overboard into the water and drowns. His family will have no case in damages; there will be no case of manslaughter brought against the officer who did this. It is a licence for official thuggery.

"The noble Earl will be aware that I am not soft on terrorism. I applauded the storming of the Iranian Embassy by the SAS and what the SAS did to those terrorists who occupied that Embassy. I rejoiced when I heard that the terrorists in Gibraltar were shot dead like rats. But broadcasters are not terrorists. What is Radio Caroline but a lot of crickets chirping in the grate? ... I know that Radio Caroline is an irritant. 1 know that it is illegal. I have a feeling that the Government will regret passing a measure of this kind. They are trying to bring down a mosquito with artillery fire. I know also that they are trying to bring it down by illegal means. There is no point in asking the noble Lord to reconsider this matter, but I ask him to

---

6. To 'break a butterfly on a wheel' means to use methods that are much more powerful, severe, etc.. than are strictly necessary to fulfill one's purpose. *Dictionary of English Idioms*, Longman. 1979, London, page 44. The English poet. Alexander Pope (1688 - 1744), made the earliest reference. In the year 1735 he wrote *An Epistle to Dr Arbuthnot*. Of Lord Hervey he said: "Satire or sense, alas! can Sporus feel? Who breaks a butterfly upon a wheel?"

7. Hansard *House of Lords Parliamentary Debates* 5 June 1990

believe that I am not pleading for an illegal radio station. Like the noble Lord, Lord Monson, from the voluminous mail I receive I am in no doubt that there are many people who listen to and enjoy that radio station. No doubt it is popular, but that is not my purpose. My purpose is to bring home to the Government and to the public that the Government are about to pass a clause which is illegal in international law and an affront to those who care about the principles of justice... I only hope that if this clause becomes law the crew of Radio Caroline will seek to obtain a craft under the flag of the United States. If they do that and the Government board and sequester that vessel, the Government will find themselves faced with the prospect of war, as in 1812, and later having to pay an indemnity, just as they did in the case of the *Alabama* in the American Civil War."

Viscount Caldecote said that it was really taking a steam hammer to crack a walnut. He went on: "Radio Caroline may be annoying, but this issue is not of such moment as to require the draconian measures that are being proposed. When a steam hammer is used irresponsibly it can do a lot of damage ... This clause sets a very bad example to others on the high seas. For example, someone like Colonel Gadaffi might well find passing near but outside his territorial waters a ship which he does not approve of for some reason. He could use this as an excuse to board it and commit piracy on the high seas, which this measure is legalising. In the past, piracy on the high seas has always been a heinous crime against which the masters of the ships have been protected by the strongest law. It is very bad to give this example which others might take advantage of for piracy on the high seas.

"Other reasons have been given, such as the view that broadcasting from Radio Caroline interferes with distress signals on the high seas. The fact is that the frequency used is well away from many of the distress frequencies used on the high seas and that argument cannot be sustained. I understand that Spectrum Radio in the United Kingdom was allocated the same frequency as Radio Caroline. There was interference and very soon another frequency was found. The fact that there are not enough frequencies available appears to be a somewhat spurious argument. That is not to say we condone illegal broadcasting and pirate broadcasting of this kind ... I urge and implore Her Majesty's Government to withdraw this clause and to look at it again very carefully. I hope that they will give an undertaking to look at it and bring back some better way of dealing with Radio Caroline than this draconian measure.

Earl Ferrers: "We are talking here about pirate radio stations. Offshore broadcasters have a colourful and romantic image. They are popularly known as pirates, conjuring up images of swashbuckling characters wearing black hats and scarves, out to tweak the tail of the authorities. They are seen by their supporters, as we have heard this evening, as harmless providers of a type of broadcasting which is not available elsewhere. On that view, the authorities who try to enforce the law against them are seen, as my noble friend Lord Caldecote said, as the sledgehammer to crack a nut, or as the noble Lord, Lord Annan, said earlier on bureaucratic killjoys out to break butterflies on wheels. The noble Lord, Lord Monson, said that what pirate stations do is innocuous. I totally disagree ... Why do they position themselves just outside territorial waters and use British frequencies if it is not to avoid British law? Unauthorised transmissions, because of their planned nature, are damaging to authorised broadcasters and other radio users. Even the safety of life services can be affected ... The noble Lord, Lord Annan, and others complained about Schedule 14 being incompatible with the law and being excessive. All states have a duty to co-operate in the suppression of unauthorised broadcasting from the high seas ... the powers we are taking are modelled on Articles 109 and 110 of the United Nations Convention on the Law of the Sea. These provide for a state to take action against broadcasters on ships of any nationality or of none which are on the high seas if their broadcasts, which are contrary to international regulations, can either be received in that state's territory or cause interference there. We do not anticipate objection from other states, although we will normally consult the flag state ... It is true that Her Majesty's Government have not yet acceded to the Convention of the Law of the Sea ... Our view is that the exercise of the powers will be in accordance with international law. That is not dependent on the convention ... Comparisons with the enforcement powers used against drug smuggling and other serious offences are oversimplified. The powers given to fight an offence are not a good reflection of its seriousness. The severity of the sentence is a far better indicator of the view taken by society of a crime. The penalties for drug smuggling far outweigh those for offshore broadcasting, and rightly so."

Lord Monson rose again and thanked Lord Annan for his powerful and detailed support. "He made only one error, but it was a significant one. Radio Caroline is not illegal because it is operated from a foreign vessel with a foreign crew in international waters. Her Majesty's Government have at present no jurisdiction over it. It would take more time than we are allowed to reply in detail to the noble Earl, Earl Ferrers, but he mentioned that the penalties against drug smugglers are greater than the penalties that are likely to be imposed on radio disc jockeys. I suppose that we must be thankful for small mercies. We are talking about overkill and about a wholly disproportionate reaction to a minor irritance, rather like sentencing someone to 14 years' imprisonment for parking on a double yellow line ... I do not intend to divide the Committee on whether the clause should stand as part of the Bill, but my noble friend and I will reserve all our fire for Schedule 14 which, I trust, will be dealt with tomorrow. I withdraw my opposition."

The following day, 26 July 1990, the debate continued.[8] Lord McNair said he wanted to preface his remarks by saying that he was speaking personally and not for the Liberal Democrats as a whole. "In 1966, I was at the Young Liberals conference at Great Yarmouth which voted overwhelmingly in favour of legalising so-called pirate radio stations. It seemed to us then, as it does to me still, a nonsense to prosecute, and to persecute, companies which gave so much harmless pleasure to so many ... The Government's attitude towards, and their actions against, the personnel and equipment of Radio Caroline in August last year went far beyond the proverbial sledgehammer to crack a walnut. An important issue of principle is involved. It seems that the more power and control that any Government have, the more they want, until situations which most would regard as outside the Governmental sphere of operation come to be regarded by a Government as a threat to that power - a state that has been called the laager mentality. The events that took place about a year ago aboard the motor vessel *Ross Revenge,* the ship from which Radio Caroline operates, were a shameful example of overkill, if the news reports are accurate. Not only was the equipment impounded, for which there could, if interference with other transmissions were a definite fact, have been some justification, but it was destroyed in the process. That, whatever the legal position, was an act of wanton vandalism and an example of the laager mentality.

Lord Orr-Ewing, one time a Parliamentary Secretary for Air, referred to remarks made about putting at risk ships at sea and aircraft in the air. He said "In 1922 a Dame Nellie Melba concert was broadcast by Marconi on the 2MT call sign from Writtle, Essex. Peter Eckersley, who later became chief engineer of the BBC, was an excellent engineer and had a good sense of drama. He hired Dame Nellie Melba to sing on the first experimental broadcast. There was a Statement in the House saying that it was outrageous that the wireless waves should be used for such trivial matters as entertainment while putting at risk ships at sea and aircraft in the air. The same phraseology has come out of the same pigeon-hole at the Home Office some 68 years later. When I first came to the House in 1950, the same row was going on. In this day and age, are ships at sea, and aircraft in the air, which have every conceivable modern technology, using telegraphy on the broadcast waves of Europe, where there are thousands of stations? After dark they all interfere with each other ... I agree that the activity is illegal, but I found it difficult to stomach the fact that we must take such absolutely amazing powers. Drug smugglers are not allowed on the high seas, but the powers to go aboard pirate radio ships appear even greater. Pirate radio operators are against the law. I wish that they paid the

---

8. Hansard House of Lords Parliamentary Debates 25/26 July 1990

musical fees for copyright. I hope those people will apply for the new wireless frequencies that will be available. They may not be on medium wave, but some frequencies will be available. As they have so much experience, I have no doubt that they would be given some of the earliest ones. Perhaps the Government might say, as a slight amelioration, that if they applied they would stand a good chance ... I hope that the Government will consider the matter more sympathetically than they have done. (Author's note: Anyone convicted of unlicensed broadcasting offences after 1 January 1989 is automatically debarred from running a legal independent radio station for a period of five years.)

Earl Ferrers replied by saying "My noble friend may find this difficult to believe, but I can tell him that if one broadcasts on a frequency which one has not been allocated one may interfere with other frequencies inland. Further, one may inadvertently combine with another frequency and mess up the beacons which helicopters in particular home in on. Therefore there is a distinct risk to life."

The Bill received the Royal Assent on 1 November 1990 and became an Act of Parliament on 1 January 1991.

The Broadcasting Act of 1990 made amendments to the Marine, Etc., Broadcasting (Offences) Act 1967 and in turn put an end to pirate radio ships off the British coasts. These amendments are reproduced on the following pages.

SCHEDULE 16   Section 171. 1967 c.41.

AMENDMENTS OF THE MARINE,
ETC., BROADCASTING (OFFENCES) ACT 1967

1. -(1) Section 2 (prohibition of broadcasting from marine structures) shall be amended as follows.

(2) In subsection (l)(a), for "external waters or in tidal waters in the United Kingdom" substitute "any waters to which this section applies."

(3) After subsection (2) insert the following subsection -

"(3) This section applies to -
    (a) tidal waters in the United Kingdom;
    (b) external waters; and
    (c) waters in a designated area within the meaning of the Continental
       Shelf Act 1964."

2. - After section 2 insert the following section -

2A.-(1) Subject to subsection (4) below, it shall not be lawful to make a broadcast which -

    (a) is made from a ship (other than one registered in the United
    Kingdom, the Isle of Man or any of the Channel Islands) while the ship
    is within any area of the high seas prescribed for the purposes of this
    section by an order made by the Secretary of State; and
    (b) is capable of being received in, or causes interference with any
    wireless telegraphy in, the United Kingdom.

(2) If a broadcast is made from a ship in contravention of subsection (1) above, the owner of the ship, the master of the ship and every person who operates, or participates in the operation of, the apparatus by means of which the broadcast is made shall be guilty of an offence.

(3) A person who procures the making of a broadcast in contravention of

subsection (1) above shall be guilty of an offence.

(4) The making of a broadcast does not contravene subsection (1) above if it is shown to have been authorised under the law of any country or territory outside the United Kingdom.

(5) Any order under this section shall be made by statutory instrument subject to annulment in pursuance of a resolution of either House of Parliament."

3. In section 3 (prohibition of acts connected with broadcasting from certain ships and aircraft, and from marine structures outside the United Kingdom) -

(a) in subsection (I), at the beginning insert "Subject to subsection (1A) below,"; and
(b) after subsection (1) insert the following subsection -
"(1A) Subsection (l)(a) above does not apply to any broadcast made in contravention of section 2A(1) of this Act, and subsections (1)(c) and (d) above do not apply to structures or other objects in waters falling within section 2(3)(c) of this Act."

4. After section 3 insert the following section -

3A.-(1) Any person who, from any place in the United Kingdom or external waters, participates in the management, stations financing, operation or day-to-day running of any broadcasting station by which broadcasts are made -
(a) in contravention of section 1, 2 or 2A(1) of this Act, or
(b)as mentioned in section 3(1)(a) of this Act,
shall be guilty of an offence.

(2) In this section "broadcasting station" means any business or other operation (whether or not in the nature of a commercial venture) which is engaged in the making of broadcasts."

5. -(1) Section 4 (prohibition of acts facilitating broadcasting from ships, aircraft etc.) shall be amended as follows.

(2) In subsection (1), after paragraph (a) insert -
"(aa) where paragraph (a) above does not apply but the broadcasts in question are made, or are to be made, from any structure or other object (not being a ship or aircraft) in waters falling within section 2(3)(c) of this Act, he does the act on that structure or other object within those waters; or
(ab) where paragraph (a) above does not apply but the broadcasts in question are made, or are to be made, from a ship in contravention of section 2A(1) of this Act, he does the act in that ship within any such area of the high seas as is mentioned in paragraph (a) of that provision; or."

(3)   In subsection (3)(e), for "or 2(1)" substitute ", 2(1) or 2A(1)."

6. -(1) Section 5 (prohibition of acts relating to matter broadcast from ships, aircraft etc.) shall be amended as follows.

(2)   In subsection (1), after paragraph (a) insert -
"(aa) where paragraph (a) above does not apply but the broadcasts in question are made, or are to be made, from any structure or other object (not being a ship or aircraft) in waters falling within section 2(3)(c) of this Act, he does the act on that structure or other object within those waters; or
(ab) where paragraph (a) above does not apply but the broadcasts in question are made, or are to be made, from a ship in contravention of section 2A(1) of this Act, he does the act

in that ship within any such area of the high seas as is mentioned in paragraph (a) of that provision; or."

(3)   In subsections (3)(a) and (4), for "or 2(1)", in each place where those words occur, substitute ", 2(1) or 2A(I)."

7. -(1) Section 6 (penalties and legal proceedings) shall be amended as follows.

(2)In subsection (l)(a). for "three" substitute "six".

In subsection (5), for "on behalf of, in both places where those words occur, substitute "with the consent of the Secretary of State or."

8. After section 7 insert the following section -
7 A.-(1) The following persons are enforcement officers for the purposes of this section

    (a) persons authorised by the Secretary of State to exercise the powers conferred by subsection (5) below;
    (b) police officers;
    (c) commissioned officers of Her Majesty's armed forces;
    (d) officers commissioned by the Commissioners of Customs and Excise under section 6(3) of the Customs and Excise Management Act 1979; and
    (e) persons not falling within any of the preceding paragraphs who are British sea-fishery officers by virtue of section 7(1) of the Sea Fisheries Act 1968;

and in this subsection "armed forces" means the Royal Navy, the Royal Marines, the regular army and the regular air force, and any reserve or auxiliary force of any of those services which has been called out on permanent service, or called into actual service, or embodied.

(2)   If an enforcement officer has reasonable grounds for suspecting -
    (a) that an offence under this Act has been or is being committed by the making of a broadcast from any ship, structure or other object in external waters or in tidal waters in the United Kingdom or from a ship registered in the United Kingdom, the Isle of Man or any of the Channel Islands while on the high seas,
    (b) that an offence under section 2 of this Act has been or is being committed by the making of a broadcast from a structure or other object in waters falling within subsection (3)(c) of that section, or
    (c) that an offence under section 2A of this Act has been or is being committed by the making of a broadcast from a ship,

and the Secretary of State has issued a written authorisation for the exercise of the powers conferred by subsection (5) below in relation to that ship, structure or other object, then (subject to subsections (6) and (7) below) the officer may, with or without persons assigned to assist him in his duties, so exercise those powers.

(3)   If -
    (a) the Secretary of State has issued an authorisation under subsection (2) above for the exercise of the powers conferred by subsection (5) below in relation to any ship, structure or other object, and
    (b) an enforcement officer has reasonable grounds for suspecting that an offence under section 4 or 5 of this Act has been or is being committed in connection with the making

of a broadcast from that ship, structure or other object,

then (subject to subsections (6) and (7) below) the officer may, with or without persons assigned to assist him in his duties, also exercise those powers in relation to any ship, structure or other object which he has reasonable grounds to suspect has been or is being used in connection with the commission of that offence.

(4)	Where -
(a) an enforcement officer has reasonable grounds for suspecting that an offence under section 4 or 5 of this Act has been or is being committed in connection with the making of a broadcast from a ship, structure or other object, but
(b) an authorisation has not been issued under subsection (2) above for the exercise of the powers conferred by subsection (5) below in relation to that ship, structure or other object,

then (subject to subsections (6) and (7) below) the officer may, with or without persons assigned to assist him in his duties, nevertheless exercise those powers in relation to any ship, structure or other object which he has reasonable grounds to suspect has been or is being used in connection with the commission of that offence if the Secretary of State has issued a written authorisation for the exercise of those powers in relation to that ship, structure or other object.

(5)	The powers conferred by this subsection on an enforcement officer in relation to any ship, structure or other object are -
(a) to board and search the ship, structure or other object;
(b) to seize and detain the ship, structure or other object and any apparatus or other thing found in the course of the search which appears to him to have been used, or to have been intended to be used, in connection with, or to be evidence of, the commission of the suspected offence;
(c) to arrest and search any person who he has reasonable grounds to suspect has committed or is committing an offence under this Act if -
(i) that person is on board the ship, structure or other object, or
(ii) the officer has reasonable grounds for suspecting that that person was so on board at, or shortly before, the time when the officer boarded the ship, structure or other object;
(d) to arrest any person who assaults him, or a person assigned to assist him in his duties, while exercising any of the powers conferred by this subsection or who intentionally obstructs him or any such person in the exercise of any of those powers;
(e) to require any person on board the ship, structure or other object to produce any documents or other items which are in his custody or possession and are or may be evidence of the commission of any offence under this Act;
(f) to require any such person to do anything for the purpose of facilitating the exercise of any of the powers conferred by this subsection, including enabling any apparatus or other thing to be rendered safe and, in the case of a ship, enabling the ship to be taken to a port;
(g) to use reasonable force, if necessary, in exercising any of those powers; and references in paragraphs (a) to (c) and (e) above to the ship, structure or other object include references to any ship's boat or other vessel used from the ship, structure or other object.

(6) Except as provided in subsection (7) below, the powers conferred by subsection (5) above shall only be exercised in tidal waters in the United Kingdom or in

external waters.

(7) Those powers may in addition -

(a) in relation to a suspected offence under this Act committed in a ship registered in the United Kingdom, the Isle of Man or any of the Channel Islands while on the high seas, be exercised in relation to that ship on the high seas;
(b) in relation to a suspected offence under section 2 of this Act committed on a structure or other object within waters falling within subsection (3)(e) of that section, be exercised in relation to that structure or other object within those waters; and
(c) in relation to a suspected offence under section 2A of this Act committed in a ship within any such area of the high seas as is mentioned in subsection (1)(a) of that section, be exercised in relation to that ship "within that area of the high seas.

(8) Any person who -
(a) assaults an enforcement officer, or a person assigned to assist him in his duties, while exercising any of the powers conferred by subsection (5) above or intentionally obstructs him or any such person in the exercise of any of those powers, or
(b)without reasonable excuse fails or refuses to comply with any such requirement as is mentioned in paragraph (e) or (f) of that subsection, shall be guilty of an offence under this Act.

(9) Neither an enforcement officer nor a person assigned to assist him in his duties shall be liable in any civil or criminal proceedings for anything done in purported exercise of any of the powers conferred by subsection (5) above if the court is satisfied that the act was done in good faith and that there were reasonable grounds for doing it.

(10) Nothing in this section shall have effect so as to prejudice the exercise of any powers exercisable apart from this section.

(11) Any reference in this section, in relation to a person assigned to assist an enforcement officer in his duties, to the exercise of any of the powers conferred by subsection (5) above is a reference to the exercise by that person of any of those powers on behalf of that officer."

The following Members of the House of Lords and House of Commons, who took part in broadcasting debates and discussion about the pirate stations 1964 - 1993, have since died:

Lord Noel Gilroy Annan 1916 - 2000
Anthony Berry, later Sir Anthony Berry 1925-1984
John Biggs-Davison, later Sir John Biggs-Davison 1918-1988
Captain Henry Britton 1914-1971
Lord Byers 1915-1984
Robert Andrew Inskip, 2nd Viscount Caldecot 1917-1999
Robert Cooke, later Sir Robert Gordon Cooke, 1930-1987
Richard Crawshaw, later Baron Crawshaw of Aintree 1917-1986
Bernard Francis Castle Floud 1915-1967
Hector Hughes 1887-1970
Arthur Irvine, later Sir Arthur Irvine 1909-1978

Captain L.P.S. Orr 1918-1990
Lord (Charles) Ian Orr-Ewing 1912-1999
Baroness Phillips 1910-1992
Christopher Rowland 1929-1967
Lord Sorenson 1891-1971
Lord Strange 1900-1982

The Palace of Westminster

Chapter Eleven

THE EVE OF DESTRUCTION

Now the "harbour light" is calling
This will be our last goodbye
Though the carnival is over
I will love you till I die.

The Carnival is Over, Seekers, 1965

JUST THIRTY months after the British pirates came on the air the Government took action to outlaw those stations broadcasting from the forts, beginning with Radio 390.

On 21 September 1966 the "sweet music station" received a summons alleging illegal broadcasting. The news made headlines in many national papers including the *Daily Mail*, "Pop Pirate Gets Summons", and the *Daily Mirror*, "War on the Pop Pirates - Radio 390 Summonsed".

David Lye, the secretary of the company controlling Radio 390, Estuary Radio of Kent, was issued with the summons by Inspector Thomas Metcalfe of the Metropolitan Police. It was returnable at Canterbury Magistrates Court on 24 November. A similar summons was issued against Estuary Radio.

The summons, which was issued at the GPO's police offices in Moorfields, London, alleged that "the station did, on 16 August 1966 at Red Sands Tower within the jurisdiction of Kent, unlawfully use apparatus for wireless telegraphy, namely a transmitter, contrary to the 1949 Wireless and Telegraphy Act."

Maximum penalty for this offence was a £100 fine, three months' jail or both.

The station's managing director, Ted Allbeury, said he would fight the case to the highest tribunal in the land because Radio 390 considered they were outside the territorial jurisdiction of Great Britain. Radio 390 would continue broadcasting until they got a decision. "But," said Allbeury, "should a court find us in breach of the Wireless and Telegraphy Act, we will stop broadcasting immediately. We will abide by the letter of the law."

Radio 390 completed one year's broadcasting three days after the first summons was issued. It broadcast from a disused anti-aircraft fort at Red Sands in the Thames Estuary, 8½ miles from Whitstable, from 6.30 each morning until midnight.

Its turnover for the first year was estimated at around £250,000 and showed a profit on the initial investment. The station cost £1,500 a week to run and had an estimated daily audience of about six million listeners.

Ted Allbeury was actually holding a press conference in a London hotel when David Lye walked in waiving a piece of paper and said "I've been summonsed." Allbeury said he expected a personal summons the following day.

And sure enough the next day, 22 September, he was personally issued with a summons from Inspector Thomas Metcalfe at Radio 390's headquarters in Bessborough Place, Pimlico. The premises where 390 were housed were owned, somewhat to the Government's embarrassment, by the Greater London Council.

Inspector Metcalfe simply said to Mr Allbeury "This is for you." The summons was identical to the one issued on Estuary Radio the previous day. It alleged unauthorised use of a transmitter.

The day Mr Allbeury received his summons, news came from Sweden of another pirate. The Court of Appeal in Malmo remitted a three-month prison sentence passed on Mrs Britt

Wadner in December 1965 for radio offences. The court substituted a suspended sentence although it found Mrs Wadner guilty of illegally transmitting from Radio Syd in the Oeresund Channel.

Mrs Wadner was in Britain when the news came through. She was arranging for the disposal of her ship, *Cheeta II*, which had been loaned to Caroline South early in 1966. Mrs Wadner said she was delighted with the news and would continue her campaign to operate from land. She also said she was interested selling *Cheeta II* which was awaiting a new transmitter from Holland. A fort-borne radio station had offered to buy it.

Many questions were asked about why the Government couldn't take the forts by force. After all, in 1964 the Dutch Government did just that to Europe's only pirate TV station, North Sea Television, which operated from a platform driven into the bottom of the North Sea five miles off the Netherlands coast. After 3½ months of profitable operation it was silenced by Dutch sailors and policemen on 17 December 1964. Police, in helicopters, dropped from a dull, grey sky on to the platform as the record *Paradiso* by a 21-year-old Dutch girl, Anneke Groenloh, was being played.

The secret operation known as "Operation Noordzee" had taken three days to plan. Two helicopters were used in the operation. The first dropped smoke marker bombs, and the second lowered a cable with two policemen onto the platform.

Meanwhile, a 360-ton pilot ship, the *Delfshaven*, was leaving the Hook of Holland with Department of Justice officials and Post Office technicians on board. When the *Delfshaven* came alongside the platform, Amsterdam's deputy prosecutor, G.R. Nube, was winched aboard. The station went off the air at exactly seven minutes past eight in the morning. The crew members on the platform were told not to oppose Government action.

Commercial television in Holland is forbidden despite a poll showing 70 per cent of the population were in favour. North Sea Television was said to have made £350,000 in its time of operation. On board they had two crews of ten. There were Swiss, Belgian, French and British personnel involved as well as Dutch. The equipment was American. The 'island' itself was said to have belonged to the Panamanians, but the Panamanian Government denied all knowledge of it. "Try the British," they said.

The platform was similar in design to the oil rigs in the North Sea and was built in eight weeks. Six stilts, 75ft. long, were driven into the sea bed. A concrete platform was built on top. Above this was a 200ft. transmitting mast. The studio and control room were housed in a two storey building on the stilts. North Sea Television began regular transmissions on 1 September 1964.

The question whether to prosecute the British forts had been under consideration by the Post Office for many months. The delay in taking action was due mainly to complex legal problems about the definition of territorial waters and, furthermore, whether the courts actually had jurisdiction over the forts.

A similar problem arose at Canterbury Magistrates Court on Thursday 24 November 1966. "Was Red Sands Tower on the high seas or was it within the jurisdiction of the court?"

Sir Peter Rawlinson, QC, former Solicitor-General in the Conservative Government, defending, told the court "Red Sands Tower is situated at sea more than three miles from the low water mark of the county of Kent and the *prima facie* case is that the tower is outside territorial jurisdiction. The county jurisdiction ends at low water mark and all beyond that is the high seas."

Mr John Newey for the Postmaster-General was in court with Admiralty charts and other papers. He said that he had been brought into court in respect of a so-called pirate radio station which had attracted a great deal of public attention. He went on "We need not concern ourselves here with whether they provide a useful public service or whether they interfere with ships' wireless and so on. Our considerations are simply whether they are offences contrary to the Act, and also whether this court has jurisdiction to hear them." The Wireless Telegraphy Act of 1949 did not define territorial waters and the law had to be looked at elsewhere. Mr Newey produced various Acts of Parliament which he said gave clues to jurisdiction. He also presented the court with a special copy of the 1958 Geneva Convention on territorial waters.

In 1878, in connection with the definition of territorial waters, the limit was laid down as three miles, but in September 1964 Orders in Council and amendments to the Continental Shelf Act were introduced to deal with the requirements of drilling for oil in the North Sea.

"The prosecution had to prove," Mr Newey went on "that wireless apparatus had been used. Furthermore that it had been used without a licence, and used at a place inside territorial waters."

He said that on 16 August the General Post Office had direction finding equipment focused on the Thames Estuary where they had picked up transmissions from a radio station that called itself Radio 390.

The following day Detective Inspector Metcalfe of the Metropolitan Police, who was attached to the Post Office during their investigations, called at the London headquarters of Radio 390 and spoke to secretary David Lye.

The prosecution was against Estuary Radio of Queen's House, Folkestone, which ran Radio 390 from the anti-aircraft forts since September 1965; Edward Theodore le Bouthillier Allbeury, the company's managing director, and David Beresford Lye, director and secretary of the company.

The two defendants and the company pleaded not guilty to the summonses.

Continuing the case for the Postmaster-General, Mr Newey said "We have to consider where England physically comes to an end."

In September 1964 the Queen made an Order in Council giving effect to the United Nations Convention. "There was now a special way of calculating limits in the case of bays and indentations in the coast," Mr Newey went on. He then defined islands, sandbanks, estuaries, and bays.

Under the Order in Council which was law, the territorial limits of a bay were found from a complex formula. In the case of the Thames Estuary one took a straight line from the Naze to North Foreland; a semicircle was then drawn seaward of the line and, if the water thus surrounded was not greater in area than that on the land side of the line, the water within the semicircle became territorial.

The hearing continued the following day, 25 November when a Customs officer gave evidence. Robert Stiff of Whitstable said that until a policy change in May 1966 Red Sands Tower was treated as being outside British territorial waters. The boat *Mallard*, which was skippered by Victor Davis, had been responsible for taking supplies to Radio 390 since December 1964. A special clearance form was completed before each trip and Mr Davis had to report to the Customs at Whitstable before leaving. In answer to Sir Peter Rawlinson, Mr Stiff agreed that a boat going from Whitstable to Greenwich would not have to fill in any forms or report to a Customs officer before leaving. The clearance which the boat *Mallard* and Mr Davis had to go through was in respect of ships leaving British waters.

Mr Newey for the Postmaster-General cross-examined Mr Stiff who said that no duty-free goods were allowed to go out to Radio 390. The captain of the *Mallard*, Victor Davis, said that the crew of Radio 390 changed every week. He had never seen any of the men who came ashore from the tower produce a passport at Whitstable. He was always asked by the Customs if he had brought in any aliens.

Sir Peter Rawlinson said that although he had every respect for Lieutenant-Commander Peter Beasley (who was head of the Territorial Waters Department of the Hydrographic Department, Ministry of Defence), it was a remarkable thing that this matter, which affected the sovereignty of the Realm, should turn on the evidence of a distinguished officer but one who only held the rank of Lieutenant-Commander.

Sir Peter went on to say that "Apparently Lieutenant-Commander Beasley had drawn the line without informing the general public. This is a very grave matter, and it is surprising that the prosecution in a case like this, where they must clearly have seen that they should produce such certificates, did not produce certificates and evidence from the highest authority."

Sir Peter urged the three magistrates at St Augustine's, Canterbury, to consider carefully the question of whether the Wireless Telegraphy Act of 1949 could give any jurisdiction by implication. He said that territorial waters could be extended by Act of Parliament. "The Territorial Waters Order of Court of 1964 had been made under the Queen's Prerogative and not by Act of Parliament."

Mr John Newey, prosecuting for the Post Office, said: "If you accept that the Order in Council is not good law and is to be treated as if it were in the wastepaper basket, I suggest that you look at the international convention which says the same thing. In my submission the order is plainly a document validly and lawfully made."

The three magistrates, Donald Andrews, Francis Gowan and Sam Brealey, then retired for thirty four minutes. The chairman, Donald Andrews, said that they had not yet reached a decision and wanted some more assistance from Lieutenant-Commander Beasley. The magistrates questioned him and then retired again, for a further thirty minutes. Mr Andrews then read a statement:

> We find that Red Sands is situated in territorial waters. The Wireless Telegraphy Act of 1949 is silent on the question of local jurisdiction but the territorial waters in question join the coast of Kent and for that reason we are of the opinion that the justices of the county of Kent have jurisdiction in this matter. On the evidence before us we find the case proved.

Estuary Radio Ltd., controllers of Radio 390, and two of its officials were found guilty on summonses that "on 15 August at Red Sands Tower in the jurisdiction of Kent, did unlawfully use apparatus for wireless telegraphy, namely a transmitter, except under, and in accordance with, a licence in that behalf granted by the Postmaster-General."

Edward Theodore le Bouthillier Allbeury, managing director, and David Beresford Lye, company secretary, were found guilty but were each given an absolute discharge. The bench made no order as to costs. Estuary Radio was fined the maximum of £100. The magistrates refused an application by John Newey for confiscation of the equipment belonging to the station.

At 11 o'clock that evening on 25 November, Radio 390 closed down pending an appeal. John Withers from the London office of Radio 390 drove down to Whitstable and made a trip out to the fort. In his pocket he had a pre-recorded taped message for the station's millions of fans. Disc jockey Stephen West broke into the programme which had included records *I Love You Samantha* and *It's a Most Unusual Day* and said "Stand by for an announcement."

Ted Allbeury then came on the air with the recorded taped message "Hello there. This is Ted Allbeury speaking. I cannot believe this is the end. I am advised that it might take three to four weeks for an appeal to be heard. If we won we would start broadcasting immediately. However, if we lost, it would mean that we should have to cease broadcasting from the fort. I should expect to make some alternative arrangements. For now all I can say is what I have always said - take care of yourselves, goodbye and God bless."

Stephen West then returned to the microphone and said "We are now closing down." The national anthem was played. West had the final word, "Goodnight." Radio 390 then went off the air from the fort.

While the appeal for Radio 390 was going through, Radio Essex faced a similar summons which was returnable at Rochford, Essex, on Wednesday 30 November. Radio Essex, owned by 45-year-old Roy Bates of Avenue Road, Westcliff, was to appear in court for operating a radio station without a licence. He said after learning of the Radio 390 verdict, "I intend carrying on with my plans to expand and I shall certainly carry on broadcasting. My case is different."

And "carry on' Radio Essex did. Roy Bates appeared in court at Rochford on 30 November and was found guilty of operating a radio transmitter without a licence from the Postmaster-General. He was fined the maximum of £100. But unlike Radio 390, he ordered Radio Essex to carry on broadcasting. But he changed their name from Radio Essex to Britain's Better Music Station.

No order was made for confiscating the transmitter which was housed on Knock John Fort, eighteen miles from Southend and nine miles from Foulness Island.

The magistrates found that under a new international law the sands were within British territorial waters, and therefore within their jurisdiction.

Mr Bates, who conducted his own case, pleaded guilty to transmitting without a licence. He asked for seven days to pay, and also gave notice of appeal. "I shall go ahead with plans to open a new pirate station at Tongue Towers, a fort about nine miles from Margate and outside territorial waters," Mr Bates concluded.

However, the appeal was dismissed by Essex quarter sessions at Chelmsford on 17 January 1967. J. Roland Adams, QC, the chairman, said that "It appears to us that Knock John Fort, the site of Radio Essex, was about half a mile inside inland waters, and within the jurisdiction of the Rochford Bench. In fact the offence was committed within the United Kingdom." Bates said he would continue with the appeal and, if necessary, take it to the House of Lords.

Disc jockey Guy Hamilton from Radio Essex remembers:

The prosecution was for illegally broadcasting in British internal waters. I was present at the court hearing, and can vouch for it being little short of a Whitehall farce. Indeed at one point the press corps was killing itself at the farcical case oilily presented by the Postmaster-General's emissary. It seemed that, despite being at least 20 miles out at sea, the Knock John Fort was 400 yards inside British waters because of the new Order in Council (i.e. legislation not requiring an Act of Parliament) declaring any bay or other indentation in the coast to be British internal waters if a line not exceeding 24 nautical miles in length was drawn across the same, and a semicircle drawn on that line's seaward side contained less water than the landward side.

Why 24 miles? Well, this was coincidentally almost exactly the distance from the Naze to the North Foreland, the extremities of the vast Thames Estuary. Why the semicircle? Who knows, but if you draw one on this particular line, it contains 1 square mile less than the water in the Estuary: however, to achieve this, the area of the River Thames upstream to Teddington was calculated and added to the area of the River Medway as far as Rochester. Thus, amidst much mirth, was the case proved. The three-mile limit was then drawn out from this line, and we were prosecuted.

So far The Post Office were winning their battle to prosecute the pirates ... Radio 390 fined £100 and now Radio Essex, £100.

On 11 December 1966 the Post Office went into action against a third pirate, but this time the case was slightly different. It was the first ship to receive a summons. Radio Scotland, the only offshore station for Scotland, was ordered to appear at Ayr Sheriff Court on 21 December accused of contravening the Wireless Telegraphy Act of 1949 by operating without a licence on 12 September 1966. The station broadcast on 242 metres from a ship anchored in the Firth of Clyde. The hearing was postponed until 13 March 1967.

On the same day that Radio Scotland received a summons, Ted Allbeury of Radio 390 announced that he was going to sue the Postmaster-General. He claimed damages for alleged malicious intimidation of customers and for "maliciously inducing them to break their contracts" with the Estuary Radio Company. Damages were also to be claimed for alleged slander, and libel resulting from a speech the Postmaster-General, Edward Short, made on 22 September 1966 at Dundee, Scotland.

Following Radio 390's £100 fine they were allowed to appeal and their case was heard on

13 December 1966. But unfortunately it was 13 unlucky. They lost their appeal and duly remained off the air. However, disc jockeys and engineers manned Red Sands Tower in the hope that they might have won the case and resume transmissions.

First, Lord Parker, the Lord Chief Justice, said he would uphold the conviction. Then Lord Justice Salmon said he would allow the appeal. That left one judge to announce his decision - he was the junior of the three. His name was Mr Justice Blain and he decided to dismiss the appeal. Mr Justice Blain said he did it with regret because it appeared wrong that a change in the definition of territorial waters should suddenly make a legal act become an illegal one.

Estuary Radio was ordered to pay the costs of the hearing which ran into thousands of pounds. Leave to appeal to the Lords was granted. However, Ted Allbeury said after the hearing "We have decided to call it a day. We shall not go to the Lords."

It appeared that a sandbank lost the case for Radio 390 ... a sandbank that only very rarely appeared ... and a sandbank which very few people have actually seen.

On 20 December the Government came out with its long awaited White Paper, the contents of which have been discussed in the previous chapter.

New Year's Eve 1966 was interesting for at 11.30pm, Radio 390 decided to resume transmissions and went back on the air again with regular programmes. The first record played had the title *This Could be the Start of Something Big*. Then Ted Allbeury said:

> It's great to be back on the air again with you all. We're back on the air and furthermore we shall stay on the air this time. We have new evidence that the fort is at least a mile and a half outside territorial waters. The survey was executed in accordance with Admiralty practice and the GPO will have to summons us again if they feel they have a case.

Many people said that Allbeury was returning to the air in open defiance of the law. But Allbeury had always been a fighting man and wanted to prove Radio 390 were in the right.

After their £100 fine in November, Ted Allbeury was reported to have admitted defeat, and the staff of the station reduced to a minimum. Estuary Radio Ltd., the company that ran Radio 390, was also reported to be winding up.

Ted Allbeury claimed that the figures which were produced in evidence against 390's position had been drawn up in 1959 and were incorrect. He and his company had employed a hydrographer to look into the case of whether there was a sandbank between Red Sands Tower and land - or not. Mr Allbeury said that the hydrographers report firmly said that the supposed sandbank was always covered with at least five inches of water at the lowest tide. The hydrographer had cost Mr Allbeury between £500 and £700.

During the five weeks the station was off the air, Radio 390 lost almost £2,000 which was paid in salaries and maintenance.

A Post Office spokesman said "We shall obviously be looking into

Ted Allbeury

the whole position of Radio 390 resuming transmissions."

And look into the position they did. On 13 February 1967 they issued a total of 28 summonses alleging broadcasting without a licence. They were issued by magistrates at Rochford and returnable at Southend on 22 February 1967.

Four summonses each were issued against Estuary Radio Ltd., of Queen's House, Guildhall Street, Folkestone, Kent; Ted Allbeury, managing director; David Lye, company secretary, and John Gething, a director. Three other directors were also issued with summonses. They were Christopher Blackwell of Colchester, John La Trobe of Ashford, Kent, and Michael Mitcham of Cambridge.

On 8 February 1967 Radio City was the fourth pirate to appear in court following a summons returnable at Rochford. They were found guilty and ordered to pay £100. Full details of the case can be found in Chapter Eight.

On Friday 17 February the Post Office was accused of 'shopping around' to find a magistrates court which would convict Radio 390. Sir Peter Rawlinson, QC, asked the Queen's Bench Divisional Court for leave to seek an order stopping magistrates at Southend, Essex, hearing the 28 summonses.

Sir Peter said that Radio 390 had been convicted by Kent magistrates in November 1966 on the grounds that Red Sands Tower was within territorial waters. The court refused to accept that the station was in a bay, but agreed it was within three miles of a sandbank exposed at low tide. After a hydrographical survey of the sandbank disputing this, the station resumed regular transmissions.

Sir Peter's application was turned down by Lord Justice Winn who said that he could not stop the prosecution taking place in any court. The Post Office said they were not 'shopping around.' They had gone to Southend because Canterbury, where the previous case had been heard, could not hear this case until April.

Ted Allbeury and his colleagues appeared in court at Rochford on 22 February and John Newey, prosecuting, said it had been found that Red Sands Tower was nearer to Essex than Kent. Therefore it was preferable that the nearest court should deal with the case. The following day Radio 390 was fined £200 and the directors were each fined £40.

Lieutenant-Commander John Mackay, commander of the Inshore Survey Squadron, said that when he reached the now famous sandbank he was able to plant a Union Jack on it without even getting his feet wet. The commander said that as he stood there taking sextant readings, the tide dropped even lower to uncover at least 600 yards of the sands.

A week before Radio 390 appeared in court at Rochford it was learned that Ted Allbeury had resigned as managing director of the station and joined the shipborne station Britain Radio as managing director. It looked as if Radio 390 would have to close down again. This was the last surviving fort as Radio City had closed down the previous week (see Chapter Eight).

David Lye, former company secretary of Radio 390, stepped in from the background to supervise the running of the station, and Josephine Lundberg and Peter James were chosen to run the London office.

Meanwhile, the House of Commons introduced a Bill into Parliament on 9 March which increased the fine for broadcasting without a licence from £100 to £400.

Commenting after he had left Radio 390 on the court cases against his former radio station, Ted Allbeury said: "They were entirely understandable from the Government's point of view. I think it was significant that they chose 390 rather than any other because they recognised our popularity and that we were beginning to matter. Also I presented a programme on a Sunday evening which criticised and exposed the lies of the second Postmaster-General with whom I had dealings. When Wedgie Benn was Postmaster-General he was absolutely civilised, made no nonsense about it all and said 'No of course these people are not criminals, they're not pirates. They're just ordinary businessmen who have found a loophole in the law, which eventually we shall close.' Those comments I found sane and perfectly in order.

"When Edward Short came on the scene it was much different. I can well see why he never proceeded beyond the rank of captain in the Army, because that was about the extent of his talent, I thought. He was a spiteful man and tried to connect Radio 390 with the murder of three policemen in Hammersmith. He did that on the day I had been summoned so I brought a libel action against him.

"As to the court cases themselves - the one at Canterbury was perfectly straightforward and dealt with by the magistrates properly, I believed. The one in the High Court was interesting because it was not an unanimous verdict. Lord Justice Summer, as he became, disagreed and said no as he found no offence committed at all. Lord Widgery sort of balanced between the two extremes and went on the basis that obviously the Government wanted us out, so if he was to overbalance one way or the other he had better overbalance for the Establishment, which is totally understandable. I said that I was always prepared to do something unauthorised but was never prepared to do anything illegal, so I arranged that as soon as that verdict was given the station closed down. I had already pre-recorded a closing-down message. I resigned and was immediately asked by some Americans to run a radio station on a ship - Britain Radio which I accepted."[1]

On 13 March Radio Scotland made its second appearance in court at Ayr charged with operating a radio station without a licence. An appeal heard on 13 December 1966 had proved unlucky. Again the 13th brought no better news as the radio station was fined £80.

City and County Commercial Radio (Scotland) Ltd., of Cranworth Street, Glasgow, pleaded not guilty to a charge that on 14 September 1966, on a hulk moored in the Firth of Clyde near Lady Isle, being in territorial waters, they used a wireless transmitter without a licence.

Tommy Shields, (45), the managing director of Radio Scotland, was found not guilty and discharged. J. Cruikshank, prosecuting, said that the hulk was at least 35 sea miles inside territorial waters - in fact in the Firth of Clyde.

Mr Hugh McCalman, defending, said that Radio Scotland had conducted its radio station in the honest belief that it was outside territorial waters. It had always been believed that territorial waters extended to three miles beyond the coast, and it was a measure of the incomprehensible nature of legislation to a layman that the company was charged with operating 35 miles within territorial waters.

Mr McCalman went on to say that the broadcasts were not offensive. They gave good clean entertainment of a kind not obtainable at present on any other Scottish station. Radio Scotland in just over a year of operation had passed on many hundreds of pounds to charitable organisations.

After the hearing Mr Shields said that their ship, the *Comet*, was being moved to a point seven miles off St Abb's Head near North Berwick.

The day after the Radio Scotland hearing, pirate news was being made in the south of England as well. Radio Dolfijn (originally 'Swinging' Radio England) and Britain Radio, the American- backed station, went broke!

The company that backed the stations, Peir-Vick Ltd., was in trouble to the tune of £110,000. This was the amount lost in just one year of the company's handling the advertising for the two stations. Accountant Martin Spencer said that creditors must be astonished to see such an amount of money lost in so short a time. There was mismanagement by the directors.

The ship from which Britain Radio and Radio Dolfijn operated, the *Laissez-Faire* broke her transmitting mast on 28 February during a gale. She sailed to Holland on 7 March to have her aerial repaired and was back in position off the Essex coast eight days later.

Charles Greville, writing in the *Daily Mail* on 15 March, said that Tory MP John Cordle was talked into joining the board of the firm, but as soon as he discovered it was a pirate

---

1. Ted Allbeury interview with *Offshore Echo's*, December 1978

Tommy Shields

radio firm he resigned. Cordle, 55-year-old MP for Bournemouth East and a member of the Church Assembly, said: "They asked me to look after Mr Vick's lease of a maisonette in Curzon Street, London. Now I am liable to pay the remaining two years of that lease. It will cost me a considerable amount." John Cordle remained on the board of Peir-Vick Ltd., for two months.

Radio Scotland came into the news again on 14 March when Mr Brian O'Malley, Labour MP for Rotherham, complained in the Commons about service commanders who had written to Radio Scotland thanking them for helping recruiting. He asked "What on earth do they think they are up to?" Radio Scotland had given the services £3,000 worth of advertising free over the air. In the *Daily Sketch* on 19 May 1967, we read "The Ministry of Defence has forbidden any member of the services to have anything to do with the pirates. This follows letters by the Army, Royal Navy and Royal Air Force to Radio Scotland thanking them for their help in a recruiting drive."

The Ministry order said "... Considerable embarrassment has been caused by these letters ... they can be made to appear to have been defying Government policy."

On 5 April it was announced that the High Court action in which the Post Office wished to stop Radio 390 operating had been fixed for 8 May 1967.

Meanwhile, on 11 April Ronan O'Rahilly of Radio Caroline was reported in the Ipswich *Evening Star* to be turning Roughs Tower, the wartime fort six miles off Felixstowe, into a heliport. But the move was denied by Bill Scaddan, Caroline's liaison officer.

Rumours circulating in Ipswich said the heliport base was being set up to beat the Marine, Etc., Broadcasting (Offences) Bill, which made it illegal for any British subject to supply or help the offshore stations.

The *Evening Star* went on:

It is believed that with the Roughs used to stockpile supplies, a fleet of helicopters will fly in food, men and equipment from Holland. Personnel working on the ships, from disc jockeys to crewmen, will fly to Holland before coming into this country. For some weeks now Radio Caroline has been broadcasting 'anti-marine offences' propaganda, and disc jockeys have declared their intention to become stateless persons.

The Roughs have been occupied by squatters for nearly two years. In January this year there was a row between Caroline chief Ronan O'Rahilly and Radio Essex man Roy Bates over the manning of the fort, but it was eventually resolved.

Since then the activity on the Roughs has hotted up. Dozens of cylinders of acetylene have been delivered, and gun mountings and superstructure on the platform on top of the towers' legs have been cut away and tipped into the sea. It is thought that the platform would be used as the helicopter landing pad, and stores could be stockpiled inside the high hollow legs of the towers to be ferried to the ships during calm weather. Stores could be winched onto the ships from the helicopters or delivered by boat.

At the same time as the heliport was in the news a GPO spokesman said it was most unlikely that a scheme for supplying the pirate radio ships would succeed. The Dutch Government was one of those which had agreed to co-operate in banning the pirates, and had been one of the first in Europe to take forcible action to seize a pirate station operating off its coast.

On 11 April Ronan O'Rahilly appeared on East Anglian TV news and denied the heliport story. He said the fort was going to be used as a health farm where rich directors could enjoy a relaxing holiday. Mushrooms would be grown in the forts' hollow legs. Needless to say this last suggestion was a little far-fetched, even if there was 'mush room' in the hollow legs!

Former *Kent Messenger* reporter David Hughes wrote an interesting article in the newspaper in April 1967 about the future of the pirates:

"We intend to stay on the air, even if it means moving our whole organisation out of the country." This statement from Frances van Staden, press officer with Radio Caroline, must be cheering news to the estimated 30 million people who daily tune into the music and gossip of Britain's offshore commercial radio stations.

Not that the pirates hold out any false hopes that the Marine etc., Broadcasting (Offences) Bill will be rejected when it reaches the House of Lords for its final reading. They are resigned to the fact that they will shortly become officially illegal, yet have found a legal loophole.

"While the Bill will make it illegal for any British citizen to work for Radio Caroline, in whatever capacity," Mrs van Staden added, "it makes no attempt to illegalise the ship itself, which, beyond all doubt, is outside territorial waters. By moving our offices to a foreign country, employing disc jockeys and other personnel who hold foreign or Commonwealth passports, and obtaining advertising revenue from abroad, we shall be able to, and intend to, continue broadcasting without moving the ship and without breaking the law."

In fact they will not have to go all the way to the Continent to find refuge, for the Manx Parliament recently rejected the bill, thus giving Caroline North, anchored in Ramsey Bay, an ideal base for its operations after the Bill has been passed.

The 20 or so British personnel currently working for Radio Caroline were last week told they had to decide between British citizenship or the station. Meanwhile Caroline's 'emigration' plans are already in full swing. They have opened an office in Baarn, Holland, and have formed an association with a French agency in Paris.

Roger Seddon, assistant company secretary with Radlon (Sales) Ltd., the organising body behind Radio London, is also confident that the station will be able to continue after the Bill has been passed. "The tender supplying the m.v. *Galaxy* is Dutch-crewed, and it will not be difficult to base it at a Continental port instead of Felixstowe," he said. "We would employ foreign or Commonwealth disc jockeys, and do not anticipate much difficulty in obtaining foreign advertising."

Mr Seddon is optimistic that such plans may not have to be put into action until late next year. "I feel sure that the Government does not intend to take us off the air until a satisfactory alternative has been found," he said. "Parliament has enough on its plate already, and I would not be surprised if the House of Lords is asked to slow things down until the BBC's planned local radio stations have been established."

Radio London firmly believes that the commercial broadcasting issue should be put to the public vote.

Added the station's programme director, Alan Keen, "The majority of the British public want free radio and I have every confidence that the wishes of the public will be carried out."

While the ships show an outward air of complete confidence and optimism, the forts will not be so lucky. Radio 390, perhaps the most popular with Kent listeners, is now the sole pirate fort still on the air, and it, too, is prepared for an early death.

"The day the Bill finally becomes law will be our final day of broadcasting," said acting managing director David Lye. "We shall not shut down operations completely however, but would hope at some future date to form a link with a foreign station which could broadcast our kind of programme to this country."

Mr Lye does not anticipate a great public outcry when 390 finally closes down. "We have at present between six and eight million listeners, many of whom are elderly or infirm. Others are hospital patients, professional men, shopkeepers, and these are not the type of people to create against the Government if we are taken off the air."

In April 1967 Radio Caroline disc jockeys were asked whether or not they wished to remain pirates and give up their British citizenship, or quit.

Disc jockey Mike Ahern and news reader Gerry Burke, son-in-law of actor Bernard Miles, later Lord Miles, stated they would become stateless. Commenting, Ronan O'Rahilly said: "It was a pretty important issue on which to ask the disc jockeys to make up their minds. But we must look to the future. The Marine Offences Bill would mean that no British citizen would be allowed to serve on the ships. We have already taken on new staff, mainly American and Canadian. One of the men, a disc jockey, has said he would not want to remain a citizen of a country which would bring in laws like this."

On 8 May 1967 the Post Office started a High Court action in a new bid to silence Radio 390. The Post Office asked Mr Justice O'Connor to order the station to stop operating. They said that Radio 390 was broadcasting within territorial waters without a licence.

Estuary Radio of Folkestone, which ran Radio 390, denied that the station was within British territorial waters. It said they were on the high seas, and they asked the judge to make a declaration that broadcasting from Red Sands Tower was lawful and did not require a licence.

John Newey, for the Post Office, said that Radio 390 had been operating between September 1965 and November 1966 and from December 1966 onwards.

The forts were built during World War II. It was claimed that they were part of Britain because they fell within internal waters. Mr Newey said the case involved the area over which a State could exercise its sovereignty. And in that area, he said, no wireless apparatus could be used without a licence.

The case was adjourned until 23 May. Mr Justice O'Connor heard a number of hydrographic witnesses, including Lieutenant-Commander Beasley and Commander Kennedy, but he was not prepared to pick and choose between technical witnesses on either side.

There was some disagreement over the figures derived from the surveys of the Thames Estuary. Detailed calculations would have to be made so that some common basis could be agreed between hydrographic experts.

From forts to ships! During their stay in the North Sea both the *Galaxy* and *Mi Amigo* had drifted, as indeed had the *Cheeta II*. Radio 227/355 appeared to be holding the record. That was until 4 May 1967 when rough seas and gale force winds caused her to drag her anchor and she drifted towards Harwich. The stations ceased broadcasting when she went inside the three-mile limit, but resumed transmissions when the ship, m.v. *Laissez-Faire*, returned to her original location.

Radio 270 came under discussion in the House of Commons on 11 May 1967 when the Postmaster-General told laughing Conservatives that party broadcasts from pirate radio stations were no laughing matter. The laughter followed a suggestion by Andrew Faulds (Labour, Smethwick) that municipal election results be declared invalid because Mr Wall (Conservative, Haltemprice) had made an illegal broadcast on Saturday 6 May 1967 on Radio 270.

Edward Short, the Postmaster-General, went on to say: "It is the first time ever in peacetime that this country has been subjected to a stream of misleading propaganda from outside territorial waters. I hope any members who may have been dragging their feet about the closing of these stations will cease to do so." The so-called illegal broadcast by Mr Wall was about future relations with Rhodesia.

On 25 May the High Court action against Radio 390 announced, after a five-day adjournment, that the station was broadcasting within British territorial waters. Mr Justice O'Connor declared the station illegal.

The judge granted the Post Office an injunction stopping Estuary Radio Ltd., of Guildhall Street, Folkestone, Kent, operating Radio 390 without a licence. A counter-claim by the company that Red Sands Tower was on the high seas and that broadcasting from it did not require a licence, was dismissed.

Mr Justice O'Connor granted a stay of execution up to the hearing of the appeal.

The acting managing director of the company, David Lye, said that Radio 390 would continue to broadcast pending the outcome of the appeal.

Mr Justice O'Connor said that Radio 390 had commenced broadcasting in 1965 but no action was taken by the Post Office until August 1966 when the company and two directors were summonsed for contravention of the Wireless Telegraphy Act. The company was fined £100. An appeal was dismissed but following a survey on behalf of the company which it thought established that the tower was outside territorial waters, broadcasting was resumed. A further summons was taken out in February 1967 and the company was fined £200 and each of the directors £40.

On 7 March a writ was taken out by the Post Office seeking to restrain the company from continuing to broadcast.

A look now at Radio Caroline. A report in a Dutch daily newspaper published in Amsterdam, *De Telegraaf*, said on 3 June 1967, that the station was going 'Dutch'.

Next month there is a new radio station for Holland - it is Radio Caroline with Dutch disc jockeys aboard. It will transmit from the British coast where it is now anchored. Radio Caroline has now moved her head office to Holland. All these measures are in connection with the Marine Offences Bill which makes pirate radio in Britain illegal .

A spokesman for Radio Caroline said "We have two ships - one in the north of England, the other in the south. We have many advertising contracts with non-British companies and we will broadcast these adverts to the British public as well as the Dutch."

Radio Caroline has a second radio transmitter for a Dutch programme. The station says that when the Bill is passed they have plenty of disc jockeys who speak English but are not of British nationality. Radio Caroline decided on an office in Paris to start with, but now believes Amsterdam is better because of the provisions and stores that have to be accounted for.

Radio Caroline has now booked two permanent rooms in an Amsterdam hotel for disc jockeys who go on shore leave.

Caroline director Ronan O'Rahilly told a correspondent of *De Telegraaf* in London that he will put an English-speaking minister on the air as a test case to measure the strength of the British law. He will start broadcasting before the Marine Offences Bill is passed and will continue broadcasting after it becomes law. For this the minister runs the risk of two years in prison and a fine of £100.

The Postmaster-General, Edward Short, speaking at the Media Executive Circle in London during June 1967, said in connection with the closing down of the pirate stations:

If private individuals are allowed to begin broadcasting without permission on any wavelength they care to choose, there will rapidly be chaos in the ether, and if we are to turn a blind eye to the ten or eleven infesting our shores we should quickly have fifty or a hundred, and other countries in the world would be similarly pestered.
The operators of these stations should have no illusions about continuing. They may try to hang on for a while, but they will certainly be put out of business.

The Dutch daily newspaper *De Telegraaf* devoted a whole page to the pirate saga on 7 June with comments from Radio Veronica, Radio Caroline, Radio London and Radio 227.

Hendrik 'Bull' Verwey, the head of Radio Veronica, said he was not worried about the English pirates broadcasting their programmes to Holland. He stated all English pirates were operating at a loss, with the exception of Radio London.

For Radio Caroline, a South African, Basil van Rensburg, who had much experience of radio acquired in South Africa, said that he believed from lawyers that should Caroline go to court they would stand a good chance of winning their case against the British Government. Rensburg said that Caroline should be able to operate at a profit with foreign commercials.

Putting the case for Radio 227 (Dutch) and Radio 355 (British), managing director Ted Allbeury said he thought the Dutch Government would take action against the stations if they all broadcast to Holland. Allbeury said that Radio 227 was operating at a loss, but 355 was making headway and helping her sister station out of difficulty. He wasn't worried about the competition from Radio Veronica.

When the Marine Offences Bill became law, Radio 355 would still transmit programmes in English and had a secret plan up their sleeve on which he wouldn't enlarge at that time.

Philip Birch, managing director of Radio London, was reported to have told *De Telegraaf* that although there was a possibility of 266 moving to Holland, no definite decisions had been made as to where the ship would broadcast. The *Galaxy* was provisioned from Holland, so there were no worries when the Marine Offences Bill became law. The station would obtain overseas advertising. British disc jockeys would, however, run the risk of £100 fine and two years in prison, so they would be replaced by foreign DJs.

As well as disc jockeys and advertisers running a risk of heavy fines and possible imprisonment, journalists were also hit by the Marine Offences Bill.

Ronald Duncan (poet and founder of the English Stage Company), writing in the *Weekend Telegraph* on Friday 23 June 1967, said that he hated pop music, and advertisements on both radio and television nauseated him. But the new Act made it an offence to write for any of the stations. Duncan went on:

Previously it had been a principle in our unwritten constitution (which perhaps needs to be set down now that our Government of grey men are whittling it away) that a writer was free to write for whomsoever he wished. There was, of course, one acceptable proviso, that he did not write for an enemy or, as the law puts it, "give comfort to an enemy during the time of war." That amounted to treason. But we are not at war with the pirate stations, and to impose this limitation on the writer in peacetime creates a dangerous precedent which must be resisted. How do we know it will stop there? If freedom of speech means anything, it means to say what you like, where you like, to whom you like, so long as you do not incite to crime or violence.

I hope many writers will join me in offering to write for any pirate stations when it becomes illegal. I am prepared to do so for sixpence, because I value very highly my freedom to write for whom I like.

There was some excitement on Roughs Tower on 9 January 1967. After flash distress signals were sent, four squatters were taken off the fort and taken ashore in freezing fog by the Walton and Frinton lifeboat (see Chapter Five).

Ronald Duncan mentioned about not being at war with the pirates, but on 27 June 1967 there was a kind of 'war' at Roughs Tower. Two armed pirates were defending the wartime fort from the threat of boarding parties. It was just over a year after Reg Calvert had been shot dead following a boarding party taking over Radio City.

This time the trouble was between Radio Caroline and former Radio Essex managing director, Roy Bates. On the fort were 15-year-old Michael Bates, son of Roy Bates, and 25-year-old David Barron (real name David Belasco). They claimed to have repelled seven raiders that evening. The so-called raiders were sent by Ronan O'Rahilly to reclaim Roughs Tower, on which he had established "squatter's rights" more than two years earlier.

One of the raiders was 36-year-old John Hoiles of Gravesend, Kent, and he was in the process of climbing up a rope-ladder to the fort. A distress call was made by shipping agent Leonard Martin and the Walton and Frinton lifeboat was subsequently launched to rescue the stranded man, who spent several hours on the ladder before being taken off. The lifeboat warned those on the fort by megaphone that they were rescuing the man and he was taken back to shore by them.

Mr Martin said, as he viewed the scarred paint on the tender *Offshore II*, "It's like a battleship. I had no idea the fort was manned and I had been asked to land two men there to

Roy Bates and his son, Michael, on Roughs Tower

dismantle equipment. One of our eight crew members was climbing up the ladder when suddenly petrol bombs burst all around us and, looking up, I saw a man and a youth shouting abuse having thrown the Molotov cocktails. I had no alternative but to pull away. It is a miracle that no one was killed. I will never let the boat near the fort again."

He said that another nasty aspect of the incident "was the manner in which they kept hidden and silent while I tried to secure a dinghy to the fort. It took some time to do this and I would have pulled away immediately if I had been warned away by the occupants. They even jeered at us after the bombardment and kept inviting us to come in and get some more. It was a baited trap and the blitz was terrifying. This sort of thing gets pop stations a bad name at a time when they could use some good publicity."

Coxswain Frank Bloom said that Hoiles had apparently avoided the missiles when suspended on the rope ladder. Hoiles had travelled out to the fort with 21-year-old Frank Heritage to act as caretakers on the fort for O'Rahilly. Heritage was reported to have fallen off the rope ladder into the sea but this was later denied.

Commenting later, Hoiles said: "We thought the fort was deserted, but in fact found it very much alive. All hell was let loose when I was about halfway up with flashes and bangs everywhere. Someone had a shotgun - another person an air rifle. The pellets bounced off my life-jacket."

Caroline's liaison officer, Bill Scaddan, also travelled out on the tender and was slightly injured when a bottle crashed on *Offshore II's* deck setting fire to the wheelhouse. Scaddan, whose jacket was set alight, said "What a foolish thing to do; throwing petrol bombs onto a tender which was carrying large quantities of fuel on board."

The captain, Dutchman Alea de Neit, said afterwards "We had to pull away very quickly in order to douse the flames."

On the fort itself there was a large anti-aircraft gun last used during the Second World War. Hoiles said that the gun was also used when he tried to climb up the fort. It was doubtful that it would have worked. Police enquiries began the following day as to why the trouble had occurred.

From a fort to a Short - Edward Short, the Postmaster-General who, on 30 June announced that the new BBC's pop music station, Radio 1, would officially open on 30 September 1967. The station would broadcast continuous pop music from 7.30am to 7.30pm, which would be followed by more light music and light entertainment shows until 2.00am.

The controller of the new station, Robin Scott, said it would be youthful, challenging and a very tuneful programme of popular music, with the accent firmly on pop. It would be a cross between Radio London and Radio 390 in presentation.

The month of July 1967 started with trouble at sea. On Monday 3 July there was a skirmish aboard the m.v. *Laissez-Faire* (Radio 227/355) when a Dutch crew member went berserk with a knife. Police refused help following an SOS call from the radio operator of the *Laissez-Faire* because the ship was outside territorial waters, anchored 3½ miles off Walton-on-the-Naze.

The Walton and Frinton lifeboat was standing by, but Frank Bloom, the coxswain, added "The police advised us not to go out to the ship."

Essex police then referred the SOS call to the Navy at Portsmouth which, in turn, put the case to the Ministry of Defence. The Ministry said they were not going to take any immediate action. The man taken off was Pete Roerrade who threatened the captain with murder. This was the second time the man had caused trouble at sea. On Christmas Day 1965, whilst serving aboard the m.v. *Galaxy* (Radio London), he ran amok with a knife and threatened a fellow Dutchman. Later, on Christmas Day Essex police came out and took Roerrade ashore, although they had no jurisdiction to take action against the man.

In charge of the *Laissez-Faire* was Captain Colin Lukehurst, an Englishman from Sittingbourne, Kent.

Radio 227/355 was controlled by Carstead Advertising and the managing director was Ted

Allbeury, former head of Radio 390. Allbeury afterwards explained "It would appear that a crewman was sacked, got drunk and then attacked the captain."

The *Offshore II* sailed from Felixstowe (skippered by the captain of *Offshore I*) and took off the drunk man who was later sent back to Holland. Commenting about the trouble on board, Roerrade said the English captain had cut down on the beer supplies to the Dutch. The *Offshore II* captain, Alea de Neit, was later sacked.

Further up the coast in the North Sea, Radio 270 was reported to be playing request records and broadcasting personal messages at a guinea (£1.05) a time. Wilf Proudfoot, a former Conservative MP for Cleveland, and managing director of the station, said the idea was no different from the personal column of a national newspaper. He denied accusations of 'payola.'

On 4 July Radio Caroline announced that they were preparing a campaign in reply to the Marine Etc. (Offences) Bill which became law in August. They said they were letting a disc jockey, a news reader and a religious broadcaster, all of them British, carry on broadcasting. The Bill, which was passed in the House of Commons on 7 July 1967, made it an offence for British subjects to work for, or to supply, a pirate station.

Ronan O'Rahilly, Caroline's managing director said: "Each broadcaster breaking the law will have to be prosecuted and arrested. I want this to take place because I will then take the case to the Court of Human Rights whose jurisdiction Britain accepts."

"Pop Pirates Walk Plank - 15th August." That was the headline of the London *Evening News* on 10 July.

In the House of Commons Edward Short, the Postmaster-General, said he hoped the Marine Etc. Broadcasting (Offences) Bill would become law on 15 August. This would take effect if the Bill received the Royal Assent on 14 July.

"After 15 August, if the Order were made on that day, the law would come into force and anyone who rendered assistance would be guilty of a criminal offence," Mr Short announced.

The 14 July duly dawned and the Bill received the Royal Assent. Thus it meant the end of the majority of radio stations at sea.

Radio 227 and Radio 355, which operated from the m.v. *Laissez-Faire*, announced that they would go off the air on 14 August. Managing director Ted Allbeury said that he recommended his shareholders not to evade the Act.

Radio 270, which broadcast from a Dutch lugger off Bridlington Bay, said they would close on 14 August. Wilfred Proudfoot, managing director, said: "We shall close down at a minute to midnight. We have not broken the law so far and we don't intend to in the future."

Radio 390, the only fort-borne station with over six million listeners, said they, too, would cease transmissions. The station's staff of 25 would be dismissed. Managing director David Lye said he hoped the station would eventually be able to establish itself abroad but this would take many months to negotiate.

Radio Scotland, which operated from the *Comet* off the Fife coast, said it was probable they would close on 14 August. Tommy Shields, the managing director and founder of the station, said "On the surface it would seem that we have lost the battle." Mr Shields added that it was a great pity if Radio Scotland had to close down as the BBC had no plan for a local station in Scotland.

The London *Evening News* wrote an editorial on 17 July 1967.

It is astonishing how a Government that wilfully inflicts the hideous sonic boom on harmless citizens should have taken so much trouble to silence the pop radio pirates. A month from now they will be outlawed and sunk without trace by a ponderous piece of legislation that turns music makers into criminals.

They were doing no harm. They gave, in fact, much enjoyment. And although they were said to be a danger to shipping, an interference with SOS calls and thieves of copyright, we have heard less and less of these complaints.

The truth is they were a nuisance to a Government that likes everything under regimental control, and a threat to Post Office monopoly in particular. And what has happened is a symbol that dreary conformity in misery is now believed preferable to allowing any one to step merrily out of line.

Proof that the pirates were performing a service (how wicked that they should profit by it!) is that the BBC launch their 'pop' channel on 30 September. But you'll pay for it!

On Friday 28 July Radio 390 announced that they would be going off the air that night. This followed the result from the Court of Appeal which they lost. In May a High Court judge's order decreed that the station must stop broadcasting as it did not have a licence, but a stay of execution was granted pending appeal.

Lord Justice Diplock, in giving the Appeal Court's judgement, said Post Office experts whose evidence was accepted by the trial judge, were naval officers whose duty was to advise the Crown not only upon its own claims to internal waters and the territorial sea but upon the recognition of claims by other states.

The court agreed with the judge's decision that Red Sands Tower from where Radio 390 broadcast was within the internal waters of the United Kingdom.

The legal battle had cost Estuary Radio about £10,000.

Just after 5 o'clock in the evening of 28 July, Edward Cole, Radio 390's chief announcer, broadcast the announcement of the station's immediate closure from the fort off Whitstable. He thanked listeners for their support since 390 went on the air in September 1965.

Mallard, the station's tender from Whitstable, sailed to Red Sands Tower to take off the staff, although three men stayed behind to ensure that no one raided the fort.

But on 6 August there *was* a raid. Five men with a sledgehammer, a length of pipe and other tools made a breakfast time pounce. They arrived in a fishing boat and tried to take control. They told the skeleton crew of Radio 390 that it was a salvage raid. The five men took lengths of copper piping, and brass fittings from radiators. Douglas Seymour, one of Radio 390's engineers, sent an SOS to his wife in Whitstable using a small transmitter. An RAF helicopter was flown out with a policeman on board.

The raiders left by their fishing boat and made for Southend Pier but were arrested by police and taken to Benfleet police station.

On 9 August the skeleton radio crew had successfully dismantled the equipment which was shipped to the mainland. The men were ordered to come ashore by managing director David Lye.

With the closure of Radio 390 all forts were now silent.

The next problem for the Government was to silence the ships. During August they were to succeed with the exception of Radio Caroline North and South.

Saturday 5 August was a sad day for all Radio 355 listeners for it was then that the station closed down. A very nostalgic programme was broadcast 'live' between 10.00pm and 12.00 midnight when all disc jockeys said their 'goodbyes' and related some of their experiences in offshore history. The disc jockeys on board were Tony Windsor, Martin Kayne, John Aston, Dave McKaye, Mark Sloane, Alan Black, and the Honourable Tony Monson whose brother, Lord Monson, fought the case on behalf of offshore radio in the House of Lords debate on the Broadcast Bill in 1990.

Towards midnight the captain of the *Laissez-Faire*, Colin Lukehurst, was introduced on air and he thanked the crew of the ship, as well as the coxswain and crew of the Walton and Frinton lifeboat and HM Coastguard. The chief engineer, Ted Walters, who had spent 3½ years in pirate radio, also spoke on the air.

The final commercial heard on Radio 355 was sponsored by Silexine. Managing director Ted Allbeury had the final few words. He said:

This is to say goodbye. You and I have seen a lot of things happen in the last two

Laissez-Faire off the Essex coast

years... the first commercial radio station serving Great Britain ... and from midnight on 14 August a new set of restrictions on the people of this country.

It will then be illegal for a newspaper to write about pirate radios, the only subject that it's illegal for a newspaper to write about. On 15 August, for the first time since the Middle Ages, there will be such a thing as an illegal sermon.

I've just come back from the United States where there are over 6,000 radio stations. In San Francisco, Dallas, New York or any other city for that matter, you can have a choice of thirteen television channels and twenty radio stations. Whether you want news, pop, or sweet music - it's there. The choice is yours, and it doesn't cost you or the Government a penny. I would like to read you two paragraphs that cover radio in the United States. They're the opening paragraphs of the FCC and the NAB rules which govern commercial radio and television in the United States:

'Any qualified citizen, firm or group may apply to the Federal Communications Commission for authority to construct a standard AM or FM or television broadcast station.'

The second paragraph goes as follows:

'We believe that radio broadcasting in the United States of America is a living symbol of democracy, a significant and necessary instrument for maintaining freedom of expression as established by the First Amendment to the Constitution of the United States.'

That sounds like real democracy at work to me!

The reasons given for closing us all down are excuses of course, not reasons - just political dogma surrounded by a tremendous element of hypocrisy. Do I believe in socialist dogma? No, not particularly. There are many so-called socialists who supported the pirates, and many who are for commercial radio. I've been a socialist all my life - up to now anyway. But I believe in freedom - freedom to choose what we want, freedom to work hard with real money in our pockets, not freedom to be unemployed. On one of my programmes way back I got a flood of mail because I played *Land of Hope and Glory (Mother of the Free)*. Are we free any more? Isn't it time to set ourselves free: free to work hard and live well, free to be entertained as we choose and free from the thousands of petty and miserable restrictions that are being placed on us, and placed on our lives, day after day. During the war we had a slogan 'Give us the tools and we'll finish the job.' We need a new slogan now - 'Give us back our freedom and we'll work hard. Set us free from the bureaucrats!'

This country, this people have a record for inventiveness, industry, commercial success, tolerance second to none, but right now we're carrying a burden that would make the strongest falter.

To all of you who have written to me, my thanks. To all who tried to help us, the thanks of all of us. Everyone of us here sends you good wishes and our hopes to be back with you some day. We'll miss you, and I hope you'll miss us. Love from Ann, Terry and myself, and goodnight and God bless.

Ted Allbeury's speech was followed by *Auld Lang Syne* and the national anthem.

Radio London and Radio Caroline interrupted their programmes to announce that Radio 355 had closed down and wished the station staff all the very best for the future - a courteous gesture.

Allbeury, who was born in 1917, and is a former lieutenant-colonel in the Intelligence Corps during the Second World War, went on successfully to full-time writing in the early 1970s specialising in crime and suspense. Since 1973 he has written more than 30 books. He also writes under the names of Richard Butler and Patrick Kelly. All his novels in the 1970s, 1980s and 1990s have been national best sellers and his books have been translated into 17 foreign languages. He has turned three of his novels into popular and highly-acclaimed radio series, and several are optioned for television and films.

The disc jockeys and engineers from Radio 355 came ashore on Sunday morning, 6 August *Offshore II*. Disc jockeys Mark Sloane and Martin Kayne joined Radio Caroline North on 12 August.

The next station to close down was Radio London. Their public execution was set for 3.00pm on Monday 14 August. It was a bleak rainy day out at sea, with rough waves. During their last day's transmission the station broadcast 'goodbye' messages from many people during the morning including the Beatles, Rolling Stones and Tremeloes. For a complete list see Chapter Six.

The final hour on Radio London was hosted by Paul Kaye and Ed Stewart who in turn introduced pop stars and former disc jockeys to say their goodbyes. Kenny Everett told listeners: "Big L will always be remembered as the fantastic radio station it is today because it is being chopped off in its prime. If people do their bit and keep on remembering Big L - keep pestering for commercial radio to come back - then the same people who are in it now will take over again, and we will get Big L, only this time, on land, so it will be clearer and better in every way."

Tony Blackburn said that he owed everything to Radio London. He went on: "It has also been a terrific pleasure working this last year with Radio London because the people connected with it are a marvellous crowd behind the scenes. It has been so nice working with people who are really enthusiastic and all with the same aim - to pioneer commercial radio." The last commercial on Big L was sponsored by Consulate Cigarettes.

In his closing speech, managing director, Philip Birch said:

It was just three years ago this month that the idea for Radio London was born. Four months after that time Radio London was on the air, and four months after that National Opinion Polls showed that it had millions of listeners. Now it's to end. During the last three years I feel that Radio London has done very little harm but an awful lot of good. During those three years it has helped organisations such as the Institute for the Blind, Oxfam, The Cancer Fund and the Lifeboat Service to raise funds for their very worthwhile causes. It has saved the life of an airman who bailed out over the North Sea and was picked up by Radio London's tender.

In closing, Radio London would like to give very special thanks to Lord Denham who fought our case in the House of Lords and to Lord Arran for all his help; to the Shadow Postmaster-General, Paul Bryan; to Ian Gilmour and the other MPs who stood up in the House of Commons and fought our case. I would like to give my personal thanks to all of the staff of 17 Curzon Street; to all the disc jockeys; to Captain Buninga and his crew; to the 1,027 advertisers who supported Radio London in the last three years and used Radio London to help sell their products. But most of all I'd like to thank you, one of the 12 million listeners in the United Kingdom and one of the 4 million listeners in Holland, France, Belgium, Germany and other countries on the Continent for all of the support you have given Radio London during the last three years.

If, during that time, Radio London has brought a little warmth, a little friendliness, a little happiness in your life, then it's all been worthwhile. As one listener put it 'The World will get by without Big L, but I'm not sure if it will be a better place.' Thank you!

Philip Birch's speech was followed by the Beatles' record "A Day in the Life Of'.

Paul Kaye, the very first and, coincidentally, last voice on Radio London, then said "Big L time is three o'clock and Radio London is now closing down." The theme "Big Lil" then followed and then there was ... silence on 266 metres.

At one minute past three Radio Caroline South carried an 'obituary'. She announced one minute's silence for the closing of her sister. Radio London. Normal programmes then followed.

To this day many Radio London listeners can remember what they were doing on the day Big L closed. Chris Cortez from Cambridge was a keen offshore radio follower. He recalls:

On that most evil of days in British history, 14 August 1967, I was travelling with my family for a holiday in the southern counties. The rear window shelf of the family car held the ever-faithful Bush tranny upon which I, like millions of other people that day, had tuned to Big L. At 1.45pm we were driving through Windsor Great Park in Berkshire. It crossed my mind that HM The Queen might be at home in Windsor Castle listening to the final day of Big L on her radio. I asked my father if he would stop the car in the park, so he could have a rest and I could listen to Big L's final hour quite clearly. He agreed and so we stopped on the grass beneath the trees. Although I was a 100% Caroline fan, I found the final hour of Radio London to be a 'real choker.' I freely admit that I was in tears at the 3.00pm closedown! I was also angry ... Angry that the MeBO Act had been devised! ... Angry that Big L had 'done a U-turn' and decided to 'take the money and run' rather than keep its promise to continue broadcasting ... Angry that apathy seemed to rule! ... Angry that Ringo Starr of the Beatles had just a few minutes earlier 'summed up' the mood of apathy by describing the need for Big L to close down as "a bit of a pity, but ...!"

The Radio London disc jockeys and engineers returned to Felixstowe aboard the tug *Ocean Cock*. They were Paul Kaye, Ed Stewart, Mike Lennox, Pete Drummond, Chuck Blair, Willy Walker, John Peel, Tony Brandon, Mark Roman, Russell Tollerfield, Dave Hawkins and Mike Howell. Programme director Alan Keen was also aboard. The thirteen men travelled back to Ipswich from Felixstowe dock after being cleared by Customs officials for the final time.

There was a small welcome for the men when they arrived at Ipswich Station as about 50 teenagers asked for autographs. It was then on by train to Liverpool Street Station in London.

From early evening a crowd of teenagers had been chanting "Big L - Big L" and by six o'clock had become hysterical. A number of former Radio London disc jockeys (including the author) had gone to welcome 'the thirteen', but the crowd went wild. The author had some of his clothes ripped off his back and was thrown against a cigarette machine which was knocked to the ground. The disc jockeys and engineers should have arrived on the 6.50pm train from Ipswich but were missing. The crowd of some 1,500, many of whom were wearing 'mourning' bands on their arms or sleeves, broke through the barriers, forced police aside and rushed the train. They clambered aboard (one compartment window was smashed), and raced along the corridors searching for the disc jockeys.

Police reinforcements dashed onto the platform to try and control the now rioting fans who refused to go home until their 'heroes' arrived. Two more trains were mobbed whilst they searched for disc jockeys. More banners flooded into the station, some proclaiming "Freedom went with Radio London", others saying "Wilson for ex-Premier". One read "266 London - Bring it Back."

One train which arrived at 7.40pm was switched to arrive at platform 14, but it didn't escape the fans who were now to be found in every nook and cranny in Liverpool Street Station.

Finally diesel locomotive No.1768 carrying the disc jockeys arrived at platform 11 and, once again, the barriers were broken and policemen and porters knocked down. Some passengers had to take shelter in the train. The disc jockeys and engineers managed to break through the crowds with the help of police who bundled them into taxis.

When the author passed by Liverpool Street at midnight there were still some 200 teenagers dancing around the station. One of them, 19-year-old Gillian Bridges of Clapham, was crying. She said: "If the Government gave us the vote at 18 we would show Wilson and his men what we thought of his killing Radio London. But we shall remember at the next election."

As the Battle of Liverpool Street was raging News at Ten was on the air being read by Alistair Burnett:

Good evening. Very soon, at midnight exactly, a way of life will come to an end for an awful lot of people. The Marine Offences Act comes into force. The Government has finally produced legislation to get rid of the pirate radio stations and force them off the air. The pirates broadcast from outside the three-mile limit so the Government has no direct power over them. What the Act says, in effect, is that anyone who in any way helps the pirates by working for them, by taking advertisements on them or supplying them with food or equipment, is committing a crime. Already at 3 o'clock this afternoon, one of the best known and most powerful of the pop pirates, closed down. Radio London, "The Mast with the Most" as it called itself, surrendered and went off the air.

Up north two other radio stations were preparing to close down - off the Scarborough coast Radio 270, and off Dunbar, Radio Scotland.

Radio Scotland ended transmissions at midnight with a bagpipe lament and a special farewell message from the managing director, Tommy Shields. His message, which was pre-recorded, was broadcast from the radio ship, the *Comet*, anchored off the east coast of Scotland and also relayed to 3,000 teenagers who attended a farewell ball for Radio Scotland at the Locarno Ballroom, Glasgow. Many of them wore black armbands.

Tommy Shields said "We in Scotland have never accepted defeat lightly in the past. Although oppressed we have always come back to win. We are Scotland the Brave. This is not goodbye, merely *au revoir*."

The *Comet* (500 tons), was later taken into Methil, Fife.

As off the Essex coast, seas were very rough off Scotland and disc jockeys and engineers were forced to stay on board until a tender could take them off.

Tommy Shields said that the ship was up for sale as was the radio equipment. He never recovered from the shock of Radio Scotland having to close down and he died in Glasgow early in 1968, aged 49 years.

Radio 270 closed down at midnight after programme director Rusty Allen had said farewell. This was followed by the national anthem.

At midnight the Marine, Etc., Broadcasting (Offences) Act became law making it illegal for any British subject to work for, supply or advertise on the pirate stations.

But defiantly Radio Caroline North and South continued broadcasting. At midnight the South ship played the civil rights song *We Shall Overcome*. Disc jockeys Robbie Dale and Johnnie Walker joined in the chorus.

On the day that all but Caroline closed down, those two had said farewell to Britain and chosen to live in Holland for at least three years.

Johnnie Walker's final announcement was "You have our assurance that we shall carry on, because we belong to you, and we love you." The Beatles record *All You Need is Love* followed and the programme carried on through the night. Both Dale and Walker acknowledged the hundreds of cars that were flashing their headlights out to sea from the Essex coast, proving they were listening to 259.

Later Walker said: "I could have got a job with the BBC, but this has become a matter of principle. I am determined to stick it out." Dale went on "Both Johnnie and I wanted to be the first to make a broadcast when we became criminals at midnight, so we have split the midnight programme up so that we can both do it ... it will be a momentous occasion."

As far as the Isle of Man was concerned the Marine Offences Act did not affect it on 14 August as the island had not received its official copy of the order banning the pirates.

At midnight on Radio Caroline North Don Allen called for two minutes' silence - but although Caroline's transmitters were silent she was jammed by a Continental station. After a series of drumbeats she introduced herself as 'Radio Caroline International'. Like Radio

Caroline South the first record played was *All You Need is Love* by the Beatles.

At Ramsey in the Isle of Man about 200 people cheered as five defiant disc jockeys, Dee Harrison, Mark Sloane, and Martin Kayne (all British), Don Allen (Canadian) and Jimmy Gordon (Australian) sailed off in the tender *Offshore III*.

Before leaving, Mark Sloane said "I am prepared to come back into England and be arrested and then go to the Court of Human Rights in Strasbourg if necessary."

The Post Office said they would not take action against people listening to Radio Caroline, although there was a fine of £50 liable if people were caught listening to pirate stations.

Ronan O'Rahilly opened his office in Amsterdam on 15 August. He said he also had offices in Paris, New York and Toronto, and would use foreign advertising. However, the station only had seven accounts compared with one hundred and seventy for a similar time in 1966. They would broadcast more religious programmes.

Paul Bryan, Shadow Postmaster-General, commenting on the banning of the pirates, said:

Despite their protests, millions of listeners will now be firmly told that they must listen to what the Government and the BBC think is good for them, and not to what they have shown they prefer.

The Socialists will not tolerate commercial radio, but the success of the pirate stations means that people want commercial radio in addition to the BBC and there is no reason why they should not have it.

It would have been perfectly possible to set up local commercial radio stations at no great cost. A great opportunity has been missed.

In August Customs and Excise officers were told to take the names and addresses of British personnel coming ashore from pirate radio ships.

On 16 August *Ocean 7* (Radio 270) sailed into Whitby harbour and was put up for sale at £25,000 - including many records.

Meanwhile, further south, Britain's lone pirate Caroline urged its listeners to vote Conservative.

Disc jockey Johnnie Walker read a message over the air from Norman St. John Stevas, Tory MP for Chelmsford, who supported free radio. "The closing down of these stations is a tragedy," he said.

Walker then said "Now you know what the Conservatives will do when they get back in power. So if you have a vote in 1970, or may be earlier, you know what to do with it!"

Trouble in the Isle of Man, which had been brewing for a week following the banning of the pirates, burst into flames on 17 August when rebel MPs from the island made new demands for independence after the British Government had rejected their protest over Radio Caroline.

An Order in Council said that Radio Caroline North must close on 1 September 1967. Charles Kerruish, Speaker of the House of Keys, travelled to London on 17 August to have talks with Alice Bacon, Minister of State at the Home Office. At the meeting Miss Bacon said that the pirate business was an international affair and not a domestic issue for the Isle of Man. However, if radio did play such a big part in the island's future she would travel there in September to see the position for herself. If it were any consolation the Government would discuss ways of improving the coverage of the island's radio.

Mr Kerruish said after the meeting that he thought it was very unlikely that Radio Caroline North would be invited to continue broadcasting from the island itself. He was saddened by the Government's decision to go ahead with the Order in Council before the Commonwealth Secretariat had discussed the Isle of Man's protest against alleged interference in its affairs.

Crowds of sympathisers with the pop pirates remained outside the Home Office all day. There were no demonstrations.

The Manx Parliament described the Marine, Etc., Broadcasting (Offences) Act as "repugnant to the wishes of our people."

In Essex a proposal was made in August for the Radio London ship to anchor near the pier at Walton-on-the-Naze to give holidaymakers an opportunity of viewing the ship. The proposal came from Michael Goss, manager and director of the New Walton Pier Company, who said he was willing to allow the use of the pier train for people to get aboard the m.v. *Galaxy*.

The chairman and secretary of Walton's Chamber of Commerce, Dudley Ward, said "As an organisation in favour of free enterprise, we would welcome the idea which would also give us the opportunity to prove Walton is still the friendliest resort in England."

However, the owners of the m.v. *Galaxy* turned down the suggestion, and on 20 August it was announced that she was in dry dock in Hamburg, Germany, preparing for a refit. Rumours indicated she would remain a radio ship.

During the month of August there were various reports in the East Anglian press about the Roughs Tower. One said that a detachment of Royal Marines was standing by to take it over. Another report said that a attractive young woman was on the tower. She had been spotted by a seaman on a British Railways ferry on the Harwich-Hook of Holland run. A Ministry of Defence spokesman said "The Roughs is definitely Crown property."

The Roughs Tower, one of the anti-aircraft forts built on sandbanks off the Essex/Suffolk coast during 1939 - 1945, had been the centre of "takeover" bids by rival pirate stations throughout 1966 and 1967.

In June 1967 a reported 'battle' had taken place in which home-made bombs had been used. A man had to be rescued by the Walton and Frinton lifeboat. Questions about this incident were asked in Parliament and Julian Risdale, MP for Harwich, called for Government intervention.

The mystery of the Roughs Tower remained. Roy Bates, the former head of Radio Essex, said that he was in charge and if anyone tried to intervene they would be dealt with.

The Government decided that they would deal with another fort off the Essex coast - Sunk Head, and on 18 August a party of servicemen and civilians went out to the tower to see how best it could be demolished.

The action was being taken in order "to deny its use to interests other than the Ministry of Defence."

The servicemen who went out to Sunk Head Tower were Royal Engineers, and they sailed from Felixstowe in the Admiralty tug *Collie*.

On the afternoon of Monday 21 August Sunk Head Tower was blown up. Eyewitnesses said there was a brilliant crimson flash and a mushroom of grey smoke with a rumbling explosion which echoed across the calm water of Dovercourt Bay 14 miles away. Windows in the town of Harwich rattled due to the explosion.

In charge of the operation was Commander Kenneth Young, and the fuse to the 2,200lb of explosive was lit by Captain Alan Cowie of 24th Field Squadron, R.E. Huge lumps of metal and concrete flew some 300ft. into the air and landed in the sea anything up to half a mile from the tower.

The men who helped in "Operation Sunk Head" were fifty sappers from the 36th Royal Engineers Regiment from Maidstone, Kent, commanded by Major David Ives.

With the successful completion of the operation there now only remained the Roughs Tower off Felixstowe. Rumours had been circulated that Radio Caroline were going to use the Sunk Head Tower as a storage base for food and equipment.

The day after the blowing up of Sunk Head Tower, there was a great deal of speculation among Walton-on-the-Naze boatmen about the motives of a group of men who had been trying to hire boats to go out to the Radio Caroline South ship.

Frank Bloom, coxswain of the Walton and Frinton lifeboat, and owner of the pleasure boat *Lady Kent* that used to visit the radio ship during the summer, said "A man approached me to take a group of men out to Caroline. He had a tape in his hand. He said he wanted to

Sunk Head Tower
Above left: Going!   Above right: Going!
Below: GONE!

go on board the radio ship. I told him that I wasn't interested."

Boatmen would make themselves liable to prosecution under the Marine, Etc., (Broadcasting) Offences Act.

In Harwich a Customs official said "The operation of pleasure boats in the vicinity of Radio Caroline is not unknown to us. Visitors like to view the ship. This is quite legal providing there is no physical contact." The Customs official said he would clear anyone wishing to go out to the Radio Caroline ship, but they would be immediately reported to Post Office authorities, who would take the necessary action.

With the Marine, Etc., Broadcasting (Offences) Act coming into force, the secretary of the Walton and Frinton lifeboat, Robert Oxley, said "Unless I receive any instructions to the contrary, I shall launch the lifeboat in any case of danger to life at sea."

Frank Bloom, coxswain, added "During the last war German pilots were rescued from the sea by our lifeboats. After all, we are an international organisation."

The Marine, Etc., Broadcasting (Offences) Act said that it was an offence to participate in any way in the activities of pirate radio stations and ships. The maximum penalty for all these offences were the same - two years imprisonment, or a fine determined by the court, or both.

The Act was in everyone's mind, especially those around the Isle of Man area, on 31 August 1967. Radio Caroline's North ship stocked up with provisions and 70 tons of fresh water on the eve of the Act's becoming law in the Isle of Man. Radio Caroline North defied the Act at midnight on 31 August and remained on the air for an extra two hours to let the British public know they wished to continue with free radio. The station opened transmission on 1 September at 6.00am, and the first commercial was heard at 6.09am which was for Kelloggs cornflakes.

Trades people in Ramsey on the Isle of Man who had been doing business with Radio Caroline North were warned by the Chief Constable and his men that it was illegal to continue doing so. Offenders could be jailed for up to two years by a Manx court.

Meantime, Radio Caroline North and South continued transmitting programmes to Britain and the Continent for the remainder of 1967. They were there until the ships were silenced on 3 March 1968.

The *Mi Amigo* and *Caroline* were towed into Amsterdam harbour by the Wijsmuller Salvage Company. Listeners were shocked by the enforced closure. They had been given no explanation. The ships were towed away by Wijsmuller's because money owed them by Radio Caroline for payment of tender services had not materialised.

Between 1967 and 1993 other pirate ships appeared including Radio Northsea International, Capital Radio, Radio Atlantis, Laser 558, and a return of Radio Caroline, but none of them had the following that the early pirates commanded. Listeners now enjoyed stereo radio both on BBC and independent radio.

Off the Dutch coast pirate ships Radio Veronica and Radio Northsea International carried on broadcasting until they were silenced after the Dutch Government had introduced their equivalent of the Marine Offences Bill which came into force on 31 August 1974.

Radio Caroline defied authority and set sail for England flying the flag of freedom exactly as she had done in August 1967. The *Mi Amigo* had sustained more than her fair share of injuries over the years. She ran aground in 1966 near Holland Haven, Essex, and on other occasions in 1974 and 1975, and had been forcibly taken over in 1968 and 1972.

She almost sank in 1979, but on 20 March 1980 in rough seas she went to her watery grave by sinking onto the sea bed close to the Long Sand Beacon. Until 1986 her 180ft. mast could, on occasions, be seen above the waves. It then keeled over and fell into the sea.

Trinity House issued the following notice to mariners on 14 August 1986 - exactly 19 years to the day since the introduction of the Marine, Etc., Broadcasting (Offences) Act.

NOTICE TO MARINERS
No. 68 of 1986
East coast of England
Thames Estuary

WRECK MI AMIGO Latitude 51 degrees 34 minutes.95N., Longitude 01 degrees 17 minutes.35E.

The wreck MI AMIGO which lies sunk in the position defined above, has been marked by means of a Buoy as follows:-

MI AMIGO BUOY:
Position: 320 degrees about 450 feet from the wreck
Description: Can: Red

Mariners are warned to give the Wreck and Buoy a wide berth. Mariners should note that the lattice mast of the Wreck is no longer visible.

By Order
J.R. Backhouse,
Secretary,
Trinity House,
LONDON EC3N 4DH.
14 August 1986

The following year Trinity House issued an amendment on 2 January to the above which said that "Mariners are advised that at the time of a recent survey the clearance depth over the wreck of the *Mi Amigo* was 2.6 metres at Lowest Astronomical Tide." The buoy marking the wreck was withdrawn.

The sister ship to *Mi Amigo*, the m.v. *Caroline*, was sold at auction in May 1972 for £3,150 to N. V. Handels-en-Ingenieors Bureau from Amsterdam who resold the ship to Rijsdijk shipbrokers from Wendrik ido Ambacht for 20,000 guilders (£7,300) then finally going to a Dutch breakers yard, where she was finally broken up in 1980.

The *Galaxy* came into the news again in 1968 when an advertisement appeared in a Hamburg newspaper which read "The motor vessel *Galaxy*, being owned by the Panamanian company Panavess Inc., Panama City, Panama, formerly registered in and since taken out of the ship's register of Puerto Cortes, Honduras, shall be brought under the hammer through the court of justice. There is a radio transmitter on board the ship. The estimated value of the ship is DM200,000 (approximately £23,000 in 1968)." A Swiss advertising agency acquired the ship and began modifying the interior. They were going to start a station called Radio Northsea International. However, the German Government hastily passed their own version of the Marine Offences Act (the Swiss agency were going to anchor the ship off the German coast). Work ceased and the project collapsed by the end of 1968. Radio Northsea International did eventually get on air, but on another ship.

Sadly the *Galaxy* is no more. Having been moved from Hamburg in 1975, the ultimate indignity came at the end of August 1986. The Big L ship had been laid up at the shipyard-harbour of Howaldtswerke-Deutsche Werft at Kiel, in the former West Germany, some years previously. Dutchman Henk Schellevis, together with a friend, Wijnand, paid a visit to Kiel on 10 November 1977 and found the *Galaxy* on the east side of the town, on the Schwentine

The Radio Caroline North ship en route to Amsterdam, March 1968

Fluss. He said: "All the equipment had been stolen or had been ruined. I found some damaged cartridges, some tapes and a pickup arm. On the floor were dozens of papers, including ship-to-shore correspondence." Trainee divers practised underwater repair work on her hull and on 20 April 1979 she sank. For seven years she laid at rest in Kiel Harbour. Local press comment alerted conservationists who believed the thirty tons of fuel which had never been removed from her tanks would eventually leak and pollute the harbour.

In August she was raised by a floating crane and the fuel was pumped out. What remained of the m.v. *Galaxy* was moved to dry land. Photographer Theo Denker visited the once proud lady. He reported in August 1986: "All that is left of her is her keel and part of her engines on the harbour side - and fond memories in our hearts. The old 'rl' symbol on the funnel was still intact, as were the dials on the transmitter cabinet." When Theo returned the following month the remains of the *Galaxy* had been broken up, and all that was left of the transmitter was its identification plate, torn away and left in the mud.

BROADCAST TRANSMITTER
Type BTA - 50H RCA   Serial BC 46327
Output 50,000 watts   Frequency 535-1620KC
Reg U.S. Patent Office.   Marca Registrada

The Radio 270 ship *Oceaan 7* sailed into Whitby following the Marine Offences Act being introduced. The ship was put up for sale. The next time she was in the news was when Radio Caroline went off the air in 1968. Ronan O'Rahilly tried to purchase her, but the sale was called off at the last minute when the Home Office pointed out to the owners of *Oceaan 7* that if she did return to the airwaves as a radio ship they would be in serious trouble. By the late 1960s the ship had been broken up.

The lightship, the *Comet*, built in 1902 and used by Radio Scotland until 1967, was towed over to Holland. Before her journey, the aerial mast was dismantled and the radio transmitter and studio equipment were removed at the port of Methil in Fife. For a couple of months, she became a houseboat in Holland before being scrapped at Ouwerkerk in 1969.

The *Cheeta II* was briefly used by Radio Caroline South in 1966 after the *Mi Amigo* had gone aground off the Essex coast. She was on loan from Radio Syd. She returned to Swedish waters until the authorities introduced legislation to close down their pirates. The *Cheeta II* was then taken to the Gambia in Africa where she was used as a broadcast base and as a restaurant. A few years ago a hurricane tore her from her moorings. The partly sunken wreck is still visible in the Gambia River.

Radio 355 stopped tranmissions aboard the *Laissez-Faire* on 6 August 1967. DJ Dave Gilbee remained on board for a week whilst the ship was at its mooring. She sailed to Flushing, Holland, on 19 August where her radio mast was removed. On 1 September 1967 she sailed for Miami, Florida, and arrived on 22 September. The *Laissez-Faire* remained there for two years. Following her departure from Miami, there was a unsubstantiated rumour that, being re-equipped by the US Government, she had broadcast programmes to US troops from the waters off Vietnam. Later she was renamed *Akuarius II* in 1970. Four years later she was renamed *Earl J. Conrad Jnr* when she became a cargo vessel. She was last heard of in 1987 working as a fishing vessel around the Gulf of Mexico. Her owners were Haynie Products of Reedsville, Ohio, USA.

The forts still stand in the North Sea, with the exception of Sunk Head which was blown up by the Army in 1967 ... Shivering Sands, Knock John and Red Sands. They are dilapidated and covered in rust. The catwalks have long gone.

In New Zealand pirate radio ended when Radio Hauraki was closed down on 1 June 1970 by the Government. However, politicians were readily made aware that Radio Hauraki had provided the listeners with the kind of radio they wanted. The New Zealand Government passed a law which allowed private stations, outside the control of NZBC, to operate. Radio Hauraki was granted a licence to broadcast from Auckland and the station went on air 26

September 1970 under the callsign 1XA, very soon becoming one of the country's top rated commercial stations.

Ten years after the Marine, Etc., Broadcasting (Offences) Act came into force I met Ronan O'Rahilly in London and asked him about his involvement in the early pirate days:

I thought 1964 was a very good year. What I had been involved in up to that point was the music business, with bands and clubs. I had pioneered the whole sort of rhythm and blues thing and I was with Alexis Korner, Ginger Baker, Jack Bruce and the Graham Bond Organisation, and clubs where we had groups like the Rolling Stones and the Who in their early days.

It was very difficult in trying to get that kind of music, especially R and B music, played on the radio. I remember very vividly recording a number with Georgie Fame, who I thought was the most fantastic thing that had ever happened at the time. We had done an independent session as none of the record companies wanted to know because, they said, you couldn't break a coloured artist in England at the time. Nobody got into explaining that Georgie Fame wasn't coloured. He was white and came from Lancashire. I went round to Radio Luxembourg with the song which was called *Let the Sunshine In*. They said they would not give it any airplay because it was not recorded by any of the major companies. So there was only one thing to do - get my own radio station.

Why did I start Caroline? Because I wasn't in any way inhibited by the idea that it was illegal or criminal or whatever. I guess there was a whole bunch of us at the time who were pretty wild, young and rebellious. I believe it was the beginning of a revolution and it was a better world for it.

We started out on the radio trying to be like a friend next door playing you some albums you know, then it became a disc jockey on the radio. It was great to have a disc jockey saying here is a fantastic record and believing it. It would have been difficult to be given a script and to play a record chosen by somebody else and be told to say it was fantastic.

Caroline was chosen as a name because at the time the biggest influence on me was John F. Kennedy. When he appeared on the scene in 1959 and became president in 1960, he had a major influence on me. He raised the expectations of people and wanted people to do things themselves. The actual moment of decision to call the station Radio Caroline was when I was flying across the Atlantic and I opened up the *Washington Post*. Right across the centre spread was a photograph of President Kennedy in his Oval Office and, climbing under his desk, disrupting the whole work of Government, was his daughter Caroline and she was smiling. That kind of imagery very much turned me on and that is the moment when I said the station would be called 'Caroline.'

There was this ship, and a bunch of young people doing their own thing fighting against the entire forces of the Establishment. It had an effect on people. It gave them hope, and it revolutionised the whole music scene and established the idea in people's heads once and for all that the listeners wanted to be able to tune into music at any time of day or night.

Many people accused us of not paying royalties. This is not so. We did pay the Performing Right people and a deal was worked out between us where we paid a percentage of our advertising revenue on a monthly basis and at the beginning of every month they got their cheque. We couldn't reach a deal with the record companies like Decca and EMI. They just didn't want to know. We had broken their monopoly.

I believe Radio Caroline was legal in 1964 and it was still legal in international law in 1967 - that's why we didn't close down like other radio stations. The Marine Offences Act made it illegal for British subjects to work for Caroline, also for a British advertiser to advertise on the station. I do not believe that law would stand up in an international court. I would love to see a disc jockey taken to court and be prosecuted for speaking over the airwaves of a radio ship. It would be a tremendously interesting court case. I would love to interview Wedgwood Benn or Edward Short or Harold Wilson of the Labour Government who rushed this Bill through Parliament, about the Act and how they themselves could make a decision to make it a *criminal* act.

Chapter Twelve

ON MY RADIO

I sit at home and watch your light
My only friend through teenage night
And everything I had to know
I heard it on my radio

Radio Ga Ga, Queen, 1984

THE POSTMASTER-GENERAL, Edward Short, announced in Parliament on 30 June 1967 that the BBC would be officially opening their new pop channel on 30 September that year. The station would broadcast continuous pop music from 7.00am to 7.30pm, which would be followed by light music and entertainment until 2.00am the following day.

The controller of the new service was to be Robin Scott who started his radio career with the BBC French Service at the end of 1942. In 1954 he composed the music to the song *Softly Softly* which Ruby Murray took to the top of the hit parade for eight weeks in 1955.

Forty-two-year-old Scott (real name Scutt - the family originated from Affpuddle in Dorset) was transferred to BBC Television outside broadcasts at the end of 1954. He was made a producer the following year and worked on programmes like the inter-region dancing series of 1956. One year later he co-produced for BBC the first 'live' underwater television outside broadcast from the Mediterranean.

In 1958 Robin Scott was appointed Paris representative and from there introduced *Report from Paris* amongst other programmes.

He came back to BBC Television in 1963, and his productions included *Come Dancing*, *Jazz 625*, *Top Beat* and *Miss England.*

In August 1966 he was appointed Assistant Head of Presentation, BBC1, and the following year took over as controller of BBC Radios 1 and 2.

On 27 July 1967 the BBC Director of Radio, Frank Gillard, announced plans to 'kill off' the Light Programme, Home Service and Third Programme. In future it was to be radio by numbers.

Radio 1 would be the new popular music service - with the accent firmly on pop.
Radio 2 would be a 'revamped' Light Programme.
Radio 3 would carry the programmes at present on the Third Programme.
Radio 4 would carry the existing Home Service.

Mr Scott said that "hundreds of would-be disc jockeys had been interviewed for jobs on Radio 1, and about twenty-five would go on the air from 30 September. The disc jockeys would come from pirate radio ships and present BBC announcers." On 4 September the disc jockeys' names were announced. The BBC went overboard for pirate disc jockeys, particularly from Radio London. The list for Radio 1 was as follows:-

Ex-Radio London
Tony Blackburn, Pete Brady, Dave Cash, Chris Denning, Kenny Everett, Duncan Johnson, Mike Lennox, John Peel, Keith Skues and Ed Stewart.
Ex-Radio Caroline
Mike Ahern, Emperor Rosko and Simon Dee.

Left to Right

Rear: Tony Blackburn, Jimmy Young, Kenny Everett, Duncan Johnson, Robin Scott (Controller), David Rider, Dave Cash, Pete Brady and David Symonds
Centre: Bob Holness, Terry Wogan, Barry Alldis, Mike Lennox, Keith Skues, Chris Denning, Johnny Moran and Pete Myers
Front: Pete Murray, Ed Stewart, Pete Drummond, Mike Raven, Mike Ahern and John Peel

Ex-Radio 390
Mike Raven.
Ex-Radio Scotland
Stuart Henry.
Non-pirate disc jockeys
Barry Alldis, Keith Fordyce, Alan Freeman, Tony Hall, Bob Holness, Jack Jackson, Ray
Moore, Johnny Moran, Don Moss, Pete Murray, Pete Myers, Denny Piercy, David
Rider, David Symonds, Terry Wogan and Jimmy Young. Miranda Ward was to become
Radio 1's first lady broadcaster.

Contracts for the majority of disc jockeys were only for eight weeks as against the usual
thirteen weeks.

Robin Scott said "We have many more disc jockeys at present than we will eventually need
to run the station. Gradually we will have a shakedown. The disc jockeys know that a weeding-
out process is certain and that only the best will survive."

The list of who was doing what, where and when on 'One' was published on 4 September
1967.

TONY BLACKBURN
He will launch the get-up-and-go 90-minute pop record show from 7.00am on weekdays.
JIMMY YOUNG
He takes over the 10.00am to noon show (Monday to Friday) with 'live' pop, discs, guests
and some friendly chat on the 'phone.
SIMON DEE, STUART HENRY, KENNY EVERETT, DUNCAN JOHNSON,
DAVID RIDER, EMPEROR ROSKO
Some familiar voices - some new ones who will take over the high noon *Midday Spin* from
Monday to Saturday.
DAVE CASH, KEITH FORDYCE, DENNY PIERCY, RAY MOORE, TONY
HALL
The pop lunchtime boys. They will introduce *Monday, Monday, Pop Inn, Parade of the Pops,*
Pop North and the *Joe Loss Show.*
PETE BRADY
He will host the 2½ hour show on weekday afternoons from 2.00pm (Saturdays 4.00 -
5.30pm).
DAVID SYMONDS
He switches from *Easy Beat* to introduce his own show from 5.30pm to 7.30pm Monday to
Friday. Show consisting of discs, 'live' pop music, and guests.
PETE MYERS, BOB HOLNESS, TERRY WOGAN, BARRY ALLDIS, MIKE
LENNOX
These are the linkmen for *Late Night Extra* from ten until midnight Monday to Friday - the
show that has pop music, news, newsmakers and the night's happenings.
KEITH SKUES
He will take over *Saturday Club* 10.00am until noon each week.
JACK JACKSON
Daddy of all the DJs. His show will consist of pop discs, with an all-star supporting comedy
cast, each Saturday at 1.00pm.
CHRIS DENNING
He will continue the Saturday afternoon *Where It's At* record show at 2.00pm.
JOHNNY MORAN
He will compère a new sixty minute Saturday *Scene and Heard* each week at 6.30pm with the
trendsetting new sounds, and news and views from the pop scene.

Dave Cash

David Symonds

PETE MURRAY

He will be on hand each Saturday night in party-going mood, with lots of pop and guests from 10.00pm.

ED STEWART

He will take over the former *Easy Beat* spot on Sundays at 10.00am. The new show - *Happening Sunday.*

PETE DRUMMOND

The anchor man for the longest (three-hour) show of the week on Sunday afternoons, *Top Gear,* at 2.00pm.

ALAN FREEMAN

He will compère Sundays' two-hour *Pick of the Pops* from 5.00pm.

MIKE RAVEN

He will introduce a new rhythm and blues show each Sunday at 7.00pm.

Radio 1 would broadcast from 5.30am until 2.00am the following day, although the first hour-and-a-half of the day, and from 7.30 until 10.00pm, would be shared by Radio 2 in broadcasting light music and entertainment.

The broadcasting day would be broken into "strips." This meant that some compères would present a show each day at the same time, five days a week. There would be jingles, station identifications and promotions for other disc jockeys - in fact a similar overall sound in presentation to the pirates ... except, of course, the added advantage of not having to cope with commercials.

Radio 1 would have its own theme tune composed and recorded by George Martin and his Orchestra and called *Theme One.* It would be on sale to the general public.

And so the great day dawned. After all the publicity and talk about the important new pop service on Radio 1, 30 September 1967 finally arrived.

At Broadcasting House in Portland Place, London, announcer Paul Hollingdale arrived for duty at 5.00am. He opened the BBC Light Programme for the final time at 5.30 with *Breakfast Special* and steered it through until 7.00am.

Meanwhile the author arrived at 6.30am in preparation for the programme *Saturday Club* which was to be the first 'live-music' show on Radio 1. He went to the small continuity suite which, at this time of the morning, one expects to find deserted except for a couple of technicians. The two studios and two control rooms were packed to capacity with a TV camera team, pressmen, photographers, onlookers, BBC staff and well-wishers.

Network Controller Robin Scott moved into "Continuity A" (the future home of Radio 1) to take over from Paul Hollingdale. Just before 7.00am he announced over the air: "Ten seconds to go before Radio 1 ... stand by for switching ... five, four, three, Radio 2, Radio 1 - Go!"

Disc jockey Tony Blackburn then took over the *Breakfast Show* which he was to present each weekday. The show ran from 7.00 to 8.30am. The biggest revolution in land-based radio had happened!

By coincidence Britain's only pirate radio station - Radio Caroline - was off the air with technical trouble on the morning of 30 September.

The very first record played on Radio 1 was *Flowers in the Rain* by The Move. It was broadcast at one minute past seven in the morning. The very first 'live' group on Radio 1 were the Bee Gees who appeared in *Saturday Club* at 10.00am.

A look now at what some of Britain's newspapers reported about the opening of Radio 1.

THE SUNDAY TIMES   1 October 1967

"Initial reaction from listeners was poor. Most people who rang up complained about Radio 1, but this was mainly because they tuned in by mistake, hoping for Max Jaffa on Radio 2 but appalled to find the DJs on Radio 1 instead. It will obviously take weeks before the country realises that Radio 1 is pure pop and Radio 2 is light music."

The *Sunday Times* went on: "As a network churning out non-stop pop, Radio 1 is bound to be a huge success. After all, the rivals have been, or are about to be, killed off."

EVENING STANDARD - Ray Connolly 30 September 1967

"For an hour today, in the pop vernacular. Auntie blew her mind with Emperor Rosko's *Midday Spin*. But for the rest it was a bit of an anticlimax, although to be fair it is early days yet."

THE OBSERVER - John Gale 1 October 1967

"Mr Scott was on hand all yesterday, and never lost his calm even when there was a short breakdown at Competition Time caused by switching from one circuit to another ('We picked up a D 17," explained an engineer 'Now it's C 37'.) But Scott went into Keith Skues, the disc jockey of the moment, and asked him to apologise for the break. Skues, who was operating with pre-recorded tapes involving intricate synchronisation, kept a pleasant grin on his runaway, streamlined face."

THE OBSERVER - George Melly   1 October 1967

"It was all go at Auntie's first freak-out. The solemnity with which the conventions evolved by the pirate stations have been plagiarised is almost Germanic in its thoroughness; the little bursts of identifying plug music, the compères gabbling over the opening bars of the records, the fake excitement, ('Beautiful song, beautiful words, must make it.') even the deliberate amateurism and fake fear of the sack, are all there. And yet somehow the effect is of a waxwork, absolutely lifelike but clearly lifeless."

NEWS OF THE WORLD - Weston Taylor 1 October 1967

"Emperor Rosko captured a fat fee from the pirate ships and at once became a controversial DJ with his souped-up voice constantly interrupting the discs he was spinning. Middle-aged listeners I consulted either switched him off or claimed he was unbearable.

"That man," said Mrs Pearl Speller of Bullsmoor Lane, Enfield, "causes an endless thump, thump on my ear drums."

My main complaints about the new network are:-
1. The endless repetition of discs by groups such as the Bee Gees, Procol Harum and other top ten favourites.
2. Ridiculous plugs by DJs for 'square' programmes (Max Jaffa and Sandy Macpherson for instance) in the Light Programme.
3. The reappearance of ageing programmes like *Saturday Club* in the new set-up."

THE PEOPLE - Jimmy Savile   1 October 1967
"Radio 1 will never be better than the pirates simply because there's only one station for us now instead of seven or eight to choose from."

THE GUARDIAN 2 October 1967
"As the sycophantic celebrations of young men whose talent lies in peddling adolescent dreams are part of a rather frenetic attempt to appear young, Fleet Street mainly welcomes the BBC's attempt to turn hip."

DAILY EXPRESS - James Thomas 2 October 1967
"Well, Auntie has lifted her skirt at last - and revealed a pair of amazing adolescent knees. Now I know how it is to be one of the Beautiful People - exhausted! I always understood the new pop channel was designed to provide an anonymous background noise considered by many to be a long-felt want. Not so. In fact the opposite. It seems that all you need to be a DJ is sheer stamina. It certainly doesn't appear to need wit above prep school level, or discrimination.

It is amazing how the professionalism and judgement of old hands like Jack Jackson, David Jacobs, and Pete Murray stand out like Sandie Shaw's feet among these noisy amateurs.

All right, they claim, we asked for it. And we have got it. And full marks to that old style announcer who brought the news flashes in the middle of Emperor Rosko's show and said in impeccable accents "Here is the news in *English.*"

MELODY MAKER - Bob Dawbarn 7 October 1967
"My own sampling of the station has so far been patchy but after some ten hours sporadic listening it seems to me that Radio 1 is still somewhat schizophrenic. Many of the shows follow the pirate format and Radio London in particular. Others - the *David Jacobs Show* for example - hardly fit the new, frantic, swinging image. But in its first week, I for one, offer cautious congratulations to Robin Scott and his team for giving us what so many people obviously want."

NEW MUSICAL EXPRESS - Derek Johnson 7 October 1967
"I listened non-stop throughout the first three days of its existence (surely a feat of endurance unsurpassed in the annals of NME history), and I have found that 247 metres was like a curate's egg ... good in parts. Undoubtedly Radio 1 is youthful, fast moving, pop-laden and a complete reversal of Auntie BBC's former image. It's all very well for the stuffy critics of the national press to look down their noses and dismiss it as tripe!

But let's face it, the station has a job to do - namely to dispense pop virtually all day long - and this it does. Relentlessly!"

DISC AND MUSIC ECHO - David Hughes 7 October 1967
"The Radio 1 blast-off left me with mixed feelings. Perhaps I had been led by the enormous advance publicity to expect too much. Perhaps my loyalty to the pirates had a biased effect, but to me Radio 1 resembled a poor Big "L" played at half speed.

So who came out best? Tony Blackburn got the most publicity; Rosko had the best show; Procol Harum, Nancy Sinatra, Bee Gees, Box Tops and Hollies the most plugs. But by Monday morning my radio dial had moved on from 247 to 259."

It was natural that newspapers would conduct a poll as to whether the new station was a success.

The *Evening News* ran its poll on the evening of 30 September, the opening day of Radio 1. Amongst the people the paper interviewed included:

Peter Elliott (17) of Willesden. "It went better than the pirates. They used to mess up things with all their talking. Today there was music and less chat, and when they did talk you could understand it."

Secretary Susan Belcher (18) of Oxford. "I won't miss the pirates. I think I will go along with Radio 1."

Caroline Booth (18), student. "I would much rather listen to Radio 1 than Caroline."

Trainee draughtsman Steve James (16) of Greenford, Middlesex. "What I heard was just like the pop pirates. Except there were no adverts - and that was better. I listen nearly all the time. And I don't want adverts."

Office junior Raymond Archer (16) of South Ockendon, Essex: "I have not listened long enough to make up my mind for certain. But what I did hear was alright."

David Lye, managing director of the now silent Radio 390, said he was disappointed with the BBC's new service. "We put out sweet, light music and it seems to me that the people who like that, and there are a lot, have not been catered for. Radio 1 may be all right to replace Caroline and London. But we were different and popular."

The *News of the World* conducted a poll on 1 October 1967 and asked the following people their views:

Ex-pirate Screaming Lord Sutch: "The BBC have copied the best ideas from the illegal stations. They've turned out to be the biggest pirates of them all."

Ted Allbeury, who was managing director of Radios 355 and 390: "The BBC have succeeded to a certain extent, but Radio 1 is like seeing your own mother dancing the frug. She may do it perfectly well, but you wish she wouldn't behave like that."

The poll in the *News of the World* was conducted by Weston Taylor who went on to say:

"Three out of four young listeners I spoke to said Auntie BBC had astounded and satisfied them."

Dave Tower, aged 20, of Isledon Road, Holloway, London, said "I was very surprised it was so groovy."

Norma Temple, aged 19, a nurse at Hammersmith Hospital, said "I thought Radio 1 would have been much stuffier."

Heather Beer, aged 20, of Highgate, said "I tuned in out of curiosity and stayed switched on because it was as good as the pirates."

Maureen O'Neill, 19-year-old civil servant, of Highgate, said "It isn't as good as Radio London or Caroline because the DJs don't sound so spontaneous."

Robin Scott, the controller of Radio 1, said after one weekend's transmission: "There has been an extremely good reaction, with hardly any complaints. I think we'll be able to hold our own with the best the pirates have ever done."

On 2 October the *Daily Sketch* conducted a poll which asked the question "What's the Verdict - Is Radio 1 switched on?"

Mary Watts of Camberley, Surrey, said "With the BBC taking over the Government's task of crushing all free radio, we young listeners have been swindled out of our enjoyment. Radio 1 is a pale imitation of the happy-go-lucky independent programmes. And millions of young people deplore their passing."

C.R. Gordon of High Street, London SE20: "Radio 1 sounds like amateur night on Radio Caroline. Since coming ashore all the BBC's ex-pirate DJs seem to be very much at sea."

The *Daily Sketch* interviewed some show business personalities.

Twiggy said "I give the gay new channel high marks. It fills in the background and puts over a lot of talent."

Norman Vaughan: "Having just finished a music series, I know some of the problems of keeping up a running high-level entertainment. Under the circumstances - early nerves and all that - these chaps are doing fine. There's something for most moods. Yes, I go for it."

Vidal Sassoon: "Radio 1 is a good idea and makes pleasant listening, but by taking over from the pirates hasn't the BBC become the biggest of them all?"

Reporters Robin Turner and Cathic Olsen of the *Daily Express* asked nine jurors - all children of show business stars - to give their verdict over lunch at the Waldorf Hotel in

London. Their views appeared in the *Express* on 2 October 1967. The overall verdict returned was **guilty** but *insane*. Guilty of being boring most of the time, but insane in between. Their individual verdicts:

Kim Braden, 18-year-old daughter of Barbara and Bernard Braden. "Radio 1 has obviously started as well as they can, and if this is the best, then I am not looking forward to the worst. They play much too much of each record. Radio 1? Miss!"

Michael Attenborough, 17-year-old son of actor Richard. "I prefer Radio 1 because there are no adverts. I think they have made a good attempt, but must make up their minds what they want to do. Radio 1? Hit!"

Carol Jacobs, 16-year-old daughter of David Jacobs. "I dislike the way they share so much with Radio 2; my father is on both tonight. Well, that's good for him, and I'm pleased, but it's not right. Radio 1? Miss!"

Nick Hawkins, 19-year-old son of actor Jack Hawkins. "I thought Emperor Rosko was great. I like those fast talking disc jockeys. But it's still the Light Programme in disguise. I hate the way the newsreaders interrupt. Radio 1? Miss!"

Nick Gregson, 19-year-old son of actor John Gregson. "If only they had tried to get away from the BBC image a bit more and given it an entirely new name so that people wouldn't link it up with 'Old Auntie.' I really thought they were going to give us an adequate replacement for the pirates - so I am very disappointed. I got a lot of illicit pleasure from the pirates. I can't get that from the stuffy BBC. Radio 1? Miss!"

Christopher Drake, 13-year-old son of Charlie Drake. "I like most of it, but the disc jockeys they got from the pirate stations are a bit too far out for me. They try too hard, I think. And some of the records they play are too wild. The BBC have done well considering their lack of experience. I am glad they have done away with the pirates and decided to keep the new station inside the country. Radio 1? Miss!"

Jane Wymark, 16-year-old daughter of actor Patrick Wymark. "The best thing about Radio 1 is that I can get it on my radio better. If they had put them in a boat on the Serpentine it might have given them a bit of the pirates' excitement. Radio 1? Miss!"

Twelve-year-old twin daughters of comedian Leslie Crowther - Liz and Lindsay. Liz. "I liked my father doing *Junior Choice* this morning, but I also like the wilder disc jockeys. I think it is much better than the old Light Programme. Radio 1? Hit!"

Lindsay: "I thought my father was very good as well. It goes a bit wild at times, but altogether I liked it. But it was touch and go whether I did or not. Radio 1? Hit!"

On 2 October 1967 David Lewin, writing in the *Daily Mail*, predicted that the top ten would no longer consist of the most popular records but rather the most popular DJs. It wouldn't be what they play, but who plays it.

Lewin thought Radio 1 was a success although he didn't like "the much touted gentleman named Rosko who seems to think that noise and raving will cover any deficiency."

Lewin asked readers to nominate their top ten disc jockeys in the first ever Radio 1 Poll. The following week on 11 October the *Daily Mail* published their results:-

1.   Tony Blackburn
2.   Kenny Everett
3.   Keith Skues
4.   Pete Murray
5.   Ed Stewart
6.   Emperor Rosko
7.   John Peel
8.   Simon Dee
9.   David Jacobs
10.   Chris Denning

Another poll undertaken by the *News of the World* on 27 October 1967 gave the following positions for disc jockeys.

1.　　　　　Johnnie　Walker - Radio Caroline
2.　　　　　Tony Blackburn
3.　　　　　Mike Ahern
4.　　　　　John Peel
5.　　　　　Keith Skues
6.　　　　　Simon Dee
7.　　　　　David Symonds
8.　　　　　Kenny Everett
9.　　　　　Pete Drummond
10.　　　　Emperor Rosko

Tony Blackburn

The *Melody Maker* ran a poll to find out whether or not Radio 1 was "One-derful" and mollified the fans for the loss of the pirates. One hundred youngsters throughout Britain were interviewed. The first question was "Are you satisfied with Radio 1?"

Fifty four of the hundred interviewees said 'Yes'. Of the rest, eleven felt they needed more time to decide and thirty five were definitely dissatisfied.

Another question the *Melody Maker* asked "Would you rather have Radio 1 or the pirate stations?"

Forty two said they would rather have Radio 1, forty two opted for the pirates and sixteen were undecided.

In summarising the survey. Radio 1 can be well pleased with the reaction. Most of the criticism (matters of individual taste) would cancel themselves out in the future.

Robin Scott, Controller of Radios 1 and 2, gave a lunchtime lecture in the Concert Hall of the BBC on 11 October 1967 about the new networks. This is part of his lecture.

It all happened last Saturday week at 7.00am. I had the privilege of launching it (they wouldn't hold me back) and, as they say, it's still happening - popular music with the accent on pop all day on 247 metres on the medium wave band. Quite a revolution for BBC Radio - which used to be called 'sound' - and even 'steam,' but I haven't heard that word bandied about recently.

Once we had 2LO and a crystal, now we have Radios 1, 2, 3 and 4 and a transistor. Some people don't like progress; they call it change and deprecate anything which upsets habits even though the habits may have become rather a bore. But one does not change for the sake of change and I think that what has been done has been done right for the right reasons.

After 2LO, which was actually one programme (and there were even some who regretted the passing of that), there were two programmes and they both were the same sort of mixture of good things and things that were good for us. There was a war and radio became part of everybody's life and a link with home - twenty five million listened regularly to *Have a Go, ITMA's* catch phrases became part of the language, the *Nine O'Clock News* was a religious ritual, Sundays were coloured grey and Vera Lynn was the Forces' Sweetheart.

Then came the Third Programme - a very good thing indeed but never destined to be more than a super service for a super minority. Later was added a good music programme, again a valuable extension to choice, but still only the choice of comparatively few (enough to fill the Albert Hall twenty five times a day). From the Fifties the audiences for radio began to diminish because the viewing habit replaced the listening habit - and this change in habit was also reflected in a reduction of listening even during the daytime. Gradually the daytime audiences became more important than the evening ones - in direct ratio to the growth of television licences, to such an extent that the total radio audience at 8.00am is now ten times larger than 8.00pm.

Those working in BBC radio during those years had to face up to the harsh fact of declining audiences, and to a rather special dilemma. Even with the near saturation of television there remained - and still remains - an important minority who do not possess, cannot afford (or perhaps do not want) a television set. This minority still constitutes the majority of the evening audience, certainly during the period from about 7.30pm, to about 10.30pm, and for this audience these are the peak hours for broadcast entertainment. This is also the period when minority interests of all kinds expect to find broadcasts addressed specifically to them - particularly if television with its eyes mainly on the mass audience can find no place in its restricted hours to cater for everybody.

The New Factor

The invention of the transistor introduced a new factor to radio broadcasting and listening. People began to carry their entertainment around with them - and what they wanted was more popular music of all kinds, background music to help them pass the time.

The Light Programme helped them to do this but it was the only network catering for the mass audience. The Home Service, with its obligations in terms of Schools Broadcasting, could not do so and the Music Programme by its very nature was not the choice for the majority. The Light Programme was still characterised by fragmented planning - with the schedule divided into short programme segments - a half-hour of this, three-quarters of an hour of that, providing a general mixture of popular and light music variously presented but without any particular continuity of style. It tried to be all things to all men and women. Its pattern was gradually evolving but it was still characterised by 'stop-go' in terms of programme flow.

The audience for daytime broadcasting began to grow again, particularly in the early morning, and well established programmes like *Family Favourites* continued to command regular audiences as high as any television programme. Meanwhile, the voice of the lobby for commercial radio grew louder; then, on a spring morning in 1964, came the first pirate broadcast - soon to be followed by others until finally three years later nine ships or forts were bombarding the country with popular music of various kinds. The most successful of these stations used formats and a style of presentation largely derived from American radio. The top 20, 30 or 40 records recur again and again in a slightly different order interspersed with old hit records and tips for the top. Such formats, and a rave style of presentation, characterise what the Americans call the "rock" type of station. In contrast, and appealing to a much smaller and older audience, were the sweet music stations which in quieter vein offered a mixture of middle-of-the-road and light music. The main attraction of these stations was that if you wanted that particular sort of music or musical mixture you could tune in any time and get it. Riding these formats were the disc jockeys with their regular daily assignments.

Outlawing the pirates

The Light Programme, in meeting this challenge, hovered somewhat uneasily between pop and sweet music carved into a fragmented pattern - though some longer 'strips' were introduced. The pirates did not individually or collectively provide national coverage, although their signal strength benefited considerably from transmission over water. Nor did they capture the majority of the audience even in the areas they served. The main inroads into Light Programme listening were at the weekend, particularly at times when the BBC as a whole did not offer a daytime alternative to talks, religious broadcasts, light music and variety. Paradoxically, the Light Programme's morning audience for the mixture format of *Breakfast Special* gradually increased and over the three years - 1964 to 1967 -rose on average by over a million, reaching a peak of about 6 million at 8.00am, whilst the Home Service was building audiences for its new style news broadcasts too. When, finally, the Government took measures to outlaw the pirates, thus confirming agreements which had been entered into at an international level, it asked the BBC to provide a service of popular music during the hours which lie outside the period of peak viewing of television. The 247 metre medium wave network relaying the

Robin Scott, first Controller of BBC Radio 1

Light Programme was to be used for this. Its coverage would be increased so that at least 85 per cent of the country would be served. In fact, the 247 metre wavelength is not in any circumstances capable of providing a 100 per cent satisfactory reception throughout the whole of the United Kingdom but the final coverage is, of course, considerably more than the combined coverage of all the pirate radios, and the engineers are still pursuing their efforts to improve it. Radio 2 - basically the old Light Programme with some changes and improvements in terms of alternatives to pop, was given the long wave of 1500 metres and the VHF network because the long wave, which was always the basic Light Programme transmitter, gives the best coverage of any single transmitter used by the BBC - about 98 per cent of the population - whilst VHF, which has been available for about twelve years, gives virtually total coverage in addition to its superior quality. Radio 2 is, therefore, the better equipped of the two networks. In fact, only a very small fraction of the population is actually deprived of the possibility of hearing such programmes as *Woman's Hour* and *The Dales*.

Meeting two needs

My aim, when I began to tackle the problem early in the spring, was to try to create as homogeneous a popular music service as possible whilst retaining the main features of the Light Programme on the 1500 metres VHF service and providing new alternatives to pop where none had previously existed. If in the process we could improve the service to those wanting continuous pop and make the alternative more attractive to the sweet, middle-of-the-road and light music audience, we should have contributed to a greater measure of enjoyment and pleasure. This would be reflected in the total audience figure for both services. If this combined total were greater than that for the existing Light Programme we would claim some measure of success. If, on the other hand, all we did was to carve up and reduce the faithful Light Programme audience, the operation would be a failure.

Keeping up the style

The challenge was therefore twofold. Given unlimited needle time and money there is no doubt what we would have liked - and would still like - to achieve with two mass entertainment radio services. The first would be a popular music and pop network, the second a sweet music service, including also the serial, magazines, and variety shows which appeal to many millions. And, although the audience is very small late at night, there should eventually be some service of entertainment music right through the twenty four hours. I was particularly concerned that the popular music service should have continuity of style, that it should not just be a series of programmes linked by announcements, that it should be attractively presented and that it should have a special image.

And what is popular music? The Government White Paper of December last did not attempt to define this and, rightly, it was left to the broadcasting authority to decide. There was indeed some idea that the new service would be for the "sweet music" audience. But there was already a good deal of this on the Light Programme and it was abundantly clear that if the new service was to be dynamic and attractive it must go for pop. There is no doubt at all in my mind that to have reduced the percentage of pop would have cut the BBC away from the majority of the audience, both existing and potential. We should not forget that the young housewife of twenty-seven - perhaps with two children or more - was a seventeen-year-old when rock 'n' roll music first hit this country and that it is nearly five years since four brilliant Liverpudlians first began to plant their imprint on the world of entertainment. Furthermore, the pirates had revealed or created needs - as so often happens with new products. Swedish radio had gone through the same experience as French radio - which, until it reorganised its France I network, was a poor third in audience ratings to its commercial competitors from across the frontiers. Competition is good for everyone, not at least to the BBC, partly because it stimulates, partly because it shows where improvements might be made - and audience statistics, whether of size or appreciation, do not always indicate this clearly. Nor does it always help to ask the audience what it wants, because the pattern of response tends to be confused. In commercial terms, to ask the public whether it wants soap of a particular colour or shape or size or smell would elicit such a mass of different answers that it might not be of much guidance to the manufacturer. But as soon as somebody offers a product of a new and different sort which captures the imagination a new need is created. The fact is that most people don't know what they need until they start needing it... and then they demand it.

The needle time problem

Satisfying any demand costs money, particularly if it is not being sold. Practically every time the BBC increases its service to the public it has to do it by further streamlining, further economies or cuts in other directions. Twenty five shillings (£1.25) per licence holder does not provide any reserve funds and there was precious little extra cash available for the new popular music service - in fact -about £400 per day 'above the line' and a top radio variety show can cost more than that - but let's not forget that a variety show may entertain an audience of nearly eight million on a Sunday afternoon and provide as many laughs for as many people as a TV show costing more than ten times as much. In addition to this comparatively small sum of money, about two hours extra needle time per day were to be available bringing the total for the two Light Programme radio services to a little over seven hours a day. Needle time is the number of hours of actual playing time of commercial gramophone records permitted by agreement with Phonographic Performance Limited - a body which represents the gramophone industry in its negotiations with the BBC. Gramophone records are copyright, by law, and their unrestricted use is illegal. The pirate broadcasters usurped the right to do so and without unrestricted use of gramophone records their programming would have been quite impossible.

Of course unrestricted, or somewhat less restricted, use of commercial records would make it comparatively easy to programme a pop network and a middle of the road/light music alternative, although the cost would be still prohibitive if the same needle time payments were applied. American observers find it difficult to understand our problem of access to recorded music and tend to forget too easily that some fifteen years ago the recording business in the United States ground to a complete halt for nearly fifteen months through union action.

The record companies are by no means sure how much exposure is good for a record - most of them did not like the over-exposure of their products by the pirate radios, though it is significant that some of the smaller companies were quite ready to pay at least one station for 'plugs' of their records on the air. Meanwhile, the Musicians' Union, whose members are largely responsible for making these same commercial records, is understandably anxious to protect their interests, and would vastly prefer continuous live performance on the BBC air to the use of commercial records. But only a small percentage of the Union's membership is up to broadcasting standards - or indeed in regular professional employment and there is little doubt that what the public wants (and is entitled to expect) is a varied diet of good popular music.

Including the news

To make Radio 1 lively and slick but informal I needed new studios and new equipment so that the disc jockey shows could be self-operated (as *Breakfast Special* always was). The continuity studios lent themselves best to modification - by the introduction of cassette machines, an extra turntable, echo, pre-fade and pre-hear facilities, and intercommunication.

Self-operation of equipment was vital to the liveliness of the Radio 1 programme. The creation of a special Radio 1 centre of operations would also help to produce the team atmosphere which any pop network needs for success.

Whilst the transmitter engineers were hard at work expanding the 247 network the technical operations staff were modifying two continuity suites for Radio 1. Their crowning achievement was to produce a special compressor/limiter which anticipates the volume of voice to be used and balances this with the music output, thus enabling voice-over-music introductions to records to be made without having to balance the two outputs by faders.

I cannot speak too highly of the work of this splendid engineering team. All programmes, with only two exceptions for foreign-based contributors, would be live on Radio 1. But a number of Radio 2's programmes would be recorded or recorded repeats - and since replay times of tape can vary up to a few seconds in sixty minutes there would be occasions on Radio 2 when a separate newsreader was necessary. This has worked surprisingly well though there has been occasional untidiness here and there. We will probably move towards a separate corps of newsreaders for Radio 1 because the news summaries should not sound like "interruptions." It is difficult to hit exactly the right compromise style for both Radio 1 and 2. On the other hand, I have resisted the introduction of dramatic sounds and frenetic reading of the news.

Are jingles fun?

We have all lived through the quite unprecedented press coverage of the plans for Radio 1, and I have lost count of the press, radio and television interviews I have given. I felt this was a most important job to do because it was essential to prepare the ground before the start of the new programme - and to get our potential audience to accept the right notion that the BBC could provide a pop music service in the right style.

And what of this style? We have been accused of imitation but in fact the pirates, as I've said, copied American formats. We already had some jingles, even on the old Light Programme - but it's difficult to sing the charms of the 'Light Programme.' 'Radio 1 on 247' lends itself much better - a pop network needs fun, and jingles are fun (as long as they are not abused) - and why can't we have fun - particularly when it helps to make things go with a swing?

Much play has been made in the press of the number of disc jockeys engaged to present the new programmes on Radio 1 and the fact that a number of them worked in pirate radio. The fact is that the Light Programme had provided few opportunities to train disc jockeys and Radio 1 needed the best people available immediately. I believe that over a hundred disc jockeys of various nationalities worked on the ships and forts. Most of them and many others went through auditions with us and were carefully assessed by the audition panel. I approved all the final choices - particularly those for the major daily programmes. I also made a number of direct nominations. Very few of the men concerned were entirely new to BBC radio. Naturally we did not give them long contracts initially because we wanted to see how they and the network shook down together. I do not foresee any drastic changes but one or two more permanent places need to be settled and this very much depends on success in terms of audience reactions - which is only right and proper.

Increasing the choice

It has been said that we have forty six disc jockeys -1 don't know who dreamed that figure up. In fact, taking the whole of Radio 1 and 2's programmes and including all the presenters of all the programmes we have a few less than we used to have on the Light Programme, and we use our staff men to better advantage - and very good they are too. Four disc jockeys carry the main weekday programme output on Radio 1 - forty three hours a week between them.

We could not have worked to a strict format of Top 20, 30 or 40 on Radio 1 because of the needle time problem. In any case I wanted a better mixture than that and the record-buying public as a whole - moreover, individual presenters should be allowed to develop their own personalities and this they are doing. I have mentioned reception problems - and in this connection the reception of 247 metres in darkness is bedevilled in some places by interference from a station in Albania. I had thought also to do jazz a good turn by almost doubling the output on Radio 1 - but Radio 1 is not relayed on VHF and there are fans who cannot receive 247 well at night. The results of the new plans will, of course, be very carefully analysed. But if the total result of the new plan is to increase the spectrum of choice for the great majority, is that not a good thing? Obviously it is a matter of concern if some sets cannot tune to both long and medium waves - it is a greater matter of concern if the signals do not reach people clearly. Everything possible must obviously be done to remedy things, but it would be unthinkable to go backwards.

Audience response

These are early days and it is too early to draw any firm conclusions from the audience survey reports on the first days of Radio 1 and 2 - but the figures are encouraging. *Saturday Club* retained its audience of about 5½ million on Radio 1 but there was a new audience of nearly 2 million for Max Jaffa on Radio 2. The combined audience from Emperor Rosko on 1 and *Marching and Waltzing* on 2 was - at over 5 million - about 1,600,000 higher than the previous Saturday average at noon.

Radio has a lot of life in it and a very lively future ahead - Radios 1 and 2 have every intention of staying very much alive, and doing everything possible to improve the service of music and entertainment to the people of this country.

Changes in the DJ line-up came within the first few weeks of operation on Radio 1.

Duncan Johnson was replaced on *Midday Spin* on Tuesdays by Tony Brandon who made his BBC début on 28 November 1967. Johnson's *Crack the Clue* programme was renamed *Star Words* and taken over by John Benson from 27 November.

Ex-Radio Caroline man Dave Lee Travis replaced Ray Moore on *Pop North* from Manchester and made his first BBC broadcast in November - Ray Moore moved to London to join the team of *Breakfast Special* presenters.

On 16 December the BBC dropped *Where It's At* introduced by Chris Denning. Kenny Everett also participated in the show which had previously run on the Light Programme. An extra edition of *What's New* combined with *Album Time* was brought into the Radio 1 schedule and introduced on Saturdays by Don Moss. Chris Denning was given Wednesday's *Midday Spin* replacing Kenny Everett. Denning continued to present *What's New* as guest compère.

Ed Stewart lost his *Happening Sunday* show from 17 December 1967. Kenny Everett vacated his *Midday Spin* and moved into the Sunday slot with a two-hour record show. Ed Stewart appeared as guest compère on *What's New* and *Children's Favourites*.

More changes! Dave Cash replaced David Rider on Thursday's *Midday Spin* when it was announced that *Monday, Monday!* had been dropped and replaced by *Radio 1 O'Clock* which, in turn, brought in ex-Radio Caroline DJ Tom Lodge from 1 January 1968. But he only remained on the programme for two months. Ex-Caroline man Rick Dane then took over the helm.

Further changes on *Midday Spin* - Simon Dee lost his only Radio 1 show to ex-Radio Caroline disc jockey Tom Edwards from 1 January 1968.

It appeared that after the initial move for ex-Radio London disc jockeys, ex-Caroline men were now being given an equal chance to demonstrate their own skills.

Chris Denning   *David Rider*

Changes on Saturdays! From 30 December 1967 ex-Radio Caroline man Rick Dane introduced a series of programmes which took the place of Saturday's *Pete Brady Show*. Brady lost his weekend commitment to bring him in line with other disc jockeys who had "strip" shows like David Symonds and Jimmy Young. Dane presented four shows. He made his BBC début for one week on *Top Gear*. Mark Roman presented a series of four weekly shows throughout February and Tom Edwards completed BBC Radio 1's second broadcasting quarter.

The Sunday programme *Top Gear* initially had a resident compère in the form of Pete Drummond and a guest DJ each week. Among those who appeared were Mike Ahern, John Peel, Tommy Vance and Rick Dane. However, in November it was decided to drop Drummond and replace him with John Peel. Ex-Caroline and London DJ Tommy Vance acted as compère number two. The three-hour show was cut by an hour from 5 February 1968 when Vance was dropped and Peel became resident compère.

The *Joe Loss Show* had a change of pace and face. On 26 January 1968 staff announcer Roger Moffat took over from Tony Hall who had regularly compèred it for three years. Hall moved to the BBC World Service and introduced *Forward Gear*.

On 3 February Radios 1 and 2 amalgamated for the *Breakfast Show* after they had decided to drop Tony Blackburn on Saturdays only, but extending his weekday show by a half-hour daily. It was also in February that Radio 1 changed around the *David Symonds Show* bringing it forward to 4.10pm and moving *What's New* back to 6.30pm.

Mike Lennox and Bob Holness were dropped from the team of *Late Night Extra* from the week beginning 4 February. Pete Myers and Barry Alldis took over. They were already presenting one show each.

Radio 1 became six months old on 30 March 1968. Given below are opinions of the new network from a range of personalities. Each person was asked the question:

"What is your verdict on Radio 1 as a pop network now that it has been on the air six months?"

DAVID MOST - Music Publisher

By introducing Radio 1 into the BBC Network it has improved the Corporation by one hundred per cent. I go along with it all the way!

IAN HOCKRIDGE - Exploitation Manager

The past five years have seen Britain leading the world with new ideas and concepts in groovy sounds whilst still lagging behind countries like the United States of America in overall exposure of new artists. This Achilles heel, the led zeppelin of British radio, has been banished and in its place has come Radio 1, filling this long-empty gap and providing for many great acts the exposure they have been seeking.

DES CHAMP - Orchestra Leader and Musical Director

As far as myself and many other musicians are concerned, we warmly welcome Radio 1. It has created a great deal of work and continues to stimulate public interest in both live and recorded music.

WAYNE FONTANA - Singer

Radio 1 is just a souped-up Light Programme.

JOHNNY WISE - Record Company Promotion Manager

I feel a lot of work has gone into the new network, and taking into consideration the very little extra needle time that has been allowed for the new programmes, I believe that Robin Scott has done an excellent job. As a promotion head I would like to see extra needle time divided into two sections, a) Radio 1 for promoting new pop records as opposed to bashing out endless top 30 material and b) To give Radio Two the chance of supplying middle-of-the-road and 'good' music for the not-so-pop-minded.

FREDDIE GARRITY of Freddie and The Dreamers pop group

Radio 1?

ROGER EASTERBY - Manager and Record Producer

Like many others, I faced the opening of Radio 1 with mixed feelings. We had just lost a very dear friend in Radio London and, quite naturally I feel, we wondered whether we were going to obtain the same sort of coverage for our artists. Now, after teething troubles, Radio 1 has settled down into a very professional and polished station. Me? I dig it!

MICKIE MOST - Record Executive

I want to know why BBC Radio 1 closes down its pop music service in the evening ... do they own Radio Luxembourg?

MIRIAM BATTERSBY - Housewife

Radio 1 has flopped because it never came anywhere near to being an adequate replacement for nine thriving pirate stations. Two or three DJs in a boat moored on the River Thames could have done a better job. Own up Auntie BBC, you're too old to mother such a lusty child!

ANDREW FAULDS - Labour MP for Smethwick

Radio 1? Is that the noisy one? Ah, yes, it's a great programme, but I can't say I've heard it!

In March 1968 the then Controller of Radio 1, Robin Scott, talking to the author said:

> There can be no real 'summing-up' of Radio 1 (and 2) after only six months of operations. Considering the limitations in terms of needle time and finance, a very considerable job of work has been done and the new networks have proved far more successful than I ever dared hope.
>
> It is understandable that whilst audiences have increased very considerably (to much higher average figures than 'pre-pirate' days) it is quite impossible with 'one-and-a-half' mass entertainment networks to satisfy all categories of taste. The job would be more effectively done if Radios 1 and 2 were completely separate for at least 12 of the 24 hours. This would eliminate the problems of compromise which I talked about in my lecture of 11 October 1967. These compromises (programmes shared by Radios 1 and 2) have caused us the biggest headaches and the solutions to them have provoked the most protest (although the weight of this protest has been far less than expected).
>
> In attempting to achieve some sort of homogeneity for Radio 1, I inevitably favoured the Radio 1 image at times when the two networks came together - even though this did not in total represent an increase in pop on the Light Programme (Radio 2). Thus *Midday Spin,* when there was only one Light Programme provoked little or no protest - but when it became a shared Radio 1 programme relayed by Radio 2 it posed the question why, if there was one programme shared between two networks, this should be pop rather than 'middle-of-the-road'. Similarly, some of the patrons of the former 'Light' who did not take readily to the *Jimmy Young Show,* preferred the old style light music programmes and *Music While You Work.* And the *Jimmy Young Show* itself, though a highly successful format, did not altogether match up to the image of a pop network.
>
> The only programme segment not to benefit from an increase in audience was *Family Choice* (ex *Housewives' Choice).* With its Radio 1 presenters and majority pop content about half-a-million of its 7-8 million daily audience were 'scared away'. This justified the inclusion of a slightly larger proportion of 'middle-of-the-road' material. Only a small minority would object to this compared with the larger audience who would derive greater enjoyment. By extending the *Tony Blackburn Show* and *Breakfast Special* to 9.00am early in 1968 I sought to increase the opportunities for alternative choice listening - between pop and 'middle and light' - and to exploit the inheritance of about 8 million daily listeners to the 8.00am to 8.30am time segment, (Radio 1 and 2 combined). In fact the total audience for what was previously the first half-hour of *Family Choice* fell very slightly - causing mo furiously to think!

Another of Radio 1's problems was that it came into being at a time when pop music was going through a period of indecision and uncertainty. The beat boom had in fact died before 1965 - with only the unique Beatles continuing to develop musical content and invention whilst retaining wide popular support. The record buying public was divided as never before into a number of different factions or "cult audiences", the most vociferous of which campaigned for more 'progressive pop' music. Much of this music was commercially unviable because its strangeness and untunefulness provoked antipathy. It was in danger of burying pop (which is *entertainment* music and *popular* by definition) in a confusing underground maze from which there seemed to be no clear way in, even if it was 'way-out'. This music had - in 1967 - associations with hippies and drug-taking and was, therefore - (fairly or unfairly) - socially suspect. It was to some extent 'drop-out' pop in that it reviled the commercial scene, yet arrogantly attacked the mass audience for not adopting it (thus depriving it of the commercial success it appeared to deplore!).

At the same time the age gap reached absurd proportions and was used by certain interests to exploit enthusiasms or hatreds for certain types of pop commercial records. The so-called 'in crowd' made it their business to dislike ballad singers and standard melodies in principle - and in so doing provoked the inevitable response. From all this confusion the tuneful ballad re-emerged as the strongest common denominator of public taste. It was at this moment that Radio 1 was born. In a monopoly position (or at least a semi-monopoly with one or both 'Carolines' on the air) it had to bear the blame for everything - from the ballad vogue to the decline of pop! In fact, Radio 1 took the pick of the best new records and its producers were usually right in their judgement of new material.

Radio 1 was also blamed for subduing disc jockeys (including the 'ex-pirate' crews) and taking the fun and enthusiasm out of 'pop.' To some extent this criticism was justified and was largely explained by the inevitable lack of homogeneity and continuous network image. Radio 1, because of its 25% to 30% 'live' music content, also had to be factory-made in a highly organised and logistically streamlined manner. Pre-planning and organisation demanded that this should be so - and thus diminished the chances for unpredictability. Obviously a legal - and a BBC - station could not have the romantic excitement of an illegal offshore station. But after six months I was exploring new ways of reinjecting some adrenalin into a baby which was still bouncing but slightly tending to adiposity.

Since those early days of Radio 1 in 1967 the network has gone on to celebrate its 1st, 10th, 15th, 21st and 25th anniversaries.

Controllers of the Radio 1 Network since 1967 have been: Robin Scott 1967-1969; Douglas Muggeridge 1969-1975; Charles McLelland 1975-1979; Derek Chinnery 1979-1985 and Johnny Beerling 1985-1993.

Johnny Beerling, arguably, has been one of the most successful and popular controllers. He was a dedicated, loyal and passionate boss, who began his radio career in the BBC in 1957. He fully understood all the practical aspects of the medium: engineering, programme operations, promotions, production and running a national network. Graduating as a studio manager, he became a producer for the BBC Light Programme in 1962, a producer for Radio 1 in 1967, later moving up the ladder to executive producer and finally, in March 1985, taking over the top job in Radio 1. He has masterminded the *Radio 1 Roadshow*, the sound for the Live Aid concert and numerous award-winning series.

In July 1993 Johnny was quoted in the national press as saying he did not wish to continue as Controller, Radio 1 when the BBC Charter came up for renewal in 1996 as he would then be aged 60 and still running a young adult entertainment network. He shocked many colleagues, both inside and outside the BBC, by announcing he was stepping down in October 1993. The job was taken over by 36-year-old Matthew Bannister, a former Radio Nottingham and Greater London Radio man. He helped the current Director General, John Birt, write *Extending Choice*, the blueprint for the BBC's future, which recommends that Radio 1 should have 'a higher speech content than commercial radio.'

Johnny Beerling, who spent 36 years with the BBC, reflected on his successful time with the Radio 1 Network:

A view from the top

Having been with the Network since it started, I produced the first programme with Tony Blackburn, and having been in charge of it for some eight-and-a-half years, I suppose I'm as well qualified as anyone to look back at the successes and failures of the station over the last 26 years.

It was in 1968, in October to be precise, that we started the first of our programmes designed to get out and about to meet our national audiences, *Radio 1 Club.* This notion was simply a daily show for club members at lunchtimes anywhere in the UK featuring live performances by local groups, records and personal appearances by recording artists. During its run, each day was presented by a different well known DJ from either a school, a ballroom, a youth club, a disco or even occasionally a theatre. As this idea ran out of steam, partly because of adverse publicity when pupils played truant to attend, I devised the logical follow-on which was launched onto the Great British Public in July 1973. This was the *Radio 1 Roadshow,* which did much the same thing as the *Radio 1 Club,* but with more fun from a specially-built mobile vehicle parked on the seafront at the country's leading resorts. Today, that show is still on the road being seen annually by about a million people. It's a tribute to the attraction of the DJs and stars that all these people turn up to see what is essentially nothing more than a man, or woman, playing records on the beach!

In April 1970, the station started *In Concert* in which a range of artists performed live in exclusive performances for the station's listeners, again a tradition which has continued up to the present. Indeed, it is one of our great strengths that no other popular music broadcaster could, or has, broadcast such a range of live music. In those early days, Elton John, Al Stewart and Fleetwood Mac were among the first performers. Outstanding highlights must be *The Summer of 84* from Wembley which gave our producers and sound balancers the experience and expertise to handle *Live Aid* in July 85 when we provided the sound for the world's media.

September 1972 was the date when we broadcast what was to be another trendsetting series, the Radio 1 documentary. The first, which I produced, was *The Beatles Story,* 13 one-hour programmes telling the story of their rise and fall through their radio interviews. This again established a pattern for story telling which has always set out to explain to the listeners just where their idols came from, and to place their music in context. Since that first series on The Beatles, most major artists have been covered, themes such as the rise of black groups have been explored and many prestigious prizes have been won by our documentary producers, notably Stuart Grundy and Kevin Howlett. DJs have come and gone by the score. People think Radio 1 is unchanged year on year, but a glance at the cast list over the years will show just how many have whispered, shouted, ranted and rapped over the years. Those no longer with us include Tony Blackburn, Paul Burnett, David Hamilton, Ed Stewart, Jimmy Savile, Terry Wogan, Noel Edmonds, Kenny Everett, Peter Powell, Mike Read, Jimmy Young, Andy Peebles and Mike Smith, all of whom made a massive contribution and then moved over to make way for today's talented bunch.

In 1986 we started the first ever broadcast initiative warning young people about the dangers of Aids. I caught the flak, and the wrath of the Roman Catholic bishops, for

Johnny Beerling, Controller, Radio 1, 1985 - 1993

allowing the programme to promote 'safe sex' using condoms. Since then our Social Action broadcasts have helped thousands of people who want information on such diverse problems as drugs, sex, alcohol, debt, homelessness, racial prejudice and so on.

In 1989 another first was the trip around the world on the surface by Simon Bates and his producer Jonathan Ruffle. They proved it was possible, by means of a portable satellite uplink, to make a programme from just about anywhere in the world and do it live. A remarkable achievement which has not been topped yet.

In September 1992 the station celebrated 25 years of popular music broadcasting with a *Party in the Park* at Sutton Park in the Midlands. 125,000 people came along to help share in the party and millions more heard the fun, topped off by Status Quo on that memorable day.

The station they said would never survive came of age and still pulls in over 18 million listeners every week despite the increased competition from local and national commercial stations, proving there is a place within the public sector for that which is innovative, original and popular. Long may it continue.

Disc jockeys from the 1970s through to the 1990s whose voices have been heard on Radio 1 include: Simon Bates, Tony Blackburn, Jakki Brambles, Bruno Brookes, Paul Burnett, Nicky Campbell, Gary Davies, Noel Edmonds, Kenny Everett, Man Ezeke, Alan Freeman, Paul Gambaccini, Mark Goodier, David Hamilton, Bob Harris, Neale James, David Jensen, Adrian Juste, Andy Kershaw, Gary King, Simon Mayo, Anne Nightingale, Dianne Oxberry, Lynn Parsons, Andy Peebles, John Peel, Peter Powell, Mark Radcliffe, Mike Read, Emperor Rosko, Phillip Schofield, Mike Smith, Ed Stewart, Peter Tong, Dave Lee Travis, Tommy Vance, Johnnie Walker and Steve Wright.

Today Radio 1, which costs £29 million a year to run, has more listeners than any other national radio station. DJs have come and gone, as have the controllers, and many 1960s pop stars no longer grace our charts, although their music lives on.

Radio 1 was renamed 1FM in 1992, due to the loss of its medium wave frequency to Virgin 1215AM.

Shortly after Radio 1 controller Johnny Beerling left the BBC in October 1993, a number of 'old faces' also departed. They included Simon Bates, Jakki Brambles, Alan Freeman, Gary Davies and Dave Lee Travis.

By the end of 1993 the only surviving former pirate disc jockey working for the network was John Peel.

Chapter Thirteen

KEEPING THE DREAM ALIVE

It's rock'n'roll and rock and rock'n'roll
It's rock'n'roll and rock keeps rolling on
Waiting all the time to find
Radio plays on Caroline.

Rock'n'Roll, Status Quo, 1981

PIRATE STATIONS POST MARINE Etc, BROADCASTING (OFFENCES) ACT

THERE HAVE BEEN four eras to offshore broadcasting: Phase 1) The Swinging Sixties up to and including the Marine, Etc., Broadcasting (Offences) Act which came into force on 15 August 1967; Phase 2) 15 August 1967 to 19 March 1980; Phase 3) 20 August 1983 to 5 November 1991, and Phase 4) Radio stations in the former Yugoslavia, the Mediterranean and America in recent times.

THE FIRST ERA in offshore broadcasting began in Scandinavia with Radio Mercur in July 1958. Later came Radio Nord and Radio Syd. Radio Veronica broadcast from off the Dutch coast but could be heard in southern England. CNBC broadcast programmes in English from aboard the *Borkum Riff* off the Dutch coast in 1961 and DCR could be heard in Denmark. DCR began transmissions on 15 September 1961 from aboard the *Lucky Star,* off Copenhagen. The station survived just four months before it merged with Radio Mercur. Radio Antwerpen made a brief appearance in 1962 off Zeebrugge broadcasting in Flemish and French, but only survived two months before its home vessel finally ran aground at Retrenchement, Holland.

Radio Caroline was the first British pirate station and began regular broadcasts on Easter Saturday, 28 March 1964. She was followed by Radios Atlanta, Sutch (which later became City), London, Invicta, KING, Essex, 390, Tower, Britain (which later became 355), England, Scotland and 270, Dolphin and 227.

The first era ended on Monday 14 August 1967. All stations, with the exception of Radio Caroline, were silenced by the Marine Offences Act. In this chapter we shall look at Phases 2, 3 and 4. Although listeners in Britain could only hear Caroline off the British shores, Radio Veronica could be heard in southern England until the IBA began testing on 539 metres in advance of the launch of the London ILR station, Capital Radio. There was a rumour at the time that an engineer on Capital was sacked for turning down the volume of the feed to the 539 metres transmitter so that 'anoraks' could hear Veronica close down when the Dutch Marine Offences Act came into force in 1974.

THE SECOND ERA of offshore pirates began on 23 January 1970 when the psychedelic-coloured ship m.v. *Mebo II* began to broadcast the programmes of Radio Northsea International. The Dutch Government had not yet outlawed the pirates and so RNI was a great success and could be heard clearly in the United Kingdom. Other pirates soon came along including Capital Radio. Radio Caroline made a brief appearance in June 1970 when RNI changed its name for the duration of the general election in Britain. Many pundits believe that the propaganda transmitted by Caroline did have an effect on the outcome of the results, which went against the Labour Government.

With the Conservative Party in power commercial radio was assured of a future and legalised independent radio began in London with LBC on 8 October 1973.

It wasn't until December 1972 that the *Mi Amigo* was to broadcast again, this time under the name Radio 199. Three weeks later, around Christmas time, Radio Caroline returned.

A new Belgian station, Radio Atlantis, appeared from the *Mi Amigo* in July 1973 with programmes in Flemish. Also, in the same month, Radio Seagull transmitted from the *Mi Amigo*.

Off the coast of Israel Abe Nathan's Voice of Peace began transmissions in 1973. Nathan was sentenced to six months imprisonment in October 1989 for having a meeting with Yasser Arafat, the Palestine Liberation Organisation leader. In 1991 he was sentenced, for a second time, to 18 months' imprisonment. He was released after serving just 9 months.

Radio Atlantis was replaced by Radio Mi Amigo. After Radio Atlantis left the *Mi Amigo* the station purchased its own ship, the *Janine*, and returned to the airwaves within a few months.

There was trouble at sea when RNI experienced a fire bomb attack on the *Mebo II*. The Dutch Government was far from amused, and within months introduced their own Marine Offences Act. Veronica, Atlantis and RNI closed down, but Caroline pulled up her anchor and sailed for the British shores. She continued to broadcast album music and remained on the air, along with Radio Mi Amigo.

Radio Mi Amigo left m.v. *Mi Amigo* in October 1978 and set up its own operation from aboard the m.v. *Magdalena*, formerly *Centricity*, on 1098 kHz, 272 metres, which broadcast from near Ostend and close to Radio Delmare which had begun transmissions a month before. Delmare had a very weak radio signal and was off the air more often than it was on. Both Delmare and Mi Amigo were silenced but Caroline soldiered on into 1980, only to be beaten by the cruel North Sea and went down to Davy Jones' locker. Thus ended the second era in offshore broadcasting, although there was a brief appearance, in 1981, aboard the m.v. *Magda Maria* off Holland, of a station named Radio Paradijs which broadcast until the *Magda Maria* was arrested by the Dutch authorities. The station had been set up by Dutchman Ben Bode, owner of the *Magda Maria*.

THE THIRD ERA in offshore broadcasting began in August 1983. Caroline returned to the airwaves with a new ship, the *Ross Revenge*. She was soon joined, in December 1983, by Laser 558. Eleven months later came Radio Monique on board the *Ross Revenge*. The third era in offshore broadcasting ended when Radio Caroline was towed into Dover harbour on 20 November 1991.

Andy Archer is the only disc jockey to have worked in offshore radio spanning three decades.

THE FOURTH ERA in offshore broadcasting took place further afield. All were heard in 1993. They included Radio Brod broadcasting off the former Yugoslavian coast. Backed by the European Community to the sum of almost £1,000,000, the ship, *Droit de Parole*, began broadcasting in April 1993. A month later it was announced that the Radio Brod organisation had spent all the money received from the European Community. At a similar time it was announced that Bernard Kouchner, at that time French Minister of Humanitarian Action, had promised 2 million French francs (£240,000). However, the money was never paid as the French Foreign Office said that the operation was against international conventions. The Voice of Peace in the Mediterranean finally closed in October 1993. The m.v. *Fury* ship in America which, at the time, had not broadcast regular programmes, was formerly a trawler with the Ross fishing fleet and built in 1965. It was reported to have two 40kW and two 10kW shortwave transmitters on board, as well as an AM medium wave and FM transmitter. Programmes were to be fed to the ship by satellite from studios in New York and re-broadcast. However the ship was raided by the Federal Communications Commission and armed police in January 1994 at Charleston, South Carolina. Radio equipment was seized.

JOHN ROSS-BARNARD
LOOKS BACK TO HIS PIRATE DAYS IN THE 1960s

I admit that I have read a few books about offshore radio, but I have never read, seen or heard a convincing explanation why anyone in their right mind would want to anchor themselves 3½ miles offshore in a rusting hulk and play gramophone records all day, in the solitude of what passed for a radio studio. What was it that drove otherwise sane (with certain exceptions!) people to indulge in this peculiar activity? Well, of course, it was all the fault of the BBC!

I think it is worth putting on the record that if you wanted to work in radio, way back in 1963, there were only two places to go, the BBC or BFBS, the British Forces Broadcasting Service, or for those with even longer memories BFN, British Forces Network.

I wanted - ACHED even - to be a broadcaster. I was an early version of the 'anorak' even if I lacked the duffel bag, bad breath and two luminous pens in the top pocket, the visible signs of a fully paid-up radio enthusiast. In the early 60s luminous pens had just been invented to match the socks beloved of the 1950s' Teddy Boys.

I shared this urge to broadcast with a number of similarly determined people. Ask the guys on Capital Gold: Ahern, Blackburn, Burnett, Cash and Everett. They will all say the same ... "they had the urge." But I was slightly different because I wanted to read "The News". Okay, so I was probably peculiar!

I wrote to BBC Appointments Department, then known as BBC Establishment. Back came the 'Roneo' reply - "No experience, no job". But where was the only place to get radio experience in the UK? Answer? The BBC.

So I couldn't get into the BBC. That left the British Forces Broadcasting Service (BFBS). I was interviewed by a man called William Cave-Brown-Cave. I passed the audition, passed the medical and waited six weeks. "Aden needs you," he cried on the telephone one day. I wasn't sure. I fancied Germany or Gibraltar. "You'll have to have injections against tropical diseases. But cheer up! We'll give you the honorary rank of lieutenant. Oh, and watch your mess bills!"

Despite having attended an Army school, Wellington, I had successfully avoided Sandhurst and, through the intervention of the calendar, National Service which stopped admissions just one month ahead of my 18th birthday.

From the North Sea, that most unlikely of locations, a revolution in radio was about to occur. A coup d'état. The metaphorical troops were surrounding the broadcasters' airport, BBC Broadcasting House. Actually Broadcasting House was shaped like a battleship, many said to insulate its admirals from the outside world. The sound of pirate radio's shots across the bows of the BBC went unnoticed.

Radio Caroline, Auntie's love-child, was born out of wedlock at Easter 1964, and of very uncertain Irish parentage. Strangely nearly 30 years later it was the Irish, in an alliance with their oldest friends, the French, who again started a radio station to compete with Radio 1 - Atlantic 252. But that's another story.

Caroline was an unruly boat-bound girl who didn't wear petticoats and behaved like the heiress who runs off with the gardener - it was all the rage to elope to Gretna Green in those days. But this young lady was no lady. If she was Auntie's daughter she was disowned, cut off without a penny. If she had parents, they were certainly unmarried. Transmitting from a ship in the North Sea she made a change to UK radio which, in impact, not even Richard Branson has matched.

Members of the broadcasting establishment were appalled. They ignored her. Spokesmen, they were always spokesmen, declined to comment publicly. Privately they thought that Caroline would be a nine day wonder. She'd be sunk by Whitsun. But just in case, behind the scenes, the BBC dirty tricks brigade began the orchestration of anti-Caroline propaganda. They were assisted in their task by the Postmaster-General and the General Post Office, the forerunner of British Telecom. Radio Caroline was "blocking emergency channels; she was broadcasting on frequencies assigned to other broadcasters", roughly the frequency for Capital Gold today. Pluggers and record companies known to provide records to Caroline were warned that their records may not receive airplay by the BBC. We were told 'the third great lie', that there were no spare frequencies for Caroline. Since then more than a hundred UK frequencies have mysteriously been 'found'. But the more the BBC contrived to blacken her name the more the press and public loved her. Here was my type of broadcaster. Radio Caroline. But she didn't do news! She, like the BBC, rejected my application. Simon Dee, where were you when I needed you?

I telephoned BFBS. Their offer still stood. Aden, Aden, Aden. "Could I have the weekend to think?" Cave-Brown-Cave, polite as ever, said: "My dear chap take the rest of your life. You need us more than we need you." He was right. I was being foolish. What a fateful weekend that was to be, I turned on the radio. Tuned up and down. DXing they call it. Through the heterodynes of Vatican Radio - still plaguing Virgin 1215AM even today - came the sound of Radio Invicta, the Voice of Kent.

The Voice of Kent it might be but I lived in Barnet and the signal sounded better than Radio Caroline to me. An address was given out for the company secretary. I jumped into the Morris Minor 1000 - and took off. David Lye was the company secretary for Radio Invicta, the man who would give me my chance. He listened to the tape. Two pairs of eyes looked hopefully towards him for a reaction - Connie, my wife, was with me and, on balance, Kent seemed a better bet to her than Aden. Anyway this was just a fad I would soon grow out of and get a proper job. Stuck in Aden that might not be so easy. No fool, Connie. She still isn't.

"Could you be in Whitstable on Wednesday?" David Lye asked. This was 1964 and Radio Invicta was already attracting press comment. Mike Raven and Mandy, his wife, did a rhythm and blues show every day. Ed Moreno and Roger Gomez were showbiz names to conjure with. I was going to be famous by association.

I went to Whitstable to pick up the fishing boat. Invicta didn't have a big posh tender like Radio Caroline. I met Bruce Holland, also a newcomer, waiting on the quay. The fishing boat used as a tender had been due to arrive the night before ... but didn't. Sadly a DJ, an engineer and the manager, Tom Pepper, together with his fishing boat, were lost at sea. Did the news of three deaths in the name of radio put a dent in my determination? Too right it did! Bruce and I went to the pub.

Another fisherman, Vic Davis, was in there with a man with a bright red beard and a matching bobble hat, his first mate, Brian. Vic, Brian and a blue fishing boat F19 had been booked to take us out instead. The journey, 12 miles, would last about 90 minutes depending on the tide. This radio station was not on a ship but was still outside territorial waters, or so we thought. It was located on wartime gun platforms which had been abandoned by Her Majesty's forces several years earlier. Not even the Army could stand the strain of peacetime-life aboard Red Sands forts.

Forty five gallon diesel drums, fresh water in old distilled-water barrels, food in crates and gallons of marine paint, lay ready, lashed to the deck - but the new disc jockeys were averse to taking risks. Playing records all day for a living was one thing but slipping beneath the waves ... Bruce and I pondered.

But then apart from our lives and a wife and two children in my case, what had we to lose? I had given up a job in retail buying, Bruce wanted to be a lawyer. He probably is by now. I haven't heard of him since 1966. Where are you now, Bruce?

It's amazing what a couple of large brandies will do for your confidence. "We'll give it a go," we said. The tide was running slow and the sea was a mill pond. Vic Davis said little on the journey out. Brian fished for mackerel. I went off to talk to Vic in the wheelhouse. "Nice weather for the time of year," I said. Always good with clichés are disc jockeys, even new ones. Vic was both chatty and cheerful. He fixed me with his one good eye. "Yes," he said enthusiastically. "It was just like this when Tom Pepper went down." Bruce and I retired and sat on the stern contemplating our present and future. We were going off the idea of being broadcasters very rapidly.

So the two new DJs arrived at the forts. One of them had pretensions to being a BBC newsreader, and what pretensions! The Red Sands forts towered out of the mist. The buoys anchored at each tower had integral bells which tolled mournfully. Cheerful faces looked down on us from many feet above. "Thank God you've come, we're down to our last kettleful of fresh water." My confidence ebbed still further.

Vic handed us leather gardening gloves. What had these to do with radio? We had been warned that we would be hoisted up to the forts, dangling over the sea on a wire hawser, one foot jammed in a metal-reinforced eye in a length of rope. Brian had had us practising on the way out. Was this a wind-up, we wondered. It wasn't. "Don't forget to put the gloves on when you get to the top." Why at the top?

We soon found out. "Get your gloves on and unload the diesel drums" Eddie Jerold, the senior announcer, barked. Not a lot of 'pleased to meet you' about him. The towers vibrated from the temporary engines which provided light, heat and transmitter power on these former ack-ack forts. Lying idle were vast War Department static engines coupled to generators which had provided the electric power for heavy ammunition to be moved into position for firing during World War II. In 1965 those sleeping generators, giants of their kind, would burst into life once again to transmit Radio 390.

The diesel drums stood 4ft. high, were rusty and could just be manoeuvred by two people rocking their half-ton contents from edge to edge. The old guard looked on -schadenfreude was their emotion of the moment. If you were going to be a disc jockey you had to pull your weight - literally. I bet Alvar Liddell didn't have this problem! Bruce and I bent our backs. We both knew that we had to bend the knee. No, this was not a peculiar ritual but a new-found skill. Our first skill-training from the senior DJ was how to move barrels of diesel oil. Rule One, bend the knee. Rule Two, protect your back. When I joined the BBC nearly three years later I was to find that those rules applied equally well, albeit for very different reasons.

The forts towered some 200ft. out of the water and were connected by 50ft. walkways which rocked from side to side in the wind. Their only support was a heavy bolt at each end. Planks were missing in places. You didn't look up to Heaven as you crossed them but you did pray.

I looked around for a lavatory. There were plenty, all marked "do not use." The end one was open. Where there had once been a lavatory pan there remained only a hole. A door propped on two jerrycans had been turned into a support for the *derriere*, and two hundred feet below the waves swallowed up my pub breakfast. The sea air whistled up my personal Khyber Pass and time spent in this Clochemerle was always kept to a minimum.

The place seemed crowded when it came to bedtime. A single bar electric fire provided the only heat in the dormitory for five DJs, an engineer and a female cook. A female cook? Yes, I didn't expect a woman either. But then it never occurred to me that food was important. A sandwich would do for a new disc jockey. I was only there to broadcast. Hollow, hollow laughter.

We all slept together. We were big on shared body heat. Not a lot of romance in radio in those days, and what there was was more in the mind, albeit at a very proper distance. Lust, yes. Romance, not quite. As I drifted off to sleep on a bed without sheets, just rough blankets, I uttered up a prayer. "Please God, one day let me join the BBC."

I had slept very soundly and for the first time in my life woke with that feeling that I had only read about in novels - "Where on earth am I?" I wasn't anywhere on earth, I was all at sea. It was 5.00am.

Cookie woke too. Where would she get dressed, I wondered. I went to turn my back. Then I noticed; only Bruce and I were wearing pyjamas the others had gone to bed fully clothed. She didn't need to get dressed. She watched me, curiously, from the warmth of her ex-Army bedstead. Should I retire to the lavatory to maintain my dignity and freeze, or stay where I was and generate yet more warmth from my embarrassment? I waited for Cookie to turn a modest shoulder. She left me in no doubt. "Get 'em off! If you're late for the breakfast show on your first morning, Eddie'll put you on moving diesel drums every day. Be careful." I got 'em off. Surely Brian Matthew didn't have to put up with this!

With not a touch of embarrassment but a lot of goose-pimples, Cookie stripped to the buff. It was my first meeting with an unnatural blonde. She threw me a towel and showed me the shower. It was fed by sea water heated by Calorgas. The shower door was pushed open. Cookie, still in the buff and with most attractive goose bumps, well two, pushed past me. "Hand me the sea-soap" she yelled above the roar of the calor heater struggling to warm the salt water. Sea-soap? Ah so that's what it was. It worked too. I stood watching her removing the grime. Despite my age - post pubescent - I felt no sense of eroticism. We were 'in broadcasting' together and having a shower in close contact, despite our different genders, was all part of the job. As I came to discover, 'broadcasting' was the excuse for having a lot of fun, the sort of fun that I was never going to experience again in my life - well, not within the corridors of the BBC's Broadcasting House anyway.

Radio Invicta was to be a short-lived station. The advertising came in for local restaurants but for not much more. Invicta needed money. New shareholders were brought in. One of them, whose name escapes me, had previously been a broadcaster in Canada. He arrived with "a concept." His concept was "KING Radio." He changed the frequency and bought with him a new and more powerful transmitter. What he failed to bring was any advertising. So he didn't last long. Then came Ted Allbeury.

He had a concept too. We changed the wavelength again, this time to 390 metres in the medium waveband where we were required to announce "Radio 390 presents Eve, the Women's Magazine of the Air." Ted had seen that radio was going towards the American model and smartly marched Radio 390 back to the Light Programme of 1946. We had *Tea Time Tunes;* we had *Evening Serenade;* we had *Masters of the Organ* - I never did master it incidentally, and we closed down at 6.00pm with *Goodnight Ladies.* Having closed down we then smartly reopened with *The World Tomorrow* with Garner Ted Armstrong, a Right wing evangelist whose job it was to prognosticate on the state of the world and invite listeners to send money so that he could go on prognosticating about the state of the world. The programme was the biggest money raiser that 390 ever had! But best of all we had producers who chose all the music and typed out the schedules. Woe betide anyone who dared to play a record not chosen by them. After two weeks the 'presenters' metaphorically threatened to throw them over the side if the programming were not improved and we were given a free choice of track once in each half-hour segment, but the producer still chose the album from which it could be taken.

An impressive line-up of talent was recruited. Edward Cole, until recently a long-serving continuity announcer on Radio 4, now with QEFM. Peter James, until 1993, with the BBC Transcription Service, now Head of ABC-FM Network in Australia. Brian Cullingford, who went on to do *Nightride* on Radio 2 for a number of years and recently applied for an Independent Radio franchise. Patrick Hammerton who later joined Radio Caroline as Mark Sloane and today, having far more sense than the rest of us, runs a very successful marketing company. Paul Beresford is now a star, I am told, on South Africa's SABC Radio. Robert

Randall, about whom many things have been said and all of them true, is with County Sound and someone who, when many of the pirate disc jockeys went to Radio 1, went to BBC Television - me!

Ted Allbeury was, and, is an author of derring-do detective thrillers. Today no airport bookshelf is complete without one of his paperbacks. He was big on marketing and sales, great at pressing the flesh, but when it came to going on boats he was one of nature's reluctants. He had never met Neptune and he had no intentions of doing so. From the day he started until the day I was fired, he never set foot on board. But he was undoubtedly good news for the station.

A few miles across the sea was Radio Caroline and one person who had been with the station from the start was Major Oliver Smedley, a former World War II Army major and Liberal MP. He had the bright idea of forming a joint venture with Radio City so that Radio Caroline could have a second transmitter on City's fort. Radio City would, meanwhile, continue broadcasting its own output on a low power transmitter. But the venture was to prove a disaster. Every step of the way the efforts of Major Smedley were frustrated. You might wonder why I am bothering to record the difficulties experienced by Caroline and City when this epistle was supposed to record the story of Radio Invicta, KING and 390? As a result of the 'Caroline Cock Up', as we called it, the men aboard Red Sands forts were to find themselves threatened with violence and shotguns and it is therefore relevant to our story.

It had been planned to put a more powerful transmitter aboard Shivering Sands fort. One day in the winter of 1965 willing helpers on Radio City accidentally dropped the crate containing the transmitter into the sea. The winchman on the fort was described as a procreative female organ and other such non-BBC sobriquets by the captain of the tug. A second attempt with a new transmitter was successfully made a few days later.

Major Smedley, having heard that his Caroline signal had been replaced by a booming Radio City output, decided he would take steps to get his transmitter back from Reg Calvert. Once again he called on his trusty tugboat captain. Full steam ahead with yet another crew of tooled-up Tilbury Tikes, he set sail for the forts. Recruitment for this little jaunt required a considerable number of approaches to be made in certain public houses, in absolute secrecy, of course. And so it came to the ears of those in charge of Red Sands forts, "KING Radio from the Nore", that the raid was to take place.

You may already have gathered Major Smedley was an Army man, not a son of the sea. Approaches to various hand-picked toughies had included the information that the raid was to be on forts in the Thames Estuary. Confusing Red Sands forts with Shivering Sands, the

home of Radio City, was a simple error. Chinese Whispers worked overtime. When this 'intelligence' reached us, the tug had already departed.

By this time I had risen to the dizzy height of 'senior announcer.' You may stand back in amazement at this point and are permitted a small genuflection. I was instructed to send various messages which were to include such lines as "We have now received the weapons and the ammunition", and "The dogs are in place but we are having difficulty controlling them." Could we take all this seriously? Believe me, we did. We had no illusions what would happen if a group of jobs-for-life dickhead dockers gained access to our station. Look outs were posted. Watches were changed every hour. Walkie talkies, our only means of station-to-shore contact, were used fort-to-fort. Terrified? You'd better believe it!

The tug came alongside at about 10.00pm. We warned them to keep off. They were not impressed. They told us so in Canning Town language which was plain and explicit. I would not like you to picture the scene. On a shelf stuck out in the sea were some half dozen broadcasters with better education than we deserved and no credit to our parents who had struggled to send us to schools where the pupils had been described by Jean Brodie as 'La crème de la crème.' Six "here-is-that-was" merchants with no more idea about a career structure than that serendipity would take them. The dockers knew the output of Radio City, cut glass accents were not a feature of Screaming Lord Sutch's radio output. We had made up some flares from sticks wrapped in old teeshirts, the ends dipped in tar, which we used to caulk the drafts in the various rusting holes in the forts. We lit them and held them aloft. They illuminated the area around us. I dropped an empty 5 gallon petrol can onto the back of the tug. I pointed out, in as posh a voice as I could muster, that the next one would be full and without its lid. We explained once again, and for the last time, that they were trying to storm the wrong forts. These were Red Sands forts. What they wanted were the Shivering Sands fort. The raiders were four miles off course. One of us, out of fear and cold, dropped one of the flares and, carried on the wind, it fell onto the sea surface just behind the tug. Now, whether it was the flare, the accents or the petrol, I shall never know but at this point with a roar of engines powerful enough to haul the QEII out of Southampton docks, the tugboat made off into the night. We maintained the watches for several days until our own tender arrived to tell us of the appalling death of Reg Calvert. We had all known Reg. He was a colourful figure, an eccentric; not exactly one of us, a bit below the salt you understand, but still an offshore radio man through and through. He and Tom Pepper both met deaths which, but for their involvement in pirate radio, would never have happened.

Although life proceeded it was always on the edge. Just as a routine was returning we were visited by one of our former colleagues, Sheldon Jay, an appealing man and a pleasure to work with. He had style, typified by the 25-year-old Jaguar that he drove. He had been a purser on cruise liners or some such and had gained great skills in calming down irate passengers. He applied these skills with a certain *élan* and I can honestly credit him with maintaining a certain calm aboard. However, as with any role in life, if you are good at something you are promoted away from it. Such was Sheldon's fate. He was transferred to Head Office in London's Pimlico. Sheldon arrived one day with the news that Radio 390 was going to be duplicated. A sister-service would start from a ship to be anchored next to Radio Caroline North a few miles from Douglas, Isle of Man. We were instructed to record every programme, remove all time checks and delete any comments which would indicate a day and date. We were not to comment on the music but limit our contribution simply to "here is and that was." Rather like London's Melody Radio today.

We were incensed! What little verbal creativity we were allowed we had guarded jealously, and now this. The announcers to a man were an anarchic lot anyway and, foolishly, I allowed myself to be their mouth-piece. We asked, very calmly, that in view of the extra exposure we would give we should have a pay rise. Pay was £28.00 per week and we dared to ask for £30.00. Sheldon, ever the gentleman, said he would consult the management. The shift changed and I left the forts for a week's leave. Little did I know that it would be forever.

Ted Allbeury reacted furiously. He regarded DJs as the lowest form of life. He made Sheldon send a letter to my home firing me for what he called "rabble-rousing." There was no appeal. I sat at home in shock at being fired so unjustly. But the shock did not last long. About an hour. I went to London and started the rounds of agents. Bunny Lewis, who had been to my old school, told me to join the BBC. He told me that I had the 'gravitas' for the job. I didn't know what he meant. "You will never make a freelance," he said. "Don't ask me to represent you because I know we'll never make any money. Go to the BBC and earn a salary. You'll never be rich but you will be secure. Stay there until you get a pension." Now this was exactly what I had always had in mind, but how? I came out of his office and chatted to his assistant, Victor Labati, a most charming man, who told me to go away and make an audition tape. Bunny would then send it to the BBC with a covering note which, if I were lucky, would get me a BBC audition. I wasn't.

I took the tape to Graham 'Spider' Webb, an Australian then in charge of news at Radio Caroline. He gave me an audition and offered me a job straight away, £30 per week, the sum that had just got me fired. He took me out to dinner. I was overjoyed. I couldn't believe my luck. But I was not to start for a month.

Across the road in Curzon Street another offshore radio man, the delightful Don Pierson who had set up Radio London, was now establishing two new stations, Radio England and Britain Radio but on the same ship. I walked in the door, more out of curiosity than anything else, and met a man called Phil Aris. Phil was a journalist, well almost, and he had the task of setting up the MOR station, Britain Radio. This was to be an exact forerunner of Melody Radio but with 'personality presenters'. Additionally Britain Radio staff would read the news on Radio England to give it 'credibility.' At the time it was staffed almost entirely by screaming American DJs who, when forced to read news, pouted. We had stories about "Lyverpool" despite the Beatles being at the peak of their fame. "War-cester-shire" grated but the news item which really ensured the removal of US jocks from news shifts was a story of a shipwreck off the coast of "Ess-cunt-thawp."

Phil heard my tape and offered me £40 per week to start the following day. What to do, what to do? I walked back to Caroline House, no more than fifty yards away. Graham Webb heard my tale. "John," he said, "You'd be a fool to turn it down. Don Pierson is one of the nicest guys in the business and he knows more about offshore radio than anyone." That was true. But Don did not know about real radio. A great big Texan from Eastland, he held several Cadillac franchises and boy was he rich! There was only one reason why Don was in radio - money! He was also bored with selling cars and liked the idea of poking the British Establishment in the eye with a sharp stick. I was to meet him the following morning on the quay at Felixstowe.

Britain Radio and Radio England were both marvellous stations. They had the best equipment, the food was excellent and the mooring was about five hundred yards from Radios Caroline and London. It wasn't the best mooring and the ship, the *Laissez-Faire*, was anchored head to wind to absorb the effect of the waves on the studios. We had those wonderful Gates turntables, later chosen by the BBC for Radio 1. The pick-up arms were two inches across. When the weather caused the needles to jump we would tape threepenny bits on the top. If we got to six threepenny bits we went over to automated tape recorders called Scullies. While playing LPs often was the time that you would put on an album at track one, the arm would jump across the record and you would back announce track six. Did the listeners notice? Too right they did. They would mention it in their many hundreds of letters which arrived weekly. And of course we were not slow to wring all the sympathy we could get from them. There were these young lads (many weren't so young) braving the winds and tides just to bring audiences the music that the BBC denied them. Strangely few of us suffered from seasickness.

The talent on Radio England was very good. We had the very best of jingle packages - "The Boss Jocks Play More Music." Within days Radio London and Caroline stole them. Tony Blackburn still uses some of them today. "Stay with the fun, hear all the hits on ..." razor blades flashed to edit on the name of whatever station was appropriate. I was always very proud of the weather jingle. We didn't just have "here is the weather"; we had a 15 second power jingle over which you had to read the copy and hit the end just right to fit the music before the Dallas choir sang all about "The Ionospheric Weather Checker." All the best jingles were made in Dallas. Radio 1's jingles are still made there to this day.

But the American jocks got bored. They had somehow been given the impression that they were going to broadcast to the whole of England, coast-to-coast. They soon realised what the deprivation of their social life meant. Within a few weeks they had mostly departed leaving Roger Day from Margate, and Johnnie Walker from Solihull. It's hard to imagine today that Johnnie Walker used to speak with a Brummie accent that would grind the rust off the bottom of the boat. But Johnnie was no fool - he still isn't. He lost his accent very quickly. The Americans who remained taught them everything they knew about broadcasting, which they absorbed like a pair of sponges!

Yes Britain Radio - "Around the clock for news and entertainment, tune to us; around the clock for sounds that will amaze you, tune to us; around the clock for sounds of the smart set. tune to us etc etc ..." as the boys and girls from Dallas sang with absolute sincerity. Britain Radio was the hallmark of quality and it was a super station. So super in fact that when the time came to leave I was not the only one to weep. Britain Radio made money. It reached those all-important 25-40-year-old big spenders. Radio England targeted 15-24 year olds. We heard the rumours that one of the stations had to close. Because Radio England was so high profile we all assumed that Britain Radio would be closed. But we were wrong. Neither station closed but Radio England was to become a Dutch service. Johnnie Walker and Roger Day were out of a job. We wept with frustration and anger. So much work had gone into making Swinging Radio England do just that - swing.

Because of the rumours I had redoubled my efforts to join the BBC. I wrote letters, sent audition tapes, but heard nothing. But fate was to take a hand. Dave Cash, then on Radio London and now a Capital Radio DJ and author, sent me to see his agent, Chris Peers. Chris had contacts in BBC TV. He got me an audition in BBC Presentation. I wrote scripts, recorded announcements, read a news script. I read in the style of BBC1, short and precise and in the style of BBC2 rambling but worthy. Another announcer, Tim Nicholls, guarded my ego and prompted me. At that point I was extremely nervous and not a little worried.

I was offered a month's trial contract with BBC Television. There was just time to return to the *Laissez-Faire* for my concluding stint on board. On the last day with Britain Radio I gave a few clues that it would be the final show in my offshore radio career. I played *For All We Know We May Never Meet Again, Bye Bye Blues*, the Peter Cook and Dudley Moore classic ... 'So long, farewell I am leaving you toodlie bye' and finally my lifelong signature tune *Happy Days Are Here Again* played by Jack Teagarden.

If anyone noticed this odd collection of titles being broadcast they didn't comment. Probably because on the same day the company dropped another bombshell for those onboard - Radio England would be transferred to a Dutch service in one month. Swinging Radio England was to stop swinging.

Bill Berry lectured the jocks: "Stations change their formats regularly in the States and jocks expect to get fired. If you want to have a career in radio you are going to have to get used to this. Go back on the air, say nothing and be professional." Johnnie Walker drew the short straw. He went into the studio, sat down and did one of his best shows. There have been many since but I have heard none to equal it.

Roger Day, Tom Hatala, Boom Boom Brannigan and the others sat in the glorious August sunshine weeping genuine tears and no one sought to stop them.

The tender stayed alongside until gone 5.00pm. I thought it would never go. I packed my gear and looked around the *Laissez-Faire* for the last time. I got to the pub in Felixstowe just after opening time, sank two large brandies and then began to think about getting home. I checked the rail timetable to London, nothing for 90 minutes, but having got there I might just make the last newspaper train to Margate.

I ordered another brandy and as the barman passed it to me a voice behind me sang very quietly "*Happy Days Are Here Again*". I turned round. Framed in the doorway stood Connie with our two children, Beverley and Niall. She had driven all the way from Margate and just caught me in time. The children had been wonderful, she said, except they had kept asking that age old question that children always ask ... "Are we nearly there yet?"

After nearly 30 years in broadcasting I keep wondering the same thing.

STEVE ENGLAND
RECOUNTS HIS DAYS ON RADIO CAROLINE
AND RADIO ATLANTIS IN THE MID-1970S

I WAS STILL at school when I became an avid listener to Radio Caroline and Radio London. My parents, who were variety artistes, moved around England and Europe. They presented a South American gaucho act and appeared at the Royal Variety performances on ten occasions. They have also appeared with Judy Garland, Jack Benny and Max Miller.

I first heard the radio pirates when living in Bristol. On one occasion I was visiting my cousin and he was listening to the radio. It was a pirate radio ship going around the coast broadcasting pop music as she sailed. It sounded very exciting. The following week when I saw my cousin I asked if we could listen to the pirate ship and he replied that it had gone north. I later borrowed my parents' radio and eventually found the station. Radio Caroline North, late at night. I also heard Radio London, but didn't know what that was. I was listening to the *Earl Richmond Show* early in 1965 and thought it was an Irish station.

Later in 1965 we moved from Bristol to Folkestone, Kent, and that is where I learned about a lot more pirates. Radio City came in loud and clear. I asked my father if he had heard of Radio City and he said "Yes, it is in New York!" So for many weeks I thought I was listening to an American station, until I saw an article in a magazine which said it was located on a group of anti-aircraft forts in the Thames Estuary.

I used to go to our local library and read all the newspapers. If there was ever a story about the pirate stations I would go and buy a copy and put it into my scrapbook. To me it sounded so romantic to be a pirate disc jockey. In my formative years, between 15 and 17, my hobby soon became an obsession. All I wanted to do when I left school was to become a pirate disc jockey.

In August 1966 I went with my parents to Clacton, boarded the *Viking Saga* and, as one of the cheering kids, sailed out to Radio Caroline and Radio London. I also used to go to London and visit the offices of pirate stations in Chesterfield Gardens, Curzon Street and Denmark Street.

Steve England

After the Marine Offences Act came into force I then listened to Radio Veronica. In February 1970 RNI came on the air. I sent an audition tape, but never received an acknowledgement. I have subsequently learned that is not the way to get a job as a pirate disc jockey. You turn up!

Radio Caroline made a return in late 1972. I had become friendly with a photographer named Martin Stevens. One day he rang me up and said he was going out to visit the ship and did I want to go along? I said yes. We had to go to Holland and take the tender from Scheveningen. Before we went on board I met Andy Archer, Tony Allan and Alan Clark. We travelled out on the tender in the middle of the night. Sadly we only spent about 10 minutes on the *Mi Amigo*. Amongst those on board were Crispian St. John and Spangles Muldoon. We returned to Holland and then back to England.

Between Christmas and New Year 1972 Martin Stevens rang me again to say he was returning to Caroline. I joined him for the journey. We eventually arrived at Scheveningen and met the Caroline crew in a pub near the harbour. The DJs were talking in a most peculiar way. Martin and I didn't know what was going on, but they tolerated our being there. We got the impression that the *Mi Amigo* wasn't at anchor. When you looked out of the window of the pub you could normally see three sets of lights ... one from Veronica ... another from RNI ... and a third set from Caroline. That night there were just two sets of lights. We later learned that the ship was in Amsterdam harbour. The crew had not been paid, so they quit the ship and returned to Holland where they hired a tug and towed the Caroline ship into port. So we got into Martin Stevens' mini and drove to Amsterdam. We got on board the *Mi Amigo*, and by this time it was New Year's Eve so the ship was deserted and in a terrible mess. Eventually Ronan O'Rahilly came on board and said "This place is a tip!" So I started to clear up, washing the plates and generally tidying away.

The following day there were discussions on how to get the ship out to sea again. If they could get the ship moved out of the harbour that day, New Year's Day, there was every chance they would not be recognised by the authorities who were on a public holiday.

Ronan arranged for a tug to tow the *Mi Amigo* through the canals of Holland to IJmuiden. Halfway through her journey the ship was stopped by Dutch police who put a restraining order on the mast and chained up the wheel. The police said the ship was unseaworthy because of a hole in the stern. Ronan negotiated that a welder would come on board and repair the hole. By now crowds of people had lined the canal banks and were cheering on Ronan, the welder and the police. It was an unbelievable and most memorable incident. Ronan came to some agreement with the Dutch police who let us continue our journey.

We all remained on board and the next morning arrived at Scheveningen. Those of us who were not employees of Caroline were then asked to climb on to the tug which would take us to the harbour. I ran to Ronan and said I wanted to stay on board. I didn't want any money and would volunteer to do the night shift. I told him how I had cleaned up the ship. He said I could stay. I felt very proud that I had finally got a job on Radio Caroline. All my dreams had come true!

I remained on the ship and was offered the 3.00am to 6.00am show. My wife at the time, Debbie, later came out and joined me on the ship where we stayed on and off for about nine months.

There was no money available; only your fare home to England when you went on leave. After you had returned home you had to be very careful because you would get a phone call saying 'don't come back!' This happened to me several times, but each time I went back to Holland and hung around the Caroline office, located near the red-light district of The Hague, until they let me go back to the ship.

During the summer I presented the *Breakfast Show* on the English language service. I decided to leave in June 1973. Throughout my time on Caroline I had not been paid and was in debt. I had done what I had wanted to but by then was very disillusioned as it was not the Radio Caroline I had known and loved in the 1960s. Most of the music we had to play on air was 'heavy' and I preferred the Top 40.

It was a peculiar time to be at sea. There were so many weird personalities on board. In my opinion most of them were homosexual. On one occasion I was on board with my wife and it was a very strange feeling. There were about 20 people on the ship and Debbie and I appeared to be the only straight ones. Many of the DJs were smoking marijuana; kangaroo courts were held on board; mock bizarre religious ceremonies took place; there were regular fights on the ship; and all the time the transmitter would be breaking down. Some of the people were schizophrenic and compulsive liars. Others were drunk or stoned. At all times there was a very peculiar atmosphere surrounding you. If this was pirate radio I didn't want to be a part of it.

Bob Noakes wrote a book, *Last of the Pirates*, in 1984 which painted an accurate picture of what was happening on the ship at the time.

Another part of my life was listening to, collecting, and producing radio jingles. In 1973 I was asked if I would like to produce the jingles for a new pirate station, Radio Mi Amigo. I was invited to Belgium to the Suzy Waffles factory which had a recording studio next door. This was the first time I had recorded in an eight-track studio. The jingles package took three days to record.

In October 1973 I returned to England and said no way would I become involved in pirate radio again. I tried to pick up the pieces of my business, ZAP Discotheques, and get out of debt as I had received no pay whilst on Radio Caroline.

Within weeks I had learned that a new pirate station, Radio Atlantis, was operating off the Dutch coast. Crispian St. John sent a message in December 1973: 'If you are listening, Steve come on over.' I had decided the answer was no. After a couple of weeks I thought maybe I will give it a try. I went out to the ship with an engineer colleague, Andy Gemmell-Smith, who was known also as Andy Anderson.

The ship was an old trawler and didn't have an engine, so was basically a hulk. There was a 1kW transmitter which was operational and had come off the original Radio Noordzee on REM Island. The ship was in a terrible condition. There were no studios, so whilst Andy worked on the transmitter, I constructed two small studios and a record library. On board were two ex-Caroline people, Crispian St. John and Gerard van Dam, but they departed for shore leave in late February 1973 and did not return. I unofficially became captain of the ship and programme controller of the English service.

During the day we would broadcast tapes in Flemish and at night there was a 'live' English service. I was responsible for ensuring that the Flemish tapes were broadcast on time and changed regularly.

Radio Atlantis was run by Adriaan van Landschoot who had made his money by his Carnaby boutiques. He also owned a publishing house and record company, Mouse Music. He couldn't get the state radio to play his records so he decided to have his own radio station, first on the *Mi Amigo* and later the *Janine*.

We had the same arrangements which were in force with Caroline as regards my wife, Debbie, together with Andy's girl friend, Lynda (later his wife), who both came out to live on board. Other people on the ship at this time were Dave Rogers (who is now Keith Rogers of ILR), Terry Davis, Dave Owen, James Rafferty and Rick Rock. Leon Tippler sent taped programmes from his home in Kidderminster. Adriaan spent a lot of money on the ship and we had central heating and hot and cold showers. During the nine months the station was on air we had a superb time. All the personnel were lovely people and they created a very friendly atmosphere which was reflected in our programmes. However, we had no Dutch crew, no Dutch captain and no proper sailors. Our average age was 21. Innocence is a marvellous thing! We tried and, I firmly believe, succeeded in recreating the sounds and excitement of Radio Caroline and Radio London of the 1960s. We were a happy little family and we had a lot of fun.

Sadly it was not to last as the Dutch passed their own version of the Marine Offences Act. We broadcast an official close-down on 31 August 1974. After we went off the air we were towed into Vlissingen harbour. As we came into the harbour there were hundreds of people on the quayside cheering. One person had come all the way from Sweden. I have to say it was a tearful time. Radio Atlantis had a sizable and very loyal audience. That evening everyone who worked on the *Janine* was entertained to a slap-up meal hosted by Adriaan, who supplied us all with a written reference for future employment. During my time with Atlantis I produced a record for Adriaan called *Russian Woman* which began life as *My Little Sister Is*

Having A Party Tonight.

I later returned to England and joined Piccadilly Radio where I worked with Philip Birch. So I was fortunate to have worked for both Ronan and Phil, my two great heros in pirate radio of the 1960s.

Nowadays I run S2Blue and produce jingles for radio stations all over the world, a job which I thoroughly enjoy.

PAUL RUSLING
LOOKS BACK AT TWO DECADES AS AN ENGINEER
AND DISC JOCKEY WORKING IN OFFSHORE RADIO

On Board: Unlike many of my colleagues, I leapt from the tender onto the *Mi Amigo* and was met by Captain Dick Palmer, a marvellous man who was often ridiculed by many (including me) down the years as being a long-haired, fun-loving headband-clad hippy. In my opinion Dick was in fact the most sensible person on the ship, if not in the entire Caroline organisation.

It was the summer of 1973. He showed me around the ship, pointing out the danger spots of the feed points for the two aerials the ship now had, and the exhausts of the generators. One was beginning to glow a dull ruby red and the heat emitted was searing, no other word is suitable. Generators were to become our source of consternation over the next few months. The original plant had given up the ghost and some peculiar replacements were obtained from a Dutch Company, called Barth Generators, who were so worried about the reliability of their machines that they supplied a man to help Dick keep them running!

Cummings Jettisoned: We heard that another generator had somehow been 'blagged' from somewhere and it would need a space in the generator room. Our acting captain, yet another hippie much given to interrupting the late night programme to read his very entertaining poetry on air, was Michael Wall-Garland. A superb character, with rivetting stories about his time in the film business in Morocco, Michael took the instruction to clear the offending generator from the hold quite literally. A two-hour operation saw four of us raise the poor old Cummins (which in reality wanted little more than new filters for its intercooler, a thorough decoke and some new injectors) out of the generator room and, to our surprise swing it over the side and unceremoniously consign it to the deep. Worth some £250 as scrap, it had years of life left - but, as I was to learn very quickly, in true Caroline spirit it was to be wasted.

Of course, without power on the ship the food in the two huge deep freezers, so recently filled to the top by our wonderful office manageress, Kate, (Chris Cary's wife) was now going off. Some of it would soon be in an inedible state, of that there was no doubt, but the Caroline answer was to throw the lot overboard.

English studio: The station was, however, on the air, not on just one but on two frequencies. Caroline was broadcasting nonstop music on two frequencies (773 kHz and 1187 kHz) as I arrived, and a new studio had been hastily constructed in the old newsroom (just for'ard of the main studio). This had two Garrard SP25 turntables, costing a mere £20 each and seen in hundreds of clubs and other low cost locations. We also had the services of a domestic reel-to-reel tape recorder on which we used to play some jingles I'd brought along; some excellent ones rejigged by Steve England and the few commercials we had.

The monitor, an old radiogram with a terrific bass sound, sat on the floor under the desk, while the mixer was a six channel home-brewed rig of dubious origin which, unlike the old Gates console in the main studio, had sliding faders. These were not very robust and soon gave up, while we were plagued by problems of feedback from the studio monitor every time we opened the microphone - it often would not mute!

The microphone was an AKG D202, one of the best available. Peter Chicago wasn't too happy to get up one morning and find me with it in pieces on the desk trying to reassemble it, but that's another story!

The following morning we ran separate tests from each studio on the two frequencies and, in the absence of other orders, began announcing ourselves as Radio Caroline One and Radio Caroline Two. No interaction of the two signals at all - the last time this had been done successfully was by Radio England and Britain Radio in 1966, with slightly more affluent resources - so the exercise was a tremendous success. The tests soon evolved into being called Radio Caroline on the 773 KHz transmitter, and Radio Caroline (with 'radio' pronounced 'rahrdeeoh') on 1187 kHz, because we now planned launching separate Dutch and English services. The plan was to have the 50 kilowatt unit on the English programmes, and the 10 on the Dutch as it easily covered Holland.

There was a deficiency in the spares department which meant the 50kW could not be moved to the 'English' frequency; indeed, it couldn't be run up to a full 50 kilowatts for want of decent tubes and the poor output from the generators.

Late on Sunday 3 June, the third tender of the day came by, this time leaving Chris Cary on board. I was pleased that we would have an extra pair of hands to carry out the test transmissions - "No chance," said Chris, announcing to the crew "Full broadcasts from tomorrow."

Andy Archer, now the head of our Dutch service which was to air easy listening music (Frank Sinatra, Peggy Lee, Ray Conniff, etc) to serve an affluent niche market in Holland, still neglected two decades later, convinced me that the Dutch TV news crews would be out to film our start early next morning. So I had an early night to get up at 5.00am, wearing my snazziest tie and a mauve three-piece suit (thank you Mecca Ballrooms for my sartorial taste!) Needless to say, the only ones to witness the birth of a 'new' Radio Caroline International the next morning were the Dutch crew, a few seagulls and some visitors from Radio Veronica, our closest neighbour.

To help out with our shortage, Andy Archer was purloined from his new position as head of the Dutch Caroline service to drive the 'Housewives' programme from 9.00am until noon; Chris did his *Spangles Muldoon Lunchtime Loonabout*. The afternoon strip was handled by Peter Chicago, and later by his new assistant, Robin Adcroft, who had joined Caroline as an audio engineer. Robin successfully rid us of the feedback and various other faults, and later became known as one of the best aerial mast climbers.

After tea I did a programme and at 9.00pm we then strapped the English service transmitter to the Dutch studio and relayed their programme, which was no longer a Dutch easy listening service.

Four Seasons of Caroline: At teatime, the Dutch service on 1187 kHz (but still announced as 259 in those days), played light orchestral music and then at 7.00pm began announcing as Radio Caroline (spoken in English) and playing classical music for two hours. I hosted this programme myself for a few days, largely because our classical collection was 99% German albums and I was the only one who could read them and pronounce the German orchestras' names! Needless to say I soon tired of the unknown works and took to playing my own Top 20 of classical 'standards' ... the *Ride of the Valkyres*, *Fire Dance*, *Pomp and Circumstance* and the old *Aluminium Chorus* from the *Messiah*, and I suggested listeners write in with their requests too! No one on board, nor in the Caroline office, listened to the classical music I'm sure, but many listeners did and a few days later a couple of dozen listeners' letters began trickling in, with requests as I'd suggested. No one was amused. It seemed it was bad form to solicit mail for classical music, and the programme was supposed to be for Holland - but it's odd to note that twenty years later, Britain's first national commercial radio station is Classic FM, something "The Lady' pioneered all those years ago as part of the Four Seasons of Caroline.

At 9.00pm, one of our English jocks, Norman Barrington, took the chair and played in classical rock music, ELO and Wakeman, and then gradually got heavier until by 10.00pm the metamorphosis was complete and we'd gone from easy listening, through Handel and Mozart to the sounds of Frank Zappa and Alice Cooper.

This was taken a step or two further when our captain, Dick Palmer, entered the fray to give us the benefit of his wisdom, philosophy and musical taste. Later this was interspersed with poetry read by crew member Mike Wall-Garland, not to mention other strange goings on and some hoots of laughter from young Rusling, despite having to be up for a 6.00am breakfast programme.

Spangles left the ship and began pre-recording his programmes in some of the studios which had been constructed on the top floor of the Caroline office in The Hague, as did Andy Archer. Many of the Dutch programmes were pre-recorded here, in the tradition of Radio Veronica, which produced most of its programmes in a superb studio complex built into a small mansion in Hilversum, near Amsterdam.

Our pre-recorded programmes were all engineer-driven for some strange reason, perhaps to eliminate the learning curve from the huge 'churn' in staff turnover? The engineers were two great guys, one called Trevor and the other a certain Brian Anderson, who had run a disco business in Kent but was as desperate as all of us to get in to radio and this was a great first step. After the demise of the English service Brian took a job on the ship as a DJ with the Radio Atlantis and Mi Amigo Dutch services, and later transferred to Radio Northsea International.

After the demise of RNI, Brian went to Radio Tees, one of the first ILR stations, and later Moray Firth Radio in Inverness. By the 1990s he had gone off to Shanghai, China to run a new radio station there - which underlines what a valuable start Radio Caroline was to so many of radio's stalwarts. It was a training ground which has, sadly, not yet been replaced.

We whiled away the days playing our way through the Caroline singles collection of about 200 items, many too dreadful to play; so awful in fact that I took out a similar number on my next trip home!

The DJ line up at the time was an excellent one, and included myself, Robin Adcroft (who also later joined the RNI circus where he became known as Robin Banks!) Peter Chicago, Andy Archer, Spangles Muldoon and Roger Day (on tape) plus Steve England and Dave West (who fell foul of the old *mal de mer*, but is now with Manx Radio on the Isle of Man). Finally we were joined by Johnny Jason who later became one of Caroline's best known names and most respected broadcasters.

Frequencies and wavelengths: Every radio station broadcasts on a particular frequency, and these are (usually) chosen by international agreement. This can also be measured in terms of the wavelength, which has a direct relationship to frequency (divide either by the velocity of propagation - the speed of light - to get the other).

In keeping with the times, for its first twenty odd years anyway, Radio Caroline didn't use the frequency name in station identification, but the wavelength. Others did too - everyone remembers Radio 1 was 247, and Luxembourg was 208. Caroline was 199 in the early days, although in reality it was either 197 or 201, but those didn't rhyme with Caroline! When the South ship moved to 1187 kHz, 252 didn't rhyme with Caroline either, so it was announced as 259. When the North Ship moved to 1169 kHz, the corresponding 256 was also announced as 259.

So, when the International service began transmissions on 773 kHz (385 metres) what else could we use but 3-8-9, which was frequently announced on air? This brought in a great deal of mail. Now the use of the frequency for identification is widespread, and Caroline imitated Laser (in more ways than one!) with its new Caroline 5-5-8 callsign used from early-1986.

The end for Caroline's International service came one Thursday afternoon. I had taken a ride on a passing boat to the Veronica ship, a mile or so away; as well as better equipment and music library, they had more beer than we had, I seem to recall. On arriving back at the *Mi Amigo* I was a little under the influence, and the captain fired me, quite rightly, as I'd left the ship without permission. I didn't mind as I knew Chris Cary would reinstate me when the next tender came out.

Sure enough, at 6.30pm the tender tied up alongside and by 6.45pm I was back on air, taking over from Steve England who was eager to get ashore for a few days. Joining me in the studio for a natter were Kate, Chris, and Leo de Laater from our Dutch service (who joined Radio Veronica a few weeks later). The lights flickered and the records slowed and wowed a few times, but we took no notice - a common occurrence at the best of times, and we did have a very sick generator - at that time cooled by seawater being sprayed over the outside of it. The captain and our Dutch engineers were already down in the generator hold, sadly shaking their heads. Dick handed control of the ship over to Mike Wall-Garland so he could go ashore and make certain the correct spare parts were obtained to repair the generator. They were never to arrive for the station was to get two brand new generators instead, skillfully negotiated as part of a deal Chris Cary did with a Belgian who wanted to operate his own radio station. He wanted the station on the International 389 channel, and IDs were made up announcing this - in fact for two weeks the station identified itself as Radio 385, before becoming Radio Atlantis. That must have been really confusing for the listeners as the transmissions went out on the Dutch transmitter - 259. Although at last the ship had full power the parts were still not available to change the 50kW unit to 389, so on 259 it stayed and carried Radio 385, later Radio Atlantis.

Wet feet again: Early in 1983 I was approached by a club DJ and car dealer, John Kenning, to set up a new ship-borne station for a mysterious Irish investor. I took Kenning to New York where we met Roy Lindau, who had been Caroline's front man there and worked at Major Market Radio, a 'radio-rep' house. These representatives sold air time on radio stations to advertising agencies. Lindau was an expert at radio sales - which were to be vital to any new offshore radio station. Lindau said he would accept a position selling the new station if a $50,000 insurance bond were put up, to which Kenning readily agreed.

After returning to England, Kenning seemed to drop the ship-borne idea and the promises of payments. On my final visit to Kenning's home in Twickenham to collect the often promised funds, I was asked to assist in commissioning an embryonic 'land pirate' station - which evolved as Radio Sovereign following the arrival of the elusive cheque. As a parting gesture,

I introduced Howard Rose into the Kenning camp.

Some time later I became involved with Kenning's mysterious backer once again as consulting engineer and later operations manager. That story of how the ship was acquired and its transformation into a floating radio station is told in my book *The Lid Off Laser 558*. The station took a long time to commission because a permanent aerial had been refused in a budget cutting exercise, a problem which was to haunt the station throughout its life.

Once on air, the station proved extremely popular due to the slick style of presentation adopted by the American DJs and the almost seamless weave of non stop music ... an idea formulated by my wife Anne and myself and based on the Sixties station, Swinging Radio England. While DJs have their own fans and some a substantial following, research by Anne showed that the majority of listeners tuned in only for the music. An automation system was considered for Laser but scrapped by Roy Lindau because his neighbour's boy, George Clissold (who had worked on a radio station as Ric Harris while at college), had been promised a job running Laser. He couldn't be a programme director on his own so a team of DJs had to be hired, and were, some nine months before the station debuted, although many left long before the station got on air.

Laser's success was due to the fact that both the BBC and ILR stations refused to play non-stop music blaming needle time restrictions, and also because Laser gave exactly what the shore stations wouldn't. Little wonder that within three months, around 5 million listeners were said to be tuning in.

The station was named after a large multinational manufacturer who wanted to make the name Laser a 'buzz word' among the affluent twenty somethings, the yuppies of south east England. They didn't want commercials on air either. The lack of commercials encouraged listeners, but worried the authorities in London.

Senior Whitehall mandarins arranged for journalists to grill Laser's front man, Roy Lindau, on the motives for the station. He made the mistake of weaving a tapestry of deceit about the source of finance by claiming a syndicate of American businessmen to be behind the station. Probably knowing that one Irishman had funded the station, the authorities suspected he was being protected for some suspicious reason, when in reality he was merely a very private person. Fearing the worst, the authorities decided that Laser had to be removed at all costs and unprecedented steps were taken to silence the station.

The Iron Lady: By 1985 I had left the Laser organisation, having realised the station was bedevilled by problems which were unlikely to be resolved. Two contacts in the record business had wanted a station of their own for record-plugging services but found themselves unable to deal with either Caroline or Laser, so a new project was assembled - to be called HITS with a sister station called GOLD. The latter station was thought to be the real money-spinner, and as one of the backers had rights to over 2,000 of the biggest chart hits of the last thirty years he was anxious to promote them by way of a radio station.

On a trip to the USA on behalf of HITS and GOLD, I visited James Ryan, the finance broker who had raised money for Radio Caroline four years before and with whom O'Rahilly had fallen out. Ryan told me a story of a huge radio and TV ship he was building for the North Sea. He invited me to a meeting with other investors which took place in Connecticut the following week. Various plans were produced at the meeting (which was attended by seven very wealthy individuals) comprising seven TV studios, six radio studios and finally a huge mock up of what was clearly an oil tanker, with one side cut away to reveal a complex of radio and TV studios and transmitter halls. On the deck was an enormous tower which, they were told, was being constructed by a yard in Norway and would be 1,200ft. high! These people were planning TV coverage. Engineers at Thomson CRF in France had confirmed that from the proposed anchorage in the English Channel they would get a signal over the Downs into London.

Nearer the bows of the ship were two more towers, a mere 350ft. high each. One was to be a 'spare' and the other used for two MW channels. There were to be three short wave transmitters too, and AM Stereo was to be used.

Of course I was quite bowled over at this wonderful looking ship which had been called the *Iron Lady*. Here was a marvellous project, and well costed out at a mere $14,000,000! A crew of 44, plus a team of 18 security guards, 'hot and cold running women,' everything taken care of, but that was not all. There were reports from the largest advertising agency in the world backing up all the figures, and documents from four banks confirming the level of their backing. I believe the backing depended upon 'seedcorn' capital of $15 million.

I had to pinch myself to see if I was dreaming, but it was all true. I brought back copies of papers, reports and huge A3 pictures - and still have them. I accepted an offer of a position with them, and returned to the UK, putting our pub on the market.

Bloody Vikings: A week later I was invited to visit the home of one of the syndicate, Carl Gjerpen, who suggested that all was not well with the *Iron Lady* project, that some of the backers had been warned off Ryan by the FBI and so on. He thought we were going too big time and that Ryan only made money from setting up projects, not from actually running them.

He said that he had always wanted a radio station in Europe, and we spent all day talking about the proposals for Scan Radio some years before. He was extremely interested, and after getting my family over to his mansion in Connecticut for a week, I sat down and planned a *Radio Viking* project. It didn't worry him that there was a *Viking Radio* newly opened in Hull, where I had gone to school. He thought that was an added bonus; we were pirates, so why couldn't we steal our name too?

A few weeks later, Carl Gjerpen's lawyer called him and said that while all the theory seemed OK, he was worried about the operation of Laser 558 and the attention it was getting from the UK Government. The illegal actions of Laser soon brought this latest project to a halt. 'Wait and see what action the British Government take,' was the verdict.

It wasn't the intervention of the Government that closed Laser, however, but a chronic lack of supplies (due more to the poor organisation rather than anything else) and total demoralisation of the crew on the ship.

Some suggest sabotage, and whether you believe the story it was perpetrated by some of the crew on board, or by 'visitors' who crept on board - quite easy to do, it happened more than once. Whether the visitors came from the Government chartered surveillance ship anchored nearby, or from a submarine - we must wait until the year 2015 to see official Government records.

The facts are that important items of equipment on the ship broke down, resulting in a total lack of power at one stage. The captain (a well-known local coaster skipper, Patrick Paternoster, who knew the waters very well) decided it was far too dangerous to keep the ship at sea under such conditions, and, despite pleas from the crew and DJs, he decided to weigh anchor and head into port. He was unable to do so without help from the 'spy ship' crew, who miraculously were able to climb on board in 'rough' weather and get the engines, steering unit and winches operational. They knew the ship well - they had crewed it just two years previously and were now to escort the ship in, for the 'spy ship' on charter was a sister ship, still owned by Gardline Surveys of Lowestoft, from whom Paul Hodge and I had bought the ship.

Once the *Communicator* arrived in port, HM Customs and Excise made a thorough inspection. They also brought out writs from two of Laser's suppliers who were owed money but could not get satisfaction - one from the Gardline Company who had sold the ship to Laser two years previously and the other from myself.

Radio Caroline took over Laser's frequency immediately, supposedly to 'look after it for them, until they return' but everyone knew the station was finished, especially when the station manager, John Catlett, told reporters he didn't know what the future held for Laser, or whether the station would be able to get back to sea. The first ever pessimist in the history of offshore radio!

Meanwhile, my other project was coming together very quickly; in fact rather too quickly, because the ship concerned was still in the UK. Apart from Marconi, my main hero was an American called Leonard Kahn, who had invented several circuits for broadcast transmitters, including a way to make AM signals stereo. I was determined to bring AM Stereo to Europe, and this latest ship project was just the platform from which to do it.

A much larger ship had been obtained, the largest ever used for radio in the North Sea. She was longer than the *Ross Revenge*, about four times the size of the *Communicator* and about eight times larger than the *Mi Amigo*.

There had been some problems with the ship's gear, and additional items were being added prior to her sailing from the UK for a port in Spain where she could legally be fitted out for her new role, as Stereo Hits 531.

Her berth in Portsmouth was ideal, convenient for Harry Pound's breakers yard, where a supply of spare anchors and chain and other maritime paraphernalia was readily available. After dry-docking, a full survey and a switch to the Hellenic Register, the ship (now named the m.v. *Nannell* after a major backer's Mum) moved into dock at Southampton, a clever move as the authorities would never suspect anyone putting a budding radio ship into a closed dock in a major UK port.

Top radio engineer Joe Vogel (whom I had hired as operations manager for Laser 558) was brought back from the USA. Unfortunately Joe phoned an old Laser buddy and reversed the charges, saying he was working for me in the UK. The Laser 'buddy', sore at Laser's being still held at Harwich for incomplete certification, guessed I was fitting out a ship there and 'grassed' the project to the DTI.

A veritable army of DTI inspectors swooped on Southampton Docks the next day, searching every ship for studios or transmitters. They got very close - and gave the owners of the *Burmah Endeavour* a hard time as she had been laid up there for some time and fitted the bill for Ryan's TV super-tanker, the *Iron Lady*.

Stereo Hits 531 was fortunate that day as Joe had recurring bronchitis (he was sadly to die of it a few years later in Felixstowe) and was so ill during the night that our captain requested that someone get him into hospital. Not wanting Joe Vogel linked to Southampton for obvious reasons, I took him across to Canterbury where he was hospitalised for three days, and he then spent Christmas in Whitstable.

Meanwhile the m.v. *Nannell* was loaded up with what equipment was deemed 'safe', including two brand new AC generators to power the transmitters and she sailed for Spain. One essential item missing from the Laser manifest, but top priority for me, was taking shape at a secret location as far from the sea as possible. This was a 250ft. mast, which was no ordinary structure and nothing like it has ever been built on a ship before or since. The tower was of enormous proportions in order to give it strength and rigidity. It was ten feet across each of its four sides, and of square section. Assembled as four telescopic sections, the mast was specially designed by naval architects and manufactured under the most rigid secrecy the plant had ever seen. Only two radio people even knew the mast was in the country, both ex-Caroline engineers. One, however, had a loose tongue and thought it best to tip off the DTI. They visited the plant and were told that the structure was a lighting tower for a football ground in Essex, but they were not convinced. They were also stupid enough to leave a message for the factory's boss advising that they'd like to come back early on the Saturday morning and get some details of the customer.

Later that Friday night, a small army of workers rapidly completed what fabrication was possible and part assembled the structure. It was then loaded on to a huge trailer and driven away at 3.00am. Due to the size of the tower, it had to have a police escort - and by 8.00am, when the DTI arrived at the factory for a better look, the mast was safely tucked up on a building site in London. It remained there for several weeks before it was taken to Plymouth and loaded onto the ferry which plies from there to Santander, the very harbour in which the *Nannell* was waiting.

Further welding had to be carried out on the harbour side in Spain, with specialists and their equipment taken out from England to Spain to carry out the work. Meanwhile I had located a 50kW transmitter at a station (WZZD, all religion) just outside Philadelphia. It was an old RCA model, but in working order, with spare tubes and all coils necessary to operate at 531 kHz. An additional Gates 10kW transmitter was located down at Fayetteville in North Carolina for operation at 801 kHz, planned to be a second outlet from the ship.

The second channel was to be operated as two radio stations - during the day it would play love songs and be of appeal to housewives, easy listening, but up to date - Alison Moyet and so on. Around teatime, this would become black, silky soul, and then the heat would be turned up and the station air black dance music all night, before slipping back into something more akin to easy listening.

Meanwhile two more ex-Caroline people had joined the Stereo Hits 531 team in the form of Stewart Vincent and Dave Richards, both from Herne Bay. Two studios were taking shape under the wheelhouse, although a lot of equipment was still awaited from the UK. Three storeys below, in the bottom of the holds, the crew were busy shovelling 1,200 tons of loose chippings and cement ballast into every nook and cranny to give additional stability, essential once the tower was erected.

Problems over finance soon turned into disputes as my partners were already looking at several 'buy-outs'. First on the scene had been James Ryan. I had collected him from the TWA First Class lounge at London Airport to discuss a lucrative advertising contract, only to find his 'investment' involved a complete take over and the usual brigade of shady American financiers.

When it was announced that the *Nannell* was to have the towers installed without guy wires, that the transmitters were not to be upgraded and that there was no more money left for other essential supplies, I reluctantly decided to accept a much more lucrative gig in the Bahamas, and two days later flew there with my family.

It was to be nine months before I returned to the UK, as the European representative of a new offshore radio venture keen to broadcast its message to the thirsty millions. This time I was 'on a mission from God' and in the pay of High Adventure Ministries of California. High Adventure already had a station in Southern Lebanon which broadcast a mixture of Christianity and country music to the people of Israel. The leader of HAM and I were to launch a floating radio station in 'another part of the world', and I knew just where I could lay my hands on a ready-built ship.

The m.v. *Communicator* was still in the Thames Estuary. Efforts to run Laser Hot Hits as a successful radio station had been thwarted by a combination of poor advertising representation in London, even poorer management (both relics of the former Laser organisation) and the loss of the 558 frequency which Caroline now occupied. Laser Hot Hits had to make do with the noisier channel of 576, which marred reception, but basically morale was low and too many people had hands in a till not very full to start with.

I brought George Otis, a former US business high flyer and one time chief executive of the Learjet company, to the UK, but the new owner of the ship, a very astute Essex businessman well known for extracting a hard deal, had done his research and saw a pot of gold behind the American religious organisation. He asked for a small fortune and even when one was offered decided he didn't want to lose his new 'toy', yearned for over so many years, just yet. There was no sale possible, so George Otis and I flew off to Holland where I knew there was another ship in apparently good condition.

Radio Paradijs was the brainchild of well known Dutch broadcaster, Ben Bode, and a team of Dutchmen who had been involved with Radio Caroline. They had equipped their ship in Dublin Harbour in 1981, but left rather hurriedly once rumbled by the authorities. In July 1981 the ship had dropped anchor off the Dutch coast and commenced test transmissions one sunny Friday morning on 1107 kHz (271 metres). The signal was quite good, in fact a little too good. Substantial publicity appeared in several Dutch newspapers on the Saturday, with some aerial photographs of the ship. Empty drums of cable left lying around on deck looked like satellite receiving dishes and one story suggested links to eastern Europe - or certainly lots of money - and within hours of its appearing the Dutch Government decided to take action.

Early on the Sunday, a fleet of Dutch Navy vessels surrounded the Radio Paradijs ship and stormed aboard, arresting all and sundry and taking the ship in tow. One thing which enabled them to do this was the fact that the over-enthusiastic crew had decided to change the name of the ship to *Magda Maria*. By just painting the new name onto their ship without correct papers, they left the Dutch a loophole.

Once chained up in port the owners first capitulated and then pursued a long tortuous case against their captors in the Dutch courts, claiming not only the ship and all its equipment back, but also consequential damages - the loss of the advertising they would have obtained if allowed to broadcast.

In January 1986, however, the Radio Paradijs ship was silent in the Entrepot haven (a Customs jail for ships!) just east of Amsterdam. Otis and I clambered on board with a TV crew purloined from a Dutch religious organisation and hung their banner over the ships bows proclaiming it *The Morning Star*, a most ideal name as anyone who has read the New Testament will agree. A full TV programme, with prayers and sermons was filmed that morning on the ship, but it was all to prove futile as the owners' representative was suddenly 'unavailable' to discuss terms and wanted to wait until the court cases were over. 'A Mission for God' or not, Otis and I were temporarily defeated. We retired to the Hotel Krasnapolski in Amsterdam for an evening's entertainment. An appropriate venue, for back in 1960, the Radio Veronica team had assembled their first group of investors there to hear a fake test transmission from 'the ship' which actually came from a building across the street!

One possibility was a ship called the *Jostrica* which had been used as a tender for Laser in the early days and was in the hands of a friend of mine named Nick Murray. We decided to call him and got a surprise - for at the very moment that the prayers had been conducted on the deck of the Radio Paradijs ship, one of the aerial masts on the *Communicator* had fallen, as if the Lord himself was casting a divine influence over the future of offshore radio.

A call to the owner of the *Communicator* to commiserate revealed that he was now interested in selling. Heavy snow was sweeping the UK and many towns and villages on the east coast were cut off for several days. I swiftly made the necessary arrangements, including bringing in a Panamanian surveyor from Singapore, Captain Fred Law, who was also supportive of the project's ideals, and soon a huge tug laden with a lawyer, engineer, surveyor and the all essential 'bagman' (a money carrier in offshore radio parlance) was heading for the dismasted *Communicator* as she wallowed helplessly in the Knock Deep.

Some element of the Laser Hot Hits management was evidenced by the fact that the would be buyers arrived before the managers and agents whose small and entirely unsuitable tenders meant they were unable to leave harbour. I had also taken the precaution of bringing along the owner of the ship, in case any resistance was encountered from the Laser crew, who would immediately guess that I hadn't just 'called by' with so many support staff. Poor old Huey, as he was known to his fellow sailors, was probably among the best known offshore radio people, but with the weakest stomach - a true sign of a totally fanatical offshore radio supporter who would give everything for the cause (including whatever he had just eaten!).

Chief engineer Michael Barrington was pleased to see me as he had experienced some problems with transmitter 'A' which had a hidden 'glitch'. As I had not only installed it into the ship in Port Everglades but had also worked on assembling it at the CSI factory in Boca Raton, Florida, I was the ideal troubleshooter and soon able to locate the problem - apparently someone had sabotaged two small components resulting in only low level modulation, thus affecting the station's coverage.

The sale, however, was not to progress as the 'Men from the Ministry' (High Adventure Ministries, the religious organisation) were unable to agree on a price for the ship - so they went off elsewhere and the *Communicator* remained on station and awaited the next supply dingy.

A few weeks later Laser Hot Hits returned on low power with a partially rebuilt mast. The owner could take no more and commissioned me to find a buyer. One person who was keen was James Ryan, and one Saturday a few months later, I drove up to Newark Airport to meet the 'King Anorak from Essex' who had just flown in on Virgin - appropriate as it was his first visit to the USA and he was going crazy flicking the dial on his radio from one station to another. It is said that he doubled his range of audio recordings for sale on that trip!

The meetings with Ryan were punctuated by frantic transatlantic telephone calls to lawyers in the UK and eventually a deal was hammered out which was abandoned at the last minute when 'Essex Anorak' and myself found that Ryan was planning to pay in junk bonds of another company he controlled - the Walker Corporation.

Some time after arriving back in the UK, I received a frantic phone call at 2.00am from the captain of the *Communicator* to say that a ship with no lights was trying to tie up alongside and invade the ship - could I help?

A friend at North Foreland Radio agreed to patch through quickly a call on the very public VHF channels, which the 'boarding' ship took and agreed to stand off until the Panamanian consul could be got out to the ship to resolve the matter, but all to no avail as a few days later a peculiar flotilla of craft (including at one stage two men in a canoe!) set sail on the orders of yet another faction, reputed to be Laser's sales manager, and successfully boarded the ship, locking the crew (two men and one very plucky woman) in their quarters. The ship's anchor was raised and she set sail for an anchorage on the Sandettie Bank, halfway between Ramsgate and Belgium.

Ryan agreed he would keep the ship supplied while the dispute was resolved, but a diet of horse flesh and weevils did little to raise spirits on board. Soon the ship was forgotten, and a crew of Belgian or Dutch anoraks eventually sailed her off to Lisbon where she rests to this day, although in far better condition than the day she left her refitting berth at Tracor Marine in Florida almost twenty five years ago.

With some excellent legitimate radio work available on land and a young family to take care of, I decided that I would take one thing from James Ryan while the man still had his liberty - some advice - 'Don't get into a pissing match with a skunk'!

Since 1987 I didn't get my feet wet again for over five years until a little project came along to rekindle the interest - but as it's still current and the legislation has a few more teeth these days, the story cannot be told for a few more years!

RADIO ATLANTIS

The station was founded by Adriaan van Landschoot, a wealthy Belgian businessman who owned 10 boutiques. His clothes were sold in 785 other shops. As early as 1962 Belgium had introduced laws forbidding its citizens to become involved in pirate radio.

Van Landschoot, who was born in 1947, reached a deal with Radio Caroline to transmit programmes from the *Mi Amigo* on 773 kHz, but this frequency was never used by Atlantis. Broadcasts in Flemish began at 12.00 noon on 15 July 1973 on 1187 kHz (252 metres). The first day was treated as test transmissions. All Flemish programmes were pre-recorded on land in studios in Oostburg.[1] The international service of Radio Atlantis, broadcast in English, captured some of the excitement of the Sixties' pirates, but at the same time still succeeded in sounding up to date. The programmes were particularly popular in Belgium, and Atlantis was the first commercial station since the demise of the offshore Radio Antwerpen in 1962.

When the mast of the *Mi Amigo* collapsed on 1 October 1973, programmes for Radio

---

1. *Offshore Radio*, Gerry Bishop, Iceni Enterprises, Norwich, 1975, p.13

Atlantis were hampered, although old music tapes were still transmitted. From time to time Tony Allan presented live music programmes as did the ship's cook, Paul Brandt. There were attempts to recommence regular transmissions, but the temporary aerial also collapsed and no more was heard of the station from aboard the *Mi Amigo*. The Belgian millionaire, Sylvain Tack, had signed a contra-deal with Ronan O'Rahilly which said that Radio Atlantis would leave the *Mi Amigo* on 15 October 1973. Tack's station, Radio Mi Amigo, was expected to go on air on 15 October 1973, but this did not happen until 1 January 1974.

Van Landschoot, who lived in a huge manor house (styled on the USA White House in Washington) in Adegem, Belgium, then purchased the ex-Radio Condor ship and renamed her the *Janine* after his wife. Test transmissions began on 270 metres on 24 December 1973 with Crispian St. John. Regular programmes began on 7 January 1974. Radio Atlantis broadcast a mixture of Flemish and English language programmes.

Steve England was the programme director on board. Ray Warner (now Ray Anderson of EAP) pre-recorded shows for the ship. Engineer was Andy Gemmell-Smith, but he also presented radio shows

including *Blast Off* and *Starshine* in addition to *Nurkorama* with Steve England. He was known on air as Andy Anderson.

The ship was reported to have been in very poor condition, but money was in no shortage. Adriaan van Landschoot was generous to a fault. Crispian St John said: "Everyone put their nose to the grindstone and made living conditions on board very pleasant. There was a lovely atmosphere for most of the time. We had a lot of fun on board."

DJs included: Andy Anderson, Brian Anderson, Lynda Anderson (former wife of Andy), Bert Bennett, Alfred van der Bos, Frans van Brugge, Peter van Dam, Terry Davis, Robbie Day, John Dwyer, Debbie and Steve England, John Harding, Tony Houston, Crispian St. John, Dave Johns, Luk van Kapellen, Mike Mourkens, Michael O. (A.J. Beirens), Gabby Hernandez Omilada (Scott Mitchell, Leon Tippler), Dave Owen, Dave Rogers (Keith Rogers), Dave Townsend, Joop Verhoof and Gerard van der Zee (Gerard van Dam).

The station closed down on 31 August 1974, due to the Dutch Marine Offences Act, and the ship was towed into a harbour in Holland. The *Janine* was sold for scrap for 25,000 guilders (1993's value £9,250) to shipbreakers Van de Marel of Ouwerkerk, the same firm which broke up the *Comet* in 1969 and the Caroline North ship in 1980.

During her stay in Vlissingen Harbour, the *Janine* was completely stripped of all her radio equipment. The harbour authorities claimed 9,000 guilders for unpaid harbour fees, and the remainder of the money was paid, not to Adriaan van Landschoot, but to the previous owner of the ship.

CAPITAL RADIO

The station was set up in 1969 by Tim Tomason, executive director of the Dutch-based International Broadcasters' Society and Paul Harris, author and publisher who worked out of Aberdeen, Scotland. Dirk de Groot, a wealthy Dutchman, resident in Switzerland, put £40,000 (1993's value: £110,000) into the project. He was working **for** a Liechtenstein-based international finance company called the Mississippi Trade

and Investment Corporation. Tomason secured £50,000 worth of advertising from a trip he made to New York early in 1970.

A special company, for Capital Radio, the Kangaroo Pioneering Corporation, was founded in Vaduz, capital of the Principality of Liechtenstein. Two lawyers from Vaduz became directors of the company. A tender which had been chained up in Groningen Harbour was purchased for 12,500 guilders. It was a 128-ton vessel built in 1916 called *Twee Gezusters (Two Sisters)*. She was renamed the m.v. *Kangaroo*.

A larger ship, which was to be the radio station, was purchased for 50,000 guilders (1993's value: £18,500) in February 1970. It was a 359-ton coaster built in 1939, the *Zeevaart*. She was renamed the *King David*.[2]

In Groningen Harbour she was fitted with a new screw and rudder and was all set to sail for the high seas, but she collided with the lock gates at Groningen, causing £2,000 worth of damage. The *King David* was detained by harbour authorities until the insurance company sorted out payment. The authorities also noticed that the ship was not properly registered, so Tim Tomason thought

it was safer to buy a flag from one of the harbour shops in Groningen. He failed to locate a Liechtenstein Government flag, so instead purchased a Swiss flag which seemed to satisfy the harbour authorities.

On 3 March 1970 the *Kangaroo* left the harbour of IJmuiden for England. Her plan was to visit Scarborough to collect transmitting equipment which had been used on the *Oceaan 7*, home of Radio 270 between 1966-1967, and which was stored in a warehouse in the town. A deal had been struck with Wilf Proudfoot, former managing director of Radio 270, to buy the RCA 10kW transmitter, two new generators and a number of electronic spares. However, due to very observant harbour officers, who suspected that the equipment was going to be used on a pirate radio station, the equipment was driven to Middlesbrough. The *Kangaroo*, a converted trawler, collected the equipment and sailed north to Aberdeen to collect more equipment. She then returned to IJmuiden, Holland.

The *King David* sailed at the beginning of March 1970 to Zaandam where transmitting equipment from the former Radio 270 was installed on the ship. Two 27kW output diesel generators had been purchased from Leonard Dale of Dale Electrics of Filey. A

---

2. *To Be a Pirate King*, Paul Harris, Impulse, London & Aberdeen, 1971, pp 42-87

The International Broadcasters' Society had its headquarters in Bussum, Holland. The society, which was formed in 1964, carried out a lot of work for radio stations. Comprising some 2,000 members from around the world, it raised money from the 'Friends of IBS' to start international activities. Each year the society presented an international shield to someone who had made outstanding contributions in the field of broadcasting. One recipient was 'Bull' Verwey of Radio Veronica for all his good work in the 1960s. Another big project the IBS started was to work in Third World countries where they set up training facilities to help people find successful careers. The founder, Tim Tomason, also helped a number of Czech broadcasters find other jobs in Europe after the USSR invaded and occupied Czechoslovakia in 1968. Another personality in the IBS was Berthe Beydals, wife of Tim Tomason, who at that time was editor of the radio and television section of Holland's largest daily paper, *De Telegraaf.*

revolutionary circular ring antenna was constructed, which had never before been seen on a radio ship. It produced a ground wave only, and no sky wave, therefore giving less chance of interference to land-based radio stations. The idea had been designed by American intelligence.

25 April 1970: The *King David* left IJmuiden Harbour for a test broadcast, but within an hour a force 8 gale was blowing. It damaged the aerial system and the ship had to return to Zaandam for repairs. The harbourmaster refused the captain of the *King David* permission to enter the Harbour as the upper structure of the ship was a danger to the safety of other vessels. The *King David* sailed to Scheepswerf Vooruit where she

successfully berthed.

1 May 1970: The ship left the Harbour for a test transmission on 270 metres, 1115 kHz. in international waters. A pre-recorded tape, which identified the BBC World Service, was broadcast. One of the technicians on board had acquired the tape when he worked for the BBC monitoring service in Kent. The signal was heard on the Dutch coast. The ship returned to Zaandam.

13 June 1970: The *King David* sailed into the North Sea and test transmissions began on 270 metres, 1115 kHz, with Handel's *Water Music* which was to become the station's theme music. Included in the crew were a number of girl sailors whom, we are told, "enlivened shipboard life."[3] In the small fishing villages on the north coast of Holland the *King David* became known as 'the sex ship of the North Sea.' All crew members became members of the Liechtenstein Navy. It has to be pointed out that Liechtenstein does not have a Navy!

The test transmission opening announcement said: "Capital Radio is owned and operated by the world body to the broadcasting profession, the International Broadcasters' Society. Capital Radio is dedicated to the saving of human lives and the salvation of human beings. Capital Radio offers an alternative radio service to the Government-controlled broadcasting stations. Capital Radio is free radio ... good radio. We hope you have enjoyed listening to us."

The Dutch Post, Telegraph and Telephone network said they were having interference problems from Capital Radio reported by Coastguards on their SOS frequencies in the western part of The Netherlands. Test transmissions continued until 26 June when one of the insulators exploded and the aerial ring was in danger of collapse.

29 June 1970: The ship's third officer, Ari van der Bent, climbed the aerial ring to investigate some burning, but he fell to the deck and was knocked unconscious. A

3. *To Be a Pirate King*, Paul Harris, Impulse, London & Aberdeen, 1971. p.58

distress call was put out and a naval search and rescue helicopter airlifted him to a hospital in Holland. His left leg was so badly crushed that it had to be amputated.

11 September 1970: Regular transmissions finally began. Broadcasts were in both English and Dutch. Advertisements, also in English and Dutch, were limited to six minutes per hour. The opening programme was at 8.00am hosted by Tim Tomason. This was followed by Paul Harris talking about offshore radio. Then followed non-stop music until 11.30am when Berthe Beydals discussed freedom and rights of the radio listener.

Programmes were middle-of-the-road in musical format and, generally, three hours in duration. Each programme had a 20-minute feature on offshore radio by Paul Harris. There were also specialist shows including country and Latin American music. A religious half hour was broadcast twice a week, on Sunday morning and Thursday evening by the Rev Dominee Toomvliet. Reception was picked up throughout Holland and Belgium and on the south-east coast of England. On Sundays classical music was broadcast from 12.00 noon to 7.00pm.

9 September 1970: A distress call was transmitted to say that an insulator had blown up, and once again the aerial system was in danger of collapse. Broadcasting ceased. The following day the tender went out to the ship with engineers to replace the insulator. The damage was more serious than at first suspected and it was decided to take the King David into harbour. However, there were problems with lifting the anchor. In a force 8 gale the decision was taken to cut the anchor chain which disappeared to the sea bed. The King David sailed to Zaandam. The following day the ship was visited by the head of inspection of the PTT, a D. H. Neuteboom, who said that the vessel had to leave harbour as they had violated the Dutch Telegraph and Telephone Law, Article 20, in which it is forbidden for anyone to have unlicensed transmitting equipment on board a ship or at home. The captain decided to leave almost immediately,

and sail to IJmuiden to collect a new anchor and anchor chain. Within a few hours a 5-ton anchor and chain were put on board. Also put on board were two Sten guns, two machine rifles, a Browning high power machine gun and a number of nerve gas bombs, all of which had been supplied by a West German firm.

The directors of Capital Radio had given authority for these to be purchased as they had been told that a pirate war off the Dutch coast was brewing after Kees Manders had tried unsuccessfully to hijack RNI.

10 October 1970: Capital Radio returned to the airwaves playing 'sweet music'.

10 November 1970: The King David lost her anchor and began drifting. A mayday distress signal was broadcast and picked up by Scheveningen Radio. The IJmuiden lifeboat was launched, together with the Noordwijk beach rescue boat, Kurt Carlsen. The crew were rescued with the exception of the captain and the electronics engineer who remained on board. The King David continued to drift and she ended up on the beach at the Dutch seaside resort of Noordwijk, only 200 yards from the Palace Hotel. Thousands of sightseers arrived in the town to view the curious sight of a crippled radio ship lying in the sand.

13 November 1970: The King David was freed by the tug, Hector, towed into IJmuiden Harbour and, one week later moved to dry dock at Amsterdam's Westerdock.

26 November 1970: Police and harbour authorities boarded the King David, served notice of the ship's arrest and chained up the wheel. They said they were acting in the name of the Wijsmuller company. The International Broadcasters' Society were having trouble obtaining money from the insurance company and were not willing to pay the Wijsmuller company for towing the King David from the beach at Noordwijk to IJmuiden.

24 May 1971: International Broadcasters'

Society, operators of Capital Radio, was officially declared bankrupt. That was the last we heard of Capital Radio. The *King David* was towed to Betuwe, part of the province of Gelderland, where she became a store ship for a steel company. In 1981 she was towed to Heerwaarden where the upper structure was broken away from the ship. The hull was filled with concrete and she was used as a floating quay and is still operational today.

RADIO CAROLINE

Disc jockeys who worked on the English and Dutch services on Caroline between 1968 and 1990 have included: Chris Adams, Glenn Adams, Robin Adcroft (Robin Banks), Ian Akres, Paul Alexander, Tony Allan, Barry Allen, Brian Allen, Dickie Allen, Brian Anderson, Ian Anderson, Tom Anderson, David Andrews, Elton Andrews (also known as Mark Summers), Andy Archer, Dave Asher, David Baker, Bud Ballou, Rex Barker, Simon Barrett, Norman Barrington, Michael Benjamin, John Bennett, Grant Benson, Stephen Bishop (Johnny Lewis), Kevin Black, Roy Black, Erwin van der Bliek, Jeff Bolan, Nick Bolland, Doctor Boogie, Kees Borell, Ted Bouwens, Andy Bradgate, Paul Brand, Peter Brian (Peter van Dam), Bruno Brookes, David Brown, Ross Brown, Max Buchanan, John Burch, Arthur Burton, Buzby (Richard Thompson), David Caine, Andy Cameron, Tony Cameron, Ben Carpenter, Chris Carson, Kelvin Carter, Rob Charles, Susan Charles, Peter Chicago (engineer), Tony Christian, Peter Clark (Peter Tait), Stuart Clark, Coconut (Mike Dixon/Mike Kerslake), Dave Collins, Steve Conway, Clive Cornell, Maurice Dancer (Roland Butter, Rex Barker and Billy Dukes), James Day, Jonathan Day, Roger Day, Ronnie Doyle, Chris Drummond, Samantha Dubois (Ellen Kraal), Mike Dundee, John Dwyer, Chris Elliot, Dave Ellis, Chris England, Debbie England, Steve England, Steve Essex, Dave Fisher, Martin Fisher, John Ford, Dave Foster, Ed Foster, Keith Francis, Neil Francis, Tony Gareth, Neil Gates, Pierre van Gent, Graham Gill, Stevie Gordon, Herman de Graaf, Paul Graham (Graham Paul), Mike Hagler, Tom Hardy, Nigel Harris, Rob Harrison, Peter Haze, Rene van Heist, Rob Hudson (Ruud Hendriks who went on to become a major name as a director of RTL4 and RTL5 Television in Holland), Douglas Thomas Ingle, Jay Jackson (Crispian St. John), Nick Jackson, Richard Jackson, Marc Jacobs, Chas James, Dave James, Tony James, Kenny James (Kenny Page), Trevor James, Dennis Jason, Johnny Jason, Robbie Jay, Fiona Jeffries, Andy 'Cosmic' Johnson, Carl de Jong, James Kay, Chris Kennedy, Steve Kent, Dennis King, Edwin King, Jamie King, Keith King, Carl Kingston, Tony Kirk, Hans van der Laan (nowadays director of Sky Radio), Stevie Lane, Diane Lauren, Mark Lawrence, Jackie Lee, Keith Lewis, Michael Lindsay, Mike Lloyd (Glen Schiller), Will Luikinga, Ian Mac, John B. Mair, Brian Marshall, Brian Martin, Caroline Martin, Frank van der Mast, Steve Masters, Bob Matthews, Mark Matthews, Roger Matthews, Melanie McArthur, Paul McKenna, Jenny McKenzie, Tony McKenzie, Fergie McNeil (Jimmy Bond), Mickey Mercer, Sue Mercer, Steve Merike, Hugo Meulenhof, Charles Miles, Ian Miles, Carl Mitchell, Phil Mitchell, Bruce Monroe, Jeff Morris, Spangles Muldoon (Chris Cary), Judy Murphy, Kevin Nelson, Alec Newman, Bob Noakes (engineer), Cliff Osborne (Martin Fisher), Dave Owen, Kenny Page, Dick Palmer, Ian Palmer, Peter Pann, Andy Parker (Joss Stick), Mark Patterson, Dixie Peach, Chris Pearson, Mike Pearson, Sebastiaan Peters, Tony Peters, Ad Petersen, Peter Philips, Steve Philips, Piet de Prater, Bruce Purdey, Peter Quinn, Brian Richards, Dave Richards, Nick Richards, Ad Roberts, Nigel Roberts, Andy Robin, Del Rogers, James Ross (Kelvin Carter), Robin Ross, Paul Rusling, Stuart Russell, Tony Scott, Dave Shearer, Paul Shelton, Tim Shepherd, Richard Staines, Don Stevens, Mike Stevens, Mike Storm, Alan Symonds, Richard Thompson, Kevin Turner, John Tyler, Graham Vega, Tom van der Velde, Hans Verbaan, Joop Verhoof, Steven Vincent, Stuart Vincent, Johan Visser, Peter de Vries, Johnnie Walker, Mark Warner, Mike Watts, Dave West, Richard West, Simon West, Alan Wheeler, Blake Williams, Mick Williams, Dave Wilson, Dave Windsor, Paul de Wit

(Erik de Zwart), Jeroen Woelwater (nowadays director of Radio 10 Gold, Holland), Marti Wright, David Wynn, Gerard van der Zee.[4]

3 March 1968: With advertisers frightened off by the new law, Caroline soon got into financial difficulties. The Wijsmuller towing company was apparently owed £30,000, and eventually took the law into its own hands. There was a disagreement between the two Wijsmuller brothers. One said "We are going on tendering the Radio Caroline ships." The other brother replied "We are not!" He went ahead and sent tugs out to both North and South ships, took them over and towed them into Holland. Following this incident both brothers went their own separate ways.

In an interview with David Hughes of *Disc and Music Echo* on 13 April 1968, Ronan O'Rahilly said he was hoping to return to the airwaves on Easter Sunday, 1968. He also said Caroline would not be using either the m.v. *Mi Amigo* or the m.v. *Caroline*. Other reports indicated that Caroline would use the *Oceaan 7*, the ship originally used by Radio 270, off Scarborough. One of the DJs, Andy Archer, mentioned this plan to a newspaper which published the story. This made it very difficult to get the ship out of Scarborough due to the problems Caroline had with the authorities who had read the story in their local newspaper.

Yet another rumour suggested that Ronan O'Rahilly might use the m.v. *Galaxy*, formerly Radio London. But as time went by it was obvious that Radio Caroline had hit various snags.

As Easter Sunday came, thousands of people throughout Britain tuned their radio sets to 259 metres. But all remained silent.

DJ Roger Day, who was one of the men earmarked to be amongst the first voices on air for the Easter 1968 comeback said: "I was told to stay in and expect a phone call on Good Friday. Then I was told Radio Caroline wouldn't be on the air after all."

Easter Sunday 1969: Radio Andorra

broadcast a special Radio Caroline tribute. A number of Caroline DJs took part in a programme hosted by 'Daffy' Don Allen.

13 June 1970: Just when everyone thought Caroline had disappeared for good, an announcement was made from the *Mebo II* radio ship by Carl Mitchell: "The impossible has happened. We're back! You're listening to Radio Caroline International."

Caroline 'took over' the RNI ship for a spell just before the General Election to campaign against Harold Wilson's Labour Government which had outlawed them in 1967. The result was a win for the Conservatives. The name Radio Caroline then reverted to RNI.

29 May 1972: The two Caroline ships were sold at auction by Wijsmuller on 29 May 1972. *Caroline* was sold for scrap. *Mi Amigo* was sold by R.W. Bais to an agent who was bidding on behalf of Rob Vermaat and Gerard van Dam, for a sum of 20,000 guilders (1993's value £7,400). Her registered owners became Vagabond Films.

During the previous year Peter Chicago and Spangles Muldoon went to Amsterdam Harbour and took away from the two radio ships studio equipment and spares for the transmitter. These were put in store in Amsterdam for when Caroline returned to the airwaves. Later Ronan O'Rahilly acquired the ship and Caroline was back on the air again on 30 September 1972, the 5th birthday of Radio 1. There were no programmes transmitted, just a continuous loop tape of *For All We Know* by the Ray Conniff Singers.

Radio enthusiast John Adamson noted in his diary for 30 September 1972: "Test transmissions (music only) have been heard on 1187kHz from the *Mi Amigo* since yesterday evening. Signal strength and modulation quality in Central Scotland is excellent during hours of darkness.

"Radio Veronica moves from 192 metres (1562kHz) to 538 metres (557kHz) at 12.00 noon. As Veronica closes, RNI immediately starts RNI 2, a new English service on 192 metres (1562kHz), leaving Dutch programmes on 220 metres (1367kHz). There are serious technical difficulties. The

4. *25 Years of Radio Caroline Memories*, edited by Hans Knot, 1989, Groningen. Holland pp 195-197

English programmes leak over the top of the Dutch service. The new English service (allegedly only put there to steal publicity from Veronica's move from 192 to 538 metres!) is suspended the following day."

2 April 1973: Force 10 gales raged off the Dutch coast. RNI dragged her anchor, but managed to return to her old anchorage; the *Mi Amigo* suffered damage to a number of portholes and the Radio Veronica ship, the *Norderney,* became stranded on the beach at Scheveningen. Both the Caroline and RNI organisations offered Veronica facilities to promote their "Keep Veronica on the Air" campaign between 10 and 18 April 1973. More than 150,000 free radio fans turned up for the demonstration in The Hague. It was the largest of its kind ever held. Radio Veronica used the transmitters of Radio Caroline. By way of thanks Veronica invested a lot of money in the *Mi Amigo* by rebuilding her studios and installing a brand new generator. The *Norderney* returned to international waters on 18 April and resumed transmissions on 558 metres.

1 June 1973: Radio Caroline transmitted two programmes from the *Mi Amigo*. Radio Caroline I, a Top 40 station on 389 metres, and an easy listening station on 259 metres being Radio Caroline II. On 389 metres Johan Maasbach was the presenter of the first religious programme to be heard, followed by Paul Alexander with the *Multi-Colour-Band Breakfast Shogramme*. Andy Archer, Steve England and Spangles Muldoon were also heard regularly. Roger Day recorded programmes on tape and was heard for the first time on Caroline since 1968. Both stations transmitted partly in Dutch and partly in English.

15 July 1973: Belgian businessman Adriaan van Landschoot put up the cash to keep the *Mi Amigo* broadcasting. New stations Radio Seagull and Radio Atlantis broadcast programmes from the ship. Van Landschoot restarted Radio Atlantis from a ship which he called *Janine* after his wife.

1 March 1974: Radio Seagull gave way to

Caroline again and Ronan O'Rahilly introduced the idealistic concept of 'Loving Awareness' to the programming. Ronan, then bearded with long silver-grey hair, had been a keen follower of Mahatma Gandhi and Martin Luther King. He said: "The concept is quite simple. If you inject love into the lives of all those you meet they will love you for it. When we brought 'The Lady' Caroline back in 1972 we decided to give it this new dimension."

21 June 1974: 40,000 attended a Midsummer's Day Radio Caroline LA Festival at Stonehenge.

31 August 1974: Holland introduced its own Marine Offences Act which saw the demise of Veronica, RNI and Atlantis. However, Radios Caroline and Mi Amigo carried on and defied the Dutch authorities. O'Rahilly had visions of the Dutch sending in the heavy brigade to silence the *Mi Amigo*, so he arranged that the ship would sail to international waters off Frinton-on-Sea, her home in the 1960s.

She anchored in an area known as Knock Deep at latitude 51 42 50N, longitude 01 35 00E. The Dutch office of Radio Caroline closed and the administration was run from Playa de Aro, Spain. The station lacked the mass appeal of the 1960s as there was more competition with ILR stations and national Radio 1 in Britain. Caroline adopted an album format to play rock music. It was described as 'narrow casting', but many listeners rejected the format and went elsewhere for their entertainment. The broadcasters were also a different breed. In his book *The Pirates Who Waived the Rules*, Jay Jackson says: "DJs sounded for the most part like stoned hippies on a trip and often the music would consist of entire album sides. The energy of Caroline in the sixties had gone."

11 May 1975: *East Essex Gazette* reported that a Holland-on-Sea man who delivered messages between people in London and others on board the pirate radio ship *Mi Amigo* was ordered to pay a total of £100 by Clacton magistrates on Monday. Peter

Jackson, who admitted broadcasting via an illegal radio system in his loft, establishing a wireless station without a licence and using a station for wireless telegraphy without a licence on two occasions, was fined £25 on each of the three cases; ordered to pay £25 costs and forfeit the equipment, which was valued at £46.10. Peter Hawkins, prosecuting on behalf of the Post Office, told the court that in November 1974 Post Office engineers discovered a station operating between the pirate radio ship *Mi Amigo*, which was anchored in the Thames Estuary, and an address in Holland-on-Sea for which there was no wireless telegraph licence in force. After obtaining a warrant the Post Office searched the Jackson house. In the loft they found an assortment of radio receiver and transmitter equipment, plus a telephone which was connected to an ordinary phone downstairs.

18 September 1975: The first prosecutions were brought under the Marine Broadcasting (Offences) Act, 1967. The first person to be fined £100 was Michael Baker for supplying records to Radio Caroline. The first disc jockey to be prosecuted was Andy Archer who was fined £100 with £50 costs for broadcasting on Radio Caroline. He was followed by John Mair who was also fined £100 with £50 costs for a similar offence. The cases were heard at Southend Magistrates' Court.

8 November 1975: Caroline drifted from her anchorage in the Knock Deep Channel. Coastguards were notified. DJ Simon Barrett presented his show whilst wearing his life jacket. The *Mi Amigo* drifted into British territorial waters and went off the air at six minutes past eleven. There were seven people on board. By 9 November a number of ships came to stand-by including the *Sun XXII* and the *Mermaid*. There was also a tug called the *MS Sauria* which stayed alongside overnight and departed early morning, 10 November. On 12 November a ship from the Port of London Authority, the *Maplin*, went alongside and the skipper asked for permission to go on board the *Mi Amigo*. This was refused. The *Maplin* stayed close to Radio Caroline for about three hours, then departed for her base at Gravesend. The tug *Egerton* also visited the *Mi Amigo*.

Finally, on 13 November a tug, arranged by Caroline, came out to help but failed to tow the ship to its original anchorage. Radio Caroline, and her sister station, Radio Mi Amigo, returned to the air.

On 14 November a police launch went out to Caroline with about 20 uniformed officers and Home Office representatives from the Radio Regularity Department. They boarded the *Mi Amigo*, having first sought permission from the captain, and four crew were arrested by Detective Sergeant Hargreaves from Chelmsford CID, and later taken to Southend police station, handcuffed, interrogated and locked in a cell until morning. On 15 November all four appeared in court charged under the MeBO Act 1967 and released on bail of £1,000 with their passports confiscated until the court case.

11 December 1975: The *Southend Evening Echo* reported that at Southend Magistrates' Court, two Caroline DJs were fined for broadcasting illegally after the pop ship broke from its moorings and drifted inside British territorial waters. The DJs were Simon Burnett (known on air as Simon Barrett), and American, Glen Schiller (Mike Lloyd on air), together with the Dutch Captain Werner de Zwart and engineer, Peter Chicago. Simon Barrett was fined £200 with £50 costs. Schiller was fined £50 with £25 costs and de Zwart was fined £100 with £50 costs. Passports, which had been confiscated a month earlier, were returned to the defendants.[5]

All had been prosecuted and found guilty of contravening various sections of the Marine, Etc., Broadcasting (Offences) Act 1967, on 13 November 1975.

A summons against engineer Peter Murtha (Peter Chicago), 27, was adjourned until 23 February after he pleaded not guilty. He was released on £1,000 bail.

23 February 1976: The *Southend Evening Echo* reported that at Southend Magistrates' Court, Peter Murtha (Peter Chicago) was

5. *SOS 10 Days in the Life of a Lady*, Simon Barrett, MRP, London. 1976, pp 1-82

Peter Chicago

fined £100 with £50 costs for repairing and maintaining illicit radio equipment.

At the same hearing DJ Don Stevens (real name Cyril Smith) admitted to having broadcast for 52 nights aboard Radio Caroline. He was fined £50 with £25 costs.

26 April 1976: DJ Johnny Jason was cleared at Southend Crown Court of taking part in an unlawful broadcast. Judge Martyn Ward stopped the hearing and ordered the jury to find Jason, real name Rudiger von Etzdorf, 27, not guilty of taking part in an illegal broadcast from the ship *Mi Amigo* while she was on the high seas, off the Essex coast. Noel Morrison reported the case for *Monitor* magazine. Edition N° 11 (1975).

The judge said the lynchpin of the case was whether von Etzdorf took part in a live broadcast, and he was uneasy about asking the jury to decide this issue from the police evidence before them. But when asked to award von Etzdorf costs, he replied: "Here is a young man who, with others, decided to cock a snoot at society. He said he was going to be a disc jockey on Radio Caroline and set about doing it. When he set foot on the ship and went into the studio, he knew he was doing something that he should not have been doing."

Von Etzdorf, of Lansdowne Road, Notting Hill Gate, London, was charged under the Marine Offences Act.

26 April 1976: A case of getting your stickers in a twist! The first prosecution of its kind for displaying a Radio Caroline sticker 'Sound of the Nation, Radio Caroline, Tune into 259 metres" in three cars, a Vauxhall Victor, registration number 3672 AR on 14 January 1975; an Austin van, 7618 TF, on the same date; and a purple ex-ambulance, ALP 546H, on the same date. In the 1960s it seemed that everyone was a pirate fan and thousands of cars across the country bore stickers proclaiming 'I Love Caroline on 199.'

The *Daily Mail* said on 27 April 1976 that Ronnie Doyle, 33, of Prescott Street, Liverpool, had first appeared before the bench in Liverpool on 17 February 1976 when he was given a dressing-down by the magistrate, Leslie Pugh, who referred to his mode of dress, a T-Shirt with skull and crossbones printed on the front. "Is it your usual practice to go around with that kind of shirt on?" Doyle replied saying that it formed part of the evidence. Mr Pugh told him "The next time you come to court you had better wear something else so your shirt can be produced as an exhibit."

Doyle faced five charges of publishing material (posters and car stickers) calculated to promote Radio Caroline. Accused with him was 27-year-old John Jackson-Hunter, who also wore a Caroline T-Shirt and James Monks, 32, manager of the Fleece Hotel, St Helens, Lancashire, who wore a dark suit. Jackson-Hunter and Monks faced one charge each. All three pleaded not guilty. The case was adjourned until 3 May. The case lasted for a week and there were 25 prosecution witnesses.

The *Liverpool Echo* said on 3 May 1976 that the bench took thirty minutes to find all three defendants guilty. James Monks, the hotel manager, was found guilty of 'indirectly publicising Radio Caroline through a foyer advertisement for a roadshow.' The roadshow consisted of a copy of the bow of the *Mi Amigo* in accurate detail with the console, turntables and tape decks, behind. The music they played was similar to that of Radio Caroline, and when dedications were read out the DJ rang a magnificent shiny bell which appeared to be

Mi Amigo, Radio Caroline in the mid-1970s

similar in design to the bell-shaped Caroline awards in the 1960s. Monks was fined £25 with £50 costs. Jackson-Hunter and Doyle were found guilty, but sentence was deferred pending 'social reports.' It is believed to have cost in the region of £4,000 to bring the case to court.

Ronnie Doyle was first in the news on 17 November 1975 when, with Kelvin O'Shea, he visited the *Mi Amigo,* became stranded, and was rescued by the Margate lifeboat.

21 May 1976: The continuing saga of the Caroline stickers court case continued in Liverpool. The *Liverpool Echo* reported the case on each of the five days. Ronnie Doyle (known as DJ Ronnie Dee) and John Jackson-Hunter (known as DJ John Shannon) had been found guilty at Liverpool City Magistrates' Court on 26 April. The two defendants again turned up in Radio Caroline T-Shirts. The sentence was announced - 'A 90-day prison sentence, suspended for 2 years, and £500 costs each!' A severe sentence in anyone's eyes. They were given 21 days to appeal against the sentence. This they did on the last day.
The appeal was heard on 29 July 1976 but the case was adjourned until 6 September at the Crown Court, Lime Street, Liverpool.

1 August 1976: Dave Hutson took out a party of sightseers to the *Mi Amigo* from Brightlingsea, Essex. On the return journey they were intercepted by an Essex police launch, the *Watchful.*

Four months later Dave Hutson of Vange, Essex, received a summons, for supplying mail and newspapers to the *Mi Amigo* and advertising the station by displaying a Caroline badge! A police officer had been aboard the 'anorak' boat disguised as a free radio fan. Calling himself Simon Martin, he was in reality Detective Constable Gary Skull. Also charged was the owner of the boat, Walter Ord. He and Hutson were asked to appear before magistrates at Southend on 27 January 1977.

6 September 1976: The Caroline stickers court case was further adjourned until 25 October 1976.

10 September 1976: The *Mi Amigo* broke her anchor chain, went adrift and grounded on a sandbank. The old vessel took in water, but was eventually mopped up and towed back into position. The Dutch crew, nervous of the British authorities who may have gone on board as they did in 1975, left the ship in a hurry and travelled to Ostend in a fishing trawler. One of the Caroline crew, Dutchman Marc Jacobs, phoned colleague and journalist, Hans Knot, to say that they would be returning to the *Mi Amigo* the following morning. Whilst in Ostend they searched the harbour for a large anchor chain and found one on an impounded oil tanker which had been chained up by the Belgian authorities. During the night they stole this large anchor chain and took it back to the *Mi Amigo* where it remained until the demise of the old lady on 19 March 1980.

25 October 1976: The Caroline car stickers appeal was heard and reported in *Monitor* magazine, Edition N° 12, 1976. The police officer who spotted the Caroline stickers in the two vehicles belonging to Ronnie Doyle and John Jackson-Hunter was Chief Inspector William Hayton. The roadshow was built in 1971. In his defence Doyle said it had no connection with the Caroline ship. He wished to draw on the nostalgia created by the name Radio Caroline. Jackson-Hunter's sentence remained unchanged, but Doyle's prison sentence was substituted by £100 fine and £500 costs. Jackson-Hunter later went to jail. He refused to pay £500 court costs awarded against him for promoting Radio Caroline. He had been sentenced to three months jail suspended for two years by Liverpool magistrates after being convicted of 'publishing advertising.' He had a Radio Caroline car sticker in his car window. The magistrates ordered him to pay £500 costs for the case, but 18 months later he still had not paid, so a warrant was issued for his arrest and he entered Walton Prison on 25 November 1977 for a sixty day term. He was released on 3 January 1978. Having served 40 days and spent Christmas in jail, he said he would continue to present his road shows around the county.

12 January 1977: Caroline DJ Samantha Dubois (real name Ellen Kraal) appeared in court in Amsterdam accused of broadcasting on Radio Caroline. She was found guilty and given three weeks prison sentence, suspended for two years. Samantha told *Monitor* magazine, Edition N° 14, 1977, she was not going to pay the fine and would return to Caroline, which is what she did in February 1978.

27 January 1977: Detective Constable Gary Skull took a pleasure trip out to see the m.v. *Mi Amigo* on 1 August 1976. He travelled under the name Simon Martin posing as a passenger. He was on duty for Essex police. Skull reported that the organiser of the trip, David Hutson, handed newspapers and mail over to the Caroline DJs. He also stated that Hutson was displaying a Caroline badge!

Hutson, 27, of Vange, Essex, appeared in court to answer these two charges. Also in court was Arthur Ord, an old age pensioner who was the owner of the boat. Both pleaded guilty. The *Standard Recorder,* reported that Ord, 68, of Brightlingsea, Essex, was fined £200 with £20 costs. Hutson was fined £125 with £20 costs.

25 February 1977: The French newspaper. *La Voix du Nord,* reported that five French businessmen were fined by a Lille court for supplying Radio Caroline with food, linen and wine. Frédéric Doucedame, Patrick Ringart, Paul Balogh, Jean-Marie Talleux and Jean-Pierre Delva appeared before the High Court in Boulogne. France had signed an agreement in 1965 with England forbidding pirate broadcasting and the supplying of radio ships. The law was passed on 29 December 1969. The charge against the accused was hiring tenders which took supplies to Radio Caroline. All pleaded guilty. Delva was fined 1,000 francs (about £110), Balogh 1,500 francs (£165), Doucedame and Ringart 3,000 francs (£330) each and Talleux 5,000 francs (£550).

27 February 1977: The Walton and Frinton lifeboat rescued 17-year-old Erik Beekman (real name Bart van Gogh), a Dutch DJ aboard the *Mi Amigo*. He was taken to Essex County Hospital, Colchester, suffering from epilepsy. Frank Bloom, coxswain of the lifeboat said: "When the lifeboat drew alongside Radio Caroline, he was lowered into the lifeboat by DJs and crew. Normally no ships are allowed near pirate radio ships unless it is a question of saving life. The boy had been ill for more than a week."

The following day he was released from hospital. His mother arrived in England by air, collected Bart, who was described as satisfactory, and returned to Holland. He travelled under heavy sedation. The story has a happy ending. Today he is a co-director of Top Format, the second biggest jingle company in Europe after Alfasound of Sale, England, run by former Caroline and Atlantis programme director, Steve England.

3 March 1977: Caroline changed her frequency from 259 metres to 319 metres medium wave, 953 kHz.

4 March 1977: Coastguards and the Calais Frontier Air Police apprehended the crew of a Boulogne trawler, *Saint-André des Flanders,* according to the French newspaper *La Voix du Nord.* The master was André Fauchet of Boulogne; his first mate was Francis Bigand of Etaples, and their crewman was Michel Delpierre of Boulogne. They were taking out provisions to the *Mi Amigo.* Mrs Oonagh Huggar, a former Caroline employee, was also accused of helping to organise the tendering service. She was now a secretary working for a Liechtenstein company. Her house was searched by six policemen and bank statements were seized. Police found documentation of a direct connection with the supplying of Radio Caroline. A court case was set for 1 June 1977 in Boulogne.

1 June 1977: At the Palais de Justice, Haute Ville, Boulogne, the court case of the four defendants named above was heard. All pleaded guilty. The French newspaper. *La Voix du Nord,* said that André Fauchet was paid 1,500 francs for each journey to the radio ship. Sentences were: Fauchet fined 10,000 francs, Mrs Oonagh Huggar 10,000 francs, and a fine of 2,000 francs against the

mate, Bigand. Delpierre was acquitted.

Mrs Huggar said after the court case she had lost her job with the Liechtenstein company. Her private address book had been confiscated by the police. She would be returning to England later that year.

5 August 1977: Peter Chicago (Peter Murtha), 29, appeared before magistrates in Norwich charged with assisting Radio Caroline, reported the *Eastern Daily Press*. He was remanded on bail of £1,500 until 9 September. Murtha was arrested in Norwich after coming ashore from a Belgian trawler at Gorleston the previous evening.

9 September 1977: The *Eastern Evening News* reported that Peter Chicago appeared before magistrates in Norwich again accused of helping to keep Radio Caroline and Radio Mi Amigo on the air. Peter Pearson, for the Director of Public Prosecutions, told the court that the ship *Mi Amigo* was stationed somewhere near the Thames Estuary. Chicago (who was charged under his real name Peter Murtha) was involved in maintenance of the radio equipment. On 4 August, he recalled, a fishing vessel entered Gorleston Harbour and three men were seen to leap ashore, run towards a public house and board a taxi which took them to Norwich. The taxi was stopped, however, and Chicago, originally suspected of having entered the country illegally, was interviewed by police. He admitted he came from the *Mi Amigo* and was in charge of electronics. Mr Pearson added that Chicago had been fined £100 and ordered to pay £50 costs on 23 February 1976, after being convicted by Southend magistrates of repairing or maintaining wireless telegraphy equipment on the *Mi Amigo*. He had also been ordered to forfeit 11 crystals and a radio service chart.

Chicago was fined £150 with £20 costs and given 28 days in which to pay.

20 October 1978: Radio Caroline went off the air and remained silent for three months. The problem was said to be lack of diesel fuel to run the generators. However, informed sources said it was sabotage done by some of the Caroline DJs. The contract with Sylvain Tack had ended and, although he could have signed another contract with Ronan O'Rahilly, there were other parties interested in hiring airtime on the *Mi Amigo* including Joost de Draayer. He was from Radio Veronica and owned several record companies and music publishing houses in Holland. He had put a great deal of money into his project for a Radio Hollandia station. The plan was to broadcast Radio Hollandia from the *Mi Amigo*. Sylvain Tack was 'not best pleased' with the idea and gave orders to those on the *Mi Amigo* to halt any plans to get Radio Hollandia on the air. Suddenly the transmitters broke down ... there was no money on the Caroline side to order new parts. Joost de Draayer became impatient and decided to look elsewhere to try and launch his radio station. He had talks with Roy Bates of the Principality of Sealand, but with little success.

19 January 1979: Caroline was still off air because of generator problems. The only power available was from a small 'Honda' petrol unit which could provide lighting but not much else. A bad storm in mid-January resulted in the *Mi Amigo* taking in more water than the limited pumps could cope with and by 20 January the ship was in grave danger of sinking. Harwich lifeboat was launched and three ships called *May Crest*, *Sand Serin* (a dredger) and *Cambrai* steamed to Caroline's position and stood by. A helicopter from RAF Manston was also scrambled and hovered over the *Mi Amigo*, but because of fading light and the 180ft. mast it returned to station. Five men, three British and two Dutch, were rescued - Frank Brooks, Brian Johnson, Tony Smith, Marcel Aykman, Bernard Gratz and Wilson, a canary. They were taken to Harwich police station where they were interviewed by Immigration and Customs officials. The *Mi Amigo* survived but had no one on board. The situation was very quickly rectified when Peter Chicago was put on board from a small trawler, which sailed from Ramsgate the following day. The weather was still very stormy and the trawler had difficulty getting alongside the *Mi Amigo*. There was no

chance she could tie up, but Chicago managed to jump aboard. His luggage was put into a rubber boat and pulled across by rope. Peter Chicago was the only person prepared to go on board an abandoned ship that was full of water and had no power. Single-handedly he saved the *Mi Amigo* and earned Ronan O'Rahilly's eternal admiration. He was later joined by others who mounted a major clean-up operation.

15 April 1979: To the astonishment of many the station returned to the air on 319 metres, 963 kHz - and with a 24-hour bilingual Dutch/English service. DJ Tony Allan played the first record, *Fool If You Think It's Over*, by Chris Rea. Tony's career on Radio Caroline was over later that year after he had brandished a knife on board the *Mi Amigo*, and frightened both Dutch and English personnel.

17 September 1979: Wilson, the bald-headed canary, died and was buried at sea with due ceremony.

21 September 1979: DJ Cliff Osborne quit the ship to help set up a cable radio station in the London Borough of Greenwich. He had been with the station since March 1978. Speaking in 1993 about his experiences aboard the *Mi Amigo* he said: "Broadcasting from a ship is a very strange experience, but in some ways better because you are eating, sleeping, breathing and living radio 24 hours a day. It certainly taught me a lot, gave me some very valuable practical experience and I will always be grateful for the opportunity Caroline gave me. It is something I am glad I did and I have some very good memories of my short time on 'The Lady.' We generally worked four weeks on board (sometimes less in the summer months) and had a week's leave. A small launch would come out from a UK port and drop us in England. I always carried my passport with me. Only once did I return to England via Holland. They were happy days."

9 October 1979: *Monitor* magazine, Edition N° 19, 1979 reported that Mike Baron and Nic Oakley of Music Radio Promotions appeared before Knightsbridge Crown Court

on 12 charges each, brought under the MeBO Act 1967.

Of the charges eight were dropped, eight not guilty pleas were accepted and eight guilty pleas entered. The four charges each that Baron and Oakley pleaded guilty to were: 1) Promoting Radio Caroline by selling a T-Shirt; 2) Promoting Radio Caroline by selling a badge; 3) Allowing an advertisement for MRP to be broadcast by Radio Caroline and 4) Publicising Radio Caroline in a magazine.

The defendants were fined £50 on each charge, a grand total of £400, and were allowed one year in which to pay. No costs were awarded against Baron and Oakley. The case had been delayed on two occasions with adjournments at Marlborough Street Magistrates' Court on 24 February and on 31 March 1978 when magistrates finally allowed the case to be heard before a jury at Knightsbridge Crown Court in London.

February 1980: The Caroline tender, the *Hosanna*, from Scheveningen, which brought out water and fuel from Holland, disappeared from the high seas. No trace was ever found of either the ship or her Belgian skipper or crew.

19/20 March 1980: At midnight disc jockeys Stevie Gordon and Tom Anderson made the following announcement:

"We're sorry to tell you that due to the severe weather conditions, and also the fact that we're shipping quite a lot of water, we're closing down and the crew are at this stage leaving the ship. Obviously we hope to be back with you as soon as possible, but we'd just like to assure you all on land that there's nothing to worry about, we're all quite safe. Just for the moment we'd like to say goodbye. Tom?"

"Yes, it's not a very good occasion really. I have to hurry this as the lifeboat is standing by. We're not leaving and disappearing, we're going on to the lifeboat hoping that the pumps can take it. If they can, we'll be back. If not, well, I don't like to say it. I think we'll be back one way or another, Stevie."

"Yes, I think so."

"From all of us, for the moment, goodbye

and God bless."

Two minutes later the transmitter was switched off for the very last time.

The ship had broken adrift after the main anchor chain broke in the early afternoon in appalling weather and the *Mi Amigo* hit a sandbank. The damage was severe and this time there was no going back. Disc jockey, Stevie Gordon, who was to be the last to leave the ship said: "We informed the coastguards out of courtesy and also because we were unsure of our position. They said they would have a lifeboat standing by."

In a force 10 easterly gale the 44ft. Waveney class Sheerness lifeboat *Helen Turnbull* made three attempts to go alongside before taking off the four DJs on board, Tom Anderson, (Timothy Lewis), Stevie Gordon (Nigel Latko) and Nick Richards (Nigel Tibbles) plus 17-year-old Dutch DJ Hans Verbaan (real name Ton Lathouwers who today is director of Sky Radio). In addition there was a canary, Wilson II. With the exception of Wilson II. they were all later interviewed by police. The Sheerness lifeboat crew were Charlie Bowry (coxswain), Arthur Lukey and Ricky Underhill (mechanics), Ian McCourt, Malcolm Keen and Les Edwards (crew members). Coxswain Charlie Bowry said: "We got a call from the Coastguard letting us know that the *Mi Amigo* had dragged her anchors to the Long Sand Bank and they asked us to launch and proceed. We got underway at 6.15pm and were with them about 8.15pm. By that time they had run aground and we had to wait two hours for her to float off. We were a bit anxious at this time because she had taken aground hard, and we knew on refloating she might have sustained some damage. We were in contact with the ship on VHF and spoke to the occupants who said they were making water. They said that the water was about six inches above the engine-room plates. I suggested at this moment in time that they abandon ship as the sea conditions out there were very confused and she was taking quite a bit of water on board. The DJs were all very good about things and did everything they were told. They wanted five minutes to collect personal belongings but, as it was

endangering the lifeboat, I asked them to scrub round the idea. The initial hesitation was probably because of the value of equipment aboard, but when she started pitching they were glad to come off." The return journey to Sheerness took three hours.

Stevie Gordon said: "We were taken to Sheerness police station where a sergeant gave us a cup of tea and let us dry out. He said the Home Office had phoned up and asked them to take down certain details from us. They wanted our names and addresses. We left the police station about 5.00am."

Stevie, Nick and Hans were free to go - but not Tom Anderson. According to the *Ipswich Evening Star* on 22 March he appeared before a special court in Felixstowe, charged under his own name of Timothy Michael Lewis, with possession of drugs. Michael Harvey, prosecuting, said the offence had taken place the previous August when Lewis was living in Felixstowe. Police had found cannabis in Lewis's car and at his Felixstowe flat. The case had been scheduled to come to court on two previous occasions, but both times Lewis had been on the *Mi Amigo*. On the date of the last hearing a warrant had been issued for his arrest. When the *Mi Amigo* sank Lewis was rescued with three colleagues, but held by Sheerness police

---

The canary, Wilson I, named after Harold Wilson, whose Government introduced the Marine Etc., Broadcasting (Offences) Act 1967, had been brought to the ship by a Dutch captain some years previously. It expired on 17 September 1979 suffering from old age, and, with due ceremony, was buried at sea. A second canary, Wilson II, was presented to Radio Caroline a few weeks later by a lady called Rosemary from Essex. After the sinking of the *Mi Amigo*, Wilson II was carried to safety and handed back to Rosemary on 21 March 1980 at the Chancellor Hall, Chelmsford.

who found out about the warrant during a check. Lewis was fined £50 and ordered to pay £25 costs. None of the DJs was charged under the MeBO Act 1967 although papers were sent to the Director of Public Prosecutions.

During the night of 20 March the *Mi Amigo* sank in 25ft. of water in the same sea which had been her greatest ally. Huge waves finished off the station's 55-year-old vessel where Government legislation and BBC competition had failed. The ship went down in raging seas just a few miles off Walton-on-the-Naze. She came to rest on the Long Sand sandbank with her tall aerial mast showing above the water line, and pointing directly and defiantly skyward.

A Royal Air Force helicopter reported *Mi Amigo* had sunk in latitude 51 35 00N, longitude 01 17 20E, at 08.33, GMT. Some superstructure was showing and 134ft. of mast. This mast stood above the waves for six years before finally collapsing into the sea in April 1986.

Coxswain Charlie Bowry was landlord of the 'Old House at Home' at Queensborough, Isle of Sheppey. The pub has a painting of the dramatic rescue showing a foundering *Mi Amigo* with *Helen Turnbull* alongside, the work of local artist, Mr G.H. Butten.

19 August 1983: After three years of rumour and speculation the station returned again. This time on a well-appointed and sturdy, former 1960-built Icelandic converted trawler called the *Ross Revenge*. The ship once belonged to the Ross Frozen Food fleet, operating out of Grimsby. She had been involved in the Cod War. She was the largest ship ever in offshore history and weighed in at 978 tons. Backed by a group of United States and Canadian businessmen, the ship, which was believed to have been sold for £30,000, had been fitted out in Santander, Spain, and took four days under tow by the tug *Aznar Jose Luis* to reach the port. The ship had a 300ft. high aerial mast. On the back deck was the logo in large letters, LA 319 CAROLINE. The *Ross Revenge* anchored off the English coast in the Knock Deep, 18 miles off the Essex coast, and only one mile from the previous anchorage of the

Mi Amigo. Test transmissions on 319 metres began on 18 August 1983. Next day programmes proper commenced. The station was opened by Tom Anderson at 12.00 noon with the famous theme tune *Caroline* by the Fortunes. She carried on throughout Eurosiege '85 and out-manoeuvred the Government, remaining on air after Laser was towed in.

TV, radio and newspapers gave the return of Caroline wide publicity. A sales office had been established in New York and everything seemed hunky-dory.

But, as Jay Jackson says in *The Pirates Who Waived the Rules*, "The opening announcement was made by a DJ who had lived through Caroline's hippy days in the seventies and he had no interest, so it seemed, in making Caroline of interest to the average radio 'punter'. If Caroline did have five million listeners at the start of the opening programme - the number must have fallen more than ninety per cent within only twenty minutes.

"The album format was there again and so were some bored DJs. They obviously didn't mean to sound bored. They played three tracks in a row. Tom Anderson, the man who made the opening announcement, became known on the ship as "Tom - name that tune - Anderson." At the same time some of the DJs wanted the station to be popular and tried many ways to get programme director, Annie Challis, to agree. It became a battle between the hippy element on the new ship, *Ross Revenge*, the programme director, the New York office and Ronan O'Rahilly. The station lacked continuity and, as a result, audience figures were not nearly as good as they could have been if the station had adopted a format of listeners' favourites."

The main transmitter was a 50 kilowatt RCA Victor Ampliphaser Model BTA 50H (Serial No 101) and used "Optimod' sound processing which enhanced the signal output and gave the station a powerful signal throughout Europe.

There were two studios on the *Ross Revenge*. Each had a 12 channel Gates mixing panel. Turntables were Russco - cartridge machine was made by Collins. Each

studio had a B77 tape machine. Later two more studios were built. One was used for World Mission Radio. The equipment came from Radio 390 which had been based on the Red Sands forts in the 1960s. The other was a production studio.

Captains who served on the *Ross Revenge* in 1983 - 1984 included Joe Woods, Martin Eve and Charles Bradley.

18 November 1983: Seven people were arrested, and later released, by Suffolk police in a swoop against Radio Caroline. Boat owner Mick East, from Melton, Suffolk, said he had brought Andy Archer and three other Caroline staff from the *Ross Revenge* to Ipswich. When the launch docked, 15 police officers were waiting, and took the DJs and crew into custody at Ipswich police station where they were questioned.

Police confirmed the raid, carried out with the assistance of Customs officers, and said a report on the matter had been sent to the Director of Public Prosecutions. The DJs had been arrested as illegal immigrants, and Mick East for aiding and abetting illegal immigrants. Sniffer dogs were also used when the launch was searched.

25 December 1983: A Caroline spokesman denied any cash problems. DJs were said to be owed wages, including Andy Archer who was extremely disillusioned with it all. He had been promised a lot of money to go back to Caroline, but he hadn't been paid since September 1983.

20 January 1984: The *Ross Revenge* ran aground on a sandbank two miles inside British territorial waters. Transmitters were switched off. Two days later the ship was able to return south to her anchorage in the Knock Deep.

Easter 1984: Caroline celebrated its 20th anniversary. A Top 500 compiled from listeners' choices was broadcast over several days. The number one record was *Imagine* by John Lennon.

20 July 1984: The *East Anglian Daily Times* reported a case at Woodbridge Magistrates' Court in which it was stated that disc jockey,

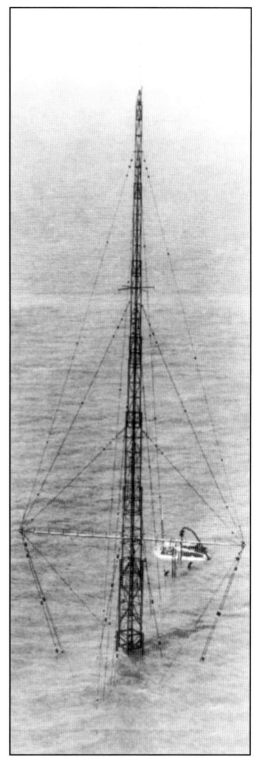

Adios Mi Amigo

Andy Archer was discovered by police hiding in the fuel tank room of a launch on her

Radio Caroline on the Ross Revenge, 1983

return to Suffolk from the Radio Caroline ship. Archer was prosecuted for broadcasting aboard the *Ross Revenge*. He pleaded guilty and was fined £500 with £100 costs. The court was told that the former Radio Orwell presenter was found on the launch when it docked at Melton. When Archer appeared in court it was said that he was working for the legitimate radio station in Surrey, County Sound. A glowing testimonial from the managing director of County Sound was presented to the bench. Michael Victor East of Melton Boatyard, Richard Jonathan Mitchell of Melton Boatyard and David Eric Stanley of Tunstall pleaded guilty to taking supplies to Radio Caroline. East was fined £60 and Mitchell and Stanley £40 each.

Autumn 1984: Caroline was experiencing financial problems and the DJs were not being paid regularly. Many went unpaid, others badly underpaid. Eventually a number of DJs left to find alternative work with land-based stations in ILR and BBC.

16 December 1984: Caroline let the 963 kHz frequency to two Dutch businessmen, Fred Bolland and Ben Bode, for programmes on a station known as Radio Monique. Caroline opened a new channel on 576 kHz operating around the clock, on a reduced power of 5 kilowatts. Radio Monique changed frequency to 819 kHz on 15 November 1987, but closed down on 25 November 1987 following a number of problems.

28 March 1985: Caroline celebrated her 21st birthday!

15 September 1985: A tribute to Ian West, 24, who was due to join Radio Caroline as an engineer at Christmas 1984, was held on the *Ross Revenge*. Ian died on 11 December before he was able to attain his lifelong ambition. He was cremated and his parents asked that his ashes be scattered at sea near the *Ross Revenge*.

Permission was obtained from both Radio Caroline and from the *Dioptric Surveyor* for this to be carried out. His parents travelled out to the *Ross Revenge* for the short ceremony. A special Caroline bell, in Ian's Memory hangs in the messroom of the *Ross Revenge* to this day.

27 September 1985: The *Southend Evening Echo* reported that three men who ferried supplies to Radio Caroline were each fined £500 with £20 costs at Southend Magistrates' Court. They admitted delivering 1,700 gallons of diesel oil to the *Ross Revenge*. The men, all from Southend, were bus driver Donald Hill, and Graham Bushell and Howard Beer, both unemployed. They were found guilty under the Marine Etc., Broadcasting (Offences) Act 1967.

Barry McGirl, for the Director of Public Prosecutions, said police at Essex Marina, Wallasea, were alerted last March when they saw oil being pumped aboard the *Aline*, a vessel owned by Bushel and Beer. A police launch shadowed her through the night to a point off the Essex coast where she tied up beside the *Ross Revenge*. Next morning the *Aline* returned to the Essex Marina where she was boarded by police. Bushell, who claimed to be the skipper, said he had been taking passengers who said they were members of the Radio Caroline Appreciation Society to see over the pirate ship. But a check on *Aline's* tanks revealed at least 1,600 gallons of the recently loaded oil were missing and Mr McGirl said "She would have needed to steam at full power for 250 hours to use up that much."

6 November 1985: Laser 558 went off the air and sailed into Harwich leaving the *Ross Revenge* alone in the Knock Deep. The next day Radio Caroline moved in and took over the 558 kHz frequency vacated by Laser.

31 January 1986: The *Ross Revenge* went adrift in a force 10 gale. Broadcasting was stopped. The ship, which had an eleven man crew, reported that her anchor cable had snapped, engines were over heating and her radar was not working. The DTI warned tug owners they could be prosecuted if they helped the ship and she returned to broadcasting. Margate and Sheerness lifeboats were launched and were ready to mount a rescue operation, but the *Ross Revenge* was brought under control and returned to near her original position 15 miles off the Essex coast. The station returned to the airwaves the following day.

10 June 1987: *Ross Revenge* pulled up her anchor and sailed out of the Knock Deep to a new position close to South Falls Head, approximately 14 miles north west of Margate. The decision to sail her to this position was caused by the forthcoming Territorial Sea Act that would extend British territorial waters from three to twelve miles.

A posse of pirates aboard the Ross Revenge
Including Dave Andrews, Mike Barrington, Andy Johnson, Johnny Lewis, Fergie McNeil and Peter Philips of Caroline; Jonelle, Erin Kelly, Tommy Rivers and Charlie Wolf from Ijiser; Ad Roberts, Walter Simons and Wirn der Valk of Monique, with Dutch crew members from Caroline and Laser.

25 November 1987: During storms the 300ft. high mast came crashing down pulling both stations off the air. Eight-and-a-half days later. Caroline was back with a temporary aerial and on very low power. In early 1988 a new lattice mast was erected and Radio Caroline was able to increase her power. The Dutch language station was still off the air and, despite numerous attempts with a new glassfibre mast, only managed to get back on air for a day and a half. On 9 May a Dutch station, to be called Radio 558, took to the airwaves during the daytime leaving 558 to Radio Caroline at night.

27 November 1987: The Southend Evening Echo ran the following story: "Following a court case in 1985 when Howard Beer was fined £500 for delivering 1,700 gallons of diesel oil to the *Ross Revenge*, he was back on the high seas within a period of three weeks taking sightseers out to visit the broadcasting buccaneers." After the first case at Southend, Beer allegedly phoned the DTI on a number of occasions seeking clarification of the legal position concerning ferry trips to the *Ross Revenge* but had received no satisfactory reply. So he pleaded 'guilty' and Judge Gordon Rice sent him to prison for nine months.

13 January 1988: The *Southend Evening Echo* reported a boat owner who broke the law by ferrying people to the Radio Caroline ship had won his freedom from a nine month sentence. Three Court of Appeal judges in London held that his sentence was too long. Beer, jailed at Southend Crown Court on 27 November 1987, was released immediately. Howard had spent seven weeks, including Christmas and New Year, in jail.

6 March 1988: A new service, World Mission Radio, was broadcast on Caroline on 6215 kHz.

30 May 1988: Start of the Dutch language programmes on 819 on *Ross Revenge*. Some of the founder members of Radio Monique started the station under programme director, Nico Volker. Today Nico is one of the directors of the satellite radio station,

Holland FM.

18/19 August 1989: Radio Caroline continued to broadcast programmes in English on 558 kHz and in Dutch on 819 kHz and 6215 kHz short wave. All remained well with Radio Caroline until 9.15am on 18 August when officials from the Department of Trade and Industry,[6] together with a representative of the Dutch radio authorities, arrived in the Customs cutter *Landward*. They said that international action was being taken to silence the broadcasts on Radio Caroline, 819 and World Mission Radio, emanating from the *Ross Revenge*. Permission to board the radio ship to discuss the future of the ship and its crew were refused by the captain. Later in the day, however, a representative from Radio Caroline went on board the *Landward* for talks which lasted for about half an hour. In the evening the *Landward* returned to Ramsgate but was back alongside the *Ross Revenge* the next morning, 19 August.

At about 12.40pm, Caroline engineer, Peter Chicago, announced: "This is a special announcement from the Radio Caroline ship, *Ross Revenge*. I am speaking on behalf of the crew and the broadcasters of the vessel, *Ross Revenge*. We've had previous warnings earlier that some kind of action was contemplated. At the moment on our starboard side, we have the Dutch tug, the *Volans*, which seems to have the intention of taking this ship, the *Ross Revenge*, from her mooring in the international waters of the South Falls Head. We'll try and let you know what's going on as the programme continues, but I have an idea that events will move very quickly. Anybody hearing this broadcast perhaps could help us by telephoning the Coastguard to register a complaint, possibly by contacting anybody in authority you think could help us. This is the radio ship *Ross Revenge* broadcasting from the international waters of the North Sea, and for the moment

---

6. The Department of Trade and Industry (DTI) are responsible for the regulation of broadcasting in Britain, and all prosecutions under the Marine, Etc.. Broadcasting (Offences) Act, 1967 must be initiated by the Director of Public Prosecutions.

anyway we'll return you to our regular programmes. Thank you."

Caroline then returned to music, but within five minutes DJs Chris Kennedy and Bruce Monroe announced that the *Ross Revenge* had been boarded by representatives of the Dutch Government. The DTI remained in low profile at the stern of the ship. DJ Nigel Harris then announced over the air "We have now been boarded by the Dutch authorities. We are in desperate need of help. They are going to shut the station down and take us all off. We are in international waters and this is a breach of this vessel's rights to be here and we are desperately pleading for help. We need help now. Caroline 558 will be leaving the air any moment now as the boarding party are finding their way to the transmitter room where they are going to dismantle all the broadcasting gear, take the studio to pieces, dismantle the generators and then incapacitate the ship totally."

Bruce Monroe returned to the microphone and invited a member of the boarding party to explain the situation over the radio, but he declined the offer and, at that moment, Radio Caroline 558 abruptly left the air at seven minutes past one on 19 August 1989. It seemed that action against the *Ross Revenge* had been planned for a number of months.

The *Volans*, a tug owned by the Dutch "Rijkswaterstaat Directie Noordzee" (Ministry of Works), from Rijswijk, Zuid-Holland, was built in 1965 by Verolme Scheepswerf Heusden N.V. The tug had a boarding party of around 30 armed men aboard including Dutch, British, Belgian and French officials. They removed all the studio equipment, records and tapes and took down the aerial array but left the towers and the new mast sections which were awaiting erection, although at one stage it appeared that they would cut down the towers. The new insulators were removed from the *Ross Revenge* and roughly thrown on to the deck of the *Volans*, causing them to smash.

The two medium wave transmitters had their valves removed before the inside of the cabinets were attacked with sledgehammers, and mountings and other components

Dutch officials on board Volans the day after the raid on the Ross Revenge

destroyed.

The ship's engines and marine equipment was left undamaged and the DC generators untouched, although one of the two AC generators was somewhat damaged. The living quarters, messroom and galley were left undamaged although some cabins were searched and items removed.

At one stage it seemed as if the Dutch boarders would cut the anchor chain and tow the ship away. The officials were in constant contact with their land-based superiors and, as a result of increasing media attention and adverse publicity, held off from acting further. They also refrained from carrying out further damage to equipment. The *Volans* left, after about seven hours, with the two Dutch citizens from the *Ross Revenge*, DJ Arie Swets, and the cook Eddie. The other crew members, all British, stayed on board.

The raid on the *Ross Revenge* was covered by all British news media. ITN news bulletins showed film of the *Ross Revenge* with the large Dutch tug *Volans* alongside. The Customs cutter *Landward* could also be seen. Caroline's founder, Ronan O'Rahilly, was interviewed and denied Dutch claims

Ronan O'Rahilly

that they were acting within international law. "Every captain on every ship all over the world would know they're talking absolute nonsense. If you board a ship in international waters, you're committing an act of piracy. There is no question about that."

According   to   Boudewyn   Dom:

"Following the arrival of a boat bringing out British press, the *Volans* left shortly after 8.00pm on Saturday evening, taking away equipment from the *Ross Revenge* and the Dutch deejays from Radio 819. The British DTI officials aboard the *Ross Revenge*, who had been trying to question staff, also hurriedly left. One of them, James Murphy, was in such a rush to leave, he even left his spectacles behind!"

In its edition of 21 August, the *Sunday Times* reported Golke Dykstra of the Radio control service section of the Dutch Ministry of Transport and Public Works as saying: "At the beginning when the boarding party of two Dutch marine police, six people from my office and nine crew from the ship that took them there arrived, things were a bit emotional. But after moments it was all friendly and they took it like sportsmen. Transmitting equipment was not smashed - it was carefully dismantled and removed". He added that because the *Ross Revenge* was not flying any flag of nationality, the vessel had forfeited the protected status of ships in international waters.

The *News of the World*, on 21 August, reported that the British Government admitted that it had played a major part in the raid, and quoted a DTI spokesman: "There was concern throughout Europe that Radio Caroline was interfering with emergency radio signals".

At noon on Sunday 20 August, Radio Caroline's directors issued a press statement saying that: "Yesterday a joint action was taken by Dutch and British authorities against the m.v. *Ross Revenge*, in the international waters of the North Sea. The radio ship was boarded by force, by 30 armed Dutch and British Department of Trade and Industry officials. Two crew members were beaten up during the boarding and crew members and radio staff, including two young women disc jockeys, were manhandled and threatened."

In a statement, the Canadian directors of Radio Caroline said that they were "shocked and horrified at this act of piracy." They said that having taken urgent legal advice, they would be bringing charges of piracy, violence, theft, misinformation and vandalism against the authorities, and against the individuals concerned. Shortly after the news of the violence on board the *Ross Revenge*, the British Department of Trade and Industry issued a statement claiming that no British officials were involved in the boarding, and that UK officials were in

another vessel keeping surveillance. Journalists who went to the scene spoke to a DTI official who identified himself as a Jim Murphy. He did so whilst he was actually aboard the *Ross Revenge* interrogating the crew. Both the Dutch and British authorities denied any use of violence.

Fraser Murray of the DTI told the author: "Our attendance was purely to mount a watching brief and DTI officials did not participate in the initial boarding. DTI officials were later invited on board the *Ross Revenge*, amongst other reasons, to render safe certain equipment. Any equipment seized was done so by the Dutch authorities. I understand that it has now been returned."

The *Ross Revenge* was first registered in Panama on 23 September 1981, but she was deleted from their registry on 12 January 1987 when new laws prohibiting unauthorised broadcasting from the high seas were passed. At the time of the raid it appears that the *Ross Revenge* was stateless because the Panamanian registry had lapsed. Thus the Dutch authorities said they were justified in carrying out their action. They also said that the 6215 kHz frequency was causing interference on a marine distress frequency on 6215.5 kHz.

DJ Nigel Harris said: "What amazed us was that we were a pop radio station and they actually sent out armed personnel which, especially as far as the two girls on board were concerned, absolutely freaked us out. To have people running around the ship with guns is not the sort of thing you see in Britain. The rest of us, being British or Irish, had no idea that this sort of thing would take place. To have armed police and coastguards running around, when all we were doing was playing pop music, was just beyond belief."

Julian Clover of *Radio and Music Magazine* said that the DTI was already beginning to distance itself from the events taking place as news of the action against Caroline broke on 19 August 1989. They took the line that they were 'assisting the Dutch in international interference complaints from the Dutch and Belgian authorities.' The Dutch also played down their involvement. "There was no damage whatsoever", said Kees Leerling of the Dutch

Ministry of Transportation. "The action was swift and efficient, and we achieved our goals. It was an illegal radio station."

The numbers who took part in the raid were less than what Caroline management stated. According to Leerling, there were six members of the PTT (Postal, Telephone and Telegraph Administrations) radio patrol service, two police officers, eight people from the ship and nine in the crew. Dutch police are armed as a matter of course.

Radio Caroline stayed off the air for six weeks. It resumed broadcasting on 1 October 1989 and stayed on air in one form or another until November 1990 when it ran out of money and closed down. The crew were rescued by helicopter on 4 November 1990. The last show had been presented by Neil Gates. Radio Caroline closed without warning. It remained at sea, off the air, with a skeleton crew until November 1991.

558 kilohertz became the frequency of Spectrum Radio (ILR). Caroline had moved to that frequency from 576 kilohertz in November 1985.

The *Ross Revenge* had been anchored at Knock Deep from 18 August 1983 to 11 June 1987 when she moved to South Falls Head off North Foreland, Kent. She stayed there until her anchor chain broke (November 1991), when she went on to the Goodwin Sands. The crew were rescued by Sea King helicopter from RAF Manston. The captain of the *Ross Revenge* was Tony Campbell. Stuart Dobson was the last man to be winched from her decks as a salvage crew from Kent pulled her into Dover's Granville Dock.

March 1992: The First CD on offshore radio, *The Caroline Legend Lives On*, was released in Holland. It was narrated by Marc Jacobs and produced by Hans Knot.

The same month there was a surprise meeting in Holland with the head of the OCD (Dutch DTI), Martin Rauman. He was invited to meet 300 attendants at an offshore radio day to tell his side of the story of the raid on the *Ross Revenge* in 1989. He also showed the official video which was produced by the Dutch authorities.

On stage Hans Knot suggested to Martin

Rauman that as the raid had happened 2½ years previously, wasn't it now time that he spoke with the Caroline organisation? As no court cases were pending, Caroline could be given back all their equipment seized in the raid. Martin Rauman said he would be pleased to chat with Peter Moore of the Caroline organisation who was also present at the conference. They agreed that the records and technical equipment could be returned to the *Ross Revenge*.

24 April 1992: Radio Caroline returned to her former frequency of 558 kHz when her old adversary, London's Spectrum Radio, offered two hours of airtime.

August 1992: Caroline celebrated the 25th anniversary of the MeBO Act 1967 by broadcasting to the Dover area of Kent under a Radio Authority restricted service licence. The station, transmitted on 101.8FM, went on the air for 28 days. Programmes came from the studios and a transmitter aboard the *Ross Revenge* in Dover's western docks. The ship had been there since being rescued after running aground on the treacherous Goodwin Sands in November 1991. In past history such a fate would have marked the end of a ship. But in the case of the *Ross Revenge* she survived and was towed into Dover Harbour.

Prior to that event the station had been at sea, though silent due to the effects of the Broadcasting Offences Act which toughened certain sections of the Marine, etc. Broadcasting (Offences) Act (1967) designed to silence Radio Caroline for ever!

The Radio Caroline transmissions were heard on Invicta Supergold as well as radio stations in Europe. During 1992 Caroline was on Quality Europe FM, a satellite radio station, from 2.00am to 6.00am.

The purpose of Radio Caroline's broadcasting from Chatham Dockyard from the *Ross Revenge* was to promote Chatham's Historic Dockyard, and the licence was granted to operate from 15 August 1992 to 7 September 1992 on 101.4FM. However it went on air late due to the Department of Transport not allowing the *Ross Revenge* to move to Chatham so it broadcast from Dover instead, linked by microwave to Bluebell Hill and directed at Chatham under the call sign Radio Caroline.

20 October 1992: The death was reported from New Zealand of former Caroline DJ Samantha Dubois, aged 38 years. She had died from a drugs overdose.

19 December 1992: The Dutch Justice department announced that the court cases against the former Radio Monique, 558 and 819 staff had been dropped and there was no longer any reason why the equipment, seized from the *Ross Revenge* in August 1989, should not be released. It comprised 12 pallets of records, studio and broadcasting equipment, and weighed some 4 tons.

The pallets were collected by Radio Caroline staff who went to a secure police warehouse at Bleiswijk near The Hague on 19 February 1993, exactly 3½ years after the raid. At this time in Caroline's history the organisation had no money to rent a vehicle to collect the equipment. The previous day there had been a phone call to Holland from Peter Moore to say they could not take the ferry across from England due to lack of money. Through the sales of the Caroline CD purchased by Dutch 'anoraks', some 2,000 guilders had been raised. This money was transferred to a bank in London to enable the Caroline team to hire a truck and travel to Holland. A very kind gesture on behalf of the Dutch offshore fans and producer of the CD, Hans Knot.

On arrival at the police warehouse it was reported that Dutch officials were singing the Caroline theme as a 7.5 tonne truck was loaded with equipment which was shipped back to England. In return for the equipment Dutch officials were presented with a copy of Peter Moore's book *Butterfly Upon a Wheel*, together with a Caroline T-Shirt.

The equipment included record decks, cartridge machines, reel-to-reel tape machines, mixers, and radio processing and general radio kit. All went back in place on the *Ross Revenge* on 20 February 1993.

June 1993: The *Ross Revenge* was still berthed at Dover costing £1,000 per month berthing fees. The owners were looking for alternative sites, which included the Essex Marina at Burnham-on-Crouch. Station manager Peter Moore said he was also examining a possibility of mooring in the Frinton and Walton backwaters. The *Ross Revenge* required 15ft. of water. The Coastguards at Walton-on-the-Naze said "It may be possible to find room for the ship in the backwaters, but it would be a very, very tight squeeze."

27 October 1993: The *Ross Revenge* left Dover Harbour under tow to the River Blackwater, Essex, within sight of the Bradwell Nuclear Power Station. Since the salvage, the ship had been detained by the Department of Transport where mooring fees, salvage costs and other expenses incurred while in Dover were paid by the support groups.

Albert Hood, a Free Radio member, told the *East Anglian Daily Times* on 28 October that the studio on board the *Ross Revenge* was in working order and had been maintained and renovated by the *Ross Revenge* Support Group plus members of the Radio Caroline Club. Although the engines were in working order and the huge mast positioned, the next major job was to repair or replace the smashed rudder.

To celebrate the 30th anniversary of the first broadcast from Radio Caroline, Breeze AM, a Southend-based ILR station, broadcast an eight-hour tribute from the *Ross Revenge* anchored in the River Blackwater. The programme featured more than 40 interviews with past Caroline staff members and was presented by former Caroline presenters Ray Clark and Peter Phillips. It also featured a very rare live appearance of Ronan O'Rahilly.

RADIO CONDOR

The station was set up by Steph Willemsen from Haarlem and shipbroker Gerrit Elfrith, although the latter did not want to be involved with the broadcasting side of Radio Condor. Mrs S. van Donsellar was employed to work with Steph Willemsen. It was

originally planned to put the station on air in May 1973, but held over as the Dutch Government were about to announce plans on the future of the offshore stations. Basically there was no future for the pirates as the Dutch introduced their own Marine Offences Act in August 1974. This did not deter Radio Condor however, who set about buying a ship and finding sponsors. The Rev Dominee Gerard Toornvliet, who had been heard on radio programmes on Capital, Caroline and Monique, put in a considerable amount of money. Known as the 'pirate vicar', he started using offshore radio in 1970. He died in 1981.

A ship was purchased and programmes for Radio Condor would be broadcast from aboard the 403-ton ex-Icelandic trawler, the *Emma IM15*. The station would go on air from 9.00am to 5.00pm daily. There would be no commercials and programmes would be of religious and humanitarian interest, illustrated by *happy* music.

The ship was built at de Dollerd shipyard in Landsmeer, Holland, in 1956. She made her maiden voyage as a fishing vessel on 1 February 1957 skippered by Johannes Blok.

In April 1964 she ceased fishing and was chartered by an oil company for drilling exercises in the North Sea. Then owned by NV Marezaten, she was sold in July 1967 to the Ouwehands fishing company of Katwijk-aan-Zee, Holland, and her name was changed to *Zeeland KW122*. She returned to the high seas fishing for herring. Three years later she made her last trip and was then taken out of commission and tied up in Katwijk herring harbour. After a further two years the *Zeeland KW122* was sold for scrap and purchased for 30,000 guilders by 48-

year-old Steph Willemsen, a TV supplier and repair man who had played with a Dutch blues band in the 1960s.

On 1 August 1973 Radio Condor announced it was still not ready for regular broadcasts, but was hopeful that test transmissions would commence in the not too distant future. Willemsen purchased and modified a 500 watt transmitter. If the station made a profit they would buy the 10kW transmitter from aboard the *King David*, which had been used in the 1960s on Radio 270.

A series of test transmission tapes had been pre-recorded by the Rev. Dominee Toornvliet.

Willemsen said he believed they would not be breaking the law once the Dutch Marine Offences Act came into force as the station was not broadcasting advertisements.

A studio was built by Steph Willemsen and DJ Ron de Loos. Also on board was a piano. The station was beset with problems. On 11 August 1973 the anchor chain broke and the vessel was towed into IJmuiden.[7] The shipping inspector said he had doubts about the seaworthiness of the ship so she was sold for scrap. However, she was towed out of harbour on 25 September into international waters and dropped anchor near the coast of Zandvoort where the waters were generally calm. At this stage the former owner of the ship, Steph Willemsen, bought her back. Radio Condor never broadcast again as the company had run out of money. However, a month later he sold the ship to Adriaan van Landschoot of Radio Atlantis for 50,000 guilders (1993's value £18,500). She was renamed the *Janine*.

RADIO DELMARE

Radio Delmare was formed by a group of people who ran the land-based pirate Weekend Music Radio in Hilversum. After they had been raided several times by the Dutch OCD they thought of the idea of operating from a ship in international waters.

Gerard van Dam and his colleague Jan de Kat, commissioned the 250-ton trawler m.v.

7.　*Offshore Radio*. Gerry Bishop, Iceni Enterprises, Norwich. 1975. p.50

Aegir named after the principal sea god in Greek mythology, and began converting the ship into a floating radio station in the summer of 1978. The 195-ton *Aegir,* which was built in 1929 at the yard of J. Koster in Groningen, was formerly the m.v. *Express.* In Holland the Dutch Marine Offences Act was now in force so the work had to be undertaken in strict secrecy. The conversion was carried out at Scheveningen Harbour. However, police at the OCD swooped on the ship and confiscated much of the radio equipment. *The Times* newspaper on 26 June reported: "Police officers, accompanied by special Post Office investigators, seized radio transmitting equipment on board a coaster lying in the harbour of Scheveningen near The Hague on Friday night. They also took possession of 10,000 records, 225 magnetic tapes and a complete inventory for two broadcasting studios. The transmitters were suitable for medium wave, short wave and VHF broadcasts and were capable of providing Europe-wide coverage, police said. The coaster's master and two technicians who were installing the equipment were detained for questioning by the police and later released. According to the ship's master the coaster had been rented by unidentified people who intended to make offshore broadcasts. The master said he had been promised a considerable sum of money once the broadcasts started." The same day as the article appeared in the *The Times,* the *Aegir* slipped out of harbour into the open sea and anchored off the coast of Noordwijk. She returned to the Dutch port of Maasluis near Rotterdam. In August she sailed out to sea once again, this time anchoring near the Belgian/Dutch border at Zeeuws Vlaanderen, twelve miles off Cadzand.

With new radio equipment Radio Delmare began transmissions on 21 August 1978 on 192 metres, 1568 kHz. Programmes were run by Gerard van der Zee, Jan Romer and Rene de Leeuw.

On 11 September a force 9 gale resulted in the *Aegir* drifting and out of control. A number of distress calls were broadcast. The lifeboats *Zeemanspot* and *Koningin Juliana,* together with the tug *Smitsbank,* made their way in heavy seas to the stricken vessel. She was taken under tow to Rotterdam Harbour by the *Smitsbank.* All on board were arrested by the Dutch authorities. The *Aegir* was later chained up in the harbour of Maasluis on the order of the Dutch Prosecutor, Mr Pieterse.

The four crew members were brought before magistrates at Rotterdam, but were released after a six-hour interrogation by the Rotterdam River Police and the monitoring service of the Dutch Post Office. Mr Pieterse called for the confiscation of the ship and the transmitting equipment.

A replacement ship, the m.v. *Epivan* (previously the *Oceaan 9* and before that, the *Helena* which began life as *Scheveningen 54),* was arrested by Dutch police in January 1979. The 500-ton ship had been built at Scheveningen in 1957. A further ship, the *Martina* (previously *Scheveningen 195)* sailed out of Jacobshaven into the high seas on 29 April 1979 and anchored off Goeree. She began regular programmes of non-stop pop music on 2 June 1979 on 192 metres and continued broadcasting until 28 September when the station closed.

Broadcasters heard on Radio Delmare included Tony Allan, Jon Anderson, Tom Anderson, Peter van der Holst, Astrid de Jager, Rene de Leeuw, Kees Mulder, Jan Olienoot, Ronald van der Vlugt and Gerald van der Zee.

LASER 558

The *Communicator* was built in 1955 by Abeking and Rasmussen at Lemwerder in West Germany. She was 177ft. long and originally designed to carry cattle. Launched with the name *Tananger,* she was converted to a survey ship in the early 1970s and renamed *Charterer.* In 1976 she became the *Gardline Seeker* and was run by a Lowestoft-based shipping company. Accommodation comprised 11 single berth cabins, 4 double berth cabins and 1 four berth cabin.

The ship sailed to America on 27 August 1983 and her conversion to a radio station took place at the Tracor Marine Shipyard at Port Everglades in Florida where she was fitted with the most up-to-date transmitting equipment. Her country of registration was changed to Panama. On 22 December 1983 she sailed into the Knock Deep and anchored near the *Ross Revenge* close to the Long Sand Head. The station was backed to the tune of US$2,000,000 (£1.4m) by a consortium of Americans. Roy Lindau was president of Music Media International of Madison Avenue, New York, which sold airtime for Laser 558. Overheads were said to be around £35,000 a month.

There were fears that the station might cause interference as it was to launch its broadcasts on a similar frequency to BBC Radio 4 on 729 kHz. The Department of Trade and Industry said there was nothing they could do against the ship itself if she kept outside British waters. But it could act against personnel who went ashore or those who took out supplies to the ship.

Disc jockeys included: Jessie Brandon, Chuck Cannon, Chris Carson, Dave Chaney, Jeff Davis, Michael Dean (the cook), Paul Dean, Ric Harris, Jonell, Erin Kelly, John Leeds, Jay Mac, Steve Masters (there were two broadcasters on Laser 558 with that name at different times - no relation), Holly Michaels, Johnny Moss (Johnny Lewis), Craig Novack, Tommy 'What a Guy' Rivers, Paul Rusling, David Lee Stone, Liz West, Charlie Wolf and Mighty Joe Young (transmitter engineer, real name Joe Vogel, died in Ipswich, 1989).

30 November 1983: The vessel, fitted out with modern broadcasting equipment, made her way across the Atlantic towards Europe, stopping off in the Azores for four days. On board were a team of American DJs including Jesse Brandon, David Lee Stone and Ric Harris. Newspapers reported the station was to broadcast on 412 metres and be staffed totally by American DJs. The transmitter power was rumoured to be twice that of Radio Caroline. The format was to be a Top 40 station.

29 December 1983: The *East Anglian Daily-Times* published its first picture of the ship.

19 January 1984: A balloon-launching platform slipped her moorings near Margate, Kent, and headed out to the North Sea. The experiment of using a helium-filled balloon had been successful many years previously when the Voice of America transmitted radio programmes from ships to Europe.

A few hours before dawn saw the entire crew of the m.v. *Communicator* out on deck holding the guy lines of the giant helium-filled balloon which was over 40ft. long and 15ft. in diameter. At 9.40am it was inflated and launched in a rather novel attempt to hoist the station's antenna as high as possible. An engineer completed some fine tuning to ensure that there was no interference to BBC Radio 4 in England. There was a loud crack on deck and cables sagged into the sea. High voltages around the end of the antenna ionised the air around a nylon securing rope which promptly melted and the balloon sailed off towards France. Shortly afterwards the transmitters were switched off.

The engineer realised there had been no insulators spacing the antenna from the balloon, and that the corona around the top of the antenna cable had ionised the air around it, thus causing the nylon tie wire to burn. When these burned through, the balloon went off on its own, dropping the cables into the sea.

21 January 1984: The second and final balloon was launched successfully and test transmissions began with non-stop Beatles music.

By coincidence, a group of Caroline fans went out in the launch *Jubilee 2* from Brightlingsea. Their purpose was to photograph the *Ross Revenge*, but the ship had drifted south the previous night after losing her anchor chain.

The radio fans were surprised to find Radio Caroline not at her normal moorings, but to see a new pirate ship flying a balloon. They thus witnessed first-hand the birth of Europe's latest offshore radio station.[8]

22 January 1984: Less than twenty four hours after it was launched, the second balloon - which, like the first, cost around £6,000 - was blown away. One source claimed they saw it later wrapped around a traffic bollard in Colchester!

---

8. *Lid Off Laser*, Paul Alexander Rusling. Pirate Publications, Herne Bay. Kent. 1984. Chapter 15

1 April 1984: Having resorted to a more conventional radio mast, the station had begun test broadcasts on 729 kHz, 411 metres. Calling itself Laser 730, Paul Rusling and Johnny Moss presented music programmes. However, a storm snapped the main anchor chain and the ship drifted until the reserve anchor was dropped.

13 April 1984: Friday the 13th! Former Laser 558 captain, David Irvine, appeared before magistrates at Sheerness and was found guilty of helping to construct Laser 558's radio mast on the Kent mainland.

Prosecutor for the Director of Public Prosecutions Gary Patten told the bench that Irvine knowingly supplied equipment to the radio ship m.v. *Communicator* knowing it intended to make broadcasts from the high seas. He said that officials had noticed the vessel *Communicator* was in a certain position some 14 miles off Clacton-on-Sea, Essex, in international waters, just outside the 12-mile fishing limit. DTI engineers had traced broadcasts on 21 January 1984 as coming from the ship.

The authorities had taken a keen interest in the ship as they knew she had experienced difficulties with aerials, and during checks on various harbours, they had discovered Irvine and several other men assembling radio masts. When arrested Irvine admitted the masts were for the *Communicator,* but claimed the vessel was a research ship which the DTI officials knew was not true. A further search of Irvine's belongings revealed technical drawings, publicity brochures about Laser, and a letter of authority signed by the owner of the vessel empowering Irvine to control the building of a new aerial system, and have access to a sum of £10,000 which had been deposited in the bank account of a local man. Irvine was fined £500 with £50 costs.

This was later quashed as a result of an error by the Director of Public Prosecutions in the wording of the initial summons.

24 May 1984: The station officially began broadcasting continuous pop hits on 538 metres (558 kHz), and claimed to be breaking no laws because the crew and

DEPARTMENT OF TRADE AND INDUSTRY

The Departments of Trade and Industry, and of Energy merged in April 1992. The role of the Radiocommunications Agency is to regulate the use of the civil radio spectrum in the national interest.

The Radio Investigation Service of the DTI's Radiocommunications Agency was created on 1 April 1990. The Agency employs 120 field officers across the country. Their remit involves regulating all categories of radio use and responding to complaints of interference from authorised users. The performance of the radio investigation service is kept under review to ensure that the service is correctly resourced.

Between 1 January 1993 and 30 June 1993, the Agency prosecuted 9 people for unauthorised broadcasting offences. In 1992 there were 536 raids throughout the United Kingdom which secured 70 convictions; in 1991 there was a total of 103 convictions. The average fine imposed was £287 and average costs of £209 were ordered to be paid. However, one person was sentenced to seven days' imprisonment. Invariably the courts ordered that the equipment used in the offence be forfeited. For the year 1992-93 with 68 convictions, total fines imposed were £4,500. Costs awarded amounted to £12,015. There were 54 forfeiture orders, 39 conditional discharges and 7 warning letters sent.

The Agency is using the new enforcement powers provided in the Broadcasting Act 1990. It targets those who manage pirate stations and those who advertise on them. Anyone convicted is disqualified under the Broadcasting Act from involvement in legitimate commercial radio for a five year period.

A DTI spokesman told the author in September 1993: "The attitude of the Agency (and its forebears) to pirate radio stations at sea was not affected by the passage of the Broadcasting Act 1990 which came into effect on 1 January 1991. Any unauthorised use of radio is unplanned and is therefore more likely to cause interference. The history of offshore radio is littered with incidents of such interference, both in the United Kingdom and farther afield. Because of this, the Agency uses the legislation at its disposal to combat the menace of unauthorised broadcasting, be it at sea or on land."

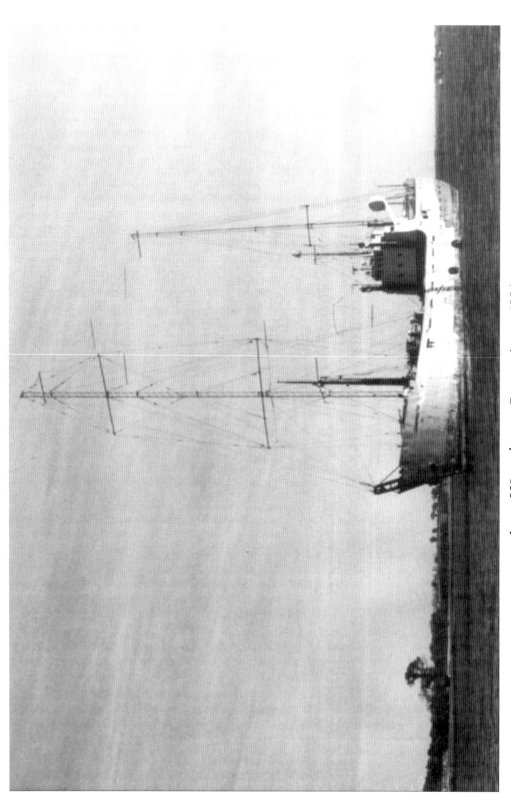

Laser 558 on the m.v. Communicator, 1984

supply sources were non-European. Signal strength showed the transmitter to be slightly less than 5 kilowatts. Ric Harris became the first DJ to announce: "This is Laser 558 - All Europe Radio."

American, Captain Tim Levensaler, was master of the *Communicator*.

Test transmissions had been voiced by Paul Rusling. Ric Harris was followed on air by David Lee Stone, Jessie Brandon and Steve Masters. The station, "All the Hits All the Time", closed at 1.00am. Paul Dean joined the team later in the week. He had worked on RNI under the name Paul May.

Three new voices appeared in June 1984, Holly Michaels, Tommy Rivers and Charlie Wolf. Holly later married Laser captain, Tim Levensaler.

Reception reports said that Laser was clearly audible throughout England, Scotland, Wales, Denmark, West Germany, as well as Belgium, Holland and France.

By an aggressive hard-sell mix of hits and self promotion, Laser, 'Never more than a minute away from music,' took Europe by storm within months and found that 5 million people tuned to the station. One had to go back to 1964 to find anything similar. Radio stations in England, including Caroline, had to change their style.

26 May 1984: In a press release from Music Media International based at 341 Madison Avenue, New York, NY 10017, USA, the worldwide sales representatives of Laser, Roy Lindau, president, said: "Unlike the pirate stations of the past, Laser 558 is a legal radio station since the ship is registered outside Europe, transmits from international waters, is owned and operated by a Panamanian corporation and staffed and supplied by citizens of the United States. The station is, in the opinion of counsel, entirely legal."

The address for record requests was given as c/o The *Communicator*, PO Box 1892, Grand Central Station, New York, NY 10163, USA.

1 June 1984: A dinghy carrying four Laser crew lost power near the ship and drifted off dangerously. A lifeboat was called for, but a fishing vessel rescued the men.

9 July 1984: DJ Tony Blackburn upset the BBC by asking Jessie Brandon to take over his BBC Radio London show whilst he toured with the Radio 1 Roadshow. Tony was quoted in the London *Evening Standard* as saying: "Laser is a brilliant station, much more fun than another pop station I don't care to mention by name. Jessie Brandon is the best girl disc jockey around at the moment and she's the ideal person to fill in for me while I am away." Predictably the BBC were not too pleased by the idea. They said that Jessie did not have the correct working papers and that Laser was an illegal set-up. They were also using a frequency already allocated to a local BBC station. In the event Tony's show was taken over by Paul Burnett.

In the ship's log there appeared an entry which recorded that "Captain Levensaler has two broken ribs on the right side from an injury received on the tug, the *Punta Torres*, which brought stores from Spain on 7 July." The tug departed on 9 July. Leftwich took up the post of master of the *Communicator* as Captain Levensaler departed on shore leave for two months.

28 July 1984: Captain Leftwich reported in the ship's logbook: "An RAF helicopter hovered alongside for 10 minutes. Crewman in hatch took photographs."

30 July 1984: Radio Telefis Eirann (RTE) claimed that they received thousands of calls from the UK regarding interference from Laser in London and South East England on 567 kHz. The complaint was passed to Roy Lindau who admitted he had received a small number of complaints about Laser's interfering with RTE. Glenn Kolk, a lawyer representing Laser in the USA, said filtering equipment would be installed on the m.v. *Communicator* which would stop the interference.

The police launch, *Ian Jacob*, out of Ipswich, circled the *Communicator* once at close range, then departed in a north-easterly direction.

31 July 1984: American mate, Shaun Moore noted in the ship's log: "Captain James Leftwich found with smell of alcohol on breath when I boarded the vessel. Moments later he severed his finger with a rope winch at 4.30pm. Twenty minutes later he was despatched by dinghy for shore. Destination was Frinton-on-Sea." The operation to sew on his finger was not successful. Leftwich returned to America.

5 August 1984: The Telecommunications Act came into force. This meant that the Department of Trade and Industry's Radio Interference Service became the Radio Investigation Service. They were given new powers and could seize any pirate radio station's equipment, pending prosecution. Penalties were increased to £2,000 fine and/or 3 months in prison, or both.

16 August 1984: The police launch *Ian Jacob* made another visit to the *Communicator* and spent 30 minutes circling the ship and taking photographs.

17 August 1984: BBC TV newsreader Philip Hayton (ex-Radio 270) visited Laser 558. He reported that the established radio stations were losing listeners to this new wave of pirate broadcasters, both offshore and land-based.

20 August 1984: The publication of Paul Alexander Rusling's book *Lid off Laser* was given huge publicity by the British media. In his book he disclosed that a wealthy Irish hotel disco owner, named Philip Smyth, helped finance and set up Laser. He owned the Sachs Hotel in Dublin.

Reviewing the book in *Offshore Echos* in October 1984, Ian Anderson said: "Rusling's book is a romance about the good knight on a white charger coming to the rescue of a radio project in distress, which has a doubtful, if not unhappy ending. The book is egocentric. He proves yet again that to be involved in offshore radio you must be tough and prepared to be ripped off, be single and preferably in your twenties."

Rusling was reported to have been owed some £7,000 consultancy fees from the Laser organisation.

President of Music Media International, Roy Lindau, objected to the book saying that Rusling's writing was not very honest and rather inaccurate. "Ten weeks after his departure from Laser, the Panamanian company, Eurad S.A. with 100% American crew and DJs, successfully launched Laser 558. Paul Rusling had absolutely nothing to do with its success. His book was like an account of a stable boy taking all the credit for a Derby winner."

Shortly after *Lid off Laser* was published, Rusling suffered a fire at his public house in Whitstable. He recalls: "I was approached by the general manager of a local ILR station who suggested that Laser was somehow behind it. She and several other ILR station managers were keen to see Laser closed down."

They wanted Paul Rusling to pass on intimate inside information. Would he be prepared to share his knowledge? Paul said "Not at first. Then about a week later I was informed that the Laser management was spreading a story that I had set fire to my own pub. I saw red and was outraged. So I hastily arranged a meeting with another ILR station manager, and former employee of the

Storm damage to the forward aerial mast on m.v. Communicator, April 1985

The Laserettes.
Left to Right: Liz West, Erin Kelly and Chris Carson on the bridge of
m.v. Communicator, 1985

1960s pirate Radio London, Eddie Blackwell, at Essex Radio. I suggested to him that I could silence Laser, which was taking his audience, providing that he would fund the operation. He said no. Blackwell had recorded our conversation and the tape somehow got to the chairman of Laser, Roy Lindau. The story was released by Laser to the newspapers."

1 September 1984: Laser '54 minutes of music every hour' was claiming more than five million listeners. There were still very few adverts however and the station was said to be losing £15,000 a week although gaining listeners all the time.

6 January 1985: Laser 558 went off the air due to generator problems. Transmissions resumed four days later, but further problems throughout the month kept the station regularly going on and off air.

February 1985: The station was plagued by serious problems with the aerial mast during bad weather, but it managed to keep going and by now had three female DJs, known as "The Laserettes." (Chris Carson, Erin Kelly and Liz West).

1 March 1985: DJ Charlie Wolf made his TV début on Channel 4's *The Tube* and spoke about Laser 558.

7 May 1985: Laser resumed transmissions after a two week silence due to storm damage to the aerial system. New American DJ Craig Novack made his début on Laser. His real name was Alan Stuart-Wortley Bishop, a distant cousin of the Princess of Wales. They share the same great, great, great grandfather. The family seat is Wortley in Sheffield. His uncle is heir apparent to Earl Wharncliffe.

24 May 1985: Laser celebrated its first birthday. More advertisements were being broadcast and a Laser Roadshow was doing the rounds, but the station's first birthday party, to be held at London's Hippodrome in Leicester Square, had to be cancelled after pressure on the venue owner, Peter Stringfellow, by the authorities. The DTI, who had been in touch with the Director of Public Prosecutions, warned Stringfellow that the party could be in breach of the law.

DJs Charlie Wolf, Tommy Rivers, The Laserettes, David Lee Stone and Ric Harris had become famous names. In February 1985 John Moss took over from Roy Lindau as President of Music Media International. Linda McCartney sent a birthday greetings tape to Laser which said: "I think you play great music. So all you disc jockeys keep having fun and keep playing all the good stuff. I listened to you a year ago. I love you. The whole family loves you. Long may you reign."

23 June 1985: DJ Ric Harris left Laser for Radio Nova in Ireland. The station was said to be in financial trouble. To date £3,500,000 had been spent on the operation. The station's main backer, Irishman Philip Smyth, was reluctant to part with more cash. Morale on the ship was said to be low. This was not helped by Laser's new policy of 'spotlighting,' under which record companies paid for plays on Laser.

26 June 1985: Laser was forced to close down its prestigious office in Madison Avenue, New York, for a smaller base. Public relations consultant Jane Norris admitted Laser owed her money and stated she was "not in the business of providing her services without remuneration."

5 July 1985: A new Laserette, Jonell, arrived on board.

8 August 1985: Euro-Siege 1985. The first moves by the Government took place when they launched a campaign to blockade Laser 558 and Radio Caroline. The purpose of the blockade was to stop vessels from British ports supplying and servicing the radio ships. The DJs on board the *Communicator* called it Euro-Siege '85 and broadcast cheeky messages, together with dedications to the DTI in the ship *Dioptric Surveyor,* which they referred to as a 'spy-ship.' The DTI said it was not a blockade. They were keeping observation on comings and goings. They referred to the pirates as 'robbers of the airwaves' who observed none of the regulations which controlled organised radio stations on land. They paid no licence fees and they were a potential danger to life. The DTI said that pirate transmissions affected not only marine distress wavebands but had also interfered with navigational beacons for

helicopters servicing North Sea oil rigs. Instead of receiving guidance signals, pilots found themselves picking up pop music.

After a visit by a helicopter which shone its searchlight on to the decks of the m.v. *Communicator,* the ship was joined by the Government's monitoring vessel, *Dioptric Surveyor.* DJ Charlie Wolf gleefully began regular Euro-siege broadcasts from on deck and sent up the Government officials something rotten over the airwaves. On Radio Caroline, DJ David Andrews said 'Hello' to the official vessel which was anchored 150 yards off their port bow. Euro-Siege '85 had begun!

12 August 1985: The *Daily Mail* reported "Pirates under Siege: Government sends out patrol ship to starve Caroline and Laser off the airwaves.

"Britain's two pirate radio stations - Caroline and Laser 558 - were under siege last night by a Government-chartered ship aimed at starving them into submission. In a major escalation of hostilities, the fast survey ship is on permanent patrol around the two vessels in an attempt to cut their lifeline of food, water and fuel supplies.

"All boats which go alongside the pirates at their North Sea anchorages off the Essex coast will be identified and photographed. They will then be intercepted by police launches if they return to British ports.

"Hired by the Department of Trade, the patrol ship has powerful searchlights to prevent supplies arriving at night. Helicopters are also being used in the surveillance operation which is understood to cost around £50,000 a month.[9]

"Caroline broadcasts from the 1,000-ton converted trawler *Ross Revenge*, and Laser, based on the 489-ton former survey ship *Communicator,* are not illegal because they are anchored in international waters. But it is illegal for British citizens to work on them, supply them or advertise on them.

"Yesterday a Trade Department

---

9. At a DTI roadshow in Chelmsford in October 1985 Dilys Gane. the director of the DTI's Radio Investigation Service, said the figure was £25,000 a month. The figure of £25.000 was also confirmed to the author by the DTI's Fraser Murray.

spokesman confirmed that the 99ft. ocean-going launch *Dioptric Surveyor* was on indefinite charter, equipped with highly sophisticated monitoring devices.

"Caroline first went on the air in 1964 and now has an adult-orientated album music format. It was joined last year by the all-American Laser 558 with a Top 40 style. Both gave New York addresses.

"The tough new moves reflect the growing alarm by legitimate British radio stations over the pirates' success.

Both have powerful medium wave signals and built up huge audiences - claimed to be

10 million - particularly in London and Eastern England.

"The *Dioptric Surveyor*, which took on supplies at Harwich, before returning to its listening post on Knock Deep, is owned by Dioptric Ltd., a wholly-owned subsidiary of Trinity House.

"Five vessels were reported to police by the Government investigators trying to clamp down on the North Sea pop pirates. Department of Trade investigators were likely 'to study with interest' reports in national newspapers. 'Five vessels have been identified. We have informed East Anglian police forces about four of them and the Dutch authorities about the other,' said a spokesman for the Department of Trade."

14 August 1985: On this, the 18th anniversary of the Marine Offences Act being introduced in 1967, Laser Radio staged an outside broadcast from its deck and DJs thanked reporters from the *Daily Star* and *Daily Mail* for visiting them.

15 August 1985: The *Daily Star* said "We waived the rules to scupper the Whitehall Wallies, bent on forcing Radios Caroline and Laser 558 off the air."

Journalist Neil Wallis reported: "We loaded a fishing boat, aptly named the *Freeward*, with champagne, T-shirts, copies of Britain's favourite newspapers and other goodies, and set sail at dawn.

"Strict radio silence was observed as we battled through a force 7 gale to reach the ships, moored a mile apart off the Essex coast.

"Petticoat Pirate Liz West whooped with joy when she got her hands on a Star T-shirt. 'I needed a new one - and this is just great.'"

The *Daily Star* spent two hours with the pirates. They were observed by the *Dioptric Surveyor*. The *Daily Star* newspaper was reported to the Director of Public Prosecutions following its trip to the North Sea pirates. A reporter and photographer were taken out to Radio Laser by Felixstowe boatman Robbie Ward aboard the *Freeward*. A spokesman for the Department of Trade said the *Daily Star* report had been referred to the DPP to see if any offence had been committed. The DPP's office said it was too early to say what action, if any, would be taken against the newspaper or the boat. Robbie Ward said on 16 August that no one from his boat had boarded the m.v. *Communicator*.

Reporter Neil Wallis was told by the DTI, on arrival back in London: "You may face two years in jail or unlimited fines. We are confident we can get you convicted."

19 August 1985: A freelance film crew, working for ITN, went out to visit Laser, but just as they were about to tie up alongside the m.v. *Communicator*, their engine broke down. An Essex police launch, *Alert III*, just happened to be passing and towed the film crew's boat into Brightlingsea.

21 August 1985: To make life difficult for the DTI officials, Laser moved to a new anchorage ten miles away so that they and Caroline could not be monitored at the same time. The *Dioptric Surveyor* followed her and indicated the authorities were especially after Laser. Two days later the m.v. *Communicator* returned to Knock Deep.

2 September 1985: Having returned to the original anchorage, Laser found that the DTI's efforts were beginning to bite. Supplies were low and money still short.

John Moss, who was owed £2,000 back pay, left the Laser operation and was replaced by John Catlett as President of Music Media International. He had previously been general manager of Laser 558 joining the company in June 1984.

Government monitoring vessel Dioptric Surveyor on Patrol near m.v. Communicator, August 1985

16 September 1985: DJs Liz West, Charlie Wolf, Tommy Rivers and Jonell left Laser. Charlie told the London *Evening Standard:* "There are only two DJs left on board and they had to play pre-recorded tapes. I've had enough. Morale on board has been very low and the food has been terrible. I am owed quite a lot of money in back pay and I can't afford to leave London until I've got it. I'm really sad about quitting. Laser is a great station but it doesn't seem to be able to generate enough cash to survive."

23 September 1985: Funds may have been low but morale was still high, however, as the Moronic Surveyors (including the Laserettes voices) released the mickey-taking record *I Spy for the DTI*. It was released on the Farce record label, number DTI 007. Those appearing on the record were singers John Wilson, Paul Young and Sad Café. Also heard were Rob Day, Liz West and Erin Kelly.

Interviewed at the Gordon Hotel, Rochester, where Laser DJs were accommodated on their way to the radio ship, Liz West appeared on TVS's *Coast to Coast* saying she was owed £4,500 back pay from Laser management. She said she was destitute with only 20 pence to her name.

19 October 1985: Day 79 of Euro-Siege. The ship was still being monitored but broadcasting continued with four new DJs. Generator problems hit the station and she began a nine day spell off the air.

1 November 1985: Two sisters met on the high seas and there was no love lost between them as the Government's crackdown on the pop pirates took on an ironic twist. The 133-ton *Dioptric Surveyor* was replaced by a new surveillance ship, the 443-ton *Gardline Tracker* which had been chartered from Gardline Surveys Ltd of Great Yarmouth. The *Tracker* was the sister ship of the *Seeker*, which was renamed the m.v. *Communicator*. The job of the *Gardline Tracker* was to continue to monitor ships that were illegally supplying Laser and Radio Caroline. The two Gardline ships were identical. A spokesman from the Department of Trade, which was paying for the siege operation, said: "You could call it poetic justice in the

North Sea." He confirmed that about 20 vessels had been reported during the three-month operation, but no prosecutions had yet been brought.

3 November 1985: The *Mail on Sunday* published a centre spread article which revealed the address of Laser's undercover London offices and the source of their supplies in Kent. Further rumours gained momentum of serious financial problems and shortage of food and water on board, as well as trouble with equipment.

5 November 1985: The ship's captain, 'Salty' Paternoster of Ipswich, apparently cried … 'Enough is enough,' after a night of terrible storms. Laser stopped broadcasting abruptly at 8.30am during the Craig Novack show and the ship headed for Harwich followed by the Government 'spy' ship. Over the airwaves the Caroline crew aboard the *Ross Revenge* wished the Laser team "Best wishes and all our love." The drama came after Laser had sent out an SOS signal on Citizen's Band radio as it was being lashed by storm force winds and blockaded by the DTI vessel which had prevented her receiving supplies from the mainland.

It was dusk when the m.v. *Communicator* arrived in the River Stour. She passed Trinity House private pier on which were a posse of police, a crowd of Customs officials and a jostle of journalists. The ship was accompanied by an Essex police launch and DTI vessel *Gardline Tracker* which followed at some considerable distance behind. The Laser ship moored near Parkeston Quay. Officials from the DTI, Customs officers and Essex police were waiting to interview those on board. The DJs and crew remained on board that night but went ashore the following morning to be interviewed by the authorities. In attendance was general manager of Laser 558, John Catlett. Later a report was sent to the Director of Public Prosecutions.

Paul Rusling, who appeared on the TVS programme *Coast to Coast,* said he was owed £7,000. He had designed, built and even conceived the station. During that period of time he had paid several bills on behalf of the station for the supply of equipment, for disc jockeys' hotel bills and transportation, even salaries for some people who worked on the ship in the very early days. Paul's solicitor instructed the Admiralty Marshal, Vincent Ricks, to serve a writ on the vessel when she docked at Harwich. This would prevent the ship from leaving port until the bills were paid. Laser's general manager, John Catlett, denied any knowledge of the debt. The Gardline Survey Company said it was owed £5,000 by Laser from when the ship was the *Gardline Seeker.*

On 8 November the m.v. *Communicator* was impounded and declared unseaworthy by Department of Transport marine surveyors. The ship had not been overhauled since she anchored off the Essex coast in 1983. A 'keeper' was put on board by the Admiralty to prevent her leaving port.

The *Dioptric Surveyor* was renamed *Surveyor* in 1986 and sold to Yorkshireman, Keith Jessop, who sailed it to the Bahamas. The *Gardline Tracker,* which had been used by the DTI to keep watch on Laser, and nicknamed 'Gardline Traitor', was also sold in 1986 and broken up for scrap. On Laser's arrival in port the ship was arrested and writs served on her.

3 February 1986: Reports in the national press suggested that a secret operation to scupper the remaining radio pirate broadcasting off the Essex coast was being mounted by the Department of Trade.

Officials refused to give details but admitted that the aim of the manoeuvre was to clear the 558 medium wave frequency allocated by international agreement to the BBC but being used by the pop pirate Radio Caroline. The BBC feared it might be forced to find an alternative and inferior frequency for its new local radio station, BBC Essex, if 558 were not cleared by the station's planned opening in late October. This could cost the Corporation tens of thousands of pounds extra.

A Trade Department spokesman explained "We are planning an operation against Caroline though we wouldn't want to show our hand just yet."

Henry Price, assistant head of BBC

engineering information, said: "No frequency is as good as 558 for Essex, and, while Radio Caroline remains there, it will be very difficult for us to provide a county-wide service.

"We couldn't hope to compete on the same frequency. Caroline puts out very heavily modulated pop music which would simply drown out the normal local radio fare of phone-in programmes and chat shows."

The BBC's hopes were raised by the apparent success of the Department of Trade and Industry's operation against the frequency's previous illegal incumbent, Laser 558, in November 1985.

When a bad storm crippled the unlicensed station, its beleaguered vessel limped to shore towed by the jubilant spy ship. But within a day, the 558 frequency had been taken over by Caroline, broadcasting with impunity just outside British territorial waters since 1964.

After seeing off Laser, the tracker ship spent a further three weeks compiling a dossier for the Director of Public Prosecutions on Radio Caroline's 978-ton Panamanian-registered vessel, *Ross Revenge*. The tracker ship was withdrawn and a dossier sent to the DPP. The four-month intelligence operation cost about £100,000, but there had been no prosecutions.

5 September 1986: The Ipswich *Evening Star* reported that an Ipswich skipper had been fined the previous day for his part in illegal broadcasts from the Radio Laser pop pirate ship, despite a bid to clear him under EEC law. Patrick Paternoster, 46, of Holbrook Road, was master of the m.v. *Communicator* when she was assisted into Harwich during severe gales last autumn, Ipswich magistrates were told.

At an earlier hearing he denied agreeing to carry wireless and telegraphy equipment in the *Communicator* knowing, or having reasonable cause to believe, it would be used for broadcasting on the high seas.

After hearing submissions from Michael Lane, counsel for Paternoster, that his client should be acquitted under EEC Law, the magistrates decided there was a case to answer. He was found guilty and fined £150 after no evidence was offered in his defence.

Nicholas Paines said that between 7 September and 6 November a Department of Trade and Industry charter ship, the *Gardline Tracker,* had been monitoring broadcasts from Laser Radio.

On 9 November the pop pirate ship started to drag her anchor in heavy seas. Later in the day her master radioed the *Tracker* and asked for assistance. He said there was a technical problem with the engines and was advised to make for Harwich, said Mr Paines.

Paternoster was charged under the Marine Offences Broadcasting Act after the vessel had anchored off Erwarton Ness. Under the 1967 Act the law has authority over anybody making illegal radio transmissions within territorial waters but only over British subjects broadcasting illegally outside territorial waters, said Mr Paines.

But the Marine Broadcasting Act had been superseded by the EEC Treaty which prohibited discrimination on the grounds of nationality. When Britain joined the EEC in 1972, courts in this country were obliged to take Community law and legislation into consideration.

Laser disc jockey Charlie Wolf had also been on board m.v. *Communicator*, but because he was American he was free to broadcast from Radio Orwell in Ipswich.

"Paternoster was on the m.v. *Communicator* as an employee. He was doing his job and yet was being charged under English criminal law," said Mr Lane. "This court has no choice but to acquit the defendant." In mitigation, Mr Lane said that Paternoster, who obtained his master's certificate 12 years previously, had been short of work following the decline in the British shipping industry. He was asked to take over the m.v. *Communicator* in August the previous year. He was paid £310 a week. At that time it was not clear to him that he was operating illegally.

Paternoster should have earned over £4,000 in the time he was master of the vessel, but the owners were "inaccessible and shadowy people" and he had only been paid £1,000 to date. He was currently

'It's all mine!' says Ray Anderson in one of the studios aboard m.v. Communicator, 22 April 1986

unemployed receiving benefits and living with his brother in Ipswich, said Mr Lane.

8 April 1986: The deadline date for which all bids had to be presented. The sale of the m.v. *Communicator* attracted a great deal of interest from would-be buyers. It was put up for sale by shipbrokers C.W. Kellock and Co. Ltd., of 27/31 St Mary Avenue, London EC3A 8AQ, brokers and appraisers to the Marshal of the Admiralty - the maritime version of the official receiver. Admiralty Marshal Vincent Ricks said offers had so far come from all sectors including ship owners and radio companies. The ship would be sold with all her radio and studio equipment on a basis to obtain the best price.

From November 1985 the ship had been under arrest, anchored up river on the Stour where a writ had been served. Government "ship-keepers" remained on the vessel guarding her, since her arrival.

21 April 1986: The m.v. *Communicator was* sold to Ray Anderson, of East Anglian Productions, whose tender was the highest of the thirteen submitted. He issued the following press release.

"Frinton-on-Sea based East Anglian Productions has purchased the ex-Radio Laser radio ship, the m.v. *Communicator*, for £35,000 from the Admiralty Marshal following the collapse of the Radio Laser company last November. The vessel has been

under arrest in the Essex port of Harwich.

"East Anglian Productions are a communications company producing many regional TV and radio commercials, corporate video productions and broadcasting equipment sales. Ironically, the company produced a documentary on Radio Laser filmed on board last September. The company's managing director, Ray Anderson, said that the £35,000 paid for the vessel represents a fraction of the ship's true worth. The vessel is equipped with two powerful 25 kW AM transmitters, studios, generating plant and a sophisticated satellite communications system. There were about 4,000 LPs and 3,000 singles on board. As a working unit, Ray Anderson said that the true worth was closer to £250,000.

"East Anglian Productions are now considering a number of legal options for future use of the vessel. One includes an outright sale to a consortium for possible use in the Mediterranean Sea as a 'summer only' English speaking radio station for tourists. Also, an international film company is producing a 'rock music' film centred around the former offshore radio station and had expressed an interest in using the vessel on a hire basis. We are also expecting some interest from the various Free Radio organisations who may wish to see the vessel turned into a museum. However, it is more likely that the vessel will be taken to another part of the world where she could easily be used as a commercial radio station and operate quite legally."

26 September 1986: Customs officers boarded the m.v. *Communicator* and removed the vessel's drive-shaft bearing. The Customs officers were acting on the authority of the Department of Trade and Industry who said the vessel was immobilised because necessary work had not been carried out and it was feared the ship was about to

slip away. Owner Ray Anderson denied this and said that thousands of pounds had been spent on necessary safety improvements. He had lodged a protest with the Customs and Excise. His solicitors threatened legal action unless the part was returned within seven days. The part was returned in October after the m.v. *Communicator* had dragged her anchor and was blown down the River Stour for half a mile. She was unable to manoeuvre.

16 November 1986: The m.v. *Communicator* was sold to a foreign buyer for a reported £130,000, complete with AM/FM transmitter and studios in working order. She sailed quietly past the sleeping citizens of Harwich and headed out to sea. By that afternoon she had safely dropped anchor in the Knock Deep, about 15 miles east of Felixstowe. The detention order, which was placed on the ship, was lifted on Friday, and on 15 November the ship was moved to the Cork anchorage off Felixstowe. The Department of Transport lifted the detention order after inspecting refurbishment work.

20 November 1986: It was announced that the m.v. *Communicator* would return to the air on 1 December 1986 broadcasting as Laser Hot Hits. The American company address was given as Suite 3600, 515 Madison Avenue, New York. The station would circumvent the law by selling advertising time through Radio Waves Inc., of 333 Irvine, Dallas, Texas, USA. The European vice-president was none other than Rob Day who had handled advertising for the original Laser 558 operation.

Meanwhile, five American DJs were waiting on the continent to board the ship. They were to be joined by Englishman, and former Radio 1 newsreader, Andrew Turner, who presented the hourly news bulletins. John Allen was also a newsreader.

1 December 1986: Laser returned to the air at 9.05pm on 576 kHz broadcasting from the Knock Deep. The first voice on the air was John Anthony's. The news of Laser's return came as an embarrassing blow to the DTI which, in 1985, spent thousands of pounds mounting a "blockade" against the station.

DJs included John 'Rock'n'Roll' Anthony, D.L. Bogart, Paul Jackson, Brandy Lee, Jim Perry, Bill Reid and David Lee Stone.

Peter Baldwin of the IBA accused the Government of an interdepartmental muddle in allowing the ship to slip away. He said "We are terribly disappointed. There appears to have been a lack of co-ordination between the various branches of the Government that has allowed the ship to have loaded up and slipped out. We have been in close contact with the Trade Department and I have no doubt we will both pursue this new Laser as vigorously as before on behalf of our legitimate broadcasting contractors."

However, problems occured on board Laser Hot Hits when the aerial mast collapsed with the result that the station was off the air more than it was on. This caused a severe loss of advertising revenue. The final broadcast of Laser Hot Hits was heard on Easter Monday, 20 April 1987. Disc jockey D.L. Bogart signed off at 8.00pm saying they would like to continue but couldn't do so without more diesel. She 'upped' anchor and sailed to Sandettie Bank off Dunkirk. However, due to severe storms she was forced to return to Harwich. By the summer of 1989 she was once again back in the North Sea before departing for Lisbon, Portugal, in July 1989.

15 November 1988: At Canterbury Crown Court four people were accused of conspiring to supply food, drink, medical aid and equipment to the radio stations moored off the Kent and Essex coasts, Radio Caroline and Laser 558. *Offshore Echo's* Edition N° 74, January 1989 reported they were Nicholas Murray, his wife Linda Murray from Minster, Isle of Sheppey, Kent; Phillip Payne, also from Sheppey, and John Cole of Newbury, Berkshire. The Murrays, Cole and DJs Robb Eden and Robbie Day - whose real name was Paul Faires - were accused of conspiring to procure the making of broadcasts from the ships.

Eden of Moreton-in-the-Marsh, Glos., was accused of inviting a holiday company to advertise on one of the radio stations.

Day of Shorne, Kent, and Roger Carr of Burnham-on-Crouch, Essex, faced charges of illegally promoting the Laser 558 Roadshow.

Robb Eden was found guilty of attempting to procure advertising for Laser and fined £250. Tug owner Nick Murray was found guilty and fined £1,000 plus £150 costs, and his wife Linda was fined £500. The couple were also fined for supplying records to Laser 558. John Cole was fined £1,500 plus £500 costs, and DJ Robbie Day was fined £1,000 plus £500 costs for supplying the ship. The case had first been heard at Sittingbourne Magistrates Court on 15 May 1987. Also named, in addition to the above, were Tony Elliot and Phillip Payne.

The case against Phillip Payne was dropped by the DPP and subsequently the case concerning the Laser Roadshow (with Roger Carr) was deferred.

The case against *Time Out* editor Anthony Elliot had been dropped because of a 'procedural technicality.'

The trial lasted several days. All

*Poster on a Kent harbour notice board
for the attention of all boat owners*

defendants were granted four months in which to pay their penalties and warned that failure to do so would result in the offender being sent to prison for a term of between 7 and 30 days. All the accused submitted an appeal, and the Criminal Division of the Court of Appeal examined the case on 19 March 1990, but dismissed it.

16 October 1989: The m.v. *Communicator* was raided by Portuguese police acting on behalf of the Dutch authorities. Studio equipment and transmitter components were removed.

20 August 1993: The Laser ship, complete with two new radio masts and a broadcasting studio, was sold to the Portuguese company who owned the shipyard where the *Communicator* was repainted. They said they were not interested in the vessel continuing as a radio station. A court case in Lisbon decided that the ship should be transferred from the former owners to Peparacoes Navais do Jego, LDA. Bills for rebuilding and repainting the ship had not been paid. The new owners said that the Honduran registration had been withdrawn in 1989. According to *Offshore Echo's*, September 1993: "The studios and technical equipment was sold off by a Dutch company. Former Panlieve SA spokesman Ben Bode claimed that he still had the official papers, and therefore considered himself the owner of the *Communicator*."

RADIO MI AMIGO

The station was founded by Flemish businessman Sylvain Tack who had observed the success of Radio Atlantis broadcasting from aboard the *Mi Amigo* in 1973. Tack rented air time from Radio Caroline and took over where Atlantis left off.

In his book *Offshore Radio*, Gerry Bishop recalls: "The station, broadcasting from aboard the *Mi Amigo*, began test transmissions on 28 December 1973. The official opening date was 1 January 1974. However, after 71 minutes the transmitter broke down due to generator problems. Programmes, which were originally in Dutch, did not recommence until 9 January.

English programmes began on 10 January 1974. The station quickly became very popular, but its life on air was somewhat curtailed because of the Dutch Marine Offences Act which was introduced on 1 September 1974. Radio Mi Amigo closed on 31 August 1974 at 7.00pm."

DJs were English, Dutch and Flemish and included: Brian Anderson, Andy Archer, Norman Barrington, Patrick du Bateau, Erik Beekman, Haike du Bois, Henk van Broeckhoven, Peter van Dam, Frans van der Drift, Ferry Eden, Eddie Emery, Herman de Graaf, Wim de Groot, Stan Haag, Jerry Hoogland, Marc Jacobs, Jos van der Kamp, Graeme Kay, Dennis King, Bart van Leeuwen, Frank van der Mast, Jan van der Meer, Michelle, Thijs van de Molen, Mike Moorkens, Bob Noakes, Norbert, Peter Pann, Ad Petersen, Ben van Praag, Ton Schipper, Paul Severs, Wil van der Steen, Dick Verheul, Joop Verhoof, Johan Vermeer, Johan Visser and Secco Vermaat.

11 May 1976: The Dutch newspaper, *Algemeen Dagblad*, reported that the Amsterdam Public Prosecutor, J.H.C. Pieterse, demanded severe punishment for two Dutchmen who went to Radio Mi Amigo; Captain Jacob Taal of Scheveningen and Koos van Laar from IJmuiden. In the case, the first of a series of six, Mr Pieterse said: "When these people are fined a few hundred guilders they would start laughing."

Captain Taal had worked on the *Mi Amigo* since 1972. In 1973 he took the ship back to the open sea after she had been captured and taken to IJmuiden by her former skipper, Captain van der Kamp. In November 1976, when the ship drifted in a bad storm, he was caught by the Authorities.

Koos van Laar, in his boat *Dolfijn*, had towed the *Mi Amigo* back to England.

Mr Pieterse said that the transmissions of Radio Mi Amigo were a "continuous, systematic evasion of the law, purely for commercial profits." He then told the court that Radio Veronica had fully complied with the new law, even to the extent of asking his advice on which was the best way to close down in August 1974.

Mr Pieterse twice demanded a suspended

two weeks' prison sentence and two years' probation against Captain Taal, and a fine of 2,000 guilders (£740). Against van Laar, 4 weeks' suspended imprisonment, also two years' probation and confiscation of the *Dolfijn* which at that time had not been seized. Her value was put at 30,000 guilders (1993's value £11,100). The sentences were to be announced on 25 May 1976.

25 May 1976: The outcome of the case was reported in *Algemeen Dagblad*: "In the first criminal case in Holland under the new Act against offshore stations, the Court of Amsterdam imposed fines and suspended imprisonments upon two people. Fiftyfour year-old Captain Jacob Taal was fined Dfl 1,000 (£345) and sentenced to six weeks' suspended imprisonment. District Judge J.A. van Waarden imposed a fine of Dfl 2,000 (£690) upon Koos van Laar and also sentenced him to eight weeks' suspended imprisonment. The Judge said he sentenced van Laar more severely than Taal because it was solely the boldness of the people who supplied the ship and transported people and goods to and from the radio ship, that enabled the people to run the radio station and continue their activities."

29 June 1976: The Amsterdam Public Prosecutor, Mr J.H.C. Pieterse, brought seven people to court, but four never turned up. Of those who appeared, two were fined 8,000 guilders with 8 weeks' suspended imprisonment each. Leunis 'T' from Gravensande said that he had worked on the *Mi Amigo* in November 1975 when the station was off the air. British police had raided the ship and removed transmitting crystals. Koos van 'D' from Hoek van Holland admitted that he had worked on the ship to repair the transmitter and other vital equipment. The Officer of Justice said that as they were the Mi Amigo's top two men in Holland their punishment must be strong, as Dutch police had also found the pair operating a regular radio contact with the ship. The third case was against crew member Jan van der 'V' who was given 3 weeks' probation and fined 1,000 guilders. The case was reported in *Algemeen Dagblad*

on 29 June 1976.

14 September 1976: The *Algemeen Dagblad* reported: "Another court case in Holland. Seven employees of Radio Mi Amigo received stiff penalties varying from between two weeks' suspended imprisonment with a 500 guilder fine and 6 weeks' suspended imprisonment with a fine of 4,500 guilders. The latter punishment was given to Donald van 'B' from Den Haag who had five times ferried people to the radio ship. Machinist Albert 'A' received four weeks' suspended imprisonment and a 1,000 guilder fine. Cooks Johan 'P' and Jozefus 'H' both from Beverwijk and Gunther de 'V' from Arnhem received two weeks' suspended imprisonment with a 500 guilder fine. A similar sentenced was served on seaman Leo 'V' of Terheide. Arie 'E' (who worked as a broadcaster under the pseudonyms of Tim Ridder and Bart van Leeuwen) was given a 6 weeks' suspended imprisonment and a fine of 2,000 guilders. Arie 'E' was not in court to hear the sentence."

September 1976: The tender, the *Hosanna*, which serviced Radio Mi Amigo was detained in Zeebrugge. Three men were arrested and later freed. The *Hosanna* was owned by Germain Ackx who also owned the fishing boat *Vita Nova* which was to be intercepted by Belgian police in April 1977 taking out provisions, water and a disc jockey to the radio ship. This vessel took Peter Chicago to England when he was arrested in August of the same year. The *Vita Nova* was chained up in Breskens harbour, Holland, for the rest of 1977.

29 September 1976: *Monitor* magazine. Edition N° 13, 1976 reported: "A court case against Radio Mi Amigo was held at the Correctional Court of Justice in Brussels following a raid by Belgian police on a number of offices in September 1974. Of the 41 people accused, 37 were present before the Judge, Anna de Molina. However, owner Sylvain Tack, DJ Peter van Dam and technician Maurice Bokkebroek and one other person were not present. Sylvain Tack faced 4 charges including operating a pirate

radio station under the law of 14 May 1930, amended 18 December 1962, which says that no Belgian person has the right to start a radio station without Government permission, even outside Belgium."

Tack had fled to Spain and ex DJ Christiaan Hendricks (also known as Patrick du Bateau) had been the new 'brain' behind Radio Mi Amigo in Belgium. Verdicts were to be announced on 12 November 1976.

12 November 1976: The Brussels Court gave the verdict of the September court case. According to *Monitor* magazine, Edition N° 13, 1976: "Owner of Radio Mi Amigo, Sylvain Tack, was given one year and seven months' imprisonment as well as a 4 million Belgian francs fine (£65,466). His brother-in-law, Christiaan Hendricks, was given seven months' imprisonment and a 2 million Belgian francs fine (£32,733). Eighteen people received prison sentences of 3 months and fines of 80,000 Belgian francs, and fifteen others were each given a one month's suspended prison sentence and a 60,000 Belgian francs fine."

20 October 1978: The station closed suddenly as DJ Marc Jacobs announced:

"We have generator problems. This is Radio Mi Amigo. We have to close down." The transmitter was then switched off. That was the end of Radio Mi Amigo after 4 years and 9 months.

6 November 1978: The Belgian newspaper *Het Volk* reported: "A number of people who worked on the tender which serviced Radio Mi Amigo appeared in court at Brugge, Belgium, in connection with offences committed in September 1977. Ostend ship owner, André van Lul (tender *Hosanna*) and shipper Hector Snauwaert received 69,000 Belgian francs fine and three months' suspended imprisonment; fisherman August Gheys, radio technician Robert Verdamme, Dutch DJs Frank van der Mast (Jan de Hoop) and Hugo Meulenhof (Jan de Boer) were each fined 12,000 Belgian francs. In addition, one months' suspended imprisonment was given to August Gheys."

15 April 1979: It was confirmed that Radio Mi Amigo had deserted the *Mi Amigo* ship for good.

27 June 1979: Radio Mi Amigo appeared again on another ship, the *Centricity,* from Cyprus. Her name was changed to *Magdalena* and she anchored off Thornton Bank, off the Belgian coast. Test transmissions carried on throughout June. Regular programmes commenced on 1 July 1979 on 1100 kHz, 272 metres. DJs were Ton Schipper, Ben van Praag (Belgian) and four Dutchmen, Wim de Groot, Daniel Bolan, Johan Vermeer and Jerry Hoogland. By August Eric Mes, Tom de Bree and Ferry Eden had joined the team.

18 September 1979: The m.v. *Magdalena* broke her anchor chain in high winds and heavy seas and drifted into Dutch territorial waters. A police launch *Delfshaven* went out, arrested her and instructed the crew that she must be towed into harbour at Maasluis. The crew were taken off the ship. The two Belgians were handed over to the Belgian authorities. Dutch DJs Ferry Eden, Wim de Groot and Eric Mes were locked up in police cells for two days and then released. The *Magdalena* was taken in tow by the tug *Furie II* to the nearest harbour, Stellendam. On 26 September she was taken to the breakers yard, Van de Marel at Ouwerkerk.

October 1979: The ship m.v. *Magdalena* was burned and broken up. She had previously gone adrift several times in August and September 1979 losing her anchor on one occasion and dragging it on another. Dutch police arrested the vessel in September 1979 and ordered that she should be scrapped immediately. She was sold for 14,000 guilders to Van de Marel who owned a salvage and demolition company on the River Lek near Ouwerkerk. He had scrapped the ships belonging to Radio Caroline North and Radio Scotland. The ship had been built at Wallsend on Tyne in 1955 and named *Centricity.* She was given the name *Magdalena* in 1978, weighed 655 tons and was 191ft. long and 28ft. wide.

11-14 February 1981: A court case was heard in Ghent, Belgium, where 118 defendants appeared before the magistrates. The case had taken 3 years to bring to court. The next appearance was to be 27 April 1981 with verdicts announced in June 1981. Eighty per cent of the defendants were advertisers, most of whom said their publicity and adverts were broadcast without their consent.

29 June 1981: Thirty people were sentenced and fined for activities involved on Radio Mi Amigo during the 1970s. All appealed.

12 November 1981: Former Mi Amigo DJ Bart van de Laar was shot dead in his Hilversum apartment. Just before his death, he had drinks with friends in a pub well-known to the Dutch broadcasting fraternity. Bart, 36, was found by friends. He was taken to hospital in Utrecht but died on 13 November. In addition to being a DJ he also discovered Belgian, Francis Goya, and made him famous. He produced the 1969 Dutch joint winner for the Eurovision Song Contest for Lenny Kuhr, and in 1981 for Linda Williams. In 1977 he had met Sylvain Tack and formed Gnome Music.

Later, a 23-year-old nurse, Martien 'H' from Baarn confessed to the murder of van de Laar. He said Bart refused a homosexual relationship with him and he killed him. He was found guilty of murder and sentenced to two years in prison.

26 November 1981: Former Mi Amigo boss, Sylvain Tack, was arrested by French police at Charles de Gaulle Airport (Roissy, Paris). He had flown in from Rio de Janeiro, Brazil, and feigned a fractured leg. Within the plaster was 3.2 kg of heroin. He had travelled on a false passport.

On 2 May 1983 the Bobigny High Court of Justice in Paris sentenced him to 8 years 6 months' imprisonment, in addition to a fine of 18 million Belgian francs (£300,000). Tack was sent to Fleury-Merogis Prison, France. Having served four years he was released at the end of 1985 and returned to Belgium where he has since written his autobiography (published 1989).

13-15 October 1982: The Radio Mi Amigo appeal was heard in Ghent, Belgium. The following sentences had been passed down on 29 June 1981. Sylvain Tack was sentenced to a year's imprisonment and a fine of 4 million Belgian francs for his Radio Mi Amigo activities between 1974 and 1978.

Marcel Sieron was given a six months' suspended sentence and 1.6 million Belgian francs fine. Patrick van Ackoleyen was given a four months' suspended sentence with a 800,000 Belgian francs fine. Jean-Pierre van Canneyt was given a two months' suspended sentence and a 400,000 Belgian francs fine; Germain Boy was given two months' suspended sentence and a 400,000 Belgian francs fine. The judge Mr van Rijn imposed fines which amounted to 20 million Belgian francs.

The case was adjourned until 23 December 1982 when all, with the exception of Tack who was in prison in France, had their suspended sentences dropped. Originally 118 people were accused of involvement with Radio Mi Amigo, but the number had been reduced to 49 by the time the case came before the Ghent Court of Appeal. Of these 30 were acquitted outright, 15 of them due to the fact the statute of limitation had expired.

Fourteen people, including singer Willy Sommers and some of the station's advertisers, had their fines reduced to 20,000 Belgian francs (about £250) each from 60,000 Belgian francs.

All jail sentences were quashed. Some of those who had received the severest sentences had only a reduced fine to pay.

Marcel Sieron, from a six months' suspended sentence and a 1,600,000 Belgian francs fine to 400,000 Belgian francs; Patrick van Accoleyen (Patrick Valain), from a four months' suspended sentence and a 800,000 Belgian francs fine to a 400,000 Belgian francs fine; Jean-Pierre van Canneyt, from a two months' suspended sentence and a 400,000 Belgian francs fine to a 80,000 Belgian francs fine and Germain Boy from a two months' suspended sentence and a 400,000 Belgian francs fine to a 80,000 Belgian francs fine.

By 1986 Sylvain Tack was back home in his native Belgium after a long run of ill fortune. He was released from prison in France in March 1986 and immediately deported to Belgium. He was the former owner of Suzy Waffles (a fast food chain), *Joepie* magazine and later Radio Mi Amigo.

RADIO MONIQUE INTERNATIONAL

The station operated from aboard the *Ross Revenge* and commenced test transmissions on 15 December 1984. Management included Fred Bolland and Mike Mourkens.

DJs who broadcast either live or on tape included: Vader Abraham, Elly van Amstel, Tony Berk, Sebastiaan Black, Erwin van der Bliek, Mark van Dale, Luuk Dardin, Joost de Draayer, Ferry Eden, Wim van Egmond, Max de Graaf, Peter de Groot, Stan Haag, Rob Hardholt, Rick van Houten, Maarten de Jong, Frits Koning, Mark van der Mast, Ronald van der Meyden, Jan Molenaar, Eddy Ouwens, Colin Peters, Ron van der Plas, Ric van Rijn, Ad Roberts, Walter Simons, Mark Stam, Pierre van der Stappen, Bart Steenman, Nico Stevens, Arie Swets, Wim de Valk, Jan Veldkamp, Ruud van Velsen, Dick Verheul, Johan Visser, Ron West, Paul Winter and Gerard van der Zee.

Religious programnmes were presented by Johan Maasbach.

On 24 January 1985 *De Telegraaf* published an article about the radio station which said: "The judiciary of Amsterdam will check up on investigations to close down the offshore station, Radio Monique. The programmes are beamed to the Benelux from a rebuilt old fishing trawler, *Ross Revenge*. This vessel is anchored in international waters off the Essex coast. Just a few days ago minister, Eelco Brinkman of WVC (also responsible for broadcasting) spoke to the British authorities and asked them to work together to ban all activities from the offshore stations transmitting off the English coast. Also, while there are well known DJs working for Monique, the judiciary will try to search for leaks in the bill to close down Monique. According to people behind the organisation of the station, which can be received from as far away as France, there will be more well known names on 319 soon. Working in any way for an offshore station is forbidden by Dutch law, but it is very difficult to take action against these people. 'We are looking for possibilities as to how to contact the station,' Mr Wooldrik of the judiciary told us. Tony Berk said that he did not work for Monique. 'I work for Belgian stations by sending programmes on cassettes. It's quite a puzzle to me how those cassettes have been played on Monique. My legal adviser will try to get action taken against the station'."

On 31 January 1985 a police launch and a Coastguard vessel sailed around the radio ship and took photographs.

On 13 June 1985 a question was asked in the Dutch Parliament about Monique. Mr van der Sanden of the CDA Party asked why the Government and judicial system were not taking action against the offshore station.

The Minister of Justice, Korthals Altes, had been in contact with British authorities and the tendering of the offshore station had been stopped. It was not possible to act against the Dutch people on board as the radio programmes were not illegal.

A listeners' popularity poll was conducted by Inter/View in June which revealed that 25% of the Dutch population had heard of Monique and 11% listened to the station, which amounted to 1,265,000.

On Friday 13 November 1987 Radio Monique announced it was closing down for a frequency change. The station returned on 15 November on 366 metres, 819 kHz. Radio Monique ceased broadcasting when the aerial mast snapped on 25 November 1987.

RADIO NORTHSEA INTERNATIONAL

The owners of RNI were Mebo Telecommunications Ltd., PO Box 113, CH8047, Zurich, Switzerland. After March 1971, record requests were sent to PO Box 117, Hilversum, Holland.

Radio Northsea International was the brainchild of Edwin Bollier and Erwin Meister who had been working as engineers on the project "Radio Gloria International" to re-launch the m.v. *Galaxy*. This operation failed as the German Marine Offences Act came into force on 2 July 1969, plus the fact that the original backers did not have enough money to re-equip the ship.

Bollier and Meister, who were Swiss, decided they wanted to begin their own pirate station. They purchased a 347-ton ship, the *Bjarkoy*, built by Tronjems M/V at Trondheim, Norway, and renamed it *Mebo* (compounded from the first two letters of their surnames MEister and BOllier. Mebo was not named after the Marine Etc., Broadcasting Offences Act!).

However, she was only a small ship measuring some 124ft. long, so the two Swiss engineers decided to buy a much larger ship, the 630-ton *Silvretta*, built in 1948 by De Groot and Vliet at Slikkerveer, Holland. Gerry Bishop, in his book *Offshore Radio* says the ship was 186ft. long, renamed *Mebo II* and converted into a radio ship at the same yard which built her. The ship had cost Meister and Bollier £25,000. Refitting her was a further £65,000.

The psychedelically-painted *Mebo II* left Slikkerveer Wharf, Rotterdam, and sailed for her anchorage off the Dutch coast on 22 January 1970. She began test transmissions on 102 MHz FM and 6210 kHz in the 49 metre short waveband. They were voiced, on tape, by Roger Day in English and Horsl Reiner in German. The medium wave transmitter on 186 metres (1610 kHz) began a series of test transmissions on 11 February 1970. Regular programmes commenced on 28 February 1970. German programmes were broadcast from 6.00am to 8.00am and from 6.00pm to 8.00pm. English

The psychedically-painted RNI ship, Mebo II

programmes could be heard from 8.00am to 6.00pm and from 8.00pm until midnight. Programmes for both the German and English services went through a number of changes in the first few weeks.

DJs included: Tony Allan, Don Allen, Ian Anderson, Brian Anderson, Andy Archer, Axel, Kurt Baer, Robin Banks, A.J. Beirens, Steve Berry, Bruno Brandenburger, Trevor Campbell, Ray Cooper, Terry Davis, Roger Day, John Denny, Pierre Deseyn, Robb Eden, Eelke, Graham Gill, Leo van der Goot, Dave Gregory, Hannibal, Peter and Werner Hartwig, Dave Johns, Duncan Johnson, Martin Kayne, Roger Kent, Steve King, Roger Kirk, Stephen Ladd, Arnold Layne, Michael Lindsay, Bob Mackey, Barry Martin, Paul May, Brian McKenzie, Stevi Merike, Carl Mitchell, Ed Moreno, Spangles Muldoon, Bob Noakes, Vic Pelli, Eva Pfister, Louise Quirk, Horst Reiner, Dave Rogers, Mike Ross, Sheila Ross, Crispian St. John, Johnny Scott, Mark Slate, Mark Stuart, Larry Tremaine, Jane Valentyne, Mark Wesley, Alan West and Jason Wolfe.

23 March 1970: *Mebo II* sailed for England, broadcasting as she travelled, and arrived off Holland-on-Sea, Essex, the following morning. The Thames Coastguard at Walton-on-the-Naze experienced some interference from RNI's medium wave transmitter. A complaint was relayed to the *Mebo II*. Transmissions on 183 metres medium wave ceased on 27 March.

10 April 1970: RNI recommenced transmissions on 190 metres (1578 kHz) but the station was soon jammed by the Ministry of Posts and Telecommunications which sent a high pitched 800 cycles per second tone from a naval station at Rochester, Kent. The British Government had acted at the request of Norway and Italy who also experienced interference from RNI. Transmissions on medium wave from the *Mebo II* ceased that evening.

30 April 1970: RNI returned with test transmissions on a new frequency, 217 metres, 1385 kHz and also 100 MHz FM.

16 May 1970: RNI tried out a new frequency on medium wave on 244 metres (1230 kHz). Czechoslovakia complained to Britain and, once again, the jamming recommenced from the naval station.

13 June 1970: RNI changed her name temporarily to Radio Caroline International in preparation for the General Election in Britain on 18 June. DJs urged listeners to vote for the party which supported commercial radio. Broadcasters were Andy Archer, Mark Wesley and Alan West.

On 14 June a large demonstration was held in London with a protest march from Hyde Park to Downing Street and thence to Trafalgar Square. It was a protest against the jamming of Radio Caroline broadcasts.

One week before the General Election, according to Paul Harris in his book *To Be a Pirate King*, a plot of land owned by the Marconi company and located near Southend Airport was taken over by the authorities. Army trucks began to pull into the empty field. Two marquees were erected and massive security precautions were put into force. In one marquee there were installed powerful RCA transmitters, and in the other, generators. Two days before the election the station came on air with an estimated 200kW (twice the power of RNI). The site was closely guarded by police, Army personnel and dogs. No photographs or observation was permitted. Any persons who loitered in the vicinity were stopped and questioned.

A Caroline bus with Ronan O'Rahilly and Simon Dee aboard toured key marginal seats. Caroline also played a send-up song, to the tune of Dad's Army, called *Who Do You Think You're Kidding, Mr Wilson?* Posters of Harold Wilson dressed like Chairman Mao also appeared on hoardings in and around London. The Conservative Party won the election with Edward Heath taking over from Harold Wilson. What sway Radio Caroline had can never be accurately quantified. However, Paul Harris, author and broadcaster, believes they did tilt the result in favour of the Conservatives. Speaking at Flashback '67 at the Centre Airport Hotel in London, ten years after the introduction of the Marine Etc., Broadcasting (Offences) Bill he said: "There is no doubt in my mind that had it not been for the intervention of Radio Northsea International (which temporarily adopted the name Radio Caroline) the Labour Government would have retained power in 1970. The swing was so marginal. It was an election in which for the first time people under the age of 21 could vote. The voting age had been lowered to 18 years. A swing of 1½% to 2% in marginal constituencies, most of which were concentrated in south-east England and around London, was enough to unseat Harold Wilson."

The *Mebo II* reverted to RNI. The jamming continued from a station at Canewdon, Essex. RNI tried a number of different medium wave frequencies, but wherever she appeared on the radio dial, there, too was the Ministry of Posts and Telecommunications jamming station. RNI accepted defeat and ceased transmissions on 23 June 1970.

24 June 1970: The *Mebo II* departed from the Essex coast and returned to Holland where she resumed broadcasting, but interference was caused to the Dutch station Hilversum III. RNI changed frequency twice, first to 217 metres, 1385 kHZ, then to 220 metres, 1367 kHZ. The jamming stopped. All broadcasts from the *Mebo II* were now in English.

29 August 1970: Trouble at sea! A launch named the *Viking* and a tug, the *Huski*, arrived at the *Mebo II*. A Dutchman, Kees Manders, formerly of Radio Veronica, climbed aboard and demanded that the ship be taken into Scheveningen. He announced that he had become commercial director of RNI on 12 August 1970. This was denied by RNI managing director, Larry Tremaine.

Kees Manders was invited by Bollier and Meister to start a Dutch service on the *Mebo II*. He was promised the post of director. Manders, who was well known in Holland, had already contacted a number of Dutch newspapers announcing his new post as Director of the Dutch Service of RNI. Nothing had been agreed on paper. Bollier

and Meister were angry that the news had leaked out and immediately ceased any agreement with Manders who became furious and hired a tug, the *Huski*. and launch, the *Viking*. Together with colleague Cor Verolme they travelled out to the *Mebo II* to try and tow her into harbour. Verolme, a Rotterdam shipbuilder, was the main backer of the ill-fated TV and Radio Noordzee from REM Island off the Dutch coast which had been closed down by the authorities in 1964.

Listeners heard a running commentary from the poop deck as to what was happening. After the *Mebo II* captain refused permission and ordered the Dutchman off the ship, Manders threatened to cut the anchor chain and tow her in. The crew of the *Huski* prepared to use water cannon directed at the aerial mast. The DJs warned the crew of the tug, over the air, that if they went ahead they would all most certainly be electrocuted. Both the *Viking* and the *Huski* later returned to Holland.

24 September 1970: RNI voluntarily closed down. An announcement on radio said it was due to the pressure from the Dutch Government to close down the offshore stations. The directors of RNI felt that it would be better for the people of Holland if RNI suspended broadcasting so that the Dutch Government would not attempt to close down Radio Veronica which had been so dearly loved by the people of Holland since 1960.

Andy Archer and Alan West presented the final hour on RNI and the station closed at 11.00am.

A Dutch crew was put on board the *Mebo II*. The following day it became known that the Radio Veronica organisation had bought out Meister and Bollier for 1,000,000 guilders (1993's value £370,000) because RNI were in debt. Meister and Bollier agreed to stay off the air for two months and not to commence a Dutch service. However, if RNI broke the agreement and resumed broadcasting the money would be repaid in full.

Meister and Bollier went out on the tender to the *Mebo II* from Scheveningen.

When they arrived at the radio ship they said to the captain: "Please go with the tender and make contact by phone with the *Mebo II* agents because they have some information about illness in your family." As the captain of the *Mebo II* was making his way down to board the tender, the captain of the tender started his engines and sailed away from the *Mebo II*. Meister and Bollier were now once again in control of the *Mebo II*.

Later that week RNI directors took the one million guilders worth of Deutschmarks in two suitcases to the Veronica offices, but 'Bull' Verway refused to accept the money.[10]

RNI began a series of test transmissions of continuous music in February 1971 for two weeks. DJ Stevi Merike announced on 14 February: "This is a test transmission from Radio Northsea International broadcasting on 220 metres medium wave band, 1367 kilocycles, and on Channel 44, that's 100 megacycles in the FM band, and short wave at 6205 kilocycles in the European band. We're very pleased to have you around. May I cordially suggest that you call up your friends on the telephone and let them know that RNI is back."

Regular programmes recommenced on 20 February 1971. The station theme, *Man of Action* by the Les Reed Orchestra, was followed by DJ Alan West who, in turn, introduced production director Victor Pelli who announced: "A new and different chapter of RNI begins at this time. On behalf of the owners, Mr Meister and Mr Bollier, 1 would like to bid you welcome to the new Radio Northsea International. In the years to come RNI will bring you the best possible entertainment." The opening record was *Nothing Rhymed* by Gilbert O'Sullivan. In addition to Stevi Merike and Alan West, also on board were DJs Tony Allan, Martin Kayne, Dave Rogers and Crispian St. John.

To begin with programmes were all in English, but Dutch language shows commenced on 6 March 1971.

A legal battle took place on 10 March in a court in Rotterdam. Veronica's legal team said they had paid one million guilders to

Meister and Bollier, and now that the station was again broadcasting from the *Mebo II* that contract was not valid. The lawyer acting for RNI said that the money, stuffed in two suitcases, had been taken to the offices of Radio Veronica as they wished to recommence broadcasting. Veronica refused to accept this money. In April the Dutch court said that no decision could be taken as all the problems occurred in international waters. As the radio ship was in the hands of Meister and Bollier they could continue with transmissions.

15 May 1971: RNI had been on the air for more than two months with programmes in Dutch from 6.00am to 4.00pm and in English from 4.00pm to 3.00am. Dutch DJs Joost de Draayer and Jan van Veen began their programmes on 6 March 1971.

Three men, including Tom van de Linden, a former captain of the *Mebo II*, climbed into a rubber dinghy and left Scheveningen at 7.40pm and headed for the *Mebo II*. It took some three hours before they pulled alongside. It was not a social visit. Two of the men climbed on to the *Mebo II* and went down to the engine room, lit a fire, returned to the dinghy and set sail for the Dutch coast. No one on board the *Mebo II* noticed any visitors. The majority of the crew had been watching television.

Within minutes there was a huge explosion which started a fire at the stem of the ship. DJ Alan West said over the airwaves "Mayday Mayday! This is the radio ship *Mebo II* four miles off the coast of Scheveningen, Holland... we require assistance urgently due to a fire on board this vessel caused by a bomb being thrown into our engine room ... Mayday Mayday! This is an SOS from Radio Northsea International."

For the next half hour listeners were given a graphic description of what was happening on board.

Captain Harteveld, the master of the ship, repeated the SOS in Dutch.

This was dramatic radio. Alan West continued "This is an act of piracy on the high seas ... you have bombed a Panamanian ship on the high seas ... we do not know how long the *Mebo II* will stay afloat ... we may

10. *The RNI Story*, Jeremy C.G. Arnold, *Monitor* magazine, undated, but probably about 1975.

Hendrik 'Bull' Verwey leaving court at The
Hague after sentencing

have to abandon ship."

Just before midnight listeners heard "The entire stern of the ship is ablaze ... we are having to abandon the *Mebo II* ... Mayday Mayday!" The transmitters then went dead.

In the early hours of 16 May the tug. *Eurotrip,* rescued ten men from the *Mebo II.* Shortly afterwards she was joined by a firefighting tug, the *Volans.* Also on the scene was the Dutch Royal Navy frigate, *Gelderland.* The captain of the *Mebo II,* together with the transmitter engineer and ship's engineer, remained on board. The fire raged for another two hours before it was brought under control by a number of ships. Damage was put at £28,000.

By coincidence neither the radio studio nor the transmitter was damaged and transmissions began again.

Dutch police began an immediate investigation and within hours three men were arrested after parts of a rubber dinghy and frogmen's suits were found on a deserted beach near The Hague. Each had been paid £3,000 to do the job. Together with Radio Veronica's sales manager, Norbert Jurgens, and a director, 'Bull' Verwey, they appeared in court at The Hague on 20 May 1971. The prosecutor said that Radio Veronica had financed the raid on *Mebo II* and the men were paid £10,000 to bring the ship inside Dutch waters. They had intended to tow her into port without damage. Veronica had not ordered the fire as they had no wish to endanger life. On 21 September 1971 Hendrik 'Bull' Verwey, Norbert Jurgens and the three divers were found guilty of the attack on the *Mebo II* and each sentenced to one year in prison.

22 November 1971: RNI lost her anchor and drifted. She stopped broadcasting as she drifted into Dutch waters. The lifeboat *Bernhard van Leer,* two aircraft and a tug went to her assistance. Later that day the *Mebo II* was towed back into international waters and broadcasts recommenced. Mike Ross and Leo van de Groot presented a live programme explaining the difficulties the ship had experienced.

30 September 1972: DJ Tony Allan announced a new service with test transmissions from RNI 2. These were heard on 192 metres (1562 kHz) after Radio Veronica had vacated its frequency and moved to 538 metres, 557 kHz. Listeners could hear a Dutch service on the original frequency and an English service on the new one. However, the English service did not survive as it was said to have brought in no money and the Dutch service director, John de Mol, sacked all the British DJs a year later in November 1973. This action did not have the approval of the directors of RNI who immediately reinstated the DJs.

23 February 1973: Once again the ship's anchor chain broke. Don Allen had read the news in the evening and during the bulletin the ship rolled a little too much. When he went up on deck, he looked out of the porthole. He recalls "It was a very clear night. I could see cars on the horizon. I was sure we were within a half a mile from shore. The captain and Mike Ross were playing cards at the time. They got up and looked out of the porthole. I went back below where the *Brian McKenzie Show* was going out. I said over the air 'we are drifting. The anchor chain has broken. We are now ceasing transmissions until we are safely in international waters.' It took about thirty six hours to get back to our original anchorage due to a storm over this part of the coast. It was all very frightening."

4 May 1973: The very first double album about pirate radio was produced in Holland by Hans Knot called *The History of RNI.* The same day some 500 Dutch 'anoraks' gathered at Scheveningen harbour to board nine fishing boats to visit the radio ships. This was the biggest party ever organised in Holland to visit pirates at sea.

21 June 1973: The campaign to "Keep RNI on the air as a legal land-based station" got underway. Free stickers were given away in town centres and on the streets. There was space on the sticker for recipients to fill in their name and address saying "I will be a member of the broadcasting society of RNI. I want to pay 5 guilders a year for my dues." Throughout Holland some 30,000 people filled in the application forms, but unfortunately there were not enough names to convince the broadcasting authorities in Holland that they should make the station land-based. A minimum number of 50,000 names and addresses were required. Radio Veronica exceeded this number and in 1975 was granted a licence to operate on land.

The company behind RNI has now been given a licence to broadcast satellite programmes from land in Holland into orbit. It is called Satellite Radio Noordzee, not to be confused with RNI programmes which are transmitted on Intelsat.

30 August 1974: RNI agreed to close shop, or should that be 'ship?' The final English programme was transmitted from 11.00pm to midnight when Don Allen, Robin Banks, Roger Kent, Brian McKenzie and Bob Noakes said their farewells. RNI closed down at midnight. The following day the Dutch service then took over until just before 8.00pm when everyone on board, including Edwin Bollier, Dutch and English, said a last farewell.

The next day the disc jockeys were taken off aboard the *Mebo I* to a hero's welcome as they arrived on land. Engineers remained on board a further week and the *Mebo II* ship sailed to Rotterdam. Customs sealed up certain sections of the ship. She then sailed on the canals to Slikkerveer. The vessel was then stripped, transmitters serviced and the studios rebuilt.

In future the ship would be known as RNI - Radio Nova International, and would anchor in the Gulf of Genoa by mid-October. It would broadcast in Italian during the daytime and in English in the evening. The new station was in honour of the Royal Park Hotel in Zurich, Switzerland, owned by Edwin Bollier.

1 September 1974: The Dutch Marine Offences Act came into force.

9 September 1974: *Mebo II* was anchored off Scheveningen for a week until towed into Slikkerveer, 25 miles inland along the Maas. The ship was put into dry dock at the De Groot en van Vliet yard where she was originally built in 1948, and where she was converted into a radio ship. Work was completed on both outside and inside the vessel in preparation for her role as Radio Nova International. Two studios were refurbished and a new one built. The record library was given a new coat of paint.

However, all this turned out to be a dream as the *Mebo II* was impounded by the Dutch police on 10 October 1974 due to the fact the vessel had radio transmitters on board. At a court hearing on 10 December Edwin Bollier was found guilty of operating a pirate radio ship and the court ordered that the transmitters should be confiscated. Bollier challenged the Dutch authorities alleging that they were illegally detaining a Panamanian ship. The transmitters were in the ship's hold and so were technically cargo. Two hearings were held on 3 and 25 March 1975 and the decision was that, after a deposit of 250,000 guilders had been paid, *Mebo II* would be free to sail. The money would be returned after two years providing that the ship did not broadcast to Northern Europe during that time.[11]

More in-fighting went on between the owners of *Mebo II* and the Dutch. The outcome was that on 2 January 1976 the company who owned *Mebo II* had to pay a 5,000 guilders fine, after which the ship was free to leave Holland. Rumours were rife that Edwin Bollier had sold the ship to an African company and so RNI would not be broadcasting to Italy.

14 January 1977: It was confirmed that *Mebo II* had been sold to the Libyans for an estimated six million guilders. There was also an extra transmitter installed on the ship near the RNI transmitters. It was a Continental Electronics 10kW transmitter formerly used by Radio Veronica which had been sold to Meister and Bollier in 1976.

The ship sailed from De Groot and van Vliet Shipyard, Holland, together with her companion ship, the *Angela*. They arrived in Tripoli Harbour on St. Valentine's Day, 14 February 1977. The Attorney General at the Court of Justice in The Hague declared that the confiscation of the *Mebo II* had been cancelled and that she, together with the *Angela*, and with the existing transmitting apparatus on board, could leave the Netherlands with due observation of the Customs control.

2 May 1977: Test transmissions began from the *Mebo II* in Tripoli Harbour.

8 August 1977: The *Mebo II* and *Angela* sailed for Benghazi, arriving on 11 August. The ships then moved on to Dema Harbour, 600 miles east of Tripoli, where the radio ship became known as the Libyan Post-Revolution Broadcasting Station. By 30 October 1977 *Mebo II* was on her way back to Benghazi. She arrived in Tripoli Harbour on 19 January 1978.

5 April 1978: An Article in *Monitor* magazine, Edition N" 18 in 1979, reported that *Mebo II* had been purchased by the Libyan Government and her name changed to *El Fatah*. The first *Mebo*, later renamed the *Angela*, became Libyan property at the same time. She then became the *Almasira*.

After six months in harbour the transmitters were taken off the ship and rebuilt in Libya. The Libyan Government had ordered a number of transmitters for land-based stations, but by April 1978 these were not ready. So the former RNI ship was used as a stopgap.

Readings from the Holy Koran were regularly broadcast.

Once the transmitters for the land-based stations had been completed, broadcasts from the radio ship ceased. By 1980 she had been stripped of all her broadcasting equipment, used as a target by the Libyan Air

Force and sunk. A sad ending to a ship which had enjoyed a colourful existence on the high seas.

RADIO PARADIJS

This radio station broadcast from aboard the m.v. *Magda Maria,* a 620-ton ship built in 1957 at Luhring in Brake, near Bremen, Germany. On 3 October 1957 the ship, then called the *Hoheweg,* made her maiden trip. She was owned by Ludwig Ras of Bremen. The ship sailed for the last time on 11 December 1979. On 19 December the vessel's owners received a freight order from the company Oltmans from Bremen. Radio Paradijs bought the ship with the help of the Baremar Shipping Company of Spijkenisse near Rotterdam, and the Chielimsky Shipping Company of Rotterdam. The ship, which was 170ft. long and registered in Panama, was operated as the m.v. *Lieve* by the company Panlieve SA and was bought in Oversthie near Rotterdam for 80,000 guilders. She was renamed the m.v. *Corunna* for two months. The ship then sailed to Cuxhaven in northern Germany where she was partly rebuilt. However, German police investigated what was going on and shortly afterwards she sailed to Dublin where three Continental Electronics radio transmitters (two 10kW medium wave and one 35kW FM) were installed, as well as two broadcasting studios and an aerial mast. Equipment for a further three studios was also put on board. By now her name had been changed to *Magda Maria* which was first used in the 1960s by Radio Nord.

During the second week of July 1981 the radio ship sailed to an anchorage off the Dutch coast, nine miles north of the REM island. On her journey, during bad weather, the ship lost 100ft. of aerial mast. She arrived on 20 July 1981.

On board was a crew of ten comprising a captain, cook and his girl friend, technicians and a deck mate. The estimate for the cost of rebuilding the ship was in the region of 5,000,000 guilders.

Programme director for Radio Paradijs was Ben Bode who employed six DJs including Tom van de Velde and Dido Dekker, both of whom had worked for a land-based pirate in Holland called Radio Mikado. The programme format was strict with no choice of music by the DJs. Speech was cut to a minimum (usually 10 seconds) with announcements after two records played back to back. Programmes were recorded on land and only the news bulletins were broadcast live from the ship.

The station transmitted on 262 metres medium wave. Two further frequencies were available for other stations to use and, at one stage, it was planned that Radio Monique would broadcast from the ship. The frequencies were 214 metres and 93 MHz FM in stereo.

On 30 July 1981, Hans Knot and colleagues from a number of Dutch newspapers hired a boat and sailed from Scheveningen to the radio ship. They were followed by the Dutch water police. Hans and his fellow journalists could not attract any attention from crew members of Radio Paradijs, so did not go on board. Three days later Hans heard Radio Paradijs broadcasting in the morning with Dutch language programmes in a series of test transmissions on 1187 kHz (252 metres). However, in spite of announcements that the station would commence regular programmes on 1 August, subsequently put back to 15 August, the station never broadcast again.

Rumours abounded that the ship was going to be raided by the Dutch authorities and so on 30 July a number of crew members were taken off the radio ship by the vessel *Maartje.*

On Friday 31 July 1981 at 11.00am the Officer of Justice in Rotterdam ordered the Dutch water police to board the ship. A marine vessel, the *Jaguar,* went to the *Magda Maria,* together with a police vessel, *RP No 3,* with a 50-strong police team on board. At 6.10am on 1 August 1981 they boarded the Radio Paradijs ship which was then towed by the *Jaguar* into IJmuiden harbour and arrived at 3.00pm. She then went to Amsterdam Entrepot harbour, arriving at 5.30pm. The Dutch authorities said that the two Dutchmen on board should be arrested as they had broken Article No A3/2O of the Dutch Telegraph and Telephone Act.

A press conference was held at The Hague on 1 August when the Dutch justice minister, Mr Doelder, said that the Dutch authorities had acted because there was a radio transmitter on board the *Magda Maria.* A Radio Paradijs spokesman said it was an act of piracy and that Holland had restarted her old hobby of taking over radio ships. They would take the case to court. Radio Paradijs hired a well-known solicitor, Mr de Gongej, and the court cases took place throughout the 1980s. The radio company managed to get back its radio ship which had been lying in Amsterdam Harbour. She was eventually broken up in 1987 at Zeebrugge. They also got back the transmitters which had been taken off the ship. These were later sold to a Belgian radio station.

Court cases were still being heard in late 1993. By the end of 1994 it was hoped an outcome would decide how much the Dutch Authorities will have to pay the Radio Paradijs company for acting illegally in arresting the ship when anchored in international waters.

RADIO SEAGULL

The radio station began broadcasting from the *Mi Amigo* on 22 July 1973 but suffered badly from gales which lasted for over a month in November and December 1973 when the mast collapsed.

The station, which was described as 'progressive', returned to the air on 7 January 1974 with transmitter power increasing to 50kW the following month. However, Radio Seagull suddenly ceased broadcasting on 23 February 1974 and was replaced by Radio Caroline.

The DJs included: Tony Allan, Brian

Anderson, Andy Archer, Baas, Norman Barrington, Peter Chicago, Peter van Dyken, Barry Everett, John Farlow, Mike Hagler, Johnny Jason, Mickey Mercer, Bob Noakes, Hugh Nolan, Dick Palmer and Phil Randall.

One of the broadcasters, engineer Michael Wall-Garland, (known on air as 'Mike the Poet') who used to read a poem on air each evening, was killed in a car crash on 17 December 1975 in Italy.

RADIO VERONICA

Preparations to operate a pirate radio ship off the Dutch coast were well advanced by 1959. It was to be called Radio Veronica and investors involved in its early days were: J. Beewkes, Will J. Hordijk, Norbert Jurgens, Max Lewin, Kees Manders, Henricus Oswald, Lambertus Slootmans, three brothers Dick, Hendrik A. 'Bull' and Jaap Verwey.

A company to oversee the project, Vrije Radio Omroep Nederland (VRON), was registered in Liechtenstein.

A former German lightship built in 1911 called the *Borkum Riff* was purchased in 1959 for 63,000 guilders (£7,000). The

Various Radio Veronica advertising stickers

Radio Veronica ship aground on the beach at Scheveningen, 3 April 1973

value in 1993 would be nearer £23,300.

There were severe problems before the station went on air. Broadcasting equipment had to go to Emden but was intercepted by both Dutch and German Customs. At that time it was illegal to transport a radio transmitter from one country to another.

The *Borkum Riff* was towed from Emden on 18 April 1960 into international waters in the North Sea by an English tug.

The station began test transmissions shortly after Easter 1960 on 185 metres, 1620 kHz. The ship was anchored in international waters off Katwijk-aan-Zee, Holland. Regular programmes commenced on 6 May 1960. At a similar time the Dutch Posts and Telecommunications (PTT) began jamming the station, so Veronica changed frequency to 182 metres (1640 kHz).

Later that month the frequency was again changed, this time to 192 metres, 1562 kHz. In November 1960 the Verwey brothers took over the running of Radio Veronica. Originally all programmes were recorded in Holland on to tape and sent out to the ship for transmission.

In 1961 the London-based company CNBC made use of the transmitters from Radio Veronica.

In his book *To Be a Pirate King*, Paul

Harris stated that: "By 1962 Radio Veronica had an advertising turnover of £1 million and an estimated audience of 5 million."

Live programming from the ship began in December 1964.

In 1965 the programme director of Radio Veronica, Joost de Draayer, had observed the success of Radios Caroline and London off the English coast and asked permission of the Verway brothers to travel to America to see how commercial radio was run in that country. He had a successful visit and returned with many new ideas for Veronica ... T Shirts, car stickers and many more promotional recommendations.

Within a few weeks Radio Veronica became very popular with the young people of the Netherlands. The programme format was changed from easy listening to Top 40 pop music. The station did away with 15-minute pre-recorded tapes and introduced 3-hour presenter shows.

In 1964 the *Borkum Riff* was towed into harbour and broken up. The old lightship was replaced by a converted trawler named the *Norderney* described as large and luxurious. The ship, which did not have an engine, was towed to a location off the Noordwijk coast. Shortly afterwards the anchor chain snapped and she drifted. She was saved by a Dutch Coastguard vessel and returned her to the original anchorage. A new anchor was attached and she survived many a storm until 2 April 1973 when she again broke loose from her moorings.

The station had its offices on the outskirts of Hilversum.

DJs included: Fred van Amstel, Anuscka, Eddy Becker, Adje Bouman, Mies Bouwman, Carlo, Tom Collins, Robbie Dale, Rob van Dyk, Henk van Dorp, Joost de Draayer, Ellen van Eck, Rik de Gooier, Stan Haag, Lex Harding, Gaston Huysmans, Karel van de Kamp, Harry Knipschild, Will Luikinga, Hans Mondt, Chiel Montange, Frans Nienhuys, Rob Out, Suhandi, Tineke, Klaas Vaak (Tom Mulder), Jan van Veen, Tony Vos, Gerard de Vries and Cees van Zijtveld.

Newsreaders included: Dick Klees, Arend Langenberg, Leo de Laater, Harmen Siezen (also a DJ) and Freek Simon.

30 September 1972: Radio Veronica changed frequency from 192 metres to 539 metres, 557 kHz, which gave a clearer signal to Holland and the eastern regions of the United Kingdom.

15 January 1973: The IBA in London began test transmissions on a similar frequency to Radio Veronica. This was in preparation for Capital Radio, the second independent radio station for the United Kingdom, the first being LBC. The strength of the IBA signal made Veronica inaudible in most parts of Belgium and England. Reception in Holland was not affected.

2 April 1973: The *Norderney* broke loose from her moorings and drifted towards the shore. The captain of the *Norderney* was Arie van der Zwaan. A lifeboat, *Bernhard van Leer* from Scheveningen, was launched. The station ceased transmissions. Within an hour and a half the lifeboat had rescued ten crew of the radio ship and returned to Scheveningen where, however, she could not enter the harbour because of severe gales. The lifeboat finally arrived in the harbour at 10.00am on 3 April. Meanwhile the *Norderney* ran aground fifty yards from the entrance of Scheveningen Harbour.

Radio Caroline offered Veronica facilities to promote their "Keep Veronica on the Air" campaign between 10 and 18 April 1973. More than 150,000 free radio fans turned up for the demonstration in The Hague. It was the largest of its kind ever held. Radio Veronica used the transmitters of Radio Caroline. The Radio Veronica organisation received over 100,000 forms from its campaign which had begun in 1972, "Veronica Stays If You Want It", signed by Dutch men, women and children. This ensured it would be given a licence to broadcast from land once the Dutch Marine Offences Act had come into force.

18 April 1973: The *Norderney* was refloated and returned to her original anchorage. She recommenced broadcasting at 10.00am. Radio Caroline also offered assistance as well as broadcasting details of the return of Radio Veronica.

28 June 1973: The Dutch Chamber of Deputies voted 95 to 37 in favour of outlawing the pirate radio stations including Veronica and RNI. The Act would become effective from 1 September 1974.

31 August 1974: Radio Veronica said it would not defy the Dutch Marine Broadcasting Act and would close down that evening at 6.00pm. DJ Rob Out said the final words: "This is the end of Veronica. It is a pity for you, for Veronica and especially for democracy in Holland." Then followed the Dutch National Anthem and the transmitter went silent.

28 December 1975: Radio Veronica's airtime on land began on Hilversum 4. In addition, shows were transmitted on Hilversum 1 and 3.

July 1976: The ex-Veronica ship *Norderney* was sold. The Veronica Omroep Organisatie (VOO) found they could no longer afford to maintain her so they accepted an undisclosed sum for her from a man in Dordrecht (a town to the south-east of Rotterdam). He signed a contract with them that he would not strip the ship, but leave her as she was. At least five people were interested, including someone from Egypt. The ship's condition was described as 'a bit tatty.'

1 September 1982: The *Norderney* was the main attraction in the small town of Zoutkamp in the province of Groningen. During the summer the ship became a 'pub' with tables and chairs set out on the bridge. Whilst in water it became a floating discotheque. The owner was Jan Groeneweg, a chef and restaurateur. He employed 15 people to run the ship.

19 April 1983: The *Norderney* was taken to Middelburg in Zeeland, Holland. The new owner was Rob Koster. The ship was described as 'a floating disco.'
Radio Veronica is now a land-based radio station operated by Veronica Omroep Organisatie. It has 1,100,000 members and is the biggest broadcasting society in the Dutch public broadcasting sector. Second is TROS with 600,000 members.

RADIO 819
This Dutch-language station was the successor to Radio Monique and operated from aboard the *Ross Revenge*. Test transmissions with Ad Roberts and Erwin van der Bliek began on 30 May 1988. The mailing address of the station was P.O. Box 146, Playa de Aro, Spain, which had earlier been used by Radios Mi Amigo and Monique. Regular programmes began on 9 July 1988. The first show was presented by Erwin van der Bliek at 9.00am followed by Fred van Amstel and Lex van Zandvoort.

DJs included: Elly van Amstel, Fred van Amstel (no relation to Fred van Amstel of Radio Veronica in the 1960s), Erik Beekman, Erwin van der Bliek, Ted Bouwens, Piet Mackenzie, Peter van der Meer, Rene de Nijs, Colin Peters, Edo Peters, Frank Peterson, Ron van der Plas, Ad Roberts, Walter Simons, Arie Swets, Mirjam Verhoef, Lex van Zandvoort

Taped programmes were recorded by Vader Abraham, Renée Bouvie, Maryke van Breeman, Raymond Bulsink, Hans Dekkers, Rev Dominee van Gendt, Johan van den Hoofdakker, Rick van Houten, Ger Lamens,

Johan Maasbach, Hendrik van Nellestein, Renée Plomp, Luv van Rooy, Ria Valk, Connie Vandenbosch, Jan Veldkamp.

17 August 1989: The Dutch police, under orders from the head of Justice in Amsterdam, raided twenty places in Holland, including studios and private houses; in conjunction with the Belgian authorities, seven in Belgium, and in Spain they visited the home of the man who operated the post office box there, Maurice Bokkenbroek. Their efforts were on behalf of Minister Nellie Smit-Kroes of the Verkeer en Waterstaat (Ministry for Transport and Waterways), which were under the control of the Opsporings Controle Dienst (Dutch equivalent of the Radio Regulatory Department of the DTI in Britain). The raids had been planned for eighteen months. With co-operation from the British and Belgian Authorities the plan was to put an end to Radio 819 once and for all.

19 August 1989: *Ross Revenge* engineer, Peter Chicago, interrupted programmes on Radio 819 and said in English: "This is a message from the crew on board the vessel *Ross Revenge*. We're at anchor in international waters of the North Sea. At the moment there is a Dutch tug, the *Volans*, which is alongside. They seem to have the intention to take this vessel from the high seas. Anybody who is hearing this message, could they please try to summon some kind of assistance for the vessel? In the meantime we continue with the programme. Over." Radio 819 continued with the programme *Texas Top 40* which was on tape, and this carried on until eight minutes to two when the programme ended. That was the last ever to be heard of the Dutch language Radio 819 from the *Ross Revenge.*

When the *Volans* left the *Ross Revenge* later that evening, DJ Arie Swets and Eddie the Cook were on board the tug. Both returned to Holland freely, having been assured by the authorities that they would not be arrested when they landed in Holland.

Various items of broadcasting equipment from the *Ross Revenge* were taken on the *Volans*, as were some 18,000 LPs and singles.

Inside studio aboard Voice of Peace

These were put into store by the Dutch authorities in Scheveningen, in the very same building to which the equipment from the REM Island had been taken by the authorities a number of years previously.[12]

VOICE OF PEACE

Not a pirate station we identify with in Great Britain. However, a number of British and American disc jockeys have served on the ship over the years.

The station was the brainchild of Abraham Nathan, born of Jewish parents in Iran in 1932. He enjoyed an exciting life as an international playboy and was one of the best known peace activists in the Middle East. In 1947 he made his name when involved in ferrying refugees in and out of India during the Indo-Pakistani hostilities. A former Israeli Air Force bomber pilot, he later opened a famous restaurant in Tel Aviv.

He flew an Auster aircraft from Israel to Port Said two days before the outbreak of the Arab-Israeli Six Day War. His mission was to try to talk the Egyptians out of provoking war. After the war he tried again and, on arrival back home, was fined for 'having contact with the enemy.' He refused to pay and spent 40 days in jail. He made yet another attempt at a peace mission to Egypt, arriving this time on a commercial flight. An Israeli court sentenced him to a year's jail sentence in his absence.[13]

It was around this time he had the idea of setting up a radio station on which both Jew and Arab alike could freely air their views.

He purchased a 570-ton Dutch freighter, the *Cito*, built in 1940, which he renamed *Peace*. It was registered in Panama. The ship had been built in Holland and was the very last vessel to get out of the Netherlands in 1940 before the Germans invaded.[14]

Dutch media authority Hans Knot remembers the m.v. *Peace* was his local playground in Groningen.

He recalls: "I was aged 12 and still at school in the early 1960s. In our local harbour were a number of vessels, including the *Zeevaart* and the *Cito* and, with my friends, we used to play on these ships. About ten years later the *Zeevaart* was renamed the *King David* and became Capital Radio off the Dutch coast, and the *Cito* became the m.v. *Peace* and sailed to the Mediterranean. It was very exciting to see these vessels as radio ships much later in my life."

In 1969 the ship sailed from Holland for the United States to be fitted out. She anchored in New York harbour. A 50kW transmitter was installed with a 160ft. aerial. The *Peace* sailed from New York on 16 March 1973. Test transmissions were tried in the Atlantic on 195 metres, 1540 kHz. There were also irregular short-wave broadcasts on 6240 kHz. She arrived in Marseilles in mid-April. The m.v. *Peace* moved around the Middle East coast, from Egypt to the Lebanon to Israel.

Regular programmes began on 26 May 1973. The majority were in English, but some were also broadcast in French, Hebrew and Arabic. The station theme was *Give Peace a Chance* by John and Yoko Lennon. The estimated audience was some 30 million covering Egypt, the Sudan, Syria, Southern Turkey, Greece, Jordan, Damascus, the Lebanon, Israel and Cyprus. Most of the music was western and the station was on air 24 hours a day. Broadcasters came from the United Kingdom, Australia, France, Holland, the United States of America and New Zealand. Special programmes were broadcast in Arabic and Hebrew.

As Abe Nathan said, the object of the

---

12. *Monitor* magazine article by Hans Knot. Spring 1990
13. *Offshore Radio*, Gerry Bishop, p.93

14. *Giving Peace A Chance*, Tony Allan, *Monitor* magazine (undated)

The Voice of Peace ship in the Mediterranean

radio was to try and bring peace to the Middle East. However, shortage of money forced the station off the air in November 1973. She moved to Marseilles.

By May 1975 rumours circulated that enough money had been raised for the ship to begin broadcasting again. Amongst the crew at this time were Bob Noakes, Keith Ashton and Bill Benson. DJ Tony Allan had left in 1973. Test transmissions were heard in the summer of 1975 but no regular programmes were transmitted.

DJs included: Tony Allan, Neil Armstrong, Dave Asher, Chris Ashley, Keith Ashton, Robin Banks (engineer), Malcolm Barry, Alan Bell, Grant Benson, Stephen Bishop, Phil Brice, Tony Britten, Nicolas Chapuis, Rob Charles, Dave Collins, Kas Collins, Peter Craig, Dave Cunningham, Mike Darby, Mike Davis, Terry Davis, Alan Dell, Rick Dennis, Ken Dicken, Paul Eaves, Alan England, Steve Foster, Paul Frasier, Matthew French, Mike Galloway, Steve Gordon, Steve Greenberg, Nigel Grover, Mark Hurrell, Richard Jackson, Tom Hardy, Nigel Harris, Tara Jeffries, John Keaton, Carl Kingston, Alex Lee, Peter Lewis, Norman Lloyd, Tony Mandell, John Macdonald, Steve Marshall, Gavin McCoy, Mike Melbourne,

John Miller, Phil Mitchell, Nathan Morley, Johnny Moss, Vince Mould, Robbie Owen, Kenny Page, Chris Pearson, David Porter, Alan Price, the Black Printz, Peter Quinn, Steve Richards, Alan Roberts, Paul Rogers (aka Dave Collins), James Ross, Steve Rowney, Phil Sayer, Rob Scott (Alan West), Dave Shearer, Bill Sheldrake, Tim Shepherd, Dave Silby, Alex Skinner, Clive St. Clair, Crispian St. John, Guy Starkey, Don Stevens, Tony Stevens, Digby Taylor, Roger Swann, Alan Symonds, Robert Talbot, Cliff Walker, Simon Ward, Steve Williams, Doug Wood, Richard Wood, Keith York and Steve Zodiac (Tom Hardy).

DJs were taken on the *Peace* ship for three months only. Many broadcasters from ILR stations went to work on the vessel, spending three weeks on board and one week ashore. They were paid US$130 a month. Airfare there and back was paid and there was a flat to use when on shore leave.

English captains have included Donald Christie and Len Clements.

16 March 1978: Fifth anniversary of *Peace* ship's first broadcast.

October 1988: The Voice of Peace was joined

by another pirate ship which anchored nearby. Arutz Sheva broadcast programmes of a right wing nature in Hebrew from the m.v. *Hatzvi*.

1 October 1993: The Voice of Peace began her last day of broadcasting. The Knesset had granted a licence for the station to broadcast from land. The station closed down at 1.56pm. The Voice of Peace ship was later towed to the harbour in Tel Aviv where she became a museum for peace in the future.

For the first time in the station's 20-year history, Abe Nathan was seen in a white shirt. Over the years he was always 'the man in black.'

MY SHIP IS COMING IN

FLASHBACK '67
To help celebrate the 10th anniversary of the passing of the Marine Etc., Offences (Broadcasting) Bill, Flashback '67 was organised by Music Radio Productions. It was held at the Centre Airport Hotel, Heathrow, on the weekend of 13-14 August 1977.

Over 40 DJs turned up. On sale were T-shirts, magazines, books, posters and badges. About 700 Free Radio 'anoraks' attended the Convention.

There were film shows featuring Radio London, Radio Northsea International, the Voice of Peace and Radio Caroline with personal presentations by disc jockeys who had worked on those stations.

ZEEZENDERS 20
Organised by Music Radio Promotions (Mike Baron and Nik Oakley) and *Freewave Media* magazine (Dutch), this event was held in the last weekend of July 1978 in Noordwykerhout, Holland, for three days.

Some 750 people attended from Holland, Belgium, Germany, Scandinavia and the United Kingdom. DJs from **all** organisations which had offshore connections attended including the Voice of Peace and Radio Hauraki. MRP did not pay the bill from the hotel and the company was later made bankrupt in England.

Between 1978-1988 there were normally two get-togethers each year for offshore radio fans. Now conventions are held annually at different locations in Holland when DJs, engineers and managers make guest appearances.

DRIFTBACK 20
This convention was held on 15 August 1987 at the Bloomsbury Crest Hotel in London. It celebrated the 20th anniversary of the introduction of the Marine Offences Act 1967. More than 30 former pirate DJs turned up. Also present was founder of Radio Caroline, Ronan O'Rahilly.

A variety of offshore films and videos were shown. A huge display of offshore radio memorabilia was assembled and many 'anoraks' wallowed in nostalgia, looking at old photographs, press cuttings, books, posters, plans and an assortment of other items of interest.

Driftback 20 was organised by the Caroline Movement, which was founded in 1977, having taken its name from the one station which remained part of the offshore radio scene throughout.

Presentation of a Harp Beat Rock Plaque to the Walton and Frinton lifeboat.
Left to Right: John Eagle, Branch President, Robert Oxley, Branch Chairman,
Ronan O'Rahilly, John Peel and Johnnie Walker

PRESENTATION TO WALTON AND FRINTON LIFEBOAT

In February 1991 disc jockeys Tony Blackburn, John Peel and Johnnie Walker, together with Ronan O'Rahilly presented a Harp Beat Rock Plaque to the Walton and Frinton lifeboat.

The inscription on the plaque, funded by Harp Lager, read: "On fourteen logged occasions between 1964 and 1967 the Walton and Frinton lifeboat answered distress calls from pirate ships, Radio Caroline and Radio London.

"Broadcasting from rusty hulks moored 3½ miles from the Essex shoreline, the flamboyant and popular pirates revolutionised music radio in Britain forever and ultimately convinced the fossilised BBC to launch their own contemporary pop music station, Radio 1. Radio Caroline began broadcasting on 28 March 1964 and has continued to broadcast ever since. Radio London commenced broadcasting on 19 December 1964 and ceased broadcasting at 3.00pm on 14 August 1967 when the Marine Etc., Broadcasting (Offences) Act came into effect."

RADIO OFFSHORE MEMORIES

Radio Offshore Memories was granted a licence to broadcast from a ship off IJmuiden, Holland, for the first time in August 1991. It was run by a local station, Radio Plus. Several former DJs from Radios Caroline and Monique took part in the broadcasts. For two days

Offshore Radio, m.v. Galexy, off Walton-on-the-Naze, 1992

they took a ship out to sea to transmit radio programmes. A similar event took place at the end of August 1992 to mark the 18th anniversary of the introduction of the Dutch Marine Offences Act. Disc jockeys who took part included Marc Jacobs, Ad Roberts and Ferry Maat. The Dutch Government would not give its permission for the radio station to broadcast advertisements.

OFFSHORE RADIO

Offshore Radio was the name of a radio station which was given a Restricted Service Licence to broadcast from 1½ miles off Walton-on-the-Naze, Essex, on 1584 kHz AM on a power of 1 watt in August 1992 for 28 days. The station was celebrating the 25th anniversary of the passing of the Marine Offences Act (1967). The air date given by the Radio Authority was 13 August 1992 to 9 September 1992 and the cost of the licence was £650.

Project Galaxy represented the closest that a group of offshore radio enthusiasts would ever get the authorities in the United Kingdom to finally accepting that pirate radio had a part to play in the development of the British broadcasting scene.

In 1980, following the sinking of the *Mi Amigo*, the Caroline Movement was in serious danger of ceasing to exist. John A. Burch was the public relations officer of CM and he had been in touch with several people who were keen to acquire the former Radio London ship, the m.v. *Galaxy*, which had lain derelict in Kiel Harbour in northern Germany. The idea was to purchase the vessel and return her to the UK as a monument to offshore radio. Thus Project Galaxy was bom. The *Galaxy* was not acquired however. As John A. Burch says in his 1993 book *Wheel Turned Full Circle* - 'It seemed that this was one World War II naval vessel that the Germans weren't going to let get away.' The German authorities scrapped the ship in 1987.

Offshore Radio 1584 broadcast from aboard the vessel *Galexy*, which had begun life as a

Tyneside ferry boat in 1940, and was anchored a mile or so offshore. It was a houseboat, once used to ferry enthusiasts to see the m.v. *Ross Revenge* and m.v. *Communicator* at anchor in 'Pirate Alley' in the North Sea. She berthed at Peter's Wharf, Wouldham on the River Medway, and later in the Gravesend Canal Basin in Kent. The *Galexy* was not a misspelling of *Galaxy*. The ship, formerly the *Tyne Princess,* was named by John Burch of the Caroline Movement after Captain Alex Pluck, who was in charge during her 28-day adventure in August 1992 - gALEXy!

Selected programmes from Offshore Radio 1584 were transmitted to 23 different countries via Euronet satellite radio. Nearly 40 helpers took part during its short life.

In addition to broadcasting around the clock, the Caroline Movement also held a convention at the Albion Hotel, Walton-on-the-Naze. The station ceased broadcasting on 9 September 1992. The service had been described both by the organisers and listeners in Essex 'as a great success.'

RADIO CAROLINE

The radio station may be silent on the airwaves but she still sails the waters of Norfolk. Melvyn Johnson was a great fan of the pirates from the 1960s through to the 1990s. As a model fanatic he decided to build a replica of the *Ross Revenge* at his home in Catton, Norwich.

The boat is 45 inches long and has a 4ft. radio mast complete with rigging lines. It took Melvyn, a carpenter, five months to construct the model complete with studio, presenters and miniature records.

The *Ross Revenge* model is wired for sound. He has installed a personal stereo in the hold. There are two speakers and an amplifier which are controlled by a hand-held control set which is also used to steer the vessel. As the *Ross Revenge* sails the lakes of Norfolk parks he plays tapes of old Radio Caroline and London programmes featuring the voices of Tony Blackburn and Keith Skues.

Melvyn Johnson also built a model of the *Mi Amigo* but, like the original it, too, has gone to a watery grave.

In March 1993 he attended the 29th birthday party of Radio Caroline in Dover where the *Ross Revenge* was docked, and showed his working model of the *Ross Revenge* to many pirate fans who attended the celebrations.

OFFSHORE RADIO, THE FUTURE:

Is there a future for offshore radio? If a new ship appeared in the North Sea broadcasting a diet of music not currently heard on either BBC or ILR, what would be her chances of surviving?

Says the DTI: "Should any radio ship begin transmitting in breach of the amended Marine Etc.. Broadcasting (Offences) Act 1967 and Broadcasting Act 1990, then the nature and extent of the Radio Communications Agency's response would be considered at the time and in the light of the facts as they may be."

In January 1994 former Caroline DJ Paul Graham, who worked on the *Ross Revenge* in 1987, and helped with Project Galaxy, said: "Pirate radio has had its day. It did what it had to do and did it well. Long may it rest in peace!"

Chapter Fourteen

THIS COULD BE THE LAST TIME

Well this could be the last time
This could be the last time
Maybe the last time
I don't know. Oh no. Oh No

The Last Time, Rolling Stones, 1965

THE SUBJECT OF pirate radio will not just lie down and die. Forty years plus after Radio Caroline began broadcasting on Good Friday 1964 there is still much interest amongst a certain band of radio enthusiasts.

Pirate radio means different things to different people. In this book we have dealt with stations surrounded by water and broadcasting from international waters either on a ship or from an old wartime fort.

Today it is impossible to set up a pirate radio station and broadcast from offshore as the authorities would pounce as soon as any signal was received on land.

Radio Caroline continued broadcasting from the *Ross Revenge* until 1990 whereas in Europe there were only two short-lived offshore stations during this decade. Radio Brod broadcast from aboard the 1986 Glasgow-built *Droit de Parole*. The ship, staffed by a group of seven well-known journalists from the former Yugoslavia, operated in international waters in the Adriatic Sea from 7 April 1993 to 28 February 1994. Offshore 98, a one-weekend-only venture appeared at Easter 1999. The station allegedly broadcast off the coast of Holland, although on-air references said they were in international waters west of the isle of Heligoland.

The ship transmitted on long, medium and short waves and was run by a group of radio anoraks. It never anchored but was on the move all the time. The ship went under the name m.v. *Morning Star*, but its real name was the m.v. *Aurora*.

Away from the British Isles and Europe we heard the Voice of Peace which broadcast in Hebrew, Arabic and English aboard the m.v. *Peace*. Owner Abe Nathan's aim for the station was to promote peace in the Middle East. The Israeli Government tolerated the station for many years, but once they signed the Oslo Peace Agreement, Abe Nathan decided his aims had been achieved and the radioship was sunk in international waters on 28 November 1993. Abe, a former World War II RAF fighter pilot, died at the Ichilov hospital in Tel Aviv, 27 August 2008, aged 81 years.

There is a daily Voice of Peace show on the Israeli local commercial radio station Radius 100FM between 1700-1900 everyday with former VoP DJs presenting.

Arutz Sheva, aboard the m.v. *Hatzvi* anchored off the coast of Tel Aviv, transmitted on

Arutz Sheva broadcast from the m.v. Hatzvi. In November 2003 the ship left its anchorage off the Tel Aviv coast to be scrapped in Turkey

918kHz on the AM band. They later broadcast on 1143AM (main AM frequency) and 711AM (religious broadcasts). Their main FM frequency was 105.2. They also broadcast on 98.7FM (religious broadcasts) and 87.3FM (foreign languages). The station was described as positive, free from controversy and very Israeli and something for which the public apparently yearned. Over the years Arutz Sheva created a listening revolution with its diet of Israeli music, Hebrew-only lyrics and soft-sell patriotism. However many would say that Arutz Sheva was without doubt a right-wing settlers' station, and it can be said that it was the only offshore radio station in the world which had mainly dedicated political aims.

Israeli police and Communications Ministry personnel raided the radio ship at 1.00pm on 24 December 2002 and stopped transmissions. The police took photographs of radio personnel and their equipment, but confiscated nothing. The ship's captain was warned not to resume transmission of the broadcasts. The raid ended at 2.15pm. Allegedly it was the first time in the history of Israeli offshore broadcasting – including 22 years of Abe Nathan's Voice of Peace ship and 15 years of Arutz Sheva broadcasts – that the police have ever made such a raid. The radio station said that not even under the Governments of Yitzhak Rabin, Shimon Perez or Ehud Barak were police ever sent to raid a ship broadcasting from outside Israel's territorial waters. Nevertheless the station kept on broadcasting until 20 October 2003.

Mike Brand is an Israeli offshore radio expert who has lived in Israel for over 30 years and challenges if the ships were in international waters. He says: EVERY offshore station that has broadcast off the coast of Israel has ALWAYS broadcast WITHIN Israel's territorial waters. This has been the silent agreement of the Government, Defence Ministry and the Ministry of Communications. This was necessary because of Israel's security needs. The Israeli navy has to know where every Israeli vessel is anchored, so if any terrorist vessel approaches they will know about it. The offshore stations (and there have been eight of them!), were in fixed positions, and the Israeli navy knew exactly where they were."

The *Israel Insider* daily news magazine (website: www.israelinsider.com) reported on 21 October 2003 ten managers, directors and broadcasters of Arutz Sheva, were convicted by a Jerusalem court of illegal broadcasting. Following the court decision, Arutz Sheva went off the air, but its broadcasts and reporting will continue on the internet. The court ruling came one day after the Government lent its support to a proposed law that would fine advertisers on pirate radio stations.

The website continued: "In a case that had been pending for five years, the court ruled that Arutz Sheva's operators had transmitted from a boat within Israeli territorial waters and from locations in the West Bank without the required Government permits during the years 1995-1998. The court also convicted station director Ya'acov Katz (Ketzaleh) on two counts of perjury after it was proven "beyond a shadow of a doubt" that he gave false testimony in affidavits stating that the station broadcast from a ship outside Israel's territorial waters......In February 1999, the Knesset passed a law formally licensing Arutz Sheva. On 26 March 2002, the High Court of Justice deemed the Knesset law null and void. It ruled that the special Arutz Sheva law harmed the country's 'rule of law' as well as the 'freedom of occupation' of potential competitors."

The m.v. Hof. Conditions on board the 91 ft vessel were claimed to be cramped. Taken from Israeli newspaper "Yediot Ahronot"

The *Hatzvi* (the deer, a traditional symbol of Israel) was much larger than most radio ships, but was broken up in 2003. Arutz Sheva may have the distinction of being the world's last-ever offshore radio station.

Other offshore stations in the Middle East included: Radio 1 aboard the m.v. *Polaris* off Haifa (1991) and Radio Hof aboard m.v. *Hof* (1993). There had been talk that the station was looking at using the m.v. *Ross Revenge*, but the idea was turned down when it was realised the ship did not have air conditioning. Eventually the m.v. *Hof* was set up as a radio station, but conditions on board were described as cramped and the studio was built from domestic and disco equipment. The station's main audience was teenagers, and many of the programmes were filled with music interspersed with teenagers calling in "on air" to send greetings to their friends. DJs were young and inexperienced and usually Israeli ex-disco DJs. At best, the station sounded very amateurish. Radio 1 is now broadcasting legally as Radio Haifa 107.5FM

Radio Hof began broadcasting in August 1993. The station manager, Barouk Ben David, said that the same commercial mistakes the Voice of Peace had made would not be repeated by his station, the advertising staff were American trained and understood how to sell "air time". The Voice of Peace ceased broadcasting on 1 October 1993 and all former staff were offered positions with Radio Hof. All personnel turned down the offer.

On 7 March 1994 rough weather caused the m.v. *Hof* to drift to a position off the coast of Herzlia, where the ship later ran aground. Rescue crews attended the stricken ship and were surprised when they found only two people on board, the captain and another crew member. This raised suspicion with officials at the Communication Ministry that broadcasts were not coming from the ship, but from a studio on land. The station manager was sacked after this incident.

The remaining staff operated Radio Hof as an unlicensed station, but transmitted on very low power. The station was raided at least twice and after December 1995 was never heard of again.

Radio Dan aboard the m.v. *Kajun* off the coast of Tel Aviv (1995) transmitted on 88.5 MHz FM and broadcast from the same ship as Radio Galei Hayam Hatichon, (Mediterranean Waves) although neither station referred to the other on air. Radio Dan broadcast continuous music with the occasional jingle. Within a month of transmissions beginning, the ship was raided by officials from the Ministry of Communications. They accused the broadcasters of transmitting from within Israeli territorial waters. Both radio stations were closed down and in November 1995 the m.v. *Kajun* ran aground and was badly damaged.

Arutz 2000 began test transmissions in August 1996 from aboard the m.v. *King David* off Jaffa Point, south of Tel Aviv. Pinchas Cohen and Nissim Avigdor, as part owners, raised funds to set up an offshore radio station. Five years previously, in 1995, the former Trinity Lightship number 3 was purchased by a scrapyard for £20,000. It was then sold to Dutch agents, headed by Herbert Visser, for £30,000 and the ship was taken for conversion to the Harry Pound scrapyard, Whale Island, near Portsmouth.

A Rhode and Schwartz FM transmitter was purchased from the German state broadcaster NDR (Nord Deutscher Rundfunk). A 20,000 watt AM Telefunken transmitter was also purchased.

The m.v. King David aground on the coast of Israel

By the end of 1995 the lightship had been painted white, aerial mast sections were stored on the rear deck and conversion work restarted inside the lightship. Ownership had now transferred to a Mauritius-based company named Blackbeard/Bluebeard who renamed the ship *King David*. It was allegedly registered in Panama.

On 6 January 2000 Mike Brand reported that the m.v. *King David* ran aground in heavy storms that hit Israel the previous day. He and a colleague Martin van der Ven had visited the ship in November 1999 when she appeared to have been abandoned with only two crew members on board. "Because of bad weather the ship's antenna had been ripped off its base, and the ship ran aground on a Tel Aviv beach", he said "so the world has only one fully-operational true offshore station – Arutz Sheva – which today continues to broadcast through the internet." Mike went down to the beach to take pictures of what was left of the *King David*. On 6 January 2000 the m.v. *King David*, ran aground in heavy storms on Tel Barach beach, south of Tel Aviv

On 30 August 2000 the *Haaretz* newspaper reported that the *King David* was towed out to sea and sunk at a cost to the state of hundreds of thousands of shekels. The ship had been a safety hazard, with children climbing aboard and diving into the water. Police were unable to locate the owners of the vessel. The work of towing and sinking the ship was carried out by the Shipping Authority in conjunction with the Environment Ministry.

Offshore Television

Syd TV was a short-lived offshore TV station that broadcast on UHF channel 41. It was the sister radio station of Radio Syd and broadcast from the m.v. *Cheeta II* anchored off the coast in the late 1950s.

TV Nordzee broadcast on VHF channel 11 from the REM Island, an artificial platform which had been built in Ireland and towed to a position six miles off the Dutch coastline of Noordwijk. The TV station, along with its sister radio station, was taken off the air by a sea and air raid by the armed forces of the Netherlands.

Tower TV broadcast on Channel 5 from Sunk Head Tower 10 miles off the Essex coast. To this day there is controversy as to whether or not the station actually went on air. It is alleged that the first transmission report was recorded on land at 4.20am on 9 November 1965. The transmitter only had a power of 10 watts.

The fort was built as an heavily armed early warning defence platform in World War II, designed by Guy Maunsell. Construction was undertaken by the Posford Company at Red Lion Wharf, Gravesend in Kent on the River Thames.

It was planned that the television station would be on air for about three hours each evening after BBC and ITV had closed down. It would cover a radius of about 25 miles and show old films, cartoons, local news and play commercials.

Television transmissions were supposed to have begun on 9 November 1965 at a power of 10 watts, using equipment built by George Short and a home made antenna system 119ft high on top of the fort. The local newspaper the *East Essex Gazette* reported that a blurred test card was seen by viewers on Channel 5 (VHF 405 lines) at Walton-on-the-Naze. The reports were unsubstantiated and may have been part of the publicity drive by Tower Television themselves. Now that over 40 years have elapsed since the transmissions were to be aired, with no-one willing to go on record having seen the television transmission it would appear unlikely that any broadcasts ever took place.

Paul Greenwald became obsessed with the idea of running his own TV station. The problem was that private radio and TV stations were banned in Israel. However, encouraged by the success of the 'Voice of Peace', he began to seek out backers for his proposed offshore TV station.

By 1980 Greenwald had purchased a ship, the m.v. *Odelia*, in Greece that had been built in 1958. He made an agreement with Nestor Pierrakios that he could become a partner in Odelia TV. Pierrakios had the ship renovated and manned it with a crew from his own firm, for a cost of about £250,000.

The following year the ship sailed to Israel and anchored about four miles offshore, and within sight of the Voice of Peace ship. A message was sent by the Israeli authorities to Odelia TV not to begin broadcasting. This advice was ignored. The test transmission went ahead in June 1981 and was successful with reception possible up to 25 miles inland.

In July 1981 the Israeli Government submitted a hastily proposed bill to outlaw the pirates. This was passed by the end of November 1981 and the Anti-Offshore law came into force. Odelia TV temporarily closed down. The following month on 9 December Israeli Police visited the ship and extensively photographed the studio and technical set-up as well as the ship's antenna. Two days before Christmas the ship set sail for Cyprus, to take on fresh supplies, never to be heard of again.

During the 1980s large numbers of pirate TV stations operated in Italy, Greece, Spain and Israel. Subsequent legislation led to the licensing of many of these stations and the closure of most of the remainder.

Radio New York International broadcast from the m.v. *Sarah* off the New York coast for a short time in summer 1987. It was raided on 25 July 1987 when a US Coastguard cutter armed with machine guns came alongside and demanded to board the radio ship. A number of US officials requested broadcasting to cease with immediate effect. Two days later RNYI began further test transmissions. The crew on board the *Sarah* were greeted by a further visit of US officials aboard another US Coastguard cutter. Armed officals boarded the *Sarah* and announced they were seizing the radio ship and arresting those on board. The three crew members were brought before a court but all charges against them were dropped. A further attempt to broadcast was made the following year, but was stopped by a legal restraining order. The station, however, continued its short wave presence into the 1990s by hiring airtime on US international broadcasters such as WRNO, WBCQ and WWCR, and Costa Rican RFPI.

A group of Chinese dissidents later planned to hire the m.v. *Sarah* and sail her to a position off the Chinese coast and air pro-democracy broadcasts. This failed to come about, but a European, mainly French-based Chinese group, put together the Goddess of Democracy project, whose ship got as far as Taiwan before falling foul of politics.

In Australia, due to strictly controlled allocation of broadcasting frequencies and tough legislative penalties, including jail, nothing happened in international waters. However, this did not stop many DJs from Australia coming over to the UK in the 1960s and making a name for themselves on British pirate radio stations.

As we learned in Chapter One, pirate radio from ships has been around for more than 80 years. In the year 2008 papers were published by the Imperial War Museum that suggested that the James Bond creator Ian Fleming, a commander in the Royal Navy, thought of broadcasting from a ship in 1939 at the beginning of World War II.

Flemimg was recruited by Rear Admiral John Godfrey, Head of Naval Intelligence, to work as his assistant. This allowed him a bird's-eye view into the world of intelligence.

One of Fleming's recommendations during the early months of the war was to locate a pirate radio ship in the North Sea pretending to be a German radio station and beam subversive propaganda to the German Navy. However, the War Office at the time did not go along with his suggestion.

Two years later a friend of Ian Fleming who was a British propaganda specialist helped to organise the *Atlantic Sender* to begin broadcasts. This was run by the Political Warfare Executive, a British clandestine body created to produce and disseminate black propaganda with the aim of damaging enemy morale. It is believed they broadcast from land and had no ship! However there was an offshore station run from a small steam-driven coal-fired fishing cutter, British registered with a crew of six, plus one broadcaster and a radio technician. The offshore station was called Sender der Deutschen Freiheitspartei (German Freedom Party Radio) and broadcast from January to 13 April 1938 on 29.8 and 38.25 metres, short-wave band. The broadcasts were made by the Deutsche Freiheitspartei (DFP, German Freedom Party), a strongly conspiratorial group formed in 1936 in London and Paris by exiled Germans from the democratic parties of the centre in the pre-Hitler Reichstag.

The announcements were: 'This is the radio of the German Freedom Party.' Then followed news, a press review (of the international press), a commentary and various items of information. Broadcast periods of thirty minutes interrupted regularly by the announcement, 'This is the radio of the German Freedom Party', with the wave length and times of the broadcast (daily from 7.30-8.00pm and from 10.00-10.30pm). The broadcasts continued for three months and were then abandoned.

Mark Stafford began his radio career in the 1970s and has worked for Atlanta Radio, the International service of Radio Boulogne, EKR, Radio Caroline's satellite service and various RSLs in this country. In August 2008 it came to his notice that Caroline House in Chesterfield Gardens, London had a link with MI5 double agent Kim Philby who defected to the Russians in 1963. Mark contacted Jon Myer of the Pirate Hall of Fame website and Mary Payne of the Radio London website and between them they found out that the previous owner and occupier, before Caroline moved in, was a Spanish-speaking officer with MI5, Tomás 'Tommy' Harris. Kim Philby was a personal friend and made regular visits to 6 Chesterfield Gardens. Harris, who was also an artist and an art dealer, was born in 1908 and died on 27 January 1964 in Majorca at the age of 56 years. His death in a road traffic accident was alleged to have been in mysterious circumstances.

Today one can take part in a 'Spies and Spycatchers' London' walk which includes 6 Chesterfield Gardens. One wonders if Caroline House was still bugged when Radio Caroline took possession in 1964.

It is impossible to list every single offshore-connected happening around the world since 1994 when the first edition of *Pop Went the Pirates* was published. We shall look at a general list of events and follow up with a selected number of anniversaries and reunions that raised particular interest at the time. There are updated photographs of some of the original pirates, many of whom are still broadcasting either in this country or in Australia, Canada or the United States of America.

OFFSHORE PIRATE RADIO - THE POST 1990 ERA

Tom Read is a mathematics teacher, musician and writer. He holds the position of Head of Mathematics at Brownhills Maths & Computing College in Stoke-on-Trent, plays bass guitar in function bands all over the North of England, and writes radio-related articles for publications including *Radcom, Practical Wireless, Radio User, Short Wave Magazine, Radio*

Active, *Communication* (BDXC) and *oMonitor* (ISWL). He also collaborated on the *Trailblazer Pennine Way* guidebook after completing the long distance trail in 2006. Tom is also a licensed radio amateur with callsign M1EYP. He is regularly heard with portable operations from the mountains and hills of the UK as part of the SOTA - Summits on the Air programme, of which Tom also serves on the Management Team. He lives in Macclesfield, Cheshire and is married to Marianne with two sons, Jimmy (who is also a licensed radio amateur, callsign M3EYP) and Liam.

Tom has prepared a detailed list of Restricted Service Licence stations linked to offshore radio that have operated from 1990 to the present day.

The original commercial pirate for England, Radio Caroline, defied the Marine Etc Broadcasting (Offences) Act of 1967 by continuing broadcasting beyond 14 August of that year. It managed to maintain an intermittent presence through the 70s and 80s. However, it was the 1990s that saw British commercial radio revolutionised again, Radio Caroline given its sternest challenges, and a surprising and refreshing new brand of offshore radio by the end of the decade, including some of those famous names not heard since 1967.

Caroline's live programmes on 558 kHz MW from the *Ross Revenge*, anchored in international waters in the North Sea, were heard regularly around the UK and Europe in 1990. Committed radio "DXers" and nostalgic enthusiasts would skilfully orient their portable radios or even configure more sophisticated communications receivers and outdoor wire aerials, still putting up with variable reception quality in order to listen to Radio Caroline. By June of 1990, the new wave of 'incremental' radio stations were appearing, and in what was arguably a confrontational move by the then Independent Broadcasting Authority (IBA), Spectrum Radio was allocated the frequency of 558 kHz – Caroline's frequency! During Spectrum's pre-launch test transmissions, Caroline broadcast its complaints of "deliberate interference by the DTI" as both stations battled it out on 558 kHz. Spectrum threatened the IBA with legal action, and was hastily assigned 990kHz as a parallel frequency. On the date of Spectrum Radio's official launch of a full programme service, 25 June 1990, Radio Caroline vacated the 558 kHz frequency.

Caroline made short returns on 558 with brief tests on 8 July and was on-air between 1500 and 1630 hours on Sunday 19 August. More substantial was the full programming from 10 to 16 September. Good signals were reported by many, but this was one of Caroline's last fleeting appearances on 558kHz. There followed broadcasting on 819 kHz from 4 October to 5 November, and further short-lived attempts to get back on the air in 1991, but these would be the last times most listeners tuned in to Radio Caroline as an illegal offshore pirate station. On 5 November 1990, Neil Gates' nighttime programme was Radio Caroline's final one from international waters!

Following storms, power failures and rescues, the *Ross Revenge* was unmanned in the North Sea between the 10 and 14 December 1990. The 1990

Peter Moore

Broadcasting Bill then became law, extending considerably the powers of the authorities and seeming the final nail in the coffin for a beleaguered Caroline. However, the Caroline management led by Peter Moore, and its supporters ensured that with determination and no little innovation, Caroline maintained its media profile throughout the next decade.

Varied and diverse methods of broadcasting were used, including Restricted Service Licences (RSL) from the Radio Authority (now Ofcom), on both FM and MW, satellite delivery, relays via short wave transmitters in Ireland, USA and England, and Internet webcasting.: A summary follows; this includes all events of which the writer is aware, but may not be exhaustive

26 March – 12 April 1991	Astra satellite
27 November 1991	Intelsat satellite
22 January 1992	via Radiofax, Ireland on 6205 and 12255 kHz short wave
7 April – 4 May 1992	RSL in Dover on 101.8 FM
19 April 1992	relayed over Astra satellite by QEFM between 1 and 5am
weekends 1992+	via Irish short wave transmitters on 6305/6295 kHz
25 August – 7 Sept. 1992	RSL in Chatham, Kent on 101.4 FM
16 May – 12 June 1994	RSL, Burnham-on-Crouch on 87.7 FM
10 Dec. 1994 – 6 Jan. 1995	RSL on River Blackwater near Bradwell, Essex
7 August – 4 Sept. 1995	RSL from North Sea, 1½ miles off Clacton, 1503 MW
6 October – 2 Nov. 1995	RSL from London Docklands on 87.7 FM
30 May – 26 June 1996	RSL in Chatham on 107.4 FM
17 Nov. – 14 Dec. 1996	RSL in Bristol on 106.6 FM
9 – 31 August 1997	RSL from *Ross Revenge* off Isle of Sheppey, on 1278 MW
regular Wednesdays 1998	Programmes via Merlin (ex-BBC) SW transmitters
14 June – 11 July 1998	RSL in Queenborough on 1503 MW
14 August 1998	Ronan O'Rahilly and Johnnie Walker on 3955 short wave (Merlin).
Nov. (and earlier?)1998	Sunday programming via EKR over Astra 1C satellite
from 20 February 1999	9am-9pm Saturdays/Sundays via Astra 1C satellite
25 July – 21 August 1999	RSL from *Ross Revenge*, Southend Pier on 1503 MW
weekends 2000	via Astra satellite (to 31/3/01), 6305 SW (unofficial) and webcast
1 – 28 October 2000	RSL from LV*18*, Harwich Harbour on 1503 MW
from 1 May 2001	via Sky Digital, programmes from Maidstone studio
mid-late 2001	via WBCQ (USA) on shortwave and Ireland (unofficial) on MW
2 - 3 February 2002	via Latvia on 945kHz
23 - 24 February 2002	via Latvia on 576kHz
August 2002 to present	via Worldspace, also Eurobird satellite and online, via Radio Monique website, and via iPhone 3G. Worldspace closed down in November 2008.
29 Feb – 27 March 2004	RSL from boat in Bristol City Docks, 87.7MHz FM.
7 Aug – 3 Sept. 2004	RSL from *Ross Revenge*, Tilbury Docks, 1278kHz AM
from August 2005	via Apple FM, Sky channel 913, weekdays 1200-1400.
12 June 2006 to present	via Sky Digital channel 0199, via Radio Monique website, and via iPhone 3G
Current	Live streaming via radiocaroline.co.uk
Current	via NTL Ireland, Dublin area, channel 927
Current	Weekends, via The Rock of Riveria, San Remo, Italy, on 88.4MHz

This, without doubt, represents a most impressive endeavour to keep Caroline alive. However, the management had been accused by some of abandoning its ideals of free radio and Loving Awareness by paying the RSL licence fees - which may, in turn, have allegedly funded Radiocommunications Agency raids on land-based pirate radio stations broadcasting at that time. Caroline was not the only organisation to arrange broadcasting events with an offshore flavour. Here is a list of all the others through the same period of which the writer is knowledgeable:

RADIO CAROLINE SALES
*148 GRANGE ROAD, RAMSGATE,
KENT, CT11 9PR, ENGLAND, UK.*

Dear, TOM.

I can verify that the reception report you sent recently is correct, Thank you for your interest in the worlds most famous Radio Station.

Best Wishes,

John Knight.

John Knight. Radio Caroline Sales.

Radio Caroline
RECEPTION VERIFICATION

DATE: 15TH AUGUST 1999.

LIVE FROM THE RADIO SHIP. ROSS REVENGE, MOORED AT SOUTHEND PIER.

1503 Khz/Power   / KW

Time: 12·03 to 12·28 BST.

PLEASE, NEVER FORGET, RADIO WASN'T RADIO BEFORE CAROLINE

QSL card received from Radio Caroline when it was moored at Southend Pier

Radio Caroline moored at Southend Pier 1999

Above: Offshore Radio poster
August-September 1992

Below: Radio England July-August 1999

13 August – 9 Sept. 1992	Offshore 1584 RSL, m.v. *Galexy*, 1½ miles off Walton, also satellite
18 July – 14 August 1997	Radio London RSL, m.v. *Yeoman Rose*, off Frinton, 1134 kHz MW
17 Dec. 1997-13 Jan. 1998	Radio London RSL, m.v. *Ocean Defender*, St Katharine's Dock, London,1503 kHz MW
4 – 31 July 1998	Radio London (Big L) RSL in Harlow on 87.7 FM
19 Dec. 1998 – 8 Jan. 1999	Radio Atlantis RSL, *Ross Revenge*, off Sheerness on 1503 MW
18 July – 14 August 1999	Radio England RSL, in Cheshunt, Herts on 1566 MW
3 – 31 August 1999	Radio Northsea International RSL, LV*18*, off Holland-on-Sea, 1575
21 – 31 August 1999	Radio Veronica, landbased from Hilversum on 1224MW
11 April – 8 May 2000	Radio Northsea International RSL, LV*18*, Harwich,1575kHz and 'net
1 – 28 August 2000	Radio London RSL, caravan on Clacton Pier, on 1143 kHz MW
31 March – 27 April 2001	Radio Mi Amigo RSL, LV*18*/Mebo 3, Harwich, 1503 kHz MW
3 – 30 June 2001	Radio Northsea International RSL, LV*18*, Harwich, 1503 kHz MW
4 – 31 August 2001	Radio London RSL from Clacton-on-Sea on 1134 kHz MW
8 Aug. - 5 Sept. 2002	Radio Mi Amigo RSL, LV*18*, Harwich Harbour, 1503kHz MW
10 – 17 April 2004	Pirate BBC Essex, LV*18*, Harwich, on 729, 765 and 1530kHz MW
15 – 18 April 2004	Radio Noordzee International, special broadcast from NL Radio 192
1 Sept. - 23 Nov. 2004	Super Station RSL, m.v. *Communicator*, Orkneys, 105.4FM and 'net
from 21 March 2005	Big L / Radio London International, test programmes on Sky Digital
26 March 2005	Pirate BBC Essex, *Ross Revenge*, 729, 765 and 1530MW and FM
14 May 2005 to present	Big L 1395 MW, studios Frinton-on-Sea, transmitter in Netherlands
14 – 23 July 2007	Red Sands Radio RSL, Thames Estuary, 1278kHz MW
9 - 14 August 2007	Pirate BBC Essex, LV*18*, Harwich, on 729, 765 and 1530kHz MW
4 - 13 July 2008	Red Sands Radio RSL, Thames Estuary, 1278kHz MW

Such was the demand from listeners, whether it be backlash or nostalgia, and the accompanying enthusiasm of broadcasters and sponsors, that the 1990s, especially the last three years, saw this remarkable revival of offshore pirate broadcasting to the English mainland. Except, that these projects were not pirates as such, broadcasting with Radio Authority licences from within UK territorial waters – or even closer to home than that! Enthusiasm from listeners, broadcasters, advertisers and project organisers alike continued, and events still occurred periodically into the new millennium. The most remarkable player on this stage turned out to be the BBC itself, putting on arguably the most successful, high profile and best received offshore commemoration projects of them all between 2004 and 2007.

Radio Caroline is in some ways, the 'odd man out' (or should that be 'odd Lady out'?) here, it being a current, ongoing, and hopefully continuing project as a 'cutting-edge' commercial rock music station. The others of course are quite the reverse, being nostalgia-based commemorations. One of the first such projects was Offshore 1584, from the m.v. *Galexy*. This ship's name was not incorrectly spelt; rather more of a tribute to its skipper – called Alex! Devised and organised by the Caroline Movement and Project Galaxy, a Restricted Service Licence was operated for 28 days from the vessel previously used to transport sightseeing anoraks out to catch a glimpse of the *Ross Revenge*, and the Laser 558's m.v. *Communicator*. An offshore convention took place in Walton-on-the-Naze within the broadcast dates.

August 1997 saw a major project, as Essex-based businessman Ray Anderson was granted an Restricted Service Licence (RSL) to broadcast as Radio London from the m.v. *Yeoman Rose* anchored one mile off Frinton-on-Sea. Ray Anderson's own business – East Anglian Productions, specialising in nostalgia, recordings and jingles from the original offshore era – was based in premises in Frinton-on-Sea. The frequency used was 1134 kHz, the current European medium wave channel closest to Big L's original wavelength of 266m. Indeed, the station was announcing '266' on-air, as well as having it painted on the side of the ship.

For those with a liking for 'free radio', or with nostalgic leanings towards that 1964 to 1967 period, Radio London 266 programmes were proving to be excellent, quite irresistible listening. The studio was authentically equipped with turntables for vinyl records and cartridge players for jingles and local advertisements. The presenters adopted the tone and pace of the original 1960s Radio London, and indeed, several of them were original presenters – Mark Roman, Ed Stewart, Tony Brandon, Keith Skues, Pete Brady and Dave Cash. These presenters were often to be heard describing the prevailing weather conditions out at sea, comparing them and recounting events from thirty years ago. Faithful to the original Radio London format, the news was carried on the half-hour, every hour.

Boat trips were available from the pier in Walton-on-the-Naze, allowing members of the public to sail out, climb aboard the radioship, and enjoy a tour of the m.v. *Yeoman Rose* and Big L studio. During the broadcast dates – 18 July to 14 August 1997 – other linked events took place, including a lifeboat/helicopter air/sea rescue demonstration, compèred by Keith Skues. The cabaret for the Staff Reunion/Summer of Love Party Night included Keith West, performer of the Big L classic *Excerpt From A Teenage Opera*.

This area of north-east Essex proved to be a popular magnet for further RSL commemorations of former offshore pirates. Of course, this was the very coast off which the majority of radioships and forts were situated back in the 1960s, but the area enjoys above average sunshine and good weather generally, as well as being home to the National Television and Wireless Museum in the port of Harwich. The museum is housed in a former lighthouse and features old televisions and radio sets, and a huge collection of offshore pirate radio memorabilia. Many enthusiasts would combine these factors to enjoy a camping holiday to coincide with one or more of the commemorative broadcasts. Those who managed to plan their holiday best were able to be in the area between 9 and 14 August 1997. A Radio Caroline RSL broadcast commenced off the Isle of Sheppey on the 9 August, while the Radio London event was due to end at 3.00pm on the 14 August – exactly 30 years after its original closedown. A few lucky holidaymakers, as well as local residents around the Essex and Kent coasts, were able to enjoy six days during which both Radio Caroline and Radio London were broadcasting from the North Sea, for the first time since 1967.

As the summer of 1999 approached, the news was starting to look very interesting again. This time, there were to be no fewer than three stations on-air, with Radio Caroline, Radio England and Radio Northsea International all broadcasting under restrictive service licences in August. The Radio England RSL took place from a static caravan in Cheshunt, Hertfordshire, so nowhere near the coast, detracting somewhat from any offshore flavour! However, the jingles and programming were clearly intended to be more faithful to that era. Loud and clear on 1566kHz in the North London area, DJ Debs presented 60s music interspersed with the famous Radio England jingles - "Remember, these golden classics... Swinging Radio England" and "The fastest thing in the air, Swinging Radio England". Regular advertisements for Cheshunt businesses and Radio England T-shirts were also carried.

The Radio England operation was housed in a static caravan outside Animal Fayre on Rags Lane. The studio and DJ were in the right-hand end of the caravan, with the other members of the team in lounge and kitchen areas getting through plenty of cigarettes and coffee! As well as the presenter Debs, other station personnel present included Mike Stevens, Steve James, Alec Hilton and Anthony Rogers.

Into the county of Essex in August 1999, both Radio Caroline 1503 (Southend). and Radio Northsea International 1575 (Holland-on-Sea) were loud and clear. Caroline was carrying rock music, advertisements for local Southend businesses and the Caroline Support Group Netherlands and trademark announcements such as "Ladies and gentlemen, the legend lives on – this is Caroline". RNI, as was the case on all its broadcasting to which I was tuned, carried an authentic 1970 format with music from that era from the original playlists.

From the boathouse at Holland-on-Sea, it was possible to buy tickets (£10 each) for the tender across to the LV18 "Mebo III". On the same tender as this visitor, was former BBC Radio 1 and television presenter Mike Read. Mike was going out to the radioship for a few days to present some programmes, his first ever offshore broadcasting. Mike recalled with affection the old Radio 1 roadshows at nearby Clacton-on-Sea. Punters were allowed to climb the rope ladder out of the tender, up the side of the LV18 and on to the deck. They were then treated to a full and detailed tour of the vessel and its radio equipment

There were two electricity generators on board, one for the studio and one for the transmitter. Working as a crew member on-board was Stuart Dobson, who was the last man to be winched from the *Ross Revenge* as it floundered on the notorious Goodwin Sands on 19 November 1991. Tuning into RNI on 1575kHz MW, it was possible to listen to Mike Read's début offshore radio programme, in which he recalled listening to RNI in the 70s himself. In later years Mike was heard in the north-west, presenting Jazz FM Manchester's breakfast programme, and winding up with the latest Ray Anderson project Big L 1395, presented from studios in Frinton-on-Sea.

On one of the broadcast days in August 1999, a large electrical storm hit the Essex coast, and both Radio Northsea International's and Radio Caroline's masts were struck by lightning. There was a period in the afternoon where both stations were off-air as a result, and further comparisons and reminiscences to the 1960s were inevitable when the stations returned to air. Caroline's ship, the *Ross Revenge* was moored at the end of Southend-on-Sea's 2.1km-long pier, thankfully served by a railway! It looked splendid, illuminated against the night sky. It actually came to the rescue on the day of the storm, when the entire electrical supply for Southend Pier was lost and Radio Caroline stepped in and powered the pier from its own generator for a few hours.

Enthusiasts going on to the *Ross Revenge* radioship and following the signs down to the mess room were met by presenter Jim Ross and crew member Bob. Sightseers were touched by how very welcome they were made to feel by the Caroline crew. Jim explained that he was originally a Caroline supporter, an increasingly active member of the Ross Revenge Support Group and ultimately now presenting the 'graveyard shift' on the Ross itself. The charge for coming on to the Radio Caroline ship was just £3, with the children free. Quite a difference to the £10 per ticket shelled out on RNI earlier, although that was contributing to RNLI funds and so couldn't be begrudged.

The tour of the ship, enthusiastically led by Jim Ross, was both lengthy and detailed. The 'punters' were shown around the transmitter, generator, engine room, galley, bridge, decks and modulator. Next was the famous Caroline record library and then the studios. There were three studios, with the first being occupied by DJ Sarah Miles who was on air at that time, playing Alice Cooper and other similar hard rock music. The second studio, adjacent to the first, looked to be similarly equipped and of a comparable size. This was the standby, back-up and link studio, and provided the opportunity for members of the public to be photographed in a Caroline studio on the Ross! A third and much smaller studio was pointed out, this being the one used to play the religious programmes of World Mission Radio, broadcast during daytimes on 6215 kHz short wave back in 1989. After midnight, this HF channel then used to put out three hours of Radio Caroline programmes. The final component to the *Ross Revenge* tour was the opportunity to purchase memorabilia from the on-board souvenir shop. An excellent tour, and Caroline presented itself extremely well.

After the excitement of 1999, the offshore scene settled back into its more usual mode of relative inactivity for a while. Radio Caroline was broadcasting regularly via Astra digital satellite and the internet, while Radio London was rocking in a caravan at the end of Clacton Pier in the summer of 2000. Further projects from the LV*18* at Harwich were being planned, to be broadcast under the names of Radio Mi Amigo and Radio Northsea International, both using 1503 kHz medium-wave. The Radio London RSL event of August 2001 was not quite so spectacular this time around, broadcasting from a hut on Clacton Pier. The frequency was again 1134kHz, or 266m medium-wave.

Listening in the car to BBC Eastern Counties, with Keith Skues presenting, brought more offshore memories and recordings. The date was 14 August, a highly significant day in offshore radio history – the anniversary of the Marine Offences Act 1967. Keith Skues had been busy during the day, and he told his BBC Eastern Counties listeners about his visit to Clacton Pier and the interviews given to various media about his offshore memories. Keith also played several recordings of note from his own time on the original Radio London, including the infamous practical joke where it seemed the Big L signal had been swamped by a new land based pirate operating on the same wavelength – Radio East Anglia! It was really a stunt dreamed up by the Radio London jocks – including Skues himself – using the voices of the ship's crew members. Such was the level of listener response and enthusiasm for the offshore nostalgia programming, that in more recent years, Keith Skues began to devote his Sunday evening show to just this, renaming it Pirate Radio Skues.

The hut from which the 2001 Radio London RSL was broadcasting was also the base of the existing Radio London shop on Clacton Pier. This RSL broadcast was also being simulcast via the internet and it was said that the webcast would become full-time – 24 hours, 7 days, beyond the MW restricted service licence.

Radio Caroline continued on Astra digital, as well as seeking out RSL opportunities. A planned Caroline RSL for August 2001 had to be shelved because Swale Sound had already been granted an RSL for the same period from the same part of Kent, and Radio Authority rules allow only one such operation at a time from a location. A project called "Pirates For Peace" was supposedly continuing preparations for an operation off the coast of Northern Ireland. The plan was to produce programmes aimed at encouraging peace in the province, and uplink and deliver via satellite, although little more was heard of this endeavour. Radio London was looking at going full-time from Clacton Pier via webcasting. However, the only "genuine" offshore broadcasting at this time was Arutz 7 (announced in Hebrew as "Arutz Sheva") off the coast of Israel, sometimes audible in the UK on 1539 kHz after midnight.

The summer of 2002 came around, and this time there was to be a Radio Mi Amigo event, using the same vessel as the RNI in 1999 - the LV*18*. This time, it was not so much offshore nostalgia, although there was still some of that, but more a trial service for Harwich Haven Community Radio. The man behind this project was Tony O'Neil, the curator of the National Wireless and Television Museum in the High Lighthouse in Harwich Old Town.

While not a former pirate nor an offshore commemoration, the RSL station Susy Radio alerted the attentions of 'offshore anoraks' in two aspects. One was that its frequency – 531kHz at the bottom of the medium-wave band allowed it to be heard throughout much of the UK at various times of the day, and was very close to the legendary 558kHz, in an area of the band rarely used by commercial radio. It also carried a special day of programmes ("Anorak Fest 2002") on 14 August to commemorate the closing of Radio London et al on this day in 1967.

In the summers of 2007 and 2008, the fort-based radio stations were commemorated. Red Sands Radio obtained RSLs to broadcast on 1278kHz medium-wave from Red Sands fort, Thames Estuary, eight miles off Whitstable, Kent. The venture was a collaboration of well-known radio man Bob Le-Roi, and Project Redsand, which is committed to the systematic preservation of what is considered to be the best of the remaining fort complexes. Another, Roughs Tower (claimed as the Principality of Sealand!) off the Suffolk coast, had been used in some kind of commercial computing venture, but never radio, apart from a dubious amateur radio event using the callsign prefix "1S". It was later reported to have been put up for sale, although the legality of that is unclear.

At Easter 2004, the British Broadcasting Corporation entered the offshore commemoration arena – and did it very well. Pirate BBC Essex was the name of a special service, featuring programmes and music of the original 1964-1967 style, presented by personalities from that era. All of the BBC Essex medium-wave frequencies were given over to the Pirate BBC Essex output, with the VHF FM frequencies continuing to carry the regular BBC Essex programmes. In addition there was a live webstream of the Pirate BBC Essex available via the BBC website, thus allowing fans and enthusiasts all over the UK and around the world to listen in and enjoy the fun.

That was to mark the 40th anniversary of the start of the British offshore era, generally accepted to have begun with Radio Caroline's launch. Pirate BBC Essex was back again broadcasting 9 to 14 August 2007, this time marking 40 years since the end of that era, generally accepted to have occurred with Radio London's final closedown, at 3.00pm on 14 August 1967. The 2004 programmes had been very impressive and popular, and so a great many people were eagerly anticipating the 2007 broadcast. 'Pirate BBC Essex' was scheduled to be carried primarily on the BBC Essex medium-wave frequencies of 729kHz, 765kHz and 1530kHz, and streaming live on the internet via the BBC Essex section within http://www.bbc.co.uk. Again, the usual BBC Essex service would continue on its FM frequencies.

The lower two of the three BBC Essex medium-wave frequencies certainly enabled many people to listen in with an analogue radio. During the daytime, these channels cover much of the south of England up to the Midlands, with just a small amount of interference. The jingles, specially recorded for Pirate BBC Essex in authentic 'PAMS' style, were catchy and enjoyable, and soon memorised! The main jingles were actually reworkings of the Swinging Radio England jingle - "Remember, these golden classics - Swinging Radio England". Now, it was "Remember, the pirate stations - Pirate BBC Essex". One would be reminded of the awesome effectiveness of this classic genre of radio jingle, first unleashed on the British listening public in the mid-1960s.

On Friday 10 August 2007, several carloads of enthusiasts drove around to Shotley to participate in the 'flashing' during Johnnie Walker's programme. It was Johnnie Walker himself who used to coordinate the famous "Frinton Flashing" during his 9.00pm to midnight Radio Caroline show in the offshore era. This was good fun, and scores were parked up around Shotley, Felixstowe and Harwich for the flashing!

Additional frequencies were announced on air, with BBC Radio Norfolk's 855 and 873kHz carrying the programmes on the Friday evening. 855kHz was just audible under strong European interference (QRM) in Shotley; a Pirate BBC Essex signal on 873kHz was not detectable. Johnnie Walker was giving requests and dedications out on-air. It was rather peculiar to hear dedications and requests coming in from all over the UK, Europe and even USA, Canada and Australia on a BBC local radio station. Some 'flashing' resumed later with Johnnie Walker and co-presenter back out on deck and soliciting votes for the 'Record of the Week'. On the voice-over station identification announcements, the line "This could be the last time", taken from the Rolling Stones track The Last Time, was often heard.

Timed to coincide with the Pirate BBC Essex broadcast was an exhibition of offshore memorabilia from a previously rarely seen collection owned by Chris and Jackie Dannatt on the Ha'penny Pier in Harwich. Pirate BBC Essex T-shirts and mugs were on sale alongside other BBC Essex merchandise on a counter at the end of the exhibition hall. Roger 'Twiggy'

Day and Dave Cash were in the exhibition chatting and posing for photographs for a while in the afternoons. Admission to this excellent exhibition was free.

Other events were taking place at the famous Electric Palace theatre in Harwich. On at least three of the broadcast days, there was a late afternoon 'Meet The Pirates' session hosted by one or more of the Pirate BBC Essex presenters. There was an admission charge for this event.

It was possible to take the foot ferry out to the LV*18*, but visitors were not permitted aboard due to health and safety regulations. The tender moored up alongside the lightship, and remained there for half-an-hour or so to allow those on board to chat with the presenters, all of whom were out on deck leaning over, chatting, exchanging banter, and signing books that were passed up to them. These included Roger 'Twiggy' Day in his trademark 'Growing old disgracefully' T-shirt, Dave Cash and Keith Skues amongst others. A large old-fashioned portable radio was on the deck of the foot ferry, providing the Pirate BBC Essex output as a soundtrack for the visit, a tame 2007 version of the 'Tender Trip'.

Back on the pier after the trip, some of the said presenters had also come ashore and were unhurriedly chatting and posing for photos with enthusiasts. It had turned out that Dave Cash's 6.00pm to 9.00pm show on the Saturday had been networked on all FM and MW frequencies. This explains why some people surprisingly picked it up around 8.00pm on BBC Radio Kent's 104.2MHz in Harwich, ahead of another Johnnie Walker 'flashing' session. The programming included The Big L Fab 40 and several (granted) requests for the famous theme tune, known as either "Big Lil" or the Big L Sonowaltz.

A pleasant interlude during the Sunday afternoon was a presenter on Pirate BBC Essex selecting more easy listening music in the style of the old Thames Estuary fort-based Radio 390.

The penultimate day of special broadcasting Monday 13 August provided some great entertainment. Gary Walker of the Walker Brothers and Bud Ballou from Radio Caroline (aka Howie Castle) were Dave Cash's special guests, while Knees Club founder Mary Payne surprised Dave with a demo recording of 'Knees' the song he recorded in 1965 with Kenny Everett.

Gary reiterated the important role that Radio London and the other pirates had played in bringing the Walker Brother's music to public attention. Howie, celebrating his 60th birthday, talked of life on Caroline post-14 August and of his long career in radio throughout the United States.

Dave Cash was followed by Graham Webb, who had travelled from Australia especially to participate in Pirate BBC Essex.

A number of music tracks were repeated several times over the few days, despite the presenters expressing their enjoyment of their freedom to play whatever they wanted. Recurrent were *I Fought The Law* – Bobby Fuller Four, *River Deep Mountain High* – Ike and Tina Turner, *Itchycoo Park* – Small Faces, *Excerpt From A Teenage Opera* – Keith West, *Carrie Anne* – The Hollies and lots of 1964 to 1967 Beatles songs! A 'novelty' record that was brought aboard by one of the presenters was *James, Hold The Ladder Steady* by Sue Thompson.

Obviously, the song's infectious amusement value reached the whole team, for it got played more and more regularly as the days of the broadcast went on. Indeed, "amusement" was clearly what the veteran team was enjoying, with the programmes increasingly being sat in on by one, two or three 'unscheduled' presenters, with lots of laughs and jokes being shared. An amusing moment occurred on one Johnnie Walker show where his wife Tiggy sat in the studio with him. Johnnie and the crew were later collapsed in hysterical laughter as they realised that his "goodbye kiss" with Tiggy before she returned on the tender to land, had been caught on the webcam, and was being shown around the world on the internet!

Between the records of the era, the classic jingles, and the occasional recordings of actual output from 1964-1967, the presenters told stories and shared memories of the events and people in the original offshore era.   A fascinating tale was revealed in an on-air chat about the Hollies' famous record *Carrie Anne*, which was heavily played by the pirates in the 1960s. The presenters told how it was originally *Marianne*, and was about Marianne Faithful, but record producers and managers involved at the time suggested that Mick Jagger may not be too impressed, and advised the subtle change to the title of the song!

The one aspect missing from the overall authenticity of the 'watery wireless' sound was the advertisements, which of course are not carried on the BBC! However, some of the famous commercials were remembered by the presenters in their chats, and one or two recordings were played.

The schedule for the final day - Tuesday 14 August – promised much.

9am - 11am	Dave Cash
11am - 1pm	Johnnie Walker and friends - Tom Edwards + Keith Hampshire + Keith Skues + Dave Cash + Ed Stewart
1pm - 3pm	Steve Scruton and Ed Stewart
3pm - 3.30pm	What Happened Next -The story of how Radio Caroline stayed on the air and Radio 1 was born.
3.30pm – 4pm	The Pirates come ashore - live from the Ha'penny Pier in Harwich.

The party atmosphere, with anecdotes, laughs and silliness prevailed in the Johnnie Walker and Friends programme, culminating in the whole packed studio of presenters singing loudly along to *James, Hold The Ladder Steady*! A more poignant and reflective tone was restored as Johnnie recounted the moment at which Radio Caroline was, once again, alone in the North Sea, after having considerable company (and competition) for most of the previous two years.

Ed Stewart was himself 'in the chair' to close down Radio London at 3.00pm on 14 August 1967. Here he was, exactly 40 years later charged with the task of doing the same for Pirate BBC Essex. In a faithful reproduction of the Big L closedown sequence of four decades earlier, the Big L Sonowaltz 'Big Lil' was followed by *A Day In The Life* by the Beatles, and the announcement "It's 3.00pm, and Pirate BBC Essex is closing down", chanted in unison by all on board. However, it wasn't quite the end, as BBC Essex broadcast *What Happened Next* - a half-hour documentary by Ray Clark about the events and changes in radio in 1967, allowing the pirates time to come ashore to participate in the outside broadcast from Ha'penny Pier, Harwich.

The documentary covered the campaign by the Wilson Government to silence the pirates, and how with English companies banned from advertising on the offshore stations, and English launches banned from tendering them, that all but one took the decision to close. The one that continued was Radio Caroline, with Johnnie Walker making the famous midnight announcement:

"Radio Caroline would like to thank Mr Harold Wilson and his Labour Government for at last recognising this station's legality, its right to exist, its right to be here and its right to provide you with entertainment, because we belong to you, and we love you. Caroline continues."

This was followed by the Beatles *All You Need Is Love* as Caroline attempted to survive in a new fugitive era.

Interviews were held on Ha'penny Pier, Harwich, as roving reporters from BBC Essex grabbed words with the 'Pirate' presenters as they were returned to land by the foot ferry in rough, wet weather that mirrored the sad day in 1967. Eventually, at 4.00pm, a more formal and less excited voice offered "It's 4 o'clock – BBC Essex News..." and it really was all over, although perhaps not with the same level of sadness felt by around 20 million listeners at the time of the original switch off on 14 August 1967.

Many share the opinion that commercial pop music radio has become bland and uninteresting. It is splendidly ironic that an antidote in the form of lively, stimulating and fun radio has been provided – by the BBC!   More or less, the opposite of what happened at Easter 1964!

The full team of presenters that contributed to Pirate BBC Essex, and a list of some of the other stations in their illustrious careers, is as follows:

Mike Ahern – Caroline North, Caroline South, BBC Radio 1, Capital Gold
Pete Brady – Radio London, Radio Jamaica, BBC Radio 1, Radio Luxembourg
Dave Cash – Radio London, BBC Radio 1, Radio Monte Carlo, Capital Radio, BBC Radio Kent, Radio Luxembourg, Invicta Radio
Ray Clark – Radio Caroline, Invicta Radio, Breeze AM, BBC Essex
Graham Cooke – BBC Radio Kent
Gord Cruse – Caroline South, Caroline North
Ian Damon – 2RG, 2LF, Radio London, BBC Radio 2, KFM, County Sound
Roger "Twiggy" Day – Swinging Radio England, Britain Radio, Radio Caroline, Radio Andorra, Radio Luxembourg, Radio Northsea International, Piccadilly Radio, BRMB, Invicta Sound, Pirate 102, Jazz FM, BBC Radio Kent
Tom Edwards – Radio City, Radio Caroline, BBC Radio Norfolk, BBC Radio 2
Tim Gillett – Essex Radio, Breeze AM, BBC Essex
Guy Hamilton – Radio Essex, Britain's Better Music Station, Radio 270, Wiltshire Radio
Keith Hampshire – Radio Caroline, CKFH Toronto
Alison Hartley – BBC Essex
John Kerr – 2PK, 2DU, 2CA, Radio Scotland, 2UE
Keith Martin – Radio Atlanta, Radio Caroline, Radio 390, BFBS
Emperor Rosko – Radio Caroline, Radio Luxembourg, BBC Radio 1, Classic Gold
Steve Scruton – Essex Radio, BBC Essex
Keith Skues – BFBS, Radio Caroline, Radio Luxembourg, Radio London, BBC Radio 1, BBC Radio 2, Radio Hallam, BBC Eastern Counties
Glenn Speller – BBC Essex
Norman St John – 3UZ, 3CS, Radio City, Radio Caroline, Radio London, Radio Luxembourg
Ed Stewart – Radio London, BBC Radio 1, BBC Radio 2, Radio Mercury
Johnnie Walker – Swinging Radio England, Radio Caroline, BBC Radio 1, KSAN, BBC Wiltshire Sound, BBC World Service, GLR, BBC Radio 5, Talk Radio UK, BBC Radio 2
Graham "Spider" Webb – Radio Monte Carlo, Radio Norway, Voice of Germany, Radio Caroline, BBC Radio 2, 2SM
Mark Wesley – Radio Essex, Britain's Better Music Station, Radio 270, Radio Scotland, Radio Northsea International, Radio Luxembourg, Radio Orwell, Radio Nova International, Capital Gold
Ian Wyatt – BBC Essex

RADIO LONDON '97 OFF WALTON PIER

The first ever offshore reunion took place in August 1997 to commemorate the 30th anniversary of the Marine Etc., Broadcasting Bill becoming an Act of Parliament. The Sunday Telegraph announced on 22 June 1997: "Radio London the pirate pop station driven off the air by Harold Wilson's Government, will make a triumphant comeback next month, broadcasting from a ship moored off Essex – just as it did 30 years ago.

"The Music will be the same, the jingles will be the same, even the disc jockeys will be the same. Well, some of them."

This time Ray Anderson of East Anglian Productions in Frinton-on-Sea had obtained a Home Office licence from the Radio Authority (now Ofcom) to operate as Radio London on

266 metres in the medium wave (1134 kilohertz), for one month from 18 July. However, the authorities only allowed them one watt of power for 28 days compared with 50 kilowatts when Radio London operated in the mid-1960s.

Ray had previous radio experience on Laser 558. He said: "The commemoration is purely an exercise in nostalgia. The Government closed down the station and signed the disc jockeys to Radio 1, thus trying to make pop music safe."

m.v. Yeoman Rose

Among the original offshore jocks who were signed up for the voyage of nostalgia aboard the 1,000 tonne m.v. *Yeoman Rose* were Pete Brady, Tony Brandon, Dave Cash, Ian 'The Wombat' Damon, Duncan Johnson, Mark Roman, Keith Skues, Ed Stewart and Dave Williams. They were complimented by a new breed of presenters Chris Baird, Tom Collins, Tony Currie, Chris Elliot, Pete MacFarline, John Peters, Steve Silby and Rob Yarnold. Some waived fees and expenses.

On board was a small studio with two turntables, a CD machine, and a triple stack cartridge machine. There was additional accommodation comprising a galley, three other crew cabins, a shower and a toilet. Two further caravans resided in the hold which provided extra sleeping accommodation.

The station began transmissions on 18 July at 5.30am and continued until 14 August 1997. It concluded with a 'rescue' staged by the Walton and Frinton lifeboat taking Skues ashore, assisted by Mark Roman and Duncan Johnson.

Some of the Big L founders came over from Texas including Anne Pierson, widow of Don Pierson, the station's co-founder and Tom Danaher, the other co-founder, together with Ben Toney, the original Big L programme director.

Without doubt the one month operation of Big L was a great success. Station boss Ray Anderson said:

There was a lot of work which had to be done behind the scenes which included researching the original Radio London Fab 40 charts, re-editing some of the PAMS jingles and locating original station promotions and trailers. A transmitter was required and a radio tower had to be welded to the deck. A studio had to be built on board which would be powered by a generator. Food and drink had to be organised

There was a great media coverage which helped us in maximizing our listener potential and ensuring Radio London was heard far and wide by a loyal audience of Big L fans, both old and new. Those 28 days were the greatest days of my adult life. It gave me the personal satisfaction of organising and running that Big L '97. Memories that I will always treasure.

Mark Roman was involved with the whole operation for a month on board and presented a daily show:

In some respects the entire month was a condensation of the days of Big L. The ship was not exactly luxurious and accommodation was in two ancient caravans in the hold, which were accessed by a single and tall steel ladder. The mess was just that, a small area populated by the jocks and the crew of two, but nevertheless it was a most memorable and enjoyable experience, especially when a chip pan caught fire, causing no damage, only drama.

The studio equipment was sufficient, none of the high tech stuff of today, proving that it is the personality of the station that is more important than technology.

The new breed of the jocks that gave their time was impressive. At first some who worked on land stations were writing carefully rehearsed ad libs and comments but after a couple

*Tom Danaher, Mark Roman and
Ben Toney aboard Yeoman Rose*

of days threw that out and flew by the seat of their pants reacting to actual events and thoughts and enjoying playing some great music much of which had not been heard by the enthusiastic audience since the sixties. Many of that audience actually came aboard to see how it was done, but that led to problems because of course the authorities just had to stick their nose in and quote health and safety regulations etc, limiting the number of people on board at any one time, and checking the transmitter wasn't exceeding its limit.

On shore the hotels, B and Bs and pier were full of fans aiding the economy of Walton-on-the-Naze, which as always was most welcoming and supportive, as were the lifeboat crew who gave a demonstration of their abilities staging a rescue with the author of this book.

The weather was kind but almost in a re-enactment of the sixties it turned and necessitated taking a short cruise to the sheltered waters of Horsey Island near the Naze Marina, but the crew of the tender continued their great support.

When the Piersons' visited together with Tom Danaher and Ben Toney it completed the picture and gave me personally a chance to meet again and thank those people who had contributed so much to broadcasting and launched me on a rewarding career. Had it not been for the opportunity they gave me I would probably have stayed in sales and not moved on to writing, producing and voicing so many commercials, and working in Australia and New Zealand.

Like so many people I have so much to be grateful for. Had it not been for the Pirates it is extremely doubtful if commercial radio would ever have come to the UK, and thus launched so many careers and personalities who are now not only household names, but international recording stars.

The *Yeoman Rose* sailed down the Black Deep and returned to Queenborough, Kent.

Following the closure of the station, a staff reunion and Summer of Love party was held in Clacton. Mark Roman presided for the evening and paid an emotional tribute to Wonderful Big L and those who had served on the ship since December 1964.

◉ Over Christmas and New Year 97/98 another RSL broadcast took place, this time from the

RNI broadcasting from the LV18

1912-built *Ocean Defender*, a converted Norwegian whaling vessel belonging to the charity Earthkind, moored in St Katharine's Dock, near Tower Bridge in London. The transmission dates were from 17 December 1997 to 13 January 1998. Those taking part in the broadcast included Ray Anderson, Chris Baird, Dave Cash, Ian Damon, Chris Elliot, Dennis Jason, Mitch, Mary Payne, Mark Roman, John Ross-Barnard, Ed Stewart, Russell Thompson, Tommy Vance and Garry Williams. The station broadcast on 1503 kHz AM

(199metres medium wave in old money!) and the signal reached out about 20 miles in the daytime, but night time reception was much more limited. Radio London was also broadcast for the first time on the internet, so could be heard around the world. It is believed that the cost to run the Restricted Service Licence station was about £10,000.

RADIO NORTHSEA INTERNATIONAL 1999

A commemorative broadcast of RNI in aid of the RNLI from the former Trinity House Lightship number 18 christened Mebo III as a tribute to the original radio station's ship of the 1970s. LV18 was moored off Jaywick on the Essex coast on a mooring laid by Trinity House. Crew had to keep a night watch and also monitor Channel 16. The station transmitted in 190 metres 1575 kHz medium wave.

Transmission took place from 3 August 1999 for 28 days, on 1575 kHz (190 metres). Former offshore people involved: Alan West (RNI 70s), Dave Rogers (RNI 70s), Norman Barrington (Caroline 70s), Dick Palmer - Engineer/DJ (Caroline 70s), Bob Noakes - Engineer/DJ (Caroline 70s), Ray Warner (aka Ray Anderson - Atlantis 70s), Phil Mitchell (Caroline 70s), Kevin Turner (Caroline 80s), Paul Graham (Caroline 80s), Dennis Jason (Caroline 80s), Stuart Dobson – Ship's Engineer (Caroline 80s), Bob Le-Roi (City 60s, Caroline 70s, 80s).

They were complimented by Chris Baird, Tony Currie, Paul MacLaren and Mike Read.

⊙ RNI also broadcast the following year 11 April – 8 May 2000 from the LV18 off Harwich, on 190 metres 1575kHz medium wave and also the world-wide web. Station manager Paul Graham said: "We brought back all the great memories of this once-loved station including the music of the early 70s when the original ship Mebo II was broadcasting. There were no computers running RNI and, unlike today's commercial stations we were 'hands-on and personal' with the listener."

The broadcasts helped raise funds for the 4th Dovercourt Sea Scouts for a new building in Barrack Lane, Dovercourt.

Presenters taking part were: Andy Archer, Norman Barrington, Dave Gregory, Bob Le-Roi, Phil Mitchell, Bob Noakes, Dick Palmer, Dave Rogers, Kevin Turner and Alan West. Former Mellow presenters Pete Edwards, Jim Gregory, Colin Lamb, Paul Maclaren and Graham Vine were also heard. Station manager was Paul Graham who also presented shows.

There are stories that that RNI 2000 was a shambles. Nothing worked properly. The ship was 'hot' as hell with stray RF all over the place and live metal work throughout the ship.

The LV18 was moored at the old Railway Jetty in Harwich Harbour.

⊙ RNI also broadcast from 3 – 30 June 2001 from the LV18 off Harwich, on 1575kHz medium wave. It was organised by Colin Lamb. Presenters were: Norman Barrington, Clive Boutell, Tony Carnell, Tony Currie, Roger Day, Jim Gregory, Dave Kent, Colin Lamb, Bob Le-Roi, Phil Mitchell, Kevin Peters, Pete Salberg, Bart Serlie and Graham Vine. The spirit aboard was described as "superb."

As with the previous year the LV18 was moored at the old Railway Jetty in Harwich Harbour.

The radio station opened and closed with the old RNI theme Man of Action by the Les Reed Orchestra.

John Edward, Ian 'Wombat'
Damon and Willie Walker with Keith Skues
kneeling at a lunchtime party in Harwich

Radio London 2001 co-organisers
Mary and Chris Payne

RADIO LONDON 2001 ATTRACTS A GALAXY OF STARS

The licence holder for this RSL was Paul Graham. The broadcasts from Clacton Pier from 4 -31 August 2001 had an interesting line-up of presenters, news readers and guests: Tony Allan, Ray Anderson, Bud Ballou, Dan Bransby, Roger Cooper, Stuart Cunningham, Tony Currie, Ian Damon, 'Fab' Alan Field, Paul Graham, Jim Gregory, Alan Hardy, Victor Hartman, Dennis Jason, David Kent, Colin Lamb, Dave Lawson, Paul MacLaren, Tony Monson, Chris and Mary Payne, Dave Rogers, Bob Le-Roi, John Ross-Barnard, Keith Skues, Norman St John, Pete Salberg, Guy Stevens, Alan Thompson, Graham Vine, Tony Weaver, Stephen Wright, Rob Yarnold and Peter Young.

Also heard during the broadcast were the voices of former watery wireless DJs Keith 'Keefers' Hampshire, Mick Luvzit, Ron O'Quinn, Emperor Rosko and Steve Young and Sixties music stars Ray Phillips, Colin Pattenden, Jackie Lynton, Karl Green and Colin Earl.

Frank Ifield's biographer, Pauline Halford guested on the Cardboard Shoes show telling how she was writing the Frank Ifield biography. She told Mary Payne after the programme: "What a thrill it was to venture amongst the ex-pirate hordes and play my part, however small, in the re-creation of those great days of REAL radio.

"Surrounded by a raft of billowing deckchairs, the blare of the fairground and the sickly-sweet aroma of doughnuts wafting in the breeze, I could almost believe I was back in my youth, dancing to the vibes from Caroline North in the teeth of a Blackpool gale. (sorry - we didn't get Radio London too well on the Lancashire coast). I never thought then that it would be me hitting the pirate air waves."

Pauline's book *I Remember Me – The First 25 Year*s was published January 2005. Sadly Pauline died in January 2009.

◖ The 2000 Radio London RSL broadcast had many of the above presenters and news readers taking part plus Don Allen, Clive Boutell, Tony Carnell, Steve James, Alan King, Phil Mitchell, Tony Randall, Alan Thompson and Alan West.

USS *DENSITY* REUNIONS

By Mary Payne, Director of Radio London Ltd.

Early in 2001, experienced model-maker and maritime historian, John S Platt, was researching ship information when a posting on a chat board caught his attention. It was by Tanya Baugus, who was organising a shipmates' reunion for the USS *Density*'s WWII crew. The *Density* is the former minesweeper that was kitted-out in Miami to become the studios and living-quarters for Radio London. When John got in touch with Tanya, he learned that the shipmates had been misinformed by the US Navy that their beloved USS *Density* (AM 218) had been scrapped. They had commenced holding crew reunions in 1965, oblivious to the fact that the battle-decorated minesweeper they had nicknamed the Mighty Little D, was in fact still afloat and commencing a new life. Rechristened the m.v. *Galaxy*, she was anchored off the coast of Essex providing a home to Radio London and its huge transmitter. Tanya's father LaVerne Bailey and her mother Marie, had organised annual reunions ever since, never knowing about Radio London until John's contact thirty-six years later.

The Bailey family was thrilled to learn of their cherished ship's second life. It cannot be understated how much the minesweeper Mighty Little D had meant and still means, to her wartime crew. Over the years, the USS *Density* shipmates, their children and many of their relatives, had been drawn together by that ship to form one big, close family. However, they were extremely happy to invite representatives of the vessel's reincarnation as the *Galaxy* to join them at their forthcoming reunion in Dallas, Texas, in September 2001 to tell them more about the Radio London story.

The Lone Star State, of course, has very strong ties to Radio London. The station founder Don Pierson and his best friend Tom Danaher, who kitted-out the *Galaxy* for her new life as a radio station, were both Texan businessman. Dallas was the home of the famous PAMS jingles company, from whom Don and fellow Texan and original Programme Director Ben Toney, had commissioned those unforgettable Big L jingles. It seemed entirely appropriate that the Radio London contingent should meet the USS *Density* shipmates for the first time in Dallas and my husband Chris and I felt extremely honoured to be invited to give a presentation about our favourite radio station.

Fate was to play another extraordinary hand. Chris and I arrived on 10 September. The following morning, I was in our room, debilitated by a migraine, when Chris came in with the terrible news of the terrorist attacks.

The mood from then on was sombre; the pain of the nation hung heavy in the air. We felt fear and uncertainty. Would there be further attacks? All aircraft were grounded, so would we be stuck for weeks in the USA?

The Baileys and all of the other reunion attendees could not have been kinder. They appreciated the predicament of two Brits, stranded far from home and welcomed us

Ron Buninga with the
former USS Density
ship's bell

The original bell which was also
used during the ship's
life of Radio London

Original crew members of the USS Density pay their respects to colleagues who were lost during World War II at a commemoration at the Admiral Nimitz Museum part of the National Museum of the Pacific War in Fredericksburg, Texas, USA. (l to r) Frank Gazafy, LaVerne Bailey, Charlie Stock, Stacey Rankin, Bill Brandstetter, Gene Barbo, Calvin Bryant

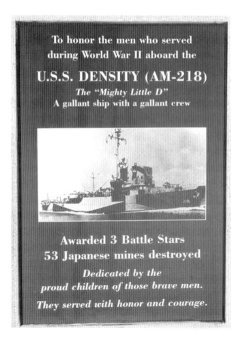

The Plaque donated to the Nimitz Museum by crewmembers' families

warmly into their close family. There was a fierce determination, perhaps understood best by wartime veterans, not to cancel the event, although it would become a much-reduced gathering. No mere terrorists could be permitted to scupper a celebration of the Mighty Little D! Many *Density* family members were forced to cancel their trip, but others determinedly got into their cars and drove to Dallas.

Although Big L DJ Norm St John, grounded at Heathrow, failed to make it to the US, Tom Danaher and Ben Toney, both Texas residents, were there to present their stories of bringing US-style commercial radio to the UK. Chris and I did our best to explain Radio London's popularity from the listeners' point-of-view. The Big L jingles proved popular immediately. It was agreed that the next reunion should be in 2003, in Branson, Missouri. There was no question of our not attending.

On New Year's Eve 2002, an e-mail dropped into Chris's Inbox, bearing the familiar name Buninga. Ron, the son of the *Galaxy*'s much-loved Captain Bill, had discovered our Radio London website. Reading our account of attending the 2001 *Density* Reunion in Dallas had prompted him to contact us. Within a few short e-mail exchanges, we found out that Ron still had in his possession the ship's bell. The *Galaxy* crew had presented it to Bill and amazingly, it had hung beside the Buninga's front door in Holland since the Sixties! It had been taken down relatively recently, when Ron's mother had passed away and the family home had been sold. Ron had attended many WWII commemorations with his late father and fully appreciated how much the *Density* meant to her crew. Very soon after our initial contact, he had made up his mind to fly to Branson with the bell, to present it to the surviving shipmates.

Bringing an extremely heavy bell all the way from the Netherlands to Branson, an exceptionally inaccessible part of the USA if you happen to be travelling from Europe, proved a huge challenge. Ron dedicated himself to cleaning and polishing it, constructing a special transportation case and clearing its passage with airlines and customs officials.

As soon as Chris and I met Ron, we became friends and naturally he was made extremely welcome by the *Density* family. He was very nervous about the presentation and asked us to check his speech to ensure the English was correct.

The ceremony returning the bell to its rightful owners was an emotional one, where Ron's kindness and dedication in bringing it to Branson was deeply appreciated by the shipmates. Everyone was thrilled to bits and naturally wanted a photo taken with the prized artefact. Tom Danaher was also in attendance. He owns a small airport in Wichita Falls, Texas and had piloted himself in, in one of his small aircraft. First thing the following morning, Ron, a great aircraft enthusiast, was thrilled to be offered a spin in Tom's plane, accompanied by reunion organisers Mary and Lanny Simmons.

The Baileys' large SUV (Sport Utility Vehicle) had sufficient room for them to carry the bell back home with them and it remained in their care until 2007. That September, the reunion was back in Texas, based in San Antonio. The main event, however, was the official presentation of the USS *Density* Bell to the Museum of the Pacific War (aka the Nimitz Museum) in Fredericksburg. This was held at 1300 on 21 September in the museum gardens, where a marquee had been erected to provide shade from the fierce sun. Seven of the surviving WWII crewmembers participated in the moving ceremony, presided over by the Reverend Richard Elwood.

Afterwards, Gibson Cushman, grandson of ship's captain Walter Smith (who had attended the reunion with his mother Eliza and grandmother, Hope Smith) unveiled a plaque on behalf of the families, commemorating the courage of those who served aboard the USS *Density*.

Visitors to the Nimitz museum are now able to ring the bell that survived the devastation of Pearl Harbour aboard the Mighty Little D, saw a new lease of life in the Sixties aboard our much-loved Radio London and enjoyed a long retirement in Holland, before being reunited with the WWII crew members, thanks to the kindness of Ron Buninga.

THE END OF OFFSHORE RADIO'S 35th ANNIVERSARY 10 August 2002

The idea of holding annual offshore reunions came from Pauline Miller, who with the late Jenni Baynton, had run the shop aboard the *Ocean Defender*. The first was held in August 1998, at The Dickens Inn, St Katharine's Dock.

The 2002 reunion organised by Mary and Chris Payne, to commemorate the demise in 1967 of all the stations save Caroline, was the biggest to date and proved to be a huge success. It was held at a private terrace overlooking the River Thames, at Doggett's pub in London on 10 August 2002 and DJs flew in especially for the occasion from Australia, Belgium, Canada, Canary Islands, Germany, Holland, Ireland and the USA.

To remind those who attended the venue was decorated with old vinyl singles, pirate flags and a host of other memorabilia.

An audio presentation was made by Chris Payne and well received by those who attended, recalling what a sad day it was on 14 August 1967 and what British broadcasting had lost with the closure of the offshore stations, all but Caroline.

Contact had been made with Steve Young in Canada. He couldn't make the celebrations but sent a recorded greeting. Ian Damon had hoped to be there but had recently undergone a serious operation and only arrived home that day. The Paynes managed to talk with him that Saturday and send greetings from all at the gathering.

Original offshore personnel who attended, were Mike Ahern, John Aston, Nick Bailey, Bud Ballou, Woolf Byrne, Gordy Cruse, Robbie Dale, John Edward, Graham Gill, Keith Hampshire, David Hawkins, Phil Jay, Duncan Johnson, Mick Luvzit, Ronan O'Rahilly, Roger

Keith 'Keefers' Hampshire

Dave Lee Travis

Ronan O'Rahilly

Tommy Vance

Willy Walker

A few of the pirate faces from the 1960s. From left to right Nick Bailey, Mick Luvzit, Robbie Dale, Keith Hampshire, Johnnie Walker, Tommy Vance, Ronan O'Rahilly, Dave Lee Travis, Mark Slione with his hand on shoulder of Keith Skues, Graham Gill, Paul Rusling, and Graham Webb with his hands on shoulder of Gordon Cruse

Scott, Keith Skues, Mark Sloane, Ed Stewart, Dave Lee Travis, Tommy Vance, Johnnie Walker, Willy Walker, Graham Webb and David Williams.

They represented Radio 390, Radio Caroline North, Radio Caroline South, Radio City, Radio England, Radio London and Radio Northsea International.

Mary Payne recalls: "When we watched the emotional reunions of shipmates who had not seen each other for 35 years, we realised our hard work and that of our kind friends had paid off a hundredfold. Outstanding memories are of Graham 'Spider' Webb travelling all the way from Down Under, misreading his invitation and nearly missing the reunion... and the surprise arrival of the notoriously reclusive Ronan O'Rahilly, who had declined to attend any previous offshore gatherings."

Graham Webb said: "I agree it was a close shave, but at least I did arrive in time to greet some of my colleagues I had not seen for years and years. Looking back on those great days in the 1960s ...the Pirates changed the face of Britain in so many ways, not just broadcasting but music, fashion, style and the people's thinking. We brought genuine laughter, mayhem, fun and games to the airwaves, not heard since the Goons. WE were PIONEERS in the true sense of the word and left a legacy which will endure."

RADIO CAROLINE 40th ANNIVERSARY CELEBRATIONS IN LONDON at the RED LION, 28 March 2004

Roger "Twiggy" Day came up with the idea of a 40th anniversary party for old shipmates from Radio Caroline. It took place on 28 March 2004, exactly forty years since the station began broadcasting in 1964. The location was The Red Lion in Waverton Street, Mayfair, London, a hostelry well-known to many of the Caroline staff and also regularly frequented by DJs from Radio London and later still by staff of Swinging Radio England. The Mayfair offices of Caroline, London and England were literally a stone's throw from the watering-hole.

Over 60 personnel from Radios Caroline North and South attended. In addition to front-line presenters, there were engineers George Saunders, Carl Thomson, Freddie Ryder and Mike Watts as well as administration and production staff including George Hare and Ken Evans.

One of those who attended was Tom Edwards. He said: "I thought the Red Lion get-together was great. The amazing thing with us pirate DJs is that we have a bond in so

A veritable Who's Who of pirate DJs past and present. See how many you recognise at Radio Caroline's 40th anniversary reunion at the Red Lion, Mayfair, London

much as we lived in each other's pockets out at sea and I found some 40 years later that our conversations just took off where we had left them … good shipmates indeed!"

"Back in the January 2004 there appeared to be nothing being organised to celebrate the actual 40th anniversary of one of the most significant events in British Radio," said Roger Day. "I thought the Caroline family should have its own party. So thanks to the wonders of the internet I just contacted all my contacts and asked them to network the news to other Good Guys who they knew. I thought the Red Lion in Mayfair was the obvious choice as it was the station's local from 64-67.

"I had no expectations or predictions of how many would turn up. But I knew it was going to be a wonderful day when I turned the corner and the first person I saw waiting outside the pub was Simon Dee. It turned out to be one of the best days of my life and still makes me smile thinking back on it. Even the reclusive Ronan turned up and was rumoured to have bought a drink. This, as we all know, is a rare event.

"It was nice to see Caroline people from all eras and all parts of the operation. A great day of spoken memories and in some cases rarely seen pictures. I don't think any other station would stimulate this response, but Caroline is a very unique station.

"The only disappointment was the people we didn't trace or who couldn't come

Ronan O'Rahilly with Simon Dee

Roger Day, Ken Evans and Nick Bailey

Mark Sloane and John Aston

Keith Skues and Ronan O'Rahilly

because of the relatively short notice. So this is advance notice we will do it all again on 28 March 2014. Next time we will do better."

PIRATE BBC ESSEX, EASTER 2004

The pirates of the radio airwaves were no strangers to new technology but when they broadcast live from a ship off the Essex coast they couldn't have imagined that 40 years on, their experiences would be re-created and broadcast live around the world on the internet.

From 10 to 17 April 2004, BBC Essex marked the 40th anniversary of offshore radio in Britain by launching their own ship-based radio station, Pirate BBC Essex. Broadcasting from the LV*18* moored half a mile off the Harwich coastline, the station transmitted sixties music and memories 24 hours a day all week.

The station's disc-jockey line-up combined some of the great broadcasting names of the pirate era with voices familiar to BBC Essex listeners. On Easter Saturday the first on air was Ray Clark. He is currently heard on BBC Essex and BBC Radio Cambridgeshire but, back in the eighties, he was on Radio Caroline where he broadcast as "Mick Williams". He was followed by Roger Day, Mike Ahern and Paul Burnett.

Other former offshore presenters and newsreaders heard on the station were Pete Brady,

Tom Edwards, Ian Damon, Roger Day, Duncan Johnson and, presenting the weekday programmes, Dave Cash and Keith Skues. One visitor to the ship was Mark Wesley, although he did not broadcast. Complimenting the original 'pirates' were Ray Clark, David Clayton, Tim Gillett, Garry Lee, Oliver Rogers, Steve Scruton, Alan Thompson, Tom Warmington and Ian Wyatt.

BBC Essex presenter Steve Scruton, who created the idea for the broadcasts, said: "The original idea was to *recreate* the sound of the pirates 40 years ago. They changed the nation's radio listening habits, giving us all day music stations for the first time. I had the chance to broadcast from a ship in the way those radio pirates did!"

As well as the broadcast being heard on BBC Essex the station was also transmitted regionally each evening from 10.00pm-1.0am. BBCTV Look East also presented one show live from the LV18.

In 1967 there were no mobile phones, computers or email. The only way to contact a DJ was via correspondence which could take up to a week for DJs to hear from listeners. In 2004 and 2007 Pirate BBC Essex had all the latest technology and the programmes were transmitted world wide via the internet.

Pirate BBC Essex Producer Tim Gillett said: "We've been amazed with the emails received from pirate radio fans from across the world. They were all asking whether it would be available on the worldwide net. I'm so pleased that with the help of the cutting edge skills of Anglia Polytechnic University's Ultralab, the answer was yes. Pirate BBC Essex was a huge success with emails, text messages and phone calls flooding in from all over the world. It was a marathon job compiling a play list for the whole weeks broadcasting and much help was given by the Oldies Project. www.oldiesproject.com The disc-jockeys all sounded like they were having a great time and the listeners certainly did."

Asked if he thought offshore radio had been successful and that his time on Radio 270 had been worthwhile, Paul Burnett said: "Of course it was all worthwhile, apart from being great fun (when I wasn't puking my guts up in a force 12!) and who at the time knew it would spawn the industry we have today, employing thousands of people.

"I do think though that the very generation that 'Pirate Radio' was created for are, ironically, being ill-served by todays radio stations! Gold stations are virtually non-existent, (should be on FM) so maybe we need a latterday Ronan O'Rahilly to come along with a pirate station for the over 50s....check out WCBS New York, an FM Gold station that returned to the airwaves with the original jocks and already number two in the ratings after only 18 months!"

Pirate BBC Essex broadcast from the LV18 - one of the last manned lightships to be built for Trinity House. She was built in 1958 and served Britain at various points around its coastline before being decommissioned in 1993 as remotely controlled lightships were established. She's now looked after by the Pharos Trust, which is carefully restoring her to her former glory.

The LV18 is moored in Harwich harbour and Tony O'Neil, trustee and founder of the Pharos Trust said: "The objective is to make the ship a tourist attraction and a lasting symbol of the town's link with Trinity House, whose national operations headquarters is in Harwich. Our endeavour is to save this historic maritime vessel for its home port of Harwich. It would also be used for educational purposes and to study navigation and maritime subjects. The ship is being loaned to the BBC for a week for the offshore celebrations."

LV18 is no stranger to radio broadcasting. In recent years several community based radio projects have won temporary licences to broadcast to the north east Essex area. The ship has two studios with the broadcast studio ideally placed with windows looking out across the harbour to the Essex and Suffolk shores.

The Harwich/Felixstowe foot ferry, which transported DJs and crew to and from the LV18, was operated by Alan Sage. He also took visitors to see the people on board the LV18, although no-one was allowed to board the ship.

◉ In October 2004 at the annual Frank Gillard Awards, given to the best BBC local radio programmes of the year, Ray Clark won a gold for his documentary about the pirates, *All At Sea*, and the team from Pirate BBC Essex won a bronze award for Best Outside Broadcast.

◉ On 26 March 2005 Pirate BBC Essex broadcast from the *Ross Revenge* on 729, 765 and 1530MW + FM. Steve Scruton, Tim Gillett and Ian Wyatt presented a four-hour show from the old studio on the ship, whereas next door Radio Caroline used the more spacious and high tech new studio. Steve Scruton interviewed Peter Moore and Roger "Twiggy" Day and Caroline engineer Alan Beech.

◉ On Friday 16 June 2006 BBC Radio York marked the 40th anniversary of Radio 270 with eight hours of special programmes. These started at 8.00am with Elly Fiorentini broadcasting live from the pleasure cruiser *The Regal Lady* on the North Sea off Scarborough, the programme included a live interview from the quayside with the stations former managing director Wilf Proudfoot. At 11.00am there was a two-hour show of sixties music from the stations studios, which included an interview with late sixties York band The Smoke. Their single, *My Friend Jack*, was banned by the BBC for drug references but extensively played by Radio 270 and other offshore stations. At 1.00pm Jerry Scott resumed broadcasting from *The Regal Lady*, onboard were fellow Radio York broadcaster Bob Preedy, author of the book Radio 270, Life on the Ocean Waves, and former Radio 270 DJ Guy Hamilton. There were also pre-recorded interviews with former 270 DJs Paul Burnett, Mike Hayes and Hal Yorke.

RADIO LONDON 40ᵗʰ ANNIVERSARY CELEBRATIONS, DECEMBER 2004

Radio London's 40ᵗʰ birthday was on 23rd December 2004. As Christmas is a busy time the celebrations, organised by Mary and Chris Payne, were delayed until a more convenient date: 26 February 2005. Even then, many of the Big L DJs found that they had other commitments which caused them to miss the party. Five original DJs, one Radio London founder from Texas, a popular steward from aboard the m.v. *Galaxy* formed a small but select group that

Left to right: Keith Skues, John Edward, Norman St.John, Mary Payne, Duncan Johnson, Tom Danaher, Mitch Philistin, Mrs Jeanne Philistin, front: Ian Damon.

gathered on board the TS *Queen Mary*, a floating bar and conference centre permanently moored on the River Thames in central London.

Tom Danaher flew in from Texas, USA and Norm St John flew all the way from Brisbane, Australia especially to attend. Many guests had not seen each other for around 40 years! A toast was made to "Absent friends." The party was organized by Chris and Mary Payne.

A RADIO LISTENER'S COMMENTS

Radio listener Mike Roberts from Chelmsford Essex looks back at events that happened since the 1990s and takes in mention of Restricted Service Licences (RSLs), satellite broadcasting, the Internet and a weekly radio programme containing the word 'pirate' broadcast on BBC Local Radio throughout the Eastern Counties from 2004-2009.

For me, the most memorable events have centred on the 40th anniversary celebrations. That includes Pirate BBC Essex in 2004 and 2007 on the LV*18*, and the special afternoon show in August 2004 on the *Ross Revenge* during one of Caroline's own RSL broadcasts. Also important is the Radio Academy Pirate Reunion event in 2007. I know there have been regular reunion gatherings, but the August 2007 one was special in that there were just so many pirates there, and listeners were welcome too.

The events that have renewed interest in 60's pirate radio are:
a) the various RSLs that have been dedicated to the pirates
b) the growth in Digital Satellite broadcasting
c) the internet, and internet radio
d) *Pirate Radio Skues*

Restricted Service Licences

The early RSLs that I remember especially were John Burch's "Offshore Radio 1584" in a boat off Walton-on-the-Naze, Essex and Radio Caroline's first RSL when it came in from the North Sea to Dover which I think was in 1992. Then there was Clacton (1995), Southend, London, Medway and Tilbury. I'm sure I've missed a few.

I remember going to the South East Boat show, around 1995, during which Caroline had an RSL. Johnnie Walker was doing a live broadcast from the Caroline Stand with ancient turntables and a dodgy microphone stand which would not keep still, yet he was still sounding as professional as ever. Tilbury 2004 (40th anniversary) from the *Ross Revenge* was one of Caroline's best RSLs.

There have been many other RSL events since then, including several from Radio Caroline, those from Radio London (1997, 1997/8, 2000 and 2001) right up to the recent fort-based Red Sands Radio. I was only able to receive a few of these as many others were well away from Essex. These RSLs all helped keep up interest in the memories.

The Radio London website gives a little more background to RSLs. It says that anyone can apply to Ofcom (formerly the Radio Authority) for a Restricted Service Licence (RSL). The RSL allows the licensee to broadcast for up to 28 days, either on FM or AM, with a very limited power output.

Mary Payne writes: "The main object of these short transmissions is for those planning to apply for a full-time licence, or community radio licence, in a particular area to 'test the water', but often stations are set up simply to cover special local activities, such as carnivals, air shows and sporting events. Most applicants are granted licences, no matter what their standard of broadcasting (or lack of), but they have to specify exactly what they intend to do for the duration. Deviation from this is not permitted. If you tell Ofcom you are going to play music from 1967, you can't suddenly decide to include a current chart show in your schedule. (Not that you'd want to, of course...) For full details of how to apply for an RSL licence and the cost, visit the Ofcom Website."

Satellite Broadcasting

Satellite Radio has long been carried on the back of TV channels, and Radio Caroline did experiment on analogue satellite for a while. Chris Cary was involved in those early satellite broadcasts, but not many Caroline people were too keen on the idea at the time. Chris also ran Radio Nova International (via the Astra satellite) using the same name of his 80s VHF and Medium Wave pirate station in Dublin.

Moving on in time, I remember Caroline taking over weekends on EKR (European Klassik Radio) before they went full time as a digital channel in their own right on Astra and Worldspace satellites. Now Caroline is established on Sky and managed to get 0199 as its channel number. During the EKR days Caroline was also on DAB, as part of the local test broadcasts, but unfortunately not many people could tune in because of the lack of receivers.

Also there was Ray Anderson's attempt to revive Big L on AM radio and satellite. It's struggled to survive, from what I read, but was quite enjoyable to listen to. Nevertheless despite the internal politics I never thought I'd be able to hear anything called Big L ever again.

Internet

Wikipedia has comprehensive entries on various pirate radio stations and DJs. The internet now also carries thousands of radio stations, which can be accessed from anywhere in the world, several of which are also pirate related e.g. Radio Caroline, BigL 1395, The Oldies Project, Offshore Music Radio, Radio Mi Amigo 259, Veronica 192, etc.

PRS

The BBC Eastern Counties programme *Pirate Radio Skues* cannot be forgotten. The programme was born out of the success of Pirate BBC Essex in 2004, as listeners clamoured for more of the same. This was the most important pirate nostalgia programme ever. And it came from the BBC, not the commercial channels that have the most to thank the pirates for. This programme regularly played jingles and promos from the pirate era and re-broadcast archives of pirate radio shows. The weekly four-hour show ran on air for five years.

DUTCH RADIO DAYS

For 30 years, the annual Dutch "Radio Day" has been a "must" for all (offshore) radio experts and enthusiasts. About 300 people normally attend the event each year in Amsterdam. Delegates come from many countries in Europe, as well as the USA, Australia and New Zealand. Events are well publicised in the excellent monthly Hans Knot International Radio Report (www.hansknot.com).

Robbie Dale and Johnnie Walker at the Dutch Radio Day in Amsterdam in 2007

The 2004 Radio Day saw the Radio Caroline 1973-74 reunion with many former deejays, technicians and crew members, and in 2005, "RNI in 1970" attracted several former Radio North Sea employees who had a magnificent discussion on the podium. In November 2006, the Voice of Peace reunion formed a major highlight, as 20 former VoP jocks and technicians got

Roger Day going Dutch, 2007

together from all over the world.

However, the biggest event ever took place in 2007 with 450 visitors. On stage were Tom Mulder (Klaas Vaak), Johnnie Walker, Robbie Dale, Roger Day and other well known DJs who told their stories about life aboard Radio Caroline after Monday 14 August 1967. In 2007 the Dutch Radio team also introduced the "Radio Day Awards" as a bi-annual event to acclaim the efforts of several special people who stood up for free radio without Governmental control.

Hans Knot, Rob Olthof and Martin van der Ven organised the 2008 event again in Amsterdam. The itinerary included "Radio Caroline in the late seventies (1977-80)" as a main topic. Three panels discussed that exciting era just before the m.v. *Mi Amigo* sank in March 1980. This included all the English and Dutch colleagues who worked for the legendary offshore radio station around 30 years ago. Again it became a big class reunion. Last but not least Sietse Brouwer presented his station Radio Waddenzee which is broadcast from the radioship *Jenni Baynton*.

Pirate Hall of Fame's Jon Myer with BBC Essex presenter Ray Clark

The official "Radio Day" website can be located at:

http://www.radioday.nl

The Three Musketeers – organisers of the annual Radio Day in Amsterdam.
Left to right: Rob Olthof, Hans Knot and Martin van der Ven. Hans is holding a precious souvenir from the m.v. Fredericia (Caroline North) which can nowadays be found in Sietse Brouwer's Radio Waddenzee ship lying at anchor in the Harlingen Harbour, The Netherlands.

RADIO ACADEMY CELEBRATION OF SIXTIES OFFSHORE RADIO, 2007

The 40th anniversary of the Marine Etc., Broadcasting (Offences) Act was commemorated on 14 August 2007. The Radio Academy hosted a celebration ten days previous at the Sugar Reef, near Piccadilly in London's West End when more than 60 former offshore personnel celebrated the achievements of the offshore radio stations of the 1960s. Members of the public were also invited to the event.

It was an afternoon of audio, movies and memories when DJs relived the golden era of music radio. Some were famous names, still successfully broadcasting today. Others moved on from radio when the pirates closed down and now work in different fields altogether. Yet they had one thing in common, fond memories of those pioneering days, and shared their stories with fans, listeners and the current generation of broadcasting professionals. Some flew in especially from Australia and Canada as well as European countries to take part.

The event was the brainchild of Jon Myer, who runs the Pirate Radio Hall of Fame website and was instigated by Radio Academy Director, Trevor Dann.

The committee that co-organised the event comprised Jon Myer, Mary and Chris Payne, Gerry Zierler, Mark Story, Brian Thompson and Tim Gillett.

A fine exhibition of offshore memorabilia was on display organised by Chris and Jackie Dannatt.

Five panel sessions were held during the afternoon:

1) **The Sound of the Nation** (Caroline) produced and chaired by Mark Story.

The beginning is in the past, "the middle is now and the end is…." Well there is no end. Forty years on those words still send a tingle down the back of radio listeners of a certain age, but what is really encouraging are the number of young people who are enthralled by the Caroline Story and want to know so much more about the "Men of a new Breed". Five of those pioneers recalled their time on Radio Caroline between Easter Sunday 1964 and before, right up to 14 August 1967. The panel were Keith Skues, Bryan Vaughan, Nick Bailey, Roger Day and Graham Webb.

2) **The Stations on Sticks** (sea fort stations) produced by Gerry Zierler and chaired by Ralph Bernard. The Thames Estuary spawned a number of stations which preferred studios and bunks that didn't move about! WWII anti-aircraft forts off the Kent and Essex coasts produced some of the earliest and, some would say, some of the most entrepreneurial of the offshore stations. Certainly, they operated on a shoestring and produced a lot of excitement

Ben Healy from Radio Scotland and Mike Ahern
Caroline North

*Newsreader John Aston who appeared on KING,
Essex, Caroline North and South, 270, 355 and 390*

*Bryan Vaughan, Radios Atlanta,
Caroline South and Scotland*

*Emperor Rosko from Radio
Caroline South*

*Mark Sloan, KING, 390,
Caroline South, 355*

Noel 'Neddy' Miller from Radio 270

Alan Turner one of the DJs to broadcast live on Radio Caroline as she sailed from Harwich to the Isle of Man

Jack McLaughlin, Scotland, 270 and 390

Tony Blackburn and Johnnie Walker with their former boss Ronan O'Rahilly

Ed Stewart and Duncan Johnson Both from Radio London

Norman St John, Caroline South and London

*Mel Howard, Caroline
South and Scotland*

*Phil Martin,
England and 355*

*Visitor, singer and artist
Rolf Harris*

and sometimes drama for those on board. The panel were David Allan (Radio 390), Brian Cullingford (KING/390), Guy Hamilton (Radio Essex/BBMS) and Mark Wesley (Radio Essex and BBMS). Tom Edwards had been booked to appear but unfortunately wasn't able to make it, which meant that Radio City wasn't represented. Former City DJ Bob Le-Roi and Candy Calvert, daughter of the station founder, Reg Calvert, were invited up on stage to redress the balance.

Paul Elvey, Radio City

Paul Elvey worked on Radio City. Reminiscing he says: I certainly do think that Pirate radio was indeed worthwhile, it broke the stranglehold that the BBC had on the music industry, it then forced them to concede and allow the public to have access to a whole spectrum of music that was not previously easily available.

The pirates attacked the establishment and won. Now we can listen to numerous stations and select any style of music - wonderful.

I'm pleased with the small part I played in the pirate radio saga, and congratulate all my old colleagues.

If only we could do a similar trick with the television medium, I really do feel that is an area that does need a shake up. But of course the cost to set up such a challenge would be enormous.

3) **The Jocks Who Rocked** (stations from the north of England and Scotland) produced by Jon Myer and chaired by Tony Currie. Although most of the offshore stations of the Sixties

were clustered round the south-east corner of England, pirate radio was not restricted to the home counties. In this session we met four DJs who worked, for at least part of their careers, further north: Mike Ahern (Caroline North), Noel Miller (Radio 270), Ben Healy and Jack McLaughlin (both Radio Scotland).

4) **It's Smooth Sailing** (Radio London) produced by Mary Payne and chaired by Radio Academy Director, Trevor Dann. Founded by Texans, Big L was the first to introduce American-style radio, complete with jingles and a Top 40 format, to British audiences. Between 1964 and 67, Radio London, with its powerful 50KW transmitter, gained millions of listeners. The panellists were Tony Blackburn (aboard June 66 - July 67), Duncan Johnson (February 65 - July 66), Norman St John (July 66 - Feb 67) and Ed 'Stewpot' Stewart (July 65 - Aug 67).

5) *No Man Shall Ever Forget...* (Caroline continues) produced by Jon Myer and chaired by Phil Martin. The panel were Mark Sloane (North), Robbie Dale and Johnnie Walker (South). The session title comes from a broadcast by Johnnie Walker in which he claimed that "no man will ever forget Monday 14 August 1967". Certainly no one in this room would ever forget it. At midnight that Monday, the new law came into effect outlawing offshore radio. Two broadcasters were on the air on Caroline South as millions tuned in to hear them challenge the legislation. And they were present to tell the tale: Robbie Dale and Johnnie Walker. Also sharing the stage was Mark Sloane (Caroline North). At first sight, former Britain Radio presenter Phil Martin might seem an odd choice to chair this panel but there was a good reason for the decision: after his offshore career, Phil Martin became a journalist with the *Daily Express*. One of his first jobs for the paper was to go out to the North Sea to interview the DJs on Radio Caroline South who had continued broadcasting despite the new law. He managed to blag his way on to the tender and got out to the *Mi Amigo* - but the DJs refused to speak to him as the interview had not been approved by the management in Amsterdam. He didn't get his interview in '67 - but he did 40 years later when he chaired this session.

Organising committee member Gerry Zieler worked under the name Guy Hamilton at Radio Essex/BBMS and 270 and later moved into independent local radio and set up Wiltshire Radio, having also broadcast on Piccadilly Radio, BRMB, Radio Orwell and Radio Hallam. He recalls: "Looking back over the (ouch) 43 years since I headed out to the Knock John Fort, I realise now how lucky I was to be around and nuts about radio (technically) at the time that wacky pirate entrepreneurs like O'Rahilly, Bates, Proudfoot and Birch were doing their thing.

"Format-wise, there's still nothing to compare - or was it the music we were all blessed with at the time? Radio Essex/BBMS's easy listening format was amazingly enjoyable but of course largely confined by transmitter power to audiophile jellyfish and the Dog and Duck pub at Pluck's Gutter.

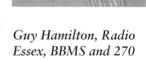

Guy Hamilton, Radio Essex, BBMS and 270

"Later on, I was proud of what we started at our little ILR at Wiltshire Radio, but have little feeling for what it became. The inevitable commercial growth of Wiltshire into GWR/GCap had a deleterious effect on content everywhere in the City-driven hunt for extra profit, though I'm immensely proud that it was my old colleagues 'what done it'.

"The last couple of years have been wonderful for pirate celebrations and reunions. I've loved it all, and was very honoured to have been asked to serve on the Radio Academy committee which organised the Pirates' 40th bash at Sugar Reef. Having said that I wish we'd staged it on HMS *President* as I wanted, especially with fantastic sunny weather we had that day. I also pulled together (or apart!) the forts panel and I'd like to say how easy and pleasurable it was. But… it was actually quite difficult to persuade those who still had functioning faculties to come to London to strut their stuff again. Some were unbelievably precious. But the crew we got had a lot of fun - even royalty attended, didn't it?! I got to meet names I'd only heard of, and later had some great lunches and get-togethers with a few reprobates: Rosko (MY teenage hero!), overseas mates like Mike Hayes and Noel 'Neddy' Miller and many more.

"We also had a wonderful trip out to the Knock John in 2006, and another Radio Essex reunion bash at Pluck's Gutter in 2008, when some of us celebrated 60 or more… We've outlasted most of our ships already, and some of us might just outlast some of the forts too!"

Dr Martin van der Ven who runs the www.offshore-radio.de website was present at the Celebration and recalls:

It was one of the few sunny weekends during the summer of 2007, that three offshore radio anoraks from the continent (Hans Knot, Rob Olthof and me) travelled to London for an exciting weekend full of memories from the golden offshore radio period in the1960s. In the beginning, we were a bit sceptical if all the well-known names having been published on different Internet sites would indeed be attending. But arriving at the venue not far away from Piccadilly Circus, we couldn't trust our eyes and ears. It was such a huge gathering of all those celebrities. For an avid radio listener in the Sixties (remember there wasn't any webcam or digital photo camera at that time!) 'your' familiar voices on the wireless didn't seem to have a face. You simply listened to them. But here in London - 40 years later - you had the chance to see them all and to identify the face behind the voice. Johnnie Walker, Tony Blackburn, Robbie Dale, Keith Hampshire, Emperor Rosko, Roger Day and even Ronan O'Rahilly - just to name a few. There were interesting panels to follow but you also had the chance to have a personal chat with all your favourite radio stars. Everyone seemed to be in such a good mood, and you had the strong feeling of a big class reunion. It was a superb event. Well done to the organisers!

Trevor Dann, Director of The Radio Academy summed up the occasion:

Our Celebration of Offshore Radio was a huge thrill for me. In my mid-teens I was an obsessive fan of the pirate ships, especially Radio London. And although I've subsequently met and worked with legends like John Peel, Johnnie Walker and Tony Blackburn, this event reminded me how important they were to my life and my career in radio. These guys were real heroes, buccaneers and freedom fighters who changed the face of UK broadcasting for good. So it was especially heartening to see so many younger people, including current DJs and radio executives, paying homage to the innovators of so much of what we all now take for granted.

List of offshore radio personnel from all eras attending the Radio Academy Celebration

Mike Ahern (Caroline North, South)

David Allan (390, 355)

John Aston aka John Stewart aka Chris Stewart (KING, 390, Caroline North, South, 270, 355)

Nick Bailey (Caroline South, North)

Bud Ballou aka Howie Castle (Caroline South and International)

'Prince' Michael Bates - son of Roy Bates (Radio Essex)

Colin Berry (Caroline South)

Tony Blackburn (Caroline South, London)

Black Printz (Real name Holman) (City, Atlantis, Voice of Peace)

Pete Brady (London)

Mike Brereton (Engineer Essex)

Woolf Byrne (City, Britain, 390)

Candy Calvert (City)

Gordon Cruse (Caroline South, North)

Brian Cullingford (KING, 390)

Robbie Dale (real name Robinson) (Caroline South and International, Veronica)

Ian Damon (London)

Roger Day (SRE, Caroline South, RNI, Caroline seventies)

Dick Dixon (City)

John Edward aka Johnny Flux (City, London)

Paul Elvey (City)

Paul Freeman (Essex) Graham Gill (London, Britain, England, 390, Caroline seventies, RNI)

Guy Hamilton (real name Gerry Zierler) (Essex, BBMS, 270)

Keith Hampshire (Caroline South)

George Hare (working on land for Caroline)

Dave Hawkins (technician on London)

Ben Healy (Scotland)

Paul Hollingdale (CNBC)

Mel Howard (Caroline South, Scotland)

Phil Jay (City)

Duncan Johnson (London, RNI)

Martin Kayne aka Michael Cane (Essex, 355, Caroline International (North), RNI)

John Kerr (Scotland)

Bob Le-Roi (City, Caroline eighties)

Dave MacKay aka Dave Gilbee (City, 355)

Keith Martin aka Gary Courteney (Atlanta, Caroline South, 390)

Phil Martin (SRE, 355)

Jack McLaughlin aka Steve Taylor (Scotland, 270, 390)

Tony Meehan (Scotland, Britain)Ricky Michaels (City)

Noel Miller (270)

Spangles Muldoon aka Chris Cary (Caroline International [South], RNI, Radio 199, Caroline seventies)

Ronan O'Rahilly (founder Caroline)

Dick Palmer (Essex, BBMS, Caroline seventies)

Mitch Philistin (chef on London)

Emperor Rosko (Caroline South)

George Saunders (engineer Caroline)

Roger Scott aka Arnold Layne (real name Greg Bance) (Essex, 270, 390, Caroline North, RNI)

Keith Skues (Caroline South, London)

Mark Sloane aka Mark Hammerton (KING, 390, Caroline South, 355, Caroline International [North])

Cathy Spence (ran the Radio Scotland Clan)

Patrick Starling (engineer Caroline South, Laissez Faire)

Ed Stewart (London)

Norman St John (City, Caroline South, London)

Ray Teret (Caroline North and South)

Carl Thomson (technician on Caroline)

Alan Turner (Caroline North)

Bryan Vaughan (Atlanta, Caroline South)

Johnnie Walker (England, Britain, Caroline South and International)

Graham Webb (Caroline South)

Mark West aka Mark Wesley (Essex, BBMS, 270, Scotland, RNI)

Stephen West (KING, 390, 355)

Dave Williams (Caroline South, North)

Penny "Wolfe" (Jason Wolfe's widow). (Jason worked on Caroline North and on RNI)

Ray Anderson aka Ray Warner on Atlantis, manager Laser Hot Hits 576)

Elija van den Berg (Caroline office seventies)

Martin Fisher (Caroline seventies)

Nigel Harris aka Stuart Russell (Caroline seventies and eighties)

Peter Moore (manager Caroline eighties until today)

Robbie Owen (Voice of Peace)

Don Stevens (Caroline seventies, Voice of Peace)

Shaun Tilley (Caroline eighties)

Mick Williams aka Ray Clark (Caroline eighties)

Steve Scruton and Dave Cash returning to the LV18

PIRATE BBC ESSEX, AUGUST 2007

Award winning Pirate BBC Essex became one of the world's favourite radio stations in April 2004 when it marked the 40th anniversary of the start of offshore radio in Britain.

Three and a half years later the station was back to mark the 40th anniversary of the offshore stations closing on 14 August 1967.

Orginal DJs from the watery wireless days of the 1960s were Mike Ahern, John Aston, Pete Brady, Bud Ballou, Dave Cash, Gordon Cruse, Ian Damon, Roger Day, Tom Edwards, Guy Hamilton, Keith Hampshire, Duncan Johnson, John Kerr, Keith Martin, Emperor Rosko, Keith Skues, Norman St John, Ed Stewart, Johnnie Walker, Graham Webb and Mark Wesley. A number had flown in especially from Australia, Canada and the USA. Steve Young was disappointed to find himself unable to travel due to passport problems, but he sent a recorded message from Canada.

They were joined by Ray Clark, Graham Cooke, Tony Currie, Tim Gillett, Alison Hartley, Steve Scruton, Glenn Speller and Ian Wyatt some of whom had appeared in the Pirate BBC Essex 2004 line-up.

Mike and Charlie were the engineers and the massive task of technical support which included disseminating emails was provided by John Lowry, Jonathan Taylor and Chris Woodward.

Appearing for both the 2004 and 2007 broadcasts was Daphne, the infamous permanent resident of the LV18. She has been called 'a loose woman' as she regularly fell to bits but continued to appear regularly on air. She even received fan mail. On one occasion Keith Skues, who had presented the late night show, returned to his cabin and found Daphne in his bunk, literally legless. He made his excuses and left the cabin.

Daphne was infact a lifesize plastic mannequin 36x25x34 with adjustable arms and legs.

Once again Pirate BBC Essex was based aboard the classic light vessel LV*18*, owned by the Pharos Trust and moored off Harwich.

Pirate BBC Essex went on air at 6.00am on Thursday, 9 August and closed down at 3.00pm on Tuesday, 14 August. Listeners were able to tune in to the radio station across the world via computer at bbc.co.uk/essex as well as via MW on 729, 765 and 1530.

The broadcasts attracted large television and radio coverage which included BBC-TV who had

Keith Skues and "Daphne"

a crew broadcasting live from the LV*18* on the first day, with coverage both on local and national news; CBC (Canadian Broadcasting Company); Meridian TV; and Sky TV. Paul Rowley provided the BBCs radio coverage, reporting to numerous local stations up and down the country.

National, regional and local newspapers also extensively gave many column inches in their journals.

Asked if he thought it was strange that the BBC were producing 'pirate' radio broadcasts, Tim Gillett said: "Yes, to the BBC hierarchy of the 1960s the pirates were the 'auld' enemy. We produced these shows as an acknowledgement of the work those young DJs did in 1964. And having some of them recreate those days was very exciting. I think they enjoyed it as well. Dave Cash even proved to all on board what a brilliant cook he was serving up gourmet dishes. Those of us who are younger than the DJs of the 1960s were privileged to work with these broadcasting legends who only did this out of their passion for radio.

"The idea of running Pirate BBC Essex was shipmate Steve Scruton's who wanted to do something to mark the offshore anniversary. I approached our then managing editor Margaret Hyde and the rest, as they say, is history. Listeners wrote to us asking if we would do another one and yes, three years later we did. Our new managing editor was enthusiastic as were the DJs and back-up staff.

"We provided the BBC with an opportunity to add thousands of new listeners who don't feel served by any radio stations on the dial. Many of these listeners were baby boomers and they came back to the BBC in force. Many would like to see a permanent radio station featuring this kind of music and played by personality DJs."

The major technical change the DJs found was instant access to and from the internet. As an example Mike Ahern was broadcasting from the LV*18*. Within minutes of his show beginning he received an email from his sons and their families who were listening in Australia. They wished him well with the broadcasts.

Now a successful presenter on BBC Radio 2, Johnnie Walker was asked if he felt all the effort of defying the law on 14 August 1967 had been worth it. "It certainly was. We attracted audiences in their millions in those days and no other radio station since has ever bettered those listening figures, apart from national radio. The very existence of Radio Caroline and other stations certainly shook up the BBC who in time were forced to provide the kind of music programming that listeners wanted to hear rather than what had gone before when management delivered programmes containing what they felt listeners ought to hear."

Forty years previously Ed Stewart had been involved with the closing hours of Radio London so he and fellow DJs brought Pirate BBC to a close on 14 August at 3.00pm. He said afterwards: "I certainly would not have predicted I would be doing a similar show 40 years on. Radio London had a winning format which does not appear to have been emulated by any other British radio station. We averaged 18 records an hour and a maximum of six minutes for commercials. One of my funniest moments on the *Galaxy* was when I had to read a commercial for the station's T-shirt. I had said 'Don't forget your Big L T-shirt. It comes in three sizes – small, medium and large, with 266 on the back and Big L on the front. The cost? A mere 12s 6d, which includes pastage and poking!' I followed this with the weather forecast and suffered another spoonerism…I said 'And there'll be shattered scowers everywhere!' By coming out to the LV*18* it has been fun to mix with the DJs, many of whom I haven't seen for a very long time."

There was plenty going on-shore as well. To coincide with the broadcast, Dave Cash and Rosko organised two "Last Time" dances while three Audiences With the Pirates raised funds for the Electric Palace Theatre.

Having only days earlier taken some of their display of amazing offshore memorabilia to the Radio Academy celebration, Chris and Jackie Dannatt were able to bring the entire collection to show in the Mayflower Exhibition Centre on Ha'penny Pier. It included original photographs, letters, records and the original Radio Caroline microphone. It attracted huge attention from visitors and some radio fans brought personal mementos to donate to the Dannatts'collection.

Tim Bishop, BBC Head of Region in the East said: "It was a moment of inspiration from the team at BBC Essex. Like many of our listeners they grew up with the pirates and it was a great idea to bring that era back to life. They say nostalgia isn't what it used to be but on this occasion everyone got such a buzz out of that shared experience of working, cooking and broadcasting together in the cramped confines of a boat that after the 2004 Pirate BBC Essex, they just wanted to carry on, so they came back and did it all again.

"And it worked even better second time around with some genuine household names bringing some of their old magic back to the airwaves. It was so good it just reminded you how much it meant to people back when the real pirates took to the air. Forty years on that excitement was reflected in an exceptional audience response to the anniversary broadcasts. Hard to beat that when the 50th comes around but I suspect somewhere someone is already plotting."

PIRATES HONOURED

Order of the British Empire
OBE
John Peel. Birthday Honours 1998 presented by HRH Prince of Wales
MBE
Keith Skues. New Year's Honours 2004   presented by HM The Queen
Johnnie Walker. New Year's Honours 2006 presented by HRH Prince Charles

Fellow of the Radio Academy
Richard Park, 1993
Ronan O'Rahilly, 2007

Radio Caroline's founder Ronan O'Rahilly was genuinely surprised and delighted to receive his Fellowship of the Academy. As GCap's Ralph Bernard said in his citation, "if we'd seen Ronan in here 40 years ago it would have been our duty to arrest him."

PRS Radio Academy John Peel Award for Outstanding Contributions to Music Radio
1990   John Peel
1991   Kenny Everett

1993   Richard Park
1995   Johnnie Walker
1997   Tony Blackburn

PRS Radio Academy Hall of Fame
Pre 2006
        Tony Blackburn
        Kenny Everett
        Stuart Henry
        John Peel
        Tommy Vance
        Johnnie Walker
2006   Tony Windsor
2007   Adrian Love
2008   Emperor Rosko

British Academy of Composers and Songwriters Gold Badge Awards
1976   Ken Evans
1977   Alan Keen
1992   Tony Blackburn
1993   John Peel
2005   Keith Skues MBE

The Biannual Amsterdam Radio Day Awards (2007)
"An Outstanding Contribution to Offshore Radio"
Bull Verweij, Johnnie Walker, Tom Mulder (=Klaas Vaak on Radio Veronica)

"Offshore Radio Top Technical Support"
Peter Chicago

"Offshore Radio Writers and Historians"
Jon Myer

"The Radio Anoraks Award"
Rob Mesander

WEBSITES FOR OFFSHORE RADIO

www.radiolondon.co.uk   www.offshoreechos.com
www.offshoreradio.co.uk   www.offshore-radio.de
www.radiocaroline.co.uk   www.bobleroi.co.uk
www.oldiesproject.com   www.offshoremusicradio.com
www.tomread.co.uk   www.soundscapes.info
www.hansknot.com   www.project-redsand.com
www.adroberts.net/andy/

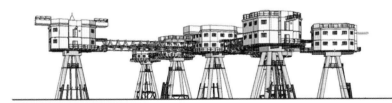

Red Sands 2007 without the radio mast

Red Sands. This formed the studio complex 2007

Members of the 2007 crew for Red Sands Radio

Red Sands 2008 with aerial and mast

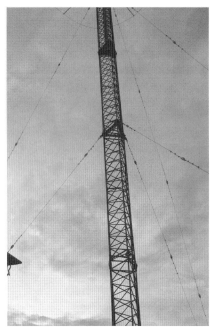

Red Sands Newsroom 2007

Aerial 2008 and flag

RADIO FROM RED SANDS YESTERDAY, TODAY and TOMORROW

Closed by the Wilson Labour Government in 1967, save for the song of seagulls that had made the fort their home. It was only as two new generators were powered up in the prevailing fresh westerly winds did Red Sands Fort stir and tremble and once again come to life after an imposed silence of 40 years thanks to Bob Le-Roi who had worked on the fort with Radio City four decades previously.

With electrical and electronic wiring complete, a modern digital studio and medium wave transmitter feeding a newly built antenna rising skyward from the top of the Gun Tower's roof the first radio signal emanated on 1278 kHz on 13 July 2007 with a positioning statement 'From the Coast to the City this is Red Sands Radio' serving Whitstable, the North Kent Coast and Thames Estuary basin with 'The Best Music of Yesterday and Today'.

Bob Le-Roi at controls of Red Sands Radio 2008

Benefiting from improved technology and a superb sea wave the signal travelled wide and far. Internet Audio Streaming enhanced output as Red Sands Radio picked up a healthy worldwide listenership. For the first time transmissions from the Fort were legal, with programmes commemorating the anniversary of the last broadcast four decades earlier and the Marine Etc Broadcasting (Offences) Act of 1967 that effectively silenced Britain's Offshore Radio.

Red Sands Radio returned again in 2008 using a brand-new substantial antenna. The generators were re-housed, and many new items of studio equipment installed. This time programmes were more locally focused and informative. The first local radio

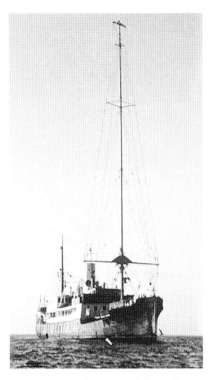

Radio Caroline North broadcast from the former Baltic ferry boat m.v. Fredericia

advertisements came to air. Unsigned artists and specialist music strands were broadcast over extended transmission hours.

Another first came, as a worldwide amateur radio station operating under the call sign GB0RSR was set-up on the Fort by the International company ICOM. It logged a phenomenal 30 counties through hundreds of live contacts.

Red Sands Radio showed over a two-year period, that even with a small onboard team, normally three living in 'Spartan' conditions supported by meagre finance, some seven nautical miles from shore and far from home comforts, radio could be local, fresh and exciting.

Programme director Bob Le-Roi said:

Despite harsh economic times we plan to continue the adventure in 2009. With overdue structural work planned on the Fort, due to commence in the spring Red Sands Radio plans to transmit from shore. In order to achieve this we need to find a suitable base for our studio and antenna. We must cover licence fees and running costs, normally through sponsorship and a small amount of local advertising. Shortfalls come from our own pocket. It's always a challenge to raise the finance but we have through sponsorship managed to maintain our seasonal operation. In addition we've had some 'material' support, i.e. web stream hosting, printing, banners and limited subsistence.

ISLE OF MAN CONVENTION, SEPTEMBER 2008

Former Radio Caroline North DJs, newsreaders and engineers returned to the Isle of Man in September 2008 to commemorate the 40th anniversary of the radio station's departure from Manx waters.

It was the first gathering in the Island of staff and fans to remember the ship that operated off Ramsey Bay between 1964 and 1968.

More than 100 delegates attended the convention, from the station's founder, Ronan O'Rahilly, and newsreader Nick Bailey to fans from across the UK. Among the DJs were Alan Turner, who was one of the three DJs who broadcast continuously on the Caroline's journey from Harwich to Ramsey in July 1964. He says:

Mention Radio Caroline to anyone old enough to remember the station and it usually brings a smile on their face, mostly associated with happy memories of those days.

Working as a disc jockey on radio was a particularly special event for DJ Mick Luvzit who married the sister of another DJ, Ray Teret, live on air in September 1966.

Ray remembers the day the former Baltic ferryboat the m.v. Fredericia sailed into Ramsey Bay in July 1964.

'Ugli' Ray Teret, Caroline North

I was having breakfast one morning and my Mum said 'There was this radio station on a ship playing rock'n'roll. It was called Radio Caroline and the DJs were playing pop music. I listened, mouth open and I said to myself 'Wow, this is the job I want.' One of the DJs on air mentioned London, so I wrote to Radio Caroline, London

Ray Teret with the Beatles in 1964

and said You need ME. Amazingly the letter got there and I had an instant reply from Chris Moore who was the programme director. I did an audition and he offered me a job right away. I was just a kid at the time. Travelling to the Isle of Man on a real plane was scary, but fantastic. I was the first Northern English DJ to be taken on with Caroline North. I was 18 at the time. It was the first time ever I had travelled outside of England. I even had to obtain a passport so I could leave the Isle of Man to go through customs, get on the tender and go three miles off the coast to go to work. Amazing! Only now after forty-odd years I still can't believe how lucky I was. It has all been brought back to me with this Amazing Exhibition on the Isle of Man.

Newsreader Nick Bailey - who now works for Classic FM - was joined by former colleague John Aston and the original chief engineer, Ove Sjostrom, flew in from Sweden to link up with past collaborator Trevor Grantham.

Alan Turner and Ronan O'Rahilly with the Caroline bell located at the Pirates of the Irish Sea exhibition at Peel, Isle of Man

Flashback to Radio Caroline North. Alan Turner in 1964

During the weekend they visited the Pirates of the Irish Sea exhibition at the House of Manannan in Peel and attended a conference at the Manx Museum where former staff shared their experiences and talked about the history of the radio station. Conference organiser Andy Wint said: 'To go to Ramsey where it all used to happen was extremely poignant for a lot of people. Some of them hadn't seen each other for 40 years. Everyone thought the exhibition at the House of Manannan was first class and was good enough to be at a museum anywhere in the world.'

The three national newspapers on the Isle of Man gave the event wide publicity.

When the UK Government announced its plans to introduce legislation to close down Radio Caroline, the Manx Government opposed it and sent an emergency delegation to London to put forward a case that the Island was exempt from the legislation. They were unsuccessful which caused a constitutional crisis.

Following political and legal pressure and unpaid bills, the radio ship was towed away in the middle of the night in March 1968 with the few remaining DJs still onboard.

PIRATE MEMORIES FROM A BBC POLITICAL CORRESPONDENT

Paul Rowley is the political correspondent for BBC Local Radio, based in London. He grew up in the North of England listening to Radio Caroline. Subsequently he has produced three radio shows heard around the country to do with pirate radio. He takes a trip down memory lane.

Paul Rowley

Pirate radio changed my life. When I first heard Caroline North as a nine-year old living in Wigan, it knocked me out. To hear pop records on the wireless during daylight hours was revolutionary. In 1964 we only had the odd smattering of pop records on the BBC Light Programme during the week, and it was only at weekends when we got Saturday Club with Brian Matthew (later to be presented by the redoubtable Keith Skues) and Pick of the Pops with Alan Freeman. You got the impression that the patrician corporation felt that pop music was a dangerous American import that would damage the health of British youngsters. We did have Luxembourg at night, but they were mostly sponsored programmes by the major record companies, and the signal always seemed to fade when they played a decent record.

My favourite DJs aboard Caroline North were Tom Lodge and Mike Ahern, and I was really upset in 1965 when they left to join Caroline South. In 1966 I desperately wanted to leave home and run away to sea to be a pirate radio DJ on Caroline North. But I couldn't swim, still can't for that matter, although my two children can, and anyway I had to do my 11-plus. My mum said it was too expensive to join the Caroline Club. It was 5/-, and I only got 1/6d a week pocket money (seven and a half pence these days). But she promised me a Caroline transistor radio if I passed. It was too great an incentive. I went to the grammar school, but my battery-operated set, like Caroline North itself, didn't last.

But it was good enough to pick up other pirate stations, beaming through at night from the south of England, even though it was 200 miles away. I loved Radio London. I thought the presenters were far more professional, and the jingles were out of this world. Kenny Everett became my hero, and I was delighted in 2002 to be nominated for a Sony Radio Award for my documentary: *Kenny Everett: The BBC Local Radio Years.*

I cried my eyes out as a 12-year-old at 1500 on 14 August 1967 when Paul Kaye said "Big L Time is three o'clock. And Radio London is now closing down".

At midnight, I was in a dilemma, trying to listen to both Johnnie Walker on Caroline South, playing *All You Need Is Love* by the Beatles, and joining Robbie Dale, singing along to Pete Seeger's rendition of *We Shall Overcome*. On Caroline North, "Daffy" Don Allen was more sedate, playing the Isle of Man National Anthem: *Oh Land of Our Birth*, a testimony to the strong affiliation that the station had with the island that had been its home for more than three years.

On August 14, 1987, on the 20th anniversary of the Marine Offences Act, I was the Political Editor of Radio City (Liverpool), and made a radio documentary *When Pirates Ruled the Waves*, looking back at those wonderful watery wireless days. I updated the programme in 1992 on the 25th anniversary, when I was by then the Political Correspondent for Independent Radio News (IRN). On the 40th anniversary, I had joined the BBC, and did a new set up of interviews for *When Pirates Ruled the Waves* (Mark 3).

As a listener I felt very fortunate to have lived through a wonderful period for radio, and for music. Pirate radio gave an exposure to artists you would never hear on the BBC at a time when there was a music explosion underway with the Beatles, the Rolling Stones, the Beach Boys, Bob Dylan, The Who, the Kinks, Dusty Springfield, the Walker Brothers, Roy Orbison, Gene Pitney, Otis Redding, Georgie Fame, and record labels like Tamla Mowtown, Stax, Atlantic, Island, Immediate, and President. On Caroline North I heard Northern Soul, Ska, and psychedelia for the first time.

I became a teenage newspaper journalist in 1974, when legalised commercial radio came to the North-West. First with Piccadilly Radio in Manchester on 2 April 1974, when Roger Day (ex Caroline South) opened the station to the sound of *Good Vibrations* by the Beach Boys. Stevie Merike (ex-Caroline) and Bob Synder (ex-270) were also on board the station, run by former Radio London boss Philip Birch. On 21 October 1974 Radio City opened in Liverpool. Within the first week I was covering sport for the station, and at the end of my newspaper indentures in 1977, I joined the station full time, staying for 10 years.

In 2008, I completed another documentary, *The Other Radio Caroline*, paying tribute to the largely untold story of Caroline North. I visited the Isle of Man for the first time, attending a special convention in Douglas organised by Andy Wint (ex Capital, Chiltern, Beacon, Manx Radio). There has also been an excellent exhibition "Pirates of the Irish Sea" at the House of Manannan Museum in Peel. The convention was attended by former DJs Ray Teret, Martin Kayne, Alan Turner and Wally Meehan, newsmen Nick Bailey and Jon Aston, and engineer Trevor Grantham. But pride of place went to Caroline's founder Ronan O'Rahilly, making his first visit to the island in 40 years.

I've now been in the business 35 years. Not quite as extensive as Mr Skues. But I owe my debt to people like Cardboard Shoes for whetting my appetite for radio. Despite making a career out of this game, I am still ostensibly a radio listener. At times I get frustrated at the way that commercial radio has gone after living (and working) in it through the glory days of the 70s and 80s. I never think of myself as a BBC man, even though I've been here for 15 years, and it's a delight to be on BBC Local Radio as its Political Correspondent with heroes like Roger Day, Dave Cash and of course, the author of this book, who has written the most definitive guide to offshore radio in Britain.

So thank you Caroline, London, England, Britain, City, 390, 270, Scotland, and Essex. You changed the face of broadcasting, and helped give a young radio lover from Wigan a career.

40th   ANNIVERSARY REUNION OF BRITAIN RADIO/SWINGING RADIO
ENGLAND, 13 May 2006

*Flashback to 1966 (l to r) Ron O'Quinn, Brian Tylney, Colin Nicol, Larry Dean, Rick
Randall, Johnnie Walker and Roger Day. At the controls, Jerry Smithwick*

**SWINGING
RADIO ENGLAND**

A Tale of Pirates, Texans and Teenagers

*At the 40th Anniversary party held in London in May 2006 (l– r) Phil Martin, Roger Day,
Johnnie Walker, Rick Randall and Larry Dean sing the Swinging Radio England jingles*

Texans Don Pierson and Tom Danaher, were instrumental in setting up Radio London in 1964. Two years later they planned another radio ship that would sail across the Atlantic. The ship, Olga Patricia, was later renamed Laissez–Faire. Two radio stations would operate from the one ship as Radio England and Britain Radio. A more detailed account of the stations' short life can be found in Chapter Four Rock Around the Clock.

Don Pierson died in 1996 but his son Grey and wife Paula organised a reunion in London attended by many of the original DJs and personnel. Grey also commissioned as a tribute to his father, a docu-drama about Don's role in offshore radio. He remembered his excitement as a 15-year old boy living in Texas who was suddenly whisked off with his family to 'swinging' London. He enjoyed the city, its people, and especially the music.

Grey's new documentary, made by Green HD Productions, concerns, "Pirate Radio in England in 1966, and more specifically Radio London and Radio England, and the Americanisation of rock music in Great Britain. Shot on location in London and Texas, this film, produced in 2008, is described as fun, hip and exciting while presenting the music of the 1960s and the history of this great rebellion in a way that will inform even the most knowledgeable of music historians."

The film is narrated by Steve England and features interviews with original DJs, including Dave Cash, Pete Brady, Roger Day, Larry Dean, Dave Gilbee, Phil Martin, Ron O'Quinn, Rick Randall, John Ross-Barnard and Johnnie Walker, interspersed with dramatisations of their tales of life on an offshore station.

FROM PRAM TO POP – the musings of a fan of 'the wireless'

Jenny Matthew is a life-long fan of radio and is herself an occasional contributor to the broadcast media. She is the author of over 60 published scientific papers plus a few book chapters and has been involved in numerous 'Healthy eating' promotions including the Fruit & Veg section of the European Commission funded 'Info 2000' project. Jenny is a serving magistrate. She helped to set up 'Magistrates in the Community', an initiative aimed at publicising the role and work of magistrates. She did a stint on the National Executive Committee of the Magistrates' Association of England & Wales and most recently she was in Cape Town, South Africa, for a meeting of the Commonwealth Magistrates' & Judges' Association. During 1996 Jenny was invited to join the BBC Local Radio Advisory Council (Norfolk), a body of which she was a member into the new millennium in the year 2000.

My mother liked relating how, as a baby sitting in a big coach-built style perambulator, I set the thing bouncing up and down whilst voicing "Moo, moo". This was not an early interest in cattle but my way of getting her to find me some music on the wireless. We are talking middle of World War II and radio was a major part of family life; I grew up in a culture of regular listening. I have early memories of both my Mum and Dad tuning across the dial to find what was available.

In my early teens the fascination was with Radio Luxembourg, much encouraged by my father who spent ages peering at the radio set's magic eye which opened and closed as one homed in on a frequency.

Luxembourg provided us with an altogether different type of programme and a much more relaxed style of presentation than that of the BBC. Then in 1964 came the age of offshore broadcasting with the arrival of Radio Caroline. I had just moved from East Anglia to work in south east London and was miffed that reception was almost non-existent in the capital.

This was true also at the beginning of the then inappropriately named, Radio London. I went back to visit friends near Ipswich as much as anything so we could listen to 'the Pirates'. My then boyfriend's mother had a battered old Baby Austin car and I had a driving licence. I would drive my beloved just far enough up the Essex coast to get a clear signal but generally stop short of putting too many miles on the clock. However, a few times, we went up to the Frinton area and sat looking out to sea to the 'Pirate' ships through binoculars. It was just such an unbelievably incredible and exciting time. Much is written elsewhere in this volume of the brief, golden age of offshore radio between 1964 and 1967, the programming style, technical aspects, DJs and other relevant history. Too much fun is not good for us, the Government of the day decided that the offshore stations had to go and the much-debated and opposed Marine Offences Act came into UK law on 14 August 1967. Radio London closed down but Caroline carried on. Up to the beginning of the 1980s friends and I would tune to Radio Caroline. BBC Radios One and Two never did match the 'Pirates' but they tried. The present Radio 1 format no longer falls within what should be funded by public subscription (Licence fee).

Fast forward to a Bank Holiday Special on 31 May 1993. I am scanning the airwaves seeking something a bit 'edgy'; I hear a voice, it is, it must be, Keith Skues, I don't believe it, but it is, falls into the 'I thought he was dead' scenario. Now commences a whole new listening experience. Credit must go to BBC Radio Norfolk boss, David Clayton, who heard RAF reservist, Keith, doing a piece to air from RAF Marham (Norfolk) and thought that he ought to get him on BBC Radio Norfolk. The rest, as they say, is broadcasting history. Keith Skues did various 'fill in' stints on Radio Norfolk and on 3 April 1995 commenced regular broadcasting across the Eastern Counties. This provided an altogether different and refreshing programming style. It was 'personality' radio with a high profile presenter who had an amazing selection of records to play and relevant chat. The Beeb did the right thing and we got Skuesy five nights a week. I truly believe that his programmes were a major part of the catalyst for the renewed interest in all things 'Pirate Radio' and led to the promotion and execution of the various reunions and broadcasts outlined in this publication.

I travelled to the East Coast for Pirate Radio related events, as listed elsewhere in this chapter, between 1995 (Radio Caroline on RSL 7 Aug to 4 Sept and still have the publicity poster on my kitchen wall) and 2007 for the fabulous BBC Pirate Radio Essex broadcasts from the LV*18* anchored in Harwich Harbour. I first heard the highly intriguing and beguiling *A Whiter Shade of Pale* whilst sitting on Clacton beach in 1967. I experienced a re-take in 1995 listening to the RSL broadcast. My regards to Janice, Mrs Ian 'Wombat' Damon, with whom I shared a perch on Harwich Pier during her husband's broadcast from the LV*18*.

Commercial local radio was slow to come, more so to some areas of the UK than others. On the whole it has proved disappointing. I used to look forward to tuning to the various local stations as I drove around the country. It's an excellent way of finding out what is going on in a neighbourhood and listening to different presenters. Now it all sounds the same. Our own Radio Broadland (Broadland FM) has been gobbled up by the Global radio network and on 5 January 2009 Broadland was renamed Heart and I no longer bother. A sad loss. In their halcyon days Malcolm James presented a delightful 'mellow music' weekend programme and we had former 'Pirate', Roger 'Twiggy' Day. I even persuaded Radio Broadland to put me on air doing a 'Magistrates in the Community' spot – a first for such a piece for them. I very much doubt that the present management would want to go 'off format'. Very, very local community radio fares better and I very much hope that it flourishes. In Norwich we had 'Crown Radio' on restricted licences for a while. That was good and another old 'Pirate', Mark Roman, who was then resident in Norfolk, made some distinguished contributions and played some ace music. I am particularly interested in 'Future Radio', in Norwich which is providing a lot of help for disadvantaged young people with opportunities to work in various aspects of broadcasting and has recording studios available for a whole range of community projects.

BBC local/regional radio has, generally, gone from strength to strength and is a major part of life in whatever area it serves. We rely on it for information at times of adverse weather and other local emergencies. Indeed, Keith Skues was instrumental in finding a person who had gone walkabout from a residential care home. No sooner had the alert gone out on air than the person was spotted.

As regards the 'entertainment' part of the BBC remit, it does not always suffice. Budgetary constraints certainly apply but managers at all

Jenny Matthew with Ray Anderson and Ed Stewart

levels are reluctant to fully take on board the wishes of listeners. Only a miniscule proportion of funds acquired via the compulsory licence fee is allocated to radio. Local/regional radio gets but a meagre amount of that. BBC local radio relies too much on 'phone-ins, fairly bland magazine programmes and football coverage. The best times are Christmas and other Bank Holidays when 'specials' are aired. At a national, regional and local level, there is still difficulty in accurately separating news, opinion and comment. A rush to analysis and opinion overtakes good reporting. Management has a controlling style but is not in control. However, the BBC is the national treasure and we should support it whilst urging better compliance with the wishes of licence fee payers.

BBC East, my own area, is bold in allowing airtime to some outstandingly individual radio presenters. These include Keith Skues and Richard Spendlove. Keith now provides Rock 'n' Roll Heaven from BBC Three Counties on Saturdays and the famous Pirate Radio Skues (PRS) across the Eastern Counties for four hours on Sunday evenings. The latter is a mix of 1960s records from the pirate era, relevant chat and archive pieces. Mr Spendlove is a truly free spirit who doesn't seem to bother too much about current 'PC' values. He plays great Rock 'n' Roll music and utterly rejects remixes. Both presenters use a lot of their own vinyl recordings of tunes of the '60s.

And what would I have done with those naughty Pirates had I been a magistrate in the 1960s and any of them came before me - declared an interest and withdrawn from the bench. The owner of the Baby Austin alluded to above and later to be my mother-in-law who worked for solicitors in the City of London, always claimed that it was illegal to listen to the Pirates. I doubt that but I don't think it was tested at law.

Internet streaming, 'listen again' facilities, pod casts and the like are all part of the current sound broadcasting scene. For myself, although computer literate and reliant on state of the art technology at work, I tend to just bung a D90 tape into my radio 'stack' to record and I have the wherewithall to set timers. Not withstanding other considerations, the over riding requirement is for outstandingly good programme making. Without the content the technology is for nought.

OFFSHORE RADIO WOULD NEVER BE ALLOWED TO HAPPEN TODAY

Writer Claire Dickenson survived the swingin' sixties observing both the forts and the ships from her shorebound base 'somewhere in Eastern England.'

During the three years of the pirate radio revolution she made regular fortnightly visits to

Whitstable and Felixstowe to ensure the safety of her kith and kin.

Standing on the quay one day waiting for the tender - and the arrival of the handsome young DJs - she overheard an excitable young...er... lady comment that the antenna on Radio London was a phallic symbol. "Big L is so sexy" she said.

Indeed Claire herself was very close to the difficulties that DJs were forced to endure. Married to broadcasting in one form or another for 50 years, this year, she wonders what she had done in a former existence to deserve such a life sentence. Here she reflects an insight into the political realities of offshore 'unlicensed' radio. Her trenchant observations, in today's context, shine a light on the real fears that our 1960s politicians and the security services suffered in deciding what to do about Auntie BBC and her unruly relatives, born the other side of the blanket on the high seas.

It would be hard to imagine, these days, that the security services would allow a foreign ship to anchor in the reaches of the Thames and pump well-aimed broadcast propaganda into the ears of susceptible youngsters. Imagine the fears. Could they be terrorists playing music designed to soften up our impressionable youth? The spooks feared hidden messages in the lyrics. Think of the paranoia. They wondered what was underlying titles like *House of the Rising Sun*. Was that something to do with Japan the old enemy? Mass immigration from the West Indies had begun so what was the code message in *Walk in the Black Forest* or *A Whiter Shade of Pale*? If you looked hard enough you could imagine all sorts of insidious messages in … *Stranger on the Shore*, *World of our Own*, *Distant Drums*, *The Carnival is Over*, *Because they're Young* and of course *The World Tomorrow* with Garner Ted Armstrong. These boat-bound invaders were Irish and Americans who owned powerful radio stations and as they saw it, pumped sectarian politico-religion into UK homes every night.

So that's how it was in 1964. Our security services had the same fears then that they (and perhaps we) have today. But in the 60s the people of England were more fortunate. Despite a world war, that had killed millions having finished only twenty years previously, we were all more realistic and objective in our fears. The enemy had been expelled and overcome. The fear of invasion had subsided, unlike today where perhaps we worry that the enemy is within our midst.

In those days there was no knee-jerk reaction to close down Radio Caroline, Atlanta, London and their imitators and successors. The Government of the day realised that the support among the young for the offshore disc jockeys and the music they played was very powerful. There were votes involved. Voters admired these young men – and the too few women DJs - who were prepared to risk their lives on the high seas just for the cause of pop music, and not only pop music either. Older family voters too turned to Radio 390, a 'sweet music' station, in their tens of thousands.

Advisors to the Government included the security services and the press. The spooks spread all sorts of rumours about the offshore stations and their motives. In this they were 'closetly' aided by the BBC but were balanced by the voices of sweet reason who questioned what if anything the pirates were doing that was so wrong. The tabloid press supported the DJs and dubbed them 'pirates' to give them glamour. Stories about pirate radio and alleged DJs' lifestyles sold newspapers! Fortunately the Government listened to the sensible side of the argument, well for at least two years. Then the owners began to fall out among themselves and that, in one case, ended in a shooting and death. The Government also recognised the threat to its own power and influence but more importantly the shortcomings of the BBC and their controlling, almost communist control of the airwaves. History took its natural course but things had to change. But if you were working in an office in MI5 or MI6 today - and in today's circumstances - what would you have advised the Prime Minister to do?

In 2007 and 2008 fortieth anniversary reunions of the American and English DJs from Britain Radio and Radio England were held in England, Amsterdam and later Dallas/Fort Worth, Texas. The English DJs that included Johnnie Walker, Roger Day, Phil Martin and

John Ross-Barnard were shocked to hear that back in the Sixties their American colleagues Ron O'Quinn, Rick Randall and others had been detained at Heathrow and threatened with immediate expulsion from the UK. Johnnie and Roger perhaps less so because they had had the courage to stay on the ships and continued to broadcast after the Marine Offences Act came into force in 1967. But Phil and John in particular thought their treatment had been quite un-gentlemanly, dammit! Phil was later to sign up with the British press as a journalist and John as an announcer on BBC 1& 2 Television. They, in their naïve way, still thought of Great Britain as a free country from which you could come and go as you pleased. They were embarrassed to hear that Ron had been treated so badly. Ron recalled that he had left his family in the UK in what he thought was complete safety. He returned to the USA to produce a new set of jingles. On arriving back at Heathrow he was taken to a room and interrogated.

Initially the officers tried to help Ron to stay in the country by making him an offer they thought he couldn't refuse. All he had to do was to resign from the radio station and promise never to work for them again. Ron was made of sterner stuff, loyal to his American employer. No limey plod was going to intimidate him. After a few hours, during which he was made to fear for his future, he was told to return to the USA immediately and warned if he refused he would be put back on a plane there and then, the implication being that he would be placed under arrest. This would make him a Federal offender on his return. Ron pleaded that his family were living in England but even a phone call to contact them was refused. Unlike today where people without identification (von papieren! Achtung! von papieren! See 1940s B & W movies starring Richard Attenborough) can be spat out on the whim of the immigration services, the interrogators were not completely sure of the legal issues involved. It was fortunate that the US owners of the radio station ship had foreseen this possibility. They had appointed an advisor to their board of management, an advisor who was not only a lawyer but also a Member of Parliament (unnamed even today).

Just as things were beginning to look pretty sticky Ron remembered this and produced a piece of paper with the all important contact details. The change in behaviour was dramatic. If the immigration officers didn't exactly bow and scrape they changed their attitude by 180°. To allow further enquires to be made they permitted Ron to enter the United Kingdom for just three weeks to collect his wife, family, chattels, old tapes, records, jingles and all the detritus that a travelling disc jockey needs to 'cart' about with him. Ron and his US DJ colleagues were only too glad to get the hell out of England. All they wanted, at that time, was to go back to a country that allowed licensed freedom of the airwaves. A country that permitted listeners to hear the kind of music they wanted, when they wanted, on the hundreds if not thousands of licensed radio stations that existed and had done so since the 1920s. That was 1966 but it would take a further seven years, until 1973, before a change of UK Government would permit the launch of commercial radio in the UK.

Ron's unhappy experience at the hands of British immigration officials was not limited to American DJs. Off the coast of the Isle of Man, in heavier seas even than the North Sea, wallowed Radio Caroline North an Irish owned ship that was twice the size of its southern counterpart. Given the height of the waves and strength of the winds it needed to be. Have you ever listened to the shipping forecast for Ronaldsway, IoM? As a BBC announcer just reading it makes you feel ever so slightly Uncle Richard.

The Irish, perhaps even more than the Americans, were regarded with fear by the security services. Just two years later in 1969 "The Troubles" were to erupt and were to last almost into the 21st century.

But as the 1967 Marine Offences Act that would force the BBC via Radio 1 to entertain its listeners as the pirates were already doing was implemented, those with the courage to continue broadcasting on Radio Caroline North were er … talked to .. when they came ashore. They were quietly confronted in the pubs in Douglas, IoM. Nothing formal but 'the frighteners' were put on them. They threw in the towel and were probably very wise to do so. Though they decline to talk publicly and in detail about their experiences, even today, the memory makes them blanche.

The Last Word

Ironically John Ross-Barnard (JRB) who had worked on Radios Invicta and KING Radio and Radio 390 and later Britain Radio and Radio England, went on to enjoy a long career in BBC TV and BBC Radio. He was head-hunted by BT/Thorn EMI to set up cable TV and later by a Capital Radio-led group for satellite stations. He was seconded to join the force of peace-keepers in Bosnia following the disastrous Balkan war between the Bosnian Muslims, Serbs and Croats where he gathered a team of media and copyright lawyers to establish the equivalent of today's OFCOM.

After working in Sarajevo for a year JRB realised that the worldwide military peace-keeping force, SFOR, thirty thousand strong at one point, had managed to control the distribution of bomb and bullet but there was no control or even influence in the use of the microphone other than political. It was the microphone that had been used to foment the wars in the former Yugoslavia following the death of Tito, the (some say) benevolent dictator who had kept the peace during thirty previous years of his rule. It was the microphone that was used to continue the dispute as the uneasy Dayton Accords' peace was maintained by the troops. It was the far-sightedness of the late Rt. Hon. Robin Cook and Secretary of US State Madeline Albright who shared the vision and voted the necessary funds for the new regulator to free the broadcasters from the political tyranny under which they had been forced to operate. Political control and censorship had once again led to many pirate stations being established. Ironically UK history had simply repeated itself in the Balkans. That Bosnian model has since been adapted and is still in use in Kosovo, Iraq and Afghanistan.

Left: Ron O'Quinn - Centre John Ross-Barnard JP - Right: Rick Randall (real name Crandall). Ron & Rick are still both in major market broadcasting and have been so since returning from Radio England in 1966. Taken in Fort Worth, Texas, at the 40th Anniversary of the start of Britain Radio & Radio England.

The Judgement of History

The same ironic pattern of history was to continue when JRB returned to the UK when he was appointed a Justice of the Peace. Among his early cases he found himself judging evidence on land-based pirate radio operators. As a magistrate you cannot pick and choose which bits of the law and cases you want to try unless you find yourself unredeemably prejudiced. On these occasions therefore JRB, with his colleagues on the bench, listened to the evidence and on more than one occasion found the pirate operators guilty - as much because they were using the power of the microphone to peddle drugs, traffic people and advertise prostitution as for broadcasting from unlicensed transmitters.

Looking back to the period 1964 – 1967 it was quite clear that Radio Caroline and her imitators were not breaking the law as it then stood. What they did was to entertain thousands if not millions. No crime in that. They were responsible for the freedom of the airwaves that led to a revolution in UK radio choice that today allows United Kingdom listeners to listen to what they really enjoy.

Accordingly he finds them NOT GUILTY.

Cue Big Lil.

The time is 3 o'clock and with much Lovin' Awareness *Pop Went the Pirates II* is closing down.

RADIO CAROLINE AT EARL'S COURT, NOVEMBER 2008

Radio Caroline made history by broadcasting from London to the world, fulfilling a pledge made by Johnnie Walker in 1967. The station sent programmes live from the centre of Sail, Power and Watersports Show at Earl's Court, London from 26 to 30 November 2008.

Caroline presenters broadcast from a replica of their original ship-based studio, containing the equipment once used by pirate disc jockeys who became household names.

It was a first, not only for Radio Caroline, but also for the veteran Caroline DJs, Alan Turner (Neddy), Tony Prince, Keith Martin and newsreader John Aston. After meeting station manager Peter Moore, they were, during the day, presented to the Caroline presenters on air. Pat Edison interviewed John Aston and later at different times John Patrick talked to Alan Turner, Tony Prince and Keith Martin. Besides broadcasting live on Sky and over the Internet the Caroline presenters also handled the show's public address announcements, quite an unusual arrangement for a broadcaster.

Alan Turner said: "On the day of our visit Mike Brill and Jim Richman were also broadcasting, and the sales side of the show stand was staffed by Phil Meek and Graham Coull.

"The technical setup of the studio was very interesting. The output was controlled through a Gates twelve-channel mixer (rotary faders), designed and manufactured long before the advent of PCs and fed from a PC using the Audio Enhance-(Digital Playout System)-Radio Automation Software. Not a piece of vinyl in sight!

"2008 proved to be a milestone in Radio Caroline's history - the first 'ex-pirate' radio station asked to participate in a show of this type and the very sucessful exhibition about Radio Caroline North run by Manx Heritage on the Isle of Man, this exhibition runs until August 2009.   Quite a tribute to the enduring appeal of Radio Caroline after 44 years!   - "Little did we realise what we were starting, back in 1964, and its eventual effect on radio and TV broadcasting in the UK."

RADIO LONDON IN THE 21st CENTURY
by Mary Payne

In March 1999, my husband Chris and I had no idea what we had started when we decided to launch an offshore website. It was called Studio Anorak, but our favourite radio station was always Big L, so we acquired the domain www.radiolondon.co.uk

and changed the site name to Radio London. Initially, we intended to devote our site to just the one station, but as the internet expanded, we found that increasingly, we were putting ex-offshore personnel from all over the world in touch with each other, no matter what station they had served on. In fact, our first contacts were with Boss Jock Ron O'Quinn of Radio England, Radio Scotland's Ben Healy and Caroline's Bud Ballou. We recognised that a strong bond existed between those who had shared the Watery Wireless experience, regardless of which ship or fort they had been aboard. We duly expanded the site to include news about internet reunions of former jocks and found ourselves receiving photos and contributions from around the globe to share with the offshore community.

Before long, we met Alan Field, who as a youngster had written down every Fab Forty, including the climbers, from May 1966 to the end of Big L's life. With Alan's enormous assistance (during which time he acquired the nickname 'Fab') we began in 2001 adding weekly Fab Forties to the Radio London site, one per week in sync with the date and month of the original broadcasts. The pages also contain information about the recording artists and snippets of news about what was happening with the Big L jocks both aboard the *Galaxy* and ashore. Brian Long, who had originally compiled an earlier version of the Fab Forties for his book *The London Sound*, was happy for us to incorporate them into our new version. With the help of contributors in Germany and Holland, we achieved a full and unique list of Radio London's original charts from January 1965 to August 1967.

The Fab Forties have proved our most popular features, especially since the Oldies Project (www.oldiesproject.com), a dedicated team of hobbyist internet broadcasters, have been airing the charts on Sunday mornings and Wednesday evenings. This began in January 2006, exactly forty years since the original ship-borne transmissions and feature the voices of original Radio London DJs. When the charts ended in August 2007, Oldies Project received so many listener requests for a repeat run, that they started again from the beginning in January 2008. The Fab Forties may never be complete, as there are often updates and amendments and new information about the music is added regularly.

In 2002, John S. Platt, who had registered the company Radio London Ltd, persuaded us to take it over. John very generously felt that the amount of work that Chris and I had put into the website, plus our involvement with the Big L RSLs and our organising of offshore reunions, had made us worthy custodians of a company bearing the Radio London name. In October 2002, having unexpectedly found ourselves directors of Radio London Ltd, Chris and I set about acquiring appropriate trade marks for our company.

We registered graphics, including the 'rl' logo, but trade marking the words 'Radio London' was to prove a very complex process, taking several years. However, the efforts and perseverance of both Chris and our brilliant Trade Mark Attorney, eventually produced success. Our company now owns and has exclusive rights to Radio London in the UK and other countries! Not only that, but legislation dictates that once a mark is successfully registered, its date of ownership takes effect from the date of application, which in our case was October 2002. The trade mark 'Big L' is also registered to Radio London Ltd in some countries.

Full registration means that our company is entitled to license our trade marks to other organisations of our choosing, as we have done with the likes of Oldies Project and Sanctuary Records and indeed with Mr Skues for this excellent tome. Our attorney has made it clear that it is also important for us to defend the marks against unauthorised use, which unfortunately, we have been obliged to do on several occasions.

The Radio London name lives on and we are proud to have custody of it.

R.I.P

Barry Ainley	1933-2003
Tony Allan	1949-2004
Ted Allbeury	1917-2005
Don Allen	1939-1995
Garner Ted Armstrong	1930-2003
Simon Ashley	1943-1964
Mike Barron	1943-1993
Paul Beresford	1939-2002
Alan Black	1943-2007
Kitty Black	1914-2006
Chuck Blair	1934-1989
Boom Boom Brannigan	1947-1967
Stacey Brewer	1927-1999
Captain Willem (Bill) Buninga	1907-1993
Gerry Burke	1930-2005
Reg Calvert	1928-1966
Tony Carroll	1942-2007
Edward Cole	1939-2003
Allan Crawford	1921-1999
Dave Dennis (aka Neil Spence)	1932-2007
Gerry Duncan	1937-1976
Kenny Everett	1944-2005
Roger Gomez (aka Roger Keene)	1942-1988
Richard Harris	1925-1993
Stuart Henry	1942-1995
Ric Jonns	1943-1985
Kerry Juby (aka Kerry Clarke)	1948-2003
John Junkin	1930-2006
Paul Kaye	1934-1980
Ted King	1929-2004
Nick Kirby	1944-1994
Paul Kramer	1947-1968
Ed Laney	1941-2002
Bob Larkins	1938-1999
Adrian Love	1944-1999
Johan Maasbach	1918-1997
Jimmy Mack	1934-2004
Allen Mackenzie	1943-2004
Tony Mandell	1945-2005
Carl Mitchell	1946-1991
Dick Morecraft	1933-1999
Ed Moreno	1933-1980
Spangles Muldoon (aka Chris Cary)	1946-2008
Jim Murphy	1940-2000
Abe Nathan	1927-2008
Martin Newton	1942-2002
Rob Out (Veronica)	1939-2003
Kenny Page	1951-2002
Brian Paull	1939-1971

John Peel	1939-2004
Don Pierson	1926-1996
Tom Pepper	1926-1964
Mike Raven	1924-1997
Earl Richmond	1928-2001
Percy (Bill) Scaddan	1908-1994
Martin Shaw	1946-1964
Tommy Shields	1919-1968
Mike Speake	1940-2008
Jack Spector	1925-1994
Crispian St John (aka Jay Jackson)	1953-2002
Screaming Lord Sutch	1940-1999
Richard Swainson	1943-2001
Gordon Swann	1947-1984
Jon Sydney	1939-2000
Sylvain Tack	1934-2006
Tommy Vance	1940-2005
Eddie White	1937-1990
Tony Windsor (aka Tony Withers)	1920-1985
Jason Wolfe	1946-1986

We have sadly lost others as well but in their cases either dates of birth or death, or both are not known. These include Guy Blackmore (Jumbo Jim Gordon) died 1997, Ralph Cooper, Tom Cooper, Alexander Dee, Bruce Holland died early 1990s, Sheldon Jay, Eddie Jerold, Sheena Russell died October 1999, John Waters and Charlie White died late 1990s.

Of the more recent offshore DJs we have lost the following: Samantha Dubois (on Caroline in the 70s and 80s) died 2 October 1992; Jimmy/Kenny James aka Kenny Page (Caroline and Voice of Peace) died 30 July 2002; Phil Mitchell (Caroline in the seventies, Voice of Peace and various offshore-related RSLs) died 25 March 2008; Mike Wall-Garland (crew member aka Mike The Poet on Caroline in the seventies) died December 1974; Peter Clark aka Peter Tait (Caroline in the eighties) died September 2002; Andy Howard alias Andy Moorcock, Bilbo Baggins, Rex Barker, Roland Butter, Maurice Dancer, Billy Dukes, etc. (engineer/occasional DJ on Caroline in the eighties) died January 2009; Fergie McNeil (cook/DJ on Caroline in the eighties) died 4 October 2008 and David Lee Stone (Laser-558 and Laser Hot Hits) died 1997.

WHERE ARE THEY NOW. A LIST OF OFFSHORE VOICES 1964-1967
A list of former Pirate DJs and their known whereabouts 2009 together with their original theme tunes, where known.

A
GLENN ADAMS (Caroline South). For the last 30 years has been an artist/potter living on the coast of New Zealand at Manukau Heads, Auckland.
MIKE AHERN (Caroline North and South). Lives in Norfolk. Still retains a great interest in the old pirate days. Theme tune: *Buckeye* Johnny and Hurricanes.

DAVID ALLAN (390/355). Announcer on the History TV Channel. Also writes a column for *Country Music People* magazine.

TONY ALLAN (Scotland). Died on 9 July 2004 in London, aged 54 years, following his long fight against cancer. Theme Tune: *Flamingo* Herb Alpert and Tijuana Brass.

TED ALLBEURY (390/355). Died 4 December 2005, aged 88 years.

DON 'DAFFY' ALLEN (Caroline South and North). Died in Ireland 13 May 1995, following a heart attack, aged 56 years. Theme tunes: *Trumpet Tramoure* Stan Reynolds and *Quite a Party* Fireballs.

MIKE ALLEN (Atlanta/Caroline South). Real name Alan Zeffert. Last heard of working in Portsmouth. Worked as a freelance writer and broadcaster on BBC Radio Solent.

VINCE 'RUSTY' ALLEN (Essex/270). Last heard of as a photographer in the West Country.

ANDY ARCHER (City/Caroline South). Real name Anthony Andrew Dawson. Presenter with BBC Radio Norfolk. Theme tune: *Soul Coaxing* Raymond Lefevre Orchestra and *In the House of the King* Focus.

SIMON ASHLEY (Invicta). Lost overboard 17 December 1964 aboard tender returning to land, aged 21 years.

JOHN ASTON (King/390/Essex/Caroline North and South/270/355). Real name John Hatt. Works in the film industry as a senior special effects technician. In recent years has worked on films *Dragonheart*, *Lost in Space*, *Enigma* (built Enigma machine with Terry Reed), *Blade 2* and was a technical advisor on *The Boat That Rocked*. John also provided all the equipment to build a replica of the Caroline North studio for the Pirates of the Irish Sea Exhibition in Peel, Isle of Man. Also heard weekly on Blast 1386, located on the Reading Campus of the Thames Valley University. Theme tune: *Bond Street*, Burt Bacharach for the 60's and *Crunchy Granola Suite*, Percy Faith Orchestra, 2004 onwards.

B

NICK BAILEY (Caroline South). Presenter Classic FM.

BUD BALLOU (Caroline South). Real name Howie Castle. Lives and works in San Diego, California, USA.

MIKE BARRON (270). Died in Florida, 1993, aged 50.

KAROL BEER (City). Lives in Paris. Has a recording studio and promotes stand-up comedy shows and concerts.

PAUL BERESFORD (390). Died of a heart attack in a Johannesburg hospital, 27 November 2002, aged 63 years.

BILL BERRY (England). Owns two radio stations, WHHO and WKPQ, in New York, USA. Now known as Wolfe Berry, presents a daily show on WHHO. Also deals in worldwide paper ephemera, especially stamps and covers, as well as books, art, records and coins.

COLIN BERRY (Caroline South). Presents weekly show on BBC local stations in the Eastern Counties and BBC Radio Kent. Also freelances with BBC Radio 2 as a newsreader.

ALAN BLACK (Scotland). Died in March 2007, following a long spell of ill health, aged 64 years. Theme Tune: *Flamingo* Herb Alpert and Tijuana Brass.

TONY BLACKBURN (Caroline South/London). Presents weekend shows on the Smooth Radio network, and weekly ones on BBC London 94.9 and Kent's KMFM. Biography published 2007. Theme tune: *Beefeaters* Johnny Dankworth Orchestra.

GUY BLACKMORE (390/Caroline North). Died of cancer in 1997 in Australia.

CHUCK BLAIR (England/London). Died of a heart attack August 1989, Maryland, USA, aged 55 years.

PETER BOWMAN (Scotland/270). Office worker for a major cleaning firm. Theme tune: *Bird Rockers* and *Pipeline* both by the Ventures

PETE BRADY (London). Works for BusinessMeetings.com Ltd, a company that processes information on hotels, conferences, convention centres, historic sites, museums and wildlife reserves. Theme tune: *Danger Man Theme* Red Price Combo.

TONY BRANDON (London). Real name John Anthony Nigel Stewart Stewart-Killick (says Tony - "a fairly compelling reason why I chose to rename myself Tony Brandon"). Lives in Haslemere, Surrey. Does occasional voice-over work. Theme tune: *Fuzz Duck* Jerry Allen Trio.

BOOM BOOM BRANNIGAN (England). Real name Robert E. Klingeman. Killed in a motorcycle accident 4 April 1967 close to the radio station for which he worked WPXI, Roanoke, Virginia, USA, aged 19 years, arguably the youngest former pirate DJ to die.

STACEY BREWER (270). Died in December 1999, aged 72 years.

ROSS BROWN (390/Caroline North/City). Lives in Canberra, Australia. Worked for the Australian Foreign Service. Theme tune: *Raunchy* Bill Justis.

ERROL BRUCE (Caroline/England). Lives in Toronto, Canada. Runs the Virtually Strange Network website, and produces a weekly podcast of his long-running UFO show Strange Days Indeed. Theme tune: *I've Got a Woman* Jimmy McGriff.

GERRY BURKE (Caroline South). Died in December 2005, aged 75 years. Theme tune: *Sucu Sucu* Laurie Johnson Orchestra.

PAUL BURNETT (270). Describes himself as 'a jobbing DJ'. Broadcasts on Hull's KCFM and Isle of Wight internet station, WightFM. Theme tune: *Perfidia* Glenn Miller Orchestra.

WOOLF BYRNE (City/Britain/390). Actor who is also heard on commercial voice-overs.

C

CANDY CALVERT (Sutch/City). Daughter of Reg and Dorothy Calvert. Was the youngest DJ at the time on Radio Sutch. Now married with two children. Spoke at the Radio Academy Celebrations 2007. Spends much of her time enjoying calligraphy and art. About to embark on a Yoga teacher training course.

SUSAN CALVERT (Sutch). Daughter of Reg and Dorothy Calvert. Had the distinction of being the first pirate female disc jockey. However, she only broadcast for one day. Author of three books and portrait artist. Has also written a play with music about Radio City.

DOUG CARMICHAEL (Scotland). Presents a weekly show for local Scottish community station, Oban FM.

TONY CARROLL (City). Died on 2 August 2007 in a car accident in Greece, aged 65 years.

DAVE CASH (London). Presents weekly shows on BBC Radio Kent and other local stations in the South and South-East. Theme tune: *Reveille Rock* Johnny and the Hurricanes and *Rebel Rouser* Duane Eddy.

ALAN CLARK (City/390). Was a journalist for Meridian TV.

KERRY CLARK (Caroline South). Died of lung cancer July 2003, aged 55 years.

EDWARD COLE (390). Died June 2003, after a long period of poor health, aged 64 years.

RAY COOPER (Caroline South). For a while lived in Barbados, but is now back in the UK. Devotes his time to painting.

CHRIS CROSS (Sutch/City). Last heard of working as a chartered surveyor and living in Hereford. Theme tune: *Struttin' With Maria* Herb Alpert and Tijuana Brass.

GORDON CRUSE (Caroline South and North). Retired. Lives in Victoria, Canada.

BRIAN CULLINGFORD (390). Managing director of Catalyst World Class Ltd., who provide speakers, entertainers and musicians for events around the world.

JACK CURTISS (England/Britain). Lives in Adelaide, South Australia. Works on his internet journalism project.

CLIFF CUTTELLE (City). Lives in Dubai and Thailand.

D

ROBBIE DALE (Caroline South). Together with his wife Stella has been in the tourist accommodation business, Lanzarote, Canary Isles since 1990. Theme tune: *I Was Kaiser Bills Batman* Whistling Jack Smith.

IAN DAMON (London). After the pirates closed down returned to Australia working in TV and radio. Returned to UK and joined Capital Radio. Has since worked for LBC, Essex Radio, Mercury and County Sound. Now lives in Norfolk. Until September 2008 presented a weekly show on Big L in Frinton-on-Sea. Theme tune: *Big Deal*, Tony Osborne Orchestra.

RICK DANE (City/Caroline South and North). Lives in Miami. Runs a company that installs audio-visual equipment to the hospitality industry, London Town Associates. Theme tunes: *In the Midnight Hour* Booker T and the MGs and *All For You* Earl van Dyke.

ROGER DAY (England/Caroline South). Presents a nightly show on BBC local radio stations in the south and east of England. Theme tune: *Green Grass* Ventures.

LARRY DEAN (England). Morning newsman on country station WSOC in Charlotte, Virginia, USA.

SIMON DEE (Caroline). Real name Carl Nicholas Henty-Dodd. Retired. Lives in Winchester. Biography published 2005. Theme tune: *On the Sunny Side of the Street* Tommy Dorsey Orchestra.

CHRIS DENNING (London). Currently in Slovakia. Theme tune *Right of Way* Andrew Oldham Orchestra.

DAVE DENNIS (Atlanta/Invicta/London). Real name Neil Spence. Died in Lincolnshire, December 2007, aged 71 years.

DICK DICKSON (Sutch/City). Recently retired from the University of Kent where he worked for some years. Theme tune: *Stars Fell on Stockton* Shadows.

PETER DOLPHIN (City). Actor. Lives in France.

PETE DRUMMOND (London). Freelance commercial voice-over man.

E

JOHN EDWARD (City/London). One of the voices on the Oldies Project Fab 40 Show. Works on his own radio project, and has written a pilot for a new Metal Mickey series.

TOM EDWARDS (City/Caroline South). Lives in Heckington, Lincolnshire. Still broadcasts from time to time. Theme tune: *Skyliner* Bert Kaempfert Orchestra.

PAUL ELVEY (Sutch/City). Works as an electrical engineer on research work. Theme tune: *Magnificent Seven* John Barry Seven.

KENNY EVERETT (London). Died of AIDS related causes 4 April 1995, aged 50 years. Theme tune: *The Stripper* David Rose Orchestra.

F

PAUL FREEMAN (Essex). Runs a department store. Also heard on a Dorset community station, Forest FM.

G

ROGER GALE (Caroline South/Scotland/270). Conservative MP for North Thanet, Kent. Theme tune: *A Walk in the Black Forest* Horst Jankowski.

GRAHAM GILL (London/Britain/England/390). Retired. Lives in Holland. Theme tunes: *Way Back Home* Junior Walker and All Stars and *Soul Coaxing* Raymond Lefevre Orchestra.

ROGER GOMEZ (KING/390/270). Died from a brain aneurysm 1988, aged 46 years.

CHRIS GOSLING (Tower). Operates an online TV service and manages a video production company

H

GUY HAMILTON (Essex/BBMS/270). Real name Gerry Zierler. Runs his own TV airtime sales companies, Zierler Media and ZMTV Ltd, selling for about 30 TV channels. Theme tune: *Iechyd-Da* (B side of *I Put a Spell On You*) Alan Price Set.

KEITH HAMPSHIRE (Caroline South). Voice over work in Canada. Lives in Ontario. Theme tune: *Sidewinder* Wes Dakus and the Rebels.

RICHARD HARRIS (Atlanta). Not to be confused with actor of the same name. Died in a motoring accident, January 1993, aged 68 years.

MIKE HAYES (City/270). Lives in Holland. From time to time works in TV and films.

PHIL HAYTON (270). Quit the BBC TV abruptly in September 2005 following a personality clash with a colleague on News 24. Theme tune: *Happy Organ* Dave 'Baby' Cortez.

BEN HEALY (City/Scotland). Retired. Lives in Vancouver, Canada.

STUART HENRY (Scotland). Died at his Luxembourg home on 24 November 1995, aged 53 years. Theme tune: *Soul Finger* Barkays.

BRUCE HOLLAND (Invicta/KING). Died following a heart attack in the early 1990s. He died peacefully at his south coast home listening to the radio. Theme tune: *Big Fat Spiritual* André Brasseur.

PAUL HOLLINGDALE (CNBC). Freelance voice-over man. Makes occasional broadcasts on BBC Radio 2.

MEL HOWARD (Caroline South/Scotland). Retired. Lives in Canada. Theme tune: *My Star* Frank Chacksfield Orchestra.

SHAUN HOWARD (City). Works as an investment adviser.

J

PETER JAMES (Caroline South/390). In 1993 went to Australia to run ABC Classic FM. Now retired.

PHIL JAY (City). Presents radio shows for the Arabian Gulf and tours the UK with his partner, Pam, singing songs from the wartime and old time music hall.

EDDIE JEROLD (Invicta/KING). Also known as Frank Smith. Died a few years ago.

DUNCAN JOHNSON (London). Worked as financial controller for David Knight Advertising in London, but retired in 2004. Lives in Kent. Theme tune: *Night Rider* John Schroeder.

JOHN JUNKIN (Caroline South). Became a successful actor, comedian and script writer for many top British comedians. Appeared in numerous films and television plays, comedies and game shows. Died 7 March 2006, Stoke Mandeville Hospital, Buckinghamshire, aged 76 years. He had been suffering from lung cancer, emphysema and asthma.

RIC JONNS (Caroline South and North). Died in a car accident in the USA in 1985, aged 42 years.

K

PAUL KAYE (London). Real name Paul Kazarine. Died on 4 November 1980, aged 46 years. Theme tune: *Town Talk* Ken Woodman and his Piccadilly Brass.

MARTIN KAYNE (Essex/355/Caroline North). Real name Andy Cadier. Works in catering and presents occasional shows for RSLs in Kent. Theme tune: *Dreamin'* Mood Mosaic.

GARRY KEMP (Caroline South/Britain). Lives in Camdenton, Missouri, USA. Theme tune: *Let's Go* The Routers and *Pepe* Duane Eddy.

DOUG KERR (Caroline South). Lives in California, USA. Now retired.

JOHN KERR (Scotland). Presents overnight show on 2UE, Sydney, Australia.

JERRY KING (Caroline South and North). Was a news correspondent for ABC Television network in USA. Now retired. Theme tune: *Tune Up* Junior Walker and The All Stars.

LORNE KING (London). Retired, living in Vegreville, Alberta, Canada.

TED KING (Atlanta). Died 10 December 2004, after a long illness, aged 73 years.

PAUL KRAMER (City/Caroline South). Died in a car accident on Putney Bridge, London, aged 21 years. Theme tune: *Kinda Kinky* Ray McVay Band.

L

ED LANEY (Invicta). Real name Eric Davies. Died very suddenly in 2002, aged 61 years.

BOB LARKINS (Caroline South). Died of cancer in July 1999, aged 61 years.

DOMINIC LEFOE (390). Runs the Players Theatre, providing a home for Victorian music hall in London.

MIKE LENNOX (London). Real name Mike Graham. Deals in real estate in Grande Prairie, Alberta, Canada. Theme tune: *I'm Getting Sentimental Over You* Herb Alpert and His Tijuana Brass.

BOB LE-ROI (City). Runs the Red Sands Radio RSLs. Theme tunes: *Some People* Ventures and *All Quiet on the Mersey Front* George Martin Orchestra.

TOM LODGE (Caroline North and South). Operates the umisatsang.org website. Lives in California USA. Theme tunes: *Rinky Dink* Johnny Howard Band and *I'm Coming Through* Sounds Incorporated.

ADRIAN LOVE (City). Died March 1999, aged 54 years.

MICK LUVZIT (Caroline South and North). Real name William Brown. Lives in Vancouver, Canada and recovered from a heart attack in August 2007. Theme tune: *Tune Up Time* X-Cops/ Junior Walker and The All Stars.

M

JIMMY MACK (Scotland). Died in his sleep 3 July 2004, following his battle with cancer, aged 70 years.

DAVE MACKAY (City/Britain/355). Real name Dave Gilbee. Retired. Lives in Essex.

ALLEN MACKENZIE (Scotland). Died, following poor health, February 2004, aged 61 years.

IAN MacRae (City/Caroline South). Presents a weekly show on 2UE, Sydney, Australia and runs the Ian MacRae Radio School.

PETER MALLAN (Scotland). Can be heard on Clyde 2 in Glasgow, and is an after-dinner speaker.

TONY MANDELL (Essex/BBMS). Died suddenly 7 April 2008, aged 60 years.

MIKE MARRIOTT (Caroline North). Lives in Northern Italy, but works in war/conflict zones for peace and reconciliation. Theme tune: *Shazam* Duane Eddy

ERIC MARTIN (City). Involved with various RSLs in Surrey and Sussex and does voice-over work. Broadcasts on Mid-Downs Hospital Radio as Richard Lee.

JOHN MARTIN (City). Runs the Mungsarin Thai Boxing Academy in Bradford. Theme tune: *You're Driving Me Crazy* Temperance Seven.

KEITH MARTIN (Atlanta/Caroline South/390). Lecturer on various media aspects.

PHIL MARTIN (Britain/355). Operates a media training business from London.

JACK McLAUGHLIN (Scotland/Britain/270/390). Lives between Scotland and Spain. Runs his internet broadcast company, Radio Scotland Worldwide. Has broadcast for Clyde 2 from both Glasgow and Marbella and occasionally heard on the internet station Radio Six International.

TONY MEEHAN (Scotland/Britain). Runs his own public relations company TMA Communications in Glasgow.

WALLY MEEHAN (Caroline North). Lives on the Costa Blanca, Spain. Presents daily Breakfast Show on TKO-FM in Spain. Theme tune: *A Swingin' Safari* Bert Kaempfert Orchestra.

STEVIE MERIKE (Scotland/Caroline South). Real name Michael John Willis. Lecturer in media and multimedia at New College, Nottingham. Theme tunes: *Billy's Bag* Billy Preston and *The Happy Organ* Dave 'Baby' Cortez.

HOWARD MICHAELS (City). Lives in Cape Town, South Africa. Does some film camera work for the BBC.

RICKY MICHAELS (City). Real name J. Patrick Michaels. Chairman and Chief Executive Officer of Communications Equity Associates of Tampa, Florida, USA.

NOEL MILLER (270). Caterer/chef. Lives in Sydney, Australia.

CARL MITCHELL (Caroline South). Real name David Carmichael. Died in 1991, after a long illness, in Menticello, New York, aged 45 years. Theme tunes: *Slim Jenkins Place* Booker T and The MGs and *In The Midnight Hour* Little Mack and the Boss Sounds.

TONY MONSON (355). Works for the internet and satellite Solar Radio.

ED MORENO (Caroline/Invicta/City/Britain/270). Real name Norman Brian Cole. Died from a massive overdose of insulin while the balance of his mind was disturbed through depression in August 1980, aged 47 years.

SPANGLES MULDOON (Caroline South). Real name Chris Cary. Died on 29 February 2008, following a stroke in Tenerife. Theme tune: *Yeh Yeh* Mark Wirtz Orchestra.

JIM MURPHY (Caroline South and North). Died in June 2000, after a long illness, aged 60 years.

N

COLIN NICOL (Atlanta/Caroline/England/ Britain). Lives in Perth, Western Australia. Has placed on record his collection of mementos from his offshore radio days. Also researches local history and writes features for local Australian newspapers. Theme tune: *Find Me a Golden Street* Norman Petty Trio.

O

RON O'QUINN (England). Presented a long running weekly oldies show on various American stations. Now retired and living with his wife in Glenwood, Georgia, USA.

P

RICHARD PALMER (Essex/BBMS). Runs an engineering company in Sussex.

RICHARD PARK (Scotland). Executive Director of Global Radio Company (formerly Capital/GWR/Chrysalis groups). Theme tune: *Wild Weekend* Rockin' Rebels.

BRIAN PAULL (Sutch). Drowned in an accident while on holiday in Greece, 1971, aged 32 years.

JOHN PEEL (London). Real name John Robert Parker Ravenscroft. Died in October 2004 while on holiday in Peru, aged 65 years.

MAC PETERS (City). Lives in the West of Ireland. Has a home studio where he makes radio commercials and jingles.

BRENDAN POWER (270). President of the Professional Speakers Association of Europe. Theme tune: *Rocking Goose* Johnny and the Hurricanes.

TONY PRINCE (Caroline South and North). Real name Thomas Richard Whitehead. Runs DMC International. Theme tunes: *I'm Coming Through/Go* both by Sounds Incorporated.

MIKE PROCTOR (City). A Christian, working in missionary radio. Manages a project making public service programmes for second language English users, broadcast on 60 outlets internationally.

HARRY PUTNAM (Essex/Britain). Has had several strokes. Lives in Pasadena, Maryland, USA.

R

RICK RANDALL (England). Recently remarried, he lives in Florida. Now retired.

ROB RANDALL (390). Showbusiness publicist. Lives in Surrey. Theme tune: *Skyliner* Bert Kaempfert Orchestra.

MIKE RAVEN (Atlanta/King/390). Real name Churton Fairman. Died on 24 April 1997, aged 72 years. Theme tunes: *Liverpool Drive* Chuck Berry, *You Can't Sit Down* Phil Upchurch Combo and *Soul Serenade* Ray Anthony Orchestra.

EARL RICHMOND (London). Real name John Dienn. Died in Thailand following a heart attack, May 2001, aged 75 years.

MARK ROMAN (London). Real name Graham Wallace. Lives in Spain. Continues with voice-over work. Theme tune: *Wipe Out* Surfaris.

EMPEROR ROSKO (Caroline South). Real name Michael Pasternak. Lives in California. Can be heard on Forest FM, KCFM Hull, Isle of Wight radio, and occasionally on BBC Essex. Theme tune: *Memphis* Lonnie Mack.

JOHN ROSS-BARNARD (Invicta/King/390/Britain). Also known as JRB, Larry Pannell, Pete Ross and Peter Barraclough. Broadcasting consultant. Lives in Coventry. Magistrate. Theme tune: *Surf del Amore* Camarata-Tutti's Trumpets.
SHEENA RUSSELL (Scotland). Died in October 1999.

S
MIKE SCOTT (Scotland). Head of Promotions for the Baeur (ex-EMAP) stations in Scotland.
ROGER SCOTT (Essex/270/390). Real name Greg Bance. Also known as Arnold Layne. Freelance voice-over man. Was not the Roger Scott on Capital Radio.
JON SEDD (London). Real name John Crosse. Retired. Spends most of his time in USA with family.
TONY SILVER (City). Real name Phil Perkins. Operates an electronics supply company.
DAVID SINCLAIR (Essex/270/390). Retired. Lives in Edmonton, Alberta, Canada.
KEITH 'Cardboard Shoes' SKUES (Caroline South/London). Presenter/producer, based in Norfolk, and broadcasting to BBC stations in the Eastern Counties. Author of various reference books. Theme tunes: *Groovin' High* Don Jacoby Orchestra and *Mr Tambourine Man* Golden Gate Strings.
MARK SLOANE (KING/390/Caroline South). Real name Patrick Hammerton. Works in the advertising industry. Theme tune: *Flamingo* Herb Alpert and His Tijuana Brass.
JERRY SMITHWICK (England). Runs the Congressional Office in Talahassee, Florida, USA.
BOB SNYDER (270). Retired. Lives in British Columbia, Canada.
JACK SPECTOR (Caroline South and North). Died of a heart attack on 8 March 1994, aged 68 years, whilst broadcasting at WHLI, Long Island, New York. Theme tune: *Hand Clapping* Red Prysock.
BOB SPENCER (City/Scotland). Retired. Lives in Helston, Cornwall.
GARY STEVENS (City/England). Runs America's most successful brokerage, handling the sale of radio properties. Between 1986 and now he has sold over $5 billion worth of radio stations.
BOB STEWART (Caroline South and North). Lives in Dallas, Texas. Theme tune: *Image* Alan Haven and *Kinda Kinky* Ray McVay Orchestra.
ED STEWART (London). Real name Edward Mainwaring. Lives in Dorset. Broadcasts on Isle of Wight internet station, WightFM. Can be heard occasionally presenting nostalgic editions of Junior Choice on Radio 2. He has also worked for Spectrum Radio in Costa del Sol, Spain. Autobiography published 2007. Theme tunes: *Drum Diddley* Joe Loss Orchestra and *Lover* Buddy Merrill.
NORMAN ST. JOHN (City/Caroline South/London). Runs his own company, Global Wire Pty Ltd, in Brisbane, Queensland, Australia and has done so for the last 16 years. Also partakes in conferences all over the world. Theme tune: *Walk In The Black Forest* Horst Jankowski.
SCREAMING LORD SUTCH (Sutch). Real name David Sutch. Suffered from depression and committed suicide. Found hanging at his Harrow home 16 June 1999, aged 58 years.
GORDON SWANN (City). Died of a heart attack 1984, aged 36 years.
JON SYDNEY (Caroline South). Real name Brian Whetstone. Died in Sydney, Australia 1999, aged 60 years. Theme tune: *Brothers Go To Mothers* Henry Mancini Orchestra.

T
RAY TERET (Caroline North). Still broadcasts and makes personal appearances. Travels the world including Indonesia, Lombok, Bali, Canada and Stoke on Trent. Theme tunes: *Jungle Fever* Tornados, *Image*, Alan Haven and *The Ugly Bug Ball* Burl Ives.
LEON TIPLER (270). Lives in Kidderminster, Worcestershire. Presents *Leon Tipler's World of Music* on Radio Maldwyn in Mid-Wales.
DAVE LEE TRAVIS (Caroline South and North). Real name David Griffin. Presents a weekend show on the Magic AM network. Theme tune: *A Touch of Velvet, A Sting of Brass*

Mood Mosaic.
ALAN TURNER (Caroline). Operates an aviation maintenance facility. Theme tune: *S'Wonderful* Ray Conniff Orchestra.

V

TOMMY VANCE (Caroline South/London). Real name Richard Anthony Crispian Francis Prew Hope-Weston. Died after suffering a stroke 6 March 2005, aged 64 years.
BRYAN VAUGHAN (Atlanta/Caroline South/Scotland). Real name Dermot Patrick Charles Vaughan Hoy. Semi-retired. Works freelance for Readers' Digest in Sydney, Australia and also as a website consultant for Australian recording artists. Theme tune: *Cheers!* Henry Mancini Orchestra.

W

JOHNNIE WALKER (England/Caroline South). Real name Peter Dingley. Presenter on BBC Radio 2. Autobiography published 2008. Theme tune: *Because They're Young* Duane Eddy.
JON WALKER (Sutch/City). BBC TV producer.
WILLY WALKER (London). Real name William Acton. Yacht captain in Fort Lauderdale, Florida, USA. Theme tune: *Maybe the Last Time* James Brown.
BOB WALTON (Caroline South/390). Musician. Lives in Bath. Writes about music.
BRUCE WAYNE (England). Real name David J. Bennett. Lives in Beverley Hills, California, USA.
BRIAN WEBB (Scotland). Retired. Lives in Spain. Theme tune: *Big Deal* Tony Osborne Orchestra.
GRAHAM WEBB (Caroline South and North). Operates Sunshine FM, a community radio station in Queensland, Australia. Theme tune: *Echo Echo Echo* The New Sound of Don Lee.
ALAN WEST (London/390/270). Real name Alan Fossey. Theme tune: *Afrikaan Beat* Bert Kaempfert Orchestra.
MARK WESLEY (Essex/BBMS/270/Scotland). Real name Martin Wesley Goble. Also broadcast under the name Mark West. Runs his own production company in East Anglia. Broadcasts on Isle of Wight internet station. Theme tune: *The Cooler Side* Dave Davani Four.
CHARLIE WHITE (Scotland). Died of cancer in the late 1990s.
EDDIE WHITE (Scotland/Caroline North). Died after collapsing at his home in Blackheath, London in 1990, aged 53 years.
DAVID WILLIAMS (Caroline North). Works in computers.
TONY WINDSOR (Atlanta/Caroline South/London/355). Real name Tony Withers. Died at St Stephen's Hospital, Fulham, London, June 1985, aged 65 years. Theme tune: *Waltzing Matilda* Frank Ifield and *Talk Town* Ken Woodman Orchestra and Piccadilly Orchestra
JASON WOLFE (Caroline North). Real name Chris Bowskill. Died of cancer, 1986.
PETER YORK (City). Works as announcer at Coventry and Birmingham Speedway and Stock Car Stadiums.
HAL YORKE (270). Real name Norman Wingrove. Lives in Hong Kong. Runs a company providing various services, including web design. Theme tune: *Man of Mystery* Shadows.
PAUL YOUNG (Scotland). Presents fishing programmes on TV in Scotland. Also acts in plays in TV and radio.
STEVE YOUNG (Caroline South). Lives in British Columbia, Canada. One of the team behind Canada's first independent web-based TV channel, EkosTV, dedicated to programmes about the Environment and sustainability resources. Theme tune: *Music to Watch Girls By* Ventures.

THE BOAT THAT ROCKED

OVER THE YEARS, many ex-offshore radio personnel and enthusiasts have penned scripts on the subject, both fact and fiction, but the movie industry showed little interest and none of them ever got off the ground. Perhaps it was felt that there was insufficient interest in events that happened in the Sixties. Award-winning writer and director Richard Curtis had other ideas.

Five years after the success of *Four Weddings and a Funeral* and *Notting Hill*, Curtis made his debut as a director with *Love Actually*. In 2007, he announced that his new project was a period comedy centred on young people of the 1960s and their obsession with pop music.

He attended the Radio Academy Celebration of Offshore Radio, accompanied by the film's associate producer, Emma Freud, and its producers Tim Bevan, Eric Fellner and Hilary Bevan Jones. The script had already been completed at this stage, but they wanted to meet some of the original pirates and get a feel for what life was really like aboard the radio ships. They have stressed that the film is fiction and is not based on any specific Sixties station or vessel.

The story follows a band of rogue DJs that captivate Britain from a large rusty metal fishing trawler moored off the coast of England. Blazing a trail for the UK pirate movement, they play the music that defines a generation, and stand up to a government that, for some unknown reason, prefers jazz.

The cast of the film includes Philip Seymour Hoffman as 'The Count', a big brash American god of the airwaves; Bill Nighy as Quentin, the boss of Radio Rock, a pirate radio ship in the middle of the North Sea that's populated by an eclectic crew of rock 'n' roll DJs; Rhys Ifans as Gavin, the greatest DJ in Britain who has just returned from a drug tour of America to reclaim his rightful position; Nick Frost as Dave, an ironic, intelligent and cruelly funny co-broadcaster.

Kenneth Branagh plays Government Minister Dormandy, a fearsome official out for blood against the drug takers and lawbreakers of a once-great nation.

"The only reason the film exists at all is so Curtis could get his hands on some kick-ass music. That's serious", Bill Nighy told MTV. "It's shameless, really. It has no other purpose but to make you laugh, and also to play all those records that charted between '66 and '67. It was a pretty good period. We've got the Beatles, the Rolling Stones, the Beach Boys and all kinds of people."

The production crew of the movie paid several visits to the *Ross Revenge*, to carry out research. Although it would have been ideal if the ship could have been used for the shooting of the film, it was not possible for various practical and technical reasons.

Filming was done aboard the m.v. *Timor Challenger* which was based, in many ways, on the external appearance of the *Ross Revenge*. From the dark red painted hull, to green aftdeck, to the twin forward and aft aerial towers, one can see that the two ships appear very similar.

External shots of the *Timor Challenger*, which played the role of Radio Rock, were filmed off the Dorset coast during the spring and summer of 2008. Internal and studio scenes were all shot in London's Shepperton studios.

Much of the studio equipment seen on board Radio Rock was loaned from the *Ross Revenge*, including turntables, tape and cartridge machines, microphones and mixing desks.

Three members of Radio Caroline spent time at Shepperton studios installing technical equipment in its temporary home. All the equipment was fully functional.

The *Timor Challenger* was formerly registered as *De Hoop*, a deep-sea fishing trawler that became a Hospital Church vessel, and finally a rescue boat for the oil rigs. Built in 1964, she is 208 feet long and weighs 1106 tonnes gross. Church services were broadcast in Dutch from the chapel on board using marine frequencies, without an appropriate licence. How strange that many years later she should be chartered to star as a Sixties pirate ship. The *LV18* spent five weeks in Portland, Dorset in 2008 and was one of the two ships involved in the filming of *The Boat That Rocked*. In her livery as Radio Sunshine she hosted the 45th anniversary of the birth of British offshore radio. She was based alongside Ha'penny Pier, Harwich over the Easter holidays, 2009.

The end of the film parodies the genuine end of the Sixties Pirates.

In an era when the stuffy corridors of power stifle anything approaching youthful exuberance, Minister Dormandy seizes the chance to score a political goal, and the Marine Etc., Broadcasting (Offences) Bill becomes an Act of Parliament in an effort to outlaw the pirates and to remove their ghastly influence from the land once and for all.

What results is a literal storm on the high seas. With Radio Rock in peril, its devoted fans rally together and stage an epic Dunkirk-style hundred-boat rescue to save their DJ heroes. Some things may come to an end, but rock 'n' roll never dies.

The film, released at the beginning of April 2009, received a flotilla of interest amongst the media, former offshore disc jockeys and pirate radio fans alike.

It certainly gave Richard Curtis the opportunity to relive his boyhood days in the 1960s, although he was only 11 when Radio Caroline began. His parents were not record collectors and only had a handful of musical soundtracks and a number of Nat King Cole songs.

Curtis admits that he did little research for the film because it was not meant to be a documentary, but a celebration of the genre. He went on to explain that he had initially written some comedy scenes involving the DJs doing phone-ins. Then Johnnie Walker reminded him that there were no direct phone line communications with the pirate stations in the mid-1960s, and mobiles (of course) were still very much *of the future*.

Reviews from newspapers
On 28 March 2008 *The Times Online* said:
'It is, to misquote Monty Python: "And now for something completely familiar" - another Curtis film with the same cast, the same jokes, the same excruciating sentimentality. I wouldn't miss it for the world. It's as comforting and truly British as a seaside postcard or a Christmas panto.'

News of the World, 29 March 2009
"With a character cull and a much sharper edit, this enjoyable, occasionally hilarious Britcom set aboard a 1960s pirate radio ship could have been another Curtis corker. As it stands, though? The boat nearly sinks thanks to its own self-satisfied willingness to drift on forever … so *The Boat That Rocked*? Not quite. It's more of a mildly exciting wobble."

Daily Mail, 3 April 2009
"This must count as one of the biggest disappointments of the year. Like *Love Actually*, The *Boat That Rocked* has multiple protagonists, but this time many of the stories and characters are clichéd, and Curtis botches his central conflict between authority and freedom… It's a lazy piece of writing that wasn't ready to go into production… Girls are seen throughout as sexual conquests, unreliable in love and dim-witted - the DJs' female fans are so excited when they get on board that they even scream at the tinned food. When yet another of these females proves to have no morals or loyalty, Curtis just makes his male characters shrug and move on… The movie fails most seriously, however, in its central conflict, which is boringly written

and wastes a valuable opportunity to tell the truth about the demise of the pirate radio stations … Curtis presents a bog-standard dated portrait of stuffy authorities versus free-thinking youth. He was only 11 when the principal events of this movie took place, but that's no reason why he couldn't have done some research. In real life, it was not the stuffy government that shut down the pirates. It was Harold Wilson's technocratic Labour government."

Sun, 2 April 2009
"If you are hoping for an accurate account of how the likes of John Peel and Tony Blackburn took on the law and lost, put those expectations aside now. This is a Richard Curtis movie, and the *Love Actually* director's specs are too rose tinted to read history books… It won't make any waves, but it is smashing and nice. Rating out of five: Four."

Daily Telegraph 2 April 2009
"Well over two hours long, the film outstays its welcome, but it does have some truly magical moments that outshine anything Curtis has done before. The montage scenes in which schoolkids, nurses, dockers, grocers and lovers are shown glowing in wonder at the tunes and monologues coming from the DJs are timely reminders of a pre-narrowcast, pre-private playlist era in which pop music had the power to unite a nation."

Press Association, 3 April 2009
The year is 1966, a golden era for rock'n'roll in this country. But BBC radio only plays a mere 45 minutes of pop music a day. Thus, around 25 million listeners tune into pirate radio stations, which devote every waking (and sleeping) minute to music. One such station is Radio Rock, under the captainship of Quentin (Bill Nighy).
    "The DJs are a motley crew of misfits with one thing in common: a passion for vinyl … *The Boat That Rocked* certainly rocks and rolls to a thumping soundtrack which includes The Beach Boys, Jeff Beck, Cream, Jimi Hendrix, The Rolling Stones and The Who. However, the script springs a leak early on as Curtis attempts to juggle too many thinly sketched characters and gradually loses ballast under the weight of its own unfulfilled ambition … Subtlety tumbles overboard as the battle between government and Radio Rock intensifies, culminating in a bizarre action-oriented finale reminiscent of *Titanic*, albeit on a budget."

Sunday Times 5 April 2009
"*The Boat That Rocked* offers a mix of British pop and patriotism, an alternative myth of what it means to be British for the pop generation, with Bill Nighy as the John Mills of louche living. Richard Curtis is celebrating the plucky, eccentric underdogs who fought the baby-boomer battle of Britain: your right to party and pig out on pop. Too bad those brave bad boys are so badly served by his film."

The Observer, 5 April 2009
"Karl Marx, fashionable once more in these times of financial meltdown, famously observed that history repeats itself, first as tragedy, then as farce. His comment came to mind as I watched the final sequence of Richard Curtis's nostalgic comedy about the era of pirate radio stations in the 1960s. In a manner reminiscent of the Titanic, the film's ship, Radio Rock, sinks in the wintry North Sea to the plangent strains of Procol Harum's *A Whiter Shade of Pale* (one of the movie's 54 golden oldies) and the Minister for Broadcasting orders that no rescue attempt be made. After two hours in the company of these DJs, we feel that Davy Jones's locker is the offshore studio best suited to their talents. But no. Dozens of little boats put out from east coast ports, steered by bunches of pubescent girls to save the heroic DJs from a watery grave. Looking back for a suitably rousing episode from our national past, Curtis has alighted on Dunkirk, a tragedy narrowly averted, which he reprises as mirthless, feelgood farce."

Mail on Sunday, 5 April 2009

Had it been made by just about anyone else, *The Boat That Rocked* might have been gently dismissed as a bit of lightweight, nostalgic fun. But the problem is that it wasn't made by just anyone; it was written and directed by Richard Curtis. As a result, it's fair to say expectations come exceedingly high. And it's also fair to say those high expectations come nowhere close to being met by a picture set in the so-called golden age of pirate radio in the mid-Sixties. It always sounded an unlikely project for the rom-com king and so it proves. It's not funny enough, there's no great central love story and the editing, for so long one of the cornerstones of Curtis's richly deserved success, is terrible.

"The script is flabby, with scene after scene adding little to the story, and some go on so long you forget what they started. As a result the film weighs in at a grossly overweight two hours fifteen minutes, half an hour longer than the flimsy material deserves."

Guardian, 7 April 2009

"The title of Richard Curtis's new film proved an irresistible opportunity for critics to reach for metaphors involving sinking, listing, foundering and capsizing. In terms of box office, it's more a case of a sputtering engine and a broken pump. *The Boat That Rocked* opened on £1.33m over the three-day weekend, £1.8m if you include previews on Wednesday and Thursday. Compared with Curtis's *Love Actually*, which opened in November 2003 on £6.66m (including £1m in previews), it's a crushing disappointment for backers Universal/Working Title. A finger of blame will inevitably be pointed at national newspaper critics for a hostile consensus likely to be at variance from the public's. But were critics really much of a factor in the box-office shortfall? *The Boat That Rocked's* lengthy running time may also have been a negative for audiences but, then again, it's almost identical to that of Curtis's earlier hit."

Daily Express, 3 April 2009

"*The Boat That Rocked* does maintain a jolly party atmosphere throughout as the disc jockeys engage in friendly rivalry, chase pretty girls, fight off the threat of closure, cavort around the decks, have a little dance to themselves and continue to spin all the platters that really matter.

"There is enough material here to sustain an Auf Wiedersehn Pet-style TV comedy through several series and maybe that's the real problem with *The Boat That Rocked*; there are just too many characters and too many incidents of schoolboy silliness to try to squeeze into one film."

Birmingham Mail, 3 April 2009

"The action begins in 1966 when Radio Rock's pirate DJs are offering the sort of pop music the BBC cannot play for even an hour a day. But, instead of giving us youthful firebrands, Curtis seems to be trying to deliver the equivalent of a bunch of fading jocks of no particular era. These guys might, for example, have lost their mojo in the '80s and '90s, and then been dumped at sea back in the '60s as punishment for landing us with 2009's bland, safety-first commercial network. All aboard? I'd walk the plank carefully if I were you."

Sheffield Telegraph, 3 April 2009

"The opening scene of *The Boat That Rocked* (Cert 15) shows a small boy secretly listening to pirate radio after bedtime and since Richard Curtis was 11 in 1967, it is safe to assume that he represents the writer-director.

"The film is a homage to the brief period when a few enterprising entrepreneurs got round the monopoly of the stuffy old BBC by broadcasting from offshore locations.

"It starts well enough with a montage of jolly scenes showing seemingly every generation of the nation crowded around their transistors, singing and/or dancing along to pirate radio, albeit a somewhat fanciful notion. Simultaneously we encounter the motley bunch of DJs cooped up on a rustbucket in the North Sea pumping out the sounds."

Bognor Regis Observer, 3 April 2009
"The soundtrack is great, comfortably the best part of the film, but the crew of pirates manning the good ship Radio Rock are individually and collectively so deeply unattractive in their variously shambolic ways that it's difficult to believe that the film does very much to honour their real-life counterparts.

"The frustration is that the film sets itself up so nicely for a couple of hours of Men Behaving Badly - style humour. The men do indeed behave badly. Very badly. But there simply aren't the laughs that would raise it to something more.

"Occasionally it's mildly amusing; and Curtis throws in a bit of sentiment to ginger it up a bit, one of the pirates managing to find first love plus his long-lost dad on the overcrowded boat.

"But the film doesn't remotely hit the heights the trailer promises - save for the soggy finale when, far too late, the film finally gets going."

The Scotsman, 3 April 2009
"Basing his story very loosely on Radio Caroline, Curtis's first love may well be pop music, but judging from his ability to convey that love on screen in *The Boat that Rocked*, he's clearly had a very shallow relationship with it over the years – and his trademark lack of grit is no excuse for refusing to get down and dirty with why music matters. Neither High Fidelity nor Almost Famous could be described as hard-edged, yet they were full of truthful observations about the extent to which music can get under a person's skin. By comparison, The Boat that Rocks tries to convey the communion-like power of pop with montage after montage of kids, teenagers, nurses, couples, pensioners, even nuns, illicitly tuning in and snickering away at their own rebellious nature."

International newspapers
Sydney Morning Herald, Australia, 9 April 2009
"Richard Curtis prepared his cast with weeks of rehearsal time aboard the boat, the aim being to engender a holiday camp atmosphere that could be transferred faithfully to the screen, and it works pretty well. The banter flows easily and when it slows, there's always the music. With more than 50 songs listed in the credits, the story doesn't really unfold, it washes over you in successive waves of nostalgia…"

The Age, Melbourne, Australia, 11 April 2009
"About the only thing with any depth in this delirious, pastel-coloured, infectiously fun tribute to the pop music and loud fashions of the 1960s is the North Sea on which the titular pirate radio station floats. Having, thankfully, shaken all the romantic comedy out of his system - writer-director Richard Curtis delivers an energetic, semi-farcical comedy romp blessed with a great ensemble cast, some gloriously tasteless jokes and a soundtrack of period hits."

Sunday Star Times, Wellington, New Zealand, 22 April 2009
"Like shooting fish in a barrel, there are so many flaws in Curtis's new film that it's almost unsporting to take aim and fire. But let's do it anyway… *The Boat That Rocked* is still a love story; primarily, with music, but also the kind that lends itself nicely to the propagation of the species.

"Curtis's passion is passion, especially between humans, which is where his new film hits rough conditions. The premise, about a rabble of loveable pirate radio DJs rocking the airwaves from a rusty boat in the North Sea in the 1960s, is great. The enemy closes in but nobody can silence the will of the people, even when Davy Jones beckons. Like American sitcom WKRP in Cincinnati, this isn't a movie about a radio station; it's about a group of people who bond as a family as they strive to stick it to the man (in this case, a very Hitleresque caricature played by Kenneth Branagh). And Curtis piles it on thicker than Thick Kevin. It's a love-in for two-dimensional characters and the audience, who Curtis treats as two-dimensional … Although *The Boat That Rocked* is an insult to the intellect of a sturgeon, New Zealand filmmakers will be kicking themselves for not getting there first with a feature about Radio Hauraki. Others may wish Curtis hadn't got there at all."

Variety, USA, 29 March 2009
"Sex, drugs and rock 'n' roll, plus a heavy dose of Swinging '60s nostalgia, fuel *The Boat That Rocked*, Richard Curtis' hymn to the wild days of U.K. pirate radio. More reminiscent of his eccentric TV comedies (*The Vicar of Dibley*, *Mr. Bean*) than his big screen romancers *Four Weddings and a Funeral* and *Notting Hill*, Curtis' second outing as writer-director throws together a large cast of wackos on a boat off the east coast of Blighty. Pic generally stays afloat on the strength of its characters but sometimes threatens to sink under its overlong running time and vignettish structure.

"Though it positively reeks of the '60s, *The Boat That Rocked* lacks the sheer grit and darker underbelly of Michael Winterbottom's '70s equivalent, *24 Hour Party People*. It also isn't quite the timely, anti-establishment comedy it promises to be at the start, but it's as close as any comedy by a middle-class entertainer like Curtis is likely to come."

What about the DJs who saw the film?
Tony Blackburn worked for Radio Caroline South, then Radio London between the years 1964-1967. He recalled:

> I enjoyed *The Boat That Rocked* and it took me back 45 years. There are some things that Richard Curtis gets right in the film. Whilst I was watching the film it took me back to Radio Caroline and the ship on which I was working in 1964, the *Mi Amigo*. It completely transformed my life. In the film the studio equipment is spot on. The correct microphone, turntables and volume controls to fade the music in and out.
> However, the film does get one or two things wrong. The film has many gorgeous girls on the ship, which reminded me of how good women looked in the Sixties. Apart from two librarians, Marion and Maureen, there weren't any women on board. So, I have to say that contrary to the racy picture painted in the film, Radio Caroline was virtually a girl-free zone.
> The film gives the popular perception that it was staffed by long-haired rebellious DJs who promoted their piratical image and played rock music between endless rounds of girls, drug and booze-fuelled parties on board. The simple truth is that, as Richard Curtis might have found if he had spent more time talking to some of us original DJs who were there at the time, this was not the case.
> These criticisms apart, and whatever you think of the film's historical accuracy, it really is an exciting film and I am sure it will go down well with the younger generation. Older viewers may have a different opinion.
> I appreciate that a bit of poetic licence is required in a film of this nature, but I was disappointed to see such an important time for broadcasting played pretty much for laughs.

Emperor Rosko joined Radio Caroline in 1966 and brought with him a personality which combined a number of gimmicks and techniques learned from American rock'n'roll radio. It was a style that British audiences had never heard before. He also had a mynah bird, Alfie, who joined him on air.

In 1967 Rosko left Caroline and moved to France and presented a daily afternoon show on French Radio Luxembourg. He later joined Radio 1 but is now resident in Los Angeles, USA. He attended the London premiere of the film and said afterwards:

Have mercy! This was a great movie. I had expected some disappointment in the film, but hey it captured the spirit of the times. It was not what I expected. You can nit-pick about the bits and pieces, but it has the greatest soundtrack you ever heard – great music of the time – which carries the movie. Apparently the Count in the film is loosely based on me. In the film he worked in a large studio. Had he been on Caroline he would have found it more difficult as the studio was only the size of a small bathroom – with only one porthole. But without doubt the highlight of the film for me was the music and I told Richard Curtis to his face. I believe he has done a brilliant job with the film which I convinced will be a box office success.

Emperor Rosko with a crowd of admirers

Johnnie Walker worked on Swinging Radio England in 1966 and later jumped ship to join Radio Caroline South and stayed with the station broadcasting illegally after the Marine Offences Act came into force at midnight on 14 August. He remained with Radio Caroline until the ship was towed into Amsterdam harbour in March 1968. He was an advisor for the *The Boat That Rocked*. His comments:

For those younger people, born after the whole pirate thing, it's an introduction to a really exciting, rebellious time in British history. If Richard had portrayed the real story, it would have been a dull film, because we lived quite boring lives on board ship. But I found the whole experience most glamorous, romantic and exciting. My first ship was the *Liassez-Faire*. The radio station Swinging Radio England was not really together and the sleeping accommodation was very basic. So basic that we did not have any bunks on board. We had to bed down in the hold in our sleeping bags. Caroline was a far better ship and we had fun on board, but not as much as is portrayed in the film. Certainly not with 100 girls on board. In summer we did see sailing boats coming alongside the *Mi Amigo* and we would certainly entertain their crews.

Dave Cash joined Radio London in 1965 and became one its most popular DJs. His take on the film:

A great romp of a romantic comedy set on a 60s pirate radio boat. It got me laughing several times and I came out feeling uplifted. Please don't take it too seriously; it's funny with good characters and a bitch sound track. What's not to like?

Bill Nighy with Dave Cash

Tom Edwards worked on Radio City and Radio Caroline South. He says:

When I first heard of *The Boat That Rocked* being made way back at the start of 2008, I 'hustled' Richard Curtis with telephone calls, emails and letters saying "I'm here. I love the movies and anything to do with films. Use me and my knowledge." He didn't even reply, which I thought was the height of rudeness, or am I just being old fashioned?

I was then prompted and helped by the editor(s) of *The Mail On Sunday* to tell my tale in print on 1st March 2009, this all going hand in hand with Curtis's production which was going to be released exactly a month later on 1st April 2009.

The hype gathered momentum. I went to see the film the week it was released. I shouted out 'YES!' when the first aerial shot of the radio ship appeared. I sat down in my seat after being told to be quiet by the audience. I was in the company of a crowd of mates - all different ages - and they thought the same.

After 20 minutes I was fidgeting, a sure sign that I was not enjoying what I was seeing. It bore none of the memories that I have. As Curtis has stated it was a fun fiction movie, not fact. I took that comment on board but the storyline(s) bored me. It seemed to be like a 'Carry On' film and I half expected to see Kenneth Williams popping up with 'Stop messin' about.'

There was no continuity in the various plots and no end to the various storyline(s). My highlight(s) were Bill Nighy who added clout, as did Kenneth Branagh, shades maybe of Ronan O'Rahilly and Anthony Wedgwood Benn? Yes, the music was great, a real memory maker.

The Boat That Rocked was a huge disappointment to me and I left the cinema in Boston, Lincolnshire very unimpressed and deflated even though the attractive female manager gave me a huge poster of the film as a souvenir.

Maybe one day a feature film will be made about the way it 'really was'. I hope I am around to see that go into production. Curtis made light of broadcasting at sea. It was damn dangerous out there, or maybe I'm living in the past too much? At least we pirate DJs were given a mention as the overlong credits rolled and I stayed until the last frame in what was by now an empty cinema, clutching my poster!

The critics also gave the film a pasting in the national press but they mean nothing to me. I had to see it for myself. It was badly directed and the editing of what I saw in the final cut was all over the place. Maybe in years to come it will be classed as film noir.

All of us were so excited for Tony O'Neil's LV*18* being used in the movie. Not a sign, except for a brief glimpse in a shower scene. Another major disappointment. I know only too well about having done something I thought was good, only to discover later it's ended up on the cutting room floor. I guess that's showbiz!

So on a scale of one to ten I would give *The Boat That Rocked* a generous three. I heard it cost millions of pounds to make and am trying hard to think where all that money went.

Curtis is a talented man and everything he has touched in the past turned into pure gold - *Four Weddings and a Funeral*, *Notting Hill*,etc etc. This was a turkey that didn't get to flap its wings.

Radio Luxembourg DJ Don Wardell
paying Tom Edwards a visit to Radio
Pontin during the summer of 1964

Tom Edwards on his 64th birthday
in March 2009

Over in Australia …

Colin Nicol served on Radio Caroline South and Swinging Radio England/Britain Radio and now lives back at his home of Perth, Western Australia. He has described the film as "Carry on Broadcasting" and says:

> The film is a fun romp, well directed and acted albeit too long by about 20 minutes. There are hints of some original pirate characters but not all the excellent dialogue can be heard.
>
> Reviews have been mixed, but just don't take it seriously. Some of the equipment is not authentic and none of the supposed broadcasting is believable.
>
> As demonstrated by the title that refers to it being a boat rather than a ship, as it should more naturally be described, the film is not really about pirate radio. That theme is just used to provide a platform for a jolly romp of a story with lots of wonderful music. But it refers to an important agent of social transition of world-wide interest and influence. What was it really like? Tough a lot of the time, tiring, noisy – and dangerous.
>
> Some would-be DJs got as far as leaving the supply tender (boat) and setting foot on the ship in order to say they made it, then greenly bounced back to port, ambitions in tatters and vowing never to return.
>
> Where are the pirates today? Household names, some. The British establishment eventually absorbs its rebels; those left meet on anniversaries to celebrate and remember. I came home to Australia.
>
> Where are the ships? Caroline North, m.v. *Fredericia* went to scrap. The south ship, my friend, *Mi Amigo*, rests peacefully in silt at the bottom of the Thames Estuary.
>
> The original creator of British pirate radio, Sydney-born Allan Crawford, died late 1999 in anonymity at a nursing home in north Wales. His nemesis Ronan O'Rahilly, at around 70, still haunts Chelsea and continues to reap the rewards and acclaim. To the victor go the spoils.

Colin Nicol rings the Caroline Bell aboard Cheeta II, 1966

Colin Nicol, 2007 in Perth, Western Australia

Legendary breakfast announcer on radio station 2SM in Sydney, Australia, Ian MacRae, spent two years of his early career working on British offshore stations in the mid-1960s. First on Radio City which transmitted from a group of derelict forts on Shivering Sands in the Thames Estuary and then on Caroline South, on a ship moored off the English coast. After seeing the movie, Macca reckons the producers have not allowed the facts to interfere with their own version of events:

In the sixties, DJs on the UK's "Pirate Radio" ships did nothing but party and have sex with the constant visiting supply of lusty young ladies. Oh yes, and present the occasional radio programme, which was totally off the cuff as no preparation was required.

At least that's what the movie *The Boat That Rocked* would have you believe.

Ian MacRae today in Australia
For a picture of Ian in 1966 see page 329

OK, you expect a movie to have a bit of artistic license and it's great that a whole generation of British kids will now be aware that it was us broadcasters who were directly responsible for forcing later Governments to legalise land-based commercial radio in the UK.

However, I squirmed for the over-long 135 minutes the movie runs watching misrepresentation after misrepresentation of what really went on.

Firstly I have to take issue with the title of the movie *The Boat That Rocked*. Radio Caroline, on which the story is loosely based, was a "ship" not a boat. People row boats.

Secondly no visitors were ever allowed on board - for insurance and safety reasons. The idea that you could invite 200 fans and have them running all over the ship is ridiculous when you have generators running and transmitters putting out 50,000 Watts. Which makes the scene where the two guys compete to climb the mast even more ridiculous.

The few visitors who did come on board were people like pop stars and entertainers, for on-air interviews, and they had to have special permission from head office in London.

The movie makes no reference to the station even having a head office, which was actually a salubrious building just off Park Lane, in London's Mayfair. The film gives the impression that the whole operation was totally run from the ship.

You'll probably be a bit confused as to what the Bill Nighy character is supposed to be. He seems to be a combined ship's captain, programme director and owner.

In real life there were two sets of crew on the ship - the seamen, headed by the Captain, and the radio station people such as DJs, engineers and technicians. Neither group had the faintest idea what the other actually did.

The movie makes it appear there was only one radio ship, which they call Radio Rock, with one DJ telling his listeners he has 25 million people listening to him. In fact there were several stations that I can think of broadcasting around the coastline, with a number positioned off London, all with a combined audience of 25 million.

The movie really totally misses the point when the police attempt to raid the ship to close it down. The vessel was in international waters and outside the jurisdiction of any British authority. A raid like that would have been real piracy by the police.

The only way the Government could eventually close the pirates down was by cutting their supply lines. They made it illegal to supply them with everything from advertising to food, water, fuel or even working for them. Come ashore and you'd get arrested.

That's when I decided two years at sea was enough and came home to Australia where you aren't a criminal if you work for commercial radio.

As for the movie, enjoy it for what it is – entertainment. But don't regard it as history.

Bryan Vaughan worked on Radios Atlanta, Caroline South and Scotland, but returned to Australia once the pirates had ceased broadcasting. He settled in Sydney, New South Wales.

For me, *The Boat That Rocked* doesn't bear close resemblance to reality but it is fun! And the music is good! It is true that the general public embraced us hugely and the government was obsessed with closing us down and both elements feature strongly. I believe the movie also captures the essence of the swinging sixties and some of the camaraderie of the DJs on board but the opportunity of getting to tell why and how we did it is lost in the sex, drugs and rock'n'roll that is promoted throughout. Maybe I'm suffering from severe Alzheimer's but the sex and drugs on board must have passed me by at the time! It may have been different when we came ashore, but that is another story!"

Graham Webb worked on Radio Caroline South from 1965-1966. He returned to Australia and is still involved in radio presentation and production. Commenting on the film *The Boat That Rocked* he says:

I LOVED the Movie! It WAS the Sixties. I think Ian MacRae has it wrong because he wanted, apparently, to see a 'Documentary' of what it was truly all about.

After the Ovation Channel flew me to Sydney for an interview by Glen A. Baker about the Pirates of Oz, I flew to Sydney at my own expense for the Red Carpet Premiere and was surprised to see Ian not there BUT all of our other "Pirates of Oz" made an appearance including Norman St John, John Kerr and Bryan Vaughan.

To me *The Boat That Rocked* was more a stylized version of what **anyone**, let alone the writer and director, Richard Curtis, **imagined** life on board the Pirate Radio Stations was like.

Sure, there was **no** "bonking in the Bunks" - too small! The *Mi Amigo* didn't sink until March 1980, but we **did** run aground in her at Frinton-on-Sea, 19 January 1966, in a very dramatic fashion. Tony Blackburn, Tom Lodge, Norman St John, Dave Lee Travis and I had to be rescued by breeches buoy.

As I am now in my 74th year, I may have forgotten some of the details but my memory of my days on Caroline North and South remain strong. I shall continue to make the re-unions, the celebrations, the commiserations, and whatever to do with what has indelibly remained in my memory **and** my life as best I can, my days on **Radio Caroline**.

John Kerr broadcast on Radio Scotland from 1966 to August 1967. He had previously worked in radio in Australia and for six years was presenter of the *Breakfast Show* on 2CA, Canberra. After the Marine Offences Act John returned to Australia and worked for radio station 2UE, Sydney where he still works to this day. He has celebrated 52 years in the world of radio. Commenting on the film John says:

I considered the film a light-hearted romp. It catches the mood accurately. The portrayal of the British public going wild for radio and the music and the government's obsession with shutting us down is true. Unlike Bryan Vaughan I won't say it was the best time of my life but it has unquestionably been the most adventurous.

I've already said it's a "light-hearted romp" which so far has given **everyone** I've spoken to on and off the air a good laugh which I'm sure was the intent of the movie-makers - they weren't out to make a documentary - they made a **movie**!

To some of my fellow 'pirates' - come on guys, lighten up! This business about the movie being incorrectly titled is laughable. Look up the dictionary and you'll find that 'boat' and 'ship' have one and the same meaning, the stronger

A young John Kerr

meaning being a 'ship' is generally an ocean-going vessel. Can't say I'd like to have actually gone to sea in The Comet - Radio Scotland's 100 foot long, 500-ton hulk. It didn't have an engine anyway!

Again, some write that the depiction of Bill Nighy's character permanently on the boat acting as sort of programme manager/ship's captain, etc is incorrect because all the stations had land-based headquarters. **Who cares** guys? - it's a movie! Do you think it would have been a better movie if they'd shown salubrious headquarters in London or Glasgow?

Some have taken exception to the movie showing lusty girls swarming all over the 'pirates' on board - "**Incorrect!**" scream some. I thought that may have enhanced your current image, seeing as we're all over 40 years older, and again fellas - it's a movie.

The Boat That Rocked shows how enthusiastically and lovingly the British public embraced all of the offshore radio stations and the significant part we all played in British radio. I'm pleased as punch the movie has been made and fleetingly, how it's drawn media and public attention in Australia back to those of us who were 'pirates'.

Norman St John worked aboard Radio Caroline South and Radio London between the years 1965-1967. After the stations were closed down by the British Government he returned to Australia where he is now a steel wire manufacturer based in Brisbane. His comments on the film:

I was fortunate enough to attend the 'Red Carpet' showing (Australian Premiere) in Sydney on 31 March 2009. Also in attendance were other 'Real Pirates', Graham Webb, Bryan Vaughan and John Kerr. I say 'Real Pirates' as they are the ones who worked on the stations, Radio Caroline, Radio London and Radio Scotland before the Marine Offences Legislation was passed. Sadly there are now only a handful of us left. Some will judge the movie harshly and I believe unjustly. In my opinion it was a very enjoyable movie based on a time in history when a few guys (there were no girls on the ships in

my time on board) braved the ocean waves to create the swinging Sixties. People I have since spoken to, who had only a little knowledge of the 'Pirates', have all said that they enjoyed the movie very much. One must remember that it was a 'movie' and like many before it was only authentic to a point in time. The producer, director and actors did a very good job and if you haven't seen The Boat That Rocked, do it and have a good laugh!

Former offshore disc jockeys with Bill Nighy. Left to right: Bryan Vaughan, John Kerr, Bill, Norman St John and Graham Webb at the Australian premiere of The Boat that Rocked *in Sydney, April 2009.*

Meantime back in the United Kingdom

Angela Lander was a 15 year-old Peterborough schoolgirl in 1964. She had been told about Radio Caroline whilst at school. She was overjoyed with what she heard and soon wanted to obtain as much information as possible. She wrote to Caroline House in London and to many of the DJs and believed that offshore radio was the best news story of the 1960s.

She kept a detailed log of events and happenings on board and on land. Her affection changed to Radio London when the station began broadcasting at Christmastime, 1964. Her favourite DJs were John Peel, Pete Drummond and Kenny and Cash. She also enjoyed tuning

in to Swinging Radio England and Radio City. Angela kept newspaper cuttings and read all the music papers of the time. In a word she was 'fanatical.'

When the Marine etc., Broadcasting (Offences) Act came into force on 14 August 1967 she retuned to Radio Caroline and recalls that the station was different from when she first heard it. Now Caroline was illegal. The music was different, as were the DJs. There was much more warmth with the presenters and she followed the careers of Johnnie Walker, Robbie Dale, 'Twiggy' Day and Spangles Muldoon. It was a sad day in March 1968 when Radios Caroline North and South were towed into Holland and the airways fell silent.

Angela Lander with Ronan O'Rahilly

Angela acknowledges that the years 1964-1967 for the offshore stations was far from normal, in fact bizarre. It was that keen interest and a realization that young people could have a say in their future that inspired her to became a journalist.

Thirty years later, Angela went to the National Archives in Kew, London to view the Whitehall Papers which are now in the public domain and was horrified to learn of all the dirty tricks the Government had orchestrated to rid the shores of the offshore stations during the 1960s.

She has retained her original log and still has an affection for the watery wireless days. Angela was excited to learn that a film about the era was being masterminded by Richard Curtis for release in April 2009. She went to see the film – twice!

> My first viewing of *The Boat That Rocked* could be summed up in one word 'disappointing' - it was factually incorrect and far removed from the pirate radio I remember.
>
> On seeing it for a second time I realized I had misjudged it. This was only very loosely based on the events during the three years of offshore radio - it was just a typical Richard Curtis comedy with plenty of sex and swearing, some nostalgic music … and a boat.
>
> What I would like to give him credit for is that he recognized how important this era of radio was and what it achieved. It kick-started a whole new era of popular radio that we are so privileged to enjoy today.
>
> However, it now leaves room for someone to make a film about the real story that led to this bizarre and zany era that has now become part of the history of broadcasting. The best attempt over the years was the documentary made for the Granada TV series *Arena* but since then the release of the Whitehall papers in 1998 has added even more intrigue.
>
> It would have to take the form of a documentary and should be done whilst most of the original cast are still breathing and before all the memories are lost.
>
> Like Curtis's film it would contain humour, risk, excitement, frustration and tears, only this time it would be for real, but as they say the original story is always the best.

Peter Moore is the boss of the present day Radio Caroline. What are his opinions of the film?

> If I savage *The Boat That Rocked* without good reason, there will surely be an accusation of sour grapes, so I will make my points very clearly.

Although the mythical station Radio Rock is a generic pirate, all of the media and therefore also the public, have concluded that this is the story of Radio Caroline. The film makers have been happy to let that image stand and to milk the additional publicity that our name still creates.

Thus, as the station in the film survives the Marine Offence Act for just a few hours before sinking, a worldwide audience will conclude that this was Caroline's fate. This is reinforced by a caption stating that the golden age of pirate radio was over by the summer of 1967.

Trevor Dann, Director, Radio Academy,
Richard Curtis and Keith Skues

The fact that Caroline never was defeated by the new law, that we continued to broadcast at sea for a further 23 years and that we still exist today, was not even hinted at. So 42 years of our 45 year history, during which time far more dramatic things happened than ever happened between 64 to 67, is utterly denied.

The media compounded this denial. The *Sun* newspaper, over a double page picture of our present ship, used the caption 'Radio Caroline's ship sinking in 1966'. The *Independent* closed a review with the comment 'The end came for Radio Caroline in August 1967'.

The other thing to regret is that, this film having appeared, it will probably close the door on the possibility of a credible and dramatic film on the subject ever reaching the screen.

I saw the film twice. The first time I walked out before the end. The second time I stayed for the credits, to look for any acknowledgement of the help we provided and the studio equipment we loaned. There was no mention.

From my viewpoint, which I admit is subjective, I wish that the film had never been made because of the damage it has done and the opportunity it may have taken away to tell the actual story of Radio Caroline.

GOODBYE MEDIUM WAVE?

During the 1960s all offshore radio stations transmitted on the medium wave band.

On 29 January 2009 the death knell sounded for AM and FM bands in a report that sets out a switchover to digital radio. The communications minister, Lord Stephen Carter's Digital Britain report says that Digital Audio Broadcasting will become the primary platform for all national and local radio services.

There have been claims that digital radio could be a waste of money. A number of broadcasters have dropped plans to expand on digital because of the very high costs. Channel 4 had planned to launch a new digital service but decided not to go ahead because of financial constraints.

Lord Carter said there was a chance that DAB and FM may co-exist for several years, but that AM (medium wave) was almost certainly doomed.

The news will upset many senior citizens who find AM (medium wave) easier to tune in with predicatable and stable reception. In addition medium wave is fitted to most inexpensive radios and can be found on most car radios. Medium wave is for range and VHF for quality. Some criticise medium wave transmissions when it becomes dark as signals fade and foreign stations take over and drown out the local station. There was the question of whether a person purchased a DAB radio in the UK then went on holiday to the continent whether or not it would work. Chances are it would not. Unlike television, where you can buy a Freeview box to receive digital stations on your old television set, nobody has yet released a device to enable people with older radios to receive digital signals.

PIRATE BBC ESSEX 2009

THE STATION RETURNED to the airwaves during Easter (10-13 April 2009) much to the delight of its numerous fans, many of whom travelled extraordinary distances to see the DJs and staff aboard the LV*18*, which this time was moored alongside the Harwich Ha'penny Pier. The vessel's bridge was converted into a radio studio and the station broadcast on 729, 765 and 1530 medium wave and on bbc.co.uk/essex online, from 7.00am on Good Friday through to 6.00pm on Easter Monday. Radio fans were truly delighted to be able to get to within a few feet of the LV*18*. The occasion marked the 45th anniversary of Radio Caroline going on air at Eastertime, 1964 and also coincided with the release of the film *The Boat That Rocked*.

"To welcome Pirate BBC Essex back within days of the film's release is just wonderful news", said Tony O'Neil of the Pharos Trust.

Prior to the station going on air, Managing Editor Gerald Main said: "In 2007 we told listeners it could be the last time for Pirate BBC Essex. Ever since, fans from Essex and across the world have been asking us to do it one more time. We've been swayed by their wishes and their ship is literally coming in."

Tim Gillett, programme producer said: "We were able to play those great pirate radio classics like *Caroline* and *A Whiter Shade Of Pale*. The most popular record played over the Easter weekend was *Paint It Black* by the Rolling Stones. In addition we spun in a few forgotten gems, songs which have not been heard for more than forty years like *That's The Way Love Goes* by Charles Dickens and *Incense* by the Anglos."

The engineers emulated the echo effect on the DJs' voices so they sounded as they were heard on several stations during those pioneering pop music pirate radio days. Listeners were also treated to '60s-style jingles.

Legendary DJ Tony Blackburn was reunited with his long-lost dog Arnold after the animal went missing more than twenty years ago. Arnold, a mongrel, was just a puppy when Tony Blackburn took him aboard the 60s pirate radio ship *Mi Amigo* in 1964.

*Tony Blackburn in
BBC London studio*

"I knew British people liked pets so I thought they'd like to hear Arnold with me on my radio shows," says Tony. He was right. It started a 20-year love affair between Arnold and the great British listening public. Children grew up hearing his famous bark.

"When I jumped ship from Radio Caroline to Radio London, Arnold came too," said Tony. "And when Radio London was forced off the air by the Government, Arnold and I opened Radio 1."

The dog can be heard barking within seconds on the official archive recording of Tony Blackburn's first show which opened Radio 1 in 1967. It was in the 80s when Blackburn moved from the BBC to commercial radio that Arnold disappeared.

"My and Arnold's jaws dropped when they told me they didn't want him," he says. "Arnold took off, leaving me in heaps of tears and I haven't seen him since." That was till March this year when Tim Gillett asked Tony to present one of the shows.

"I asked him whether he would be bringing Arnold aboard the LV*18* in Harwich and he told me how he had lost the poor dog," says Tim. "So I made it my challenge to find him. I got in touch with Mark Punter a colleague from the world-famous BBC sound archives in London and was stunned. Within an hour he came back with the good news that that he had found him."

Keith Skues

"Arnold was lurking behind one of the shelves of 60s archive recordings," says Mark Punter. "He was asleep, though his nose was twitching."

Tony Blackburn said that one thing was for sure. "Arnold still had his bark." – and he brought him to Harwich to prove it!

The DJ team

Original Sixties DJs appearing on Pirate BBC Essex in 2009 were Mike Ahern, Tony Blackburn, Paul Burnett, Dave Cash, Roger Day, Tom Edwards, Paul Freeman, Steve Merike, Emperor Rosko, Keith Skues, Norman St John, Alan Turner and Johnnie Walker.

They were complimented by Ray Clark, Steve England, Tim Gillett, Dave Owen, Mark Punter, Steve Scruton, Stuart Smith, Jonathan Taylor, Gary Walker (of the Walker Brothers) and Ian Wyatt.

Comment

Tom Edwards said after presenting his show:

> I thought this was the biggest and best ever Pirate BBC Essex. The year 2004 was good so was 2007, but this time it had the 'edge' I feel the reason was because we could see and meet some of the audience as the LV*18* was moored at Ha'penny Pier. It added more clout and atmosphere. I loved every single moment of my far-too-short stay at The Pier Hotel and it was such a delight to be able to chat with fellow broadcasters old and new.
>
> I am humbled by the folk who have followed us for well over forty years. One lady brought her grandchildren to meet me. Pirate radio being handed down by generations was such a compliment.
>
> I thought the atmosphere together with great weather was fabulous. All the guys from BBC Essex - Tim Gillett, Steve Scruton, Ian Wyatt, plus Chris, Mark and Jonathan were so helpful and friendly, so rare these days in the media world.
>
> Ian 'guided' me through my two-hour show, Easter Sunday lunchtime. We had worked together before and I asked for him especially. An absolute joy to work with. I wanted to go on for another twelve hours! Not only are these guys colleagues but they have also become fine friends too. As for us pirate DJs again I have to say we pick up on a conversation from last week, last year or four decades ago. These are friendships that were first cemented out there in the North Sea in the Sixties. I am chuffed to have played such a minor role in it all. Also thanks to Tony of the LV*18* Pharos Trust. What a smashing fellow!
>
> I have told the BBC bosses to put my name down for the 50th anniversary in 2014. I am determined to be there, but that's something out of my control. Pirate radio - the 50th? I am excited already!

◉ Various BBC and independent stations produced tribute programmes over the Easter period to mark the 45th anniversary of offshore radio.

A FEW PHOTO MEMORIES of PIRATE BBC ESSEX
August 2007 and Easter 2009

Left to right: Duncan Johnson, Keith Skues, Johnnie Walker, Norman St John, Tim Gillett (back), Ed Stewart (front) and Dave Cash. Looking out of the door is Mike Barrington.

Above left: In the studio aboard the LV18. Roger Day and Johnnie Walker with Keith Skues behind and Charlie Wallace at the back.
Above right: Returning to the shore after the closure of the 2007 broadcasts aboard the foot ferry to Harwich. Left to right: Norman St John, Gordon Cruse (back), Johnnie Walker, Steve Scruton, Ed Stewart, Keith Skues and Dave Cash.

Above: The LV18 appeared in the Radio Sunshine livery for the 2009 broadcasts from Pirate BBC Essex.

Johnnie Walker wired for sound

A motley crew of radio 'pirates' on the deck of the LV18

Roger Day presenting the Breakfast Show

Mark Wesley

The Two Steves. Steve Merike (left) interviewed by Steve Scruton.

Crowds swell Ha'penny Pier to see DJs

David Owen (left) with Steve England

Elaine and Alan Turner

Ian Wyatt

Norman St John

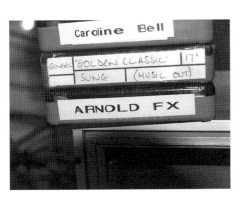

Jingles used in programmes

Roger 'Twiggy' Day

Tony Blackburn and Johnnie Walker talking about their days on Radio Caroline South

Gary Walker of the Walker Brothers

Mike Barrington

*Ray Clark interviewed by
Mary Payne and John Sales*

*Steve Scruton being filmed
by Chris Woodward*

*Emperor Rosko planning for
'Pick of the Chops'*

Tom Edwards

Presenters meet their audience on Ha'penny Pier

*Arnold the Dog
with official BBC pass*

Tim Gillett takes a break for fresh air

*Night time on Ha'penny Pier, but Pirate BBC Essex
continued to broadcast 24 hours a day*

AND FINALLY

Many of us who helped pioneer the days of 'watery wireless' in 1964, only to have the Government close us down, have dreamed of a return to the golden days of pirate radio. It would be true to say that we now believe that those halcyon days of fun and excitement have gone for good.

Ironically, it's the new media of satellite and the internet, powered by a loyal band of enthusiasts, that are 'keeping the dream alive'. *The Boat That Rocked* seems set to ignite a new wave of interest in the subject of 'watery wireless', both by invoking some happy memories for the older generation and educating a new one.

I, for one, hope the reunions and anniversary celebrations will continue for as long as any of us are fit enough to attend.

BIBLIOGRAPHY

Since the author wrote the original manuscript in the 1960s a number of books and magazines have been published about the offshore era and early days of Radio 1 which are well worth a read. The author consulted all these books and magazines whilst updating *Pop Went the Pirates* and is grateful to the publishers where appropriate for allowing extracts to be used. They are listed below in chronological order.

Radio Caroline
John Venmore-Rowland, Landmark Press, 1967 (now Terence Dalton Ltd)

Radio Onederland
Keith Skues, Landmark Press, 1968 (now Terence Dalton Ltd)

Monitor Magazine
Benfleet, Essex, 1972-1990

Offshore Radio
Gerry Bishop, Iceni Enterprises, 1975

SOS - 10 Days in the Life of a Lady
Simon Barrett, Music Radio Promotions, 1976

Broadcasting From the High Seas
Paul Harris, Paul Harris Publishing, 1977

Pirate Radio Now and Then
Stuart Henry and Mike Von Joel, Blandford Press, 1984

Last of the Pirates
Bob Noakes, Paul Harris Publishing, 1984

The Lid off Laser
Paul Rusling, Pirate Publications, 1984

The *Pirates Who Waived the Rules*
Jay Jackson, Now Radio Communications, 1985

Offshore Echo's
1986-2009

25 Years Radio Caroline Memories
Hans Knot, Monitor Magazine, Benfleet, 1989

The Radio Companion
Paul Donovan, HarperCollins, 1991

Selling the Sixties
Robert Chapman, Routledge, 1992
Radio Magazine
1992-2009

Butterfly Upon the Wheel
Peter Moore, Offshore Echo's Magazine, London, 1992

Wheel Turned Full Circle
John A. Burch, Caroline Movement, Grays, Essex, 1993

All Night Long
Dave Cash, Mandarin, 1993

The Wonderful Radio London Story
Chris Elliot, East Anglian Productions, 1997

Radio 270 Life on the Oceaan Waves
Bob Preedy. www.yorkshirebooks.org.uk, 2002

Radio Caroline
Ralph C. Humphries, Oakwood Press, 2003

Radio Caroline North Rockin' and Rollin'
Bob Preedy. www.yorkshirebooks.org.uk, 2004

Wet and Wild History of Radio Caroline 1964-2004
Edited by Hans Knot. P.O. Box 53121, 1007 RC – Amsterdam, Holland, 2004.

Out of the Stewpot
Ed Stewart. John Blake Publishing, 2005

Making Waves
Edited by Bob Le-Roi. Photoradio, Whitstable, Kent, 2005

Margrave of the Marshes
John Peel. Bantam Press, 2005

Poptastic! My Life in Radio
Tony Blackburn. Cassell Illustrated, 2007

The Autobiography – Johnnie Walker
Johnnie Walker. Michael Joseph, 2007.

INDEX